THE GREAT WAR

VOLUME 7

This Volume Combines Volume 7 & Volume 8
of an Original 13 Volume Set.

Reprinted 1999 from the 1916 & 1917 editions
TRIDENT PRESS INTERNATIONAL
Copyright 1999

ISBN 1-582790-28-0 Standard Edition

Printed in Croatia

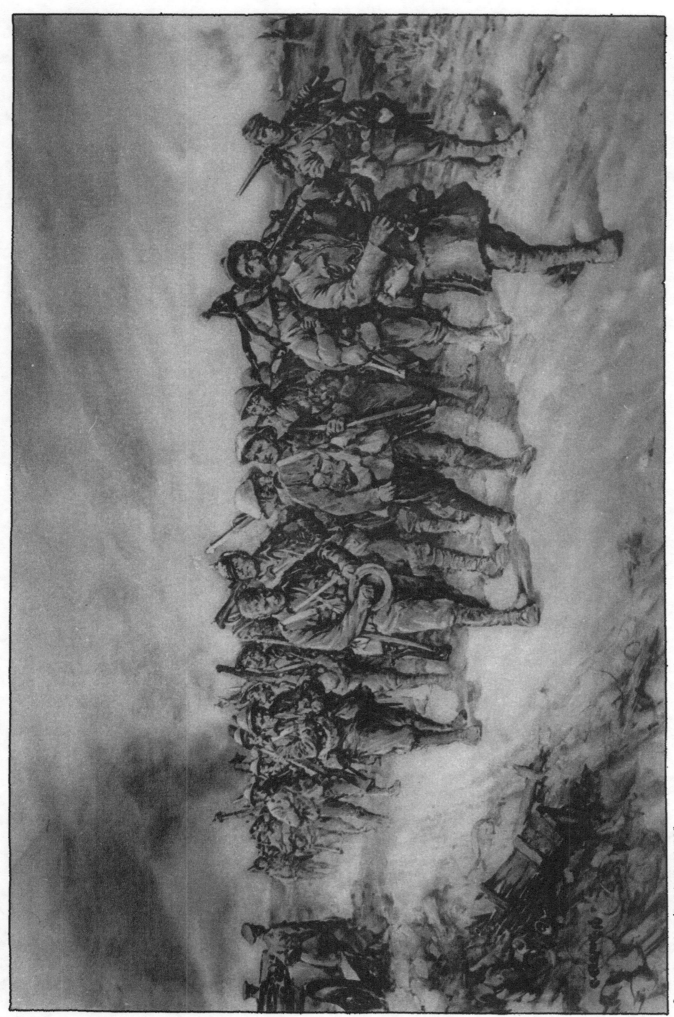

From the Drawing by CHRISTOPHER CLARK.

Dublins and Munsters Returning from the Victory at Ginchy.

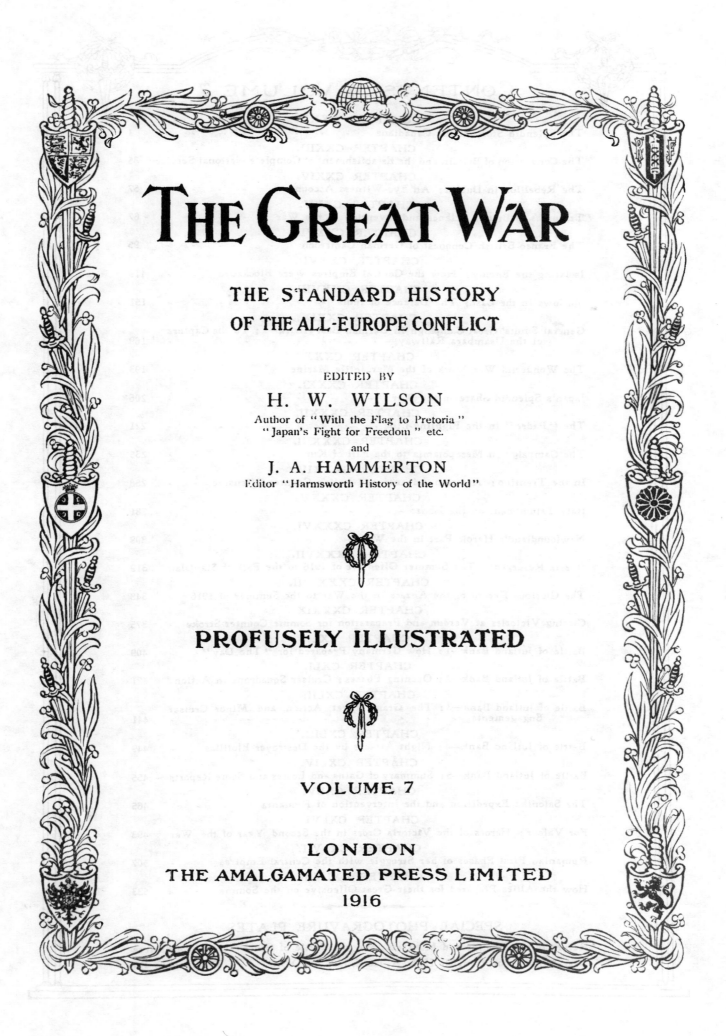

THE GREAT WAR

THE STANDARD HISTORY
OF THE ALL-EUROPE CONFLICT

EDITED BY

H. W. WILSON

Author of "With the Flag to Pretoria"
"Japan's Fight for Freedom" etc.

and

J. A. HAMMERTON

Editor "Harmsworth History of the World"

PROFUSELY ILLUSTRATED

VOLUME 7

LONDON
THE AMALGAMATED PRESS LIMITED
1916

CONTENTS OF VOLUME 7

SPECIAL PHOTOGRAVURE PLATES

THE GREAT WAR

THE STANDARD HISTORY OF THE ALL-EUROPE CONFLICT

VOLUME 7

CHAPTER CXXII.

THE SPLENDID STORY OF THE CANADIANS.

By F. A. McKenzie.

Expectations with which the First Canadian Contingent went to France in February, 1915—Dreary Winter Warfare in the Trenches—Discipline and Soldierly Qualities of the Men—They Take over Part of the Line round Ypres from the French—Ypres in April, 1915, and the Great Bombardment—Germans first use Poison Gas and Rush the French Position—The Canadians at St. Julien—Four Days' Murder—How the Canadians Saved the Situation—General Alderson's Speech to the Troops—The "Princess Pat's" Prove their Quality—The Orchard at La Quinque Rue and "Bexhill"—The Battle of Givenchy: "Stony Mountain," and "Dorchester"—The Canadian Army Corps in 1916—Some Names in the Honours Lists—St. Eloi and the Fighting for the Mine Craters—Hooge—Canadian Trench Journalism—Canadian Philanthropy, Organisation, and Medical Aid—General Hughes—The Spirit of the Canadian People—Rapid Increase of the Army—"Can't We Do More?"—The Canadian Soldier—His Characteristics—Sir Robert Borden's Declaration.

I N February, 1915, when the First Canadian Contingent, after a winter of training on Salisbury Plain, proceeded to France there was universal confidence that it had gone to take part in the great drive that was to hurl the Germans back to the Meuse and back to the Rhine. The only nervousness of the Canadian soldiers was lest they should be too late to share in the decisive battles. A travelling kitchen had been prepared for their general in command, to follow him as he moved forward with his troops from point to point in the "great push." It remained for fifteen months in the same place.

The Canadians were not alone in their belief. It was shared by all ranks of the British Army. Official despatches encouraged it. "Eye - Witness," attached to Headquarters, wrote in mid-April that the feeling that we were growing stronger every day, while the Germans were becoming less strong, was the chief factor responsible for the undoubtedly excellent state of the high spirits of our forces.

[*Official photograph issued by the Press Bureau.*]
CANADIAN LANCE-CORPORAL RECEIVES THE D.C.M.

At this stage of the war we were ignorant of both our own deficiencies and the enemy's resources.

The Canadians immediately found themselves taking part in one of the dreariest and most trying forms of war—the winter occupation of the long lines of trenches. We British understood comparatively little of trench warfare in winter time, and we had to acquire our knowledge at considerable cost. We lacked skilled miners for the necessary tunnelling operations. We were short of searchlights, short of high explosives, and—above all—short of big guns, and without an adequate supply of shells. We understood so little of trench construction that many of our trenches were nothing but long, sodden lines of mud, in which men stood up to their middles hour after hour, sometimes day after day, in the ooze, with the very minimum of protection from the enemy's fire. Our men were not properly clothed for such work, and they lacked even waterproof boots. The result was that disease from the cold—more particularly foot diseases such as trench foot—swept our ranks, and in some

A

THE DUKE OF DEVONSHIRE.
Successor to the Duke of Connaught as Governor-General of Canada.
His appointment was announced on June 28th, 1916.

THE DUCHESS OF DEVONSHIRE.
A charming photograph of her Grace, who before her marriage was Lady
Evelyn Fitzmaurice, daughter of the Marquis of Lansdowne.

cases put out of action over two-fifths of the men of the new battalions within a few days of their arrival at the front.

The enemy had worked out in advance this form of warfare as we had not. The German officers and men in their lines had well-drained and boarded trenches, sometimes even lighted by electricity. They had dug-outs which defied our shells. The Canadians suffered in common with the rest of the British forces from the weeks of work in the sodden and miserable country. They tackled the problem of the trenches, however, with **Canadian resource** great enthusiasm. Canadian doctors, **and spirit** familiar with frost-bite in their own country, were able to devise new means more successful than any yet known for dealing with trench foot. Men from the West, whose ingenuity had been sharpened in earlier years by work in a semi-developed country, started systematically improving their trenches. The Canadians quickly acquired a reputation for having some of the best trenches in the British lines, a reputation which they showed they deserved more and more in the months ahead.

It must be remembered that when the First Contingent of thirty thousand Canadians went to the British front the Canadians were still regarded by many military authorities as a very doubtful factor in war. No one questioned their courage, their willingness, or their ingenuity, but many military men did question if they would show a sufficient sense of discipline to fit themselves into the regular organisation of the British Army without much trouble. They were much better paid than soldiers who enlisted in the United Kingdom; the traditions of the West made for individual independence; and exaggerated stories of the doings of a small section in the camps on Salisbury Plain had been taken to apply to all. In the early weeks of 1915 those who knew what the Canadians were and what they could do found themselves called upon time after time to defend them against foolish

and ill-informed criticism. No one who had seen the work of the Canadians at first hand doubted for a moment but that they would make splendidly good. They were soon to show that the confidence of their friends was more than deserved.

The first experiences of the Canadians in Flanders have already been described in Chapter LIII. in this history. Early in April the Canadians moved up to take over a portion of the lines around Ypres from the French. The British position around Ypres at this time ran from Hill 60 in the south in a big salient running around from near Hollebeke to a point fronting the village of Poelcapelle. From here the French held the line to Steenstraate on the Yser Canal. The big salient, jutting out as it did over five miles in one direction from the city of Ypres, was from a military point of view an exceedingly dangerous and difficult place to hold. The Germans had it hemmed round in a semicircle. They could pour an enfilading fire on many of our positions. Their big guns could bombard Ypres itself. Sir John French had by the utmost gallantry saved Ypres from the enemy in the autumn of 1914, but it still presented a weak point in our lines where the enemy could attack with everything in his favour.

The population of Ypres, who had fled from the city during the first battle, had largely come back again. To the Canadians, as to the **Animation** other British troops in the front trenches **at Ypres** of the salient, Ypres itself at this time appeared like a city of refuge. It is true that the Cloth Hall had been almost destroyed by the purposeless vengefulness of the German gunners and that many parts of the city were in ruins. But the civilian population, hardened by experience of war, had come to treat occasional shell fire almost with indifference. Ypres, despite its ruins, presented during April, 1915, a picture of great animation. The civilian population was chiefly engaged in the work of catering for our men. Numerous tea-shops were running;

amusements were afoot ; baths were open—an unspeakable luxury to men soaked for days with trench mud. Here were warmth, comparative comfort, and dryness. And even the constant procession of the wounded being carried through the streets could not for long dull the cheerfulness of the men resting there.

Some of the Canadians moved out of their former billets north-west of Neuve Chapelle only a few days before the great fight they were soon to take part in. They marched through Poperinghe and through the square of Ypres out along the canal. They remarked on the Cloth Hall, then being used as a hospital. Many of the houses they passed had been repaired, others still had gaping holes from the shells. The boys knew that they were going to a part of the line where they were to have a hard time. They moved through Ypres singing. Some troops stationed in the city itself cheered back at them. "That's right, boys!" they called. "That's the spirit to go into the trenches with." But the stories that reached them as they marched out were not of a kind to encourage high spirits.

"As we came out of the street into the market-place," wrote one Canadian soldier home, "suddenly down the street a Red Cross motor came. By the driver were three poor fellows, two with heads and arms bandaged and a third with trouser legs ripped from the thigh down and showing the discoloured bandage below. Inside the waggon the same sorry sight. They all seemed able to sit up, but were sorely wounded. It brought such a lump to one's throat. Presently along the road in twos and threes came a mournful little procession of men, who were more or less wounded, but still able to walk. I spoke to three of them, and one, a sergeant, gave us some particulars, his trembling lip showing the tremendous strain he had been under. He spoke of ill-made trenches taken over from the French, of the horrors of a night's shelling, of the wounded out there in the No Man's Land between the trenches, being unable to help themselves and no one being able to go to their aid. He

spoke of a temporary shortage of bandages owing to the number of wounded, and still there shone such pluck and courage in his eyes that once again speech was taken away from me, and I was glad to look away and let him talk. I thought of his wounds, and advised him to go and rest now with his chums, and he said good-bye, and the trio moved away." But the Canadian finished up with : "All goes well. We are happy, looking forward to doing good work in the future and the speedy end of this ghastly dream."

On April 18th the German artillery fire began to increase. On the afternoon of April 22nd a hurricane of shells suddenly burst upon Ypres. The people of the place were too accustomed to shells to take notice of a few explosions, but this was beyond anything they had known or dreamed of. Shells came by the dozen, sweeping every street, smashing building after building, killing and wounding people in all directions. Troops were hastily ordered out of barracks into the fields beyond the city. The civilian population started an almost blind rush to escape. Weeks afterwards, when this writer visited Ypres, it was possible to see even then the signs of the sudden panic of the people. In one house the music still stood on the open piano, with the high stool for the pupil and the chair for the teacher close by. Pupil and teacher had

FAREWELL SCENES IN THE DOMINION.
Part of Canada's Second Contingent leaving an inland town to embark at Halifax, Nova Scotia, for the Home Country.

fled out of the room, moved by a common impulse to escape death. In another house a little girl had taken her darling treasure, her doll's perambulator, a few steps from the door and then had to drop and leave it, whether because she herself was killed one could not say. Here were the papers on an open desk in another house. The man had been making up accounts and had stopped midway in his figures. Men, women, and children hurried into the streets. Some big men fought their way, disregarding everybody, down the Rue d'Elverdinghe or down the Rue au Beurre to the open. Mothers clasping their children to their arms, and white with terror, hurried on.

FROM THE OLDEST BRITISH COLONY TO THE FLANDERS LINE.
Newfoundland furnished a quota of splendid fighters. This illustration shows men of the First Regiment embarking on the transport Calgaria in St. John's Harbour.

SHORT SHRIFT FOR ALIEN ENEMIES IN CANADA.
German and Austrian civilian prisoners proceeding under armed guard to the eating-house of the internment camp at Petawawa. The services of these enemy aliens were utilised in road-building and clearing the land.

In these moments nothing that they left behind seemed to matter, whether gold or clothes, or great treasures. Here and there some man or woman burdened him or herself with the first thing they picked up in their rooms, some dainty wear, or the like. But most of them soon dropped it, unwilling to burden themselves with anything. The Canadian Provost-Marshal in the city did his utmost with the men under him to lessen the panic and to shepherd the people into safety, but with the rain of shells ever increasing, with the buildings tumbling into ruins all around, with the heavy detonations shaking even the old Flemish houses, calm was difficult.

Ypres was transformed in less than an hour from a busy, cheerful war city to the home of desolation which it was to remain for many and many a month to come.

One Canadian battalion stationed outside Ypres was having its afternoon sports of that day in its rest camp. The men noticed that the firing around St. Julien was unusually heavy, and some of them, gazing curiously over the fields, saw in the distance a low bank of what they thought was a yellow-greenish haze.

A few minutes later some French transport waggons which had gone slowly up the road came back at a terrific gallop. They were followed by a British motor despatch-rider tearing along, who shouted as he passed that the Germans had broken through the French lines and were using poison gas. Then came hundreds of French Colonial troops hurrying back in frenzied retreat, **The first taste of gas** their faces working spasmodically as though in terrible agony. They were all that were left from the men in the trenches who had been engulfed in the gas. As they hurried by they were gasping and spluttering in their agony. "Save yourselves," called some. "Allemands!" called others. "What a sight there was to behold," wrote one of the Canadian soldiers afterwards, "soldiers, hatless, coatless, without rifles or equipment, men on horses whose traces had been cut—utterly demoralised—and men, women, and children, all carrying packs—some few precious things they had hastily grabbed up. They went flying past, and as the evening came on still they came unceasingly, the old people plodding along

as best they could, and many carrying babes and children. It was awful to see their distress."

Following the heavy bombardment that afternoon the Germans had attacked the French division on the left. Two simultaneous advances had been made east of the Ypres-Staden railway, both preceded by asphyxiating gases. These gases were so virulent and the troops were so unprepared for them that the French division was virtually wiped out of action at a stroke. A new form of death had come, a form so surprising that people at first could not realise what it meant. The smoke blew over the lines. Hundreds of men collapsed as it passed them, and the whole position with its fifty guns had to be abandoned.

As General French pointed out in his subsequent report, the French division could not in the least be blamed for this unfortunate incident. No man could stand up before the smoke. "After all the examples our gallant allies have shown of dogged and tenacious courage in many trying situations in which they have been placed throughout the course of this campaign," wrote General French, "it is quite superfluous for me to dwell on this aspect of the incident, and I would only express my firm conviction that if any troops in the world had been able to hold their trenches in the face of such a treacherous and altogether unexpected onslaught the French division would have stood firm."

The Germans swept on beyond the French trenches. There was a British battery—the 2nd London Heavy—of four 4·7 in. guns in a wood behind the French lines. Survivors told afterwards how the British gunners refused to run away when the Germans came **Germans sweep forward** on. They stood by their guns, fighting with bare fists and with anything they could pick up until almost every man was bayoneted or killed.

The position of the 3rd Canadian Brigade on the left of the British line was very serious. The collapse of the French had left it without any support to one flank, and the Germans were quickly advancing onwards behind its lines. When the Germans occupied the wood there was great danger that the 3rd Canadians would be surrounded and cut off. They quickly readjusted their position, forming themselves into an acute angle, facing the Germans on either side. Every effort was made to hold the village of St. Julien, behind the original brigade lines, a village which quickly became the most important centre of the fighting.

The Canadians were greatly outnumbered. There were at least four divisions attacking them. The Germans continued to use poison gas. The Canadians held on, and hastily devised methods to enable them to resist it. Men took off their socks, tore pieces off their shirts, dipped them in whatever liquid they could obtain, bound them around their faces so as to cover their noses, and fought on. The Germans were supported by a very heavy fire of artillery. The British artillery was weak in numbers and had inadequate shell supplies. Our men fought under almost every disadvantage.

That night the road to Ypres lay open to the Germans. The 3rd Canadian Brigade was desperately holding its own in the position fronting St. Julien. The 2nd Brigade was closely engaged to the right. The 1st Brigade in

General Sir Sam Hughes congratulating officers of the Canadian Contingent stationed at Shorncliffe.

Reviewing Canadian troops in England. General Sir Sam Hughes (second figure from the right).

March past of Maple Leaf men before General Hughes, who is seen again in the third illustration standing underneath the Union Jack.

CANADIAN TROOPS UNDERGO INSPECTION BY GENERAL HUGHES AT SHORNCLIFFE.

forward and was in the front ranks of the charge, armed only with a walking-stick. They told, too, how the colonels led their men foremost in the fighting. Most of these soldiers here saw close fighting for the first time. Old British Army men who were with them could not speak too highly of them. "They went up like old-timers," said one. "They were steady, calm, and dependable. It was something to be proud of."

The Canadians recaptured the woods. From there they attempted to go still farther. They now found themselves out in the open, too much weakened to continue the attack. They were unsupported on the flank, and the Germans were **German advance held up** developing a strong advance there. It was impossible for them to bring back the guns, which were virtually destroyed, and a little later they had to fall back from the wood into the trenches, where they waited all day. But they had done their work. They had held up the German advance.

When daylight broke next morning the Canadians everywhere could see that they were faced by almost overwhelming forces of the enemy. "The most surprising thing," said one of the men afterwards, "was the terrific numbers of German troops that came on like a swarm of bees. We shot them down, line after line, but all our firing seemed to make no difference to their numbers. It was as though when they fell each sprang up again. There were times when there were fifty to one against us on particular points. Ten to one seemed the common rule."

The Germans evidently thought that they still had French Colonial troops against them, and they were apparently somewhat surprised when the Canadians got among them once or

A SERGEANTS' MESS.
Meal-time outside wood-constructed billets in France. One Canadian is holding a "mascot."

reserve was hurrying up to the support of the others. Why the Germans did not move straight in and occupy the place that night has never yet been explained. It, however, was one of the most striking examples this war afforded of how, time after time, the Germans for the moment exhausted their effort in the first part of their push and remained passive when the fruits of victory were almost within their grasp.

The Canadians threw themselves into the gap. They were determined to get back the guns, and during the night two battalions, the 16th and the 10th, moved out to attack. The 10th were Western Canadians, and the 16th were the Canadian Scottish. They marched through the darkness of the countryside under a heavy bombardment from shrapnel and "Jack Johnsons." When, as they believed, they were in the neighbourhood of St. Julien they were told that the Germans were holding the wood some hundreds of yards away. They crept on in the darkness. They first attacked a hedge barricaded with barbed-wire, which they captured. The Germans now were concentrating machine-guns on them.

Captain MacGregor's heroism Nevertheless, after pausing to gather strength, they forced their way through the hedge and made straight for the wood, about a hundred yards off. Men fell like flies, but still the Canadians kept on. The Highlanders, shouting, yelling, triumphant, reached the German position. The German soldiers, after firing a volley, tried to retire. The Highlanders were too quick for them. Now came a brief spell of deadly bayonet work. Here was ample occasion for great heroism. The soldiers loved to tell afterwards how Captain MacGregor, their paymaster, a non-combatant officer, left his books, joined the battalion as it went

USE OF THE GRENADE.
Officer in charge of a Canadian bombing-party about to fire a rifle-grenade.

NEWS FROM LONDON.
Canadian infantrymen in a muddy trench reading the London papers for news of the war.

twice with their bayonets. On the Friday morning, noting the steady attempt of the Germans to move farther and farther to the left and so completely outflank the Canadians, a fresh counter-attack was resolved upon. Two Ontario battalions, the 1st and the 4th of the 1st Brigade, which had now come up from reserve, were given the post of honour, a British regiment, the Middlesex, acting as their support.

The attack seemed quite hopeless. The Canadians were at this point a considerable distance from **Jokes under** the Germans, with about eight hundred or **murderous fire** nine hundred yards of absolutely open ground to go over. The German trenches were on a slope and there was no shelter whatever between the attacking troops and them. As the Canadians rushed forward the Germans raked them with machine-gun and rifle fire. Men started dropping before the 4th Battalion got properly started. The advance was made in short rushes, two sections at a time. There was no cheering, no shouting, nothing but whispered words of command. The troops made short charges down a ravine and up a slope, dropping to the ground after each rush. There was no hesitation, no bravado, no hanging back. The machine-guns swept over the glacis. The German gunners timed their shrapnel so as to burst over the ranks. The German companies lining the trenches picked out their men. The British artillery did all it could to cover the advance, pouring shrapnel fire on the hill crest where the Germans lay dug in. Sometimes, when a heavier blast of fire than usual struck our ranks, the men joked together. "Say, boys, there seems to be a war on here," one remarked when things were hottest.

"Believe me, if hell is anything like Friday, I am

ON THE TRENCH SEAT.
More types of Britons in Flanders. A restful snapshot from the region of strife.

for reforming," wrote one young soldier to his family afterwards. "How I lasted as long as I did, I hardly know, as at every rush the fellow next me 'copped it.' Once, when we were lying down, the man next to me got it square through the head. Only one sergeant and four men, including myself, out of our platoon got up to within two hundred yards of the trench, when the fellow next me was hit in the arm. I sat up beside him to get out his bandage to tie him up, when I got hit myself through the back, and the next fellow got it in the shoulder. Only two were left. I suppose they got it later." His experience was typical.

Lieutenant-Colonel Burchill led the 4th Battalion. He carried nothing but a light cane. He moved ahead of his men almost as though on parade, cheering, inspiring—I was going to say encouraging—them, but they needed no encouragement. In six hours the men, or what were left of them, advanced about seven or eight hundred yards, finally reaching to within **Colonel Burchill** a hundred yards of the German trench. **avenged** Then Colonel Burchill fell dead at the head of his battalion. That was the last touch. His soldiers, stung to fury by the loss of their beloved commander, made one final effort to avenge him. They flung themselves through the last hundred yards, despite the direct rifle and machine-gun fire. How a single man got through it is scarcely possible to understand, for by all the laws of war every one should have been wiped out long before. Possibly the sight of the yelling, cheering, infuriated men shook the nerves of the Germans, as well it might. The Canadians reached the trench and swept through it like fury, bayoneting, shooting, overcoming every German there.

A TRIO OF "TROGLODYTES."
Corner of a British trench along the first line, where men grew accustomed to the life of cave-dwellers.

IN WINTER KIT.
Three Canadian soldiers, during the work of consolidating their position, pause to glance at the photographer.

WINNIPEG RESERVE BATTALION BIVOUACKED IN A PLEASANTLY WOODED CORNER OF THE WESTERN FRONT.   (*Canadian official photograph.*)

The 4th Battalion had won, but at a great price. It was reported at the time that only one officer and twenty-five men were left. The colonel, the adjutant, and several officers were killed outright. But the 4th had covered itself with eternal glory.

Many of the officers and men afterwards tried to describe the scenes during these fierce days. "It was just hell," said more than one tersely, unable to find adequate words for it. "How anyone came out of those days, especially April 23rd, 24th, and 25th, can only be ascribed to a merciful Providence," wrote General Mercer, himself to be lost in the fighting a little over a year later in that very Ypres salient. "Shells fell like rain, and machine-gun and rifle fire was almost incessant, while gas bombs and trench gas appliances liberating poison fumes blinded and rendered the strongest as helpless as little children."

"It required all one's self-possession to keep control and give encouragement," wrote Colonel Rennie, who gallantly led the 3rd Battalion in some of the hardest fighting. "The days were bad enough, but the nights were the worst. So much work to be done, and so few hours in which to do it. The men all behaved splendidly. Not a man faltered where movements under fire had to be made, and the cheerfulness and willingness to share the work of relief to the suffering of other (British) battalions was marked, and filled me with pride."

"It would be useless to try to describe in detail," wrote another. "It was four days of murder, that's all it was."

The 7th Battalion, from British Columbia, was in rest billets behind the village of St. Julien when the fighting broke out. It promptly moved up in support of the 3rd Brigade, arriving under heavy artillery fire and digging itself in, in a position just on the right of the road to St. Julien. It was soon ordered to retire, and proceeded to take up another position some distance away on the right. Next day it moved on again, and dug itself in in a mangold field under heavy rifle fire, which, however, did very little harm, owing to the enemy being over the crest of the hill. Then, shortly after daybreak on the morning of the 23rd, it received orders to double across the road and line the cross-roads. A German aeroplane, flying very low, gave signals by dropping smoke bombs. These apparently informed the German artillery of the British Columbians' position. "It seemed as though Hades had broken loose," one soldier told me afterwards. "It also seemed as if nothing could live in this terrific artillery fire, shells dropping closely all around us, but fortunately slightly to our rear. Notwithstanding the terrific din, we did not suffer such very heavy losses. We stayed in that position until dusk."

Gallant rescue under fire

That afternoon the commander of the regiment, Colonel Hart McHarg, a Vancouver lawyer, Major Odlum, a Vancouver newspaper proprietor—who was soon to make a brilliant record as a soldier—and Lieutenant Mathewson, of the Canadian Engineers, moved out to reconnoitre the ground, in order that they might decide on the position of fresh trenches. They suddenly found themselves within a hundred yards of a large body of German infantry, who could see them quite plainly. They at once threw themselves on the ground. The colonel and major rolled into a shell-hole and the junior officer rolled into a ditch, while the Germans opened rapid fire upon them. The colonel was shot, and Major Odlum, leaving the lieutenant to look after him, raced away for medical aid, running uphill under fire. The doctor and a sergeant of the Red Cross came back with him. Captain Gibson and Sergeant J. Dryden their names were. They deserve to be named. They went under heavy fire right to the shell-hole and removed the colonel into the ditch. Later on he was carried back to Battalion Headquarters and to hospital, only, however, to die there a few hours later. The battalion found itself in a very perilous position. It had the enemy on two sides of it, and its ranks were cut down to about one hundred men. It had eventually to fall back.

These words only faintly convey a blurred impression of its experiences. Let us give what actually happened in the words of one of its own soldiers, who was wounded and made prisoner there and who described the scene when he returned home to England.

7th Battalion's experiences

We were told that our colonel had been shot through the breast and was not expected to live, and had received his wound a considerable distance in advance of our position where he had gone to reconnoitre. We felt his loss very keenly, for he was a very brave man.

We—No. 4 Company—moved across the road about 7 o'clock that evening, and dug ourselves in by platoons. We were told that the enemy was only a short distance away from us, and we must hold this position at all costs. We made ourselves as strong as possible, placed barbed-wire in front, and sent out patrols. Our task was completed shortly before dawn and then we took some rest. On the extreme right of the trench of No. 4 Company was our machine-gun section, in charge of Sergeant Peerless, who won the D.C.M. for his splendid work. Shortly after dawn the enemy aircraft again came over us and dropped some more smoke bombs, giving the range of our position to the German guns. They proceeded to open up an exceptionally heavy bombardment. It seemed as though they must have had hundreds and hundreds of guns. I asked my officer, Captain Haynes, if there were any orders to retire as yet. His reply was, "Our orders are to hold the trench at all costs." Word came from No. 3 Company to keep a sharp look-out to the left, and looking over the trench I noticed that quite a number of Germans were coming up on our left flank. These men were promptly cut down by our machine-gun, which was being fired by Private Ross. Ross showed special bravery, sticking to his gun when it seemed that he could not live owing to the number of rifle bullets whizzing past his head.

poor fellow would get hit and quietly slide to the bottom of the trench we could hear his mates say, "Poor old Harry is done." In the next instant the mate would be asking for a cigarette, and swearing because his lighter would not work. One young fellow, who had the evening before received a large cake from home, calmly proceeded to cut up the cake and pass it around among his comrades.

No. 3 Company sent time after time for reinforcements. "Send us reinforcements, we are hard pressed," came the message. "Send us someone to take charge. All our officers and non-coms. have been killed," word came a little later. Captain Haynes turned to me and ordered me to take the two sections of my platoon across the road to reinforce No. 3 Company. The enemy had three machine-guns playing on this part of the road, making it very difficult to get across. We rushed over, but lost a number of men in doing so. The men seemed to be dropping like leaves off a tree. I shall never forget one moment shortly after I had got across the road and laid down, one fellow turned to me as he was about to lie down by my side, placed his hand on his breast and gently sank down. I saw blood trickling from his lips. He said, "I think I am hit." I told him to cheer up, we would get back shortly. "Do

ARRIVAL IN THE HOME COUNTRY.
Men from Calgary marching with full kit along the road leading from Plymouth.

you think I have done my duty?" he asked. "Why, of course you have." He then proceeded to give me a message for his mother. He must have been badly hit, for he died with that word on his lips—"Mother."

After we had lined this hedge we proceeded to cross the road and get up on the trench beyond. We were flanked both right and left, and the Germans were playing machine-guns on us from an enfilading position. We had now but very little ammunition left, and the enemy were preparing to make a bayonet charge. We gathered all the ammunition we could find from the dead men lying around and fired a volley into them just as they were about to make their charge. They recoiled for the moment, then they seemed to come on in thousands. They seemed to spring up from everywhere. "Are we ever going to retire?" I heard one man ask. His chum intent on firing, paused and replied, "To hell, you say."

A KHAKI ASSEMBLY AT TORONTO UNIVERSITY.
One thousand five hundred members of the Canadian Officers Training Corps on their way to the Convocation Hall of the Toronto University.

I told him that he had better keep under cover or he would get hit. "What the hell are we here for but to get hit," he answered. I do not know what has become of him, but if any man deserved a decoration for bravery Ross was that man.

Their artillery seemed to be trying very hard to locate our machine-gun. Every minute a shell would break in the near vicinity, covering us with a mud bath. Shells were clipping off huge big trees, and these were falling across the road and across our trench. When things were hottest some of the boys would shout, "Are we downhearted?" The remainder would reply, "No." Everyone wanted to know when we were going to get at them with the knives. "I believe we'll have to give these sausage-eaters a licking before we are through," one lad would joke with another. Then as some

Some Turcos were trying to make their way across the open space to our rear. I crossed the trench for a moment to direct them. Forgetting where I was, I stood in front of a huge gap made by a shell in a hedge.

Someone who had been wounded and was lying on the ground, said, "Don't stand there, old chap, six men have been killed there already." He had hardly finished the words when I received five bullets from that machine-gun in my left arm, and till I glanced at my arm and saw the streams of blood coming out I could hardly realise that I had been hit. I felt a weakness coming over me, and felt myself falling. The next thing I remember was being pulled by soldiers under cover of the hedge. I looked up and found one of the signallers in my company bending over me to give me a drink.

B

REST TIME BEHIND THE RAMPARTS.
Three typical Maple Leaf men whose nonchalant attitudes and genial expressions are typical of the spirits of Canadians on active service.

against their position. A machine-gun had been sent up, and was reported to have made deep lanes in the ranks of the enemy. The other troops could see considerable forces moving on these trenches, but it was not possible to send up support in time to render aid when most urgently required. "You must hang on," the message was sent to the major. "We are holding on very nicely," he replied. "Every time the enemy starts something he goes back before he comes close. But we have been lucky, as the enemy's artillery has left us alone fairly well." His position grew more and more critical. The Germans continued to attack in considerable numbers, moving from north to south on St. Julien. His flank was being turned. Soon he had to report that the enemy had secured all the front trenches in St. Julien. He suggested that they should drop back on their right flank and hang on. "Don't lose touch with St. Julien," came the instructions to him. "Hang on, a counter-attack is being made on your right."

Hard pressed at St. Julien

To quote from a Canadian description published at the time:

At two o'clock, however, it was realised that the gallant C and B Companies had done all that was humanly possible to stop the onrush of the Germans. With the air east of St. Julien laden with poison gases and the 3rd Brigade compelled for the time being to turn its left flank, Major Kirkpatrick's body of men was in a precarious position. He was, therefore, instructed to fall back to the newly-formed General Headquarters line, about twelve hundred yards to his rear. When the order to retire was received the platoon on the right (nearest St. Julien and the most advanced) was first withdrawn. The enemy concentrated his

Here the man lost consciousness. The next thing he remembered was the Germans swarming over the parapets by hundreds, yelling like fiends. He saw several slightly wounded men, who had put up their hands in the air as a token of surrender, being bayoneted by German soldiers. He himself had a narrow escape of instant death as he lay there helpless, and had many hard experiences before he was taken back.

The 3rd Battalion, the Toronto regiment, played a splendid part in the fighting. It was in rest camp with the remainder of the 1st Infantry Brigade when the fighting started, and it hurried up that night to assist. At four o'clock on Friday morning the order was received by telephone to send two companies in haste to hold the line from the left of St. Julien to the wood a thousand yards to the west. Major Kirkpatrick moved out in command of the men. Then the remaining companies and machine-gun detachment were called upon to support the 2nd Battalion of the Buffs in an attack. Major Kirkpatrick lost rather heavily in moving up. The Germans were found to be occupying the north end of the wood, considerably reinforced. The British artillery opened fire on them. Major Kirkpatrick dug in, held his position, and fought hour after hour, almost exhausting his supply of ammunition. Fresh supplies were sent up to him.

Early on the Saturday morning the Germans opened a heavy bombardment on the 3rd Brigade Headquarters. This brigade lost so heavily that it was compelled to fall back from St. Julien east of the town. It was a case where every man was wanted, and even the bandsmen and orderlies of the Headquarters Staff were ordered to the trenches. The falling back of the 3rd Brigade left Major Kirkpatrick and his men almost isolated. The Germans noticing this, launched attack after attack

Toronto men splendid

READY FOR GERMANS—AND GAS.
Impression of a Canadian in full fighting kit, including the respirator and rifle, to which is affixed an unusually long bayonet.

fire on the trench to prevent the movement, with the result that a number were wounded while getting out of the trench, and only a few came away. Only two reached Headquarters unhurt. Hard pressed as never men were before, the survivors of the two companies endeavoured to carry out the order of the retirement, but they were cut off.

Here let the official report take up the story. "From the trenches on the left could be seen a tremendous force moving on the trenches held by the two companies of the 3rd Battalion, under Major Kirkpatrick. But the reinforcing brigade was not near enough to render aid when most urgently required. No further report has been received from Major Kirkpatrick as to the position of himself or his command." The major and several of his officers were captured and taken as prisoners of war to Germany.

How Major McCuaig held on To attempt to tell the story of all the heroic deeds in this great fight is impossible. Every battalion that was engaged distinguished itself. All Canada rang with the story of Major McCuaig, who took charge of the Royal Highlanders of Montreal when other officers were shot, and held an important position against enormously superior German forces from the afternoon of the 22nd until the morning of the 23rd. His communications were cut, and he was without artillery support. Had the enemy advanced they must have overwhelmed him. By sheer bluff he held on, and eventually, when daylight showed the Germans his weakness, got his men away, protecting their retirement by heavy machine-gun fire. He even carried his wounded off. He himself waited with the rearguard to see the last man

A VARIANT TO OFFICIAL VICTUALS.
Canadian, in the interval of sniping Boches, secures a rabbit by way of an additional item to the front-line menu.

CLEAN TOWELS FOR CLEAN FIGHTERS.
Going up to "Dug-out Town" with a welcome load of towels, which had been hung out to dry in the camp laundry.

back in safety, and while he was thus waiting he was shot down and made a prisoner.

The 3rd Brigade, which had so brilliantly held the left of the position, was forced steadily back by the overwhelming nature of the sustained German attacks. It held on to each point to the last possible moment. Battalion after battalion was wiped out. Had we had adequate artillery fire, even now the situation might have been saved. But it was impossible for the Canadians to continue for many days with enemy shells raining on every spot they held and with our heavy guns few and inadequate. When the 3rd Brigade retired, the 2nd Brigade, to the right, now found its position seriously threatened. By Sunday, as already told, the village of St. Julien was in German hands. Fresh troops were now hurrying up. Two British brigades came to the help of the Canadians, and attempted by a brilliant counter-offensive to save the village. The 2nd Brigade, exposed to the full fury of the German attack, had in turn to repeat many of the experiences of the 3rd Brigade. **Canadians save Ypres** In the end it had to take up a fresh line. Here the troops, worn out by their days and nights of ceaseless fighting, were gradually relieved by fresh regiments coming up from the British front, and on the Wednesday they moved back to billets in the rear. The brigades had suffered heavily. The 3rd Brigade had battalions almost wiped out. The 2nd Brigade was little more than a quarter of its original strength. The 1st Brigade had paid a very heavy score; but the Canadians had done their work. They had saved Ypres. It is not too much to say they had saved the whole British position in the north, and they had given the Empire a story of great heroism that will be told to rising generations as long as Britain endures.

When the details of the great battle became known the whole Empire was swept with a wave of mixed admiration

FROM THE PRAIRIE TO THE FIELD OF WAR.

Canadian scout on duty in a wood. One who brought his experience of prairie life to the task of defeating the Hun.

and grief. Canada had lost the very pick of her young manhood. Hundreds of her best families were in mourning. Every great city was in mourning. But for every man who fell, ten promptly volunteered, and recruiting throughout the Dominion received an impetus which lasted for many months to come. In London a memorial service was held at St. Paul's, which gave the British people an opportunity, of which they gladly availed themselves, to show their feelings. In the Army it was felt that the Canadian soldier had won for all time his right to an honoured place in British fighting ranks. Sir John French, in an official message, made full acknowledgment of the Canadians' service, declaring that "the Canadians saved the situation." General Alderson, the commander of the Canadian Division, in a speech to the troops, said:

I tell you truly that my heart is so full that I hardly know how to speak to you. It is full of two feelings—the first being sorrow for the loss of those comrades of ours who have gone; and the second, pride in what the 1st Canadian Division has done.

General Alderson's fine tribute As regards our comrades who have lost their lives—let us speak of them with our caps off—my faith in the Almighty is such that I am perfectly sure that when men die, as they have died, doing their duty and fighting for their country, for the Empire, and to save the situation for others—in fact, have *died for their friends*—no matter what their past lives have been, no matter what they have done that they ought not to have done (as all of us do), I am perfectly sure that the Almighty takes them and looks after them at once. Lads, we cannot leave them better than like that.

Now I feel that we may, without any false pride, think a little of what the Division has done during the past few days.

I would first of all tell you that I have never been so proud of anything in my life as I am of my armlet with "Canada" on it. I thank you, and congratulate you from the bottom of my heart, for the part each one of you has taken in giving me this feeling of pride.

I think it is possible that all of you do not quite realise that, if we had retired on the evening of April 22nd—when our allies fell back before the gas and left our left flank quite open—the whole of the 27th and 28th Divisions would probably have been cut off. Certainly they would not have got away a gun or a vehicle of any sort, and probably not more than half the infantry would have escaped.

This is what our Commander-in-Chief meant when he telegraphed as he did, that "the Canadians saved the situation." My lads, if ever men had a right to be proud in this world you have.

I know my military history pretty well, and I cannot think of an instance, especially when the cleverness and determination of the enemy is taken into account, in which troops were placed in such a difficult position; nor can I think of an instance in which so much depended on the standing fast of one division.

You will remember that the last time I spoke to you, just before you went into the trenches at Sailly, now over two months ago, I told you about my old regiment—the Royal West Kents—having gained a reputation for never budging from their trenches, no matter how they were attacked. I said then that I was quite sure that, in a short time, the army out here would be saying the same of you.

I little thought—none of us thought—how soon those words would come true. But now, to-day, not only the army out here, but all Canada, all Britain, and all the Empire are saying that you, too, stand fast.

There is one more word I would say to you before I stop. You have made a reputation second to none in this war; but, remember, no man can live on his reputation. He must keep on adding to it. And I feel just as sure that you will do so as I did two months ago, when I told you that I knew you would make a reputation when the opportunity came.

I am now going to shake hands with your officers, and as I do so, I want you to feel that I am shaking hands with each of you, as I would actually do if time permitted.

A few days after the attenuated ranks of the First Contingent had reached their rest camp, the Canadian regiment at that time outside the contingent, Princess Patricia's Light Infantry, was called **Ordeal of the** upon to give full proof of what it could **"Princess Pat's"** do. The "Princess Pat's," as they were commonly called, was a regiment specially raised at the entire cost of Mr. Hamilton Gault, a Canadian millionaire, who himself became a major in the corps. It consisted at first almost wholly of old soldiers of the British Army, and it was its boast that more men in it had seen actual war service previous to this war than perhaps any other British regiment. The Patricia's were in barracks at Ypres, in mid-April, when the Germans began shelling the town with their heavy guns. They were moved to a wood to the north-east, and held the line there day after day against the German advance, the Germans attempting to drive them farther to the right at this point and to cut them off from the Canadian front.

During the heavy attack upon the remainder of the Canadian lines they were mainly called upon to hold their trenches, under almost continuous shell fire. Their turn for more active work was soon to come. On the night of May 6th the battalion, after a few days of duty as reserve, relieved the King's Shropshire Light Infantry in the trenches. Early next morning a tremendous bombardment opened out on it. The Germans began at 4.30 with some ranging shells. An hour later the real bombardment began. Seventy-eight heavy guns kept up a continuous fire from three different sides, with high explosives, upon the section. The guns enfiladed the Patricia's lines. By six in the morning every telephone wire was cut and all direct communication with other parts of the line broken. The Patricia's, seeing their desperate state, called every man to the trenches, from the cooks to the orderlies. Soon the lines scarce deserved the name of trenches, for the German shells had flattened them out. There was nothing to do but to lie still in the craters and shell-holes and wait. Then the Germans came out and tried to storm the Patricia's position. They expected no resistance. They were soon undeceived, for the men who were left opened a steady rifle fire on the advancing lines and swept the enemy back. Time after time the enemy tried to come on. Time after time the ever-dwindling band of Patricia's met them firmly.

The second advance was attempted at nine o'clock in the morning. Most of the Germans who set out fell, and those not shot down staggered under the heavy Canadian fire, reeled, broke, and hastily retreated.

Machine-guns were buried by the exploding shells; men dug them out again. Officers and soldiers who were shot

After Langemarck, April, 1915: Playing the Canadian Scottish through Ypres.

Lieutenant Campbell and Private Vincent, Canadians, at "Stony Mountain," May, 1915.

How Private Smith, Ontario, took bombs to his comrades at "Stony Mountain."

Canadians cheered, after their great stand at St. Julien, April, 1915, by the relieving West Kents.

continued to fight on and do their work after their wounds had been bandaged up. By noon the small-arms ammunition was beginning to run short. There were many ready to go over the shell-covered ground behind the trenches to bring fresh ammunition back. By early in the afternoon less than two hundred men were left. By now the Rifle Brigade arrived to help the Patricia's. They needed it. Almost every officer had been shot or wounded. There was only a subaltern in command. The Patricia's were almost wiped out. They had gone into the fight six hundred and thirty-five strong; they moved back to the reserve trenches that afternoon with only one hundred and fifty left. It is worth noting that the officer who commanded them as they marched back was Lieutenant Papineau, descendant of the famous Canadian rebel, himself living evidence that in Canada all races and all sections were now one for the Empire.

"It was slaughter," said one of the surviving officers, when afterwards describing the scene. "But we Patricia's stood firm throughout. We held our lines."

Three Canadian V.C.'s Three Canadians received the Victoria Cross for the deeds during the Ypres battle, and seventy other Canadian officers and men were decorated on the recommendation of Sir John French. Captain Francis Scrymgeour, of the Army Medical section, a son of the Principal of the Montreal Presbyterian College, was given the cross for heroism. On April 25th he was in charge of a dressing-station for the wounded that was being heavily shelled. He directed the removal of the wounded with great coolness, and personally carried a badly wounded officer to a stable. He attempted to reach a safer place, but found this impossible, and remained with the officer, facing a terrible shell fire for several hours until assistance came. Colour-Sergeant Hall, the second of the three, made two attempts to aid a wounded man near Ypres on April 24th, though under heavy fire. He dragged a British soldier to within fifteen yards of the British trenches on the first attempt, and called for help. When aid was not forthcoming he stooped to lift the wounded man, and was himself shot in the head and mortally wounded. Lance-Corporal Fisher was only nineteen years old at the time of the battle. He was attending the engineering school at the McGill University when the war began, and was well known in college athletics as a football and hockey player, playing in University teams in the Intercollegiate Rugby and Hockey Leagues. He was in reserve at St. Julien, and when the French retreat began he brought up a gun and covered the retirement of a battery of heavy guns. He then borrowed four machine-guns and reinforced the 14th Battalion by a deadly fire, enabling it to retake a trench. He set up a gun to protect another machine-gun section which was being shelled, and enabled it to retire safely. He was shot through the heart while working his gun.

If the Germans thought that they had eliminated the Canadians by the fighting around Ypres, they were soon to find their mistake. The skeleton battalions were reinforced by heavy drafts from the Canadian troops under training in England. On May 17th the battalions again took up their position at the front, the division being moved into the First Corps area, under Sir Douglas Haig. The Canadians found themselves face to face with an orchard held and entrenched by the Germans. They had a small post in front of La Quinque Rue, which the Canadians captured on the night of the 19th and 20th.

The Canadian Scottish on that night crept up to a deserted house close to the German lines and occupied it with a garrison of thirty men and two machine-guns. This was done so quietly that the Germans evidently had no inkling of what had happened. Our artillery directed a heavy fire upon the enemy position in the orchard, and the Germans replied. But although they maintained a continuous fire against the Canadian lines, the house near them with the troops in it was left untouched all the next

CLEARING UP DEBRIS ON THE BATTLEFIELD.
Canadian soldier shovelling debris into an improvised incinerator erected just behind the foremost line in Flanders.

day. Early in the evening our artillery fire suddenly ceased, and two companies of the 16th Canadians rushed out of their trenches on the Germans. Simultaneously the two machine-guns in the house opened out. The enemy greeted our advance with a very heavy fire. Our men kept on unflinchingly. Some officers of the Coldstream Guards near by, who watched the move, paid the Canadians the highest compliment they could. "Short of the Guards," they said, "we would rather have the Canadians behind us in a hard fight than anyone else."

The Canadians reached the edge of the orchard. Here they came upon a deep ditch with a hedge, well protected with barbed-wire at the opposite side. They plunged through the ditch and made for some broken points in the hedge, where they got across. Soon they were in the orchard itself. They went through it at one great rush. The Germans occupied a formidable position twice as strong as our own men. They were hopelessly defeated, and in the end the orchard remained in our hands. A **Progress at La Quinque Rue** number of prisoners and some machine-guns were captured, and the German line was pushed considerably back. The Canadian losses were naturally heavy, but the result of Festubert gave great satisfaction to the whole division.

The troops were justified in some self-congratulation. To advance in broad daylight on an enemy position, to rush it under the fire of modern rifles and machine-guns, and to force a way over open ground through a ditch and through barbed-wire entanglements held by a stronger foe was a high military exploit.

Doubtless the success of our troops was due to good discipline, to great rapidity of movement, and to the exact timing of artillery fire which continued to the last possible moment. But, above all, it was due to the high temper of the men, eager to avenge recent losses.

Another attempt was made about the same time to capture a German position near by, known as "Bexhill." This was not at first a success, the machine-gun fire of the enemy being so overwhelming that the companies which tried to face it on the left were practically wiped out. Our men on the right, however, did succeed in reaching the enemy's trench lines to the south of the position, and drove them four hundred paces down the trench, there building a barricade to hold what they had won.

The attack on "Bexhill" was renewed on May 23rd. This time part of "Bexhill" was taken after a very brave advance. The attack was renewed on the following day with strengthened forces, and now succeeded. "Bexhill" had cost us dearly. When it was in our hands it was found that it was very difficult and costly to hold. The German positions around us were such that it was impossible to make further progress. Our men were exposed to an exceedingly galling fire. Several days of heavy fighting followed here. One battalion alone was under continuous fire for ten days and eleven nights.

On May 31st, in the language of the official report, "the Canadian Division was withdrawn from the territory it had seized from the enemy and moved to the extreme south of the British line."

In June there came another outstanding fight in which the Canadians took a prominent part—the Battle of Givenchy. Sir John French in his official report dismisses the matter very briefly, saying that, "By an attack delivered on the evening of June 15th, after a prolonged bombardment, the 1st Canadian Brigade obtained possession of the German front-line trenches, but were unable to retain them owing to their flanks being too much exposed."

The 7th British Division was ordered to make a frontal attack on a strong enemy position known as "Stony Mountain," and the 1st Battalion, from Ontario, commanded by Lieut.-Colonel Hill, was directed to secure the lines of German trenches stretching from "Stony Mountain" to another German position known as "Dorchester." The Ontario troops were reinforced by men from the Edmonton Fusiliers. The Canadians knew some hours before that they were picked for this dangerous advance, and waited in their trenches, eager for the onslaught. Two **The Battle of Givenchy** 18-pounder guns were planted in their own front trench, and played havoc in the German ranks for a quarter of an hour before the advance began. "We could see portions of their trenches falling in and accoutrements flung in the air," said some of the men when describing the scene afterwards. Two minutes before the hour fixed for the advance a mine exploded under the first German trench. As the débris and dust were still in the air, the Canadians leapt from their trenches and rushed straight across the seventy yards between them and the enemy. The German guns fired among them, but nothing could stop them. They had agreed on a battle-cry, "Gas devils!" and they hurled the words out in bitter shouts as they rushed along. The Germans fired on the Canadians until they were quite near; then some tried to escape while others remained, and as the Canadians jumped into the trenches threw their arms up with the call of "Kamerades!" The trench was soon in our hands. The Germans now concentrated their artillery fire on this captured front trench. From it the

ARRIVAL OF STRETCHER CASES AT ST. CLOUD.

Arrival of a wounded soldier at the Hippodrome, St. Cloud, in France, which was converted into a hospital for Canadians. Many of the most distinguished medical men in the Dominion abandoned private practice to serve with the troops abroad. Circle: On June 22nd, 1916, the King invested Sister D. E. Winter and Sister M. K. Lambkin, Canadians, with the Royal Red Cross conferred upon them in the Birthday Honours List.

WELL-EARNED REST.
Canadians resting in the lovely grounds of the Massey-Harris Convalescent Home at Dulwich.

Canadians rushed the second trench and captured it. The German fire grew heavier and heavier, and our men in the trenches attempted in vain to secure some shelter for themselves. Their supply of bombs ran short, and one lad, Private Smith, son of a Methodist minister of Southampton, Ontario, volunteered to go back for some more. He went back singing, was caught by a mine explosion and buried. He dug himself out, gathered a number of bombs from dead and wounded bomb-throwers around him, and returned to the second trench with them. He repeated this five times. It is said that the fire was so hot that several times he could not get into the trenches of the men who needed them most, and had to lie down and toss the bombs to them. But even with the work of such as Smith, enough bombs could not be had. Men who tried to bring them up were nearly all of them killed. The British advance had been held up by the strength of "Stony Mountain." The Canadians held their position as long as they could, but in the end had to go back.

From division to army corps
From the Battle of Givenchy for many weary months to come the Canadian troops now found themselves engaged in the routine of what was virtually siege warfare. It was their business to hold a section—an ever-growing section—of the British lines, to keep the enemy engaged, to prevent surprises, and wherever possible to surprise the enemy. The one original division grew, as further reinforcements were sent to the front after training in England, to a Canadian army corps.

By early in 1916 the Canadian Army Corps consisted of three divisions, with General Sir E. A. H. Alderson in command. The 1st Division was under Major-General Currie, and its three brigades were commanded by Brigadier-Generals Garnet Hughes, Lipsett, and Leckie. This division included the 1st, 2nd, and 3rd Brigades. The 2nd Division was under Major-General Turner, V.C., and his brigadiers were Generals Rennie, David Watson, and Kitchen. The 3rd Division, with the 7th, 8th, and 9th Brigades, was under Major-General Mercer, with Brigadier-Generals John Macdonald, Victor Williams, and Hill under

SHEARING SHEEP WITHIN SIGHT OF ST. PAUL'S.
In 1916 the Massey-Harris Company, a prominent Canadian business organisation, presented and maintained an estate on the southern heights of London, as a Convalescent Home for wounded Canadians.

him. While the supreme command of the Canadian Army Corps was given to a general of the Imperial Army, the divisions were all placed under Canadians, and the brigadiers were in nearly every case Canadians. These officers were drawn from the most varied ranks of civilian life. General Turner, who had won his V.C. in the Boer War, and who proved time after time at the front his splendid abilities as a military leader, was in times of peace a wholesale grocer in Quebec ; Garnet Hughes, brother of the Canadian Minister of Militia, was a railway engineer ; David Watson was a newspaper proprietor ; Mercer was a lawyer.

What was true of the generals was equally true of other ranks. The officers were, as a rule, business men, lawyers, engineers, bank managers, and the like "Look for officers among those who are able to handle men well in their own business," was the general principle. **Business men as officers** "They will be able to handle men well in the field.' The 39th Infantry Battalion afforded a typical example of this. When this battalion arrived in England the officer commanding was a lawyer. The second in command was a retired business man. One major was a financier, two were farmers, one a builder, and one an express agent. One captain was a railway engineer, another a real-estate agent,

ONE WHOM HIS COUNTRY DELIGHTED TO HONOUR.

In the presence of troops and of a large crowd of spectators assembled in Alexandra Park, Montreal, Corporal E. Casstles was presented with the Distinguished Conduct Medal conferred on him for gallantry at Ypres. Left : Corporal E. Casstles. Right : The 5th Pioneers cheering the hero.

a third a business man, and a fourth a Y.M.C.A. worker. The case of two of the lieutenants of this regiment shows the difference between the Canadian and the Regular Army. These two lieutenants were ordered to remain behind when the regiment started from Belleville to England. They dressed themselves in privates' uniform and joined the train. They were discovered and ordered back. They disobeyed, tried to go forward once more, and were again caught. Finally they hid themselves in the transport as the troops were embarking. Luck was apparently against them, for they were hunted out once more. General Hughes, the Canadian Minister of Militia, was there bidding the soldiers good-bye. The colonel hauled the two incurable offenders before him. General Hughes looked at them, and his eyes twinkled as he heard the story of their crime. " Let them go along with you," he said. And they went.

These men proved their capacity on the field, and they and many of the younger men under them demonstrated how wide-spread real fighting ability is among classes of our countrymen at ordinary times largely or wholly removed from military influences. It might have been expected that in an army such as this, officered largely by men whose traditions up to a few months

HONOURED BY TWO COUNTRIES.
Corporal W. H. Baker, of the 10th Battalion, Canadians, won the French Croix de Guerre and the British D.C.M.

before had mainly been civilian, would have been some-what amateurish in its methods, and that while the men might have fought bravely, there would have been a slackness in the routine details of army administration. This was certainly not so. The condition of the trenches, the health of the men, the excellence of their equipment, the regularity of their food supplies, the steady discipline, and all those great qualities which make an efficient army

and not a mob, were found among the Canadians in a very high degree. This was the considered opinion of every competent military man who studied their work.

It was during the months of long waiting that some of the best qualities of the Canadian troops revealed themselves. It is one thing to take part in a brilliant dash against the enemy. It is quite another to sit down day after day, week after week, in the exacting monotony of trench warfare when occupying the front trenches under shell fire, when the main tasks are the taking of fresh trenches, bringing up supplies, watching for the enemy, sniping, and attempting little raids. In time work such as this grows drearily dull, and nothing but a strong sense of discipline and of duty sustains the zeal of the men. The Canadians adapted themselves splendidly to the hard conditions. They became noted all along the lines of the Allies as trench-builders.

Each brigade pitted the excellence of its trenches against all comers. The old shallow, muddy, irregular lines of earth that in the earlier months had done work for our troops as trenches, gave way to splendidly arranged lines, giving the maximum of protection. Dug-outs were so solidly constructed that they would stand anything save direct blows from heavy shells, and some of them, it was claimed, would stand even that. Trenches were so well drained that the troops stood on firm emplacements even in the wettest weather. A trench school was established, where selected men from the different battalions went for training. Every new device was examined, tested, and, if of any use, adopted. Western ingenuity came well into play here.

A FIELD-AMBULANCE WARD.
(*Official Canadian photograph. Canadian Government copyright reserved.*)

A BOMB-PROOF TESTING STATION.
(*Official Canadian photograph. Canadian Government copyright reserved.*)

At the beginning many Canadians were victims of German snipers, whose ingenuity and resource drew unwilling admiration even from our men. But before many months the Canadians turned the tables here also. They developed special groups of snipers, adepts at concealing themselves, men who never fired but to hit ; who would lie hour after hour, and if necessary day after day, for a single sure shot. The Canadians, like every other part of the British Army, developed bomb-throwing to an amazing extent.

In one special line of trench warfare the Canadians gave a lead to the whole of the allied armies. Colonel Odlum, who had distinguished himself prominently in the fighting at Ypres, worked out a system of night raids on the enemy lines that for some time kept the Germans very uneasy.

The British and the German lines were separated by a space of land generally known as No Man's Land, and called by some Canadians " the Great North-West." In this long stretch, varying in depth from thirty or forty yards at some points to two hundred yards and more at others, both British and Germans had protected themselves by long stretches of barbed-wire—thick, strong, and deep. In some threatened points the Germans had two tangles of wire, the first sixteen feet deep, the other forty feet deep, and between these two their patrols would move at night-time to prevent the possibility of their being surprised. Colonel Odlum planned a regular method by which raiding parties would go out at night, wriggle silently to the enemy wires, make a way through the entanglements with wire-cutters, throw themselves into the enemy trenches before the Germans had realised that they **Raiding " the Great**
were there, capture the men, destroy the **North-West "**
machine-guns, and go back with their
prisoners before it was possible to capture them. These reconnaissances were repeated time after time by the different brigades at the front. They gave opportunity for the display of great individual heroism. In one case a young officer led his men into the trenches, emptied his automatic pistol twice, firing from the hip, then sprang at a German, wrenching his dagger out of his hand and flinging it in the face of another, and finally returned with his men and his prisoners, himself the last to leave the trench. When he reached the safety of our own lines it was found that he had received nine wounds.

The Honours Lists gave many examples of individual heroism among the men. It is only possible to mention

LITTLE USED IN THE SIEGE WAR, BUT READY FOR EMERGENCIES.
Canadian cavalry undergoing a severe test during a practice ride. The smaller illustration depicts a group of mounted officers taking a fence in splendid style during manœuvres somewhere in England preparatory to their departure for the western front.

CAMP COOKERS FROM CALGARY.
Camp cookers of a Calgary battalion. (*Canadian official photograph. Crown copyright reserved.*)

a few. Captain E. C. Jackson, of the 5th Battalion, received the D.S.O., Lieutenant Kenneth Taylor-Campbell received the Military Cross, and several of the men were given the D.C.M. for their conspicuous coolness, courage, and gallantry in attacking an advanced German barricade on the Messines Road in December. Six men of the 7th Battalion were given the D.C.M. for conspicuous gallantry on the night of November 16th-17th, 1915. near Messines. They worked for four hours in the bright moonlight cutting lines in the wire close to a heavily-manned German trench. They then placed a bridge over the Doube River about sixteen yards from the enemy's parapet, and guided bombing-parties through the lines they had cut.

Lieutenant Chetwynd, of the Engineers, received his commission and was given a D.C.M. for his conspicuous gallantry and ability on many occasions. He had frequently, as a non-commissioned officer, prepared bridges for demolition and carried out difficult engineering work under heavy shell and rifle fire. On one occasion he was present as a volunteer in an attempt, with a detachment, to link up the Canadian lines with the advanced line, and, after the non-commissioned officer in charge and many men had been killed and wounded, he rallied the survivors and led them forward with great bravery and skill under an intensely heavy fire.

Names in the Honours Lists

Sergeant Ferris, of the same company of Engineers, received his decoration for a deed of great bravery. While in charge of a detachment he was ordered to advance on a prearranged signal to link up communications between trenches. The signal was given, and he attempted to do what he was ordered in face of very heavy fire, the German trenches at this point being only one hundred yards from our own. Several men were killed in the attempt to carry a line through. Then Sergeant Ferris advanced alone. He had barely set out before he was shot through the lungs; but he kept on, found out what was wrong, struggled back, and made his report. Sapper Harmon, of the Engineers, was decorated for constructing a barricade with sand-bags across a road under heavy fire, and keeping it repaired when apparently demolished by heavy shell fire. The same man accompanied the assault on another occasion in charge of a blocking-party to barricade trenches when gained. The first line of trenches was taken, and nearly all of the party killed or wounded. Then Harmon

A GAME OF CARDS.
Men of a Winnipeg battalion on the western front. (*Canadian official photograph. Crown copyright reserved.*)

AMMUNITION LORRIES IN WAITING.
A line of lorries ready to take ammunition to the firing-line. (*Canadian official photograph. Canadian Government copyright reserved.*)

23

ALL SMILES.
Members of a Calgary battalion as they appeared after leaving the trenches.

third line of trenches some eight hundred yards behind these, with communicating trenches connecting them. This third line remained in German hands.

On the night of April 2nd-3rd the 6th Canadian Infantry Brigade relieved the British troops in the new line. As they advanced they saw a party of German prisoners, three officers and one hundred and twenty men, being taken back. These German prisoners declared that the British artillery fire against their position had been so well directed that it had been impossible for them for three and a half or four days to bring up any supplies of food. They were caught in a crater, and kept there starving until they had

armed himself with bombs and continued to force his way forward, in spite of the fact that he was severely wounded in several places, until his supply of ammunition was exhausted and he could get no more.

There were no fewer than eighty-seven names of Canadians in one list alone published in March, all decorated for deeds such as these. This was only one list out of several.

In the early summer of 1916, Lieutenant-General Alderson retired from the command of the Canadians and was succeeded by Major-General the Hon. Sir Julian Byng. The Canadians parted with General Alderson with great regret. From the days when he took charge of the 1st Canadian Division on Salisbury Plain, in the autumn of 1914, he had held unbroken the confidence, affection, and respect of his men. "General Alderson is a human being, not a ramrod," wrote one soldier home. Frank, open, cheerful, with a gift for saying the right word at the right time, he showed great tact in dealing with the prejudices which existed among some Canadians at the beginning against an Imperial commander. He took every opportunity to keep himself in real touch with his men and to show them how he appreciated their services. "I love these men," he said once, before the Canadians had proceeded to the front. "They are always cheerful and willing, in spite of the discomforts they have on Salisbury Plain, and I know they will make splendid soldiers."

Move towards St. Eloi

Early in April the Canadians moved up towards St. Eloi from positions they had held farther south. A British division immediately on the left of the Canadians exploded several mines under the German lines and advanced, capturing two lines of German trenches for a length of about six thousand yards. One of these lines of trenches was about twenty yards behind the other. There was a

[Canadian official photographs. Crown copyright reserved.
ON THE FRINGE OF WAR.
This photograph has more the appearance of a Thames backwater than a scene within sound of the guns. Here members of the Calgary battalion performed their ablutions after leaving the front line.

finally climbed up from the crater and surrendered. The Canadians in the new lines found themselves in an exceedingly difficult position. Our own artillery was active, but that of the Germans was equally so. A terrific fire was concentrated on the craters and on the trenches which our troops occupied. In ordinary times it is not usual for more than a few trench-mortars to fire into a position during the day. Now it seemed as though all day long trench-mortar shells were hurtling through the air. It was estimated that in two hours alone there were two hundred of these great bombs falling around our lines. Every form of shell came—high explosives battering the parapets, trench-mortar projectiles bursting all around.

The Canadians had to hold the craters made by our mine explosions. The whole neighbourhood was one mass of mud and dirt. The troops could only approach the craters during darkness, often crawling along with mud up to their ankles.

It soon became evident that the Germans were making supreme efforts to recapture the craters and their lost trenches. The prisoners brought in said that troops had been brought from Verdun to make the attempt.

Early on the Tuesday morning a terrific artillery fire opened on the Canadian lines. After slackening for a few hours it was renewed with redoubled force. Parapets disappeared under it. The troops made every effort to strengthen their positions and to bury some of the British dead still lying around. Aerial torpedoes, "Jack Johnsons," weeping shells, and apparently every other kind of shell, now fell. Men caught in this raging hell of fire at first thought that all was finished. It seemed as though no man could hope to live. Here it was, however, that discipline told. They automatically and coolly continued their work, even when death seemed inevitable. Some in the

ISSUING RATIONS.
Canadian official photograph of the issue of rations to men of a Winnipeg battalion.

WHERE "SOMEWHERE" WAS REALLY LOCATED.
A Canadian field post-office on the western front. (*Canadian official photograph. Crown copyright reserved.*)

craters climbed up the steep sides to fill trench-bags and put them in position, forming fresh parapets. Bombers crawled out for counter-offensives. In the line of communicating trenches Canadians and Germans met time after time—met and died. It was in the craters that some of the most terrible aspects of war were seen.

Day after day and night after night this ding-dong fight continued, swaying now this way and now that. The Canadians would advance through the mud at every opportunity, bombing the enemy; the enemy would rush back, bombing them. Now a crater would belong to one, now to another. Time after time the Germans made rushes forward, only to be met, as they drew near, with our machine-gun fire, which swept them wholesale away. Soldiers who witnessed some of these rushes declared afterwards that they would retain to their last days impressions of men staggering, reeling, rushing into inevitable death.

If the German shell fire was terrible, that of the British was soon more so. As the fight developed the British brought more and more artillery strength on this point. "This seems like heaven," said one German prisoner

when dragged into our lines. "If you want to know what gun fire is, go into our lines when your shells are coming in."

In one case the Germans made a great attack upon two central craters, covering their advance by a heavy curtain of fire. These craters had already suffered heavily, the dead lying thickly all around. The defenders, almost stunned and deafened by the concentration of shell fire, suddenly found Germans among them. Men climbed over the bodies of fallen comrades to reach the enemy. "I shot one, clubbed another, tried to use a bayoneted rifle against a third," said one survivor, "and then——" And then the crater was in the enemy's hands!

The two craters were seized. Our men who were left were hopelessly outnumbered, and a gap had been made in our front lines through which it seemed that the enemy might come right back again. Then it was that the Canadians from other points redoubled their efforts, holding the enemy in check. "Men climbed on to the parapets and parados," said an official account, "the better to fire at the advancing foe. Machine-guns were lifted into the open and worked with desperate courage, until they became clogged with mud **In the Ypres** splashed on to them by exploded shells, **salient** or else were smashed and buried." Again the craters were recaptured. When early Saturday morning came the brigade was able to hand every crater over to its successors. The Canadians had lost severely, but they had held their own against heavy odds.

Soon afterwards they were to face a still more dreadful experience. They had now moved up to the foremost point in the Ypres salient, and they were holding the line between Hooge and the Ypres-Menin railway. Shortly after nine o'clock on the morning of June 2nd, Major-General Mercer, accompanied by Brigadier-General Williams, was visiting the front lines held by the 4th Canadian Mounted Rifles when an artillery fire of the most severe nature covered the entire Canadian front of some three thousand yards. Simultaneously a great line of shells fell continuously far behind the front lines, making it impossible to bring up reserves. The artillery fire at St. Eloi had been severe, but it was almost as nothing to the rain of shells here. Men who had been in both called the first "child's play." The Germans had care-

Caught by a rain of shells

fully and secretly accumulated a great force of guns—such strength of guns as probably never previously existed in the history of war. The Canadian troops caught in the front lines could do nothing to reply. They could not advance. They could not retire. For any man to show himself was to seek immediate death, and had he shown himself he could have done nothing against the enemy. In this rain of shells trenches disappeared, parapets were wiped out, and the British front was reduced to little more than a blurred and broken line. Some of the troops got into tunnels and into dug-outs waiting for the fire to die away. Other troops in reserve, some eight hundred yards behind, were hastily

called upon to dig themselves in, for it was seen that the front lines would form little protection against the enemy.

General Mercer, who had done such brilliant service in former battles, apparently went into the battalion head-quarters dug-out, accompanied by his two A.D.C.'s. General Williams, wounded in the face, went into a trench called the Tunnel, slightly to the north-east of the headquarters dug-out and running towards a still deeper trench known as the Tube. General Williams was accompanied by the commander of the battalion, Colonel Ussher, and a considerable number of men. The shell fire soon blocked the Tunnel and the men inside it were nearly suffocated before it was possible to dig their way out again.

After several hours of this artillery fire the Germans came up to our lines. They were so satisfied that no man could be living that they approached without any great haste, some smoking cigarettes and all carrying heavy packs. One Canadian corporal and a few men had got into an excavation at the bottom of a trench and had dragged in a machine-gun with them. Here they lay low during the firing. When the German shell fire suddenly ceased they crawled out and looked around. They saw the Germans coming up.

Mystery of General Mercer

They placed their machine-gun in position, waited until the enemy were comparatively close, and then poured their fire into them. Many of the Germans fled and very many fell.

But incidents like this could not affect the final result. The Germans reached the trenches; they came to the Tunnel and apparently all inside it were captured. General Mercer, after staying in the battalion head-quarters dug-out for a considerable time, started to walk back in the direction of Maple Copse through Armagh Wood. It was his frequent custom to stride in front of his aides, leaving them to follow him as best they could. Apparently he did so this time. It was said

HARDY SONS OF CANADA PREPARING FOR FLANDERS ON THE PLAINS OF ABRAHAM.
Men of the 33rd Battalion, Canadian Contingent, passing through the St. Louis Gate of the old fortifications of Quebec, which were built by the British regulars after the occupation of 1759. The smaller illustration depicts men of the 57th Battalion in training on the historic snow-covered Plains of Abraham, the scene of the Battle of Quebec.

for the retention of Ypres. From some of their new positions they commanded vital sections of our lines, and it was plain to every man that we must drive them out. The Canadians had lost very heavily indeed. Their record further showed many instances of their splendid gallantry, but no one denied that the Hooge fighting was for the moment a German victory. This thought itself added bitterness to the grief for the brave men who had fallen.

Two of the corps that had suffered most were the Canadian Mounted Rifles, drawn from all parts of Canada, and the famous Princess Patricia's Light Infantry. This latter regiment, after having been almost wiped out at Ypres a year before, had for a time seemed in danger of extinction. Then the Universities of Canada, more particularly the Universities of the West, had given the pick of their young men as recruits for it. It had become in the main a great University Corps. Now hundreds of its men were among the killed and wounded in the Hooge fighting.

The losses at Hooge

The British steadily brought more and more artillery to bear upon the captured trenches. Day after day a

SIMPLICITY AND STRENGTH.
Sleds of simplest design and stoutest build were fashioned on which to draw fallen trunks from the forest.

that he had been rendered stone deaf, but whether as the result of a blow or merely from the noise of the shock of the shelling was not clear. First reported wounded and a prisoner, he was on June 19th "unofficially reported" killed.

Some details of what happened during this fighting in the front lines were obtained shortly afterwards from German newspapers. According to these, many a nest in the front lines contained Canadians who defended themselves desperately, refusing quarter, and who had to be overcome with hand-grenades. One paper told of a general, possibly General Victor Williams, who was caught in the Tunnel. He drew his sword and struck the sergeant who summoned him to surrender in the face, whereupon the infantryman attacked the general, who, in the language of the Germans, was fighting like a madman, and ran him through. Numerous other officers, so the report stated, were killed because they refused to surrender.

The Germans, by the explosion of mines, still further wrecked the Canadian position. It was impossible either to hold the front lines or to rescue the men there. A fresh line was hastily constructed, but in attempting to bring troops forward to support it we suffered heavily, for the German artillery was playing now far back, not only in Ypres but beyond it. During the night the Canadians launched attack after attack upon their old position. A party of German bombers had got through as far as Zillebeke. All of them were destroyed. Some of the old British trenches were recaptured, but it was found impossible to hold them, the German artillery fire being at this stage stronger.

The end of it all for the moment was that we held our new line and the Germans held our old trenches, with important positions such as Sorrel Hill, Observatory Wood, and Maple Copse, all of the utmost importance

CANADIAN LUMBERMEN IN WINDSOR GREAT PARK.
Vast quantities of timber were required for the construction of the trenches in France, and Canadian lumbermen were formed into a Forestry Battalion to fell fir-trees in England for that purpose.

heavy bombardment was maintained. The 1st Division, the veterans of the Canadians, was brought up for the attempt that was to be made. The weather now was in our favour—wet and cold, an ideal condition for attack. Day by day the Canadians lay in their new trenches waiting their opportunity.

Late on the night of Monday, June 12th, a heavy British bombardment was maintained for two hours. After a brief pause the bombardment reopened. Then it paused again, thus keeping the Germans in a state of nervous anticipation of an attack. Soon after midnight the Canadians moved into position and the British artillery opened up in full force. German prisoners afterwards said that they had never experienced such gun fire. Heavy shells swept the whole position at intervals of a few yards. While the artillery was firing, the Canadians crept up through the rain in the darkness. The move was so exactly timed that the troops were almost on the trenches before the British gun fire ceased. Then, before the Germans had time to recover, they were in among them. It was a grim business that night, men moving through the trenches, exploring every corner, bombing wherever they suspected the enemy, and clearing the Germans out of line after line at the point of the bayonet. The whole final move from first to last took about twenty hours.

Four German officers and one hundred and thirty-one men were made prisoners. The Canadians were delighted to find some of their own wounded from the earlier days were still left in the trenches and had been well looked after and kindly treated. One of them had a label on him, " We do not kill the wounded."

The loss of life, considering the importance of the operation, was comparatively small, yet some of the battalions that took a foremost part in the fighting suffered very heavily in proportion to their numbers. The Toronto Regiment, which had already distinguished itself in the great Battle of Ypres, at Festubert, and at Givenchy, once more played a prominent part. Its casualties amounted to over fifty per cent., and out of twenty officers engaged, seventeen were killed or wounded. One small section of twenty men mounted a hill at the final objective of the advance; five were killed and ten wounded. The old British front trench was reoccupied in the early hours of the morning. It was difficult to recognise it. It had been crushingly bombarded, first by the Germans against the British, and then by the British against the Germans, and shortly before the big advance the British guns had planted a line of 12 in. shells twelve yards apart along the entire trench. The Canadians, after capturing this front trench, held it for several hours under an almost overpowering German shell fire, while certain readjust-

Journalism in the trenches

ments were made immediately behind. Then they fell back to our new permanent line, about forty yards behind. The old trench front was untenable by either side, and had to be left. The bodies of many gallant men, friends and foe alike, lay there.

No account of the Canadian troops would be complete that did not touch on two aspects—both of them outside the usual routine of their military life—trench journalism, which flourished among the Canadians as it did in perhaps no other section of the British Army, and the liberality of all classes of Canadians in providing supplementary comforts for the men and special accommodation for the wounded and convalescent.

During the first year at the front no less than ten Canadian regimental or brigade papers were issued. Their titles ranged from " The Listening Post " to " The Dead Horse Gazette," and from " The Growler " to " The Brazier." The Canadian Medical Service alone had three separate papers : " The Iodine Chronicle," " The Splint Record," and " Now and Then," which were eventually amalgamated under the title of N.Y.D " The Listening Post " was generally accorded premier place by reason of seniority and a very bright editorial management. As with nearly every other paper, jokes, chaff, and merriment

filled most of its columns. It was typical of the high spirits of the fighting men.

Some of the matter, full of brigade and battalion allusions, was not easily comprehensible outside—for example, " Is the R.Q.M.S. still in love with the girl in Bailleul ? " But most appealed to a wider public. Take, for example, these directions for the game of " Craters." " This fascinating pastime is now (May, 1916) in full swing at the Ypres salient. Crater parties are organised nightly both by the British and German Governments. As bombs and blighties are issued free of charge the game is becoming popular. The rules of the game are simple. According to Hoyle, it is a mixture of hop-scotch and checkers." **The game of " craters "**

Here and there men allowed their real selves to be seen. Take, for instance, an extract from some verses, " To Ypres, May, 1916 ":

> A year has passed, and still your battered walls
> Spell grim defiance to the crouching Hun ;
> He lying in waiting, seeing your mighty halls
> Standing in ruins, thinks the time has come
> To strive once more, accomplish his desire :
> Kill your defenders, and work out his will.
> Fear not, brave City ! We have faced the fire,
> And will again ; Ypres, we guard you still !

High spirits were even more pronounced, if that were possible, in the note of " The Brazier." Its manager, a full private, was in the days before the war a publisher of newspapers in British Columbian mining camps. Its compositor, a Highland drummer, was once an expert linotype operator on a great Vancouver paper. Its pressman, a Highland piper, was in civil life a partner on a Manitoba newspaper. These three leased the use of a French jobbing office, and turned out a very creditable production. Two or three extracts will show the note of its contents. Here is a menu of a Hogmanay Eve dinner for the Machine-gun Section :

Olives, celery, salted almonds.
Soups : Puree of Mud, Cream of Tomato.
Fish : Salmon Croquettes à la Hand Grenade.
Entrees : Macaroni au Pull-Through, " Colt " Mutton.
Roasts : Turkey and P.P. Sauce, Old English Roast Beef and Yorkshire Pudding. The function of the turkey is to transmit motion and energy to the mechanism of the M.G. Section.
Salad : A la German Kultur (Boche !).
Game : Sniper, potted au Telescope Sight.
Vegetables : " Bombardier Fritz " (fried potatoes), Carrots, " Shrapnel " (shelled peas).
Sweets : " Belt-fillers " with Ammunition Sauce (plum pudding), " Jack Johnsons " (a trifle ?), " Bomb Proofs " (mince-pies), Cheese, Nuts and Raisins.
Coffee.

One " Brazier " story was of a junior Staff officer who was asked to interrogate some German prisoners in the absence of the official interpreter. The youthful officer jumped at the opportunity of displaying his linguistic talents, and addressing the nearest Hun, he politely asked : " Parlez-vous sprechen the Allemands ? " Even the Hun grinned. Another story was of General Alderson. The first commander of the Canadian Army Corps was in the habit of getting around everywhere, and seeing things for himself. On one occasion, looking over some transports, he congratulated the driver on his well - combed and well - kept team. " Thanks, cap," the Westerner replied. " A little encouragement once in a while don't do a fellow any harm."

KILTS IN THE DOMINION.
Squad of the 5th Royal Highlanders, forming a guard at the headquarters of Valcartier Camp, the Canadian Aldershot.

There were many accounts in some papers of sports and amusements. The 3rd Infantry Brigade had been given a moving-picture machine. There had been field sports galore at the rest camps, football matches, boxing contests, and baseball. Great things were to be done by the Soccer League. "We shall attempt to prove that it is not only in the rebuilding or destroying of obsolete or tottering trenches that we hold the palm." There had been a big entertainment at the Y.M.C.A., with a boxing contest and singing, dancing, and piping. The guest of the evening was a hero from Ypres, who had been away for months wounded, and had now come back as camp commandant His voice had been badly damaged by his wound, and the paper told how, since he was unable to make himself heard, someone else had to repeat his speech for him.

But it was not the chaff and merriment of "The Brazier" that made the most lasting impression on the reader. In number after number glimpses were given of the tragedies and the horrors of war. Sometimes it was simply the "In Memoriam" list of the officers of their battalions killed in action. "Few indeed of the original 16th, or for the matter of that the first draft, are now with us," wrote the editor. "But this is war." Then in one number there came a description of

GETTING READY FOR BUSINESS.
Canadian Highlander cleaning his rifle.

the actual life of the men in the camp, grimly realistic. The camp was lying in a hollow, surrounded by low hills, topped here and there with fringes of trees stripped bare of foliage. On the other side was the "front," a bleak and wintry aspect, forming a very fitting background to the great drama of Armageddon.

Human endurance seems to gaze with equanimity on the daily deluge of high explosives, machine-gun and rifle fire under the pitiful shelter of parapet, trench, and dugout. But with the elements also to combat, life at the front takes on a greater physical strain. For these temporary earthworks and shelters have indeed suffered more severely from the elements than from the enemy's cannon. Due to the continuous rain, communication trenches, dug-outs, and even massive parapets constructed of many thicknesses of sand-bags have collapsed, and for days on end miles of parallel and connecting subterranean passages have been temporarily rendered useless in places, through being undermined by the running water. Happily the weather god plays no favourite, and the Huns' earthworks have during this trying period suffered equally as much as our own."

In the most prominent place in one issue were two quotations printed in the biggest type, quotations which typified the spirit of Canada. They were headed "Lest we Forget." The first was part of the declaration by Sir Robert Borden: "The sword, which we reluctantly drew, will not be sheathed until the triumph of our cause has been full and unmistakable." The

MEAL-TIME IN THE CANADIAN TRENCHES: A MID-DAY IMPRESSION FROM THE WEST FRONT.   D

second was words by Sir Samuel Hughes: "Canada demands that the war shall be continued not to a draw, but until the Hohenzollerns have been humiliated and the world has been freed from the menace of Prussian militarism."

"N.Y.D.," the amalgamated organ of the medical service, admirably sub-edited and printed, was equally typical of Canada, and its sometimes mocking, sometimes serious, pages were by no means confined to the medical aspects of the army's work.

When war broke out the people of Canada, more particularly the women of Canada, came together to help by personal service and personal gifts all engaged in **Gifts from Canadian women** the war. One of the first Canadian moves was to send a great national present of foodstuffs to the people of England to meet anticipated distress. These foodstuffs were in part sold, and the proceeds used later on to relieve some of the great distress on the East Coast. Canadian women formed local working associations in every city and in every village. They produced comforts for the troops in such quantities that at one time it was difficult to know how to deal with them. The Canadian troops at the front were amply supplied with everything they could want, and so much was left over that it became possible to distribute great quantities of goods among other less fortunately placed soldiers.

The Canadian community in London formed itself into a War Contingent Association. It opened a hospital at Beachborough Park, Shorncliffe, a fine old house placed at the disposal of the Canadians by Sir Arthur Markham, M.P. Sir William Osler, the Canadian Regius Professor of Medicine at Oxford, supervised the medical, and Colonel Donald Armour, the well-known Canadian consulting surgeon, supervised the surgical side. Beachborough Park was of great use in the early days of the war, and its accommodation grew as the demand increased. Mr. Astor, M.P., placed the house and magnificent grounds of Taplow Lodge at the disposal of the Canadians, and a

very large military hospital under Canadian nurses and Canadian doctors was built there. The Ontario Government, as a gift to the Empire, built a large temporary hospital holding some 1,200 men at Orpington, and sent a Canadian staff to man it. It was the justified boast of the Ontario authorities that everything had been done to make this hospital one of the most completely equipped of any in the country.

A new departure, even in Canadian philanthropy, was made in the summer of 1916, when a prominent Canadian business organisation, the Massey-Harris Company, presented and maintained a convalescent home at Sydenham for Canadian soldiers. This home, planted on the southern heights of London, with all the metropolis stretched out as a vista in front of it, consisted of a splendid mansion in the midst of thirty acres of pleasure ground. It would have been difficult to imagine more handsome surroundings for men fresh from hospital.

The Canadian Red Cross, the main Canadian organisation for the collection and distribution of gifts for the sick and wounded, established a headquarters in London in the late autumn of 1914, under the direction of Colonel Hodgetts, and from there it directed a shower of gifts not alone on the Canadian troops, but on the British also. It equipped the hospital at Taplow. It presented tens of thousands of pounds to the British Red Cross, it helped to provide British hospital trains and ambulances, it brought large numbers of Canadian doctors and also nurses to England for **Canadian doctors on Empire service** service, and it also distributed tens of thousands of other gifts in kind.

A word may well be added about the prominent services of Canadian medical men. Canadian doctors were foremost even among the people of the Dominion in volunteering their services for the Canadian Medical Department, under the direction of Surgeon-General Carlton Jones. It would be invidious to select names, but it will be enough to say that a number of the best known and most highly placed

HOW THE 16TH CANADIAN SCOTTISH AND 10TH INFANTRY SAVED YPRES IN THE SPRING OF 1915.
Owing to the Germans using poison gas the Canadians had temporarily to abandon a battery of 4·7 in. guns, but they rallied, and with incredible courage recaptured the weapons at the point of the bayonet. The action took place at midnight amid the tall trees of a wood in the neighbourhood of Ypres. In the words of the official record, " the Canadians undoubtedly saved the situation."

HOW THE CANADIANS RETOOK LOST TRENCHES AT YPRES.

In June the Canadians won fresh laurels by their heroic recapture, under heavy enemy fire, of lost ground in the vicinity of Ypres. The fighting was of the fiercest character, and though our men lost heavily the ground was covered with German dead.

surgeons and consultant physicians throughout Canada—men at the very height of their practice and in the fullness of their fame, distinguished medical professors at the universities, and leading specialists—abandoned their private practice to serve with the troops at the front or in the base hospitals of England. The list of great Canadian doctors who swept their private practice on one side to serve the Empire at war was a long and distinguished one.

The Canadian Expeditionary Force began in the early days of the war as a single division. Twenty thousand men were asked for, but before the expedition had left Canada its numbers had increased to thirty-three thousand. By the summer of 1916 there were over three hundred thousand in the Canadian ranks, including a complete army corps in Flanders and large reserves in training centres in England. Sir Samuel Hughes, the Minister of Defence and Militia—an office corresponding in Canada to that of Secretary for War in England—announced the intention of the Government eventually to increase the army to half a million men.

General Sir Samuel Hughes

This is the more remarkable when it is remembered that up to the outbreak of the war Canada was one of the least military nations of the world. Its population was almost wholly absorbed in commercial and agricultural expansion, and in conquering the West for civilisation. There was no national military training as in Australia, and the only military organisation to hand was the old militia, a small regular army, and an allied semi-military body, the North-West Mounted Police.

Much of the credit for the way in which Canada rose to the situation must go to the one man whose name has been previously mentioned, General Sir Samuel Hughes. When, some years before war began, Sir Robert Borden was elected to power, he chose Colonel Hughes, as he then was, as his Minister of Militia. Colonel Hughes was well known as a man with a hobby, his particular hobby being the duty of the Dominions to render military assistance to the Motherland in war time. Politician, editor, a noted amateur athlete when young, a university lecturer, and a militia officer, he had seen service and done good work in the Boer War. He had travelled throughout the Empire, preaching his gospel of unity for Imperial defence. His bitterest enemies could not deny him the possession of a forceful, magnetic, and very unusual personality. Big, blustering, indifferent to critics and criticism, more concerned to get things done than about the way they were done, he started years before the war to make Canada ready. His militia officers were sent to Aldershot for training. He fought hard for efficiency. On one occasion, in the autumn of 1913, he took a number of commanding officers, hired a fleet of motor-cars, and conducted them over the Belgian, German, and French frontiers, the very land soon to be the field of war. He knew that war was coming, and he thought it wise to let his officers learn something in advance of the ground over which they would have to fight. When news went abroad of what he had done, politicians were aghast. "Sam Hughes' joy-ride" was denounced almost everywhere. Even some of his colleagues thought that he had gone too far. But Hughes did not mind.

This was typical of General Hughes. When he was satisfied that a thing ought to be done, he had it done, and left explanations until afterwards. This sometimes left him open to criticism, which culminated in the early summer of 1916 in a very serious charge of corruption in the issue of war contracts brought against men for whose conduct he was responsible. Sir Samuel—he had been knighted a short time before—had arrived in England for **Facing the music** a short visit to the Canadian troops training in Britain at the time when the charges were made. He promptly closed up his work in England and returned to Canada to face his accusers. A judicial committee had been appointed to investigate the matter. General Hughes handed over the external duties of his office to the Canadian Premier. Then, even while the commission was busy with its inquiries, he continued his work of military expansion.

"A man who has been scrutinised by two Judges and eight millions of his fellow-citizens because he has been

THE INEVITABLE AFTERMATH.
The first casualty after an advance being put on board a horse ambulance which waited for the wounded under cover of a farmhouse on the western front.

THEIR "LITTLE GREY HOME" IN FLANDERS.
Canadian Highlanders regaling themselves with some official beverage. One of them seems to have felt the need of special covering for his lower limbs.

[Canadian Government photographs. Copyright reserved.
CLEANING THEIR KILTS.
Canadian Scottish engaged in an essential, if officially unrecorded function, preparatory to being inspected. An unkilted critic is watching the operations with interest.

assailed in Parliament is usually regarded as being under a cloud," wrote Mr. Arthur Hawkes, one of the most brilliant Canadian journalists, at the time. "Sam, when this particular cloud hove into sight, was relieved of his duties as Minister of Militia. Any other Minister of the Crown so situated would observe a discreet reticence about his situation. Not so, Sam. He assumes a garment of praise for the spirit of heaviness.

"Cloud, is it? Cloud did you say? All right, it shall be a pillar of cloud to let the whole world see where he is. Cloud? Nay, verily, no cloud, but a shekinah."

And everyone, whatever their side of politics, apart from a very small clique, was more than glad when the judicial committee cleared those involved in its inquiry of the charge of personal corruption.

It would be a mistake to suppose the Canadian people, glad as they were of what they had been able to do, were by any means satisfied with what they had done. They measured their duty not by what had been done, but by what needed to be done. Thus it was that many of the most influential newspapers in Canada led, in the summer of 1916, a soul-searching inquiry into the questions, "Can't we do more?" "Are we playing at war?" One **Canada asks to do more** prominent Toronto newspaper asked—Toronto, be it noted, the city that had given more of its sons to the war than perhaps any other in Canada—" Is Canada mobilised at all as she should be?" Then it framed its indictment: "Wherever you turn what strikes you is that we have not begun to organise; we have not begun to appreciate what we mean when we say we are fighting for national existence. We are so fighting, but, as heaven is above, we do not seem to know it. We need a few Zeppelin raids to wake us up. We may not be to blame for what we do not know, but the people who do know are blind or foolish or wicked if they do not tell us that we are foozling around the edge of a precipice without direction, without inspiration, without humility, or without justice to ourselves or to our future." And so it was that the Canadian people, whose sacrifices and endurance had aroused the admiration of the whole Empire, felt themselves not proud at what they had done, but humiliated that they had not earlier tackled the things waiting to be done. It was fit mood for ultimate victory that the Premier of the Oversea Dominion should, in the hour when she was reckoning her wounded sons by the tens of thousands, dash away the tears of grief, fight down the exultation over great deeds well done, and sturdily prepare herself for yet greater sacrifices that the Empire in which she formed so big a part might attain to victory, and that the freedom of all humanity for all time might be made permanently secure.

At the beginning of the war some extraordinary misapprehensions prevailed in England about the character and personnel of the Canadian Army. It was believed by many in England that this army was mainly made up of cowboys, pioneers, backwoodsmen, trappers, and hunters. The British military authorities evidently entertained this notion, for they planted the 1st Canadian Division down for some months in the bleakest and most inhospitable plain in England, under conditions which permanently wrecked the health of many men. This was a great misapprehension. To quote some words written at the time : " All these—cowboys, trappers, and hunters—are found in the ranks, but none of them represents **A great** the typical Canadian soldier. There are **misapprehension** the thick-limbed giants from the Yukon, and others who abandoned their traps and their dog-trains in the northern hills, and hurried post-haste to the Peace River when they heard that war was declared. There are French Canadians, speaking with musical accent, men whose forefathers fought against Wolfe and who led the rebels in the early struggles against British rule. A Papineau, directly descended from Papineau, the splendid rebel, was one of the heroes of the great stand of the Princess Patricia's. A Riel, close relation to Louis Riel, the half-caste hanged for treason a little over thirty years ago, was one of the first to join the Winnipeg Regiment.

You will find in the Canadian ranks lumber-jacks from the Soo, pioneer farmers from New Vermilion, and many young Americans who crossed the border and concealed their nationality to get a chance of fighting for the Old Land. But these are the picturesque elements rather than the basis of the army."

The First Canadian Contingent was largely composed, so far as the rank and file were concerned, of young immigrants from England and Scotland who had spent a few years in Canada and had become Canadian in spirit and in aspiration. The most of **Part of the** these were townsmen. To them had to be **Highlanders** added the splendid Canadian stock found in such corps as Strathcona's Horse, and found especially in the North-West Mounted Police, the picked irregulars of the world. It was estimated at the time that at least sixty per cent. of the First Contingent of the Canadians were British born, particularly Scottish born, for the Highland regiments played a very large part in the Canadian ranks. A large proportion of these British-born men came from the West, and in the West the young Englishman or Scotsman soon learns a resource and adaptability not always fully brought out in the Homeland. In the subsequent contingents this major proportion of British born did not hold, for many of the battalions now were overwhelmingly composed of Canadian-born units.

At the time when the Canadian Army had reached its 300,000 figure the army represented no group, no section, and no particular interest in the country, but it represented faithfully the whole Dominion ; every class shared alike in the duty and glory of service. Canada's purpose was well expressed by Sir Robert Borden, the Dominion Premier, in words quoted earlier in this chapter : " The sword, which we reluctantly drew, will not be sheathed until the triumph of our cause has been full and unmistakable."

PANOPLY AND CIRCUMSTANCE IN MODERN WAR.

Canadian Highlanders cheering the King on his arrival at their part of the front. Though a utilitarian sameness of dress prevailed among the fighting forces of the belligerent nations, the kilt and glengarry introduced an element of picture and romance even into the drab landscape of siege warfare.

Teaching rapid firing under active service conditions.

Training at home for serious work at the front.   Officers of the Royal Engineers receiving instruction in the very necessary art of bomb-throwing.

Engineers constructing and placing obstacles to protect trenches.

Practising trestle bridging.   Floating a trestle on a barrel pier raft.

THE HANDYMEN OF THE ARMY: ROYAL ENGINEERS AT HOME PREPARING FOR ACTIVE SERVICE CONDITIONS.

CHAPTER CXXIII.

THE CONVERSION OF BRITAIN AND THE ESTABLISHMENT OF COMPLETE NATIONAL SERVICE.

Creation of a Field Army of Two Million Men—Britain Prepares to Shoulder a Larger Burden of the Land War—Cabinet Minister Organises Opposition to Conscription—Approaching Crisis in the Coalition Government—Labour Conference at Bristol Votes Against Repeal of Military Service Bill—Reasons for Prejudices of Trade Unions—Rate of Production in Some War Factories Still Unsatisfactory—Strikes on the Clyde and in Belfast—Unpatriotic Organisations for Covering "Slackers"—Conscientious Objectors and the Cant of Non-Resistance—The Philosophy of Decadent Cowardice—Suffragettes Try to Hold a Peace Meeting in Trafalgar Square—Trouble with Surplus of Starred and Badged Men—Unexpected Call on Married Groups—Attested Married Men Agitate for Equality of Sacrifice—Grand Crisis in the Cabinet—Compromise Bill Rejected by House of Commons—Bill for General Compulsion Passed by Large Majority—Great Speech by Mr. Lloyd George—Influence of Labour Premier of Australia on British Working Men—First Direct Step in Conscription of Wealth: Government Call for £200,000,000 American Securities— Compulsion Extended to Early Rising in Summer—Call to Married Groups and Upheaval of Home Life—Fear of Conscription in Ireland—Farmers Flock Into the Sinn Fein and Priests Advocate Revolt—Mr. Birrell Afraid to Disarm the Disloyalists— Nationalist Leaders Advocate Policy of Inaction—Our Government Continually Warned of Increasing Dangers—How the British Navy Smashed Up a Rebellion—Ammunition Ship Captured and Casement Made Prisoner—Effect of Insurrection on British Policy—Compulsory Service Established in Britain as Result of German Intrigues in Ireland.

DURING the apparent deadlock on all fronts in the early spring of 1916 the domestic problems of Great Britain attracted the attention of both friend and foe. Even when the Germans tried to put an end to the deadlock by their great thrust towards Verdun the new military situation only intensified the general interest in our home affairs. There was, indeed, a strong probability that the persistence and ferocity of the enemy's offensive movement against the French lines were related to the revolution of ideas which was taking place in Britain. The passing of the first measure of compulsion for unmarried men, which was arranged to come into force on March 2nd, 1916, had seriously disturbed the General Staff of Germany and also the German people. It was clear to them that our nation was at last moving in the direction of a system of general compulsory military service. Tardily and reluctantly did our Coalition Government arrive at the decision to make this critical change in our national condition. For long the enemy had thought that so profound a transformation in the structure of British

CYCLISTS IN THE TRENCHES.
Divisional cyclists receive training in rifle shooting in a properly-constructed trench.

society was impossible by reason of financial difficulties, of strong-rooted political prejudices, and the habit of insular egoism.

The Germans always reckoned that we should conduct our part of the war in accordance with our traditions of the seventeenth, eighteenth, and nineteenth centuries. That is to say, they expected we should throw our full fighting power mainly into naval operations, and employ in land warfare a force of quite secondary strength when compared with Continental standards of military power. They had been disagreeably surprised when, by a tremendous voluntary effort, we increased our Army from a total of twenty-six divisions in August, 1914, to seventy-one divisions in the autumn of 1915. Our Army of seventy-one divisions was then augmented by twelve divisions of British stock from the Overseas Dominions, making eighty-three divisions in all, numbering some two million men. Moreover, a further reinforcement of our military power had been obtained from India by a splendid volunteer movement among the Indian races, which was checked only by our incapacity to supply large numbers of new officers with a knowledge of native ways and speech. Our complete naval and military enlistments, including the forces existing at the outbreak of war and, it is believed, men who offered themselves but were rejected, exceeded at last 5,000,000 men.

No doubt our enemy hoped that this enormous growth of our forces was all that he would have to contend against. But in July, 1915, a Cabinet Committee, presided over by Lord Crewe, had reported that the weekly inflow of recruits was becoming insufficient to maintain the strength of the new British Army of seventy divisions. And by September, 1915, Mr. Lloyd George, the most energetic and foreseeing man in the Cabinet, was convinced that a general system of compulsory service would be necessary to end the war in a victorious peace.

Dawn of compulsory service

The terrible blows which Russia had received had temporarily reduced to a very serious extent the great army with which she had invaded Prussia, Austria, and Hungary. In addition, the Russians had lost millions of rifles, thousands of machine-guns, and a very large number, of pieces of artillery. Their munition factories were woefully inadequate to their needs, and the process of building up another immense army, with the help of Japanese, American, and British armament firms, was likely to take a considerable time. Meanwhile, the reserve forces of France were coming almost within sight of exhaustion. Austria-Hungary, it is true, was in a worse condition than France, but this did not alter the main situation. Germany was still extremely formidable in both men and armament. Her artillery was more powerful than it had ever been. She was replacing her outworn field-guns of 3 in. calibre by new standard guns of 5·9 in. calibre, and her control of shell production had been developed in a tremendous manner, until it reached a daily output of 400,000 shells. Our Army Council could see that, if the Germans continued to hammer at Verdun in order to deplete the French reserves, at any sacrifice to themselves, our country might have to shoulder at last the main burden of the land war as well as maintain a Fleet of predominant strength while financing allied and friendly nations.

And the trouble was that it was not a matter of immediate danger. The sense of immediate, overwhelming danger would have excited to intense effort every true man of our race. It was only a danger seen from afar by special observers, and requiring hard and vehement preparation to counter it in time. There was a temptation for us to gamble on the chance of the Germans being unable to exhaust the French reserves and on the possibility of Russia regaining strength to break the Austro-German lines. Some members of the Coalition Government were at first inclined to abide. by the method of the older and younger Pitt, and maintain fully our export industries at the cost of restricting our military power, and rest contented with giving our Allies naval and financial help of the first class, with military assistance of the second or third class.

Such had been the policy of Sir John Simon, one of the leading members of the Cabinet that had engaged our Empire in the war. Happily, he resigned; but after his resignation he publicly stated that there still remained in the Cabinet members who fully shared his views. This appeared to be the case, for, in the House of Commons on March 9th, 1916, Mr. R. McNeill drew attention to a statement reported to have been made by the member of Parliament for Tottenham, Mr. Percy Alden, to the effect that he had been asked by a member of the Cabinet to organise opposition to the Military Service Bill. According to the reported statement, this extraordinary thing occurred shortly before the introduction of the Military Service Bill of January, 1916, which was designed to carry out the pledge given by the Prime Minister to attesting married men that single men should first be brought into the Army. So to many persons it appeared that, while the Cabinet as a whole was loyally preparing to redeem the Prime Minister's pledge, one member of the Cabinet was using Mr. Alden to organise opposition in the country against the action of the Cabinet.

Crisis in the Cabinet

Wide and indignant attention was given to this revelation, which was made quite inadvertently by Mr. Alden when trying nervously to excuse himself at a meeting of

SMART YOUNG BRITONS EAGER TO DEFEND THEIR COUNTRY.

March-past of the Sussex Yeomanry Cadets at an inspection at Preston Park, Brighton, by Colonel Rawson, V.D., M.P. They were taken over by him on behalf of the Sussex Yeomanry. Many looked to a development of the Cadet movement to furnish universal training for the youth of Great Britain.

MOTOR MACHINE-GUN BATTERY IN READINESS FOR THE FRONT.

One of the most effective of the new units was the Motor Machine-Gun Corps, a battery of which is here seen photographed prior to its departure for the front. This particular battery had the reputation of being the best that ever left the headquarters of the corps.

his supporters for the opposition he had organised against the Government Bill. It shocked the country. Attempts were made in the House of Commons to obtain the name of the Cabinet Minister who had organised opposition to a Cabinet measure. The design, of course, was to compel the resignation of the unknown Minister; but after some weeks of baffled inquiry and smothered discussion the extraordinary affair merged into a general Cabinet crisis in regard to the problem of conscription.

The crisis had inhered in the general situation since July, 1915, and the solution of it was only delayed by the series of inadequate measures of palliation extemporised by the strong middle party in the Cabinet. Between the compulsionists and the anti-compulsionists the balance was held by a section of Cabinet Ministers, largely of Unionist principles, who were apprehensive of a great strike movement by the trade unions. On January 27th, 1916, the Labour Party held a conference in Bristol. At this conference a card-vote division on conscription resulted in 219,000 votes in favour of universal military service, and 1,796,000 votes against it. The Bill enforcing compulsory service only on single men was favoured by 360,000 votes and opposed by 1,716,000. But a proposal to agitate for a repeal of the Bill was opposed by **Trade unions** 649,000 votes and favoured by 614,000 **and conscription** votes. There was thus a majority of 35,000 votes tacitly consenting to the compulsion Act for single men being put in force. As one representative put it: "These divisions mean we Labour men are very angry, but don't intend to do anything."

The fact was that the Labour delegates, especially those representing 600,000 miners' votes, were uncertain of the feeling of the trade unionists. The trade unions had supplied most of the men of the new armies. And the men who had volunteered for military service and left their dependents to struggle along on a small Government

allowance were not anti-conscriptionists in 1916. At first all our trade unionists had been bitterly prejudiced against any form of compulsory service, and many of the finest and most thoughtful spirits among them had given up valuable skilled work for the country and entered the recruiting offices in the hope of making any measure of conscription unnecessary. Their great fear was that the system of conscription would remain in force after the war, and that justifiable strike movements would then be dishonestly defeated by calling the men up as soldiers and making them obey the will **What Labour** of their employers by means of military **feared** discipline. A French Minister, M. Briand, had used the conscription service in this manner in order to break the great strike of French railwaymen during one of the very critical periods of tension with Germany. Our trade unionists did not then know how perilous was the European situation and what part German agents had played in paralysing an important section of the French railway service. They saw only that the instrument of conscription had been apparently perverted in a great democratic State and used to quell what seemed, on the surface, to be a fair, legal attempt on the part of French working men to improve their conditions of work.

None of our statesmen took the trouble to meet the British trade unionists in a frank manner and explain the secret history of M. Briand's action in the somewhat too notorious French railway strike. Our Government might have brought M. Briand himself over, when he became Prime Minister in succession to M. Viviani, to explain to our working men the reason why he had used the instrument of conscription in what had appeared to be merely an ordinary economic struggle. As it was, the field was left open for pro-German agitators of the pseudo-Socialistic or the falsely pacifist school continually to suggest, with an increasing virulence of expression, that the movement towards compulsory military service in our country was the consummation of a great plot to reduce the working classes to impotence after the war and make it impossible for them ever to come out on strike, no matter how just were their grievances. The pro-German agitators also went on to develop the still wilder and more fantastic theme that military conscription was only a step to industrial conscription, and that when the war ended the employing class would have the working class reduced to a condition worse than that of ancient serfs.

Attitude of railway workers The British railwaymen seem to have been the most important body of labour with a dread of the industrial aspect of conscription. The men themselves were splendid ; they were working our lines at an unending high pressure, feeding the fleets and the armies and saving the civil population from a famine of both materials and food. In spite of the great strain upon them day and night, railway accidents remained small in proportion to the enormous traffic, and, though the men themselves worked as hard as any other war workers, and received some increase of wages to balance the higher cost of living, they were not repaid for their intenser labours in the way that many skilled men were. Perhaps it was the long stress of their

FLIGHT ! A NEW VERSION.
Army Service Corps motor-cycle despatch and test rider making a jump test with a new machine, prior to its being sent on foreign service.

work that made them a little nervous and fanciful. A heart-to-heart talk with M. Briand might have done them good, for it was his action during the Morocco crisis that weighed upon their minds.

The miners, as they had shown in their great consenting vote, were in a warlike mood. One of the great mining constituencies had returned a Labour member distinctly in favour of conscription, and in the front of battle, where many of the miners had become tunnellers, they were among the keenest fighters in the world. Some of the Socialists among the miners had been inclined to make difficulties, with a view to bringing about the nationalisation of the mines, and a large number of men were indignant at the high price at which coal was being sold, and anxious either to force the price down, or at least to get a larger share of the profits they thought were being made. The Amalgamated Society of Engineers, representing a great and important body of highly-skilled men, was somewhat disturbed by sinister agitation. It was among them that the friends of Germany created the phantom menace of

a system of industrial conscription, which was used to hinder the work being done by the Ministry of Munitions in the great number of controlled factories working for the Army and Navy.

Even in the spring of 1916 the speed of production in some of our war factories was not satisfactory. Some trade unionists, men with years of experience, were outpaced in their special work by women, who had picked up their skill since the outbreak of war. The trouble on the Clyde, engineered by the Clyde Workers' Committee, became serious in March, 1916, when men engaged on heavy guns urgently needed by the Army in the field came out on strike. One of the Clyde agitators was the chairman of the Independent Labour Party in Scotland. Some of the ringleaders were deported, and about a score of men fined, and the strike ended on April 3rd, 1916. The vital problem of the dilution of skilled labour by new and half-trained or untrained men and women also produced a strike at the Harland & Wolff yard in Belfast at the end of March, 1916, and in other places the hesitation of some sections of trade unionists to co-operate loyally in the general interest with the new-comers in the shops and factories delayed the development of our warlike strength. On the other hand, skilled mechanics, urgently needed at home, were doing ordinary infantry work in the Army ; and, as was said at the time, boilermakers were tending camels in Egypt. Magnificent as the results of our voluntary enlistment had been, it had seriously interrupted the expansion of our vital war industries.

Great as was the worth of a trained soldier, the value of a man skilled in armament work was greater. France had for months been " combing out " her armies to recover all her first-rate mechanics, and it looked as though our country would also have to revise the mistakes made in our first great burst of recruiting energy, which had impoverished our workshops. There had been no forethought and no organisation of the nation's energies during the volunteer movement. Tens of thousands of men had become tyros in war who were already, without knowing it at the time, the finished pillars of our military and naval power. It was because so many highly patriotic men had left the Clyde yards for the barracks that the work of the sinister agitators there went on with such increasing virulence. In the trenches there were many men who began to desire to return to the shop and the yard, not because they were tired of fighting, but because they longed for an opportunity to discuss **Agitation on the Clyde** matters by coming into personal contact with some of their former shopmates.

The leaders of the trade unions were not unaware of the angry feeling pervading the very large section of trade unionists who had enlisted for military and naval service. The leaders knew also that the majority of men remaining at home were anxious to win the war at all costs, and that only a small, noisy minority of born "slackers" and ca' canny working-class profiteers, with hopeless cranks, fishers in troubled waters and agitators of a dubious sort, were, when matters came to the ultimate test, ready to help Germany by preventing us from becoming a great military Power on the Continental scale.

From the point of view of those Labour leaders who were supporting the Coalition Cabinet, the difficulty was that they represented a most important class that still needed to be educated in the matter of national service. We may fairly say that no effective strain of insular egoism remained in our country. Members of Parliament of the pro-German school now and then proclaimed to the world that their design was to save the loss of British lives ; but the people of Britain did not agree that French, Italian, and Russian conscripts ought to be allowed to fight to exhaustion for the freedom of civilisation while the fine volunteer British Army grew smaller in the autumn of 1915 because our casualties could not be made good by compulsory service.

With the 3/19th London (St. Pancras) Regiment bomb-throwing from practice trenches.

Instruction in machine gunnery at the famous Eastern Command School of Musketry at Hythe.

Squad of A Company, 8th (Service) Battalion the Leicester Regiment, digging trenches at Wokingham.

THREE PHASES OF BRITAIN'S MAMMOTH MILITARY MACHINE IN THE MAKING.

A great effort was made in February, 1916, to bring in sufficient "unstarred" (*i.e.*, not employed in munition factories or in indispensable trades) single men as volunteers to make the Military Service Bill, that came into operation on March 3rd, 1916, a dead letter. Mr. Redmond issued a manifesto to young Irishmen calling them to the Colours, and Lord Derby addressed a personal letter to every single man of military age who was liable to service. But the single men began to search for cover. In one district in London—Islington—it was found that some thousands of single men had departed, leaving no address. Published reports of proceedings at the Military Service Tribunals also exhibited a deplorable amount of tragically farcical cowardice on the part of a great number of conscientious objectors. Too long a start had been granted to the unpatriotic organisations which worked to discourage recruiting and to instil conscientious objections into "slackers" searching for any excuse to escape the risk of death. These organisations had practically covered England, Wales, and Scotland with their branches, and when the Military Tribunals were opened it was alleged that one

Appeals to the single men

that the meek should inherit the earth. The Quakers themselves, some of them men of wealth, who increased the funds of the unpatriotic associations, were also inclined to expand the very small and doubtful part of the Gospel that suited them, and to overlook the fact that Christ used force to drive the money-changers from the Temple and was far clearer in His condemnation of rich men than He was of soldiers.

The Society of Friends was on its trial before the nation during the spring of 1916. Some of its members were doing noble work at home and abroad and maintaining the glorious traditions of practical humanitarianism. But the general feeling was that the Friends had flourished for centuries in trade and finance under the protection of forces which they had no right to contemn. There was no question of their sincerity, but considerable doubt of their bias and narrowness in interpreting the Christian Gospel. It was felt that the primitive Christianity which they professed to restore went with personal poverty and a community of goods. They had totally disregarded Christ's attacks on wealth, and, while themselves growing one of the richest bodies in the kingdom in proportion to their numbers, had escaped the ultimate duties attaching to their wealth by exaggerating, in such a way as to pervert it, the doctrine of non-resistance. Christ Himself certainly resisted evil. Some of our modern Christian sects do a partial amount of good by emphasising neglected aspects of the Gospel, but it cannot be said that those members of the Society of Friends who helped in organising the movement to evade the duty of military service established by Act of Parliament did any benefit to the general cause of religion. Had they, like St. Francis of Assisi, carried out the spirit of Christ's teaching in regard to the possession of wealth, the quality of the conscience that made them object to war service would have been more generally respected.

Oxford and Cambridge, having poured their stores of virile and gallant youth into the Services, were strangely stricken by the blight of conscientious objection. Cambridge produced in Mr. Bertrand Russell the philosophic pillar of the new doctrine of

PRACTICE SHOOTING IN THE TRENCHES.
Members of the 69th Divisional Cyclists at practice shooting in the trenches. During the long months of siege warfare the cyclists to a great extent played the part of "cavalry" scouts.

anti-conscription society arranged a mock tribunal for coaching curs in all the arts of pious humbug by means of which they might be able to escape the drill sergeant.

The reports of proceedings at the Military Service Tribunals helped to augment the extraordinary number of able-bodied young men belonging to the new school of religious hypocrites. Amazing conversions occurred when ordinary "slackers" read in the newspapers the excuses brought forward by trained evaders belonging to fellowships and societies that had made a long study of the craft of evading legal military duties. Men with as much pluck and brains as the rabbit and as much conscience as the skunk became of a sudden philosophical disciples of Tolstoy, who was himself a genius, but at the same time the promoter of some of the most theatrical insincerities in modern life. Young infidels of the Agnostic sort also became suddenly converted to a new form of Quakerism, that did not require any belief in God, but only a belief that the man who would not fight could steal the job of the man that did—which was a new version of the beatitude

pacificism. He was able to give the convenient dogma of non-resistance a larger scope than Christianity afforded, and so make it a weapon to the hand of every pro-German agitator of an irreligious cast of mind. Another light of Cambridge, Mr. G. Lowes Dickinson, who had been working in the interests of the Union of Democratic Control, also became the intellectual guide to all the young men of Britain whose attitude encouraged the view that they would rather be ruled by the Kaiser than fight against him. A considerable strain of decadence in the educated English middle-class was revealed by the organising energy of the leaders of the conscientious objectors. A century of naval supremacy and unparalleled prosperity had produced a kind of sickly idealism and rhetorical sentimentalism which enabled some men and women to enjoy roast lamb and mint sauce while condemning the brutal work of the butchers who fed them.

All the routine, regular work of slaughter underlying our food supply was passed over by the new race of genteel

The dogma of non-resistance

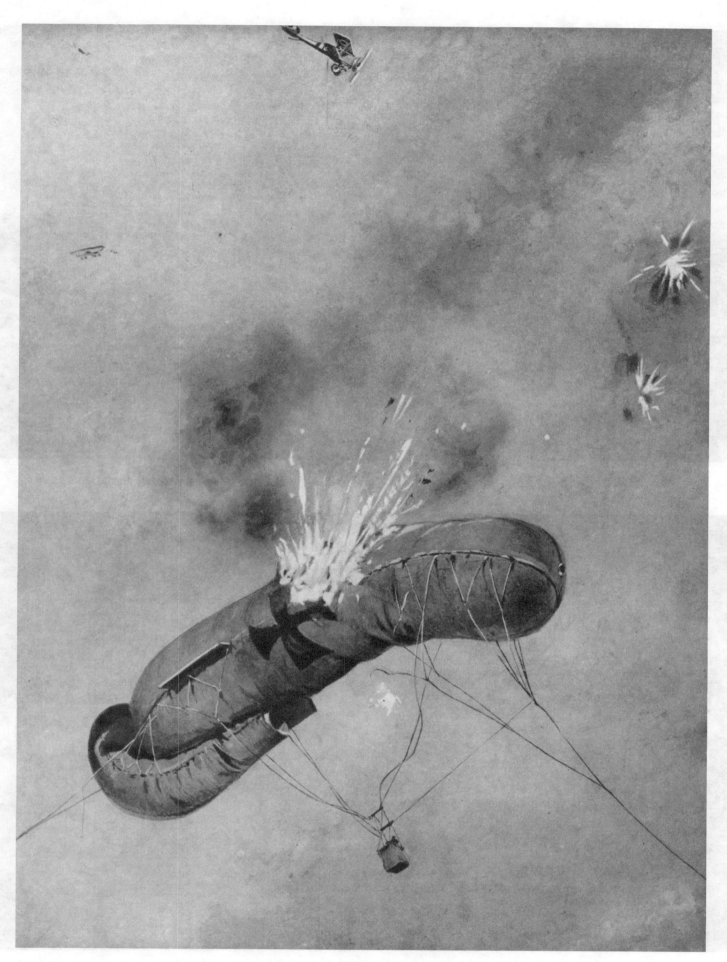

German observation balloon destroyed by bombs dropped from an aeroplane.

Great British howitzer, on railway mounting, in action on western front.

"Lucky Jim": British heavy howitzer well screened from the enemy.

Gun team ramming home shell in heavy howitzer seen firing in opposite photograph.

One of the many big guns in action on the western front. (Official photographs.)

Canadian officers training in the art of "sniping."

Soldiers being instructed in "sniping." (Official Canadian photographs.)

minds that fed on meat three times a day and discussed over the dinner-table Tolstoyism and the Higher Thought, with remarks about Futurist art and the last play by Bernard Shaw. In the highly organised world in which they lived the fundamental realities of life had been divorced from the graces of civilised intercourse. That section of our enriched middle-class, which neither had to work for its living nor take any active part in administrative and directive labours of the Empire, was the chief source of all the symptoms of decadence seen in our civilisation since the days when Oscar Wilde walked up Piccadilly with his sunflower. It incarnated all the fatal elements of sentimentalism that George Meredith had first clearly discerned as the gravest danger in our national life.

The terrible shock of the war saved many members of this class from perishing through fatty degeneration of the **The Non-Combatant** soul. But there still remained a consider-**Corps** able body of sentimentalists, whose spirit was so weakened by their long divorce from the realities of life that they succumbed to the menace of the armed power of Germany. At heart they were ready to remain at peace on any terms that the enemy cared to impose upon them. It was, indeed, from them that the Germans had obtained the idea that we should stand out of the war and gradually decline to a position of vassalage, and become in the greater Teutonic Empire what the Greeklings had become in the Roman Empire.

Such was the class that provided the larger number of conscientious objectors of the intellectual type, who joined forces with some members of the Society of Friends and with some Nonconformist congregations, though moved by no religious principles themselves. It was only the immediate selfish value of the doctrine of non-resistance that inclined this last rally of decadents to interest themselves in religion. Most of them, however, were put in the way of salvation by the Military Service Tribunals, through which, to their indignant surprise, they were passed for duty in a new Non-Combatant Corps. By the end of the spring of 1916 there were grounds of hope that many of them would be made into real men after working behind the battle-front, for a large proportion began to volunteer for the work of fighting.

A somewhat unexpected reinforcement to the party of conscientious objectors was the East London Federation of Suffragettes, which, led by Miss Sylvia Pankhurst, tried to hold a peace meeting in Trafalgar Square on April 9th, 1916. The meeting, however, was broken up by a large crowd of soldiers and civilians, and Miss Pankhurst and her supporters were collected by the police and moved from the danger zone. On the same day, at a meeting of the No-Conscription Fellowship in the Friends' Meeting House in Bishopsgate, the chairman, Mr. Clifford Allen, was alleged to have declared that young recruits who deserted would be received in the homes of married men in sympathy with the no-conscription movement. Then, amid much cheering, Mr. Clifford Allen went on to say that the only alternative to conscription allowed by the conscientious objectors was that the Government should immediately enter upon peace negotiations. This statement lent colour to the suggestion that the unpatriotic movements were not entirely disconnected with the German intrigues for bringing about a premature truce which the German war leaders required to enable them to reorganise their resources for a greater effort.

But all this agitation to impede the development of our national strength was but the buzzing futility of some flies round the wheels of our new war machine. A very strong majority of the people of the United Kingdom and the Overseas Dominions was determined to win a lasting, victorious peace. The only difficulty resided in the attempts made by some of the civil departments of the Government to maintain our commerce even at the expense

CHIEF OF THE STATE WITH THE CHIEF OF THE IMPERIAL GENERAL STAFF.
Notable photograph of his Majesty the King talking with General Sir William Robertson in the grounds of the Royal Pavilion at Aldershot.

of our military power. An Interdepartmental Committee existed for the purpose of representing the industries of the country against the War Office, and marking what men were indispensable. At the time when the National Register was made, in August, 1915, the reserved occupations—the workers in which were starred—were munition making, certain branches of agriculture, coal-mining, railway work, the merchant service, and public utility services. These were presumed to represent four-fifths of the exemptions of men of military age, while the remaining fifth was reckoned to be made up largely of men in export trades. When **Lord Derby and** Lord Derby made his report as to the **Lord Selborne** numbers of men available for service, he had a fairly precise idea of the number of starred men, but he was mistaken in regard to his calculations of the number of men in certified trades.

He afterwards discovered that the number of men who were able to get into reserved occupations between November, 1915, and January, 1916, was much beyond his estimate. The result was that the Military Service Bill for single men did not produce the recruits needed by the War Office. The whole cause of the shortage was the reserved occupations list. Lord Derby appealed to the Interdepartmental Committee to reduce the number of starred men and remove certain industries from the reserve list. He approached Lord Selborne, President of the Board of Agriculture. But Lord Selborne would not agree to the proposals, as he regarded the men engaged on the food resources of the country as absolutely indispensable. In Germany in times of peace the number of women

AIMING AT AN INVISIBLE
TARGET.
Firing a rifle-grenade at a bombing
school somewhere in France.

engaged in agricultural
pursuits was about eighty-
nine per cent., and in France
before the war the percentage of woman workers was
sixty-seven per cent. But
in England and Wales, in
the same circumstances, only
eight per cent. of women
workers were engaged in
agricultural pursuits. Lord
Selborne would not admit
that, when the need arrived,
our women also could look
after our farms while our
men fought.

But men had to be got
for the Army, and as Lord
Derby could not get the
Interdepartmental Com-
mittee to unstar some men
and remove some trades
from the reserve list, he

A WEAPON OF PRIMITIVE
TIMES.
Catapult used for hurling bombs
from trench to trench.

made a direct appeal to the Government to take action.
The result was a conference, under Mr. Walter Long, the
President of the Local Government Board, and attended
by the Secretary of State for War, the President of the
Board of Trade, a representative of the Board of Agricul-
ture, the Home Secretary, and other representatives of
Government departments. But while the

**Single men
" slackers "**

conference was trying to obtain more men
from the reserved industries and the
munition works, Lord Kitchener stated on
March 15th, 1916, that he would need more groups of
married men than he had expected. He also went on to say
that, even if he had obtained all the single men anticipated
from the Group System, he would still have required
a large number of married men in the spring of 1916.

By this time there was considerable unrest throughout the country in regard to the married men who had
attested under Lord Derby's scheme. The immense
number of homes that would be broken up by calling the
married men up for service made the women of the nation
angry about the large exemptions that had been given to

single men. Lord Derby candidly admitted that the Military Service Bill had only carried out the letter of the Prime
Minister's pledge. There were 1,100,000 men of military
age unattested, and the number of single men among
them was very large. Some forty per cent. of the 1,600,000
munition workers under Mr. Lloyd George's scheme were
reported to be single men. Doubtless a large proportion
of these bachelors in our war factories were skilled mechanics
who could only be gradually replaced,
but tens of thousands of them had fled
to the war factories for refuge since the
making of the National Register.

**Injustice to

married men**

On March 4th, 1916, the first call on attested married
men was made. Proclamations were posted in regard to
the eight groups, Nos. 25-32, referring to married men
between the ages of nineteen and twenty-six. April 7th
was the date fixed for their calling up, and it was reported
that nine more groups of married men, between the ages
of twenty-seven and thirty-five, would be called by proclamations to be posted in the middle of March. Thus,
only six groups of married men would be left in civilian
life, and it was stated that all attested married men would
be serving long before the
autumn. The unexpected-
ness and sweep of this
recruiting measure shook
the country. The attested
married groups held mass
meetings and protested
against the injustice being
done to them. They quickly
formed themselves into a
National Union of Attested
Married Men, and strongly
agitated by letters to members of Parliament, by
public meetings, and by
deputations to the leading
men in the Government.

They had two principal
grounds of complaint. In
the first place they argued
that their homes were being
broken up in order to fill

THE CATAPULT AT WORK.
The bomb fuse having been ignited, the missile was released. For the
perilous work with the bombs men were selected and carefully trained.

THE BOMBS EXPLODE.
Taking cover in the deep trenches after hurling bombs on to an imaginary enemy position. The natural instinct of self-preservation was developed by special training.

BOMBS AND BAYONETS AT THE READY.
Soldiers in training getting ready to advance against a hostile position—the most thrilling moment in warfare.

the ranks at a time when hundreds of thousands of single men in the flower of their strength were escaping from military service. In the second place they called attention to statements made, apparently upon official authority, during the working of Lord Derby's scheme, which had led them to think that if a married man did not attest he would have no right to appeal. The representatives of the National Union stated that many of the married men had attested on the understanding that there would be compulsion for all. They also accused Mr. Asquith, when he received a deputation from them, of not having fully carried out the pledge given in regard to compelling single men to serve before married men were called up.

Call for equality of sacrifice The National Union of Attested Married Men made a stand upon the principle of equality of sacrifice. In other words, the attested groups asked for a general system of compulsory national service for all men of military age. Their grudge, of course, was heaviest against the single men who had escaped service, but they also wanted to include all available married men who had not attested. There were reckoned to be 1,029,231 unattested single men and 1,152,947 unattested married men. The two groups were estimated to be capable of yielding together more than 800,000 fit recruits. The feeling in the attested groups ran deep and strong, and practically every member of Parliament felt some of the stress of it from his electors. Mr. Asquith had a somewhat angry interview with a deputation of the National Union on April 12th, 1916, but he was not inclined to adopt their policy of conscription for every fit man up to the age of forty-one.

Two days before the deputation to the Prime Minister, Sir William Robertson, our Imperial Chief of Staff, made his final report to the Cabinet in regard to the number of men needed to end the war. Then, at a Cabinet meeting on April 15th, which was held in consultation with the military authorities, a decision was arrived at not to pursue a national policy of compulsion. A sub-committee of the Cabinet, composed of Mr. Asquith, Lord Lansdowne, Mr. McKenna, and Mr. Austen Chamberlain, was reported to have gone thoroughly into the question of recruiting, and to have discovered that the men needed by the Imperial Staff could be obtained by three methods. The first was the compulsory enlistment of all lads reaching the age of eighteen, the second was the "combing out" of some 300,000 single men from reserved occupations, and the third was the embodiment of all attested married men.

This scheme did not come into operation. A strong

THE BRITISH COMMANDER-IN-CHIEF IN LONDON.
General Sir Douglas Haig photographed leaving the War Office on the occasion of his last visit there before the British offensive opened on July 1st, 1916.

the Coalition Government by surrendering for the moment their principles.

A secret session was a novelty in our Parliamentary history, and it was not regarded with favour. Among the thousand men who listened to the secret revelation of our military position and our military needs were some notorious persons who had paraded their disinclination to co-operate towards a decisive close of the war. It was, besides, against the spirit of our system of Government to hold a secret session, and members of Parliament felt uncomfortable while listening to information they were bound not to reveal. In the secret session the Prime Minister impressed the majority in the House with the fact that the military situation was such as demanded a change of policy. He made an especial attempt to win the general consent of the representatives of organised labour, to whose anti-conscription views, he afterwards publicly admitted, he attached great importance. He proposed a plan

party in the Cabinet, headed by Mr. Lloyd George, stood out for the principle of equality of sacrifice. The dispute turned largely upon the point whether the attested groups of married men should bear all the burden of service, leaving a very large body of unattested fit men of military age free from the obligation of training for battle. The lowest estimate of the number of married men of military age fit for service and unattested was given by Mr. Asquith as 200,000. But Mr. Lloyd George reckoned that a considerably greater number than 200,000 could be spared from munition work and other vital industries and brought into a general scheme of compulsion.

For some days neither party in the Cabinet would yield. April 17th, 1916, was the first day of public anxiety, and the tension continued until April 19th, when Mr. Asquith announced :

There are material points of disagreement in the Cabinet, and if these points cannot be settled by agreement, the result must be the break-up of the Government. The Cabinet is united in believing that this would be a national disaster of the most formidable kind. It is in the hope it may be averted by a few days' more deliberation that I shall propose that this House, at its rising to-day, adjourns till Tuesday.

But on the afternoon of April 20th the Cabinet came to an agreement upon the proposals to be made to Parliament upon the subject of recruiting, and it was arranged that these proposals should be submitted to a secret session on Tuesday, April 25th. The fact was that under the influence of Mr. Arthur Henderson, President of the Board of Education and sole Labour member in the Cabinet, Mr. Lloyd George and his group had made concessions in order to save the Coalition Government. Bitter attacks were afterwards made upon Mr. Lloyd George in two of the principal organs of the Radical-Liberal school of politics. The famous Welsh democrat was charged with personal treachery and treachery to the cause of democracy, and with various other sins. His former friends and admirers attacked him in a vein of virulent meanness that defeated itself and merely revealed the depth of character in a certain class of political writers, for Mr. Lloyd George and the other members of the Cabinet who agreed with him in regard to the necessity of general compulsion had saved

Secret session of Parliament

that did not involve immediate compulsion, but carried on the scheme of getting recruits by instalments if they could be got to come forward in requisite number by the dates required by the military authorities. Four weeks of voluntary recruiting were arranged, as had been proposed by the Labour member of the Cabinet, Mr. Arthur Henderson. Then, to meet the immediate needs of the situation, the Government put forward a measure to keep time-expired men in service until the end of the war and to transfer Territorial troops into Regular battalions where needed, and also to apply conscription to all lads reaching the age of eighteen.

Mr. Stephen Walsh's protest

These proposals were embodied in a Military Service Bill, which was brought before the House of Commons on April 27th, 1916. Mr. Walter Long asked leave to introduce the measure, and the result was an astonishing situation, for which no parallel can be found in recent times. The bill was killed before it was born. In the debate not a voice was raised except in criticism or condemnation, and the strongest attack was made by Mr. Stephen Walsh, the Labour member who represented a large body of miners. He said that there was no fair play in the measure, and that the Prime Minister had led the Labour members to understand he would resign if a measure of the nature of any compulsion was introduced. Yet Mr. Walsh went on to say that if a scheme of general compulsion were introduced he would now vote for such a measure.

Why temporise any longer ? It is simply fooling with the whole business. When the last Military Service Bill was before the House I suggested that men who had gone into reserved occupations since August 15th should be brought within its scope. Now, several months after, the Government are endeavouring to "comb out" those who ought never to have been there. We were told this was being vigorously done.

I know something of the area in which I act as miners' agent, and there not a single man is being brought out of the mines. That is the vigorous way in which the process is going on ! Not a single one ! Papers have been supplied and have been filled up, but not a single person has been brought out, though there is the very best ground for believing that at least 3,000 men between eighteen and forty-one, who never worked in mines before, have gone into mines for the purpose of escaping their military obligations. And that which is true of my part of Lancashire is true, I believe, in a greater degree of the whole area of Great Britain.

The rights and privileges of citizens have been advanced. I know nothing that gives me a right to skulk in safety at the expense of others. Let us have a straightforward Bill. Let the Government take its courage in both hands and say, " This necessity has arisen and must now be resolutely met." If it make an appeal such as that to the country it need not despair of a response.

It was clear that the proposal for general compulsion was the only measure which the House would support. Mr. Lloyd George and his group, whose resignations had been expected ten days before, proved to have a majority in Parliament as well as overwhelming support in the country. It was the Cabinet group that had not agreed to equality of sacrifice, and had threatened to break up

SIR CHARLES WAKEFIELD (IN MOURNING) CONVERSING WITH A GENERAL OFFICER.

the Government rather than consent to it, which was patently without either national or Parliamentary support. In these circumstances Mr. Asquith accepted the defeat of the Cabinet Bill—which in peace time would have meant the defeat of the Government—and arranged to bring in a measure for general and immediate compulsion.

The Prime Minister asked leave to introduce the Bill on May 2nd, 1916. In his speech on this occasion he summarised some of the reasons given in the secret session for the necessity of obtaining more recruits. The forces of the Empire consisted of forty-two Regular and twenty-eight Territorial divisions, with one Naval division and twelve Dominion divisions, which, excluding India, made eighty-three divisions. The average number of men in each British division was 25,000. For the purpose of maintaining a British Army of seventy divisions a weekly inflow of 25,000 to 30,000 men had to be obtained. The provision of at least 200,000 recruits from the unattested married men class was, the Prime Minister stated, of vital importance to the maintenance of the strength of the Army in the field, in view of the contingencies of the summer and autumn campaign. Moreover, the number of men needed could, it was estimated, be spared from industry without crippling our financial power, our output of munitions, or the maintenance of our sea-power and ocean transport.

The new Bill laid down that every male British subject between eighteen and forty years of age was to be deemed to be duly enlisted in the regular forces for general service, unless he came within the exceptions set out in the schedule to the Military Service Act of January, 1916. Time-expired men were to be retained in service for the duration of the war. **Parliament and compulsion** Members of the Territorial force were to be transferred to the Regular forces if the Army Council so required, and the Army Council was given power to review the medical certificates of men who had been rejected for unfitness since August 14th, 1915. The main outlines of the Bill were not altered in its passage through Parliament, except that time-expired men over military age who had done twelve years' service were exempted, and men dismissed from certified occupations were given two months' grace instead of being made liable to be called up in two weeks. This step was taken to avoid the appearance of industrial conscription and prevent employers from threatening to turn men quickly into the Army if they did not give way on some disputed point. On the second reading of the Bill, on May 4th, 1916, Mr. Lloyd George made a speech of striking vigour and sweep in support of it. He stated that the Imperial General Staff had made an irresistible demand for every available man to be called up and trained for the field, and he asked his critics if they could bring forward some ground of principle that would override even military necessity.

THE LORD MAYOR OF LONDON AT THE FRONT.
Sir Charles Wakefield visited the front in June, 1916, taking a message of good cheer from the metropolis to men of the City regiments. He is here seen inspecting trenches.

He pointed out that every great democracy which has had its liberties menaced has defended itself by resort to compulsion. Washington won independence for America by compulsory measures, and Lincoln kept democracy alive by conscription. He maintained that when his critics said that conscription was contrary to the principles of liberty they were talking in defiance of common-sense and the whole teaching of history. Even if **Mr. Lloyd George** the measure produced only 200,000 men, **and his critics** which was an underestimate, that meant ten divisions of infantry. In the first critical Battle of Ypres, when the troops on both sides were at last exhausted, a single fresh British or German division would have meant victory to the country that could bring it up. The Minister for Munitions went on to say that we might even have to take greater risks in regard to our financial power and form a larger Army should certain contingencies arise.

Then the Labour Minister, Mr. Arthur Henderson, frankly admitted that of all members of the Cabinet he had hitherto been the greatest drag-weight on the question of compulsion, but now that compulsion had become a military necessity he stated he was convinced that the alternative of conscription or defeat would unite and not divide the nation. He pointed out that, owing to the rough-and-ready system of voluntary recruiting, men from skilled trades had gone into the Army, and thereby

directly created our grave difficulty in regard to a shortage of merchant ships. He agreed with Mr. Lloyd George that considerably more than 200,000 unattested fit men of military age could be spared from industry in order to increase our means of making a victorious peace. The House then divided on the Bill. There were only thirty-six votes against it, while the votes in favour of it were 328.

Mr. Lloyd George addressed a meeting of his constituents at Conway after his great victory in the House of Commons. He said that he had 300,000 women in his munition works, engaged upon tasks which no one before the war assumed a woman was capable of discharging—such as metal-work, chemical work, and other heavy labour. In his young days, he observed, a far larger proportion of women were engaged in agricultural work than was now the case, and, if the need arrived, women could still look after the farms and let the men fight. He remarked that the colossal effort made by Lord Derby to **"Time not** recruit the men in groups had a mixture **an ally"** of compulsion in it, and a great many disadvantages of both conscription and voluntaryism, without the advantages of either. He stated that, while working harmoniously under the Prime Minister, he had had some differences of opinion with his chief, and he asked what use he would have been if he had not stated his views freely, frankly, and independently. Free discussion was wanted in the council chamber—counsellors were not

ONWARD—EVER ONWARD—FOR THE GLORY OF BRITAIN!
The tramp of armed men livening a deserted village street in the Somme district. With steady step and stern resolve a regiment of Britain's new citizen soldiers is seen advancing to take up its position in the great allied offensive of July, 1916.

merely penny-in-the-slot machines, and, if the nation required only automatons, Mr. Lloyd George said he would not be one of them. In a very remarkable passage he observed :

I want to say one thing : time is not an ally. It is a doubtful neutral at the present moment, and has not yet settled on our side. But time can be won over by effort, by preparation, by determination, by organisation. And we must have unity among the Allies, with design and co-ordination. Unity we undoubtedly possess. No alliance that ever existed has worked in more perfect unison and harmony than the present one. But there is still left a good deal to be desired in regard to design and co-ordination. Strategy must come before geography. The Central Powers are pooling all their forces, all their intelligence, all their efforts. We have the means. They, too often, have the methods. Let us

THE PUBLIC SCHOOLS AND THE WAR.
General Broadwood inspecting members of the Westminster School O.T.C. at St. Vincent Square.

AFTER THE REVIEW.
General Broadwood (next to the Headmaster of Westminster School) with Captain Trench, A.D.C., and Captain Willett, of the Westminster O.T.C.

apply their methods to our means and we shall win. I believe in the old motto, "Trust the people." Tell them what is happening. There is nothing to conceal. They are a courageous people, but they never put forward their best effort until they face the alternative of disaster. Tell them with what they are confronted, and they will rise to every occasion. You can trust the people. I read a story the other day about a mining camp at the front of a black mountain in the Great West. The diggers had been toiling long and hard with but scant encouragement for their labours, and one night a terrible storm swept over the mountain. An earthquake shattered its hard surface, and hurled its rocks about, and in the morning, in the rents and fissures, the miners found a rich deposit of gold. This is a great storm that is sweeping over the favoured lands of Europe. But in this night of terror you will find that the hard crust of selfishness and greed has been shattered, and in the rent hearts of the people you will find golden treasures of courage, steadfastness, endurance, devotion, and the faith that endureth for ever.

On the platform at Conway beside Mr. Lloyd George was another famous Welshman, Mr. W. M. Hughes, Prime Minister of the Labour Cabinet of Australia. The arrival of Mr. Hughes in Britain during the crisis over compulsory service was a fortunate thing for the Motherland. Mr. Hughes was the first Labour Premier in the history of mankind, and the working men from whom he had sprung

regarded his views with a peculiar consideration for of all the leading men of the Anglo-Celtic race he could least be charged with working in favour of the employing classes. He dragged the modern German system into the full light of democratic criticism, and showed it to be the abnegation of every democratic principle—an unholy alliance between a caste of aggressive conquerors and a powerful organisation of Trust magnates who aimed at the economic conquest of the world. In speeches of clear eloquence and telling feeling, the leader of democracy in Australia pointed out that the German capitalists had prepared for a victorious war by getting a monopoly over some of the most important pivotal industries connected with warlike manufactures.

Mr. Hughes was principally concerned at the time in inviting such arrangements in regard to the working of the resources of the Empire that German intriguers could never again control the spelter market and other pivotal trades. But, at the same time, he urged the working classes of Britain to organise all their forces for victory. "Time is the essence of the contract, and if we now fail, then surely as I live, and as the Lord our Saviour lives," he said at Conway, "we shall go down to hell." He meant an earthly inferno on the Prussian model, with two or three hundred Trust magnates dominating the workmen, grinding them into economic serfdom, and calling on a military caste to shoot the populace down if they tried to rise and strike for industrial and political liberty of action.

Battle-cry of Mr. W. M. Hughes

In January, 1916, there had been some talk of civil war occurring if a general measure for compulsory service were passed. Even Mr. Stephen Walsh, who afterwards became so impassioned an advocate of the principle of equality of sacrifice, was inclined at the beginning of the year to think that an attempt to carry out the Prime Minister's pledge to attested married men might bring about a great strike leading to a revolt. Then, Mr. J. H. Thomas, one of the leaders of the railwaymen, was still more openly afraid of some great national disturbances if general compulsion were used. Indeed, Mr. Thomas's language became, at times, almost menacing towards the Coalition Government. Other Labour members were still more hostile, and some of them seemed to work rather with a view to make things easy for the German capitalist and military castes by enabling them to secure the peace that Germany wanted than to ensure the triumph of the root principles of every form of free life. Against the agitation of this latter group of strangely doubtful working-class representatives the influence of the Labour Premier of Australia told with quelling effect.

The new Military Service Bill received the Royal assent on Thursday, May 27th, 1916. Thus was accomplished the greatest revolution in our social system since the institution of feudalism under William the Conqueror. The nation had reverted in the great crisis of its fate to the method of Saxon and Norman times, when the king had a right to take for the purpose of national defence every man, ship, and available chattel in his dominion. In English history this ancient right to press men, ships, and wealth continued in a vague and indefinite form through the feudal era, and became the ground of the common law tradition for our old press-gang system. It was not until the merchant ship became absolutely inferior in fighting power to the warship that the king's right to collect all the available merchant marine for the purpose of defence became vaguely obsolete. But some modern authorities maintained that the common law right of the monarch to call up every man to defend the country still survived from the days of Alfred the Great; compulsion for home defence was enforced by Pitt.

Soon after general conscription was revived in a modern form in regard to persons, our country took a direct step in regard to the conscription of wealth, which had already begun with the very high income tax.

Conscription of men and wealth There were some two hundred million pounds' worth of gilt-edged American securities held in Great Britain in the spring of 1916. The Chancellor of the Exchequer had then been engaged for nearly six months in mobilising American stock in order to obtain ready capital in the United States to pay the debts of Britain and her Allies. The vast orders for munitions given to American firms by Russia, Britain, and France required vast payments. It was impossible for us to develop our exports to the United States into the enormous volume of commerce required to balance the amount of food and manufactures pouring from American ports into the ports of the Grand Alliance. Despite the gold we sent across the Atlantic, the rate of exchange fell against us, until the British pound sterling could not purchase anything like five dollars' worth of goods. We therefore had to sell to the Americans more of our holdings in their joint-stock concerns.

But in May, 1916, Mr. McKenna, our Chancellor of the Exchequer, was not receiving at the National Debt Office the amount of American securities he needed. So on May 29th he proposed to establish a special tax on American securities which had not been lent to the Government. A preliminary tax of two shillings in the pound was fixed to come into operation on July 1st, but the Chancellor frankly explained that, if this tax did not bring in the securities he needed, it would be increased even up to twenty shillings in the pound. It was, of course, understood that nobody lost the value of the securities he lent to the Government. It was only a kind of forced loan under the threat of an overwhelming tax. But the menace of taxation began to produce the desired effect upon British holders of American securities, and at the beginning of June, 1916, the clerks in the National Debt Office had to work at high pressure collecting the two hundred million pounds' worth of American stock that had been skilfully conscripted for Government requirements.

Daylight saving introduced

About the same time a still more extraordinary form of compulsion was instituted by the Government. Practically everybody was compelled to rise an hour earlier and work longer in daylight, in order to save the lighting resources of the country. An ingenious scheme of daylight saving had been proposed some years before by a London master-builder, Mr. William Willett. In our conservative country, in the lethargic days of peace, Mr. Willett was regarded partly as a crank and partly as rather too clever a man of the employing class, who wished to get more labour out of his workmen. But his brilliant idea of reverting in industries, during the long summer days, to the ordinary conditions under which agricultural work was done, was taken up in Germany and reduced to practice. All the clocks were put on an hour in summer, so that the ordinary day's work should end at evening in full daylight, thus saving the expense of lighting, and obviating the fatigue due to lessening natural light at the close of the day.

Many millions of pounds were, it was estimated, being saved in Germany by the adoption of this English idea. In times of peace we should have gone on, no doubt, neglecting our own discovery as we had formerly neglected our dye discoveries, our electrical discoveries, our vacuum-flask invention, and various other British ideas which the Germans had annexed and then energetically developed. But during a great war we could not allow the enemy to win over us the advantage of saving an annual sum equal to the interest on a £400,000,000 war loan by monopolising

GAS DRILL, AN ESSENTIAL DUTY OF BRITISH SOLDIERS IN TRAINING.
How a regiment before its departure to the front underwent a severe course of training in the application of respirators.

FROM AUSTRALIA TO FLANDERS VIA GALLIPOLI.
A column of the splendid Anzacs on their way to the trenches.

Mr. Willett's idea. So our Government brought in the Daylight Saving Bill, which received the Royal Assent on May 17th, 1916, and at 2 a.m. on Sunday, May 21st, the nation temporarily lost an hour in summer-time, and had to rise an hour earlier and labour every full working day an hour in brighter light.

Meanwhile, the calls to the remaining groups of attested married men, which had been postponed during the great agitation in March, were gradually posted by the military authorities. Groups 33-41, including men of from twenty-seven to thirty-five years of age, were called up by proclamation at the end of April, and on May 29th these married men went out to join the Colours. June 24th was fixed as the date for the calling up of all remaining married men, and July 24th was the ultimate date for all men to report at recruiting offices.

It was a profound upheaval of home life in Britain. Though the men came up with brave faces, attended sometimes by their wives and children, there was deep anxiety of mind in all the emptied and emptying homes. The only class of married men in uncertified

Great upheaval of home life

occupations who were likely to be released from military duties were those who were the sole head of a business with a family of three persons depending on them. These men, according to instructions sent to the tribunals, were to be released in the national interest by reason of their value as contributors to the national revenue. The State had made certain special allowances to the new married recruits. Besides the usual cost of their upkeep on military service and the ordinary allowance to their families, there had been established a system of Government relief to meet the rent, insurance, and other liabilities of married recruits up to the sum of £104 a year. Then in order to prevent the permanent breaking up of the homes of the wives and children, the Local Government Board, towards the end of May, 1916, empowered all local authorities to make arrangement for the storage of furniture belonging to men serving in the forces. The plan was intended to apply, in particular, to married men whose wives and children were preparing to live elsewhere during the absence of the breadwinner. The local authorities were permitted to incur reasonable expenditure in storing the furniture of recruits, though they did not seem to move very quickly in the matter when the first new groups went into the recruiting offices. All this tended to increase the cost to the nation of the services of married men at the very time when their value as contributors of revenue

THE BROAD SMILE OF ANZAC.
Confident expressions of Overseas Britons, men who came from the ultimate end of the earth to help shoulder the Empire's burden.

BUSY MOMENTS IN THE NEW ZEALANDERS' TRENCHES.
Consolidating a position on the firing-front with stones and wire.
(Official photographs. Crown copyright reserved.)

53

AT THE MILITARY TAILOR'S.
Scene in a workshop where thousands of uniforms were turned out to
clothe some of the magic millions of Britain's fighting men.

many of their farm hands with them.

This class used the Sinn Fein simply as a shield against military service. A considerable number of young officials in the Irish Post Office and other Government offices also joined the movement, seemingly with a wild desire to be in any shindy that was preparing. Ireland, however, was fairly quiet in the early part of the war, and it was principally alien enemies and bribed traitors that helped the German submarines with oil supplies. The police noticed, in both Galway and the south, that certain men in poor circumstances suddenly and strangely acquired more money than they could handle

was· annulled. But so urgent was the need of more soldiers that the process of gathering in the married men went on with great speed in order to recover the time lost during the final agitation for general compulsion.

The people of Ireland had from the beginning been left out of all schemes for national service. For the trouble was that a considerable body of men in the Catholic regions was not merely hostile to all recruiting schemes, but actively disloyal. In Galway the Clan-na-Gael, the Irish-American secret society of murderers, maimers, and terrorisers, still maintained an active branch, which was connected with the Sinn Fein. The Sinn Fein had started long before the war as a literary-political association, which was chiefly remarkable for promoting the spread of Gaelic speech and encouraging the study of the ancient literature of Ireland and Gaelic Scotland. There was a good deal of fanciful amateurishness among the early Sinn Feiners in Dublin, who were drawn largely from the middle-class followers of the Irish literary movement, but this little local back-wash of æstheticism became a potent source of trouble when the Sinn Fein was organised into con-

**German Intrigue
in Ireland**

nection with the Clan-na-Gael and the powerful Teutonic-American forces working in preparation for the Great War.

Certain Sinn Feiners in the United States boasted, at a convention held in New York in the first week of March, 1916, that they had submarines of their own. Before this the Sinn Feiners probably had petrol supply bases for German U boats along the Kerry coast. According to an allegation afterwards made before the Royal Commission in Dublin, a German, who managed a large number of hotels owned by the Great Southern and Western Railway, filled the hotels with alien enemies, escaped internment, and worked around Killarney in the interests of Germany. The man appeared to have powerful friends, and was allowed to remain in the area scheduled under the Defence of the Realm Act. Throughout Catholic Ireland certain of the young priests helped in promoting a movement of rebellion, and in some cases urged their congregations to acts of bloodshed. Then there were a great many farmers' sons enjoying extraordinary prosperity owing to the high rise in the price they were getting for their crops and cattle. They wished to avoid military service for purely mercenary reasons, and, probably without intending to resort to acts of war, joined the Sinn Fein and brought

RECLOTHING A NATION.
Automatic packing of a dozen Army greatcoats to be sent to the men in the
expeditionary forces overseas.

with discretion. But for nearly twelve months recruiting for the British Army went on with good results, especially in the towns. The proportion of recruits in Catholic Dublin was only about half that in Protestant Belfast, but, owing to the appeal made by Mr. John Redmond, even Dublin produced nearly a division of men.

The establishment of the National Register and the stoppage of emigration of men of military age, however, produced a bad effect on the Catholic population. The fear of conscription then led a large number of men to join the Sinn Fein movement. and many people who at first rather favoured the British cause began to sympathise with the rebel movement. Sinn Fein organisers became extremely active in many parts of the West and South of Ireland, and in January, 1916, some of the young priests began to deliver seditious sermons, calling on the people to arm with any weapons they could find, even axes. Sir Neville Chamberlain, the Chief of the Irish Police, reported to the Under-Secretary for Ireland, Sir Matthew Nathan, that the arms and explosives in the hands of the extremists were a public danger, and he urged that all persons unconnected with the Crown should be compelled to get a permit to carry arms. But the warning and recommendation of the Inspector-General of Constabulary were disregarded, and the Irish constables were discouraged in their activities and inclined to turn their eyes away from what was going on.

The fact was that Mr. Augustine Birrell, the Secretary of State for Ireland, was largely governed by the views of Mr. John Redmond and Mr. Dillon. The leaders of the Nationalist Party were in many ways the chief opponents of the leaders of the Sinn Fein. It was against Mr. Redmond and Mr. Dillon that the heads of the Sinn Fein directed their most virulent abuse and their subtlest intrigues. For the Irish Nationalist Party, with its largely successful programme of reform by constitutional means, was the grand obstacle to the desperate futile scheme of the rebel chiefs. The general body of the people of Catholic Ireland was fairly well contented with the work done by Mr. John Redmond, and the farming class, that was merely using the Sinn Fein as a shield against conscription, did not dream of losing their best market and being over-whelmed in the horrors of a civil war in which the Protestants of Ulster would have struck with all their might by the side of British troops.

WINTER WEAR ON THE WAY.
A.S.C. men moving cases of winter service caps to a motor-waggon.

Mr. John Redmond would seem to have miscalculated a problem which he should best have been able to solve. He despised the Sinn Fein as a picturesque and noisy futility, that seemed only to cover the serious disinclination of the farming classes to recruit for the war. The Nationalist leader did not allow for the blind passion of violence in his countrymen, which makes a good many Irishmen willing to join in any sort of a shindy for pure love of fighting.

Among such a race there was little consideration for the issue of a rebellion. With the exception of the farmers, who had a clear but limited end in view, towards which they worked with the political talent that had long distinguished them, the Sinn Feiners

desired a fight. They had the spirit of first-rate fighting men, if not the training, and the poor, undeveloped lads of the Dublin slums, who had been drawn into the movement of rebellion by Socialistic propaganda, were still wilder for an affray of some sort. Neither the village boys, nor the amateur intellectuals of the middle-class, nor yet the transport workers, weighed the chances of revolt.

The only practical way in which the hopelessness of their aim could be brought home to them was a display of overwhelming force from the British Government, and following this display of force there should have been a general disarmament. Lord Midleton, acting as the mouthpiece for an influential section of Irishmen in Dublin and the south, pressed Mr. Birrell to disarm the Sinn Fein Volunteers, and bring to trial the men who were making seditious speeches. But Mr. Birrell said that the Sinn Feiners were to be laughed at   **Irish Secretary's** and not taken seriously. Hearing more   **inaction** grave reports in January, 1916, Lord Midleton had an interview with the Prime Minister, but could not convince him the situation was dangerous. Again, in February, March, and April, Lord Midleton collected evidence of German intrigue and German help in arming and maturing the preparations of the Sinn Feiners, and placed this evidence before Mr. Birrell and the Under-Secretary for Ireland. The Under-Secretary became alarmed at last. To the end, however, Mr. Birrell held to the policy of non-intervention, and he was supported by both Mr. Redmond, who regarded the Sinn Feiners as practically harmless, and Mr. Dillon, who regarded them as dangerous.

The policy of non-intervention, it seems, was not a Cabinet decision, but the personal decision of Mr. Birrell, swayed by Mr. Redmond and Mr. Dillon. He knew there was a good deal of tinder in Ireland, but thought that nothing except bomb-throwing was likely to occur unless a German army landed: On the other hand, he was afraid to take strong action and order a general disarmament. The Ulstermen would have laid down their arms, and so would the National Volunteers, but it was possible that blood would be shed in disarming the Sinn Feiners, and Mr. Birrell was lacking in the strength of character needed at the time in any Secretary for Ireland.

FROM THE CONTRACTOR TO THE FRONT.
Each consignment is about to be sent to some regiment somewhere on Empire duty—France, the Balkans, the Persian Gulf, or elsewhere—according to the stencilled addresses on each case.

He was a good-natured, easy-going barrister, with a mind that played wittily over the surface of things and never penetrated deeply. He had won his way to power by his connection with Nonconformist interests and his literary fame as an essayist of the lighter sort. Personal charm was his only distinction, and he had been a political cement of great party value in the Liberal Cabinet, when the Imperial Liberal Leaguers and the Little England Radical group had come together in a state of great friction. He was the incarnation of all the virtues of soothing syrup, and it was by reason of his soothing power that he had been made Secretary for Ireland in succession to Lord Bryce.

British Fleet's preparedness Naturally, when strong yet only anticipatory measures had to be taken, Mr. Birrell flinched. It was beyond the power of his nature to adopt what the enemy calls the offensive-defensive, and, rather than provoke a few unimportant riots by disarming the Sinn Feiners, he practically allowed Mr. Redmond and Mr. Dillon to direct the larger affairs of Catholic Ireland without saddling them with any responsibility for the results. Mr. Dillon was afterwards able to make in Parliament an extraordinary accusation, winged with wild passion, against the military authorities who were putting down the insurrection, which had happened through following out the policy of non-intervention for which he was practically, though not constitutionally, responsible. Such was the way in which Ireland in the crisis of her fate was vaguely governed.

Happily, the British Fleet covered Ireland, and by some mysterious means penetrated into the enemy's designs in regard to the Sinn Fein movement. On April 17th, 1916, the Admiralty obtained information that a German ship, accompanied by German submarines, was due to arrive at Ireland on April 21st. A steamer, showing the Norwegian colours, crossed the North Sea at the time appointed, and was met by one of our patrol boats north of the Faroe Isles. After an examination of the ship's papers the vessel was apparently allowed to pass as a neutral trader. She then shaped a new course towards the south-west of Ireland, and was met again by another patrol, H.M.S. Bluebell, some one hundred and thirty miles west of Queenstown and ninety miles from the nearest land, and ordered to Queenstown for further search. She was the expected German ammunition ship, a Wilson liner captured by the Germans and renamed the Aude. She contained twenty thousand rifles, a million rounds of ammunition, bombs, firebombs, and ten machine-guns, hidden beneath a layer of merchandise.

The Norwegian crew was really composed of twenty-one picked men of the German Navy, commanded by a lieutenant, with a junior officer as his second in command. Off Daunt's Rock, near Queenstown Harbour, the disguised German auxiliary ship suddenly hoisted the German flag, and the crew put off in boats, were fired on by way of warning by the Bluebell, raised a flag of truce, and were captured. But before leaving the liner they lighted the fuse of a powerful bomb which blew the ship up.

While this remarkable incident was taking place, one of the German submarines that had accompanied the ammunition ship approached Tralee Bay, in Kerry. Early in the morning of Good Friday, April 21st, three men landed near Ardfert by means of a collapsible boat. The first man was Sir Roger Casement, a leader of the Sinn Fein, who had been staying in Germany; the second was a mysterious man called Monteith; and the third was a

ROGER CASEMENT.
The Irish traitor.

soldier of the Royal Irish Rifles, Daniel Bailey, who had been captured by the enemy at the front and afterwards released and sent to Wilhelmshafen for the submarine voyage to Kerry. Casement had apparently arranged for the three to be met. But some Sinn Feiners, driving in a motor-car to the rendezvous among the dunes, had an extraordinary accident on Good Friday night. The car jumped a bridge near Castlemaine Bay, twenty miles from Tralee, and its occupants were drowned. This seems to have broken an important link between various arrangements. Casement was taken prisoner by the police in the brushwood of an old Irish fort near the shore; Daniel Bailey was arrested on his way inland; and only the man of mystery, Monteith, evaded the searching constables.

It afterwards appeared that the destination of the German ammunition ship was Fenit, in Tralee Bay, in the neighbourhood of the spot at which Sir Roger Casement and his companions had landed from the German submarine, and not far distant from the apparent destination of the Sinn Feiners who were drowned in the motor-car. One of the prisoners said that the ammunition ship had not been due to come in and unload its deadly cargo until Easter Monday morning, and that a pilot-boat was to be lying outside and showing two green lights.

On Easter Sunday, according to a statement made before the Royal Commission in Dublin, some three hundred and sixteen Sinn Feiners mobilised in Tralee, apparently to assist in the landing of arms. But no rising took place, as the rebel leader in Kerry had been arrested at the same time as Casement was taken. Some of the Sinn Feiners complained that the German ammunition ship had thrown everything out by arriving too soon off Ireland. On the other hand, we have seen that our Admiralty authorities knew that the ship was coming on April 17th. So, in any case, the situation seems to have been mastered by the British Fleet some days before any danger arose.

But matters did not go so well in regard to the British military surveillance of the Sinn Fein insurrectionary movements. There was a terrible outbreak in Dublin, and smaller risings elsewhere, the story of which, related by an eye-witness, forms the succeeding chapter.

Casement was tried for high treason in London, found guilty, and sentenced to death on June 29th, 1916. Then on July 3rd, 1916, the Royal Commission on the Irish Rebellion—composed of Lord Hardinge of Penshurst, Sir Montague Shearman, a Judge of the High Court, and Sir Mackenzie D. Chalmers—published its finding that Mr. Birrell had been "primarily responsible for the situation that was allowed to rise, and for the outbreak that occurred."

Yet the German agents, with their German-American and Clan-na-Gael assistants, who engineered the futile rising of the Sinn Feiners, only achieved the final and definite strengthening of the armed forces of the British Crown. Our powerful organisations of working men **Royal Commission's finding** were even more shaken than the Coalition Government by the trouble in Ireland, and the remarkable vehemence with which leading Labour members of Parliament advocated the establishment of general compulsion during the debates in the first week of May, 1916, was a telling testimony of the effect produced on the mind of our public by the events in Ireland. Once more German intrigue had issued in a great result exactly contrary to that at which the intriguers and their dupes had aimed. The British Empire was stronger than ever.

THE REBELLION IN DUBLIN: AN EYE-WITNESS ACCOUNT.

By Warre B. Wells, Assistant Editor "Irish Times."

Dramatic Opening of the Irish Rebellion of 1916—First Shot Fired Before Dublin Castle—The Insurrection Foredoomed to Failure from the Outset—A General Rising an Integral Element in the Rebel Plans—The Latter Briefly Reviewed—The Outbreak Takes the Authorities by Surprise—Many Civilians Killed on the First Day of the Rising—Rebels Seize or Attempt to Seize Dominating Points in the City—Countess Markievicz in Command of a Rebel Force.—Provisional Government of the Irish Republic Establish their Military Headquarters at the Post Office—Telephone Girls' Fine Courage—Centre of Dublin in Rebel Hands on Easter Monday—Thrilling Story of Defence of Trinity College—Dublin in Effective Rebel Occupation from Easter Monday to Wednesday.—The City Cut Off from the World—Citizens Welcome Troops from England—Decisive Action Develops on South Side of the City—Heroic Work of the Dublin Volunteer Training Corps—The Sherwood Foresters in Action—Strong Military Cordon Thrown Round the Whole City—Rebels Evacuate St. Stephen's Green—Sniping from the Roofs—Artillery in Action—Reducing the Area Around the Post Office—"Liberty Hall," the Headquarters of James Connolly's "Citizen Army," Captured—Great Conflagration Breaks Out—Connolly Wounded, and P. H. Pearse Surrenders—Organised Resistance Ends on Saturday, April 29th—Loss of Life and Material Damage—Fifteen Rebels Shot and Many Imprisoned.

THE first shot in the Irish Rebellion of 1916 was fired shortly after noon on Easter Monday, April 24th. It was fired, with a fine sense of the dramatic, before the seat of Imperial authority in Ireland, Dublin Castle, and killed an unarmed policeman on duty. The act was an epitome of the rebellion—a rising spacious and in a sense sublime in its conception; murderous and, by contrast with that conception, petty in its execution. The insurrection was foredoomed to failure from the outset. It proposed, as an indispensable complement to the seizure of Dublin, a general rising throughout the country. Such a rising was an integral element in the rebel plans, and the nature of those plans must be briefly reviewed if the progress of events in the capital is to be made intelligible. The seizure by a surprise stroke of the capital—the Government buildings, the strategic positions, the nodal points of communication, physical and other—was, immediately, to a large extent successful; but it depended for its ultimate success on other factors. It demanded a larger rebel force than was at once available, and it required that while this larger force was being concentrated the forces of the Crown should be prevented from a rapid and effectual intervention. The concentration of this larger force in turn depended on such a general rising throughout the country as would not merely put the Irish provinces in rebel hands and disperse military forces to deal with the provincial risings, but would also enable surplus rebel troops to be made swiftly available for the reinforcement of the bodies holding Dublin. It depended, that is to say, upon a wholesale arming of rebel forces for which, despite months of secret preparation, no adequate provision existed in the country. It presumed the immediate landing from overseas of a great quantity of arms and ammunition. The interception, three days before the rebellion, of the vessel carrying these warlike supplies was the ultimate cause of the speedy collapse of the insurrection in the capital. This implied that the provincial rising must be largely abortive. The miscarriage of the provincial rising was ensured by the confusion which prevailed at the rebel headquarters on the receipt of the news that the vessel was lost, in which confusion the orders to the

REPRESENTATIVES OF THE IRISH GOVERNMENT.
Mr. Birrell (Chief Secretary) and Sir Matthew Nathan (Under-Secretary), right and left respectively, leaving the Commission House, Dublin, after a meeting of the Royal Commission on the Rebellion.

MR. SHEEHY-SKEFFINGTON (wearing a trilby hat).
The officer responsible for his death was found guilty of murder, but insane, and was sent to an asylum.

provinces were first cancelled and then, too late, confirmed. The rebels struck in Dublin, therefore, in circumstances which prohibited them from expecting on the one hand any material reinforcement from the country, and from anticipating on the other hand any serious obstacle to the rapid concentration of military forces upon the capital. They struck with a strength probably inadequate to the task to which they immediately set their hand, and certainly inadequate to the lengthy prosecution of that task.

The shot fired before the Castle was the signal that set in operation in Dublin various bodies which totalled rather less than three thousand men. The outbreak took the authorities completely by surprise. Dublin Castle itself was garrisoned by three soldiers with blank cartridges. Many officers of the troops in Dublin were absent at a race meeting in the vicinity. Unarmed soldiers were everywhere about the streets with no suspicion of the instant danger in which they stood; for from the moment of the rising soldiers, whether armed or unarmed—many convalescent wounded were in the streets—and policemen were shot at sight by the rebels without challenge. Many civilians were killed on the first day of the rising, but in the majority of cases they were not fired upon deliberately; the action **Rebel occupation of the capital** of the rebels was directed against uniformed representatives of the Imperial authority. The scattered and helpless soldiers and police were rapidly withdrawn from the centre of the city, into effective occupation of which the rebels entered without serious opposition. Their operations proceeded upon an exact and admirable strategic plan. They seized, or attempted to seize, every dominating point in the city. At the Castle, which would have fallen an easy prey, they refrained from attack, expecting a ruse, until the garrison of three was so strongly reinforced as to make the attempt hopeless. The rebels occupied, however, a newspaper office commanding the Castle Yard, from which they assailed the troops with rifle fire and bombs. Out from the centre of the city, houses commanding most of the canal bridges on the south side were occupied and garrisoned in strength. Beyond the canal, houses

commanding the junction of the roads from Kingstown were similarly seized; the occupants, in all these cases, were summarily ejected. Nearer the centre of the city a rebel force, commanded by Countess Markievicz, entrenched in St. Stephen's Green, an ornamental park dominating an extensive grouping of road communications. Other bodies occupied and organised for defence adjacent buildings and Messrs. Jacobs' great biscuit factory, and, nearer the river, Boland's Mills at Ringsend. The north side of the river did not offer such a simple scheme of points of strategic advantage, but on this side also every suitable position was occupied.

The efforts of the rebels to seize the arteries of communication were less successful. The General Post Office in Sackville Street was taken at once by a large force, which expelled the staff, some of whom were in league with them, at the point of the bayonet, and **Seizure of the G.P.O.** all telegraphic communication was promptly cut. At the General Post Office the rebels, under command of P. H. Pearse, "Commandant-General and President of the Provisional Government of the Irish Republic," established their military headquarters. For the rest of the week Dublin was completely isolated, except for the telephone system. The rebels committed a grave blunder in their neglect to seize the Central Telephone Exchange. This was protected by the ruse of an old woman, who informed the force detailed to seize it that the building was full of troops It was, in fact, garrisoned by nothing more formidable than twenty girl operators, who stood to their posts with a fine courage throughout the rebellion. The maintenance of telephone communication was of the first importance to the military authorities in the development

ARMS SURRENDERED TO THE CROWN.
British soldier proceeding along a Dublin street, carrying a number of arms surrendered to the military by the Sinn Feiners.

of rapid and effective measures to suppress it. The railway-stations also were largely immune from the rebel efforts. On the south side the two stations of the Dublin and South-Eastern Railway were both seized; but one of these was found to be unsuitable for defence, and was almost immediately evacuated. Both the terminus of the Great Southern and Western Railway and that of the Great Northern were strongly held by soldiers, and no effort to capture

THE COUNTESS MARKIEVICZ.
An extreme Sinn Feiner. Her death sentence was commuted to penal servitude for life.

VISITING IRISH PRISONERS.
Relatives of the Sinn Fein rebels who were interned in the Richmond Barracks, Dublin, submitting parcels for examination before being allowed into the rooms.

DISILLUSIONED ENTHUSIASTS.
Types of Sinn Fein prisoners in one of the rooms of Richmond Barracks. They all expressed themselves contented with the treatment meted out to them.

either was made by the rebels, who had the terminus of the Midland Great Western within the area of their occupation. They attempted to destroy the railway lines some miles out from the city, and were so far successful in these attempts that no trains except troop trains were able to reach Dublin for the rest of the week. By the afternoon of Easter Monday the whole centre of the city was firmly in rebel hands, with a strong cordon of fortified posts in the suburbs, which the more or less abortive risings in the vicinity of the capital were intended to strengthen further with an outer cordon.

One place alone in the central area of the city stood like a rock in the surge of revolution. That place was Trinity College, and the story of its defence is the most stirring chapter in the history of the insurrection. Trinity College occupies a commanding strategic position in the city, and formed a rallying-point of capital importance in the operations for the suppression of the rebellion. To its defence

JAMES CONNOLLY.
One of the seven signatories to the "Irish Republic Proclamation," who paid the death penalty.

during the first days of the rising was wholly due the fact that the city's commercial centre on the south side of the river was spared that visitation of fire and sack which later obliterated its commercial centre on the north side. The College, a massive pile of grey stone, towering high above the surrounding roofs, completely dominates in front the Bank of Ireland and Dame Street ; to the left Grafton Street (leading up to St. Stephen's Green) ; and to the right Westmoreland Street (leading to the river and across the bridge to Sackville Street)—the three streets which contain the bulk of the banks, the insurance offices, and the important business houses of South Dublin. Its possession by loyal forces effectually prevented the extension of the rebel operations from Sackville Street across the river into the commercial area on the south side, or any serious outbreak of looting in this area ; and it prohibited communication by the most direct routes between the rebel headquarters in the Post Office and the outlying rebel bodies in St.

SINN FEINERS IN CUSTODY AT RICHMOND BARRACKS, DUBLIN.
Going to their morning bath. Within less than a week the outbreak of Sinn Feinism was quelled, and several hundred rebels surrendered to the authorities. A large number of these men were deported to England. This photograph shows some more of the actors in the Dublin tragedy.

Stephen's Green and elsewhere on the south side. These important results were secured in a manner which added an heroic page to the history of Ireland's ancient University. The call to arms overseas had drained the strength of the Officers Training Corps to the utmost ; only those members remained behind who for sufficient reasons could not obey it. When the rebellion broke out the members of the Officers Training Corps in the College mustered an exiguous garrison of thirty rifles. The senior officer **How Trinity College** in charge, Captain Alton, a Fellow of **was defended** the University, promptly organised the defence. It was decided to hold only the main block of buildings, dominating the three streets in front and commanding an open field of fire in the rear across the College park towards one of the Dublin and South-Eastern railway-stations, which the rebels held in force. During the night of Easter Monday a picket was posted in the College park, close enough to the station to hear the challenges of the rebel sentries and the frequent exchange of the password, " Limerick," but this picket was

INGENUITY TO BAFFLE THE REBELS.
Improvised armoured car, constructed from locomotive smoke-boxes hastily fitted together in Guinness' Brewery Yard. A unique vehicle in the streets of the Irish capital.

withdrawn before dawn. The gates were shut and barricaded ; sand-bags were placed in the windows and on the parapets of the roof, and a brisk fusillade was exchanged on the right with the rebel positions across the river. A few soldiers in the neighbouring streets and in the Central Soldiers' Club opposite the College, including some Anzac sharpshooters, were summoned to strengthen the garrison in the defence. Fortunately the rebels were impressed by its parade of strength, and were ignorant of its actual poverty. Trinity College was, perhaps, the one place in the city where no spy was present to aid the rebels. One daring spy did gain admission in the disguise of a soldier, but he was detected before he succeeded in escaping to betray the situation. The rebels, in consequence, made no actual attack on the College. Action was continued with the positions beyond the river ; looting in the streets under fire from the College was prevented ; several rebel despatch-riders on bicycles who attempted to run the gauntlet were shot ; the sharpshooters made good practice on snipers on the surrounding roofs. The garrison held the commercial

centre of Dublin on the south side in trust until the advance of the troops into the city relieved it.

The city, except for the area dominated by Trinity College, remained in effective rebel occupation from Easter Monday, throughout Tuesday, into Wednesday. During this period and the subsequent days of desperate street fighting until the end of the week, the social and economic life of Dublin was completely paralysed. The chief business quarter of the city was inaccessible. No trains ran into the city ; no trams ran through it. The supply of gas and electric power was cut off as a measure of precaution. The food problem early became acute, and was growing desperate when the rebellion collapsed. Prices rose quickly to a famine level, though the actual shortage was not, in the great majority of cases, aggravated by any attempt of the shopkeepers to mulct the people in their necessity. With all ordinary means of vehicular communication about the city suspended, the citizens, in high station and in low, went foraging for their own supplies. The behaviour of the crowds, in the entire absence for a considerable period over wide areas of any authority, was remarkably orderly ; the amount of looting, in view of the unique opportunity which the rebellion presented, was surprisingly small. Dublin was cut off from the world, without letters, and without newspapers, save one. The exception was the " Irish Times," which enjoyed an advantage over its contemporaries in that it possessed a suction gas plant of its own, and was not wholly dependent for its motive power upon the city gas supply.

Its office lay in No Man's Land between Trinity College and the rebel positions across the river, and here, under a state of siege, it was published daily until the Friday of Easter week, when mechanical difficulties interrupted its issue until the following Monday. Dublin's only newspaper, however—no newspaper from outside was able to circulate during the week—was prohibited from publishing anything but the official communiqués and proclamations. Nobody knew how serious the rebellion might be. Nobody knew the state of the provinces. There were rumours of risings here, there, and everywhere, of large rebel forces marching on Dublin, of a German landing in Kerry. But, as the days passed and the fighting spread, and the great fires, whose glare by night was visible for miles around, broke out, though there was growing strain, there was always calm and nothing in the nature of panic. The people of Dublin kept their heads and went their way with a nonchalance not generally attributed to the Irish temperament. In spite of the military **Calm of the** restrictions on movement, under martial **populace** law, the citizens followed the progress of the fighting with a close interest that often came near to foolish recklessness, and sometimes paid its extreme penalty. They gave the troops from England a welcome which vastly surprised these unfamiliar men, who imagined at the outset that every inhabitant of the city was a potential enemy. Food was short ; but with the soldiers arriving in the city from Kingstown, citizens cheerfully shared, or surrendered to them altogether, the last square meal which they had in immediate prospect. Women and girls

Ruins of the Imperial Hotel, Dublin, as seen from the top of the Nelson Pillar. Not a room in the building remained intact.

The portico of the gutted Post Office—another scene of devastation. Photograph taken from the lofty Nelson Pillar.

Firemen engaged in the work of putting out the great conflagration during the Sinn Fein outbreak.

Greek bas-reliefs, which adorned the walls of the Dublin Art Gallery, damaged by shot and shell during the rising.

DUST, DEBRIS, AND DESPAIR: SCENES IN DUBLIN AFTER THE SINN FEIN REBELLION.

ran out of houses in the suburbs during the hottest action to give food and drink to the troops, or help the wounded into shelter.

On the south side of the city, where the decisive action developed, the advanced guards of the Territorial battalions —railed across England, packed in transports across the Channel, and tramping from Kingstown into Dublin —reached the suburbs on Wednesday morning. They were thrown immediately on their arrival, in an advanced stage of exhaustion, into desperate street fighting of the most hellish kind. Their marching van, a battalion of the Sherwood Foresters, came under heavy rifle fire from strong bodies of rebels posted in the corner houses commanding the junction of Haddington Road and Northumberland Road.

Here, on the afternoon of Easter Monday, a body of the Dublin Volunteer Training Corps, composed of professional men over military age, returning without arms from a route march in the Dublin mountains, had been ambushed by the rebels. Six of its members were killed and ten wounded. The Volunteers made their way to Beggar's Bush Barracks, reinforced the besieged garrison with nine officers and eighty-one men, and helped splendidly in the defence of the barracks until the arrival of the troops from Kingstown. Thus the Irish Rebellion made history for more than one branch of the armed forces of the Crown. The Trinity College Officers Training Corps was the first university corps that has been required to defend its own university from attack; the Dublin Volunteer Training Corps comprised

LOYAL MEN AND TRUE.
Irish Volunteers, many of whom assisted the troops in the work of restoring order in Dublin. This photograph shows them marching on St. Patrick's Day, 1916.

the members of the first Volunteers in the United Kingdom who shed their blood in their country's cause; and the military operations in Dublin in Easter week were the first operations conducted almost exclusively by units of the Territorial Force and New Army, the Regular Army being represented scarcely at all except in the higher command. The Territorial battalions first engaged fought under the most trying conditions with a cool courage and an indomitable cheerfulness. The Sherwood Foresters, who came under a sudden and heavy fire at the junction of Haddington Road and Northumberland Road, suffering several casualties, immediately took such cover as was to be found behind walls, and proceeded in a businesslike fashion to the reduction by rifle fire and bombing of the houses in which the rebels were posted. Their colonel, meanwhile, rode his white charger up and down the open street, smoking a cigarette, and by a miracle escaped untouched. With the reduction of this first rebel outpost by the Sherwood Foresters the relief of Dublin had begun.

By this time (Wednesday, April 26th) a military cordon, composed on the north side of reinforcements from the Curragh and the North and on the south side of troops landed at Kingstown, had been thrown round the whole city, inside the wholly ineffective outer rebel cordon, and in immediate contact with the strong inner cordon of fortified posts. From this date the weakness inherent in the rebels' situation operated progressively towards their downfall. Their numerical deficiency, actually for the execution of their plan of campaign and relatively in

BARRICADE OF BEER BARRELS.
Rifles of Government troops firing on the rebels from behind a rough but effective barricade across a Dublin street.

THE OTHER SIDE OF THE BARRICADE.
Kneeling soldiers taking aim. Much fighting of a guerilla character took place in the narrow streets and alleys.

"Liberty Hall," a squat stone building facing the river, the headquarters of James Connolly's "Citizen Army," reduced to ruins.

The havoc at Clery's Stores and the Imperial Hotel, Sackville Street. The Munster and Leinster Bank, to the left, was entirely gutted.

Interior impression of the General Post Office, with troops in possession. On the left is an instantaneous photograph of the collapse of a house in Liffey Street.

General view of Dublin after the rebellion. Many of the landmarks of the city were wrecked as well as a large number of private dwellings. Property to an estimated value of two millions sterling was destroyed, apart from individual private losses.

CAMERA VIEWS OF THE IRISH CAPITAL AFTER THE INSURRECTION OF APRIL-MAY, 1916.

DUBLIN, MAY, 1916: THE PRICE OF THE SINN FEINERS' EXTRAVAGANT IDEAL.

proportion to the military forces arrayed against them, made it impossible for them to maintain their internal lines of communication. In the result, the isolated strategic points which they had seized became so many traps into which they were gradually penned. Heavy fighting was necessary, however, before this decision emerged. From Wednesday the cordon drew in gradually towards the centre of the city, enclosing the main body

St. Stephen's Green cleared

of the rebels within it, and leaving behind it detached bodies to be surrounded and submerged. The cordon closed more steadily and against a more obstinate resistance on the south side, where it was further removed at the outset from the centre of the city. By Thursday, St. Stephen's Green, the seizure of which was apparently intended by the rebels to cover the approaches to the city over the southern canal bridges, was cleared by an operation independent of the main operations. Their occupation of this park was the most faulty piece of rebel strategy. The Green was dominated throughout by the upper stories of the square of houses which encloses it. It was commanded in particular by the towering building of the Shelbourne Hotel, situated at a corner of the Green. This was the most fashionable hotel in Dublin, and its visitors throughout the week experienced a strict siege. The windows were plentifully riddled with bullets by the rebels, but no casualties were recorded. On the roof of the hotel a small force of soldiers early in the week mounted a machine-gun, which raked the Green from end to end. The rebels soon found their position untenable and, having suffered considerable loss, evacuated the Green, retiring to the massive building of the Royal College of Surgeons, upon which the machine-gun from the Shelbourne Hotel continued to play.

After this clearance, the military cordon closed in on the

south without encountering much opposition. Fierce fighting meanwhile developed on the north side, where at one point a day and a night were spent in an advance of a hundred and fifty yards down a narrow street. The most determined fighting of all, however, occurred in forcing the approaches from Kingstown on the west, by way of Haddington Road and Northumberland Road, towards the heart of the city. For a distance of half a mile every other successive house was a fortress, which had to be reduced by rifle fire and bombing before the advance could proceed. Behind the advance accurate sniping from the roofs broke out as the troops moved forward, and it was long before the lines of communication were wholly cleared of hidden irregulars. The troops pushed steadily on, not without considerable loss, over Baggot Street and Mount Street canal bridges. They were very desperately engaged in the warren of mean streets inside the latter bridge on the right of the line of advance. Here, against Boland's Mills, a high stone building overlooking the basin of the Grand Canal, artillery was brought into action for the first time in the course of the operations. A nine-pounder, smartly handled by naval gunners, did good work in enabling a close cordon to be drawn round the Ringsend area towards the mouth of the river, while the main advance proceeded. By Thursday, pickets had

Naval gunners' effective work

penetrated into the heart of the city, and communication was established between the advancing bodies and the garrison of Trinity College, which, with its academic cloisters packed with horse, foot, and artillery, became the advanced base of the military operations.

From this point, while fighting continued against isolated rebel positions, the main operation consisted in the reduction of the area around the Post Office, the chief rebel stronghold, the seat of the "Republican Government," and the headquarters of the rebels' military command. In this operation the military tactics were varied. Whereas there was fighting of the closest kind in the earlier phases of the action, now the rebel defences were methodically reduced by more distant artillery, machine-gun, and rifle fire. From Trinity College to the Post Office in Sackville Street is a distance of some five hundred yards. The Liffey, crossed by O'Connell Bridge, intervenes. At the end of Sackville Street abutting on the bridge, the rebels occupied houses and shops immediately commanding the bridge, and bringing the two streets—Westmoreland Street and D'Olier Street—which converge upon it from the College under a searching fire.

On the left of these rebel positions, facing the river, "Liberty Hall," a squat stone building, the headquarters of James Connolly's "Citizen Army," could bring enfilade fire to bear on O'Connell Bridge and direct fire on Bl·tt Bridge, the lowest of the river bridges. This rebel outpost, however, was early reduced by the combined operations of a gunboat lying in the Liffey off the Customs House and field-pieces manœuvred from Trinity College into the adjacent streets. With the destruction of "Liberty Hall," forces were able to move, though still not without considerable risk, across the river, and the operations of the troops on the south side were closely linked up with the operations of the troops pressing in on the north side. The rebel positions immediately commanding O'Connell Bridge were riddled and rendered untenable by artillery and machine-gun fire, largely directed from the roof of Trinity College, and by Friday the military lines had been advanced right down to the river by way of Westmoreland Street and D'Olier Street, in the block between which, however, persistent sniping was continued by one or more elusive rebels, the last of whom was not accounted for until several days later.

Meanwhile, on Thursday evening, the great fire had begun. How it originated —whether through the shelling from Trinity College, the explosion of a rebel ammunition store, or some accident of looting—will probably never be known. It broke out on the west side of Sackville Street, immediately in rear of the rebel fortified post fronting on the bridge, and raged and spread without ceasing from Thursday evening throughout Friday and Saturday, until Sunday. The military operations made it impossible, except at long intervals, for brief periods, and at certain times, for the Dublin Fire Brigade to attempt to cope with the conflagration. The fire, fanned by a breeze from the sea, spread from the west side of Sackville Street, where it had devastated a wide area, across to the east side. The whole of the west side of Sackville Street, comprising forty-seven buildings, was gutted. In all, here and

Buildings gutted by fire in the surrounding streets, some two hundred and thirty buildings were demolished. They included two churches, a Presbyterian and a Methodist, as well as a Church of Ireland Mission to Seamen church, four hotels, several banks, the bulk of the important business houses, and the Royal Hibernian Academy. Fortunately, few residential houses were within the devastated area, although it contained some tenements, and the loss of life directly due to the fire was small.

On Saturday, April 29th, there came the end of the criminal adventure which had wrought this widespread havoc and destruction in the heart of Dublin. The area of the Post Office was by this time closely invested, and early in the afternoon the rebel headquarters was itself in flames. James Connolly, the military director of the rebel

operations, although P. H. Pearse was in nominal command, had been seriously wounded on the Thursday, and his injury contributed largely to the disintegration of the rebel defence. Hopeless as their situation had become, the leaders displayed at the end a cool courage worthy of a better cause. P. H. Pearse spent the closing hours in the Post Office in writing a vindication of the rebellion; Connolly, on Friday, although there was by this time little or no chance of getting it circulated, composed a heartening "Order of the Day" to the rebel forces. Driven out of the Post Office by the flames, the rebel leaders with the garrison retired to the block of buildings fronting on the river, where the Law Courts are situated, known as the Four Courts. The exits from the Post Office were under **Rebellion's final phase** military fire. To draw this fire and cover their escape, the rebels sent out first about a dozen officers whom they had captured on Easter Monday and kept in close but not harsh confinement during the week. Some of the officers thus sent out were wounded by their comrades' fire, but fortunately none was killed.

The rebel leaders, having made good their temporary escape, held a council of war. Of the fighting which attended this final phase of the rebellion no clear account is possible. It was a confused and desperate affair of ambuscades and sniping in streets and alleys where the glare of the fires paled the sun and the crash of falling masonry mingled with the roar of artillery and bombs, the vicious knocking of machine-guns, and the rattle of musketry. The rebel remnant, surrounded by the soldiers and the flames, fought with the courage of despair. The inevitable end came early in the afternoon, when P. H. Pearse went out under a white flag and, after an offer of surrender on terms, which was at once rejected, agreed to unconditional capitulation. He then issued the following document: "In order to prevent the further slaughter of unarmed people, and in the hope of saving the lives of our followers, now surrounded and hopelessly outnumbered, members of the Provisional Government present at headquarters have agreed to an unconditional surrender, and the commanders of all units of the Republican Forces will order their followers to lay down their arms." The "cease fire" was sounded to the military forces throughout Dublin, and one by one, as the news of the surrender at headquarters was confirmed, the various detached bodies of the rebels about the city made their submission. By nightfall on Saturday, April 29th, although single snipers still haunted many roofs, all organised resistance to the forces of the Crown was at an end, and Dublin emerged from a week of revolution to contemplate its destruction and bury its dead. The Irish Rebellion of 1916 had passed into history.

Both in loss of life and material damage it had been a costly business. Property was destroyed to an estimated value of two million sterling; but this sum, of course, did not include the loss of individual property, due to robbery and loot by the mob while still out of hand. Among the military and police the casualties were one hundred and twenty-five killed and four hundred and five wounded; among civilians they were one hundred and eighty killed and six hundred and fourteen wounded, according to the hospital returns; while a number of snipers—how many perhaps will never be exactly ascertained—were buried by their friends in cellars, and only discovered and disinterred later as their secret graves were located. Besides these, fifteen rebels were shot by order of court-martial, while more than a hundred were sentenced to varying terms of penal servitude and imprisonment.

LORD WIMBORNE.
The Lord-Lieutenant of Ireland, who resigned after the Dublin Rebellion.

German corpse covered by a greatcoat, a last tribute either from a retreating comrade or some sensitive Briton who passed it during the great advance of July, 1916.

A shell apparently hit the loopholed plate behind which the German was engaged in preparing a bomb fuse. His dead fingers still hold the wire attached to the missile.

Dead German soldiers prostrate before the entrance to their dug-out. A British shell exploded immediately above them, killing them together before they could seek refuge underground.

British soldier making notes in enemy trenches which were completely flattened out by the shells. In the background are the stakes which supported the German wire.

THE REALM OF KING DEATH: IN THE GERMAN TRENCHES AFTER THE BRITISH ADVANCE ON THE SOMME.

GALLANT WORCESTERS ON

CHAPTER CXXV.

THEIR WAY TO BATTLE.

TRIUMPHS OF BRITISH SCIENCE AND INVENTION IN THE WAR.

By Edward Wright.

Modern War Entirely an Affair of Applied Science—British Race More Inventive than the German—The Battleship a Symbol of Our Dominion in Scientific Power—We Defeat Germany Without a Struggle by Our Inventiveness—Cordite and the Failure of German Chemistry—How France Benefited by Our Victories in Steel Invention—Great Guns Only Last Three Seconds—Why Our Expeditionary Force Started Only with Field Artillery—Lack of Watch and Clock Factories Hinders Our Production of High-Explosive Shell—Britain Still Holds the Key Industry in Gun-Making—Germans Imitate Our Smoke Method—Germany's Monopoly of Coal-Tar Industries and Its Military Results—How British Men of Science Overcame the German Monopoly in Antiseptics—Conquest of Enteric and the Struggle Against the Horrible Crimes of German Bacteriologists—The Epidemic in Serbia and in Wittenberg Camp—Our Crowning Misfortune of Government Without Knowledge—How the Men of Science Who Saved Us from Defeat Had to Struggle against Reactionaries—Optical Glass and the Peril to Our Armies—Corporal Beach and His Periscope Rifle—German Control of Base Metal Manufacture—Tungsten Smelting in Relation to Zeppelin Bombs—How We Broke the German Monopolies—Our Equipment Difficulties in Machine Tools and Jigs—Heavy Calls on Our Factories by France and Russia—Reinforced Aluminium in the Conquest of the Air—Telephonic Invention and Its Influence on Warfare—Three Thousand Guns Controlled by Telephone—Effect of Electric Means of Communication on Naval Tactics—Possibility of Wireless Packs for Infantry—Inventions in War that Make for Increased Economic Power in Peace.

I N our praiseworthy desire to stimulate ourselves to the fiercest activity we have sometimes been inclined to attribute to the enemy more genius than he possesses. The world has rung with the marvellous applications of science to warfare made by the German, but the work of the Briton in the same field of technical invention is probably superior in quality to that of the Teuton. Indeed, if we put together all the modern warlike inventions of the Anglo-Celtic races and compare them with the war machinery of the Central Empires, we shall probably find that the Germanic races occupy the second or third place in the intellectual field of warfare. A complete comparison is impossible at the time of writing, for if it were attempted too much would be revealed to the enemy. We must, therefore, restrict our survey to matters of published facts, and of these we can only give a small selection.

The mass of detail would fill many volumes. For modern war is entirely an affair of applied science. The soldier is in himself no more powerful than the

primitive savage of the Stone-Age. His terrible strength is due to the fact that behind him are the coalfields, iron-mines, steam-engines, factories, chemical works, power lathes, electrical shops, and a vast host of highly trained workers, researchers, mathematicians, and other men of science. Science is the child of war. The first tool man ever made was a chipped flint for killing his fellow-man and conquering a larger hunting ground with a more abundant food supply. For some hundred thousand years of human history we can trace the very gradual development of the human mind only by the stone weapons of slaughter unearthed from the deep dust. From the beginning man has put all he knew into his instruments of war, and the more his knowledge increased, the more terrible became his conflicts.

War remains the most intense display of a nation's scientific activities, with the general result that the people which in time of peace has applied science most thoroughly to the needs of its life will prove the most powerful on the field of battle. This is, in fact, what the Germans continually proclaimed throughout the

THE GRIP OF THE ALLIES.
General Sir Douglas Haig receiving General Joffre at the British Headquarters immediately before the concerted allied action on the Somme.

war, but they have been much too ready to assume that they are incontestably supreme in scientific activity. We have flattered their self-conceit in the matter by our peculiar habit of taking some enemy or rival as a standard in some achievement, and whipping ourselves up to surpass him in the points in which he seems better than us. Our turn for self-castigation is not wholly to be condemned. It preserves us from overweening pride, keeps us alert and enterprising, and bent on bettering the progress we have accomplished. On the other hand, we must not allow ourselves to be misled by the ideal of German efficiency in all things, which is only the fabric of a vision that we began to construct towards the close of the Victorian era in order to escape from the errors of mid-Victorian self-complacency.

Birth of the Dreadnought

In our special field of war we have continually shown more inventiveness than the Germans. In the days of peace we were mainly a nation of well-trained mechanics and designers of machinery, and instead of building up an

Crown copyright reserved.]

AN ENGINE OF DESTRUCTION.

Heavy British howitzer which helped to prepare the way for the British forward movement on July 1st, 1916. The weapon was dug into its emplacement and screened in an ingenious way from hostile aircraft.

army of millions of men, we defended ourselves chiefly by our mechanical skill and our talent for devising new machinery. When Germany directly threatened our life we did not create new army corps, each of which needed 40,000 men, but we built a low grey hull with no sign of life visible on it, that floated about the sea like the dismantled wreck of some tramp steamer. Into this sombre raft of steel went everything that modern science, modern invention, and modern industry could devise for the dreadful purpose of human slaughter. Only a thousand men, most of them trained in intricate scientific work or highly skilled industrial labour, manned the floating raft of steel and looked after its steam-engines, electrical dynamos, compressed-air engines, and hydraulic plants. Scarcely anything was done by hand power ; electricity, hydraulic power, compressed air, and an enormous force of the energy born of oil, moved the vast and exquisite masses of metal. We continued to call the men sailors, but they were really engineers and engineers' mates, and many of them were as highly trained as a scientific specialist

in a university. Among them were experts in refrigerating processes, who kept the ammunition cool, and experts in X-ray work, not only for surgical purposes on the day of battle, but for studying the quality of cordite by which the guns were fired. Other men were as keenly practised in the use of elaborate optical instruments as any astronomer, and the general knowledge of practical mathematics among the officers was such as could not have been found in any average group of graduates from Oxford.

All this knowledge and skill were employed on a war machine, the most dreadful and complete in the world. Ten large guns and some twelve or sixteen quick-firers, with tubes for firing automobile mines from the bowels of the floating machine, constituted its striking power. But the thing could move as fast as an ordinary train, and if the thousand men in it caught 40,000 hostile soldiers near the shore with their ordinary field-artillery of one hundred and seventy small guns, the land force would be outranged and scattered by the great guns on the floating steel platform that we call a battleship. The gunners of the Queen Elizabeth have been known to sink an enemy troopship at a range of fifteen miles by firing over a mountain into a sea they could not discern.

When, in the year 1912, the Germans saw that we were determined to maintain a superiority in battleships, they modified for the time being their plans. They could see that in a duel between Britain and Germany alone we should win. They had an Army capable of being expanded to eight or nine millions of soldiers, while our chief defence consisted of about 120,000 sailors, living in floating steel gun platforms known as Dreadnought battle-ships and Dreadnought battle-cruisers. We had other warships assistant to our great new ships, but it was these new war machines that daunted the Germans, and made them see that their Army of millions was powerless against us. With our Dreadnoughts we could have cut Germany off from the sea and forced her to trade through neutral ports at great expense and increasing difficulties. We should have had less trouble with hostile submarines then, because they were not at the time in such a highly developed state.

Instead of accepting the silent, bloodless defeat we inflicted on them, by showing more inventiveness, enterprise, and mechanical skill, the Germans prepared to conquer a large part of our friends' and Allies' territory in Europe, as a preliminary to engaging us at sea with all the industrial resources of Belgium, France, Austria, and Polish Russia. In other words, they admitted that they could not at the time surpass us in the application of science to warfare, but they aimed at making up, by vaster material resources, larger supplies of trained labour, and a more tremendous production of naval war material, for their lack of inventiveness. German brains had been beaten by British brains, so the German made war on the rest of Europe with the ultimate view of bringing all the mineral resources, steel-making plants, and machine tools of Europe against the British Isles.

Germany's ultimate objective

We need not then abase ourselves any longer before the idol of German scientific efficiency. The German organises.

Nerve=racking work : Heavy British howitzer on rail emplacement bombarding the German positions.

Paving a way for the advance of 1916: Monster British gun in action.

Gun emplacements in Sanctuary Wood: A paradox in nomenclature.

Desolation in No Man's Land: A scene of the British advance, July, 1916.

Where the wrath of Mars descended: A ruined village near Mametz.

A new version of the forest giant: Mammoth French howitzer articulates the will of France.

but he does not invent, and even his modern power of organisation is based on an adaptation of the American Trust system in industrial matters. It is easier to organise than it is to invent, and an inventive race like ours, surrounded by the wealth and power it has won, is apt to await the pressure of circumstances before using the genius it possesses. By the middle of the nineteenth century we had manifested a wealth of inventive force that could not in every case be turned to profit. We had founded steam-power civilisation, discovered the electric telegraph, the principle of the dynamo ; we had laid the foundations of the science of chemistry, gained some idea of the ultimate mystery of the material universe, discovered the ether and the electrical foundation of matter, established geology, and ascertained the main outlines of the evolution of living forms. The impetus to this unparalleled explosion of national genius was given by our struggle for existence against Napoleon.

The Napoleonic impetus

The great French captain had roused us from our leisurely graces and dilettante researches of the eighteenth century, and compelled us to use the entire force of our mind to preserve our independence, maintain our food supply, and increase our wealth as a weapon of war. We fought Napoleon with our new steam-engine as well as with our direct new instrument of victory, Major Shrapnel's shell, which did almost as much as Wellington to win Waterloo.

Again we have been roused, after a Continental peace of a hundred years, to display the quality of mind inherited from our forefathers. We must admit that we have inherited a much larger wealth of science than our ancestors possessed. But, on the other hand, we share our science as fully with Germany as we do with France. The leading nations have equal opportunities in winning and developing that knowledge which is power, and we have not in reserve so mighty and tremendous an instrument as James Watt, of Glasgow, gave Britain in the days of her last great struggle for life. We have only the same prime movers that Germany has, and our new steam-engine, the turbine, invented by Sir Charles Parsons, is used in Germany as well as in Britain. Moreover, the Germans are able in one way to match our latest invention in steam-power by means of the new German prime mover, the Diesel oil-engine. It owes its origin to the inventiveness of an Austrian engineer and the enterprising spirit of the German firm of Krupp.

In some technical industries, such as the manufacture of steel castings, optical glass, and coal-tar products, in which we once excelled, the Germans far surpassed us. In the old days, when the resources of the world were undeveloped, we were the kings of coal and iron, and with our steam-engine, Bessemer process and Armstrong gun, iron steamers and ironclads, we dominated the earth. We were the first of all nations to create an industrial State, and until our American kinsmen and the Germans copied us and built up great scientific industries, we were beyond attack. Simply by our inventiveness and enterprise we held the greater part of mankind in economic dependence upon one small island lying off the coast of Europe.

Trafalgar and Waterloo were only small military incidents in the generally peaceful process by which the power of Britain was maintained and extended. Even our possession of coalfields and iron ore was but an incident in the expansion of our influence. Other nations had coal and iron, and had been using them for thousands of years. But, first of all men, the Anglo-Celt made a machine that could do the work of thousands of men. He harnessed this machine to his tools, looms, mills, vehicles, and ships, so that the comparatively small population of parts of England, Wales, Scotland, and Ireland acquired a productive power greater than that of the rest of mankind put together. In other words, it was our inventors that made us great. Nelson and Wellington kept the foe from our shores, but it

A RELIC OF THE SOMME ADVANCE.
German trench loophole plate riddled with bullets. In spite of countless experiments, no infallible bullet-proof shield had been invented.

was not their victories that enabled us to overshadow the world for a hundred years. No fleet could provide us with the food we needed in order to expand our numbers, so as to people the larger part of the United States, Canada, Australia, New Zealand, and part of South Africa. It was James Watt and the men who followed him who gave us our industrial supremacy, and, by binding the agricultural nations to us by our extraordinary commercial power, achieved the incomparable expansion of the Anglo-Celtic races.

We are good fighters, all of us—English and Welsh, Scottish and Irish. But there were kings before Agamemnon, and there were first-class fighting races before the amalgam of Angles, Celts, and Norse settlers of the British Isles took to interfering with their neighbours of Western Europe. It is the genius of our race which gave us greater power in the world than the Romans. In the Middle Ages we produced Roger Bacon, and soon afterwards we applied our budding talent for science to matters of war, and used Bacon's invention of gunpowder in cannon in 1327, the first recorded date in history of ordnance being employed. And since our invention of modern artillery we have usually marked our great wars with some improvement in ordnance unforeseen by our enemy. Since the fifteenth century we have been less engaged in national struggles for existence than our neighbours on the Continent, and have, therefore, had less urgent stimulus to warlike invention. Nevertheless, when we have taken the field we have often shown the old powers of mind. In the Napoleonic era, when warships carried only small guns, Gasgoyne, of the Carron Ironworks in Scotland, invented

British genius for invention

(Official photograph.)

PANORAMA OF THE BATTLEFIELD AT LA BOISSELLE, CAPTURED BY THE BRITISH ON JULY 3RD, 1916. IN THE FOREGROUND IS THE ORIGINAL BRITISH FRONT LINE.

the carronade, with which our naval victories were won. These pieces were lighter than the ordinary gun, but threw a shot twice as heavy as the enemy's missiles, and produced such a devastating effect on enemy ships that our sailors called them " smashers." In the Crimean War we made a 36 in. gun, throwing a ton shell. Then the modern built-up gun was invented and developed by our race, which also discovered the method of making large steel castings that Krupp introduced into Germany. In regard to ammunition, the shrapnel shell, as we have seen, is a British invention. It was the chief instrument in saving our line around Hougomont on the field of Waterloo, and our military gunners have ever since had an especial affection for it.

Picric acid, a mixture of carbolic acid and nitric acid that looks like honey, is another British contribution to the science of war. One of the Fellows of our Chemical Society demonstrated its warlike use at Woolwich testing grounds in 1871, and some years afterwards sent his article on this coal-tar high explosive to M. Eugene Turpin, of Paris, who worked up the acid into the new compound known as melinite, lyddite, or shimose. After the war broke out M. Turpin discovered a high explosive of greater power than melinite, and it was partly due to his invention that the army of Verdun made so magnificent a resistance; for, with the new explosive, a comparatively small French shell had greater smashing power than a heavier German shell, so that it is reported that a French shell of about six inches charged with the new chemical produced on the German trenches more effect than a German 8 in. shell produced on the French trenches. M. Turpin thus, by a small discovery in chemistry, increased the power of the French artillery in an extraordinary way. Searching for means to attain a greater smashing effect, the German armies seem to have neglected the construction of 3 in. guns and concentrated the larger part of their armament plant on turning out heavy **The power of** 5·9 in. pieces. Naturally, these heavy **French artillery** pieces took longer to construct than light field-artillery, and the French armament firms, relying on the increased power of their new high-explosive shell, continued to produce light guns in vast numbers, while maintaining a very considerable output of giant howitzers. They fought their enemy by a scientific invention, in such a way as to keep up with the enormous mineral resources that the Germans temporarily won in Northern France, Belgium, and Russian Poland.

As regards our progress in artillery during the war, detailed information cannot be given at the moment of writing; but there is the patent fact of our victorious battleship squadron, carrying a gun much more powerful than that carried in any enemy squadron, and bringing it to bear with greater speed than that at which the battleship force of any other nation can steam into action. From the outset of the war there was a great deal of talk about the Austrian 12 in. Skoda howitzer and the German 16·8 in. Krupp howitzer. But we continued to make as powerful guns as either friend or foe possessed.

The monster siege artillery which the French brought into action in the summer of 1916 was made of a new steel alloy. In size the new French howitzer excelled Krupp's giant weapon, and, by reason of the strength of the steel employed, more muzzle energy could safely be generated inside the new French ordnance. The result was that a greater range was obtained, together with a higher throw of the missile and a more tremendous smashing effect. It is only just to add that the French metallurgists were at least good seconds to our leading men.

The significance of this fact was brought out by the terrible prolongation of the war. The life of the finest British high-velocity gun was only three seconds. For three seconds did the great power-heat engine known as a big gun perform its work with accuracy. At the end of three seconds the erosion of the rifling rendered it necessary to withdraw the inner tube and fit a new tube—a process occupying several weeks. Of course, the extraordinarily short life of three seconds meant in practice weeks or months of actual use, for each shot required work lasting only a minute fraction of a second. But the general result was that the life of the inner gun-tube became amazingly short when the Germans and Austrians made drum-fire tactics the decisive feature of the battle. and went on prolonging the hurricane fire from massed parks of artillery, first for days, then for weeks, then for months. The incessant internal pressures, even with the low muzzle energy with which the Teutons were contented, rapidly

WAY FOR THE CAVALRY.
Bridge constructed by the Fort Garry Horse. An officer is about to test the strength of the structure.

RAPID ENGINEERING. [*Canadian Government copyright photographs.*]
Royal Canadian Horse Artillery crossing a bridge erected in the record time of one and a half minutes. Two soldiers are holding it in position by means of ropes.

ate up the brief life of the gun-tubes. Guns built on the British model could much more easily be re-tubed.

If our blockade had succeeded in depriving the enemy of the rare metals needed in making very high tensile and hard and high-speed steel, our skill in metallurgy would have told with overwhelming effect. The enemy was only beyond the attack of a vigorous blockade in regard to manganese ore. His nickel mines in Saxony were inadequate to his needs, while the French possessed in New Caledonia vast deposits. Britain and her Overseas Dominions had abundant supplies of most rare metals needed in the finest steel-making, and laws against the export of these scientific necessities in modern warfare helped to impede the labours of the enemy. What we did with our illimitable resources, our science in steel, and our fertilising collaboration with our brilliant French and Belgian allies forms a story of high technical interest which cannot yet be told. It will make an inspiring romance of science for our boys when they crowd into those improved and numerous institutes for secondary technical education which will consolidate the work of improvisation carried on during the war.

Meanwhile, it may be well to point out that our metallurgists and artillery engineers never failed our Army from the beginning. Our first five divisions were equipped for a battle of manœuvre, though for this they were very short of motor-transport and machine-guns. If siege operations against German fortresses were required, the French siege train was to undertake this work. We had a quick-firing 5 in. howitzer, and a quick-firing 5 in. field-gun, and it was probably because of our example that the Germans introduced giant howitzers and heavy guns into the equipment of their field army. Our French allies had followed our example in regard neither to our 4·5 in. field-howitzer nor our 1910 model 5 in. long-range gun, for they held that their "75" quick-firer was all that would be required in mobile warfare. They thus left themselves at a great disadvantage, and in the first battles they were surprised, outranged, and badly shattered.

Along the Aisne and at Ypres our guns were completely outranged, but this was due to the fact that our mobile field force on the Aisne plateau was opposed by part of the great German siege train brought from Maubeuge, while around Ypres the Austro-German siege train that had smashed the forts of Antwerp was brought against our men.

Our chief artillery defect

Our chief defect from the artillery standpoint was our lyddite shell, the fuse of which was not as fine as the French fuse. We had been the first nation to employ high-explosive shell. The fuse we employed was at first faulty, so that the shells sometimes exploded when being carried along rough roads, and this prejudiced some of our artillery officers against lyddite. They relied more on the sweeping fire of shrapnel, while both the French and the Germans, who had very safe and effective fuses, employed high-explosive blasts even in open field warfare. When our field army learnt by terrible experience the need for a larger proportion of high-explosive shell there were apparently two obstacles that delayed the improvement of our munitions. In the first place, soldiers of experience in the War Office retained their faith in shrapnel and a certain distrust of the high explosive, acquired from observation of our old type of lyddite shell.

Watch-makers and fuse-making Then, our shell-making plant, though expanding with the expansion of our forces, was planned to supply the needs of an army fighting in the open. That is to say, it was planned to supply shrapnel in much larger proportion than high-explosive shell, and the plant for making the high-explosive fuse remained comparatively small.

We had not workers in sufficient number expert in fuse making. It was an exquisite kind of labour, like fine clockmaking, and we had no large body of men who could be turned on to it without training. The French, whose fuse factories were from the beginning on a Continental scale like those of the enemy, obtained valuable assistance

In exquisite trueness the English lever watch and the first-rate English clock, the English sporting gun, chronometer, and many English scientific instruments of delicate precision are famous throughout the world. Even in the heavy work of shipbuilding the engine needs as fine work almost as a watch. The amount of research and experiment expended in our country on turbine blades, to take one example from our heaviest kind of engineering work, shows that the genius of the British race is as good at fine detail as it is at huge construction.

Indeed, we have continually progressed during the last generation in quality of work. In the industry on which our modern power was first built—iron and steel making— we have been overtaken in the rate of production by the United States and Germany. But we have used our ancient genius in science to make certain steel manufactured in our country more valuable than any steel that America or Germany produces. Sheffield steel, especially, played in the Great War a part like that which our early steam-engine played in the Napoleonic War. Germany uses the power-lathe we invented and the high-speed steel

BRITISH BOMBARDMENT OF FRICOURT, CAPTURED DURING THE FIRST WEEK OF JULY, 1916.
Sir Douglas Haig attacked on either side of Fricourt, and all but surrounded the village. The German line was broken in two places and such enemy reinforcements as entered the village were caught in a trap. This photograph shows the panorama before Fricourt and British shells bursting on the enemy position.

from the watchmakers in the French-speaking districts of Switzerland, and the Germans organised their clockmakers of the Black Forest and built huge new factories for them. We suffered from relying, in the days of peace, on American clock factories and Swiss watch factories. There were no great plants in our country for stamping out the delicate mechanism of the fuse, and no large bodies of trained assemblers who could be rapidly instructed in putting fuses together.

All this lack of means for making high-explosive shell in enormous quantities can scarcely be said to tell against our scientific genius for war, though some French critic remarked at the time that our temporary set-back was due to the fact that we had developed the heavy side of engineering, while the French had specialised in fine and exquisitely true work, such as distinguished the French motors used in light vehicles and flying machines. Yet the workmanship of the mechanism of a Rolls-Royce car was surely as good as anything made in France, and the new Coatelen engine of the Sunbeam Company did not seem to be very much inferior to the French aerial motors.

tools we elaborated. But Sheffield still held some secrets of steel manufacture likely to tell on the problem of the duration of the war.

Even the poisonous chlorine gas, which the Germans inhumanly introduced as a weapon of warfare, is a British invention. For a considerable period we have held almost a monopoly of one of the most important fields of industrial chemistry, based on the breaking up of common salt into soda and chlorine. In recent years a couple of British inventors worked out an electrical method of reducing salt to chlorine, which was used for bleaching purposes, and to soda, which was employed in soap-making and a score of other manufactures. Some of the German chemical works adopted the British invention, and by means of it produced the terrible fumes against which the Canadians had to fight at Ypres. It was in no way a triumph of a diabolical kind for German science. We possessed the infernal weapon of chlorine gas at the beginning of the war, but we refrained from using it because it did not simply kill. but produced prolonged agony.

The use of chlorine gas

Phosgene—a union of carbon monoxide and chlorine—which the Germans used in their dyeworks, and then employed as one of their poison gases on the battlefield, was discovered by Sir Humphry Davy. And it may be remarked that French and English discoveries of bromine and benzine were the foundation of the benzil-bromide shells used by the Germans to produce inflammation of the eyes and blindness.

Germany's diabolical weapons Even after the Germans used such diabolical weapons, our Government was averse to making use of our great alkali and refrigerating industries. Our refrigerating trade had the tens of thousands of gas cylinders needed. The cylinders were being used for gas required in the freezing process, and could quickly have been charged with chlorine at our alkali works. But apparently our Government was too tender-hearted to turn against the enemy the dreadful weapon he employed, though we had everything in our favour—the prevailing westerly wind, the greatest alkali plants in the world, and a large number of gas cylinders with the plants for making more. In other words, we had in this branch of technical science a great advantage over our fiendish enemy, and we refrained from using this advantage for unknown reasons. When we were at last compelled to use gas, we produced a heavy vapour of a harmless, intoxicating quality that merely stupefied the enemy and allowed him to be taken if his position were reached.

The employment of thick smoke from destroyers as a screen for battleship movements is another thing that

SONS OF THE EMPIRE.
Young Anzac officers in a merry mood before going up to the zone of operations.

the Germans learnt from us. They were clever pick-brains rather than original thinkers, and even their intense activity in developing the ideas they picked up was due rather to the fact that they were energetically working up for a great war, than to any naturally sustained alertness of intellect.

In their use of chemistry for war purposes the Germans certainly had some

AFTER THE TURK—THE HUN.
Splendid types of British soldiers from overseas congregating in a village behind the line in France. Most of these men had seen service in Gallipoli before getting to hand-grips with the real enemy.

advantage over us, but it was largely from the fundamental work of British men of science that they derived their main processes. For example, they were able to replace the nitre that they could not obtain from the nitre-fields of Chile by extracting nitre from the air by means of an electric arc—the old invention of Henry Cavendish. We, on the other hand, neglected our native sources of nitrates because we could rely upon the Chilian fields. But when our troubles over freightage became acute and the need for economy in the use of our cargo steamers grew urgent, our chemists were equal to the occasion. We had an enormous supply of ammonia, produced as a by-product in our gas and coke ovens, and by an oxidation process we were able to convert this by-product into concentrated nitric acid. It was also discovered that British gas companies were wasting a very large amount of ammonia, which could be recovered without difficulty. The by-product and **Utilisation of** the waste were sufficient to cover all **by-products** our requirements for high explosives.

Germany was producing half a million tons a year of nitric acid by the arc process and the cyanamide process, because she could not get Chilian nitrate of soda; and by the spring of 1916 it looked as though we should have to get our nitrates from our coal-mines, and thus unintentionally help to diminish the value of the one great source of natural wealth that Chile possessed. After the war the nitrates would be used for fertilising purposes in agriculture, and the chief belligerent countries, with their great new plants, would

ROUND THE VILLAGE PUMP.
Anzac soldiers filling their flasks at a village tap before going up to the trenches. With their slouch hats and loose-fitting tunics, the Anzacs were quite conspicuous.

A GREAT FRENCH POLITICIAN ON THE BRITISH FRONT.
M. Briand, the French Premier, studying a military plan on the occasion of a tour of the British lines made by him under the personal guidance of General Sir Douglas Haig. M. Briand appeared to be much impressed by his visit.

make the by-product of their gas and coke works into a permanent national source of nitrate supply. The farmers would then maintain a great industry needed for war.

From the gas and coke ovens of Germany and England also came picric acid and toluene. Here we had suffered a serious loss of warlike power by allowing Germany to develop the discovery of coal-tar dyes made by an English chemist. The enemy had the practical monopoly of coal-tar antiseptics, needed by our surgeons, coal-tar dyes, required for our khaki uniforms, and—what was of most importance—coal-tar high explosives of the safest, most lasting, and powerful kind. From their coke ovens the Germans obtained the toluene which they nitrated, also with a product of their gas ovens, and made into trinitro-toluene. Before the war this chemical had been offered by a German firm to our Government for use in torpedoes and floating mines. It had a more shattering effect than gun-cotton and did not deteriorate in water. But our Government did not adopt the new explosive. The German Government, however, did. For it was found that T.N.T., as trinitrotoluene is familiarly called, had some points of superiority over lyddite and other picric-acid explosives as a bursting charge in shells. Picric acid, obtained by boiling carbolic and nitric acid, must not be allowed to come into contact with metals, as it forms highly sensitive compounds. A varnish is employed to prevent it from blowing up its users, as it blew up some of our troops in the South African War. T.N.T., on the other hand, is more stable.

Coal-tar and high explosives In the form of " Jack Johnsons " and other terrible shells, T.N.T. was pitched into our lines while we were still mainly employing shrapnel because of our difficulties with picric-acid fuses. But the British chemists soon worked out a process for T.N.T. and another new high explosive. Practically all the toluene from our gas and coke factories was commandeered by the Ministry of Munitions. Then the benzole, from which the toluol had been extracted, was also taken over by the Government. Before the war our country manufactured annually about ten million gallons of benzole from the waste of gasworks and coke ovens. A large proportion of this by-product used to be sent in peace

time to Germany, there to be manufactured into coal-tar dyes, drugs, and scents, and what then remained of the benzole was employed as a spirit in motor-car engines. But our war chemists, towards the close of 1915, began to turn our ten million gallons of coal-tar spirit into another new high-explosive, popularly called T.N.A. This was short for tetranitraniline, made by nitrating aniline, and is a solid high explosive, the most powerful of its kind. But about this time a Swedish engineer, Mr. W. Normelli, was reported to have invented a new form of nitrated ammonia from coke oven by-products which had twenty-five per cent. greater bursting effect than any other explosive. If the facts of this invention were truly stated, normellite promised to have a great influence on naval warfare, for our chief chemical problem, as the leading naval Power has been for many years the armour-piercing shell.

We learnt from a Russian experiment, in the days when we were hostile to Russia, how to make a bolt of forged steel that would break through heavy armour. An ingenious Russian had discovered that a steel bolt needed, paradoxically, a cap of soft iron over its nose to prevent it from smashing against armour. We fitted soft iron caps to our armour-piercing shells, but were perplexed to find the devastating high explosive that would withstand the tremendous shock of the impact of the shell on the armour and explode inside the stricken ship. Nearly all the high explosives detonated on the armour-plate as this was being pierced, and did little **Discovery of** damage. For some time we used black **normellite** powder in our armour-piercing shells, because this old-fashioned and feeble explosive could be made to survive the smash on the armour, and burst a fraction of a second later inside the pierced ship. Normellite, it is stated, is as stable as black powder, in addition to doing more damage than lyddite or T.N.T. Propelled with sufficient force, it will go through any armour without detonating in the terrific shock, and then explode by its own fuse when travelling in a pierced turret or below a deck.

In regard to the German monopoly in certain coal-tar antiseptics, needed in vast quantities on the battlefield, this was overcome by British men of science with extraordinary rapidity. In the first place, Professor Lorraine Smith and Dr. Dakin found, in our great chemical factories of bleaching powder, the means of making a new antiseptic, which was both cheaper and stronger than carbolic acid and lysol. But long before this important newer antiseptic industry was established, the greatest of all our medical men of science, Sir Almroth Wright, discovered that our old slave-traders in the West Indies in the eighteenth century knew more about antiseptics than any modern German chemist. When a slave tried to escape and received a severe lashing, they used to rub his broken skin with a mixture of sea-water and lemon-juice. Sir Almroth Wright studied the effect on the blood of a solution of common salt and lemon-juice, and discovered that while ordinary antiseptics killed the injured tissues, the old slave-traders' remedy caused the injured parts to be bathed in healing fluids coming from the rest of the body. So, during the war, the wounds of our soldiers and sailors twice with their bayonets. On the Friday morning, noting the steady attempt of the Germans to move farther and farther to the left and so completely outflank the Canadians, a fresh counter-attack was resolved upon. Two Ontario battalions, the 1st and the 4th of the 1st Brigade, which had now come up from reserve, were given the post of honour, a British regiment, the Middlesex, acting as their support.

The attack seemed quite hopeless. The Canadians were at this point a considerable distance from the Germans, with about eight hundred or nine hundred yards of absolutely open ground to go over. The German trenches were on a slope and there was no shelter whatever between the attacking troops and them. As the Canadians rushed forward the Germans raked them with machine-gun and rifle fire. Men started dropping before the 4th Battalion got properly started. The advance was made in short rushes, two sections at a time. There was no cheering, no shouting, nothing but whispered words of command. The troops made short charges down a ravine and up a slope, dropping to the ground after each rush. There was no hesitation, no bravado, no hanging back. The machine-guns swept over the glacis. The German gunners timed their shrapnel so as to burst over the ranks. The German companies lining the trenches picked out their men. The British artillery did all it could to cover the advance, pouring shrapnel fire on the hill crest where the Germans lay dug in. Sometimes, when a heavier blast of fire than usual struck our ranks, the men joked together. "Say, boys, there seems to be a war on here," one remarked when things were hottest.

"Believe me, if hell is anything like Friday, I am

Jokes under murderous fire

A TRIO OF "TROGLODYTES."
Corner of a British trench along the first line, where men grew accustomed to the life of cave-dwellers.

for reforming," wrote one young soldier to his family afterwards. "How I lasted as long as I did, I hardly know, as at every rush the fellow next me 'copped it.' Once, when we were lying down, the man next to me got it square through the head. Only one sergeant and four men, including myself, out of our platoon got up to within two hundred yards of the trench, when the fellow next me was hit in the arm. I sat up beside him to get out his bandage to tie him up, when I got hit myself through the back, and the next fellow got it in the shoulder. Only two were left. I suppose they got it later." His experience was typical.

Lieutenant-Colonel Burchill led the 4th Battalion. He carried nothing but a light cane. He moved ahead of his men almost as though on parade, cheering, inspiring—I was going to say encouraging—them, but they needed no encouragement. In six hours the men, or what were left of them, advanced about seven or eight hundred yards, finally reaching to within a hundred yards of the German trench. Then Colonel Burchill fell dead at the head of his battalion. That was the last touch. His soldiers, stung to fury by the loss of their beloved commander, made one final effort to avenge him. They flung themselves through the last hundred yards, despite the direct rifle and machine-gun fire. How a single man got through it is scarcely possible to understand, for by all the laws of war every one should have been wiped out long before. Possibly the sight of the yelling, cheering, infuriated men shook the nerves of the Germans, as well it might. The Canadians reached the trench and swept through it like fury, bayoneting, shooting, overcoming every German there.

Colonel Burchill avenged

IN WINTER KIT.
Three Canadian soldiers, during the work of consolidating their position, pause to glance at the photographer.

TRENCH CARPENTRY.
Australian soldiers repairing a
communication trench.

profession in regard to his discovery of a preventive against enteric. It was not until Lord Kitchener undertook the reorganisation of the Indian Army, recognised the merits of the new vaccine, and had it tested in a decisive manner, that the prejudices of ignorance were overcome. At the outbreak of hostilities not more than eighty men in this country were fully trained in the new methods of treatment of bacterial disease developed by Sir Almroth Wright. Hence, perhaps, the breakdown in our measures of prevention in Meso-potamia and Gallipoli.   But, on the other **Antiseptic progress in** hand, small as was our band of medical   **France** men of science of the new school, it was larger than that possessed by the Central Empires.   In the winter of 1914 the Austrians suffered horribly from a general lack of modern medical science.   Germany had one man of great distinction, the brilliant Jew, Paul Ehrlich, of Frankfort.   He was bound by ties of common admiration to Wright and the leaders of our London and Liverpool schools for the studies of tropical diseases.   His personal troubles during the war killed Ehrlich, for he was a Jew more of the type of Spinoza than of Ballin and Dernberg.   Ehrlich's death robbed the Germans of their greatest active mind.

were not generally treated with coal-tar antiseptics in such a way as to hurt the tissues, but were kept free from germs by the Almroth Wright solution.   At the same time as the wound was being dressed in this new way a vaccine was injected into the wounded men, which prevented any suppuration from occurring.

The old, elaborate lint bandage and wool frequently acted as a deterrent to the discharge of lymph, which cleansed the injury, and formed sometimes a breeding place for germs.   The removal of such dressings, too, occasioned considerable suffering to the wounded man.   The saline solution irrigation dispensed, to no small extent, with the cumbersome surgical dressing.   Another advantage of the non-application of coal-tar antiseptics and bandages was that the injured and exposed periosteum (sheath of the bone) was in no way irritated.

THE QUICK AND THE DEAD.
Grave of a British soldier only a few
yards from a first-line trench.

France, to whom the need of conservation of life was of supreme importance, was in as fortunate a position as Britain.   Pasteur left behind many heirs of his genius, and at the Pasteur Institute and elsewhere there were hundreds of finely trained minds working on the problems of military injuries and diseases. Wright's work on the new antiseptic was taken up, thoroughly examined, proved, and then developed, with results that were soon to be seen by the public in ordinary surgical operations.   Enteric was fought

In spite of all the loud advertisements of the achievements of German medical science, our country at the outbreak of war was in the happy **A preventive against** position of possessing the greatest living **enteric** master of ordinary germ diseases.   Sir Almroth Wright and a large part of his laboratory staff joined the Army, and helped to safeguard the bodily strength of all the fighting men of the western line.

It was in Sir Almroth Wright's laboratory at St. Mary's Hospital, Paddington, that enormous quantities of enteric vaccine were prepared, with which first the British troops and then the French, Belgian, and Russian troops were safeguarded from the most deadly of all battle perils.

After the South African War, Sir Almroth Wright continually struggled against the inertia of the medical

[*Official photographs.*
AFTERNOON TEA IN SPITE OF THE WAR.
Anzac soldiers lined up for a can of tea, one of the most popular beverages
in the first line.

CATERING ARRANGEMENTS UNDER DIFFICULTIES.

Just behind the Anzac trenches. Headquarters of the cook, who was in the act of preparing a meal for his comrades. Shells had snapped off many of the tall trees in the vicinity. Four of the men are wearing the excellent steel helmet which saved so many valuable lives.

[*Official photograph.*]

by vaccination, and the strange outbreak of spotted fever, which seems first to have occurred in our Canadian Division, was combated by American, British, and French research. We have no wish to paint the devil blacker than he is, but having regard to the known fact that cholera from an Austrian source was deliberately spread among the Belgian troops and also among the Russian troops, we must point out that the germ of spotted fever was only clearly discovered at the beginning of the war. Months passed before any well-tested method of treatment could be devised. The germ was first discovered in the United States, and it was brought into our country and then into France, by infected Canadian recruits. Then it strangely appeared in a great, overwhelming, horrible epidemic in Serbia, where it largely contributed to the enfeeblement of the Serbian people and the sapping of the last reserves of strength of the Serbian Army.

The germ of spotted fever

We possess a large mass of definite Russian evidence that drinking vessels containing cholera cultures were placed for Russian troops to use. There are, therefore, grounds of suspicion that German bacteriologists, profiting by the discovery of the new spotted-fever germ, employed this deadly microbe for the same purpose as German chemists employed chlorine gas. In any case, cholera germs were certainly employed in the Teutonic method of warfare, and round Ypres and in German South-West Africa the enemy poisoned the water with arsenic, after the manner of the lowest savages. But because the German used his knowledge of bacteriology in order to spread diseases among his foes, there is no reason to allow him any superiority in scientific skill.

Britain and France possessed together more knowledge and probably larger equipment, but they kept wholly to preventive and to healing work, while the Teuton used the mind and common heritage of medical knowledge of civilised men to attempt atrocities beyond the dreams of the most blood-maddened savage, and, if Milton's view of Satan is correct, lower and viler than anything imagined by the devil. We have yet to learn how the horrors of Wittenberg Camp originated. It would be easy for a skilled bacteriologist of the German school to murder prisoners by having them first kept in such a condition that they were plagued with vermin, and then deliberately introducing among them either a stricken patient or an unconscious plague-carrier. Professor Huxley used to discourse very eloquently on the ennobling effect of scientific studies. He should have lived to see what the Germans did after studying certain medical branches of knowledge, which they lacked the genius to originate, but developed with ant-like industry when they saw the practical value of the new discoveries. It was a war of annihilation that German men of science of the materialistic school tried to wage against Russia, Belgium, Serbia, France, and Britain. They endeavoured to sweep all the allied populations away by means of a revived form of a "Black Death." The very instrument of research which Pasteur, Lister, Metchnikoff, and Wright developed for the cure of human weakness and suffering was perverted into the most ghastly of all weapons of general slaughter by the bacteriologists of Germany and Austria-Hungary.

This matter is of supreme importance. It goes down deep into the ultimate problem of the human race. We are a collection of frail creatures, living, each for a brief span of time, on a clot of substance whirling round the gas-jet we call the sun. It seems to have taken us about a million years to climb out of a purely animal stage of existence, and become, in varying degree, instruments of the Divine power that labours through the universe. It is scarcely more than ten thousand years since civilisation was established, and the work of collecting a permanent body of knowledge in a form that could be handed down from generation to generation and spread and developed among and by all classes was begun but four thousand years ago. The great increase of human power, born of science, has taken place in the lifetime of men and women still living. Our power over the agents of disease is still imperfect, and the knowledge underlying this power is a technical and

Scientific crime of the Teutons

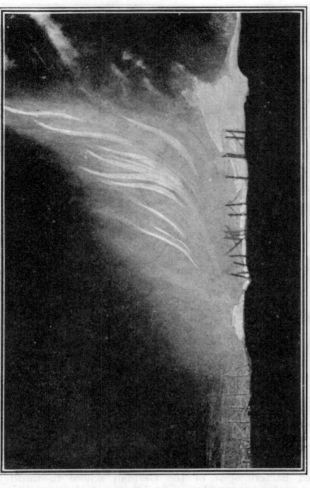

Flame night attack on the British trenches. The neutral zone became one great blaze, and the photograph was secured simply by this light.

Testing a new type of respirator. Perilous work of British officers. After the Germans introduced gas into warfare several types of respirators were used at the front.

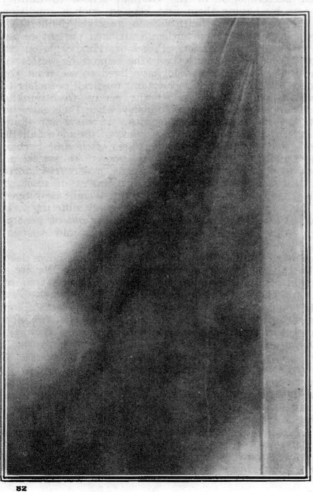

Veritably the inferno of war. Flame attack by day which was accompanied by huge clouds of black smoke intended to veil enemy movements.

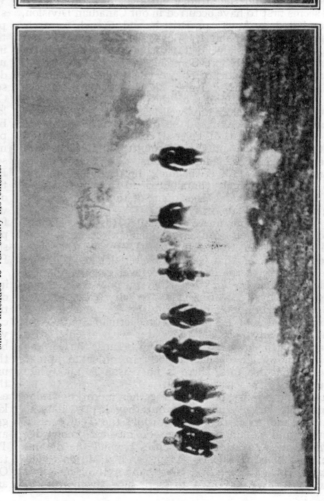

British officers wearing respirators running through a gas cloud. The poisonous atmosphere was so weighted as to creep along the ground, not unlike a mist on the moors.

FLAMES AND FUMES: THE NEW ELEMENTS INTRODUCED INTO WARFARE BY THE ENEMY.

abstruse thing, of which scarcely more than one person in forty thousand Britons has a comprehensive grasp.

Thence arises a state of popular ignorance concerning the terrible crimes of the German bacteriologists, which helped the enemy. Our public does not appreciate the quality and scope of the scientific crime of the Teutons. As a nation we are too much lacking in uncompromising trenchancy of intellect to attack and solve the problem of the future struggles of the human race which Germany has raised. Our public does not understand what the Germans actually attempted. Had any people attempted to do to the Germans what the Germans tried to do to the Allies—and sometimes succeeded in doing—there would have been such a propaganda of scientific enlightenment that the oldest and most illiterate peasant in the Black Forest would have been made clearly to understand the terrible significance of the event.

The majority of our people, however, appeared likely to go through the war and then settle down to the work of peaceful reconstruction without facing the present and future possibilities of bacteriological warfare. It is now possible for a very skilful bacteriologist to prepare a practically new form of death and elaborate at the same time its antidote. It is possible for him, with the assistance of his Government, to use the antidote on all his countrymen and make them immune from some deadly disease, and then secretly and thoroughly spread this disease through a neighbouring nation by means of assistants working in the large cities of the country attacked. Yet there was every probability that the Allies would at last make peace with the Central Empires without paying the slightest attention to the awful problem of the future means of protection of the human race which German and Austrian bacteriologists have raised during the present war. The crime against civilisation committed by the Germans in regard to the employment of poisonous gas is utterly unimportant in comparison with their subtler devilry in spreading deadly infectious disease germs. It used to be fancied that some insane Anarchist with scientific knowledge might possibly pervert the great discovery of Pasteur into a means of attempting to depopulate the earth. It was no utter madman that attempted this ultimate crime, but some of the cool-headed men of science attached to German universities and paid by the German Government. And when peace is established no guarantees will be obtained that war will not silently break out in a strange, secret, fiendish way that is likely to find the attacked nations all unprepared.

Awful problem of the future

It has been said that evil is wrought by want of thought as well as by want of conscience, and it is our crowning misfortune that we are governed by men none of whom has any first-hand knowledge of science. And behind these men are four or five party machines, run by governing castes which are either dull or unenlightened.

A small band of true lovers of human wisdom proved our salvation when the great ordeal by battle opened. Probably a majority of them were men of private means, who

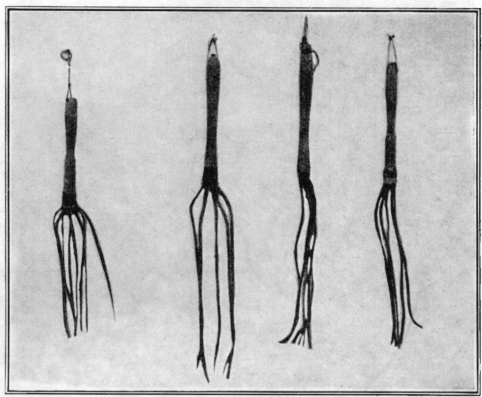

[*Official photograph. Crown copyright reserved.*

DISCOVERED IN THE ENEMY'S FIRST LINE.
Cat-o'-nine-tails found in the German trenches. Four sinister implements which fell into British hands on the occasion of the general move forward on July 1st, 1916.

pursued in their own homes the work that German men of science undertook with Government funds in magnificently equipped laboratories. Others were captains of industry, like Sir Robert Hadfield, of Sheffield, who ran important factories, and for pure delight in research work built private laboratories in their works, and held all foreign competitors at bay by an astonishing stream of discoveries. Then some of our intellectual leaders, like Sir Almroth Wright, began their fine work in universities and Government positions, fought for years against official stupidity and jealousy, abandoned their posts and their salaries, and at last by great labour attracted the admiration of generous rivals abroad and slowly rose, through foreign recognition, to a position of authority in their own country. Extremely rare were well-endowed centres of research like the Cavendish Laboratory at Cambridge, founded by the Duke of Devonshire, in which British men of science could pursue their studies with as great a wealth of appliances as German and American professors possessed.

Even for military purposes our Government, Conservative or Radical, would not provide proper funds for scientific research. To take an apparently small example of Government indifference: We were in a perilous position in regard to the manufacture of glass for scientific purposes. The glass we required for vaccinating our troops against enteric and suppurating wounds, and for scientific researches in factories and laboratories where great heat was used, was a German monopoly. The Germans also controlled the production of the optical glass required in increasing quantity by our Navy and Army for submarine periscopes, gunnery sights, and range-finders, field-glasses, and other warlike purposes. We had inventors able to provide us with periscopes and range-finders—in fact, the submarine periscope was an Irish invention, and the range-finder of Messrs. Barr & Stroud was the mother instrument of all similar devices used at home and abroad. The advantage of inventive genius rested with us.

Government and scientific research

"PRESENT KUKRIES!": UNIQUE FORM OF DRILL IN THE HETEROGENEOUS FORCES OF THE EMPIRE AT WAR.
Kit inspection of Gurkhas, some of the fierce warriors from India. Each is displaying his kukri, a steel weapon which gave the Germans considerable anxiety in the early part of the war. The rest of the Gurkhas' outfit is placed neatly on the grass.

All that the enemy possessed was the advantage of manufacture. He had in the Thuringia Forest fine glass industries of larger scope than he required, and his great optical glass and instrument factories produced in peace time more articles than his Army and Navy needed. It was foreseen that when war broke out Germany would turn her monopoly in optical and heat-resisting glass against us, and provide her gunners, sharpshooters, and observing officers with an extraordinary number of ingenious optical devices, while leaving us with no immediate means of supplying the growing needs of our military and naval forces.

Five years ago, some of our men of science pointed out to our military and naval authorities and to the Board of Education that, in the event of a European war, our import of glass for binoculars, gun-sights, range-finders, and many other instruments would be suddenly stopped, and that we must, for the sake of the safety of the country, learn to make the necessary glass ourselves. It was proposed to establish an optical institute **Germany's glass** in connection with the Northampton Poly-**monopoly** technic in Clerkenwell. When the military and educational authorities were asked to contribute some financial aid to the capital cost of the building the answer given was: "No item in the Parliamentary estimates." So the scheme could not be carried out, although another notable band of men of science, attached to the Imperial College in Kensington, agreed to direct the higher work of the institute. The result was that we paid in blood for the blindness of our caste of professional politicians.

In the end it was our inventors who saved us and stopped the wastage of life along our battle-front. A group of men in our Chemical Society energetically tackled the secrets of German glass, and with remarkable rapidity discovered the formulas and gave them to our manufacturers.

In optical glass there was considerable difficulty in getting the exquisite moulds by which the Germans standardised their output. We turned to America for some of our searchlights and optical instruments, and, happily, one of the principal **Power of the** German-American firms was strongly in-**periscope rifle** dignant over the wrong done to Belgium, and worked for our forces with magnificent energy. A long time passed before our snipers were provided with sights such as German sharpshooters used. But again the inventive talent of our race helped us out of our difficulties. In the Gallipoli campaign, for instance, the moral superiority of the Anzac force was largely due to a clever device worked out on the spot by Lance-Corporal W. C. D. Beach, of the 2nd Australian Battalion. Using his shaving mirror, Beach constructed a periscope rifle, with which he was able to fire over the parapet while remaining completely hidden. Sir William Birdwood quickly appreciated the strange power of the periscope rifle. He denuded all the transports of their looking-glasses, and with the help of Corporal Beach constructed some two thousand rifle periscopes, with which the Turks were kept completely under throughout the campaign. The invention was sent home, but apparently some time elapsed before the simple and ingenious periscope rifle was introduced into France and Flanders.

A still more remarkable example of the British faculty of meeting a great need by inventiveness occurred in connection with another German monopoly of a key industry. The most subtle and far-reaching of the enemy's preparations for war was his control of base metals and rare metals. Zinc, for instance, was badly needed by us as the chief naval Power and shipping Power. Our Army needed zinc for making cartridges, but our large steamers and warships also required it in vast quantities. For instance, a single Atlantic liner needed every year a supply of fifty-eight tons of zinc to protect her boilers from corrosion. The zinc she required every twelve months was sufficient to make the brass for seventeen million cartridges. The zinc in one of our latest fast battleships probably represents the base metal required for 20,000,000 cartridges. So as the war developed, zinc rose tenfold in price and became scarce. The Empire had an abundant supply of the metal in Australia, but there were no works, either in Australia or in Britain, for getting the spelter out of the ores. A German ring, with factories in Germany and in the occupied part of Belgium, controlled this great key industry. The ring took the ore from the Australian mine, roasted the zinc out of it, and, when war broke out, kept the zinc in Germany. We had no works of any importance for zinc-making. But an inventive Englishman, Mr. Elliott Cumberland, helped to save the use of zinc in the ordinary boilers of our land and marine steam-engines. It was known

The German spelter ring that the corrosion of boilers was due to electro-chemical action. Mr. Cumberland introduced two iron points into a boiler, and sent a ten-volt current of electricity from point to point. It was such a current as could be obtained from a small dynamo used for lighting purposes—something both small and cheap. But the electric current proved sufficient to take all the corrosive elements from the interior of the boiler and deposit them on the iron point, together with all grease, oil, and other impurities from the boiling water. Instead of a large fast steamer needing fifty-eight tons of zinc a year to keep her boilers clean, she required only a few iron points, costing perhaps less than ten shillings, annually.

This great saving in one of the most useful of base metals related to our Navy and our mercantile marine, and to all works in which power was derived from steam. Naturally, old-fashioned large boilers were easier to save from corrosion than the modern tubular boiler. But Mr. Cumberland's little anti-corrosion current promised to upset one of the most important markets of the German zinc ring.

The German base-metal ring was further defeated by another British invention. There was a large British factory troubled with a useless waste product, consisting of calcium chloride. This **Circumvented by** firm used its waste as a source of chlorine **British invention** for getting the zinc into a liquid form. The roasted ore was brought into contact with chloride waste, with the result that the mineral in it was dissolved. An electric current was then sent through the chloride of zinc, producing a superb result—a 99·96 pure zinc. As at Broken Hill, Australia, there were the vastest zinc deposits in the world, the new British method of smelting and refining, which completely superseded the laborious German method of spelter-making, broke the enemy's monopoly, endowed us with a great key industry, began to give us some of the zinc we needed, and made things look very bad for the German metal ring. For the Prime Minister of Australia offered to arrange for zinc production to be established on a great scale in the Empire.

Among the other key industries we recaptured from the enemy was tungsten-smelting. Most of the tungsten ore was obtained from British territory, but the Germans, having patented a process for producing the tremendous heat of 3,000 degrees Fahrenheit, by the action of aluminium power on the oxides of metal, smelted the tungsten by this thermit treatment. It may also be remarked that the aluminium powder and oxide process, employed by Goldschmitt and the German metal ring for the production of pure metals, was afterwards used against us in our homes in the shape of thermit incendiary bombs from Zeppelin airships. We needed tungsten urgently for fine steel-making and electrical purposes.

UNLIMITED SHELLS: A WELCOME SIGHT FOR BRITISH SOLDIERS IN FRANCE.
German officers' reports on the British bombardment north of the Somme in July, 1916, left no doubt as to its devastating character. This official photograph, issued by the Press Bureau, shows some of our soldiers watching the British shells bursting over the enemy lines.

BOMBERS GOING TO THE FRONT LINE.
The roads were so cut up, that they rendered the going very arduous for men so heavily burdened.

OFF TO PUSH THE ENEMY YET A LITTLE FARTHER BACK.
Hand-to-hand fighting with bomb and bayonet was incessant during the first fortnight of the July advance. The men of our New Army were too much even for the Prussian Guard.

The Germans had practically all the stock of pure metal and the plant for making more, and there was a risk of our munition work being seriously impeded by this foresightful piece of scientific strategy on their part. But our metallurgists quickly discovered an improved method of getting pure tungsten, and under the stimulus of our military needs our possession of the principal tungsten mine made us supreme in the manifold tungsten industries, such as the manufacture of tungsten wire-drawn electric lamps, tungsten-steel, and other tungsten alloys.

With respect to nickel, first used in steel-making by a Glasgow firm, whose ideas were borrowed by Krupp in his nickel-steel guns, there was another difficulty in addition to that of escaping from the power of the German metal ring. There was not enough nickel in the world for the needs of ourselves and our Allies.

Canada's great discovery Canada here came to our assistance in an indirect but effective way. In North Ontario was the only important source of cobalt in the world, but except for the production of cobalt-blue the metal was a nuisance. It was obtained as waste when extracting silver. But the Canadian Department of Mines instituted researches into the production and applications of metallic cobalt. As usual, Sir Robert Hadfield, of Sheffield, was foremost in the study of its possibilities. He found that, like nickel, it raised the elastic limit and maximum stress of steel. Cobalt-steel high-speed tools were then obtained by a simpler, cheaper method than that needed for the high-speed tools of other alloys. Cobalt also promised to be a better plating material than nickel, with the result that the British Empire acquired, under the stimulus of war, another great key industry. Cobalt-steel was especially valuable in war time, in that it accelerated our output of munitions.

The list of our amazingly rapid conquests and reconquests in the scientific field of warlike activities could be extended through many more pages. But we shall only refer to one more key industry—the manufacture of magnesium. As usual, the Germans controlled the output of this metal, and used it largely in flares on the battle-front at night, as all the allied troops knew only too well. Owing to their monopoly they had an enormous supply of flares. The reduction of magnesium was a British invention and had been an important British industry; but the enemy blocked our trade by tariff duties and then used his deposits of easily-worked ore to ruin our plant. But the indomitable British genius for invention discovered a cheap process of dealing with refractory ores, and a large new plant was laid down capable of supplying the needs of the world. And these needs are vital. For the oxide of magnesium—magnesia—is one of the most infusible of substances. It withstands almost every practical heat except that of the electric arc, and is therefore an important element in the making of crucibles and firebricks. It is largely required in steel-making plants.

Manufacture of magnesium

It is impossible not to admire the infinite pains the Germans took to monopolise the chief means of war. They could not equal us in inventive power, but they tried to prevent us from getting the alloys and crucibles we required. Even when a material like tungsten was only to be found in bulk in British territory, the enemy so absorbed the means of dealing with the ore that, like the Australians, who had vast mines of zinc but could get no zinc for love or money, we were left impoverished amid our natural riches.

All that could be done by small patented technical improvements, powerful financial enterprise, and a mighty international organisation of control, the Germans accomplished. But one thing escaped their business-like, yet narrow, calculating minds. This thing was a spiritual quality—genius. They overlooked the genius of the British race, even as the military and political leaders of Germany overlooked the spirit of determined courage that inhered in our people.

Genius versus patient industry All that the Germans achieved by patient, industrious talent, by the endowment and development of scientific research, by intensive methods of education, by the organisation of Trust systems of industry with research departments, and by the very skilful use of finance, was overcome by the British people when the British gift for invention was violently brought into action. We may admit that, as a nation, we scarcely deserved the results obtained by our men of science when they were abruptly asked to help us in our need. Science, like poetry, had been, from generation to generation in Britain, the cult of a very small number of men, who laboured to hand down the torch transmitted from their great predecessors and delight their own tastes in life rather than to win public appreciation. Not the slightest breath of national inspiration helped them in their task. There was no popular interest in their work.

At the time of writing we have still some leeway to recover against both Germany and the United States in the matter of certain technical equipment and certain branches of organised research. We have, for example, suffered greatly from allowing both the German and the American to surpass us in the production of machine-tools. Our new munition factories, in December, 1915, could not be supplied with all the machine-tools required, although the power-lathe and similar devices, together with high-speed cutting steels, were originally British inventions. First the Americans and then the Germans had become leaders in the machine-tool industry. Instead of making our own machine-tools, we began to buy German tools because they were both cheap and ingenious. This enabled the German firms to extend their plants, with the result that the German equipment for munition-making became enormous. The number of their war factories was limited by the skilled and semi-skilled hands available, and not by any practical limit in machine-tool production. We, on the other hand, had a large supply of skilled labour and vast sources of trainable labour, but we lacked machine-tools for our great army of munitioneers.

We also lacked jigs, gauges, and similar instruments of standardised production in which the Americans excelled. It was by means of jigs that the Americans had developed and monopolised the cheap motor-car industry and many other standardised mechanical manufactures. During the war they applied the jig system **Britain's threefold** to shipbuilding, and began to produce on a **burden** wholesale scale the cheap, standardised steamer. Gradually, however, we partly made and partly imported the machine-tools, jigs, gauges, and other guides for apprentice hands who diluted our host of skilled mechanics. While supplying France with fine steel for her new heavy artillery and helping also to re-arm Russia, we increased the daily output of war material for our mighty New Army and our enlarged Fleet, and drew near to the industrial and scientific output of war material in

"FRANCE'S DAY," 1916: THE GREATEST NATIONAL FÊTE IN PARIS SINCE THE FALL OF THE BASTILLE.
Memorable scenes of enthusiasm were witnessed in Paris on the occasion of the March of the Four Nations along the Boulevards, on July 14th, 1916. All Paris turned out to give French, Russian, Belgian, and British troops a glorious welcome. President Poincaré presented diplomas, crosses, and medals to the representatives of the first five hundred officers who fell on the field of honour, while an officer announced the name of each family in turn, a public honour conferred on the great dead of France, with a charm and dignity which only the Latins can express.

THE "EYES" OF THE ARTILLERY.
Kite-balloons ascending on observation work. This type of balloon was much used by all the European belligerents by reason of its stability in the wind, obtained by the sausage-like appendix seen on the left.

Germany. In the matter of artillery, for instance, Germany was helped by Austria, whereas Britain used a considerable part of her steel-making plant to assist France, who had lost her chief coal and iron fields. We also made plant, steel, and weapons for Russia, and provided Italy with coal and other material.

Our energies were not devoted entirely to our own needs. We gave to our Allies larger aid in war material than Germany, with the help of Austria-Hungary, gave to Turkey and Bulgaria. And though we purchased help from the armament firms of the United States, our native effort for the munitioning of our own forces increased in formidableness. By midsummer of 1916 neither our gun nor our shell output had surpassed that of Germany. But Britain and France then began to rival the common enemy in the power of his armament on the western front. And our Empire was still developing its warlike resources. We promised, indeed, to become stronger in peace than we were in war. For in war we were continually improvising better methods and making small and large discoveries to overcome the difficulties that we encountered. It was reported that some German manufacturers were preparing to recover and extend their foreign markets, by dumping accumulated stocks of articles at prices defying competition. But we, without deliberately designing it, were also to some extent preparing for the coming economic struggle with the foe by enormously increasing our plant, by speeding-up production, and devising superior processes.

There seem to have been only two branches of science of great value for war in which we were excelled by hostile or neutral States. The Germans maintained the immense lead in the technique of fast, large, rigid airship construction, which they had fairly won by costly research and courageous experiment before the war. Yet the aluminium alloy used by Count Zeppelin for the framework of his airships was a British invention, and in 1915 we improved upon this aluminium alloy of remarkable tensile strength, and invented a reinforced aluminium, cast by a very ingenious system of centrifugal pressure in moulds containing strips of high-tensile steel. By means of this combined structure of steel and aluminium we were endowed with a new weapon for conquering the air. The material was a union of lightness and strength, from which both flying machines and dirigible balloons of the rigid type could be constructed

Where the Germans led

with an important saving in weight. Aero-motors could also be lightened so as to give more horse-power in proportion to weight, by using reinforced aluminium for pistons and other freely-working parts not subject to severe strain. But, for some reason, there was no determination on the part of our Government to surmount the difficulties of providing our Fleet with wide-ranging scouting airships of a powerful sort. We had started with a heavy bias towards heavier-than-air machines. Our Royal Aircraft Works were strangely laggard even in aeroplane design, and for long gave us no machines by which we could raid the German coast. Fortunately the spirit of invention abode in our private aircraft manufacturers and aero-motor makers, and their productions gradually supplied our aeroplane deficiencies.

Meanwhile, we had been surpassed—happily by a friendly neutral country, the United States—in telephonic invention. The Americans were able to achieve a supreme feat in wireless electrical communication and transmit speech for thousands of miles without wires. But for the war they would have bridged the Atlantic Ocean with electric waves, enabling men in London and Paris to talk with men in New York. Some years before the outbreak of hostilities the problem of long-distance wireless telephony had been approaching solution. Music and speech had been transmitted for hundreds of miles, and means of conversing over considerable distances from trains and motor-cars going at high speed had been practised. During the war some Swedish inventors perfected a system of wireless telegraphy requiring such small instruments that messages could be sent from travelling motor-cars, and the Americans accomplished the first known practical system of talking by electric waves over a space of thousands of miles.

Long-distance wireless telephony

Our men of science, associated with Lieutenant Marconi, devoted the greater part of their energy of mind to the solution of smaller but more urgent problems in wireless research for military purposes. They extended the range of messages sent from aeroplanes, so that while United States pilots in the summer of 1916 could only transmit over a distance of fifteen miles, our scouting military and naval pilot could "wireless" information over a range of one hundred and fifty miles. The Allies badly needed a receiving instrument that would withstand the extraordinary vibration of an aeroplane in full flight, and allow the pilot to receive as well as transmit messages. A marked improvement in the aerial services was, therefore, effected when the difficulty of the vibration of the machine was overcome, and the pilot was enabled to converse with the gunners and his various headquarters possessing wireless installations. His messages were made clearer, for he could be asked to repeat or extend them. In cases of emergency his orders could be varied with decisive effect. One of the principal advantages of the Zeppelin in scouting work was that it provided a steady platform, from which wireless messages could be both sent and received. But the aeroplane and seaplane at last won the power of wireless conversation, and though their range of transmission remained comparatively limited by reason of the small space available for the instrument, the main deficiency in their scouting faculty was supplied when their pilots were

Type of captured German trench-mortar mounted on a heavy wooden emplacement.

German machine-gun and automatic rifle, the latter being supported by two steel rods.

77 mm. field-gun, which corresponded to the French "75," but was inferior to the famous Déport invention.

German 10 cm. gun, which fell into British hands during the "great push" in July, 1916.

Enemy trench-mortar fitted on a revolving platform, captured by the British.

Another type of German trench-mortar, which hurled an enormous projectile.

Machine-guns, ammunition, and German helmets—relics of the great British advance.

(Official photographs.

German 10 in. mine-thrower, consisting of a timber barrel bound round with galvanised wire.

DIVERSE WEAPONS CAPTURED FROM GERMANS IN THE GREAT BRITISH ADVANCE IN 1916.

enabled to hear as well as speak by wireless. Everything else was merely a matter of developing the lifting power and the horse power per pound of engine weight, thus increasing the fuel capacity and range of action of the flying machine to enable it to do all the work of the Zeppelin, and do it better. This was our objective in aircraft science, to develop the flying machine into a better aerial vehicle than was the rigid dirigible balloon. The aim was certainly a sound one, but all the same it would have been more practical for urgent war purposes to have taken up Zeppelin construction for the benefit of the Navy, while we were gradually working our way towards the great flying machine of the future.

As was seen in the Battle off Jutland, the bomb-dropping power of the Zeppelin was not so important as its wireless range. The part played by the science of electrical communication in warfare continually increases in both strategic and tactical value. Telegraphy and telephony, with and without wires, form the master means of control for the modern commander. In naval warfare, electrical communication with coded signals is an essential weapon of

THE LANDSCAPE OF WAR: A CAMP IN FRANCE.
British camp behind the lines in France, adjacent to the scene of the 1916 summer advance. Wooden frameworks had been covered with tarpaulins and served as tents. In the background a troop of transport horses had been left to graze.

tactics. Submarines, destroyers, light cruisers, and aerial scouts are linked with battle squadrons by wireless communication, and in actual battle wireless communication continues in use until the apparatus is damaged by hostile shell fire. Recourse then has to be had to the old-fashioned and limited, but still useful, method of flag signalling and light signalling, though small spare wireless installations of comparatively short range can be **Telephony and** employed even when the main aerials have **fire-control** been shot away. Modern fire-control systems, as we have seen, are based upon telephonic communications, with ordinary voice tubes as a standby in case of damage to the wires, and with electric firing wires running from the guns to the fire directors' station. When all the outer wireless and inner wire means of communication of a fighting fleet remain fairly intact in an action, the conduct of the operations forms a system approaching perfection. Centralisation combined with team

work results in a wonderful machine-like ease of control. The mind of one man plays with almost instantaneous effect through the fleet; for the progress of scientific invention in naval warfare increases instead of diminishes the responsibility of the commanding admiral. His orders are now winged with electric energy, and all his organs of information are winged also with the same mysterious force. All the marvellous control over the material that men of science have accomplished for him serves only to make the experience, talent, **Modern Jupiters** and quality of his mind bear more **in action** immediately on the issue of the battle. His power of intellect and his strength of character mould the situation more directly than in the days of Nelson.

Instead of the modern accumulation of an intricate variety of machinery dwarfing the directive genius of an admiral, it rather simplifies the circumstances of his position, and in the heat of battle brings his spiritual faculties, unhampered, into play with swift effect. Presence of mind is useful in a cavalry charge, but it is still more decisive in the swifter manœuvring of great naval forces. Many of the men are reduced for the time to human machines. Their duty is to keep fearlessly steady at routine work, and labour in semiautomatic fashion on the machinery working around them. They have simply to "stick it," and work at top speed on tasks they have learnt in battle practice. But the fighting officers—gunnery and torpedo lieutenants, navigating commander and captain, fire-control officers and gunlayers —have the personal exhilaration of armoured knights of the Middle Ages intensified a hundred thousand fold. Their machinery and their highly-trained men enable them to fight like mundane Jupiters with thunderbolt and earthquake. Science has endowed them with superhuman powers, and at the same time made their personal qualities of mind, character, and trained experience the decisive elements in the battle.

Naval warfare in its latest form is the perfection of scientific tactics. Land warfare, as its instruments and methods improve, approaches the naval standard. Since German and Belgian rifles and 3 in. quick-firers rattled and roared against each other around Liège, at the beginning of August, 1914, the power of the individual soldier has tended to diminish as the importance of war machinery has tended to increase, and the responsibility of the army commander has augmented. Probably, the first great Battle of Ypres, in October and November, 1914, was the last soldiers' battle in warfare on the Continental scale. Soldiers now are like sailors in a battle fleet. They are becoming human machines, and their capacity to stick at their tasks and do their work until they are put out of action is of more value than the old qualities of dash, vehemence, and even enterprise. The heavy gun, the telephone, wireless communication, and other forms of war machinery make an army corps fight somewhat like a battleship. The guns do the principal work. They wreck the enemy's defences and demoralise his troops, and the infantry of the attacking side go forward to annex the wreckage.

It is possible we may yet live to see armoured and gunned vehicles acting somewhat like a land fleet, though land

When the army went into action the guns of each battery generally separated and sought concealing cover, and then connected up by field telephone for the purpose of fire control and massed fire effect. A near shot against a German gun was not likely to damage another unit of the battery, for as much space as possible was left between each piece of artillery. The field telephone had become the instrument of concentration and control, and in the crisis of battle a general check could often be inflicted by damaging an attacker's telephone wires without doing any serious injury to his batteries. At Neuve Chapelle, for instance, our advance was completely stopped by a long, violent curtain of shrapnel fire that destroyed our telephone wires more quickly than we could repair them. The enemy's last line consisted of fortified buildings and machine-gun redoubts, against which our charging infantry was powerless. Our guns could have reached the sand-bagged and cellared buildings, but our forward observing officers, owing to difficulty in extending our telephone communications, could not direct the batteries exactly on the hostile points of resistance.

The check at Neuve Chapelle

In the near or distant future the small portable wireless telephone is likely to change this circumstance of the battlefield. But as we have yet only got so far as the Swedish invention of motor-car wireless installations, the wireless pack, light enough to be carried by an infantryman over parapets and through a maze of trenches, has yet to be produced in as enormous quantities as the ordinary small telephone receiver and transmitter. But when the light, portable wireless telephone comes into use, it will greatly increase the power of that army which possesses a superior gun power. By means of it all the movements of troops will be

Crown copyright.]
NATURE TO THE AID OF SCIENCE.
Army transport conveying branches of trees to be used as screens for the big guns on the British front.

mines are likely to be a greater hindrance to vehicles attacking than they are to fleets in action. At the time of writing, the war on the western front between the most highly industrialised nations of the world rages almost motionless between fortified lines. We cannot foresee clearly what new instruments and methods may come into play in a quick-moving battle of manœuvre between an allied force of two or three million soldiers and an enemy force of some two million men. Indeed, if we knew anything definite concerning the introduction of new machinery of mobile war, we should either remain silent or give misleading suggestions.

But, as has already been explained in a previous chapter, electrical communication between an army commander and his batteries is a striking feature of the latest form of warfare. In the French system the forward observing officers and some thousands of guns are linked directly with Army Headquarters, and the guns are often fired in massed parks by the commanding general. At the outbreak of hostilities the Germans had a glimmering of the possibilities of centralised telegraphic and telephonic control. Their scouting cavalry carried reels of light uninsulated wire, and this wire was rapidly strung along trees and hedges in an advance, so as to keep the mounted troops in instant electric touch with their main force. Then every march of the main force was marked by the establishment of central exchanges for electric communication between army groups and General Headquarters. Underground telephones, overhead wires, and wireless plants were employed on a grand scale.

German use of the telephone

Crown copyright].
POWER OF THE NEW SHELLS.
Scottish officers examining shell craters in a shattered town along the line of the British advance.

FIELD-ARTILLERY IN ACTION. [*Crown copyright.*
British gunners at their work. Four of them had donned respirators in anticipation of poison gas. An observer is scanning the sky with his glasses for hostile aircraft.

The consumption of ammunition by the mortars used in trench warfare was enormous. These official photographs show how the ammunition was stacked in the trenches ready for instant use, and, on the right, a reserve accumulation of it behind the lines.

How many million miles of wire were used in entanglements can never be computed. Above a wiring party is seen going up to the lines.

Left : Bringing in a wounded man. Right : A patrol crawling up towards the German trenches. Both these official photographs are of men actually under heavy fire.

SCIENTIFIC WARFARE ON THE WESTERN FRONT.

OBLITERATED! MAMETZ, JULY, 1916.
Effect of the British bombardment on Mametz, captured in the early days of the summer offensive, 1916. The whole village was practically reduced to atoms.

interests of the cause of civilisation. Because of this political failure in the way of preparation, German science and German technical activity won great advantages over us. But after we were aroused to the height of our creative power, it did not appear that the enemy had any faculties of mind likely to annul our recent achievements in the application of science to the machinery of war. He temporarily acquired vast resources of coal and iron. He also had a very large number of Russian prisoners and Polish, Lithuanian, and Belgian workmen, who enabled him to release quite an extraordinary proportion of his own population for war work. He had not to pay for the help he obtained in this manner, as

strictly controlled by the commanders. The fog of battle will be dissipated, and then the scientific soldierman will require as long, intensive, high training as the scientific sailorman already does. It will certainly come about in the present generation. We shall see in every country signallers with a wireless pack on their shoulders and a receiving flap on one of their ears. They will be divided into company signallers, battalion, brigade, divisional, corps, and army signallers, each section having its special length of electric wave with, no doubt, secret codes. It will be an intricate piece of organisation, requiring much practical intelligence in the signallers to link every part of a moving army firmly together by wireless messages, which the enemy will attempt to jam in moments of crisis.

Thus, when the white races of the British Empire were getting fully into their stride the enemy was left with no advantage in scientific talent and technical skill. In the greatest of war industries — fine steel-making — he was outclassed from the beginning. His
German steel-makers outclassed striking power depended chiefly upon the enormous quantity of his weapons, and his superiority in regard to quantity was due to circumstances over which our nation had no control. We fully carried out our first part of the common duties of the Entente by surpassing the enemy in naval war material and organising our Expeditionary Force.

Our Government lacked the strength of character and fearlessness of mind to put all the facts before the people and establish national service. We seemed so safe against our Continental foe that our politicians of both parties thought they would lose all hope of office if they asked the people to adopt a system of conscription in the

ANOTHER IMPRESSION OF THE SHATTERED VILLAGE.
Mametz as it fell into British hands. An idea of the destructive power of the British high-explosive shells, millions of which were rained on the German positions before our infantry went forward.

we and our Allies had to pay for the industrial and agricultural products we obtained from neutral States by our practical command of the seas. We were, therefore, faced with the great problem of meeting the enemy's quantity of military resources by the quality of our inventions for speeding-up and standardising production. Not only did the effect of our great effort tell on the course of the war, but the results will form, for at least a generation, a mighty instrument in our hands in the economic struggle.

Still more majestic shalt thou rise,
More dreadful from each foreign stroke ;
As the loud blast that tears the skies
Serves but to root thy native oak.

Germany has strengthened and spread the roots of our native genius. Unless by political weakness or indecision we consented to a peace without full settlement, the great ordeal by battle seemed likely to leave the British Empire, despite its heavy losses of fine virile blood, so fortified in mind and character that the Anglo-Celtic Federation would last and develop beyond the range of our vision of the future.

Gate of Garua. Protected by forts on adjacent heights and itself most scientifically strengthened, Garua was a great entrenched camp that was deemed impregnable. Nevertheless, on June 10th, 1915, the German garrison was compelled to surrender unconditionally.

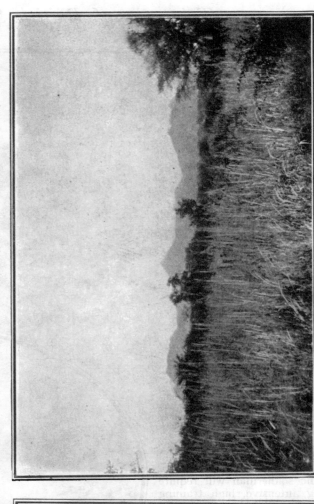

Typical grass country over which the British and French troops operated during the conquest of German Cameroon, with the Kaa Chiu hills in the distance. Although native troops were employed almost exclusively, the climatic conditions made the campaign exceptionally arduous.

View of the fortified palace of the Sultan of Gulfei, an important personage in Northern Cameroon. The figures in the foreground were a group of dancing women. But for their ill-treatment of the natives, the German Cameroon Army might have held out until the end of the war.

German native troops belonging to the garrison of Garua with a field gun. When the fortress was surrendered five Krupp field-guns were captured, ten Maxims, several hundred rifles, and half a million rounds of ammunition.

CAMERA VIEWS OF THE CONQUERED GERMAN COLONY.

THE FRANCO-BRITISH CONQUEST OF GERMAN CAMEROON.

German Position in a Fortress Country on Interior Lines—Disposition of the Nigerian Frontier Force—Intervention of the Belgian Congo Government—Belgians on the Luxembourg Support General Aymerich in Successful Attack on Ndzimon—Franco-Belgian Occupation of Molundu, Dume, and Bertua—German Machine-Gun Equipment—Prussianisation of the Bantu of West Africa—German Abuse of the Natives and Its Nemesis—Practically Impregnable German Positions at Mora, Garua, and Yaunde—Animal and Insect Terrors of the Campaign—General Cunliffe's Capture of Garua—The Franco-British Drive Along the Midland Railway—Colonel Mayer, Checked by Sickness and Commissariat Difficulties, Withdraws to the Kele River—General Cunliffe Attacks Mora, the Gibraltar of Cameroon—The Reason for Its Abandonment—Captain Fowle and His Nigerians—General Cunliffe's Attack on and Capture of Banyo—The Allies Begin to Close In on Yaunde—Sir Charles Dobell Operates Towards Wum Biagas, Colonel Mayer Towards Iseka—Gold Coast Regiment Surprises the Enemy at Muin—A Trap that Sprang too Soon—German Retirement from Wum Biagas—Colonel Mayer and His Splendid Senegalese—Zimmermann's Desperate Resistance—The 1st Nigeria Regiment Storm an Entrenched Ridge—Captain Balder's Fine End—Capture of Ngung and Jang Mangas—The Allies Converge on and Occupy Yaunde—Surrender of Captain von Raben with all His Troops—What the Loss of Cameroon cost Germany.

IN the concluding part of Chapter LXXXVII. we sketched some of the opening incidents of the campaign in Cameroon. The publication of despatches from Major-General Sir Charles M. Dobell and from Brigadier-General F. J. Cunliffe now enables us to fill in the outlines of our previous chapter, and to relate the story of the victorious close of the combined operations of British, French, and Belgian troops. We entered on the struggle against the Germans in West Africa in much the same way as we began the contest with the enemy in East Africa. In both cases we first employed a small force with inferior equipment against a large hostile army which had prepared by years of organisation to master any attack we might make. All that can be said on our behalf is that our Government never intended any aggression against Germany and her colonies, and was not convinced that Germany intended any invasion of our African dominions.

Many of the British officers in Nigeria, however, had reasons for believing that German Cameroon was a great fortress country, destined to be used as a base of operations against us and the Belgians and French. The

Germans had begun to construct strategic railways in Cameroon. The Northern track was planned to envelop our Nigerian frontier and enable the Germans to mass an overwhelming force against any part of the line their commander selected. Then there was a Midland line running towards the Congo, by which the German native army could be concentrated against the Belgian and French forces. The Germans thus occupied their favourite position of interior lines. They could swing nearly their whole force against the separated native regiments of the Allies, and thus defeat these in detail. As already related, the Nigerian frontier force was arranged in three columns, each of which suffered a reverse.

The northernmost column, based on Maiduguri, and under the command of Major R. W. Fox, crossed the frontier on August 25th, 1914, encountered a German force near Mora, and was defeated in an attempt to dislodge this force, but was strengthened on October 13th, 1914, by a French force which had come from Fort Lamy and captured on its way the German post, Kusseri. The middle Nigerian column was based on Yola, and under the command of Lieut.-Colonel P. Maclear. This column also crossed the frontier on August 25th, 1914, and was heavily defeated in

A COOL CORNER OF CAMEROON.
British officer and native soldier contemplating the rapids at Dipikai, Cameroon. Parts of the colony abound in great rivers and cataracts.

THE FRENCH OCCUPATION OF YOKO.
Lieut.-Colonel Brisset (marked with a ×) in command of the French Eastern column, standing with members of his staff before the German fort of Yoko, Cameroon. Colonel Brisset entered the town on December 1st, 1915, encountering slight opposition from the enemy garrison, and the Tricolour was soon flying over the fortifications, as seen in this photograph.

a strict neutrality, and not to take part in the French and British action against Cameroon. But after the invaders of Belgium had extended to the Congo the systematic atrocities they had practised in Europe, the Congo steamer Luxembourg, mounting three guns and a machine-gun, turned northward up the Sanga River to co-operate with the French attack. The Belgian force was at first small, consisting only of a detachment of one hundred and thirty Belgian colonial infantry. But as this detachment had a good steamer, with three quick-firers and a machine-gun, it proved a powerful support to the French Equatorial Force under General Aymerich. Indeed the Belgians in their steamer were mainly responsible for the opening victory of the Allies on the southern line of the enemy's country. In the last week of October, 1914, the Luxembourg was boldly worked along the Sanga to the German stronghold at Ndzimon. The vessel steamed along the bank at a distance of less than one hundred and fifty yards from the German entrenchments, and then, with the French steamer Commandant Lamy in support, fought down the fire of the opposing troops in an action lasting seventy-six hours. A splendid bayonet charge by the Belgian and French troops, delivered over a river swamp against machine-gun fire, compelled the Germans at last to evacuate the position.

The Germans at the time were invading the Congo State from East Africa as well as from West Africa. The Belgian native infantry was only a widely scattered police force, with the main detachments separated from each other by vast spaces of tropical jungle. But in spite of these difficulties, the force based on the Sanga River, and co-operating with the French, was increased by January, 1915, to five hundred and eighty men, with a very considerable number of guns. In the early months of 1915 the combined Belgian and French force, under General Aymerich, worked along the western tributary of the Sanga towards the German frontier post of Molundu, which was occupied after a hard struggle. The **Machine-gun** Germans, however, were strongly en- **traps** trenched in this corner of their dominions, in a land of hills and branching streams. The small Franco-Belgian force had to battle for months in order to penetrate some fifty miles into Cameroon, for the Germans transformed the tropical jungles into machine-gun traps, each of which was surrounded by a pathless tangle of growth. The tracks made by elephants and buffaloes to their drinking-places by the rivers were often the sole means of traversing the Equatorial wilds. Natives of Cameroon watched all these tracks for the enemy, who also employed gangs of blacks by the thousand in digging pits, trenches, and machine-gun redoubts.

a night attack on the German post of Garua on August 30th, 1914. It fell back to its base, half shattered. Then the advanced troops of the southern Nigerian column, based on Ikom, and under the command of Lieut.-Colonel G. T. Mair, were enveloped by a larger German force on September 6th, 1914. The German encircling movement took place at Nsanakang, and resulted in the practical annihilation of our advanced troops. Only two officers and ninety native rank and file broke through the German lines in a bayonet charge. After this series of enemy successes, the Germans began to raid our territory along the Benue River. Our Nigerian troops had to stand on the defensive, and bring up their reserves along the Benue line. The immediate result of the disasters was that the Nigerian force designed for the direct attack seaward upon Cameroon had to be diminished in both men and guns.

Meanwhile, a German column had struck out from the southern frontier of Cameroon, and made an attack upon the Belgian Congo station of Lukuga. It had been the intention of the government of the Belgian Congo to maintain

In the Somme Valley, summer 1916: British transport on the move.

Into battle: East Yorks going up to the fighting front, July, 1916.

At the outset of the "big push": British advancing over the captured German trenches on the Somme, July, 1916.

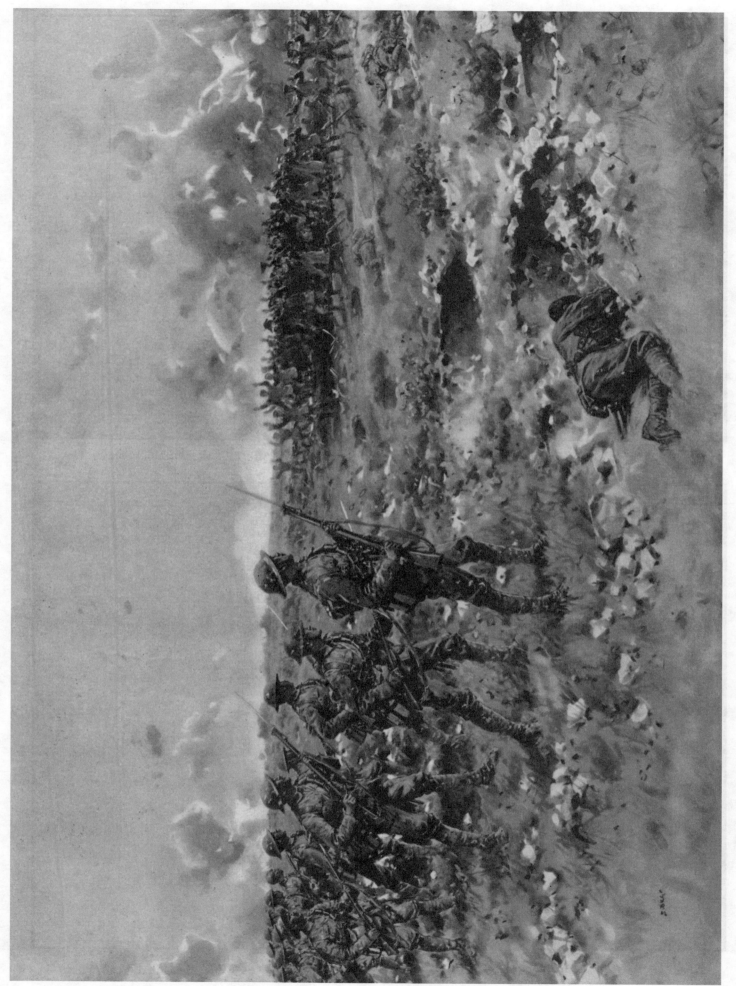

Their last hope: Demoralised German soldiers implore clemency from advancing British troops.

Eve of battle: Lancashire Fusiliers being addressed by their divisional commander.

After the victory: Roll=call in the captured trenches on the memorable 1st of July, 1916.

General Aymerich seems at first to have thought that his progress would be easy. He sent a mission to Duala to arrange a scheme for a combined advance against Yaunde, which was the enemy's central base. The mission arrived at Duala from Equatorial Africa on March 12th, 1915, and asked the allied Commander-in-Chief, Sir Charles Dobell, to attempt a great thrust towards Yaunde. But General Aymerich soon discovered that his Franco-Belgian force could not make the movement he intended. Towards the end of April, 1915, the Belgians and French were severely checked not far from their side of the enemy frontier. As had happened on the Nigerian side, the Allies had to bring up reinforcements and alter their plan of operations, and it was only late in the summer of 1915 that General Aymerich got well inside the German Cameroon territory, west of the Sanga River line, and seized the posts of Dume and Bertua.

The secret of the extraordinary strength of the Germans was their machine - gun equipment. For some years they seem to have been storing machine-guns by the hundred, with millions of rounds of ammunition. In some of the enemy raids there was one machine-gun to every four white men. Thousands of carriers followed each detachment, carrying boxes of cartridges and other war stores and food. The Bantus, forming the larger proportion of the Cameroon population, had been severely Prussianised. Thousands of the strongest men had been transformed into first-rate soldiers, who feared their officers more than they feared any enemy, and marched and fought with wonderful endurance. In one raid into Nigeria, for example, the Bantu troops marched for twenty-eight hours without a halt, through the steaming, tropical paths made through the thickets by wild animals. In the middle of this march they fought a violent action with one of our frontier posts, and then, by avoiding all known roads, escaped the cutting-off movement we made against them.

In the Bantu of West Africa the Prussian found a cannon-fodder suited to his brutal but effective methods of discipline. He liked best the tall, fierce blacks of the highlands, who had been converted by the Senussi's missionaries and transformed into temperate, clean-living, and fanatical Mohammedans. He taught his great black garrison machine-gun tactics and also hand-grenade fighting. Our Nigerian force, like the French and Belgian black force, was composed of riflemen, who had practically no appreciation of the effects of machine-gun fire. This, indeed, seems to have been the chief reason why all our first series of operations ended in disaster when the enemy opened a sweeping machine-gun fire against our black troops. Many of these belonged to ignorant pagan tribes, and the

Black cannon-fodder

HAUSA HEROISM AT THE BROKEN BRIDGE.

On December 6th, 1914, Lieut. Luxford, 1st Nigeria Regiment, Sec.-Lieut. Schneider, R.E., Capt. Charnley, 1st Nigeria Regiment, and Private Minoni, Luxford's orderly, were reconnoitring a bridge at Nlohe, in Cameroon, when a murderous machine-gun fire was opened on them. Schneider was killed and Luxford wounded ; Private Minoni remained by his officer under heavy fire for two hours, and then brought him in, being promoted lance-corporal for his heroism.

scything rain of bullets surprised and dismayed them. Their officers, of course, had to lead them in the attack, and when the officers fell they broke and scattered. To our officers also the extraordinary number of the enemy's machine-guns was a surprise, and we scarcely seem to have been prepared for the German tactics of using machine-guns as a distinct armament, instead of employing them merely to strengthen the fire power of an infantry line. The Germans appear to have deliberately rejected the use of any considerable number of mounted guns. They selected the easily carried Maxim as their main weapon in jungle warfare, and they employed the Maxim corps to form traps, towards which their manœuvring infantry often endeavoured with success to allure the allied troops.

Long after Sir Charles Dobell seized the port of Duala, on September 27th, 1914, the Germans in the inland wilderness continued to regard themselves as unconquerable. In fact, they boasted they could easily hold out until the war in Europe was decided. Even when they were forced away from their two railways, the Northern

ON OBSERVATION DUTY.
Allied officers of the Nigeria Regiment who participated in the conquest of German Cameroon.

and the Midland lines, not only did they not lose heart, they even continued to act like men sure of eventual victory. The most important of their acts of braggart strength was their conduct towards their own native subjects. They used the natives, as we have remarked, in slave-gangs of thousands in fortifying the country and constructing immense mountain strongholds. Any native chief who refused labour or food was murdered. Carriers who were too slow or weak for their work were lashed for their first offence in failing to keep up with the column, and then shot. The commandeering of huge quantities of native food and large herds of native cattle led some of the chiefs to send messages for help to the nearest French or British force.

But as both the French and British forces were at first weaker than the German black army of Cameroon, many of the chiefs could not obtain assistance in time, and were killed. The Chief of Mubi, for example, was pursued into British territory and killed some miles above Yola. All the horrors of the German campaign against the Hereros in South-West Africa and against the Masai in East Africa seem to have been outdone in Cameroon. The strange, ghastly, decadent turn for useless **Decadent turn for** cruelty that some Germans showed in their **cruelty** days of transient victory in Belgium and Northern France was given fuller play in the sombre mountains and jungles of tropical Africa. When a European, at the head of a first-rate fighting black force, consisting largely of pagans with a thirst for diabolical blood-rites, gets diseased in mind and soul and goes "fantee," the result is more horrible than that which a blood-mad negro chief can produce.

The most ignorant of pagan Bantus, however, is a human being, and with regard to human beings there is a limit and a reaction against the most atrocious system of terrorisation. In regard to the native population of Cameroon the point of reaction was quickly reached. Men and women did not care whether they lived or died, if only they could do some harm to their white oppressors. The consequence was that the British and French commanders obtained from native enemy sources valuable information about the movements of the German forces. The Germans, on the other hand, were often given by their own black spies misleading intelligence of our movements. In the

CHAMPIONS OF CIVILISATION IN WESTERN AFRICA.
Officers' tent in the rough country of Equatorial Africa, a crude shelter from the fierce rays of the sun. The circle illustration shows three officers of the Nigeria Regiment, together with a native French African soldier, standing behind a stone barricade in the region of military operations.

TROPICAL VEGETATION AND MASSIVE BOULDERS.
Native encampment in Cameroon. Men of the Nigeria Regiment who were about to advance on the enemy. The illustration gives an excellent idea of the rough country which formed the theatre of this campaign.

immediate neighbourhood of any German garrison there was a condition of complete terrorism in native villages. If any important movement of a German force occurred, some man or woman would slip at night into the thicket and get into touch with our native watchers. This is the explanation of the remarkable statement in Sir Charles Dobell's despatch concerning the great German attack on our main force: " I had obtained some knowledge of the German commander's intention."

Such was the retribution that overtook the officers of the new Attila when they gave full play to that quality in them which their War Lord had long since admired and commended. It may fairly be maintained that the Germans in Cameroon might have made good their boast and held out until the end of the European War if they had not starved, tortured, and killed their black fellow-subjects. For the positions which the Germans held were practically impregnable. Commandant Zimmermann was Commander-in-Chief. In his northern province, looking towards Lake Chad, the local commander was Captain von Raben.

Raben occupied the Mora mountain, that covered a rough circle about thirty miles in circumference and rose in cliffs to a height of 1,700 feet. In only a few places could the top be reached by men using both hands and feet in climbing, and in the rare breaks in the cliffs where this could be done, the slopes were covered with huge boulders that gave magnificent shelter for a defending force. Raben had water cisterns, cattle, preserved food supplies, and apparently an inexhaustible magazine of ammunition on this mighty land Gibraltar of Northern Cameroon. In his circuit of thirty miles he had pasture for his herds of cattle, a good supply of wild game, ample water, and such a system of defences as would require a Continental army to blockade and besiege. From his great mountain fastness Raben raided Nigeria and French Equatorial Africa.

Von Raben's position

About one hundred and fifty miles south of Mora was another great mountain fortress, Garua, on which two thousand native labourers had worked for nearly half a year. They had turned it into an entrenched camp that would have done credit to the engineers of a European battlefield. Here Captain von Crailsheim dominated the Nigerian line of the Benue River, with five guns, an unknown number of Maxims, and a large force of riflemen. A line of communications connected him with the Banyo mountain in the centre of Cameroon. This height, rising

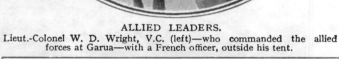

ALLIED LEADERS.
Lieut.-Colonel W. D. Wright, V.C. (left)—who commanded the allied forces at Garua—with a French officer, outside his tent.

AN OUTPOST OF THE EMPIRE.
Tea-time on the Cameroon front. British officer inside his tent, which boasted a folding chair and the proverbial pot of jam.

twelve hundred feet above the small hills of the surrounding country, was covered with large boulders, which were linked together by some three hundred sangars. Every prominent commanding point was strengthened by a small fort. On the summit were cement reservoirs for water, brick-built houses with glass windows, forty tons of grain, a good herd of cattle, poultry-runs full of chickens, and large quantities of various stores. Connected with this fortress was a mountain stronghold on the Ngaundere plateau.

Then in the heart of the broken highlands was the main German base, Yaunde, from which roads and paths radiated to entrenched heights and fortified fords in the country going

"The Fortress Country"

down to the coast and to the Congo and its tributaries. The labour and the organisation displayed by the enemy led some of our officers to call Cameroon "the Fortress Country." There was good reason for Commandant Zimmermann to look without anxiety at our capture of the port of Duala in September, 1914; for between Duala and Yaunde there was the mightiest system of defence existing in the world. It consisted first of a belt of estuary swamps, from which grew a deadly mangrove forest. Above the great fever belt a primeval tropical forest rose in terraces of stifling gloom, extending for a depth of eighty miles at the narrowest to a depth of two hundred miles at broadest, into the inland plateau.

When the plateau was reached, the forest sent seams of thicket growth into the ravines, and between the thickets there was often a jungle of elephant grass eighteen feet high, which only blended into fine, good prairie land in the region where the Germans were concentrated. Wild animals abounded, but did not impede our operations by charging our columns and motor-cars with the frequency of the rhinoceroses and lions in German East Africa. The river crocodiles, watching by the fords and snapping at the feet of the troops, were the principal animal allies of the Germans.

But all the big beasts were of very little importance compared with the insect terrors of the Cameroon jungles. The huge ants, that swarmed on the men and tried to eat them to the bone, were an agonising pest, especially if they could not be shaken off by a dive in the water. Then there were tropical biting flies of the tsetse kind, with mosquitoes that rivalled the tsetse in infecting the troops with fevers which have turned the great forest into the white man's grave. In spite of the fact that we employed troops of tropical or semi-tropical origin—tattooed Hausas from Nigeria, strong and sinewy coast men from Sierra Leone and the Gold Coast, with some Indian light infantry— our force was seriously incapacitated by disease. For the climate of the great forest belt was the very worst in the world. There were two long rainy seasons that turned the jungles into steaming swamps and so soaked the ground that the forest continued to steam in the hottest month of the year—February.

We have already related the story of the first success of Brigadier-General Cunliffe, who took over the command of the allied forces in Northern Cameroon on February 5th, 1915, and captured the great enemy fortress of Garua on June 10th, 1915. General Cunliffe had two thousand native infantrymen, mainly from the Hausa tribes, one company of native mounted infantry, three guns, and nine machine-guns. With this Nigerian force there were seven hundred and fifty French native infantry, a squadron of cavalry, two guns, and two machine-guns. The French force was commanded by Lieut.-Colonel Brisset and the British column was under Lieut.-Colonel W. I. Webb-Bowen, both of these officers being under the orders of Brigadier-General Cunliffe.

The fall of Garua

The fall of Garua was brought about by a mutiny of the German black force. The enemy held out strongly until the last week in May, and not only defended himself, but sallied out over the frontier and attacked our force at Gurin. The German treatment of the natives of Cameroon was the immediate cause of the fall of Garua. In the last week of May, Brigadier-General Cunliffe, relying on the profound indignation of the Bantu tribesmen, shifted the position of his troops. He moved from the south and south-west to the fortified heights round to the north. In spite of

CAMP OF THE BRITISH NIGERIA REGIMENT AND (ABOVE) A MACHINE-GUN IN ACTION IN CAMEROON.

WOUNDED NATIVE SOLDIERS ON THEIR WAY TO THE BRITISH BASE IN CAMEROON.

the long time it took to carry all the French and British material and stores on the shoulders of our native carriers and haul the guns through the wilderness, the German commander remained ignorant of the change in the direction of our attack. In other words, the natives he sent out as spies refused to serve him. Then on May 28th, 1915, three days after the attacking force had shifted to the north, Lieut.-Colonel Brisset received one heavy French gun, a 3·6 in., which outranged anything the enemy possessed.

So long as the Germans had been stronger in weapons than the Allies, their system of inculcating discipline by fear had kept their native troops well in hand. But when the new French shell swept the forts and the hostile native troops saw that their white officers were powerless to reply to the new gun, the Cameroon troops began to get out of hand. On the night of June 9th some of the German officers tried to turn the mutineers into a forlorn hope, and, telling them they would be killed if taken prisoners, induced them to make a last sally over the Benue River. But the river was in flood. Most of the men who attempted to cross it were drowned, and others were driven back by the fire of our infantry at Bilonde. The German native troops then got quite out of hand, and to save **German troops** themselves from being attacked and **mutiny** killed by their own men, Captain von Crailsheim and his thirty-six fellow-Germans surrendered, with two hundred and twelve native soldiers, five guns, and ten Maxims, on the afternoon of June 10th, 1915

Many natives managed to escape by stripping themselves of their uniform and taking to the bush. Lieut.-Colonel Brisset, with the French force, remained at Garua to watch over Northern Cameroon, while Lieut.-Colonel Webb-Bowen's column pursued the fugitives towards the Ngaundere highlands. In addition to the German force holding Garua, there had been outlying detachments linked with the mountain fortress and other points in the German system of defence. These detachments were included in the pursuit, and some were driven towards Banyo, after actions at Koncha and Maio Kelah on June 27th. Then, on the other wing of the movement of pursuit, a British advance guard under Captain C. H. Fowle reached the steep paths leading up to the Ngaundere plateau on June 28th. One of the terrific tornadoes of **Discipline and the elements** tropical Africa smote both the British and German forces, and amid this appalling tempest the two very different methods of discipline employed by the contending forces were put to a supreme test. Our West African troops, inspired by trust and admiring loyalty to their white officers, charged through the whirlwind and completely surprised and overwhelmed all the black German rearguards holding the great cliff paths. Our men climbed up on the wings of the tempest, and with scarcely any loss captured the town of Ngaundere in the evening. During the night, when the tornado had blown over, the German officers succeeded in bringing up their main force and collecting their other scattered troops, and made a counter-attack upon our small and heroic advance guard. But the German native troops had no energy or courage left. Their assault was broken at a loss to us of only five native soldiers and one native non-commissioned officer wounded. The tornado charge, ending in a great strategic victory on an almost inaccessible plateau, deserves to rank among the finest feats in our Colonial wars. Lieut.-Colonel Brisset quickly arrived at Ngaundere from Garua and, with his comparatively strong body of French troops, firmly established the important new line won by Captain C. H. Fowle.

AMPHIBIOUS BRITISHERS IN CAMEROON.
Armoured barge which was used with much effect against the enemy in Cameroon. Apart from the complement of the vessel, all armed with rifles, the craft carried machine-guns, and was protected by steel-plating.

This, however, was the last of our important successes for some months. It had originally been intended that Brigadier-General Cunliffe's forces should cease operations in Northern Cameroon, and, leaving only an investing force round the great frontier fortress of Mora to check Raben's raids, turn south and help to close on all the main German positions. The great enveloping scheme had been proposed on March 12th, 1915, by General Aymerich. Cunliffe's attack on Garua and Ngaundere had been carried out in harmony with this scheme. But, as already related, the main actions in this combined operation did not prosper. Only Brigadier-General Cunliffe achieved success on his lines, and he was held up in the north until September, 1915, when the combined movement of a second general envelopment plan was resumed.

In the first and fruitless attempt to encircle the German main force it had been arranged that Brigadier-General Cunliffe should break into Garua, storm the Ngaundere plateau, and then move southward and unite near Yaunde with the forces under the command of Sir Charles Dobell and General Aymerich. General Aymerich, however, could not make the progress he had expected, and he remained for some months in the south-eastern corner of Cameroon with the enemy posts of Dume and Lomie strongly barring his way. There was, however, another strong French force of fine Senegalese troops, under Colonel Mayer, acting with the troops under **Fighting in the** Sir Charles Dobell. Mayer's troops and **fever belt** Dobell's troops were in the fever belt along the coast, and suffering severely from disease. The British general did not want to move, as the great rains had begun in March and the forest tracks were difficult. On the other hand, while General Aymerich was attempting an advance against the other side of the fortress country, he could not allow the enemy to throw his full weight against the Franco-Belgian column. So to make at least a diversion, and compel Zimmermann to divide his army, Sir Charles Dobell undertook the operation to which he had demurred.

On April 7th, 1915, a British native force under Lieut. Colonel Haywood moved along the Midland Railway to Edea, to co-operate with the French native force under

Colonel Mayer. The aim was to force the line of the Kele River, and from there to fight through the jungle, by Iseka and Wum Biagas, towards Yaunde. In a series of fierce actions the British and French columns took the line of the Kele River in April, and then found themselves opposed by the main German army. Zimmermann had so completely checked the Franco-Belgian column four hundred miles away, that he was able to withdraw troops towards the coast to resist the Franco-British advance.

On May 1st, Colonel Mayer's little army moved along the railway line to Iseka, and in spite of broken bridges and machine-gun ambushes, torrents of rain and great sickness, captured Iseka on May 11th. Meanwhile, along the line of the road from Duala to Yaunde, Lieut.-Colonel Haywood, with two battalions of the Nigeria Regiment, made a drive north of the Midland Railway, to outflank the enemy's main position on the permanent way. The road and railway were the only clear wide paths in the vast forest, and if the Germans had not built these tracks the Allies would not have been able to reach Yaunde before the European War was over. Where we had to cut down the trees and make a road to advance our progress was despairingly slow. For **Sharpshooters in** while our men were felling trees and **the jungle** building a motor track for supplies, the enemy's sharpshooters, having a life-long knowledge of the jungle paths, were apt to work around the head of our column and snipe our labourers and carriers. Our column had to cut through the bush, ford rivers waist deep, and storm fortified mission-houses and wayside posts in order to get an outflanking position on the Kele River, by Wum Biagas, which was on the Yaunde road. Then in a magnificent assault, in which both our officers and men suffered very heavily, the entire position of Wum Biagas was stormed on May 4th.

The Nigerians were splendid. They lost many of their white leaders, and yet fought up the steep ridges steadily and coolly, and though their victory left them with their two battalions badly shattered, they held their ground, and the French force at Iseka moved off and joined them. Colonel Mayer then took over the command of the allied column, and stores and supplies were sent forward by road, together with a naval 12-pounder gun. On May 25th, Colonel Mayer with all his force rapidly weakening by sickness, tried to push on before the heaviest rain fell and made the bush impenetrable. By this time it was known that General Aymerich's advance, four hundred miles away, had failed. There was only a bare fighting chance that the coast column might be able to win through the great fever belt into the healthy, dry highland country before Zimmermann could bring practically his entire main force against it.

But Colonel Mayer could not win through. In the first place Sir Charles Dobell, supporting him from Duala, could not get food supplies up. There were only three motor-cars available, and the ordinary carriers were suffering from sickness and also from hostile raids, for the German native troops soon worked through the jungle and raided our line of communication, forcing us to send food and war material under armed convoys, and place guard posts along the track. At the same time the head of the Franco-British column was swept by machine-gun fire at every turn of the road, so that at every bend the troops had first to cut through the bush and outflank the hostile gunners. One mile a day was the average rate of progress of the allied column from May 25th to June 5th. In the wet, steaming chaos of trees, swamps, and entangled bush, disease continued to spread among both natives and Europeans, and in the first week of June a general epidemic of dysentery broke up the whole expedition.

Epidemic of dysentery

Half-starved by raids on its line of supplies, shaken with fever and weakened by intestinal trouble, the Franco-British force drew back to the Kele River. A great raid on our most important convoy of five hundred carriers was the immediate cause of Colonel Mayer's retirement. He had to race back to save his men from starvation. Sir Charles Dobell hurried up the last small force of troops in Duala, and after fierce and incessant rearguard fighting, the Kele River line was regained on June 28th. In the rearguard actions the Allies were badly harassed but never broken, and as they in turn used machine-guns

in continual ambushes, they inflicted heavy losses on the attacking force. But our casualties were serious, a quarter of the entire Franco-British force being either killed or wounded, and nearly all the rest being weakened by sickness.

The great rains had begun to fall during the retreat, and for some months the extraordinary tropical torrents continued to wash through the forest. This, however, was an advantage to the Allies, as the downfalls checked the raiding operations of the victorious Germans. But our misfortunes were not at an end. The rains which prevented all operations in Southern Cameroon did not hinder the movement of men in the north. Brigadier-General Cunliffe remained, therefore, free to attempt to extend his field for victories. The central German fortress of Banyo was the point of greatest strategic importance in his sphere of operations. But he knew that

Operations stopped by rain

if he attacked it while General Dobell and General Aymerich were standing on the defensive, Zimmermann would swing his main force round to the central fortress and make it practically impregnable.

There remained the northernmost stronghold of Mora,

DEBRIS OF A GERMAN BLOCK-HOUSE, WHICH CAME UNDER A HEAVY BOMBARDMENT FROM THE ALLIED ARTILLERY.
The enemy forts at Garua, which were captured by the allied troops in June, 1915, were remarkably strong, and every device known in field fortification was adapted. Underground passages, moats, a formidable ring of wolf-pits, bristling with poisoned spears, etc. In this illustration the wolf-pits are clearly seen on the left, and no advance could be made in the vicinity of the fort without probing the ground with a stick.

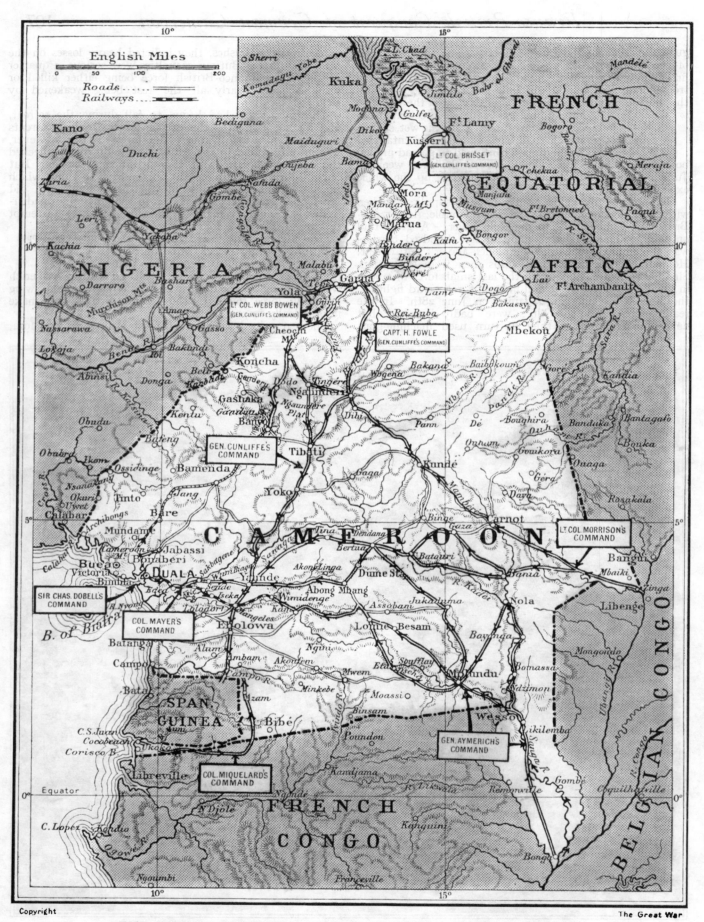

THE FRANCO-BRITISH CONQUEST OF THE GERMAN CAMEROON.

The country conquered by the Franco-British forces commanded by Major-General Sir Charles M. Dobell, K.C.B., is some 306,000 square miles in area, or, roughly, one and a half times the size of the German Empire. Duala and Bonaberi surrendered on September 27th, 1914, and by the middle of February, 1916, the territory was cleared of the enemy. Our map indicates the localities of the several British and French commands.

CAPTIVE GERMAN SOLDIER-COLONISTS.
Group of German non-commissioned officers taken prisoners at Mora Hill—types of the leaders who kept up a resistance to the allied forces in Cameroon for over a year and a half.

which had been cut off from Zimmermann's army by the capture of Garua and Ngaundere. Under the arrangement which had been made after the failure of the main expedition, Brigadier-General Cunliffe's force was not wanted for any general enveloping movement until November, 1915. So the brilliant and victorious brigadier reckoned that he would be able to operate for three months against Mora. Towards the end of August he spent some days travelling round the mountain and reconnoitring for the easiest slopes on which his men could fight their way up. He decided to attack from the north. Here we had already won a hill almost level with the northern end of the Mora mountain, and separated from it by a deep valley some six hundred yards wide. In the first week of September our two or three mountain guns were hauled up the hill, and then, under cover of artillery fire, the 1st Nigeria Regiment made three gallant attacks across the valley and up the mountain side.

In the final advance the Hausas, fearlessly led by their officers, reached the summit of the Gibraltar of Cameroon, and were then stopped by machine-gun fire fifty yards from the German redoubt. For forty-eight hours our native troops clung to the Mora summit, near the dead body of Captain R. M. Pike, who had led the charge. No food or water reached the men, for the German machine-guns swept all the slopes by which the supplies were bravely but vainly carried forward. On

the second night Brigadier-General Cunliffe had to order his swarthy heroes to retire as best they could from the mountain across the valley. He had been unable to help his men because his artillery ammunition had run out, and he could not shell the machine-gun redoubt that hung up his force. But he still felt certain that victory was within his reach as his guns commanded the northern end of Mora. He resolved to sap across the valley, so as to provide his troops with cover from the German machine-guns, and he sent an urgent telegram to Lagos, asking for shells to be sent to him up the Benue River.

But, on September 15th, Sir Charles Dobell and General Aymerich held a conference at Duala, and the two commanders then decided to resume the general enveloping movement against Yaunde early in October instead of in November. As Brigadier-General Cunliffe's force was needed to close the northern and north-western sectors of the great ring of enemy territory, the attack against Mora had to be abandoned after the first reverse.

On the orders of his chief the victor of Garua and Ngaundere left merely an investing force at Mora, and resumed his main operations in the Middle Cameroon. Captain C. H. Fowle, the tornado charger, had improved our Ngaundere line on July 23rd by breaking and scattering a German force from Tibati.

He was in an entrenched position when the Germans attacked him, and after staying their assault his men, on their own initiative, leapt from their trench with the bayonet and raced down and killed their assailants. They were a tempestuous band these tattooed Nigerians under Captain Fowle.

LAST SCENE AT MORA.
Captain von Raben (third figure from left) at the moment of surrendering to the British officer in charge of the operations against Mora Hill. Note the two canine occupants of the enemy stronghold.

BLACK WARRIOR PRISONERS.
Surrender of Mora Hill, Cameroon. German native prisoners and a collection of arms and ammunition in the valley.

In order to carry out the great sweep from the north, Brigadier-General Cunliffe had to capture a knot of fortified mountains some hundreds of miles in circumference. Towards the middle of October he flung half his force towards the Sanaga River and the highland country round Ngaundere, in order to hold back Zimmermann's central forces. Then, with two columns, he directed in person an advance from the north and north-west on the mountain knot round Banyo. All the German garrisons on the southern Nigerian frontier rallied round Banyo for the coming conflict. Intercepted letters showed that they were inspired by an absolute confidence in their ability to hold out to the end of the war. In the mountain they had herds

Village of Banyo occupied

of cattle, a magnificent water supply, large stretches of tilled ground, and all the implements for farming, and they looked forward to withstanding a long siege in perfect comfort.

Towards the end of October, however, they lost two of their main outworks by a surprise attack. A British column under Major Mann advanced from Gashaka, and, after a most arduous climb, overwhelmed and routed the German force holding the Gandua Pass. At a considerable distance to the north was another pass, where the enemy had prepared a system of trenches and redoubts to hold back Brigadier-General Cunliffe's main column. But when Major Mann took the more southern pass he got so close to the rear of the force opposing the British main column that he threatened to envelop it. The enemy, therefore, retired in extreme haste, and Brigadier-General Cunliffe's men had only a long, hard climb to the evacuated fortifications on the plateau. For a few days the advance continued across open rolling grass lands, and though the Germans tried to hold some isolated kopjes all their positions were successfully turned with no loss to our

troops. At the end of October the village of Banyo was occupied, and the German garrison retired some three miles away to their great mountain fortress.

It was a grim, stupendous mountain, from which rocky boulders stood out prominently up to the summit. All down the steep slopes sangars had been built, with loopholes for the defending riflemen. Between the lines of stone ramparts connecting the boulders were masses of thorn-bush, and in some places a hedge of prickly pineapple served instead of barbed-wire entanglements.

It seemed as if a large army were needed to capture the stronghold. Brigadier-General Cunliffe had only 1,250 infantry, and he

ASSENT TO AN ARMISTICE.
Answering the German sign of truce from one of the British forts—an incident in the fighting for Mora Hill, Cameroon, just prior to the enemy's surrender of this valuable position. Huge boulders had been used as a barricade.

was still short of shell. But hearing that two hundred more rounds of gun ammunition were on the way to him, he determined first to snatch all the advantages he could by an infantry attack, and afterwards to use the three screw guns he possessed in the critical part of the mountain battle.

He arranged his five companies of infantry on the northern, north-western, and southern sides, and spread out his mounted troops widely eastward to check there any attempt by the enemy to break out. On November 2nd our infantry began to work over the foot-hills, but their great attack was postponed in order to allow time for the new shell supply to arrive. At dawn on November 4th the Banyo mountain was shrouded in thick fog, and the British commander resolved to push up at once as far as the fog allowed, without waiting for shells to smash up the sangars. In the fog the different sections could not assist each other, but on the other hand the enemy machine-gunners were practically blinded.

All round the mountain there was fierce hand-to-hand fighting amid the boulders and sangars, in a series of pure soldiers' battles, where the Staff and commander could do practically nothing to control the situation. For no section knew what was before it until it got almost within bayonet thrust of the next line of loopholed stones. One company of Nigerians, under Captain Bowyer-Smijth, had amazing luck and amazing disaster. The company had been one of the most successful under General Cunliffe's command, and had conquered Gashaka the previous August by a great fighting climb that lasted twelve hours. Now the same company, while battling in the fog, found a weak point in the enemy's defences, and by noon it had smashed its way right up to the summit of Banyo mountain. By this time, however, the fog had cleared off and the enemy's reserve caught the victorious company under a cross fire of maxims and musketry. Captain Bowyer-Smijth, one of our most able officers, was killed, and his shattered company forced back to the foot of the mountain.

The other four companies, however, found themselves, when the fog lifted, half way up the mountain slopes, and within thirty yards of one of the enemy's main systems of defences. Nothing more could be done in the clear tropical sunshine but to hang on to all the conquered positions and wait for our three guns to get the shells they needed. When night fell, allowing food and water

VICTORS AND VANQUISHED.
British native troops of the Nigeria Regiment guarding a group of disarmed German native soldiers after the surrender of Mora Hill to the British.

and cartridges to be brought up to the men, the enemy tried to light up every line of advance by fire-balls and rockets. Then rain fell, making the steeps like slides; but profiting by the storm, the Nigerians reached the enemy's entrenchments and hugged the southern wall of his great sangar as a defence against his fire.

Captain Schipper, the German commander of Banyo, was, however, an ingenious and foreseeing man. He had prepared hundreds of dynamite bombs, and these novel and dreadful weapons were dropped upon our men with alarming effect. To many of the pagan tribesmen of Nigeria the dynamite bombs, by reason of their

terrific explosions, seemed to be magic of the blackest sort. No discipline based on fear could have made them withstand the pots and tins of dynamite that were rolled down upon them, but our British officers, by their cool, laughing and jesting courage, rallied the tribesmen, and induced them at last to see that the bombs made more noise than damage. When day broke the great sangar had been carried, and the advance slowly continued until the afternoon. Then it was that our gunners got their fresh supply of two hundred 2·95 in. shells. With these projectiles the three mountain guns began to smash sangar after sangar, and make a shrapnel curtain before each main advance of our thousand troops. When night fell on November 5th a violent thunderstorm broke over the mountain, and the enemy, with all his courage knocked out of him, divided into small parties and tried to escape on the eastern side.

Most of the fugitives, however, were captured by our posts of mounted infantry, and at dawn the white flag of surrender could be seen flying on the fort on the mountain top, with our victorious troops silhouetted against the misty sky-line. The German commander had been killed, and all his men, white and black, had been **The white flag of surrender** completely demoralised by the resolute advance made by our Nigerian troops. The tribesmen of Nigeria had reason to be proud of the soldiers they had produced. At Banyo these soldiers had carried out a task which would have tried the finest troops in the world. The entire system of defences on the mountain had been most carefully thought out and executed. Banyo seems to have been designed as the final impregnable place of retirement of the main German forces in the south. The position was lost because the German black troops, either through lack of nerve or from disgust with their masters, did not shoot well. They had line

CAPTURED WEAPONS OF THE GERMAN COLONISTS.
German rifles, machine-guns, ammunition, etc., which fell into British hands with the fort of Mora. The enemy had no dearth of armaments throughout the whole Cameroon campaign. In fact, both Cameroon and German East Africa were well prepared for "The Day."

ENTRY OF THE FRANCO-BRITISH FORCES INTO GARUA, JUNE 10TH, 1915.

An attack on Garua during the early days of the war revealed the considerable strength of this German fortress in Cameroon, and it was not until May, 1915, that the allied troops resumed the offensive in this region. On the last day of the month a heavy Franco-British bombardment began which brought about the unconditional surrender of the fortress, which was found to be consolidated with every device of fortification, and well armed with eleven machine-guns, six field-pieces, and a large quantity of shells and small-arms ammunition.

upon line of loopholed walls running up to the mountain top, and had they shot straight and used their dynamite bombs well in the fog battle, they would have been able to smash up a far larger force than that which Brigadier-General Cunliffe employed.

After the capture of the greatest stronghold in the fortress country, Brigadier-General Cunliffe made a broad-winged movement southward with his four victorious columns, which included the French force under Lieut.-Colonel Brisset. Every time the Germans tried to make a stand they were outflanked by a column next to that against which they were directly acting. No struggle of any importance, therefore, occurred during the sweeping operations of the northern allied force. The enemy was always retreating at the utmost speed, in order to avoid being enveloped, and in the first week of January, 1916, the middle British column **Outflanking** of the northern force, under Lieut.-Colonel **the enemy** Webb-Bowen, entered Yaunde, and there met the French column under Lieut.-Colonel Brisset, the Franco-Belgian column under General Aymerich, the main Franco-British force under Colonel Gorges, and the Senegalese force under Colonel Mayer.

But in this great closing movement on the new German capital of Yaunde the northern force under Brigadier-General Cunliffe played only a subsidiary part. The main work of smashing and routing the principal German force was done by the forces directed by Sir Charles Dobell and General Aymerich. As already stated, the two commanders met at Duala on August 25th, 1915, and made a plan for a new campaign for the conquest of Cameroon. By this time General Aymerich's troops, by very hard fighting, had captured the south-eastern German posts of Bertua and Dume. The French commander could, therefore, promise to make strong thrusts from Bertua and Dume towards the central German position at Yaunde, and he also arranged to send a third trench column under Lieut.-Colonel le Meillour to the Campo River, in the south-western corner of Cameroon, to cut off the German retreat to Spanish Guinea.

Sir Charles Dobell was much strengthened by the arrival of the 5th Light Infantry of the Indian Army. He also received more carriers from Nigeria and the Gold Coast, and trained some five hundred and thirty-six recruits enlisted in Nigeria. Also his full requirements in regard to motor transport were met, which enabled him to lighten the work of his carriers in the terrible forest region and thus accelerate his advance. The operations began in the first week of October, 1915, and followed the lines of the unsuccessful expedition of May. The French column under Colonel Mayer moved southward towards its former objective, Iseka, **Native and Indian** while the British column moved along **reinforcements** the Yaunde road to the scene of its former pyrrhic victory, Wum Biagas   Naturally, the Germans had not been idle during the six months that had elapsed since the last expedition.

The high position at Wum Biagas was transformed into a great system of earthworks, from which fortifications extended for miles. Our Nigerian force strongly demonstrated against this practically impregnable position, while three hundred men from the Gold Coast Regiment attempted a turning movement on the left flank. For two weeks the little Gold Coast force cut its way through the bush, forded rivers, and made one of the most terrible marches through the forest known to men. On the way the troops took a German mission-house which had been fortified, and then came to the Kele River, there hoping to get unexpectedly on the enemy's flank.

The Germans were surprised at a place called Muin, where they had constructed rows of beautifully constructed trenches, which they abandoned without a struggle. Recovering, they tried to attack our rear, but were beaten off. Not a man did we lose in this action.

It looked as though the enemy would be outplayed. The last march the Gold Coast force did was appalling in its natural difficulties. After fording a river five feet deep, the troops had to go down the side of a mountain, along a path with five inches of mud on the surface and sloping steeply to an edge. At this edge was a tremendous precipice, falling sheer into an unknown depth. Twenty of our loads fell into the abyss, and it took the troops eight hours to cross. Then they heard firing on their right, which indicated that the push against Wum Biagas had begun.

At midday the Gold Coast force cleared the mountain precipice, and entered a bush path, with rising ground to the right and a steep hill to the left, both covered with a tangle of tropical growth. Everything looked quiet and peaceful as the officers went forward to spy out the land. They found in front a deep river, on the opposite side of which was a cliff. But the land going down to the river on the side of their advance was as clean as an English meadow. All the trees had been felled and the brushwood cleared away. But a great bluff across

An uncomfortable silence

the water was still clothed in trees and undergrowth, and our scouts were able to spy the loopholes of a block-house and a longer series of loopholes running across the ridge. It was afterwards discovered that the river was only fordable in a line with the block-house.

There was still no sign of an enemy, black or white, but the silence was uncomfortable. Obviously the Germans had engineered a great trap, and some of our officers thought that they had skilfully prepared and abandoned their forward position at Muin in order to make us think that we should find the stronger position also evacuated. Sounds of the main battle at Wum Biagas came across the bush, helping to make our little flanking column think that the Germans had abandoned the trap they had prepared in order to reinforce their centre position.

Gold Coast men trapped

Happily, the commander of our flanking column was a man of great prudence. He brought up his little mountain gun, two machine-guns, and most of his men, hid the gun in the nearest clump of trees and then sent out the troops in artillery order. As soon as the men were clear of cover, and visible in the open ground prepared by the enemy, there was a terrific burst of fire, not only from the block-houses and the loopholed ridge, but from trenches along the river bank and from both flanks. And this was not all. There was a line of flame also in our rear.

The Gold Coast men dropped like logs, every man lying on his stomach and knowing he had been trapped. But our tiny mountain gun, with our two Maxims and our small reserve in support, had been able to get the range of the enemy when he made his great burst of fire. The German commander had been too quick. He should have waited until our troops were swimming about the river and trying to find the ford. As it was, we got in a swift and accurate fire, with the result that the German

WEST AFRICAN NATIVES WHO WERE MENTIONED IN DESPATCHES.
Both Major-General Dobell and Brigadier-General Cunliffe praised in their despatches the work done in the Cameroon campaign by the native carriers, "patient and amenable men," who "toiled incessantly under heavy loads and at times under heavy fire to keep the troops supplied with food and ammunition."

NATIVE CARRIERS ON THE MARCH IN CAMEROON.

Transport difficulties seriously hampered the Franco-British operations in Cameroon. Almost impenetrable bush exposed the long convoys of carriers to constant attack, and they further suffered heavily from sickness. But they responded bravely to the encouragement of the British officers, and did work without which the operations could not have been successful.

black troops lost their nerve. Their firing went to pieces and their bullets flew well above the heads of the men in our advanced section, who were shooting at every rifle flame that they saw in front of them.

We sent men out on our flanks and rear, and finding that the point of least resistance was on our left, the commander of the little column threw his main force there. After a fierce little battle, lasting four and a half hours, the Gold Coast force managed to threaten the enemy's left flank. For some unexplained cause the unknown German commander then hurriedly retired. There was no apparent reason why he should have done so. On the bluff across the river our men found trench after trench hidden in splendid cover, with accommodation for six hundred native troops and sixty white officers and non-commissioned officers. There were also trenches on the steep hill on our left, and on the rising ground on our right. As the total strength of our flanking column was only three hundred men, the enemy must have greatly outnumbered it, and they should have been able, not merely to hold up our force, but to annihilate it. Some of our officers thought that our deadly mountain gun was the victory maker. In firing its small shell this little quick-firer made a most furious and alarming rattle, and it is presumed that its terrific bark frightened the tribesmen of Cameroon just when they were beginning to suffer from the good marksmanship of the Gold Coast riflemen.

When the enemy's flank was thus turned by a small but quite extraordinary victory, he hastily retired from his main position at Wum Biagas, where the gallant Nigerian troops were making fine headway. Ten miles farther down the Yaunde road there was a wooded ridge, where the road bent between two ravines. Here the Germans had built another system of earthworks. But before attacking, the main British column sent a force southward to assist the Senegalese troops under Colonel Mayer. Colonel Mayer had not been able to reach Iseka and help

Germans' amazing retreat

LT.-COLONEL A. H. W. HAYWOOD, D.S.O., R.A.
An officer "who experienced the brunt of the hard fighting" in Cameroon, and whose judgment and discretion were never at fault.

us at Wum Biagas as he did in the former expedition. The enemy had again been using gangs of thousands of natives to make line after line of fortifications across the railway track. Colonel Mayer had to carry widely extended positions at every rise of ground and bend of the permanent way. Walled in by the primeval forest, and anticipated in every attempt to make a flanking movement with the axe, his task was extremely difficult. By reason of a swifter advance the British column was soon in a position to outflank southward, from the Yaunde road, the German troops defending the railway line; and after great trouble in crossing the flooded Kele River, our flanking forces came to the help of the French. Colonel Mayer was then able to make a strong thrust on Iseka, with his Senegalese fighting at the top of their form. They captured a considerable amount of rolling-stock which had been left behind in the previous advance, and as our supply of engines and waggons was small, the recovered additional spoil greatly helped to improve the transport of supplies. The bridges between Duala and Iseka had partly been rebuilt, and the work of making good all this section of the Midland Railway was rapidly carried on during the first three weeks in November. Our motor track along the Yaunde road was also much improved, and some seven thousand carriers, each carrying from fifty to sixty pounds on his head, served as means of communication off the two main lines of motor and rail traffic.

We pushed our camp a little way beyond Wum Biagas to Angas. Thence a Nigerian force, under Colonel Gorges, moved against the enemy's position on the Yaunde road, while the French column under Colonel Mayer advanced along the railway towards the point at which another road from Kribi ran upward to Yaunde. In effect, however, the two forces, British and French, combined into a main body with two wings that swept towards the German base on a wide front. The German Commander-in-Chief, who was fighting at the same time the Franco-Belgian force

Allied forces converge

under General Aymerich and the French column near Spanish Guinea, could no longer bring against all the main allied forces in the south a superior or even equal number of troops. On a very small scale, he was in the same position as the armies of the German Empire afterwards were. He held the interior lines, but instead of being able to swing his main force from side to side and defeat each enemy in turn, he had to fight hard and incessantly on all fronts. Northward, Brigadier-General Cunliffe was closing in upon him; eastward, General Aymerich was stubbornly and victoriously advancing; and southward, two French forces were moving along the Spanish frontier and towards the station of Ebolowa.

Zimmermann decided to use his most powerful force in holding Colonel Mayer on the railway. Colonel Mayer was indeed held up in a most violent fashion. Only the remarkable gallantry of his Senegalese troops enabled him **Cheery, courageous** to win through. **Senegalese** The Senegalese lost heavily in a struggle that lasted five weeks, but all the time they gave more punishment than they received, and at last smashed their way through broken entrenched country to Mangeles. Against Colonel Mayer, Zimmermann was fighting for his life, and he knew it. If the French column,

[*Underwood & Underwood.*]

THE KAISER'S REPRESENTATIVE.
Herr von Ebermeier, who abandoned his governorship of German Cameroon to the allied authorities, the German forces having evacuated the territory for neutral refuge.

which was immediately acting with our Yaunde road column, had carried out the plan of Sir Charles Dobell and swept on Yaunde from the south, the principal German force would have been completely enveloped. In conjunction with the weaker French forces in the south, Colonel Mayer's column was closing the only road of escape to Spanish Guinea.

Zimmermann saw this, and therefore fought against Colonel Mayer with his main strength. Sir Charles Dobell **Lack of** tried to answer **communication** this movement by combining the Senegalese, Nigerian, and Gold Coast troops into a single army acting on a connected front. But the lack of transverse roads through the bush prevented the British commander from transferring forces quickly from wing to wing. All that could be done was for the northern British wing, under Lieut.-Colonel Cockburn, and the British centre, under Colonel Gorges, to drive hard and incessantly at Zimmermann's flank and centre in order to compel him to weaken his attacks against Colonel Mayer's column.

In all that follows it must, therefore, be remembered that though Colonel Mayer made less progress than his British comrades-in-arms, he had the hardest task of all. His slow yet magnificent pushing movement was the pivot on which depended the victories of the British, French

BRITISH NATIVE TROOPS FOR THE CAMEROON FRONT ABOUT TO LAND ON THE WEST AFRICAN COAST.

Equatorial, and Belgian Congo forces. Sir Charles Dobell, in his despatch, especially remarks upon the help he received from Colonel Mayer, not only in the skilled leading of the brave and cheerful Senegalese, but in the perplexing strategical problems of the expedition.

While Colonel Mayer was desperately fighting from the railway towards the Kribi road, the Nigerian troops made their main thrust on Yaunde along the upper road. The column set out on November 23rd, met the enemy's patrols the next day, worked past two German machine-gun parties, skirmished until November 26th in the rubber plantations, maize fields, and banana orchards along the road, and followed the enemy into the jungle beyond the clearings.

Bondage of natives Then, after topping a wooded ridge, the Nigerian column found the enemy's battle position. At a point where the road sharply turned to the right the German force had lined up on a range of steep, heavily wooded hills, which they had previously deeply entrenched. The Germans must, in the previous six months, have worked thousands of the native population to death in preparing earthworks. All that could be effected in defensive spade-work by a native population of three and a half millions, Zimmermann and his engineers had planned with care and carried out with intense energy.

In the present case the Germans held advanced positions by two ravines, that opened on either side of the Yaunde road and left only a little neck of land running towards the entrenched heights. Three companies of the 1st Nigeria Regiment were ordered to take the ridge. The attack was opened by the second and third companies, commanded by Captain Balders and Captain Giles. The attack was apparently not a success. On both

flanks we were held up all the morning by the two gullies on each side of the road, and the sweeping machine-gun fire of the enemy broke our sections up terribly. Captain Balders fell when leading an attack against the main ravine, where the enemy had a machine-gun less than a hundred yards from our thinned and despairing line. One of our Maxims had been pushed forward across the gully to help the two advanced sections. But these sections suffered such losses that there were not more than a dozen rifles left in the line after seven hours' fighting. Of four British officers two were killed and one wounded. Lieutenant Ford, who was left in command, was inclined to retire with his twelve men to save his machine-gun from being rushed. But he hung on because Captain Balders, before falling dead with a bullet through his neck, had said : "This is a case where we've got to do or die." And almost by a miracle the handful of men won through. Suddenly the enemy's fire slackened and then ceased. He was evacuating the ridge. By amazing and almost hopeless tenacity a small British force, that had been reduced to

PICTURESQUE VILLAGE SCENE AT SAVA.
View of a native village near Mora Mountain, Northern Cameroon, with troops and horses of the Nigeria Regiment Mounted Infantry. The village was occupied by the British during the attack on the German position.

twelve men and a Maxim, frightened one of the two most important German forces in Cameroon out of a high fortified position. As the Germans were retreating, another company of the 1st Nigeria Regiment came up as a support, but merely helped to quicken the general withdrawing movement of the enemy.

The enemy, however, only fell back to another entrenched ridge, and fighting went on furiously, over position after position, until the station of Ngung was conquered on November 30th. By this time the main British force was nearing the open and cultivated country. Only a narrow belt of bush remained, and the enemy, knowing that he would be

FUGITIVE GOVERNOR OF A LOST PROVINCE.
Herr von Ebermeier, formerly Governor-General of German Cameroon, surveying the beauties of the colony before its loss, from the heights of the volcanic Cameroon range—a captured German photograph. The ex-Governor was interned in Spanish Guinea with a remnant of German troops who escaped with him.

outmanœuvred when the clear ground was reached, made desperate efforts to snatch a decision in his last patch of wooded jungle land. Our column stayed for some days at Ngung, in order to bring up supplies and clear its line of communication from hostile parties raiding through the jungle. Then, on December 7th, 1915, the advance was resumed, with a small part of the Gold Coast Regiment, under Captain Butler, acting as an outflanking force and cutting its way through the bush. Captain Butler, by the arduous work and the intrepid spirit of his men, succeeded in turning the last great German fortified position in the bush.

Our main column then burst into the open country and captured Jang Mangas on December 17th. The British column had by this time got well in advance of the French column under Colonel Mayer. The orthodox thing to do was for the British force to establish a base at Jang Mangas, wait for the French force to advance, and help this advance by a flanking movement southward.

VIEW OF MORA MOUNTAIN, NORTH CAMEROON.
Germany's strongest entrenched position in North Cameroon, on this mountain crest, was surrendered to the Franco-British troops on February 18th, 1916.

Sir Charles Dobell, however, reckoned that the condition of mind of the German native troops was the ruling factor in the situation. In a previous expedition from the end of the Northern Railway we had halted for sound reasons near the rail-head in order to strengthen our line of supplies and amass material. But this necessary postponement of our pursuit had put heart into the routed German native forces and had given them time to recover from their demoralisation.

At Jang Mangas the principal British column had again got a large force of Germans and natives in a fugitive and demoralised condition. Sir Charles Dobell, therefore, resolved not to wait for the co-operation of Colonel Mayer, but to thrust forward towards Yaunde with a view to preventing the Cameroon tribesmen from regaining confidence in their German commanders. It was this psychological movement, seemingly against the principles of good strategy, that completely shattered the German system of resistance. For as the British column advanced along the Yaunde road in the third week of December, while Brigadier-General Cunliffe's northern force also converged towards Yaunde, Zimmermann could not keep his native troops in hand.

Our Yaunde road force found position after position with strongly entrenched works abandoned, and on January 1st, 1916, the head of the Yaunde road column, under Colonel Gorges, entered Yaunde. The enemy **The Allies enter Yaunde** was completely crushed by the pressure brought against him from all sides. During the first week in January troops from Brigadier-General Cunliffe's command, with troops from French Equatorial Africa and the Belgian Congo, began to arrive in Yaunde. As Sir Charles Dobell remarked in his despatch : " It is a remarkable feat that troops that had fought and marched for a period of seventeen months should have converged on their objective within a few days of one another." The country in which they operated was one and a half times as large as the German Empire, and consisted largely of a roadless, tropical wilderness belted with jungle growth and topped by fortified mountains. The immediate effect of the occupation of Yaunde was to relieve all pressure on Colonel Mayer's heroic force, which reached the Yaunde-Kribi road early in January;

for Zimmermann was flying at utmost speed towards Spanish Guinea, preferring internment to capture by the Allies. The French and British forces swept south to Ebolowa and Kribi, picking up remnants of the scattered German garrison. Then Colonel Morrison, taking command of a strong French **Capt. von Raben's** force, spread it out like a net towards the **surrender** Spanish frontier, and, linking with the French force operating from the Campo River, cleared Cameroon of Germans by the middle of February, 1916. At the beginning of this month Brigadier-General Cunliffe, having completed his sweep on Yaunde, turned back to the northern Gibraltar of Cameroon—the great mountain of Mora—and brought up guns and shells to the hill level with the first ridge of the enemy's position. But the affair ended without a battle, as the German commander, Captain von Raben, surrendered with all his troops on February 18th, 1916.

With the conquest of Cameroon the enemy lost a territory 306,000 square miles in area, on which he had expended great sums of money and thirty years of steady work. The Woermann line, that carried the Cameroon produce, lost most of its steamers; so that the conquest of the great colony was as complete as possible. With the exception of the help of one Indian battalion, the native forces of Nigeria, the Gold Coast, Sierra Leone, Senegal, French Equatorial Africa, and the Belgian Congo carried the operations to a victorious close. In this matter it must be remembered that Cameroon was a fortress country specially organised for the conquest of the surrounding British, French, and Belgian colonies. If the Germans had treated their own natives fairly and had used more humane methods in both government and discipline, their strength of resistance in a country of such immense natural difficulties and intricate fortifications might have proved insuperable. In Cameroon the German fell unwittingly by his own hand, because he was a most brutal exploiter and not a civilising, colonising power. On the other hand, the difference between the spirit of the natives of the Belgian Congo in the days of King Leopold and their spirit in the days of King Albert, the great reformer, was marked by the number of fine, gallant native recruits whom the Belgians rapidly trained for victory with General Aymerich's column.

LONDON COLLIER WANDLE SUCCESSFULLY ENGAGING A GERMAN SUBMARINE IN THE NORTH SEA ON APRIL 29TH. 1916.

German submarines, though armed with the latest guns and torpedoes, frequently encountered effective opposition from their would-be victims. On April 29th, 1916, the collier Wandle, belonging to the Wandsworth, Wimbledon, and Epsom Gasworks, was attacked by a U boat with torpedoes and gun fire. The former missed their mark, whereupon the collier opened fire with her sole gun. After the sixth shot the German submarine suddenly disappeared, and Captain G. R. A. Martin brought the Wandle safely back to the Thames. He was subsequently awarded a silver medal for his brilliant exploit.

CHAPTER CXXVII.

ISOLATING THE ENEMY : HOW THE CENTRAL EMPIRES WERE BLOCKADED

Difficulties in the Way of Exerting Naval Pressure Against the Commerce of the Enemy States—Direct and Comprehensive Methods of Blockade in the Napoleonic Wars and Their Effect—Abraham Lincoln and the Doctrine of " Ultimate Destination "—Development of the Policy of Blockade into Our Most Important Weapon of Attack—German Fear and Denunciation of the American Doctrine of Blockade as Developed by the Spanish-American War—Lord Fisher's Preparations for a Naval War with Germany—German Astuteness and British Obtuseness Exposed by the Declaration of London—German Misconception of Britain's Real Attitude—Resumption of Our Full Sea Rights Required as Punishment for Germany's Violation of Belgium—Strict Blockade at the Outset would have Exhausted Germany's Energy within Two Years—Why Sir Edward Grey Declined the Responsibility—The French and the Russian Position—Italy—The United States—Sweden and the Open Route to the Baltic —Cotton—British Coal as a Factor in the Situation—The German Submarine Campaign and the British Retaliation—Dutch and Danish Commerce with Germany—Incompleteness of Our Counter-Blockade in 1915—Sweden and the Allies—American Criticism of the British Blockade and Sir Edward Grey's Reply—Sir John Jellicoe's Opinion—The White Paper of January 4th, 1916, and Lord Beresford's Alternative Statement—Pressure of Public Opinion on the Cabinet—The Black List—Lord Robert Cecil Appointed Minister for Blockade—Abandonment of the Declaration of London in July, 1916.

IN no other branch of the war were there such difficulties and perplexities as in the exercise of naval pressure against the commerce of the enemy States. From the first the British and the French Navies in the North Sea and the Adriatic interfered with the sea-borne trade of Germany and Austria-Hungary. At a later date the Fleets of France and Great Britain, reinforced by the Navies of Italy and Russia, operated against the maritime traffic of Bulgaria and Turkey, while maintaining their watch on the coasts of the Central Empires. Trade in the Baltic was not interrupted seriously until the autumn of 1915, but all other seas adjacent to the enemy States, and also to the neutral States through which sea-borne goods could be transported by rail and road, river and canal, to enemy destinations, were dominated by the warships of the Entente Powers. From the beginning of the war Britain could have sadly disturbed the transit across the Baltic of goods bought or sold by Germany and Austria if our submarine flotillas had been sent through the Sound.

Had we retained and developed the direct, simple, and comprehensive methods of blockade of the days of Nelson and of the American Civil War, there would have been no immediate difficulties or perplexities for our sailors

THE SEA'S DEADLY HARVEST.
Iron model of a German submarine erected on a pedestal, which consisted of a British mine washed up on the shore, at Hornum, Island of Sylt.

in the days of Jellicoe. A hundred years ago we used our power on the sea as Napoleon used his power on land. All military conquerors have practically an entire dominion over the territories to which their striking force reaches. They stop and divert trade in those territories as they wish, and they can even require neutrals to modify the course of their commerce, as Germany did during this war in the case of Switzerland. Napoleon's grand scheme for preventing all trade between the Continent of Europe and the British Isles is the classical example of the exercise of blockading power by a military empire. It was mainly because Napoleon tried to exert greater pressure on Russia than his military position allowed that his scheme ended in disaster. Had he been the actual conqueror of all Europe, his Continental system might have been worked for what it was worth.

For many reasons such a system was not as effective as our naval blockade. The discovery and colonisation of the New World, together with the discovery of the sea route to India, and the establishment of trading stations and plantations in the East, gave our country enormous resources. Our sea-power enabled us to collect against the enemy the wealth of the world, for we were then the only nation employing power and machinery in our manufactures. Moreover, there was only one extra-European country

119

READY FOR EMERGENCIES.
All in the day's work aboard a
destroyer. British Marines scouring
a torpedo.

that approached us in
energy—the United States—
and its population, manu-
facturing capacity, and mercantile marine were greatly
inferior to ours. Our Government was able to apply
against the great land
empire of Napoleon a larger
measure of restriction in
trade than Napoleon used
against us. Even when the
United States went to war
against us, partly in the
interests of its trade with
France and French territory,
we held to the blockade
system established by our
Orders-in-Council, and in the
treaty of peace concluded at
Ghent in 1814 there was no
mention of any limitations
of our right of blockade
in the interest of neutral trade.

ALL IN ORDER.
Naval picket-boat making its way
back to a warship after inspecting
the papers of a vessel under
suspicion.

The most important section
of the American Republic, the New England States, had
shown some sympathy with the British Government and
had been lukewarm in the struggle.
Naval blockade   Had the war lasted longer, New
precedent   England might have seceded, and the
English-speaking races might even have
been reunited. The exercise of the blockading power of
our Fleet may, therefore, be said to have been a great
and general success in this case. The pressure we exerted
caused discord between Napoleon and his chief allies, and conduced to his defeats in Russia in 1812 and at Leipzig in 1813.

Our blockading methods were turned against us during
the American Civil War. Abraham Lincoln declared the
staple produce of the Confederate States—cotton—to be
contraband, though it was not then used for any warlike
purposes. His reason was that it supplied his enemy
with the sinews of war. The United States President
also extended the blockade from enemy ports to neutral
ports through which goods were passing by land to the
Confederates. If, for instance, a ship went to Matamoras

a port in Northern Mexico, with a cargo destined to be
transported by land to the Confederates, the cargo could
be seized under the doctrine of "continuous voyage" or
"ultimate destination" (which means that goods could be
condemned if they were ultimately intended to reach the
enemy). Our Lancashire cotton operatives suffered cruelly
from lack of cotton, but both they and our Government
acquiesced in this extraordinary extension of the law of
blockade. What we then lost as a neutral trading State
was felt to be more than balanced, in the event of a naval war,
by our gain as the greatest sea Power. The
greater the restrictive force allowed by   **Law of**
international convention against neutrals   **compensation**
and enemies, the stronger became our
position against any possible foe who possessed highly
developed industries and large oversea trading interests.

The policy of blockade, indeed, seemed to be developing
through the nineteenth century into our most important
weapon of prolonged attack. In purely military operations
our Fleet, if kept at great strength, could only save our
shores from invasion, our sea-borne commerce from interruption, and our transports
from destruction, thus playing a defensive part. But
when agricultural States,
such as Germany, entered
upon a period of intense
industrial activity, with vast
sea-borne imports of raw
material and vast sea-borne
exports of manufactures, the
scope of our sea-power began
to trouble our future foes.
Treitschke was then openly
proclaiming in Berlin that
the Germans had settled
accounts with Denmark,
Austria, and France, and
they would in due time
settle accounts with Britain,
as Britain was the last great
obstacle to that dominion
of the earth towards
which they were working.

MANNING THE PICKET-BOAT.
Petty-officer, men, and an interpreter about to leave a British warship to
inspect papers of a suspicious ship.

"GERMAN BATTLESHIP FIRING BROADSIDES IN THE NORTH SEA."
This picture had much popularity in Germany, where it was described as above. While undoubtedly a photograph of an actual occurrence, the practice was one in which German battleships indulged by preference where defenceless towns rather than British battleships formed their objective.

The prospect of the indirect pressure of our sea-power, by such a blockade as Abraham Lincoln had established against the Confederate States, perturbed the Germans and led them to spend some three hundred million pounds in trying to outbuild us in battleships. The leading German authority in the matter was Vice-Admiral Baron Curt von Maltzahn, professor of naval strategy at Kiel. In his work on "Naval Warfare," written in November, 1905, he violently denounced the American doctrine of blockade as further developed during the Spanish-American War of 1898:

The United States hold that if the commander of a vessel, which might be thousands of miles from its destination, can be proved to have had the intention of entering a blockaded port, he is guilty of trying to run the blockade. In other words, the United States hold they would have been justified in stationing their cruisers at the mouth of the Elbe to keep watch over German ships sailing from our harbours, lest these ships should be bound for the blockaded port of Havana.

Admiral Maltzahn, doubtless, had in mind the defence of the German coast against a British blockading squadron by German submarines. If, after the American doctrine, our blockading squadrons could act hundreds or thousands of miles away from the blockaded coast, submarines could not seriously impede a blockade. The submarine of 1905, for instance, could not have interfered with a British blockading squadron operating in the Northern Atlantic. The bold and enterprising policy of the United States inflicted serious loss on us when we were neutral, but served our larger interests as a great sea Power by its sensible and well-founded insistence on the fullest right of blockade. For the United States remained the dominant extra-European trading nation, and in the event of a European war its own practice and doctrines would apply to Americans as neutrals.

Unfortunately, in December, 1908, we went widely out of our way in order to deliberately create enormous difficulties in the exercise of economic pressure on an enemy by means of our Fleet. At that time Germany directly threatened us at sea. All our measures against the increasing aggressiveness of our future foe were restricted to naval preparations. Far-seeing men anticipated a naval war between ourselves and Germany, and our First Sea Lord of the period, Lord Fisher, made ready as best he could to meet a sudden attack upon our Navy and mercantile marine.

Lord Fisher, however, had to struggle against a party of immense influence in the Liberal Cabinet. This party was strangely hostile to any adequate preparation for the war which was being openly planned by the sovereign who called himself "Admiral of the Atlantic." When Kaiser Wilhelm II. began an enormous programme of battleships and battle-cruisers, there remained a very strong British political group which violently agitated against the maintenance of the strength of our Fleet. Lord Fisher and the other Sea Lords had to threaten resignation in 1909, and all but gave effect to their threat, before the wiser members of Mr. Asquith's Government could obtain a Cabinet decision for the maintenance of our battleship strength. In other words, they had to menace their colleagues with the break-up of the Government and the publication of the news of the resignation of the Sea Lords before they could persuade them to agree to steps being taken to prevent the people of the British Isles from being beaten at sea and starved into surrender.

Lord Fisher resumed his control of our naval preparations, but friction in the Cabinet apparently prevented him from obtaining all that the Admiralty required. The result was that he received insufficient money, built only the battleships necessary to counter the German menace, and failed to get the cruisers and destroyers needed for the Fleet.

Lord Fisher had attended the First Hague Conference in 1899, and had then made a resolute stand against the subtle intrigues of Germany. At the Second Hague Conference of 1907, from which Lord Fisher was absent, numerous conventions affecting naval war were signed—providing amongst other things for the creation of an International Prize Court. Our Government convoked the leading naval Powers in London in 1908, in order to settle the rules which this International Prize Court was to apply. Nothing quite like the Conference of London is to be found in history. The British lion, half dazed and half alarmed by the threats of the Prussian eagle, invited his rivals to convince themselves that his intentions were perfectly peaceable, and allowed them—with his eager consent—to clip his claws.

Blindfolding Britannia

With a genius for management unexcelled by Bismarck, the German representatives affected to work in our interests, and professed their eagerness to safeguard our necessities as the greatest merchant shipping nation. They proposed that certain raw materials, largely imported by this country, should be included in a list of goods which could

" except within the area of operations of the warships detailed to render the blockade effective." This very vague and ambiguous phrase seems to have been meant to forbid anything like a long-distance blockade, enforced by warships some hundreds of miles from the enemy's coast, such as had been carried out in the American Civil War by the United States. Thus Germany hampered the British Fleet in every conceivable manner.

It was a marvellous triumph for the German diplomatists. Britain, who could not live on her own produce, was to be deprived of foodstuffs for man and beast by enemy cruisers raiding her trade routes ; while Germany—who wanted raw cotton for her smokeless powder, oil for her nitro-glycerine and dynamite, jute for her sandbags, iron, copper, nickel, tungsten, and other ores for making fine steel for guns, rifles, bayonets, shells, and other munitions of war, rubber for her military motor transport, and wool for the clothing of her troops—was to get all these things without interference from our Navy. Under the Declaration of London all these war stores were practically to be allowed to enter Germany, provided they were carried by neutral vessels.

But a hundred of our admirals opposed this surrender of our ancient sea rights. The Unionist Party, under Mr. Arthur Balfour, voted against the Naval Prize Bill which put the Declaration of London into force so far as this country was concerned. Though the Liberal Government forced the measure through the House of Commons by a straight party vote, the House of Lords saved the Empire by defeating the Bill.

It was one of the luckiest strokes in our history that the Declaration of London was defeated. It was born of the faltering, hesitating, half-frightened, and half-incredulous policy of the Cabinet then in power. Instead of meeting and answering the German menace firmly and bravely, the British Government tried first to disregard it, and then to dodge it.

LIFEBOATMEN "DOING THEIR BIT."

The use of mines and the absence of navigation lights at sea resulted in a number of wrecks round British coasts, augmenting the duties of lifeboatmen. This illustration shows the Spurn lifeboat on an errand of mercy, supported by a railway company's tug.

never be declared contraband or liable to seizure in neutral ships by belligerent cruisers. Among the articles which the Declaration of London placed in this free list were raw cotton, jute, flax, hemp, silk, and wool, copra, oil seeds and nuts, rubber, raw hides, iron, copper, nickel and other metallic ores, wood-pulp, bleaching powder, ammonia, and such curious things as office furniture. On the other hand, foodstuffs, forage, and grain could be treated as contraband of war.

In addition to these extraordinary inclusions in and exemptions from the list of contraband, it was agreed that if a neutral vessel was found to be carrying contraband to a neutral port she could not be seized. Her papers, whether true or false, were to be accepted as evidence of the destination of the goods.

Perhaps the master-stroke of the German delegates was the first chapter of the Declaration, laying down an entirely new law of blockade. Its very first article forbade a blockade extending " beyond the ports and coasts of or occupied by the enemy " (such a blockade as we must establish in case of war). Other articles forbade the blockading forces to " bar access to neutral ports or coasts," and prohibited the capture of neutral blockade-runners

The actual result of our continual weakness was that Germany concluded we should never go to war with her in any circumstances, if we could by any sacrifice of honour or interest avoid the struggle. And it was because our real attitude was then misconceived that the enemy afterwards attributed to us a Machiavellian genius in diplomacy in forcing him to enter the European War with the odds against him. There was no shadow of scheming in the matter on our part. Our Government had in it so large an element of feebleness that our politicians really acted as ostriches, instead of pretending to do so. Only our professional soldiers and sailors saved us, and at times by a very narrow margin of power.

Our sailors had had to submit to the ideas of our politicians with regard to the Declaration of London. When **Golden opportunity missed** we were involved in a war on Germany, Austria, and Hungary, with Continental allies on our side, the most energetic action was required. Had the British Liberal Government possessed downright courage and the presence of mind born of courage, it would have kept clear of the Declaration of London—which was null and void—have proclaimed a strict blockade, and enforced the doctrine of " ultimate destination " when the German invasion of Belgium stirred the conscience of the whole world.

If our resumption of our full sea rights had then been

SUBMARINE WAR ON NEUTRALS.
Torpedoed neutral vessel sinking in the North Sea. On the right a lifeboat, which was lowered from the British vessel in the foreground, was conveying the crew of the neutral steamer to safety.

BRITISH SHIP TO THE RESCUE OF A NEUTRAL CREW SOMEWHERE IN THE NORTH SEA.
The U pirates' victim the moment before she foundered. The small illustration indicates some of the neutral steamer's crew swimming to the British vessel. Sailors were about to assist them to board the rescuing ship.

READY TO SINK OR TO SWIM.
Newfoundlander on a transport prepared to sink any submarine sighted.
He wore a lifebelt in case a pirate should get a torpedo home.

established as a direct punishment of Germany for her atrocious conduct in Belgium, there is but little doubt that we could have greatly helped to exhaust the warlike energy of the Teutons within two years. In particular, we could have prevented a very large part of the American cotton crop of 1914 from passing into German powder factories, for transformation into the propellant for all German and Austrian guns, howitzers, machine-guns, and rifles. We could have stopped the enemy from getting fat for nitro-glycerine, considerable quantities of ore for fine steel manufacture, copper for cartridges and shell-bands, and large quantities of food. American cotton was the decisive article of contraband, because without it Germany and Austria-Hungary would soon have run short of powder. They would have had to resort hastily to wood or other inferior cellulose material. Large new plants would have been required; every gun, howitzer, Maxim, and rifle would have needed different sights; and then all these weapons would have been diminished in carrying power and in regular precision.

Fear of powerful neutrals Sir Edward Grey, however, would not accept the risks of a severe blockade. In his view, as he afterwards explained in public, any attempt on our part to prohibit neutral commerce with Germany would have led to some of the principal neutral Powers joining Germany and Austria, and declaring war upon us and our Allies. It is possible that France and Russia may have strongly influenced our decision. Both the French position and the Russian position remain, at the time of writing, very obscure. But it is clear that Russia needed free transit of war stores and general material through a friendly Sweden. Sweden, on the other hand, was agitated by a strong and energetic pro-German party, known as the Activists, that eagerly sought for any fairly popular motive for bringing their country into the field against Russia and invading Finland. Had we confiscated in the Channel

and the Atlantic all cotton, copper, lard, ore, and other cargoes of materials capable of military use, in Swedish vessels and shown to be eventually destined for transhipment to Germany, the Activists might have fomented the discontent of the Swedes regarding this restriction of their carrying trade until war resulted.

The French Government was anxious as to the attitude of Italy. At the beginning of the war Italy was friendly, and allowed the French Army along the French-Italian frontier to be moved against the Teutonic invaders. Nevertheless, German financial, commercial, and political influences permeated the entire fabric of Italian life. It was questionable whether the French blockading squadron in the Mediterranean could seize Italian ships, containing cotton, copper, and other war material, consigned to agents who were engaged in transporting the goods into Austria or into Switzerland for **Italy and** despatch to Germany. For many years **the tariff** Italy had retained a grudge against France, and fought her in a tariff war. It was quite possible that the severe methods of a full blockade, with their general interference with Italian shipping and their restriction of trade between Italy and Germany, would alarm the Italians, spread a belief that the French were jealous of Italy's extending commerce, play into the hands of the Teutonic intriguers, and thus keep the Italians from extending their sympathies with the Allies to the point of joining them in the war.

Finally, we had our own special risk of troubles with the United States. Since they fought us in 1812 the Americans had enormously increased their trading interests. But, on the other hand, they had themselves established a precedent by making cotton contraband and by their doctrine of "ultimate destination" against imports passing through neutral ports to an enemy. Further, as Admiral Curt von Maltzahn pointed out in 1905, they had extended the range of blockading operations to a distance of hundreds of miles from the blockaded ports. Moreover, if Abraham Lincoln could place cotton exported from the South in the contraband list, the way seemed open for us to place manufactures of all kinds exported from Germany in that list, to say nothing of the wheat and meat which she imported.

For Germany was a nation in arms, with no distinction between her combatant and non-combatant population. In fact, many of her non-combatant adults were engaged in the manufacture of munitions and general material of war, and were, therefore, assisting the forces in the field. The great naval Powers of the world had agreed at the Conference of London that foodstuffs for man and beast could be declared contraband without notice. Generally speaking, therefore, the United States was bound, by its own precedents and by its contraband doctrine, to acquiesce in a long-range blockade of the German coast.

There remained, however, the open sea route in the Baltic between Sweden and Germany. Had we from the beginning closed this route by submarines, the blockading operations would have been technically complete. But as we did not wish to give the Activist party in Sweden any excuse for beginning a war with Russia, our blockading operations were at first confined to the main Atlantic routes. As Sweden remained free to trade with Germany, the United States might have argued that the blockade was not effective, because it was not applied "impartially" to the ships of all nations, and might have made this a ground for war.

We might have overcome the fears of Italy by specially considerate treatment, and have supplied her with all the war material her Government needed for its work of preparation. But unless Russia was willing to face the risk of Sweden joining Germany, and unless she was capable of permanently holding back the Swedish Army among the Finnish lakes, and dispensing with the stream

Chasing an enemy submarine: Patrol work of the R.N. Motor Boat Reserve.

P   125

On the alert for the furtive foe: Scene in a submerged British submarine.

Sentinels of the Grand Fleet: Patrol boat overhauling suspected blockade-runner.

Courage and skill overcome mine peril: Exploding infernal machines brought to the surface by trawlers.

of supplies that flowed from Britain and America through Swedish channels of communication, a strict blockade was dangerous.

At the outset, however, we could have blockaded the German Empires much more effectively if we had had the courage and the energy. International law is a whole. Its fabric of conventions stands or falls as a system. One belligerent cannot infringe international law in an important particular, and then maintain the validity of some separate articles of international convention which subserve his purpose. By treacherously invading Belgium, and then aggravating this infringement of treaty and neutral rights by deliberate and systematic atrocities which outraged every line in the Hague Conventions, Germany made the system of international convention invalid **Germany's** in every particular. Its validity would **blood-guiltiness** only have been maintained if all the States which signed the Hague Convention had forthwith taken steps to preserve international law against a country whose professed aim was to tear up all "scraps of paper."

We, at least, as the only active and professed defender of the treaty rights of Belgium, must have been granted an open field, had we immediately applied the severest naval pressure against the brutal and uncivilised disrupter of those universal conventions on which modern civilisation rests. When Germany reverted to the savage conditions of the Thirty Years' War our powers were no longer limited by the surrenders we had made of our sea rights in the past. In 1856, for instance, we had, for no visible reason, surrendered our right of taking enemy goods in neutral ships and neutral cargoes in enemy vessels.

The Cabinet in August, 1914, was completely unequal to the occasion. In it there was no man of dominating influence and genius for war. Rhetorical talent was abundant, but the strength of character, the presence of mind needed to seize an unexpected opportunity and use it to strike a swift and stunning blow—these qualities were lacking. Sir Edward Grey was amiable and gentle, but not a man to "ride in the whirlwind and direct the storm," and as Secretary of State for Foreign Affairs he had a ruling voice in determining our blockade policy. At the Admiralty were Mr. Winston Churchill, who had more energy than knowledge, and Prince Louis of Battenberg, who was a capable officer of trained talent but without the fire of genius and masterful strength of Lord Fisher. And even Lord Fisher would not have been able to revive the sea rights of Nelson's day without a desperate struggle and a Cabinet crisis when Sir Edward Grey so greatly feared complications with powerful neutral States.

The upshot was our Government did the very weakest thing possible—played for safety and went to the limit of its powers of surrender. Illegally and unconstitutionally the Cabinet resurrected the Declaration of London, which the Peers had rejected, and temporarily adopted most of its principal features. No constructive idea whatever can be traced in this extraordinary act. Possibly it was thought that, as the war was going to be very short, the code of sea law could not greatly affect it. Only Lord Kitchener, who was not at first a member of the Cabinet, had foreseen for some years that the war would be long, needing millions of British soldiers.

One step we did take. By an Order-in-Council, which showed the range of intellect of our administrative minds, the list of contraband in the Declaration was extended to aircraft. Nothing else of importance was done for months.

In November, 1914, when the enemy had just lost his first wind after being brought up between Dixmude and Arras, he, too, realised that the war would be long, and increased his output of munitions enormously. Everything he wanted was reaching him by sea—cotton and nitrates for making the propellant (or powder) for his

PIRATES POSING BEFORE THE CAMERA
The old pirates of the Spanish Main were not more ruthless than their modern German types, some of whom appear in this photograph.

guns and rifles, metallic ores for his new weapons, wheat and meat for his troops. Under the Declaration of London, most of these things were exempt from seizure. On October 29th, 1914, some keen intellect under the Liberal administration discovered that copper could be made into shell-bands and cartridge-cases, and that barbed-wire was useful in warfare, and had, in fact, been in common use since the South African War. Then the British Government declared that copper and barbed-wire, aluminium, lead, and sulphuric acid were contraband. Copper had been a war material for centuries, and the Austrians were still using bronze guns. The framework of Zeppelin airships was made of aluminium, and the gas with which they were filled was generated with the aid of zinc; bullets, moreover, were cast of lead—but the British advisers had seemingly never discovered these facts.

The British public never appears to have grasped what was happening. The previous agitation over the Declaration of London had been largely confined to naval experts and pacifist politicians. The people did not grasp its military signifi- **The public in** cance. They thought that we were acting **the dark** as we did in the days of Nelson, and exerting a strangle-hold upon all the import and export trade of Germany. Indeed, the general, uninformed opinion was that the Grand Fleet under Sir John Jellicoe was beginning to starve the Germans into surrender. This ignorant, unfounded, popular view was strongly and strangely supported by Mr. Winston Churchill in a speech he made as First Lord of the Admiralty at the Guildhall banquet on November 9th, 1914. In effect, Mr. Winston Churchill definitely assured the British naton that a naval blockade was in operation, and he stated that at the end of twelve months the resulting economic stringency would achieve the doom of Germany. His words ran as follows :

SIX HUNDRED LEAGUES UNDER
THE SEA.

The German submarine Deutschland
reached Baltimore from a German port
on July 10th, 1916, after a voyage of
4,180 miles, of which she travelled 1,800
miles under water.

It is very difficult to measure the
full influence of naval pressure in the
early stages of a war. The punishment we receive is clear and definite.
The punishment we inflict is very
often not seen and even when seen
cannot be measured. The economic
stringency resulting from a naval
blockade requires time for it to reach
its full effectiveness. Now you are
only looking at it at the third month.
But wait a bit. Examine it at the
sixth month, and the ninth month,
and the twelfth month, and you will
begin to see the results—results which
will be gradually achieved, and silently
achieved, but which will spell the
doom of Germany as surely as the approach of winter strikes the
leaves from the trees.

THE CAPTAIN OF THE SHIP.
Captain Paul Koenig, of the Deutschland, with Paul Hilken, of the
North German Lloyd Agency, Swedish Vice-Consul at Baltimore.

This statement was made by Mr. Winston Churchill
in the presence of Mr. Asquith, Lord Kitchener, and Mr.
Balfour in circumstances of historic solemnity. Therefore,
all the people of the British Empire believed as a fact in
the economic stringency we were producing in Germany.
All the vain and misleading prognostications of the growing
enfeeblement of the enemy's strength in war materials
and even in food can be directly traced to this speech.

The enemy was not blockaded. His ocean-going
steamers were driven from the sea, and he was unable to
ship direct a few articles which he could
Copper wrapped   produce in vast quantities in his own
in cotton   country. Copper was the only thing he
seriously lacked, and when it was made
contraband in October, 1914, he imported it wrapped up in
cotton. The great American cotton harvest—which our
Government might have bought up without any resort to
our old sea rights or Abraham Lincoln's precedent—poured
so fast into Germany that the Germans could not store it.

No explanation of the attitude of our Government in
regard to the cotton question is yet available. It cannot
have been a matter of pure, blind, hopeless, utter ignorance.
Mr. Winston Churchill, as the Cabinet spokesman of the
Board of Admiralty, must have known that the Germans
did not want cotton merely in order to weave pinafores
for babies and summer dresses for women. Sir Edward

Grey was presumably assisted
by experts, so it is difficult to
suppose that lack of knowledge
prevented our executive from
putting cotton on the contraband
list. It has, however, been
suggested that somebody in
authority had a slight acquaintance with chemistry and an
extreme fear of exasperating the
German-Americans who controlled
the American cotton market. The
suggestion was that it would have
been useless to stop cotton passing
into Germany, because German
experts could have used wood to
make all the powder required by
their armies and fleet.

One of our most eminent men
of science, Sir William Ramsay,
pointed out that smokeless powder
made from wood would lack the
precision and uniformity of
nitrated cotton fibre, and would
also be less powerful. The vast
German and Austrian plant
designed for cotton powder would
have had to be remodelled in part,
in order to deal with cellulose
obtained from wood. The
essential thing, therefore, was
for us to act quickly and stop
cotton imports into Germany
and Austria, either by making
cotton contraband and removing
the cargoes from all neutral
vessels, or by buying the crop.
In this case the Germans and
Austrians would have had to
save their existing stock of
powder, and refrain from any
great offensive while they were
re-sighting their weapons,
practising with wood powder,
and establishing their new plant.
During their difficult transition
from a cotton to a wood propellant there would have been
a period of weakness, and this period of weakness would

MERCHANTMAN OR MAN-OF-WAR?
Some of the crew of the Deutschland. The boat carried seven hundred
and fifty tons of dye-stuffs as cargo, and, according to Mr. Ryan, the
Collector of the Port, conformed to all the requirements of a merchantman.

CAUGHT BY A BRITISH DESTROYER.
German submarine mine-layer UC5 in distress off the East Coast. Her crew abandoned the craft and were picked up by a British warship's whaler.

have coincided with the first French attack in Champagne, the British attack at Neuve Chapelle, and the Russian sweep over the Carpathians. It is difficult to see where Mackensen and Hindenburg would have obtained the powder for their grand phalanxes, with their million of shells daily, if the Central Empires had been abruptly and unexpectedly deprived of the cotton they had ordered from the United States.

No doubt if the enemy had been given time he would have made use of the wood substitute. Possibly he afterwards tried to do so, when our Government was being slowly compelled by public agitation to include the cotton crop of the late autumn of 1915 in the list of contraband. Success in catching the enemy with depleted powder resources depended entirely upon surprise. We needed a man of genius and knowledge to foresee the part that cotton would play in the war, and to make effective plans to stop the supply from reaching the Teutons at a time when they possessed no proper plant for dealing with inferior wood fibre.

Unless at a later date information becomes available showing things to be entirely different from what they seem, the failure of the Liberal Government to revise the Declaration of London in the late autumn of 1914 and make cotton contraband then, will be regarded by all impartial historians as the greatest blunder in the conduct of the war. It appears to have been well within our power to cripple the fighting arm of the enemy. Why we failed to do this is the great mystery of the war.

The great mystery of the war

It is commonly said that a nation has the Government it deserves. In our period of slackness between the South African War and the European War we displayed, in the ruling majority of our elected representatives, a degree of weariness for which we had afterwards to suffer. On the other hand, we can justly claim that when we were at last aroused we showed a direct power of popular control such as is not to be found elsewhere in history. The people pushed the Government along the path towards efficiency and strength. We educated our masters ; but the process of education was slow and troublesome. And in the meantime the figureheads of our Empire created difficulties for our sailors.

The chief difficulty was the vast mushroom growth, in almost every important neutral State, of powerful vested interests concerned in producing or conveying war material for the enemy. On the resurrected corpse of the Declaration of London battened a medley of parvenu traffickers who became in many cases the outer tentacles of the Germanic octopus. The new millionaires had large funds to spend on political intrigues among their own people, with the result that Germany was able to intensify her well-known methods of pacific penetration in some of the neutral States she was enriching by her diverted sea-borne imports and exports. Strong new interests, broadly established on a gold basis, arose among neutrals who had deeply and passionately sympathised with the Allies in August, September, and October, 1914. Sometimes the voracious and poisonous Germanic tentacles went too far

TAKING POSSESSION OF THE PRIZE.
British sailors aboard the UC5. The German commander attempted to destroy the craft with bombs, which exploded ineffectually after the crew had abandoned it.

LONDON'S UNIQUE TROPHY.
The UC5 in dry dock. She was only eighty-five feet long, and carried twelve mines on each trip. The submarine was exhibited to the public at Temple Pier, London, in July, 1916.

in sucking at the independent life of neutral countries; and as happened at last in Holland, for example, the drain of both imported and home-produced food menaced the common people with famine, and compelled them to agitate vehemently against the newly created pro-German commercial and political interests.

Yet our Government had extraordinary powers of control over the general situation, which it was cravenly allowing to develop to the disadvantage of the cause of the Allies. In addition to our lost sea rights as a blockading Power, we possessed in our incomparable mines of hard steam coal a peaceful and yet crushing instrument against pro-German shippers. All German coal was poor in quality and unsuited for use in steamers. Moreover, during the first month of the war the Germans, like the French and the Russians, called most of their miners of military age to the Colours, and only dug enough coal for their own limited purposes. Nearly all the shipping in the Eastern Atlantic depended for motive power on British coal. Also, Dutch, Greek, Scandinavian, Italian, and Spanish cargo boats trading to the Orient or rounding Cape Horn depended upon coaling depôts scattered about the world and controlled and supplied by Britons. Even the United States did not possess as good steam coal to meet the need of the neutral shippers who kept Germany supplied with war material and food ; and from our coaling port at Jamaica we could have controlled many American ships trading to South America. Everybody with a steam-engine in Western and Southern Europe looked to our coal-mines for fuel. Only Switzerland depended upon German coal, and she did this merely because her difficulty in land situation made the import of fine British coal too costly. Wherever a ship could go, our coal had gone for the best part of a hundred years, and even in Northern Germany British coal had remained more important in steam-power industries than was the cheaper, but inferior, German coal.

The British coal factor

A TROPHY FROM TIRPITZ.
Sentry on guard over a faulty German shell. As many as two hundred and forty residences in Lowestoft were damaged by the German bombardment.

By watching neutral ports in Scandinavia and Holland, and blacklisting all ships that helped the enemy and everywhere refusing them coal, we could from August, 1914, have established a virtual blockade by purely economic means.

Naturally, our politicians did not, before or at the outbreak of hostilities, appreciate this great governing factor in the European situation. We were in reality an industrial oligarchy with a democratic colour, but we had maintained, throughout our change from a Government of landowners to a Government of professional orators, the showy amateurishness characteristic of an age of

transition. In the eighteenth century the landowning oligarchy knew a good deal about its own special productive interests of farming, but neglected the new national interests represented by the creators of our industrial power. The industrialists, thereupon, fought for freedom of private development in their own sphere and overthrew the landowners in the struggle to get cheap imported food for the urban working classes, but remained content to be governed by orators without knowledge, so long as these human gramophones did not seriously interfere in the fundamental work of the nation. Some industrial groups that were directly subject to Parliamentary control established in turn a certain amount of control over Parliament by giving directorships to politicians. But it was only the great transport corporations that obtained by private efforts some power of direction in the Government. None of the chief productive groups, which in a loose, free way controlled us economically, troubled to organise political

WASTED EFFORT.
Part of a house in Lowestoft struck by a German 11·7 in. shell that failed to explode. Two soldiers were examining the damage.

power. Mr. Joseph Chamberlain tried so to organise this, but he was defeated by the shipping interests, the international finance interests, and the international industrial rings largely concerned with Germanic trade.

Generally speaking, our Government, Liberal and Unionist, was composed of men who possessed power and lacked knowledge. Some were a remnant of the old landowning oligarchy ; others were retired traders, manufacturers, and bankers, using Parliament as a ladder for the society ambitions of their wives and daughters ; and many were professional politicians of the new school, ready to take up any little popular domestic grievance likely to attract votes and enable them to increase their standing in their party. The sincerest men among them were entirely immersed in the vast problems of social reform, which overtaxed the powers of mind they possessed, as these powers of mind were not usually remarkable. Behind the Parliamentarians was an army of administrators, with generally as large a breadth of outlook as a mole. Their highest duty was to play for safety, and to avoid exposing their Parliamentary chiefs to awkward questions. Since the industrial revolution the nation had made itself, while Parliament acted only as a buzzing fly above the great wheels of invention, industry, labour organisation, and popular movements of gradual reform of the social structure. The utmost that Parliament did was to register by legislation the evolution of national tendencies. It created

An easy target for German naval gunners. Two women and a special constable were injured here. The firing lasted about half an hour.

Damage done to small houses as a result of the German raid on Lowestoft with four battle-cruisers, light cruisers, and destroyers.

Convalescent home at the East Coast resort which was shattered by Hunnish "frightfulness."

Large residence on the front reduced to ruins by German shells.

Shell-shattered business premises in one of the main streets of Lowestoft.

Room in the Lowestoft convalescent home where the matron was sleeping. In spite of the great damage wrought by a shell explosion, she escaped uninjured.

House on the front wrecked by German gunnery. Four inhabitants were killed and some twelve were wounded by the enemy's fire.

"FRIGHTFULNESS" AT A POPULAR EAST COAST RESORT: LOWESTOFT AFTER THE GERMAN NAVAL RAID, APRIL 25TH, 1916.

nothing, and it fostered none of the growing forces. The people as a whole worked out their own destinies; they led and their so-called leaders followed.

And so it was throughout the war. From the beginning, the spirit, the courage, the instinct, and the diffused knowledge of the people were much superior to those of members of the Government. But unfortunately the people did not have all the facts before them. For example, as we have seen, they thought we were rigorously blockading Germany and stopping all war supplies from reaching her, when Germany was getting everything she wanted except copper. And even then copper and other additional contraband continued to pour into neutral ports connected with Germany and Austria-Hungary, if the cargoes were consigned to a neutral merchant.

U.S.A. and the copper question

It was only when a ship's papers showed that an enemy agent was the direct consignee, or the name of no consignee was given, that the cargo was stopped. Yet certain copper interests in the United States began as early as September, 1914, to bring pressure to bear upon various Senators. The Senate passed a resolution calling for information from the Secretary of State in regard to our interference with shipments of copper from America for Rotterdam. It was admitted by the Americans that this copper was being sent through Rotterdam to the Krupp works. We paid for the copper cargoes we intercepted. Yet the American Senate, touched to action by the far-reaching tentacles of the Germanic octopus, tried to intimidate our Government in this matter.

As a matter of fact, in our parody of a blockading operation, from August 4th, 1914, to January 3rd, 1915, we placed in the Prize Court only eight out of seven hundred and seventy-three ships that had cleared for the United States for Holland, Denmark, Norway, Sweden, and Italy. One of the eight ships was released by our Prize Court, and

only forty-five whole or part cargoes were stopped by us and bought up at a fair price. Reckoning the cargoes that were only stopped in part, we probably intercepted, during the most critical months of the war, when Germany was getting her second wind and storing the new cotton crop in millions of bales for powder-making, less than half a day's imports usually received by the enemy—twenty to twenty-five whole cargoes in all.

Happily, if our Government was weak and timid, the German Government was insanely arrogant. Instead of letting matters drift on with immense benefit to them and profiting by the resurrection of the Declaration of London, the German authorities moved all the machinery of the German Press, at the beginning of 1915, to agitate against our inhuman method of starving the German non-combatant population. Unless the customary food of the men, women, and children of the Germanic Empires was copper, lead, iron ore, and rubber, it is difficult to see how they were being starved. We were even admitting these articles of contraband freely to Norway, Sweden, and Denmark in November, 1914, on a guarantee by the Governments of these countries that the contraband material would not be re-exported to the enemy. Italy was also allowed to receive all the copper cargoes consigned to her. Not only were foodstuffs pouring into Germany owing to our considerate treatment of neutral States, but the Beef Trust of Chicago was trying to arrange to supply tinned meat to the German and Austrian Armies, one of the heads of the Trust being in close personal communication with the Austrian Ambassador.

Germany's insane arrogance

The fact was that Germany wanted a pretext for starting her murderous submarine campaign against our mercantile marine and against all neutral shipping trading to French and British ports. As no pretext existed, and the entire spirit and letter of international law were dead against

BRITISH MONITORS IN ACTION WITH THE ENEMY BATTERIES ASHORE.
Monitors did excellent work not only in the Dardanelles, but also off the Belgian coast, where they constantly harassed the German right flank. The two shown here were engaging the enemy at long range, while the crews of their small guns stood by to repel possible submarine attacks.

such a method of wholesale murder of non-combatants and innocent neutrals at sea, a pretext had to be laboriously invented. Especially was it necessary for the German Government to prevent any of their own people from opposing the new system of atrocities intended to terrorise the British nation. In the case of the military policy of atrocities applied in Belgium, what conscience the German nation possessed was deafened and drugged by loud lies as to the torture and murder of German soldiers by Belgian women and girls. In much the same way what remnant of conscience the German nation possessed in February, 1915, was again put out of working order by a vast machine-made Press campaign concerning the hundreds of thousands of German infants who were dying under the non-existent British blockade. An attempt was also made to soothe in advance the indignation likely to occur among the "unhyphenated" part of the population of the United States when American citizens were murdered. This was done by developing a great organisation among American women for supplying starving German babies with food. More than a year passed before some German newspapers revealed that the infants of Germany in war time were better fed and better tended than they had been in peace time. Hundreds of thousands of good-natured American women and girls wasted a great amount of agitated sympathy upon the babes of Germany, but their stir of emotion produced the effect intended by the German minds that did the stirring. It helped to assuage and keep within controllable bounds the genuine storm of passion produced by the torpedoing of the Lusitania.

When the German Government proclaimed that the waters around the British Isles formed a war zone in which all merchant ships would be torpedoed by their submarines, our Liberal Cabinet had

S.S. AVOCET ATTACKED BY THREE GERMAN AEROPLANES.
The s.s. Avocet, when off the West Hinder lightship, October 30th, 1915, was attacked by three aeroplanes, which bombed her heavily for half an hour. So well was she handled that no bomb hit her. Before flying off one aeroplane hit her with a machine-gun, but wounded none of the crew.

full opportunity to redeem its mistakes, bury once more the Declaration of London, and exert a complete naval pressure against the outlawed nation of assassins that was running amok among both neutrals and combatants. The new vested interests in the huge diverted trade going through neutral ports to the Central Empires could then have been uprooted with comparative ease. According to our old and proper sea law, confirmed by the practice of the United States, we could stop the contraband trade by seizing the instruments of it. We could confiscate all neutral vessels carrying cargoes destined for the enemy, and use the confiscated ships for our own purposes. This had been found the only way of teaching blockade-runners that the risks of their game

Vested interests and ocean trade

were equal to their profits. They were often able to buy a steamer out of the profits of a single voyage.

But our Government thought that some neutral States would rather go to war with us than let their blockade-running ships suffer the proper penalty of confiscation. And in our Declaration of March 15th, 1915, announcing a counter-blockade by way of reprisals for the German submarine campaign, it was expressly stated that neutral ships carrying goods of enemy destination, ownership, or origin, would not be confiscated, unless they were liable to condemnation, under the futile Declaration of London, for trading directly to a German port. In the same Order, enemy cargoes were likewise to be free from confiscation and liable only to be intercepted and bought at a fair market price by British authorities.

As Sir Walter Runciman, M.P., afterwards pointed out, we were crippling our present and future shipping resources to a considerable extent by imposing penalties upon our mercantile marine, and allowing at the same time neutral shipping to escape confiscation when running valuable cargoes of contraband likely to make the fortunes of their owners. The consequence was that neutral shipping lines, greatly enriched by their successful voyages with contraband, and unpunished for their unsuccessful attempts, were growing into most menacing competitors of our half-commandeered and wholly overworked mercantile marine, which was also most exposed to the murderous, destructive operations of German and Austrian submarines.

Eight months too late

A formidable element of competition is being nourished in neutral countries which will test all our financial and productive resources when the war is over. It would be all to the national good if a less benevolent scope of brotherhood were manifested towards neutral shipping, and the war brought to an end by a *merciless blockade* on all supplies filtering through neutral ports into Germany.

There was, however, promise of a veritable stoppage of supplies to Germany; for in our Declaration of a counter-blockade it was stated that we had been " driven to frame retaliatory measures in order to prevent commodities of any kind from reaching or leaving Germany." The blockade-runners were to play their millionaire-making game without risk to their ships and without loss to the owners of their cargoes, but our Government apparently intended to prevent, in a very mild and gentlemanly manner, anything whatever getting into Germany along the Atlantic and Mediterranean trade routes. The cotton crop had gone through, and immense quantities of other war materials had reached the enemy. We were eight months too late. As we had not had the presence of mind to declare even a similar blockade as a reprisal for the invasion of Belgium, the numerous and powerful new vested interests in general contraband traffic began to tell widely and heavily against us. The fact that we apparently lacked the courage to apply the old method of confiscation against their cargoes and their ships seems to have made them believe we could still be daunted. But our Government had at last gathered a certain degree of courage, and it began in March, 1915, under the strong pressure of public opinion, to undertake what had become a ticklish task.

Government and public pressure

In the first place, it was very doubtful if we could seriously injure Germany by stopping her food supplies. In this connection we were perhaps rather misled by the success which Abraham Lincoln had achieved in the Civil War. The Confederate States were not self-supporting, but Germany was very nearly so. The Confederates had few iron foundries and still fewer machine shops. Their railways and rolling-stock could not be renewed when worn out, and rails had actually to be taken up from the less important railways and relaid on the main strategical lines which were in constant use. Germany, on the other hand, had immense steel and machinery works, and was in this respect much more powerful than all the Allies combined.

SCENES ABOARD MEN-OF-WAR, BRITISH AND GERMAN.
Another photograph which had much popularity in Germany under the title " Clearing the decks for action in the North Sea." Above: Some of the wholesome, cheerful boys of the British Grand Fleet greasing and coiling up a wire hawser.

COALING A WARSHIP AT SEA.
With the British Navy's happy knack of imparting interest to an otherwise unpleasant duty, coaling ship is made a matter of keen competition.

TAKING BIG SHELLS ABOARD.
Great dexterity, as well as great strength, is required in the manipulation of these monster projectiles, some of which weigh more than 1,400 pounds.

Then—in a matter of still more importance —the Confederacy did not manufacture arms and munitions. The Federal blockade therefore destroyed the efficiency of the Confederate armies. Germany, on the other hand, still traded in munitions and arms. Her output, with that of Austria-Hungary, was said to be greater than the entire output of the Allies plus that of the United States. Not only was she making, with Austria, nearly half a million shells a day, but she still produced more guns than she needed for herself and her allies. By quite an extraordinary display of intensified warlike industry she went out of her way to supply Switzerland with new 6 in. guns. This is something for our munition workers to

Germany and her food supply

ponder over. It was a glorious gesture of braggadocio on the part of the Germans to supply the Swiss with new heavy artillery when they had Bulgaria and Turkey to munition and Austria continually to strengthen on three fronts.

In regard to food, Germany and her allies produced, before the war, four-fifths of the food needed by their combined populations. Even if Russia, Italy, France, and Great Britain could have stopped grain, meat, and fish from entering the Central Empires, the Germanic population, which used to overfeed itself, would only have had to go without one-fifth of the normal quantity of food. But it was impossible for the Allies to stop the entrance of this one-fifth of food imports. Adjoining Hungary, and connected with it by railway, were the rich wheat-lands of Rumania, and a considerable part of the Rumanian harvest of 1915 passed through Hungary towards Germany. Then adjoining Germany was the famous dairy-farm country of Denmark, which increased its commerce with its neighbours, so that the price of Danish bacon rose tremendously in the hungry British market. Germany was also closely connected with

Holland, a country which in peace time had provided the British market with pork.

Dutch pork became strangely rare in our country, and the Dutch pig industry, which we had almost entirely fostered by our patronage, was transformed into a weapon against us. We could not get Dutch pork when we most needed it, because the agents of Germany were buying it up.

Here are some figures, published in a Dutch newspaper, the "In-en Uitvoer," showing how Holland starved Great Britain and fed Germany. The exports are given in metric tons of about 2,200 lb.:

—	Jan.-May, 1914.	Jan.-May, 1916.	—	Jan.-May, 1914.	Jan.-May, 1916.
BUTTER.			POTATO-FLOUR.		
To England .	2,495	63	To England .	6,005	747
To Germany .	5,860	14,805	To Germany .	13,491	50,115
			FRESH BEEF.		
EGGS.			To England .	5,043	236
To England .	3,708	572	To Germany .	2,574	13,643
To Germany .	4,736	17,136	FRESH MUTTON.		
			To England .	1,181	—
CHEESE.			To Germany .	33	1,112
To England .	7,178	528	FRESH PORK.		
To France .	1,310	423	To England .	20,484	32
To Germany .	5,708	34,520	To Germany .	1,647	10,281

PATHETIC HUMILITY OF THE CAPTURED SEA-HUN.
Crew of a German submarine captured in the Channel. Apparently the men were not over-willing to face the camera. Having lost their boots, their French captors presented them with sabots, prior to placing the men under a well-deserved, if perhaps too lenient restraint.

By our policy of Free Trade we had enabled the Danes and the Dutch to expand their production of food at the expense of our farmers, with the result that the bacon, pork, butter, and cheese supplies upon which we relied were largely withdrawn from our markets, to our grave injury and to the benefit of the Germans, who in peace time had maintained a high tariff wall against Dutch and Danish farmers.

Our farmers had given up pig-raising, partly because of sanitary restrictions in regard to the position of sties, but mainly because Danish bacon and Dutch pork came freely into the country. The foreigners at first undersold our producers and then, having won a practical monopoly, kept the prices as high as ever they could without exciting us to breed our own pigs. Still all went well in the days of peace. But in the days of war many of us had to go without pork or bacon while the Germans, who had formerly closed their markets to the Danes and the Dutch, reaped much of the benefit of that famous General Election of ours which the Free Traders had won with their cry of "Your food will cost you more!" Our food would have cost us less in the years of the great crisis if we had maintained our farming industries at the expense of the Dutchmen and Danes and had looked on the slight rise in prices as an insurance for ampler home supplies in war time. It is only fair to say that Denmark at least tried hard to maintain her ordinary supply of bacon and butter to the country whose Free Trade policy had made her prosperous. But Holland, as has been already stated, sent at last so much food into Germany that her own population began to famish, and the Revolutionary Social Committee held meetings of protest against the Government foodstuff policy.

In addition to the help she received from Holland, Denmark, the rich mountain pastures of Switzerland, and the wheat-fields of Rumania, Germany acquired, in the summer of 1915, all the fertile loess plain of Poland, which is one of the most productive stretches of earth in Europe. Multitudes of experienced Russian peasants were captured and set to work like serfs on the old and new farmlands and potato-fields of the Central Empires. There were also thirty millions of subject populations in Poland, West Russia, Belgium, Northern France, Serbia, and Montenegro, many of whom were compelled to toil in the German service at vast State farms.

The only article of food that Germany began badly to lack was pig's flesh and pig's fat. She entered upon the war with an enormous number of pigs, whose flesh has been for hundreds of years the principal meat of the Germanic races. The German eats little beef and little mutton. Though he has acquired somewhat of the Austrian's relish for calf's flesh, the calf remains a middle-class and aristocratic article of diet in the form of *Wiener-schnitzel*, while the working classes obtain from the pig the fat sausage stuffs from which their working power is largely derived. A panic in regard to the food available for fattening pigs led to some very foolish German expert giving an order for the rapid destruction of millions of pigs.

At the time when Germany was crying out to the world that she was being starved, the grand slaughter of her pigs was producing a glorious time for all sausage eaters. The Germans then were on the whole better nourished than ever they had been. It was only when the gigantic stock of sausages began to diminish, owing to the need of millions of unproductive soldiers working in the open air and developing great appetites, that the problem of the pig began to engage the attention of the German Government. Then it was that the young pigs of Holland and the old hogs of Denmark were reduced to trainloads of carcases and sent over the frontier. The fat part of them was needed in German munition works, and most of the fat of all the German pigs that could be spared by the breeders was required for making nitro-glycerine and tallow lubricant for heavy machinery in war factories.

German sausages, therefore, became horribly dry. as only the lean of the meat was used in making them. But, after all, this was only a discomfort, like the mixture of potato starch with rye flour in the German war-bread. There was always enough rough and somewhat unpalatable food in Germany to prevent the working power of the nation from any dangerous enfeeblement. Only the

138

arrant stupidity of some of the leading ration organisers and the arrogant avarice of many of the German land-owning magnates led at times to serious temporary deficiencies in the victualling of some of the great cities.

During the Napoleonic Wars certain of the great Prussian landowners kept their wheat back until the price of it rose enormously, and enabled them to emerge at the end of the struggle with new wealth. Many of the fortunes of the Prussian nobility were based upon the holding back of corn from their own starving people during the struggle with Napoleon. And the same method of making money was generally pursued by the large modern German landowners. They skilfully assisted Admiral Tirpitz in swelling the early baseless agitation against the starvation policy of our country in order to divert popular attention from their traditional method of making money out of the semi-famine they were producing in the urban population. The potato-bread spirit, as Mr. Lloyd George justly remarked, was indicative of the patriotic heroism of the German urban populace. But it was countered and partly defeated by the selfish, price-raising policy of the old

Prussia's land-owning oligarchy
German landowning oligarchy which, by means of its sons, controlled the Army, and by means of its poor relations dominated the German bureaucratic machine. Despite all appearances, the old landowning oligarchy was more powerful than the German Emperor.

It governed him in devious and subtle ways, through members of his Great Staff, through many of the leading men in his bureaucracy; and though the German Navy was not generally officered by the poorer kinsmen of the landowning magnates, they established a working alliance with the heads of the Marine Office. They also had an understanding before the war with a majority of the leaders of the German industrial and financial organisations. But during the war the great captains of industry began to see that good and cheap food for their working people was a most pressing necessity, both in maintaining the warlike power of the country and in preparing for the international economic struggle that would follow the war. There then occurred a rift between the two classes of Germans who had formerly combined in an attempt to win dominion over the earth. Herr von Bethmann-Hollweg became the leader of the somewhat despondent and dis-illusioned industrialists, who also drew towards them some of the most influential German-Jewish financiers.

A rift in the German lute

Our blockade helped to intensify this domestic tension in regard to the distribution of food supplies and the general discontent of the urban working class and their powerful leaders with the high prices maintained by the leading agrarian magnates. Even our domestic troubles with reference to the rising charges made by shipowners for bringing food and forage to our islands helped in-directly to increase the pressure upon the German urban working classes. When the price of food went up enor-mously in our country, the merchants of pork, bacon, butter, and cheese in Holland and Denmark increased their prices in their German markets. The great Greek land-owners in Rumania studied the price that wheat was securing in Western Europe, and held back their trainloads of corn until German buyers were willing to give even higher prices than wheat was fetching in Liverpool. The Rumanians went so far as to arrange to send their wheat

U BOAT CAUGHT IN A NET, SUNK BY HER CAPTAIN, AND AFTERWARDS REFLOATED.
Captured German submarine in a French dry-dock. The U boat was caught in a net somewhere off the French coast. On coming to the surface her captain, realising his predicament, surrendered, but managed to sink his craft. The French naval authorities, however, soon raised the vessel.

round to Great Britain by Archangel and Kola, if the Teutons would not give in gold a remarkably high price for it. For the Greek magnates of Rumania rather sympathised with the Allies, and especially with France, and though they hesitated to declare war upon Austria-Hungary, they wrung the last possible ounce of gold out of the Germans.

The Danes were not so harsh in their terms for feeding Germany, though they hated the conquerors of Schleswig-Holstein quite as much as the French hated the conquerors of Alsace and Lorraine. But the Army of Denmark was much weaker than the Army of Rumania. It could not threaten to take the field with any immediate disastrous effect for Germany. Its numbers were small and its artillery was exceedingly feeble in comparison with the monster pieces of ordnance which the Germans had unexpectedly brought into use and developed with astonishing productive energy. Denmark was overborne by her great bullying neighbour, and almost forced, as Switzerland also was, to feed as many German mouths as possible. Holland was stronger than Denmark, but she had no grudge against Germany as Denmark had, and no large unredeemed and oppressed mass of countrymen waiting for a war of liberation as Rumania had.

Many of the Dutch farming and merchant classes threw themselves with their old cynical commercial zest into the work of making money out of Germany's necessities and out of Great Britain's stupidities. The Dutch imported American fodder in extraordinary quantities. They promised that none of this animal food should be re-exported to Germany. They merely fed their cattle on the stuff, bred calves, and increased their milk resources for cheese-making, butter-making, and skim-milk feeding for pigs. It was the pork, butter, cheese, and veal which had been produced largely by means of American fodder that were turned into German gold. Oils and fats imported under our blockade into Holland were also retained in the country in accordance with the letter of the guarantee against re-exportation. But until our surveying authorities became interested in Dutch margarine, and began to wonder if most of it was going into Germany, the oil and fat cargoes reaching Dutch ports underwent a transformation that enabled large quantities eventually to pass the German frontier.

American supplies through Sweden Our Declaration of a counter-blockade in March, 1915, designed to prevent commodities of any kind from reaching or leaving Germany, failed of general effect. American lard for the manufacture of nitro-glycerine in dynamite went to Sweden and thence passed into Germany. All the cotton Germany needed she received directly and indirectly. By April, 1915, the quays of Gothenburg were congested with bales of cotton, nominally belonging to the common stock of Sweden, at a time when some of the Swedish cotton spinners were stopping work because they could not get cotton. This condition of things was officially set forth by our Secretary of State for Foreign Affairs in April, 1916, in his note regarding the allied blockade, addressed to the American Ambassador in London. Many

of the consignees in Sweden of American cargoes of contraband were ridiculous, covering figures of straw ; among them were Swedish dock labourers, lightermen, and other extraordinary examples of penurious hypocrisy.

In our own country there were also men who went on supplying the enemy with commodities after our Declaration of a rigorous counter-blockade. For example, we had managed during the war to annex the great cocoa trade of Hamburg, and our imports of cocoa rose from seventy-eight million pounds in 1913 to one hundred and eighty-seven million pounds in 1915. We consumed about half of our increased cocoa imports, but certain of our countrymen, engaged in the newly-enlarged trade, sent cocoa to the enemy through neutral ports. **British exports** This fact was admitted by a leading **of cocoa** member of the Coalition Cabinet, Lord Lansdowne, in January, 1916. He stated that cocoa was not added to the list of restricted goods until January, 1915, and the restriction then was only limited to cocoa powder. It was not until July 30th, 1915, a year after the outbreak of the war, and more than five months after our Declaration of a rigorous counter-blockade, that the export of British cocoa indirectly to the Teutonic Empires was prohibited.

We seem also to have supplied, through neutral agents, considerable quantities of tea to the enemy, and there can be little doubt of other large leakages from our own country to the countries we were pretending to starve into surrender. In the test case of cocoa our Government publicly admitted the facts, but the country was not informed what politician and what administrator was responsible for permitting the export to the enemy of a British foodstuff containing a stimulant most valuable to soldiers in action. The condition of mind of officers and seamen of our blockading squadron when they found that they could not interfere with British cocoa going to Germany through Sweden may be better imagined than described.

THE SOWER OF MINES.
German submarine mine-layer UC5, an enemy photograph taken on a previous trip to that in which the craft was captured by a British ship, as shown on page 131.

Denmark and Norway, according to Lord Lansdowne, shared with Sweden the profits of the cocoa traffic.

Sir Edward Grey at last devised a serious and well-considered plan to stop neutral countries adjacent to Germany from acting as funnels for German and Austrian commerce. Calculations were carefully made of all the imports each neutral funnel State needed to supply the wants of its own population. It was allowed that the interruption of Germanic and Russian supplies should be made good by supplies from the United States and other productive nations. Also a very liberal additional surplus was allowed to the funnel States, in order to cover all possible expansion of their legitimate requirements. Holland, of course, received an enormous supply of imports, by reason of her multitude of Belgian refugees and the requirements of the American Commission which was feeding Belgium by supplies imported through Dutch channels.

When the British authorities had worked out all their figures, the delicate and most difficult task of inducing the funnel States to agree to the proposal was tactfully started and very gradually carried out.

Powerful corporations, representing the chief commercial interests in Switzerland, Holland, Denmark, and Norway, were organised under British and French influence, and entrusted with the work of receiving and distributing the legitimate imports of their country. No shadow of threat of warlike action was made by the Allies. Peaceful inducements of an economic kind were mainly employed. In some cases shipping lines were asked to give guarantees against indirect contraband traffic with the enemy, in return for a full and constant supply of Welsh steam coal. In other cases the unavoidable delay in stopping ships on the high seas and bringing them to British ports for search was mitigated if shipowners agreed to give a guarantee against contraband traffic. According to American reports, agents of our blockading squadron developed a secret service system in the principal American ports from which neutral vessels were conveying contraband to enemy agents in neutral States. If this were so, we had **Our secret service in the U.S.A.** a double check upon neutral shippers who attempted to act against their guarantee. We might obtain information at the neutral port from which the errant ship cleared, and perhaps from the intermediate neutral port at which she discharged or merely stopped to coal. And over all this was the exercise of our right of search, with stoppage of the ship at sea and thorough examination of the cargo in port.

Our position was thus a powerful one. For in addition, the wide dominions of our Empire and the great dominions of our Allies contained many substances of great value that neutral States could hardly do without. Canada, for example, had a practical monopoly of nickel, which was required by almost every steel manufacturer in the world. The American steel industry was dependent upon Canadian nickel and hungry for Canadian iron ore. In Burma was the greatest mine of tungsten, quantities of which were required by all high-power **Pressure on the funnel States** steel-makers and electric-bulb makers. Australia was the mistress of the zinc trade. British steam coal was needed throughout Western Europe, and Australian wool controlled the winter-clothing markets of the world.

Thus, without the slightest threat of war, we were able to exercise considerable industrial and commercial pressure upon the funnel States. Switzerland, Holland, Denmark, and Norway at last agreed to our plan for national import distributing agencies, after making alterations in detail in our proposals. Human nature being what it is, none of the distributing organisations worked perfectly. In Holland, in particular, the smuggling of contraband across the German frontier went on to an enormous extent, and, according to a Dutch paper with strong Belgian sympathies, a very powerful Dutch corporation maintained a great contraband commerce with Germany.

The Dutch possessed in the Orient important petroleum wells, tin mines, tea, coffee, sugar, and rubber plantations. A good deal of Dutch rubber went into Germany by parcel

JUSTICE AND POWER BEFORE WHICH HONESTY NEVER HAD TO QUAIL.
The British Navy conducted the blockade with absolute justice, but with a stern authority that brooked no nonsense. This official photograph shows the officer in charge of a naval search-party making exhaustive inquiry into the character of a sailing ship.

post and by frontier expeditions in which the guards were either dodged or bribed. At last the military force along the frontier was increased, but whether every soldier was averse to making money by helping the Germans is a matter of speculation. If we were to accept as evidence statements made in Dutch papers sincerely sympathising with the cause of the Allies, the corruption of the Dutch conscience by German gold was such as to make it seem that the great republican race that once lighted the torch of liberty in modern Europe, and inspired our people in the age of Elizabeth, was in danger of growing corruptly weak in spirit. But, it must in justice be remarked that towards the summer of 1916 the Dutch Government began to take steps to divide between Great Britain and Germany what exportable food supplies remained in the Netherlands.

Dutch conscience and German gold

Sweden withstood our attempt to form even a transit company for the protection of material on the way to Russia. Our Fleet, however, established a virtual blockade of the Baltic by means of submarine operations in the autumn of 1915, and so increased the insurance rates on contraband cargoes passing from Sweden to Germany that Germany was bled of money and deprived temporarily of certain war material. Swedish iron ore, however, continued to flow into German foundries. The most remarkable feature in this class of contraband trade was the continual and regular passage of iron-ore steamers from the Gulf of Bothnia to Rotterdam. The steamers kept within the territorial waters of Sweden, then crossed the Sound into the territorial waters of Denmark, skirted the fortified coast of Germany, and hugged the territorial waters of the Netherlands. At Rotterdam the iron ore was transhipped into river boats and conveyed to Krupp's works on the Rhine. Ore from Norway also passed through Rotterdam to Krupp's works at Neuwied; and according to a statement made in the House of Lords by Lord Devonport in January, 1916, some iron ore from Spain, which had to cross the Bay of Biscay and meet our blockading ships, reached the German agents at Rotterdam.

From August, 1914, to December, 1915, a million and a half tons of ore entered the port of Rotterdam. After the declaration of a counter-blockade in March, 1915, the Dutch iron-ore imports—mainly from Sweden, but also in part from Norway—did not diminish, but increased. Obviously, the ore could not be converted into pig-iron in Holland; for, as Lord Devonport observed, there was no coke in Holland and not a single blast furnace. The Norwegian mines, from which ore was also sent, were owned by the Hamburg-Amerika line. In the Baltic the old line of traffic between Sweden and Germany from Trelleborg to Sassnitz was found to be inadequate, and goods traffic was arranged to be directed from Malmö to Stettin at a conference between Swedish and German railway representatives.

Sweden and the Allies

In the spring of 1916 there seemed a certain amount of tension between Sweden and the Allies. Our country stopped the import of Swedish chemical wood-pulp, and influenced the Swedish match-making industries by putting a tax on matches. Swedish and other timber was also placed upon the list of prohibited British imports, and Canadian lumbermen came to our country to cut down wood needed by our mines. According to Norwegian rumours, there was in May, 1916, some danger of the

REAR-ADMIRAL ARTHUR CHRISTIAN
(On left) leaving Buckingham Palace after being invested by the King with the insignia of Companionship of the Bath, July 29th, 1916.

STOKER DAVIS AND BOATMAN WHITE.
Decorated with Board of Trade Medal for saving life. Circle Capt. C. Fuller, who received C.M.G., D.S.O., and Medal for saving life.

Activist Party in Sweden intriguing their country into a war with Russia, with a view to helping Germany. But whatever danger there had been appeared to have been dissipated by July, 1916, by the negotiations of the Russian Foreign Office. But no agreement in regard to the restriction and distribution of imports was arrived at between Sweden and the Allies. Swedish publicists went so far as to deny the validity of the American doctrine of ultimate destination, and only the Socialist Party in Sweden showed any sympathy with even Belgium or France.

The stand made by Sweden against the blockading policy of Great Britain and France was naturally used as an effective lever against the Allies by the Government of the United States. In a Note against the blockade,

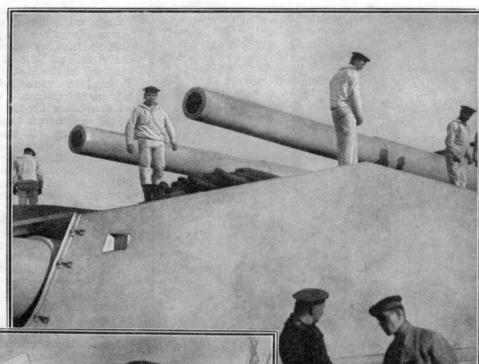

BEFORE THE JUTLAND BATTLE.
Aboard a German warship in the Kiel Canal. Enemy sailors at work among the guns.

Scandinavian and Danish ports. It is an essential principle, which has been universally accepted, that a blockade must apply impartially to the ships of all nations. This principle, however, is not applied in the present British blockade, for, as above indicated, German ports are notoriously open to traffic with the ports of Denmark, Norway, and Sweden.

Sir Edward Grey's answer to this objection was well based and masterly. In his Note in reply, published on April 25th, 1916, the British Secretary for Foreign Affairs showed for the first time in his treatment of our blockade problems a touch of constructive power. It is not extravagant to say that a considerable part of the American people was pleased to see the British Minister slowly rise to the height of common-sense that Abraham Lincoln and his Secretary of State, William H. Seward, attained at once in the blockade disputes of the Civil War. Sir Edward Grey did not

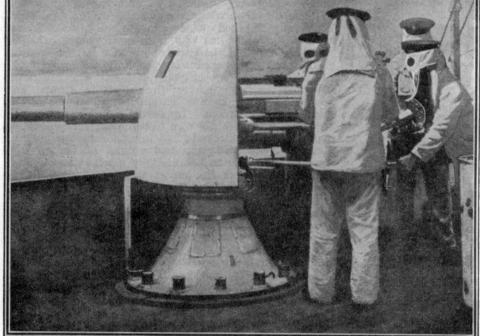

MASQUERADERS OF THE ADRIATIC.
Weird appearance of Austrian naval gunners equipped with respirators against the effect of poison gas generated by the explosion of their shells. The part of the Hapsburg Navy in the war appears to have been practically negligible. Austrian war vessels ventured even less frequently beyond their bases than did the German ships, though Austrian submarines emulated their policy of piracy in the Mediterranean.

delivered in London on November 5th, 1915, and hailed in Berlin as the international Magna Charta of the seas, the American Ambassador denounced our methods of naval pressure as "ineffective, illegal, and indefensible." Amid a mass of detailed objections there were two principal contentions against our blockading operations. One was that no proper blockade of the Germanic Empires existed, as we did not regularly maintain a cordon of intercepting ships in the Baltic waters. The other was that delay was caused by our new methods of search.

It is common knowledge, ran the American Note, that the German coasts are open to trade with the Scandinavian countries, and that German naval vessels cruise both in the North Sea and the Baltic, and seize and bring into German ports neutral vessels bound for

work from text-books of international law. He was no longer like a lawyer trying to win over the rather prejudiced mind of other legal men sitting in judgment over him, but a great legislator of international rules of the sea, creating a new order of governing ideas to meet the new conditions of the world. His success in getting his new ideas accepted depended of course upon the justice and reasonableness of the ideas. He first went back to the basis of American thought in the matter, and cited a remarkably profound and comprehensive passage in a letter from W. H. Seward to the American Ambassador in Paris in 1863: "The true test of the

Sir E. Grey and the Blockade

THE SUMMER SEASON—OSTEND, 1916.
Ostend, the erstwhile resort of fashionable Europe in the summer days preceding the war, became a scene of German naval activity. A torpedo-boat is here seen signalling its departure from the harbour.

efficacy of a blockade will be found in its results. Cotton commands a price in Manchester and in Rouen four times greater than in New Orleans. Judged by this test of result, I am satisfied there never was a more effective blockade."

Thus the great rise in price in Germany of many articles most necessary to the enemy in the prosecution of the war was the fundamental test whether our blockade was "ineffective." From this point of view, the British Minister dealt with the geographical problems of the blockade. He insisted that the sea traffic across the Baltic was of no more decisive importance than the land traffic over the Danish and Dutch frontiers. As his reply ran:

Commerce from Sweden and Norway reaches German ports in the Baltic in the same way that commerce still passes to and from Germany across the land frontiers of adjacent States; but this fact does not render less justifiable the measures which France and Great Britain are taking against German trade. . . . If the doctrine of continuous voyage may rightly be applied to goods going to Germany through Rotterdam, on what ground can it be contended that it is not equally applicable to goods with a similar destination passing through some Swedish port and across the Baltic, or even through neutral waters only? *The best proof of the thoroughness of a blockade is to be found in its results.*

Doctrine of continuous voyage

A marked impression was made on American opinion by the statements of Sir Edward Grey, and the view that our blockade, though perhaps loose in style, was generally sound in principle, appears to have gained strength in influential quarters in the United States.

Yet President Woodrow Wilson and his Secretary of State, Mr. Lansing, stubbornly objected to our method of search. They averred we had broken the settled law of nations by refusing to search ships at sea and taking them into port for thorough examination of the cargoes. An American official in London, according to general newspaper report, had informed the American Government that

this method of delaying American shipping was a subtle British trade device, designed to prevent the American mercantile marine from growing powerful enough to compete with the British mercantile marine. The point was raised in the American Note of November, 1915, but it was not rebutted in the British reply of April 1916; for, as Sir Edward Grey remarked, it had been completely settled by interim negotiations. We had been able to prove there was no foundation for the suggestion made by the American official, and he was removed from the position he occupied in our country. It was his baseless, deplorable allegations which had created smouldering, dangerous resentment against us throughout the United States in the early period of the war, when we had resurrected the Declaration of London and were exerting no effective naval pressure upon the enemy. All the apparently academic protests by the American Government were charged with an invisible heat of passion, by reason of the suspicion that we were interfering with American shipping for unfair purposes of commercial rivalry.

Rise in American export trade

Our Secretary of State for Foreign Affairs was, however, able to convince the American Government that their agent in London had been completely mistaken in his view of the blockade. At the same time, there was an enormous rise in the export trade of the United States in 1915, surpassing all previous records, and making it evident to the American people that our methods of blockade were not injuring them. By repressing the Germans we were directly making the fortunes of the Americans. Too deeply absorbed ourselves in war work, we could not capture the world markets from which our blockading squadron excluded the enemy; so that large new fields of enterprise were opened to the people of the United States. It was the grand age of gold for them. The Americans redeemed the larger part of their debts to Europe, and became a leading creditor nation instead of one of the principal debtor nations. Important American newspapers began to ridicule their own Government for pretending that the British blockade had injured American oversea commerce, and with the real ground of tension thus removed the situation became very much easier.

At the same time, the important point in regard to our new method of search was developed by us in an unexpected manner; for Sir Edward Grey, in this technical affair, called to his aid Admiral Sir John Jellicoe. A report from the commander of the Grand Fleet was forwarded to the American authorities. The report of the British admiral was, like most of the work of our leading sailors for generations, a creative piece of legislation in international sea law, animated with such soundness and justice that every blockading Power was almost certain in time of need to adopt it. That is to say, Sir John Jellicoe did not speak merely in the immediate interests of his own blockading squadrons and his own nation; he showed there were reasons of permanent and universal force in our methods of search. It was, of course, the newly-extended power of the submarine that brought about the new developments. Also, the increased bulk of cargoes in large modern ships and the ease with which concealment could be made of small parcels of exceedingly valuable metals for high-speed steel alloys made examination in port necessary. Sir John wrote:

I dispute the contention, advanced in the American Note, that there is no difference between the search of a ship of 1,000 tons and one of 20,000 tons. The fallacy of the statement must be apparent to anyone who has ever carried out such a search at sea. There are other facts which render it necessary to bring vessels into port for search. The most important is the manner in which those in command of German submarines . . . attack and sink merchant vessels on the high seas, without visiting the ship, and therefore without any examination of the cargo. This procedure renders it unsafe for a neutral vessel, which is being examined by officers from a British ship, to remain stopped on the high sea. *It is therefore in the interests of the neutrals themselves that the examination should be conducted in port.*

Surely the hammer-stroke of that last sentence is a masterpiece. Robert Louis Stevenson should have lived to read it. He had a high opinion of the powers of expression of our old fighting admirals, and it would have kindled him to find that our new fighting admirals could fire out ideas as well as they could fire out shells. After this reply to American contentions the genuine current of public opinion in the United States turned in favour of our methods of blockade, and the only remaining criticism of importance was that our Government should bury the Declaration of London, use the incomplete old British doctrine of continuous voyage in its complete American form of the doctrine of ultimate destination, and proclaim and exercise the most rigorous blockade possible.

The Declaration of London

For many months, however, the new Coalition Cabinet of Great Britain remained apparently attached to the Declaration of London. Despite the Declaration of March, 1915, for preventing commodities of every kind reaching Germany, cotton was not listed as contraband until August 20th, 1915. According to a passage in Sir Edward Grey's reply to the Government of the United States, cotton had continued to enter Germany up to June, 1915. The fact seems to have been that our Foreign Office and its assistant committees were averse to using direct blockading methods, and content with the very slow and very

HOW A GERMAN SUBMARINE MINE-LAYER WORKED IN THE HIGH SEAS.

Sectional drawing of the captured German submarine mine-layer UC5, indicating the method of sowing mines in the track of hostile shipping. One of the most interesting features of the UC5 was the jumping wire, to facilitate the submarine's passage through net defences and entanglements under water. The upper illustration shows a released mine rising from the sea bed, while its carrier-cage remains stationary to anchor the machine.

FOILED! A DESTROYER FLOTILLA CAUGHT BY SEARCHLIGHTS WHEN ON THE POINT OF SUCCESS.

Battleships lying at anchor off a naval port are always liable to attack by enemy destroyers. The operation is a dangerous one for the destroyers, but that fact only adds zest to it as an exhilarating adventure. In this spirited drawing Mr. Padday gives an impression of a destroyer flotilla being detected and foiled when on the very point of success. Baffled by the beams converging on them from searchlights at sea and on shore, and made an easy target by them for the battleships' heavy guns, the destroyers have no choice but to make a run for it. The sailor astride the torpedo-tube is looking through the range-finder.

leaky methods of getting guarantees from the neutral funnel States by means of coaling arrangements and other economic factors.

In a White Paper published on January 4th, 1916, it was stated that the enemy's export trade had then been practically stopped, and that with the curtailment of his credit in neutral countries his imports from such countries would automatically diminish. No figures were given in connection with German export trade from August, 1914, to February, 1915—the months in which Mr. Winston Churchill said that we were exercising such economic pressure against Germany that she would be helpless by November, 1915. It was, indeed, admitted that neutrals had freely been ordering German goods in the first seven months of the war, and receiving them under the terms of the Declaration of London. But it was stated that from March, 1915, to September, 1915, German and Austrian imports into the United States had fallen to the value of £4,400,000, as against a value of £24,800,000 obtaining before the war. It was also stated that the latest returns showed a great diminution of Germany's commerce with the United States to only eight per cent. of its peace-time volume.

The writer of the White Paper then pointed out that the plan of drawing up agreements with importers in Norway, Denmark, Holland, and Switzerland was being put into execution. Even in Sweden bodies of merchants had come to terms in regard to particular commodities of special importance, such as cotton and rubber. Undertakings backed by pecuniary penalties had been given, and many shipping lines had entered into engagements not to carry for enemy agents various articles of contraband. Rubber, copper, wool, hides, oil, tin, plumbago, and certain other metals were largely controlled by British authorities, with the result that their import into Germany had been stopped for some months without any serious friction with any neutral Government.

The other side of the case, however, was presented on January 24th, 1916, by Admiral Lord Beresford, in a letter from which we extract the following passages :

The conviction is gaining ground that had the Navy been allowed to act, and had we used our legitimate rights as a belligerent, the war would have been ended some months ago. We have neglected to use the tremendous force ready to our hands represented by the power of the Fleet.

I acknowledge there are difficulties now, but they are of our own creating. Preferential and permissive agreements with some neutrals have caused, and will cause more, difficulties. An effective blockade is impartial. Owing to want of decision and prompt action at the beginning of the war, we are now in a hopeless muddle and an inextricable tangle.

The following short summary of contradictory Orders-in-Council and Proclamations since August 4th, 1914, accounts for the position :

The Proclamation of August 4th, 1914, made eleven articles absolute contraband and fourteen articles conditional contraband, among the latter being foodstuffs, etc.

The Order-in-Council of August 20th, 1914, substituted the lists of the Proclamation of August 4th, 1914, for those of the Declaration of London.

Contradictory Orders-in-Council The Proclamation of September 21st, 1914, added nine more articles to the list of conditional contraband.

The Proclamation of October 29th, 1914, withdrew the list of September 21st, 1914, and made the whole of the previous articles mentioned in former Proclamations absolute contraband.

At the same time the Declaration of London Order-in-Council No. 2, 1914, annulled and replaced the earlier Order-in-Council of August 20th, 1914.

The Proclamation of December 23rd, 1914, again withdrew the list, and fresh lists of absolute contraband were published.

The Order-in-Council of March 11th, 1915 (owing to public pressure after murder and piracy on the high seas), added a large number of articles to the list of absolute contraband. With regard to this Order, the Prime Minister stated that "commodities *of every kind* were to be prevented from leaving or entering Germany." This intimation was received with acclamation throughout the country. The neutrals regarded this Order as a reprisal not coming under international law.

The Prime Minister stated one thing, the Order-in-Council stated another.

The Proclamation of May 27th, 1915, added some articles to the list of absolute contraband, and some articles to the list of conditional contraband. What becomes of the Prime Minister's statement that "commodities *of every kind* were to be prevented from leaving or entering Germany " ?

On August 21st, 1915, raw cotton was added to the list of absolute contraband, although all commodities were to be prevented from entering Germany after the Order-in-Council of March 11th, 1915. Thousands of bales of cotton, which are necessary in the manufacture of high explosives, entered Germany between March 11th, 1915, and August 21st, 1915. No wonder the end of the war is not yet in sight.

War is won by fighting ; not by confusing Proclamations and Orders-in-Council or the appointment of countless committees. Unshackle the Navy, and the result will be apparent in a few weeks.

It is reported that new orders have been issued to the Fleet this month (January, 1916) to the effect that German-Americans bearing American passports are not to be interfered with. The effect of this order, if true, will be to allow reservists once more to proceed to Germany.

Lord Beresford and public opinion The action of the Navy appears to be controlled by three different departments—the Foreign Office, the Board of Trade, and the Admiralty. Executive orders are given to the Fleet contrary to directions conveyed in Orders-in-Council. When is this foolery going to stop and the Navy be allowed to put a paralysing grip on Germany ?

If the Government wish to end the war, firm measures must be taken. Orders should be given to the Fleet immediately to exercise to the full its legal and legitimate use of sea-power, the only measure for bringing the war to an end, and the best assistance we can offer to our Allies. Why should not the four Navies of the Allies have a broad strategic plan of blockade and put it into action at once ?

The people have a right to demand that our rulers shall use the means they possess of beating the enemy. We cannot afford to throw away the powerful advantage we hold. Ship after ship has been captured by the Fleet, brought in for adjudication by the Prize Court, and released by order of the Foreign Office without coming before the Prize Court at all.

Can anything be more heartbreaking for officers and men of the Fleet than to feel that their power is crippled at such a time, knowing that if left to them the end of the war would soon be in sight ?

Lord Beresford did not speak for himself alone. Behind him an important current of public opinion made itself felt against the shackling of our blockading squadron

CAPTAIN CHARLES FRYATT, OF THE S.S. BRUSSELS.
On July 27th, 1916, with the Kaiser's personal sanction, Captain Charles Fryatt, captured on his ship Brussels, was put to death by the Germans in revenge for his legitimate defence, in March, 1915, of his ship from German submarines, for which he had been rewarded both by the G.E.R. Company and by the British Admiralty.

ON DANGEROUS DUTY IN THE DARDANELLES.
Two naval officers fishing a mine from the Dardanelles, apparently unconcerned that the machine might explode at any moment.

by the Foreign Office. At a meeting of City men in London, on February 14th, 1916, Lord Devonport was strongly supported when he, too, stated that the blockade was not being conducted in a satisfactory manner, and that the Foreign Office system of allowing contraband to enter Holland and Scandinavia, under guarantees from distribution agencies, was resulting in an immense amount of smuggling. In the House of Lords, a few days later, Lord Sydenham also pleaded for a closer blockade, and much discontent with the Foreign Office control of our naval pressure was expressed in the House of Commons.

Yet still both the Liberal-Radical and the Unionist party leaders remained bound to the decayed and offensive corpse of the Declaration of London. Sir Edward Grey had as Under-Secretary Lord Robert **Germany's sub-** Cecil, who at first fought with brilliant **marine operations** dexterity against the abandonment of the old peace-at-any-price Declaration and against the carrying out of the policy of a rigorous blockade, under the terms of the Declaration of March, 1915.

It is, of course, possible that the British Government was in a somewhat similar position in blockade affairs to that of the German Government. The German authorities had given their people to understand that the submarine campaign against our shipping would so reduce our strength as to compel us to sue for peace. First Mr. Winston Churchill vaguely, at the Guildhall banquet in November, 1914, and then afterwards Mr. Asquith definitely, in his speech on retaliatory measures against the enemy's proclamation of a war zone for submarine operations against our sea-borne commerce, had given our public to understand that Germany's economic strength would be sapped by our naval pressure. We know the German Government was prevented, by circumstances over which it had no control, from fulfilling its promises in regard to its submarine blockading campaign. But lacking the courage to acknowledge defeat by British force of arms, the directors of Germanic policy pretended to their people that they had abandoned submarine pressure out of consideration for President Woodrow Wilson's feelings. This left the German public much dissatisfied over an apparently weak political surrender to a neutral State in a matter of vital military importance.

In the case of the British Government we know that no hostile force of arms prevented our Navy from carrying

out the proposals made by our leading statesmen at two critical periods of the war. Our public, therefore, receiving no explanation of the delay in using the full restrictive power of the Fleet, grew restive and worried. According to Mr. Rudyard Kipling, our sailors were still more perplexed and upset. He who never hopes never despairs. If great expectations had not been excited by men in authority, profound disappointment would not have followed. Certain political considerations appear to have led to the abandonment of our declared policy of a rigorous blockade.

Yet the agitation of the public mind produced some effect. Our Foreign Office, into which the leader of our blockading squadron, Rear-Admiral Sir Dudley De Chair, went as naval adviser in February, 1916, invented a new instrument of restriction in the black list. Beginning in February, first with Egypt, then with Greece, Holland, Scandinavia, Portugal, **New instrument** and Spain, the leading agents of the **of restriction** Germanic Empires were entered on black lists and all consignments to these persons or firms were liable to capture. In March, enemies and neutral agents of enemies in Argentina, Uruguay, Brazil, Ecuador, Peru, Central America, East Indies, and the Philippines were blacklisted. And finally persons and corporations in the United States engaged in contraband commerce with the Germanic Empires were entered on the list, which practically covered all the important productive centres of the world. Violent protests arose from the German organisations in the United States, but "unhyphenated" American opinion did not appear to be deeply perturbed.

Lord Robert Cecil was made Minister for Blockade, with Sir Dudley De Chair as his adviser. The poor harvest in Germany in the autumn of 1915 began to tell on the

THE MESSENGER OF DESTRUCTION.
Hoisting a live torpedo aboard a warship by means of a hand crane. A stalwart seaman is keeping the weapon steady with a rope round the stern.

condition of the enemy urban classes of the humbler sort. The potato crop especially had been scanty and bad in quality, as it was in our islands, and the great German landowners did not relax anything in their methods of wringing wealth out of the misfortunes of their country. A new food dictator, Count von Batocki, had to evade fighting the dominant Prussian oligarchy by bringing pressure upon the peasantry of Bavaria, Saxony, and Würtemberg. But none of these semi-sovereign States of the Empire would release its peculiar food resources for the benefit of the great Prussian cities. There was still no peril of famine ; but food grew scarcer in the interval of anxiety between the ending of the old supplies from the harvest of 1915 and the beginning of the

[Official photograph.
AN OBJECT OF PARTICULAR CURIOSITY.
Submarine patrol overhauling a suspicious sailing craft in a suspected area along the coast.

UP FOR A PIPE AND A BLOW. *[Official photograph.*
Interesting impression of the wake left by a submarine when under gas motors ; the above-water speed of such craft is about twenty knots.

new supplies from the harvest of 1916. There was just enough general discomfort to aggravate the gloom of the national mind when military affairs on both frontiers were unsatisfactory.

In an atmosphere of victory the Germans would scarcely have felt the power of our Fleet in the restriction of their food supplies. The loss of the ordinary imports of Russian fodder, cheap Russian eggs, and grain was a more direct blow than our blockading operations inflicted. By partly keeping from the enemy, in the summer of 1915, the wheat

and meat of Argentina and the United States, and raising throughout the civilised world the price of all foodstuffs, we helped our eastern allies in making things somewhat uncomfortable for the munition makers and transport workers of Germany. Yet it is doubtful if we diminished in an appreciable degree the productive energies of the classes that armed, manœuvred, and served the German fighting men. At times the enemy seemed to consider it worth while making us fancy he was weakening from lack of proper nourishment. This was usually a sign that he was about to renew his submarine attacks on combatant and neutral shipping, or a symptom that a surprise was intended in some sudden, furious offensive movement. When neither of these alternatives obtained, the organised outcry about **Cry of "Starving** food was a Prussian device for attempt-   **Germany"** ing an increased control over Bavarian domestic matters, for the energetic Prussian believed in trying to make even an ill wind turn some of his windmills.

Happily, our new Minister for Blockade and his new naval adviser continued to work with quite a Prussian-like energy over the problems of their work. An Order-in-Council, issued on March 30th, 1916, removed some of the diplomatic fetters from our Fleet. Both conditional and absolute contraband were made liable to capture if found on a neutral vessel bound for a neutral port but destined for the enemy. Goods consigned to a person known to have forwarded goods to the enemy were also made liable to condemnation. No vessel or her cargo was to be immune from capture for breach of blockade, simply on the ground that she was at the time on the way to a non-blockaded port.

This made a great rent in the Declaration of London, and at last, after nearly two years of debilitating and hesitant timidity, the codes of rules which never had any legal force and which were injurious to the interests of our country were completely abolished. In July, 1916, the Declaration of London was abandoned by an Order-in-Council reviving our maritime rights. The confiscation of contraband cargoes and of neutral ships carrying contraband was to take place if more than half the cargo were contraband. Any neutral ship carrying goods indirectly to the enemy and running the blockade was made liable to capture and condemnation on her next voyage. The principle of ultimate destination was made applicable to cases of contraband and blockade. Hostile destination of contraband articles was to be presumed to exist, unless the contrary were shown, in all doubtful cases.

Thus the British and French Fleets were set free to use their full force of economic constriction against the enemy. Whether popular agitation gradually produced this desirable result may be doubted, though the student of the history of true democratic control of national destinies would like to think so. It is just possible that the military and naval successes of the Allies in the summer of 1916 removed the obstacles that had been dreaded by our Foreign Office. What those obstacles exactly were will not be fully known until the great struggle is ended. Meanwhile, we would again point out that only cotton, of which the enemy had obtained a vast store, was a decisive article of contraband. By July, 1916, all opportunity had passed for surprising him with a shortage of powder material and with no plant for any substitute. Lost was the chance of bringing about a sudden collapse of the Germanic Empires by an extraordinary manœuvre of blockade. Yet one of the greatest of English poets had the courage to say of God :

> But Thy most awful instrument
> In working out a pure intent,
> Is man arrayed for mutual slaughter :
> Yea ! Carnage is Thy daughter !

If Providence presides over the ghastliest fields of battle as well as over the happiest scenes of home life, we may be, in our apparently great mistakes, directed towards some dreadful yet purifying work by ways we cannot trace in advance. Perhaps Germany—the modern Assyria—could soon have recovered from a short, disastrous war, and would have once more become a menacing force. Perhaps only a long, wearing struggle could so completely exhaust her as to make her permanently impotent for evil.

Slow pressure of sea-power

The pressure of sea-power has always worked very slowly. A century ago it failed for twenty years to reduce France directly by exhaustion. Napoleon was really brought down by great military defeats—Moscow, Leipzig, and Waterloo—though the British Navy prepared the way by intercepting foreign trade, and causing discomfort and restiveness throughout the territories dominated by the great hostile captain. At the present time sea-power has lost much of its old bite. When we last used it in a large way, land transit was slow and costly. Armies could be moved more quickly by sea than they could by land, with the result that the power of the impending stroke resided in Great Britain. But railways and modern large canals have modified the situation.

"The power of the impending stroke," as a wise thinker has pointed out, has, to a considerable extent, passed from our Fleet to the Armies of the highly-developed Central Empires. The magnificent German railway system has worked in war time as punctually as in peace time, with a scarcely reduced train service. Strengthened by the German canal system, it fights against our marine system of transportation practically from Rotterdam to Bagdad. Better guns were able to be transported by rail and road to the Turkish forces at Bagdad than we were able to carry by sea and river to General Townshend at Ctesiphon.

Mercantile marine on war service

As we have pointed out in a previous chapter, for nearly a year we blockaded ourselves more than we did Germany, by diverting nearly half of our mercantile marine to warlike services, especially in connection with our diverse gambles in oversea expeditions. The extraordinary rise in our cost of freightage at first more than balanced the slight economic inconveniences which the enemy suffered direct through the pressure of our Fleet. For all we did under the Declaration of London was to restrict German shipping to the Baltic and the territorial waters of Sweden and Norway, Denmark and Holland, and close German ports to a small and extremely inadequate list of contraband cargoes. For many months neutral ships were able to enter German ports with general cargoes of war material. Though the freights were heavy, the goods had afterwards to bear only the minimum rates of the German State railways and canals.

When we gradually increased the stringency and scope of our blockading action the enemy was controlling in Europe a population of nearly 140 millions, in an area of 650,000 square miles that included some of the best wheat-producing lands on the Continent. He was in railway communication with countries in Asia Minor, giving him tropical or sub-tropical produce, and he possessed a very great number of steam-ploughs, and an inexhaustible monopoly of potash that could fertilise almost any land into crop production. With a conquered population of more than thirty millions to act as her helots in agriculture and manufacture, Germany was practically secure from swift collapse through our blockade.

THE FRENCH NAVY IN ACTION IN THE MIDDLE SEA.
The "75" gun on an unusual element. The celebrated French ordnance engaging a German submarine in the Mediterranean, from a transport laden with French Colonial troops from Morocco. A great quality of the "75" was its mobility and lightness of construction.

INDIAN BATTERY IN ACTION.

IN GERMAN EAST AFRICA.

SHADOWS IN THE EAST: THE DEFENCE OF INDIA.

By F. A. McKenzie.

Why Frontier Trouble was Anticipated—Growing Unrest—How the Tribes were Armed—Rumours of British Defeats—The Amir of Afghanistan's Attitude—The Position of Aden—The Attack on Shaikh Sa'id—Importance of Lahaj—The Abdali Sultan—Battle of Lahaj—The British Retire—Difficulties of Climate—Loss of Prestige—General Younghusband Appointed to Aden Brigade—Desert Skirmishes—False Turkish Claims—Fighting Around the Gulf of Oman—Arab Revolt against Turkey—Grand Sherif of Mecca's Position—Importance of the Revolt—Trouble in Upper Burma—The Kachin Uprising—No Trifling with Treason—Position on the North-West Frontier—The Jehad of the Khostwals—How Captain Jotham Earned his V.C.—The North Waziristan Militia—Trouble with the Mohmands—The Raid on Shabkadar—Influence of the Fakirs—Some Examples of Fanaticism—The Malakand Column—Fighting around Shabkadar—The Battle of September 24th—A Terrible March.—The Charge of the 21st Lancers—Colonel Scriven's Splendid Example—An Outbreak in Swat—Minor Troubles—How the British Soldiers Fought—Facing Hardships Gladly.

MANY people acquainted with the conditions of life on the mountain borders of India assumed, as a matter of course, that the outbreak of war between Britain and Germany would be quickly followed by serious disturbances in Central Asia and in Arabia. It was well known that Germany had for some time previous to the war been carefully preparing for a propaganda among the Mohammedan peoples with a view to starting a Jehad, or Holy War, against the British. But the real reasons why trouble on the frontiers was anticipated almost as a matter of course went much deeper than any external propaganda. For generations unrest had swept periodically over the Mohammedan tribes of the mountainous North-West Frontier. They are naturally robber tribes, living in mountain fastnesses and preying as opportunity offers on their weaker neighbours. Independent, hating control, warriors by birth, by training, and by instinct, fighting is their normal life, and it was only the fear and authority of the British Raj that kept many of them temporarily at peace.

The history of the Indian Frontier for half a century before the war broke out was one long record of wars, raids, and punitive expeditions. For every raid that took place a score or more were prevented by the prudence,

the diplomacy, and the able management of the British Political Agents on the border. What was true of the Indian North-West was true at least in equal degree of South-West Arabia. The British held on to the rocks and barren sands of Aden and its neighbourhood. Beyond that, they tried by friendly arrangements with some of the many sultans in the desert lands to maintain cordial relations. But Southern Arabia claimed the distinction of being, with Central Formosa, the most perilous and the least explored territory in the world. The traveller who moved among the tribes did so at hourly risk to his life. Racial antipathy, fierce religious hatreds, and centuries of carefully fostered fury against white civilisation had made Southern Arabia one of the danger-spots of the world.

Before the outbreak of war there were various indications of growing unrest on the Indian Frontier, unrest quite independent of any disputes between European nations. "Conditions on the British side of the frontier are arousing much uneasiness," wrote the Bombay correspondent of the "Times," in February, 1914. Lawlessness and insecurity prevailed to a greater extent than for many years. Robber bands from the mountains achieved such success in their raids that in case after case villagers harboured them, bribed them, and shielded them to secure their protection. It was evident that the

INDIA'S FIGHTING PRINCES.

[Official Photograph.

Lieut.-General Sir Pertab Singh with (on his right) his son Maharaj Kumar Dolat Singh, and (on his left) the Rajah of Rutlam.

Now, surely, was the opportunity of the North-West. Now, if ever, was the time to strike a united blow.

It was at this moment that the British were to reap the fruits of the many years of just, conciliatory, and sympathetic dealing with those troublesome clans. The Amir of Afghanistan, whose position gives him the religious standing of a King of Islam among the North-West tribes, declared himself to be a friend of Britain, and kept true to his declaration. He and his advisers were not going to allow themselves to be the tools of a German campaign for world conquest, however well disguised under the plea of a Holy War of Mohammedan nations. Several of the most powerful tribes, which in former years had been active against us, also refused to attack the British. The result was that what might well have been a serious and concerted campaign by the Central Asian Mohammedan tribes degenerated into a few sporadic and apparently unconnected risings, which could be dealt with in detail, not without trouble and some hard fighting, but without any really considerable effect outside their own territories.

Shortly after the outbreak of war with Turkey, on October 31st, 1914, it became clear that the Turks, in co-operation with a number of the Arab tribes were preparing an advance against the Aden Protectorate. The Turks had gathered in some strength on the Shaikh Sa'id Peninsula, which runs out to the south of the Red Sea towards the Isle of Perim. The 29th Indian Infantry Brigade, under Brigadier-General J. H. V. Cox, C.B., then on its way from India to Suez, was

[*Official photograph. Crown copyright reserved.*

SIR DOUGLAS HAIG INTRODUCING LIEUT.-GENERAL SIR PERTAB SINGH TO
GENERAL JOFFRE.

native tribes were acquiring far better weapons than they had previously possessed. The trade in arms along the Persian Gulf continued, despite the utmost vigilance of our naval patrols. Weapons landed on the coast by European agents—weapons, some of them it is feared made in England by manufacturers whose greed killed their patriotism—were taken through Persia and Baluchistan to the Himalayas, and found a ready market among the tribes. Other weapons were made in Afridi factories. Mullahs—fierce preachers of Mohammedan intolerance— were at work provoking discontent and stirring up revolt.

It can readily be imagined how news of the outbreak of war and of the result of the first battles spread among the tribes of the North-West. Tales of the German occupation of Belgium, of the retreat of the British Army from Mons, of the German advance almost to the gates of Paris, of the heavy losses of the French, and of the Russian disaster in North-East Prussia were carried up by fakirs and pilgrims from the bazaars of the Indian cities to the village headquarters of the tribes. It was known that Britain had called on India to help her, and that regiments of the Indian Army were leaving in great numbers for Europe.

ordered to interrupt its voyage to capture Shaikh Sa'id and destroy the Turkish works, armaments, and wells there. On November 10th transports conveying three battalions of the 29th Indian Infantry Brigade and the 23rd Sikh Pioneers arrived off the coast of the peninsula. They were accompanied by H.M.S. Duke of Edinburgh, which opened fire on the Turkish defences while the transports were seeking a satisfactory landing-place. The point that had been at first selected proved impossible on account of the weather. The troops landed a little way off, under cover of the fire of the warship. They stormed the Turkish positions and compelled the enemy to retreat, leaving his field-guns behind. The sailors took active part in the fighting with the troops, and a naval demolition party assisted, on November 11th, in destroying the Turkish works. Having accomplished its task, the British force re-embarked and continued its journey. It was not considered advisable at this time to push an expedition into the country to attack the Turks there. The Turks, consequently, remained in some force on the northern boundary of the Aden Protectorate.

Reduction of Shaikh Sa'id

Off Schleswig: British destroyers and seaplanes in action during a storm, March 25th, 1916.

Off Jutland: Lucky shot destroys German torpedo and saves a British warship.

Camera impression of the great sea fight of Jutland Bank : B

troyers in hot pursuit passing a sinking German light cruiser.

Daylight signalling in the British Navy: Heliographing a long=distance message by the aid of a searchlight.

Seven months later they reoccupied Shaikh Sa'id and endeavoured from there to effect a landing on the north coast of the Isle of Perim. This attack was successfully repulsed by the garrison of the island, the 23rd Sikh Pioneers.

In the spring of 1915 a Turkish force from the Yeamana district crossed the frontier of the Aden Hinterland and advanced towards Lahaj. Lahaj was at this time one of the most important towns in Southern Arabia. Placed in an oasis, surrounded by a fertile plain with the deserts beyond, it was the centre of trade between Aden and the Hinterland, inhabited by a prosperous agricultural people, the Abdali. Its Sultans formerly claimed rule over the Aden Peninsula, which Britain took from them in

Turks advance on Lahaj

1839 as punishment for an outrage on a shipwrecked British crew. For some years after our occupation of Aden there had been frequent fighting between the British and the Abdali, the latter seeking to reconquer their lost port. In recent years our relations had been friendly, the British paying the Abdali Sultan a subsidy for the occupation of certain land in the interior and protecting him and his agricultural people against the fierce desert tribes who hemmed them in.

Under our protection the Sultan of Lahaj had waxed very prosperous. His city, with its palace, its gallows—built for ornament rather than use—its purely Oriental life, its fine horses, its little show army, and its constant traffic in camels and caravans, seemed like a vision out of the "Arabian Nights." When war broke out the Abdali Sultan proved that his loyalty to Britain was real. Though other tribes turned against us he came to our side and prepared to help us. He soon made himself an object of special

PATHANS IN A WARM CORNER. *[Crown copyright.*
A German shell bursting in front of a sector of trench on the western front held by the Pathans.

detestation to the Turks and to many of the surrounding tribes by his open and unwavering friendship for Britain.

The Sultan sent word to General D. S. L. Shaw, commanding the Aden Brigade, that the Turks were advancing from Mawyiah to attack him, and asked for help. General Shaw ordered the Aden Movable Column, under Lieutenant-Colonel H. E. A. Pearson, towards Lahaj. The Aden Camel Troop was despatched to reconnoitre. It discovered a strong Turkish force beyond Lahaj, supported by a large number of Arab tribesmen. The Camel Troop fell back on Lahaj, where it was reinforced by the advance guard of the Aden Movable Column, numbering two hundred and fifty rifles, with two ten-pounder guns. This advance guard had moved up under most

trying conditions. The heat was intense, **Intense heat and** there was great shortage of water, and **no water** it was difficult to make any progress over the heavy, sandy plains. The main body of the Aden Column was so delayed by difficulties of transport and by shortage of water that it did not reach Lahaj at all.

Our force in the Sultan's capital found itself faced by several thousand Turkish troops, with twenty guns. In addition, Arab tribesmen had rallied by the thousand to help the Turks. We on our part were backed by a few hundred men, the Sultan of Lahaj's little native army. Our troops were suffering terribly from the climate and from the shortage of water. It seemed as though they must be wholly swallowed up. To add to the difficulties, the Arab camp followers of the Aden Troop deserted them in a body at the most critical hour and took with them all their camels.

Fighting opened on the evening of Sunday, July 4th. Time after time the enemy attacked our front, and time

LINKING-UP IN THE ADVANCE.
Signallers of an Indian regiment putting up a telephone wire in a French village communicating with headquarters.

WITH THE ROYAL FLYING CORPS IN INDIA.

War took the aeroplane to practically every corner of the world, carrying men over almost every water—the Hellespont, the Tigris, the Congo, and the Nile. The aeroplane seen here was photographed when crossing Kabul River, soaring above the pontoon bridge near Peshawar.

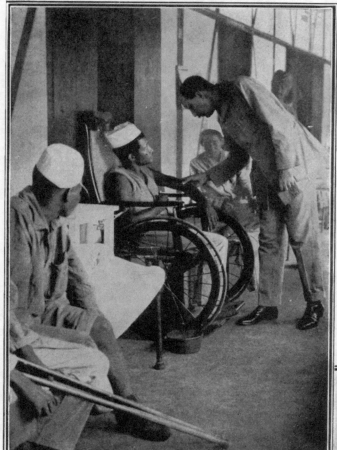

THE NATIVE HOSPITAL, BOMBAY.
Wounded Indian soldiers on the veranda.

prepared us for the difficulties which every experienced traveller knew we would have to face. In the official report on the operations issued by the Government of India much stress was laid on " the intense heat, sand, and shortage of water." " The desertion of the camel-drivers and the severe climatic conditions so delayed and distressed the main body as to necessitate a withdrawal from Lahaj," the report stated. But the severe heat of the climate, the potential treachery of hired Arabs, and the shortage of water were all of them factors which had been familiar from the beginning to the Indian authorities, and, one might suppose, ought to have been allowed for.

Reinforcements for Aden

The British force fell back on the Kaur, immediately outside the Aden Peninsula. The Turks followed them up and occupied Shaikh-Othman, a town about two miles inland from Aden Harbour. This place was formerly part of the Sultanate of Lahaj, and was now within the British Protectorate. The Turks at this stage held practically the whole of the Aden Hinterland, except immediately around the peninsula. They had reoccupied Shaikh Sa'id and had destroyed Lahaj. Some appreciation of the real perils of the situation apparently reached the Indian authorities, and it was decided to increase the Aden garrison. Major-General Sir G. J. Younghusband, a soldier with a distinguished career, succeeded for a time to the command of the Aden Brigade. General Younghusband was a man who had won fame both as a soldier

after time they were driven off. The Turkish artillery was much stronger than ours, but the men of the Royal Artillery strove, by courage and skill, to make up for the inequality in numbers. They showed a devotion to duty which afterwards drew a warm tribute from the general commanding the Aden Brigade. Before long the Turkish artillery had kindled fires in different parts of Lahaj, and our men were in danger of being outflanked and cut off by the flocks of Arab horsemen. The Sultan was killed with many of his men. Our troops struggled to defend the capital as long as they could, hoping every hour for the

THE LADY HARDINGE WAR HOSPITAL, BOMBAY.
Exterior view of one of the finest buildings in the magnificent capital of Western India. The hospital was planned and organised on a scale that did honour to the British Raj.

arrival of the main body of the Aden Column. Hour after hour they waited in vain. Relief did not come. Next day there was nothing to be done but to fall back from Lahaj towards Aden.

Our losses included three British officers wounded. But our main loss was not so much in men as in prestige. A friendly Sultan had been killed, his town captured by the enemy, and his Sultanate swept away. The news of what had happened spread abroad throughout Arabia and inflicted a very serious blow on British authority. Our men at Lahaj had fought splendidly, but their task had proved beyond their strength. We had not been able to send forward an adequate number of troops to meet the Turks, and we do not seem to have made such arrangements for transport and for water supply as would have

and as an author. Since 1878, when he served in the Afghan War, he had shared in many campaigns. He was in the Sudan in 1885 and in the North-West Frontier War of 1886. From there he had gone to the Burma War, and in due course he made one of the Chitral Relief Force, writing a notable book on that campaign. He was in the fighting in the Philippines, in the Spanish-American War ; he was severely wounded in South Africa, and later on he shared in the big punitive expedition against the Mohmands on the Indian Frontier.

It would have been difficult indeed to find a soldier more adept in the warfare and diplomacy now necessary in this region.

On July 20th, 1915, troops from Aden, the 28th (Frontier Force) Brigade, a battery of Royal Horse Artillery, and a

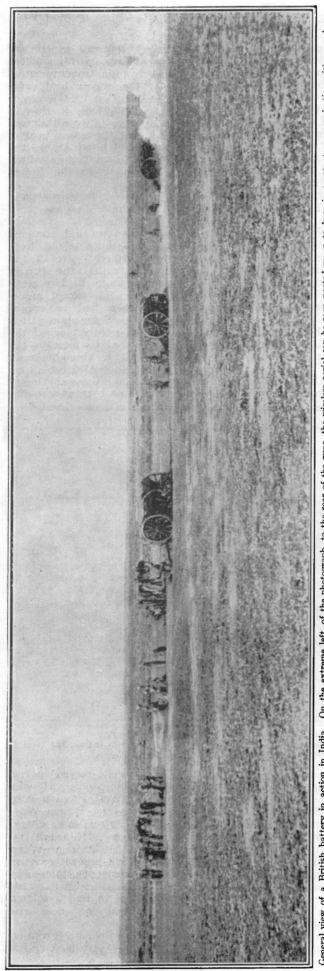

General view of a British battery in action in India. On the extreme left of the photograph, to the rear of the guns, the wireless aerial can be seen posted so as to keep in constant communication with aeroplanes that directed the fire from above.

Gunners making signals to acknowledge a wireless message received from an aeroplane. Broad strips of white cloth, plainly visible at a great height, were stretched on the ground and arranged variously on the principle of the arms of a semaphore.

WITH THE INDO-BRITISH FORCES IN INDIA : AIRMEN AND ARTILLERYMEN ACTING IN CONCERT.

detachment of Sappers and Miners, under the command of Lieut.-Colonel A. M. S. Elsmie, a soldier well trained in frontier fighting, surprised the Turks at Shaikh-Othman, completely defeated them and drove them out of the place. Between fifty and sixty Turks were killed and wounded, and several hundred men, mostly Arabs, were made prisoners. This success was followed up in the following month by an attack by a small column on a Turkish post between Lahaj and Shaikh-Othman. The Turks were driven from the town. Another attack in a different direction was equally successful. Reports reached Aden that the Turks were preparing to retire from Lahaj itself, and in September a column under Colonel Elsmie set out in the direction of Waht. Here it surprised a force of seven hundred Turks, with eight guns, who were supported by about a thousand Arabs. The Turks were driven back, and Waht fell into our hands. The troops were greatly aided both on sea and land by the co-operation of H.M.S. Philomel, under Captain Hill-Thompson.

A series of minor engagements and skirmishes between the Turks and Arabs and our own troops followed. It was found impossible for us to hold the country far inland. Early in 1916 the Turks claimed that the British had been

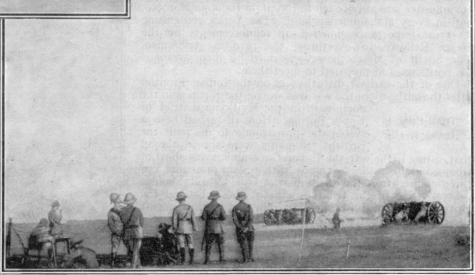

RIDING PILLION.
A British and an Indian soldier enjoying a ride on a camel, with an amused escort on foot.

driven back on to Aden itself, and had retreated as far as where they were covered by the fires of the warships, where they had been inactive for some months. Many of the Turkish claims were greatly exaggerated, and some wholly false. In February, 1916, Major Newman asked in the British Parliament for any information about the fighting near Aden. Mr. Chamberlain said that the Turkish claim of success which had recently been put forward would seem to have been founded on an engagement which took place on January 12th between a reconnoitring column of the Aden garrison and a Turkish force in the neighbourhood of Shaikh-

Othman. The loss on our side was one British officer and thirty-five Indian rank and file killed, and four British and thirty-five Indian rank and file wounded. The enemy losses were severe, amounting to about two hundred killed and wounded. The British column was neither annihilated nor defeated, but withdrew when the purpose of the movement was completed.

Later on, the Turks officially claimed to have scored a substantial victory in further heavy fighting around Shaikh-Othman and Bir-Ahmad. This was a sheer invention. In January, 1916, the Aden Movable Column moved out to protect some friendly troops to the east of the Aden Protectorate against Turkish troops who had been sent to coerce them. Our column located the Turkish force near Subar, and defeated it. The general position was so unsatisfactory, however, that in April, 1916, it was decided, on the suggestion of the Government of India, that ladies should not be allowed to land at Aden without receiving permission from the Commander-in-Chief in India.

In the region around the Gulf of Oman there was considerable Arab unrest, and early in January, 1915, some three thousand Arabs attacked our outpost lines. The entire available British force promptly moved out against them, attacked and defeated them, and compelled the Arabs to flee into the interior with a loss of over three hundred killed and wounded. In April and in May, 1915, there were two other attacks, one against the British post at Jask, and one against the post at Chahbar; both were driven off with loss.

Three thousand Arabs defeated

In the summer of 1916 the situation in Arabia was suddenly and startlingly altered by a revolt by the Arabs of the Hejaz against Turkey. The independence of Arabia was proclaimed. Jedda, the port of Mecca, was seized, and the Turkish garrison compelled to surrender, and the Turks were turned out of the Holy City of Mecca itself. The Grand Sherif of Mecca openly renounced his allegiance to the Sultan. He was supported by the Arabs of Western and Central Arabia. The causes of the revolt were various. The Arabs believed that Mehmed V., Sultan of Turkey, was really in the hands of the Germans —as he was—and that the Germans were using him and his religious position for their own purposes. It was said that Enver Pasha, who had recently visited the Mecca district, had aroused intense anger by inaugurating a

FOLLOWING THE "EYES" OF THE GUNS.
Battery of British guns in action in India, their fire directed by an aeroplane hovering overhead. At the table in the foreground wireless operators were engaged in taking down the instructions transmitted to the battery by the aeroplane.

FIRST-AID FOR THE FIRST WOUNDED.
Indian casualties, some walking, others being conveyed by stretchers to a regimental aid post, consisting of a picturesque old farmhouse. A doctor was receiving the patients, and gave them temporary treatment.

number of drastic anti-Arab measures—hanging, shooting, and imprisoning a number of Moslem Arabs. It was also believed that the Turks, who had issued false statements throughout the world that the British had shelled certain sacred Mohammedan shrines, had actually done this themselves. This revolt of the rulers and people of the sacred cities of Mohammedanism had far more than a local effect. Its influence was at once felt in Egypt, in India, in Morocco, and in every Mohammedan land. The Turks, recognising its great importance, hurried up reinforcements by the Hejaz Railway to overthrow the revolting tribesmen. The Sherif of Mecca, however, armed his men, arranged his positions, and prepared to meet them.

One of the earliest disturbances on the Indian Frontier after the outbreak of the war was among the Kachins in the

Tribal rising on Indian Frontier

north-east, in the Myitkyna district of Upper Burma. Here there had been a systematic propaganda to discredit the British. Rumours were spread abroad that, owing to the war, the Indian Government was short of troops, and the headman Thama, with a Shan pretender and three followers from the Katha district, tried to bring about a general rising of the tribes. Some of these, beyond the British administrative border, joined in, and for the moment the prospect looked somewhat black. A detachment of a hundred men of the 64th Pioneers, accompanied by Mr. F. C. Lowis, executive engineer in charge of the Myitkyna-Putao road, was attacked by the people of Wawang on January 29th, 1915. The troops at once cleared the district. The Kachins fought obstinately, holding each point of vantage as long as they could, and then retiring to another along a very steep and thickly-wooded road. But they were driven in turn from place after place. They

made a final stand at a hastily built stockade. The Pioneers drove them from that at the point of the bayonet. Two headmen were killed.

A British movable column was subsequently formed and travelled through the disaffected country, stamping out any signs of rebellion wherever seen. Our troops, moving in detachments quickly from point to point, broke the back of the uprising and gained a complete success. The Shan pretender, accompanied by some of his followers, fled across the border, but villagers beyond our frontier captured him and brought him in. Three Kachin leaders were arrested and sentenced to transportation for life.

The Indian authorities showed clearly in dealing with the Kachins that they did not intend to treat lightly any disloyalty in those hours of crisis for the Empire. The strongest influences were used to pre-

No clemency for the rebels

vent the headmen from turning against us. Where these influences failed, punishment was prompt and severe.

In the north-west trouble first came to a head in the Tochi Valley, in the strip of mountain land between British India and Afghanistan. It became evident towards the end of 1914 that great attempts were being made to stir up the frontier tribes, and to enlist them in a Jehad against the British.

Some of the most influential Mullahs in this strip of independent territory called the tribesmen together and led 2,000 of the Khostwals into British territory. On November 29th, 1914, a portion of the North Waziristan Militia, under Major G. B. Scott, attacked and defeated the tribesmen and drove them back in a demoralised condition. The action reflected great credit on the militia

THATCHED COTTAGE-HOSPITAL IN FRANCE.
Severely wounded Indian soldier leaving the aid post on a stretcher to be put aboard a motor-ambulance. After having had his injuries dressed he was sent down to the base.

GURKHAS CAPTURING A GERMAN TRENCH: THE FIRST LINE.

The Gurkhas inspired the Germans with particular dread, not only by their courage, but also by their silent movement and the deadly use of their peculiar weapon the kukri. This photograph shows first-line Gurkhas capturing a trench.

MAKING GOOD THE CAPTURE: THE SECOND LINE.

Second-line Gurkhas rushing up through the wood amid shell fire to win the trench. The smile on the face of the officer in the foreground suggests that the conduct of his company met with his complete approval.

hills and to threaten our frontier. Late in March, between 7,000 and 8,000 Khostwals assembled together and threatened Miranshah. The Bannu Movable Column and a portion of the North Waziristan Militia again moved out under the command of Brigadier-General V. B. Fane. The British force was directed with great skill. One part of it, under Major Scott, made a long night march and gained a position in the rear of the enemy. Another portion, under Lieut.-Colonel H. E. Lowis, of the 10th Jats, made a direct frontal attack. The British were completely successful. Our troops struck at the enemy in the front and in the rear. On our right **Eight thousand** there was a force of cavalry to guard our **Khostwals surrounded** flank. Our attack was supported by the fire of a mountain battery of artillery. Two hundred Khostwals were killed and three hundred wounded, and those left hastily retreated. It was officially stated afterwards that our success was largely due to the skilful manner in which the column under Major Scott had gained its position during the night in rear of the enemy, in time to combine with the frontal attack.

For some months after this there was peace along this part of the frontier—an armed peace however, where the tribesmen were restrained by the sound common-sense of our civil authorities, and where a force of troops waited behind, ready to deal with trouble immediately it came to a head.

At the end of 1914 reports were received from different quarters of serious trouble brewing in the Mohmand country. The Mohmands are a powerful Pathan tribe, living partly in Afghanistan and partly in the districts around Peshawar. They are turbulent, fanatical, and quarrelsome; ready subjects for fiery Mullahs to stir up to revolt. Long before the outbreak of the war they had been in repeated conflicts with the British. Between 1872 and 1908 there had been several expeditions against them. In January, 1915, there came a raid in the neighbourhood of Shabkadar, a fortified post eighteen miles north of Peshawar, but it was easily driven off. In April it was reported that the Mohmands were collecting with a view to raiding Shabkadar. It was evident that a serious blow was now being planned, and the British forces in the district were greatly strengthened. The Khyber Movable Column was brought up and other troops held in readiness. On April 18th the tribesmen attempted to advance, but were met by our troops and driven back to the hills, where the British did not attempt to follow them.

GURKHAS IN BOMB ACTION.
Gurkhas bombing their way along a German trench in France.

and on the officer in charge of the small force. Fresh troops were sent up, and Major-General H. O'Donnell proceeded with the Bannu Movable Column and part of the North Waziristan Militia to keep the tribesmen in check. On January 7th, 1915, the militia, after a long march, came in touch with the enemy, and despite the fact that odds were greatly against them, immediately attacked with the greatest enthusiasm. Some fifty or sixty of the enemy were killed, and the Khostwals were driven in confusion over the frontier. Among the many brave individual deeds of the British troops during this fight one specially stood out. Captain E. Jotham was in a desperate situation. He was practically surrounded at close range, and was under orders to run for it with his party. As he was falling back with his men, he noticed that a wounded sowar had lost his horse. He stopped to help him, and tried to carry him into safety. Both were killed. Captain Jotham subsequently posthumously received the Victoria Cross. Dafadar Darim took up a position by himself half way to safety and fought single-handed to cover the flight of his comrades.

The tribesmen, driven back on their own territory, had not yet had enough. They continued to gather on the

CLEARING OUT THE CAPTURED TRENCH.
That the task accomplished was a difficult one is proved by the still figures lying in the undergrowth.

died down for a time, and some of the troops were temporarily withdrawn. But it was soon abundantly evident that the Mullahs did not mean to allow things to rest. All possible religious pressure was being brought on these Mohammedan tribes to make them fight again. There were large tribal gatherings in which fanatical preachers played on the feelings of the assembled hillmen and roused them to fury, painting in glowing colours the possibility of success, and promising Paradise to those who fell in the battle between the Crescent and the Cross. The Ramadán fast, in July, brought a temporary respite, but throughout the whole summer the British Movable Columns were kept constantly on the alert, and the troops had always to be ready to resist an advance. In August, Haji Sahib of Turangzai, a notorious anti-British Mullah, gathered several thousand men around him in the Ambela Pass, and prepared to invade British territory. The men he had assembled around him were not to be despised. The majority of them were Pathan hillmen, trained in fighting from boyhood. Scattered among them were a group of Hindu fanatics. Then there were fakirs of many kinds, reputed miracle workers, men of extraordinary austerity—fierce, lean, keen religionists, who showed the marks on their own bodies of the tortures they had delighted to inflict on themselves to prove the sincerity of their faith. Every factor that in previous generations had made the Mohammedans so tremendous a force in warfare in semi-civilised lands was embodied here. Each man was taught that Heaven itself would help him in the fight, that angels would come to strengthen his arm, and that Paradise was his.

The British authorities knew better than to underestimate the menace of a tribal Jehad. Nineteen years before in this very region a fakir, known as the Mad Bareheaded Mullah, had stirred up the country-side to revolt. Coming from Kabul he had gone among the tribes, assuring them that he was sent from Heaven to tear the infidel out of the hills and hurl him and his armies back into the plains of the Punjaub. He declared that he was backed by untold hosts of horsemen and footmen concealed in the hills, men fed with food from Heaven. He did not want other men to assist him, he declared. That was not necessary. He himself could go single-handed, if need be, against the Infidel, for even though he went alone there would be armies of angels of Heaven on either side of him, making him invulnerable and invincible.

In scores of hillside villages he preached his message, and soon crowds of tribesmen rallied around him. He promised them plunder such as they had never dreamed of, loot in abundance from the stores of **The Mad Mullah** the British rulers, treasures on earth, and **from Kabul** undying bliss after. He worked the people up to such a state that he brought about a great rising, in which the Mohmands fought against British forces with almost incredible fanaticism. Peasant boys with stones rushed against our fine Indian infantry; men with sticks tried to fight troops with modern rifles, confident that Heaven was with them. The whole country-side was ablaze, and after our troops had fought back the Mohmand advance it was necessary to organise a punitive expedition to sweep through their country to teach them our strength.

That was in 1896. There had been other trouble since then, and now Haji Sahib was doing the same work of stirring up the people against us as the bare-headed fakir had done a generation before.

On August 17th a hostile gathering of 3,000 or 4,000 tribesmen came down from the Ambela Pass towards Rustam. It was reported that another force was coming to support them. British troops at once pushed up to attack the Ambela Pass party before it was reinforced, and drove it back with great loss. The 91st Battery Royal Field Artillery came up during the course of the action after a forced march, its shells doing great execution. A brigade was now concentrated at this point, and wherever the tribesmen appeared it attacked them. In the latter part of **Enemy driven to** August there were three fights between **the hills** our troops and the tribesmen, and on each occasion the enemy was driven back into the hills, and the villages which had sheltered him were destroyed.

A still more formidable gathering of hillmen under a fakir, known as the Sandaki Mullah, advanced down the left bank of the Swat River to invade the Lower Swat. This force was reported to be between 17,000 and 20,000 strong. The Malakand Movable Column took up a position on the left bank of the river on a ridge known as the Landakai Ridge, which gave them a great advantage of position in meeting the hostile advance. The tribesmen attacked our outposts in strong force on the evening of August 28th and 29th, but were driven off. Next day the Malakand Column moved out, destroyed a fort, and shelled several villages held by the enemy. The tribesmen scattered, and for the time their offensive was broken

The fanatics were at work on the Mohmand border, and the reports from here were so threatening that two brigades and a mobile column were ordered up to Shabkadar with a mounted column and divisional artillery, while a mobile column was formed at Mardan and subsequently moved to Abazai. Other troops were held in readiness to proceed to the Mohmand front if necessary. There had been various large tribal gatherings in the Mohmand country, and early in September considerable numbers of the men moved down to the foot-hills and prepared sangars in the vicinity of Hafiz Kor. The movements of these tribesmen were carefully watched, but for the moment they were left alone, our aim being to permit them to come down from the mountains on to the plains where our troops could deal with them. The enemy grew in numbers until by the evening of September 4th they totalled fully 10,000. Then Major-General F. Campbell, commanding the British troops, determined to attack. The battle that followed was the biggest that had taken place on the North-West

GALLANT SIKHS WHO GATHERED LAURELS IN FRANCE.
The Sikhs have always been famous as warriors. The men shown here, returning from the trenches to their billets in France, were the company of the 15th Ludhiana Sikhs commanded by Lieutenant John G. Smyth, who won the Victoria Cross at Festubert, May 17th, 1915.

Frontier since 1897. Some of the British and Indian troops that took part in the engagement had reached their positions after record journeys. A British and Indian force covered a thirty-four mile march to Abazai, where the revolting tribes were reported in strong force, in ten marching hours, travelling at night and going over roads described by one officer who took part in the fight as "the most appalling I have ever seen." The dust was two feet deep. "You can imagine what this was like with cavalry on ahead of us and all our transport. I shall never forget the march as long as I live, nor will the others, and added to the dust was the frightful stifling heat. Not a man fell out, which is an extraordinary performance, especially as the last nine miles from Zearn to Abazai were done in the hottest part of the day— 12 to 3 p.m.—arriving at Abazai, the hottest and most mosquito and sandfly-ridden place on the frontier. The weary soldiers were bitten all night."

Those troops were then ordered on to Matta, a levy post on the Shabkadar-Abazai road, where our outposts had already been heavily engaged and had been driven in, Mohmands estimated at 3,000 strong having practically surrounded them.

The troops who were engaged in this fighting with the Mohmands and their neighbours included many notable corps —the famous 21st (Empress of India's) Lancers, Skinner's Horse, Lumsden's Guides, Watson's Horse, the 14th Lancers, the Liverpool Regiment, the Royal Sussex **Famous corps fighting Mohmands** Regiment, the North Staffordshires, and the Durham Light Infantry, besides Punjabis, Rajputs, Gurkhas, the Guides, the Sikhs, and the Dogras. Nor must we forget the Royal Artillery, who did very notable work.

On the morning of September 5th the tribesmen, who had come down from the hills by the Kuhn Pass, advanced right in the open nearly down to the Shabkadar village. As they approached, the British howitzers and field-guns opened on them, but the tribesmen kept on, threatening our left. Thereupon two squadrons of the 21st Lancers, one squadron of the 14th Lancers, and one squadron of a mounted battery of the Royal Horse Artillery moved

QUAINT TRAPS TO CATCH THE WANDERING BREEZE.

Hyderabad has the reputation of being the hottest city in India. The houses are fitted with air-shafts and ventilators, not unlike the funnels of a ship, and these give a fantastic, decorative appearance to the roof-lines of the famous capital of the Nizam's dominions. Above: A steamer unloading at the harbour of Karachi, the chief seaport of Sind, in the North-West Provinces of India.

ON THE SUMMIT OF THE PASS.
View of Kohat Fort, commanding the Kohat Pass, on the North-West Frontier of India. Armoured cars did excellent service against the recalcitrant Mohmands.

LOYAL DEFENDERS OF THE BRITISH RAJ.
A group of tribesmen from Kohat Fort who did not revolt. The taller of the two British officers is Captain Clifton, who was in charge of the armoured cars.

out to meet them. Our troops moved out around Shabkadar village and occupied some foot-hills to the north. The Mohmands, ignoring the Indian Cavalry, concentrated their fire upon the British Lancers. The gallant 21st were eager to distinguish themselves, for it was then within two days of the anniversary of their great charge at Omdurman in 1898. The Mohmands were entrenched in their sangars and in the nullahs (deep, dry ditches) along the foot of the hills. The 21st Lancers charged full against a large force, went through them, and turned straight again into a dense mass of Mohmands. At one point they were charging over what they thought to be level ground when a blind nullah intervened. To quote the description of one soldier of the Royal Sussex Regiment: " The 21st Lancers charged what they thought to be a small belt, but came suddenly on a big ditch, and a lot of horses and men fell in. Then out of the grass on the other side about 3,000 Mohmands came. The only thing they could do was to charge. They went right through them, turned round, and charged back again. One chap, about nineteen years old, just out from England, killed five with his lance, leaving it sticking in the fifth one, and two more with his sword."

The British cavalry came out splendidly.

21st Lancers in glorious charge Emerging from the bed of the Minchi-Abazai Canal they came under very heavy fire at close range. They charged the enemy a third time, and in this charge, which really decided the battle, they suffered heavily. Many stories of the fighting were afterwards told by the survivors. Lieut.-Colonel Scriven led his squadron in the charge, and did great execution with his sword until his horse was shot and fell upon him. Two of his lance-corporals assisted him to his feet. Shortly afterwards he was shot through the heart and fell, shouting, " Go on, lads. I'm done." Two men guarded his body until they were rescued. Captain Anderson who had been severely wounded, fought desperately with his revolver until he was shot dead. Lieut. Thompson was so severely wounded that he died in the evening. Of five officers who rode in the charge three were killed and one wounded, the adjutant alone coming out unhurt. He, however, had his horse shot from under him, and was only fifty yards from the enemy when he was rescued by a shoeing-smith. One sergeant was unhorsed, and after killing two natives, grappled with a third huge native on the ground. Each man had his hand at the other's throat, when another sergeant came up and shot the native. At the same moment he himself was shot and severely wounded.

All the troops engaged did well. The Sussex and the Staffordshires were engaged in fierce hand-to-hand fighting with the enemy. But it was undoubtedly the charges of the Lancers that saved the day. Their tremendous courage and irresistible élan cowed for the moment even the fanaticism of the Mohammedan tribesmen. After some hours of fighting the Mohmands broke and the cavalry pursued them to the hills.

Although the Mohmands and their neighbours were thus repulsed, they were still not wholly broken. The Mullahs made fresh efforts to stir them up, and early in October some 9,000 men again gathered in the neighbourhood of Hafiz Kor.

The British forces under Major-General Campbell, which had been strengthened by the addition of another brigade, took the offensive against them. The enemy fought well and offered strong opposition, but in the end was defeated. This occasion was especially notable because armoured cars were used for the first time in actual fighting in India, and **Armoured cars** proved of great value. They were exceed- **in action** ingly successful both in reconnaissance work and in covering some of the movements of our cavalry. This fight practically brought the unrest among the Mohmands to an end.

In October there was an outbreak in Swat, when 3,000 Bajauris advanced towards Chakdara to stir up the troops of Dir and Swat to attack the fort there. Lieut.-Colonel C. C. Luard, of the Durham Light Infantry, who was then temporarily in command of the Malakand Movable Column, decided to attack the enemy. He did so with the utmost vigour. He drove them back, pursued them, captured a standard, and gave them a lesson which evidently went right to their hearts, for months afterwards it was officially reported that there had been no further gathering of the tribes on that border.

There were some more minor troubles along the frontier, but little, if any, more than would have happened at ordinary times. In Baluchistan one chief looted the treasury of the Khan of Kalat, and it was feared that the trouble might spread, but a column visited the district, and things rapidly settled down. There was an attempt to raise a Jehad among the Black Mountain tribes in the summer of 1915, but it came to nothing. Peace was maintained on the British side of the border of the Shan States, but the French experienced some trouble on their side. Their post at Samenna was attacked and looted by a strong band of Chinese. Troops were hurried to the scene. The marauders were intercepted, and two hundred killed in action. Another band of considerable strength had also to be broken up. But these disturbances were really due not so much to the European War as to the fact that a large number of disbanded Chinese soldiers, with no money and no means of returning to their homes, had become brigands and were ready for any trouble.

It is difficult to convey to readers unacquainted with life in Northern India any idea of the great hardships gladly endured by the British troops in the frontier campaigns during the war. Young British soldiers found themselves exposed to great variations of climate, to tremendous heat, to nights of bitter cold, to shortage of supplies, and to physical efforts of the most exhausting type. Thrown into mountain country, pitted against tribesmen of magnificent physique, who were fighting on their own territory and accustomed to mountain war, with little public appreciation and with the knowledge that their own countrymen knew little of what they did, they fought their **Privations of heat and cold** lonely fight with a magnificent endurance that was the admiration of all who knew of them. Some idea of the physical trials of our troops was obtained by the British public by the report of one ghastly journey of troops moving from Karachi to Peshawar in June, 1916. They had to travel through one of the hottest regions in India, where the shade temperature is constantly above 120 degrees. A large number of the men collapsed, and nineteen deaths were officially reported. In this case the great strain on the men was accentuated by amazing official neglect, a neglect for which three high officers were subsequently dismissed from their posts. Such neglect was exceptional, but severities of heat and biting cold almost undreamed of in England were, time and again, the inevitable lot of the soldiers who so bravely kept the peace for Britain on the Indian Frontier.

WHERE AND WHY HELMETS SUPERSEDED THE TURBAN.

Masked in anticipation of a gas attack, these Indians on the western front would have been indistinguishable from their white brothers-in-arms but for the turbans which a few of the men left uncovered by the protecting hood. Only the iniquitous devices of Teuton Kultur could have availed to persuade the Indian to hide the distinctive head-dress of Oriental civilisation. Above : Indian natives making roofs of mud, after their immemorial practice, for the transport sheds of the most modern branch of armies, the Royal Flying Corps, on service in India.

CHAPTER CXXIX.

GENERAL SMUTS' GREAT CAMPAIGN IN GERMAN EAST AFRICA.

I.—To the Capture of the Usambara Railway.

By Robert Machray.

German East Africa " the Jewel of all Germany's Foreign Possessions "—Geographical and Historical Survey—The Treaty of 1890 and the Creation of German East Africa—Opening of the Campaign with the British Bombardment of Dar-es-Salaam, August 13th, 1914— German Successes at Tanga and Jasin—British Occupation of Mafia and Complete Blockade of the Coast—Indecisive Fighting During the Summer Campaign of 1915—Lieut.-General Smuts Appointed to the Supreme Command—The General Military Situation on his Arrival at Mombasa, February 19th, 1916—Magnificent Preliminary Work Done by Major-General Tighe Recognised—General Smuts Decides to Occupy the Kilimanjaro District Before the Rains—The 1st Division under General Stewart Advances from Longido—The 2nd Division under Major-General Tighe Bombards Salaita—General Van Deventer's Column Occupies Taveta—The Fight for Latema Nek—The Advance on Kahe—General Van Deventer Crosses the Pangani River and Occupies Kahe Hill and Kahe Station—General Sheppard's Fight at the Soko-Nassai River—The Conquest of the Kilimanjaro-Meru Area Completed, March 21st, 1916—General Van Deventer's Rapid Advance Along the Central Railway— General Smuts' Advance Along the Usambara Railway—Capture of Mombo—Capture of the Usambara Highlands—Capture of Handeni—Defeat of the Enemy at the Lukigura River—General Smuts Announces that he has Effective Possession of the Entire Usambara Railway, July 21st, 1916.

EARLY in the spring of 1916 the course of the war brought it about that the territory known as German East Africa was the last colony that remained to Germany, not only out of her once immense and potentially magnificent African empire, but in the whole world. And it was just at that time that the Allies, with General Smuts in command of their principal forces— which were British—began, after previous reverses under other leaders, their sustained and successful campaign for the conquest of this most important area.

In this case the special tragedy for Germany was that as this was her last colony, so also was it her largest and best. To quote the words of a prominent German writer, who was well acquainted with it : " German East Africa was the jewel of all her foreign possessions," or, to vary the metaphor, it was like a darling son, for whom nothing was too good, and Germany complacently stated that by comparison the neighbouring East African protectorates on the north appeared to be treated by Great Britain as if they were unwanted and unwelcome step-children. Upon her favourite Germany poured out money without stint. All that the

COMMANDER G. B. SPICER-SIMSON, R.N.
The officer in charge of the motor-boats' expedition to Lake Tanganyika, an account of which romantic episode will be found on page 180.

patient but prodigious skill of her administrators could accomplish had been done for it without a grudge.

Here in this tropical semi-savage land, if nowhere else on the globe, the Germans displayed a real genius for colonisation, evincing the keenest intelligence alike in the development of its resources and in their dealings with its native population. A series of able officials had given, in the thorough German fashion, the closest study to its problems, and had sedulously tried all manner of experiments to ascertain its agricultural, commercial, and other possibilities. Numerous plantations had been started in suitable localities and many industries organised throughout the country. Cities and towns of characteristic German solidity had been built, harbours made and railways and roads of a permanent nature constructed. In a word, nothing was left undone to open up the entire region and put it on a prosperous basis. The Germans, moreover, had managed, though not without occasional grave failures, to conciliate and even make friendly the bulk of the natives. In a large measure they had put down slavery and brigandage

When the war broke out, German East Africa was unquestionably a great and a growing success. One of the little ironies to which that fateful

U   169

NAVAL EXPEDITION'S OVERLAND TRIP THROUGH AFRICA TO LAKE TANGANYIKA.
Armed motor-boats were conveyed from Cape Town to Lake Tanganyika, travelling 2,800 miles over-land. Roads and bridges had to be made for their passage through the bush. Above: Two of the boats on the lake preparing for action.

August of 1914 gave grim point was that the Germans had planned and advertised, far and wide, a large exhibition, which was to be held in that very month at Dar-es-Salaam, its capital, to exhibit its products, announce its facilities for settlement, and draw attention to it generally as a shining example of the power, adaptability, and persuasiveness of German Kultur.

Without a shadow of doubt Germany firmly believed that her possession of this area would endure for ever more, and she had dreamed brilliant dreams of its future —to give her her due, she had gone some way towards their realisation by governing it well. But when she invaded Belgium, and consequently Great Britain declared war upon her, the doom of her colonial empire immediately came into sight, and its passing into other hands became inevitable.

Geography and inhabitants Germany had been in undisputed occupation of the country for about a quarter of a century. She obtained, when Africa was divided up among the Great Powers of Europe, a considerable share of the continent, both west and east. Part of the plunder was the spacious territory subsequently known as German East Africa. Bounded on the north by British East Africa, on the south by British Nyasaland and Portuguese Mozambique, on the east by the Indian Ocean, and on the west by the line of the great lakes, Nyasa and Tanganyika, and the small lake of Kivu, it was over 384,000 square miles in extent, or twice the size of Germany herself. It was upwards of 60,000 square miles bigger than German South-West Africa, the colony whose forces had surrendered unconditionally to

General Botha on July 9th, 1915. Its native black population was seven and a half millions, and several of the tribes were of a superior type, some of them being half-civilised; there were, and had long been, many Arabs in the country, and their influence on it was marked.

Over this vast region Germany first flew her flag in 1890, but it should not be forgotten that this region was part of an enormous tract of land, usually and compendiously described as East Africa, which had had an interesting history long before her traders ever touched its coast. There can be little doubt that the Phœnicians and their allies in Southern Arabia sent their questing ships thither more than two thousand years ago, and it is on record that about the commencement of the Christian era the Arabs had posts and stations on the island of Zanzibar and the mainland behind it.

Coming to later dates, both Arabs and Persians in the twelfth century were settled at Zanzibar, Mombasa, and Kilwa. At the last-named place, which was situated in what very much later was called German East Africa, an Arab State, with all the characteristic **Ancient Arab influence** features of Arab civilisation, flourished for a lengthy period. All along the coast from Somaliland southwards the Arabs held sway over the blacks, and, favoured by the monsoon, despatched gold, ivory, and other merchandise to India and the East—slaves, too, where there was a demand for them. In the fifteenth and sixteenth centuries the Portuguese, the daring navigators of their day, arrived upon the scene and, ousting its Arab sultan, made Kilwa their headquarters. But in their turn they were deprived of a large share of their conquests by fresh incursions of Arabs from Asia, and afterwards by hordes of negro warriors—the Jagas, from the Congo—who laid Kilwa in ruins. The Portuguese were pressed back to the south side of the Rovuma River, which, however, remained their northern boundary; above it the Arabs gradually regained all the ground they had lost to the blacks.

It was not till the beginning of the nineteenth century that the British paid any particular attention to East Africa. By that time they occupied the Cape of Good Hope, and they were bent on frustrating certain schemes of the French, who had garrisons in Madagascar, and then owned Mauritius. The British Government fitted out an expedition which, in 1804, sailed round the Cape and up the east coast of Africa for the purpose of entering into diplomatic relations with its Arab rulers. Later, an important British consulate was established at Zanzibar. At that period Zanzibar and all the other Arab possessions in East Africa were governed from Muscat, the capital of Oman, at the mouth of the Persian Gulf, and the British were on the most friendly terms with its sultan. In those days everything went well for Great Britain in these regions.

Very little then was known to the outside world of what lay behind the coast, and one of the most fascinating chapters of all history was that which narrated the adventures and experiences of the explorers who, from about the middle of last century, penetrated into the interior. It started in humble, evangelical fashion with the opening of missions at Zanzibar and on the littoral of the mainland, by representatives of the Church Missionary Society of England, and they, curiously enough, were men of German birth. But they heard from the Arabs amazing and well-nigh incredible tales of gigantic snow mountains far within that torrid land, and of enormous lakes hundreds of miles to the west. Fired by what they had been told, two of these missionaries, Krapf and Rebmann, natives of Würtemberg, travelled inland, and were rewarded by the discovery of the majestic mass of Kilimanjaro, one of the greatest mountains in the world and, for the most part, a wonderland of beauty. Their accounts of what they had seen inspired other explorers, among them Burton and Speke, the latter of whom discovered Lakes Tanganyika and Victoria Nyanza. The remaining portion of the chapter was glorious with the names of Livingstone, Stanley, and Commander Cameron. In this absorbing story British explorers easily came first, but French and German travellers also played some part in it.

A wonderland of beauty

In the second half of the nineteenth century Great Britain was fortunate in having a really remarkable man as Consul-General at Zanzibar—Sir John Kirk, G.C.M.G. Possessed of extraordinary political grasp and magnetic in personality, Sir John, who had served as surgeon in the Crimea, and had accompanied Livingstone on his Zambesi expedition, spent over twenty years in East Africa. Known and trusted by the Sultan of Zanzibar and the Arab chiefs, who governed themselves by his advice, he became the virtual ruler of the whole immense area from Somaliland down to the territory of the Portuguese. His main preoccupation was the extension and consolida-tion of British influence, and next to it was the suppression of the slave trade. To a large extent he was successful in attaining both objects. He induced the Sultan of Zanzibar to prohibit the traffic in slaves, but in the purely political field he encountered the opposition of France, who had established a rival consulate at Zanzibar ; and with her there were treaties in existence which tied his hands.

Great Britain and France, in the period of the Second Empire, had agreed, in order to avoid a conflict, that neither of them would bring under her control politically the Muscat territories in East Africa or the lands which belonged to the Sultanate of Zanzibar. There was, however a good deal of competition between the two Powers, but no disturbance of the existing *status quo* took place, and the Arabs retained their possessions. Then another Power stepped in, and soon brought about a radical change in the situation. That Power was Germany, eager for her " place in the sun," and not too particular as to the means of getting it.

Arabs retain their independence

THE LONG ARM OF THE NAVY PENETRATES INTO REMOTE AFRICA.

A traction-engine taking a motor-boat across one of the rivers encountered on the way. Above : Removing a boat and its crew from the railway truck at the point on the line whence the naval expedition began its long trek through the bush.

German traders appeared at Zanzibar as far back as 1846, but it was not till some years after the unification of Germany was accomplished that Kaiser Wilhelm II. and his Ministers entered on that policy of expansion which aimed at the establishment of a great German colonial empire. All the globe had been pretty thoroughly parcelled out with the exception of Africa, and it was natural, no doubt, that Germany should turn her attention to the opportunities presented by that continent. A move was made in 1884 by sending Dr. Karl Peters to East Africa, where, according to the German version, he acquired some treaty rights from the native chiefs, and in the following year the German Government gave him and his associates in this enterprise an "Imperial Charter of Protection." In 1885 Germany declared a protectorate over the independent State of Witu. In 1886 Great Britain and Germany came to an understanding that the Sultan of Zanzibar's dominions included Zanzibar, Pemba, and the Lamu archipelago, in addition to a ten-mile belt along the coast from Tungi Bay to Kipimi and some northern towns—much less, in fact, than these Zanzibar princes had claimed.

Meanwhile the British, who scarcely had made as good use of their chances in East Africa as they might have done, had formed a chartered company, the British East African Association, to offset the activities of Dr. Peters' company and counteract German intrigue, which was incessant all over the country. In 1887 the Sultan of Zanzibar granted a lease of his mainland

Rise of German East Africa

possessions between the Umba River and Kipimi to the British company, but in the succeeding year he made similar concessions to its German rival with respect to his territories south of the Umba. As was to be expected, there was much jealousy and considerable friction between the British and the Germans, and with a view to terminating this unsatisfactory state of things, a treaty was signed on July 1st, 1890, by Great Britain and Germany, to which France was also a subscriber.

This treaty created "German East Africa." By its terms Germany withdrew from Witu, and resigned her rights, which more properly might have been designated pretensions, to other lands north of her new colony, but now she received its definite cession. (It may be recalled that Heligoland was included in the bargain.) Great Britain established a protectorate over Zanzibar and Pemba and the regions north of the new German zone up to Somaliland, reaching westward from Mombasa as far

inland as Uganda. By the treaty Germany recognised this British sphere. France obtained recognition of her claims to Madagascar, the Sahara, and the Nigerian Sudan. Great Britain afterwards organised three protectorates in the area assigned to her—the East African Protectorate which included Witu, the Uganda Protectorate, and the Zanzibar Protectorate. The Governor of the East African Protectorate was High Commissioner for Zanzibar, but in other respects their administrations were separate and distinct.

Situated on the island of the same name, the city of Zanzibar was by far the greatest town, and its harbour was much the best in East Africa. Nothing in the country given over to Germany was of anything like the same immediate im-

Enemy competition and enterprise

portance or value, and there was no little discontent among the colonial party in Berlin and Hamburg when the details of the treaty were published. But the Germans at once went to work to find other ports, and discovered them in Tanga and Dar-es-Salaam. From the former, in 1891, they set about building a railway, known as the Usambara Railway, into the Usambara Highlands and on to Kilimanjaro, and from the latter they subsequently constructed a line right across the whole breadth of their territory to Lake Tanganyika, its terminus being Ujiji where, in 1871, occurred the strikingly dramatic meeting between Livingstone and Stanley. At the outset of the war the Usambara Railway from Tanga stretched as far west as Moshi, a distance of over two hundred miles from the coast, while that called the Central Railway,

IN MEMORIAM.
The cross amid the thorny vegetation of an East African battlefield. The lonely grave of Lieut. W. T. Dartnell, V.C., 25th Royal Fusiliers ("Frontiersmen"), who fell in action in September, 1915.

running from Dar-es-Salaam to Ujiji, which was only completed in February, 1914, was seven hundred and eighty miles in length. These ports and railways were what might accurately be termed the vitals of German East Africa, and it was certain that if the Germans lost them to a vigorous enemy, no long time would pass before there would be an end of their power in this territory.

Although Germany had set such store by this her premier colony, settlement had gone into it very slowly. It was estimated that

THE CEMETERY BEYOND THE HILLS.
Graves of British patriots who fell in the service of the Empire fighting the Germans in Equatorial Africa. Each grave was marked out with white stones, and inscriptions appeared on every cross.

After hours of marching through East African desert and bush, a British column has discovered a water-hole, the only one within a radius of fifty miles. This illustration, reminiscent of a prairie scene, shows some of the men and mules refreshing themselves before advancing farther.

So overjoyed were the troops at their timely find that they drove their tired and dusty steeds through the whole extent of the pool. One of the difficulties in the way of concentrating a large force at Mbuyuni was the absence of water in this district.

THE POOL IN THE DESERT: BRITISH EAST AFRICAN TROOPS STRIKE THE ONLY SPRING WITHIN A RADIUS OF FIFTY MILES.

NATIVE TROOPS ENTRAINING FOR THE FRONT.
The enemy made numerous attempts to blow up more than one of our railways, but these were all frustrated.

for its fate. On the contrary, it was her intention to carry hostilities into the British territories, which were unprepared for defence or attack, and on the north offered in the Uganda Railway, running from Mombasa to Lake Victoria Nyanza, a conspicuous mark for hostile operations. This line lay almost parallel with the German frontier, the distance between them varying from fifty to a hundred miles, and their Usambara Railway from Tanga to Moshi gave the Germans a quick and easy means of concentrating troops against it. The plans of Germany included an assault on

in 1913 its entire white population was under six thousand, or only about a third of the white population of German South-West Africa. All its males of military age, however, were trained soldiers, and when the war began their numbers were increased by the arrival of German reservists in the East until they mustered a strength of about 3,000 men. They had plenty of machine-guns, rifles, and other munitions. Further, they were sup-

German Reservists for the East ported by several battalions of askaris— blacks, partly from the Sudan and partly from their own Masai and Manyumwezi tribesmen—to the number of six or seven thousand men, who, fortified by German discipline, and well armed and well led, were excellent fighting material, particularly in such a tropical country. After the war had started the Germans recruited thousands more of the natives.

Apparently it had never entered into the mind of Germany that she might be forced to relinquish her East African domain, which she prized so highly. She was well aware that the British forces in the protectorate were so insignificant as to be practically negligible, and calculating that the war would soon be over, she felt no great concern

RESERVE WATER SUPPLY TANKS.
General Smuts' forces required several hundred thousand gallons of water daily. The watering arrangements were so carefully worked out that not a single hitch occurred.

it by land, with the cruiser Königsberg (sister ship to the Emden) co-operating from the sea, by the bombardment of Mombasa, as well as invasions from her southern boundary of Nyasaland and Northern Rhodesia.

In point of fact, when war was declared the British in East Africa were in a serious position. They were able to put into the field hardly more than a thousand men during the first month of the struggle. In British East Africa and Uganda they had the 3rd and 4th Battalions of the King's African Rifles, but these were not in full strength, and at the moment the majority of their effectives were in the north of the protectorates and in Jubaland, where, as luck would have it, a punitive expedition was going on against the Somalis. But the troops were immediately recalled, and some five hundred King's African Rifles concentrated. About two hundred police defended the railway. Two corps of volunteers, the East African Mounted Rifles and the East African Regiment, were raised among the white settlers, and the existing Uganda Railway Volunteers were called out for the

NATIVE CARRIERS ON THE TREK WITH MACHINE-GUNS.
In many parts of the area of General Smuts' operations there were no roads at all, and native porters exclusively had to be relied on.

protection of the bridges on the line. The total number of men in these three forces was perhaps five hundred, the Mounted Rifles mustering four-fifths of that figure.

As regards quality, the King's African Rifles were splendid fighting men, and, want of training excepted, the same could be said of the Mounted Rifles, who were composed of young British settlers, in whom the sporting instinct was strong, and of Boers from Uasin Gishu, whose deadly skill in shooting was an important asset. But it was obvious that the whole British East African Army was far outweighted by the German, which, however, failed to take full advantage of its opportunity in the north during August, 1914. The Germans attacked the British in the south at Karonga, on Lake Nyasa, and in the west at Abercorn, near Lake Tanganyika, but gained little or nothing by these attempts; indeed, in this area the British held or repulsed the enemy. If the Germans had at once advanced in force on the Uganda Railway, they in all probability would have achieved a striking success. Beyond seizing Taveta, and Vanga, on the coast south of Mombasa, they allowed August to elapse, and it was not till the close of the first week in September that serious operations

NEW LINE LAID THROUGH JUNGLE TO KAHE.
The work of our railway engineers was particularly fine. At one point they actually laid a mile of line a day through virgin jungle.

German steamer Von Wissmann, named after a really great German administrator of the colony, and captured her captain and crew—this was near Sphinxhaven, on the eastern shore of Lake Nyasa.

August passed, and on September 3rd reinforcements from India reached the small British force in the north. They consisted of the 29th Punjabis, a battalion of Imperial Service troops, a battery of Calcutta Volunteer Artillery, some maxims, and a mountain battery. With them was Brigadier-General J. M. Stewart, and he assumed command of the entire British forces. Even thus strengthened, the British in the north were still hardly in sufficient numbers effectively to resist the Germans if they attacked in any decided strength, but, thanks to German inactivity in August, they were now in a much better position. The country there, which, generally, is a waterless desert covered with dense and thorny scrub, was also in their favour so far as defence was concerned. On one occasion a party of Germans, who crossed the frontier with the design of blowing up the railway at Maungu, got lost, missed the water-holes, and were all captured.

Waterless desert land

MAGNIFICENT MASAI WARRIORS.
Scouts and guides of the Masai tribe, some of the tallest and finest natives of Africa.

against the railway were begun. In East Africa the campaign of the Allies commenced on August 13th with the bombardment of Dar-es-Salaam, the German capital, by a British cruiser. The port was shelled, landing-parties were sent into the harbour, and a new wireless installation was destroyed. The German ships were dismantled, and the Möwe, a survey ship of six hundred and fifty tons, together with a floating dock, was sunk. The British Tars performed very thoroughly the work they were given to do. On the same day, in the far south-west, the British steamer Gwendolen took by surprise the

NATIVE WARRIORS EMPLOYED AS SCOUTS AND GUIDES.
German askaris captured by British troops. Askari signifies a native of any African tribe who has been specially trained by Europeans for service as soldier-scouts.

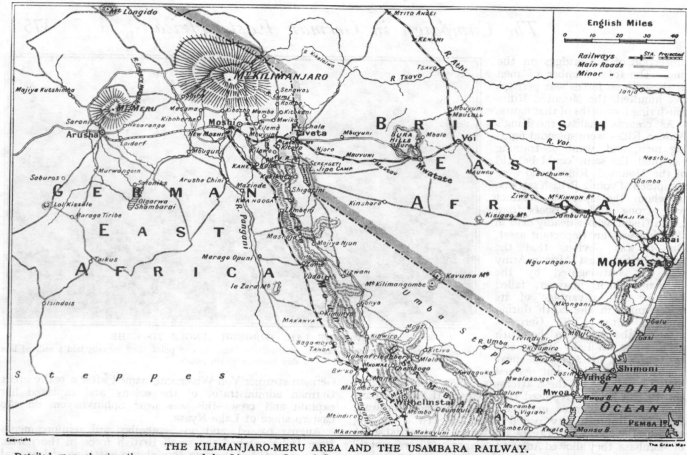

THE KILIMANJARO-MERU AREA AND THE USAMBARA RAILWAY.
Detailed map showing the area covered by Lieutenant-General Smuts between February 12th, 1916, when he assumed command of H.M. Forces in East Africa, and April 30th, 1916, when he sent home his despatch announcing the capture of the Kilimanjaro-Meru district and his effective occupation of the entire Usambara Railway.

During September the enemy made several advances against the Uganda line, three of them being in some strength. In the first of these he was held and finally thrown back near the railway bridge over the Tsavo River by some companies of the King's African Rifles and a half battalion of the Punjabis. In the second some of the King's African Rifles, close to Lake Victoria Nyanza, drove him out of Kisii, which he had succeeded in occupying, and then, aided by the steamers Winifred and Kavirondo, forced him from Karungu on the lake itself, compelling him to fall back across the frontier. His third advance was the most dangerous, and its route was from Vanga up along the coast to Mombasa. It was with this expedition that the Königsberg was to act in combination.

According to schedule, the Königsberg was to bombard Mombasa, which stood on an island connected by a bridge with the mainland, and then capture it, the German land forces having meanwhile destroyed the bridge. But the schedule was not carried out, for the Königsberg was unable to appear at the appointed date—British sea-power saw to that. Nor, for that matter, were the German land forces up to time. They had been checked and held at Gasi by some of these redoubtable King's African Rifles,

Native sergeant saves the day

supported by an Arab company. The fighting was desperate. All the white officers were wounded, and the situation was saved by the courage and coolness of a native colour-sergeant of the Rifles, who took command, and headed the charge which routed the enemy. On October 2nd some Indian troops came up, and this at one time menacing advance definitely failed. Throughout October the Germans retained Taveta, some seventy miles from the line, and one or two other posts equally distant from it, but the British, considering the circumstances in which they were placed, had done very well, for they kept their railway from destruction or even damage, and gained time for the arrival of much-needed reinforcements.

A second force from India reached the coast on November 1st, and, escorted by two gunboats, lay off Tanga next morning. It was commanded by Major-General Aitken,

176

and consisted of the 95th and 101st Indian Regiments, together with the 63rd Palamcottah Light Infantry, the 61st King George's Own Pioneers, some detachments of Imperial Service troops, and two mountain batteries, besides one British battalion—the 1st Loyal North Lancashires. Tanga was summoned to surrender, but when the officer in charge asked for some hours' grace for the purpose of communicating with the Governor, who he said was absent, his request was granted. On the expiry of the time specified, an extension was given of some hours more for the same reason. It was a pretext of the rankest kind, for he employed the day in bringing up soldiers from the interior by the **Treacherous German** Usambara Railway and in increasing and **armistice** strengthening the defences of the town.

In the evening the British landed one and a half battalions which, after advancing towards the town, were compelled to fall back to the shore. The rest of General Aitken's troops disembarked next day, and the attack was renewed on the 4th. After heavy fighting the British succeeded in reaching Tanga itself. Among the foes they had had to overcome on the way were swarms of infuriated bees. Hives of these insects had been hidden in the bush and along the paths, and concealed wires had been fastened to their lids, which were pulled off as the British came up, with the result that many of the soldiers were stung severely. From one man of the North Lancashires over a hundred stings were extracted. With great determination the North Lancashires forced an entrance into the town on the right, while the 101st Indian Regiment attacked with the bayonet on the left. But in the streets they came under so heavy a fire from the houses that they were unable to advance farther, and were compelled to retire to the shore and re-embark. Their losses were serious, being some eight hundred casualties, including one hundred and forty British officers and men. An attack on Longido, which the Germans had occupied, failed on the same day with considerable losses, but the enemy abandoned the place a fortnight later, and the British took possession of it again. In the third week of November the Germans

Under the broiling sun, along a plain devoid of vegetation, a British 4 in. gun is being towed into action by an erstwhile motor delivery van.

Troops of the Loyal North Lancashires on the march. The heat was so intense that the men discarded their tunics, working only in shorts and shirts.

Men of the King's African Rifles, which regiment took part in the attack on Latema Ridge, co-operating with the Rhodesians and Baluchis.

British 4 in. gun in action. To the left of the weapon is seen the brushwood shelter of the gunners.

ARTILLERY, LOYAL NORTH LANCASHIRES, AND KING'S AFRICAN RIFLES MOVE INTO ACTION.

A RELIC OF THE ELUSIVE KÖNIGSBERG.
Destruction of one of the German 4 in. guns which were dismounted for land warfare from the enemy cruiser Königsberg. It will be recalled that this ship sought refuge in the Rufigi River, and was subsequently destroyed by British monitors, July 4th, 1915.

it was evident that, unless Germany was absolutely victorious in the other theatres of the war, German East Africa was now straitly and hopelessly besieged. In January, Dar-es-Salaam was bombarded a second time. In July the Königsberg, which for months past had been sheltering up the Rufigi, was destroyed by indirect fire from the monitors Mersey and Severn, directed by aeroplanes. But the Germans managed to preserve some of her guns, and these reappeared later in the field elsewhere.

At the end of April, Brigadier-General Tighe, with the rank of major-general, was given command of the British in East Africa. While there was much de-sultory fighting, the summer campaign of 1915 contained no incident of the highest importance. German attacks on the **Enemy defeated at Bukoba** Uganda Railway were made repeatedly in the course of the year, but were uniformly unsuccessful. On Lake Victoria Nyanza an expedition commanded by General J. M. Stewart, and consisting of detachments of the Loyal North Lancashires, the Legion of Frontiersmen (25th Royal Fusiliers), and King's African Rifles, defeated the enemy at Bukoba on June 25th. In the south of the country, four weeks previously, a naval force under Lieutenant-Commander Dennistoun, with field-artillery and some King's African Rifles, captured Sphinxhaven, a German town on Lake Nyasa. In June and July the Germans, in considerable strength, attacked Abercorn, a few miles south of Lake

THE RED CROSS IN CENTRAL AFRICA.
Hospital waggon crossing the Wiri Wiri River, East Africa. The arduous work of the Red Cross in Equatorial Africa can well be imagined. Surgeon-General G. D. Hunter, C.M.G., D.S.O., medical officers, and personnel were specially praised in General Smuts' despatch.

invaded Uganda and captured Fort Kyaka, but were repulsed elsewhere in that protectorate.

January, 1915, saw another unfortunate affair for the British on the coast, up which the Germans, after their victory at Tanga, had advanced into the territory of the former. The invaders were checked and thrown back across the frontier, losing Jasin, twenty miles south of it. On the 20th of the month, however, the enemy, with a force of over 2,000 men, attacked this post and compelled its surrender next day. It had been held by three companies of Indian infantry, and they did not give in until all their ammunition was expended. Help, **Indians' splendid resistance** which was attempted from the north, was unable to reach them owing to the superior strength of the Germans. But they put up a splendid defence, and this was acknowledged by the enemy permitting the two British officers in command to retain their swords. About two hundred and forty men were made prisoners. Some twenty of the Kashmirs fought their way out of the place, and one of the King's African Rifles, a negro, succeeded in bringing his machine-gun into the British lines, humbly apologising for having had to leave its tripod behind.

After the loss of Jasin the British retired from other outlying positions on the mainland of German East Africa—for a time. They, however, occupied Mafia, the island lying opposite the mouth of the Rufigi River, and on February 26th began a complete blockade of the whole coast, neutrals being allowed four days to clear. The Germans in the colony thus were entirely cut off from outside assistance. and British sea-power remaining supreme

BRITISH PIONEERS OF CONQUEST IN A SYLVAN CORNER OF GERMAN EAST AFRICA.
British engineers rebuilding a bridge over a river for the advancing troops, a picturesque impression of the scenery typical of Germany's last colony. The enemy had spent lavish sums in the exploitation of this territory, and had governed the natives with an unusual intelligence and resource.

Tanganyika, but the British received reinforcements in time to beat them off. In this southern area the British forces were drawn mainly from the Northern Rhodesia Rifles and the Northern Rhodesia Police.

During the campaign the British suffered greatly from flies and other tropical pests, to say nothing of having to be on their guard against lions, hippopotami, and other wild beasts at all times. Malaria and such diseases as prey on a white man in a black man's land were prevalent. A British officer wrote home that it was the devil's own country, swarming with tsetse and every known form of insect, in addition to several varieties peculiar to itself of astonishing viciousness, and it also was subject to sleeping sickness and nine kinds of fever, each worse than the one before.

Towards the close of August the Germans retired from Lake Victoria Nyanza. Early in September they advanced in the south from Bismarckburg and New Langenburg against Rhodesia, but were held up. However, in November, on the north, they regained Longido, and took Serengeti, east of Taveta; in the following month they rushed the small post of Kasigau, seventy miles west of Mombasa. They were again menacing the Uganda Railway.

Meanwhile, intense dissatisfaction had been expressed throughout Great Britain with regard to the failure of the British to achieve any vital success in East Africa. Questions were put in Parliament, and the newspapers urged the Government to bestir itself and display much greater energy in the operations in this quarter. Fresh troops were despatched, and in

WELL SINKING IN DESERT TERRITORY.
Boring for water at Serengeti Camp. The Serengeti Plains were practically a waterless desert.

December the announcement was made of the appointment of the veteran General Sir Horace Smith-Dorrien to the chief command. Particularly in South Africa, whose soldiers had returned from their triumphs in German South-West Africa, had there been much comment of an unfavourable character. It was proposed that South African troops should be sent to the scene of action, and with this, prior to the appointment of Smith-Dorrien, was coupled the suggestion that they and the other British forces should be led by General Smuts. General Botha's name also was mentioned in this connection, but he let it be understood that he considered his proper place now was in the Union itself, of which he was still Prime Minister. A strong recruiting campaign was organised in South Africa, and enthusiastic meetings were held to promote it. The movement spread, and many thousands enlisted. It was not to be expected that the campaign against East Africa would attract as numerous recruits as that against South-West Africa, in which the interests of South Africa were much more direct. The number, however, was great. In a proclamation General Botha stated that 35,000 men had come forward. Several infantry and mounted regiments were despatched in the winter of 1915-16 to Mombasa.

General Smith-Dorrien duly set out for his new post, but he was attacked by pneumonia on the voyage. On February 10th the War Office stated he had retired because of ill-health, and that Lieutenant-General Smuts had been chosen to succeed him. The news that this distinguished South African soldier (see Chapters LII. and LXVIII.) was to assume the chief command was hailed with delight both in the Union, which appreciated the compliment to itself, and throughout the British Empire generally. It was pointed out that the appointment was appropriate, as South Africa was contributing large contingents to the forces in East Africa, and that the general's special experience in war, together with his great powers of intellect and insight, could not but prove invaluable. He left Durban for the front immediately, and arrived at Mombasa on February 19th, where he was met by General Tighe, who had been conducting the operations against the Germans.

WHERE DANGER LURKED.
An enemy machine-gun hidden where the figure stands did much harm before it was located.

the supreme desideratum in this desert area. The camp, however, needed 100,000 gallons a day, and the difference was made up by using railway and storage tanks. Transport also was seen to on a huge scale, between two and three thousand motor-lorries and waggons being accumulated, with plenty of petrol. A push forward was imminent.

Such was the situation on the north. In the west the British, with the assistance of the Belgians—who from the beginning of the war had done what they could from the Congo side—made themselves masters of Lake Tanganyika. This fine result was mainly the work of two armed motor-boats, with a complement of twenty-seven officers and

A GERMAN POM-POM POSITION IN THE SCRUB.
In German East Africa, as in Cameroon, the British troops had to advance against strongly entrenched positions cunningly concealed in jungle and scrub, and well supplied with machine-guns of various kinds.

Shortly before the appearance of General Smuts in East Africa, the British in the northern section had been successful in repulsing hostile attacks at several points, and the smart recapture of the Serengeti Camp and of Longido was auspicious in the last week of January. A prominent feature of the fighting in these affairs was the splendid work done by the naval armoured cars, which the natives called the "rhinoceroses that spit bullets," an armoured car in motion somewhat suggesting a charging rhino. Early in February the Germans evacuated Kasigau, having held it for about sixty days, but they still retained Taveta. And a British assault on Salaita on the 12th of that month failed, with about one hundred and seventy casualties. But the whole British position in that region had greatly improved. Large reinforcements from South Africa had arrived under trusted leaders, and additional troops had come from India in the shape of Pathans, Baluchis, Bhurtpores, and mountain batteries. The construction of a branch line from the Uganda Railway at Voi had been successfully completed, in spite of German attempts on it, as far as Njoro, past Mbuyuni, at which place arrangements had been made for concentrating a large force. A pipe-line was laid from the Bura Hills to Serengeti, which gave a daily supply of 40,000 gallons of water,

men, which had been brought all the way from the Thames into the heart of Africa. Leaving England on June 12th, 1915, these vessels, which were named Mimi and Tou Tou, travelled out to Cape Town, and thence were conveyed by rail to Fungurumee, the terminus of the Rhodesian line nearest the lake, to whose waters they were hauled by traction-engines for many miles over roads hewn out from the bush by the axemen of the expedition—the whole in its way a record achievement. They promptly showed their power by forcing the surrender of the German steamer Kingani after an action which lasted only ten minutes. Her captain, who had belonged to the Königsberg, and her other German officers were all killed in this engagement. On February 9th, 1916, the gunboat Hedwig von Wissmann was destroyed by them with Belgian aid, and Lake Tanganyika was freed from the Germans.

The motor-boat miracle

General Tighe explained to General Smuts how matters stood in the northern area, and detailed the preparations he had made for an offensive, before the setting in of the rainy season, from Mbuyuni on the east and Longido on the west, against the Germans in the Kilimanjaro district. Smuts forthwith went with Tighe to see for himself the two proposed lines of advance, and this personal reconnaissance

Major-General Sir Michael Joseph Tighe, K.C.M.G., C.B., C.I.E., D.S.O.
Who did brilliant work in the earlier stages of the East African campaign.

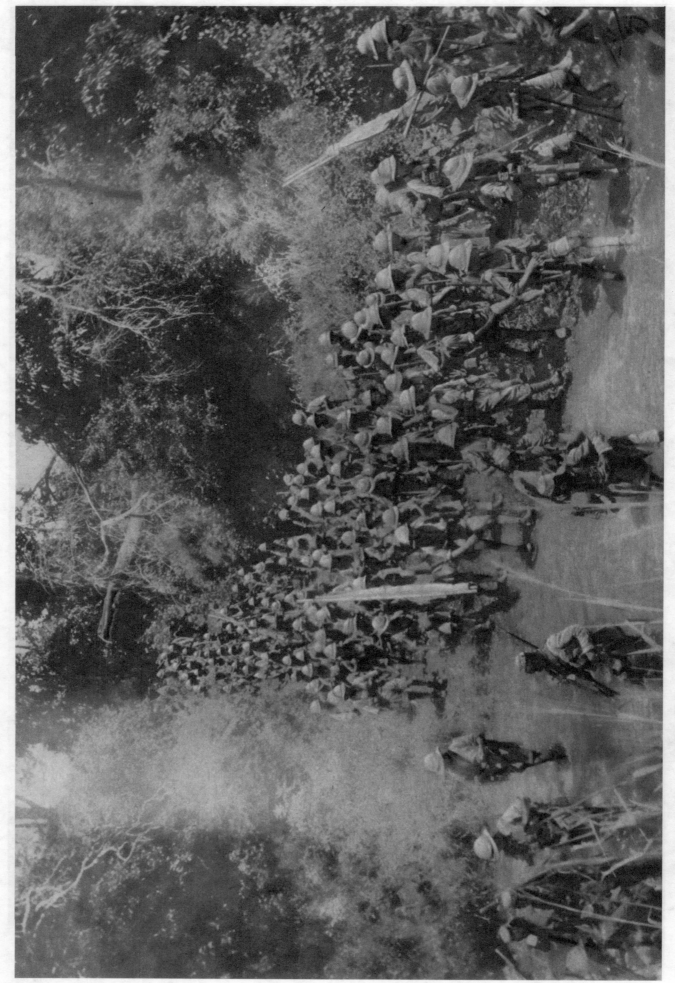

To Kilimanjaro and victory: Troops of General Smuts' command crossing a river in East Africa.

Keeping its place in the Kilimanjaro column : 13-pounder gun treks on three wheels and a tree trunk.

General Smuts surveys an East African battlefield from his armoured car.

determined him to attempt the conquest of this portion of East Africa at once. So complete had been the organisation and preparation for the campaign by Tighe, that Smuts, who cordially recognised the excellence of the measures which had been taken, was able from the start to devote his whole energy to active operations. In a despatch, dated April 30th, 1916, to the War Office, General Smuts said he could not "speak too highly of all the preliminary work done by General Tighe," and handsomely admitted that the subsequent success of his own operations was to a great extent due to General Tighe's foresight and energy. Major-General Tighe, who was already C.B., C.I.E., D.S.O., was promoted K.C.M.G. on March 29th, in acknowledgement of his services in East Africa.

General Tighe's great work

General Smuts arrived at headquarters at Nairobi on February 23rd, telegraphed to Lord Kitchener his belief that the occupation of the Kilimanjaro district before the rains was a feasible operation, and two days later received the sanction of the British Government to undertake it. No time was lost in putting matters into shape for the advance, and, early in March, Smuts' considerable force was strengthened by the coming of the 3rd South African Brigade, the 1st and 2nd Brigades being already on the ground. By March 4th all was ready. His army was disposed in two divisions—the 1st Division at Longido, and the 2nd Division at Mbuyuni and Serengeti, but from the former he had taken the 1st South African Mounted Brigade, which he added to the latter. The army artillery was with the 2nd Division. He now transferred his headquarters to the field at Mbuyuni, retaining with himself as a reserve force the 2nd South African Brigade, and one field and one howitzer battery.

Believing in having an adequate, and even more than a sufficient number of men, General Smuts led an army which decidedly outclassed that of the Germans, whose total strength in the Kilimanjaro district was estimated at 6,000 rifles, with sixteen guns and thirty-seven machine-guns. On the other hand, if Smuts was in superior numerical strength, the enemy had selected his defensive positions carefully and well, and further was protected by the difficult nature of the whole region. To attack him successfully meant having greatly preponderant strength, and the coming of the wet season, which was expected about the end of the month or the beginning of that following, necessitated the conducting of the operations with all possible celerity. It should be stated, however, that the term division, which in European armies connoted 12,000 effectives and upwards, did not imply anything like the same number of men in the army of General Smuts, his two divisions comprising in infantry and cavalry, besides details, only about 17,000 men at the outside. It was a small army, as armies went in the war. He had, in addition, to place many men along the frontier from the coast to Lake Victoria Nyanza to guard it from attacks, and his line of communications as he advanced absorbed many more.

General Tighe's plan had been to make a converging assault from Longido and Mbuyuni with the 1st and 2nd Divisions respectively on the Kilimanjaro area, Kahe, south of Moshi, on the Usambara Railway, being the objective. In the main General Smuts followed it, but altered certain dispositions to avoid expensive frontal assaults on entrenched enemy positions in the dense bush, and also to secure that rapidity of movement which was essential in the circumstances. This was why he transferred the 1st South African Brigade from the 1st Division at Longido to Mbuyuni. The strategy of the campaign was at once simple and sound. The 1st Division was to advance from Longido to the River Engare Nanjuki, across thirty-five miles of desert to the south, and thence between Meru and Kilimanjaro to Boma Jangombe, from which it was to march to Kahe and cut the Usambara Railway. The 2nd Division was to advance through the gap between Kilimanjaro and the Pare Mountains against the enemy's

Sound and simple strategy

CROSSING ONE OF THE LUMI RIVER'S LITTLE TRIBUTARY STREAMS.
British troops crossing a drift of the Lumi River on their way to Taveta. General Smuts paid special tribute to the work of the Supply and Transport Services in keeping open and available roads which often were mere clearings through jungle.

THE LAST OF HER LOST COLONIES: GERMAN EAST AFRICA.

main forces concentrated at Taveta, Salaita, and behind the Lumi River. The 1st Division was allowed a start of two days, so as to time up with the 2nd Division later when they would converge and come into touch with each other. The 2nd Division had the much harder task, and nobly did it accomplish it. The 1st Division was delayed, and did not join up with the 2nd till after the other had completed its work.

Under General Stewart, the 1st Division began the advance from Longido on March 5th, and encountered only slight opposition, as the enemy in this quarter was taken by surprise. It crossed the thirty-five miles of waterless tract in safety, and on March 8th reached Gera-ragua. On the 9th it halted to let its supplies come up, and allow the general to reconnoitre. There was trouble in finding a road, and the ox transport was exhausted. On the 10th a track was found, and three days afterwards the division arrived at Boma Jangombe, the six companies of the Germans, who had resisted it but feebly, having retired before it to New Moshi on the 12th. When the division got up to New Moshi on the 14th, it discovered that the town was already in the possession of the 1st South African Mounted Brigade and the 3rd South African Infantry Brigade under General Van Deventer, who had started out with this column from Mbuyuni and Serengeti on the evening of March 7th for Chala, which lay to the north of Salaita and Taveta, and after heavy fighting, in company with the 2nd Division, had occupied the place on the 13th.

Occupation of Chala

General Deventer's column and the 2nd Division took a prominent part in the keen and bitter struggle which was waged for the possession of the Kilimanjaro area.

Setting out from Mbuyuni and Serengeti on the evening of March 7th, General Deventer marched northwards all night, and a hard march through the thick bush in the ghostly darkness it was. Early next morning he reached the Lumi River at two points, one, with the 1st South African Mounted Brigade, at the south end of the Ziwani Swamp, and the other, with the 3rd South African Infantry Brigade, at the crossing of the stream east of Lake Chala. With swift success the ford was seized with insignificant loss; the rapid movements of Deventer surprised and confounded the enemy. Next, having made good the plateau lying between Chala and Rombo, he directed a converging advance on the position of the Germans at Chala, meanwhile sending out patrols to cut off retreat to the south. Thus threatened, the enemy fell back on his chief supports at Taveta, pursued by the South Africans, who, when they found their opponents in considerable force, halted before nightfall and retired to concentrate near Chala. During the afternoon a body of Germans to the number of several hundreds, which had been isolated from the rest by Deventer's unexpectedly sudden coup, attacked his outposts, but was easily repulsed.

While all this was going on, the 2nd Division, under General Tighe, was bombarding Salaita, and the men of its 1st East African Brigade advanced against the place, and dug themselves in to be ready for the assault next day, March 9th. In the meantime something important had occurred.

At dawn Deventer with his mounted troops occupied the road between Taveta and Moshi, with the immediate result that the enemy evacuated the former town. Later in the day he gained possession of the bridge over the Lumi east of Taveta, and the Germans taken on both flanks, forthwith retired from Salaita. On the morning of March 10th Deventer entered Taveta, forestalling a strong German detachment which had evidently been despatched with the intention of reoccupying it. After a fight this German force was driven back towards the Latema-Reata Nek, west of the town. The 2nd Division marched to Taveta on the same day. The initial moves of Smuts' campaign here had been most successful in strategy and inexpensive in casualties, notwithstanding the difficult country. Within three days the Germans were forced from their strong position behind the Lumi, though it was covered by miles of jungle, and turned out of their entrenchments at Taveta and Salaita at slight cost in spite of these having been most carefully prepared.

Two days afterwards came the real struggle, and it was stubbornly contested, fortune swinging backwards and forwards for many hours from one side to the other.

ABOVE THE CLOUDS ON PARE HILLS, EAST AFRICA.
The district of Kilimanjaro as seen from an aeroplane flying over Ngulu Pass. The Pare Hills are seen in the immediate foreground.

The Germans had withdrawn to formidable positions in the Kitovo Hills, which were densely wooded and easily capable of defence. On the morning of the 11th the British made a general advance, in the course of which the 4th South African Horse and the 12th South African Infantry captured East Kitovo Hill after a brisk skirmish while the mounted troops of the 2nd Division reconnoitred the Latema-Reata Nek, where they found the enemy in force. The 2nd South African Infantry Brigade, with artillery, was then being brought up from Chala to Taveta. General Smuts now determined to take the Latema-Reata Nek, and for this purpose sent forward, under General Malleson, a mixed force consisting of the 3rd King's African Rifles, the 130th Baluchis, the 2nd Rhodesians, Belfield's Scouts, the Mounted Infantry Company, and field and howitzer batteries, besides machine-guns, including those of the Loyal North Lancashires. About noon General Malleson advanced to attack the spur of Latema, which commanded the nek from the north, but made little

Advance on Latema-Reata Nek

ENEMY STRONGHOLD IN BRITISH POSSESSION.
Captured German fort on the Rhodesian border. A British force under Brigadier-General Northey operated at the southern extremity of Lake Tanganyika, and on June 8th, 1916, a column under Colonel Murray occupied Bismarckburg, the only German port of any consequence on this part of the lake.

REMINISCENT OF EUROPEAN TRENCH WARFARE.
British native soldiers on guard at a look-out station in East Africa. The edifice was constructed with wattles, mud, and stones, and a number of loopholes were left for rifle fire. On the right of the photograph a British officer, in shorts and a pith helmet, was also on observation duty.

headway. The enemy had plenty of cover, and from the bush-clad slopes of the hill maintained so severe a gun and rifle fire that the British were held up.

In the middle of the afternoon General Tighe took command of the operating force, as General Malleson had become seriously ill. About the same time the 2nd South African Infantry Brigade reached Taveta, and Smuts ordered its 5th Battalion forward to reinforce the fighting line. On its arrival Tighe assaulted the Latema Ridge with the Rhodesians and **Gallant but** the King's African Rifles, the Baluchis co-**ineffective onslaught** operating on the right. This attack was, in the words of General Smuts, " gallantly pressed home, especially by the Rhodesians, but failed to make good the ridge." Those splendid warriors, the King's African Rifles, were hotly engaged, and had the misfortune to lose their leader, Lieut.-Colonel Graham, and several other officers. The Baluchis, heavily pressed, had to be strengthened with half of the 5th South Africans. At eight o'clock in the evening the 7th South African Infantry came up as a fresh reinforcement. Tighe now determined to try to carry the nek by sending up the two South African battalions with the bayonet by night.

Led by Lieut.-Colonel Byron, commanding the 5th

South Africans, the 7th South Africans formed the first line, with the 5th in support. Advancing with great dash through the dense thorn bush, which was partially illuminated by a young moon, they steadily drove the enemy to the crest, where, however, they were checked. It was about midnight when Colonel Byron, with only twenty men, reached the nek within thirty yards of the Germans' main position. Some of his men had got lost in the scrub, and he had encountered fierce opposition. At one point the **Holding on till** brigade-major, Major Mainprise, R.E., **dawn** and twenty-two men had been killed by the concentrated fire of three machine-guns. Being unable to advance or even hold the ground he had won, Byron was reluctantly compelled to withdraw. But part of his force had done very good work. He had given orders that when the crest was reached, Lieut.-Colonel Freeth, commanding the 7th, and Major Thompson, of the same battalion, should occupy the heights north and south of the nek respectively, the hills Latema and Reata. Freeth fought his way up the steep sides of the former till only eighteen of his men remained, but being joined by some Rhodesians and King's African Rifles, who had clung on to the top of the hill since the earlier assault, he held on till daylight. Major Thompson, with one hundred and seventy men, secured an advantageous position on Reata, where he dug himself in.

With the fighting so much scattered in a night that now had become dark, General Tighe found it almost impossible to keep in touch with his attacking troops, but, getting requests for reinforcements, he sent up the Baluchis, who fell in with Colonel Byron and his small force retreating. Tighe thereupon entrenched astride the road to await daylight. Hearing from him of what appeared to be the unpromising position of the battle, General Smuts considered it to be prudent not to press the attack farther, preferring to see what would be the result of a turning movement which he had ordered for the next morning. He accordingly directed General Tighe to withdraw before daybreak to a line more distant from the nek. This retirement was actually in progress when it was reported by scouts that both Latema and Reata were in the possession of the British and, more important still, that the enemy was in full retreat from the nek towards Kahe to the south. The struggle was over—finished. It cost the British about two hundred and seventy casualties but the Germans suffered much heavier losses in men, besides losing a 2.4 in. gun and three machine-guns, a quantity of rifles and ammunition. So, on March 12th, the Kitovo position was occupied. The same day General Van Deventer, on Smuts' right, advanced to the bridge over the Himo, on the road from Taveta to Moshi, meeting with small resistance, and on the 13th he entered Moshi unopposed, the enemy having retired the previous night on Kahe. And there Deventer remained for a week.

Kahe now obviously was Smuts' next objective. From March 13th to 18th was spent in reconnoitring towards it, in bringing up supplies, reorganising transport, and in mending roads. So far General Smuts had succeeded in driving the Germans out of British territory, and in taking from them the greater part of the important districts of Kilimanjaro and Meru. As the 1st Division, under General Stewart, had now joined up, his whole army was available for operations. But he had to negotiate formidable natural obstacles in the Ruwu River, the upper part of the Pangani, and the dense tropical forest lying immediately north of it. On March 18th he ordered a general advance towards this river, and that day his infantry occupied the line Euphorbien Hill-Unterer Himo with-

Dense bush impedes operations out difficulty, while some of his cavalry marched from Mue along the road towards Kahe. The advance was continued on the 19th, but little progress was made through the thick and well-nigh impenetrable bush which fronted the German position on the Himo about Rasthaus. On the following day he directed Deventer, with the 1st South African Brigade, the 4th South African Horse, and two field batteries, to march from Moshi, cross the Pangani, and get in rear of the enemy at Kahe. Deventer found the crossing of the Pangani far from easy, but by noon of the 21st he had taken both Kahe Hill and Kahe Station with slight loss. Kahe Hill was the key of the Ruwu position, and the Germans made several

determined efforts to recapture it, all of which failed. As soon as General Smuts knew that Deventer was nearing Kahe he gave orders to General Sheppard, of the 1st Division, to advance with the 2nd East African Brigade, the 2nd South African Brigade, the East African Rifles, the 1st King's African Rifles, field, howitzer, and mountain batteries, and two of the naval armoured cars. Sheppard's march lay along and on both sides of the road from Masai Kraal, south of Mue, to Kahe. But he had gone on only a short distance when he was checked by a large force of the enemy in a strong position between the Soko Nassai and the Defu Rivers. **Germans retreat over the Ruwu** His attempts to advance were met and repulsed by rifle and machine-gun fire in front and on the flanks. A turning movement made by the Baluchis, across the Soko Nassai, was unsuccessful. In his full report to the War Office, General Smuts said that "the whole force was ably handled by General Sheppard, and the men fought like heroes, but they were unable to turn the enemy from his strong position." Sheppard dug himself in, purposing to renew the attack next morning, but at dawn his scouts discovered that the Germans had retreated under cover of the night across the Ruwu and were falling back along the road to Lembeni. Such had been the effect of Deventer's fine turning movement from the right. In the Soko Nassai fighting the British casualties were two hundred and eighty-eight, but the

IN BUKOBA, LAKE VICTORIA NYANZA, BEFORE THE VICTORIOUS BRITISH ATTACK.
German soldiers and natives of Bukoba, which was captured by the British forces in June, 1915—a photograph discovered in a colonist's house The smaller illustration depicts natives repairing an East African rail-track after an accident which occurred within thirty yards of a bridge.

enemy also suffered severely. During the battle he had used two of the 4·1 in. guns of the *Königsberg*, and one of these he lost.

Arusha, west of Moshi, and an important centre, was occupied by some of Smuts' mounted scouts on March 20th, the German force which had held it being dislodged and driven in a southerly direction. This put the finishing touch to the conquest of the Kilimanjaro-Meru country, "probably," as the general stated, "the richest and most desirable district of German East Africa." Lord Kitchener telegraphed congratulating him and all ranks on the brilliant success which they had achieved, and on the dash and energy of the operations in a region whose difficulties were not unknown to him (Lord Kitchener). This phase of the campaign, though brief, had been a trying one, by reason of the long marches in the hot sun and in occasional heavy rains, and there were **Great hardships** times when rations ran short. General **cheerfully endured** Smuts bore witness that all hardships were endured with unfailing cheerfulness. Having transferred his headquarters to Moshi, and placed a chain of outposts along the Ruwu, he set to work to reorganise his forces for the next move, concentrating the troops as far as possible in healthy localities to give them a rest after their trials. Meanwhile the rainy season supervened, and it was not till towards the end of May that General Smuts began his second advance, which ended in the occupation of the Usambara Railway.

In another part of the field, however, he achieved results of importance during April. Having gained the western terminus of the Usambara Railway, he proceeded to strike a blow at the Central Railway, which ran from Dar-es-Salaam to Lake Tanganyika. This movement also had the effect of tying up the Germans in that area, so that they could not send reinforcements to their friends in the north. Its conduct was placed in the capable hands of General Van Deventer. Moving from Moshi to Arusha, Deventer concentrated **Cavalry success** at the latter place, at the end of March, **at Kissale** a considerable body of mounted troops, with the infantry and artillery of the 2nd Division, mainly drawn from the South Africans. Advancing with great rapidity, his mounted forces defeated the Germans at Kissale on April 4th and 5th, and marching south-westerly occupied Köthersheim, or Umbugwe, as the natives called it, on April 12th, and Salanga on April 14th, capturing many prisoners and driving the rest of the enemy's forces southwards. On the 17th he was in the neighbourhood of Kondoa Irangi, one hundred and twenty-five miles from Arusha, and one hundred miles from the Central Railway. At this point, which was the centre of several main roads, the enemy offered a stubborn opposition, but Deventer overcame it, and took Kondoa Irangi on the 19th. This success was gained, it was reported, by the employment of typical South African tactics, the centre being firmly held while the flanks were enveloped, but the enemy broke away before the process was completed, and retreated to a strong position in the hills to the south-east of the town.

Doubtless, the disconcerting rapidity with which Deventer had struck at Kondoa Irangi had much to do with the defeat of the Germans, who, as soon as they had somewhat recovered themselves, proceeded to effect a great concentration about Kilimatinde, on the Central Railway, with a view to opposing his farther advance, and to forcing him out of the town. In the first week of May they displayed some activity in the direction of the place, and on the night of the 9th of the month, after a heavy

THE LABORIOUS WORK OF CONVEYING SUPPLIES TO THE EAST AFRICAN FRONT.
East African natives carrying ammunition in the rear of an advancing column. Owing to a lack of road communication through the thick bush, and a scarcity of water, the difficulties of conveying supplies from place to place were considerable. The smaller illustration depicts a water supply column on its way to the front from an outpost in the desert.

A LONELY LOOK-OUT IN THE EAST AFRICAN BUSH.

British observation post in Kilimanjaro, an illustration giving a good idea of the tall jungle grass and other tropical vegetation abounding in this region. General Smuts began his vigorous offensive on February 25th, 1916, and by the end of March the whole of the Kilimanjaro-Meru area, which is described in his despatch as "probably the richest and most desirable part of German East Africa," was under British occupation.

bombardment in which another gun of the Königsberg took part, they delivered a heavy attack on Deventer, which was repulsed with severe losses to them. During the next two days the enemy, who was led by General von Lettow-Vorbeck, the German Commander-in-Chief, persistently assaulted the British positions, making in particular, on May 11th after the sun had set, a great effort against the left flank of Deventer, but without success. This effort was the last of importance for about two months, during which the South African general, with occasional fighting, held up—"contained"—a very considerable enemy force. But as it drew on towards the close of July he received reinforcements, and was able to resume his advance, occupying Dodoma, on the Central Railway, on the 29th. More than a week before that date General Smuts announced that he had got the whole of the Usambara Railway in his hands.

Last enemy effort for two months

As the rainy season came to an end in May, General Smuts, who meanwhile had rested and reorganised his troops in the Moshi-Kahe area, resumed his offensive for the occupation of the northern railway. Despite the torrential rains and the flooding of the rivers, there had been no failure in supplies, and thorough preparation had been made for the energetic prosecution of this part of the general campaign. He had now a distinct advantage in having railway communication all the way from the Uganda Railway, the branch line from Voi being completed by the beginning of May to Moshi, where it was linked up with the rail-head of the Usambara Railway.

For this fresh advance against the Usambara Railway Smuts had at his disposal the 1st Division, now commanded by Major-General A. R. Hoskins (General Tighe had gone back to India), with Generals Sheppard and Hannyngton as brigade commanders, as well as other forces, including South Africans. By May 25th his advanced troops had moved along the line, and occupied Lembeni, twenty miles south of Kahe, and Ruwu Lager, on the Pangani River, twenty-six miles south-west of Kahe. By the same date he was in Ngulu, in the Ngulu Pass, lying between the Northern and Central Pare ranges, eight miles south-east of Lembeni. He entered all three places without opposition. East of the railway his line of march led through a region

of hills rising in places to a height of three thousand feet, and covered with forests, and still farther on he had to negotiate the Usambara Highlands. It was in this area, which provided positions of great natural strength, that he expected to find the most determined resistance. On May 25th he reached Zame, on the railway, and with another column moved down the Pangani River, by way of Marago Opuni, eighteen miles north-west of Zame, to Le Zara. The enemy had retreated southwards to Mikocheni, a fine defensive position at the southern end of the Pare Mountains which lay between them and the river, with the railway in the middle. The Germans had entrenched, and were strongly placed to defend the bridge over the Pangani; the thickness of the bush was also in their favour. After a reconnaissance on the 29th the British assaulted and carried the enemy's trenches next day, with slight loss. On the 31st he was in full retreat, and, coming under the fire of a flanking movement from the hills, had many casualties.

Smuts gave the Germans no rest. Pressing on he arrived at Mkomazi, on the railway, where he found a train had been left behind by the retreating foe, who, however, had destroyed the bridge as they had destroyed that at Mikocheni. From Mkomazi he marched on to Bwiko, a station midway between the Pare Mountains and the Usambara Highlands, which gave the name to the district and the railway. On the morning of May 31st his left column, which had advanced through the Gonya Gap from Zame, reached the Shegulu Bridge over the large tributary of the Pangani called the Mkomazi, ten miles north of Mkomazi Station, and progressed southward along that stream.

Capture of Mombo

After halting for a few days, during which he bridged the Pangani at Mikocheni, he again had his forces in rapid motion. General Hannyngton, whose troops were operating along the railway, was at Mazinde, twenty miles south of Mikocheni, on June 8th, and on the following day he captured Mombo, eight miles farther on, dislodging the Germans who had tried to hold it. This was an important success, as from Mombo there ran a light railway south to Handeni, forty-five miles away, and this line, the existence of which had not been generally known

SPICK AND SPAN ON THE EQUATOR.

British officers selecting an outpost position near the German East African frontier. Pith helmets and shorts seem to have composed the most comfortable uniform in this tropical region of the world-war.

before, became an avenue for a second British advance towards the Central Railway.

From the station of Mombo a good road zigzagged up the slopes to the capital, Wilhelmstal, which lies in a pleasant valley four thousand feet above sea-level and surrounded by mountains. Wilhelmstal was a favourite health resort. When within the next week of the advance the British were in possession of this town, they found that the wives and families of many Germans had been left confidently to their care.

Crossing to the right bank of the Pangani, at Mikocheni, General Hoskins' forces marched down to Mkaramo, where the light railway from Mombo passed over the river fourteen miles south-west of the junction, and there had a sharp fight with a considerable body of the enemy, which ended in the Germans being driven off to the south, while Mkaramo was occupied, with insignificant casualties to the British. Both at this point and at Mombo the enemy had severe losses. By June 13th Hannyngton was at Makayuni, eight miles from Mombo, and two or three days later, by gaining Korogwe, only forty miles distant from Tanga, the coast terminus of the railway, and the second town in Usambara, he made Smuts practically master of the whole of the Usambara Highlands. It had been a quick and, everything considered, an inexpensive conquest. Nowhere had the Germans really availed themselves of the splendid opportunities for defence presented by the district. The Highlands had been outflanked, and the enemy had, in fact, come to the conclusion, which was abundantly justified, that he would not be able to retain the railway, and that his further efforts to beat the British— or at least to hold them off as long as possible. with the

Enemy in full retreat

other Allies, from taking the country, for he could look for nothing else in the final issue—must now be made south of the line.

Although the Usambara Railway was not yet wholly abandoned by the Germans, they had now withdrawn their main forces from it, and had taken up positions between it and the Central Railway. When General Hoskins forced them out of Mkaramo, an event which took place on June 10th, they retreated along the light railway towards its rail-head at Handeni, forty-five miles away, and there threw up entrenchments. Between the two places the country was dense jungle, and movement through it was almost impossible. Besides, water was very scarce. And no doubt the enemy laid his account with delaying a hostile advance because of the difficulties which Nature had interposed, while in the meantime he would have time to concentrate his men and prepare strong positions. To a certain extent he was right. Yet on June 15th the part of Hoskins' division which was commanded by General Sheppard succeeded in arriving at Kwedizwa, only six miles from Handeni, and on the morning of the following day pushed on through the bush to the village of Kilimanjaro, close to the German camp. Having regard to the obstacles the troops had to overcome it was a wonderful march.

Port of Tanga captured

Handeni was a settlement which contained several German plantations, and from it a good road went east to the port of Pangani, at the mouth of the river of the same name. It also had a water supply, and the German forces were entrenched in its vicinity. Other troops belonging to General Hoskins came up, and on the 19th the place was taken, the enemy retreating south to the Lukigura River, after incurring some losses in a rearguard action. Four days later the British got close to the Lukigura, and on the 24th a battle developed. The enemy was attacked by three columns. One, under the personal command of General Hoskins, by an arduous night march, enveloped the Germans on the flank. The second, led by General Sheppard, made for and held the bridge across the river, attacking frontally. The third, composed of South Africans, engaged the enemy on the other wing. After considerable fighting the enemy was heavily defeated, and drew off in the direction of the Central Railway, having lost many killed and wounded, some machine-guns and a pom-pom, munitions, and numerous prisoners, including several Germans. The British losses were trifling. The Germans managed to get away their Königsberg gun, shelling the British with it, in the words of Reuter's correspondent, "erratically, sullenly, and at random through the darkness."

While this second advance in the direction of the Central Railway was successfully going forward, General Smuts completed and consolidated his conquest of the Usambara Railway. As far back as June 13th it had been reported that the enemy had evacuated Tanga, the terminus on the coast. From Korogwe, occupied by Hannyngton on the 15th, the British marched along the line down to the sea, but found that the statement of the evacuation of Tanga was incorrect. The port, however, was captured on July 7th after a brief resistance by the Germans, who destroyed the waterworks before retreating. The country in the neighbourhood was not yet cleared of all hostile bands, and these gave some trouble by endeavouring to cut the railway and Smuts' communications between Korogwe and Tanga, but they were driven down the Pangani, with the loss of a field-gun, and then forced south of that river. On July 21st General Smuts announced the occupation by him of Amani and Muhesa, the former some miles north of the line, and the latter a little south of it, and stated that he had taken effective possession of the whole of the Usambara Railway, which was being repaired by his engineers. Thus triumphantly came to an end this stage of his campaign.

BRITISH SUBMARINE CREW | CHAPTER CXXX. | GREETS CHANNEL STEAMER.

THE WONDERFUL WAR WORK OF THE MERCANTILE MARINE.

By Percival A. Hislam.

Our Right to the Dominion of the Sea Proved by the Rally of the Mercantile Marine to the Service of the Flag—Naval Reserve Called Out August 2nd, 1914—Magnificent Response of the Merchant Service—Their Work on the North Sea Patrol—Beaching of the River Clyde at Gallipoli—The Mercantile Marine and the Blockade—Rear-Admiral Sir Dudley De Chair's Tribute—Utility of the R.N.R. Man's Special Knowledge of Merchant-Ship Construction Illustrated—The Trawler Section of the R.N.R.—Work with the Dover Patrol on the Belgian Coast—Vice-Admiral Sir Reginald Bacon's Tribute—Distinguished Service off Gallipoli Praised by Vice-Admiral Sir John de Robeck—Peaceful Pursuance by the Merchant Service of its own Vocations—Rise in Freights Owing to Depletion of the Mercantile Marine—Failure of the German "Submarine Blockade" to Affect British Merchantmen Infuriates the Germans—Captain Charles Fryatt, of the s.s. Brussels, Evades Submarine Attack, March 3rd, 1915—Captain Fryatt Tries to Ram another Submarine, March 28th, 1915—The s.s. Brussels Captured June 23rd, 1916, and Taken to Zeebrugge— Court-martial on Captain Fryatt at Bruges—Murder of Captain Charles Fryatt by the Germans, July 27th, 1916—Other Merchant- men's Encounters with Submarines—Adventures of the Lady Plymouth.

NOTHING that occurred in the course of the Great War was more significant of the latent strength of the British Empire, or provided a stronger proof of our inherited right to the dominion of the seas, than the magnificent rally of the mercantile marine to the service of the Flag. In every department of naval activity the ships, officers, and men of the merchant service fought side by side with the specially designed ships and the professionally trained personnel of the Royal Navy, and distinguished themselves to a degree that challenges comparison with the Navy itself. Outside the actual fighting-line — in which the deeds of the Carmania, the Alcantara, and the Engadine will always be remembered with pride—the merchant service provided us with everything necessary for the maintenance of the enormous transport services involved in the prosecution of a gigantic and almost world-wide war; it was solely responsible for the performance of many auxiliary duties without which the fighting fleet could have had neither mobility nor efficiency; and, finally, the ships and men that were left behind to pursue their "lawful occasions" as in time of peace, carried on with their work under the highest possible pressure, and in circumstances which made their existence from day to day hardly less perilous than that of a regular warship and her crew. Indeed, it might be urged with some show of reason that the lot of the merchant seaman was the more perilous, for while the enemy's submarines were not long in coming to recognise the neighbourhood of a regular warship as a rather unhealthy one, they were able to give their attention to our helpless trading steamers with something approaching comparative impunity.

It is well that there should be set on record, however inadequately, something of the debt which the British Empire and the cause of civilisation generally owe to the splendid fellows who, in normal times, fill our larders, provide work for our factories, and are responsible for more than a half of the carrying trade of the world. A little over three hundred years ago the rôles of trader and warship were interchangeable; for, since the trader had, for her own protection, to be armed against the attentions of pirates and privateers, the Sovereigns of those

MOMENTS OF LEISURE ON A BRITISH PATROL SHIP.
Not on the look-out for submarines or Zeppelins, merely watching a spirited sailor boxing bout aboard a British warship at sea.

AN ALLIED WAR VESSEL,
steaming at a moderate rate, as she appeared in the North Sea from a friendly
hydroplane.

So far as ships are concerned, these were the only arrangements of this kind that had been made by the Admiralty with a view to war. That may have been an instance of official short-sightedness, especially in view of the fact that when war actually came the Admiralty found it did not really require the services of either of these fast and gigantic ships. At the same time, it throws into stronger relief the extraordinary rapidity with which a great fleet of liners was fitted out for war service. Had the Navy been maintained on a wholly adequate basis, it would never have been necessary to reinforce it from the ranks of ships that were urgently needed to meet our requirements in other directions—that is, for transport services and the carriage of munitions—but when the authorities found themselves face to face with the crisis they met it with a highly commendable promptitude. Our greatest need was for cruisers—moderately armed vessels of fair speed and great staying power for the patrol of the trade routes and the defence of our floating commerce against the enemy's raiders. For many years before **Dangerous economy** the war, Governments had been **in cruisers** saving money on these ships.

distant times found it economical—as well as very sensible—to do without a fleet until a war came, when they would simply hire from the shipowners as many ships, with crews and guns complete, as they thought would be necessary for dealing effectively with the enemy.

As the science of shipbuilding and of gunnery advanced, however, this interchangeability ceased to be possible save in a very limited degree ; but the British Admiralty still retained the system in a sort of tentative way. In the official Navy List, as it existed at the outbreak of war, there will be found a list of vessels " held by the Cunard Co. at the disposal of the Admiralty." The " list " contained only the Lusitania and the Mauretania ; but a note was added to the effect that in return for the annual subsidy paid in respect of these ships, the Cunard Company held the whole of its vessels at the disposal of the Admiralty, for hire or purchase, whenever the need should arise.

They " dressed the window "—and very effectively—with Dreadnoughts, and saved a few millions of pounds upon ships which, however essential to the successful conduct of war, would not be missed by anyone who had not made a close examination of our position.

No sooner, then, did war come than the Admiralty were compelled to fall back upon the mercantile marine to make up our obvious deficiencies. War was declared on August 4th, 1914. Within a fortnight, twenty-two liners—including such well-known vessels as the Alsatian, Aquitania, and Oceanic—had been put into commission as auxiliary cruisers. In nearly every case the whole of the ordinary crew of the ship volunteered to remain for war service under the Admiralty, and were transferred to the Naval Reserve, and the Navy itself was represented only by the commanding officer, one or two juniors among the executive officers, and a stiffening of Navy-trained

" MOSQUITO " CRAFT " GUARDING THE ACE."—
The great work of the destroyers became prominent in the Jutland Battle, but apart from their supreme importance in action, these splendid craft had a vital work to perform in what is known as " guarding the ace "—a nautical expression signifying battleship. No battleship ever proceeded to

men among the rank and file. The number of these auxiliary cruisers steadily increased as the war progressed, and by the end of the second year of hostilities more than a hundred of them were on active service, sharing with the Navy the distinctions and the dangers which attached to the maintenance of the command of the sea against the world's second strongest naval Power.

The fighting work of these vessels is described in its proper place in this history, but in such a general survey as this it will not be out of place to make a passing reference to it. Take, for instance, the case of the Carmania. In peace this Cunarder was commanded by Captain James Barr, who held a commission in the Naval Reserve as a commander. On August 4th, 1914, she was commissioned by Captain Noel Grant as one of his Majesty's ships, and was promptly sent westward into the Atlantic to assist in the protection of our commerce. Within six weeks she had distinguished herself by defeating and sinking in single combat the German auxiliary cruiser Cap Trafalgar, a new Hamburg-South America liner of 18,500 tons that had been **Triumph of the Carmania** specially designed to take her share in the destruction of British commerce in war. As a matter of fact, she was sent to the bottom before she had accounted for a single British tramp steamer, and Commander Barr was decorated with the C.B. for the part he played in winning the action.

It would be out of place here to traverse the whole of the ground covered by our converted merchant ships in the course of the war—and, indeed, our theme lies rather with men than with ships. Never in any great war have we been found at the start with sufficient seamen for our needs. In the old days we met the difficulty either by offering a liberal " bounty " to men who would volunteer for service, or else by the persuasive agency of the press-gang. In recent years, however, the Admiralty had taken time by the forelock by instituting the Royal Naval Reserve, a force composed of officers and men belonging to the seafaring profession who undertook to put in a

CLOUDS OF ILL-OMEN AT SEA.
As in land warfare, the Germans are known to have made use of gas at sea, this being generated by shell explosion. The above illustration, secured from a British warship, shows German gas clouds on the horizon.

certain amount of training with the Fleet each year, and to place their services unreservedly at the disposal of the authorities in war. On August 2nd, 1914, the Naval Reserve was " called out "—mobilised—and the Admiralty at once found itself the richer by some 20,000 officers and men. It was useful, but it was not enough. The regular Fleet itself was expanding rapidly under the stress of war and the feverish energy of our shipyards, and it was a physical impossibility for the Admiralty to turn out trained officers and crews as fast as they were turning out ships, to say nothing of the steady appropriation of additional vessels from the mercantile marine.

It will readily be seen that in circumstances like these the mighty products of our shipbuilding yards would have been little more use than scrap-iron unless the authorities had had a reservoir upon which they could draw for an

—HOW A BATTLESHIP PROCEEDED TO SEA AND WAS SHIELDED FROM ENEMY SUBMARINES.
sea without a cordon of destroyers ahead and astern in close line, all on the alert with guns at the ready to open an effective fire on hostile periscope or conning-tower that showed itself on the surface. Thus a torpedo attack on first-class battleships was rendered practically impossible.

LOOKING FOR MURDEROUS CONTRABAND: INSPECTORS SEARCHING BALES FOR BOMBS WITH THE AID OF X RAYS

So many efforts were made in America by German intriguers to place bombs aboard steamers bound for allied ports, that the authorities examined all cargo destined for Europe, particularly cotton bales. The inspectors resorted to X rays, looking through a fluoroscope, and wearing a rubber apron impregnated with lead oxide, to protect the wearers from the heat. This photograph shows the ingenious method in operation.

adequate supply of trained seamen. Call after call was made upon the merchant service as the needs of the Navy grew, and every call was answered with a promptitude which reflects eternal honour on that splendid force. Exactly how the breaches were filled it is still too early to tell in detail, but it is possible to give some idea of the extent to which the merchant seamen responded to the call of war. In July, 1914, the number of executive officers enrolled in the Naval Reserve was 1,288. At the end of the second year of hostilities the number had increased to 4,435—and over a hundred had laid down their lives for their country. The number of engineer officers increased in the same period from 318 to over 2,000. There is good reason to believe that the total strength of the Naval Reserve in the first two years of war was multiplied at least ten times.

Naturally, all those who were specially entered were not trained for war work, but they were expert in the duties relating to the handling of their own ships. From truck to keelson they remained responsible for everything concerned with navigation, seamanship, and engineering, and all the Navy had to do was to put in a commanding officer who knew how to get the best out of the ship as a fighting unit, and a few specialists to take charge of the fighting equipment. Thus it happened that, when the Admiralty armed and commissioned a great liner for service in the blockading squadron that held so effectively the northern outlet from the North Sea, **Into the greatest danger** they found ninety per cent. of the crew already at their stations, trained and seasoned to their work, leaving only the expert members of the guns' crews and two or three officers to be provided out of the established strength of the Navy.

It seems most anomalous that men who came into the fighting service of the nation under these conditions should be described as members of a "reserve." They stepped straight from their civil occupations into the line of greatest danger, remaining not for one moment in any position that could be described as a reserve. From the day they went into the service of the nation they were constantly on active war service, and nothing but war brought them into the service. There is nothing in our military organisation which is called a "reserve," with the exception of

those " veteran " corps which undertake to perform combatant work in the almost impossible event of a hostile army landing on our shores, and it seems altogether out of place to apply the term "reserve" to a body of men who, day in and day out, faced the treacherous perils of the North Sea Patrol.

In the early days of the war the ships that were specially commissioned for this service suffered rather heavily. In September, 1914, the famous White Star liner Oceanic was stranded and wrecked **Losses among liners** on the Scottish coast. The Viknor (ex-Viking) and the Clan McNaughton were lost respectively in January and February, 1915, because of the fierce storms which they encountered off the North of Ireland, or, as was alleged both at the time and subsequently, because their guns had been mounted on the upper decks with insufficient regard to the effect which the added weights at such a height would have on their stability. On March 11th, 1915, the Bayano was torpedoed and sunk in the Irish Sea ; but from then until the end of the second year of the war the only armed merchant vessels lost on the patrol service were the Ramsey, the India, and the Alcantara. The Ramsey was sunk in fair fight with the German mining-ship Meteor ; but the latter was detained so long on the job that she was overhauled before she could get back to shelter, and had to be sunk by her own crew to avoid capture. The India—a P. and O. boat—was torpedoed off the Norwegian coast on August 8th, 1915 ; while the Alcantara met her end in nipping in the bud an attempt on the part of the enemy to get the disguised raider Greif out on to our trade routes.

So magnificent was the response of our merchant officers and seamen to the call of the Admiralty, that a large surplus was available after every provision had been made for the manning of the specially commissioned liners. To nearly every ship throughout the Service a proportion of "reservists" was drafted, relieving the enormous drain made by the war on the regular personnel of the Fleet, with the result that the merchant marine had no small share in every victory that we won.

The magnificent story of the beaching of the transport, River Clyde, at Gallipoli, will always be remembered with especial pride by those who sail under the Red Ensign.

The officer in charge of that perilous, disastrous, and yet glorious expedition was Captain Edward Unwin, who went straight into the Navy from the merchant service, as a supplementary lieutenant, in 1895 ; and of the six Victoria Crosses awarded in connection with that stupendous exploit one went to him, another to Midshipman G. L. Drewry, of the merchant service, and a third to Seaman George Samson, of the Royal Naval Reserve. No other incident of the war brought out so fully the magnificent fighting stuff of which our merchant seamen are made.

Outside the actual fighting-line, the merchant service performed innumerable services without which the Fleet could not have existed. The Navy, like the rest of us, is dependent for its daily bread upon supplies brought into the country from oversea, and of the dangers which our merchant ships cheerfully and successfully faced in maintaining those supplies more will be said anon. At the end of the second year of war well over a hundred cargo-boats had been put into commission as " Mercantile Fleet Auxiliaries," charged with the duty of keeping the Fleet supplied from day to day with everything it could possibly require. Petroleum for our oil-fired ships had to be brought from the termini of pipe-lines in Persia and Mexico. Coal had to be ferried round from the Welsh ports to the Fleet bases away in the north. Ammunition, ranging from the 3-pounder of the semi-automatic gun to the 1,950 lb. shell of the 15 in., had to be delivered with such regularity that no ship, within

CAPTAIN SCOTLAND, OF THE CLAN LINDSAY.
Early in 1916 the Clan Lindsay was attacked in the Bay of Biscay by a German submarine. Captain Scotland replied to the fire so hotly that the pirate disappeared.

twelve hours of the end of its latest fight, had a depleted magazine. For all these things, and many others, the merchant service was solely responsible. After the great and exhausting action off Jutland, Sir John Jellicoe reported that " at 9.30 p.m. on June 2nd " the Grand Fleet was fuelled and replenished with ammunition, and " ready for further action." It is well that we should realise that this remarkable performance, accomplished within thirty-one hours of the Fleet's departure from the scene of its victory off the coast of Denmark, was rendered possible only by the regular and efficient services of the mercantile fleet auxiliaries, which are manned almost exclusively by officers and men of the Naval Reserve. In spite of the thousands of voyages which these vessels made, only one was lost in the first two years of the war, the Fauvette, 2,644 tons, which was mined in the North Sea on March 13th, 1916, with a loss of two officers and twelve men.

To maintain the commercial blockade we relied almost entirely, as well for men as for ships, upon the mercantile marine. When Rear - Admiral Sir Dudley De Chair took the blockade squadron to sea from Queenstown in August, 1914, it consisted almost entirely of ancient cruisers manned for the most part by immature ratings under training. It was a false move, sacrificing efficiency to expediency, and it was not long before the Admiralty effected a thorough modification of their arrangements. In December, 1914, the admiral commanding the blockade

THE BRITISH WAR-FLAG WHICH NO STRANGER SHIP DARED TO IGNORE.
All round the British coasts all ships were challenged by destroyers belonging to the Examination Service. These flew a distinguishing flag, white and red horizontal, surrounded by a blue border, and a blue ensign ; also three red vertical balls (lights at night) if the port were closed.

INVALUABLE SERVICE OF THE " YACHT PATROL" : STEAM-YACHTS ESCORTING BRITISH TRANSPORTS CROWDED WITH MEN BOUND FOR THE FRONT.
Every kind of craft that floats was offered to the Admiralty when war broke out, and the services of many were promptly accepted. An idea of the help they were able to give in matters of the very first importance is conveyed by this picture of two large steam-yachts escorting three transports laden with priceless lives, alert to mark and charge any lurking submarine.

squadron transferred his flag from the twenty-two-year-old cruiser Crescent to the Allan liner Alsatian, and within a very short time the whole network of warships patrolling the area between Kirkwall, Iceland, and Norway was composed of converted merchantmen.

Speaking once to an interviewer regarding the nature of his work, Admiral De Chair said : " Although there is an adequate sprinkling of Royal Navy men in command, by far the majority of blockade officers are drawn from the Royal Naval Reserve. These men, many of whom have had splendid careers in the British mercantile marine, are peculiarly fitted for blockade work. They are accustomed to manifests and ships' papers ; they know how to make a quick, comprehensive, and judicial inspection of cargoes." The admiral might have added that it really takes a merchant service officer to see through such tricks as Germany and **What the** her friends devised in order to smuggle **merchantman saw** past the blockade the goods of which the enemy stood most in need. It is no disparagement to the British naval officer to say that he would have been wholly taken in by many of the devices which the mercantile man detected with very little trouble, thanks to his deeper knowledge of merchant-ship construction. To give but one instance of this : A ship was stopped one day on her way from America, laden to all superficial appearance with cotton (this, by the way, was in those times of folly when the Government declined to class cotton as contraband, and so permitted the enemy to receive vast quantities of material necessary for the manufacture of explosives). The ship's manifest said she carried cotton. A few bales were hauled out of the hold, opened, and found to contain nothing but cotton. The boarding-party was about to leave, satisfied, when a Naval Reserve man suggested to the officer in charge that for a ship loaded with nothing but cotton, which is very light in comparison with the space it occupies, she was lying strangely low in the water.

The naval officer took a glance at the ship's side, and his suspicions were aroused. He ordered the stranger to make another dip among his cotton bales ; and when one was brought up from the lower layers it was found to contain practically nothing but copper. There were, in fact, several hundred tons of the metal on board, and it would all have got through to Germany if that Naval Reserve man had not brought to bear his special knowledge of the characteristics of merchant ships.

It is a remarkable testimony to the efficiency of the blockade, and of the merchant service officers and men who were mainly responsible for its maintenance, that in two years of fighting only one enemy ship, submarines apart, managed to get out of the North Sea. The Möwe, blatantly disguised as a neutral trader, managed to sneak out into the Atlantic in the midwinter of 1915-16, when the hours of darkness in the northern latitudes where the patrol worked are abnormally long and fogs are frequent. The only other known attempt was that of the Greif, a similar vessel to the Möwe, **Only three blockade** which was rounded up and sunk on **breakers** February 29th, 1916, by the converted Royal Mail liner Alcantara, which in turn succumbed to a torpedo fired just as the German was about to go under. To be strictly accurate we probably ought to include among the enemy vessels that slipped past the blockade the " Norwegian" ship Aude, which convoyed the submarine in which Roger Casement travelled from Germany to the coast of Tralee ; but as the Aude was quietly shepherded by the British Fleet for the whole of her journey, and, when her object was partly accomplished, was duly taken in charge by the armed sloop Bluebell, she is hardly to be reckoned as a blockade-breaker.

In no department of our glorious naval service has the merchant seaman shone more conspicuously than in the manning of those almost innumerable groups of steam trawlers and drifters upon which the Navy largely depended

PLEASURE YACHTS ON SECRET SERVICE.
Much work of a serious kind was done for the Admiralty by little sailing yachts, once attractive features of summer-time regattas.

for its protection against mines and submarines. Rudyard Kipling once put into his inimitable verse the forecast that, when the time came for the British Empire to reassert its claim to the dominion of the seas, our great liners would be ordered to preserve themselves in the security of safe harbours while the Navy would have to "up and fight" for the cargo-boats upon whose coming and going we depend for our daily bread. The liner never for a moment succumbed to the stay-at-home idea. Those that did not put on war-paint in one shade or another were called upon to redouble their energies in the carrier service on the high seas; and if, here and there on the map of the world, the Royal Navy was called upon to settle an account with the enemy on behalf of the "little cargo-boats," the debt was surely repaid a thousandfold.

We have it on the authority of Mr. Balfour that when war came there was not a single harbour on the East Coast of Great Britain where the Grand Fleet could lie in safety from submarine attack. It was a defect **Lack of East Coast** that was quickly remedied in various **harbours** ways, with which Germany, doubtless, became familiar as speedily; but from the very first day of the war the Fleet found itself most severely handicapped not only by the absence of protected harbours, but by the serious lack of small craft capable of countering the only methods by which Germany was able to carry on the war in the North Sea. Our enemy showed his hand very clearly on the first day of hostilities, when the disguised mine-layer Königin Luise was discovered pitching mines over her stern within a relatively short distance of the East Coast. By the indiscriminate scattering of loose mines and the surreptitious laying of anchored fields in areas likely to be traversed by our warships, a great part of the North Sea was rendered altogether too perilous for our heavy vessels to enter; and when, at the end of three months of war, our losses through mine and submarine in the North Sea alone had run up to ten ships, with a death-roll of close upon 2,500, there were many who felt that we were confronted with a state of affairs

which might conceivably bring disaster in its train. But the men who man the smallest of our "little cargo-boats"—the hard, incomparable fishermen of the English and Scottish coasts—were already getting the situation well in hand. A few years before the outbreak of war Lieutenant (afterwards Captain) Donald Munro—himself an ex-merchant service officer—had laid before the Admiralty a plan for utilising steam-trawlers for dealing with the menace of the mine which he could see was bound to arise in the event of a war with Germany. Lord Beresford, then in command of the Channel Fleet, was ordered to carry out the necessary tests, and he reported on the scheme most favourably. A few trawlers were bought and attached to the Fleet, and a number of old gunboats adapted as mine-sweepers; and in 1911 a special branch of the Royal Naval Reserve was formed with the object of putting at the disposal of the Admiralty in time of war a large body of seamen inured to the handling of small craft in all sorts of weather, and, in particular, expert to the last degree in everything   **Great rally of** that appertains to the handling of nets   **fishermen** and the trawling up of submerged objects.

The Trawler Section of the Royal Naval Reserve was not a great success to begin with, and in the three and a half years from its establishment, at the beginning of 1911, to the outbreak of war only one hundred and eleven "skippers" enrolled themselves; but, whatever may have kept them back, it was certainly not lack of patriotism, for with the first blast of war the crews of the fishing fleets all round the coast began to roll up to the naval recruiting offices in their hundreds. The Admiralty hired or purchased the trawlers and drifters from their owners; they parcelled off the North Sea into areas, and to each area they allotted a division or a group of these little patrol craft to trawl up the lurking mine and ensnare the elusive submarine. In the whole theatre of naval warfare there was none in which monotony was so subtly combined with ever-present danger. The light draught of the trawlers enabled them to steam in safety over the average mine-field; but their

MINE-SWEEPERS' "ADMIRAL" IN THE VAN.
Flotillas of mine-sweepers were led by an "admiral," the ship carrying the officer in charge, usually a lieutenant of the Royal Navy.

work lay not so much in saving themselves from destruction as in destroying the mines laid for the destruction of others, and many a gallant little vessel was lost through the explosion of a mine fished up in her own trawl. The work was done well beyond the range of public vision. An occasional honours' list reminded the country of the existence of these craft, plodding away day in, day out, to clear the sea routes for the passage of the British Fleet and of the merchant ships that used our ports; but far

Unsung heroes of the R.N.R. more frequent was that brief official statement, lost in the confusion of the day's news, which recorded the unsung death of a skipper and a dozen men of the Trawler Section of the R.N.R., blown up in the execution of their duty by a mine laid for the destruction of a super-Dreadnought with a crew of a thousand souls.

The work of the drifters was even less generally recognised than that of the mine-sweeping trawlers, for it was the particular business of the former to protect the Fleet by an "offensive defence" against hostile submarines, and how they did it, and where, and the measure of success that came their way, could not be known until the time

FISHING FLEET AT FLUSHING IDLE THROUGH FEAR OF MINES.
The Germans' indiscriminate mining of the North Sea had military results quite incommensurate with the enormity of the offence, but it crippled neutral fishing industries. This fishing fleet was laid up at Flushing.

was past for Germany to gain anything by the knowledge. Throughout the first two years of war the splendid work of the drifters only once received any measure of public recognition. Whenever the Admiral of the Dover Patrol took his monitors across to the Belgian coast to bombard the enemy's positions and bases there, he always took in company a great flotilla of trawlers and drifters to clear away the enemy's defensive mine-fields and to protect the heavy ships against submarine attack, for which all the conditions were intensely favourable. In penning his first despatch to the Admiralty, dated December 3rd, 1915, Vice-Admiral Sir Reginald Bacon wrote as follows: "Their lordships will appreciate the difficulties attendant on the cruising in company by day and night under war conditions of a fleet of eighty vessels comprising several widely different classes, manned partly by trained naval ratings but more largely by officers of the Naval Reserve, whose Fleet training has necessarily been scant, and by men whose work in life has hitherto been that of deep-sea fishermen. The protection of such a moving fleet by the destroyers in waters which are the natural home of the enemy's submarines has been admirable, and justifies the training and organisation of the personnel of the flotilla. But more remarkable still, in my opinion, is

the aptitude shown by the officers and crews of the drifters and trawlers, who in difficult waters, under conditions totally strange to them, have maintained their allotted stations without a single accident. Moreover, these men under fire have exhibited a coolness well worthy of a service inured by discipline. The results show how deeply sea adaptability is ingrained in the seafaring race of these islands." Coming from Sir Reginald Bacon this was, indeed, high praise, for no man was ever more sparing in the distribution of compliments, or a greater stickler for the prestige of the regular naval service.

This chapter does not aim to be a record of events, but rather a general survey of the contribution made by the merchant service—both in ships and in men—to the winning of the war. It would, however, be incomplete if no mention were made of the work our fishermen did outside the North Sea. During the operations off Gallipoli, and particularly after the arrival of the first German submarines in May, 1915 their vigilance and promptness in action saved the Fleet from many a disaster, and when, in the spring of 1916, the King bestowed the Distinguished Service Cross on three skippers, on the recommendation of Vice-Admiral Sir John de Robeck, it was officially noted that the men had "performed long, arduous, and dangerous duties, and are specially selected from over a hundred names.' In such a case as this, therefore, less than three per cent. of those who were recommended were rewarded, or even given the honour of a public "mention in despatches." The country, too, knew nothing of the work of our "fisher patrols" in the Adriatic until the Astrum Spei and the Clavis were sunk by an Austrian cruiser in July, 1916.

So far mention has only been made of the work of the merchant service in close and active co-operation with the fighting Fleet, but in the peaceful pursuance of its own vocations it exhibited a courage and an indifference to danger worthy in every way of our highest traditions as a maritime nation. Germany had long perceived—and, indeed, we ourselves had recognised—that our greatest danger in a war with a first-class naval Power would lie in the possibility of our merchant shipping being so seriously disturbed as to dislocate our industries and force the prices of the necessaries of life up to famine figures. The Germans traded from the first upon what they believed to be the weakest link in our Imperial organisation, and the needs of our own case were such that we were compelled, in meeting our immediate naval and military requirements, to give the enemy a substantial start in the direction he desired to travel. One of the very first steps taken by the Government when war was seen to be inevitable was the re-**Conversion of merchant shipping** quisitioning of a great number of ships for service as cruisers, transports, hospital ships, and for various other services. As the war progressed the proportion of shipping thus taken away from its ordinary employment increased rather than diminished, with the result that in the summer of 1916 the tonnage taken by the Government "for the naval and military and essential civil needs of the allied countries" amounted to forty-three per cent. of the whole, while another fourteen per cent. was occupied in "carrying foodstuffs and raw materials on behalf of the Government and its Allies."

If the German Fleet never experienced the joy of a great sea victory, enemy torpedo-boats at least enjoyed the exhilaration of sea-power in holding up neutral steamers. Frequently Dutch craft came under this surveillance in the North Sea, and such an incident is illustrated above.

German submarine raiders about to shell a peaceful liner on the high sea. With feverish haste the gun is being brought to bear on the steamer, and perhaps a torpedo was being launched simultaneously. The German commander was giving orders from the conning-tower. (From an enemy painting.)

EASY PREY FOR THE GERMAN TORPEDO CRAFT AND SUBMARINE.

In other words, only two ships were left to do the work for which five were previously available, and, with the withdrawal also from the world's carrying trade of large proportions of the French, Italian, and Russian mercantile fleets, and the entire suppression of the German and Austrian, each ship remaining in ordinary service represented a correspondingly more important factor in the economic structure. The operation of the law of supply and demand sent freights up to a staggering height—over £5 a ton was asked and paid for carrying coal from the Tyne to Genoa, as against a normal peace quotation of 4s. 6d. or 5s. Ships, earning sufficient in a couple of voyages to pay for their cost and provide their owners with a profit, changed hands at fabulous prices, the ultimate burden falling, of course, upon the purchasers of the goods which the ships carried.

It was upon a mercantile marine thus already depleted of three-fifths of its ships that the Germans turned with their methods of barbarism in order to frighten the remainder out of their legitimate business. The more or less cleanly-played game of the Emden and her fellow-corsairs on the high seas had failed completely, and when the German Naval Staff found that the military effectiveness of their submarines was undergoing a similar process of strangulation, it determined to change its objective and see whether the U boats could not be employed successfully to scare the British merchant seamen off the seas.

The full story of the " submarine blockade " is told elsewhere in this work. It had no effect whatever on the British mercantile marine, beyond the bare record of ships

The German U boat bogey sunk. Never after the first week of the " blockade's " existence was there the slightest trace of the moral of our merchant seamen being affected. Ships entered and left our ports with their old regularity, and, subject to the demands of the Government, in their old numbers. Many were sunk, for the threat of the German Naval Staff was far from being an empty one ; many, when attacked by hostile submarines, were handled with such skill by their captains that they succeeded in escaping even after rapid-fire guns as well as torpedoes had been brought to bear on them. Such cases were usually rewarded by the Admiralty with a gold watch for the captain, together with an expression on vellum of their appreciation of his seamanship, while the owners usually liquidated their indebtedness to the officers and ship's company in coin of the realm. As time

went on, the authorities extended very largely the practice —begun, as a modern measure, a few months before the opening of the war—of giving our merchant ships one or two light guns, with a competent gun-layer for each, as an additional means of defence against submarine attack, and in many cases these were used with considerable effect. The practice of the Admiralty in withholding all information relating to the destruction of U boats prevents us for the time being from appreciating as fully as we otherwise would do the useful part which the merchant service has played in this direction.

The nonchalance with which the British merchant service pursued its normal courses, in spite of the fiercest and most barbarous efforts of the Germans to drive it off the seas, roused the enemy to a pitch of frenzy which led them into the commission **Running the gauntlet** of perhaps the most dastardly crime that **to Rotterdam** lies even to their discredit. Nothing in the whole war story of the mercantile marine can have been more galling to Germany than the continuance of the British steamship service between our own East Coast ports and Rotterdam. The nearest German naval base to the north of the River Maas, on which Rotterdam stands, is only one hundred and fifty miles distant, while Zeebrugge, to the south, is only fifty miles away. Both Emden and Zeebrugge were bases for German torpedo craft, both surface and submarine, and yet, in spite of their proximity to the line of route, steamship communication with the Dutch port was maintained—not, indeed, regularly, but with sufficient frequency to expose the impotence of the Germans and the absolute failure of their methods of " frightfulness " as aimed at our merchant seamen.

Captain Charles Fryatt had been running the Great Eastern Railway steamer Brussels on this route since the outbreak of war, and the Germans had made many attempts to intercept and destroy his ship. In the month of March, 1915—a month in which no fewer than nine merchantmen were torpedoed by German submarines without the slightest warning being given—two separate and determined attempts were made by the enemy to get rid of the obnoxious Brussels. On the 3rd of the month Captain Fryatt successfully dodged an attack and brought his ship safely into port, and was presented by his owners with a gold watch in appreciation of his seamanship. On the 28th a further attempt was made to sink the vessel ;

MOTOR-BOAT PATROL RETURNING TO THE DEPOT SHIP FOR ORDERS.
The motor-boat patrol was a new branch of the Service, organised to deal with any emergency as naval initiative and resourcefulness might suggest. This illustration shows two of the boats returning to the depot ship for orders.

WITH THE MOTOR-BOAT PATROL: VERY IMPORTANT INTELLIGENCE.
One of the most responsible of the motor patrol's many duties was to attend transports and keep them safe from submarine attack. Inset: A fisherman telling a motor patrol he had sighted a submarine just previously, heading in a certain direction.

but when Captain Fryatt saw the U boat come to the surface so as to get a proper line of fire for her torpedoes, he swung his helm over and bore down on the would-be assassin with such speed that she was compelled to dive in precipitate haste in order to save her own skin. Indeed, it is not altogether certain that she did save herself. The submarine dived on the starboard side of the Brussels and came up on the other—so close, as Captain Fryatt said, that "you could easily have hung your hat on the periscope as she lay alongside us." Then she suddenly disappeared and was not seen again, and as there were some members of the Brussels' crew who reported having felt a shock while the U boat was submerged, it is quite within the bounds of possibility that she sustained an injury that sent her to the bottom. The Admiralty on this occasion presented a gold watch to Captain Fryatt, the chief officer, and the chief engineer.

For another fifteen months the Brussels, still under the same commander, continued her trips between England and Holland, until she was at last trapped by a flotilla of German torpedo craft, making one of their periodical midnight excursions from Zeebrugge. Treachery is believed to have played its part in the misfortune—at any rate, one man who was on board at the time of the capture was treated with marked consideration by the enemy. However that may be, the Brussels found herself, in the early morning of June 23rd, 1916, in a ring of German torpedo-boats. There was nothing for it but to submit to the inevitable. The steamer was captured and taken into Zeebrugge.

Captain Fryatt's tragic fate

The sequel—though it was but the murder of one man—sent a wave of indignation through the world that was not outdone in intensity by the wholesale massacre of the Lusitania. In doing his best to save his ship from being sunk on sight by a German submarine, Captain Fryatt had acted in strict accordance with the law of nations. He had done nothing whatever to controvert even those "maritime laws" which Germany had framed principally with a view to the protection of her own interests. Most particularly of all, it was distinctly laid down in these German laws that if enemy merchant seamen were captured after offering armed resistance to German warships, they were to be treated strictly as prisoners of war. Judged by any and every conceivable standard, therefore, Captain Fryatt should, at the least, have been assured of an honourable captivity—the more honourable because of the success with which, for nearly two years, he had pursued his dangerous calling, almost, as it were, between the lines of the German Navy. It was for just such a reason that the British people had loaded almost unreasonable praise upon Captain von Müller, of the Emden, though he had destroyed millions of pounds' worth of our property and sunk a Russian cruiser and a French destroyer.

With Captain Fryatt in their hands, however, the Germans threw all laws and all honour to the winds. They regarded him only as an object upon whom they might vent the hatred they felt towards the whole of our merchant marine—a non-fighting service that had pursued its way without fear and without wavering in despite of the policy of organised assassination which had been adopted towards

CHANGING THEIR COLOURS: ARMED BRITISH LINERS BEING PAINTED MAN-OF-WAR GREY AT LONDON DOCKS.
The great work of the mercantile marine constituted a strong aid to sea-power. When war broke out, many of the largest liners put on war-paint, mounted quick-firers, and generally made ready for all emergencies. The London Docks presented a scene of unusual animation, all the ocean liners changing their colours to "man-of-war" grey before proceeding on their various and perilous voyages.

it. Captain Fryatt was brought to trial before a so-called court-martial at Bruges. The only business of a court-martial is to administer military law, and the German law in this case was as plain as daylight. Captain Fryatt had defended himself against the attack of German warships, and the German law said quite unequivocally that any merchant seamen who had done that were " to be treated as prisoners of war." The court-martial overrode and ignored the law it was supposed to administer. It condemned Captain Fryatt to death as a franc-tireur. The " trial" took place on July 27th. He was murdered the same evening, the sentence being " confirmed "—as it had, in all probability, been ordered—by the Kaiser himself.

The Kaiser's part

Words altogether fail one in the attempt to describe so foul a crime. It was committed under no misapprehension. The whole thing was done under the cloak of the law, and with the express sanction of the German Emperor —and, indeed, no one but he could have authorised such a contravention of German law as was involved in the murder. There is no imaginable code of punishment that fits such an atrocity as this ; but Mr. Asquith voiced the unanimous feeling of the British people—and, indeed, of the whole civilised world—when he declared that " his Majesty's Government desire to repeat emphatically that they are resolved that such crimes shall not, if they can help it, go unpunished. When the time arrives they are determined to bring to justice the criminals, whoever they may be, and whatever their station." " The Government are determined that this country will not tolerate a resumption of diplomatic intercourse until reparation has been made for the murder." The German Government allowed it to be stated that this atrocity marked a precedent, and that any other British seaman who deliberately tried to save his ship from destruction and his own and his crew's lives from murder at the hands of a German submarine, would be murdered in cold blood at the first available opportunity. It was another attempt to frighten the British merchant seaman off the seas ; and it was a more hopeless and ignorant attempt than any that went before it. Nothing the Kaiser could have dreamed of could have so steeled the nerve and the determination of the whole of our maritime services as the doing to death of

Captain Fryatt. It may have been something of an omen that just a week after this murder Captain David Thomson, of the steamship Strathness, reported that he had sunk a large German submarine in the Mediterranean on July 15th.

It must not be supposed that the only exciting experiences met with by our merchant ships were occasioned by direct encounters with enemy submarines. It would be altogether impossible to recount these other experiences in anything like detail, but a brief resumé of the adventures of a single steamship, the Lady Plymouth, will give a very good idea of the exigencies that befall a British merchant vessel in war time. On March 26th, 1915, this vessel left the Clyde on her maiden voyage, bound for Buenos Aires. When two days out of port the lookout sighted a lifeboat crowded with men and women, and although the sea was so rough that oil had to be pumped out to quell the waves, she succeeded in rescuing the survivors of the steamship Aquila, which had been sunk twelve hours before by a German submarine. The occupants of the boat were well-nigh exhausted, and if the Lady Plymouth had not run across them it is doubtful if any of them would have survived. On November 5th, 1915, the same steamer came across a boat empty of life, but well stocked with fresh provisions—the only remaining evidence, possibly, of one of those cases where the Germans had attacked a ship and sent her to the bottom before the passengers and crew had time to get into the boats that were lowered. Later in the same day a raft bearing the name Calvados was sighted, but no trace of life was found on or near it. The Lady Plymouth proceeded on her way, and an hour or two **Adventures of the** later came across another raft, this one **Lady Plymouth** laden with French soldiers. They had been on board the Calvados, which, having embarked some hundreds of French troops who had for fifteen months been fighting on the Belgian frontier, was torpedoed by an enemy submarine when within twenty-five miles of her destination—the port of Oran, in Algeria. Captain J. K. Watson, of the Lady Plymouth, took the soldiers aboard—they had been adrift for twenty-four hours—and shortly afterwards another raft was sighted with a load of fifteen men. The steamer stood by to pick them up, and while she was in the middle of the work the periscope of a submarine was sighted. There is little doubt but that the submarine was only waiting a favourable opportunity for torpedoing the Lady Plymouth and sending her to the bottom with the men she had rescued ; but, thanks to vigilance and good seamanship, the steamer got safely away after taking all the soldiers on board. At two o'clock the following morning, while Captain Watson was going the rounds to see that all the men he had saved were comfortable, two shots were fired at the Lady Plymouth, one passing over her amidships and the other dropping a hundred yards astern. No craft was sighted, but there is no doubt that the U boat was still in chase. However, the vessel got safely into Algiers, having on board fifty-five French soldiers—all that were saved out of some nine hundred who were on board the transport Calvados when she was torpedoed. Captain Watson was awarded a gold medal by the French Government for his services on this occasion.

In February, 1916, when the Lady Plymouth was in the Atlantic south of Gibraltar, she was hailed by a suspicious vessel who made signals for her to stop. German submarines had been active in that neighbourhood for some time, and were known to have disguised themselves as tramps, with dummy funnel and upper works. Besides, it was not long since the raider Möwe had passed through the same region. So, when Captain Watson found the first signals followed by a gibberish which he could not comprehend, he came to the conclusion that someone was trying to lure him close enough to be destroyed with the minimum of trouble ; and, putting on full speed, he signalled in the international code, "I cannot understand your message, and thank you."

In the following April, those on board the Lady Plymouth heard the sound of firing, and, though they could see nothing, distinctly counted thirty-one shots. The vessel kept on her course, and about an hour later sighted the Russian barquentine Imperator. There was no one on board ; the sails were flapping aimlessly about ; and the

Ignoring the bait

vessel, loaded with timber, was on fire. A boarding-party was despatched to endeavour to put out the fire, and the Imperator was taken in tow ; and then, shortly after midnight, a red flare was observed which, on investigation, was found to come from a lifeboat containing twenty-four officers and men of the crew of the steamship Angus, which had been sunk by a submarine a few hours before. A few days later the Lady Plymouth skilfully avoided the deliberate attempt of a submarine to torpedo her in the neighbourhood of Gibraltar, and in June, 1916, an attempt was made by German agents to blow her up as she lay in an American port awaiting her cargo. The incendiaries endeavoured to get on board and drop their infernal machines into her open holds, and were only deterred when the night watchman opened fire on them.

A charmed existence

Such is the bare record of fifteen months' experiences of a British merchantman in war time—a vessel of whose name not one person in a thousand is aware. It is typical in a way of the extraordinary work that was done by the mercantile marine as part of its daily and nightly routine. The risk of sudden death moved alongside our merchantmen wherever they went, and the most outrageous punishments were held out in prospect by the Germans if ever a man who had avoided a submarine attack should fall into their hands. Nothing, however, succeeded, and nothing is ever likely to succeed, in disturbing the equilibrium of the British merchant seaman. Calmly and quietly he proceeded with his own business, in the face of perils far greater, far more subtle, and certainly no less inhuman than any trader faced in the heyday of the Barbary pirates.

Whether fighting in advance of the Navy on the North Sea Patrol, shoulder to shoulder with it in all its fights from Coronel to Jutland, or following up in its rear to clear the seas of mines scattered by a retreating enemy, the merchant service proved itself worthy to rank with the greatest of our fighting sea kings.

HOW ENEMY SUBMARINES WERE PACKED FOR TRANSPORT OVERLAND.

To avoid a long sea passage, the peril of mines and hostile ships, smaller German submarines were occasionally transported overland from Kiel and Wilhelmshaven to Zeebrugge, whence they were able to pursue their policy of piracy on the high seas. This illustration, though not taken during the Great War, shows how U boats were packed for transport, to be fitted on arrival at their destination.

CHAPTER CXXXI.

JAPAN'S SPLENDID SHARE IN THE WAR.

By Robert Machray.

Japan Declares War on Germany, August 23rd, 1914—Capture of Tsingtau—Japanese Navy Takes Possession of Micronesia—Co-operation of Japanese Navy with British Warships—Baron Ishii on Japanese Co-operation in the War on Land in Europe—Elimination of Germany in the Far East the Primary Japanese Object—Japan a Member of the Entente—German Overtures for a German-Japanese Entente—German Intrigues in the Orient—Work of the Japanese Navy in Protecting British Littorals and Convoying Troops—Restoration of Russian Warships to Russia—Supply of Munitions to Russia—The Effect on the Campaigns Conducted by the Grand Duke Nicholas and General Brussiloff—Russian Imperial Mission to Tokyo—Russo-Japanese Convention of July, 1916—Chagrin in Germany—The Effect of the Convention upon the Anglo-Japanese Alliance—German Intrigues in China—Friction Between China and Japan—Japanese Triumph over German Intrigue—Japan's Financial Position—Japan's Disinterested Financial Assistance to the Cause of the Allies.

ORIENTALS have always been credited with an infinite capacity for silence—which, according to circumstances, might cover a very great deal, or mean no more than that there was nothing worth talking about. In her war with Russia, Japan showed how well she could hold her peace and keep her own counsel, when it seemed good to her to be taciturn; but she generally had excellent reasons for her temporary inarticulateness. For one thing, it made her enemy imagine she was inactive, while all the time she was exceedingly busy.

After her capture, in conjunction with the British under General Barnardiston, of Tsingtau and the district of Kiao-chau, of which that town was the capital, in November, 1914 (see Chapter L.), so little appeared in the Press, or otherwise came to light—at least up to the close of the second year of the war—respecting what Japan was doing towards the prosecution of the whole colossal conflict that, misled by this silence, it was widely supposed that, with the expulsion of the Germans from the territory which they had forced China to "lease" to them, she

practically had ceased to take any further important share in the struggle.

THREE JAPANESE NOTABILITIES.
Count Okuma (left), Prime Minister, and Baron Kato, Minister of Foreign Affairs. Mr. J. Okuma (standing), the Premier's heir.

But this was very far from being the case; for Japan, though she kept quiet about it, continued to contribute most materially to the common cause—not so much by actual fighting as by assisting in the most splendid and wholehearted manner the other Allies to fight. This she did chiefly in two ways. She helped the Russians in the field in Europe directly by providing them with an abundance of the munitions of war which they lacked, but which were vital to them, and to a very large extent she relieved the British, French, and Russian warships in the Indian and Pacific Oceans, and set them free for service elsewhere, while she herself kept watch and ward over these immense water areas. She also did all that was possible to her financially to aid the Entente Powers, and instead of seeking loans from them, took up part of their loans, or assumed obligations which had the same effect.

Japan declared war on Germany on August 23rd, 1914, and on the following day the Emperor of Japan issued a proclamation to his subjects, in which he defined her attitude towards both Great

Britain and the enemy. He spoke of her desire for peace—no country in the world had a greater interest in maintaining tranquillity, especially, of course, in the Far East. He said that Germany was making warlike preparations in Kiao-chau which were a threat to British and other shipping in the Eastern Seas, and he pointed out that the action of Germany had compelled Japan's ally, Great Britain, to commence hostilities. He therefore commanded all his people, high and low, to make every effort, in accordance with international law, to defeat their common enemy, and placing no limit to the part Japan was to play, ordered his Army and Navy to carry on the war with "all their might."

Tsingtau was the striking and almost immediate result. By its capture from Germany a heavy blow was dealt to her prestige in the Far East, which had been very considerable owing to her success in intimidating China into what amounted to the surrender to her of Kiao-chau, and because of her incessant intrigues and the vainglorious self-advertisement of the strength of her military power. But Kiao-chau was not the only, though it was the most important, territory that was wrested from Germany by Japan. Some thirty years before, Germany, casting about all over the world how to make good what she called her "place in the sun," had seized a number of islands in the Western Pacific, to which no other Power had laid claim, and on one of these, named Jaluit, she established a naval base.

Germany in the Western Pacific

These islands lay, roughly speaking, between Japan and Australia, and in the hands of a strong empire, such as Germany, could be made to possess a high strategic significance. As Germany had also occupied the northern portion of New Guinea, as well as the Bismarck Archipelago, farther south, she had substantial interests in this quarter of the globe. The Japanese turned their attention, however, to the islands which have just been referred to. Grouped under the general title of Micronesia, they were known as the Marianne (or Ladrones) Islands, the Marshall Islands, and the Caroline Islands. For the most part they were coral atolls, slightly raised above high water, and none of them was large. Of these the most easterly were the Marshalls; there were some twenty-three of them in all, and Jaluit, the best, though not the most populous of them, became the headquarters of the Germans, with an Imperial commissioner in command.

Her surrender of Micronesia

A squadron of the First Fleet of the Japanese Navy, questing in these waters for enemy ships, visited Jaluit on October 6th, 1914, and the Germans gave up the island without resistance. Japanese marines destroyed all the German military establishments and seized their munitions and supplies. About the same date Japan in the Carolines took Yap Island, the local seat of the German Government in that area. Before the end of October, 1914, all Micronesia was in the hands of the Japanese. There was no fighting, as Japan displayed to the discomfited enemy naval strength far more than sufficient to render any real

SECTION OF THE ILTIS FORT, TSINGTAU, AFTER CAPTURE BY THE JAPANESE.
The Iltis Fort was one of the capital defences of Tsingtau on the land side. At dawn on October 31st, 1914, the Japanese began their bombardment with siege-artillery, and on the night of November 6th they carried the position.

THE SHELL-MAKERS OF TOKYO.

To cope with the ever-increasing demand by Russia for shells, as many as forty thousand workers were engaged day and night in the Japanese arsenals at Tokyo and Ostaka.

opposition impossible. Forthwith she set about re-organising the government of the islands, and according to a statement made on July 17th, 1916, in the British Parliament by Lord Robert Cecil, as Foreign Under-Secretary, she was at that time administering the Carolines and all the Marshalls with the exception of Namu.

If her operations in Kiao-chau and in Micronesia exhausted the list of the military achievements of Japan in the conquest of the territory of the enemy, her Navy constantly co-operated with the British warships in Far Eastern seas. When this chapter of THE GREAT WAR was written the vast extent and extraordinary value of that co-operation was but little understood among the people of the Allies. It had not transpired, for instance, how much the Japanese Fleet had done in the hunt for the Emden, or in helping to round up Von Spee's vessels, which had escaped from Tsingtau on the outbreak of the war, and finally were destroyed in the Battle off the Falkland

Japan's naval co-operation
Islands; but it was known that the Japanese Navy had something to do with these events, both of which were notable. In addition to her obligations to Great Britain under the Anglo-Japanese Alliance, the implementing of which was a matter for arrangement between the two Powers subscribing to the treaty, the supreme consideration of Japan in the war was the extirpation of German influence and the shutting down of German military or commercial activity in Eastern Asia, with the complete cessation of all their disturbing effects. Her idea was the elimination of Germany in the Far East; and regarding the Far East as primarily and chiefly her military sphere, she in the main kept to it, nobly fulfilling her share in the general, world-wide campaign of the Allies against the Central Powers.

In the first months of the war the view found expression in England that Japan should be invited to co-operate with the other Allies by despatching an army to Europe, and the figure of half a million men was sometimes men-

tioned in this connection. At that time Great Britain had hardly begun to raise and equip the mighty armies which later she placed in the field, and there was a holding back on the part of some of her people. Over in Japan this greatly puzzled the Japanese, who could not understand how they should be asked to send soldiers to Europe when there were thousands upon thousands of young men in the United Kingdom who were not in the British Army, and apparently had no intention of joining the Colours. However, in a remarkable interview which Baron Ishii, the Foreign Minister of Japan, gave to the correspondent of a French journal in November, 1915, official Japan said that Japan would send a very strong army to Europe if it seemed to be desirable, but that she had not yet even considered such an eventuality. By using the word "desirable" in this statement, Baron Ishii showed Japan's willingness to assist the Allies with her troops in Europe.

Japan was in thorough sympathy and in complete accord with the Entente Powers—nay, she herself was a member **Problem of military aid** of the Entente Group. Besides her Alliance with Great Britain, she had ententes with both France and Russia, though they did not go so far as did the Alliance, which, initiated in 1902 and revised and extended in 1905 and 1911, provided, among other things—such as the independence and territorial integrity of China—that if Great Britain or Japan were involved anywhere in a war, arising from unprovoked attack or aggressive action by any Power or Powers, the other party to the treaty should at once come to the military assistance of its ally. In 1907 Japan formed ententes with Russia and France. All the while a rapprochement was going on between Japan and Russia, and this found expression in an agreement or convention in 1910, which pledged the two Powers to the maintenance of the *status quo* in China, leading the way in 1916 to another agreement, which was tantamount to a formal alliance; but it may be questioned whether anything of the kind would have come about so soon had it not been for the magnificent manner in which Japan assisted her old foe as regards munitions during the war.

Though Japan was thus allied with Great Britain and on the most cordial terms with the other two Entente Powers, it should not be forgotten that she might conceivably not have joined in the war in their favour. She might have declared her neutrality. Indeed, there was a current of political opinion that was not friendly to the Anglo-Japanese Alliance, affirming that that treaty circumscribed far too much Japan's action, particularly with respect to China. Moreover, there were some of the Japanese who believed that Germany would emerge victorious from the conflict. But neither of these was the view of Japan as a nation, nor was official Japan in the least responsive to them. On the contrary, Japan never hesitated, but from the outset sided with the Entente.

Had she been content to remain neutral, and given no support to Great Britain, France, and Russia, the position of the Allies would have at once become most grave. The first would have had to keep a fleet at least equal to that of Japan (which at that time totalled upwards of half a million tons) for the protection of India, Australia, and New Zealand, not to mention the coast of Western Canada. This would most seriously have affected the British naval dispositions in the North Sea and in the Atlantic, and have been of the utmost benefit to the German Navy. The second would have been forced to place in Asia several army corps, besides warships, for the defence of her Indo-Chinese possessions. The third must have retained at least a million troops in Siberia, and thereby her armies in Europe would have been that much the weaker. Japan knew all these things very well, as did Germany, but she had made her choice.

Germany had courted her in the past, and German jingoes, like Count Reventlow, had frequently and clamorously asserted that Germany should come to an

Organising victory for the Great Republic: General Joffre at work in his Headquarters.

Boulevardiers of the moment : Jubilant heroes from the trenches on leave in Paris.

Hero-worship in a French newspaper printing works : A soldier-printer visits his old comrades of the machine-room.

"Into the jaws of death": *French officer about to convey a message under heavy fire.*

understanding with her, and make an entente. But long before the war Japan had made up her mind that her real friend, on every ground, was Great Britain and not Germany, though the latter posed in that rôle. Her eyes were opened to the want of sincerity in the protestations of Germany in 1894, when, after the Treaty of Shimonoseki, by which China had ceded to her Southern Man-

Kaiser's intrigues against Japan churia, including Port Arthur, the German Kaiser induced France and Russia to join him in strong diplomatic and menacing action that resulted in her retroceding to China the Manchurian territory she had won in war. The Anglo-Japanese Alliance of 1902 was in itself a blow to his ambitions and intrigues, which, however, were again apparent when two years later he urged Russia, whom he desired to keep occupied outside Europe, on the course of policy in the Far East that brought about her unfortunate war with Japan.

Japan had never forgotten what the Kaiser had done in these matters, and she was well aware that Germany was incessantly intriguing against her in China and, farther afield, in the United States. In 1908 the Kaiser nearly succeeded in placing China in direct and open hostility to the Anglo-Japanese Alliance, though that treaty was the best guarantee of the independence of China and the inviolability of her territory. His plan was to form an alliance of China, the United States, and Germany against Great Britain and Japan. It failed, but his machinations and plots continued, and it was largely owing to them that China was a prey to unrest and internal disunion, with something approaching anarchy, during 1915 and 1916.

The struggle between the Entente and the Central Powers was foreseen by the sagacious statesmen of Japan, and they knew perfectly on which side she would stand when it broke out. In their opinion her action was the logical outcome of her policy during the years that had preceded the war, and they never wavered. A rumour was long current that at the start the Kaiser sent a despatch to the Emperor of Japan asking him to throw in his lot with Germany, and promising whatever he wished; but it was false, as was stated on authority later. The Kaiser could not but be aware how vain and fruitless such a request would be, and certainly nothing of the sort reached Japan.

In the eyes of Japan the capture of Kiao-chau, though it was undoubtedly a fine achievement, did not appear a great feat of arms in comparison with the main events and incidents of the war; but that which pleased her about it was that its moral effect in Eastern Asia was very great in the undoing of German influence, to the utmost benefit of the Allies both by land and sea in the Far East. Another important feature of her operations in Kiao-chau was that the Siege of Tsingtau immobilised several of the German gunboats, besides an Austrian cruiser, which otherwise might easily have perpetrated raids and done much mischief to such British centres as Hong Kong and Singapore. The rest of the German Asiatic Fleet, which had got out of Tsingtau, was quite prepared to attack Australia and the islands belonging to the Entente Powers in the southern

seas, but both Great Britain and Japan took action, described earlier in others parts of this history (see Chapter XLVI.), which within a few months rid the oceans of this peril.

From the beginning of the war Japan's part in it from the naval point of view was of exceptional importance, and continued to be the same, all the multifarious services rendered by her warships being performed with remarkable energy and the highest efficiency. In the first year of the struggle Japanese vessels protected the coasts of Australia, New Zealand, and British Columbia at a time when German cruisers still roamed the Pacific. The Parliament of British Columbia, indeed, placed on its records a public acknowledgment of the work done by the Japanese Navy in the interests of that province of Canada. After all the German warships had been swept from the Indian and Pacific Oceans, and the enemy merchant marine in these waters had been either captured or bottled up in neutral ports, such as those of the Dutch East Indies, the Navy of

DISAPPEARING GUN IN THE BISMARCK FORT, TSINGTAU.
The formidable Bismarck Mountain position was destroyed at the beginning of November, 1914, by the British pre-Dreadnought H.M.S. Triumph. Her shooting was so good that she put the fort out of action with seven shells.

Japan was never idle, though little was heard of its many activities. It was natural that, with the main concentration of the British Navy in the North Sea, with British patrols all around the shores of the British Isles and out into the Atlantic, and with the French and, later, the Italian Fleets guarding the Mediterranean, the charge confided to Japan should be the Eastern Seas and the great ocean routes from Hong Kong to Vancouver, from Singapore to Suez and Zanzibar, and she remained primarily responsible for them.

Troops from Australia and New Zealand were convoyed to the Red Sea with the assistance of Japanese cruisers, not once but frequently. **Japanese cruisers** Now and then a glimpse of what was going **as convoys** on in this way was obtained by the general public, who else knew nothing about it, as when a notice appeared in the Press of a presentation by members of the New Zealand Expeditionary Force of a silver model of a Maori war-canoe to Captain Kato, of the Japanese warship Ibuki, which had been one of the squadron

FRIENDS AND ALLIES.
The Russian Grand Duke George Mikhailovitch reviewing the Japanese Imperial Guards Division.

protecting the transports bound for Egypt. Part at least of the Russian soldiers, who in 1916 were fighting in the trenches by the side of the French and the British on the western front, were embarked from Dairen, the Japanese port in Manchuria and the terminus of the Japanese railway which connects with Russia's great trans-continental line across Siberia.

A wider and better notion of what the Japanese Navy was doing on the oceans of the East was obtained from a speech made in the Japanese Parliament by Admiral Yashiro, the Minister of Marine. He said that, subsequent to the occupation of Kiao-chau, the strength of the Japanese warships which were constantly employed in co-operating with the British Navy was 225,000 tons, or, expressed in another form, was equal to nearly the total naval strength of Japan in the Russo-Japanese War. In carrying out the task that had been committed to her capable hands of guarding the Indian and Pacific Oceans, Japan used a naval strength double that of the British Eastern and Australian Fleets prior to the war. When the war broke out the Navy of Japan was most formidable, its total strength being about 650,000 tons, and all this was at the disposal of the Allies, if required; Japan put more than one-third of it as one of her contributions to the common cause. This took no account, furthermore, of the activities on the same behalf of her merchant marine.

Japanese goodwill to Russia

There was a report at one time, which was spread by German newspapers, that after the sinking of two of her big passenger liners by enemy submarines in the Mediterranean she stationed cruisers in the Mediterranean, but this statement was incorrect. Though the activities of the Japanese Navy were so incessant and so various, they fortunately did not cost her much in ships, her only losses, and these of comparatively small consideration, being incurred in the Kiao-chau operations. During the

Siege of Tsingtau a third-class cruiser, the Takachiho, one destroyer, one torpedo-boat, and three steamers employed as mine-sweepers were destroyed by mines or gun fire.

In March, 1916, Japan performed an act which at once reflected credit upon her, and at the same time showed how utterly former animosities had disappeared. This was the return to Russia of the two battleships Sagami and Tango and the armoured cruiser Soya, vessels which had taken part on the Russian side in the Russo-Japanese War under the names of the Peresviet, Poltava, and Variag. These ships had been sunk by

JAPANESE AT THE ITALIAN NAVAL SCHOOL, MODENA.

the Japanese during that conflict, but they had been raised by patient Japanese skill, refitted, rearmed, and transformed into fine fighting units. Japan did not hand back these warships to Russia without receiving value for them, but by restoring them she gave Russia a navy in the Pacific, and demonstrated afresh the goodwill she bore to that empire.

This was a striking instance of her friendship with Russia, yet it almost dropped into insignificance when compared with the vast and continued services which she ungrudgingly rendered to her old antagonist in the making of all kinds of munitions for the Russian armies. Russia, however, was not the only member of the Entente combination to whom she gave arms.

In the early days of the war Japan was not so badly prepared for it as were most of the Allies, and she threw open her very considerable military stores for the common benefit. Thus, a part of Kitchener's new armies was furnished with Japanese rifles, and all the Allies except Italy had certain rifle supplies from Japan, who also provided some guns for the British Navy. But it was on behalf of Russia that she worked wonders in manufacturing munitions, invoking for the prodigious effort all her industrial resources, and keeping at work, day and night, every available mill and factory in the country, besides the Government arsenals.

Japan began to send munitions to Russia from the very outset of the war. As far back as September, 1914, the correspondent of the London "Times" in Petrograd reported that heavy siege-guns, purchased from Japan on the outbreak of the war, were already in position on the Russian front in Europe. In proportion to the enormous scope and protracted duration of the stupendous conflict which the ambition and arrogance of Germany forced upon the world, Russia was but poorly supplied with munitions. She possessed no such resources, either in her Government works or in her industrial communities, as were at all equal to what she required, but her lack of arms and supplies was not at first evident.

Baron Ishii's revelation It was only when it was known that the retreat from Galicia and Poland of her armies, as brave as any that ever fought on any stricken field, which began in May, 1915, and continued into October of that year, was entirely due to her shortage in shells, rifles, and other munitions that her tragical deficiencies came to be understood. Yet prior to the fall of Warsaw in August, 1915, Japan had sent to Russia, to speak of rifles alone, a number sufficient to arm no fewer than fifty-two divisions, or, put in another way, something like three-quarters of a million of rifles. She had also despatched to Russia a considerable quantity of field-artillery and of heavy guns.

It was after Warsaw had passed into the possession of the enemy that Japan, at the urgent request of the other Allies, so greatly expanded her munitionary capacity, and mobilised all her mills, factories, and plant of all sorts that was of use. In November, 1915, in the course of the interview already quoted, Baron Ishii, after mentioning that two Japanese arsenals were constantly employed in producing to their full power munitions for Russia, stated that of the troops Russia had mobilised or was mobilising at that time only one-third was armed, and that Japan was arming the rest. It seemed a tall order, even for the devotion of the Japanese, but it was filled.

During the summer of 1915 Japan had experienced a political crisis connected with her domestic affairs which left its after effects. The Marquis, then Count, Okuma, one of the most distinguished and far-seeing among her leaders, was forced to resign the Premiership, but the country rallied round him, and he came into power again. Yet, however much her politicians quarrelled among themselves, and feeling ran high in her Parliament, the making of munitions went on just the same. In October of that year the coronation of the Emperor Yoshihito took place with all the time-honoured, beautiful, and stately ceremonial of Japan, but the flow of arms into Russia never stopped for a moment. And all through the winter of 1915–16 and the following spring, munitions in extraordinary plenitude were poured into the ports of Vladivostock and Dairen, and long processions of trains loaded with them were daily to be seen hurrying across the great Siberian plains to the Russian depôts in Europe and the Caucasus.

Magnificent results were almost immediately apparent when in January, 1916, the Grand Duke Nicholas inaugurated his campaign in Armenia and Persia, driving the Turks out of their stronghold of Erzerum in the one region and from their headquarters in Kermanshah in the other. But they were still more strikingly exhibited

in the succeeding June of that year when the brilliant Brussiloff, carrying out the plans of Alexeieff and the Russian High Command, began his splendid offensive against the Austro-German armies between the marshes of the Pripet and the Pruth. The speedy and wonderful success of his brave soldiers was prepared chiefly by the guns and shells that had been sent to him in such prodigious quantities for months past by Japan. Nothing on such an overwhelming scale had been expected by the enemy, and his front was broken to pieces. Japan's silence had borne amazing fruit.

In 1915 Japan furnished Russia with munitions to the value of two hundred millions of yen, or in English money rather more than twenty millions sterling, and in the first half of 1916 her production was of even greater value. Besides guns of all calibres, rifles, bayonets, and ammunition, Japan

SONS OF THE TWO ISLAND EMPIRES.
Japanese sailors at gun practice. Above: British sailors landing at Tsingtau after the capitulation. The ships bombarded Tsingtau effectively from the very long range of nine miles.

also sent large quantities of cloth and hundreds of thousands of boots for the Russian soldiers. In 1915 she provided for Russia ten million yards of cloth, eight millions of which were made in Japanese mills, the rest being taken from the Government stores. In many other ways she rendered prompt and efficient aid, and among them was the coining of silver into Russian roubles and smaller pieces in immense numbers.

Not the least item in the account of all that Japan did for Russia was the comparative cheapness of the munitions and other articles which she sold to the latter Power, and this important feature came from the low cost of labour among the Japanese—Russia got the benefit of it to the full. When the manufacturers of the United States supplied the Allies with munitions it was at a much higher figure, because

WESTERN WARFARE IN THE ORIENT.
Portable Japanese trench-mortars, used by our Far Eastern ally in the approach trenches around Tsingtau. The mortars shown in the illustration have their muzzles covered to keep out damp.

THE MORNING TUB—JAPANESE STYLE.
Japanese warrior bathing in the special tub, typical of Far Eastern army equipment—an impression from the Kiao-chau area of hostilities.

everything was much dearer there than in Japan. For example, Japan was able to let Russia have rifles at about seventy shillings each, whereas rifles in America cost something like twice as much. And there was this further difference between the United States and Japan. In the case of the former, private firms and establishments, spurred on principally by the desire for commercial profit, made the munitions; but in the case of the latter, it was the Japanese Government itself—or that Government standing behind and urging on, by giving assistance in cash or with practical advice, the private manufacturers of Japan—that directed, controlled, and ensured the tremendous output that was so necessary for Russia.

Russia, as well she might be, was exceedingly grateful. She showed her keen appreciation of Japan's prodigious efforts on her behalf by an Imperial Mission, headed by the Grand Duke Mikhailovitch, a near relative of the Tsar, to Tokyo, where it arrived in January, 1916, and was enthusiastically welcomed by the Japanese. The visit was naturally an occasion for the display of all the courtesy and fine manners that are immemorial in Japan, and the Russians fully responded. The Emperor was present at a banquet given to the guests, and in toasting Russia, spoke with confidence of her future and that of the Entente Powers. The Grand Duke Mikhailovitch in reply said that Japan's sympathy for Russia, and the immense assistance Japan had given to the Russian armies throughout the war, had created a feeling of unbounded gratitude in his country, and guaranteed a lasting friendship between the two great empires.

But more lay behind this Russian mission than thanks, however sincere and profuse, or an exchange of compliments, however pretty and deserved, as was seen when, in July, 1916, it was announced **New Russo-** that a convention had been signed in **Japanese agreement** Petrograd by the two Powers which blended their efforts to secure and preserve enduring peace in the Far East. By this agreement Russia and Japan undertook two things. First, each of the subscribers agreed not to become a party to any arrangement or political combination directed against the other. Secondly, they pledged themselves, in the event of the territorial rights or the special interests in the Far East of either, which were recognised by the other, being threatened, that they would take counsel together with regard to the adoption of measures for safeguarding and defending those rights and interests. It was understood at the time that the two Powers had come to an arrangement respecting various definite matters of importance, and no surprise was excited when the further announcement was made in August that Russia, in recognition of the invaluable help Japan had rendered to her, had consented to make over to Japan that portion of the Chinese Eastern Railway which ran from Changchun to Harbin, and also had settled in favour of Japan a question as to the rights of Japanese shipping in the Sungari River, which had been in dispute since the Portsmouth Treaty of 1905.

As affecting the course of the war, the outstanding result of the convention was that it put an effectual stop to Germany's attempts to seduce either Russia or Japan from the number of the Entente Powers or from the Pact of London, by which these Powers covenanted to make peace only by common consent. Germany had offered, not once but several times, a separate peace to both Russia and Japan, and this fresh agreement between these two empires was their crushing reply. Great were the disappointment and chagrin of Germany. In her characteristic way, she tried to sow discord among the Allies by representing that the convention was a blow at Great Britain, and by suggesting that it might be looked on as replacing the Anglo-Japanese Alliance—instead of its being the corollary and complement of that treaty, as in fact it was.

The truth was that the convention had been made with the full knowledge and the complete approval of Great Britain, who had no interest stronger in the Far East than a lasting friendship between Russia and

German efforts to sow discord

Japan. The terms of the convention, when published, were received with pleasure in the United Kingdom. But in this attitude towards them Germany pretended to see nothing but the "usual British hypocrisy." German comment, as expressed by the "Cologne Gazette," a leading and typical German journal, and in close touch with the Kaiser and the German Government, said that while the convention strengthened to an extraordinary degree the position of

Japan in the Far East, and by forestalling Russian opposition made it much easier for her to exploit China, the real sufferer was Great Britain, together with the United States, and that it was absurd for the British people to profess to welcome it, when it was plain that British, like American, influence in China was being steadily reduced more and more by Japan. Yet in reality what the convention brought about was a further cementing of the alliance of Great Britain with both Japan and Russia, all indissolubly united in the one great purpose of over-throwing Germany. That disturber of

Renewed intrigue in China

the world took very good care to say nothing regarding the blow to her hopes which the convention was, nor did she succeed in causing ill-will among the Allies, though she went on, as before, to do her utmost through China.

Under cover of China, who had declared neutrality at the beginning of the war, Germany continued her incessant and unscrupulous campaign of intrigue against the Entente Powers. She bought up and edited Chinese newspapers, which she filled with reports, many of them false, of her victories, and with slanders of the Allies. From her concessions in the bunds of the various treaty ports she conducted a propaganda of lies and distorted statements to impress the Chinese and any other people she could reach. She egged on the Chinese Government, then presided over by Yuan Shi-kai, to oppose the Japanese in particular, and when the latter, after the wresting of Kiao-chau from the Germans, declared that by their conquest of the district they were entitled to fall heir in that area to all the German rights and privileges, including the railway which the Germans had built, she stirred up China to protest and take measures injurious to Japan.

ON WAR SERVICE IN THE FAR EAST: JAPANESE SAILORS CLEANING THE GUNS ON A BATTLESHIP.

JAPAN'S PART ON THE EASTERN FRONT.

When the Germans took possession of Brest Litovsk a number of Japanese cannon used by the Russians were captured. Some of these are seen in this illustration, together with ammunition waggons which, it will be noted, are marked with Japanese characters.

This action of China led to a grave crisis in 1915 in the political relations of the two countries, and for a time it looked as if war were inevitable between them—which was exactly what Germany had been playing for, with a view to the embarrassment of Japan and of the other Allies through Japan, for it was clear that if Japan had to fight China she would not be in a position to do so much munitionary and other work for her friends. The situation was greatly strained for some months, but Japan was firm, and in the end China gave way. As results of the negotiations that then took place Japan secured valuable concessions, such as ninety-nine year leases of the South Manchurian Railway and the Antung-Mukden Railway, to which she already had an excellent title. She also had demanded from China an undertaking that the latter would not cede or lease any portion of her coastline or

AFTER TEN YEARS.

The complete reconciliation of two honourable foes. Photograph taken by a Russian officer, showing some of the Japanese and Russian soldiers in company.

any of her islands to any Power except Japan, but on China issuing a proclamation that she would not alienate any part of her coastline or any of her islands to any Power whatsoever, Japan was content. The German-fomented agitation had done no good to either Germany or China.

Japanese jingoes, who disliked the Anglo-Japanese Alliance, asserted that China had been let off far too lightly, and hinted that it was because of Great Britain. But the statesmen of Japan replied that they had no wish that Japan should pose as dictator in China, and that her policy remained based, as in the past, on the independence and territorial integrity of China, which was guaranteed by Japan and Great Britain, and virtually by France, Russia, and the United States. The business of Japan, they said, was to help China to get on her

ENEMY FIND AT GRODNO.

German soldiers unearthing a 28 cm. howitzer of Japanese origin, buried at Grodno before the Russian retreat, August, 1915.

feet, and to free her from pressure from outside, but meanwhile Japan could not afford that China should drift into anarchy. China was too near to herself for her to permit a state of chaos in that country, in which she also had large interests.

Japan had to conserve her interests in China and elsewhere, for she was not a rich country in the same sense that Great Britain and France were rich. Her war with Russia had imposed on her a debt of two hundred millions, and the interest on it, together with the upkeep of her national services, had seriously burdened her people, some of whom complained of the necessary taxation, and protested that this or that service might be managed at less cost. It **Japan's financial resources** so happened that Japan, when she declared war on Germany, had a surplus in her treasury of ten millions sterling, which had been acquired by the most rigid economies spread over three years, and had involved the retirement of three thousand functionaries. Financially, Japan was not a Great Power, and these ten millions, so hardly come by, were a vast sum to her, but she devoted it to the war, and never asked her wealthy Allies for money. It also was the case that the general position of her trade and commerce was one of depression at that time, but there was a marked improvement, which set in during the

COMMANDER SHIMOMURA.
Lost with the Queen Mary in the Jutland Battle.

ADMIRAL KATAOKA AND HIS STAFF ABOARD THE FUSÉ.
On the occasion of the Coronation Naval Review at Tokio.

latter half of 1915, owing to the large sums derived from the sale of munitions and from her shipping, though, as in other lands, some industries suffered considerably from the war. The national gold reserve increased rapidly, and thus, instead of it being necessary for her to receive financial·help, she was able to give assistance in the financing of her Allies which, taking into account her comparative poverty, was on a considerable scale, and was as much as was within her limited power.

Great Britain experienced a good deal of difficulty in paying in America for the enormous quantities of munitions and supplies which she had bought there, and the rate of exchange fell. Now, Japan had twelve millions in gold deposited in New York, and she transferred the whole sum to Great Britain by taking British Treasury bonds in London against the amount. The financing of Russia was also one of the difficulties of the Allies, and Japanese bankers helped by buying five million pounds' worth of Russian bonds, and by promising to take a similar sum later. Japan also did something for France, for her Budget for 1916 set aside five millions for the redemption of Japanese railway bonds, which had been placed in Paris before the war.

Unlike that of her Allies, the debt of Japan decreased during the war, and by the end of the second year of the struggle her gold reserve had grown to sixty million pounds. Of this immense sum she kept more than one half in London—which was at once an assistance to British finance generally and for the prosecution of the war, and a remarkable proof of the confidence she reposed in Great Britain.

THE MEETING OF "THE TWAIN": WESTERN ROLLING STOCK AND EASTERN BANNERS.
There is a curious blending of East and West in this illustration of Japanese school-children cheering the Mikado's soldiers on their way to Tsingtau. While the flags and some of the costumes are essentially Japanese, the locomotive and sheds are incongruously Western.

FORTIFIED WITH THE BLESSING OF THE CHURCH: ABSOLUTION BEFORE BATTLE.

It was the invariable custom of French Roman Catholic soldiers going into action to present themselves before a priest, and their confession, by ecclesiastical authority, having been taken as heard, receive absolution and the blessing of the Church on the self-sacrificing duty before them.

THE "PADRE" IN THE FIGHTING-LINE.

By F. A. McKenzie.

The Chaplain-General's Department at the War Office—Harmonious Co-operation of the Churches at the Front—The Rev. Lionel Studd—Army Chaplains at Mons—The Rev. O. S. Watkins Accompanies the Retreat to Tournan—Heroic Chaplain Wins the D.S.O.—Work of the Chaplains on Gallipoli—The Rev. J. A. Luxford at Anzac—Burial of the Dead—Death of the Rev. William Grant—Prayers at Walker's Ridge Gully—Armistice Day—The New Zealanders and their Padre—Suvla Bay—Mr. Luxford Loses a Leg—The Dean of Sydney holds Communion Service under Shell Fire—Service in a "Jack Johnson" Shell Hole—Colonel McKenzie, of the Salvation Army, Wins the Military Medal—Twenty Weeks in the Trenches—The Rev. A. G. Parham Wins the Military Cross—Canadian Chaplain Buries Comrades in No Man's Land Single-handed—The Rev. Edward Noel Mellish Wins the V.C.—The Battle of Loos—Chaplains of the Highland Brigade—Service in a Cellar at Ypres—Father William Finn at Seddul-Bahr.

EARLY in the Great War even the newest and youngest British soldier learned to call the chaplains by a special name, padre—father. It was a significant title, sure proof that the chaplains had won the affection and confidence of the men. What the chaplains did, how worthily they carried out their high task, can be judged to some extent from the official honours' lists. One chaplain—a South London curate—won the Victoria Cross, while many were given the Military Cross and other decorations for gallantry in the field. The long list of clergy killed and wounded in the war tells its own tale—the naval chaplains who sank with their ships; the workers with the Army wounded in the trenches of Flanders, torn asunder by shells in the advance on the Somme, or cut down while comforting the dying in the Dardanelles. But the crowning testimony to their work came from the men among whom they laboured. It is not too much to say that thousands of our men had their whole pur-

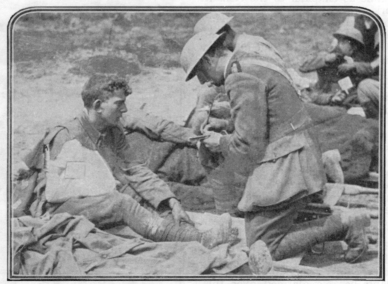

THE MINISTRY OF KINDNESS.
A British chaplain writing a field postcard for a wounded man whose right arm had been disabled.

pose of life turned by the lessons learned from the simple services in the gullies of Gallipoli, in barns and dug-outs in Flanders, or in open-air gatherings, where the ceremonies of faith were ever liable to interruption from chance shell or gas attack.

The work of the Churches in the British Army is controlled by the Chaplain-General's Department at the War Office. At the beginning of the war one chaplain was allowed to each brigade; but this number was found inadequate, and was later on considerably increased. In addition to the regular chaplain of the brigade—Anglican for English regiments, Presbyterian for Scottish, etc.—other Churches could obtain the right of appointing chaplains under certain conditions. The British chaplains were drawn from the Anglicans, Presbyterians, Roman Catholics, Wesleyans, a Nonconformist Board, and Jews. With the Dominion forces the field of selection was even wider. Thus the Australian Government appointed thirteen Salvation Army officers as military chaplains

THE CHAPLAIN-GENERAL TO THE FORCES. [*Russell.*]
The Rt. Rev. John Taylor Smith, D.D., C.V.O., appointed Chaplain-General in 1901. He accompanied the Ashanti Expedition in 1895, and afterwards was Bishop of Sierra Leone.

The Chaplain-General to the Forces, Bishop Taylor Smith, had, before joining the Services, done distinguished service in West Africa, first as Canon Missioner in Sierra Leone, and subsequently as bishop of that diocese. He acted for a time as chaplain to the Ashanti Expedition, when his work brought him in touch with Prince Henry of Battenberg during his last illness. He brought back Prince Henry's last messages to his wife and to Queen Victoria. He was appointed one of the honorary chaplains to the Queen, and when the bishop retired from his see in Africa, he was appointed to control the religious work of the Army. Next to him were the Rev. Dr. Simms, a Presbyterian minister, principal chaplain on the western front, and Bishop Gwynne of Khartoum, appointed to control the Church of England clergy at **Christian Union in** the front. Both of these held the rank **the field** of major-general in the Army.

At home there was at first some difficulty about selecting the chaplains so as to give proper representation to the different Churches and in adjusting their ranks. At the front there was little or none of this. Every Church worked together in almost complete harmony. Men sank for the time their differences. Catholic helped Congregationalist in works of mercy; Methodist and Jew co-operated; the Presbyterian assisted the Catholic priest in some of his duties, and the priest reciprocated by visiting and taking comforts to the Presbyterian's flock. A religious journal in England became alarmed over this, and complained that the distinct lines of denominational positions were being wiped out by the men in the trenches. One chaplain admitted that this was true. "We have all seen a regiment come out from England, every man decked

out like a Christmas-tree, with writing-cases, Thermos flasks, and all kinds of fal-lals pressed on them by friends at home," he said. " Meet that same regiment a week or two after, when it has been in action. All the Christmas decorations have gone. The boys have learned that they have quite enough to carry without them, and have got down to bare essentials. So it is with us chaplains. We find in the stress of war that all we carry are the essentials of our faith."

One of the warmest eulogies of the work of the Y.M.C.A. was passed by the head of the British Jewish Church; and the senior chaplain at the front, a Presbyterian, asked the Bishop of London for his blessing when the bishop was leaving after a service in the fighting-lines.

When war broke out, ministers of every Church volunteered to serve as chaplains. Comparatively few could be accepted. Others determined not to be denied. Scores of Presbyterian ministers enlisted in the ranks or obtained commissions, since there was no other **Ministers in the ranks** way. One of these resigned his charge to take a commission, because he said that he could not look the lads of his congregation in the face if he did otherwise. He died soon afterwards, leading his men at Loos. Many Church of England curates were anxious to enlist as private soldiers. Here, however, their bishops intervened, and forbade them. It was not the work of a Christian minister, they declared, to fight. He must continue his work at home, or at the most, he must go as an ambulance worker with the Red Cross. Most of the clergy unwillingly submitted; some put on khaki and could be found in the months that followed driving motor-ambulances, organising ambulance squads, or serving in other ways behind the lines.

THE RT. REV. MONSIGNOR BICKERSTAFFE DREW. [*Elliott & Fry.*]
Began his long service as Army chaplain (R.C.) in 1886. He was twice mentioned in despatches during the Great War.

The Rev. R. J. Campbell told how, on one of his visits to the front, " one West of England vicar introduced himself to me and laughed at my bewilderment when I looked at his grey hairs and then at his private's uniform. ' Oh, yes,' he remarked, ' I am over age right enough, but not for my particular job. I drive an ambulance out here; at home I am a parish priest, but in both places I have the cure of souls.' "

A few Anglican clergymen, who deemed themselves fortunate indeed, enlisted at the very beginning, before the bishops' prohibition was known. One of these, the Rev. Lionel Studd, was the first English clergyman to be killed in the war.

The Studds are a famous English family of country gentlemen and cricketers. In the days when Moody and Sankey first visited England, Mr. Studd, the grandfather of Captain Studd, came under their influence. Up to this time he had been distinguished as a leader in every kind of sport; now he won fame of another kind. He joined with Quintin Hogg at the Polytechnic in Regent Street, London, the most successful religious institute for young men in Europe. Mr. Studd's sons followed in his footsteps. The Studd brothers were among the finest cricketers of their day. One of them went as a missionary to China; the other took the leadership of the Polytechnic when Quintin Hogg died. The grandson, young Lionel Studd, maintained the family tradition. He was keen on games; he was an active Territorial, and he was also strongly religious. On Trinity Sunday, 1914, he was ordained as a clergyman by the Bishop of London. That summer he worked as a curate in the parish of Holloway. Then came the call of war. He had not yet resigned his place in his old corps, the 12th Battalion of the London Regiment. For a moment he hesitated as to what was his duty. But not for long. His curacy was given up, and he joined his regiment.

Early in 1915 he and his battalion were in the trenches outside Ypres. Their position was being heavily

Cricket and cure of souls

BISHOP OF LONDON ABOARD A DREADNOUGHT.
In July, 1916, the Bishop visited every battleship and battle-cruiser.

BISHOP OF LONDON HOLDING A CONFIRMATION SERVICE ON H.M.S. IRON DUKE.
The Bishop pronouncing the blessing at the end of a Confirmation service for officers and men of the Grand Fleet, held July 23rd, 1916, on H.M.S. Iron Duke, when he confirmed two hundred men. In circle: The Bishop walking with Admiral Sir John Jellicoe.

bombarded, and he had some narrow escapes. "The thing that strikes me most is that it seems the most natural thing in the world to be here," he wrote. "It doesn't seem either heroic or terrifying. In fact, we were shelled last night again, and I slept peacefully through the whole shelling. After all, what is there to be afraid of? If one is killed it is merely the beginning of a life far fuller than the present one

On the next day he was again in the trenches, when he was hit on the head by a shrapnel bullet, and died a few hours later. He never recovered consciousness. He had given a fine example of the parson as the fighting man in the trenches. If he was the first English clergyman to die in this way, there were soon many to follow him, and his little grave outside Ypres, with a simple wooden cross over it, recalls a young life well spent and bravely ended.

The work of the Army chaplains in the early days around Mons is a romance of itself. One of the most vivid accounts of their experiences was given by **Army chaplains at Mons** the senior Wesleyan chaplain, the Rev. Owen Spencer Watkins.* Mr. Watkins was first attached to the 14th Field Ambulance. He arrived at the front just as the retreat from Mons had begun. The ambulance, after forming a dressing-station, was ordered to retire, with the rest of the army. "In haste the Red Cross flag was hauled down, the waggons packed, and even as we moved out of the yard round the buildings we had occupied as a temporary hospital the

* "With French in France and Flanders." By Owen Spencer Watkins. London: C. H. Kelly, 1915.

shells began falling, and in half an hour the place was a smoking ruin."

For three days he retreated with his comrades to Le Cateau, three days in which they had only six hours' sleep and two real meals. During the day the heat was almost tropical; at night it was fiercely cold. Rain came on— freezing rain. Men dozed as they stumbled along; some fell and had to be left where they lay; padre and private were happy when they **The retreat to** could pause for a brief spell and rest on a **Le Cateau** pile of corn sheaves in the open field in the rain and cold. At Le Cateau our army turned on the enemy, and the immortal battle followed. After a time the approaching German batteries made it necessary for the ambulance to move still farther back. To the chaplain was given the work of shepherding the wounded who could walk, and seeing them safe to Busigny railway-station. "I never want such a task again," he wrote. "Up and down that road I galloped, urging one poor fellow to hop faster, expostulating with another who, seated by the road-side, declared he could go no farther, and that to fall into the hands of the Germans would be no worse than the agony he endured as he walked. At last I came across a farmer's cart, and taking the law into my own hands, commandeered it, and made the man come back with me and pick up all who could walk no more. Time and again there would be a burst of shrapnel in the road, but as far as I could see nobody was injured. Just off the road the cavalry were at work, doing their best to guard our flank as we retreated. for now I learned we were in full retreat.

DRUMHEAD SERVICE IN THE GROUNDS OF THE GENERAL HOSPITAL, BIRMINGHAM.
Dr. Wakefield, Bishop of Birmingham, visited the front on several occasions and paid high tribute to the devoted work of the Army chaplains.
On the second anniversary of the declaration of war he conducted a special drumhead service at the General Hospital, Birmingham.

THREE SONS OF FRANCE BAREHEADED BEFORE A BROKEN ALTAR.

On the outbreak of war a large number of French priests forsook the pulpit for the trenches, and thus were able to administer spiritual consolation to their countrymen. A Red Cross priest is seen praying before the débris of a church that had been shattered by enemy guns.

Amongst the cavalry the casualties were heavy. Such as we could reach we carried with us. At last, to my infinite relief, Busigny was reached, and I was relieved of my charge."

The retreat went on. At Roumont Mr. Watkins found not only the church but also a neighbouring school packed with wounded. "The scene presented was such that I will not harrow your feelings in attempting to describe it. I passed down the lines of broken men, saying such words as God gave to me, but not daring to tell them that we should have to leave them where they were." Still on! The dreadful night that followed left its mark on all who passed through it. Aching in every nerve and in every bone, thirsty beyond words, so long without food that they had forgotten to be hungry, they pressed on. At one point the padre paused and dismounted, feeling that he could go no farther.

In four days he had only had ten hours' sleep and three proper meals. He sat by the roadside holding his horse, and once went off to sleep. He reached soon after sunrise an ambulance-waggon, with a water-cart. The water was wanted for the wounded.

Wounded men first Just then a battalion of exhausted infantry came up, saw the cart, and made a dash for it. Thirst had now reached a point where it was torture. Mr. Watkins spoke to the men and explained that there was very little water left in the cart, and that it was wanted for the wounded. "I'm thirsty myself," he said, "and I'm awfully sorry for you chaps, but you see how it is; the wounded must come first." "Quite right, sir," the men replied at once. "Didn't know it was a hospital water-cart." And parched as they were, they moved on.

The retreat continued until September 6th, when the troops paused at Tournan, south of Paris. Then they turned on the enemy. "At dawn on Sunday, September 6th," wrote the chaplain, simply and nobly, "we turned our faces north once more, and thanked God that we were able to do so. It was another Sunday without public services, but it was rich in private communion on the march, in bivouac, and ambulance-waggon, and as at the close of the day I wrapped myself in my greatcoat to sleep in the long grass by the roadside, I thanked God that He had honoured me by calling me to such high service."

There were many chaplain heroes in the great retreat. Here is the story of another. A party of British wounded were hidden in a cave. Word was brought to a brigade, and a chaplain headed a rescue-party. The party found that the only road which approached the cave was being heavily shelled by the Germans. The chaplain ordered his companions to halt. He was on horseback, they were on foot. "You stay where you are," he said. "I will ride through. Wait ninety minutes, and if I don't return, report to headquarters." He started off before they could stop him, right through the death-laden zone. Time after time it seemed as though a shell had got him. Time after time he escaped as it were by a miracle. Then they lost sight of him.

The ninety minutes passed, and the padre had not returned. The stretcher-bearers went back and reported. They were ordered to return and wait for half an hour more, and then, if the chaplain had not arrived, to go into the cave. At the end of twenty-five minutes the chaplain appeared riding as coolly as though out for an afternoon trot, taking no notice of the shells whistling all round. He had found that the wounded there had already been attended to by a retreating company. He had remained on to minister to them. The chaplain was given the Distinguished Service Order; the soldiers who had witnessed his bravery declared that he ought to have had the Victoria Cross.

Heroes of the retreat

The Gallipoli campaign illustrated another side of the life of the chaplains.

Here was an army called upon to endure the worst that war can give. Day and night, in the trenches or behind the lines, the men were never out of reach of the enemy fire. Weakened by disease, working perpetually at the highest strain, crowded together in a small space for months amid fierce tropical heat, with little shelter and no comfort, they were constantly called upon to undertake the most desperate ventures. How they fought and how they died the world knows.

Attached to this army were a number of chaplains, Catholic, Anglican, Presbyterian, Baptist, Methodist, and Salvation Army. If ever men were called upon to prove their faith by works, these were. Their parishes were the trenches; their church services had to be held under the shrapnel fire of the enemy; their very Communion gatherings were frequently broken into by enemy snipers or spattered by enemy shells. It was their daily task to be among the reeking dead, to rescue the wounded under fire, to endure to the full the dangers and discomforts of the men. They more than rose to the occasion. Catholic priest and Salvation Army brigadier, Methodist padre and Presbyterian minister alike, showed as splendid examples of supreme courage as any recorded in the history of the Christian Church. The experiences of the Rev. J. A. Luxford, senior chaplain with the New Zealand contingent, were typical. He was at the great landing of the Australian and New Zealand troops at Anzac on the morning of April 25th, 1915, going ashore with a field-ambulance. There was already plenty to do. While the fighting was continuing a little way ahead, men were bringing the wounded in. The doctors had everything ready, and there on the beach, amid the crack of bullets and the din of shell fire, they hastily rendered first-aid. As the Anzacs pressed farther on, they brought their wounded back by every possible means—on donkeys, on the backs of their fellows, on improvised stretchers, bearing the mangled men through the gullies and down the cliffs as best they could. The sea around was literally red with the blood of the wounded men—blood from the bandages, the stretchers, and the dressings rinsed in it.

First-aid on Gallipoli

Picture the chaplains busy at first-aid; busy, too, administering the last consolations of their faith to dying men. A few hours later another duty called them. There were many to be buried. Dead bodies cannot be kept for long in this climate. The ministers wanted to give them Christian burial, but how could it be done? Everywhere they were exposed to snipers from the hills around.

For a few men to gather together even for a funeral would mean that they would be picked off, one by one, by Turkish riflemen with telescopic sights, concealed in sheltered positions behind.

It was resolved to wait till midnight. Graves were dug, and the little party moved out quietly to perform the last rites. There were two chaplains, a Catholic priest and Mr. Luxford. Bodies were gently lifted in and the service had begun, when suddenly a Turkish machine-gun opened out on the position. There was no time to discuss what should be done. The burial-party took cover. The two clergymen jumped into the grave and, lying low, finished their service while the bullets swept overhead. Some of the soldiers had gone on to the hills that evening and had gathered a number of wild flowers, and when the Turkish machine-gun fire ceased they came back again and scattered flowers over their comrades' graves.

Burial scenes at midnight

It was a grim introduction to a grimmer time. The little foothold won by the Anzacs at tremendous cost consisted in the main of one valley: Shrapnel Gully with lines of posts and ridges on either side of it—Steele Post, Courtney Post, Quinn's Post, Pope's Hill with the direful Deadman's Land around, and Walker's Ridge. The Australians and New Zealanders here were never out of reach of the enemy's fire. In most campaigns the man who leaves the trenches can obtain some rest behind the lines. At Anzac there was no rest. Snipers were a special plague. When the Turks retired they left behind them picked marksmen hidden among trees and behind rocks, covered with branches or bushes or in other ways, so as to be invisible, and provided with a stock of ammunition and some provisions. These marksmen would lie still and wait, and, unseen themselves, would pick out and shoot down man after man. The only way to locate them—save when someone saw the flash or the slight haze from the fire of their rifles—was to note the direction of the bullets and to follow them up, a very difficult work. Death was always in the midst of the Anzacs. It was a pilgrimage of death and pain.

One of the most frequent tasks of the chaplains was to give Christian burial to the bodies of men who were killed. In the European field of war some endeavour was made to keep trace of the graves of the soldiers. In Gallipoli it was practically impossible, save in exceptional cases. The strain was so great, the work so tremendous, and the danger so constant that all that could be done was to try by some means and in some way to inter near where the brave had fallen, and to hold an abbreviated service over the remains of all that could be reached. Hundreds lay beyond the lines, whom even the boldest could not get at

FATHER ANTHONY.
Roman Catholic Naval Chaplain. He was wounded while saving two sailors from a warship during the Battle off Jutland.

THE REV. B. P. PLUMPTRE.
Curate of Bermondsey Old Parish Church. Awarded the Military Cross for gallantry and devotion in the field, July, 1916.

THE REV. J. G. TUCKEY.
Senior Chaplain, Third Army Corps. Served in South African War (despatches). Mentioned in despatches from the western front by Viscount French.

The British and the Turkish lines almost touched one another at some points. There were places where the British held the first part of a trench and the Turks held the end, a barricade separating them. It was here that one chaplain, the Rev. William Grant, a Presbyterian minister from New Zealand, died. He was up in the front trenches, and had reached a barricade across them when he heard moaning on the other side. He looked across the barricade; a wounded Turk was lying there in agony. By some oversight the chaplain had not been warned that the Turkish troops were on the other side. He walked round the barrier, raised the Turk and started tending his wounds. Two Turkish soldiers peeping round the corner saw a man in a British officer's uniform. They did not take time to observe what he was doing, but shot him dead on the spot.

A FESTIVAL ON THE FIELD OF WAR.
A "Slava," or name-fete day, with the 1st Regiment of Serbian Cavalry. A priest is blessing a cake, while the choir sings. Above: French priest officiating at the interment of fallen soldiers. Each grave was marked with the metal tricolour cockade of Liberté, Egalité, Fraternité.

Religious services were held wherever possible, now among a company just going out into battle, now under the shelter of a small hill, now with the aeroplanes buzzing aloft and the bombs dropping near by. On one occasion a battalion at Walker's Ridge Gully was going out on a desperate endeavour, and before it started Mr. Luxford came up to it. The chaplain suggested that they should have a prayer together. The major in charge eagerly assented. Picture the scene! The men amid the fierce heat wore a very minimum of clothing. They were in their shirt-sleeves. Athletes' " shorts " left their legs bare. As they stood up under the evening sun the chaplain started the hymn, " Abide with me," in which all joined, and then he read from the Prayer Book the beautiful prayer to be used before a fight at sea.

O most powerful and glorious Lord God, the Lord of Hosts, that rulest and commandest all things; Thou sittest on the throne judging right, and therefore we make our address to Thy Divine Majesty in this our necessity, that Thou wouldest take the cause into Thine own hand, and judge between us and our enemies. Stir up Thy strength, O Lord, and come and help us; for Thou givest not alway the battle to the strong, but canst save by many or by few. O let not our sins now cry against us for vengeance; but hear us thy poor servants begging mercy, and imploring Thy help, and that thou wouldest be a defence unto us against the face of the enemy. Make it appear that Thou art our Saviour and Mighty Deliverer, through Jesus Christ our Lord. AMEN.

Then they sang " Rock of Ages," and moved out to battle, fighting none the worse for their prayer. Out of a thousand men who went out, only one hundred and fifty answered the roll-call a few hours later; most of the remainder lay wounded, dying, or dead on the rocky front. The major was one of those who did not return.

Then came armistice day, a day as dreadful as any. Large numbers of dead were lying between the lines of the Turks and the British. Their bodies in the tropical climate were decomposed, spreading disease around. Both sides agreed on a truce to bury the dead. A line was drawn along the centre. The Turks were not to go beyond this on one side or the British beyond it on the other. The Turks were to hand all the British dead to their comrades and the British to do the same with the Turkish fallen. The British parties came in their shirt-sleeves, stained and wearied with much fighting. The Turks sent their companies up clad in fresh uniforms of clean khaki. The contrast between the two was very striking. The officers on either side talked together. The British had a very genuine respect for the Turks, who they felt fought bravely and fought cleanly, and the Turks reciprocated the feeling. It was soon seen that all hopes of sorting out the dead were impossible. They could not be moved, for often they fell to pieces when touched. Hour after hour during that long day the chaplains, amid the reek of indescribable corruption, performed the last rites over hundreds of graves. At times the decomposition was almost too much to be endured, and then it was the business of the chaplain with a word of encouragement to nerve the burial-parties to go through with their direful task.

One group of three dead figures was found, a major in the centre, a sergeant and a corporal supporting him. It was

A day in Dead Man's Land

AUSTRIAN SACRILEGE ON THE EAST FRONT.
The Austrians, like the Germans, showed no respect whatever for churches, and adapted them, whenever possible, to military needs; in the case illustrated digging a trench through the building.

in many a way their appreciation of their padre. He had a dug-out on the hillside. Some of them, passing, noticed it. "That's not far enough in, padre," they said. "A fragment of shell might get you there." And so they set to work and dug it farther in, to be safe from shrapnel bullets. Then, while the padre was away on one of his tasks, they gathered sprigs, branches of trees, and green leaves to make it cool, soft, and attractive. At another time Mr. Luxford was carrying a wounded man on his back from the trenches. "I won't have that!" said one burly soldier, coming up and endeavouring to relieve him of his burden. But the chaplain who would not carry a wounded man on his back, go into the front lines with words of consolation, or advance if needs be with charging men, would have been little use at Gallipoli.

Then came the final crowning experience at Suvla Bay. A great blow was being struck that would, it was hoped, end the campaign and give Britain the Dardanelles. The Anzacs started from Suvla Bay, attacking with the utmost gallantry the Turks on Sari Bair and Chunuk Bair. The ground was one vast labyrinth of trenches, saps, and traverses. Barbed-wire entanglements were erected at every spot, shells were bursting, bombs exploding, and innumerable machine-guns were planted where they would do most damage to the attacking troops. How the Anzacs landed, how they cleared point after point, and then how victory was at the last moment taken from them by the failure of some other groups to advance from Suvla Bay, has already been told in this history. Their failure was one of the most glorious failures this world has known.

easy from the positions to reconstruct what had taken place. The major had fallen, shot in the leg; his sergeant and corporal had picked him up, and were bearing him back through the zone of fire when all three were shot down and died where they lay.

It was one work of the chaplains to take the identification discs from the dead soldiers and to preserve and gather up any little things, like letters or photos, likely to prove of interest to friends. In one man's pay-book, still clutched in his dead hand, they read the beginning of a letter which he had written as he lay dying. It was to his mother. "Dear Mother, I am hard hit. I shall never see you again. God——" And then the letter ceased.

Summer was coming on. The great heat was growing more and more unendurable, yet it had to be endured. The flies were an indescribable plague. Every man—chaplain, officer, private alike—had to do everything he could for the wounded and the sick. Disease, due to the closely packed positions of the men and to the insanitary surroundings, eventually carried off even more than the enemy's bullets and shells. The New Zealanders showed

Three of the chaplains accompanied the New Zealand troops who took part in the first landing. Others came later. They all endured to the full the danger, the thirst, and the misery from heat and flies, of their comrades. They went out into the gullies, seeking their wounded and helping them when found. Mr. Luxford was one of the three. Hour after hour he kept on.

After one speciallytrying experience he sat   **The Dean**
down for a moment on a stone, tired out.   **of Sydney**
As he paused there a Turkish bullet struck
his leg severing the femoral artery, deflected, and travelled around the leg, inflicting a terrible wound—a wound which, in spite of every endeavour, made it necessary to amputate the limb.

The Dean of Sydney accompanied the Australian troops to Gallipoli. At the commencement, the soldiers were not quite sure whether they liked the Dean or not. He was a Talbot, a member of one of the great territorial families of England, and possibly they thought him a little stiff. What first won them to him was his absolute coolness during times of peril. For example, on one occasion he was holding a Communion Service on the side of a hill. For a Communion cloth he had a Red Cross flag. There was nothing else to be had. A little congregation gathered around him. The service had barely begun before the Turks opened out with their heavy guns on that part of the line. Shells were bursting all around. The soldiers, accustomed as they were to·shell fire, looked nervously up, and would not altogether have objected to an announcement that the celebration was postponed. The Dean took no notice. He did not show by so much as the flicker of his eyes that he heard or saw the shells or was conscious of the danger. The ceremony proceeded steadily, solemnly, without abbreviation, to its close. And no one was injured.

"There's a man!" said the Australians. When, a little later, the Dean was caught by a bullet as he was carrying up surgical supplies for the wounded at the front and was nearly killed, the men's confidence in him was confirmed. In his dug-out on the torrid hill-sides of Gallipoli he organised his little church. By a hard squeeze half a dozen men could get in his bomb-proof apartment at once. It was vestry, choir room, oratory, and a spot where many an anxious soul found comfort. The soldiers organised a choir for him. They dug a trench near to his abode— "Ambulance Trench," it was called. The choristers even ambitiously trained themselves in the intervals of fighting in anthems and part-singing. When at the end the Dean left them, no one held more firmly the affection and confidence of the men.

Services under shell fire

The Dean's Communion Service under shell fire did not stand alone. The Army chaplain had to hold services wherever he could and however he could. In Flanders the chaplains sometimes gathered the men in shell-holes. "I had a very interesting service with the men of one battery," wrote a chaplain with the North Midland Division. "The only secluded spot we could find was a large 'Jack Johnson' shell-hole. Fourteen of us gathered in it, and we had a good time there, conversing of things concerning the Kingdom. Firing was going on all round us, but it only served to intensify our assurance of the promise, 'I am with you—even to the end.'"

Another noted Gallipoli chaplain of a very different type was Brigadier—afterwards Colonel—McKenzie, of the Salvation Army, who won a high reputation among the Anzacs for absolute fearlessness. On more than one occasion he led the charges of the troops against the Turks, himself unarmed. He declared to the soldiers that he had prayed with them and preached to them, and he would be **Fearless Salvation Army colonel** ashamed not to share their danger with them when they were in a tight corner. His distinguished bravery was recognised by the Government by the bestowal of the Military Medal.

McKenzie reached the front with the 1st Brigade of the Australians at the end of the first week of May. At the spot where he landed the Turkish trenches were within fifty yards. There had not been as yet any chaplains there, but there was abundant need for them. The troops had been paying very dearly for their boldness. Attacking the Turks without guns, armed only with rifles and bayonets, and facing a deadly hail of shrapnel and machine-gun fire, they had carried trench after trench, at a cost of over 5,000 casualties.

McKenzie's first work was to conduct the funeral service of the colonel of the 4th Battalion.

BLESSING THE TRICOLOUR: AN ITALIAN SCENE.
Italian priests blessing and kissing the tricolour, held in position by the officer commanding a new regiment to which the flag is being presented. Above: Celebration of Mass for Alpine soldiers at an altar, formed of ice-blocks, three thousand metres above the sea.

"THE DEFENDER OF THE FAITH" WITH HIS FAITHFUL SOLDIERS.

King George paid another visit to his soldiers on the western front during August, 1916, and saw every phase of their life. He did not fail to attend Divine service, and this photograph shows his Majesty at church, among his troops.

We found our colonel's body, he said, lying in an exposed position. We buried him at 9 p.m., and had to lie crouching to read the service, the bullets meanwhile whistling over my head by the hundred. I thought I was nearly "outed" on four separate occasions, twice with shells and twice with bullets. The first shell fell three feet behind me, and I threw myself flat on the road. I got covered with oil thrown up by the shell. The second shell fell the next day while I was conducting a funeral service. There were twenty of us, and the shrapnel fell all around and even into the grave, although by a miracle none of us were hit. One bullet grazed the top of my head and the other my right ear.

In ten days he had to read the Burial Service over one hundred and seventy men. Then came armistice day. Even he described it as "the most trying experience I have ever had. Many bodies had been robbed by the Turks and their identification discs taken off, and quite a number had to be buried 'unknown,' or 'unidentified'." Even here his faculty for making friends stood him to good purpose. He established cordial relations even with some of the Turks on that day. One Turkish doctor gave him his visiting-card and told him if ever he was taken a prisoner to show it and he would come to him. He invited him to afternoon tea in Constantinople when he was taken there. The Turks thought they were sure to get him and all the other British troops at Gallipoli. "What a pity," said the Turkish doctor, "that so many fine young men should come from Australia just to be killed!" The thing which the chaplain particularly missed was water—water to drink and water to wash with. He and his comrades dreamed of a bath, and dreamed of the luxury of being able to take their verminous clothes off and change them, as other men dream of great bliss.

Army chaplain and Turk

September found him with the rest of the Australians at Suvla Bay, and here he had some of his hottest experiences. In one of the biggest charges, where he advanced with the troops, his cap-cover was pierced in three places, his hand was hit, and a spent bullet penetrated his right side. But wounds in hand and spent bullet in side did not stop him. He reached the Turkish trenches with the rest of his brigade. Here he found a veritable shambles, with dead Turks piled up in places four and five deep. For twenty-four hours together he searched through these trenches, piled with dead and dying and badly wounded, to find his own Australian comrades. Some of them had lain wounded there amid the terrible heat and torturing thirst for twenty hours and more. Wounded men were weighted down with the bodies of the dead, and from among these tangled masses came the groans and cries of the smothering broken men.

Oxford chaplain's heroism

For forty-eight hours he and his fellow-chaplains worked without any cessation—the most awful forty-eight hours they had ever lived. For five days he kept going with brief snatches of rest. Besides helping with the wounded, he had to conduct Burial Services over hundreds of men during these days, parties of men being buried in great groups While conducting a burial of fifteen, a bullet whizzed by within half an inch of his right ear while he was praying, and killed a man standing by his side.

He had been with his regiment for twenty weeks in the trenches without a break, and the great fight had come immediately on top of that. The regiment itself had been reduced to one hundred and eighty effective men. Even his iron frame almost broke down under the strain, the want of sleep, the want of food—still worse, the want of water and the sight of the agony which he could do so little to alleviate.

Among the chaplains who did noted service at Gallipoli, the Rev. A. G. Parham, precentor of Christ Church, Oxford, received a Military Cross for heroism. He was attached to a brigade that was in the attack at Suvla Bay on August 21st. The shrubs on the Anafarta

Plain caught fire. Helped by his servant, he carried a number of the wounded men to safety. On the following day he obtained a number of volunteers as stretcher-bearers and carried out the wounded from Chocolate Hill. After the battle he remained with the brigade in the trenches for ten weeks under shell fire.

When the rival armies settled down in the autumn of 1914 to the long trench warfare in France and in Flanders there was not for some time much opportunity for chaplains to distinguish themselves by special gallantry. One young clergyman, Mr. Guinness, the first to win a military decoration in the war, gained his reward by courage and initiative under very dangerous circumstances. But the ordinary life of the padres in Flanders during these months was full of danger. They had long lines to serve, and, in the course of duty they were constantly under shell fire.

With the padres in Flanders They had to make their homes mostly in broken-down houses, probably partly wrecked and torn by enemy fire. The noise of the aeroplanes overhead, the whistle of the approaching enemy shells, the sounds of battle, going on unintermittently, day and night, told of the reality of danger.

One young Canadian clergyman did a deed of courage in the No Man's Land between the British and the German lines which well deserves to be recalled. No Man's Land was blocked with dense masses of tangled, barbed-wire fronting either side. It was swept day and night, particularly at night-time, by the fire of machine-guns and by individual marksmen. Every night British and German scouting parties crept forth from the shelter of their parapets, repairing torn wires, seeking for enemy scouts, or raiding the opposite trenches. Frequently big attempts were made to rush the enemy's front, and although careful preparation before the advance was made many fell. Every effort was made to get the wounded back into shelter again, but it **Canadian clergyman's courage** was not always possible to carry out the dead. In many points in this No Man's Land one could see black forms lying amid the wires—the unburied bodies.

A Canadian battalion had fought fiercely over one section and had lost a number of men in No Man's Land. Every attempt to get in their bodies failed. A young chaplain often visited the front lines and often looked at these black figures. Some of them had been his old comrades. There was one group which specially affected him. Little but the skeletons were left now. These at least he determined should not be left to the sport of the winds.

Choosing a specially dark and wet night he crept out from under our own trenches towards the listening-post. Then lying low and going carefully he crawled from shelter. Every now and then the Germans sent up flares into the sky, flares which lit the whole heavens around. As soon as he heard the preliminary hiss of the flare he would drop and lie low, rigidly still. Every now and then there came the crack of a rifle overhead, or the clatter of a machine-gun opened out by the Germans at any point where they thought the British might be.

" A FOREIGN FIELD THAT IS FOR EVER ENGLAND."
One of the most frequent tasks of the chaplains was to give Christian burial to the dead. Sometimes this was done under fire, as at Anzac, where two chaplains actually took cover in the grave, and finished the service while bullets were sweeping overhead.

Crouching, making no sound, he stealthily dug into the damp earth. With infinite pains he scooped out a shallow grave. At any second the enemy might discover him. If they did so, that second would be his last. He knew it, but still he kept on. Then reverently he lifted up the remains of his old friends, placed them in their last resting-place, read the form of Christian burial over them, covered them up, and still in the utmost silence crept back to the shelter of the front-line trenches again.

It was on the western front that a clergyman gained the Victoria Cross, the second time since that great Order was instituted that it was bestowed upon an Army chaplain. The Rev. Edward Noel Mellish, curate of St. Paul's, Deptford, had the Cross bestowed upon him on April 20th, 1916, for most conspicuous bravery. The official account thus described his deed:

During heavy fighting on three consecutive days he repeatedly went backwards and forwards, under continuous and heavy shell and machine-gun fire, between our original trenches and those captured from the enemy, in order to tend and rescue wounded men. He brought in ten badly wounded men on the first day from ground swept by machine-gun fire, and three were actually killed while he was dressing their wounds. The battalion to which he was attached was relieved on the second day, but he went back and brought in twelve more wounded men. On the night of the third day he took charge of a party of volunteers and once more returned to the trenches to rescue the remaining wounded. This splendid work was voluntary on his part and outside the scope of his ordinary duties.

Mr. Mellish had already proved his courage. At the time the Boer War broke out he was only seventeen years old. Yet he went out with Baden-Powell's Police and did good work in the **The Rev. E. N.** later guerilla stages of the war. He **Mellish, V.C.** then settled at Jagersfontein, where his qualities as a leader of men were noted   He was induced to enter the Church and became a curate at Deptford, where he remained until the call of the war took him away. His old friends at Deptford were the least surprised of any at his decoration. They knew him, and knowing him were prepared to expect the best from him. At the Battle of Loos he was able to help with the wounded under fire.

This battle gave many of the padres the opportunity to prove their qualities. The Gordon Highlanders, who took a prominent part in this fight, were given the order to charge with the Staffordshires straight at the German lines. As they

AT A HOSPITAL FOR DISTINGUISHED HEROES, ST. CLOUD, NEAR PARIS.

St. Cloud, the picturesque environ of Paris, boasted a war hospital unique among the hundreds throughout the fighting area. Every patient had been wounded in the performance of some noteworthy deed. The hospice, which was primarily for Canadian soldiers, was administered by Dominion officials. Our illustrations show the curé of Troyon, who had won the War Cross, addressing some of the patients and chatting with officers.

PRAYERS NEAR THE SITE OF THE GARDEN OF EDEN.
A chaplain with the force that tried to relieve General Townshend at Kut-el-Amara holding an open-air service in Mesopotamia. The suggestion of the early Paradise given by the sunlit, palm-fringed lawn contrasts with the view of the trench in the foreground.

dashed from their shelter the German artillery opened on them with high explosives and shrapnel, the German machine-guns blazed out, and the German infantry kept up a tremendous fire. The men fell almost in lines, but for every one who fell another dashed . up behind, despite the fire. One company and part of another reached the German trenches. Unfortunately for them, the other half of their regiment and the Stafford-shire Regiment accompanying them found, when they moved forward, that the heavy British artillery fire had not succeeded in destroying the German barbed-wire entanglements. They cut and hacked and fought to get through, but the thing could not be done.

Endeared to the Highlanders

The soldiers afterwards told how, in these heroic and desperate hours, when their regiment was largely wiped out, the chaplains showed their mettle. One chaplain, famous among the men for his cheerfulness and activity, crept out in the darkness beyond the trenches amid the heaps of dead. He was searching for the body of the colonel of the Staffordshires. Then, despite the fact that the machine-guns were firing constantly over him, he glided from spot to spot, securing identification discs of soldiers who were dead, and seeing if he could do anything to help those in whom a spark of life remained. One Gordon officer writing home at the time told how, " This young chaplain, an Anglican, had endeared himself to these Highlanders, how he crawled out into the danger zone collecting identification discs from the many gallant

fellows who had been lying dead there, and how whatever was going on there (and there was usually something), he made a point of going round the firing-trench every day, doing much appreciated work among the men." " The padre," said another in writing of him, " is a jolly good fellow. We have just returned from a three days' trek. I saw no other chaplain marching with our brigade, but this one did the whole march with us ; he walked every step of the way, carrying a pack like the rest of us, and also lending a hand with a rifle or two towards the end of the day. And he is entitled to a horse, too. He would not even take a turn on mine, which was otherwise most useful for the cripples."

Four Scottish chaplains attached to the Highland Brigade also had moving experiences. On the night before the attack they held special services both with the Royal Scots and the Gordon Highlanders. That night in their tents the chaplains waited while one by one officers and men came shyly in with letters and keepsakes to be sent home if they themselves fell. A little time later they listened while the colonel of the Gordons, in brief, stirring words, told his men what they had to do, and bade them " remember the name of the regiment." They cheered him to the echo. Then the chaplains waited at the advanced dressing-station—the dressing-station for the wounded immediately behind the front line. It was here the wounded passed through their hands ; here the dead that could be recovered were brought in ; and here all the

At the dressing-station

agony and torment that followed the great glory of the battle was witnessed. The scene was thus described by one of the chaplains :

All that day I was engaged in burying the dead. Through the following night the wounded came streaming in faster than they could be evacuated. Their condition was pitiable, for a cold, clammy rain had fallen persistently all day. Yet I never heard a murmur. Yes, I heard one. A young Aberdeen student, with a finely-chiselled face, lay on the table while the surgeon tried to give him unavailing relief, and as I held his hand he moaned out his sorrow over the failure of his battalion to hold the trenches they had won. I saw a Scot lying on the ground, plastered from head to foot with mud as with a trowel. I thought I recognised the yellow stripe in the tartan, and stepping gently over an unconscious form between, I touched him and said : "Are you a 1st Gordon, my lad ?" His arm was crushed, his leg was twisted, but the white of his eye gleamed through the mud that caked his face as he answered with an unmistakable grin, "A wis this mornin', and A think A'm a half yin yet." And then in a moment he knew me, and reaching out his only hand he gripped me tight, and said, "Oh ! minister, it's you. Ye might write to my wife, and dinna frighten her. A'll be a' richt yet." What a superb spirit ! A jest for his own misery and the tenderest consideration for those at home. Such are the men who are bearing all for you on those grim fields in Flanders.

A cheerless dawn was breaking as I left that dreadful place. I noticed the stains upon my boots, and thought of Barbour's terrible phrase—"reed wat shod." And I went to meet the Gordons returning. Grim and stern and silent they marched in, but still they held their heads high, as well became the "Gay Gordons." At the head of the column strode a young captain with the purple and white ribbon of the Military Cross gleaming on his breast (a year ago he was a divinity student of the Church of Scotland), and as I listened to him speaking a last word to the men as gently as a mother putting her children to bed, there was revealed to me something more of the nobility of the men with whom I had to do.

Private Ernest King, of the Northumberland Fusiliers, told in a letter home another story of an Army chaplain at Loos. King was a transport driver, and halted close to the range of rifle fire.

While standing there (he writes) I was patted on the shoulder by my chaplain, a big, fine, resolute man. After the exchange of a few words we parted, I to the left, where a heap of dead lay, and he to the right to the trenches. Early next morning we had run short of ammunition, and if it had not been for the tremendous energy put forth by the chaplain more men would have gone under.

Through shot and shell at Loos

With resolute courage he did the work of a dozen men, carrying close on fifty boxes of ammunition, one box in each hand, each box weighing six stone. In journeying to the trenches he had to go through a murderous rifle and shell fire. Then we saw him carrying the wounded and dead as fast as he could, and then burying the dead. For hours he worked at it incessantly, and was still hard at it when I was relieved. Afterwards I learned that he had worked incessantly all through that night, burying the dead and tending the wounded.

I have thought, in looking over the events of that horrible battle, it might have been a whole battalion wiped out had not our chaplain worked so nobly.

Many are the stories the chaplains told of the interesting conditions under which they held their services, sometimes in tunnels, sometimes in dugouts, sometimes in the open, sometimes amid the tottering walls of broken buildings in ruined cities such as Ypres.

What more impressive setting could there have been for a religious service than amidst the ruins of Ypres ? Here was a city in ruins, a city where every house was a wreck, where every wreck bore witness to the prosperity of yesterday and the destruction of to-day. One chaplain, visiting Ypres, found his passage through the streets and through the great squares disturbed by the sustained shell fire of the enemy. A

A SHATTERED SANCTUARY.
Ruins of a church at Fleury, in the Verdun sector. This village was retaken by the French during the third week in August.

42 cm. shell — the biggest shell then known — burst so near to him that it cast up the soil two yards from his feet. He joined a company in some cellars, and found they belonged to his old battalion. The dark, smoky cellar rang with song until midnight, when the soldiers moved out to their work. "Next morning," he wrote at the time, "at 11.45 I had one of the finest services of my life with this company in a tunnel-shaped cellar, fifty feet by twenty feet, three lines of men sitting along each side, leaving a narrow aisle down the centre. As deeply reverent as any service ever held in a cathedral it was also hearty, homely, happy. I found it was easy to speak 'home to the heart.' We sang 'Lead, kindly Light,' 'Peace, perfect peace,' 'Through the night of doubt and sorrow,' in that order. Every word of each hymn had in it a living message, and was sung with solemn meaning in the very words :

Amidst the ruins at Ypres

> Yea, though I walk in death's dark vale,
> Yet will I fear none ill,

when I heard the whistle of a shell behind me. It grew louder and louder, rushing like a railway train overhead, and burst with a crashing roar half a mile away, near where the 4th Gordons were bivouacked. It was an occasional visitor from a naval gun which Tommy had christened with characteristic felicity the 'Ypres Express.' But I remember thinking at the moment that the most gifted organist could not have achieved with all the resources of his art such a solemnising accompaniment as it provided for the words we were singing. But not a man in the ranks before me moved a muscle. and I hope the padre kept his countenance, too."

The Roman Catholic priests earned the confidence and respect of the whole army by their great devotion and self-sacrifice. One in particular must be mentioned, Father William Finn, who met his death at Seddul Bahr, in Gallipoli, in the great landing there. When the ship in which he arrived with the troops approached the shore he was urged not to attempt to land with the men under the shell fire of the enemy. "A priest's place is beside the dying soldier," he replied. As he stepped on to the gangway he received a bullet through the chest. He kept on, notwithstanding, across the lighters, when two more bullets struck him, one in the thigh and another in the leg. To quote the description of a special correspondent who was present : "By the time he reached the beach he was literally riddled with bullets, but in spite of the great pain he must have been suffering he heroically went about his duties, giving consolation to the dying troops. It was while he was in the act of attending to the spiritual requirements of one of his men that the priest's head was shattered by shrapnel."

Working under war conditions, the list of deaths of chaplains at the front was naturally a long one. In July, 1916, the Bishop of London said that sixteen chaplains had been killed, and that between five hundred and fifty and six hundred of the best of the younger clergy of the Church of England were then serving at the front. This list was soon augmented, one of the later victims being famous as a leader of the Y.M.C.A. movement in England, the Rev. E. J. Kennedy; he endured such hardships during his year as chaplain that a few weeks after he returned home he passed away.

CHAPTER CXXXIII.

THE CAMPAIGN IN MESOPOTAMIA TO THE FALL OF KUT.

The Development of Mesopotamia by Railway Originally a British Project—Opening of the Suez Canal Secures Alternative Route to India and Leads to Decline of British Influence in Turkey—Germany Seizes her Opportunity—Gradual Extension of German Influence over Turkey—The Bremen-Berlin-Bosphorus-Bagdad Bahn—All-Important Question of Eastern Terminus on Persian Gulf—Mission of German Consul-General Stemrich to Purchase Site for Station at Koweit—Fidelity of Mobarek, the Koweit Sheikh, to Great Britain—Germany Pulls the Wires Through Constantinople—Successful Counter-moves by Great Britain—Basra, the Port on Shat-el-Arab, Finally Selected as Terminus of the Bagdad Railway—History of the Campaign Continued from General Townshend's Retreat upon Kut-el-Amara after his Brilliant Victory at Ctesiphon—Immediate Investment by the Enemy—Difficulties of River Transport—Exploits of Armed Tugs and Gunboats under Captain Nunn, R.N.—Want of Cohesion between Home and Indian Governments—Unsatisfactory Rumours and Reports as to Conduct of Campaign by Authorities—Admission by Mr. Austen Chamberlain, Secretary of State for India, that Indian Organisation was at Fault—Heroic Defence of Kut Continued—Brilliant Sorties by Garrison—Gradual Reduction of Rations and Consequent Privations—Strenuous but Unavailing Efforts of the Relieving Force to Break Through Enemy's Lines—Final Surrender of General Townshend from Hunger, after Holding Out for One Hundred and Forty-three Days—World-wide Admiration for his Magnificent Resistance.

EFORE carrying on the story of the Mesopotamian Campaign from the points previously reached in our history (*vide* Chapters LXVII. and XCIV.), it will be helpful to the complete understanding of the position, as between Germany and Turkey on the one hand and Great Britain on the other, briefly to set out the story of Germany's varied efforts before the war to intrigue her way to "a place in the sun" in the Persian Gulf.

In order fully to appreciate the measure of sanity which seasoned "the Mesopotamian madness," as the campaign in many quarters was regarded, it is necessary to look backward over a considerable number of years. Time was, well within the memory of the middle-aged, when the Euphrates Valley Scheme, as it was originally called, precursor of the Bagdad Railway, loomed large in the purview of current politics. In some shape or other during the latter half of the nineteenth century it was continually coming to the fore, and received serious, if intermittent, attention from more than one British Administration.

The idea of opening up the rich but undeveloped countries constituting Asia Minor, of making Mesopotamia "the granary of the world," and conferring the boon of Western civilisation upon the inhabitants—none of whom had the slightest desire to adopt or capacity to appreciate it—was not made, though it certainly matured, in Germany.

A purely British project in conception, it harked back to the 'fifties, contemporaneous with Lord Stratford de Redcliffe, "the Great Elchi" at Constantinople, and the Crimean War—a muddle indeed, beside which the Mesopotamian Campaign shines as a miracle of management. Germany as an empire was neither born nor thought of. Turkey was then the friend, Russia the bugbear, of the moment—and not only the bugbear of the moment but the nightmare of the future; for it was an article of faith with every well-brought-up Briton most fervently to believe that she cherished sinister designs upon India. Any scheme, therefore, of rapid transport from Europe and across Asia which tended to strengthen the British position against Muscovite malevolence was of a nature to attract and rivet popular attention. The Suez Canal scheme was still germinating in the fertile brain of M. Ferdinand de Lesseps, and the only route to India lay round the Cape. Obviously then, the projection of a railway from Constantinople to the Persian Gulf possessed an element

ENEMY STEAMER ARRIVES AT KUT-EL-AMARA.
Turkish doctor and officer landing from a Turkish steamer at Kut-el-Amara followed by their veiled wives.

WHENCE OPERATIONS WERE DIRECTED.
Norfolk House, a sort of Eurasian edifice, which served as the British Headquarters at Kut-el-Amara.
Note the wireless apparatus which was installed on the roof.

The aim of the Kaiser's policy, as soon as he had acquired undivided control of the German ship of State by dismissal of "the Pilot" in 1890, was gradually and insidiously to gain ascendancy over the Sultan, a matter not easy, but most important of attainment.

Abdul Hamid was no fool. Not without reason had he been dubbed the acutest and least scrupulous of living diplomatists in embassy chancelleries. In vulpine qualities he out-Heroded Herod—whom, indeed, he excelled in other respects. To promote and foster a revolutionary spirit amongst his people, to stir up the mud that Germany might fish in troubled waters, were aims no less essential. Control of Turkish trade, and finally of the Turkish Army, were, with equal assiduity, to be angled for. These measures, comprehensive as they were of revolution and deposition, took years to accomplish; but German policy neither faltered nor failed. The Old Turks, the dominant class, dignified, conservative, slow to move, and procrastinating to the crack of

of superlative attraction to the British public. The prospect of obtaining the much-coveted firman lured many a concession-hunter from the Thames to the Bosphorus, where he was fooled to the top of his bent by wily Turkish officials, and afforded ample opportunity of realising with chastened spirit and lightened purse the truth of Solomon's assertion that "hope deferred maketh the heart sick."

The British Embassy restricted or extended its support with the ebb or flow of opinion in Downing Street; but no firman was ever forthcoming, though the money spent and the energy wasted in endeavours to acquire it, would have constructed a considerable portion of the line.

Times changed and policies with them. The opening of the Suez Canal (originally opposed by Great Britain) in 1869, the acquisition by Disraeli of the Khedive's shares— a masterstroke of genius (176,602 for £3,976,582)—in 1875, the lease of Cyprus from Turkey in 1878, and the occupation of Egypt in 1882, had brought about a change in the spirit of the British dream. The new waterway to India, far more effective than any land-laid line, which could never be an "all red" route, was for all time secure.

To these and other causes, not germane to the present issue, the wane of Britain's influence in Turkey was mainly due.

The Kaiser in Constantinople Her influence, which for generations had been paramount (the Sublime Porte trembled at Lord Stratford's nod), gradually declined. Its final withdrawal was the signal for Germany's advance. One of the first visits paid by the Kaiser in 1889, the year after his accession, was to Constantinople. During his stay were sown the seeds of a most unholy alliance, which increased the sum of human wickedness to a greater extent, and added more to the burden of human suffering, than any collusion between the powers of evil in the annals of recorded time. "Mercy and truth had met together; righteousness and peace had kissed each other." The pact between Kultur and Kismet was destined later on to become complete. Abomination of desolation lay in its train. Amongst its first fruits was the massacre of Armenians on a truly Imperial scale. Its aftermath was the monumental monstrosity of the world-wide war.

doom, did not accord with Teuton ideas or fall into line with Teuton methods of progression. They saw, with uneasiness, the steady growth of German influence, and recalled the story of "Sindbad the Sailor" and the "Old Man of the Sea." **Old Turks and Young Turks** They were mindful, too, of the dictum of Fuad Pasha, one of the few statesmen their country had produced, that in Turco-European relations, "C'est toujours la Turquie qui paie."

They stood, an inert mass, desirous only of being left alone to misgovern as they chose, in the path of the Kaiser's ambition, and had consequently to be negotiated out of the way. So it came to pass, after many days and infinite vicissitudes, that the Young Turks, with all the vices and but few of the virtues of the "old" ones, pursuing a policy shaped and guided by the unseen hand in Berlin, attained the ascendancy and ruled in their stead.

Eventually, throughout the length and breadth of the Sultan's domains, which from the religious aspect stretched as far afield as the British dependency of India—the objective point—German influence reigned supreme. German finance asserted itself on the shores of the Bosphorus and German money flowed freely through all the arteries of Turkish trade. All valuable concessions went to Germany, amongst them, in due course, the right of construction of that hoary-headed yet evergreen project, the railway line to Bagdad. The Turkish Army, second to none in fighting material, was handed over to German instructors to be taught the parade-step and moulded on the German pattern with a thoroughness typically Teutonic.

Meanwhile, Great Britain gave no sign. To all appearances she was an entirely indifferent spectator of the growing German grip upon the throat of Turkey, and Germany laughed aloud.

When railway development was taken in hand, the work proceeded apace and with characteristic energy. German engineers, artisans, and contractors scoured the country, surveying here and levelling there, and boring through the burial-grounds of a civilisation nobler far than their own The trail of the serpent was over it all.

Major-General Charles Vere Ferrers Townshend, C.B., D.S.O., defender of Kut-el-Amara.

Along the strand at Basra: Indian transport in the City of Sindbad.

Roll-call before the advance: Inspection of Indian warriors in Mesopotamia.

Abandoned trenches in an immemorial battlefield: Earthworks along the Tigris.

Economy in metal: Gathering old shell cases at a depot near the river bank.

'Mid sequestered palms and waterways: Indian transport on a Mesopotamian river.

A vital need: Pumping water from the Tigris into portable filters.

By 1899 the project had assumed shape definite enough to warrant allusion by the Kaiser, in terms of alliterative grandiloquence, to the "Bremen-Berlin-Bosphorus-Bagdad Bahn" (railway). A year later it became apparent that the moment was opportune to secure a suitable site for the eastern terminus of the gigantic undertaking. Obviously a trans-continental line of this importance, which lacked an outlet at either extremity to the sea, lacked all; and therefore, with admirable forethought, it had been decided that the Oriental terminus should be situated on the Persian Gulf—for choice, on the shore of a natural harbour deep enough to allow vessels of the largest tonnage, actual or potential, to load and discharge their cargoes at its wharves.

Curiously enough, the Persian Gulf is singularly ill-provided with natural harbours answering to this description, and possesses only one, Koweit, on the north-west coast, within convenient distance of the mouth of the Shat-el-Arab, which conforms to

BRITISH SOLDIERS RESTING IN THE OLD TRENCHES AT ABU ROMAN, MESOPOTAMIA.

it. Its area—some four hundred square miles—is sufficient in extent to contain the navies of the world. It was an ideal location for the terminus of the great railway. Upon Koweit, in consequence, the choice of the German Government naturally fell. Selection of any other place would have been short-sighted and foolish, not at all in accordance with procedure in Berlin.

To Herr Stemrich, German Consul-General at Constantinople, was entrusted the task of purchasing the requisite amount of ground—four hundred acres, or thereabouts, in extent —for the site of the terminus. During his voyage from the Bosphorus the distinguished delegate enjoyed plenty of opportunities for reflection on the far-flung and ubiquitous nature of the British possessions. He possibly caught a glimpse of Cyprus in the offing. He certainly steamed through the Suez Canal, in which the British holding was no less than forty-four per cent. of the entire capital. He noticed that the island of Perim commands the entrance to the Red Sea, and that Aden, some miles farther east on the opposite coast, occupies a position of vantage. He must have passed various men-of-war of different shapes and sizes on his way up the Persian Gulf, for the illicit gun-running trade kept them constantly on the qui vive. It certainly did not escape his notice, while he scanned the horizon in vain for a sign of the Imperial flag, that they were all flying the White Ensign.

But the mission which had been confided to him was fraught with possibilities of a nature to induce stupendous change. The moment Germany acquired a vested interest on the Persian Gulf its days as a "British lake" would most assuredly be numbered. Indeed, a beginning had already been made. Some time previously (in 1897) a German Vice-Consul had been appointed at Bushire to promote and safeguard the interests of precisely six German subjects. The Hamburg-Amerika line, in consideration of a Government subsidy, had established a service between its home port and Aden, Muscat, and the Gulf. The first steamer, on its initial voyage, had called at all the ports it could possibly enter, while its band, grouped on the bridge,

Herr Stemrich's mission

played "Deutschland über alles," and, as an afterthought, "God save the King." Truly an excellent start.

It was, therefore, with sentiments akin to elation, possibly enhanced by the fact that Great Britain had her hands full at the time of the South African War and might therefore be left conveniently out of account, that the Consul-General and his suite arrived at Koweit. He lost no time in opening up negotiations with Mobarek, the native and principal sheikh, who exercised more or less despotic sway over the 200,000 members of the Uttub tribe, mostly shipbuilders by trade, in which they had attained no slight degree of proficiency. He explained, quite possibly in Mobarek's own language, that he had come all the way from Constantinople, on behalf of the All-Highest the German Emperor, to purchase some four hundred acres of land abutting on the harbour, which had already been selected, and asked Mobarek to name his price. Mobarek, with befitting humility, expressed himself as only too willing to comply with the august wishes of the All-Highest the German Emperor, and admitted that the question of price could easily be arranged but for the intervention of a slight and, as he feared, an insuperable difficulty. Of what nature? he was haughtily asked. The representative of the All-Highest the German Emperor had arrived just a little too late. How too late? Only the year previously Mobarek had entered into a convention, signed, sealed, and delivered, whereby he was precluded from selling even a square inch of ground in the territory of Koweit without the consent of the other contracting party. And who might the other contracting party be? His Excellency the Viceroy of India. And what was the consideration received? The protection of the British Empire.

Fidelity of Mobarek

That heartfelt prayer, the German soul's sincere desire, "Gott strafe England!" had not yet found its way into public utterance, but it requires no great stretch of the imagination to conceive of the fervour with which Consul-General Stemrich gave vent to its nineteenth-century equivalent. Germany ceased to laugh.

The inference, "Thus far shalt thou go and no farther," was perfectly plain. Great Britain, despite preoccupation of a somewhat pressing nature in South Africa, notwith-

THE CENTRE OF INTEREST IN MESOPOTAMIA.
Kut-el-Amara as seen from the roof of the British Hospital. For one hundred and forty-three days General Townshend's resistance to starvation held the admiration of the world.

standing her seeming indifference to German expansion in Asia Minor, had neither slumbered nor slept. She had, on the contrary, kept very wide awake. She had been fully cognisant of and alive to the all-important issues at stake. She had stolen a march on the All-Highest. In a word, she had quietly locked the door of the projected terminus and put the key in her pocket. Threats and cajoleries, blandishments and bribes, were of no avail. Mobarek had not been brought up in an atmosphere of Kultur nor trained to regard treaties as binding only to the extent which suited his personal convenience. Versed probably in no philosophy save the precepts of the Koran, he yet entertained the clearest possible notions on the sanctity of contract. He had given his word, and that ended the matter.

The mission of Consul-General Stemrich thus resulted in a fiasco of the very first order. His report to the Embassy in Constantinople, no doubt, made interesting reading. What to do now? Clearly to induce the Sultan to exercise his right of sovereignty over Koweit and make things as unpleasant as possible for Great Britain through the medium of Mobarek. This was accordingly done, and in the following year, after numerous pourparlers, during which Mobarek, in his endeavours on the one hand to smooth the ruffled feathers of Ottoman dignity and on the other to maintain the advantage of British protection, frequently found himself "between the devil and the deep

sea," the Sultan, prompted from Berlin, took a hand in the game and played what looked like a winning card. The sudden appearance of an Ottoman transport crowded with troops in the harbour of Koweit boded ill for Mobarek.

Fortunately, and by the happiest coincidence, one of those White Ensigned gunboats which the Consul-General had had occasion to note on his trip from Constantinople "happened" to be in port at the time. Its captain intimated politely but firmly to the Turkish commander that it would be to the latter's advantage, and prevent all sorts of unpleasant complications, were he to forgo his intention of landing troops and immediately to leave Koweit. The Turkish commander, whose instructions did not cover any contingency such as that which had unfortunately arisen, **Turkish commander's discretion** there and then, with commendable discretion, weighed anchor almost as soon as he had cast it, and steamed away, leaving the score distinctly in favour of the White Ensign. The Sultan's lead had been roughed in the first round.

A few months later the Porte made another move, this time of a less bellicose nature, and sent a special representative to treat with Mobarek and bring him to terms. The emissary of the Sultan was given courteously to understand, on behalf of the senior British naval officer on the station (a sub-lieutenant would have served), that he could attain no useful object by making any prolonged stay at Koweit. He speedily came to the same conclusion—indeed, there was none other to arrive at—and his sojourn consequently rivalled in brevity and result that of the Ottoman transport.

Abdul Hamid, never at a loss for an expedient, then turned his attention inland, and instructed one of his Arabian henchmen, Ibn Rachid, with a horde of native swashbucklers, to attack Mobarek from the desert. When Ibn Rachid arrived on the scene the first sight which met his view was that of an array of funnels which sprang from the decks of three cruisers in the harbour, whose guns gave him furiously to think. They also were flying the White Ensign. As no mention had been made of the possibility of an encounter with the British Navy in the programme which Ibn Rachid had engaged to carry out, he wisely emulated the example of the Ottoman commander, beat an instant retreat, and headed full gallop for Central Arabia.

The Sultan, urgently pressed by Berlin, replied to this, the third, "retort courteous" which had been addressed to him in his endeavours to assert his sovereignty over

THE COMMANDER-IN-CHIEF IN MESOPOTAMIA AND HIS STAFF.
Lieut.-General Sir Percy Lake, K.C.B., K.C.M.G., and his Staff at General Headquarters, Basra. Sir Percy Lake (the fourth figure from the right in the centre row) succeeded Sir John Nixon in the Mesopotamian Command in January, 1916.

Mobarek, by occupying the Bubian Islands, situated to the north of Koweit. Great Britain took no exception to this move beyond affirming that the position as regarded Mobarek remained unchanged, and that he still enjoyed her protection.

Prince von Bülow, the then German Chancellor, had been at some pains meanwhile publicly to declare, "We never for a moment entertained the absurd idea of seeking to acquire a port on the Persian Gulf." Herr von Schoen, his subordinate, was equally emphatic. "The German Government is absolutely opposed to the acquisition of a port in this inland sea." Those grapes were very sour.

Frustrated in their endeavours to secure a foothold for their terminus on deep water, the Germans cast about for another site. Obviously the line could not stop at Bagdad. With equal futility might the Canadian Pacific Railway come to an end at Kamloops, or the Paris, Lyons and Mediterranean Railway at Tarascon. Basra, a well-sheltered port, forty-five miles up the Shat-el-Arab, was the next alternative which suggested itself. The bar at the entrance offered a serious but not insurmountable objection. It could be overcome by dredging, and, as things were, vessels drawing sixteen to seventeen feet of water passed over it easily. Basra, moreover, lay within undisputed Turkish territory, where the question of British protection, with concomitant and disconcerting British cruisers, could by no possibility be raised.

The final decision was, however, not yet. Protracted diplomatic negotiations ensued arising out of Turkey's desire to increase her customs dues. Great Britain demurred. In 1913 Hakki Pasha was sent to London on behalf of the Porte with the object of getting her objection removed; but so long as the Ottoman Government continued its policy of undermining and counteracting British influence in the Persian Gulf, Downing Street remained adamantine. It was, moreover, an open secret that the additional custom-house receipts were to be applied to the construction of the Bagdad line and its extension to the shores of the Gulf. Unless British interests in these waters were protected by treaty there could be no approval by Downing Street of the proposed increase in the Turkish dues.

Anglo-Ottoman agreement

Finally it was agreed that the Sultan should exercise sovereign rights over Koweit, subject to full recognition of British protection to Mobarek; Turkey abandoned the Bahrein (pearl fishery) Islands to Great Britain and accorded her the sole rights of buoying, lighting, and policing the whole of the Persian Gulf, which, as a matter of fact, she had long exercised.

Basra was thus promoted to the dignity of the terminus of the Bagdad Railway, but no extension beyond that point

THE COMMANDER OF THE TIGRIS CORPS.

Lieut.-General Sir George Frederick Gorringe, K.C.B., and his Staff at Field Headquarters in Mesopotamia. Sir George Gorringe (the second figure on the left in the front row) in April, 1916, succeeded General Aylmer in command of the Tigris Corps that attempted to relieve Kut-el-Amara.

was to be undertaken without the consent of Great Britain. The latter claimed no participation in the construction of the line from Bagdad to Basra, but two British delegates were to have a seat on the board of administration of this section. On these terms the desired increase of four per cent. in the Turkish custom-house dues was agreed to.

The outbreak of war brought the Anglo-Ottoman agreement to an end. It also freed Mobarek from Turkish sovereignty, but left him undisturbed in the protection of Great Britain. In March, 1915, the Viceroy of India, Lord Hardinge, traversing the territory won from the Turks, personally conferred upon him the Grand Cross of the Indian Empire in recognition of his loyalty to the Crown. It certainly merited the distinction. Nothing but a scrap of paper bearing the seal of an untutored Mohammedan sheik stood in the way of the accomplishment of German designs (Prince von Bülow's disclaimer notwithstanding) upon a port on the Persian Gulf. The bond held.

Owing to a variety of causes, some due to climatic conditions and therefore unavoidable, others of a nature within the scope of human intelligence to foresee and consequently to counteract, the Mesopotamian expedition was extremely badly executed. It served, while bringing into the boldest possible relief the gallantry of men and officers in the field, as a monument to the inefficiency, short-sightedness, and lack of co-ordination on the part of supreme authorities. A long series of blunders, alike difficult to understand or excuse, culminated through want of support in the surrender of a larger garrison of troops under the British flag than had so far found record in the history of the Empire.

Townshend's retirement to Kut　　We may now resume the thread of our history of the Mesopotamian Campaign at the point where it was dropped at the close of Chapter XCIV.

By December 7th, 1915, just a week after the victor of Ctesiphon, when almost within sight of Bagdad, had been compelled by lack of reinforcements to fall back upon Kut, where it had been decided that his retirement should end, the investment of his position was complete. The Turks, their line of communications fully open behind them, had hurried heavy bodies of troops down the river and completely surrounded the place. Then began one of the most heroic, gallant, and long-drawn-out defences ever set down to the credit of British arms.

During the fateful seven days which had wrought such a momentous change in General Townshend's fortunes, he had taken every conceivable precaution to minimise its effects. Defences had been improved. All shipping, with sick and wounded, together with the 1,350 prisoners captured at Ctesiphon, was despatched to Basra. The only vessel retained was the armed tug Sumana, which had rendered invaluable service during the retreat to Kut, and she was reserved for use as a ferry.

The heterogeneous river fleet commanded by Captain Nunn, D.S.O., often under fire from both banks of the river, afforded inestimable assistance in protecting the steamers and barges and refloating them when they took the ground, a matter of frequent occurrence. The shifting shoals and shallows of the treacherous Tigris served the enemy well. The Shaitan had stranded on the evening of November 28th, and defied all efforts of the Firefly and Shushan to get her off, though they were fortunately successful in salving all her guns and stores. The hull, however, had eventually to be left.

On the morning of December 1st the Firefly, in company with the Comet, after making good practice with lyddite on the occasion of the Turkish attack at Umm-el-Jubail, received a shot in her boiler which completely disabled her. Her consort the Comet (Captain Nunn) immediately took her in tow; but luck was against them. As they were turning down stream in the narrow river both vessels grounded. The strength of the current, combined with the dead weight of the Firefly, which was pressing against her, forced the Comet more and more deeply into the bank. Finding that his own position was hopeless until

ENERGY IN THE SULTRY EAST.
Making a new pier at Basra. British
engineers pile-driving in the Tigris.

assistance arrived, Captain Nunn devoted all his energies to getting the Firefly clear, and finally succeeded in sending her careering down stream in the forlorn hope that she would escape disaster.

The Sumana speedily came to the Comet's assistance, but all efforts to dislodge her proved unsuccessful. Meanwhile the enemy's fire had increased greatly in intensity. Several field-guns had been brought up within short range and directed upon the devoted ships. They were, moreover, the target for the Turkish infantry, which poured volley after volley into them and the

"H.M.S. BELLUM" ON THE TIGRIS.
Cheery Britons learning to master the native craft known as the "bellum." The nearest of the R.A.M.C.
vessels by the shore was named after Florence Nightingale.

Firefly (which had speedily taken ground again) at a distance of fifty yards. Very soon it became evident that the Firefly and the Comet would have to be abandoned, for each was badly damaged and in flames. Under an inferno of shot, shell, and rifle fire, the operation of rendering the guns useless and transferring the crews and stores to the Sumana, which seemed to bear a charmed life, was coolly and successfully accomplished.

On the same day, December 1st, a fine feat of endurance was performed by the mixed brigade commanded by Major-General Sir Charles Mellis, V.C., consisting of the 30th Infantry and 1/5th Hants (Howitzer) Battery R.F.A., and the 16th Cavalry Brigade. It had been sent on, after taking part in

DAYYIR, IN SOUTHERN PERSIA.
Dayyir, in the Persian Gulf, used by British ships as a port of refuge during winter storms.

animals was marched to Imam Ali Gherbi, some fifty miles down the river, there to be reinforced by infantry and guns from Basra. They fought a rearguard action all the way, but fortunately with few casualties. Behind this detachment a force under Lieut.-General Aylmer, V.C., was collected with the object of relieving Kut as soon as concentration had been completed.

At Kut the Tigris takes one of its innumerable bends in the shape of the letter U. Upon the peninsula thus formed, of about a mile in width and less than three-quarters of a mile in depth, General Townshend occupied an entrenched position, the village—it scarcely deserves the designation of a town—lying at the most southerly end. He also held the liquorice factory situated on the

WIRELESS STATION: JASK, IN THE GULF OF OMAN.
Jask stands on the Cape of that name, jutting out into the Gulf of Oman. An important wireless station is established there on a site in a British concession.

right bank, which he fortified and garrisoned with two battalions. To the east lay a bridge of boats covered by a bridge-head detachment on the right bank. **Hopes of prompt relief** The besieged were well supplied with stores and ammunition.

the engagement at Umm-el-Jubail, to deal with hostile mounted troops which were interfering with the passage of steamers at Chubibat, some twenty-five miles below Kut. It became necessary to recall them, the increasing strength of the enemy rendering General Townshend anxious to concentrate his forces. So the mixed brigade retraced its steps, having marched eighty miles in three days, during one of which they had been engaged in fighting, without the loss of a single prisoner. To cover over twenty-six miles in a day over Mesopotamian tracks for three days, and arrive at the end of it, as Sir John Nixon, the then commander-in-chief, says in his report, with their valour and discipline in no way diminished, is no mean testimony to grit and physical fitness.

On the day previous to the completion of the investment (December 6th), the cavalry brigade, with the exception of one squadron retained at Kut, and a convoy of transport

General Townshend had confidence in himself and his troops, and looked forward to being promptly relieved. He therefore returned a determined refusal to Nuredin Pasha's summons to surrender. So certain was the Turkish commander that the besieged force must as speedily give in that he transmitted this summons, after a heavy bombardment, on the day immediately following the investment —December 8th. On the 9th he delivered a fierce attack upon the bridge-head in sufficient force to oblige the defenders, who of necessity were compelled to husband their resources, to retire. On the following night, December 9-10th, the bridge itself was destroyed by a party gallantly

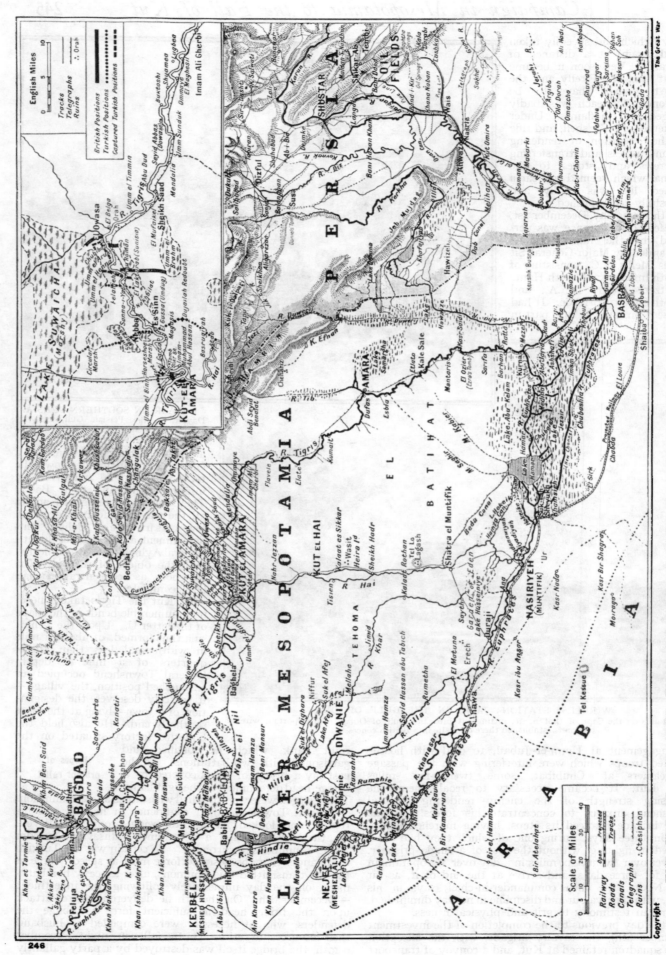

Copyright

THEATRE OF THE OPERATIONS BETWEEN BASRA AND CTESIPHON, UP TO THE SURRENDER OF KUT-EL-AMARA.

Map of Mesopotamia, showing the area covered by the British forces up to the date of the fall of Kut-el-Amara, April 29th, 1916. The enlarged inset shows the position of the British and Turkish armies on the day when starvation compelled General Townshend to surrender. The relief force was then within eleven miles of Kut-el-Amara, but was held up before the impregnable Turkish position at Sanna-i-Yat.

The Great War

led by Lieutenant A. B. Matthews, R.E., and Lieutenant R. T. Sweet, of the Gurkha Rifles.

During the next three days a continuous bombardment ensued, and a series of attacks were delivered, all of which were successfully repulsed, particularly on December 12th, when the enemy's casualties in two days amounted to a thousand men. So far the casualties of the besieged force had only amounted to four hundred and seventy.

Of the difficulties in the path of the relieving force the chief was the question of transport on the Tigris. The carrying capacity of the river, notwithstanding the ever-increasing number of craft of all descriptions and sizes which crowded it, was still insufficient to the exigencies of the campaign. As far as Kurna, where the Euphrates joins it and they together flow seaward under the name of the Shat-el-Arab, the Tigris is navigable for ocean-going steamers of moderate draught; but once above it, troubles not only begin but multiply. A draught of anything over five feet means certain and constant grounding, a source of interminable delay, and progress except in the flood season is a matter of impossibility at night. To tie up alongside the dreary stretch of mudbank as soon as it is dark and wait patiently for the dawn is the only course open.

The transports upon which the carriage of stores depended were mostly paddle-steamers drawing between four and five feet of water with a capacity of about five hundred tons. Each of them towed a couple of lighters, and together they moved no faster than the army which it was their business to keep supplied with the necessaries of life, to say nothing of the innumerable other things constantly required by troops on the march. To every brigade was allotted a parent ship

GALLANT DORSETS MAKE HISTORY AT KUT-EL-AMARA.
One of the splendid charges in the history of the Mesopotamia Campaign was that of the 2nd Dorsets at Kut-el-Amara on September 28th, 1915. Their task was the difficult one of storming the redoubts on the extreme left of the Turkish position, and before coming to the enemy's trenches the 2nd Dorsets had to hack their way through a forest of unbroken wire.

Difficulties of river transport
which met its wants, and was in turn supplied by attendant mahailas, craft peculiar to the river, and presenting with their high-sloping masts, lateen sails, pointed bows, and lofty stern an exceedingly picturesque appearance. They again were fed by bellums, also indigenous, long, narrow boats shaped like canoes propelled by pole or paddle, the caiques or gondolas of the Tigris, and capable of anything, except upsetting, when managed by their owners. They were frequently used with great effect for the transport of troops over the reedy marshes contiguous to the river and occasionally were even armour-plated.

The call made upon the Indian authorities for vessels of any description suitable to the navigation of the Mesopotamian waterways resulted in a collection of the most heterogeneous craft ever brought together. One in particular, named the Aerial, is worthy of description. Her

hull hailed from Brahmaputra, she was fitted with an air propeller, a fifty horse-power Diesel engine, and heralded her movements with a din like unto that of a general bombardment. She once plied as a shikar boat in Assam, where the Government's necessity proved her owner's opportunity, so she changed hands, and found her way to the Tigris under her own steam, a feat of navigation far excelling that of the famous Deutschland. She did great service during the advance upon Ctesiphon, was "stormed at with shot and shell" on more than one occasion, had many hairbreadth escapes, and was finally promoted to the position of an official ferry plying every hour between the field ambulance and the hospital camp "somewhere in Mesopotamia."

Anything that will float can be turned to account on the spur of necessity by the officers of the Royal Navy or Indian Marine. It is not surprising, therefore, that they should have enlisted the services of the gufar, which lays claim, not without justification, to be considered the oldest craft in the world. The gufar is built on precisely the same principle as the Welsh coracle, but is completely circular in shape. An enormous basket covered with skins, or plastered with pitch, answering neither to the impulse of sail nor the control of rudder, it is cast upon the waters at any point between Tekrit and Amara—where it immediately assumes a dual motion analogous to that of the earth—and finds itself after many days. Urged downward at varying degrees of speed by the current, it spins its way to its destination carrying a cargo according to its capacity and a complement of two men. Sometimes a donkey is thrown in as ballast. On arrival, the cargo is disposed of, and the crew wend their way homeward either afoot or on donkey back. Unless, indeed, it be skin-covered, in which case the hide may possibly serve the captain and crew with a shelter by night, the gufar itself is not worth transporting. One skin will outlast several generations, and time is of no value in the eyes of the Mesopotamian. He has practised this form of transit from the beginning of the ages.

The oldest craft in the world

Gufars went spinning down stream from Nineveh to Babylon in the days of Herodotus, and will in all probability so continue to spin until they have been swamped for ever by the remorseless and ever-rising tide of Western civilisation, together with other quaint relics of an interesting past. That their owners, of their own free choice, will elect to abandon them in favour of an up-to-date motor-boat making thirty knots is a contingency so improbable that it need not be taken into account. They regard all such modern inventions in the light of Sheitanlik (wiles of the devil), most religiously to be eschewed, as fraught with danger to peace of mind in this world and chance of salvation in the next.

Results of divided control

It became apparent at an early stage in the Mesopotamian Campaign, that the relations between the Home and Indian Governments were not tuned to the same note of mutual understanding and co-ordination which—none too soon—had been struck with such admirable precision in the concert of the Allies. The inevitable result—discord in lieu of harmony—ensued. It is a far cry from Delhi to London, however rapid and easy telegraphic communication between them. Two heads on occasion may be considerably worse than one. As regards the medical service, the lack of co-operation between the two centres of authority was particularly and painfully noticeable. Statements were freely made and passed without contradiction that the whole organisation of the medical department was deficient ; that field hospitals were too few in number, while those which did exist were inadequately equipped and completely undermanned ; that both doctors and nurses when most needed were rarely to be found, for the simple reason that

ARAB COOLIES UNLOADING A BARGE UNDER DIRECTION OF BRITISH OFFICERS.
Arab coolies naturally furnished much of the labour involved in bringing the British forces to the scene of operations in Mesopotamia. They are good-tempered men, but naturally indolent, and required careful and tactful supervision by British officers to keep them to their work.

A MESOPOTAMIAN BY-WAY.
A striking contrast between east and west in the Tigris Valley.

IN THE FOREFRONT OF DANGER.
A machine-gun outpost in direct touch with the enemy on the south (left) bank of the Tigris.

they did not exist in sufficient numbers to be able to meet the calls made upon them from all points of the compass and at once.

Demand considerably exceeded supply. At Ctesiphon the available medical staff could give adequate attention and assistance to five hundred men. Nine times that number, 4,500, urgently clamoured for both. Appalling accounts came to hand of the condition of the wounded, owing solely to lack of medical and nursing aid. Case after

Appalling lot of the wounded case was reported of officers and men, under the most trying climatic conditions, whether of heat or of cold, being left for days with no attention to their injuries beyond that of the first dressing in the field, sometimes barely that ; thrown into the same barges as stores, munitions, and horses ; as many as six hundred under the charge of a single doctor and one orderly. That these two did their duty nobly went without saying, but what were they among so many ? Time and again the Tigris tugs, their decks thickly packed with sick and wounded, hurried down stream to the base unprovided with any means of protection for the men against the bitter cold of a winter's night. The same stricture was applied to the ocean-going steamers which transported the wounded from Basra to Bombay, where they arrived in a pitiable condition. Injuries originally slight in nature had been rendered gangrenous by exposure in torrents of rain or mud-sodden trenches and camps. Precious lives were lost or permanently impaired by neglect, which in turn was engendered by faulty organisation.

The enormous demands made upon the R.A.M.C. from the various centres of war in France, Egypt, and the Dardanelles, which in every instance had been responded to in a manner beyond all praise, had depleted the ranks of available medical officers, and the Indian medical service, all-sufficient in time of peace, proved inadequate, as regards numbers, to the strain put upon it in time of war.

The same spirit of lamentable parsimony and optimism, which characterised the conduct of operations at the outbreak of the Boer War, seemed to colour the counsels of the Indian Government. **Indian Government's** It learnt nothing and it forgot nothing. **mistake** It made the fatal mistake of underestimating the powers of resistance of the enemy. The relief of Kut was regarded in the light of a walk-over, and, from the nature of the medical arrangements made, it almost looked as if the wounded were expected conveniently to limit their numbers and requirements to the capacity of the existing medical staff. The usual penalty was paid, and, as usual, by the innocent for the guilty.

An officer writing home said :

What a number of reasons will be given for our failure ! Weather has been against us several times, but our worst enemy has been the utter gross slackness, stinginess, and lack of foresight of the Government at home and in India. The latter still firmly believes that we are scrapping with a few wild savages instead of with a fine lot of very brave Turks who probably have not their equals as trench fighters.

Candid opinions such as these, which appeared in the newspapers from time to time from those in a position to form them, did not make pleasant reading or encourage feelings of public confidence. **Public confidence shaken** Complaints, however, were not restricted to the insufficiency of medical officers, nurses, and supplies. They applied in ever-increasing volume to the deficiency of munitions, bombs and hand-grenades in particular, which played so prominent a part in the war, and whereof the troops in Mesopotamia stood badly in need. When they did arrive, at irregular intervals, their quality left much, if not everything, to be desired, and reflected seriously upon the source of their manufacture.

About other matters of grave import, uneasiness was

Commons was eagerly looked for, had but cold comfort to give. Speaking on March 22nd, 1916, he gave it as his opinion, after paying a deservedly fitting tribute to the valour of the troops engaged, that there had been a lamentable breakdown on the part of the Indian organisation, its only excuse being the extraordinary difficulties attending the conduct of the campaign. He believed that there had always existed an abundance of medical supplies at Basra, but a grave and, as he thought, an inexcusable want of them higher up, due mainly, he did not doubt, to the Gordian knot presented by the problem of river transport.

Boats had to be of exceedingly shallow draught, and were not easy to obtain in anything like sufficient numbers. Many had been requisitioned from as great a distance as Egypt, but were lost en route by perils of the sea General Bingley and Sir William Vincent, distinguished soldier and civil servant respectively, had been sent by the Government of India to investigate matters on the spot, and report upon medical arrangements in connection with the campaign. The advance on Bagdad, Mr. Chamberlain informed the House, had been agreed to by the Home and Indian military authorities, and in addition had met with the approval of the officer commanding in Mesopotamia. He begged members to keep an open mind upon the subject until such time as the report he alluded to had been received and t h e information before the House was more reliable and exhaustive than that which it then possessed.

The hope previously entertained that the officer commanding had exceeded his instructions (in view of the difficulty of believing that they could have emanated from concerted authority) was thus rudely shattered by the Secretary of State, and the opinion, openly expressed in the House, that an advance upon Bagdad with a handful of twelve or fourteen thousand men savoured of insanity, was fully shared outside. There was nothing for it in the circumstances, however, but to make fresh demand upon the national stock of patience and still further

NATIVE PRESERVERS OF THE PEACE AT BASRA.
The Commissioner of Police, Basra, inspecting some of his men. The story of its native police work in every corner of the world is one of the romances of the British Empire.

felt and questions were asked to which a satisfactory reply never seemed to be forthcoming. How came it, for instance, that there was such a deplorable shortage of transport on the Mesopotamian rivers ? Flat-bottomed boats of the particular nature required were not difficult to build, and took no great length of time in construction. Had the dockyards at Bombay, Calcutta, Madras, and other Indian ports been utilised for this purpose ? Had no attempt been made to turn to account the railway material, left by the Germans at or near Basra for the construction of the Bagdad line, while the Turks were laying down their rails below Ctesiphon at the rate of a mile a day ? Was there no telephonic communication at the engagement of Sheikh-Saad between the Headquarters Staff and officers commanding in the field ? Had the signalling apparatus been despatched in as many as eleven separate steamers, reaching their destination on as many different occasions ? Was there a dearth of supplies where they were most needed, and a surfeit where least required ? In a word, had the organisation of the Indian Government completely broken down ?

The Secretary of State for India, Mr. Austen Chamberlain, whose announcement on the subject in the House of

to " wait and see," though the public was getting well-nigh sick unto death of the threadbare policy of shutting the stable door after the steed had been stolen.

To return to the beleaguered garrison at Kut. On December 14th, 1915, the two battalions occupying the liquorice factory rushed the enemy's trenches, which were only two hundred and fifty yards away. Three days later a sally resulted in the bayoneting of thirty Turks, the British loss being only one man slightly wounded. As Christmas approached, the **An unforgettable Christmas Day** fury of the enemy's attacks increased. He had received a formidable addition to his strength by the arrival of the 52nd Division, which had won its laurels in the Caucasus. Christmas Day saw the besieged hard pressed indeed. The garrison of the fort was unable to withstand the furious attack, which was delivered in vastly superior numbers, and had to evacuate its position ; but not for long, as a determined counter-attack, in which the enemy was repulsed, enabled the British to regain the lost ground.

Fighting of a desperate nature went on during the whole of Christmas Day, and was continued far into the small hours of the following day. Shortly before midnight

Men of our splendid Indian Army in readiness to leave a Mesopotamian base.　Left : Indian ambulance awaiting the signal to fetch in the wounded.

British and Indian soldiers getting a gun over a ridge, preparatory to shelling the enemy positions.　An incident in the Mesopotamian field which the camera has succeeded in describing with unusual force and reality.

SAHIB AND INDIAN TOILING TOGETHER FOR THE WELFARE OF THE EMPIRE.

SAVING THE STORES.
Troops removing baggage to higher ground, out of reach of the rising Tigris.

flour was now the difficulty. Grinding operations for so large a force were beyond the capacity of the solitary mill. The problem was solved by the simple expedient of calling down a rain of millstones from the sky. Friendly aeroplanes dropped them into soft places of special selection.

Oil stored in the naval barges supplied the deficiency of fuel, which by this time was running short. General Townshend, with admirable forethought, had planted vegetable seeds three days previously (January 26th), anticipating that he would shortly have to cope with the scourge of scurvy. So, indeed, it proved; and by the first week in February, by which time the stores of green food, rice, and sugar had run dry, and the milk at the hospital was reduced to a supply for ten days, the garrison was forced to add the bane of this disease to the sum of its sufferings.

a fierce onslaught was made on the northern bastion and a temporary footing secured. Forced to retire with heavy losses, the enemy came on again and again, striving to rush the breaches which had been made in the walls, and hurling bombs innumerable. To no purpose. To their indomitable courage was opposed valour greater still, and as the day broke they withdrew. That Christmas Day was likely to linger long in the memory of the garrison of Kut. On the 24th and 25th the British had lost over three hundred of their already depleted numbers. On the other hand, the enemy's losses were sufficiently heavy to warrant his asking on December 29th for an armistice to enable him to bury his dead and remove his wounded, who lay in heaps in front of the fort. Of course, the request was accorded. During the first month of the siege the British casualties were 1,840 ; the Turkish could not well have been less than 4,000.

IN AN INTERVAL BETWEEN THE FIGHTING.
Some of the smart and soldierly men of our army in Mesopotamia. The flat ground was a heavy handicap in the advance, as it presented no barrier to the spreading floods.

Finding it impossible to take the position by assault, except at a sacrifice of life which he **General Starvation** was not prepared to make, Nuredin **called to help** Pasha changed his tactics, and prepared to reduce it by starvation, keeping up a bombardment of an intermittent nature, principally at night, with his heavy guns.

The grim spectre of hunger had not yet made an actual appearance, but its shadow was gradually creeping over the devoted defenders of Kut. Hopes of speedy relief still ran high within its walls, and of rations, if on a reduced scale, there were yet enough to go round. There were always the horses. Fortunately, on January 24th, a large quantity of privately stored grain was discovered. The find proved of incalculable value. To reduce it to

The British troops were then receiving a twelve-ounce loaf of mixed wheat and barley flour, one pound of meat, a few dates and groceries per diem. The rations for the Indians were a pound of flour, half the usual allowance of tea, turmeric chillies and ginger, and a handful of dates. On this small scale the groceries were eked out until March 5th. From that time onward, as the prospect of relief grew less, the rations were gradually and systematically reduced, General Townshend and his Staff sharing every privation with the men.

On April 8th there was no further possibility of running the mill, which had to stop work owing to lack of fuel, though fortunately there was a stock of flour in hand to last another week, when the rations had to be cut down to a quarter of a pound per man per day, British and Indian alike.

Many, and amongst them several successful, attempts at escape were made by Arab inhabitants after food became scarce. One man, a particularly strong swimmer, aided by inflated bladders, was reported to have made the journey down stream to the British camp at Kurna.

Another—sole survivor of a party of eighteen—arrived, wounded in the leg, on a raft. These men brought first-hand news of the condition of the besieged, all of whom, they said, were in cheerful spirits, fully confident that relief would yet reach them. Their respect for General Townshend, who seems to have been endowed with the same capacity for arousing and maintaining enthusiasm in his men as the hero of Khartoum, amounted to veneration.

On April 24th a final attempt was made to get supplies through, and the Julnar, laden with stores of every sort and kind, left Basra, bent **Capture of the Julnar** on running the blockade. Her mission, however, had been an open secret for three weeks before she started, and the Turks, through Arab sources, knew as much about her every movement as the British authorities. She, consequently, fell an easy prey into the enemy's hands, actually within sight of Kut. To render the process as dangerous as possible by shell fire was their only consolation, but it was not of a satisfying nature.

Attempts to replenish the failing supplies of the garrison by aeroplane had been frequently made, but, except in a few cases—the millstone episode amongst them—had proved unsuccessful. The Turks boldly claimed that the superiority of their battle-planes enabled them " to shoot down the old British machines one after the other."

The efforts made by the relieving force were alike indicative of the gallantry of the officers and men composing it and of the insufficiency of the means supplied for the accomplishment of their task. Despite temporary and, on occasion, brilliant success, it speedily became evident to those who followed their movements that nothing but a large and immediate accession to their numbers and armament could enable them to overcome the resistance which the enemy was capable of offering.

The odds, almost invariably, were against them at the rate of five to one, and that the Turks were foemen worthy of their steel on even terms had been already demonstrated at Gallipoli. No fewer than a dozen different attempts to break through were made over a period of four months, practically the whole duration of the siege. On January 7th the Turks were attacked and forced to retreat from their position at Sheikh-Saad, situated due east of Kut on the south bank of the river, some fifty miles down stream. This success enabled an advance to be made a fortnight later on the still stronger enemy's entrenchments at Umm-el-Henna, twenty-seven miles higher up the river. This venture, unfortunately, did not meet with success, the enemy being in too great strength ; and until March 6th no further attempt was made.

On that date an attack was directed against Es Sinn, still higher up stream, almost within sight of Kut, but here also the enemy was in **General Gorringe's** considerably superior force, and it was **appointment** found impossible to dislodge him. Three weeks elapsed, during which the command devolved upon General Gorringe, in place of General Aylmer. He moved against the formidable position of Umm-el-Henna on the north bank of the river, where the British had failed to gain a footing in January. The only line of progress open to him was by frontal attack, as, indeed, had been the case

FLOODED AREA IN A PALM GROVE ON THE TIGRIS BANK.
Floods seriously impeded the operations of the British force in Mesopotamia, and added incalculably to the misery of the campaign. The beauty of this scene cannot blind one to the discomfort that must have attended encampment at such a spot.

BACK TO THEIR OWN PEOPLE.
Hospital ship drawing in to Felahieh. After Kut-el-Amara surrendered, the Turks allowed the sick and wounded to be sent to the British lines.

in all prior advances. Outflanking operations, owing to the condition of the country on both sides of the river, were impracticable. He had to move along the strip of high ground contiguous to its banks. The marshes, flooded to the full, extended far on each side. Beyond the marshes lay the desert, firm enough for transport or foothold, but waterless save for a few isolated wells totally inadequate to the necessities of troops and known only to the Arabs. Good progress had been made during a week's fighting by the 13th Division, which had so conspicuously distinguished itself at the Dardanelles and lost 6,000 officers and men out of a total strength of 10,500, thereby disproving the German axiom that no unit could survive the loss of twenty-five per cent. of its strength. The men of the 13th had supported a drain of more than twice that amount, yet showed no sign of reduced vigour. Though in seven days the distance which separated them from Kut had only been reduced by eight miles, they had fought for and carried every inch of the way.

Progress of the 13th Division

Trenches had been pushed forward by means of saps to within one hundred yards of the enemy's position at Umm-el-Henna, where he was strongly entrenched in places as deeply as nine feet. At 5 a.m. on the last day of March, the leading battalions of the 13th Division rushed the first and second trenches in quick succession under the support of concentrated artillery and machine-gun fire. Another hour saw them in possession of the third line, and by 7 a.m., after two hours' furious fighting, during

A LESSON IN SEA-POWER TO FRIENDLY NATIVES ALONG THE TIGRIS.
Retainers of the Sheikh of Mahommerah about to inspect H.M.S. Espiegle. This armed sloop, together with the Odin, covered the disembarkation of the original Mesopotamian Expeditionary Force at Fao. Above: Enemy patrol-boat sunk by the Espiegle. The craft was eventually salved.

A NEW RECRUIT TO THE A.S.C.
Landing a large motor-lorry from a river barge, somewhere on the Tigris bank. On the right of the illustration another automobile can be discerned under the awning.

which they drove everything before them, they occupied the fourth and fifth line. Information was then received by scouting aeroplanes that the enemy was strongly reinforcing his positions both at Felahieh and Sanna-i-Yat, three and a half and seven miles away up the river. As the approach lay over very open ground farther advance was deferred until nightfall. At 8 p.m., after a well-earned rest, the forward movement was continued on the left (north) bank, and the Felahieh position was successfully carried in the darkness. The 3rd Division in the meanwhile, under General Keary, had pushed on upon the other bank and had met with equal success in capturing the enemy's trenches opposite Felahieh, and consolidated the position, despite a strong counter-attack.

General Keary's advance

On April 9th General Gorringe pressed on to Sanna-i-Yat, but here he found the enemy entrenched in such strength that he had to fall back. General Keary, on the right bank, met with less resistance, and he was able to press onwards until, by April 17th, he had reached a point within eleven miles of Kut. On that and the following day the Turks delivered furious counter-attacks which, at a computed cost of 3,000 casualties, forced the British to retire. A bombardment of Sanna-i-Yat was followed by a fresh assault on the 23rd, but again the position proved impregnable, and once more the British had to fall back.

So in storm and rain and flood, with ever-decreasing forces opposed to ever-increasing numbers, the relief force found itself within eleven miles of Kut, whence the beleaguered British, now in the last extremity of hunger, could see the flashes of its guns.

On April 29th the limit of endurance was reached and the doom of Kut sealed. An ominous message from General Townshend, received by wireless at half-past eleven

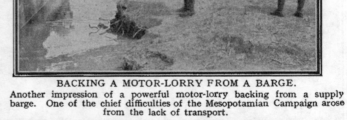

BACKING A MOTOR-LORRY FROM A BARGE.
Another impression of a powerful motor-lorry backing from a supply barge. One of the chief difficulties of the Mesopotamian Campaign arose from the lack of transport.

THERMOS FOOD-SAFE AT THE KUT-EL-AMARA HOSPITAL.
Ingenious arrangement for keeping food either hot or cold for the patients.

PRISON COMPOUND ON THE ROAD TO KUT.
Prisoners of war taken by the force that tried to relieve Kut-el-Amara
under guard in their wire-fenced compound.

on the morning of that day at the British Headquarters,
stated that he had surrendered.

I have destroyed my guns and most of my ammunition is being
destroyed. Officers have gone to Khalil Pasha, the Turkish Commander-in-Chief, who is at Madug, to say that I am ready to surrender. I must have some food here and cannot hold out any
longer. Khalil has been told to-day, and a deputation of officers
has gone in a launch to bring food from the Julnar, the ship
sent by the relief force on the night of April 24th to carry supplies
to the garrison of Kut.

Shortly afterwards came another message :

I have hoisted the white flag over Kut Fort and town, and the
guards will be taken over by a Turkish regiment which is approaching. I shall shortly destroy wireless. The troops go at 2 p.m. to
camp at Shamran.

The news, to a great extent discounted by the tenor
of the messages from General Townshend intimating
that the end was in sight, was received throughout the
Empire with profound sorrow. In Great Britain regret
was tempered with indignation, for a strong and justifiable
feeling existed that the reverse need never have been
sustained. Allied and neutral countries were unstinted
in their sympathy and admiration. In hostile camps the
announcement was hailed with expressions of extravagant
delight. Berlin, in delirium of joy, claimed the credit

for General von der Goltz and the scientific training which
the Turkish Army had received at his hands. Of the fact
that never before had so large a British force as 9,000 men
capitulated to an enemy the most was naturally made.

Khalil Pasha received the envoys of General Townshend,
for whom he expressed unbounded admiration, with the
proverbial courtesy of his race. He was specially desirous
that the garrison, after all the privations it had undergone,
should be generously provisioned, and regretted that his
own stores were not sufficiently plentiful to enable him to
furnish what was requisite. As soon, however, as the iron
pressure of the blockade had been removed, supplies poured
into Kut from British sources.

General Townshend, who was permitted to retain his
sword, was shortly afterwards sent to Constantinople,
where quarters were assigned him at Prinkipo, the principal
amongst a group of islands in the Gulf of Ismidt. He
carried with him into his enforced retirement the sympathy,
respect, and admiration of his country-
men. For nearly five months he and　　**An immortal**
the troops he so ably commanded had　　**story**
acquitted themselves under conditions
of the utmost difficulty and of a nature to test character,
whether in bravery or endurance, to the core.

The story of Kut and its gallant resistance will never
die. It may well inspire the pen of a great poet in the
future, even as the defence of Lucknow impelled that
of Tennyson in the past. Lucknow held out for eighty-
seven days, Kut-el-Amara for one hundred and forty-three.
To the survivors of the historic siege in Oude, after all
their sufferings—

Heat like the mouth of a hell or deluge of cataract skies,
Stench of old offal decaying and infinite torment of flies—

came final relief at the hands of Outram and Havelock,
and, as a fitting climax, the supreme consolation that

Ever upon the topmost roof our banner of England blew.

No such happy issue out of all their afflictions was in
store for the heroes of Kut. For them, despite privations
even greater, though endured with the same magnificent
fortitude for nearly half as long again, was reserved the
crowning humiliation of being forced by hunger alone
to lower the flag.

MAHAILAS: TYPES OF ANCIENT RIVER CRAFT ON THE TIGRIS NEAR SHEIKH-SAAD.

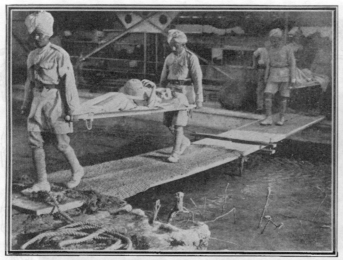

A member of General Townshend's immortal band. A sick hero of Kut returning to the British lines and on his way to hospital.

Indians who fought at Ctesiphon and Kut leaving the hospital ship wounded, emaciated from lack of food, and needing assistance over the gangway.

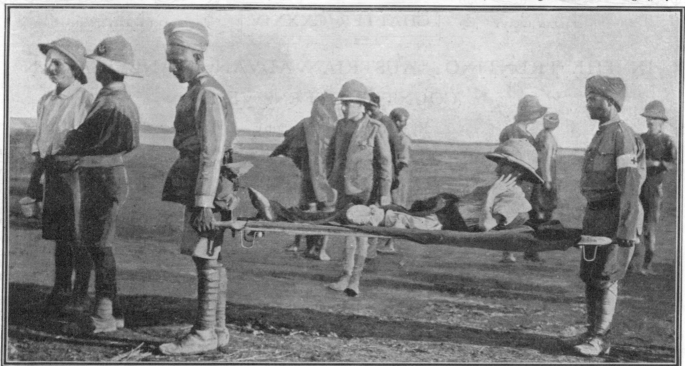

Conveying a wounded soldier to the ambulance. After the fall of Kut-el-Amara the Turkish commander, behaving with a chivalry seldom displayed by his German ally, allowed sick and wounded Britons and Indians to be sent down the river to the British lines.

Thoroughly worn out with their ordeal, a batch of Indian soldiers, carrying a few personal effects, landing from a hospital ship.

Less than a week after leaving Kut. Convalescent British soldiers eating bread-and-jam outside a hospital at Basra.

THOSE WHO CAME BACK FROM KUT: SICK AND WOUNDED SENT DOWN THE TIGRIS BY A CHIVALROUS FOE.

ITALIAN HEAVY

CHAPTER CXXXIV.

ARTILLERY TRANSPORT.

IN THE TRENTINO: AUSTRIAN ADVANCE AND ITALIAN COUNTER-OFFENSIVE.

By Dr. James Murphy.

Austrian Preparation for the Great Trentino Offensive—Constitution and Grouping of the Austrian Forces—Geographical Character of the Austro-Italian Battleground—General Plan of the Offensive Prepared before the War by General Konrad von Hötzendorf—Political and Tactical Mistakes in the Plan—Slav Refugees Herald the Attack—Bombardment of the Whole Line from Rovereto to Val Sugana, May 15th, 1916—The Battle for Cima Maggio—The Adige and Terragnolo Sector and the Battle of the Buole Pass—The Armentera to Val Sugana Sector and the Fight for Ospedaletto—The Terragnolo and the Astico Sector and the Fight for Borcola and Asiero—The Asiago Plateau Sector and the Struggle in Sette Comuni—The Battle of Novegno, June 5th to 24th—Austrian Retreat begins June 25th—Review of the Strategical Situation since May 15th—Organisation and Disposition of the Italian Defensive Forces—General Pecori-Giraldi—General Cadorna Begins the Counter-Offensive—The "Austrian Drive" Ends in the "Trentino Races" and an Austrian Debacle.

WHEN, in May, 1916, Italy was preparing to celebrate the first anniversary of her entry into the European conflict, in circumstances set out in Chapter CXIX., Austria launched a colossal offensive in the Trentino. Equalling, if not in many respects outstripping, the magnitude of the German preparations for the attack on Verdun, the Trentino offensive was the most formidable undertaking that had yet been organised by the Austro-Hungarian Staff. It was the long-delayed counter-attack against the positions which Italy had conquered from Austria during the first weeks of the campaign; but it was more than a counter-attack. The purpose of the expedition had been preached and advertised throughout the Dual Monarchy. It was a sort of sacred crusade for the just punishment of a "faithless" ally. No Austrian harboured the thought that the expedition could fail. And certainly the time, pains, and material which had been expended in organising it warranted strong faith in its success.

PREPARING FOR ALL CONTINGENCIES.
Headquarters Staff on one of the Italian fronts in consultation before an expected Austrian attack.

With characteristic Teutonic thoroughness, the Austrian Staff devoted several months to the preparation of its great *coup de main*. The fundamental idea of its plan was to amass large bodies of well-trained troops close to the line of attack, so that no time should be lost in bringing up reserves. Eighteen divisions of infantry, selected from the best troops on the Balkan and Galician fronts, were transferred to the Trentino, grouped and distributed so as to form three armies, two of which were intended for the front line, while the third was to be held in reserve. The supreme command was entrusted to Archduke Karl Franz Joseph, with General Konrad von Hötzendorf, Chief of the General Staff, acting as assistant. The respective armies were placed under the immediate control of three famous generals— Dankl, who had command in Galicia during the early part of the war; Kövess, who had been victorious in the second invasion of Serbia; and Boróvic, who had so stoutly defended Gorizia against the Italians in 1915. The number of men enrolled in the three armies amounted to over 400,000. They were supplied with stores of food, clothing, tenting and barrack material, hospital provisions, etc., sufficient to last them six months.

The method followed out in the constitution and grouping of the forces is extremely interesting. An Austrian division normally consists of four regiments, each regiment being made up of four battalions of a thousand men apiece. But for the purposes of the Trentino campaign the number of regiments in a division was raised to six. Two of these constituted what might be called a movable depot. As units they were not meant for the fighting-line, but were to fill the breaches occurring in the front-line regiments during the course of the struggle. By this system each division was enabled to make up its losses automatically, so that it could keep a steady pressure on the foe.

Plans of the Austrian advance

The enormous amount of artillery placed at the disposal of the different divisions and army corps affords another striking example of Austro-German faith in weight of metal. The allotment of machine-guns accredited to each battalion was raised from the normal number of eight to the extraordinary number of thirty-two—or, in other words, seven hundred and sixty-eight machine-guns to a division. In addition to this several regiments were supplied with a number of small mountain guns (42 mm.) drawn by dogs, which had been trained to follow the troops into the most advanced positions.

The artillery of medium calibre was supplemented in similar proportion. At the beginning of the war each Austro-Hungarian division possessed six batteries of "seventy-fives" (3 in.), each battery containing six pieces. Two batteries of a heavier type (4 in.), each battery also containing six pieces, completed the divisional equipment.

In the Trentino six additional batteries of heavy field-guns containing six guns apiece, were allotted to each division. The normal equipment in medium artillery of an Austrian army corps amounts to eight 6 in. guns, arranged in two batteries of four guns each. For the attack in the Trentino the number of 6 in. guns was raised from eight to twenty-four; and an additional allotment of thirty-six field-guns, of a calibre a few degrees larger than the "seventy-fives," was given to each army corps.

Totalling up the number, and leaving out of count the supply of machine-guns, we find that each division possessed eighty-four pieces of light and medium artillery. Taking account of the additional artillery at the disposal of an army corps, we find that each army corps, when composed of two divisions, was supplied with two hundred and twenty-eight pieces; and when composed of three divisions, the number was increased to three hundred and twelve. Over and above all this was the great supply of heavy guns and the enormous stores of ammunition placed at the disposal of the expedition. The formidable train of siege-artillery consisted of forty 12 in. howitzers of the Skoda type, four 380's, and four 420's (15 in. and 16.53 in. respectively).

I have dealt with these figures somewhat in detail, because not only are they an index of the immense importance attached to the Trentino exploit by the Austrian Staff, but they also throw an instructive light on the state of affairs in other war theatres. Having succeeded in obtaining an accurate estimate of the enemy's strength on the Trentino frontier, the Italian Staff was in a position to afford information which turned out to be of immense service to the allied cause. The purpose of the Central Empires was laid bare. In the hope of anticipating the

The enemy's objective

THE SENTINEL OF THE PASS: AN EMBATTLED HEIGHT THAT FELL TO ITALIAN PROWESS.
One of the Austrian heavy guns in position on a snow-capped peak. Before the war the Austrians held all the geographical advantages in a mountain campaign, but General Cadorna's strategy and troops were not to be denied.

ROCKET APPARATUS AT A SIGNALLING POST.
Rocket apparatus to light up enemy positions and detect any advance attempted under cover of darkness was in constant use on all fronts.

combined offensive of the Allies by crippling the Italian Army for the time being—and this became a pressing necessity now that the same plan had miscarried at Verdun—Austria threw every ounce of her strength against her former ally. In desperate straits because no help could be afforded her by Germany, she had seriously weakened her eastern front in order to strengthen her Trentino phalanx.

Now was the time for Russia to strike. The first blows revealed Austria's weakness. It is interesting to note that though General Brussiloff captured 366,000 prisoners between June 4th and August 12th, the number of guns captured amounted only to four hundred and fifty-one. If we reckon exclusively on a basis afforded by that number, we shall find that no more than twenty guns were allowed to each Austrian division in the east. But the artillery equipment on the Russian front must be estimated on a wider basis—namely, on a basis which takes into consideration not only the number of prisoners captured, but also the losses in killed and wounded. Thus considered, the disproportion between the supply of men and guns becomes still more striking. Evidently Austria had staked her Imperial fortunes **Austria's desperate** on the success of the Trentino offensive. **throw** The desperate throw was destined to result, both directly and indirectly, in the most tragic episode that had yet darkened the tragic history of the Hapsburg Monarchy.

Before coming to the story of when and how the attack was launched, it is necessary to call special attention to the geographical character of the Austro-Italian battle-ground. A knowledge of its peculiar configuration is indispensable, if one would follow intelligently the fortunes of the campaign. Here the rules which govern the struggle are almost entirely different from those which are applicable on the plains of France and Flanders.

Comparisons and analogies are misleading, because what seems essential to warfare in an open and undulating country is only of secondary importance in mountain battles. For the mountain and valley take active part in the struggle. Therefore, the strength of many positions depends not on the number of men who hold them, or the guns that guard them, but primarily on the advantages afforded by the terrain. Consequently, the importance of battles must not be judged by the numbers employed. It often happens that vital points are held by small forces,

CHEERFUL AND SMART ALTHOUGH ONLY JUST OUT OF THE TRENCHES.
Italians coming out of the trenches. The men of General Cadorna's armies, like the French and British, were supplied with steel helmets as protection from head wounds. In circle : One of the famous Bersaglieri scrutinising a position which his transport had to pass.

SUMMER QUARTERS OF THE ITALIAN SECOND LINE.
Campaigning among the Italian mountains had its attractive aspect in the summer. These were the quarters of the troops of the second line.

and it has happened more than once that the fortunes of some of the most decisive battles in the Italian campaign—Pal Piccolo, for instance—have been in the hands of a few thousand troops.

The worth of a victory, then, being relative to the damage inflicted upon the enemy, must be estimated in relation to the strategic value of the terrain from which he has been dislodged. For instance, if he be forced to withdraw from a point where a few hundred men have held some thousands at bay, he will now have to employ thousands instead of hundreds, whereas his conqueror can dispense with numbers correspondingly large. Of course, all these truths are applicable to every form of warfare, but they play a specially dominant part in the Austro-Italian war.

This becomes very clear in the case of the Trentino campaign. The ordinary map is of very little use in following the movements and manœuvres which take place in so complex and varied a territory. One must make a mental sketch of a contour map in which serrated peaks and towering blocks of mountain stand in irregular and intricate formation, as huge sentries watching over innumerable valleys and passes. Pushing southwards from the main ridge of the Alps, the Trentino forms a colossal triangular bastion. It is a wedge-shaped block of mountains, the narrow point of the wedge penetrating far into the great expanse of Italian lowlands which lie between the Alps and the Appenines. From time immemorial this has been the starting-point of countless attacks against Italy. The triangle is cleft through its centre by the Valley of the Upper Adige, along which runs the southern portion of the Brenner Pass. For our present purpose we shall have to extend the political confines of the Trentino and speak of it in terms of the whole of Southern Tyrol, from the saddle of the mountain range to the Lombardian Venetian plains.

The Swiss frontier cuts into the western side of the triangle at a point about one-third of its length from its

Configuration of the Trentino

WIRE INSTEAD OF CONVOLVULUS AND VINE.
Miles of wire ran like insidious bindweed creeping round the stakes that were thick upon the hillsides.

GENERAL HEADQUARTERS BENEATH THE CHESTNUT-TREES
Italian General Headquarters, pleasantly situated under chestnut-trees: no more pretentious than the bungalows allotted to the rank and file.

TO GORIZIA: THE PENULTIMATE STAGE.
Communication trench on Monte Podgora, the hill from which the Italians
debouched to ford the Isonzo and carry Gorizia by storm.

base on the north. Farther south the Toscolano Valley leads into Lombardy at a point which seriously threatens the main railroad from Milan to Verona. Moving northwards along the eastern side of the triangle, the first valley of importance is Vallarsa, the opening of which is controlled by Monte Pasubio, 7,325 feet high. Farther north is the Valley of the Astico, with the Cima di Campolongo and Monte Verena at its mouth. And still farther north the important Valley of the Brenta leads into the Italian plain, dominated on its southern side by the towering heights of the Cima Dodici. In this sector, between Vallarsa and the Brenta, the great attack was launched.

The district is made up of innumerable valleys and passes amid serrated mountains. Mule-paths wind in and out on the shoulders of the hills, and carriage roads follow the serpentine courses of the mountain torrents. Towards Trent these valleys converge, so that it stands to them in the relation of a hub to the spokes of a wheel. It was possible to amass immense quantities of war material here, because even if the Italians were successful in stemming the onrush of the Austrian tide, there would be no need of a serious retreat on Austria's part, the mountains acting as fortress walls for the protection of men and material within. The most the Italians could hope to do would be to compel the enemy to withdraw within the outer defences of his fortress.

Where the attack was launched

From the Austrian positions on the protruding bastions of South-Eastern Tyrol to Vicenza is a distance of some thirty miles. Vicenza stands in the centre of that neck of lowland which extends from the mountains to the Venetian shore and through which the Italian railroads pass on their way to the north-eastern arm of the Venetian Plain. If the Austrians should succeed in breaking through they would completely cut off from its base of supplies the great Italian army operating in the Dolomites, in Carnia Cadore, and on the Isonzo front. If the purpose were but partially carried out it might eventually succeed in forcing General Cadorna to employ the main body of his army for the defence of the Italian plains, and thus abandon the idea of an offensive on the Isonzo.

The general plan of the offensive was not due to any decision arrived at in Austro-German war councils during the course of hostilities. Before the outbreak of war it had already been prepared, under the influence and direction of General Konrad von Hötzendorf and the late Archduke Franz Ferdinand, as part of the war treacherously premeditated against Italy. A series of fortifications were built at Folgaria and Lavarone, dominating the Upper Valleys of the Astico, Assa, and Brenta. The whole territory between Vallarsa and Val Sugana was organised and militarised, with no other purpose than that of making it the starting-point of a gigantic offensive against Italy at one of the most vulnerable points of her frontier.

A pre-war project

In the immediate planning of the attack it is not difficult to follow the mental workings of the Austro-German Staff. Verdun would forestall the allied offensive in the west, the Trentino would cripple Italy, and the victorious armies of the Central Empires would be free to attend to Russia before the armies of the Tsar would be ready to move. But also from the more restricted viewpoint of her Italian campaign there were pressing reasons why Austria should undertake a strong offensive against her southern enemy. The Austrian position in the Trentino was one which insistently called for betterment. Cadorna's troops were pressing closely on the great fortress city. Rovereto was already under the control of their guns. Should they push their successes farther north Austria would lose her only chance of organising a serious offensive against Italy. The Trentino position was the most vulnerable point of the Italian line. Here the Austrian position was specially favourable to the launching of an attack. If the advantage were not now taken, the Dual Monarchy would be compelled to confine itself to a defensive war on the Italian front.

Military critics have written at length about the great blunder made by Konrad von Hötzendorf. He could not have hoped, it is pointed out, to lead a triumphant army into Venezia, for he must have known that Cadorna could mobilise upwards of a million men against the Austrian attack. That criticism is sound, so far as it goes; but it should be remembered that Konrad's purpose would have been successfully carried out if he could dislocate the existing disposition of the Italian forces, and compel General Cadorna to keep a large army on guard in the Trentino sector. This would relieve the pressure on the Isonzo, and paralyse, at least for the present, any Italian attempt at a grand offensive.

Konrad's blunder was of another and more elementary nature. He did not prepare for eventualities. Underestimating Italy's military resourcefulness and misinterpreting the political situation, Konrad's Staff staked everything on the success of the Trentino adventure. Furthermore, the tactical mistake was plain even to the man in the street. General Cadorna's army was operating within an arc, which formed well-nigh three-fourths of a complete circle. In order to counteract an Italian push on its south-eastern end, Austria opened an offensive against the extreme south-west. The movement of Italian troops took place along internal lines, or cords, whereas the Austrians were compelled to mobilise along the circumference. Besides, Austria had difficult mountain roads to traverse, and only one railroad, whereas Italy had the plains and a network of railroads. And, further, the Italians in the neighbourhood of Monte Croce began to control the railroad through the Puster Valley, with the result that Austria could not withdraw troops or material from the Trentino front unless by moving northwards into the Valley of the

In complete contrast to the attractive aspect of the campaign among the mountains in summer-time, these photographs show its forbidding and formidable aspect during winter. The men are seen advancing at a height of 3,000 metres.

Advances were made at the expense of extraordinary physical energy, the men trudging heavily along the steep sides of the mountains often more than knee-deep in snow, hooded like monks for protection against the biting winds.

Fatigue-parties, laden with fuel for fires and timber for making barricades for their positions, toiled painfully up the heights, zigzagging upwards in Indian file where the acclivity was too sheer to be compassed direct.

NATURAL DIFFICULTIES OF THE ITALIAN CAMPAIGN UPON THE SNOW-COVERED ALPS.

Inn, and thence by a most roundabout and tortuous route, in her effort to reach the Isonzo. Should the Trentino offensive be held up, it was clear that in the race for the Isonzo Italy must be days ahead of her enemy. The alert Latin mind would never allow such an opportunity to go by the board. And this explains the sudden and triumphant character of the subsequent Italian move.

These preliminaries are indispensable to a clear understanding of the military situation. It is true that the Russian offensive helped Italy; but it is more true that Italy mainly owed the success of her defence and attack to the close co-operation of all the Allies, as well as to the military genius of her commanders and the valour of her troops.

A rather dramatic incident heralded the attack. In the early hours of Sunday morning, May 14th, 1916, the Italian sentries on duty in the advance positions overlooking Val Terragnolo noticed three strange forms moving along the mountain side. Towards the Italian barbed-wire defences they came, pausing and peering round at **A dramatic** every step. Through **incident** the half-opaque atmosphere they seemed like wanderers lost on the mountains. The sentries challenged. Immediately six arms were lifted upwards in sign of surrender. And yet it was not the sign of surrender, but that of pleading for deliverance. It was an impressive and solemn gesture, like that of a Mohammedan who turns his face to Mecca and raises his hands in prayer to Allah. They were Slavs who had escaped from their Austrian taskmasters and sought deliverance at the hands of the Italians.

"The attack against the Italians is arranged for to-morrow," they said. "It will commence with a bombardment lasting from dawn till evening. At six o'clock in the evening the infantry will attack."

The information proved to be entirely exact. On the Monday morning, as the sun's rays were tipping the Dolomite peaks and the lower hills lay hidden in the darkness of night, one 15 in. naval gun opened fire on the little village of Asiago at a range of ten miles. Following one another at intervals of twenty minutes, five massive shells fell in the narrow streets, excavating immense craters, smashing the windows of the dwelling-houses, and creating general consternation amongst the inhabitants. It was the signal for the general outburst. Along the whole line, from Rovereto to Val Sugana, the Italian positions were smothered by an avalanche of fire and flame. On a front of some twenty-five miles two thousand guns were in action. Austrian aeroplanes hovered overhead, directing the fire of the artillery by means of wireless appliances installed in the machines. Many of the shells burst above the clouds, creating opaque masses of flame, as if some Olympic artillery had begun to thunder from heaven itself. Down the mountain sides came the rain of splintered shells. It was the most awe-inspiring spectacle that had yet been witnessed in the Great War.

During the bombardment Italian officers succeeded in locating many of the heavier Austrian batteries. By a careful examination of the shells it was ascertained that one of the mammoth 420's (16·53 in.) had been installed on Monte Costa Alta, in the Asiago sector, another on the high table-land at Folgaria, and a third at Rovereto. Following out this method of location it was possible to find the key to the grouping system adopted by the enemy. Owing to the difficulty of quickly transferring heavy batteries over any considerable distance in this intricate and difficult region, there was little likelihood that any surprise manœuvres would be attempted by the enemy. Consequently, the Italians were enabled to form a rather safe opinion as to the points where the series of infantry attacks were likely to be made. The conduct of the Italian war being essentially a question of strategy, it constantly called for the exercise of that intuitive faculty which enables a military commander to read the mind of his enemy and arrange his plans accordingly. That power of psychological insight is a gift which is almost omnipresent in the Latin mind but lacking in the Teuton. In the military sphere Italian commanders seem to have displayed it in its highest degree. Cæsar had it. So had Napoleon. Throughout the course of the present war it has been strikingly displayed by General Cadorna and his Staff.

Towards the evening of May 15th the infantry attack was launched. At all the points along the whole line, from the Adige to Val Sugana, the offensive was simultaneous. Against the Italian position on Zugna Torta, which stands between the Valleys of the Adige and Vallarsa overlooking Rovereto, a tremendous assault was made. There the Italians were not well established, because for a whole twelvemonth their trenches had been under fire from the Rovereto forts. Still they boldly held their ground, forcing back avalanche after avalanche of the oncoming foe. Five times the Austrians charged up the mountain; five times they were hurled back, their ranks depleted by the fire **The assault on** of the machine-guns. **Zugna Torta** Hundreds of their dead lay torn and massacred amid the barbed-wire entanglements, and hundreds more rolled down into the Adige. Still they came on, reinforced at each charge, until the Italians were forced to abandon the hill, their trenches having been utterly ruined by the terrific bombardment.

Up the Valley of the Terragnolo—a tributary of the Adige, joining the Vallarsa north of Zugna Torta—another avalanche poured. There the positions were rather thinly held by the Alpini, and it was evident that only a short stand could be made. But the longer the Austrians were held at bay the more time would be gained for the bringing up of the reinforcements. Having delivered several counter-attacks with the bayonet, the Alpini retired to the defensive line, Milegna-Soglio d'Aspio, which runs from Val Terragnolo to Val Astico, a few miles westward of the old frontier line. This line follows the watershed, resting on a series of mountain rests, which vary from 5,000 to 6,000 feet in height. Several streams have their sources here, one set running westwards to join the Adige and another flowing eastwards towards the Adriatic.

GENERAL COUNT GUGLIELMO PECORI-GIRALDI.
General Pecori-Giraldi, then in command of a division on the Carso, displayed such military genius by his capture of Sei Busi, July 25th, 1915, that on August 10th he was given command of an army corps, and on May 10th, 1916, was promoted to the command of the First Army on the Trentino front.

Discovered ! Barbed=wire cutters taking cover. *Italians consolidating a captured trench.*

Mat screens for exposed roads : A device employed by the Italians advancing upon Gorizia.

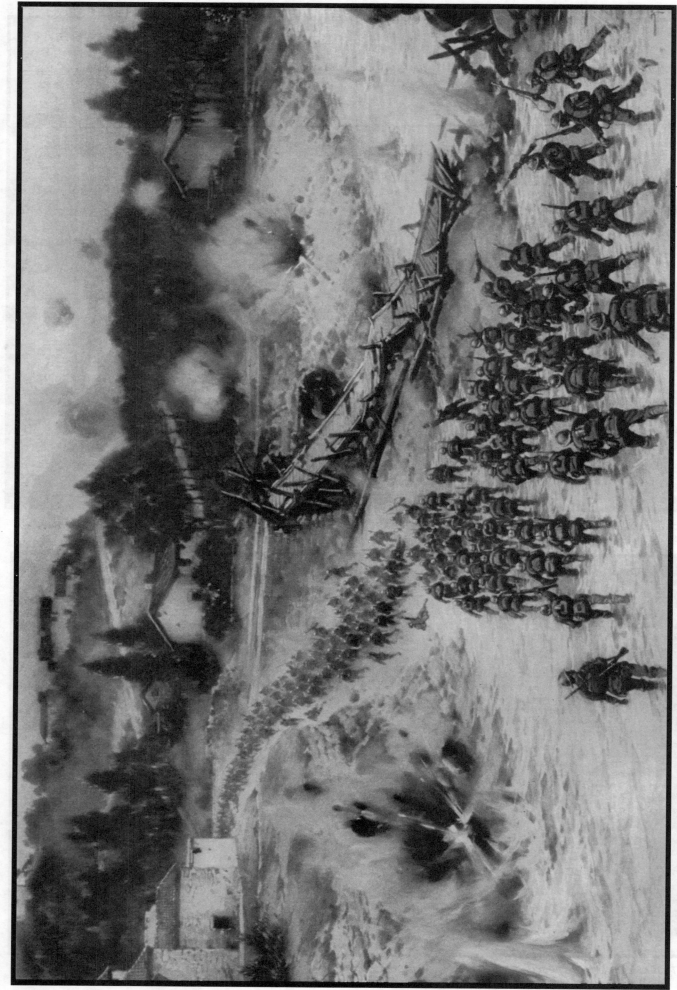

In July, 1916, the Italians recaptured Arsiero in the Trentino, fording the Posina at Ponte Rolto with superb intrepidity.

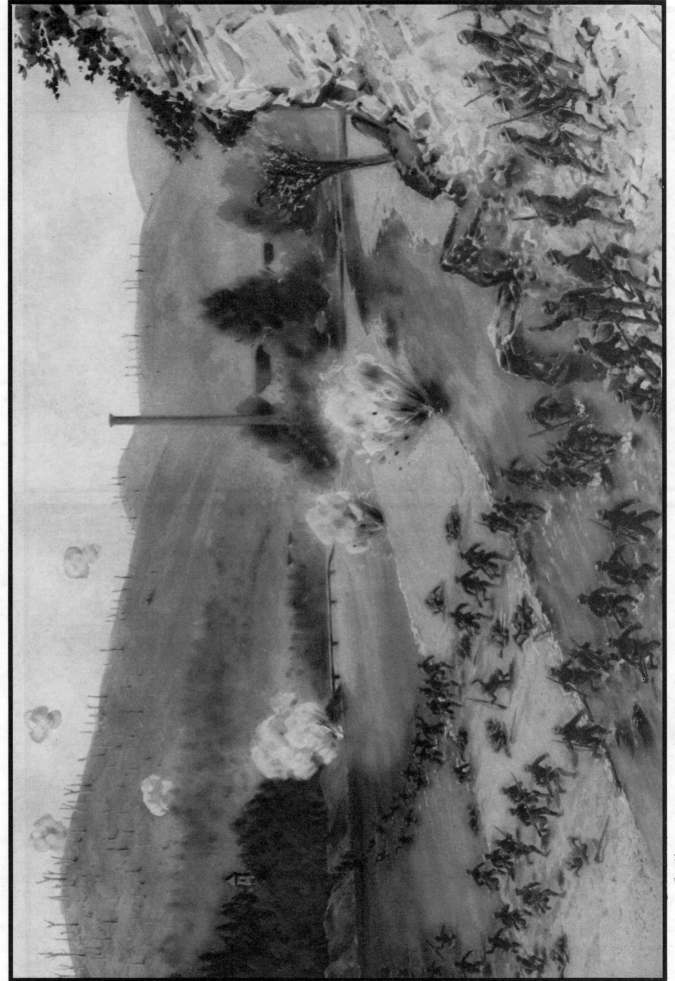

Italian troops crossing the Isonzo under a hail of shrapnel during the storming of Gorizia, August 9th, 1916.

"Carry the position": Italians salute their dying colonel's order.

Cavalry pursuit of Austrians in the Sette Comuni.

In the intricate network of valleys, peaks, and passes, sometimes enveloped in heavy storm-clouds, or high in the luminous air amid glittering ice and snow, the struggle assumed an almost supernatural character. Though not strongly reinforced, the Alpini held the vantage points and were well supplied with machine-guns. The slaughter of the Austrians was appalling, yet they still came on. Owing to the system of attaching supplementary regiments to each division, which had been employed by the Austrians, the line was being constantly reinforced automatically. The clouds blanketed many of the positions, so that much of the firing on the part of the artillery was wild and blind. This was specially detrimental to the advancing troops the nearer they got to the Italian trenches. Several combatants have given their impression of the struggle as one of the most cruel and awe-inspiring that the mind can conceive.

An awe-inspiring struggle   Meanwhile, on the extreme left of the advance, another army moved down the Brenta Valley. The left wing of this army attacked Monte Colo, on the northern bank, while the right pressed on towards the high tableland of Asiago, attempting to encircle Monte Verena and enter the Valley of the Assa. Clad in white shirts, the moving troops seemed part of the snow-covered mountain. They crept along silently, without a whisper of command being spoken. Along the shoulder of Monte Vezzena on the north and across the Valley of the Torra on the south they came, scaling the mountain to a height of some 5,000 feet, where the Italian outpost was entrenched. Not a sound from the sentries. Closer and closer the Austrians drew. But the whisper of the Italian sentries had passed along the telephone wire. When the Austrians were within close range the machine-guns opened fire. The enemy replied with a volley of hand-grenades. Again and again he was driven back, but he returned persistently to the attack, each time in undiminished strength. Five attacks had been repulsed, and now came the dawn. Viewing the masses of their dead which lay on the mountain, the Austrians lost heart and returned to their trenches on Busa di Verle and Palauro.

On the northern bank of the Brenta a like struggle went on. Again and again the phantom-like army attacked Monte Colo and Sant' Anna, but the Alpini drove back each assault. When the first streaks of dawn appeared no appreciable advance had been made, and the Austrians withdrew to their original lines.

Pivoting their phalanx on Monte Armentera and Cima Panarotta they moved forward once again, under cover of their artillery. But the Alpini jumped from the trenches, scaled the peaks and crags, bayoneted the enemy, and drove him back to his cover. The struggle was waged above the clouds amid peaks that glittered like polished silver in the morning sun, while the valleys still lay in darkness. The Austrian attempt was suspended for the moment, and this sector of the front remained comparatively quiet during the 16th, 17th, and 18th.

The Austrian plan was now plainly revealed. It became evident that the attack in the Upper Brenta Valley was of a preparatory character, and that the enemy intended opening three roads farther south—namely, along the Valleys of the Astico, Posina, and Assa. The southward advance along the Valley of the Adige was rather of a defensive nature. The capture of Monte Zugna Torta and Monte Coni Zugna would relieve the Italian pressure on Rovereto, and thus obviate the danger of an attempt at an encircling movement by General Cadorna's troops.

Along the centre of the new line taken up by the Italians, the struggle grew more intense and concentrated, the objective of the enemy being the high tableland between the Astico and the Assa, known as the Sette Comuni. This mass of territory projects as a sort of bastion into the Venetian Plain and completely dominates the mouth of the Astico. In order to move along the Posina and reach

LIEUT.-GENERAL EMILIO BERTOTTI.
Commanding the Italian army at Valona, a port of great strategical importance with the finest harbour on the Albanian coast.

Arsiero, where the Valley of the Posina joins that of the Astico, it was necessary to secure control of Cima Maggio, the key of the Borcola Pass in the Upper Valley of the Posina. Here an epic struggle took place. During a three days' combat the mountain changed hands several times.

For two days the heavy artillery kept up an incessant bombardment. At intervals the whole mountain seemed aflame, a mammoth tongue of fire cast up from the mouth of a volcano. Trenches were utterly destroyed, steel and concrete parapets shattered, the pathways and aerial railroad pillars reduced to a mass of debris. The Alpini abandoned their position, which was immediately seized by the Austrian troops. When the Austrians were grouped and massed on their new ground the Alpini returned to the fray. This time it would have been suicidal for the enemy to use his artillery; and his soldiers were no match for the Alpini with the bayonet. Once more Cima Maggio was in Italian hands.

Again the Austrian artillery thundered. The mountain was now torn and gored, as if devastating lava had deluged its sides. The intense heat melted the snows, so much so that survivors say **Fire that melted** they found the water boiling and steaming **the snows** in some of the gorges. Once again the Alpini retired and the Austrians reoccupied the shell-riven crest. But the thought of Cima Maggio in the enemy's hands was too sad a one for the mind of the Alpine soldier. He returned to the combat and drove out his conquerer at the point of the bayonet. During this last struggle another company of Alpini succeeded in scaling Height 1869, which also controls the Borcola Pass; so that though the possession of Cima Maggio eventually rested with the Austrians, it was robbed of its strategic effectiveness.

GUNNERS PASSING DOWN A VILLAGE STREET.
Officers and men were as interested in the photographer as the pretty girl
under the artistic iron balcony was interested in them.

COVERED TRENCHES VERY NEAR THE ENEMY.
An Italian trench on the Lower Isonzo well screened and stoutly protected
from an enemy position dangerously close at hand.

North of Cima Maggio, on the heights of Monte Coston
and Monte Costa d'Agra, a similar battle was fought. On the
18th the positions finally fell into the enemy's hands ; and
then it was no longer possible to hold Monte Coston d'Arsiero,
which had been one of the pivotal points in the first line of
the Italian defence. The Italian centre was now withdrawing to its main line of defence.

In order to follow clearly the further developments of
the struggle, it is important to remember that the line
of battle was not continuous. It divided itself into four

distinct sectors which were not in actual touch with each
other, though they were the scenes of concerted operations.
The first sector extended from the Adige to the Terragnolo,
the second from the Terragnolo to the interwoven series
of valleys which form the sources of the Astico, the third
along the high tableland of Asiago, the fourth from Armentera to Monte Colo, on the banks of the Brenta in
Val Sugana. The different sectors have their different
battle-histories. We shall consider them separately.

The movement in the Adige Valley brought about the
fall of Zugna Torta ; but the Austrians were unable to press
farther south, owing to the Italian resistance on Monte Coni
Zugna. Realising the extreme importance of preventing
the Austrians from moving down the
Adige Valley or up the Vallarsa, Cadorna   **How Monte Pasubio**
ordered Monte Coni Zugna to be held at   **was held**
all costs. On the northern bank of the
Vallarsa is Monte Pasubio, which towers to a height of
7,325 feet, and dominates the valley. Directly westward of
Monte Pasubio, on the opposite bank, the Pass of Buole
leads into the Valley of the Adige, south of Monte Coni
Zugna. If Monte Pasubio could be taken the Pass of Buole
would fall into the hands of the Austrians and Monte Coni
Zugna would be turned. An enormous number of heavy guns
were brought into action against Monte Pasubio, and a
bombardment kept up without a moment's breathing
space, day and night, for three weeks. From May 26th to
June 1st violent infantry attacks were delivered against
the Italian positions, but they were only successful in
driving the Alpini to the higher crests of the hill. From
there all efforts failed to dislodge them. Deeming it
possible, however, to gain possession of the pass, even

270

though the high crests of Monte Pasubio still remained in Italian hands, the Austrians decided to make a blind drive and break through by sheer force of numbers.

As a saddle on Monte Coni Zugna rests the Buole Pass. In order to understand the importance of its position, imagine the mountain cast in the mould of a gigantic horse. His head faces north-west, towering high in proud defiance. His brow is Monte Coni Zugna, gaunt and bare to the north but sloping and wooded along its southern declivity. At his shoulder stands Monte Salvata. He has a pair of outstanding hips—Monte Mezzana on the left and Parmessan on the right. Standing between two valleys, the Adige on the left and Vallarsa on the right, you must vault over his saddle if you would pass from one valley to the other. His saddle is the Pass of Buole.

In the hope of attracting the main strength of the Italian resistance towards Monte Coni Zugna, **Monte Coni** the Austrians attacked the central Italian **Zugna** positions on the high mountain. Then, by a quick manœuvre, they sent forward large detachments to push up through Vallarsa and thence over the pass, thus encircling Monte Coni Zugna. The first stages of the manœuvre were carried out successfully. Mounting the hillside, towards the saddle, the Austrian troops covered the first few hundred yards of the ascent without let or hindrance on the part of the defenders. Faster and denser they came, now full of the spirit of victory and confident that their plan would be successful. But the Latins were on the alert. When the enemy was about halfway up the ascent the defenders opened fire. A hail of machine-gun and rifle bullets poured into the breasts of the attackers. Immediately they wavered, but the shrill whistles of the officers in the rear warned them that death awaited them

OUT ON THE "DEATH PATROL."
"Death Patrol" was the name given by the Italians to the men who went out at night to cut passages through the enemy wire.

if they dared to return. Once more they attempted the ascent, only to realise the utter impossibility of moving forward in the face of the Italian fire.

But the Austrians had sworn that they would retake Ala on the anniversary of its fall into Italian hands (May 27th, 1915). An airman had already flown over the town, dropping missives which announced the benevolent intention of Francis Joseph's troops, and also plainly hinted that a dose of frightfulness might be expected if Ala would not willingly surrender herself to the embraces of her former master. One of the missives ran thus: "We shall take Ala on the anniversary of her fall; but if within two days she does not become thoroughly Austrian we shall bombard the city." **"Konrad's sausage-** The anniversary was now at hand. **machine"** But the Pass of Buole still barred the way to Ala. "Hack through at all cost" was the order given. Believing that if dense masses were rolled upwards towards the breach all could not be destroyed, and that some at least would succeed in getting through, the Austrians advanced in massed formation, taking advantage of the cover given them by the wooded glens. They brought a supply of small machine-guns which could be manipulated by one man. Having arrived near the crest of the mountain, where the woods cease and the rugged steeps stand out bare and gaunt, the troops began to pour into the pass. The Italian machine-guns mowed them down. Those that escaped were massacred in the bayonet charge of the Alpini. Still they came, so quickly and regularly that it seemed as if they were being poured forth from the mouth of some monster machine. "Konrad's sausage-machine is at work," said the Italian soldiers to one another. Platoon after platoon

PROBING THE SECRETS OF THE HILLS.
Powerful "75" searchlight brought up among the mountains by the Italians to discover any enemy movement during the night

WITH THE ITALIAN GENERALISSIMO.

General Cadorna, eager and well satisfied, watching an artillery duel and pointing out details to his keenly interested Staff.

40,000. A rather pathetic phase was revealed when the prisoners began to tell of their experiences. For days their food had been failing, as the guns on Monte Coni Zugna had interfered with the transport of supplies from Trent. The soldiers were hungry and parched with drought. But their officers had kept urging them on, saying: "Break through—break through! There is plenty of food in Italy."

The left wing of the advance met with a similar fate. At first the onrush was successful, and succeeded in driving the Italians from their advanced positions in Val Sugana. The principal line of the Italian defence in this sector extended from Ospedaletto, on the northern bank of the Brenta, along the western crests of the Cimon Rava group. On the southern bank of the river it rested on Monte Civaron (3,600 feet), the Cima Undici (7,300 feet), and the Cima Dodici (7,660 feet). But the advanced line was about seven miles westward, running from Monte Colo on the north of the river to the eastern crests of Armentera, on the southern bank. For two days this line withstood the Austrian advance; but during the **Road to Asiago opened** 17th and 18th it was forced to withdraw. The Austrians occupied Borgo on May 19th. They crossed the Brenta and drove the Italians from Armentera on the 21st. Crossing the Moggio on the 22nd, they occupied Monte Civaron, and on the 25th the Cime Undici and Dodici fell into their hands. Thus they opened the road to Asiago. But this movement brought the extreme left of the advance into the territory of the centre. Instead of moving directly down the Brenta it struck against the

forced its way into the pass, but the Italians mowed them down as fast as they appeared. The anniversary was over, and the road to Ala still barred.

For four days more the battle raged. Austrian artillery swept the whole sphere, reducing to a mass of atoms the beautiful little hamlets that overlook the Adige. Each day operations culminated with an assault against the defenders of the pass, but the Italians would not yield an inch. Blasting quarries into the side of the mountain they tore loose the jagged crags and hurled them downwards on the oncoming foe. Through all its tragedy and grim horror the battle assumed a character that was heroic and sublime. It had something of primeval barbarism in it, recalling the time when the Cymbri of old attempted to pass through on this same spot; and in the evening, when rocks were no longer available, their women threw the children against the faces of the Roman defenders.

On May 31st the final assault was made. A whole division was hurled to the charge. Having clothed themselves in the uniform of Italian soldiers, several detachments of Austrians rushed from the edges of the woods, crying out: "Don't fire! We are Italians!" But the "melon heads" belied the disguise. Shouting their false chorus, they were mowed down mercilessly by the machine-guns on the crest. Throughout the whole day the slaughter in the pass continued. At last the division rolled backwards, leaving 7,000 of its dead on the battle-ground. Thus ended the Battle of the Buole Pass, and with it the Austrian hope of breaking through to Ala. A conservative estimate of the losses suffered by Konrad's troops in this sector alone places the number at

MOUNTAIN GROTTOS TURNED INTO FORTRESSES.

Almost every crevice where protection could be found was seized upon by the Austrians, built up with concrete, and turned into a fortified grotto. Before the outbreak of war the whole territory between Vallarsa and Val Sugana was organised and militarised, with a view to making it the starting-point of a gigantic offensive against Italy at a vulnerable point of her frontier.

AUSTRIAN TROOPS AMID THE MELTING SNOW.
With the beginning of the melting of the snow, great holes were perforated through the tracks, and miniature avalanches made the Italian counter-offensive all the more noteworthy.

SETTING OFF ON THE TRAIL.
Column of Italian infantry with pack-horses going up to the front, the long line curiously suggestive of Indians on the trail.

Italian position on Ospedaletto and was "cannoned" towards the centre. On the 27th a frontal attack was launched against Ospedaletto, but it was utterly unsuccessful, and cost the Austrians dearly. From this date onwards no farther advance was effected in Val Sugana. Here the Italians stood deeply in Austrian territory. They held their principal positions through the whole encounter, and succeeded in carrying out Cadorna's plan of holding the wings at any cost. The advances which would now take place in the centre must necessarily be robbed of their ultimate effectiveness.

In the sector between the Astico and the Terragnolo the southern half of the Austrian central column was engaged. Having succeeded in driving the Italians from their advanced positions to the first line of defence, the Milegna-Soglio d'Aspio position, they followed up their advantage by bringing into play an enormous mass of artillery. A violent artillery attack was made against the positions on Monte Pasubio (7,325 feet), the southern peak of the Pasubian range. This chain of mountains runs from the Vallarsa to the Astico. In the centre stands Cima Maggio (6,150 feet), outside the Italian frontier, and thence in a north-eastern direction runs the line Maggio-Toraro-Spitz. Between Cima Maggio and Monte Pasubio is a depression known as the Borcola Pass, leading from the head of the Terragnolo Valley to that of the Posina Valley. Borcola is thus a key position. The Terragnolo flows westwards into the Adige and the Posina flows south-eastwardly into the Astico. By coming up the Terragnolo and crossing through the Borcola Pass into the Posina Valley the way to Arsiero is opened, and thence the great channel to Vicenza. The Italians held their ground on Monte Pasubio, but were forced to give up the Coston dei Laghi (Hill 1,859) and retire to the Toraro-

Austrians occupy Arsiero

Campomolon position. Firmly hinged to Monte Pasubio as to the pillar of a gigantic gate, the line swung still farther backwards, until it finally ran from north to south on the range of mountains which form the southern ramparts of the Posina, its extreme right now resting on Monte Novegno. Here they made a desperate resistance from May 31st to June 15th, beating back attack after attack and inflicting heavy losses on the enemy. In the retreat to Monte Novegno Arsiero was evacuated, and occupied by the Austrians on June 1st.

Meanwhile the northern half of the Austrian centre was moving forward on the Asiago Plateau, sometimes called the Sette Comuni position. From May 15th to 21st the Alpini withstood the onslaught of the enemy, and on the 21st were forced to retire to the Verena-

The battle-line of the Italian centre formed two sides of a right-angled triangle. Originally it was straight as a taut string, bound firmly to Monte Pasubio on the south and Ospedaletto on the north. During the offensive the centre of the line had been pushed in a south-westwardly direction, while the ends remained firm. Immediately within the angle thus created stood Arsiero. The left wing ran almost directly westwards, from Monte Novegno to Monte Pasubio, the right from Monte Novegno along the Canaglia Valley and the Sette Comuni Plateau to Ospedaletto. If the Austrians could burst through at the vertex of the triangle, the Astico Valley and the road to Vicenza would be open to them.

Being now the most important pivotal point in the defence, Monte Novegno became the immediate objective of the Austrian attack. **Attack on** It is the strategic key to the whole **Monte Novegno** series of military positions here. A continuous row of hills runs from the plain to Monte Pasubio, forming a sort of turreted fortress wall. Monte Novegno is the great bastion on the eastern end, Monte Pasubio on the west. The intervening hills are Cogolo, Alba, and Forni Alti. North of this chain is the Astico and south of it is the Leogra Valley, joining one another at Schio, whence a short railroad runs to Vicenza. Should Monte Novegno fall, the secondary hills must needs follow the same fate.

An immediate attack was the main hope of the Austrian cause. Every moment's delay meant the heaping up of new obstacles; for the Italian railroads were busy day and night bringing masses of troops and material to the defence.

On the afternoon of June 5th the battle commenced. From the roof-tops of their homes the inhabitants of

VEDETTE POSITION ON THE CARSO.
A picturesque vedette position in the area of the fiercest fighting on the Carso, and the entrance to an Italian trench.

Campolongo line. But the territory here was of the most difficult character, constantly under fire from the enemy's great forts and affording very few facilities for the bringing up of reinforcements. The Italians farther retired to the Valleys of Galmarara and Assa, eventually evacuating Asiago, which was occupied by the Austrians on June 1st. The Austrian centre was now well into Italian territory.

After evacuating Asiago and Arsiero the Italian centre fell back on its last line of mountain defence, which ran along the Sette Comuni Plateau from the southern banks of the Posina to the Brenta. During the retreat Italian rearguards kept the enemy constantly engaged in the Upper Astico and Assa Valleys, with a view to hindering and delaying his advance as much as possible. In the meantime the centre of the defensive line was being strongly reinforced, especially in the Astico Valley. For it was now a certainty that the Austrian centre would concentrate its full energy on an attempt to break through here.

From the Plateau of Arsiero to the Venetian Plain there is only one outlet. It is the Valley of **Defence of the** the Astico. South of Arsiero, where the **Astico Valley** Posina joins the Astico, the valley becomes deep and narrow, winding in and out among soaring cliffs which sometimes reach a height of 7,000 feet. Here are the last defences which guard the entrance into Venezia. Having reached the Arsiero Plateau it is as if one stood upon the ramparts of a great mountain castle. Looking out over the plain beneath you see the church-spires of Vicenza and discern with the aid of glasses the long, serpentine trains entering and leaving its great railroad junction. The European War would assume a new aspect if the Austrians could reach that railroad centre. And now it seemed so near.

MOVING THE GUNS ALONG A MOUNTAIN SIDE.
The task of moving artillery about the mountainous terrain of the Trentino was so difficult that, had it not been accomplished, it might have been thought impossible.

STRENUOUS TEAM WORK FOR MEN AND HORSES.
Another impression of the extraordinary labour that fell to the lot of the Italian field-artillery in moving its guns about the mountainous area of operations.

Vicenza could see the Austrian shells breaking over the hill-crests. At least twenty heavy howitzers had been brought into play against the Italian positions, together with upwards of a thousand guns of medium and smaller calibres. For four hours the bombardment continued, completely demolishing the parapets of the trenches and the barbed-wire entanglements. During the bombardment Italian airmen hovered over the enemy's lines and discerned countless trains of ammunition-waggons bringing food to the guns, while the massing and grouping of infantry went on on a colossal scale. Austria was concentrating all her might against the gate which barred the way into the Astico Valley.

The battle-cry, At seven in the evening the artillery **"Avanti, Savoia!"** fire abated and the enemy moved to the attack. Everything was silent for a while. The infantry swarmed around the mountain range, making a simultaneous attack from different points. The wooded slopes of Monte Novegno and Monte Cengio offered them excellent cover. Suddenly the Italian artillery rang out at short range, plunging a hail of shell into the woods. But the Austrian supply of human material seemed as illimitable as its ammunition. They came on in massed formation, crying out to one another through the darkness. The enfilading fire from the Italian guns was unable to keep them at bay. They reached the trenches, struggled through the battered terrain, and it seemed for a moment

HEAVY FIELD-ARTILLERY IN POSITION.
One of the 149 mm. (6 in.) howitzers of the heavy artillery of the Italian field army ready for action.

as if they would hold their ground on Monte Novegno. But suddenly the cavities of the mountain are bellowing forth loud cries: "*Avanti, Savoia! Avanti, Savoia!*" as the Alpini fall upon their foe.

Before morning dawned the Austrians had been driven back into the woods, and again the artillery preparation began. Eighteen days the struggle lasted, sometimes waged with sustained fury, at other times weak and spasmodic. But the Italians did not cede a yard of ground. Many of the prisoners taken told harrowing tales of the sufferings they had endured. The supply of water had run short, the food was scanty and bad. The supply of ammunition was inexhaustible; but an army cannot live on ammunition

THE DUKE OF AOSTA.
The Duke of Aosta, cousin of King Victor Emmanuel III., commanded the Third Army, which captured Gorizia, August 9th, 1916.

that the Italians were suffering an unexpected set-back. To the general public, whose eyes had been so long riveted on the Franco-British and German fronts, a retreat of a few miles was a matter of the first importance. It was natural, therefore, to look upon the retreat of the Alpini, over a distance of seven or eight miles during the first days of the onslaught, as a rather serious reverse for General Cadorna's troops. Serious, in many senses, it certainly was ; for it is always a serious matter to be forced into abandoning positions which have been won at great cost. But the span of the retreat was no index of its importance, for in mountain warfare distances cannot be measured in miles, and it threw no light either on the weakness or strength of the Italian defence.

These facts become quite clear when one remembers that the Italian line on the mountains is a line that has been established by an invading army. The advance-guard always occupies positions **The strategic** which are not meant as points d'appui, but **situation** are held simply with a view to keeping the opposite armies in touch. In the case of a serious attack it is the duty of the advance-guards to play the part of covering troops, and delay the progress of the enemy. That is what happened in the case of the Tridentine offensive. Retreats on the mountain being from one strategic line of hills to another, once the outposts began to retire they could not come to a halt before reaching the next strategic line.

In the farther withdrawal of his troops General Cadorna was bowing to the necessity imposed upon him by circumstances, while at the same time preparing for his counter-offensive. Between the Terragnolo and Val Sugana the mountain region which forms the watershed of numerous streams, and is torn and twisted in most fantastic

alone. It needs bread and water, especially water. On the arid heights of Asiago, beneath a blazing tropical sun, Austria's army was without water. Worse than all, the troops had been drugged with lavish doses of alcohol and ether, the German professorial substitute for wholesome food and manly courage.

Giving details of the condition of things which prevailed behind the Austrian lines, the prisoners explained that they had been led to believe that the right wing of the army of invasion was already in Verona. In order to uphold its honour and earn the supply of medals promised by his Kingly and Imperial Majesty Francis Joseph, the central army must push on to Venice before the regiments of the right wing would have the chance to enter. One poor delirious fellow, as he was being tended by **Tide of Austrian** Italian surgeons, asked : " How many **invasion turned** hospitals are here ? Isn't this a small hospital for a great city like Venice ? " They had been told that Venice was just beyond the crest of the mountain. " When you enter Venice we shall make peace," said the officers. Naturally, the prospect of a speedy return to their homes, a square meal, and a jug of beer or fresh water from the spring had an inspiriting effect on the minds of simple peasant soldiers.

On the morning of June 24th Italian airmen reported that the enemy was in flight. The battle of the forty days was over. Austria's army of invasion had turned homewards. The Italian counter-offensive had already begun.

Here it may be well to consider a few of the main features of the strategic situation which had come into prominence since May 15th. During the Austrian advance in the Trentino, it was commonly believed, especially by outsiders, that the invaders were having the best of the battle, and

IN MEMORY OF THE BRAVE DEAD.
Gabriele d'Annunzio, national poet of Italy, reciting his three " Hymns for the Dead " to the troops at Aquileia at a memorial service for the dead.

AN ITALIAN "149."
Italian 6 in. howitzer at the moment of discharge.

A FLYING FORTRESS ON THE ITALIAN FRONT.
An Italian armoured car with quick-firing guns in action during the struggle for Gorizia.
(Drawn by a soldier, Plinio Codognato.)

fashion, forms very difficult terrain. The advantage of position lay entirely with the Austrians. They were provided with the great series of forts, Lavarone and Folgaria, which had been erected in time of peace, and they were convenient to their base of supplies. It was impossible for Cadorna to think of holding them at bay from the outset. He could not stop the initial stages of their advance but he could force it in a direction which would enable him to deal with it later on.

The Italian commander ordered that the wings were to be held at all cost. "Remember that here you defend the soil of your Fatherland. These positions must be held to the last," was the majestic message he sent to his troops. And they obeyed him. Every attempt on the part of the Austrians to break into Val Sugana, on their left, and the Adige Valley, on their right, met with utter failure. Cadorna was preparing for his favourite strategy of piercing the wings so as to compel a retirement in the centre. For those who were familiar with the tactics of the Italian chief it was possible to foretell, with a fair degree of confidence, that the decisive blow against the Austrians would be delivered from the two pillars where they had been held stationary since the start.

It would not have been wise or possible to attempt to withstand their advance in the centre. In rapidly pushing forward they were coming into territory where the manœuvring of large bodies of troops is a matter of utmost difficulty. For that reason the Italians had never held the positions between the Terragnolo and the Brenta with large forces. The ground is barren and waterless, and almost entirely without roads. By withdrawing towards the edge of the plateau they were coming nearer to their bases of supply, and approaching the verge of a territory which is well watered and well supplied with facilities for transport. Of course it is also true that, being unable to detach from other parts of their front an amount of artillery equal to that which the Austrians were employing, the overwhelming mass of material against them made a retirement an absolute necessity for the Italians.

It is interesting to study the methods adopted in organising and disposing the defensive forces. Every phase of

General Pecori-Giraldi

the gathering storm in the Trentino was well known to the Italian Staff. A few days before its outbreak General Pecori-Giraldi was given control of the forces operating in the Trentino sector. He was the right man in the right place. At the beginning of the war Pecori-Giraldi was simply a divisional general, directing a small body of troops in the Carso region ; but he displayed such quick initiative, sureness of insight, and thoroughness of execution that he was made general of an army corps a few weeks after the outbreak of war. Like his chief, he had had his political enemies. Five years before they succeeded in enforcing his retirement from the Army, the judgment of the State Council against him being that he did not have the ability to command a division either in peace or in war. But Cadorna, who had no illusions about the military genius of politicians, placed Pecori-Giraldi in the foremost rank of military commanders. On May 10th he was made general of the Italian army operating in the Trentino. Events proved the wisdom of the choice.

A few days after General Pecori-Giraldi had taken up his new duties all the roads in Italy led to the Trentino. A pressure was put upon the railroads such as they had never borne before, exceeding by one-third their scheduled capacity. Over half a million men were almost instantly mobilised, with their full equipment in artillery, food supplies, ammunition, mining and railway-building appliances, Red Cross stores, etc., besides a complement of 75,000 horses, mules, and oxen, and 15,000 waggons of

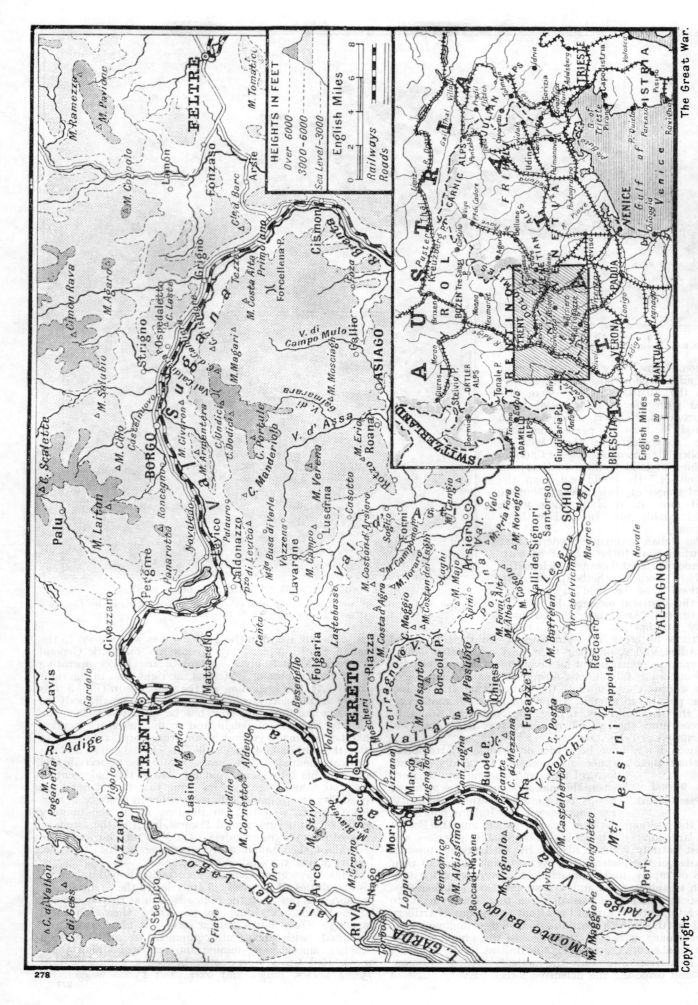

HEIGHTS IN FEET
Over 6000
3000—6000
Sea Level—3000

English Miles
0 2 4 6 8

Railways
Roads

English Miles
0 10 20 30

The Great War.

Copyright

MAP OF THE SOUTH-EASTERN TRENTINO SHOWING THE AREA FOUGHT OVER IN THE AUSTRIAN OFFENSIVE IN MAY AND JUNE, 1916.

Area of operations in the Trentino covered by the Austrians in their offensive from May 15th to June 25th, 1916, sometimes called the Battle of the Forty Days, by which they sought to break the Italian defensive and penetrate through Vicenza into the Venetian Plain. The key map on the right shows the portion dealt with in this chapter in its relation to the entire Austro-Italian battle-ground.

every description. One of the outstanding features of this improvised mobilisation was the enormous number of motor-cars employed. Each car averaged about one hundred and thirty miles per day, and the whole motor-transport service accounted for the mobilisation of 100,000 men. Perhaps that does not look a very large number on paper, accustomed as we now are to thinking in millions, but when one bears in mind the conditions under which the transport was effected, the achievement is remarkable. Most of it had to take place under cover of the night, over roads which were no better than mule-paths, crossing bridges and viaducts which were being constantly destroyed by the enemy's fire and constantly rebuilt by Italian engineers. Many of the drivers did not leave their cars for six days and six nights, getting food as best they could, and snatching a few moments of sleep between the fitful pauses in their work. But Italians have a gift of taking such burdens as a matter of course; for they have an intense sense of solidarity, working with an enthusiastic self-sacrifice when some general cause inspires them. Those

PREPARING A WARM RECEPTION.
Anti-aircraft gun being put hurriedly into position by Italian troops to repel attack by an Austrian airman of whose approach warning had been given.

of us who experienced the difficulties of civilian travel in Germany during the weeks of mobilisation were astonished to find that during this crisis in Italy passenger traffic followed its normal course, except for the short period of two or three days.

Everything in readiness, his armies disposed, their ammunition and food supplies measured, grouped, and allotted, General Cadorna ordered the counter-offensive on June 2nd. One section of the new army moved up Val Sugana, while another advanced through the Adige Valley. Much preparatory labour had to be expended in making the terrain suitable for the transport of troops and supplies. The engineers laid a system of aqueducts which brought fresh water to the arid heights from the pumping-stations in the plains beneath. With drill and dynamite they excavated new roads for the motor-waggons and guns, and erected aerial railways for the bringing up of ammunition.

On June 11th the new army was in touch with the enemy; but as yet the troops were unused to the mountain, and a few days more were spent in reconnoitring and light skirmishing. On the 17th Malga Fossetta was attacked and won. Monte Magari and the Cima d'Isidore followed immediately. On the 24th they had conquered the Cima Manderiolo and were at the head of the Campo Mulo Valley. Meanwhile, the extreme Italian left had driven back the Austrians from the farther side of Monte Coni Zugna. They had swept through the Buole Pass, taking Parmessan and laying siege to the Austrian positions on the northern slopes of Monte Pasubio. The Italian pincers was bending inwards the Austrian wings. On the 24th the Austrian generals learned of the Italian preparations for the conquest of the Cima Dodici. But one road of retreat lay open, the Valley of the Assa. A few days more and the great army of invasion would have been entrapped. Realising how critical their position was, the Austrian generals ordered an immediate retirement. On the 25th they were in full retreat.

In the event of the Austrians breaking through the Italian defence and entering the Venetian Plain, General Cadorna had a second army in readiness to receive them. To this force was attached all his available cavalry, who could be employed to immense advantage in the open country. The sudden Austrian retreat would have left the cavalry without any immediate prospect of a fight had it not been for the extraordinary order given, that they were to chase the

The invaders in full retreat

WHERE ONLY MAN-POWER AVAILED.
Frequently on the Carso only man-power could be used to bring the heavy artillery into position.

enemy through the mountains. This was work very much to its heart's liking, for the Italian cavalry is justly proud of its prowess in negotiating difficult territory. There was a ring of exultation in the address which the divisional commander delivered to his troops :

" Fellow-soldiers, to you and your companions falls an honour which will be received with choruses of joy. The Austrian invaders would descend upon our plains. They would bask in the sunshine of this glorious land which is as a benediction before our eyes. On our country, our homes, and our maidens they looked with greedy eyes. But now they are in flight. So swift is their course that our infantry finds the pace too fast. You are called upon to lead the hunt. You will scale the mountains on horseback. To-morrow the whole of Italy, and the world at large, will marvel at this strange feat you are about to perform. They will say it is a fantastic dream, but you will show them that it is a reality. *Allora, avanti, la Cavalleria !* "

Before the onrush of the cavalry and Bersaglieri cyclists the enemy retired hastily. His great concern was for the salvation of the guns which had been

Austrians' stubborn retirement

brought into position after so much labour and sacrifice. On the Asiago Plateau the situation was critical, and no time could be lost ; but once within cover of the Lavarone and Folgaria forts it was possible to offer resistance to the pursuing foe. Therefore, though the first stages of the retreat seemed to verify the prophecies of the Italian wags, who had already named it " the Trentino Races," it must be admitted in justice to the Austrians that they were very well commanded and that they fought stubbornly as they retired. Realising the danger of being outflanked, large bodies of men and artillery were sent to defend the Adige and Val Sugana positions. The Italians were already on Monte Zugna Torta, and were pushing down the Vallarsa towards Rovereto. In order to counteract this pressure and offset a danger which might soon become imminent for Trent, it was absolutely necessary for the Austrians to take up once

more the positions which they had held before the advance. During the first few days of the pursuit the Italians recaptured most of the towns which they had lost. By the end of July the Austrians were well back within their old quarters, retaining, however, a few of the outstanding positions which they had conquered during the advance. Manifestly, a full pursuit on the part of the Italians was out of the question. The Trentino zone does not afford possibilities for the manipulation of large armies ; so the rest of the fighting was left to the Alpini. In the skirmishes carried out from day to day they would eventually win back all the territory they had lost. Anyhow, as matters stood, the enemy had suffered a serious disaster.

Serious disaster for the foe

He had come into Tyrol with bands playing and banners flying. It was the first time in the Austro-Italian war that the Royal standards had been borne at the head of the troops. So confident were the Austrians of victory that they gave to their first attacks the character of a triumphal procession. But when their standards trailed in retreat and the roll-call of their heroes was ordered, it was found that of the 400,000 who had gone forth only 240,000 returned.

Meanwhile, Cadorna's artillery was shelling the railroad which runs through the Puster Valley, making it impossible for the Austrians to withdraw from the Trentino by the ordinary route. The Italian commander was now in the enviable position of having more troops at his disposal than he needed for present emergencies. Had the Austrians delayed a day or two longer in the Asiago Plateau they would almost certainly have fallen a prey to the Italian strategy. A stand of another two days would have made it extremely difficult for them to withdraw in time to save the wings, one of the greatest *coups de main* would have been effected, and Cadorna raised to the dignity of a super-hero.

But a good sportsman does not quarrel with his luck. If not Trent to-day, then let it be Gorizia to-morrow. His army was ready to march to the Isonzo. In the next chapter of THE GREAT WAR we shall deal with the Isonzo victory.

GLIMPSES OF THE PAGEANT OF WAR IN RURAL ITALY.
Field-artillery marching through a village. Each Italian army corps had six batteries of six guns besides heavy batteries.

DESTROYED ISONZO BRIDGE

CHAPTER CXXXV.

REBUILT BY THE ITALIANS.

ITALY TRIUMPHANT ON THE ISONZO.

By Dr. James Murphy.

Fundamental Purpose of Austria's Trentino Offensive (the Removal of Italian Pressure on Gorizia) Defeated by General Cadorna's Superior Strategy—Main Characteristics of the Terrain of Operations around Gorizia—Strategic Value of the Mountain Positions along the Isonzo Valley—Gorizia the Key to Trieste—Formation and Characteristics of the Carso—Italians Attack the Austrian Southern Defences on the Doberdo Plateau, August 4th, 1916—Italians Carry Monte Sabotino, August 7th—Bitter Struggle for Monte Podgora—Capture of the Austrian Positions on Monte San Michele and the Carso Ridge—Italians Cross the Isonzo and Enter Gorizia, August 8th—Gorizia Occupied and the Italian Flag Hoisted on the Castle, August 9th—Scene of Desolation in the Town—Gorizia " Renews her Baptismal Vows," August 13th—The History of Gorizia, a Vital Strategic Spot where the Frontiers of Three Races Meet—Possession of the Isonzo Line Essential to the Defence of Italy—The Conquest of the Carso—Italian Expeditionary Force Joins the Allies at Salonika, August 11th, 1916—Political and Military Reasons why Italy did not Intervene in Macedonia Earlier—Italy Repudiates the Commercial Treaty with Germany—Italy Declares War on Germany as from August 28th, 1916.

A S we have attempted to show in the preceding chapter, the fundamental purpose of Austria's Trentino offensive was to dislocate the existing disposition of General Cadorna's troops and force him to make redistribution. If that purpose could have been carried into effect, it would have wrecked the Italian project of a gigantic offensive on the Isonzo. All the drum-beating and banner-waving which announced throughout the Dual Monarchy the starting of the "Strafe Expedition," and all the high-flown talk in the German newspapers about the "Los von Italien," must be relegated to the region of advertisement.

It is impossible to believe that in the minds of General Konrad von Hötzendorf and his Staff the inspiring motive of the undertaking was not of a genuine military character. They must have been aware of the Russian preparations, for in modern warfare movements of such enormous proportions cannot go on in secret ; but Austria could not prepare to withstand the Russian attack while the Italian menace on the Isonzo remained active and pressing.

LEADERS WATCHING TIDE OF BATTLE.
Two Italian generals at an observation-post following operations north-west of Gorizia.

Now, the south-western sectors of the Italian line had been lightly held since the beginning of the war, while the bulk of the Army was concentrated on the Isonzo. Therefore, if the impression could be created in the minds of Victor Emmanuel's Staff that the Trentino salient was a serious and constant menace on their flank, the military centre of gravity must necessarily be moved to a point nearer the geographical centre of the line. This would relieve the pressure on Gorizia and give Austria a freer hand to attend to the Russian danger. From that point of view it was calculated that even though the army of invasion failed to reach the Venetian Plain, its mission would still have been successful. Expounded from the professional pulpit, the wisdom of the plan was indeed incontrovertible.

But in the game of war pre-calculations often go by the board. Cadorna did not play the hand which was called for by the Austrian lead. In re-organising his forces to meet the Trentino attack he was careful not to weaken his front where he had intended it to remain strong Not only that, but the sudden mobilisation of fresh forces which the crisis

I I **281**

TRANSPORT TROUBLES.
Accidents to the artillery transport were inevitable in the Gorizia sector, where it was easy for tractors to get overturned.

necessitated admirably suited his plans. Though his projected advance had been delayed some five or six weeks, he had a surplus army now on his hands which he could transfer to the Isonzo almost immediately. Thus he would considerably increase the striking power of his offensive.

That is the outstanding fact which throws light on the Gorizia victory. There are no grounds for believing that Austrian troops were withdrawn from the Isonzo to withstand the Russian attack. What happened was something quite different. Believing that their Trentino exploit had achieved its main purpose, and that the Italian military machine would need a serious overhauling before it could be again set in motion, the Austrians began to send their effectives to Russia, and neglected to make special preparations for the coming storm at Gorizia. The Italian commander seized his opportunity. He knew that the forces with which he now had to reckon were those that still remained in Trentino, and he knew that in the race for the Isonzo he could easily outstrip them. To **Knowledge of** make assurance doubly sure, by taking **enemy movements** good care that they should be seriously handicapped, he ordered his long-distance guns to pound the railroad in the Puster Valley at Toblach, Innchen, and Sillian, thus blocking the ordinary route from Tyrol to Austria.

To prevent the transport of troops from Salzburg, Villach, and Klagenfurt, the junction at Tarvis was vigorously bombarded. Tarvis is a vital joint in the railroad system which connects the Drave Valley with that of the Save, whence the Isonzo Valley is supplied. Imagine a gigantic fire-tongs laid on the map. Its head rests on the Italian frontier at Pontebba; its left leg stretches north-

eastwardly along the Drave, and its right south-eastwardly along the Save. The intervening space is filled by the towering range of the Karawanken Mountains. Tarvis is the joint. Along the northern leg of the tongs an important railway system runs. It rounds the western heights of the Karawanken range at Tarvis, and sharply turns south-eastwards into the Save Valley. This is the most important system which connects Western Austria with the Save and Isonzo **General Cadorna's** Valleys. By destroying Tarvis, the whole **skill** system was shattered, and only one railroad now lay open to the Austrians—namely, the Gratz-Marburg-Laibach-Trieste-Gorizia line.

It is well to bear this fact in mind, for it is vital to an appreciation of the Italian tactics. The success of the Isonzo operations cannot be attributed, even in a minor degree, to any factor of a haphazard or accidental nature. General Cadorna's triumph was the reward, not merely of talented generalship within the area where the actual battles were waged, but also of an elaborate and well-planned organisation for the military control of the vast territory which lay at the rear of the enemy's forces.

Before treating of the operations around Gorizia, it will be well to point out the main characteristics of the terrain. Here, as in every other sector of the Austro-Italian battle area, in order to understand the grouping and estimate the relative strength of the armies engaged, the strategic value of mountain positions must form the basis of our reckoning. In Chapter CXIX. the salient features of the Isonzo line were pointed out, and the plan of campaign adopted by General Cadorna explained. Here it will be necessary to give a more detailed account of the position at Gorizia.

TRIUMPH OF THE TRANSPORT MEN.
The tractor ready for business again, but with its shell cargo still strewn around. In circle: How the indomitable Italians hauled it upright.

ADVANCING AT THE DOUBLE ACROSS A SHELL-SWEPT PLATEAU.

Italian infantry doubling across a field exposed to Austrian gun fire. They were on their way to relieve comrades who had spent many hours in the trenches. The undulating ground is typical of the Isonzo district, where this photograph was taken.

Moving down the Valley of the Isonzo from Tolmino, as we approach Gorizia two massive hills stand on either hand, Monte Santo (2,230 feet) on the left, and Monte Sabotino (2,000 feet) on the right. As Alpine hills go, they do not tower to great heights, but their bulk is huge, and its surface is gored by great furrows which create a veritable chaos of ridges, valleys, and spurs. Monte Santo is the chief Austrian position on the left bank of the river. In days of peace it was a favourite pilgrim resort. Leading up the mountain side from the town of Gorizia the road is fringed with many shrines and wayside Calvaries, where devout pilgrims rested and prayed as they toiled along their Via Crucis towards the summit of the " Holy Hill." The venerable convent is now roofless and battered. Its church-tower and the windows of its dormitories afforded observation posts for Austrian officers, and each grotto by the wayside enshrined a howitzer. From here there was full command of the Gorizia position on the south, and until the Italians captured the bridge-head it was the main support of the Austrian lines on Sabotino. On our right as we move downwards the southern slopes of Sabotino assume the form of a Gargantuan staircase. The chief landings along the descent are San Valentino, San Mauro, Oslavia, Peuma, Grafenburg, and Calvario. At the foot of Sabotino stands the isolated mound called Podgora by the Slovenes, and Piedimonte by the Italians, which in English means " the foot of the mountain." All this region from Podgora to the summit of Sabotino is often called the Hill of Death, for it has been from time immemorial the scene of many dreadful combats.

Hill of Dreadful Strife As we reach Podgora the Vipacco Valley opens on our left. Approaching the river it forms rather an extensive plain about six or seven miles in breadth. Gazing eastward we can see where it narrows into an avenue and winds onwards amid the hills. The avenue leads into the Plain of Laibach, a distance of about forty miles. Laibach lies on the main road connecting the Danube with the Adriatic, and is therefore a very important centre both strategically and commercially. Opposite Podgora, on the left bank of the river and within the breach of low ground formed by the mouth of the Vipacco, Gorizia stands.

It is a city of 30,000 inhabitants, and therefore of no outstanding importance from the political or commercial viewpoint, but it would be impossible to overestimate its military value. In a strategic sense the Gorizia position is the key to Trieste. And that is so for two reasons. Once in control of the Gorizia defences, an army has the choice of two roads to Trieste ; it may follow the Vipacco Valley at the rear of the Carso, or it may move southwards on this side of the Carso through Monfalcone and Duino, following the shore road from Duino through Nabresina and Prosecco. **Strategic value of Gorizia** Along each route a railroad runs. If an invading army choose the former route, the possession of Gorizia is necessary for its forward march ; if it choose the latter, the possession of Gorizia is essential to the defence of its rear. Along either route the distance is about thirty-five miles, though as the crow flies Gorizia is only about eighteen miles from Trieste. The shore route has manifest advantages for armies approaching Trieste from the Italian side. They can begin their journey at Monfalcone, thus lessening the distance to about twenty miles, and greatly facilitating the transport of supplies. But in order to safeguard the flank and rear, the possession of the Carso is essential.

Leaving Podgora on our right, and moving southwards on the Isonzo, Monte San Michele rises on the left. It is the northern spur of the Carso, dominating Gorizia from the south. We now have the grotesque-shaped bulk of the terrible Carso lying on our left along the whole way from Gorizia to the sea. As is the case with so many mountains and rivers in this region, the original form of the name is Celtic, meaning " a heap of stones." It suggests to the mind the picture of a mound or cairn raised by a race of primeval giants over the grave of some Celtic hero. The pall of death lies over it. Its stony wastes are without vegetation, and save in a few isolated spots there are no trees to be found. The north wind, or Bora, sweeps mercilessly across its barren brow, making the cultivation of the soil and the raising of crops an impossibility.

Sometimes the inhabitants build huge stone walls to break the force of the wind, in the hope of securing a secluded spot where crops may be grown. These enclosures, whose walls are sometimes of Cyclopean character, afforded excellent cover for the Austrian armies. And there is another freak of Nature in evidence on the Carso which makes it almost impregnable against an attacking foe. Huge depressions of various grotesque shapes are to be found all over the terrain. By the Slovenes these are called "doline," and the name seems to have been adopted by the Italians, though the Venetians call them "inglutidori." They sometimes present the appearance of amphitheatres surrounded by rows of seats. When the rain falls these

"Gluttens" of the Carso

doline swallow it up—hence the name inglutidori (gluttons) — but it quickly percolates through the porous limestone, leaving a deposit of mud at the bottom of the pit.

These hidden spots are carefully cultivated by the inhabitants, and sometimes rude cabins are built within the enclosures. Beneath its crust of indentations and corrugations the Carso is gored by a subterranean network of channels and caves. Scores of streams flow in buried corridors, which sometimes have openings on the surface, forming a series of caves where very beautiful stalactites often abound.

Such being its formation and characteristics, all can

A sudden and extraordinary increase in railroad activity marked the prelude to the offensive. On July 27th orders were given for the immediate transference of large bodies of troops from the Trentino to the Isonzo front. Within a week, from July 27th to August 3rd, the railroads transferred across the Venetian Plain 7,000 officers, 300,000 men, 60,000 animals, 10,000 waggons, 800 pieces of light artillery, and 500 pieces of medium and heavy calibres. This huge bulk of traffic was further increased by the number of motors employed. Many newspaper reports, written immediately after the battle on the Isonzo, sought to explain the sudden triumph of the Italians by referring to a series of ruses which were supposed to have been employed by the Commander-in-Chief. It was said that his transport trains moved in one direction by day and in the opposite direction under cover of night, with the result that the Austrians were utterly deceived as to his purpose.

Needless to say, such a performance is impossible in modern warfare, where huge bodies of men and material are employed. What happened was not abnormal; but the abnormal swiftness with which the movement was carried out, and the advantage of position on the Italian side, made it impossible for the Austrians to cope with it. As I have already said, the Italians had the advantage of the cords, whereas the Austrians were condemned to operate along the arc. By leaving his surplus army on the fringes of the Trentino until the last moment, and then suddenly transferring it to the Carso, the Italian commander had held the enemy's forces at the south-western extremity of the arc, and outstripped them in the race for its south-eastern extremity. Furthermore, the larger portion of this army did not take an active part in the onslaught that swept the defences of the Isonzo, but was used as an army of invasion to drive the Austrians to their subsidiary lines of defence at the rear of Gorizia and the Carso. It was an ingenious and able manœuvre, the success of which was in large degree due to the energetic co-operation of the railroad and motor-transport organisations.

A FLASH OF MERRIMENT IN A CARE-CLOUDED DAY.
Delightfully human snapshot of General Cadorna suddenly amused by a humorous remark from the officer whom he was interrogating—one of the unexpected flashes that can brighten a grey day.

readily understand what a terrible obstacle the Italian troops had to face. The doline concealed innumerable batteries and whole regiments found shelter in the caves. No portion of the mountain rises to a height of more than a few hundred feet, but there is a row of peaks along its summit which resemble a series of heavy bastions protruding from the wall of a colossal fortress. Moving from north to south these are Monte San Michele, Monte San Martino, Monte Sei Busi, Selz, and the Rocca di Monfalcone. They are key positions, in so far as there can be any key positions in so torn and tormented a terrain. The reader is referred to Chapter CXIX. for an explanation of the position held by the Italian troops at the end of May on the Carso, Podgora, and Monte Sabotino.

Throughout June and July the line remained stationary, the Austrians still holding the greater part of Sabotino, the western heights of Podgora, and the whole series of positions along the western bank of the Isonzo, which formed the bridge-head of Gorizia. To drive the Austrians from Monti San Michele, Podgora, and Sabotino, and cross the Isonzo in front of Gorizia, was the task set before the Italian army on August 6th, 1916.

General Cadorna's plan was to open the attack in the southern section of the line. With an intense eagerness the soldiers had awaited the order to advance. For them it signified the hour of liberation from the monotonous torture of warfare on the Carso. It must be remembered that since the opening of war the Italian line in this sector had never been stationary. Yard by yard the soldiers had fought their way up the side of the hill. They were constantly under fire from the guns on the summit, and the ground did not afford them an opportunity of digging themselves in. It was impossible to organise defences in anything resembling a straight line.

A miracle of endurance

Toiling uphill in serpentine fashion, dragging huge baskets of limestone rock to build their barricades, they constantly threw forward salients in the hope of gaining a footing on some little hillock and enfolding a few yards of the enemy's trenches. Whoever has not seen this dreadful form of warfare cannot experience the sense of horror and utter helplessness which it engendered. When I saw them blasting the rocks and toiling up the hillside with their ugly burdens, pushing their trenches forward like an army of Sisypheans, I could think of no language adequate to

CALABRIAN INFANTRY SAVING THE GUNS.
An Italian battery, surrounded on Mount Mosciagh on the Asiago Plateau, was saved by Calabrians of the 141st Infantry Regiment.

TO THE VICTORS THE SPOILS.
Italian soldiers collecting the spoils in an Austrian trench which they had rushed and captured shortly before.

HEAVY ITALIAN FIELD-ARTILLERY.
An Italian 305 mm gun in action. There were two or three batteries of heavy artillery to each army corps of the Italian field army.

TRENCH WARFARE ON THE CARSO.
Italians watching a mine explosion in the enemy trenches. Directly it occurred they sprang up to rush and occupy the crater.

describe the scene, except that of Dante in the seventh canto of " The Inferno " :

Come fa l' onda là sovra Cariddi,
Che si frange con quella in cui, s'intoppa,
Così convien che qui là gente riddi.

Qui vidi gente più, che altrove troppa,
E d' una parte e d' altra, con grandi urli,
Voltando pesi per forza di poppa*

It was natural that they should look forward with yearning to the hour of the general attack, when they might leap forward and gain the summit of the hill.

*E'en as the billow on Charybdis rising,
Against encountered billow, dashing, breaks.
Such is the dance this suffering folk must lead.

There saw I people, more than elsewhere, many,
On one side and the other, with great howls,
Rolling weights forward by main force of chest.

On the morning of August 4th the artillery opened fire against the Austrian positions on the Carso directly opposite Monfalcone. Running from the south-east of Cima Debeli along the Rocca di Monfalcone to Duino, this line formed the southern defence of the Doberdo Plateau. Following a bombardment which lasted about six hours, small bodies of troops were sent forward to test the strength of the enemy's resistance. They found that extensive breaches had been made in the front line, and a small number of soldiers who still remained in the trenches readily surrendered. Believing that the Italians intended launching an important attack here, the Austrians quickly brought up heavy reinforcements. Save for the incessant artillery duel, no fighting took place throughout the night or during the following forenoon; but on the evening of the 5th

Capture of Hill 85

the Italians attacked again and succeeded in capturing Hill 85, east of Monfalcone, taking a few hundred prisoners.

This was the prelude to a general onslaught on the Doberdo positions. Under the impetus of the first success the troops were borne forward through the principal line of the enemy, their advance being greatly facilitated by an entire company of Hungarians who had thrown down their rifles and refused to fight for Austria. While the infantry encircled Cima Debeli three regiments of Bersaglieri cyclists rode along the shore road from Monfalcone and seized Hill 121, the position which had controlled the approaches and dockyards of Monfalcone since the outbreak of war. Hills 85 and 121 were pivotal points of the Austrian line, which had formed a half circle around Monfalcone, cutting

IN POSSESSION: VICTORIOUS ITALIANS IN THE HEART OF CAPTURED AUSTRIAN TOWNS.
Alpini in occupation of a newly-captured town in the Trentino receiving congratulations from elated officers. Above: Italians at the portico of the Town Hall, Gorizia, so soon after capture that the police notices printed in German had not been removed.

VICTORY OVER MOUNTAIN AND FLOOD.
Mountain batteries proceeding across a temporary bridge on the Isonzo on their way to the occupation of Gorizia.

across the railroad and highway that lead to Trieste. In the course of the operations in this section, 3,600 prisoners were taken, together with valuable booty.

The attack on Doberdo was in the nature of a diversion, intended to deceive the Austrians as to the location where the main offensive had been prepared. At first sight it looks somewhat strange that, with all the modern means of observation at their disposal, the Austrians did not realise the extent of the preparations which were being made against them; but when one realises how the Italians took pains to conceal every movement, the Austrian lack of information is not remarkable. Owing to his advantageous position on Monte Santo, which dominated the immediate neighbourhood of the Friulian Plain, the enemy had been able to shell all approaches to the Italian line. Wherever a white cloud of dust arose above the hedges **Under the enemy's eye** it signalled the passage of transport waggons, and drew a hail of shells from the Austrian batteries. The movement of troops along the main roads was constantly carried out under the eye of the Austrian gunners. Expert snipers had been placed in the observation-posts, so that even a solitary pedestrian on the Gradisca or Monfalcone road risked his life at every step.

To contend with this difficulty effectively and entirely escape observation the Italians decided to build a series of new roads. While carrying out these operations a system of blindfolding the enemy was adopted. Airmen constantly accompanied the engineers and labourers, hovering overhead and warding off hostile aircraft. Whenever captive balloons ascended a direct attack was made against them. Meanwhile the engineers worked with drill and dynamite, and the pick and shovel of the peasant hacked and levelled the rough pathways on the hills. Long stretches of road were tunnelled through limestone rock. At the points where they emerged into the open and followed new routes which had been excavated on the crust of the mountain, a system of artificial foliage was employed to screen the passage of guns and troops. Hedge-rows were erected, tall pines grew in a night; and in some parts sheets of straw matting were hung on wires that stretched from tree to tree. To this ingenious inventiveness

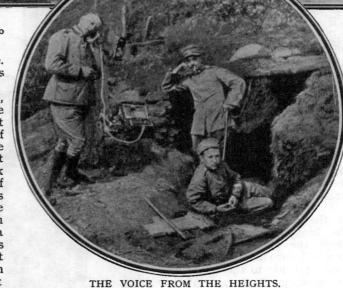

THE VOICE FROM THE HEIGHTS.
Italian telephone exchange situated in a remote part of the mountains. An operator is communicating with headquarters.

WALKING THE PLANK.
Italian infantrymen crossing a stream by means of an improvised bridge, in reality a precarious tree-trunk.

LABOUR OF HERCULES.
One of the miracles of the mountain war
was the transport of the heavy guns.

whole area was a holocaust of fire and flame. Hitherto the Italians had scrupulously spared Gorizia, but now they picked out and marked the buildings where the several departments of the Austrian Headquarters Staff had their offices. Each one of these buildings was demolished, the telephone communications destroyed, and the surrounding streets rendered impassable. Still farther in the rear of the town the roads and pathways were torn by an incessant hail of heavy shells The purpose of this bombardment was to destroy the communications between the offices of the Staff and the headquarters of the divisional commanders, thus throwing the whole organisation into chaos.

Shelling Austrian headquarters

Those who are familiar with the system of inter-connecting the fighting-line and the bases of supply, the reserve depots, and the Staff offices on the Franco-British front, will think it strange that the artillery of one army could so easily get into touch with the vital communications and headquarters of the other ; but the Austrian position in Gorizia had been so protected by the surrounding hills as to be considered absolutely impregnable. Therefore, it was not a want of foresight that betrayed Konrad's Staff into fixing its headquarters in the town. A striking example of their sense of security was given by two of the leading Austrian commanders during the few days that preceded the Italian offensive. Major Moraht, one of Germany's leading military lights, had solemnly announced that the Italian army was like a mosquito ; it could bite and sting, but not destroy.

Archduke Frederick, the Commander-in-Chief of the Austrian Imperial Army, had declared to his troops, in July, 1916, that the Austrians could check the Italians

and untiring energy in execution the Italian army owed much of its success.

At six o'clock in the morning of the first Sunday in August the heavy artillery opened fire along the whole length of the Lower Isonzo line. It sounded like a prelude to the celebration of some great festa. At ten o'clock the infantry attacked the formidable line of Austrian trenches on Sabotino and Calvario. As they advanced two screens of curtain fire preceded them, one ravaging the Austrian trenches in the immediate foreground, the other pounding the bases so as to hinder the bringing up of reinforcements. Lest they might become the victims of their own artillery, the Italian troops carried a number of long poles to the ends of which polished discs were attached. This sparkling ribbon marked their advance. With panting breath it was watched by the observers and Staff officers and the rank and file of the reserves. Amid the clouds of smoke, the deafening thunder of the guns, and owing to the rugged character of the terrain, it was impossible to follow the actual combat ; but the gleaming discs marked every yard of ground gained.

The long-range guns pounded the bridges and the Austrian approaches on the further side of the river. This

BRIDGE WHICH THE AUSTRIANS BURNED BEHIND THEM.
Bridge over a river destroyed by the Austrians in the precipitate retreat with which they concluded their great Trentino offensive, June 24th, 1916.

when and where they wished. The great Konrad von Hötzendorf had pretended to look upon the whole affair with an intermingled feeling of pathos and annoyance, in much the same light as the ladies of a West End salon consider the spectacle of the street organ-grinder. " You will defend the Empire against this army of mandoline-players," said Konrad to his troops at the commencement of the war. What wonder if lesser lights than Moraht and Konrad allowed themselves the comfort of that same transcendental sense of security. General Borövic, who had defended Gorizia during the October-November battle,

1915, and in whom the hopes of beating back the Italian attack once again had rested, was away in Carlsbad. General Zeissler, to whom the immediate control of the defences of the town had been entrusted, had betaken himself to his villa in Villach. This state of affairs, and the measures which the Italians adopted to take advantage of it, accounts in no small degree for the sudden disorganisation and ultimate paralysis of the Austrian defence.

But it must not be supposed that the Italians were having a walk-over, or that their enterprise was anything in the nature of a ruse. The individual sectors of the line offered a stubborn and well-organised defence. As the troops moved forward on Monte Sabotino they were met by a murderous hail of shells from the heavy batteries on Monte Santo. At closer range the machine-guns and trench mortars mowed them down. The barbed-wire entanglements and the thick brushwood were littered with explosives. Yard by yard the Italians advanced, losing very heavily. Even when they had conquered the crest, the enemy still lay hidden in the inner recesses of the mountain.

The exposed trenches were taken at the point of the bayonet; but the Austrians had built a series of catacombs in the limestone rock, and had fortified the openings with walls of concrete and steel. Into these they retired, belching forth clouds of poison gas and hurricanes of machine-gun fire on their foes. "Come out! Lay down your arms!" shouted the Italians. But the Austrians still held their ground. They had hoped that reinforcements would eventually come, and that the counter-attack would drive the victors back. Hand-grenades and machine-guns made no impression on them. Then the Italians brought up huge quantities of petroleum, in the hope of smoking the enemy out. This plan was successful, but the chief garrison in the caverns occupied by the divisional commander on Monte Sabotino steadfastly refused to surrender. Only when **Honours to a brave foe** his catacomb was a stifling mass of petrol fumes, and fire was already issuing from its ventilators, did he come forth, followed by hundreds of his men. "He is a brave soldier," declared the Italian colonel in command of the attacking party, "and I order that his sword be returned to him and to his officers." He had resisted throughout the day and night. On the morning of the 7th Monte Sabotino was in Italian hands. The Hill of Death, which had claimed so many brave lives during the bitter struggle that had been waged there incessantly for fifteen months, had been conquered at last.

The northern portion of the bridge-head was now in Italian hands. Throughout the day the fight still raged on Oslavia, Peuma, and Podgora. In the evening Oslavia and Peuma had fallen; but Podgora still resisted. Directly opposite Gorizia, Podgora shuts out the view of the town

LIKE SOLDIERS OF THE MIDDLE AGES.
Steel helmets, breast-plates, and even chain mail were worn by Italian soldiers engaged in the perilous work of destroying the Austrians' barbed-wire defences. This illustration might represent some incident in mediæval warfare.

from the plain of Friuli. It is a low hill, its highest point being about eight hundred feet, with a flat surface. It rises gradually towards the east, and then falls precipitously on to the bank of the Isonzo.

At the opening of the offensive the Italians had already gained the greater portion of the hill at the cost of immense sacrifices, but the Austrians were still entrenched on its eastern slopes. At first sight Podgora appeared to be the key of the whole position. And so it was in former wars. But the modern epoch of howitzers and high explosives had given a leading advantage to towering hills and commanding views. Podgora was therefore a supporting point for infantry and light artillery. It had to be won before the Isonzo could be attempted. And it had to be won under a converging fire from the guns on the higher hills.

Throughout the night of the 7th the battle for Podgora continued. As dawn broke the decisive phases began to be reached. Instead of wholly trusting to the advance on the ridge the Italians initiated a supplementary movement along the right bank of the river. The Austrian trenches had been entirely screened from artillery fire, and were supported by a labyrinth of spacious corridors and caverns built in the interior of the mountain. Moving

K K

The Great War.

AREA OF GENERAL CADORNA'S SUCCESSFUL OPERATIONS AGAINST GORIZIA, AUGUST, 1916.

The Isonzo Valley forms the eastern line for the defence of Italy, and its possession was essential to the realisation of Italian ideals. Gorizia, its main strategic position, was captured on August 9th, 1916, by the Italians, who thus secured possession of the key to Trieste.

ON THE FIELD OF VICTORY.
Scene at Monte Podgora immediately after
the battle of August 8th, 1916.

supported by their companions in the rear, while the enveloping column, which had advanced along the river-bank, drew the fire of the machine-guns, and died as they crawled to the mouths of the caves. About two o'clock the enemy's resistance grew spasmodic, and a last wild rush swept the trenches like a whirlwind. Podgora was in Italian hands.

While the centre of the attacking forces was operating opposite Gorizia the right wing toiled upwards along San Michele, in an effort to reach the crest that controls Gorizia from the south. If this move were not successful, the fall of the bridge-head would have been ineffective, for Gorizia would have remained under the double fire of both pillars, Monte Santo on the north and Monte

along the surface the Italians had to fight blindfolded, casting their bombs at a dead angle and trusting to luck for the effect. As the encircling troops approached the mouths of the caves they were met by jets of poison gas and machine-gun fire. Bayonet and bomb were of little value to the attackers. The enemy was deeply entrenched in his cave, and had to be drawn forth somewhat as a terrier draws a badger.

Again and again the attack from the river-bank was driven back; but the Italians re-formed, reorganised, and returned to the charge with unabated vigour. Meanwhile their comrades on the crest were toiling as best they could. Volumes of asphyxiating gas issued from the mouths of the caves, ascending above the crest of the hill

Bitter struggle for Podgora in wreaths of sickly yellow and green. At every onslaught hundreds were stricken down. Several times the trenches were entered and desperate hand-to-hand struggles took place. Sometimes friend and foe rolled to the river-bank, locked in deadly embrace. Podgora had seen some of the most terrific fighting of the war, but survivors said that this last struggle was the bitterest of all. About midday the end came in sight. The men in the trenches were creeping slowly towards the brow of the hill; and now they could see the church-spires of Gorizia gleaming from across the river. It was the vision for which their eyes had longed. A wild hurrah rang from the foremost line. They swept over the crest of the hill and began to descend its steep side towards the river. But here the foliage and brushwood, which had been sheltered from the artillery since the start, concealed a hidden forest of barbed-wire network, rendered still more deadly by the layers of explosive bombs embedded in the thick grass. The first battalions suffered heavily, but they were vigorously

AFTER THE TIDAL WAVE OF WAR.
The field of battle beyond Podgora after the fall of Gorizia, a desolation of blasted trees, litter of sand-bags, and tangled wire.

San Michele on the south. Fully realising that their positions on the bridge-head could not be held if Monte San Michele should fall into the enemy's hands, the Austrians had built their most formidable defences on this hill. The brow of the mountain is crowned by four angry peaks, one of which juts like a bastion towards the west, giving a full view of the Italian lines on the side of the Carso. Three lines of trenches were constructed, connected by underground passages, and supplied from subterranean caverns where food and ammunition had been stored.

The first line was built on the shoulder of the eastern crest, the second stood higher up on the southern bastion. This encircled the whole brow and overlooked the trenches of the first line. Corridors were tunnelled through the rock, forming connecting cords with the circumference of the outer circle. This system enabled the defence quickly to mobilise its artillery and infantry on the sectors of the trench which happened to be in greatest danger during the course of the struggle. The third line ran on a higher level, about three hundred yards distant from the first.

A GARIBALDI TO THE FORE.
Group of Italian officers, among whom is Colonel Peppino Garibaldi, grandson of the great Italian patriot. He enjoyed the distinction of planting the tricolour on the Col di Lana, in that part of Italia Irredenta captured from Austria in the summer of 1916.

All three defences were constructed of reinforced concrete walls, which were sometimes three yards in depth. Against these even the heaviest artillery could not prevail. They might be battered and disfigured, but they could not be destroyed. No account has been given of the sacrifices which have been made on this spot. Since the beginning of the war the Italians had made upwards of a dozen organised assaults against it, and sometimes succeeded in reaching the summit, only to be driven back with tremendous slaughter. It is interesting to note the large number of medals which were conferred for bravery on San Michele. The famous Regina Brigade lost its bravest and best, but won undying honour here. The same is true of the Brescia, Ferrara, and Perugia Brigades, and the 2nd Regiment of Bersaglieri.

At half-past three on the afternoon of August 6th, while the attack on Sabotino was developing, the troops in the San Michele sector received the order **Austrians shoot their** to advance. In the course of the first on-**own men** slaught an unforeseen incident helped to bring about the fall of a large section of the Austrian trenches. The portion of the line facing south was controlled from the Austrian lines on San Martino, on the Carso, so that if the Italians should succeed in reaching San Michele they would immediately come under fire from San Martino.

While the right column was advancing, the attacking forces on San Martino succeeded in gaining some trenches and making prisoners. As the prisoners left the trenches, with uplifted hands, the Austrian commander was seized by a violent attack of rage and ordered the machine-guns to turn their fire on them. The momentary distraction

caused by the action of the enraged colonel was providential for the Italians. They seized the western trenches of the San Michele line and had firmly established themselves while the machine-guns on San Martino were mowing down Austrian prisoners.

Having once got a footing the Italians clung to their gains with desperate tenacity. They fought yard by yard, almost inch by inch. Having reached the second line of trenches, which constituted the principal defence of the crest, they succeeded in forcing the Austrians to withdraw to the caves. And now began the gruesome business of smoking them out. As on Podgora, the enemy made lavish use of asphyxiating gas, and his machine-guns guarded the mouth of each cave. Realising how hopeless was the Austrian position, and wishing to spare the slaughter which the resistance would necessitate, the Italians called upon their foes to surrender, promising that every honourable consideration would be shown The enemy, however, would lend no ear. An Austrian prisoner volunteered to take a message to his comrades and explain to them the recklessness and crime of their resistance. A few minutes later the report of a revolver was heard from the interior of the caves. They had shot the messenger of peace. Bales of cotton which had been **Messenger of Peace** soaked in petroleum and set alight were **shot** now thrown into the cavities, but the labyrinthine system was so spacious that the enemy was able to barricade himself against the fumes. Mountain cannon were used, but to little effect.

When deadlocks of such a type occur in ordinary warfare it is a simple matter to cover the position with masking troops while the main forces continue the advance. But in mountain warfare the operation is not so simple; for the advance is upwards, not onwards. At length, after siege operations of the most extraordinary type, lasting throughout three days, the second line of trenches was occupied; and on the 9th the whole position fell. The Italians were now in possession of the Carso ridge from Gorizia to the sea.

With the range of hills from Podgora to the summit of Sabotino now in their hands the Italians were masters of the whole bridge-head, and were ready to cross the Isonzo. There are two bridges in the immediate neighbourhood. One of these is a modern metal construction over which passes the main road from Lucinico to Gorizia. The other is the railroad bridge, rather monumental in its aspect. It has a series of majestic arches which remind one somewhat of the great aqueducts one sees on the Roman Campagna. Both structures had been more or less injured during the Italian bombardment, and both still remained under the fire of the Austrian guns on Monte Santo.

The army of invasion was now gathered on the outskirts of Podgora and Lucinico and along the roads leading to Gradisca and Cormons, its infantry fully accoutred, its cavalry mounted, its artillery trains in line, its commissariat stocked and ready. As it waited for the order to move, a mournful procession was seen leaving Gorizia.

Konrad's Staff was departing. Along the road to San Daniele and through the Tarnova Wood a dense trail of dust marked the passage of the transport and gun waggons, heavy howitzers drawn by long teams of oxen, Staff motor-cars, and mule-carts piled high with every species of military furniture. The lumbering teams of oxen being a good mark for the artillery, the guns on Podgora and Sabotino were enabled to inflict considerable damage on the howitzers which the enemy dragged in retreat.

Believing that Cadorna's troops intended to effect a grand crossing in processional style, the Monte Santo guns busily watched the right bank of the river between Carinzia and Campagnuzza. But the Italians had decided to go slowly and carefully, picking their steps and making sure of the conditions on the opposite bank before risking their troops in the open stream. It was surmised that the

With the enemy: Austro=Hungarian night patrol among the Dolomites.

Italian troops assembling in Gorizia before the assault on Monte San Gabriele.

In the captured city: Italian cavalry occupying the streets of Gorizia, August 9th, 1916.

Italian outpost above the snow line over the Austrian frontier and in captured territory.

The Duke of Aosta entering Gorizia. In background the bridge over the Isonzo.

How the Italians drove the Austrians out of burning Asiago in June, 1916, and stayed their thrust towards the Venetian Plains.

Austrians had mined the bridges as they retreated. Italian gun fire had already exploded one of these mines, damaging a portion of the metal bridge. To cope with this danger, small bodies of engineers crawled along the girders, carefully removing the unexploded shells which had been hidden there. As this work went on their companions mended the broken section under the fire of the enemy's guns; but the gunners on Monte Santo did not now have **The victors enter** so free a hand as before, for the Italian **Gorizia** occupation of Sabotino made it possible to bring heavy howitzers into play against the enemy's batteries beyond the river.

The infantry did not intend to await the reconstruction of the bridges. Nor would it have been wise, for the dense massing of large bodies which such a method of crossing would entail might bring about disastrous results. Accordingly, it was decided to build rafts and send the troops across in small batches. On the first raft twenty foot-soldiers of the Casale Brigade embarked, but the fire from Monte Santo searched them out and depleted them severely. However, they succeeded in reaching the opposite shore. It was evident that the experiment did not recommend this method as a general means of crossing.

The officers hesitated and consulted, many of them casting thoughtful glances at their men. Not a word of command was given, but the soldiers understood. Directly opposite the mouth of the Vipacco, between Sant' Andrea and Mainizza, a portion of the river which had as yet escaped the enemy's attention was selected for the crossing. Here the river runs shallow, and the formation of the foreshore makes the launching of rafts impossible. Hence it was an excellent spot for fording. From Peuma and Oslavia and San Floriano and Lucinico, chanting *sotto voce* the "Hymn of Mameli," the troops marched to the appointed rendezvous.

The leading battalions were soon in the water, wading bravely across, their rifles lifted high in sign of triumph and exultation. Luckily the big guns of the enemy were busy elsewhere; but his snipers turned their rifles against the advancing column. The firing, however, was fitful and blind, owing to the curtain fire of the Italian artillery from this side of the river. Within about half an hour the leading battalions had reached their goal. It was the signal for a triumphant cheer from the men who stood along the conquered bridge-head. At half-past four in the afternoon of August 8th—a date which will be memorable in Italian history—the soldiers of Victor Emmanuel III. entered Gorizia. The first to set foot in the city were the advance guards of the Casale and Pavia Brigades.

Some Bohemian and Hungarian regiments still held the town. The Bohemians readily surrendered and welcomed the invading troops, many of them offering their rifles to help the cause of Italy. But the Hungarians stubbornly held out. From their places of ambush in the houses, well barricaded and supplied, they peppered the streets heavily when the invading troops appeared. As the main body of the infantry arrived dusk had set in and the great searchlights began to play on the town. The task of clearing the houses now began. Doors had been well barred and windows barricaded, offering excellent shelter for the enemy. This portion of his troops, which formed

the rearguard of the retreat, had orders to hold out as long as possible, in the hope of delaying the Italian advance, thus affording opportunity for the removal of material and the establishment of the new line in the mountains at the rear of the town. The Italians swarmed through the town, however, with unexpected rapidity. When morning came they had already driven the enemy from most of his hiding-places.

Meanwhile the cavalry and artillery had been getting ready to cross the river. Having reconstructed the shattered sections of the metal bridge, the engineers gave the signal for the advance. The light artillery teams passed over at a fast trot, the drivers holding their horses by the bridle-rein and shouting words of encouragement to their beasts as the hail of shrapnel fell on the river. The officers who had control of the traffic stood on the roadside with watch in hand. They knew the location of each gun on Monte Santo, and they had calculated the intervals which must elapse between the volleys. Small detachments of cavalry volunteered to rush the bridge and draw the enemy's fire. Immediately the explosion was heard the gun-waggons rattled over. On the whole the number of

A DISTINGUISHED NEAPOLITAN: THE ITALIAN MINISTER FOR WAR.
General Paolo Morrone (third from left) with officers of the Headquarters Staff of his army corps in the field. General Morrone succeeded General Zupelli at the Italian War Office in April, 1916.

casualties was remarkably small, considering the position of vantage which the Austrians occupied on Monti Santo and San Gabriele.

Taking turn about with the artillery, the cavalry, mounted police, and Bersaglieri cyclists succeeded in reaching their goal. Once in possession of the town, and a considerable section of the artillery at hand, the invaders succeeded in silencing the secondary positions on Monte San Gabriele. Only the long-range guns could now search out the river, and their fire was necessarily a long-drawn-out staccato. This immensely **Spirit of death over** relieved the pressure on the bridge, and **the town** made the crossing a matter of routine— always, however, with a sufficient spice of danger to make it exciting. Large supplies of bridging material had already arrived. Throughout the morning several other crossings had been constructed by means of pontoons, and large streams of material were now pouring into the captured city.

The scene within Gorizia was one of utter desolation. The spirit of death and silence brooded over the town. The inhabitants had long ago fled from their homes. No

IN OCCUPATION OF GORIZIA.
Italian cavalry riding along Franz Josef Strasse (renamed Via Luigi Cadorna), Gorizia, whence the Austrians precipitately retreated.

CAVALRY DESPATCH RIDER.
Over rough ground. Nowhere else in the battle-zones did cavalry encounter greater difficulties of progress than on the Italian front.

provisions remained in the cellars or store-rooms. The electric plant and water supply had been destroyed. Great tufts of grass flourished in the crevices of the side-walks, and the foliage of the well-trimmed gardens had grown wild. Broken gun-carriages, the dead bodies of horses and men, the debris of shattered churches, monuments, and public buildings lay strewn in chaotic confusion. Gazing on the scene, the spirit of cheering and exultation was smothered in the breasts of the soldiers. The Austrian Nice was another Pompeii. It seemed as if many centuries must have passed since its normal life had been brought to a close.

Deeper in the valley lie the ancient sections of the city. There the houses are of older design, somewhat like those in old Venetian towns. In this quarter the majority of the

298

inhabitants were Italians, and not a few had remained throughout the martyrdom of the bombardment. Being stoutly built of solid stone, the houses had resisted the devastation of the guns. From the cellars and covered passages women and children came forth, fearful and trembling, their nerves shattered from the dreadful experiences they had endured, their faces furrowed deep with sorrow; for their husbands, fathers, and brothers had been either interned in Austrian prisons or sent to fight a friendly foe on the plains of Galicia.

On the night of the 9th two Gorizian ladies who had remained in the city throughout the whole reign of terror made their way to the Castello. Austrian shells were pouring on it in a veritable hailstorm, the purpose of the gunners being to prevent the Italians from planting the tricolour on the tower. **Austrians shell** Through the clouds of smoke and mael- **the Castle** strom of powdered masonry the two heroines made their way. Scrambling up the old stone staircase, they reached one of the portholes of the tower. In a few moments the Italian tricolour was waving aloft, high above the smoke-clouds of the shells, its red and green standing out dramatically against the lambent rays of the searchlights.

Before retiring, the Austrians had ordered the civil population to evacuate the city. Terrifying stories of the treatment that might be expected from the invaders had been circulated through the poorer districts. Orders had been given that women and children should take the road to Laibach, trusting for food and accommodation to the generous consideration of the Austrian Staff. Believing the stories that had been told them, and yet reluctant to trust to the proffered hospitality of their rulers, old men and women and children fled to the surrounding hill towns. Collecting their few little belongings and family treasures, they set out for Tarnova, Vertoiba, and Aisovizza in the hope of finding shelter. But the Italian curtain fire blocked their exodus. In fear and trembling, with uplifted hands and prayers for mercy on their lips, they returned.

One needed to have seen the Italian soldiers in the towns that they had already captured to realise their gentleness towards the inhabitants. Food and drink were readily given to the returning Gorizians. The first acts of kindness seemed to have a magic effect through the city. From their hiding-places in cellars and caves the people rushed forth waving handkerchiefs and shouting evivas in the language of the conquerors. But it was no more than a remnant of Gorizia. Of its thirty thousand inhabitants only seven thousand had remained. They told vivid stories of the life which had been endured in the city during the long months of war. Many had hoped that the Italians would arrive sooner, but dared not express their yearning even to everyday friends. The slightest suspicion of Italian leanings would have entailed removal to a concentration centre in Poland or Bohemia. When Italian wounded or prisoners were being brought in any show of sympathy from the inhabitants was forbidden under penalty of death. Public notices announced the rigour of the enactment. Numbers of these placards were taken by the victorious troops, to serve as unassailable testimony for future chapters in the history of Gorizia.

That the enactments had been carried out according to the spirit as well as the letter was only too plain. In a few of the houses the Italian soldiers found a number of their wounded comrades who had been taken prisoners on Monti San Michele and Sabotino during the fighting. For two days they had been without food or drink, and even first-aid had not been rendered them. Among **Premature Austrian** the relics secured one of the most interest- **triumphs** ing was a huge notice printed in display characters, intended for the announcement of the great victories which were to be won during the Trentino offensive. In the printing of the text a space had been left vacant for the insertion of the names of the cities. Doubtless these would be Vicenza, Verona, Venice, and Milan. For the benefit of the Italian section of the population a special version had been prepared in their own language. It ran as follows :

Concittadini. Esultate ! La città di ——— é stata presa da noi austriaci. Incrollabili nella fede nell'avita fedeltà ed attaccamento alla sacra persona dell'Augustissimo' nostra Imperatore Francesco Giuseppe I e alla Patria, dimostrate il vostro giubilo per questo fatto storico e glorioso del nostro esercito esponendo dalle vostre case vessilli e drappi.
Dalla residenza Comunale, Gorizia.

Firmato : Dandini.*

Among the other interesting documents collected were bread tickets and meat tickets, official communiquès announcing bogus victories in Russia, permits for the supply of soap, shopkeepers' **A campaign of** lists of prices, and a host of popu'ar **slander** pamphlets, lampooning, libelling, an attributing imaginary crimes to the soldiers of the Allies. It would be senseless to suppose that these did not have an important effect on the minds of the people. Supplementing the long campaign of slander against the Italians, which had been carried on for years in Gorizia, the more recent outbursts of Austrian vilification fell upon ears that had already been attuned to the cry. While it is true that many of the inhabitants of the city received their deliverers with open arms, it is also true that many looked upon them in the light of unwelcome visitors. Many months, perhaps years, must pass before the effects of the slanderous campaign can be rooted out.

In preparation for their flight the Austrian armies destroyed whatever supplies they could not bring away. Petroleum was poured on the food that could not be removed. Shopkeepers stood mutely by and watched the soldiers destroy their stock of goods. Interference was forbidden under penalty of death. From house to house officers led their bands of organised marauders, crying out at each door, " Nothing must be left for the Italians. The city is lost for ever. If goods are still

---

* Fellow-citizens,—The city of ——— has been captured by us. You whose fidelity and devotion to the sacred person of our Most August Emperor Francis Joseph I. and to the Fatherland is unconquerable, let it be made manifest how you glory in this historic and majestic achievement of our army by waving flags and banners from your houses.
City Hall, Gorizia.

(Signed) Dandini.

INSPECTION OF ALPINI BY THE ITALIAN GENERALISSIMO.
General Cadorna was ubiquitous and indefatigable in his tours of inspection at the front. On this occasion, accompanied by officers of the General Staff, he was reviewing the Fourth Regiment of the incomparable Alpini.

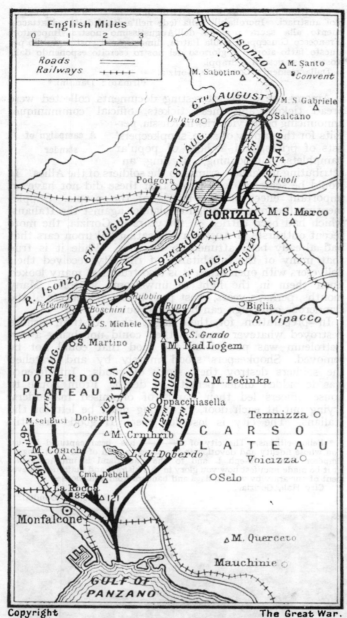

ITALIAN DISPOSITIONS ROUND ABOUT GORIZIA.
Sketch plan showing the Italian lines of progress described on page 302. The town was captured on August 9th, and after August 15th the positions remained practically unchanged until the end of the month.

concealed in your homes, give them up or destroy them ; if not, we shall blow up the house." The mayor and municipal officials fled with the retreating troops. Only the town-clerk, Signor de Vecchi, remained. He at once unfurled the Italian banner from the balcony of the City Hall and offered his services to the invaders. Bands of Carabinieri and Red Cross officials were soon organised to care for the inhabitants and wounded soldiers. Food supplies were distributed, engineers began to repair the water and lighting systems. A census of the population was taken, and those to whom suspicion might reasonably point were sent to Italy. In searching for the records which might have been left in the City Hall it was found that the Austrians had forgotten to take the cash-box. Fifteen thousand crowns (about £500) still remained in the safe.

On August 13th a ceremony took place which had by then become part of the regular ritual in the Italian Army. In the picturesque Italian phrase, Gorizia made the renewal of her baptismal vows. On the morning of the 13th Signor Carlo Banelli, formerly member of the municipality of Trieste, arrived in the conquered city.

Entering the City Hall, where a number of Gorizians had assembled to greet him, he unfolded a silken tricolour. It was received by the assembly in the name of the city of Gorizia. At the sight of the Italian national symbol tears welled into many eyes.

The bitter fortunes of war and the tyranny of rulers had already removed many who would have rejoiced to welcome the Latin deliverers. The banner was unfurled from the flagstaff of the City Hall. It was the official declaration that Gorizia had taken her rank among the cities of the Motherland. A little later the mayor of Cormons, who had been appointed head of the municipality of the newly redeemed city, arrived on the scene. Along the Via Francesco Giuseppe (renamed Via Luigi Cadorna) and the Via Giuseppe Verdi the doors were unbarred and the windows thrown open. In a few days civic life had resumed its normal course. On August 20th the King of Italy paid an official visit, and was received triumphantly by the inhabitants.

Though the name of Gorizia figured largely in the Press of the world after the commencement of the Austro-Italian war, its story is not widely known. Situated at a vital strategic spot where the frontiers of three races—the Teuton, the Slav, and the Latin—join, it has been the scene of political and military conflicts from time immemorial. Throughout the long series of barbarian invasions, when the Huns, Goths, and Vandals swept down upon the Roman Republic and Empire, Gorizia saw their banners flutter in the breeze. Again and again the troops of the Empire made their last stand on the bridge-head of Gorizia. When they went down before the invaders the Valley of the Po was lost.

From the south-western slopes of Monte Sabotino Attila is said to have watched the burning of Aquileia. In mediæval times it was the scene of endless conflicts between the Venetians and the Austrians. So fully did the Venetians realise the importance of holding the gates of the Isonzo line at Gorizia that, in 1344, the Republic **Sabotino's storied height** censured and exiled its leaders, Morosini and Grimani, because, having conquered the Counts of Gorizia, they did not insist upon the necessity of establishing the Venetian frontier beyond the hills that lie to the east of the city. While Gorizia remained in Teuton hands the enemy was considered to be within the walls.

In 1469, when the Turks made their onslaught on Western Europe, they succeeded in coming through the Vipacco Valley and crossing the Isonzo, because they had secured as allies the Slav nations whose territory joined that of the Venetians on the Isonzo. Six years later, on their return attack, the Venetians met the Turks at Gorizia, taking their stand on the same bridge-head where the decisive battles of August, 1916, were fought. That history consistently repeats itself is probably true of military history more than of any other. One of the old Venetian chronicles gives a description of the battle-ground and the disposition of the opposing forces, which might apply in all its details to the history of the twentieth century battles on this spot. "They made a trench near the bridge of Gorizia," he says, "in that part of Friuli which borders the Isonzo. From Gradisca the trench extended and ran along the river-bank for six miles on the one side and eight miles on the other."

During Germany's bid for domination over Italy in the later Middle Ages the control of Gorizia was persistently regarded as indispensable to their programme of world domination. In modern times the writing on the old palimpsest has stood out clearer than ever. Already in 1866, when the Garibaldian troops threatened the Isonzo city, the shrewd Bismarck saw that if the Latins once got a footing on the farther side of the river their position would form an impregnable bulwark against future attempts to spread the reign of German Kultur beyond the Alps. Accordingly, arrangements were made, under the dictation of

PLIGHT OF GORIZIA: OLD CASTLE AND PIAZZA IN THE THROES OF ITALIAN BOMBARDMENT.

Prussia, for peace between Austria and Italy. In deciding on the terms of the agreement, care was taken that the Teutonic frontier should embrace Gorizia and the Isonzo.

During the twenty-five years preceding the war the Teutonising of Gorizia was part of the general programme in vogue in Istria and Dalmatia. The Italians were systematically ousted from their positions in the municipality. In trade and commerce German tradesmen thrived while Italians suffered. Every conceivable means was employed to ban Latinism in schools and public offices. But the spirit of Irredentism grew more intense under the persecution. At the opening of the European War several young men escaped from the city and enlisted as volunteers in the armies of the Allies.

In looking back over the series of battles which culminated in the conquest of the city, it is impossible to give an estimate of the sacrifices which were made on either side. The Italians must have lost very seriously during the **The price of victory** struggle. For, although the heavy fighting lasted only three days, General Cadorna's troops had to face obstacles such as no other army encountered. The Italian Supreme Command, which gained a world-wide reputation for the laconic and conservative wording of its communiqués, spoke of the struggle as one of the bitterest which had been experienced in the European War. In the communiqué of August 9th the heroism of the soldiers was extolled, and particular reference made to the generosity with which they had offered their lives. From these phrases one may safely conclude that the struggle cost the victors dearly.

On September 2nd the Supreme Command published an authoritative account of the number of prisoners and amount of booty captured in the Gorizia zone and on the Carso during the series of battles which opened on August 4th and closed with the fall of Doberdo on August 10th. According to this report the number of prisoners taken amounted to 393 officers and 18,365 men. **Prisoners and booty taken**

The mass of artillery captured consisted of the following pieces : One 6 in. howitzer, two howitzers, two field cannon and one mortar, each 105 mm. (3·93 in.), one 5·51 in. mortar, eight "seventy-fives," and three of a calibre 2 mm. larger than the "seventy-five," eight mountain cannon, four 37 mm. guns, 63 trench-mortars, 92 machine-guns, and 12,225 rifles.

The amount of ammunition captured consisted of three thousand shells, five million cartridges, sixty thousand bombs and hand-grenades, three thousand bombs for bomb-throwers, 190 boxes of ammunition, 378 cases of grenades, 34 cases of rockets and fuses.

The war material included 5,906 shields, one auto-train, two heavy oil drills, several miles of telephonic and telegraphic wire, several hundredweight of engineering material, two thousand chevaux de frise, 112,000 labourers' tools, 442 wire-cutting pincers, 276 rolls of barbed-wire, 1,337 blankets, one complete dressing-station, one carpentry-shop,

PASSING OF AUSTRIA FROM GORIZIA : A SYMBOLICAL IMPRESSION.
The body of an Austrian soldier killed during the bombardment of Gorizia. It was left lying at the corner of Franz Josef Strasse, one of the most imposing thoroughfares of the city, the Austrians retreating so rapidly that they had apparently no time to bury their dead.

and forge, tailors' supplies, cooking utensils, an enormous quantity of explosives, one asphyxiating-gas apparatus and 68 carboys, five liquid-fire throwers, numerous " tear " bombs, spiked clubs for murdering soldiers and prisoners, and heavy daggers for piercing breastplate armour.

Because of its historic associations the conquest of the Gorizia bridge-head was hailed throughout Italy as a racial triumph. At an hour when Europe had been called upon to decide whether she would have Latinism or Teutonism as the inspiring ideal of her civilisation, there was a dramatic fitness in the answer given by the children of the Romans on the spot where their fathers had so often contended for the same ideals against the Teuton hordes of the North. And there is a further sense in which the victory is of

True heirs of Ancient Rome importance. When writing and speaking of modern Italy, one must set aside the idea that it is the child of mediæval romance. Its ideal is far different. The modern Italians are the heirs of the ancient Romans; and the great ideal that inspires them in their struggle for the unity and integrity of their country is the ideal bequeathed them by their fathers.

Now, one of the leading dogmas of Roman statesmanship was that the Isonzo line is essential to the defence of Italy. The Danube was the first defensive line of the Roman Empire, the Isonzo the last. As part of the system which ensured the safety of their frontiers the Romans built three great military cities close to the Isonzo and the circle of the Alps. These were Trent, Aquileia, and Trieste. To the outsider they are mere names of cities, to the Italian they are symbols of national security. As long as they are in the hands of the stranger Italy is not mistress in her own house. From Aquileia the forces of the Empire went forth to defend the Isonzo. It was then a city of a million inhabitants, rivalling Rome in wealth and importance; but to-day it is a lonely street, with only about two hundred houses. In 452, when the Huns swept away the Isonzo defences, Attila burned Aquileia. With the Isonzo once in his hands Rome easily became his prey. The defence of Rome, therefore, is on the Isonzo. That is an important dogma of modern Italian statesmanship. With the wresting of the Isonzo from the Teuton the ideals of the Risorgimento became established for the first time on an abiding foundation.

On August 10th the Italians completed the conquest of the western ridge of the Carso. Had it not been that the glamour of the Gorizia victory was still in the public mind, the conquest of the Carso would have been hailed as one of the most important events of the war. From the point of view of sheer fighting it probably offered more difficulties than even Podgora or Monte Sabotino. When Lord Kitchener passed along the battle-line of the Carso and saw the positions of vantage which the Austrians held, he declared : " The army that conquers the Isonzo defences may account itself the greatest fighting force in the world."

The system of defence which ran from Monte San Michele to the southern limits of the Doberdo Plateau was intended as the great barrier on the road to Trieste. Therefore it had for years engaged the attention of the Austrian Staff. A line of fortifications was constructed on the Doberdo Plateau, supporting the positions on Monti San Martino and Sei Busi. An intricate series of trenches, large sections of which had already been built when war broke out, extended along the whole crest of the mountain. They were connected by a series of underground passages supplied from spacious caves, where artillery and food and supplies had been stored. In the minds of the Austrian Staff there always had been a suspicion that the Italians might decide that the capture of Gorizia was not indispensable to their advance on Trieste. Therefore, no pains were spared to make the Carso line independent of the Gorizia defences.

On the night of the 10th the Austrians retreated across the Vallone and took up their new positions on a line that

THE CASTLE, GORIZIA.
Gorizia, situated about twenty-two miles north-west of Trieste, is a thriving centre for cotton and silk spinning. The majority of its inhabitants have always been Italian.

runs along the hill-crests on the other side of the valley. This Vallone is of immense military importance on the Carso. Running almost directly north and south, it is a sort of low pass leading from the Vippacco Valley to the sea. Opposite the Doberdo Plateau, on the hills beyond the Vallone, Oppacchiasella was attacked and won on the 12th. The Italians were now pressing their enemies backwards into the hills, in an effort to clear the way to Trieste. By the end of the month their lines ran from Hill 85, east of Monfalcone, to the high tableland of Pecinko, north-east of Oppacchiasella, thence in front of Vertoiba and along Monte San Marco to Monte San Gabriele and Monte Santo.

Two weak spots still remained in the line. The Austrians had held their ground on Monti Santo and San Gabriele, thus enabling them to annoy the Italian supply trains and troops passing over the **A programme** Isonzo by the Gorizia bridge. It also gave **of destruction** them the opportunity of destroying the city, just as they destroyed Monfalcone from the Carso. That they ntended carrying out a programme of destruction was made only too plain by their action during the first days of the Italian occupation. From this point of view the victory was not complete. The whole block of mountains that stand between the Idria and the Vippacco would fall into Italian hands if Cadorna's troops could bring about the fall of Monte Santo and Tolmino. As they stood at the end of August they formed an ugly menace on the flank of the advancing armies. The possession of this block of hills might not be considered indispensable, but certainly it would be very desirable.

The great series of battles which swept away the defences of the Carso and the Gorizia bridge-head opened a new phase in the Italian military situation. King Victor's Staff could now begin to feel that they were masters of their task. Hitherto, their march had been uphill and gruelling. They had commenced the struggle with slender forces, poorly supplied with artillery and only half prepared for the type of warfare which had to be undertaken. Yet they had to fight against one of the best-equipped armies in Europe, and on most difficult terrain, where all the odds were against them.

The first victories cost the Italians dearly. But lives could not then be counted, because stern necessity called for the most generous sacrifices. Throughout the winter and spring all their resources were engaged in fighting the elements. As spring advanced a great **Italian valour and sacrifice** army appeared on one of the most dangerous sectors of the line, and threatened not only the most vital military lines but also the invasion of the country. Throughout this period it was utterly impossible for the Italian Staff to think of withdrawing some of its divisions and sending them into other war theatres. That is the commonplace fact which accounts more eloquently than all other explanations for the Italian delay in sending troops to join the Allies in the Balkans.

But now that the enemy had been driven from his most threatening positions, and that the threat of invasion had been effectively removed, it was possible for Italy to carry out a programme which she would have carried out long ago had not stern necessity prevented her. In the chaos of thought created by the European upheaval there were moments when even careful writers and speakers blamed Italy for her hesitancy about joining in the Balkan campaign. In some quarters it was actually suggested that she was fighting a war of her own, and did not

MAKING GOOD A NEWLY-CAPTURED POSITION.
Organisation of a position follows immediately upon its occupation. These trenches were being made by the Italians on ground which they had only just won.

feel called upon to take active part in the full programme of the Allies. The strange feature of that view was that it had left out of count the main historical fact which brought about Italian neutrality and subsequently forced Italy into war with Austria. That fact was the Austrian attack on Serbia. In August, 1914, Great Britain declared war on Germany because the neutrality of Belgium had been violated. On the same date Italy severed herself from the Triple Alliance and declared her neutrality, because Austria had vowed the destruction of Serbia. This formed part of the basis on which she later made her declaration of war.

The stern logic of her position, therefore, made it incumbent upon Italy to join in the Macedonian Expedition. And she seized the earliest possible opportunity of carrying out an essential part of the programme which her action in 1914 called for. On August 11th the first battalions of the Italian Expeditionary Force landed in Salonika, to take **Italy to the Balkans** their place beside the French, British, and Russians in re-establishing the fabric which Germany had destroyed. General Carlo Pettiti di Roreto, who had given distinguished service during the Trentino offensive and counter-offensive, was in command of the troops.

This move brought Italy into direct conflict with Germany. Hitherto open hostilities had not been declared between the two countries, though Italy was at war with Germany's ally. To attempt an adequate explanation of the situation would involve too many hypotheses and surmises. Even when the diplomatic history of the period becomes known the mystery will probably remain. And, as in the case of many another mystery, it is possible that the key is a very simple one. Once Italy had declared war

BRIDGE-BUILDING COVERED BY ARTILLERY.
Italian engineers spanning a bridge across a river under cover of their artillery and of the trees on the opposite bank.

ASHES OF ASIAGO: AN ALPINE CITY DEVASTATED.

General view of Asiago, situated amid the Venetian Alps in the Trentino. The town was more or less destroyed by Austrian gun fire, and presented quite as melancholy an appearance as any town caught between the lines on the western front.

GORIZIA, WHICH FELL TO ITALIAN SKILL AND PROWESS, AUGUST 9TH, 1916.

Picturesque view of Gorizia as seen from Podgora. In the foreground houses typical of this region of the Isonzo are seen, while in the middle distance a large modern factory is discernible.

against the Dual Monarchy. Germany was bound, by the stern logic of the situation, openly to come to her ally's assistance. But she failed to do so. In November, 1915, Italy signed the London Pact, whereby she officially declared herself bound to the programme of the Allies. Yet Germany did not retaliate. This probably accounts for the anomaly of the situation.

Not being in contact with Germany on any section of her frontier, the declaration of war on Italy's part would have remained a dead letter, at least as long as the political and military situations of May, 1915, remained. The German declaration not being forthcoming, Italy naturally took the stand that by concentrating her energies on the Austrian frontier she would be doing the best service in her power to the cause of the Alliance. Without Austria, Germany cannot stand. Therefore, if Austria were brought to her knees, and the discussion of peace terms refused as long as she did not consent to sever her relations with Germany, the European problem would have been solved. One may safely say that that was the idea in the minds of Italian states-

ISONZO VALLEY.
Panorama of the Valley of the Isonzo with the Salcano Railway Viaduct in the foreground.

AL BRIDGE, NEAR GORIZIA.
Fierce fighting took place for possession of this fortified bridge-head near Gorizia.

men. And the position which they had adopted was undoubtedly logical.

But people at large are not governed by logic, especially in crises where great issues are being decided not by words but by blows. The absence of open hostilities between Germany and Italy was a constant source of uneasiness among the people of the Alliance. In the eyes of the man in the street no amount of argument could explain or justify it. And the Italian populace were at one with the Allies in that view. Yet there were weighty reasons which bade the Government to go slowly and securely. The financial conditions of the country were almost hopelessly intertangled with German interests. It took many months of weary work before Italy could make her reckoning and decide where she stood. Then she could show her accounts to her friends and arrange terms whereby they might be adjusted. All this necessitated heavy and painstaking work and a wholehearted co-operation on the part of the other members of the Alliance. With the betterment of the financial situation it was a more simple matter for Italian statesmen to embark upon a bold course.

In July, 1916, the commercial treaty which had existed between Germany and Italy was denounced. The denouncement of it logically followed Germany's

THE CASTLE ON THE HILL, GORIZIA.
Modern artillery had deprived the Castle Keep of its fortress value, but it remained the symbol of its holder's power. The Italian flag replaced the Austrian on Gorizia Castle, August 9th, 1916.

BEFORE PROCEEDING TO THE PRISON CAMP UNDER A VIGILANT GUARD.

In the course of a barbarous Austrian Army Order the following significant statement appeared : "The good wine and beautiful women of Italy await us." Doubtless these few hundred Austrian prisoners arrived in their detention camp in distinctly chastened mood. All were captured in the summer fighting of 1916.

VICTORS ADVANCING AND PRISONERS RETREATING ALONG THE SAME ROAD.

Unique illustration showing steel-helmeted Italian infantry going forward into action considerably heartened by the sight of a column of dejected Austrian prisoners who were descending the mountain-side, having been captured in a recent engagement.

REST AFTER THE FIGHT.
Bivouac of Italian infantry among the pines near Asiago. Evidence of artillery bombardment is seen on the farmhouse.

Government to hand to the Imperial Government of Berlin. Among the causes stated in the Note as justifying and impelling their action the Italians accused the Kaiser's Staff of open and organised hostility. Germany had systematically supplied guns for the Austro-Italian front. She had sent some of her best-trained officers to serve in Francis Joseph's army. She had counselled the Trentino offensive and sent the higher members of her military Staff to examine the territory and help to draw up the Austrian plan of campaign.

"For these reasons above set forth," the document concluded, "the Italian Government announces, in the name of his Majesty the King, that from August 28th Italy will consider herself in a state of war with Germany." On August 27th the Italian Minister at Berne presented the document to the Swiss Government with a request that the Swiss Government forward it to the Imperial Government at Berlin.

The last shreds of the Triple Alliance were now gone. The lifework of Bismarck had been undone. No more even outwardly an ally of Teutonism, Italy had fully taken her stand by the side of the nations that were struggling to uphold and safeguard the ideals which were first established in Western Europe by the valour and genius of Roman civilisation.

action towards Italian creditors. According to an agreement, signed by Prince von Bülow and Baron Sonnino, it had been stipulated, in May, 1915, that each country should respect the proprietary rights of the citizens of the other. This document was not drawn up with the foreknowledge that war would not be declared between both countries. On the contrary, it was a document intended for use in the event of war breaking out.

It is well to remember that point, because the document is often taken as a proof that when they declared war upon Austria the Italians had already known what course Germany would take. As a matter of fact, a similar document had been presented to the Austrian Ambassador, but he refused to make the arrangement.

Italy scrupulously kept her part of the bargain, but the Berlin authorities violated it consistently. Though German creditors were allowed to sue Italian debtors in Italian courts, no such permission was given to Italian creditors who had German debtors on their books. Furthermore, the money which was owed to Italian labourers in Germany was refused. And when the test cases were brought into court it was officially declared that Italians in Germany were to be treated as alien enemies.

This act was tantamount to a declaration of war on Germany's part. Hence the Italian Government immediately decided on a retaliatory course. They prepared a formal declaration of war, which they asked the Swiss

A "GUN CARRIAGE" IN THE ALPS.
In certain sectors of the Italian line mules were the only means of transport, and both belligerents resorted to these sure-footed, if sometimes refractory, quadrupeds. Such a military mule is here seen, laden with rifles, in charge of a Bersagliere.

NEWFOUNDLAND'S HEROIC PART IN THE WAR.

By F. A. McKenzie.

The "Merchant Venturers" and Terra Nova—Poverty and Hardihood of our Oldest Colony—Development of the Colony under Sir Robert Reid—The Anglo-Newfoundland Land Development Company—Sir Edward Morris—the Colony Undertakes, August 7th, 1914, to Supply a Force of One Thousand Naval Reservists for Naval Service Abroad and of Five Hundred Efficient Men for Land Service Abroad—Departure of the First Contingent for England—The 1st Battalion Leaves England for Gallipoli, August 15th, 1915—Landing at Suvla Bay—Attached to the Immortal 29th Division—The Fight for Donnelly's Post on Caribou Hill—Evacuation of Suvla Bay and Cape Helles—The Newfoundland Regiment in France—The Battle of the Somme, July 1st, 1916—Out of Eight Hundred and Eleven Men only Ninety-seven Left Unwounded—General Hunter-Weston's Praise—Sir Douglas Haig's Message to Newfoundland—Newfoundland's Answer—Sir Edward Morris Visits the Newfoundland Regiment at Beauval—Congratulations from the Colonial Secretary, and from the President and the Premier of the French Republic on Behalf of France.

THE story of the Newfoundland Regiment presents a splendid page in the story of the world-war. Here was a small dominion, for long looked upon as the Cinderella of the Empire, with a population numbering not more than a quarter of a million. Its resources in money and in men were limited, but it showed from the first a spirit of valour, a willingness to sacrifice all, if need be, for the Empire's liberty, and a steady endurance under heavy loss which won it the esteem of all the allied nations. Twice in the first two years of the war its troops in the fighting-line were almost wiped out, once by battle and disease in Gallipoli, and next in a brief charge against desperate odds on the Somme. It then began again with fresh reinforcements to win still further honours.

To understand the position of Newfoundland in the war, it is necessary to go back for a brief space. Terra Nova, "the oldest colony," as it was long known, was discovered five years after Columbus first set foot in America, by John Cabot, a Venetian mariner who had been sent out on a voyage of exploration by Henry VII., at the instigation of a group of merchants at Bristol. A century afterwards the Bristol merchants attempted to make the best of Newfoundland's great fisheries, and from then until close on the middle of the nineteenth century there followed one of the most amazing chapters in British Colonial history.

The "Merchant Venturers" and their successors did not desire a permanent settlement of Newfoundland. Their aim was rather to keep it as a fishing station. The fishermen, who formed almost the whole of the population there, were ruled for a century and a half by captains of merchant ships, who administered justice as they pleased. Men were forbidden to settle within six miles of the coast. People who came to Newfoundland—despite every possible discouragement—were, wherever possible, expelled. Spain and France fought with Britain for the possession of the Newfoundland fishing rights, thus adding external troubles to internal ill-treatment. Despite everything, the British population, hardy men of the west, grew. The present colony of Newfoundland was the result.

In time, the Newfoundlanders secured self-government. But they were still greatly hampered by faulty international agreements to which the Imperial Government had assented, and by disputes with France over fishing rights. Newfoundland was out of the current of world travel. Few visited there. Few knew of its great natural wealth. Investors passed it by. It was a little world of its own, poor and struggling, in some years scarcely able to pay the cost of its own administration, yet noted for the hardihood of its men, for its high standard of life, and for its sturdy simplicity. Serious crime was unknown among its people.

Then a new chapter in its history opened. Sir Robert Reid, a famous Canadian contractor,

[Elliott & Fry.
NEWFOUNDLAND'S FOREMOST STATESMAN.
The Right Hon. Sir Edward Patrick Morris, K.C.M.G., P.C.,
K.C., D.C.L., LL.D., Premier of Newfoundland since 1909.

NEWFOUNDLANDERS IN TRAINING.
Eight weeks after the declaration of war five hundred Newfoundlanders embarked for England to complete training. Ninety-eight per cent. were Newfoundland born.

took over the railways of the island, transformed them, and further enormously improved communications by opening a series of steamship services. The Anglo-Newfoundland Development Company, founded by Lord Northcliffe and owned and directed by the Amalgamated Press and allied organisations, secured a large area of land around Grand Falls, and built there a modern town and one of the largest paper and pulp mills in the world. General attention was in consequence directed to the potential wealth of the island, and other large industrial enterprises soon followed. The country was fortunate in the important years that followed in having Sir Edward Morris at the head of affairs as Prime Minister, a statesman of broad views and great energy. Sir Edward Morris threw himself into the work of fostering the industrial growth **Newfoundland's** of the colony. Fresh enterprises were **instant rally** opened in many directions, agriculture was developed, mining was encouraged, trade commissioners went abroad to learn the best methods for the island trades, the lesser fishing industries were fostered, and the administration improved in every department. Newfoundland, the Cinderella of yesterday, soon found itself enjoying hitherto undreamed-of prosperity.

The war turned the entire energy of the colony from industrial development to fighting. News arrived in the night of August 4th, 1914, that there had been a declaration of hostilities between Great Britain and Germany. All parties in the island came together, political differences were forgotten, and on the 7th the Ministry, expressing the determination of the entire community, undertook to supply a force of 1,000 efficient Naval Reservists by October 31st, available for naval service abroad, and to raise an efficient local brigade of five hundred men for land service abroad.

At this time, it is important to bear in mind, Newfoundland was probably the least military part of the British Empire. In olden days the British Government had maintained a garrison at St. John's, but in 1868 the Gladstone Government had ordered its withdrawal. The colony then offered to meet the cost of the troops itself, but its offer was refused. The soldiers were shipped away, and their barracks remained a ruin for many years, until they were finally burnt to the ground. From that date until the beginning of the war no British troops of any

description had landed in Newfoundland, and the vast majority of the inhabitants had never seen a soldier, save in pictures. The military education of the community had to start at the beginning. A prompt commencement was made, and the people at once began to train themselves in the art of war.

In naval affairs Newfoundland was more happily placed. For many years before the war the Legislature annually voted a sum of money to train Royal Naval Reservists to man the Dreadnoughts of Britain. In 1892 the Imperial Government handed over the Calypso, an old cruiser, for the purposes of training Newfoundland fishermen as Naval Reservists, so that if an emergency

SUN HELMETS FOR WEAR IN GALLIPOLI.
" Just the men I want for the Dardanelles," Lord Kitchener said ; and on August 15th, 1915, the 1st Battalion of Newfoundlanders left for Gallipoli.

like the Great War arose, they would be able to assist in maintaining the supremacy of Britain on the seas. Ever since that day, five British officers lived on board the Calypso, and every year there passed through that ship hundreds of fine young Newfoundland fishermen, between the ages of sixteen and twenty-four, who received their training, first on the Calypso itself and then by voyages in the ships of his Majesty's Navy.

Thus, when war was declared in 1914, there was a force of trained naval men ready for the Empire's call. They dropped their nets and their fishing gear and abandoned their boats, and before the war was two years old 2,000 Newfoundland fishermen were serving in the King's ships. Within that time over one hundred of them had perished. Twenty-five went down in H.M.S. Viknor on June 30th, 1915 ; on February 15th twenty-two Newfoundlanders were drowned when H.M.S. Clan MacNaughton was lost. On March 17th eleven were lost in H.M.S. Bayano. Several of the Newfoundland men in the Royal Naval Reserve were mentioned in despatches for bravery, including William Peddle and Leander Green.

Newfoundland had resolved to raise a force for land service: The men were quickly recruited, and hundreds more clamoured to be allowed to serve. Fishermen, hunters, trappers and lumbermen, lads from universities and high schools, the sons of politicians, professional and business men, every section of the community was represented in the regiment. The ages of the recruits averaged between twenty-three and twenty-four, the ideal age for a young soldier. Newfoundland had no officers of military experience, so men were selected from the local cadet corps, the Church Lads' Brigade, the Catholic Cadet Corps, the Methodist Guards, and the Highlanders. Committees were appointed for the examination of volunteers, for instruction in musketry, and for equipment and finance. One voluntary organisation, which afterwards did great service, undertook to look after the comfort of the lads when overseas. Within eight weeks the first contingent of five hundred embarked in a Newfoundland ship for England, to complete their training there. This **The first five hundred** first contingent was to grow in the months ahead to several thousand fighting men.

On first arriving in England the Newfoundlanders were sent to Salisbury Plain, and were quickly transferred to Fort George, in Inverness-shire, an old barracks built immediately after the Rebellion of 1745, and rich in historical associations. English and Scottish people were at first apt to confuse the Newfoundlanders with the Canadian Contingent, which arrived about the same time, greatly to the annoyance of the Newfoundlanders, who were intensely proud of their land of origin. They belonged to their colony in reality as well as in name, ninety-eight per cent. of them being Newfoundland born.

Now followed a wearisome time of preparation and waiting. From Fort George the young soldiers were sent for a time to Edinburgh, and then to Aldershot. Their strength was being **Chafing for the fight** steadily increased by fresh drafts from home. News came that the Canadians were off to France. Still the Newfoundlanders waited on, chafing at the delay. The war would be over, many of them feared, before they could strike a blow. They had only been asked to enlist for a year. Ten months of it were already over, and still they were in a peaceful camp in Britain, doing routine duty.

Then came a memorable day when Lord Kitchener came to review them and pronounced them, "Just the men I am wanting for the Dardanelles." The soldiers were offered the choice between going back to Newfoundland, at the end of their year of service, and re-enlisting for the period of the war. Every man re-enlisted. Their only fear was lest they should be kept from the front. On August 15th, 1915, the 1st Battalion, now numbering about eleven hundred men, the flower of the manhood of Great Britain's oldest colony, left Aldershot for Gallipoli.

One little incident serves to illustrate the spirit of the

GERMAN TRENCH AT OVILLERS AFTER BOMBARDMENT BY THE BRITISH ARTILLERY.
Ovillers, a small village lying on the north of the main road from Albert to Bapaume, was the scene of some of the fiercest fighting at the beginning of the great advance in July, 1916. It did not pass wholly into British hands until July 15th, 1916.

Newfoundlanders. Among the men in the ranks was a private, Gallishaw by name, formerly private secretary to two members of the Cabinet, and at the time war began a special student at Harvard. Private Gallishaw was selected by the commander to keep the records of the regiment in London, instead of proceeding to the front with the others. He had enlisted to fight, not to work as a clerk in London. When the regiment embarked he smuggled himself on board the transport, remained in hiding until the boat had left Malta and there was no chance of his being put back, and then came out and reported himself. He was pardoned for his insubordination, put in the fighting ranks, and was wounded in Gallipoli, but recovered.

The regiment landed at Suvla Bay on September 16th, and was at once attached to the 29th Division, replacing the 1/5th Royal Scots, who had suffered heavy casualties in recent engagements. The fact that they were selected to take the place of so famous a corps was regarded as a signal honour. "It was far beyond our expectations," wrote one of the officers. "Although we felt that we would be able to pull our own weight, and more, when the time came, yet, as untried soldiers, we realised that we would have to make no mean effort to attain the standard and uphold the glorious traditions of the incomparable 29th Division."

The Turks were apparently lying in wait for new arrivals. The men landed in lighters in the dark, jumping over the sides as the boats grounded and wading ashore. As daylight came on it showed that they were on a steeply sloping beach with cliffs around.

"A short distance up the hill we could see our battalion digging themselves in," wrote one of the soldiers afterwards when recalling the scene. "To the left I could see the boats of another battalion. Even as I watched, the enemy's artillery located them. It was the first shell I had ever heard. It came over the hill close to me, screeching through the air like an express train going over a bridge at night. Just above the boat I was watching it exploded.

A few of the soldiers slipped quietly from their seats to the bottom of the boat. At first I did not realise that any one had been hit. There was no sign of anything having happened out of the ordinary, no confusion. As soon as the boat touched the beach the wounded men were carried by their mates up the hill to a temporary dressing-station.

"The first shell was the beginning of a bombardment. 'Beachy Bill,' a battery that we were to become better acquainted with, was in excellent shape. Every few minutes a shell burst close to us. Shrapnel bullets and fragments of shell-casing forced us to huddle under the baggage for protection. A little to the left some Australians were severely punished. Shell after shell burst among them. A regiment of Sikh troops, mule-drivers, and transport men were caught half-way up the beach. Above the din of falling shrapnel and the shriek of flying shells rose the piercing screams of wounded mules. The Newfoundlanders did not escape.

"That morning 'Beachy Bill's' gunners played no favourites. On all sides the shrapnel came in a shower. Less often, a cloud of thick, black smoke and a hole twenty feet deep showed the landing-place of a high-explosive shell. The most amazing thing was the coolness of the men. The Newfoundlanders might have been practising trench-digging in camp in Scotland. When a man was hit some one gave him first-aid, directed the stretcher-

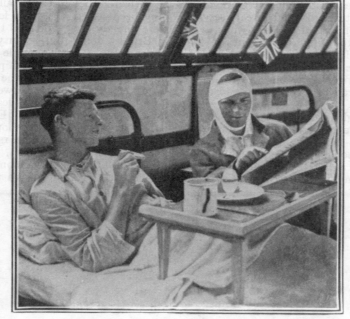

"RESTING"—BUT KEEN ON THE PROGRESS OF EVENTS.
Two men of the Newfoundland Regiment in Wandsworth Military Hospital reading the news of the great advance from which they were knocked out.

bearers where to find him, and coolly resumed digging. In two hours our position had become untenable. We had been subjected to a merciless and devastating shelling, and our first experience of war had cost us sixty-five men. In a new and safer position we dug ourselves in."

Among those severely wounded was the adjutant of the regiment, who had been hit by the first shell.

Following the usual routine, the Newfoundlanders were scattered among different regiments for their first spell in the trenches, in order that they might learn actual fighting conditions. It was impossible to advance during the day, but towards dusk the senior company, under

FOUR MEMBERS OF ONE FAMILY WHO FELL ON THE FIELD OF HONOUR.
Four members of one Newfoundland family, two brothers and their two cousins, fell in France on July 1st, 1916. From left to right they are: Capt. Eric S. Ayre, Newfoundland Regt.; Capt. Bernard P. Ayre, Norfolk Regt.; Sec.-Lieut. Wilfred D. Ayre and Sec.-Lieut. Gerald W. Ayre, both of the Newfoundland Regiment

THE TRENCH IN THE HOP-FIELD.
Any little obstruction encountered in the course of trench construction was soon disposed of by the aid of high explosive. Such an operation was being carried out when this illustration was secured.

HAZARDS OF BOMBARDMENT BEHIND THE LINE.
German shell, having gone fairly wide of its mark, nearly falls by accident into a British rest camp situated some distance behind the lines. The white ridges seen in the illustration indicate the communication trenches.

the command of Captain George Carty, the "father of the regiment," moved forward in single file, followed in due course by the remainder. Great honour had been given to them. They had been sent to what was pre-eminently the danger-spot of the perilous Gallipoli line. The division they had come to join had won high fame at heavy cost. Sir Ian Hamilton himself described it as the "Incomparable 29th Division." The New-foundlanders were to form—with the Dublins, the Munsters, and the King's Own Scottish Borderers—the 88th Brigade. They moved that night through the underbrush to join their new comrades. All along the line they could see in the darkness the white crosses marking the many graves of the men who had fallen.

Nearest to Constantinople In due course the battalion moved from the front lines to the dug-outs in reserve for "rest." This rest consisted chiefly of trench digging and trench strengthening. Parties of one hundred men were constantly at work from 7 p.m. until dawn, and to use their own phrase "the soil of Gallipoli made hard going." The Newfoundland digging-parties soon became famous on the Peninsula, and it was said that they could do more in four hours than most men could accomplish in double that time.

After this first experience the regiment went into the trenches as a distinct unit, responsible for its part of the line. Save for one vigorous attempt at an attack by the Turks, the situation had now reached the stage of what might almost be described as siege warfare. Each side kept the other ever in view, shelling where possible, sniping, mining, standing steady under aeroplane attack, ever watching the foe and improving its own position. The Newfoundlanders were well up in front, and they were able to boast afterwards that they approached nearer to Constantinople than any other troops on the Peninsula.

It was deadly monotonous work, hard, exacting and dangerous, with each day's routine much like that of the day before. The men longed for active fighting. When there came any rumour of a raid, everyone volunteered. All longed for the command to jump over the trenches and storm the enemy lines.

One brief spell of excitement came over the capture of Donnelly's Post, on Caribou Hill—as it was afterwards called—the foremost point on the British lines. The Newfoundlanders had suffered a great deal of annoyance and some loss from a group of Turkish snipers who established themselves on a knoll looking down into the line. It was decided to take the hill and to clear the Turks out. On November 4th Lieut. Donnelly, after a careful reconnaissance, went out with a party of eight men and took possession of the knoll while the Turks were away. They had scarcely occupied it before a party of Turks approached and made a desperate attack on them. The Newfound-landers succeeded in driving them off, but not before they had suffered some casualties.

Later on, Lieut. Ross, Sergeant Greene (afterwards given the D.C.M.), and six men, set out to strengthen the original party. As they were crawling through the No Man's Land they came upon a platoon of twenty Turks who were endeavouring to surround Lieut. Donnelly's group. A hot fight followed. Three of the Newfoundlanders fell wounded, one of them being hit by four bullets, one by five bullets, and the third by shrapnel. Lieut. Ross was wounded in the forearm near the shoulder.

In the end he had only a sergeant and two men left, and had to retire. Lieut. Donnelly's party returned at daybreak, **Capture of Caribou Hill** but went out again the next night and held the hill till the end. The knoll was afterwards called Caribou Hill in honour of the regiment, whose badge was the deer's head.

The work of two soldiers in this little expedition won great credit among their fellows. One of Donnelly's men, Jack Hynes, moved away from his comrades on the first night to a point two hundred yards to the left. He remained there, single-handed, keeping up a rapid fire all night and making the enemy believe that the spot was held in force. Next morning Hynes saw Sergeant Greene moving back time after time, carrying wounded men to the

313

LIEUT.-COLONEL C. W. WHITAKER.
Commanding the 2nd Battalion of the 1st Newfoundland Regiment.

rear. To distract the attention of the Turks from him Hynes started back, purposely exposing himself and stumbling as he retired. Both Greene and Hynes were given the Distinguished Conduct Medal. Lieut. Donnelly was decorated with the Military Cross.

This was the first real engagement in which the Newfoundlanders had taken part. They were soon, however, to undergo a much more severe experience. Towards the end of November the Gallipoli Peninsula was swept by a storm of rain, wind, and snow. Trenches and dugouts were flooded. Men were overwhelmed where they stood, or frozen as they strove to struggle along. Hundreds of our troops were drowned in the flooded trenches ; others died from exposure. In many parts of our lines it was impossible to remove the sick men to the clearing-station on the beach, and those who tried to crawl there were often overwhelmed on the way. This November storm remained for long a horrible nightmare to all who were in it. The spirit of the Newfound-

Ordeal by storm landers, however, was by no means broken. Reduced to short rations, chilled to the bone, with every garment soaking, and almost exhausted for want of sleep, they yet managed to rebuild their parapets, clear the communication trenches, and " carry on " until the storm was over.

Then came the evacuation of Suvla Bay and Cape Helles. At Suvla Bay part of the Newfoundland Regiment was in the rearguard covering the retirement at Cape Helles ; other companies did great things in building roads and bridges and loading transports on W and V Beaches. Shells were raining death and destruction, but they kept on in such a way as to earn very high praise from the general officer commanding the division. The Newfoundlanders had landed in Gallipoli without having heard a shot fired in war. Within three weeks they were veterans, and in the short, trying experience their capacity for hard work, their readiness, resource, and courage had earned them the goodwill of all. They had started out eleven hundred strong. It was said that when the roll was called at Lemnos Island the day after they left the Peninsula there were only one hundred and seventy to reply.

About the middle of January the Newfoundland Regiment landed at Suez and encamped in the desert, where it began a system of training which was to stand the men in good stead when they were called upon to show for the second time their mettle.

From Suez the 1st Newfoundland Regiment moved on to France, and here it was soon to undergo an experience that will long be remembered in the history of the colony and of the Empire. It was moved down to the neighbourhood of the Somme, to take part in the great advance. On the night of June 25th, 1916, a party of fifty men, under the command of Captain Butler, attempted to raid the German lines, but did not succeed, although it partly succeeded in cutting the German **In the Somme** entanglements. The effort was repeated **advance** on the following night, and the men, carefully making their way through the German entanglements, found that the Germans were ready for them. Machine-guns were fixed at places to sweep the paths through which they must go, and the trenches were strongly held. Captain Butler and his men rushed forward before the machine-gunners could get to work and hurled bombs on them. Some of the party leapt into the German trench and some placed themselves so as to cover the entrances to the dug-outs, killing the Germans as they emerged. One German machine-gun began to work, but a private named Phillimore threw himself on to the machine-gun party and stopped them at the cost of his own life. In the end, however, the raiding-party had to retire, but only after all their bombs had been used. All the officers had been wounded and some six men killed and thirteen wounded.

Then came the great Battle of the Somme. On the night of June 30th-July 1st the regiment marched eight miles from its billet to its allotted place in the trenches. Its actual strength when it set out was twenty-six officers and seven hundred and eighty-three rank and file in the front, with fourteen officers and seventy-five rank and file in reserve. The regiment reached its position about 2 a.m. on the morning of July 1st. Everyone knew that the mighty blow for which we had been preparing for months was now about to be delivered. For a week the ears of the soldiers had been deafened by the noise of the terrific British bombardment. All that night it continued. In the morning, from six until half-past seven, there came a hurricane of fire which made even what had gone before seem mild and ineffective. Surely, men said to one another, nothing could survive a rain of death such as that.

The Newfoundlanders were at a position south of the village of Beaumont-Hamel, over the ridge flanking the River Ancre. The Ulsters had advanced astride the Ancre, and the Inniskillings were attacking to their left. But where it was hoped the Germans had been all killed, men suddenly emerged from dug-outs. They put their machine-guns in position even before our artillery had ceased. They met our men with a withering fire before which none could live. Two British regiments moved forward, one after another. Both failed, not through any weakness or lack of dash, but simply because the German fire was irresistible. Our own men were the first to admit that for once the enemy surpassed anything we had known of their fighting power. The bravery on either side was as great as anything seen in the whole war.

The first two attempts had failed. The Newfoundlanders were to have been used to push home the victory obtained by the first attacking parties. In place of that, word was sent that they were to make the third attempt to break the enemy line. Victory was crowning our arms at point after point ; we must not fail here.

There came a pause in which our artillery spoke again. A heavy fire was concentrated on the German lines, and now came word for the Newfoundlanders to advance. Their colonel called the company commanders together, and told them what was before them. There was no hesitation.

With a cheer, every man jumped over the parapet, with the colonel in the van. Again the German lines suddenly swarmed with men. They emerged once more from the dug-outs in which they had remained sheltered. It seemed as though every concealed spot had a machine-gun behind it, and every machine-gun was firing at once on our men.

Success was impossible. The terrific machine-gun fire was soon followed by shell fire. The men continued to move forward at a rapid pace, without flinching. They fell by the units, by the scores, soon by the hundreds. A few reached the beginning of the enemy's entrenchments, only to die there. They had not even an opportunity to strike a blow at the foe. The whole thing was over so quickly that it seemed impossible that in a few minutes a gallant regiment should thus have been wiped out. Yet when the roll was taken afterwards it was found that out of a total of eight hundred and eleven Newfoundlanders engaged, only ninety-seven were unwounded, two officers, the commander, Lieut.-Colonel Hadow, and the adjutant, Captain Riley, and ninety-five rank and file. The bodies of ten officers and forty-six men killed were recovered;

Great and glorious effort fourteen officers and four hundred and forty-two men came in or were brought in wounded, and two officers and two hundred of other ranks were missing. Some of them had fallen, killed or wounded, too close to the German lines to be recovered.

"When the order to attack was given," the corps commander, Lieut.-General Sir Aylmer Hunter-Weston afterwards wrote to Sir Edward Morris, "every man moved forward to his appointed objective in his appointed place, as if on parade. There were no waverers, no stragglers, and not a man looked back. It was a magnificent display of trained and disciplined valour, and the assault only failed of success because dead men can advance no farther. They were shot down by machine-guns brought up by a very gallant foe under our intense artillery fire. Against any foe less well entrenched, less well organised, and—above all—less gallant, their attack must have succeeded."

Many were the stories told afterwards by the survivors of what their comrades had done. One captain, when leading his men, was hit by a bullet in the hand. **"Go on with it, boys"** Some of his men moved to go to his aid. He ordered them on. "Go on with it, boys, I will be with you in a minute." Then he stepped back to a dressing-station, had his bandage fixed, and doubled back, urging on his men till he fell with another wound.

Captain J. A. Leddingham, the youngest captain in the regiment, while leading his company in a charge, fell wounded in three places, and crawled into a shell-hole, where he lay, barely conscious, for five hours. Aroused by the moaning of a comrade, he peeped over the edge of his shelter and saw an old chum, Lieut. Robertson, lying a few yards away, helpless. Hardly able to move himself, he crept out of his shelter, hoisted his comrade on his back, and crawled along with him to the British lines. One young private, going into the firing-line for the first time, approached near to the German front. All his comrades were shot down, and he fell into a shell-hole. For four days he lay among the dead, with the fire continuing ceaselessly around. All the food and water that he had was taken from his dead comrades. He did not know

A BRITISH CAMP IN FRANCE ON THE EVE OF THE GREAT OFFENSIVE.
[*Official photograph.*]
Great activity prevailing at a camp prior to the advance of July 1st, 1916. The dusty road was alive with movement and preparation, transport horses and mules going to and from the base, and men collecting their equipment for the coming ordeal.

where he was. At the end of the fourth day he crawled out, selecting his line of route by chance. Fortunately it led him in the direction of the British patrol.

The story of the Newfoundland men sent a thrill through the Empire. General Hunter-Weston, addressing the survivors said, "Newfoundlanders, I salute you individually. You have done better than the best." In a letter to Sir Edward Morris, written shortly afterwards, the general repeated in even more emphatic terms his praise. Some part of that letter has been already quoted in this chapter. The remainder is well worth reading. "The Newfoundland Battalion covered itself with glory on July 1st by the magnificent way in which it carried out the attack entrusted to it. It went forward to the attack when two other attacks on that same part of the line had failed, and by its behaviour on that occasion it showed itself worthy of the highest traditions of the British race and proved itself to be a fit representative of the population of the oldest British colony.

"As it was, the action of the Newfoundland Battalion, and the other units of the British left, contributed largely to the victory achieved by the British and French farther south, by pinning to their ground the best of the German troops, and by occupying the majority of their artillery, both heavy and field. The gallantry and devotion of this battalion, therefore, was not in vain, and the credit of victory belongs to them as much as to those troops farther south who actually succeeded in breaking the German lines. An attacking army is like a football team; there is but one who kicks the goal, yet the credit of success belongs not alone to that individual but to the whole team, whose concerted action led to the desired result.

"I should like you to let my fellow-citizens of the Empire in the oldest overseas portion of the British Realm know how well their lads have done, both officers, non-commissioned officers, and men, and **Praise from** how proud I, as their corps commander, **Sir Douglas Haig** am to have had such a battalion under my command, and to be a comrade of each and all of them."

Sir Douglas Haig was equally emphatic. In a message to the Government of Newfoundland he wrote: "Newfoundland may well be proud of her sons. The heroism and the devotion to duty they displayed on July 1st has never been surpassed. Please convey my deep sympathy and that of the whole of our armies in France in the loss of the brave officers and men who have fallen for the Empire, and our admiration of their heroic conduct. Their effort contributed to our success, and their example will live."

When the news of the fight reached Newfoundland, the little colony was torn by conflicting emotions of pride and grief. There was scarcely a family of prominence

THE "HIGH-EXPLOSIVE EXPRESS": TYPE OF GREAT BRITISH GUN IN ACTION.
From the size of the cloud of smoke and debris raised by the explosion of its projectile, some idea may be gleaned of the power of this huge engine of war, the destructive capacity of which was enhanced by its mobility. It ran, like a colossal locomotive, on wheels—an ammunition waggon being coupled to it, as seen in the smaller photograph.

THE ASSAULT ON LA BOISSELLE.
Our troops got into the village on July 1st, but did not finally master the
defences until July 3rd, 1916.

that had not lost one near and dear to them in that fierce
advance. "The soldiers of Newfoundland have won the
highest praise which sons of Britain can ever earn,"
said the governor. "The glory of it can never fade.
July 1st, when our heroes fought and fell, will stand
for ever as the proudest day in the history of the loyal
colony." Grief for those who had fallen meant no looking
back.

The men of the Newfoundland Regiment who were
quartered at Ayr, in Scotland, under training, sent a
message home, "Unanimous message from Ayr boys. Our
ranks are thin. Come all who can and help us to defend
the safety and honour of the Homeland
and Empire, and avenge our gallant comrades who have fallen at the post of duty."
On the second anniversary of the war,
while still in the first flood of their sorrow, the people of
the island held public meetings, and there solemnly resolved
that Newfoundland's part in the war should continue,
that recruiting should go on, and that the public credit
was pledged till the final issue resulted in victory for Britain
and her Allies.

**The message
home**

The remnants of the regiment at the front did not
repine. "The Newfoundland spirit is indomitable," wrote
an observer a few days afterwards; "already the regiment
is reshaping itself. For every man who fell in that glorious
fight there are two others willing and anxious to take his
place, and all burn with a desire to avenge the comrade,
the brother, and the cousin who fell." Volunteers
went out soon after the fight to gather in the dead
under heavy German fire, and they gave them Christian
burial behind the lines. "Our comrades sleep easily,"
they said.

Shortly afterwards, Sir Edward Morris, who was then
visiting the British front in France, went to Beauval, where
the remnants of the Newfoundlanders were stationed.
The regiment, numbering four hundred and fifty—having
been increased by drafts from its British depot—was then
resting in billets. Sir Edward Morris's own description
of his visit, taken from a published official report to the
Governor of Newfoundland, is well worth giving. "The men,
four hundred and fifty in number, were parading, and
through the courtesy of the colonel I was afforded an

MAKING THE BEST OF IT.
French troops having exploded a mine in the enemy first line, the Germans
organised it into the defensive position here shown.

opportunity of addressing them. I told them how much
we appreciated their work, and especially their action of
July 1st; how we had followed their career with
interest from the day they had left our shores.

"I told them what we thought of their conduct in
Gallipoli, and in France, and how we rejoiced in the splendid
name they had won for themselves and their country;
how their example had fired the patriotism of their brothers
and relatives in their far-off home, and that while I spoke
a leviathan of the ocean was ploughing her way through
the Atlantic, followed by a keel-compelling breeze from
their own shores, carrying in her cabins five hundred and
fifty of their brothers to reinforce their ranks and prepare
them for the day if they should ever be called upon to
again go into action.

"I told them of the letter addressed to them by their
lieutenant-general; how it was an heirloom that each man
would transmit to his children, a legacy establishing the
honour, patriotism, and character of their fathers, of more
value than gold and precious stones. They in no way
appeared to be cast down by the losses of July 1st.
On the contrary, there was a light in the face of every
man of them, and a ring of determination in the voices of

all; they appeared to long only for the hour when they would have an opportunity of getting at the insolent foe and avenging the death of those of their comrades who had fallen.

"And yet, I could not but feel sad to see only four hundred and fifty of that splendid battalion, that to us represented and meant so much. I had **Sir Edward Morris's** seen them grow from the enlistment of the **tribute** first man; it seemed a part of myself. But they had died for their country; their death was like the death of those bright stars whose death is day. The war training had developed them; they had become magnificent men. Of the eight hundred that had gone into battle that July morning the average age could not have been more than twenty-four, and this in itself made it particularly sad to think that the course of so many of them should have run at so early an age.

> "It is not growing like a tree
> In bulk, doth make Man better be;
> Or standing like an oak, three hundred year,
> To fall a log at last, dry, bald and sere:
> A lily of a day
> Is fairer far in May,
> Although it fall and die that night—
> It was the plant and flower of Light.
> In small proportions we just beauties see;
> And in short measures life may perfect be."

Of the many messages sent in from all parts of the allied fronts in praise of the Newfoundlanders, only a few can be given. The Colonial Secretary cabled his intense admiration for the gallant deeds of the contingent, and his warmest sympathy with the relatives of those who had suffered in the fight. The President of the French Republic sent his congratulations in the name of France through Sir Edward Morris to the people of Newfoundland and the valiant army. Monsieur Briand declared "Their courage has called forth the admiration of all who have seen them in action."

In a memorable tribute in the House of Commons, Mr. Steel-Maitland, Under-Secretary of State for the Colonies, said that Newfoundland, with a population less than half of that of Wandsworth, had not only contributed to the land forces which had **Spirit of Drake** fought so nobly in France, but had **and Hawkins** furnished more daring seamen to the British Fleet and British trawlers during the present struggle than all the other Dominions combined. "It seems to me it must be something in the blood. Newfoundland is largely peopled by the descendants of those who set out from Barnstaple and Bideford in the days of Drake, Frobisher, and Hawkins."

To the people of the Empire the story of the Newfoundlanders' great sacrifice was a stimulus. To the people of Newfoundland itself it was an inspiration. It was felt that the island had now to maintain the reputation of the brave boys who had thus given their lives, and to send others to replace them. Newfoundland set about living up to the ideal it had raised for itself.

[*Official photograph.*

RUINS OF MONTAUBAN: "A TRIUMPH FOR OUR ARTILLERY."
Nowhere was our artillery fire more destructive than in Montauban. In one almost impregnable position our heavy guns left nothing whole, not even the elusive machine-gun. The honour of being first to enter the place in July, 1916, fell to certain battalions of the Manchesters.

CHAPTER CXXXVII.

RUSSIA RESURGENT: THE SUMMER OFFENSIVE OF 1916 TO THE FALL OF STANISLAU.

By Robert Machray.

How Russia Astonished the World in General and Germany in Particular—Vain Boasts of the German Chancellor—Russia's Great Spirit—Her Lack of Munitions Remedied—Positions of the Russian and Austro-German Armies in June, 1916—The Rival Generals—How Brussiloff Prepared his Offensive—Attack Along the Whole Southern Front—Smashing In of the Enemy's Lines—Capture of Lutsk—Inspiring Message from the Tsar—Kaledin's Wonderful Fighting Advance—Fall of Dubno—Lutsk Salient Formed—Enemy Counter-Offensive—Its Success and Failure—Sudden Appearance of Lesh's Army—Decisive Effect—The "Iron" and "Steel" Divisions—Sakharoff's Splendid Victories and Triumphant March—The Taking of Brody—Pressure on Bothmer from the North and South—Collapse of the Austro-German Line—Shcherbacheff's Advance—Fresh Austro-German Efforts—How Lechitsky Contributed to the Russian Triumph—Penetration and Conquest of Bukovina—Capture of Czernovitz—Fall of Kolomea—Weather Interferes with Operations—Advance Resumed—Retreat of Bothmer—Capture of Stanislau—Colossal Number of Prisoners Taken—Russia's Asiatic Front—Fall of Trebizond and Erzingan—The Situation in Armenia and Persia—A Turkish Counter-Offensive.

AMONG the great surprises in which the war abounded none was more unexpected in its occurrence or astonishing in its result than the resurgence of the armies of Russia that was manifested, to the delight of her friends and the confusion of her foes, in the summer of 1916. Even those of the Allies who were acquainted with her vast resources in men, and understood something of her infinite capacity for sustained effort and ungrudging self-sacrifice, were amazed. The well-informed correspondent in Petrograd of a London journal stated, when in England on a holiday in January of that year, that no movement of vital importance could be looked for from Russia for at least the next twelve months. Similar pessimistic views were general, because of the grave losses which she had undergone in 1915, and of her tragical deficiencies in munitions. But to the Central Powers the resilience and the recovery of Russia were a staggering blow.

Germany had declared, and apparently with conviction, that Russia was so completely defeated as to be practically negligible. As narrated in Chapter CIX., entitled "The Renewed Russian Offensive and the Fall of Erzerum," there were signs that the German estimate that Russia had been reduced to a condition of collapse was another of the fond delusions to which the enemy

GENERAL ALEXEI BRUSSILOFF.
General Brussiloff's drive through Volhynia in 1916 signalised the resurgence of the Russian armies.

was a prey. Yet Germany still retained her belief in the impotence of her big neighbour; though she ought, it might have been supposed, to have known better.

Two months after the capture of Erzerum by the Russians, Bethmann-Hollweg, the Imperial German Chancellor, said, when addressing the Reichstag, that the fortress had been taken because of the numerical superiority of Russia's forces in that area, but that Turkish reinforcements would speedily give a different complexion to the situation in Armenia and Persia. He then went on to boast that the Central Powers would find no difficulty in keeping all the territory of Russia which they occupied. Never again, said he, was she to be permitted to rule over the Poles, Lithuanians, Balts, and Letts who had been set free by Germany and her allies, nor ever again would the land of the Vistula be used for an assault on "unprotected Germany." He spoke with derision of the attempts of Russian storming columns to drive "Hindenburg and his brave men" from their trenches.

Such was the attitude of official Germany to Russia, and it also was that of the German people. Bethmann-Hollweg's speech was delivered early in April, and it might have seemed a warning to German arrogance when the Russians, of whom he had spoken so contemptuously, took Trebizond a few days later. On the other hand, the position on

319

LEADER OF THE RUSSIAN ADVANCE IN VOLHYNIA, JUNE, 1916.
General Alexei Brussiloff first saw active service in the Russo-Turkish War of 1877. He led the Russian dash over the Carpathians in 1915, and in 1916 commanded the four armies of the Russian left wing which hunted the Austrians out of Russia.

nearly all fronts, as late as the beginning of June, appeared to be so favourable to Germany that there was some excuse for the complacency with which she regarded the outlook. Nowhere were the Entente Powers genuinely forging ahead. At Verdun the French, in spite of almost unimaginable heroism, were scarcely holding their ground, and the brave Italians had been compelled to retire for several miles in the Trentino. The Austrian offensive against Italy in itself indicated how scanty was the regard paid to Russia. In Armenia the Russians had been thrown back by the Turks, though they had made some progress in Persia, and in Europe their success had not been conspicuous.

Indecisive winter battles Along her European front Russia had gained little or nothing positively by the battles that had taken place during the winter. In some of these the fighting was of the most desperate description. After the spring thaw had passed, and the terrain had become practicable for the marching of armies, the struggle was resumed about the beginning of May, when, in the district around Lake Naroch, east of Vilna, the Russians, who had made a slight advance in this quarter, were heavily checked by the Germans, who claimed to have captured upwards of 5,000 men and four guns. About this time experts in Petrograd expected that the enemy would make a powerful attack on the Russian positions in the north. Artillery actions were incessant on the Riga-Dvinsk line, and in the second week of the month a violent contest developed in the vicinity of Jacobstadt on the Dwina, but with indecisive results. And whatever was the plan that had been evolved by Hindenburg, who was in chief command of the German

operations in this region, it was paralysed by the need of reinforcements at Verdun by his compatriots, which deprived him of several divisions, weakening him materially. During May artillery duels were almost continuous on the Oginski Canal, north of Pinsk, and south of the marshes there was considerable cannonading. But nothing in this period even faintly suggested the prodigious change that so soon, and with such dramatic suddenness, was to come over the scene. Surprise, with the success attending it, was the chief note of the great Russian offensive that began in June.

Germany and Austria, stultified by their overweening pride and their confidence in their power easily to hold and deal with Russia, were fooled to the top of their bent. They had thought that Russia was finished. Their mistake was to cost them dear. Nothing in the whole war, with the exception of the splendid way in which the civil population **The enemy's fatal pride** of the British Empire rallied to the Flag, was more remarkable than the recovery of Russia, as shown by the formation of immense new armies during the months that had elapsed since the preceding October.

The heart, the spirit, the soul of Russia were in the business, and this national feeling made tremendous and terrible her inexhaustible strength in men, to which a German statesman had referred, not without foreboding, shortly before the war broke out. Not even in the dark days when Napoleon strode on to Moscow was Russia so united, so inflexibly determined. Throughout all the vastness of the Russian land no one talked of anything but the war. Every town, village, and hamlet had its wounded back from the front, and everyone knew that a part of the soil of Holy Russia was in the remorseless grasp of the most brutal of invaders. Horrible, true stories of the hideous treatment meted out by the Germans to Russian prisoners circulated from mouth to mouth. Russia was thoroughly roused from one end to the other. Therefore, willingly and gladly did the Russians in their millions drill continually all these months, inexorably resolved to defeat and conquer their enemy.

The man is more than the machine. It was this marvellous outflow of national feeling, with all its quickening and vitalising influence, that accounted for the extraordinary resurgence of the Russian armies, and explained the magnificent, unquestioning heroism which they displayed when the offensive started. Naturally, there were other factors that made for success. The retreat of the preceding year had not been brought about by any wonderful generalship on the part of the Germans or by lack of courage on the side of the Russians—when it became known, the story of the unfaltering bravery shown in the retirement of the Russian armies thrilled the world. The retreat was caused solely by the shortage of guns, rifles, and other munitions. When the Russian people understood that this was the case, they threw themselves into munition-making with a perfect frenzy of enthusiasm.

Russia, however, was unfortunately but poorly equipped from the industrial point of view, yet she mobilised all her mills, factories, and everything that could be pressed into service. More than that, she called on Japan—lately her foe, but now her friend—to assist her, and that strong, young old giant of the Far East wrought mightily on her behalf, sending to her millions of rifles and bayonets, besides large numbers of guns of all calibres with the proper ammunition, to say nothing of clothing and boots in prodigious quantities. (Chapter CXXXI.) Her other allies also helped her in various ways; among them, Belgium supplied her with a fleet of armoured cars.

Russia, when the brilliant Brussiloff commenced operations against the Austro-Germans, was stronger than she had ever been in all her history. And she had learned much, taken it to heart and profited by it. If she was terrible in man-power, she was truly formidable in all the grim machinery of war, and she was great in hardly-won

Fodder for horses and guns: Provision train en route for the front.

Watering horses by the roadside: A restful interlude in the daily toil.

Historic meeting in France: King George, Sir Douglas Haig, and Sir Henry Rawlinson.

Royal interest in trench drill: Watching the Anzacs at work in France.

During the third Royal visit to the front : The King follows the Poziéres fighting.

[Official photographs.

King George and the Prince of Wales inspect the calcined ruins of Fricourt trenches.

323

Derelicts of Contalmaison: German prisoners proceeding to the base via a trench.

The day goes well! First batch of prisoners on the memorable First of July, 1916.

knowledge. She was fortunate, too, in her generals, who, at any rate in Alexeieff and Brussiloff, already had proved themselves to be soldiers of the highest class, and as her offensive progressed other names sprang into fame.

As June opened the Russian armies in Europe were disposed in three groups, strung along a front of about eight hundred miles in length from north to south. The northern Russian armies, composing the first group, and temporarily under General Kuropatkin, well known from his connection with the Russo-Japanese War, stretched along the Riga-Dvinsk line. The central Russian armies, forming the second group, were under General Evert, who had shown distinguished ability in the great retreat, and they took up the line from Dvinsk to the Marshes of the Pripet.

The southern Russian armies, the remaining group, stood on the front from the marshes to the Rumanian frontier, and they were led by General Brussiloff, a man of exceptional capacity, as was evinced—even when he was retreating, under General Ivanoff, in Galicia the previous year— by the defeat she inflicted on the enemy. All three groups were under the command of General **Rise of** Alexeieff, who was subordinate only to **Brussiloff** the Tsar himself. In the preceding October the total strength of Russia on her whole European front was perhaps a million men ; by June, 1916, it had probably been nearly tripled, with plenty of reserves at the depots in the background.

Over against the northern and central Russian armies lay the eastern German armies, including one Austrian army corps, led by various generals, but all under the supreme command of Marshal Hindenburg, whom Germany still regarded as her best soldier. Opposite the southern Russian armies five Austro-Hungarian armies, with which were incorporated several German divisions, stretched down from the Pripet Marshes through Volhynia, Galicia, and the duchy of Bukovina to Hungary and Rumania. These armies were commanded by the Archduke Frederick, the one member of the House of Hapsburg who was a professional soldier, but of no particular distinction in that rôle. His headquarters were at Lemberg—or Lvoff, as the Russians called it—and he held a Royal court in that ancient city, which, after its occupation for nine months by Russia, had resumed its old life as if there had been no interruption.

Though the fact was not known till the middle of June, the chief command in Volhynia was in reality in the more efficient hands of General Linsingen, a German officer with headquarters at Kovel, a railway centre and strategically important as the point of junction between Hindenburg and the Austrians. But whether the Austrian prince or the German soldier were in charge, both firmly believed that their line was impregnable and absolutely secure against the assaults of Brussiloff.

From the Pripet to the Pruth, the boundaries north and south of the area in which Brussiloff was about to spring his offensive on the enemy, the battle-front was nearly two hundred and seventy miles in length, over a country that did not rise into considerable hills or steep eminences till the Carpathians were reached, but was rendered difficult by its being broken by rivers and streams with lake-like expansions and marshy tracts, as well as

ALFRESCO HAIR-DRESSING : A SIDE-LINE IN THE WAR.
Russian soldiers having their hair cut before proceeding to take a bath. Although the operation frequently had to be performed in the open air, military organisation had not omitted to supply mechanical appliances.

by broad belts of forest. Below the Pripet it passed through Volhynia along the Styr to Chartorisk, thence over open, undulating ground to Olika, to the west of the fortress of Rovno, struck south to the east of the fortress of Dubno, on the Ikva, into Galicia, where it lay on the Strypa, west of Tarnopol and east of Buczacz, and crossing the Dniester at Uscieczko, which the Russians had retaken in the winter, swung eastwards to the Dniester again, and, lower down, to the Pruth in Bukovina, with Czernovitz well to the south-west of it. Both combatants had strongly fortified it. With communication trenches in between, trench succeeded trench, the first in each case being protected by row after row of savage wire entanglements ; mortars were abundant ; field and heavy guns and howitzers, with vast stores of shells and bombs, had been accumulated at the best points ; machine-guns bristled everywhere. Probably the Austro-Germans possessed the stronger "machinery," and they certainly enjoyed superior facilities as regarded railways. From Kovel they had constructed a new line which ran through Vladimir Volynsk and Sokal to Rawaruska, where it linked up with the line from Lemberg, itself a great railway junction, and this gave them the enormous advantage of a line of communication laterally behind their whole front.

On the Russian side of the front the four armies of General Brussiloff's command were, from north to south, respectively, the Eighth Russian Army under General Kaledin, in Volhynia ; the Eleventh Russian Army under General Sakharoff, in Volhynia and Galicia ; the Seventh Russian Army under General Shcherbacheff, in Galicia ; and the Ninth Russian **Russia's estimated** Army under General Lechitsky, in the **strength** region of the Dniester. Of these armies Kaledin's had been Brussiloff's own before his appointment two months previously to the leadership of the whole southern group, in succession to General Ivanoff, who had gone to the Imperial Headquarters to act as military adviser to the Tsar. A German estimate, published a few weeks prior to the start of Brussiloff's offensive, put the total strength of the forces at his disposition at forty-one infantry and fourteen cavalry divisions, or not far short of a million men, if the divisions were at full strength. A very large proportion of them were, however, young, untried troops, whose training had begun in the preceding winter, but all were animated with the same sublime spirit of devotion.

On the German side of the front two Austro-Hungarian armies held the part of it which lay in Volhynia and bent down some distance into Galicia. The Fourth Austro-Hungarian Army, under the Archduke Joseph Ferdinand, stood on the line from the Pripet to about Chartorisk on the Styr. Next came the First Austro-Hungarian Army, under General Pulhallo von Brlog, with Lutsk and Dubno in its possession, and facing Rovno, held by the Russians—the three fortresses formerly termed the Volhynian Triangle. South of Pulhallo lay the Second Austro-Hungarian Army, under General Böhm Ermolli, with its right north-west of Tarnopol. Below Böhm Ermolli, the German General Count Bothmer, with forces predominantly Austrian, held the west bank of the Strypa and the line to a point north of Buczacz, where he connected up with the Austro-Hungarian army of General Pflanzer-Baltin, whose troops occupied the remainder of the front to the Dniester and Bukovina

The total strength of these five armies was about forty-one divisions, including three German divisions, and about ten divisions of cavalry, or very much the same number of men as Brussiloff had. The enemy would have been far stronger in this whole area but for the requirements of the German offensive at Verdun and of the Austrian in the Trentino. Just as Hindenburg had been weakened in the north by the one, so were the Austrians in the south by the other.

Diversions for Verdun and Trent

These armies were composed mainly of Austrians and Hungarians, most of the Slav elements of the Dual Monarchy having been stationed on the Italian front.

These two opposing groups of armies were so nearly balanced as regarded their numerical strength that there was little or nothing to choose between them. Among their leaders, however, Brussiloff was the general who had most distinguished himself in previous operations in the war, but then only in the subordinate capacity of an army commander, and it remained to be seen what figure he would present as the commander of a group of armies. Unlike Ivanoff, who was of peasant descent, Alexei Brussiloff came of noble stock. Slim, of medium height, with a clear-cut, aristocratic face, Brussiloff was now sixty-three years of age, but had lost none of his early vigour. He said himself that he abhorred "lulls," and an aggressive energy was characteristic of him. His appearance indicated the cavalry soldier. Ten years before he had been appointed to the command of the 2nd Cavalry Division of the Guard, and in 1911 was placed

MASKED FOR ATTACK.
Russians preparing to attack Germans in the north-west.

RUIN AND DESOLATION IN THE DUCHY OF BUKOVINA.
Russian scouts observing the enemy from the useful shelter of a shattered mill. In circle: Flooded trenches in Bukovina. No scene could better suggest the desolation through which the Russians advanced.

at the head of the army corps stationed in the district bordering on Galicia. When the war broke out he was selected, as was natural, to lead the army which invaded that Austrian province, and during the first months of the struggle his achievements were most remarkable.

Forced to retire from the Carpathians in May, 1915, along with the other commanders under Ivanoff, Brussiloff made every foot of territory he yielded up extremely expensive to the enemy, whom he more than once turned on and severely defeated. It was he who, as the great retreat came to a close, retook Lutsk in September, 1915, though lack of munitions prevented him from holding it. His fine counter-offensive at that time helped, however, to retain Rovno for Russia. Meanwhile, he had perfected his knowledge of the country, and obtained as thorough a knowledge of Linsingen, Bothmer, and the Austrian generals against whom he later was to pit himself. General Lechitsky, too, knew the terrain well, and, besides, had taken the measure of Pflanzer-Baltin, before whom he had been compelled to withdraw during the general retreat, but whom he was now about to engage on more equal terms.

Russia superior in leadership On the Austro-German side Marshal Mackensen, the leader of the tremendous offensive of 1915, and to whose ability much of its success was due, had disappeared from this theatre, and none of the subordinate commanders he had left behind him was of outstanding merit. Man for man the Russian generals in this portion of the field were superior to, or quite as good as, those of the enemy. And it was doubtful whether Germany possessed in her High Command a strategist or a tactician of the genius of Alexeieff, whose was the brain that worked behind that of Brussiloff.

Extensive and careful preparation was made for the new offensive. The Staff organisation had been greatly improved; weak elements were weeded out; better men with better methods supervised and worked out details. For months munitions had been pouring in; there was no shortage of guns or ammunition, and every soldier had a rifle—in 1915, when not more than half of the men in the firing-line had rifles, all had been very different. Transport and the means of communication had been seen to, speeded up, and rendered efficient as never before. Every feature of the attack had been studied. The Russian guns by their fire had learned the ranges on the enemy's front to a nicety.

One of the open secrets of the success of the Germans had been their power to move forces swiftly from one point where nothing was

ABANDONED.
Broken guns abandoned by the Austrians in Bukovina.

COGS IN THE GREAT RUSSIAN WAR-MACHINE.
Motor-cycles on the Russian front. Vast numbers were employed in the war, regardless of bad roads or lack of roads. In circle: Wounded Russians at a rest camp near Riga.

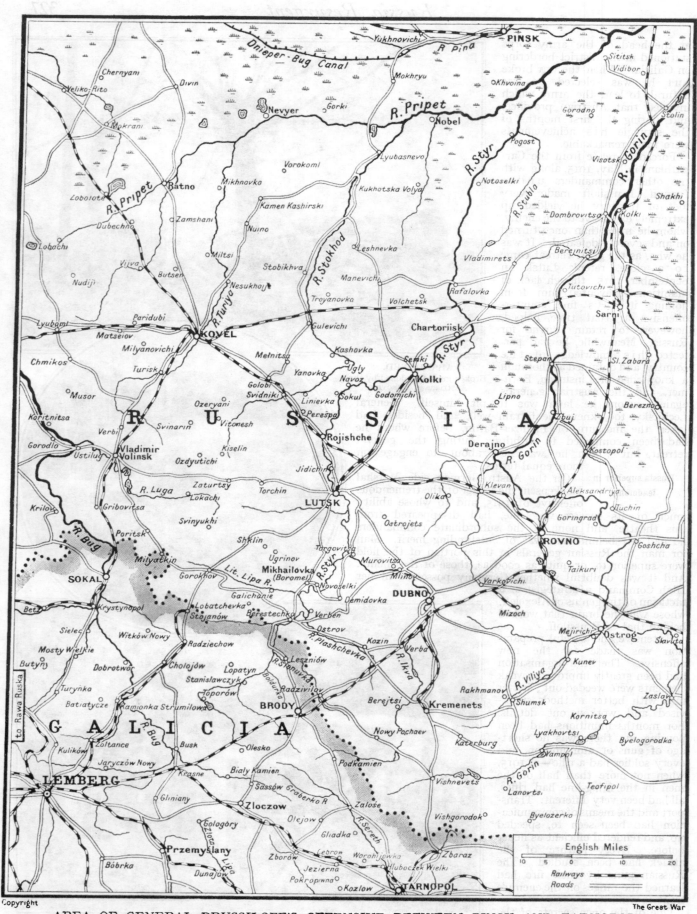

AREA OF GENERAL BRUSSILOFF'S OFFENSIVE BETWEEN PINSK AND TARNOPOL.

Region of operations in June and July, 1916, of the armies commanded by Generals Kaledin and Sakharoff. These armies formed half of the Russian left wing under the command of General Brussiloff, whose vigorous offensive marked the resurgence of Russia in 1916.

The Great War

doing to another which was being heavily assaulted. Seeing this, the Russians determined to deprive the enemy of this advantage by taking the offensive over so long a front that it would be excessively difficult, if not impossible, for him to work on his old plan. So Brussiloff attacked the Austro-Germans not at one point, or at several points, but at every point of his two-hundred-and-seventy-mile line. He applied on his whole front that unity of attack which the Allies, only in May, 1916, came to understand and agree was absolutely essential on all fronts for the triumphant prosecution of the war.

On Sunday, June 4th, an official Austrian communiqué gave the first news of Brussiloff's offensive to the world, which little suspected

FEEDING THE CAPTIVES.
Some of Russia's thousands of prisoners waiting for rations.

TEA-TIME: RUSSIANS PREPARING TO BREW THEIR NATIONAL DRINK.
Russian soldiers in camp in France drawing their supply of hot water for tea. The British soldier came to regard tea rather as a necessity than a luxury; to the Russian it was indispensable.

how important was the information. This statement said that in the morning the Russians brought their artillery into play against the whole of the Austrian north-eastern front, and that their fire was especially violent on the Dniester, on the Lower Strypa, in the region north-west of Tarnopol, and in Volhynia, where the army of the Archduke Joseph Ferdinand near Olika, covering a front of seventeen miles, was being subjected to a severe bombardment. After mentioning that a Russian gas attack on the Dniester had failed to do the Austrians any harm, it concluded with the remark that everywhere there were indications that assaults by infantry were imminent. Next day the Russian Chief Headquarters reported in somewhat laconic sentences that fighting had begun the previous morning " from the Pripet River front to the Rumanian frontier," and that the Russians had won considerable successes in many sectors, capturing 13,000 prisoners, besides guns and machine-guns. It was added, however, that the struggle was developing further, and the manner in which it was developing was shown by the significant words, " Our artillery is progressively demolishing the enemy's works and shelters, and as the success of ·the artillery preparation becomes evident, our infantry advances and captures the enemy positions."

These despatches.but dimly suggested what was happening and was about to happen. Later on June 4th, in a second

communiqué, the Austrians claimed that Brussiloff's offensive had been expected for a long time by them, but in reality they looked for nothing so tremendous as actually occurred, or they never would have started their drive against Italy. Towards the end of May, Vienna had announced some attacks by the Russians on the Bukovina frontier, and bombardments of the Volhynian front; it noted what it called an artillery battle along the whole line on June 1st. These operations may have prepared them to a certain extent, but certainly gave them no uneasiness.

In the west it was almost universally believed that Russia was only making a gallant attempt to relieve the pressure, then very formidable, on the Italians in the Trentino, but it soon was apparent that it was ever so much more than that. When on June 7th Petrograd stated that the Russian operations had resulted, up to noon on the preceding day, in the taking of upwards of 40,000 prisoners and nearly eighty guns, with fifty trench-mortars and over one hundred and thirty machine-guns, it was everywhere seen that Brussiloff must be moving on a very large scale, and that great events were in the wind.

Early in the morning of June 4th **Brussiloff's terrific** the deep roar of the Russian guns was **blows** heard all along that southern front.
Particularly heavy fire was directed on selected strategic points, where the ranges had been got, the heaviest being poured on the Olika-Dubno sector in Volhynia and the Okna positions in the Bukovina, but it was heavy everywhere. This intense bombardment lasted for twelve to thirty hours on the various parts of the Austrian line, according to circumstances. Here and there the trenches of the enemy were completely flattened out, as at Okna, but the general effect of the Russian artillery preparation was to cut great openings in his barrier wire entanglements, and provide avenues for the advance of the Russian infantry and, where possible, cavalry.

As these big breaches in the ramparts of wire were disclosed, the Russian foot, regardless of the storm of bullets from the hostile rifles and machine-guns, swarmed up to and through them, and with their bayonets made short work of their adversaries, who, deprived of support from their second line, and unable to retire on it, owing to the curtain of shrapnel interposed by the guns in the Russian rear, had no choice but death or surrender. Then the Russian cavalry pushed forward, and rode on through the gaps.

By this action of the Russians numerous enemy first-line trenches and deep dug-outs, all of which had been constructed with the most sedulous care, and **Enemy trapped** fortified with sand-bags, large beams of **but courageous** wood, and cement, were turned into so many prisons. The Austrians were trapped, but during the first hours, at least, of the offensive they fought with furious courage and the utmost determination, the bravery of the Hungarians being especially noticeable. In and about a front of trenches only a very few miles long the Russians buried 4,000 of their foes—a fact which clearly told of the strong resistance they met and overcame. The second communiqué, issued by the Austrians on June 4th, spoke of a bitter struggle at Okna, and mentioned that stubborn fights were continuing around Olika, but even on that day Russian infantry and cavalry had swept beyond the latter town and were miles on their westward march, carrying all before them. Here not only was the enemy's first line shattered, but all his lines were destroyed: his front was completely broken.

It so happened that, by one of the many minor ironies of the war, June 4th was the birthday of the Archduke Frederick, the Austrian Generalissimo, and celebrations of the event were being held at his headquarters and elsewhere. The Russian offensive, with its deep smashing in of his front, was Brussiloff's present to him. Tidings of what was going on, particularly at Olika, in which they were vitally interested, broke in on the Archduke's commanders at Lutsk as they were feasting in his honour, and before they realised it, their fortress was in dire peril. They could not at first believe that their heavily-fortified entrenchments had been destroyed, and though they made a belated effort to stem the Russian flood, it was of no avail. In this sector Lutsk was the immediate objective of the Russians, and they were not to be denied.

On June 5th and 6th Brussiloff's offensive began really to develop amazingly. On the former day the Austrians were forced to withdraw for three miles from their first-line trenches at Okna, on their extreme right flank, thus preparing the way for the triumphs of Lechitsky in Bukovina. But also on that day and on the next the Russians under Kaledin's leadership made even more sensational progress in their advance from Olika towards Lutsk. Here the assaults of the Russian troops proceeded in waves of thousands of men, fresh forces being thrown into the fighting masses as opportunity offered. A few miles lower down in the same district they were marching victoriously upon the same goal from the direction of Mylnoff. All this region was of extreme significance strategically, as the Austro-German bases and railways lay behind it. No great distance away, west of Lutsk, was the Vladimir Volynsk base on the railway from Kovel to Rawaruska, and north-west of the fortress was Kovel itself, where the railways from Rovno and Sarny met and joined up with other important lines. Vladimir Volynsk and Kovel were the obvious Russian objectives, with Kovel much the more valuable of the two. Rushing on rapidly and irresistibly, and corralling thousands of prisoners as his main columns converged on Lutsk from the east and south-east, Kaledin captured the stronghold in the evening of June 6th without having to beat down any serious resistance there, so demoralised had the enemy become.

Lutsk was once more in Russian hands. It had powerful defence works, and its capture should have given Kaledin much trouble, but practically it was taken by surprise, owing to the panic caused by **Broken Austrians** the impetuous energy of the Russian **panic-stricken** advance. So great were the dismay and confusion of the enemy that in his wild retreat he left intact a considerable number of 4 in. and other heavy pieces with their charges still in them, and in many instances cases of shells newly opened were discovered beside the guns. In Lutsk the Russians found large quantities of military stores in excellent condition, besides hundreds of wounded, as the Austrians had not had time to clear their hospitals.

Within little more than sixty hours of the initiation of his offensive, Brussiloff was able to report to the Tsar and Alexeieff, both anxiously awaiting news at the Imperial Headquarters, this very substantial success, together with other, if less striking, gains on his whole front. Late that

EFFECTS OF GENERAL BRUSSILOFF'S GREAT OFFENSIVE: RUSSIA INVADED BY ARMIES OF TEUTON PRISONERS.
Thousands of Austrian prisoners on their way to a Russian internment camp. These men were captured during General Brussiloff's great offensive in Volhynia in the summer of 1916.

evening the Tsar telegraphed to Brussiloff in reply to tell his beloved troops that he was watching their bold deeds with pride and satisfaction, and, appreciating their dash, to express to them his heartfelt gratitude for their splendid achievements. This inspiring message from their "Little Father" kindled fresh flames of devotion in the breasts of the Russian soldiers. The taking of Lutsk was an encouragement to all the Allies, and a correspondingly heavy blow to the Central Powers.

From his starting-point Kaledin had advanced no fewer than twenty-five miles in about two and a half days, and he had been fighting all the way. On June 7th and 8th his forces were crossing the Styr and its tributary the Ikva at many points, and hotly pursuing the beaten Austrians, who, however, made an attempt to check him at some places. By this time German detachments, sent in great haste by Linsingen or Hindenburg from the German front above the Pripet, had begun to come. upon the scene and stiffen the Austrian resistance. On the 8th and 9th a sanguinary battle raged at Rojishche, thirteen miles north of Lutsk, and the town at which was the chief passage over the Styr.

In this desperate affair the youngest Russian soldiers, who had been with the

FLEEING FROM THEIR NATIVE LAND.

In ramshackle farm-carts, old men, women, and children made their way out of Czernovitz as the Austrians entered the town. Most of the refugees found asylum in Rumania.

Colours only two or three months, greatly distinguished themselves, their deeds of valour vying with those of men belonging to war-seasoned regiments. Russian Territorials drove the Austro-Germans, by dint of sheer hard fighting, from the strong bridge-head at Rojishche, captured the town, and took about 2,000 prisoners, most of whom were Germans, besides two guns, several machine-guns, and much other booty. It was a wonderful feat of arms on the part of Russia's young troops, and the place was important both as a military base of the enemy, and from its position on the Rovno-Kovel railway, the light railways from Lutsk on the south and Kolki on the north joining the main line there.

Of even greater importance than Rojishche, and equally important with Lutsk, was Dubno, the southernmost fortress of the Volhynian Triangle, and there also the Austrians, with German supports, made a determined stand in order to prevent the Russians from crossing the Ikva; but they failed utterly, though not without first exacting a heavy penalty from their conquerors. This region was one of oak forests, and easily capable of the most formidable defence; the enemy took every advantage of the natural difficulties of the position,

REFUGEES FROM CZERNOVITZ.

Refugees from Czernovitz awaiting a train at Burdujeni Station. Czernovitz changed hands several times in the course of the war. In circle: Distributing bread to the weary, hungry fugitives from Czernovitz.

A NIGHT ATTACK: RUSSIANS AND GERMANS DIVIDED ONLY BY THE PERMANENT WAY.

On a certain front a detachment of Russians held a village through which a railway ran on a slight embankment. The Germans attacked at night, and a sharp engagement resulted, in which the opposing forces were separated only by the width of the permanent way. The Germans sent up rockets which burnt in great flares, while the Russians used rockets which burst in innumerable stars and kept alight for about five minutes but was unable in the end to withstand the fierce and prolonged Russian assaults, and the fort and town of Dubno fell on the same day as Rojishche. The Russians had never relinquished Rovno, and now they had regained possession of the two other fortresses of the Volhynian group—Lutsk and Dubno. Westward of Dubno they marched on, forcing the enemy back continually, and occupied Demidovka. Southward, on June 13th, they had got as far as Kozin, nearly twenty miles from Dubno, in the direction of Brody on the Rovno-Lemberg railway, and on the 16th entered Radzivilov, some miles closer to Lemberg. In this region, where Kaledin's army joined up with that of Sakharoff, the front of the Austro-Germans had first been deeply pierced and then rent to pieces, while Lemberg though still some distance off, was threatened.

Those swift and crashing successes of Brussiloff's offensive, with the menace they necessarily implied to vital Austro-German centres, could not but attract the most earnest attention of the German High Command, and several German divisions were railed **Kaledin's** down from the north and thrown into the **irresistible advance** conflict. But in spite of the increasing numbers of Germans hurried forward to the assistance of the discomfited Austrians, Kaledin for some days longer continued his advance towards Vladimir Volynsk and Kovel after the capture of Lutsk and Rojishche.

On June 12th he took Torchin, on the high-road from Lutsk to Vladimir Volynsk, and rather more than half-way between the latter centre and Olika, where he had first broken through the enemy's front. On the following day he was fighting at Zaturtsy, still nearer Vladimir Volynsk. He had advanced nearly forty-five miles due west, and the Austrians had retired from the Styr to the Stokhod. With another column he struck up from Rojishche along the Rovno-Kovel railway towards the latter river, but some miles lower down that stream, the course of which flowed to the north, and on June 16th he reached Svidniki, some twenty-one miles from Kovel. It was obvious that Germany would have to make very great efforts if Kovel and Vladimir Volynsk were to be saved, and from her point of view it was essential to retain them.

What was known as the Lutsk Salient had now been formed. On the north it began at Kolki in a tract of marshy land, on the east side of the Styr. In this district fighting had been desperate. On June 10th the Austrians, who were in superior numerical strength, attacked the Russians as the day dawned at Semki, east of Kolki, and under cover of a concentrated fire forced Kaledin's troops across the Styr, but there the enemy was held up. Three days later Kaledin took Kolki, and afterwards advanced to Godomichi. From Kolki the salient ran along the Styr, through Sokul to Svidniki on the Stokhod, and thence went on to Zaturtsy, on the road from Lutsk to Vladimir Volynsk, where it reached what might be called its apex. South of Zaturtsy it was bounded by the line Lokachi-Svinyukhi, whence, bending eastward to the Styr again, it crossed that river and travelled along the Plashchevka, an eastern affluent of the Styr to Kozin. Roughly speaking, it was a semicircle, of which Olika was the centre, its radius being about forty-five miles.

UNLOADED HAY AT A RAIL JUNCTION.
Scene at a supply section in Galicia. In the middle distance, placed on a truss of hay, is an accordion, a favourite musical instrument of the Russian soldier.

The Austrian positions on the Plashchevka had been stormed by Sakharoff on June 15th, after a terrible battle, in which, according to the Russian communiqué, a young Russian regiment, led by Colonel Tatarnoff, after a fierce fight, forded the deep river, with its waters rising to the chins of its men. "One company was engulfed, and died an heroic death, but the valour of their comrades and their officers resulted in the disorderly flight of the enemy, of whom seventy officers and 5,000 men were taken prisoners. Two guns, a great many machine-guns, thousands of rifles and cartridges, and enormous reserves of barbed-wire were captured."

It was chiefly against the Lutsk Salient that the Germans, under Linsingen, who relegated their defeated Austrian and Hungarian friends to an entirely subordinate position, now proceeded to start a powerful and for a while not unsuccessful counter-offensive, beginning about June 16th. It was certainly high time for the Germans to bestir themselves. Kaledin was only some twenty miles from Kovel and Vladimir Volynsk, and Sakharoff about sixty miles from Lemberg. In the course of the twelve days of his advance Kaledin had taken nearly 72,000 prisoners including over 1,300 officers, eighty-three guns, two hundred and thirty-six machine- **German reserves** guns, and a vast quantity of all kinds of **from all fronts** material. These large figures pointed to the thorough beating he had given his opponents, and were eloquent of the condition to which he had reduced them. To restore the situation, which was equally bad for their ally on two other parts of the front, and promised well nowhere, the Germans now brought reinforcements from France, amounting to four divisions, with all possible speed. According to a memorandum found by the Russians in the note-book of a dead Austrian officer, a whole German army corps was transferred from Verdun to Kovel in six days. At the same time the Austrians withdrew all their reserves from the Trentino, thus weakening their offensive against Italy. They even brought up troops from Serbia and Albania. Taking full advantage of his superior railway facilities, the enemy in one way or another succeeded in concentrating forces to attack the Russians and, with his heavier artillery, to check them.

Severe fighting developed on the whole of the Lutsk Salient during the next week, slackened off for a few days, and then broke out with fresh fury towards the end of the month. It was reported that Hindenburg, alarmed by the Russian victories, had sent General Ludendorff, his Chief of Staff, and generally believed to be due the credit for most of his triumphs, to Kovel to superintend the counter-offensive of Linsingen, but his name did not appear in the despatches. Two or three days earlier the old Field-Marshal had tried to relieve the pressure on the Austrians by launching a series of local assaults on the Russian front from the Baltic to the Pripet, but four of these completely failed, and only the fifth made slight temporary progress. On June 16th Vienna, however, plucked up a little heart, announced that in Volhynia " new fighting " was developing along the entire front, and asserted that the Russians had been repulsed with severe losses. What had happened was that at Sokal, north of Rojishche, the Austro-Germans were on that day defeated, with a loss of nearly two thousand prisoners, and were equally unsuccessful at other points on the salient. But it was the case that Kaledin had to slow down his advance in presence of the vastly augmented numbers and better fighting quality of the German element of the enemy forces.

Godomichi village, near Kolki, on the northern flank of the salient, was the scene of violent encounters, in which the Russians broke the enemy's front and took hundreds of Germans prisoners. But for several days the chief centre of the struggle, brought about by Linsingen's counter-offensive, was Svidniki, which had just been captured by Siberian troops, assisted by the famous Hussars of White Russia, who charged through three extended German lines and sabred two companies. On June 17th and 18th the Germans made furious attacks on the town, being greatly helped by fire from an armoured train, but the Russians defeated them, sotnias of Cossacks making a flank assault that threw the hostile ranks into great disorder.

The most that the official German communiqué asserted was that Russian attacks in this district were " partially repulsed." But in the region of Lokachi the Germans on the 19th scored a success, asserting that they took 3,500 Russian prisoners there. The result was the other way in a san- **Russian success at** guinary battle between Vorontchin and **Vorontchin** Kiselin, which occurred on that day, and on the 22nd German attacks on Vorontchin were overwhelmed, the enemy being put to flight. Some miles farther south the Austro-Germans were routed near Sviniuky. Meanwhile, stubborn fighting continued near Godomichi, the village of Gruziatin, two miles north of the former place, changing hands several times. But in all this area the Russians found the general pressure of Linsingen so heavy that they could not advance, and deemed it wise to retire from some of the positions on the Stokhod and make a fresh alignment on the Styr. They also withdrew from Lokachi for a distance of four to six miles in an easterly direction on the Zaturtsy-Shklin-Lipa line. The Germans had succeeded, at least for the time, in forcing Kaledin back from both Kovel and Vladimir Volynsk.

For the next few days there was something in the nature of a lull in this part of the salient, now somewhat flattened

CUT OFF BY ARTILLERY FIRE: A LARGE HAUL OF TEUTON CAPTIVES.
Russian sentries escorting a batch of Austrian prisoners to the rear. The total of Teuton soldiers captured by our ally was numbered in hundreds of thousands. The smaller illustration shows three artillery officers directing a bombardment from an advanced trench in Bukovina.

RUSSIAN CHARGE UNDER COVER OF SMOKE.
Smoke clouds, to evade or conceal attack, were employed with good effect in the warfare on the Russian front. This illustration shows Russian infantrymen charging the enemy lines under such improvised cover.

SCATTERING DESTRUCTION IN THE VOLHYNIAN FIELDS.
This photograph, taken outside Dubno when the Austrians were in possession of the town, shows a shell bursting in the long grass in which Russian troops were taking cover.

out by the German counter-offensive. Then the enemy attacked again, and with redoubled fury. He had now railed up many heavy guns of various calibre, including 8-in. cannon, and large quantities of explosive shells. On June 28th Berlin announced that the Germans had stormed and captured the village of Linievka, which lay west of Sokal and about three miles from Svidniki. In the first days of July there were violent battles, fought with great fury on both sides. From Linievka the Germans, under cover of an extremely heavy fire, started an offensive movement, but it was held up, with a loss to them in prisoners alone of over eight hundred, **Futile Austrian** besides nine machine-guns. Near **massed attacks** Zaturtsy the Austrians, in massed formations, delivered a powerful assault on the Russians along the Lutsk-Vladimir Volynsk road, but they were checked and thrown back.

In the neighbourhood of Ugrinov, between Shklin and the Styr, the Austro-Germans, who had been reinforced, pressed the Russians closely, but at a critical stage of the encounter relief came to Sakharoff's troops from a flanking charge of Cossacks led by their colonel, Kortchenoff. The enemy immediately gave ground, and the Russian infantry advanced, capturing nearly a thousand prisoners. The contest throughout this portion of the salient was of the most savage character. The usually merciful Russians had been infuriated by the German use of explosive bullets, and were not disposed to be easy with their foes. Fresh troops were now arriving to reinforce them. On July 6th the Petrograd communiqué spoke of the "most desperate battles" between the Stokhod and the Styr, and of the "extreme tenacity" of the enemy on the Lipa, another of the Styr's tributaries. Germany was, in fact, making a supreme effort in this area, and the result seemed to hang in the balance.

But in the meantime fresh features had developed, both above the Pripet on the main battle-front and on the northern flank of the salient. More influential still, through its effect on the whole war, the Franco-British offensive, which had begun on July 1st, was progressing favourably on the Somme in France. These three new factors, together with what had gone or was going on on Brussiloff's front below the Lutsk Salient (about to be recorded), finally prevented Germany from sending further formidable reinforcements to Linsingen and the other commanders opposed to the Russians in the south, or to anyone on any front whatsoever. She no longer was in a position to do anything to help her allies with large masses of troops swung from one front to another, and, indeed, from this time onward practically her sole preoccupation was to defend herself. She strove to mend matters, as against Brussiloff, by putting Hindenburg in command of all the Austro-German forces, with the exception of a small part which, to save the face of Austria, remained ostensibly under the control of the Dual Monarchy. Moreover, she ordered the Turks to despatch assistance to the Austrians in Galicia and the Carpathians, and they complied by transferring three divisions from Thrace, but their appearance in the Russian theatre could have no decisive effect. The tide had turned definitely—away from Germany. In that first week of July, 1916, the aspect of the entire colossal conflict, east and west, was changing completely.

The first of these fresh features was a strong offensive on the front above the Pripet by the Russians in the neighbourhood of Baranovichi, a great railway junction and a place of cardinal importance to the Germans. With a view to relieve the pressure on the Lutsk Salient, General Alexeieff instructed General Evert, in command of the central Russian armies, to attack in force on July 3rd the enemy south of Tsirin, some miles north of Baranovichi. At the same time the Russians attacked Hindenburg at other points farther north. At Tsirin, Evert broke through two lines of the German defensive organisation, capturing eleven guns and nearly 3,000 prisoners. Severe fighting took place near Smorgon, on the Minsk-Vilna railway, and at Tcherneshki the Russians **General Evert** carried part of a German position. South **engages Hindenburg** of Lake Naroch a portion of the enemy's first-line trenches was stormed with the bayonet. It looked as if Evert were making a great bid for both Baranovichi and Vilna; in reality, he was keeping Hindenburg too busy to dream of sending many fresh troops to the aid of Linsingen. For about a week a series of extraordinarily violent and sanguinary battles raged in this area, with daily offensive and counter-offensive movements of extreme ferocity. Evert was at pains to maintain the illusion he had created; then, when Alexeieff was satisfied with affairs

335

below the Pripet, the Russians withdrew to their original front, and the struggle in these sectors died away.

Kaledin, although holding the Austro-Germans well on the line to which he had retired on the Lutsk Salient, required reinforcements in order to resume his advance towards Kovel and Vladimir Volynsk. The sudden appearance of a large army on his northern flank, on and above the Sarny-Kovel railway, was the second of the new features alluded to above. This was the Third Russian Army, under General Lesh, which had been stationed above the Pripet. Lesh had won distinction in the Russo-Japanese War, and had been in command of the Russian forces opposing Mackensen on the Lublin-Cholm line in August, 1915. He was regarded as one of the ablest of the generals of Russia, and events soon proved the accuracy of this estimate. He took the field above Kaledin, first in the region of the Lower Styr, between the Pripet and the Sarny-Kovel railway, and struck shrewdly and swiftly towards the Stokhod. In this area the enemy's troops were partly German, belonging to the command of Prince Leopold of Bavaria. Lesh had not been expected by the Germans, perhaps on account of the difficult swampy country, which in anything but a very dry season made

ETERNAL PROBLEM OF DEFENCE.
Russian soldiers erecting rough wooden screens from shell fire. These consisted of tree-trunks consolidated with mould.

WITH THE RUSSIAN ARMY AERONAUTS.
Type of captive balloon used on the Russian front for the purpose of artillery observation. Hidden in a wood, the envelope had been partially deflated, and was guarded by sentries.

military operations on a large scale well-nigh impossible. The weather, however, had been hot, and the small streams, lakelets, and marshes in which the district abounded had become negotiable.

It was on July 7th that a Petrograd communiqué first gave news of the activities of Lesh and his army, by remarking that the battles to the west of the Lower Styr continued with much success for the Russian arms. In the region of Volchetsk, Lesh drove the Germans and the Austrians from their fortified positions, and put them to flight. In the course of the fighting the Russians took a battery of six Krupp guns, which, in the words of the communiqué, "had hardly time enough to fire a few shots." By that date Lesh had advanced from his starting-point a distance of eleven miles, driving the enemy out of Manevichi, a station on the Sarny-Kovel railway, and capturing in the pursuit seven guns, four of which were heavy pieces. Immediately to the south of the railway the troops, after a sharp fight, occupied the village of Kamaroff.

After dislodging the Austro-Germans from many points south of Nobel on the Pripet, Lesh marched on towards the Lower Stokhod, and on July 8th reached Leshnevka, a few

miles from that river. On the same day, another column gained possession of the enemy's well-organised entrenchments east of the small towns of Ugly and Navoz, and pressing on the heels of the retreating foe crossed the Stokhod near the former place.

Up to this date Lesh had "bagged" upwards of 12,000 unwounded prisoners, forty-five guns, big and little, as many machine-guns, and huge quantities of munitions and supplies, including forage. His soldiers fought with wonderful dash. The speedy capture of the passage of the river near Ugly was due to the courage of Colonel Kautseroff, of the 283rd Pavlograd Regiment, who, rushing to the head of his men, and calling on them to follow him, crossed the bridge, which was in flames, and got to the other side safely, in spite of heavy artillery and rifle fire.

Presently the Russians were lined all along the Lower Stokhod, which was Lesh's immediate objective, with Kovel behind it. On the 11th and for some days afterwards there was heavy fighting on the river, as the Germans had brought up some troops and many big guns, but the Russians maintained themselves in the positions they had conquered. **Crossing a flaming bridge** Once the enemy succeeded in getting to the right-hand bank near Gulevichi, but was repulsed, with a loss in prisoners of eight hundred men.

Not only was Lesh successful in this local offensive, but his action, by indicating an enveloping movement from the north on Linsingen's forces who were attacking Kaledin, had at once a beneficial effect on the struggle of the Russians on the Lutsk Salient. It speedily was clear that the German counter-offensive was able to make no farther progress, and for a little time, along portions of this area, the fighting took on the character of trench warfare.

The great fact remained that Linsingen had failed, although for his effort, which was very determined, he had had the support of very many heavy guns and of the famous 20th Braunschweig Division, dubbed by the German Kaiser the "Steel Division," on account of its exploits in France. By a coincidence, this division was confronted by a Russian force known as the "Iron Division," which for four days withstood all the attacks of the Braunschweigers, finally repulsing them. It was stated that during a pause in the contests between the two the Germans put up a placard on which was inscribed : "Your Russian iron is not worse than our German steel, but for all that we shall smash you." In reply the Russians exhibited a rival bill, having written on it : "Well, then, German sausage, just try !"

But the trench warfare did not last long, for on July 8th Kaledin broke through his opponents' line, and two days later was fighting with success a pitched battle on the Rovno-Kovel railway at Svidniki. At Kiselin he put the enemy to flight by a sudden blow. A week later, near Svinyukhi, he thrust back by a vigorous **Germans admit** counter-offensive a German attack in **serious defeat** massed formation. On the 20th Lesh defeated a formidable assault on his lines near Ugly. The middle of the month was marked by heavy rain, which flooded the marshy reaches of the Stokhod, prevented movements in force, and gave the enemy an opportunity of strengthening his defensive works in the region of that river.

Towards the end of the month, however, Kaledin once more advanced and was not to be gainsaid. Fighting with great energy, he pushed Linsingen out of his heavily fortified entrenchments at Trysten, a pivotal point about four miles from the Stokhod, and forced him to the opposite side of the stream. It was a serious defeat for the Germans, who admitted it in an official communiqué by stating, "North-west of Lutsk, after severe unsuccessful attacks, the enemy succeeded in penetrating our lines at Trysten, and obliged us to evacuate the positions we still held in front of the Stokhod." Not often was Berlin so truthful.

At the beginning of August there was tremendous and widespread fighting, particularly strenuous at Stobikhva and Lyubashevo, north of the Sarni-Kovel railway, in all this part of Volhynia, but in the upshot the Germans, under the unrelaxing pressure of Kaledin and Lesh, were compelled to retire from **Pressure of Kaledin** most of their ground on the left bank of **and Lesh** the Stokhod, including the bend formed by that river where it approaches the Styr. At that time the Russians were about twenty miles from Kovel, north, east, and south of it, the point they held nearest it being Vitonesh, eighteen miles south-east, this town also being about the same distance from Vladimir Volynsk. On August 3rd they were on the Stavok, a western tributary of the Stokhod. The general position a week later in this northerly part of the Lutsk Salient—to retain that name, though there was no longer really a salient—was that the Russians, having driven the Austro-Germans from the western bank of the Stokhod, after overcoming as stubborn a resistance as any seen in the war, had no great natural obstacle to surmount in their advance on Kovel or Vladimir Volynsk, to both of which their menace was now very direct.

On the southerly face of the Lutsk Salient the Russians, under General Sakharoff, did even greater things. In the first week of July the counter-offensive of Linsingen was directed in this area from Shklin, almost due south of Torchin, Ugrinov, and the little River Lipa flowing into the

PAIN AND PITY FOLLOW ON THE HEELS OF VICTORY.
Wounded soldiers, Russian, Austrian, and German, awaiting attention by Red Cross men. At dawn of the summer day in 1916 when this photograph was taken the Russians under General Sakharoff had made an attack which resulted in an advance of seven miles.

AT THE END OF THE WIRE.
Russian soldiers receiving messages by telephone from their officers, who were observing the enemy movements from a point of vantage between the forks of a great tree.

Upper Styr. For it he had concentrated strong forces in the neighbourhood of Stojanow, the terminus of a railway from Lemberg, and Gorokhov, a few miles east of Sokal on the railway from Kovel to Rawaruska. His intention was to strike up at Lutsk from the south-west, and he hoped that under cover of his attacks west and north of that fortress he would be able to distract the attention of the Russians from this sector, but in this he was wrong, for Sakharoff, who opposed him here, showed himself far more than equal to him. Sakharoff, Chief of Staff to Kuropatkin during the Russo-Japanese War, proved both a strategist and a tactician of the highest order. Guessing what was the German plan, he anticipated and absolutely thwarted it, with disastrous consequences to the enemy.

Sakharoff's front in July extended from about Svinyukhi, south-west of Lutsk, across to the Lipa, **Sakharoff's brilliant** along which it lay, thence passed over the **offensive** Upper Styr, and continued along the Plashchevka to Kozin, on the Rovno-Dubno-Brody-Lemberg railway. The part of it north of the Lipa was heavily bombarded by Linsingen on July 14th. Two days later, with a fine prescience of the scheme of the enemy, which was on the very eve of maturing, and knowing that the best way to defeat it was to forestall it, Sakharoff suddenly attacked him. The Russian general struck unexpectedly at both of Linsingen's flanks, drove them in and crumpled them up. The Russian Main Headquarters afterwards characterised Sakharoff's action as a "clever manœuvre"; and so it was. East and south-east of Svinyukhi his "brave troops," in the words of the Petrograd communiqué of the 17th, "broke the resistance of the enemy," taking at Pustomity, near Svinyukhi, many guns and prisoners—this was on Linsingen's left wing. He

also advanced, notwithstanding desperate opposition, near the mouth of the Lipa, cleared the Austro-Germans from his side of that stream, and in places drove them in confusion and rout across it—this was on Linsingen's right wing.

Berlin's singular comment on this battle, which the Russians denominated the Battle of Mikhailovka, was: "South-west of Lutsk the Russian attack was arrested by a German counter-attack, and thereupon, in order to strengthen our defence line, our troops were withdrawn behind the Lipa without being molested by the enemy." Fighting continued next day, with the advantage to the Russians. Linsingen's counter-offensive was not only foiled, but smashed up. He **Surrender of Austrian** now had to stand on the defensive. In **Landwehr** these two days Sakharoff captured about 13,000 men, thirty guns, of which seventeen were heavies, thousands of rifles and shells, and an abundance of other war material.

On July 18th Sakharoff was bombarding the new German line on the Lipa with some of the big guns he had taken on the 16th, and was using the German shells. Having recovered somewhat, Linsingen, two days afterwards, attempted to advance on the line Zviniany-Elizaroff, but was quickly checked by Sakharoff, who on that same day and the following fought and won a great battle termed by the Russians the Battle of Berestechko, in this area. While making a feint on his left against the strong Austrian position at Ostrov, he delivered a powerful and successful assault from Novoselki on the flank of Linsingen, many of whose troops fled in disorder. In the vicinity of Verben the 13th Austrian Landwehr Regiment surrendered in a body.

RUSSIA'S ALLIES IN A NOBLE CAUSE.
Nurses and doctors of the British Field Hospital attached to the Russian Army operating in the region of the River Stokhod at lunch in the open. Note the Union Jack, which flies suspended from an adjacent tree.

BARRICADES ON THE RIVER BANK: SOME SPADE-WORK AT DUBNO.
Russian soldiers consolidating their position along the bank of the River Ikva, in the vicinity of Dubno. The Austrians were driven out of this town after hard fighting from house to house and garden to garden. Note the effect of shell fire on a large building to the left.

Consequent on the success of the 20th, the Russians advanced from Ostrov, and next day took by storm the town of Berestechko. While this operation was proceeding Colonel Tataroff, who was leading his men, was hit by a shell and fell from his horse, exclaiming that he was dying, but, raising himself by a supreme effort, he shouted to his troops to advance, and then expired. A splendid soldierly end in the midst of victory. In this battle Sakharoff added to his list of captures 15,000 men and ten guns. Berlin explained away this defeat by the statement that "after Russian attacks between Verben and Korsov (about twelve miles north of Brody) had been brought to a standstill, our salient jutting out towards Verben was withdrawn in view of enveloping attacks."

With scarcely a halt, Sakharoff continued to make marked progress. On July 23rd, after fierce, sanguinary encounters in the streets, he dislodged the Germans from the village of Galichanie, on the south bank of the Lipa. He began on the night of the 24th the third of the series of his great operations by breaking through the Austrian front, which was protected by rows of wire entanglements, on the River Slonuvka, an eastern tributary of the Upper Styr, in the Galician part of its course. To cover his real attack, which was directed towards Brody, Sakharoff attacked fiercely at Leszniow, farther west, and there the Austrians claimed some success, but it was only in appearance. All day long on the 25th the **Austrians routed on the Slonuvka** Russians in vast numbers pressed on across the Slonuvka, driving the routed foe before them and inflicting heavy losses. Next day they were fighting for the possession of the fords of the Boldurka, a more southern affluent of the Upper Styr, which it joined about nine miles north of Brody.

Vienna spoke of Russian repulses between Radzivilov and the Styr, but Sakharoff went on gaining ground. On the 27th the Russians were well on their way to Brody, and as they approached the town they heard explosions and saw fires breaking out in it. Their aeroplanes reported that processions of goods trains were leaving the place. The enemy was, in fact, preparing to evacuate Brody,

and was destroying such of his stores as he could not save. Early in the morning of July 28th Sakharoff captured the town. At the end of the month he had reached the Upper Sereth and its tributary the Graberko, from ten to sixteen miles south of Brody.

Sakharoff's magnificent contribution to Brussiloff's offensive, which in the north now embraced the entire area between the Sarni-Kovel railway and the Rovno-Lemberg railway, as well as the district above the former to the Pripet, was of the greatest tactical and strategical importance. The German troops under Linsingen and the Austrians under Böhm Ermolli had been thoroughly thrashed, with a loss to them, from July 16th to **Heavy enemy losses** 28th, of upwards of 40,000 prisoners, fifty guns, more than double that number of machine-guns and an enormous quantity of booty of all kinds. Sakharoff had victoriously advanced from forty to fifty miles, and his line of march south and south-westward menaced both the Rovno-Lemberg railway, with Lemberg itself, and the Austro-German army of General Bothmer, on the Strypa, west of Tarnopol. His successful offensive on the Sereth, which was beginning as July closed, continued into August, and threatened Bothmer with envelopment from the north.

In the first week of August the Austrians fiercely resisted his progress, which, in any case, was impeded by the marshy nature of the terrain, made all the more difficult by reason of heavy rains at the time. The enemy counter-attacked him many times on August 4th as he was crossing to the right bank of the Upper Sereth, but his efforts were of no avail, as the Russians occupied Zalose on August 6th, and moved on, though slowly, taking numerous prisoners, nearly 9,000 men being captured between August 4th and 6th. In this region the gallant troops of General Ekk, one of Sakharoff's army commanders, took between August 4th and 10th upwards of 14,000 prisoners, 5,000 of them being captured on August 10th. As the result of the victories of the Russians, the enemy was compelled to retreat from his fortified positions at Gliadki and Worohijowka, and on the 12th had to retire from a

The Great War

SOUTHERN AREA OF GENERAL BRUSSILOFF'S VICTORIOUS ADVANCE IN THE SUMMER OF 1916.

Galicia and Bukovina, where the Russian armies under Shcherbacheff and Lechitsky operated during the summer of 1916. These forces were the
southern half of the four armies constituting the Russian left wing, of which General Alexei Brussiloff was in supreme command.

string of other villages, which he tried with extreme desperation to hold, only three or four miles from the railway.

Sakharoff's enveloping movement now was of material assistance to General Shcherbacheff, who had been standing for about two months—or from the commencement of Brussiloff's offensive on June 4th—over against Bothmer, on the Strypa. On August 12th the Russian High Command issued a statement, which announced that the celebration by the valiant soldiers of Russia of the birthday of the Tsarevitch Alexis, who was sojourning in the theatre of war, happily coincided with the fall of the last sector of the powerfully-fortified rampart which the enemy had erected from the Pripet as far as the Rumanian frontier during the preceding

BIVOUAC AMONG THE TREES.
Russian infantry at ease on a farm near Czernovitz. A picturesque corner of one of the most sanguinary battlefields in the whole theatre of war.

CUMBERSOME VEHICLE OF AGGRESSION.
Type of Austro-Hungarian armoured train used on the eastern front. The armoured train, like the armoured motor-car, hardly realised expectations on either the eastern or the western front.

winter. "To-day," it added, "as the result of seven weeks of persistent effort on the part of the glorious troops of General Sakharoff and Shcherbacheff, under the direction of General Brussiloff, the fortified villages of Gliadki, Worohijowka, Cebrow, Jezierna, Pokropiwna, and Kozlow, the powerfully-organised wood of Burkanow, and the whole line of the River Strypa fell into our hands. The whole sector of the winter base position established by the enemy in front of Tarnopol and Buczacz is in our possession."

Naturally this great event, which was the completion of the first stage of Brussiloff's campaign, was the occasion of much rejoicing to Russia and the Allies. It, however, had been brought about not only by Sakharoff and Shcherbacheff, but also by the astonishingly brilliant offensive of General Lechitsky in Bukovina and in the whole region of the Dniester and the Pruth, which more than once held for a time the attention of the world and extorted its admiration.

Shcherbacheff's share in driving the Austro-Germans from their winter front was for several weeks somewhat negative, but in the start of the general offensive he was

successful in the sector of which Buczacz was the centre; opposite Tarnopol he failed to make any considerable impression. On his part of the line, as on every other part of it, the Russians, after an intense artillery preparation, attacked the enemy on June 4th in force. Their main assaults were in the direction of the three railways leaving Tarnopol for the west. These were the Tarnopol-Lemberg railway, which joined the line to Lemberg from Rovno, via Dubno, at Krasne; the Tarnopol-Lemberg railway running through Brzezany to Chodorow, where it linked up with the line from Stanislau and Halicz to Lemberg; and a third railway that went due south from Tarnopol on the east side of the Sereth to Czortkow, whence it turned west through Buczacz and Nizniow, reached Stanislau, and connected with the system from Lemberg.

Russian assaults on the railways

Of these railways the first, which was part of the Berlin Odessa line, was the most important. That the Germans attached special significance to it and the district was evident from the fact that the Austro-German forces had as their leader the German soldier Bothmer, supported by two German divisions, one of which was probably the 3rd Division of the Prussian Guard. Immediately west of Tarnopol the Austrian positions had been made exceedingly strong, and the country north of it to the head-waters of the Sereth and the Strypa, well-wooded and marshy, lent itself readily to defensive measures. From Zalose southward the line of the Strypa formed the front between the Russians and the enemy.

The struggle between Shcherbacheff and Bothmer fell into two sectors, the Forest of Burkanow lying in the middle. On June 4th the Russians penetrated the Austro-

ADVANCE GUARD OF GENERAL BRUSSILOFF'S VICTORIOUS ARMIES.
Russian cavalry scouts making their way across country on their small but wonderfully trained horses. Conditions of fighting on the eastern front, where the opposing lines moved to and fro over large stretches of territory, gave cavalry greater opportunity than it had on the less mobile western front.

German trenches north-west of Tarnopol at various points, but were unable to maintain their ground, and at Kozlow their attacks broke down in front of the wire entanglements under withering Austrian fire. Their assaults, which for a time were incessant, were carried out with the most reckless courage, but in this region did not prevail, though they were supported by some of the Belgian armoured cars. South of Burkanow the Russians were much more successful. On June 8th the Petrograd communiqué announced that on the Trybukowce-Jaslowiec front, which lay a little north of the Dniester, Russian infantry, under cover of artillery, carried by a vigorous blow several strong positions and had got quite close to the Strypa. They crossed the river on that day, entering Buczacz at dawn, and developing an offensive along the Dniester, carried after bitter fighting the village of Scianka, and in a battle of equal intensity took the village of Potok Zloty, both of these places being on the west side of the Strypa, the one eight and the other four miles beyond the stream.

Among the many captures they made was an artillery park with great quantities of shells at Potok Zloty, a battery of 4 in. howitzers at Ossowice, north of Buczacz, and a large number of prisoners, with the Staff of an Austrian battalion. Of the struggle in this sector Vienna

admitted in its communiqué of June 10th that on the Lower Strypa strong Russian forces "drove our troops from the eastern to the western bank." Higher up, near Tarnopol, Bothmer held firm, though his front from Buczacz to the Dniester had been completely broken. On the 11th, near Bobulince, north of Buczacz, the Austrians, assisted by German troops which had been brought into the district, forced the Russians back in a contest of the most terrific kind, nor were the latter able to regain the line which they had attained.

By an heroic effort Shcherbacheff over- **Shcherbacheff's**
threw the enemy on the 15th at **heroic effort**
Hajworonka, on the west bank of the
Strypa, but the Austrians rallied and put up a determined resistance, which was not ineffective. Nor was there much change during the rest of the month.

Fighting of an indecisive character continued throughout July on this part of the front, the Russians attacking near Gliadki in the northern sector, and lower down on the Strypa ; in the second week of the month stubborn combats took place at various points, in the course of which the Russians captured several thousand Austrians and Germans, besides guns and machine-guns. As the month drew to its end the Russians were on the Koropiec, south of Buczacz, but their gains had been small, and Bothmer maintained himself in what practically was his old position west of Tarnopol. He had, however, increasing reasons for uneasiness, for Sakharoff, to the north of him, had routed his friends, taken Brody, and was pressing downwards on his left flank, while on his right the progress of Lechitsky upwards was not less dangerous. As August began, Germany showed the apprehension with which she viewed the general situation by placing the whole eastern front under Hindenburg, with the exception of that portion of it on which Bothmer still stood, and also that which had been commanded by Pflanzer-Baltin. The part excepted was left in charge of Austria in the person of the Archduke Charles, heir-presumptive to the Emperor Francis Joseph, but Bothmer was responsible for it in reality.

Things grew worse and worse for the German general. In the second week of the month

KEEN EYES AND EARS.
Inside a Russian observation-post improvised in a tree. Two Russian officers were scanning the enemy position, while a third transmitted information by telephone.

Sakharoff, as has been narrated, had forced the Gliadki-Worohijowka sector, and Lechitsky was on the Koropiec, near the Dniester; thus both of Bothmer's flanks were enveloped. Thus threatened, the German commander, who had stubbornly held out on the Strypa since the start of Brussiloff's offensive ten weeks before, withdrew from his winter front on that river, and on August 12th retired to entrenched positions about ten miles west on the line of the Zlota Lipa, which he had had plenty of time to prepare. Next day Sakharoff was in Jezierna, and Shcherbacheff, who had captured upwards of 56,000 men, 55 guns, and over 200 machine-guns from the retreating Bothmer, was in Podhajce, close to the latter's new front, while lower down Russian troops were crossing the Zlota Lipa.

Splendid as the success of Sakharoff had been, it would scarcely have made Bothmer retreat from the Strypa had it not been for the not less splendid success which had attended the operations of General Lechitsky in Bukovina and in the region lying between the Dniester and the Pruth. Lechitsky had to negotiate most difficult country—more difficult, indeed, than that on any other sector of the front as it existed at the commencement of June. From the north it was protected by the formidable line of the Dniester, on which only one **Lechitsky shares** bridge-head—that at Uscieczko—was in **the laurels** the hands of the Russians when the great offensive began, and it offered no facilities for an invasion on a large scale. South-eastward, however, they held the north bank at Usciebiskupie, in Galicia, from which a road went south to Okna and Czernovitz, in Bukovina.

Below this crossing the mountains of the Berdo Horodyszcze walled in the east side of the duchy from the Russian province of Bessarabia, and below that again lay the then neutral frontier of Rumania. Thus the front of the Austrians under Pflanzer-Baltin was exceedingly strong by nature, and all that military science could do had been done to strengthen it. Yet Lechitsky not only forced it but broke it in pieces. Perhaps the Austrians believed that their positions were impregnable here also,

BRITISH MISSIONERS OF MERCY IN RUSSIA.
With a Red Cross field hospital on the Stokhod. A wounded Russian soldier was being put into the ambulance by the orderlies and a nurse.

and did not pay sufficient attention to them, in that arrogance of confidence which was their ruin; but they seemed to have been caught napping, or, at all events, insufficiently prepared.

There was one spot—for it was hardly more—and one spot alone, where Lechitsky had a chance; though it was little short of desperate, he took it. Into the Dniester flowed from the south the little stream called the Onut, and it made a cleft and a tiny valley among the hills of the Berdo between Okna and Dobronowce, in the north-east corner of Bukovina. On May 10th, 1915, it had been the scene of some wonderful exploits of the Cossacks of the Don. This spot was commanded by the Russian guns stationed on the high bank of the Dniester on the north side, and after being shelled was turned into a means of access into the duchy. On June 4th and 5th, as was related earlier in this chapter, Lechitsky launched his soldiers across the Dniester and took Okna. At the same time he attacked the Austrians south-east of it at Dobronowce, and after four days of terrific battling captured it.

The nature of this victory was explained in the Petrograd communiqué of June 11th, which announced: "In spite

REDOUBTABLE COSSACKS MOVING AGAINST THE RETREATING FOE.
Knee-deep in the long grass, a troop of Russian cavalry were moving forward in pursuit of fugitives of Bothmer's battalions. By the middle of 1916 the Russian Government had completely reorganised the Army. Munitions, guns, and trained men were forthcoming in quantities incredible to the Central Empires, whose leaders imagined that Russia had been practically vanquished.

of a desperate resistance on the part of the enemy, a violent flanking fire, and even curtain fire, and the explosions of whole sets of mines, General Lechitsky's troops took the enemy's position south of Dobronowce, fourteen miles north-east of Czernovitz." It added that in the region of this struggle the Russians captured 18,000 men, of whom three hundred and forty-seven were officers, and ten guns, while more prisoners were "still streaming in in large parties." Lechitsky had driven a wedge deep into the Austrian front.

Bukovina open to Lechitsky In their retreat the Austrians blew up the railway bridge at Jurkowce, and by June 10th had been driven out of Zaleszczyki, the most important bridge-head on the Dniester, where both a road and a railway crossed the river, and which had been the theatre of the most sanguinary and even ferocious fighting in previous phases of the war.

By the same date, or a day later, Lechitsky had entered Horodenka, the meeting place of several roads, and all Bukovina was open to him. Pflanzer-Baltin's beaten and disorganised forces fled partly up the Pruth, and

AUSTRIAN GAS APPARATUS IN RUSSIAN HANDS.
After the Germans first used poison gas at Ypres it had to be adopted by all the belligerents as a weapon of war. This Austrian apparatus was captured by the Russians.

partly towards Tysmienica and Stanislau. Advancing with great rapidity, Lechitsky was in Sniatyn on June 13th—this was the third time the Russians had occupied it since the war began—and was marching along the railway in the direction of Kolomea.

To the east he was fighting his way across the Pruth to Czernovitz, the doom of which was already sealed. He was held up for a while south of Bojan, and the strong line of the Pruth gave him a good deal of trouble; but at four o'clock in the afternoon of June 17th he captured the Czernovitz bridge-head on the left bank of the river by assault, and after bitter fighting at the fords—the bridges having been blown up by the Austrians—occupied the city, which now changed hands for the fifth time, the first being as far back as September, 1914. During these fluctuations most of the cosmopolitan people of the capital of Bukovina had adapted themselves with apparent aplomb to the changes which took place, and no later than a fortnight previously the town had been gay with flags in satirical commemoration of the time of its Russian occupation; it received the returning Russians with expressions of joy.

One of the curious things about the struggle for Czernovitz was that the city itself was only slightly damaged, and not more than six civilians were wounded. Sensational tales of the unnecessary, not to say reckless, destruction wrought by the Russian guns on the town were spread by Austrian and German journalists, but these stories were contradicted by one of its most prominent citizens in a Vienna paper. The main railway-station had been shelled and ruined, but otherwise the damage, which was not considerable, was confined to some streets near the river. The Russians had brought with them a Rumanian barrister, who had been mayor of Czernovitz during their second occupation of the place, and he was again installed in that office by the conquerors, now come to stay so far as could be foreseen.

With the capture of Czernovitz that portion of Pflanzer-Baltin's army which had been on the Pruth was thrown back upon the Carpathians, and Lechitsky lost no time in pursuing it and completing its defeat. Crossing the Bukovinian Sereth, one of his columns took Radautz on June 21st, having marched thirty miles south, and less than twenty-four hours later was in Gora Humora, twenty miles farther in the same direction. By the night of June 23rd it was in Kimpolung, but not till after a fierce struggle in which it captured over 2,000 Austrians. This movement, taken in connection with other of Lechitsky's movements in the same area north-westward, made him master of Bukovina, a land more than half the size of Wales, in nineteen days. It was the largest conquest of enemy territory the Allies had had to their credit for a long time in Europe.

Meanwhile other portions of Lechitsky's army were advancing westward. The town of Kuty, on the borders of Bukovina and Galicia, lying on the Czeremosz, a southern tributary of the Pruth, was taken after a fight on June 23rd, and the Russians advanced from it along the road to Pistyn, a few miles south of Kolomea, on which more of his columns were converging from the east and the north-east. Pressing on from Sniatyn, the Russians stormed the heights overlooking the Rybnica, another affluent of the Pruth, and on June 28th fought a great pitched battle on the ground lying between the Dniester and the Pruth, on a front bounded on the north by the Czortowiec, a southern tributary of the former river, and on the south by the Czerniawa, a northern tributary of the latter. Victory once more crowned the Russian banners, and in the course of this fighting about 10,500 Austrians were taken prisoners, as well as a battery of four heavy guns intact, horses and all, besides other guns. The enemy fled panic-stricken, abandoning large quantities of war material, and **The fall of** Kolomea, the centre of four railways, fell **Kolomea** to Lechitsky on the last day of the month.

Obertyn, thirteen miles north-east of Kolomea, was occupied, after an engagement, about the same date.

As July opened, Lechitsky pushed on westward. The Austrians, who had received reinforcements from the Italian front, made a stand seven miles beyond Kolomea, but were defeated with a loss of over 2,000 prisoners, most of whom, according to the Petrograd communiqué of July 2nd, were drunk. Here the Russians took seven guns. At Tlumacz, twelve miles to the east of Stanislau,

While one Russian soldier was intent upon his laundry, another was engrossed in fishing along the bank of the Stokhod.

Cossacks watering their horses at a river on the eastern front, whence the Austrians retreated before General Brussiloff's hammer blows.

PEACEFUL SCENES AND INCIDENTS IN THE ENVIRONMENT OF IMPERIAL ENMITY.

DIVISIONAL HEADQUARTERS OF A RUSSIAN ARMY.
Some Russian officers at Staff work in a residence adjacent to the firing-line. Throughout the war both the strategy and tactics of the Russian Staffs were of the highest order.

Bothmer, now in command of the enemy's troops in this sector, checked Lechitsky and threw him back for some distance. This, however, did not interfere with the main movement of the Russian general, and on the 4th he captured Potok Czarny, only six miles from Delatyn, and fifteen from Kolomea. Bothmer was again tackled both north and south of the Dniester, and this time with success, his forces in this region being overwhelmed and put to flight. Lechitsky's cavalry made a dash for the railway running from Delatyn south through the Jablonica Pass into Hungary, and on the 4th seized the small town of Mikuliczyn and cut the line, thus making it impossible for Austria to transfer forces from the south to this area. On the 5th a score of Cossacks swam the Dniester, took the village of Dolina, and captured over a hundred of the enemy and a gun. A terrific combat took place on the right bank of the big river near Zuyaczow on the same day, and after yet another desperate contest, in which Russian heroism and contempt for death were characteristically displayed, Lechitsky on the 8th occupied Delatyn, an important road centre and railway junction.

This marked an advance of nearly seventy miles from his starting-point five weeks before, and during that period he had fought and won many an engagement, and at least three really great battles. The name of Pflanzer-Baltin now disappeared from the story, its place being filled by that of General Kövess, who with Mackensen had been in charge of the Austro-German campaign against Serbia and Montenegro during the preceding autumn and winter. Bothmer remained in command of such of Pflanzer-Baltin's troops as had escaped westward from Lechitsky, and Kövess was at the head of the rest of the defeated Austrians in

Russians approach Hungary the Carpathians and Southern Galicia, who had been reinforced with drafts from the Trentino and Isonzo fronts, as well as part of some Turkish divisions, the balance going to Bothmer. Having compelled Bothmer to fall back at Nizniow to the north side of the Dniester, Lechitsky, with that river on his right and the mountains on his left, was secure on both flanks. In the far south of Bukovina his cavalry were scouting near the Kirlibaba Pass and striking into Hungary in the third week of the month, while fighting for the crests of the Carpathians was going on in other districts.

As the situation stood, Bothmer, thus deeply outflanked on his right, hunted off the Koropiec, and hearing of the victorious march of Sakharoff and his soldiers on his left, must have withdrawn from the Strypa, on which he still held a front of about twenty-five miles, had it not been the case that Lechitsky was unable to move. For days rain fell in torrents in this region, as in that of the Lutsk Salient, and snowstorms swept the Carpathians, jeopardising his communications and forbidding advance. Both the

Dniester and the Pruth were flooded, the former rising ten, and the latter sixteen feet. For two or three weeks Lechitsky was condemned to inaction, but on July 28th he threw the enemy back by a dashing coup in the direction of Stanislau, while the division of natives of the Caucasus charged and captured Jezierzany on the Tlumacz road, eighteen miles east of that city. In the beginning of August Berlin announced some successes for the enemy south of Jablonica in the mountains, an area in which German troops had made a reappearance. The Russians admitted that their advanced cavalry patrols had retired a short distance there. But for the moment the Carpathians interested Lechitsky very little, as his objective lay elsewhere.

Following up his attack along the Tlumacz road and to the north and south of it, he successfully advanced, in spite of the fiercest opposition, on a front of sixteen miles, on August 7th, stormed his way through Tlumacz to Tysmienica, took Nizniow on the Dniester, and entered Ottynia, farther south on one of its tributaries. The ground he gained was about seventy-four square miles in extent, and in these operations and in those of the next day, which gave him Tysmienica, he captured 7,500 men, nearly half of whom were Germans, five guns, and 63 machine-guns. More than that, Stanislau was appreciably nearer. On the 9th his troops occupied the right bank of the Bystrzyca, and took the joint railway-station at **Lechitsky captures Stanislau**

Chryplin, only two miles from Stanislau, which held the same position in the south with respect to Lemberg that Kovel did in the north; in other words, it was of immense strategical significance in that area of the war.

The Bystrzyca alone stood between Lechitsky and the town. The enemy had blown up all the bridges, and was arrayed on the opposite bank. There was an obstinate fight, but the Russians triumphed, and, on the 10th Stanislau fell into Lechitsky's hands, the Austro-Germans making off northwards in the direction of Halicz in full flight. No fighting actually occurred in Stanislau itself, for the enemy, seeing that the game was up in this quarter, had evacuated the town, which the Russians reported "untouched and in good order," with the exception of some parts of the railway. So, for the third time since the outbreak of the war, Russia held this extremely important Galician town. Fourteen months had elapsed since Lechitsky had yielded it up to Pflanzer-Baltin; that Austrian general was now in deep disgrace and a broken man, while his rival was in possession of it again. In the first ten days of August, Lechitsky's "bag" was over 10,600 Austro-German officers and men, with nine guns, many machine-guns, and other plunder. Lechitsky next turned his attention to the Carpathians, and on August 12th was pushing Kövess back at Jablonica once more.

With the retirement of Bothmer from the Strypa, as the result of pressure from Sakharoff and Lechitsky on his wings and Sncherbacheff on the centre, Brussiloff's marvellous offensive, as conducted by these three generals and Lesh and Kaledin, reached a definite stage. In seventy days the Russians had advanced on their whole southern front from ten miles in the middle to sixty and eighty miles respectively on the flanks, and, including Bukovina, had reconquered several thousand square miles of territory. Their capture of prisoners was simply colossal, and it was difficult to understand how Austria-Hungary could long survive such losses. According to an official Petrograd statement, which gave the figures up to August 12th, Kaledin and Lesh took 2,384 officers, 107,225 rank and file, 147 guns,

459 machine-guns, and 146 bomb and mine throwers; Sakharoff took 1,967 officers, 87,248 rank and file, 76 guns, 232 machine-guns, 119 bomb and mine throwers, and 128 powder-carts; Shcherbacheff took 1,267 officers, 55,794 rank and file, 55 guns, 211 machine-guns, 29 mine and bomb throwers, and 129 powder-carts; and Lechitsky took 2,139 officers, 100,578 rank and file, 127 guns, 424 machine-guns, 44 bomb and mine throwers, and 35 powder-carts. The total of prisoners was nearly 360,000 men, and of guns over four hundred, in addition to vast quantities of every description of war material, including twenty miles of light railways. The moral of the enemy was thoroughly shaken, while that of the Russians continued superb, though their wonderful victories were not achieved without commensurate sacrifices. It was estimated that the total losses of the enemy were not far short of a million men. One very great result of Brussiloff's success, coupled with other factors all making in favour of the Entente Powers, was that Rumania, towards the end of that August, threw in her lot with the Allies, declared war on Austria-Hungary, and forthwith invaded Transylvania.

The fall of Erzingan

While Russia was achieving so much in Europe, she also was active in Armenia and Persia, where the Grand Duke. Nicholas conducted her operations, his chief executants being General Yudenitch in the one area and General Baratoff in the other. In Asia the struggle was chequered. Russia's conquest of Erzerum and her march west of that stronghold aroused Enver Pasha and the Turkish governing clique to fresh efforts, and in April and May the Grand Duke was confronted by greatly augmented Turkish forces. But he captured Trebizond on April 18th, after winning a two-days' battle on the Kara Dere, in which the Russian Black Sea Fleet gave material assistance.

During May, however, the Turks were strong enough to take the offensive against him, and in the course of that month drove him back at Askala and Mamakhatun. Throughout most of June the Russians stood on the defensive, retiring in some cases from positions they had conquered, and the Turks pressed on towards Erzerum. It was not till July that Yudenitch was in a position to renew the attack. The first intimation of the progress he was making was given on the 12th of that month, when it was announced from Petrograd that he had recaptured Mamakhatun, taken nearly 2,000 prisoners, and was marching on to Erzingan, while the Turks were repulsed

in the mountainous region of the Chorokh. A further success was chronicled on the 15th in the capture of Baiburt, midway on the Erzerum-Trebizond road, and ten days later all Russia rejoiced over a more important and striking triumph in the fall of Erzingan itself, a considerable military station and otherwise of strategic value. With the taking of this centre the conquest of Armenia was practically complete, and the Tsar sent a telegram in which he congratulated " with all his heart " his brave Army of the Caucasus on the victory.

But the Turkish offensive was not thoroughly overcome, for on other parts of Russia's long Asiatic front it was continuing and even making headway. The Turks, in their general plan of campaign, which had been brilliantly worked out for them by a young German officer of talent, struck along the whole of the Russian line. After some success they failed, as was seen, on the Grand Duke's front from the Black Sea to Erzerum, but in the south-east, in the district of Lake Van, they took from him the towns of Bitlis and Mush in the second week in August, and for some time the aspect of affairs in this region was unpromising for the Russians, who also had been forced to retreat from Mesopotamia into Persia. In May it had been thought among the Allies that the Grand Duke, through Baratoff, was in a position to attack Mosul, and perhaps cut off the Turks at Bagdad.

Events utterly belied these anticipations. On June 8th the Russians were defeated at Khanikin, less than a hundred miles from Bagdad, on the Teheran-Hamadan-Bagdad road, and driven across the mountains into Persia. In July they lost Kermanshah, and about August 12th had to evacuate Hamadan. Farther north, on the Teheran-Lake Urmia-Mosul road, they had to abandon Rowanduz, only eighty miles from Mosul, retire across the passes, which were infested with hostile tribesmen, and withdraw to the south of Lake Urmia. These successes of the Turks were somewhat alarming, especially in such a distracted country as Persia, many of whose people were pro-German in their sympathies. But as August went on the situation was once more got in hand by the Grand Duke, who had been reinforced. Mush and Bitlis were captured again, and the Turks checked and caused to turn westward on both of the Persian caravan roads mentioned above. It was to the last degree unlikely that the Turks, in these circumstances, could have anything but the most fleeting success in all this area.

Successes of the Turks

RUSSIAN WOMEN AND CHILDREN RETURN TO THEIR HOMES ON THE TIDE OF VICTORY.
For many months the seesaw-like result of fighting on the east front kept the civil population on the move. According to the fortune of war, the peasants retreated and advanced from and to their own homes. This illustration shows Russian women and children coming back to their villages, which were recaptured in General Brussiloff's offensive.

| CHAPTER CXXXVIII. |

THE GLORIOUS RECORD OF THE ANZACS IN THE WAR TO THE SUMMER OF 1916.

By E. C. Buley, Author of "Glorious Deeds of Australasians."

Military and Economic Efforts of the Southern Dominions—Australian Preparedness Justified by the Existing Nucleus of an Efficient Army and Navy—New Zealand Captures Samoa—Australia Captures German New Guinea and the Bismarck Archipelago—The Australian Navy—Conditions of Service with the Expeditionary Force—Forty Transports Put to Sea, November 1st, 1914—Gallipoli and the Landing at Hell-fire Spit—The Attack Upon Krithia—Sir Ian Hamilton's Cablegram to the Australian Prime Minister—"Anzac"—Enemy Attack on Anzac Cove and Rout of the Turks, May 18th, 1915—Australia and New Zealand Call for More Recruits—"Wallaby Marches" to the Tune of "Waltzing Matilda"—The Landing at Suvla Bay—The Fight for Lone Pine Plateau—Sacrifice and Daring of the Australian Light Horse and the Mounted Rifles of New Zealand—Gallant Behaviour of the 21st Battalion in the Southland, Torpedoed near Lemnos—The Evacuation of Gallipoli—The Visit of Mr. Hughes, Prime Minister of Australia, to Great Britain in 1916—Anzac Day, April 25th, 1916—Anzacs Transferred to the Western Front, 1916 —Reconstitution of the Anzac Force and Transfer of its Base and Training Quarters to England—Anzacs in the Trench Raids on the Western Front—Anzacs on the Somme—The Four Battles for Pozieres—Generosity of the Southern Dominions and their Moral and Material Support of the Empire.

THE part played by the Commonwealth of Australia and the Dominion of New Zealand in the single-minded prosecution of the Great War has necessarily been the subject of frequent and extended reference in this work. It will now be convenient, and indeed necessary, to collocate all the mighty exertions of these two young nations, so that the sum of their effort may be presented in the mass.

How many people realise that out of a population of 6,000,000 Australasia, in the first two years of the war, equipped no less than 300,000 fighting men of the first quality for Europe? The despatch of this force over the longest sea route the world knows—no army had ever before travelled so far to fight—and its maintenance in Europe involved the people of these Oversea Dominions in an expenditure which exceeded, per head of population, the financial burden laid upon the Mother Country itself. Yet this daily-increasing liability was cheerfully borne by the people of Australasia.

348

THE "SOUL OF ANZAC" IN A NEW ZEALAND CAMP.
General Birdwood walking with Sir Thomas Mackenzie, High Commissioner for New Zealand.

These sacrifices indicate but one direction in which the Southern Dominions applied themselves to the task of war-winning, to the exclusion of all else. Their economic effort has also to be known in order to be fully appreciated. Nowhere among the Allies was the concentration of national resources for the one essential purpose so rapidly and thoroughly effected. At the very outset of hostilities the vast food supplies of these countries were laid at the disposal of the Imperial Government in their entirety. The meat, sugar, wheat, wool, and other invaluable commodities at once passed under Government control—a control so exercised that these stores became available for the great cause with the least delay and the greatest possible facility. Steps were immediately taken to extend the production of such necessities as wheat, with the result that in the second year of the war Australasia was able to place 90,000,000 bushels of wheat at the disposal of the friendly European Powers needing it.

Besides the concentration of its military and economic force, Australasia was prompt to act in other directions. Quick attention

Bringing up heavy howitzers during the Somme advance of July, 1916.

Big gun on a railway mounting: Ramming home the shell.

"Forward, East Yorks!" Camera impression of the British advance.

London Scottish marching to the trenches on the Somme.

Cheering their way to victory: How the Worcesters went forward on the Somme.

In a trench at Ovillers: On the look-out while his comrades rest.

The hour has struck! British first line of attack taking up position in front of their barbed=wire defences, July 1st, 1916.

was given to the suppression of all trade likely to benefit the enemy in any direction. War charities were organised; thought was taken for the needs of the Empire's soldiers when the war should be finished. Their probable desire to colonise, instead of returning to sedentary occupations, was taken into account and preparation for an influx of soldier immigrants was at once begun.

The details of these military and economic preparations, conceived in a spirit of unflinching **"The last man and** resolution during the first days of the **last shilling"** war, and carried forward with purposeful steadfastness, make the war record of Australia and New Zealand one of absorbing interest.

The brightest moment in those dark days in which the war opened was that in which the Oversea Dominions and Dependencies, without hesitation or division of opinion, ranged themselves in the ranks of Empire. The unforgettable scene enacted in the Commonwealth Parliament when war was declared will live for ever in one comprehensive promise that was made then, and continued to be honoured in the letter and the spirit ever after. It was announced, amid cheers, that Australia had placed her warships at the disposal of the Empire, and had offered an expeditionary force of 20,000 men. Both offers had been graciously accepted. It was then that Mr. Andrew Fisher, Leader of the Opposition, spoke for the Labour Party and the solid, united ranks of the Australian working men. "The last man, and the last shilling," he said, "would be spent by Australia to defeat the tyranny of German militarism." Australia adopted the phrase as its war motto, and never swerved from the pithy promise.

In the New Zealand Parliament the members rose and sang "God save the King" when the Prime Minister, Mr. Massey, announced that New Zealand's offer of 8,000 men as a preliminary expeditionary force had been accepted. Nowhere was any voice raised in criticism or opposition. Both these young nations went to work with a single and unanimous purpose.

Before the war could be carried into the Old World there was much work to be done in their own neighbourhood. Germany's colonising ambitions, a generation before, had inflicted the red, white, and black flag upon several large stretches of territory in the South Seas, in spite of the earnest but useless protests of Australasian statesmen of the time. Samoa, part of New Guinea, and several important groups of islands had been Germanised. There were coaling and wireless stations near at hand, and ports where the German war cruisers could lurk for a dash at Australasian ports.

Forthwith, the Southern Dominions reaped the reward of a preparedness which had at one time involved them in much searching criticism. In both Australia and New Zealand systems of compulsory military training for the youth had been enforced for some years. Australia had a military training college, organised at a place called Duntroon by General Bridges, the efficient soldier who commanded the First Australian Expeditionary Force, and who lost his life at Anzac. There was abundance of trained men and efficient young officers available at once for expeditions against these German settlements.

Australia had more; she had a small but invaluable fleet of modern warships. A few years before, when Europe was shuddering on the brink of war in consequence of the Agadir incident, a German fleet had been waiting within easy striking distance of Australia, ready to swoop upon her great ports and coveted coal supply. Nothing could have saved Australia had war broken out then.

Australia took the lesson to heart. When the crisis again arose, the Scharnhorst and Gneisenau, with their 8·2 in. guns, the Leipzig, Nürnberg, and Emden, all fast cruisers, were again on the spot. They dared not strike. Why? "We did not raid any Australian port, nor sink any Australian shipping," explained one of the officers of the Scharnhorst, after that vessel had been sunk by Admiral Sturdee at the Falkland Islands, "because we knew our 8·2 in. guns were no match for the 12 in. guns of the Australia."

After the war began no British ship was sunk or even attacked in Australasian waters. On the other hand, a large number of German mercantile vessels were promptly captured in and about Australasian ports, and Von Spee's

AUSTRALIAN IMPERIAL FORCES HEADQUARTERS STAFF.
Back row (left to right): Lieut. Sherington, Col. Forsyth, Col. Kendall, Capt. Butler, Major Maxted, Lieut. Clark, Capt. Donnelly. Middle row: Col. Anderson, General Sellheim, Col. Johnson. Front row: Lieut. Evans, Col. Millard, Major Miller, Lieut. Murphy.

cruiser fleet was impotent to help them. Nor could it interfere with the expeditions that were sent with amazing despatch against Germany's South Sea colonies.

New Zealand struck the first blow by equipping a force of 1,300 men against Samoa. The work was done with surprising rapidity, and before the war was a fortnight old the Union Jack was flying at Apia, the German capital of Samoa; and on August 29th the place had passed into British hands. A fortnight later the Gneisenau and another **New Zealand's** warship appeared off the harbour, but **first blow** they were fugitive vessels before the Australia and the Japanese Pacific Squadron. They had to steam away without firing a shot.

Early in September, 1914, the Australian expedition was despatched against New Guinea and the Bismarck Archipelago. The details of the expedition include the capture of Rabaul, Toma, and Friedrich Wilhelmshaven, and the destruction of several wireless stations scattered about the islands near New Guinea. Before the month of September had expired the work was finished, and at a cost of a few men 100,000 square miles of colonial territory had been wrested from our chief enemy.

The efficient little fleet that made these things possible consisted of one battle-cruiser, the Australia, 19,200 tons, armed with eight 12 in. guns and sixteen 4 in. guns ; three light cruisers, the Sydney, Melbourne, and Brisbane (incomplete at the opening of the war), each of 5,600 tons, with eight 6 in. guns ; six destroyers of a modern type, and two submarines—AE1 and AE2.

The Australia, after the island expeditions were completed, joined in the great sweep which drove the German

cruiser squadron to its doom at the Falkland Islands. She covered 48,000 miles and, among other services, captured and destroyed a big German liner laden with supplies for Von Spee. Then she joined Admiral Jellicoe's North Sea Fleet, and had the misfortune to meet with a slight accident which prevented her taking part in the Battle of Jutland. In that battle the Dreadnought New Zealand, the gift of the Dominion to the Imperial Navy, played a gallant part.

The Sydney, while escorting the Expeditionary Force to Egypt, encountered and destroyed the notorious German sea-raider the Emden, as recounted in Chapter XLVI. of THE GREAT WAR. Of the submarines, AE1 was sunk in the course of the operations against German New Guinea. AE2 was sent to the Mediterranean, making a record distance for a submarine cruise. After splendid service about the Dardanelles, AE2 was sunk in an attempt to enter the Sea of Marmora, and her company fell into the hands of the Turks. **Compulsory military training**

Australia's Naval College, situated at Jervis Bay, on the coast of New South Wales, was the only college of the kind in the Dominions, and afforded instruction to its full complement of one hundred and fifty picked lads, who were trained, kept, and even provided with pocket-money by the Commonwealth while they were being fitted for the fine career of officers in his Majesty's Australian Navy. One could linger over the democratic system on which these boys were selected, and a sketch might be given of the ambitious shipbuilding programme to which the Commonwealth stood pledged. The actual record, however, must be pursued.

The compulsory military training in force in Australasia carried an obligation for home service only, so that it was necessary, before the despatch of an expeditionary force, to call for volunteers to serve abroad. The response to the call was magnificent ; so widespread, that in Australia and New Zealand alike, the selection from such a wealth

BRITISH WOMEN AND CHILDREN'S GIFT TO THE AUSTRALIANS.
In July, 1916, the Princess Royal presented to the General Officers commanding the Australian Forces in England a flag and shield, gifts from British women and children. The ceremony took place at Wellington Barracks, under the auspices of the League of Empire. These illustrations show the Princess Royal with Mr. Andrew Fisher.

ANZACS AND POILUS FRATERNISE AT A WAYSIDE STATION.

Before the war Australia must have seemed a very remote country to many Frenchmen. Within two short years the pick of this island continent were fighting shoulder to shoulder with their Latin allies. The men were able to study the characteristics of each other from personal contact.

of fine material was an embarrassment. Conditions of service were liberal, as may be gathered from the following summary of Australian conditions, which differed in no essential from those of New Zealand.

Rates of Pay.—Lieutenant, 21s. per day; sergeant, 10s. 6d. per day; corporal, 10s. per day; private, 6s. per day.

Separation Allowance.—Married members receiving less than 8s. per day—(a) for wife living at home, 1s. 5d. per day; (b) for each child under sixteen years of age, 4½d. per day. A similar allowance as in (a) is paid to the mother of a member who is solely dependent upon him for support.

Pensions.—Payable to widow on death of member of the forces or to a member on total incapacity: Lieutenant, £91 per annum; sergeant, £70 per annum; corporal, £68 per annum; private, £52 per annum. In addition, on the death or total incapacity of a member, for each child under sixteen years of age, £13 per annum. In the case of total incapacity, the wife in addition receives half the rate specified above for the respective ranks.

Within a marvellously short space of time all the men required were in training camps, and the work of fitting transports for them and providing their equipment was proceeding apace. By the end of October all the men and horses were aboard ship, and had kept the rendezvous at the West Australian port of Albany. On November 1st the long line of forty transports put to sea.

Let it be realised that one hundred years before the white inhabitants of these countries numbered a few scanty thousands, and the sense of pride and adventure which thrilled Australasia can be measured. **Men worthy of their mission** These new lands, which never knew war, were sending a fine army on a journey of 12,000 miles to fight for right against might amid the battle-scarred nations of the Old World. The men were worthy of their mission. The average height of the 20,000 Australians was five feet eight inches, while the New Zealanders surpassed that average by an inch all round. Quite fifty per cent. of the men and the majority of their officers had seen service in South Africa. They

were tough, high-spirited, enterprising; a force fitted in every way to initiate Australasia's great adventure.

The story of that long journey across the Indian Ocean, and of the ocean fight between the Sydney and the Emden, which so gloriously broke its monotony, has been told in Chapter LIII., where are also detailed the reasons which dictated the debarkation of the Australasians at Egypt for training, instead of carrying out the original plan of sending them on to Great Britain for ultimate service on the western front. **Memorable scene at Colombo**

One incident of the journey, however, must be recalled here, since it serves to indicate the spirit in which these crusaders from the South went forth to fight. When the Sydney detached herself from the convoy to engage the Emden there was naturally great excitement among the soldiers in the transports. The occasion was a remarkable one. For the first time a vessel of Australia's maiden navy was going into battle. Twelve hours later the news was spread through the fleet that the Emden had been destroyed, and the jubilation was proportionately great. The fleet proceeded steadily on to Colombo, and anchored there to await the victorious cruiser.

Before she arrived an order was communicated to all the transports. The Sydney was about to arrive, but on board she had wounded prisoners, German sailors who had fought gallantly, and who were now in a critical state from the injuries received. Therefore, Captain Glossop, of the Sydney, begged that there should be no noisy demonstration. Soon the Sydney came steaming proudly through the long double line of ships she had so ably protected. The deck of every transport was crowded with soldiers, who stood, hat in hand, in solemn silence. This mark of consideration overcame the German prisoners when they were made to understand its full significance, as well it might.

STRIPPED FOR THE FRAY.
In France, as on Gallipoli and in Egypt, the Anzac gunners worked stripped to the waist.

Three months of stern training followed the landing in Egypt, and during this period the men gained not only supreme physical fitness, but the invaluable discipline which it was thought they needed when they left Australasia. Early in April, 1915, the infantry of Australia and the whole New Zealand force again embarked for a final course of training on the islands of Imbros and Lemnos. The men knew the day of battle was now at hand, and that they were to form part of the British force which was about to be landed on the Peninsula of Gallipoli in order to assist in the attempt to force the passage of the Dardanelles.

MUSCULAR YOUNG MANHOOD.
The Anzacs were the pick of the manhood of Australia and New Zealand. Their physique was as superb as their spirit.

The spot chosen for the Australasian landing was the most northerly of the British landing-places. It lay in the Gulf of Saros, about a mile north of the hillocky promontory of Gaba Tepe, on which stood an old Turkish fort. Still farther to the north was Suvla Bay, and back from the coast between these two landmarks frowned the hill mass of Sari Bair, reaching the height of nine hundred and seventy-one feet at its highest point in Koja Chemen.

The 3rd Brigade of Australian Infantry supplied the actual landing-force of 1,500 picked men, under Colonel Sinclair MacLagan, D.S.O. These steamed down to the Gulf of Saros on the evening of April 24th, followed by the New Zealanders and three more brigades of Australian infantry in transports. They passed the British fleet in the darkness, and heard the roar of its guns as it bombarded the forts at Cape Helles, preparatory to the British landings there.

Before day broke the men of the 3rd Brigade were in the boats, and the pinnaces began to tow them shorewards as silently as might be. By a piece of good fortune, the tows got off the line laid down for them, and neared the shore at a point considerably north of the selected beach. It was afterwards discovered that the Turks were entrenched in some force at the selected point, and that barbed-wire had been laid under the water in considerable quantities.

At the place where the actual landing was made the beach is a strip of sand some ten feet wide, from which cliffs rise precipitously for forty or fifty feet. On the top of the cliff were trenches held by the Turks with machine-guns. As the boats neared the shore these Turks opened fire upon them, and the fort at Gaba Tepe sprayed them with shrapnel, as did some guns placed in the hills to their left. Rifle fire broke out from all points in the hills, where snipers had been posted, and amid this galling fire the first three boats reached the beach.

The men jumped out into water breast deep, and made for the land by twos and threes. They waited for no orders, but scaled the cliff like goats. More boats beached, and their occupants poured up that upright wall of rock, facing a deadly fire from above. No man waited, each acted on his own initiative. The result was a triumph for Australian daring and enterprise. Troops better accustomed to waiting for the word of command might have been shot down, while pausing to take the regulation order. These raw troops were at the cliff-top before the Turks could realise what they were doing.

When it came to hand-to-hand fighting the Turks could not stand before the picked giants of Queensland, West Australia, and Tasmania. The men made instinctively for the machine-guns and bayoneted the gunners. By order, not a shot was fired, but in a minute a cheer was raised by them that reached the anxious watchers on the ships, and informed them that the landing had been secured.

Now dawn was breaking, and from all the transports boats might be seen putting out for the shore. The other brigades were following the 3rd, and were taking greater risks. The guns in the fort played sad havoc with them; the snipers seemed innumerable, while shrapnel coming from all quarters proved that the hills concealed many guns commanding the bay and the landing-beach. One spit of sand was swept from all quarters at once, yet the boats had to beach there. Before the landing was twelve hours old that spit of sand had received its baptism of blood and the name it now bears of Hell-fire Spit.

As the men landed they scaled the cliff and pressed inland through country as rough as any of the wild gullies of their native lands. They drove the Turks over three successive ranges of hills, each **The landing at** higher than the last, and pursued them **Hell-fire Spit** through winding valleys with precipitous sides, which were covered with a dense growth of holly bushes taller than a man. Here was good cover for snipers, and the impetuous invaders passed many of these, leaving them to shoot them down from behind at their leisure. The valleys were strewn with dead and wounded men, Turks and Australasians side by side. And still they pressed on. They had no artillery support except a few mountain guns of an Indian battery and that which came from the warships. The nature of the country rendered the ships' guns useless to the men who had worked their way inland, except for the moral effect of their firing, for they all declare that the sound was most encouraging.

The tragedy of that landing soon became apparent to every man among those bold pioneers. They drove the Turks before them like sheep, and with adequate support would never have stayed in their forward progress until they had crossed the few miles that separated them from the Dardanelles. They were, however, too few in number. Turkish troops were hurried up to meet them from Maidos and other camps in the vicinity, and before night fell the Australasians were falling back in little groups, hopelessly outnumbered.

As they fell back, fighting stubbornly and losing heavily, the little scattered bands began to coagulate, and to stiffen with the supports that were still hurrying forward from the landing-places. By dusk they had fallen back to a place from which it would have been dangerous to give ground further. There they dug in, a semicircle of desperate men, with their backs to the sea and the cliffs up which they had climbed, and their faces set against a foe who occupied ground above them in numbers much greater than their own.

All night they fought, consolidating their precarious positions. They had become hopelessly mixed, and fought, not in companies and battalions, but as they found themselves; men from New Zealand with strangers from Queensland and Victoria. It was five days before the Turkish pressure slackened, and the scattered **Anzac heroism** battalions were re-formed. They were **on Gallipoli** sadly depleted in numbers, and almost exhausted from lack of rest and proper food. They had, nevertheless, hung on to the bit of ground they had won, less than a square mile of the roughest portion of the rugged Peninsula of Gallipoli.

In the meantime the British landing at Cape Helles had been followed by stern fighting, which had brought the invaders to the foot of the great Turkish mountain fortress of Achi Baba. Sir Ian Hamilton was determined to press on at all costs, and was mustering all his forces for a grand assault on the strongly held village of Krithia, situated on the very slope of Achi Baba itself. His force was so inadequate to the task that he had recourse to the thin garrison of the Australasian holding, detaching from them the 2nd Brigade of the Australian Infantry and the New Zealanders as well. These troops were embarked in trawlers, in order to join the main British force at Cape Helles.

Thus it came that Australians and New Zealanders were included in the composite army that delivered an attack upon Krithia on the evening of May 8th. French, English, Scottish, and Irish troops were concerned in that attack. A naval brigade took part, and a variety of coloured soldiers, including negroes and Arabs from the French African Colonies, and Sikhs, Gurkhas, and Pathans from India. The Australasians at last were fighting side by side with other soldiers, and their comrades-in-arms included men of many continents and shades of colour.

In the afternoon of May 8th the Australian 2nd Brigade was posted on the extreme left of the British line, supporting a naval division which held the advanced line of trenches. To their right, across the main road to Krithia, were their friends **Up the slope to** from New Zealand, similarly supporting **Krithia** the 88th British Brigade. Right of them were Indians and more British troops, while on the extreme right of the allied line were the French troops.

From the guns of the warships and the field-artillery a rain of shell was being poured upon the Turkish trenches. Suddenly the roar of the guns hushed; it was the signal to go. Australians and New Zealanders, Frenchmen, Irish, and Indians all sprang forward together. Led by their Brigadier, General McCay, the Australians swept up to the front line. "Go on, Australians!" he shouted, and without pause they passed through the sailors and rushed on up the slope to Krithia.

The New Zealanders had reached the first line in the same moment, and had been checked for an instant. When, however, they saw the Australians pressing on so gallantly, they advanced again, racing their neighbours up the bare slope. Six hundred yards away were the positions where they were instructed to dig in, and the way thither led up a slope quite bare of all cover. It was swept by the shrapnel of the Turkish redoubts and by a withering rifle fire from the Turkish infantry, steady as usual in the cover of their trenches.

The spectators in the warships held their breath in view of that glorious rush through the storm of shot and shell that tore down the slope. The Australasian troops might have been performing on the stage of a great theatre, so plainly were they to be discerned on the bare hillside. They could be seen advancing at the double, then checking to a quick walk, only to run forward again with another rush. But they never turned back a yard, or even paused in their rapid advance. Australians and New Zealanders

[*Official photograph.*]

THE HALL-MARK OF FITNESS IN MEN AND HORSES.
Anzac heavy gun on its way to the front in France, drawn by a team of powerful Shire horses. An impressive illustration secured by the official photographer on the eve of the great Somme offensive, July, 1916.

AN INTERNATIONAL MATCH: CANADIANS, AUSTRALIANS, NEW ZEALANDERS, SOUTH AFRICANS, AND IMPERIALS.

were racing for the positions under Krithia village. Groups of men melted away from the hillside under the fire they endured, but the rest went on. The Australians reached their objective first, and threw themselves down on the ground, each man scraping for himself a shelter there in the open. The New Zealanders were hot after them, and they, too, dug in. They stayed until they were relieved.

Perhaps it was " gallery " play; for they knew that the eyes of the world were on them. Away to their right the line lagged hundreds of yards behind. The losses the Australasians incurred were too heavy, **Ian Hamilton's** even for the object they had in sight. **eloquent tribute** But the reputation of the Australasian soldier was made. He had made good in a public trial; and General Sir Ian Hamilton was able next day to cable to the Australian Prime Minister: " May I, out of a full heart, be permitted to say how gloriously the Australian and New Zealand Contingents have upheld the fine traditions of our race during the struggle still in progress. At first with audacity and dash, then with sleepless valour and untiring resource, they have already created for their countries an imperishable record of military virtue."

They returned to the Australasian holding covered with glory, but sadly diminished in numbers. The 2nd Brigade had only 1,600 effectives left of the 4,200 men who mustered for the landing; 2,600 losses in little more than a fortnight's fighting. The New Zealanders had suffered in the same degree. They found on their return that they had on their patch of cliffside not only a local habitation, but a name. The strip of beach they had left was now Anzac Cove.

Under the cliff were piled thousands of cases, holding munitions and stores; and on each was stencilled in bold letters the initials of their title—Australian and New Zealand Army Corps—A. N. Z. A. C. The recurrence of those letters had given an idea to their commander, General Sir William Birdwood, when he was asked to supply a handy telegraphic address. Long before they had left Egypt, cables to their headquarters were addressed to Anzac, Egypt. When the choice of a name for the

cove where they landed on Gallipoli was entrusted to the general, Anzac Cove leaped to his mind as a matter of course. In a few more days the whole location was Anzac, and the men who held it were referred to all over the world as the Anzacs.

The title was joyously accepted by the men themselves, even before an interpreter made it clear that the word is good Turkish. That it should mean " wholly just " seemed to them a good omen and typical of their cause. The people who sent them into the arena of battle were equally glad of a word which might take the place of the unsatisfactory term " Australasian." The world's newspapers and headline writers jumped at it, and in a few weeks it seemed that they had always been Anzacs, so general had the use of the word become.

The men did not return from Krithia one day too soon. In their absence the weakness of the little Anzac garrison had been discovered, and violent assaults had been made upon it. General Bridges, the deeply-honoured soldier who had led the Australians across the seas, had been so severely wounded that he afterwards died of his injuries; and General Sir William Birdwood, " the soul of Anzac," had himself been wounded.

Moreover, General Liman von Sanders, the German general who directed the Turkish defence of Gallipoli, was even then preparing for a grand attack, which, in his own inflated words, was to " drive them into the sea." Regiments from the élite of **Von Sanders'** the Turkish Army had been brought up **inflated boast** from Constantinople; the observers could see their natty light-blue uniforms in the crowded trenches, contrasting vividly with the mud-stained garb of the troops who had hitherto been opposed to the Anzacs. There was a stir of munition trains, and all the other signs that indicate preparation for a big offensive were discernible.

The attack was delivered in the evening of May 18th, and its dramatic failure has been described in Chapter LX. The whole Anzac force answered nobly to the emergency, displaying qualities of steadiness under shell fire and in the face of advancing forces hugely outnumbering their own, which valuably supplemented the reputation for dash and daring that they had already gained.

The brunt of the attack was borne by the 4th Brigade of Australian Infantry, which kept the line from the Bloody Angle through Quinn's Post to Courtney's Post, where the fighting raged most fiercely. The 4th was a brigade despatched from Australia after the departure of the First Expeditionary Force. Commanded by Briga-dier-General Monash, it had joined the main force in Egypt, and took its worthy part in the landing of April 25th and the days which followed. The 4th, with the New Zealanders, formed the command of General Sir A. J. Godley, who expressed his opinion of these men in a speech he made to them at Anzac on June 2nd. From it the following words may fitly be quoted :

Yours is a fine record, and one of which you yourselves and the whole of the people of Australia have the fullest reason to be proud. You have made, and are making, the military history of Australia, a history equal to that of any other brigade or body of troops in the Empire, or in the world ; and you have performed deeds and achieved successes of which the Commonwealth will surely be proud. Pope's Hill position is named after the gallant commander of the 16th Battalion, which held it so long against such odds ; Courtney's Post will for ever be associated with the 14th Battalion, which has defended it against all attacks for the whole period ; the most difficult post of all, Quinn's Post, is named after Major Quinn, who died bravely at this post in the service of his country, and who, I am sure, would have preferred no more glorious death. This post will be for ever associated with the name of Lieut.-Colonel Cannon and the 15th Battalion. Nor will be forgotten the gallant behaviour of the 13th Battalion, under Lieut.-Colonel Burnage, who, among many other fine performances, held on for a night and a day in a difficult advanced position which they had stormed, and from which they did not withdraw until ordered to do so in view of the subsequent course of the operations.

Anzac ascendancy over the Turk

The Turkish rout of May 18th-19th gave the Anzacs an ascendancy over the Turk which they turned to excellent account. A request for an armistice was the immediate outcome of that engagement, the Turks finding no other way to accomplish the burial of their dead, which were heaped in hundreds in the narrow lane of No Man's

Land that separated the lines at the spot where the battle was thickest. Nor did they again engage in any elaborate offensive move against the Anzacs as long as they remained upon Gallipoli Peninsula.

The invaders wrought incessantly and skilfully to make their holding impregnable. By miracles of energy and engineering skill pieces of artillery were dragged up the steep hillsides and posted at spots that looked impossible. The engineers and miners were constantly at work, making covered ways so that the area of occupation might be furnished with paths proof to the shells which fell every day and at all hours of the day. The inventive Anzacs, by many ingenious devices, emphasised the mastery they had won. One such contrivance was the periscopic rifle, a combination of the service weapon and the periscope, by means of which a good marksman could make excellent practice from the safety of a deep trench. Such skill

SIR IAN HAMILTON INSPECTING ANZACS WHO FOUGHT UNDER HIM IN GALLIPOLI.
Going down the line, he had a cheery word and handshake for each one of them. Above : "Three cheers for Sir Ian !" Men who went through the glorious but ill-fated campaign cheering their appreciative commander.

"PROSPECTING" FOR THE EMPIRE.
Stripped to the buff, Australian pioneers are here seen doing a kind of work of which they had already considerable experience.

was developed in the use of this device that not a Turk ever ventured to show his head. Men landed at Anzac, fought in the trenches, were wounded by shell fire, and left the Peninsula to confess they had lived at close quarters with the Turks for weeks but had never seen one.

During this period the main British force at Cape Helles made several important attacks upon the Turkish lines there. At such times, in order that the Turkish forces before Anzac might not be drawn off to help in the defence, it became necessary for the Anzacs to make demonstrations against them. These operations were carried out with striking audacity, the men leaving their trenches and advancing against the Turkish positions with a daring that may have been their best defence, for the losses incurred were remarkably light when the risks run are taken into consideration.

In this way the weeks slipped by. Spring merged into summer, and the Anzacs met the tropical weather by stripping to the buff, going about their **Cable message** tasks arrayed only in the shortest of **from the King** "shorts," boots, and pith helmets. They were in magnificent condition, burned a dark brown by the sun, and hard as nails. The stalemate their position implied did not please them. They could not be shifted, it is true; but they felt that they could not enlarge their little holding or fight to any effective purpose.

Early in 1915, when it was known that their men had arrived in Egypt, Australia and New Zealand began to look for tidings of their exploits on the battlefield. The first news to reach them was a cable message, graciously despatched by his Majesty the King to the Prime Ministers of Australia and New Zealand after the landing on Gallipoli had taken place. "I heartily congratulate you on the splendid conduct and bravery displayed by the Australasian troops in the operations at the Dardanelles. They have indeed proved themselves worthy sons of the Empire."

This was the first news received of the despatch of their force to the Dardanelles; it was quickly followed by extended cables, relating the miracle of their landing, the glory of their charge at Krithia, the blow they dealt Liman von Sanders when he planned to drive them over the cliff-edge into the sea. The news thrilled the Continent

of Australia from its populated coastal regions to the sparsely-inhabited plains of the interior. It ran like wildfire through the flourishing settlements of New Zealand, and all Australasia stirred with pride and consciousness of achievement.

Surely no countries ever entered the lists of war in such a blaze of glory!

There were dark moments for the Southern Dominions as well. In seven weeks the Anzacs had lost 14,000 men—one-half their number. Households that had never dreamed of war and loss by war rested under the dark shadow of irreparable loss. But they wore their mourning with a proud grief in Australasia, taking thought only of filling the gaps in their lines and of doubling the strength of their fighting force.

[*Official photographs.*
FOLLOWING UP WITH A "FLYING PIG."
In the course of the summer offensive, 1916, Anzacs loading a trench-mortar, known among the soldiers as a "flying pig."

Their instinct was backed by the warnings of the Imperial Government. The difficulties of the Dardanelles enterprise were now measured, and it was recognised that more men, and more men still, would be needed if the attempt so gallantly begun was to be carried to a successful end. In Australia the call was made to increase their quota for service overseas to 250,000 men, while New Zealand undertook to complete a force of 50,000.

The call for recruits rang through the great seaport cities. It spread beyond the mountain ranges to the agricultural uplands; it ran like a fiery cross to every remote settlement in the far interior. The response was magnificent. The State of Victoria, with a population of something over a million, yielded one thousand suitable men a day for a fortnight. That is only a sample of what was done throughout Australia and New Zealand. The recruiting agencies, operating in the cities and towns, received the best the country had to offer; but the bush gave of its best without the intervention of any agency.

From the fastnesses of the interior there began spontaneous pilgrimages to the sea-coast that were like nothing seen on earth since the days of the Crusaders. They were called "Wallaby Marches," and their course from

Right Hon. W. M. Hughes in the robes of LL.D. of Edinburgh University.

Lord Mayor of Cardiff presenting the freedom of the city to Mr. Hughes on the occasion of his visit to the Welsh capital.

Mr. and Mrs. Hughes chatting to a wounded Anzac at the Australian Convalescent Home, Harefield. On the extreme right is Mr. Fisher, and Mrs. Fisher is seen standing next to the nurse.

Mr. and Mrs. Hughes. A photograph taken after their visit to an Anzac Camp, just prior to their return to Australia.

Anzacs march past before the Right Hon. W. M. Hughes, Prime Minister of Australia. No politician ever had the pleasure of reviewing a finer body of soldiers than were raised in the Commonwealth. A number of British officers and the admiring inhabitants of a small French café were also spectators of this interesting event.

THE VISIT OF THE RIGHT HON. W. M. HUGHES, PRIME MINISTER OF AUSTRALIA, TO THE MOTHERLAND.

the centre of Australia to the sea was like the gathering of a mighty river from the conjunction of numerous little streams.

Somewhere in the heart of Australia, hundreds of miles from the railway terminus farthest inland, and scores of miles from any road, some young fellow would tell his neighbour—anyone within ten miles is a neighbour in such places—that on the morrow he would take the Wallaby Track. The neighbour, as likely as not, had the same intention. In the morning, with a "swag" containing clothing, blankets, and food for the journey on his back, each man would set out, the pair meeting where the bush track forked to their two holdings.

A CHOSEN SON OF THE EMPIRE.
General Birdwood decorating Sergeant Watson with the D.C.M. on the occasion of his visit to a New Zealanders' camp in England.

A few miles down the track they would find Bushman No. 3, equipped like themselves for a long tramp. They would swing along the track to the bush road, where a little school, a public-house and a police-station marked the locality of a bush township. Here were a few more adventurous souls; and they would all join forces and move along seawards. By night they slept under their blankets in the open air; by day they pressed on, growing in numbers as they marched forward.

The news of their coming preceded them to the little towns by the road, and more men would be added to their number. The good folk made ready for them, providing the best food and beds the place afforded, and encouragement of every possible nature. Girls on horseback escorted them along their path; and as they tramped they sang the song of the Wallaby Track, which is called "Waltzing Matilda." Matilda, it must be understood, is the Bushman's facetious name for the heavy "swag" he carries on his back; and when he prepares for the Wallaby Track he says that he is about to "waltz Matilda." So they sang:

Waltzing Matilda, waltzing Matilda!
Won't you go waltzing, Matilda, with me?
He sang as he sat by the edge of the waterhole,
"Won't you go waltzing, Matilda, with me?'

SEEING FOR HIMSELF.
The Right Hon. Andrew Fisher, who succeeded Sir George Reid, M.P., as High Commissioner for Australia in London, inspecting some of the Anzacs.

And so, in the end, they came to the railroad, a couple of hundred strong, to find a recruiting depot, where they exchanged their bush clothes for the good brown khaki which made them Anzacs and heirs to a tradition already glorious.

Such enthusiasm permitted Australia to have another division training in Egypt by the end of July, and yet further divisions in camp in the Commonwealth. New Zealand's efforts corresponded; and in both cases the new men were of the same high quality as their predecessors. The end of July marked a new era in the course of the Dardanelles operations, for then Sir Ian Hamilton began to act upon his scheme for transferring the main theatre of fighting from Cape Helles to Anzac.

The story of the Suvla Bay landing and of the part played in it by the Anzacs is told in Chapter CVII. It was, perhaps, the greatest of Anzac exploits to hold all the Turks in fight, while the British force was landed unopposed at Suvla Bay, and it was certainly the most costly in life and limb.

Here the 1st Brigade of Australian Infantry came into the limelight. The 3rd Brigade had led the way at the landing; the 2nd Brigade shared with the New Zealanders the honours of the Krithia charge; while the 4th Brigade had made a mock of the grandiose threat of Sanders Pasha. Now the 1st had its **Fight for Lone Pine Plateau** hard-fighting chance, for upon this brigade was cast the responsibility of opening the ball by charging the well-nigh impregnable position of Lone Pine. Later, on the western front, the same gallant brigade led the way into Pozières, and fought the Germans up and down the streets amid the ruined houses and into dug-outs fifty feet down in the earth. But the men will say that nothing in Pozières approached the fight for Lone Pine Plateau.

The trenches they charged were roofed over with heavy balks of timber, and when the Anzacs leaped down into the obscurity below, the Turks for the first time stood and fought them with the bayonet, amid the gloom and the reek of their long occupation of these fetid dens. For days the fight lasted. Seven Victoria Crosses were won in that network of trenches, and countless deeds of heroism passed unnoticed. By such sacrifice was Lone Pine added to the area under Anzac occupation.

When they left Egypt for Gallipoli the Anzacs had left their cavalry behind them. It consisted of three brigades of Australian Light Horse and units of Mounted Rifles from the various provinces of New Zealand. The whole formed a cavalry force which, for its size, could not be bettered on the face of the earth. For certain kind of work, as subsequent events in Egypt were to show, it could not be approached. Men and horses alike were of the highest quality, perfect horsemen superbly mounted, and trained to meet any emergency and endure any hardship.

Deathless fame won at Suvla

When, however, the news of the Anzac landing reached them, and when they saw the first of their wounded limping to a Cairo hospital, the horsemen of Australasia were not content to be out of it. They volunteered as one man for trench duty, and their offer was accepted with a promptitude which showed how welcome it was. As foot soldiers they showed themselves the equals of the infantry through the months which preceded the Suvla Bay fight. In that fight they won deathless fame.

Mr. Hughes, the Prime Minister of Australia, in one of the stirring speeches which electrified Great Britain during his visit in 1916, immortalised the Australian Light Horse in a passage in which he told of the daring and the sacrifices made by the Australian Light Brigade. The occasion was in the early dawn of August

7th, when the 1st and 3rd Brigades had to attack the Turkish trenches opposite the left of the Anzac line.

The 3rd were stationed on Russell's Top, and had long looked up the slope inland at the series of trenches the Turks had made there. They knew these works, protected by well-posted machine-guns and ranged by artillery; in short, they recognised that under Anzac conditions they were unassailable. Now they were ordered to charge this position. Without hesitation the 8th Battalion sprang over the trenches into a stream of bullets—only one man returned unwounded. The 10th Battalion followed, and lost more than half its number in a few seconds. The Turks were in great force opposite them,

WARRIOR SCIONS OF BRITAIN FROM THE ANTIPODES.
Anzac artillerymen awaiting to embark for the front. In the foreground a number of munition and baggage waggons line the quay ready for the transport. Above: Happy group of the First Australian Contingent, including two motor despatch-riders.

and ready to move off to oppose the British landing. It was no useless sacrifice that pinned them to the spot ; and it was the nobler for that.

To the right of the 3rd Brigade the 1st Brigade of Light Horse was duplicating their experience. They charged across Bloody Angle from Pope's Post and Quinn's Post to the Turkish positions on Dead Man's Ridge, and in time came back from untenable trenches they had captured, sorely depleted in numbers. They, too, had gained the end for which they were sent out.

The Mounted Rifles of New Zealand equalled, if they did not surpass, the feats of the Light Horse. They were concerned in the direct attack on the mountain mass of Chunuk Bair, which intervened between Anzac and the road to the Dardanelles and the British objective at Maidos. The Wellington Mounted Rifles stormed a hill known as Tabletop, the angle of ascent being " impracticable for infantry " ; but, in Sir Ian Hamilton's words, " neither Turks nor angles of ascent were destined to stop Russell or his New Zealanders that night."

Near by the Otago Mounted Rifles carried a similar stronghold, called Bauchop's Hill. The Auckland mounted **Prowess of** men had captured another outpost, and **New Zealand Rifles** on the next day took a part in the great effort of New Zealand, which won the crest of the great hill and a view of the promised land beyond. That position was lost later in the fight, but not by the men of New Zealand.

The Suvla Bay fighting, which began on August 6th, ended on August 27th with the capture of Hill 60, an operation which established sound communication between Anzac and Suvla Bay, and consolidated the British holding along the sea-coast ; but the hopelessness of the operation had now been recognised, and no further attempt to force a path across the Peninsula was made.

During the latter days of August the 2nd Australian Division began to arrive at Anzac from Egypt, and one battalion, the 18th, took a gallant part in the capture of Hill 60. The work which fell to the lot of the 2nd Division was far from being as showy as that performed by their forerunners. They had to sit tight in their trenches and endure the constant and persistent hammering from the Turkish guns, which was part of the daily routine of Anzac. Before the entry **" Beachy Bill's "** of Bulgaria into the war this daily **deadly fire** bombardment had been limited by the need for economy in Turkish munitions. Much old and faulty material was hurled upon the area, the old-fashioned weapons in the Dardanelles forts expending their ancient shells in this fashion.

When the railway communication between Berlin and Constantinople was restored by the perfidy of Tsar Ferdinand of Bulgaria the Turkish bombardment assumed a more serious aspect. The modern weapons, which had been deprived of half their sting by lack of munitions, were now dangerously effective ; and shrapnel and high explosive were showered upon Anzac from all quarters.

One battery, concealed in the mangrove swamp beyond the fort of Gaba Tepe, acquired a sinister reputation among the Anzacs, to whom it was known as " Beachy Bill." Scores of attempts were made to silence these guns by cruisers, which turned their heavy guns on to the emplacements. Sometimes they would do enough damage to keep " Beachy Bill " quiet for two or three days ; but invariably the damage would be repaired, and he would begin to talk again.

[Official photograph.

A SYMBOL IN SILHOUETTE: ANZAC SENTRY ON GUARD FOR THE EMPIRE IN FRANCE.

He ranged the greater part of Anzac Beach, and aroused enmity in the minds of all by his interference with sea-bathing, a necessity there because of the waterless nature of the area. An Anzac statist made an estimate of the casualties due to this battery, and set the figure at over 1,500. "Beachy Bill" retained his effective measure of the beach until the very last day at Gallipoli.

This was only one among many quarters from which shell was rained upon Anzac. On the Asiatic shore, near Chanak Fort, was a battery of big guns which changed ground every day, the weapons being moved along a light railway. From this source came the "Sunrise and Sunset Hate," which were part of the Anzac daily round. Quick-firers were also posted about the hill mass of Sari Bair, so that there was little respite at any of the Anzac posts.

As the autumn advanced the sanitary conditions deteriorated notably. The soil became thoroughly infected, and an epidemic of dysentery afflicted the men. It was spread by the swarms of flies, which did more than anything else to make life intolerable and all food suspect. The lack of water, always a notable hardship, was felt the more keenly as the few wells the place boasted had to be condemned. When the torrential rains that ushered in the winter began to fall, the trenches got the drainage from the high ground above them and became almost untenable. Amid all these disadvantages the newcomers held on tenaciously and uncomplainingly, proving themselves to be of metal as good as their comrades who had preceded them to Anzac.

One battalion of the 2nd Division—the 21st—added to the fame of the Anzacs by an exhibition of discipline and steadfastness in extreme danger which has justly been compared to the glory won by the troops in the Birkenhead. On the last Monday in August, 1915, the 21st sailed from Egypt for Gallipoli in the transport Southland. At this time German submarines were very active in the Ægean Sea, and as the officer in command of the division, General Legge, and his Staff were also on board, special precautions were taken against attack. Boat and lifeboat drill occupied a good part of each day of the voyage, and this care on the part of the commanding officer of the battalion, Colonel Hutchinson, had its reward in the sequel.

Parade on sinking transport On Thursday, four days after sailing, the Southland was nearing Lemnos, and the tension on the ship's officers was beginning to relax. Many of the men were on deck, preparing their equipment for the landing. Suddenly a voice called, "God! Is that a torpedo?" Many caught sight of the weapon just before it struck, blowing a hole thirty feet in diameter in the side of the Southland. Above all the din that resulted the ship's siren could be heard blowing the signal, "Abandon ship."

The men of the 21st behaved as though at one of their daily ship drills. They lined up on deck as if on parade,

every man calm and collected, not one missing from his place. They watched the men from the engine-room rush on deck and lower boats, without any apparent concern. Their own business was to stand at attention, and wait for a lead from their officers.

General Legge and his Chief of Staff, Colonel Gwynn, were standing together, chatting and surveying the scene with apparent interest. The general, booted and spurred in the ordinary way, **Discipline preserved** was smoking a cigarette. Their men, **to the last** who were recruited from country farms in Victoria, only knew as much about boats as they had learned in boat drill, and many of them could not swim. But every man scorned to betray any more emotion than the general was showing.

They showed to less advantage, perhaps, when they were set to the work of lowering boats and launching life-rafts. They were just as cool as ever, but the work was new and unfamiliar. One or two boats were upset as they were lowered into the sea, and what lives were lost were mainly lost through such mishaps. Among the dead, unfortunately, was the brigadier of the 6th Brigade, Colonel Linton, who was upset into the water, where he died of heart shock.

The captain of the Southland and his officers had behaved with wonderful promptitude and presence of mind in the face of the mishap. The magnificent steering of the captain enabled the wounded ship to escape the second torpedo launched at her, while the engineers at once saw to the closing of bulkheads and portholes. While the Anzacs were busy with boats and rafts the captain conceived the hope that his ship might be navigated to Lemnos under her own steam, and resolved to make the attempt.

He made a call, therefore, for volunteers from among the Anzacs to replace his stokers, most of whom had already left the ship. The response was so splendid that he was able to select, from among some hundreds, men who could claim previous experience in stoking. With the help of his officers and these volunteers he succeeded in beaching the Southland upon the island of Lemnos. The men who were in boats and rafts, and those swimming in the sea, were picked up by hospital ships, destroyers, and other British craft which hastened to answer the wireless call made by the operator of the Southland when the vessel was struck.

The Anzacs preserved to the last the discipline and cheerfulness which had marked their conduct from the moment the vessel was hit. As soon as all were again collected, General Legge issued an order congratulating them in high terms upon their conduct in this emergency.

Their arrival at Anzac was followed by a commendation from General Birdwood himself, worded as follows:

On behalf of all the comrades now serving on the Peninsula, I wish to convey to the Australian unit concerned our general feeling of admiration for the gallant behaviour of all ranks in the Southland. All the troops of the army corps have heard with pride of the courage and discipline shown at the moment when the nerves of the bravest

FIVE PROVED FIGHTING MEN.

Anzacs leaving London on their way back to the front after short leave granted to some sixty of their number in appreciation of a dashing raid into German trenches on the western front.

AUSTRALIAN CHEERS AND SMILES FOR THE KING IN FRANCE.

[Official photograph.

On one of his visits to France in 1916 the King had a full-hearted greeting from some Australian troops. The men were lined up by the roadside and cheered him enthusiastically, to the evident pleasure of his Majesty.

are liable to be so highly tried. Not only was there not the slightest confusion on the part of the troops, who quietly fell in and prepared to meet whatever fate might be in store, but later, when there was a prospect of the Southland being able to make way under her own steam and stokers were called for, the men at once came forward and successfully helped in getting the Southland into port.

The supreme courage displayed by the 21st in the face of imminent danger was shared by the whole Anzac force— a statement warranted by the behaviour of the men when the risky business of the evacuation had to be faced.

Quarrel of the "Diehards" The steps by which the decision was taken to evacuate Gallipoli, and the success attending that remarkable operation, have been detailed at length in Chapter CVII. The most delicate part of the whole scheme had to be entrusted to the Anzacs, for they held the extreme outposts of the British area on the Peninsula.

One little mistake would have involved the men who held these advanced posts to the last in a rearguard action, in which they would probably have been called upon to sacrifice themselves to ensure the safety of the scheme. The men selected for this danger were known at Anzac as the "Diehards," and there was a great deal of heartburning there, because only a limited number might aspire to the honour. Men who had landed on the first day, and who were still at the post of duty after eight months of continuous danger, went to their commanding officers with tears in their eyes, to urge their claims to this distinction. The men quarrelled about it as they had never quarrelled before ; for every Anzac wished to be a "Diehard."

The sacrifice they offered was not called for ; for it is now a matter of history that the miraculous evacuation was accomplished without any loss of life whatever. So the Anzacs turned their back upon the place where they had won so much glory, as well as a title which will abide with them for all time. If they had any regret in leaving a place where they had endured so much to such little direct purpose, it was centred in the lonely plot of ground which held the mortal remains of their gallant dead ; but they took comfort in the thought that the graveyard on the rugged Gallipoli hillside would be respected by a foe of whose chivalry and honour they had formed the highest opinion.

Among the many great services rendered by Australia and New Zealand to the Empire during the Great War, none will do more to strengthen the warm sentiment that

unites the scattered Dominions than the forbearance from criticism or complaint in this moment of trial. Through no fault of theirs, the first great warlike enterprise in which they were intimately concerned had ended in ghastly failure, and the sacrifices they had made had come to naught. The total number of Australians and New Zealanders lost on Gallipoli may give some measure of the extent of that sacrifice. The figures are :

AUSTRALIA :

Killed..	Officers 350	Ranks 6,750	—	7,100	
Prisoners	,, 6	,, 52	—	58	
Sick and Wounded	,, —	..	—	30,000	
Total Australian Casualties				37,158	37,158

NEW ZEALAND :

Killed	Officers 116	Ranks 2,625	—	2,741	
Prisoners	,, —	,, 22	—	22	
Sick and Wounded	, 210	,, 4,691	—	4,901	
Total New Zealand Casualties..				7,664	7,664
Grand Total of Anzac Casualties					44,822

The Empire waited for Australasian comment upon the evacuation, and thrilled to the unanimous voice of both Dominions. "It is a blow, but it will only serve to nerve us to greater efforts." Whatever criticism may have been hurled at the conception of the Dardanelles adventure, and whatever comment may have been passed upon its execution, no word of the kind was heard in the Antipodes. Later, when the High Commissioners of Australia and New Zealand were invited to sit upon the Commission of Inquiry into the operations in the Dardanelles, there were voices raised in protest from Australasia. The people of "Down Under" did not wish to appear as questioning in any way the Imperial authorities, to whom they entrusted their share of the direction of the war with supreme confidence.

The debt of the Empire to Australia was augmented by the war services **The genius of Mr. Hughes** rendered by the Prime Minister of the Commonwealth, the Rt. Hon. William Morris Hughes, P.C., during a visit paid to Great Britain in the spring of 1916. The mission which brought Mr. Hughes to London was of vital Imperial importance. He came, in the first place, to represent the feeling prevailing in all the Dominions Overseas that, just as they had borne their full share in the prosecution of the war, so were they entitled to be heard with attention when the time should come for the consideration of terms of peace.

Another object he had in view was the re-establishment of the Australian industry for producing the baser metals, which had been in German hands until the outbreak of the war. The decisive steps Australia had taken to close all business dealings with the enemy had put an end for ever to this profitable connection for Germany. Mr. Hughes succeeded in re-establishing the industry on an Imperial basis. He had other objects as well, such as the provision of cargo vessels to carry the abundant wheat of the Commonwealth to the Allies' markets in Europe.

His coming aroused a moderate amount of interest and enthusiasm, which he rightly attributed to the reputation the Anzacs had won on the field of battle. "I feel," he said, in one of his first speeches to a British assembly, "that I stand before you to-night in the reflected glory of the Australian soldier." But the man himself, his fiery earnestness, his singleness of purpose, and the eloquent gravity of the message he had to deliver soon captured attention. In a few days his words were on the lips of the people, and were accepted with approval and gratitude as the sentiments of the average British citizen.

Mr. Hughes made vocal the uneasy feeling that most men cherished, not as to the result of the war, but as to the course of events after the war should be ended. He said what everybody was thinking vaguely and formlessly; he crystallised the national resolve that Germany should never again enjoy the easy tolerance **An Imperial** which had reared her into the most **warning** stupendous danger that civilisation had ever encountered.

From the capture of London, Mr. Hughes turned to a triumphal tour of the provinces. Great and ancient cities competed for the right to entertain him, and to present to him their prized civic freedom. Honours were showered upon him by the seats of British learning; he went from place to place advising, warning, and prophesying. He was invited to take a seat at the historic Economic Conference of the Allied Powers in Paris, and helped to draft the solemn resolutions which, if faithfully carried out, doomed Germany to the position of a second-rate trading Power for generations to come.

After that conference had concluded its labours, Mr. Hughes returned to take up his arduous task in the Commonwealth, leaving the Motherland stimulated and cheered by the evidence he had given of the zeal and unshaken resolution with which the Southern Dominions were animated.

Before he left he was able to visit a great Australian training camp on Salisbury Plain, where a new Anzac division was already quartered, and where accommodation was provided for training as many men again for service on the western front. For more than a year the Anzac soldier, with his slouched hat, lean, brown face, and wiry, athletic figure, had been a **Twenty thousand** familiar figure in the streets of British **wounded Anzacs** cities. His appearance dated back to the days that followed the first Gallipoli landing, when the wounded Anzacs were sent to Great Britain for the period of their convalescence. After the Suvla Bay fighting they came in their numbers, and at one time during the latter months of 1915 there were twenty thousand wounded Australians and New Zealanders recuperating in England.

Their presence necessitated the establishment of military offices, hospitals, convalescent camps, and training establishments by both Dominions in London and the neighbourhood. The men were the recipients of a hospitality they would remember all the days of their lives, a hospitality acknowledged by them so warmly in their letters home that it formed the subject of gratified comment throughout Australia and New Zealand. They were invited to British country houses and treated as honoured guests; friends they had never before seen called at their hospitals with motor-cars and took them out to see the sights; they were given free seats in the theatres, and the best seats at that; finally, when Christmas came round, any man of them might have eaten a dozen Christmas dinners had he felt so disposed.

The men themselves strove hard to live up to the high standard imposed by their new title of Anzac. They displayed an attention to smartness of appearance and correctitude of behaviour which surprised and gratified even their best friends. Their officers had always a strong hold upon them by appealing to the good Anzac spirit, the heritage they had won so gloriously and were to keep unsullied for Australasia.

[*Official photograph. Crown copyright reserved.*

AUSTRALIANS RETURNING FROM THE TRENCHES THROUGH LANES OF BROTHER ANZACS.
Anzacs distinguished themselves by their dash and initiative in trench raiding. They showed equally praiseworthy steadiness and endurance under the torment of bombardment from heavy howitzers to which their own trenches were frequently subjected.

The pontoon bridge is the only one which is carried with an army. All other forms have to be constructed by the Engineers. These two photographs show a tidal ramp rise bridge in the making to enable troops to cross over on a tide.

Left: Building a bridge for heavy material. The maximum load such bridges are usually constructed to bear is five hundredweights per lineal foot for infantry, and four and a half hundredweights for field-artillery with two horses per gun. Right: Making thin wire rope. AUSTRALIAN ROYAL ENGINEERS IN TRAINING IN ENGLAND: LEARNING TO BUILD BRIDGES AND SPIN ROPE.

Their crowning debt to the sympathetic Mother Country was incurred when April 25th came round, and Australia and New Zealand celebrated their new and solemn holiday of Anzac Day, a day to be observed for ever by the young nations who were first tried and found worthy of their nationhood on that day. It was a day set apart to the memory of the Anzac dead, when all work ceased throughout Australia and New Zealand, and the citizens met in concourse to mourn with a sad pride that was half exultation.

The Anzacs in England wished to hold a celebration also, and cast about for some means. They found the way made marvellously easy for them. Westminster Abbey was lent them for the asking, a noble setting for their memorial service to their fallen heroes. More than that, London, which had given its streets up to no warlike demonstration since the day when war was declared, made an exception in their favour, and **Homage to the great dead** cleared its main streets of traffic that they might march through them to the Abbey.

It was a memorable scene when the veterans of Anzac passed through the cheering London crowd on that glorious spring morning. The sun washed the grey streets of London with lavish gold, and the men, only two thousand all told, gloried openly in the flowers that were thrust upon them and the loud praise that was shouted at them. They were joined in the Abbey by the King and Queen, by Mr. Asquith and Lord Kitchener, by their Australian Prime Minister, Mr. Hughes, and by their trusted leader, General Sir William Birdwood. Those who had lived both in Australasia and the Motherland recognised that the boundless sympathy displayed with the Anzacs in their solemn celebration of the first Anzac Day was another symbol of the indissolubility of the great Empire bond.

By that time the transfer of the Anzac infantry to the western front, decided upon early in the year 1916, had already been accomplished. The men, rested fully after their arduous experiences in Gallipoli, were already pining for action again. Their ambition had always been to fight against the Germans and by the side of the Canadians, South Africans, and other troops from overseas. The wish was an easy one to gratify, and in April, 1916, the transfer of the infantry began.

A notable feature of the journey to Marseilles was an address delivered by General Sir William Birdwood to three thousand men in one of the transports, the text of which was afterwards communicated to the whole Anzac Force. It ran as follows:

Now that we are proceeding to France, I am republishing Lord Kitchener's message to the troops of the British Expeditionary Force, which was originally issued to the Australian and New Zealand Forces before their departure from their homes in October, 1914. I feel that it is hardly necessary for me to emphasise to all ranks how sincerely I trust that they will bear in mind all that Lord Kitchener says, and do their utmost to live up to the ideal which he has placed before you.

Since the Australian and New Zealand Forces left their respective countries you have made for yourselves a national reputation as good fighters, which has earned for you the esteem of your comrades, alongside of whom we will shortly be fighting. The training that you have had will, I hope, enable you to utilise your fighting qualities to advantage. But, in addition to these two qualifications, there is still a third which is essential to success—discipline; and it is the greatest of the three, for without discipline the best fighting troops in the world will fail at the last to achieve success.

You will undoubtedly be faced with temptations in France, for we shall probably have to pass through and be billeted in densely populated French villages. Drink will, I am afraid, be obtainable, while villages will mostly be full of women and children whose fathers, husbands, and brothers are fighting for their country in the trenches against our common enemy. That you will respect the women I have not the slightest doubt, because I well know how absolutely repugnant the idea of any offence against a defenceless woman is to every Australian and New Zealander. It is against drink, however, that I particularly wish now to warn you, and to implore you to take hold of yourselves, and in the case of every man absolutely to make up his mind and determine for himself that he will not give way to it, and that he will remember that the honour of either Australia or New Zealand is in his personal keeping. In saying this you all know that I am only referring to a very small

[*Official photograph.*
WHERE THE PERISCOPE WAS INDISPENSABLE.
Turkish snipers were deadly on Gallipoli, and the Anzacs made good use of the periscope, which they were the first to adapt to the service rifle.

proportion of your numbers. The great majority of you want no such warning, for I know you will already have made up your minds on the subject, and all such I earnestly beg to do what is in their power to look after their comrades who may not have the same strength of mind as they have.

Remember that a few black sheep can give a bad name to a whole flock; so let there be none such among us, and let us make up our minds that the Australian and New Zealand Forces are going to prove themselves second to none in the way of discipline, as they have already done where sheer hard fighting was concerned.

See to this, boys! You know you are capable of it, if you will only determine that it shall be so, and if you will do this you will be able to return to Australia and New Zealand after peace and victory with an unsullied reputation, which will go down for all time in your home.

Early in April, 1916, the first bands of Australians began to arrive at Marseilles, where they were received by the French citizens with a cordiality which gave them an ineffaceable impression of the strength of the bond by which **France smiles on Anzac** the Allies were united. They made the journey north by train, through the wonderful Rhone Valley in all the beauty of its spring verdure. Many of these men had never before gazed upon the landscape of an Old World country. After the sombre foliage of Australia and its sun-baked plains, the yellow desert sands of Egypt, and the scrub and mangrove of Gallipoli, the smiling vineyards and green fields afforded a memorable contrast. " What a country to fight for ! " was the remark by which they translated their sense of its beauty and fertility.

Some of them had the honour of passing in review before General Joffre himself and of fraternising with the Russians, the selection for the post of Commandant of Commonwealth Troops in Great Britain of Brigadier-General Sir Newton Moore, a former Premier of Western Australia, who had been for some years Agent-General of that State in London.

When the convalescent men from Gallipoli had first been sent to Britain he had organised and created for them a training depôt, and his firmness and understanding of the men had been instrumental in the success which attended these preliminary measures. The establishment on a much larger scale upon Salisbury Plain was evolved with a similar success, the men of the 3rd Australian Division settling down there automatically upon their arrival from Australia. The administrative work of the Military Office in London, which had been ably organised by a civil controller, Mr. H. C. Smart, now passed into the hands of General Sellheim, and after him into those of General Anderson.

At the same time New Zealand stepped into training quarters and a London Military Office, the whole establishment being controlled by General Richardson, a very distinguished New Zealand soldier. From the very outset New Zealand could point to its camps as models of order

STRENGTH AND TENDERNESS.
Transferring a patient from an emergency sling to the regulation stretcher of the ambulance-waggon.

who arrived at nearly the same time. Then they settled down in their new quarters in the neighbourhood of Armentières. It must be understood that a reconstitution had been effected while they were resting in Egypt. The 4th Brigade, formerly attached to the New Zealanders, was now to form the nucleus of a fresh division, known as the 4th. This, with the 1st and 2nd Divisions, which had served on Gallipoli under General Sir William Birdwood, constituted the First Australian Army Corps.

The New Zealand infantry had been augmented to form a division, and with the 5th Australian Division, which had been in training in Egypt, and the 3rd Australian Division, then on its way from Australia, made a second Anzac corps, commanded by General Sir Alfred Godley.

Men from each battalion were selected for special training to form trench-mortar sections, etc.; and every care was taken that each brigade, in equipment and fighting capability, should conform to the high standard of the British Army. One practical step, **Anzacs reinforce** attended with excellent results, was the **new battalions** distribution, where possible, of the veteran fighters of Gallipoli among the men of the new and inexperienced battalions. This, and the admirable training many of them received in France at the famous "Bullring," ensured that the Anzacs, when they again took the field, were a fighting force equal to the task of maintaining the high reputation they had already earned.

The transfer of the Anzacs to the western front involved the shifting of the Anzac base and infantry training quarters from Egypt to England. The Imperial authorities put at the disposal of the Australian and New Zealand Governments a number of camps on Salisbury Plain, and the new drafts of troops were sent by direct route from Australia and New Zealand. Australia was fortunate in

TRAINED SKILL AND INGENUITY IN THE FIELD.
The Anzacs included a notably fine corps of mounted ambulance men. One is shown here rendering first-aid to a wounded man while his comrades turn a saddle blanket into an emergency sling.

and efficiency. Thus England became the base of Anzac military operations, and the Anzac soldier, with his distinctive uniform, became an established street figure in the Old Country.

The Anzacs quickly signalised their presence on the western front by their prominence in those dashes upon the German trenches which characterised the British fighting in the days immediately preceding the "great push." The object of the raids in question was twofold— the capture of prisoners, so that the regiments in the opposing trenches could be identified, and the assertion of a mastery in fighting which was maintained throughout the subsequent offensive with such excellent results.

The typical raid was preceded by an artillery bombardment, which ensured, among other effects, that the barbed-wire protections should be broken and made negotiable. Then the trench-mortars were brought into play, demoralising the Germans still further. Working on a carefully-prepared time-table, the raiders dashed forward, covered the stretch of No Man's Land at top speed, and for eight minutes busied themselves with the enemy in his own trenches. Prisoners were seized and rushed back to the British lines, and war material of any kind was picked up and removed. Everything was done at top speed, for at the end of the eight minutes the artillery was due to recommence its bombardment.

This was work which appealed to the Anzac soldier. The men laid themselves out in the most painstaking manner for its performance, considering every trifle that might make for efficiency. The finest athletes in each battalion were selected as raiders, and they trained for the work as though for an athletic meeting. They sprinted over hurdles, developing their leaping capacity so that such trifles as standing barbed-wire might not check their rush. They were rubbed down and dieted with strict care, and when the night came for the actual raid were as fit as hands could make them.

Then, with blackened faces and the minimum of equipment—though each man carried a revolver—they sprinted across the No Man's Land on their audacious errand. One of the first successful raids was carried out by some of the men of the 7th Brigade, who came back without the loss of a single man, and brought six German prisoners with them. When they burst into the German trenches the enemy, terrified by their blackened faces, set them down as Australian aborigines, and the legend of Australian coloured troops persisted in the German papers for long afterwards. The raid of the men of the 7th Brigade was the model for many succeeding raids, carried out with the best results.

Unflinching under heavy fire In the trenches in the neighbourhood of Armentières the Anzacs made acquaintance with many aspects of trench warfare to which their Gallipoli experience had not accustomed them. They proved themselves unflinchingly courageous on many occasions under the torment of a heavy bombardment, directed upon some section of trench from the heavy howitzers which were the mainstay of the German artillery.

One notable instance was that of the 11th Battalion, one of the veteran regiments concerned in the initial landing on Gallipoli. The steadiness of this battalion under a shell fire which caused over three hundred casualties in a few hours was the subject of special commendation in an army order issued by General Birdwood in the month of May. Such visitations were not at all uncommon, and the experience was repeated by other battalions in the weeks which followed. On every occasion the Anzacs showed a steadiness and endurance corresponding to the dash and initiative they displayed in such work as the trench raids.

On the Somme front Early in July the First Australian Army Corps, consisting of the 1st, 2nd, and 4th Divisions, was entrained for Amiens, and during the next three weeks moved by forced marches to various points in the neighbourhood of the Somme front. At the end of this period of final training they found themselves near Albert, the point from which the British troops started upon the offensive movement which began in July, 1916. From Albert they moved up to a position known as "Sausage Valley," opposite the village of Pozières, then strongly held by the Germans.

Northward was the village of Thiepval, the strongest point held by the Germans along that portion of the Somme front attacked by the British. Thiepval was strengthened by the famous Leipzig Redoubt, and its stout resistance was delaying the whole British advance. A necessary preliminary to its envelopment was the capture of Pozières, which had resisted five successive attacks by British troops. South of Pozières was another stronghold, Guillemont, afterwards brilliantly taken by British troops; while the road from Albert ran straight through the village of Pozières over the highest ridge in the Somme Valley to Bapaume, ten miles farther on. It was for an attack upon Pozières that the Anzac mobile column had been moved from Armentières.

The attack upon Pozières was opened from the south-west by the Anzacs, and from the north-west by some British troops (London regiments), in the early morning of July 23rd. The heroes of Gallipoli, the 1st Division

THE ROAR OF THE LION'S CUBS: AUSTRALIAN GUNNERS IN ACTION. *[Official photograph.*
Stirring scene on a sector of the line on the Somme held by the Anzacs—Australian battery galloping up to a point where one of their heavy guns
was already bombarding the enemy.

of Australian Infantry, were chosen to open the ball, and after a bombardment from the British artillery, which exceeded anything the Anzacs had ever before known, they went out along the Contalmaison road to the assault of the first German line. A second wave charged beyond this to the second line, which ran along a light railway the Germans had built before the village.

Successes in the "Great Push" This position was carried by assault, and further waves of Anzac braves rushed beyond it to the storming of the village itself.

In two hours from the initiation of the movement the Anzacs were digging in along the Bapaume road, on the north-easterly edge of Pozières. North of them, but some three hundred yards away, the British troops had also established themselves. By midday the Anzacs had consolidated the positions they had gained, and by night were enduring a heavy bombardment from the German guns. These had been moved over the ridge beyond Pozières, but as the British airmen permitted the enemy flying men to make no observations, the shell fire was not entirely effective. More damaging was the enfilading fire from the direction of Thiepval, and during the ensuing days the Anzacs suffered heavy casualties from this source.

At Pozières the Anzacs made acquaintance with some of those remarkable dug-outs constructed by the Germans

capture, the 2nd Australian Division was sent forward against the German trenches below the ridge, and carried them after a stiff fight, in many respects more protracted and stubborn than that by which the position was gained. This success was followed up on August 5th by the 4th Division, which carried the Anzac lines to the flank of the high ridge.

A week later the ridge itself was taken by another great assault, the fourth battle the Anzacs had fought in the neighbourhood of Pozières in three weeks. When it was over they had the ridge won. In the distance they could see the German guns which had been bombarding them for twenty days retreating down the slope, far away in the neighbourhood of Bapaume. Before them was the village of Martinpuich, a German stronghold that had still to be attacked, while far on the left they could discern the British lines drawing in around Thiepval.

Those four battles for Pozières and the ridge were the greatest battles in which the Anzacs had ever fought. "I do not know," wrote Mr. C. E. Bean, the official historian of the war for the Commonwealth of Australia, "if it is realised what tremendous fighting all this is. The series of battles now being fought by the Australians is the biggest in which our troops have ever been engaged, and they have fought in a manner beyond all praise. It is

ON LEMNOS: AN ISLE OF GREECE HENCEFORWARD LINKED WITH THE HISTORY OF AUSTRALASIA.
In April, 1915, the infantry of Australia and the whole New Zealand force arrived at Lemnos and Imbros for final training before landing on Gallipoli. Off Lemnos the 21st Battalion won immortal honour by its courage and discipline in the torpedoed Southland.

on lines that rendered them impervious to the worst shell fire. These constructions were thirty feet and more under the earth, spacious and well furnished, giving an air of permanence never hitherto encountered in trench warfare. They had to be captured one by one, and as many of them were connected by underground passages, the Anzac bombing-parties spent many exciting hours in the smoking-out of this rabbit-warren. In this work they found their gas bombs, charged with innocuous but vile-smelling fumes, of the greatest assistance.

It was long before they exhausted the wonders of those subterranean dwellings. Several had periscopes, similar to those in use on submarines, so that the occupants, lying snug thirty feet down, could see what was going on upon the surface of the earth. More than one had an automatic lift, for the purpose of moving machine-guns and other heavy things up and down. All were well stocked with luxuries, including abundance of liquid refreshments ; some were papered with wallpaper ; and in one, at least, was found a large walnut wardrobe full of women's attire, with other signs to show that the occupant's wife shared the dangers of warfare with him at the very front of the German line.

Having once got their feet in Pozières, the Anzacs remained proof against a series of German counter-attacks which were made on the place. Indeed, a week after its

sufficient to say that it is becoming recognised by their fellow-soldiers here that the reputation won by the troops of the Anzac Corps in Gallipoli was not exaggerated."

The tremendous nature of the fighting was indicated by the Anzac casualty lists. In a few weeks they had lost more men by far than the total number of their Gallipoli losses. The proportion of serious wounds, however was much lower than that to which their first experience of fighting had accustomed them, and, like the British troops everywhere upon the western front, they **Splendid in attack or defence** found their mortality appreciably reduced by the steel helmets they wore.

In the days that followed their consolidation of the position they had won upon the high ridge the British took Guillemont upon their right, and began, with the French, to close in upon Combles. This movement the Germans sought to stultify by desperate efforts to recover the lost ridge. In the incessant counter-attacks they were called upon to meet, the Anzacs had once more the opportunity to show that they had endurance as well as dash, and that they could hang on to position as well as carry it by assault.

Other battalions were moved from Armentières to assist in carrying on the movement so splendidly initiated, and among them the celebrated New Zealanders. They,

March-past of an Australian battery on the occasion of a review of the Anzacs by the King on Salisbury Plain, September, 1916.

His Majesty receiving C.O.'s and Staff officers after the review of the Australian and New Zealand troops on the historic Wiltshire plain.

THE SPREADING HOSTS OF ANZACS UNDER ROYAL REVIEW ON SALISBURY PLAIN.

too, set the seal on the fame they had won on the crest of Sari Bair by their exploits between Pozières and the German lines, shining by their valour in three desperate fights for Mouquet Farm, afterwards won and held by the Canadians. Enough had already been done to make the name of Pozières as closely associated with the prowess of Anzac troops as Ypres is with the undying glory of the Canadians.

Having raised by voluntary effort a force of some 350,000 men, Australia and New Zealand were still anxious to accelerate the great effort they were putting forward, in common with the rest of the Empire, to secure victory and an honourable and speedy peace. The example of compulsory service abroad, set by the Mother Country in the early months of 1916, was held before the eyes of these patriotic young nations, and New Zealand first decided to follow it. With very little opposition or comment the principle was adopted and put in force by the Dominion in June, 1916.

New Zealand decrees conscription

In the Commonwealth action was delayed by the absence of Mr. Hughes in Great Britain; but immediately upon his return the question engaged his attention and that of his Cabinet. The proposal for compulsory service abroad encountered more opposition in Australia than in New Zealand, and it is noteworthy that the opposition was well represented in the Labour Ministry, at the head of which Mr. Hughes stood. The formulation of a scheme involved long and anxious consideration by the Cabinet as well as a secret session of the National House of Representatives.

In the end it was announced that the final decision of the question would be left to the people. Arrangements were made for taking a referendum of the nation upon the subject, special interest and importance attaching to the fact that the men already serving with the Colours were given an opportunity of voting, as well as the adults of both sexes who had remained in Australia.

It has to be borne in mind that the whole cost of these extensive and far-reaching military operations was borne by the Dominions themselves. Local war loans provided a very gratifying proportion of the huge sums that had to be provided, the citizens of Australia and New Zealand shouldering the cost in the same cheerful spirit as the home-keeping British people.

The remarkable generosity shown in the support of all war funds was characteristic of the Australasians. In the first two years of the war the benefactions of the Commonwealth population reached the total of £6,000,000 in cash, in addition to valuable gifts in kind, a system initiated in the first days of the war, and steadily maintained throughout its course. New Zealand, as usual, bettered Australia in proportion to population, and in two years provided £1,500,000, in round figures, for war charities.

One heard a great deal of the great sympathy for Belgium shown by the United States since its occupation by Germany—a feeling crystallised in the oft-repeated phrase that "America has fed the Belgians." It is interesting to note, in the light of this belief, that every New Zealander gave six shillings to the Belgian Relief Fund, and every Australian nearly five shillings. The total of the American benefaction, if spread over the population of the United States, shows that each American citizen subscribed but sixpence to this fund.

Such is the record, in brief outline, of the service rendered to the Empire and the allied cause by Australia and New Zealand in the first and second years of the war. Some emphasis was laid in the opening paragraphs upon the readiness and preparedness of these two Dominions to begin the fight; but time and disappointment had no effect upon the stern resolve with which the Southern Dominions entered the lists, except to stiffen them to greater effort and higher resolve. It was no momentary enthusiasm, expending itself by its own vehemence, but the sturdy, continuous manifestation of a deep conviction, shared by two nations unanimous in their opinion.

Australasia's noble record of service

The moral support derived from this attitude of two of the greatest of our self-governing Dominions was only second to the material support they gave from the first day of the war, and steadily increased throughout its progress. The inspiriting promises made in August, 1914, by the leaders of Australasia were honoured beyond all conception then formed of the amplitude of their meaning. That is their record of service—a noble chapter to be set alongside others equal in grandeur, and headed Canada, South Africa, and India.

A TEMPLE AMONG THE ROCKS: AUSTRALIANS AT SUNDAY PRAYERS ON GALLIPOLI.
Religious services were held regularly wherever possible on Gallipoli, under the shelter of any hill or heap of rocks, often with shells and bombs dropping near by.

CHAPTER CXXXIX.

THE CLOSING VICTORIES AT VERDUN AND PREPARATION FOR THE SOMME COUNTER-STROKE.

By Edward Wright.

Falkenhayn as the Grand-Vizier of the Teutons—His Personal Struggle against Hindenburg and Bethmann-Hollweg at Verdun—Position of France under the Tremendous Strain—General Joffre's Marvellous Patience and Tenacity—M. Briand Frustrates Intrigues against the French Staff—Terrific German Flank Attacks End in a Decisive French Victory—Rise of General Nivelle and the Glorious Defence of Dead Man Hill—Three Frenchmen Defeat Thousands of Germans—Extraordinary Swarm Attacks Broken by French Fire—Germans Lose a Hundred Thousand Men in One Day—General Mangin Recovers Douaumont Fort and Relieves Pressure on Dead Man Hill—New Direction of Enemy's Storming Attacks—Struggle in the Ravine of Death—Immortal and Incomparable Defence of Vaux Fort—Its Effect upon French Opinion and the Directing Power of the Parisian Mind—French Provinces at Last Convinced and Confidence in the Government Fully Restored—Germans' Drive Through Thiaumont into Fleury—Superb Recovery of the Thiaumont Garrison—More than Half the German Forces in the West Lost in the Furnace of Verdun—Decisive Difference between the French and German Handling of Infantry—Every Dead Frenchman Takes Three Germans With Him—General Nivelle Recovers Thiaumont and Intimidates the German Staff—His Threat to the Lorraine Ironfields Assists the Franco-British Operations on the Somme.

IN Chapter CXIII. Lord Northcliffe has given a description of the struggle around Verdun up to the close of March, 1916. Much that he knew at the time of writing he could not reveal to the public; but now that the tension at Verdun has been relieved by the Franco-British offensive on the Somme, it may be admitted that the peril to France and her Allies during the German thrust at the Meuse was extreme. General von Falkenhayn robbed all his fronts of men and shell in his endeavour to break a path by Verdun. The great eastern offensive, which Hindenburg and Ludendorff had arranged, was not merely postponed; it had to be abandoned owing to Falkenhayn's desperate persistence at Verdun. Ludendorff at last resigned his position as Hindenburg's Chief of Staff, and implored Hindenburg also to retire from active command in the German Army. But the old Field-Marshal grimly remained at his weakened and useless post. No doubt he foresaw the swift approach of the day when he would be

GENERAL NIVELLE.
In June, 1916, General Nivelle (on the left) took command of the Army of Verdun, General Pétain having been appointed to the command of the armies of the centre.

avenged upon Falkenhayn and Falkenhayn's puppet, the Crown Prince, with General Mudra and Field-Marshal von Haeseler and all the other supporters of Erich von Falkenhayn. Falkenhayn was using up the German reserve with terrible speed in a supreme endeavour to retrieve the grand mistake in his strategy.

The German commander had made no mistake in selecting Verdun for attack. In May, 1915, six of the largest industrial and agricultural associations in Germany demanded that Verdun should be captured. They pointed out that this strong salient in the French front was a great menace to the ironfields of the Briey basin, from which Germany was obtaining nearly eighty per cent. of the steel required for guns and shells. The Briey mines were scarcely twenty miles from the fortified line of Verdun, and France had been allowed to retain them after the Franco-Prussian War because the iron was of such poor quality as to be practically worthless. An English invention, however, made the ore of high value, and for this reason the strongest German army under the Crown Prince

THE FRENCH HERO OF FORT VAUX IN GERMAN CAPTIVITY.
Major Raynal (marked with a cross) photographed with his adjutant after their capture. The defence of Fort Vaux was one of the sublime achievements at Verdun. When thirst compelled Major Raynal to surrender, June 6th, 1916, the French Government appointed him Commander of the Legion of Honour.

co-operated with the army of Metz in springing upon the ironfields in the early days of the war, and securing twelve million additional tons of steel for the manufacture of guns, shells, tractors, and rails. The conquest of the Briey basin was the chief economic factor which made it possible for Germany to continue the war. The Germans expected that France would launch her supreme offensive movement towards the Briey basin. Therefore, General von Falkenhayn erected a semicircle of monster guns round the ironfields and, anticipating a French advance, tried to hack his way into Verdun. As we have seen, he was caught and held round Douaumont, and he could not then break off the battle because the German Emperor had, with extreme rashness, deeply involved the military prestige of his Empire in the aborted Verdun operations.

Falkenhayn's personal pride was also implicated in the affair. Besides having an embittered rival in Hindenburg, the Chief of the Great Staff had a formidable opponent in the Imperial Chancellor, Bethmann-Hollweg, who wished to subordinate all large military questions to certain political views. Supported by many of the principal German industrial and financial magnates, who were thinking of the huge task of reconstructing German foreign trade after the war, Bethmann-Hollweg had some very serious differences with General von Falkenhayn and with Falkenhayn's men on the Great Staff. Bethmann-Hollweg would have been glad to help Hindenburg and Ludendorff to get supreme control over all military **Feud among German** operations. Falkenhayn, of course, was **leaders** well aware of this, and it was one of the motives that induced him to keep hammering at Verdun until he lost more than half a million men. Success at any cost would enable him to maintain his position, and prevent the military policy of the Great Staff from being subjected to political control. First as Minister of War and then as Chief of Staff, Falkenhayn outplayed Bethmann-Hollweg and had overthrown the tradition established by Bismarck, who had repeatedly restrained Moltke. The power of the Great Staff became practically despotic, and so long as Falkenhayn could manage the Kaiser he

was in a position similar to that of one of the old fighting Grand-Viziers of the Ottoman Empire. He controlled the lives of all the men of the Germanic Empires and all their resources that could be used in war. So, for personal as well as dynastic and national r e a s o n s, this hard, desperate, brilliant courtier-soldier fought against the enemies in his own house by flinging lives away by the hundred thousand at Verdun.

We must think of the position of Falkenhayn before Verdun when we sadly ponder the mistakes made by Great Britain and France in the early phases of the war. Large, loose, half-organised modern democracies, governed by committees of orators, tend to compromise over grave military difficulties instead of driving quick and straight towards some solution. They often move slowly when time is of the essence of success, and they hesitate when quick decision is needed. There have been occasions when Great Britain could have retrieved her great mistakes if only she had strongly and swiftly persisted, when by sheer stubbornness she might have made her errors good.

This is the reason why the republicans of ancient Rome put themselves under a Dictator when their national life was in great danger, and it is reported that Mr. Joseph Chamberlain used to think that the loose democracies of the British Empire could only weather a great Continental war by following the old Roman model.

But from the case of Falkenhayn we can now see that the unity of decision and control of all human and material resources, which is the chief source of strength of a temporary or permanent **Weakness of** military despotism, has special weaknesses **despotism** of its own, which tend to balance the weaknesses of the Parliamentary system of managing a war. A German Cabinet, responsible through Parliamentary representatives to the German people, might have broken off the attack on Verdun in time, as the British Cabinet broke off the attack on the Dardanelles. The grounds of the quarrel between Falkenhayn and Hindenburg would have been ventilated, and though the Great Staff would have lost some of its power, it would not have been at last overthrown completely by a man of such low general calibre as the wooden idol of Berlin.

This point is one of supreme and lasting importance. Germany's main advantages were derived from the fact that she possessed the most efficient system of despotic control known in history. She was the practically perfect incarnation of all the political, social, economic, and financial forces of despotism traceable elsewhere only in plutocratic Trust systems without military power, in military tyrannies without great economic strength, and in social systems of caste lacking an emperor behind them. Germany combined, in a strongly modernised form, all the elements of despotic power. Even her sham revolutionary working classes were chained to the vast war-machine of the Great Staff of which Falkenhayn was in single-handed control.

Falkenhayn was himself a miracle of adjustment. He had such soldierly qualities as made him the choice of the able military experts of the Great Staff, and when at last he fell no eminent German could be found of such proved

On the field before Douaumont: French officers watching artillery fire.

"Fall 'midst the ruins rather than surrender!"   Motto of Fort St. Michel, Verdun.

Shattered houses along the Meuse: Verdun Cathedral in the background.

Effect of German long=distance bombardment on the ancient part of Verdun.

French soldiers testing respirators before advancing to the first line.

Field kitchen hidden among the pines in the environs of Verdun.

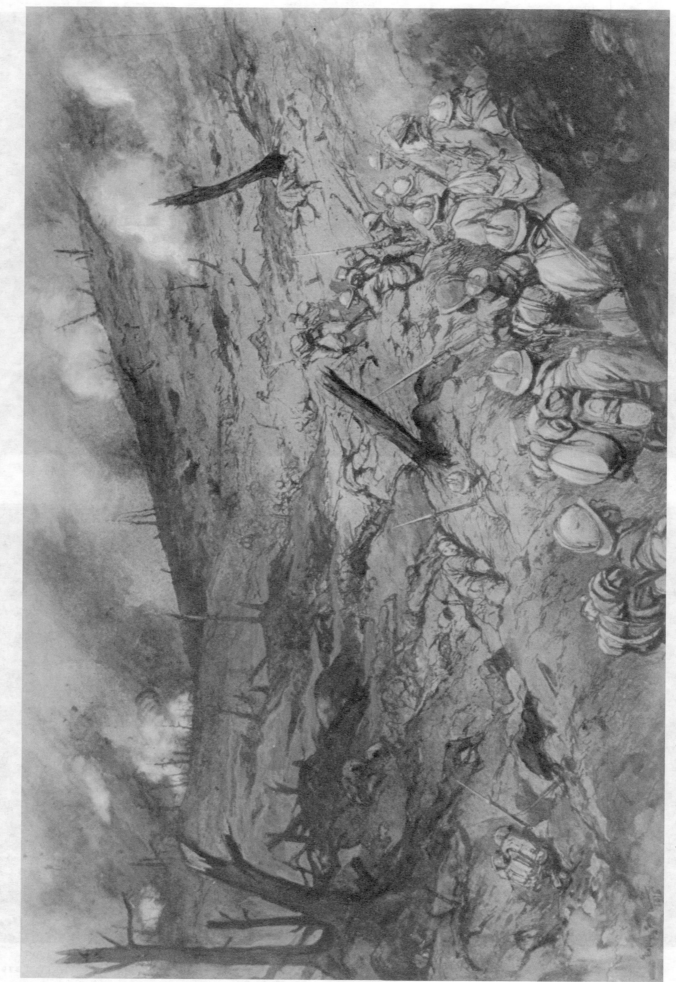

A maelstrom of the Meuse: French infantry debouching to attack a flaming ridge near Douaumont.

ability as was this man of Austrian stock. But in addition to his soldierly qualities Falkenhayn possessed a remarkable power of personal charm, which subdued the Dowager Empress of China some years before it mastered the Crown Prince and the Kaiser. Vivacious, amusing, subtle, and diplomatic as beseemed an Austrian nobleman, Falkenhayn was also a general of the grand school, eclipsing the younger Moltke, Haeseler, Heeringen, Hindenburg, Kluck, and other northern Germans of some renown. He was likewise a statesman, thought by the Great Staff and by the Prussian aristocracy to be better than Bethmann-Hollweg. And in so far as his plans for the reconstruction of Europe were carried out by him at the point of the bayonet they were certainly realisable. But the trouble was that this extraordinary man, exercising a combination of military force and industrial power unimagined by any other despot from Hammurabi to Napoleon, was an underling and not a born war lord. At each step he had to justify himself by success. He could not withdraw from Verdun, or Hindenburg and Bethmann-Hollweg would have overthrown him. Yet, owing to the immense power that had been given to him, this persuasive, influential, intriguing upstart could go on sacrificing large armies, month by month, in an endeavour to maintain his position.

The ordeal of France during the frantic explosion of German energy that Falkenhayn directed was terrible and tragic. Every French hamlet had to send forth men to die at Verdun. The German Chief of Staff transformed the struggle into an incomparable test of the staying power of the German and French races. On all fronts there was a great pause, while Gaul and Teuton rocked in slow, deadly wrestle on the Meuse. The Russians attempted a movement of relief on their southern front, but it was little more than a demonstration. Not only did it fail to carry any enemy trenches, but it convinced the Teutons that Russia was still too weak to do anything. The British Army did not move, the Italian Army remained practically stationary, and the Franco-British force at Salonika attempted no diversion. Falkenhayn, therefore, was able to concentrate his strength on the narrow sector of Verdun. German troops were taken from various points on the Russian front, and there replaced by Austrian troops. Siege-guns were moved even from Serbia towards Verdun, and except for the store of shell which the Austrians were accumulating in the Trentino, and the diurnal numbers of rounds needed for defensive purposes on all fronts, the grand stream of shells and guns from the Germanic war factories poured into the rail-heads near the Meuse.

There was no art or science in the desperate attacks that Falkenhayn prepared from his Staff Headquarters at Charleville on the Meuse. His method was plain, simple, and brutal. It was the method of the bull rush. He massed his guns first on one point and then on another, sending out the Germans to die in divisions so that he might put the French out of action in brigades. He sacrificed three Germans to kill one Frenchman. His idea was that France would not stand the incessant strain. No doubt his spies in France informed him that certain sections of the French race were beginning to weaken. A few French Socialists, who remained in touch with the treacherous leaders of the German democrats, arranged to meet some of the Germans in Switzerland and discuss a European peace. An agreement was signed in Switzerland by certain French and German Socialists. In the French Parliament there were intrigues against M. Aristide Briand, the Premier, who was personally responsible for launching the expedition to Salonika and thus apparently wasting a large, fine French force that was bitterly needed at home. M. Georges Clemenceau, the notorious breaker of Ministries, was one of the men who wished to recall the French troops at Salonika. Among the French

France in the balance

FOR VERDUN THE GLORIOUS.
Decorations of seven Powers for Verdun. At the top: Cross of St. George (Russia). Left to right: Military Cross (Britain), Legion of Honour and War Cross (France), For Military Valour (Italy), For Military Bravery (Serbia), Cross of Leopold (Belgium), Gold Medal Chilitch (Montenegro).

peasantry there were grumblings about British slackness in not coming to the assistance of the hard-pressed army of General Pétain.

France certainly felt the strain. Russia seemed to be too much weakened to assist her. Indeed, the Russians could not apparently hold the main Austro-Hungarian Army and relieve the pressure against the Italians in the Trentino. Great Britain had been boasting to all the world about her five million recruits and her enormous new munition plants; but Sir Douglas Haig, who in the previous autumn had relieved the pressure against the Russians by his offensive at Loos, remained strangely quiet, while Germany, who was maintaining an output of nearly 400,000 shells a day, bent all her forces to the task of annihilating France.

Had it not been for General Joffre, an influential part of the French people might have lost faith in victory. Thanks, however, to the reputation he had won on the Marne after a period of horrible anxiety, General Joffre exercised, without speaking, a marvellous ascendancy over the soul of his heroic commonwealth. Despite the intrigues in Parliament against the Premier, despite the intrigues in Switzerland against the future of humanity, and despite the vague, wide grumblings against the mysterious policy of the egotistical Britons, and the general feeling of despair in regard to Russia, France as a whole stood as firm as a rock, because of her confidence in her quiet Commander-in-Chief.

Joffre restores French confidence

General Joffre's immediate plan was very simple. It was to hold out. As was afterwards revealed, much to the satisfaction of the French people, Sir Douglas Haig had placed himself completely at the service of the French Commander-in-Chief, and had suggested that he should use the British Army to weaken the thrust at Verdun.

But General Joffre had refused the proffered help. No man knew better than he what his country, with its exceedingly low birth-rate, was suffering on the Meuse. He had but to send a telegram to British Headquarters, and a million Britons, with thousands of heavy guns, would fling themselves upon the German lines and compel Falkenhayn to divide his shell output, his heavy artillery, and his millions of men between Verdun and the Somme. But General Joffre, instead of sending the telegram in question, merely despatched officers to British Headquarters to assure and calm the chafing Scotsman commanding the military forces of the British Empire.

In the matter of tenacity of

THE DESERTED CITY.
Ruins of Verdun. Much of the débris was arranged alongside the roadway.

A DEVASTATED VERDUN STREET.
A German onslaught on Verdun was always a foregone conclusion, but no citizen could have visualised its enormity, and no war expert could have foretold its abject failure.

character, it may be doubted whether any ancient commander has shown the power of General Joffre. There have been many great captains to inspire fighting races to struggle to the death rather than give in. But has there been any other leader in war who has watched his fellow-countrymen fall by the hundred thousand and ordered them to go on falling, when he could have saved them by allowing a million foreign soldiers, all passionately eager to help, to join in the struggle? No such leader can be found in history. Up to the present time every race, however honourable and chivalrous, has in a period of dire national necessity been moved by national egotism. It has faithfully combined in operations with allies, as British and Dutch did in the age of Louis XIV., as British and Prussians did in the age of Frederick the Great and Napoleon. But every country fought for its own immediate interests, and, except where protected by sea-power, entered into negotiations for peace when left single-handed to face the shock of an overwhelming attack. This was what Erich von Falkenhayn relied upon. He felt sure that he had only to persist in massing his entire forces around Verdun and hammering

there for months in order either to induce France to make peace or to bring the British Army also into the furnace of battle.

General Joffre's position was very difficult. He did not possess any such despotic power over his country as Falkenhayn possessed over Germany and Austria-Hungary. No dynastic and caste interests were involved in the stand he was making. Yet he could not reveal to his fellow-countrymen at large the reason why he used only Frenchmen to resist the tremendous German pressure. He represented an alert, expressive, cultivated democracy that liked to think out things for itself, and keep its Government strictly in the position of an executive of its ideas and desires. During the ten years before the war several powerful groups of French workmen had been breaking away from State control and developing an intensified form of particularism based upon a new guild system. Neither in ancient Athens nor in mediæval Florence was the spirit of personal liberty so highly developed as in the French Republic of the twentieth century. Yet these Republicans, with their fine intelligence, their passion for reasoning out everything and actually governing themselves, had to submit to fall at Verdun without understanding why they fell. And it was because they could not understand why General Joffre did not ask Sir Douglas Haig to help them that the Chamber of Deputies became restive, and strange rumours about the intentions of Great Britain spread and grew embittered as they spread.

General Joffre had to resist considerable pressure from his own countrymen while withstanding enormous pressure from the enemy. Yet this wonderful man—surely the supreme flower of modern European democracy—displayed on his bluff, quiet, fatherly face no shadow of anxiety. At various times he had made three plans for a general

Public opinion mystified

THE MARK OF THE BOCHE.
French soldiers amid the ruins of a
thoroughfare at Verdun.

cold, serpentine, egotistical strategy of the British Empire. By many subtle channels the French were informed that unless they accepted a fragment of Southern Alsace and made a friendly peace with Germany, strong, idle, selfish "England," who was continually accumulating men and munitions, would become master of the world without the trouble of striking a blow.

Happily, in this turmoil of battle and intrigue, General Joffre and his Staff did not stand alone, as did General von Falkenhayn and his Staff. The French Premier, M. Briand, brought the most valuable assistance to General Joffre during the critical period when General Pétain's army was

offensive movement by all the Allies. First, he had sent his right-hand man, General Pau, to Italy, Serbia, Rumania, and Russia to arrange for a simultaneous movement against the Central Empires. Pau's arrangements fell through owing to the Russian retreat. Then in February, 1916, under General Joffre's directions, General Castelnau had collected the finest French forces under a new general of the young school, General Pétain, as the French spear-head in a general allied attack planned in December, 1915, to take place in the spring of 1916. This attack Falkenhayn had again frustrated by employing on the Meuse the same terrific hammering tactics as he employed on the Dunajec and Biala. General Pétain's force had to be diverted to Verdun, in order to prevent the Germans from breaking through.

There then remained to the hand of General Joffre, as an instrument for a third attempt at a general allied offensive, the great new British Army, under Sir Douglas Haig. And this Army, General Joffre was determined, should not be diverted from the task to which he had assigned it. The French people murmured, the British people chafed, but General Joffre remained inflexible.

Britain's Inexplicable In Russia a powerful body of politicians
Inaction and courtiers began to despise the New Army of Great Britain that did not come to the help of heroic and desperate France. Certain Russian newspapers openly jeered at the sorry part which the Britons seemed to be playing. They attributed selfish designs of a most sinister cast to the British Cabinet, and advocated that peace should be made with Germany and Austria, in order to prevent the British from standing at last victorious over the exhausted Germans and French, without having struck one great blow on land during the struggle. All the neutral Press in Europe that did not sympathise with the Allies was full of calumnies about the

[*French official photograph*

WANTON DESTRUCTION BY THE ENEMY.
Beaurepaire Bridge and Place Chevert, Verdun. Several houses of business were shattered here. In the distance is seen the Bell Tower of the Hotel de Ville.

absorbed in the Verdun struggle. M. Briand knew very little about military matters. He had entered on his political career as a Socialist, with much of Mr. Lloyd George's old passion for despoiling the rich in order to help the poor to attain a decent standard of life. But, like Mr. Lloyd George, the French social reformer was a man with a remarkable open mind and a remarkable gift of persuasion. In other words, he was a born diplomatist, and after becoming convinced of the necessity for a very strict combination of all the allied forces, he set himself to win over Italy and Russia to the third French plan for a combined movement. The British Staff seems to have been in the happy position of needing no persuasion in military affairs. It was at the service of France, and it had followed her even when it thought she was wrong, as at Salonika—where, as a reward, it was afterwards found that she was brilliantly right. In regard to a combined economic policy, which was part of M. Briand's far-reaching plan of co-operation, the British Cabinet of Free Traders and Tariff Reformers was harder to convince. But M. Briand succeeded in burying some of the dying Free Trade traditions, and making the British Empire the supreme

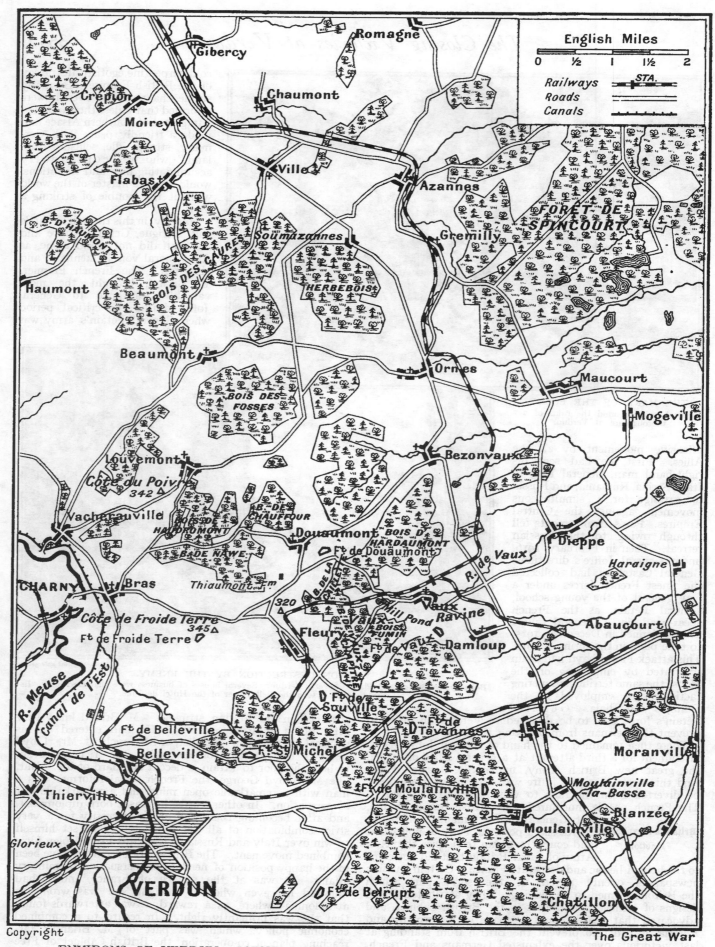

ENVIRONS OF VERDUN: SCENE OF GERMANY'S GREATEST EFFORT IN THE WEST.

Map of the east bank of the Meuse, indicating the towns, villages, ridges, woods, and forts involved in the German attempt to capture Verdun. Within a few days the enemy had swept all before him up to Douaumont and Vaux, an achievement fully commensurate with his stupendous preparation and sacrifice of effectives. Then came the glorious French defence, loss, and recapture of Douaumont, where the Bretons saved the day, and the equally splendid effort at Vaux, lost and regained several times. From March, 1916, what progress was made by the Germans cost them losses fatally disproportionate to the territory occupied, though at one time the French Staff did not consider the fall of Verdun impossible.

factor against the Teuton idea of a tariff union of Central European States.

Then Italy, who was linked to Germany by industry and finance, and inclined to confine herself in her own way to a struggle against Austria, was won over by M. Briand in March, 1916, and excited to generous emulation in all allied matters of co-operation by the gallant vehemence with which the Russians, under General Brussiloff, relieved the pressure of the Austrian advance in the Trentino. In order to assist the Italians, the Russians undertook a grand offensive some months before their process of re-armament was completed. This superb example of fidelity to the common interest of the Allies deeply moved the Italians, and made them incline in magnanimous mood to the advances made by their old rivals in the Mediterranean, the French.

To all her Allies France could say : "Consider Verdun." Single-handed the French were resisting the entire attacking forces that Germany could bring to bear against all the Allies. Naturally, the Allies recognised the incomparable self-sacrifice that France was making in the common interest. By the end of April, 1916, General Joffre's new plan was accepted. Great Britain was not to move, but to conserve her men and accumulate shells and guns. Italy, in spite of being hard-pressed in the Trentino, was to make a grand attack against Gorizia, in order to compel the Germans to use more of their reserves in helping the Austrians against the Russians. The northern Russian front was to remain idle like the British front. Then when Falkenhayn had exhausted himself at Verdun, the British Army was to move together with a fine French force that General Joffre was withdrawing from Verdun and holding in reserve. Nevertheless, it was agreed that, despite all this successive outbreak of strong and interlocked activity on the part of the Allies, there was to be no general offensive during the summer of 1916. In a general offensive the enemy's lines are assailed practically everywhere. He is entirely held by an attacking movement, even in places where no decisive break through is attempted. Nothing of this kind was arranged by the Allies. Their plan was to imitate Falkenhayn's action at Verdun, and select two or three weak spots in his western, eastern, and southern lines and hammer methodically and persistently at each of these sectors with a million or more men. The idea was to exert a general pressure, until the reserves of Germany and Austria-Hungary were exhausted. Only when complete exhaustion was evident was the real general offensive to take place. No date for it was, therefore, fixed. It depended entirely **Masterly French** upon the course of events and the **plan** progress of munition-making in Great Britain and Russia.

As Lord Northcliffe explained at the time, the French Staff did not consider it impossible that Verdun would fall. Of one thing only they were certain—which was that the enemy would have to pay a fearful price for the capture of the positions along the Meuse. The French soldiers took as their battle-cry the now famous phrase : "Ne passeront pas !" (They shall not pass!). But the French High Command, while inspiring their soldiers with an incomparable spirit of valour, recognised that the Germans might pass across the Meuse if they sacrificed everything. Towards the end of March, 1916, Falkenhayn imposed upon his local commanders a new plan of attack. He had first tried to pierce the French front on the north-east of Verdun, and then he had endeavoured to drive in both the French wings. After the failure of these two manœuvres on a grand scale, the German commander tried a third method, and, instead of launching the great simultaneous attack, he began a series of local assaults.

These were generally conducted by the effectives of a single division, with the **Minor German** object of dividing the French reserves and **successes** securing advantageous positions for another general offensive. The Germans carried the remains of the original first French line on the left bank of the Meuse, at Malancourt, Haucourt, and Béthincourt, these three hamlets lying below the northern slopes of Hill 304 and Dead Man Hill (le Mort Homme.) They also captured Avocourt Wood, which gave them a line of attack towards the rear of the principal French line of defence at Hill 304 and Dead Man Hill. Then, on the right bank of the river, they won a part of the Vaux Ravine and a patch of forest, Caillette Wood, commanding one of the slopes of the ravine. But

EASY MOMENTS FOR MEN WHO KNEW NO FEAR.
French infantry for the first-line defence of Verdun resting to the rear of a temporary aircraft hangar before proceeding to the terrible scene of conflict.

the Avocourt, Vaux Ravine, and Caillette Wood positions were recovered by superb French counter-attacks in the first week in April, leaving the enemy little to show for the loss of hundreds of thousands of men since the last week in February. "Nibbling" having proved unsuccessful, the enemy returned to the method of flank attacks in force.

A vast mass of men, with some thousands of guns, was concentrated among the forested heights on the left bank of the Meuse, from Cumières Wood to Béthincourt Wood. The French lines were scarcely more than nine miles long. They were drawn around Dead Man Hill, rising a hundred feet above the woods occupied by the Germans, and around Hill 304, the summit of which was only sixty feet above the highest part of the wooded ground held by the enemy. Between the two principal heights round which the French were established there ran a valley road southward to the hamlet of Esnes. This valley dipped about a hundred feet between Dead Man and Hill 304. The German siege-guns bombarded the nine-mile front with unparalleled fury, the tempest of shell being more terrible than that which swept away the first French

AT THE MOMENT OF FIRING.
Type of French cannon that helped to hold the enemy from Verdun. The numerous woods and ridges in the region of Verdun afforded ample cover for batteries defending the fortress.

hundreds of guns upon the grey masses, smashed them up completely, and followed them into Crow Wood (Bois des Corbeaux) and Cumières Wood until the entire force went to pieces. The German commander then brought up a fresh force that crept over the water meadows between the Meuse and the slopes of the Goose Crest (Côte de l'Oie) and tried to rush the ruins of Cumières village. Advancing along the open field of fire by the grass flats, the Germans were caught in a terrible way by shrapnel, machine-gun bullets, and musketry fire, and smashed back with very heavy loss.

In the afternoon two more masses of forty thousand men each were launched westward against Hill 304 and eastward against Dead Man. Towards the end of the day a German brigade managed to take some trenches near Avocourt, but the position was recovered in the twilight by a French counter-attack. On the eastern side the enemy won five hundred yards of advanced trench at the base of the Dead Man, and succeeded in retaining this unimportant bit of low ground for some days. It had cost Falkenhayn the best part of a hundred thousand men to take five hundred yards of advanced French trench. His losses were as heavy as those the British Army had incurred during its entire operations at Loos, yet the Germans had not made the least impression upon the French defences. It was one of the greatest defeats in the war, and in a special Order of the Day General Pétain informed the soldiers of Verdun that they could now be confident that victory was achieved.

The battle of April 9th was practically decisive, in that it proved that the forces of the French defence were very much stronger than the forces of the German attack.

defences at Verdun in February. Then, on the morning of Sunday, April 9th, 1916, some forty thousand Germans came out of the woods of Béthincourt and Malancourt, and stormed up the long western slopes towards Hill 304. The grey figures advanced in dense and very deep formation, by columns of companies, the intention being to choke the French guns by sheer numbers.

But the wonderful French quick-firer, which was used like a machine-gun by General Pétain's soldiers, broke every German column within a hundred yards of the French trenches. Then as the grey flood ebbed from the western slopes of Hill 304, a stronger German attack was launched against Dead Man Hill on the eastern side of the nine-mile front. Here the Germans had only seven hundred yards of ground to take, in order to reach the high northern boss which the French used as an observation-post. Another forty thousand German troops charged from the woods in dense columns, but General Pétain, working on his central telephone control system, turned

All the elements of General Pétain's new system of resistance had been tested to breaking-point, and it was the Germans who were broken. General von Falkenhayn could not for some time maintain an ordinary amount of pressure against Pétain's lines, for the German reserves before Verdun were exhausted. But instead of letting the battle die down, General Pétain began to force the pace of it. He pressed the Germans back at Douaumont, and in answer to his pressure two fresh German divisions were brought from another part of the front and launched in a general attack between Douaumont and the river. The French guns and machine-guns broke the attack in a scene of ghastly slaughter, and all that the Germans won was a small French advanced position in Chauffeur Wood. The Teutons also made a strong local attack on Dead Man, where they were again defeated. The Battle of Verdun was clearly won, and at the beginning of May General Pétain relinquished his command to one of his

General Pétain's counter-attack

brilliant subordinates, General Nivelle, and took over the control of all the French centre from Soissons to Verdun.

Pétain had proved himself equal in genius to Foch, and was entrusted with power similar to that of the man who broke the German centre on the Marne. Foch controlled all the Belgian-British-French front down to the Aisne, while Pétain controlled the great and important armies on the Aisne Plateau, the rolling downs of Champagne, the forests of Argonne, and the eastern and western banks of the Meuse. The southern French forces from Toul to Alsace apparently remained in the command of the tried and victorious commander, General Dubail. General Castelnau, at the head of the French Staff, directed the larger elements of strategy and co-ordinated the efforts of Foch, Pétain, and Dubail. General Joffre harmonised all the French efforts, including that at Salonika, and acted as the leading strategist of the Grand Alliance on the Board of Strategy which directed the combined movements in France and Flanders, in Italy, Greece, Rumania, and Russia.

General Nivelle was, like General Pétain, a colonel at the outbreak of the war. Married to an English lady, he was, indeed, in July, 1914, staying at a southern **Nivelle's rapid promotion** English watering-place, where some of his children were being educated. After ably commanding the 5th Infantry, he was promoted brigadier-general in October, 1914, and divisional commander in December, 1915. He came to Verdun at the head of the Third Army Corps, and there distinguished himself so greatly that General Pétain selected him as

his successor. A man of sixty years of age, trained at the Ecole Polytechnique, he had the advantage of having been in the artillery before he was given the command of an infantry regiment. He was able to assist General Pétain in organising all the guns around Verdun into one mighty instrument for battle by means of telephone communication. Both the British and the German Armies appear to have antici- **Annihilation by telephone** pated the French in the establishment of a system linking thousands of guns together by a central telephone exchange. But General Pétain and General Nivelle worked out, first in Champagne and then at Verdun, some important refinements in this new method of handling massed parks of artillery, and they made the French gunner at last a wonder and a dread to the Germans.

For a month Falkenhayn kept his thirty battered divisions at Verdun engaged in little local attacks and little local counter-attacks. General Castelnau was able to get Pétain and Nivelle to give up their finest body of troops, the Twentieth Army Corps, under General Balfourier, which had broken the first great German attack on the Douaumont Plateau and saved Verdun. Although neither the Germans nor the peoples of the Grand Alliance knew it at the time, the position around Verdun had become one of secondary importance. Though the losses among the defenders had been heavy, they were much less than the Germans estimated. The Germans were inclined to think that, if they had suffered most terribly, their opponents with a smaller population had suffered at least equally. This was not the case. Only in the

[*French official photograph.*]

WAR MATERIAL IN RESERVE AT A DEPOT OF THE MEUSE SECTOR.

French transport arrangements to and from the region of Verdun were a marvel of organisation, and contributed in no small measure to our ally's success. A network of light railways as well as scrupulously good roads disgorged everything needed to carry on the great defence. Depots, such as the one seen in this illustration, were never allowed to run short of barbed-wire and other necessities of trench construction.

THE CROWN PRINCE MOTORING ON THE VERDUN FRONT.
The disaster of Verdun will ever be associated with the Crown Prince, who was nominally in charge of the colossal operations. For his lack of success after the greatest numerical losses of any one failure in military history the Hohenzollern heir was awarded the Oak Leaves of Merit.

battles of February, 1916, had the French lost men in as great a proportion as their enemy. After General Pétain re-established the French lines and greatly increased the French gun-power, France had saved the lives of hundreds of thousands of her children by means of an enormous expenditure of shell. The French infantry in the fire-trenches were always comparatively few in number, well dug in and armed mainly with hand-grenades and machine-guns. In General Pétain's system the rifle became for the time almost obsolete. The work of the bullet was done by the machine-gun, and the work of the bayonet by the hand-grenade. The "75" French quick-firer, that could send its shell in a curve with something of a howitzer-like effect, was used in the manner of a super-machine-gun. It was hidden in batteries on the slopes of hills behind the front French trenches, and by indirect fire at short range it broke up the German infantry masses. Machine-guns cannot fire over a hill, but the French quick-firer could spout shrapnel and high explosive over Dead Man Hill and Hill 304. It, therefore, became the supreme weapon of the French trench defence, and smashed up the grey German masses, while the heavy howitzers beat down the fire of the German batteries, which were trying to put the French field-guns out of action, and also kept up a curtain fire in the German front line and the German support line and over the German communications.

At the beginning of the war the French had thought that their quick-firer, by far the best of its kind in the world, would prove an incomparable instrument of attack. It was, however, beaten by the slower but longer-ranged heavy artillery of the enemy. Even at the Battle of the Marne the French suffered very seriously from a lack of mobile, heavy guns, and it was because the army of Paris, which tried to turn Kluck's flank, lacked the heavy pieces with which Kluck defended himself that the army of invaders was saved from a rout. France had to construct hundreds of very heavy pieces of artillery before she could thrust well into the German lines. By the spring of 1916 the French output of heavy shell was nearly fifty times as large as the output in August, 1914. The output of heavy guns was about thirty-five times as much as that at the beginning of the war. Yet the manufacture

"75" fails for attacks

of French light field-guns also increased in a remarkable manner, the number of "75's" being twenty-three times as great as that obtaining when the Germans made their abortive rush on Paris. This extraordinary increase in 3 in. guns was due to the fact that their terrific rate of fire, combined with their handiness and their semi-howitzer effect, made them master instruments in defensive warfare. In attacking trenches the new quick-firing mortar, that pitched a big mass of high explosive for a short distance, was more useful than the "75." But for breaking up either massed columns of men or drenching with shrapnel attacking lines of men in open order, the "75" remained a most murderous weapon, as it could be employed in hilly country where machine-guns, with their direct fire, had only a very limited range.

In local attacks, such as those by which the French recovered all Dead Man Hill on April 22nd, 1916, the innumerable "75's," pumping up fountains of fire from hidden slopes southward, forced the German infantry to keep under cover until the French infantry arrived with their hand-bombs. Machine-guns could not produce this effect, because every machine-gun that could be brought into play was situated on the northerly slopes of the rounded boss of Dead Man, and clearly exposed to the direct fire of hostile artillery. At the beginning of May, 1916, the French made an evening attack on the German positions south-east of Douaumont Fort and captured five hundred yards of trenches. This was a masterly example of the semi-howitzer effect of the "75." The flame of the light guns could be clearly seen through the darkening air, but as many of the pieces fired from hollows, only a German airman could have marked their positions for attack by the 12, 15, and 16·5 in. guns at Spincourt. One of the first things General Pétain had done when he arrived at Verdun was to recover the mastery of the air from the enemy, so that the Germans usually had to go by direct observation from heights and from captive balloons far in their rear in order to trace the position of French batteries.

French aerial ascendancy

Hill positions had lost nearly all their old military importance. Neither side entrenched a large force of infantry along the crest of a hill in order to shoot down an attacking host. Hill-tops were occupied only by artillery observers, sitting in a deep hole at the end of a periscope and a telephone wire. French observers on Dead Man Hill, and the line of Charny Ridge some miles south of Dead Man, watched every movement of Germans near the Meuse, and brought howitzers by the score or by the hundred to bear upon the moving target. Dead Man, rising nine hundred and sixty-eight feet above sea-level, was the dominating French observation point. Eastward it overlooked all the German positions facing the Douaumont front, and northward it dominated all the woods occupied by the Germans from Forges to Cuisy. But it was the eastward outlook, on the German attacking positions immediately north of Verdun, which made the Dead Man an objective of the highest importance to the German commander. He could not make a frontal attack on Verdun with any chance of success until he had captured the Dead Man and had thrown back the numerous French batteries that enfiladed from across the Meuse every German advance on the Pepper Hill (Côte du Poivre)-Thiaumont-Douaumont line.

So all through May and the greater part of June, 1916, Falkenhayn, through his subordinate commanders, directed a series of terrific attacks at the Dead Man Hill. Some assaults were made directly against the long undulating plateau rising northward in the round boss above Béthincourt. Other attacks were planned to turn the Dead Man Hill positions by flanking movements westward. For three days and three nights all the ridges and slopes for miles around Dead Man Hill were swept by heavy shell fire, and on Sunday morning, May 7th, a mass attack was delivered on a two-mile front between Dead Man Hill and Hill 304. The hillsides and the mouth of the valley between the crests glimmered with advancing grey waves. Some five brigades tried to storm the heights, but they were broken one after the other before the cross-fire of the French batteries and machine-guns, and when evening fell only one communication trench on the west side of the valley had been won by the Germans. This trench was dominated by higher French positions both east and west, so that, costly as it had been to win, it was still more costly to hold. In the night the French recaptured it, and then held and smashed up every counter-attack. When dawn broke the French still held their recovered trench, and the Germans had only tens of thousands of dead and wounded to show as the result of the fourth great battle for Verdun.

On the east of the Meuse a Prussian division tried to break through the Thiaumont Farm on the Douaumont Ridge, while the French enfilading forces around Dead Man Hill were held up by the direct assault made upon them. The Prussian division advanced with admirable steadiness, and though battalion after battalion was shattered, a few hundred survivors succeeded towards the evening in taking five hundred yards of the French line. But, courageous as the Prussians had proved themselves, they were no match against the French in scientific warfare. The victorious remnant of the division was pounded all Sunday evening by hundreds of French guns, and then, by certain means, a small fresh French force was brought through the curtain of fire the Germans maintained around Thiaumont, and in a swift counter-attack nearly all the lost ground was retaken. The Germans had spent nearly a month in the preparation of this new offensive movement, yet after expending millions of shells, wearing out guns by the hundred, and losing men by the thousand score, they

TO AND FROM THE INFERNO OF VERDUN.
Wounded German infantry on their way back from a fruitless attack on Verdun. They were about to be transported to a base hospital. The smaller illustration shows a group of first-line German troops lined up for inspection in a French village street before being ordered to the attack.

ALL THAT REMAINED OF MURMURING TREES AND LUXURIANT VERDURE.

Corner of the Caillette Wood, near Verdun. Little of the original landmarks survived the deluge of conflicting shells. In fact, many of the woods along the Meuse Valley, so prolific in timber and foliage, were transformed into rubble heaps, a few gaunt trees shorn of their branches emphasising the melancholy of the scene.

won nothing. As a French officer sardonically remarked : " The cost of ground around Verdun was rising."

Under the explosions of innumerable shells the north and north-western slopes of Hill 304 were churned into a chaos. All the northerly slopes of Dead Man ridge were likewise ploughed up. The French infantry sheltered on the southern slopes, the summits being defended only by crossing fires from French batteries. Thereupon, the tide of battle was turned by Falkenhayn still farther westward. He had begun by attacking Dead Man in order to turn Cumieres Wood ; then he had attacked Hill 304 in order to turn Dead Man, and on May 10th he attacked the height west of Hill 304 in order to turn Hill 304. The attacked height, known on the map as Hill 287, and called by the Germans White Ant Hill, is an elevation with gentle slopes lying midway between the main French position and the westerly woods occupied by the Germans. It was enfiladed by French batteries in Avocourt Wood in the same way as Avocourt Wood could be enfiladed **Splendid artillery** by French batteries in the next westerly **positions** sector. All the French positions interlocked, so that any German frontal attack upon one or more of them came under a cross-fire. Yet two German divisions endeavoured to storm White Ant Hill. One advanced from the western woods and another from the northern valleys. The western division was caught on two sides by gun fire, and broken before it arrived at the French trenches. Sections of the northern

division reached one of the slopes held by the French, only to be driven out by a counter-attack.

This waste of the forces of an army corps was followed by another pause. The Germans replaced their worn-out guns, and filled out with young drafts their wasted infantry forces. Then on May 17th, after another long, terrific bombardment, a general attack was delivered against the French line on the left bank **Germans** of the Meuse from Avocourt to Cumières. **await reinforcements** Avocourt Woods, from which the French guns had enfiladed the assault on White Ant Hill, were first attacked by strong German forces at six o'clock in the evening. The struggle raged with extreme fury all night, the successive waves of German infantry being thrown back with terrible losses. Towards dawn on May 18th the French commander felt the enemy weakening, and suddenly launched two charges, one against a German position north of White Ant Hill and the other against a fortified post on the north-east slope of Hill 304 held by Pomeranian troops. Both of these German positions were captured. The defeated enemy commander, therefore, moved his point of attack towards the Dead Man, and, under a hurricane of shell, sent two fresh divisions forward. These, however, were broken by French gun fire, their only gain being a small position by White Ant Hill near the road leading from Haucourt to Esnes. Thereupon, Falkenhayn resolved to overwhelm the French with shell fire. For two days and two nights the boss and the plateau

SHATTERED BUT UNCONQUERED: FORT SOUVILLE, WHERE THE GERMAN DESIGN FOR A FINAL GENERAL ASSAULT ON VERDUN WAS CHECKMATED.

Fort Souville occupied a dominating position overlooking the plateau of the tableland of Vaux. The stream of attack which the Germans were planning against this strong though dismantled fort was checked by General Nivelle's men who, on June 30th, 1916, rushed and recovered the outflanking Thiaumont Work. This feat marked the final passing of the initiative in attack from the Germans to the French.

of Dead Man smoked and flamed under the concentrated fire of hundreds of heavy German and Austrian howitzers. When the north-western and north-eastern slopes of the Dead Man had been made uninhabitable, two swarms of German infantry attacked on either side in an endeavour to envelop the salient height.

Shattered by flanking fire The eastern division, that came from Crow Wood, swept over the remnant of French machine-gun sections who valiantly tried to hold the fire-trench, and in large numbers climbed up to the French second line. But on the height they were met by flanking counter-attacks from the French lines at Cumières. Though the German commander flung another division into the battle, he could not make any headway. The French forces by the Meuse continued to take the Germans in the flank with gusts of artillery fire, machine-gun fire, and bayonet and bomb attacks. All the spear-heads of the German thrust were cut off and destroyed.

On the western slopes of Dead Man Hill, however, the enemy succeeded in winning a position round the dominating boss of the hill. The boss itself was swept by the fire of French and German guns, and transformed into a No Man's Land, the French garrison being driven down into the shallow depression on the plateau. The French trenches were wiped out, and all the ground on the height for a depth of nearly two miles was covered by a curtain fire from the German batteries. Yet French reinforcements,

coming up in motor-lorries, pushed through the tempest of death, and leaping forward from shell-hole to shell-hole, arrived at the ruins of the first-line trenches. There the fresh French troops, sadly diminished in numbers, broke back two waves of enemy sharpshooters, and then held up the driving massed columns of double companies, by means of which the German commander tried to conquer the lower southern ridge of Dead Man Hill. As the German columns were held by rifles and machine-guns, the flanking French batteries caught the checked, grey masses and mowed them down in ghastly swathes.

Soon the Germans had ramparts of their own dead to serve as cover in their rushing mass attacks. On both Dead Man Hill and Hill 304 the grey piles of dead, wounded, and stunned men formed barriers some yards in height. In their counter-attacks the French took prisoners from these stacks of corpses. For it often happened that men who had not been hurt were knocked down and buried under the falling wall of their slain or wounded comrades. Most of the men thus recovered seemed to be dazed, partly by shell shock but largely by **Alcohol and** a drug mixture of ether and alcohol. A **German courage** good deal of Dutch courage was thus combined with the remarkable iron discipline, under which mass after mass of German infantry climbed up the slopes to die. Still, there was something sublime in the absolute disregard for death displayed by the Teutonic swarms. Their cohesion and drive, under appalling losses, exceeded

THREE GREAT FRENCH SOLDIERS.
General Joffre with General Fayolle, who planned the French offensive
on the Somme, and General Balfourier, whose Bretons trapped the
Brandenburgers at Fort Douaumont.

trenches, running across the Esnes Valley, connected the French organisations on the Dead Man Hill with their system of trenches on the western slopes of Hill 304. On this height the French positions now formed a salient in the large horse-shoe curve which the Germans had won round the base of the hill. The crest of Hill 304 was still held on May 23rd, 1916, by our ally, in spite of the fact that the Germans in their official communiqués claimed to have conquered it. As a matter of fact, the enfilading fire of the eastern French batteries at Cumières had become a greater obstacle to the German advance on Dead Man than the batteries south of Hill 304. Cumières and the woods around it formed the extreme northern point of the defending armies around Verdun. As the guns in the wood were linked by telephone to the central exchange in Verdun, as well as to the army exchange on the left bank of the Meuse, their fire could be directed against the Bras-Douaumont front as well as against all German movements on the eastern slopes of Dead Man Hill. Cumières, therefore, became the main objective of Falkenhayn's next general attack.

On May 23rd the French line was again buried in shell and cloaked in smoke. French airmen, sent out to reconnoitre the movements of German infantry, flew perilously near the ground **Falkenhayn's** but could see nothing. A great cloud of **suicidal persistence** smoke, six hundred feet thick, blanketed the scene. The smoke was so dense that the flame of the high explosives could not pierce it, and into this hell of death and torment the German commander sent his waves, lines, and columns of cannon-fodder. His main attack was delivered on the centre at Hill 304 and Dead Man Hill and on the right wing at Cumières.

But the smoke was not all German smoke. Every French gun and howitzer that could bear maintained a barrage of fire over the German positions and the No Man's Land between the trenches. It was not until the evening that the German infantry could get through the curtain of high explosive and shrapnel and reach the French trenches between Dead Man Hill and Hill 304. Having at last got within striking distance, the Germans brought up a detachment of flame-throwers, and with torrents of liquid fire burned the French out of their lines as twilight was falling. Just before nightfall the French returned, and in a charge of terrible fury stabbed and bombed the flame-throwers and the supporting enemy troops out of the lines and recovered all the position.

Liquid fire is like poison gas. It is calculated to frighten savages, but when used against an army of disciplined civilised men it rouses them to such a pitch of fury that they overthrow all the calculations of their enemy. In half an hour's nocturnal fighting the Germans lost all the ground they had won at the cost of tens of thousands of men, and only a small remnant of them escaped back to the trenches from which they had advanced. But on the wing at Cumières the German effort was more prolonged and more successful. The ruins, lying in the great loop of the Meuse, were bombarded for some hours and then attacked by waves of infantry. The small French garrison armed with machine-guns held out in cellars and shell-holes until May 24th, but then some Thuringian regiments, by means of a long, violent alternation of battery and assault, broke through the village and stormed along the water meadows of the Meuse towards the railway-station at Chattancourt.

This was a very important advance for the enemy. It brought him a mile behind Caurettes Wood, in which the French batteries were sited, and south-east of Dead Man Hill. But the French commander had the situation well in hand. All the low land by the river which the Germans had won was under the fire of French guns on either side of the river. A tempest of shell was poured upon the Thuringians, and a fresh French force, brought up in the night, was launched in a counter-attack.

all old Prussian records of tenacity in attack. But the brutal manner in which Falkenhayn's commanders sacrificed their men did not shake the spirit of the thin, advanced lines of French infantry that clung to shell-holes and fragments of trench in a noble spirit of alert and intelligent self-sacrifice. Each Frenchman could see what a tremendous price the Germans were paying for every yard of ground they won, and he, therefore, knew that his steady individual effort would not be wasted by his commanders, even though he fell in one of the wild swarm attacks made by the enemy.

Innumerable were the deeds of heroic initiative performed by French non-commissioned officers and privates. The machine-gunners especially were magnificent. Only a remnant of them survived each great bombardment that ploughed up nearly every **Three great** front dug-out. But those who did survive **machine-gunners** fought until they received the order to retire. To one patch of wood, which was thought to have been conquered by the enemy, no order was sent, and the three Frenchmen who remained alive in it beat back every attack and saved the position. The French did not need to be drugged in order to carry on to the edge of doom. Their keen intelligence, the finest example of democratic culture in history, nerved them to a high-conscious individual effort, against which the mob-like, semi-collectivist spirit of the Teutons broke in vain. At the end of the battle the French still held the southern slopes of the Dead Man Hill, where they were solidly entrenched, and their positions ran in a horse-shoe curve round the eastern and western slopes.

The Germans had won a salient on the northern face of the height, but could not get any farther. Communication

By the river the Germans were pushed back a mile to Cumières village, and then from Caurettes Wood they were assailed by another French force. When day broke on May 25th one point of the French pincers was thrust into the cellars and rubble of the village eastward, and another point of the pincers closed westward on the Germans above Caurettes Wood. The enemy commander had then to free his trapped and half-scattered force, and by hammering for the greater part of a week against the left point of the pincers he compelled the French force in Caurettes Wood to loosen its hold on Cumières.

It is, however, to be observed that the French commander controlled the situation from the night of May 24th to the morning of May 31st. All this time he held the survivors of the Thuringian regiment in a vice, and compelled the enemy to launch from the northern wood mass after mass of infantry against the terrific fire of the French guns. The original French garrison of Cumières was very small, and though the counter-attack was made by a larger force, its first victory was won at no great loss, **Enemy's compulsory** and the enemy was then forced to **sacrifice** sacrifice his men in divisions during a week of tremendous gun fire defence.

By this time the French had brought out a new missile of attack against the line of German observation balloons that dominated the hills on either side of the Meuse and directed the fire of thousands of German guns. A new kind of French bomb destroyed the floating "sausages," and left the German gunners in a condition of great disadvantage. The French airmen were masters of the air, and were able to trace the direction of the flow of German ammunition and German reinforcements, spot for their own guns, and protect their own observation balloons. Meanwhile, General Nivelle was in a position to make his preparations in secret, and when Falkenhayn was bringing all his available forces to bear against Dead Man Hill and Cumières a surprising answering move was delivered by the French commander on the other side of the Meuse.

Here the main French positions had scarcely altered since the Twentieth Army Corps flung the Brandenburgers back on Douaumont Fort. The fort was a ruin hemmed in by new French trenches and **Under wings of** dominated by French howitzers. But as **victory** the German Emperor had staked the military prestige of his empire on the possession of the fort, General Nivelle selected this point for attack, with a view to lightening the enemy pressure against the French positions across the Meuse. His direct object was to relieve the pressure against the Dead Man Hill by compelling the Germans to bring large reinforcements across the Meuse. A single French division was assigned the task of making a diversion, but it was a famous division—the 5th—under a famous commander, General Mangin, who with his men had broken all the attacks made by the enemy the previous April on the Douaumont-Vaux sector. In their first Verdun battle the troops of the 5th Division had killed or captured every German who reached their trenches, and had stormed every position they were set to attack. "You march under the wings of victory," said General Mangin in April, when he gave his men a furlough for a month while the division was being strengthened with new drafts.

In the third week in May the troops came back from their homes, with their ranks brought up to full strength,

CONTRAST IN TRANSPORT: WHEEL-LESS TROLLEY AND HORSELESS CARS NEAR VERDUN.
Simple but effective water-cart in use near Verdun. It would be difficult to imagine a better illustration of the contrast between the old and the new than this horse-drawn trolley without wheels halting beside the wheeled vehicles without horses.

FIRE AND DESOLATION IN VERDUN.
The town of Verdun suffered terrible material damage in the epic siege, and many fires raged in its forsaken residential quarters.

to all the world. Under a blasting shell fire of three-quarter-tons and half-tons of metal and high explosive they dug deeper into the caverns the Germans had made, watched by their telephones and periscopes, and sought for rest from the monster guns at Spincourt by closing with hand-grenades on the remnant of the German garrison in the north-eastern corner of the fort.

But in the night came the furious mass attacks of the disconcerted and frightened German commander. His position was already menaced by the surprising French success. If he could not hammer the 5th Division from the fort the position of Falkenhayn himself would not be safe. In fact, the Hohenzollern dynasty

and at dawn on May 22nd Douaumont Fort looked like a volcano in eruption. The French artillery was completing its methodical bombardment, and as soon as the air brightened a squadron of pilots flew over the lines and exploded six of the German observation balloons. Having thus " bandaged the eyes of the Boche," as the French soldiers put it, the 5th Division began to advance from shell-hole to shell-hole at ten minutes to twelve in the morning. One regiment skirmished forward through the Caillette Wood towards the right side of the fort. Another regiment made a frontal attack in the centre, while the third regiment converged on the left near Thiaumont Farm. The Germans, divining their danger, drenched all the ground with shrapnel, but the veterans of France went through the hail of lead and over three lines of German trenches.

Just at noon a French aerial pilot reported by wireless that a Bengal fire was burning on Douaumont Fort. It had taken the 129th Regiment a little under eleven minutes to break into the fort. Bengal fires also appeared on the western side among the shattered masses of concrete, indicating that the 36th Regiment was succeeding in its flanking attack on the west. When the north-western and northern angles were reached, machine-gun sectors and

French checked at Caillette sappers began to move about the ruined masonry, constructing redoubts against the coming counter-attacks. But the French thrust from the Caillette Wood, in which the 74th Regiment was engaged, was shattered by a flanking fire from some German communication trenches. This check prevented the swift enveloping movement from being completed, with the result that the north-eastern angle of the fort remained in the hands of the Germans. Nevertheless, the two victorious regiments bombed their way into nearly three-quarters of the entire position, and in half an hour captured more than a hundred prisoners.

General Mangin had remarked to his men before the operation started : " If we do get in, we must look forward to having not a moment's rest." But the veterans of the 5th Division had fought in the labyrinth of Artois, under General Foch, long before they came to fight under General Pétain and General Nivelle at Vaux and Douaumont. They understood what would happen to them if they captured the fort about which the German Emperor had boasted clamorously

THE PIT WHERE MAJOR RAYNAL WON RENOWN.
Vaux Fort as the Germans received it from Major Raynal when thirst at last compelled him to capitulate.

was vitally concerned in the matter, as General Nivelle had calculated. An enormous number of infantry was collected east of Haudromont Wood, and by sharp bombardments alternating with mass attacks the French line in front of Thiaumont and east of the fort was slightly pressed back. But in the fort itself the 129th Regiment resisted in a marvellous manner. Instead of giving ground, its men somewhat increased their gains. At dawn on May 23rd the German fire on the fort became appalling. The trenches had for months been battered by heavy French shells, and now that the Germans again turned their parks of artillery upon the ruins, tearing the concrete into more murderous splinters and excavating the ground to an extraordinary depth, it seemed that nothing could remain alive amidst the choking, smoking poison fumes. But the masked men of the 129th Regiment, though falling in hundreds, continued to break up every charge. Some of their grenadiers went berserker, ran out to meet the German attacks, bombed their way round the fort, broke into the German lines, and came back unhurt. The miracle was how the regiment managed to save any machine-guns and bombs in their front lines during the terrific bombardments, seeing they had had only a few hours in which to prepare their position against the very heaviest shell fire. When the regiment was relieved in the early morning of May 24th it had not lost a yard of the ground it had captured. But afterwards two fresh Bavarian divisions were launched through the broken remains of the first great counter-attacking force, and by the evening the ruins of Douaumont were recovered by the enemy.

Nevertheless, the operation was a telling success for General Mangin and his chief, General Nivelle. By employing only 12,000 bayonets in an abrupt, unforeseen attack upon the most ticklish point in the enemy lines, the French commander had compelled Falkenhayn to bring at least four times the number of bayonets for a counter-attack. Falkenhayn had been collecting a large general reserve, which he intended to use in a grand, decisive frontal attack on Verdun as soon as he had won the positions round Dead Man Hill from which General Pétain had enfiladed all his previous frontal attacks. He thought that he had at last reduced the French Army to a condition of grim, passive resistance ; but General

by a single division produced any marked result, whereas one French division in artillery order threatened to shake the entire fabric of Falkenhayn's plan.

In these circumstances, the German Chief of Staff determined to make a general attack on Verdun itself, and press it with hundreds of thousands of men while he still remained master of life in the German and Austrian Empires. The French Government had published the news that General Pétain had been given the command of all the armies in the centre, and from this fact Falkenhayn no doubt concluded that another strong spear-head French force was preparing to break into his lines. The Press Bureau of the German Staff fed the German public with news about the utter exhaustion of French reserves, but we may fairly suppose that the German Intelligence Department was under no illusion in the matter. The mistake it afterwards made was in concluding that General Pétain, the hero of the last **German Staff** campaign in the Champagne sector, **misled** was placed in control of the Champagne front and the sectors east and west of it in order to make another thrust towards Vouziers. This seems, indeed, to have been the impression the French Staff desired to create by publishing the news of General Pétain's promotion.

It will be remembered that one of the reasons why Falkenhayn attacked Verdun in February, 1916, was to anticipate and divert a forward movement by General Pétain's First Army. This army had been diverted to the defence of Verdun, as Falkenhayn intended, and towards the end of May the desperate and distracted German Chief of Staff spent his last available forces in an endeavour once more to attract to Verdun the fresh troops which he supposed General Pétain designed to employ in Champagne.

By a fateful miscalculation the German commander withdrew two divisions from the Sixth Army facing General Foch's army on the Somme, and weakened the reserve at Cambrai, near the British front, by taking two more divisions. Another fresh division, making five in all, was obtained from the Champagne sector. Heavy guns by the hundred were also shifted towards the left bank of the Meuse, and, after a bombardment, the first of the new divisions advanced from Crow Wood on Dead Man Hill in the evening of May 28th, 1916. Broken by

VIEW FROM FORT SOUVILLE.
Devastating shell fire was poured on Fort Souville at the end of June, 1916, but the position remained in French hands.

Mangin's alarming thrust into Douaumont Fort taught him that the offensive spirit of the French infantrymen was still as violent as ever. The French had been able to advance under heavy fire in open order, after standing the strain of more than ninety days' resistance in the trenches. On the other hand, even the best German troops were beginning to break and falter unless they were kept in a terribly expensive, close formation. In short, the French people, whom Falkenhayn was attempting to daunt, were at last clearly seen by him to be wearing better than the German people under the superhuman strain of four months' incessant slaughter. No German attack in open order

COMPOSED DIGNITY IN THE MIDST OF DESTRUCTION.
The shattered Rue Jeanne d'Arc in Verdun. The decent orderliness in which the debris was arranged gave the street a quiet dignity of its own.

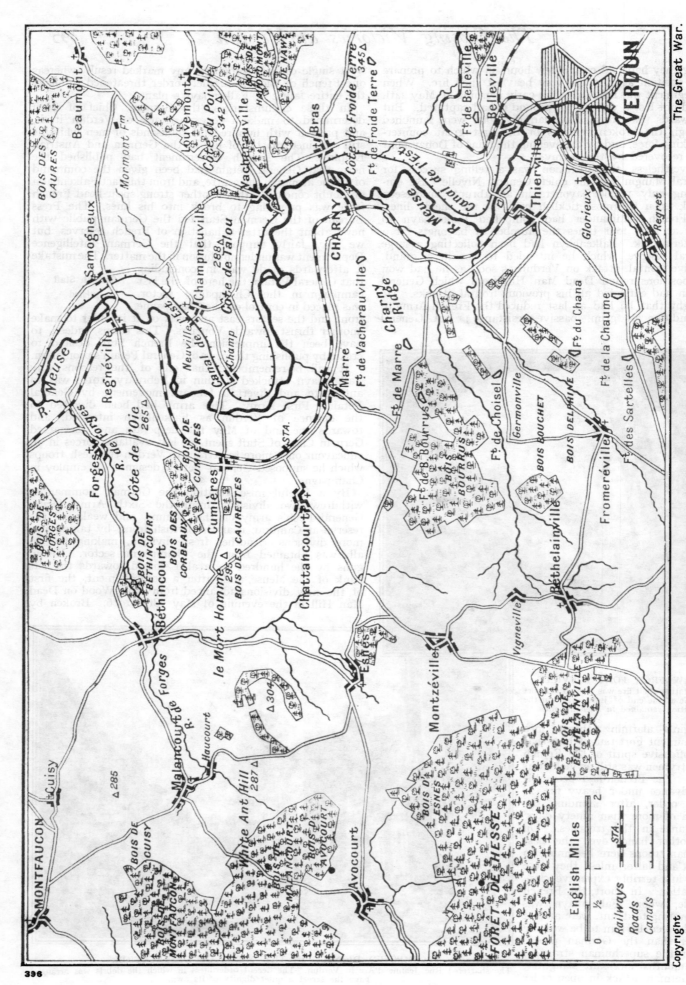

AREA OF THE TERRIBLE DUEL ON THE WEST BANK OF THE MEUSE.

The Great War.

When the initial German onslaught on Verdun received a check at Avocourt, the enemy began an equally vigorous offensive on the west bank of the Meuse.

were scenes of the most fearful carnage in the great struggle. Later heavy fighting took place at Douaumont and Vaux, the French, however, always making the Germans pay a ruinous price for every inch of ground occupied. Béthincourt, Cumières, and Le Mort Homme

the French curtain fire, the division fell back, re-formed, and attempted another advance at midnight, which was again shattered. Finding that the preliminary bombardment had not weakened the French defence, the German commander marked the hundredth day of the Battle of Verdun by an unparalleled storm of heavy shell fire.

For twelve hours the nine miles of front from Avocourt to Cumières were subjected to a bombardment far exceeding in violence that which had first broken the French front north of Verdun. Then by terrific blows of massed brigades the French positions from Dead Man Hill to Cumières were hammered in with fearful waste of life. The French trenches were erased along the high-road running from Béthincourt past Dead Man Hill to Cumières, but the advanced French forces retired to the high-road and there resisted every hammer-blow. The German infantry could not get through the French artillery fire. The position was indeed an extraordinary one. Practically the whole of Dead Man Hill had been conquered by the German gunners, who kept two hundred and fifty heavy howitzers playing on this small stretch of high ground. Very small French forces of infantry were holding out in shell-holes and broken trenches on some of the east, west, and southern slopes. It seemed to require only one charging German regiment to take and occupy the position. But though the enemy commander sent out divisions instead of regiments, his troops could not sweep up the ruins of the French position. The guns of France dominated the field of struggle. Far from being the queen of battles, the German infantry could no longer complete the work of the German artillery. Hill 304, against which a fierce assault was also delivered, remained impregnable, and on the left bank of the Meuse the French were still holding out on their old lines on July 1st, when the Franco-British offensive on the Somme opened.

As General von Falkenhayn failed to push back the French positions on the left bank of the Meuse, which enfiladed across the river all his frontal drives against Verdun, he had to abandon the short road towards the fortress town. He turned away eastward, towards the right wing of the French defences at Vaux. Here there was a natural line of attack which had allured Field-Marshal von Haeseler during the first phase of the Verdun operations. From Vaux a great ravine ran from east to west as far as the village of Fleury, providing cover for a large attacking force directed against the last fortified heights around Verdun. On the north of the ravine was Caillette Wood, which the French had captured on March 31st and lost on April 2nd. South of the ravine was the broken mass of Vaux Fort, empty of its guns and defended only by a small force of infantry with machine-guns and grenades. It was only four miles from Vaux Fort to Verdun, and owing to the long ravine a considerable part of the distance was sheltered from direct fire and ordinary observation. The French heavy guns on the left bank of the Meuse could give practically no assistance against an attack along the Vaux ravine, and the wonder is that Falkenhayn did not concentrate continually against Vaux, instead of wasting men by the hundred thousand on the enfiladed Douaumont front and on the impregnable and secondary western Heights of the Meuse.

East of Douaumont Fort the Germans had possessed for months, in Hardaumont Wood, an excellent means of approaching to the ravine, for a number of smaller ravines ran from the wood down into the long, deep gorge. But the French were so firmly established from the south-east of Douaumont to the Vaux gorge that the area of attack was practically reduced to the mouth of the ravine. On May 31st a grand bombardment began on ground already churned and pitted by months of fierce artillery fire. Strong German detachments, which had been working round the flanks of Hardaumont Wood, made raids to test the defences

Falkenhayn's new move

of Vaux village, and piled the French barricades with their dead. The woods up the slopes on the left became alive with crawling foes, while the hostile artillery continued to shell the village. Then, when the strain upon the defenders had become intense, two fresh German divisions made a terrific rush attack. Each mass took a side of the ravine. One division on the left won a footing on the slopes of the promontory occupied by Vaux Fort, while another division on the right drove through the French barricades in the valley, carried the church and the group of houses round it, and stormed the larger part of the long street. This result was due largely to the skill of the German artillery observing officers watching the struggle from the northern slopes. They brought their gun fire down in hammer-strokes, with terrible precision, on the houses and gardens

[*Official photograph.*

MR. LLOYD GEORGE IN FRANCE.
Mr. Lloyd George paid many visits to France during the war as Chancellor of the Exchequer, Minister of Munitions, and Secretary for War. This photograph shows Sir Douglas Haig explaining to him a point made by General Joffre, while M. Thomas, French Minister for Munitions, lent an attentive ear.

where the French tried to make a stand. But there were French observing officers on the southern side of the gorge, and when their infantry was driven from the village to the mill-pond the French heavy guns then smashed up what remained of the village. The French infantry, who were fighting with machine-guns behind an old mill, then charged back with amazing dash and pluck, recapturing the village street, and pushing the Germans back to the ruined church at the eastern end. All day and all night the small band of Frenchmen, after their wonderful recoil against the blow of an entire army corps, fought like men possessed and broke every charge made by the enemy.

For three days and three nights the awful struggles at the mouth of the gorge went on, and as the German commander threw fresh divisions into the shamble of ruins, the fight swayed up and down the village street till the little brook in the ravine ran red and the living fought behind mounds of dead. On the south-east of Douaumont Fort the French Alpine troops broke every German attempt to get at Vaux village from the rear. On the glacis of Vaux Fort a Saxon division, which had made the first mass attack on the left, came upon a sunken line of barbed-wire entanglements which had been missed by the German shells, and were there held and slaughtered by the thousand. The steep slopes of the promontory were covered with a mass of writhing figures unable to advance and unable to escape. The French had a long field of fire down the incline, and with bombs, musketry fire, machine-gun fire, and a curtain of shrapnel they caught the Germans, front and rear, and annihilated them.

Saxon division annihilated Half-way between the fort and the village there was one small trench held by the 101st French Infantry Regiment, and only forty yards away were the German entrenchments. The French trench was smashed up by salvos of 11 in. shells, and by maintaining a continual fire with packets of ten of these shells the Germans prevented the position being repaired. But the weakened regiment held out and stopped an enemy advance through a neighbouring wood, and then, cut off from food and water, fought on all night and all the next day and broke an enemy charge in the evening. An order was then given to send up a rocket, asking the French gunners to put a curtain fire over the retreating Germans. But, unhappily, the rocket burst before it rose, and set fire to all the stock of rockets. The trench filled with fire and smoke, and French artillery observers on the height above thought that the enemy had conquered the position by a liquid-fire attack. At the end of two hours the flames were got under and the stock of grenades prevented from exploding. Sixteen pints of water were then got through the German curtain fire to the survivors of the regiment, enabling each man to have one mouthful.

In the darkness of the early morning of June 3rd the Germans made another attack in force. "Let us be more patient this time," said the captain who remained in command. "We were too quick before." So the Germans were allowed to get within fifteen feet from the trench, and were then shattered by hand-bombs and rifle fire. Soon afterwards it began to rain, much to the relief of the defenders. Spreading out canvas, tins, and other receptacles, they at last obtained a good drink of water. As the torture of thirst had troubled them much more than the shell fire and the infantry charges of the enemy, they became more confident. A rain of smaller shells, 4 in. and 5 in., fell upon them like tropical showers. Some Germans, hanging on to the slopes by Vaux Fort, enfiladed them with a machine-gun on the right, and another party of Germans who had got into Fumin Wood brought a machine-gun against them on the left. Then, after being sprinkled with shells of all sizes for six hours, they were attacked by wave after wave of grey figures. Yet once more they threw back every attack.

All night they were again bombarded with extreme

violence, and just before dawn the German troops again attempted to rush the shell-holes in which the battered regiment was sheltering. But when the relieving-party managed to get through the German fire on June 5th the enemy was still held off the north-west slope of Vaux promontory. It was an extraordinary defence.

And so was the defence of Vaux. The torn and twisted fort had been pounded with heavy shells since March, 1916, an average of eight thousand shells falling on the ruins every day for nearly three months. The entrance was blocked up, and only one wicket in the north-western corner remained for bringing in supplies and keeping up communications. The trench held by the heroic 101st Infantry Regiment had protected the movement through the north-western wicket-gate; hence the extraordinary resistance which the men there maintained for five days. Within the fort was a tiny garrison of one hundred and fifty men under a fine French officer, Major Raynal, who had been twice badly wounded, and came out of hospital unfit for service in the field. He applied for the command of Vaux Fort in May, pointing out that his injuries would not impede him in directing the defence of the ruined mass of concrete. Sleeping in a cavern and hobbling among the broken masonry, the gallant major so arranged his machine-guns and stock of grenades that the fort, which was absolutely useless as an artillery position, became a magnificent machine-gun post.

It rose in the north-eastern angle of a little tableland, stretching eighteen hundred yards above the great gorge. On the eastern side the plateau was cut by another ravine that ran towards the south-east. On both these steep sides the little garrison, with its machine-guns and hand-grenades, had a tremendous advantage over the attacking forces; and though outnumbered often by a hundred to one, they rolled the Saxon division down the crest, two hundred yards from the wall of the fort, and broke another division that climbed up the south-eastern ravine. As the Germans had proved at Douaumont, a modern fortress of armoured concrete when hammered into absolute ruin makes a superb machine-gun position. **A German death-trap** It needs only a small garrison, who have profound caverns in which to shelter; and long periscopes help to make the work of observation safe against anything except a direct hit by a heavy howitzer shell.

Vaux Fort, however, was more than a machine-gun redoubt defending two of the principal ravines of the Verdun district. Owing to its position on the edge of the plain stretching to Metz, it was the principal observation-post of the Eleventh French Army. It overlooked the lowland eastward and north-eastward of Verdun, and afforded such information of the enemy's movements as no balloon observer or aerial scout could obtain. Major Raynal had only a hundred and fifty men with him as a garrison on May 31st, but the next day some four hundred wounded troops, caught in the terrific rain of German shells, retired into the fort for shelter. This was the chief reason why the fort fell, for there was not enough water for five

FLEET OF AMBULANCE CARS PRESENTED BY LLOYD'S TO THE ARMY OF VERDUN.
Twenty ambulance cars, costing over £40,000, were presented by members of Lloyd's, the great British association of marine underwriters, to the French Army. King George inspected them at Buckingham Palace before they were despatched on their beneficent mission behind Verdun.

hundred and fifty men. Practically nothing could be got through the wicket-gate after June 2nd, even despatch-bearers being brought down by the enemy's fire. The shower of rain that saved the 101st Regiment, holding the trench between the fort and the ravine, was of little use to the garrison. They were too furiously busy fighting on all sides to make arrangements to get water for half a battalion. They had to contend against liquid flame, poison-gas shells, and innumerable assaults. There were eight or nine attacks in force every day, with only one pause on June 3rd, after four divisions had been broken in the ravine and round the promontory.

On June 4th, however, the German commander made a new concentration of his guns, drawing on Metz and increasing his fighting power on the Woevre Plain. He drove an advanced French force back from its dangerous position on the edge of the plain at Damloup, south of Vaux, and then, with an enormous crescent of guns firing north, north-west, and east of the promontory, he smashed up all Major Raynal's outer defences, and ringed the entire fort with an incessant fire.

Surrender of Vaux Fort Then it was that the handful of heroic Frenchmen began to weaken from thirst. A few daring men succeeded in getting in with a tiny supply of water, but all outside attempts made to get a large supply into the fort failed. By an encircling movement the German infantry won the wall of the fort and tried to rush across the courtyard, but were shot down. They climbed on the shattered roofs and, with a rope, lowered baskets of high explosives through the windows, dropped in time-fuses, and swung the charges against the French sharpshooters in the rooms. Still the garrison fought on. But, owing to lack of water, the situation became hopeless on the morning of June 6th. One private, Vanier, a stretcher-bearer who had worked nobly among the wounded and gone out continually to fetch water for them, was told that the remnant of the garrison would have to surrender. "I would rather die than be taken prisoner by the Boches," said Vanier. And with some of his wounded he crawled through the German lines, and though several of his companions were killed, Vanier led the others into the distant French trenches. Major Raynal then surrendered with his handful of exhausted men. Even the Teuton was moved when he saw how small and how enfeebled by thirst was the force that had for a week resisted the attack of his great army, and Major Raynal was allowed to retain his sword. By the French Government the defender of Vaux Fort was created a Commander of the Legion of Honour, and, in special recognition of his historic feat in delaying the German advance for a week, the insignia of his new rank were conferred upon his wife at a review in Paris.

In an ordinary way the fall of the valuable observation-post at Vaux might have produced upon the French public as staggering an effect as the fall of Douaumont Fort. But in the extraordinary circumstances in which Major Raynal, with one hundred and fifty men, broke tens of thousands of Germans, the final surrender of Vaux thrilled France with heroic resolve. It illustrated vividly the military gospel of the French High Command—that the enemy was paying a terribly excessive price in man-power for every yard of

WITH THE FRENCH ARTILLERY NEAR FORT DOUAUMONT.

Two "75" guns in action immediately to the rear of Fort Douaumont and working on a revolving emplacement. These guns proved most effective in defence. Every battery was connected with Headquarters by telephone, and the whole mass of artillery could be concentrated on one point at the general's command.

ground he won. The French peasantry, who controlled the master current of general opinion and often went strongly against the official view obtaining in Paris, became convinced that, in spite of the sacrifices they were making at Verdun, France was gaining in power upon her eternal enemy.

Ever since 1870 the Press and the leaders of opinion in Paris had been robbed of all real powers of national control by the French peasantry of the provinces. Paris in vain tried to continue the war of 1870; the people of the provinces would not accept her leadership in the matter. By compelling her to make peace they brought about the insurrection of the Commune, and after sternly putting it down, kept the Parisians under control for forty-five years. Paris under the Third Republic ceased to rule. All the excerpts from the leading Parisian newspapers which appeared in our Press during the early phases of the present war were often indicative only of the minority opinions of the leaders of the dethroned metropolis. The flight of many well-to-do members of the Parisian population just before the Battle of the Marne did not tend to augment the directive power of the capital. The French peasant, the most alert and intelligent man of his kind in the world, continued to follow his own train of thought, and give the governing quality to the national cast of opinion. His frame of mind was as grimly resolute as that of an ancient Roman farmer; but under the first shock of the breaking of the northern lines at **Power of French** Verdun he seems at times to have thought **peasantry** about trying to recover something from the wreck. In short, Paris—indomitable, resilient, incomparable Paris—seemed again to be rising to a greater height of soul than the provinces that had abandoned her in the last generation. But as the awful struggle at Verdun went on the ancient heart of France, by means of thousands of subtle veins of radiating emotion, poured her intensity of spirit through the provinces.

When the attack on Vaux began the French Chamber of Deputies was in a condition of extreme agitation. There was a strong party forming, apparently, against the French High Command and moving for an immediate inquiry concerning Verdun. Alongside this dangerous movement against General Joffre and General Castelnau and their Staff, which was largely inspired by opinion in the provinces,

A CORNER NEAR SOUVILLE.
Fragments of a shattered ammunition-waggon. The recovery of Thiaumont Works outflanked the German attack on Souville and saved the position.

there was a movement of one section of the French urban working-class Socialists towards resuming friendly relations with the treacherous leaders of the German Social Democratic party. No doubt Teutonic intriguers, working by hidden and devious means, had some influence upon these agitated currents of opinion. The Frenchman is a born sceptic, and his personal knowledge of the losses incurred among his people during the stupendous effort to put out of action half a million Germans made him distrust the estimate of comparative losses given by the French Command.

The great episode of Vaux reassured him, and in the first secret sitting of the Chamber of Deputies on June 16th, 1916, the sombre movements of agitation were stilled, and finally, in both the Chamber and the Senate, confidence was fully restored, and the position of the Government and the Staff strengthened and well assured. In other words, the chief aim of all General von Falkenhayn's operations and intrigues from February to June, 1916, was completely frustrated; for he had mainly

Falkenhayn's intrigues frustrated intended to produce an overwhelming moral effect upon the French public. He could not stagger and dishearten the French Commander-in-Chief and the French Staff. They would have withdrawn the army of Verdun across the Meuse and continued the struggle with cool and deadly skill, knowing they were exhausting the general German reserve and winning advantages in the common interests of the Grand Alliance. Yet they had to contend against a natural feeling of depression among their own people, and it was for this reason that they held with superhuman tenacity to Verdun.

With the fall of Vaux, however, all the tension was relieved. For while the struggle was raging around the promontory on June 3rd, 1916, General Brussiloff's armies began that marvellous Russian advance in Volhynia and

Bukovina which broke the main forces of Austria-Hungary, brought Rumania into the Grand Alliance, and compelled Germany to divert troops, guns, and shells to the assistance of both Austria-Hungary and Bulgaria. Thus, all that General Joffre, General Castelnau, and the French Staff had striven for at Verdun was attained. Nevertheless, General von Falkenhayn made one desperate, tremendous effort to snatch a tactical local victory from his general strategic defeat.

After vainly battering along the ravine from Vaux to Fleury, which the French soldiers had named the Ravine of Death, the German commander made a thrust northward at Thiaumont. The Thiaumont Works lay on a long ridge connecting the Douaumont Plateau to the height of Froide Terre, rising by the Meuse immediately north of Verdun. On the right of the Thiaumont ridge was another height, Hill 320, that dominated the eastern end of the Ravine of Death, the gorge being also commanded by two wooded promontories known as Vaux Chapitre Wood and Fumin Wood. On June 12th the Germans drove in on Thiaumont on a front of three miles with three divisions, and after dreadful losses they got a footing on the slope

Germans rush Thiaumont

west of Thiaumont. There followed a long pause of eleven days, that clearly showed the condition to which the three attacking divisions had been reduced. It almost looked as though Falkenhayn, perplexed by the break-up of Austria on the Russian and Italian fronts, was about to abandon the attempt to reach Verdun. As a matter of fact, the long pause of the German commander was indicative of the labour required to bring up the enormous forces he was concentrating at Thiaumont. And on June 23rd he made his supreme attempt with six divisions of infantry, launched in dense columns like incessant battering-rams, against the

SHELL-WROUGHT HAVOC IN CAILLETTE WOOD.
Caillette Wood, north of the ravine between Vaux and Fleury, was the scene of terrific fighting in the Battles of Verdun. In circle: Heap of French shell-cases collected near Souville.

Thiaumont ridge. The ridge was carried with its earthworks, after a Rhenish division had been thrown back from the western slopes of the ridge, for a Prussian reserve corps simultaneously pushed down eastward from Douaumont and, after hours of fighting, reached the Thiaumont earthworks and pierced the French line.

To avoid being cut off by the forces closing on it eastward and westward, the small French garrison fell back rapidly on Fleury village by the end of the ravine coming from Vaux. The victorious Germans stormed into Fleury village, but again there was seen the surprising and magnificent power of recoil of apparently beaten French troops. Fugitive and seemingly routed, the defeated garrison of Thiaumont turned in the village, smashed the Prussians out of the houses they had won, and then chased them northward up the road to Bras.

Thereupon the German commander threw in his last reserves, making in all a hundred thousand men launched on a sector only three miles wide. In a fierce hand-to-hand struggle with bomb and bayonet the French were again pushed out of the northern end of Fleury village. French forces, however, still occupied the southern **German prodigality** promontories of the Ravine of Death **of man-power** running from Fleury to Vaux, and a small wood south-east of the fort was also held by our heroic allies against all attacks. Every line of approach from Verdun was crossed by converging fires from powerful hidden French artillery positions. All the German attacks coming from Fleury, for example, were taken in flank by tempests of shell directed from the observation-post at Fort St. Michel, while attacks coming from Vaux were taken in flank by a tempest of fire coming from Fort Tavannes. Then directly facing the enemy was Souville Fort on the right of the line, a dominating position overlooking the plateau of the tableland of Vaux and about equal in height to Douaumont. None of these French forts was an artillery position. The old 6 in. guns had been removed, and far more powerful howitzers, with quick-firing action, were concealed around the southern slopes of the heights. As in the case of Vaux, the old battered forts were merely observation-posts and machine-gun redoubts, manned by a couple of hundred men. The main French forces sheltered in large caverns and moved into action by way of tunnels and deep communication-trenches.

The design of the German commander was to press a converging attack upon Souville Fort, eastward from Vaux and northward from Thiaumont. In four months' operation he had captured a mile and a quarter of ground, at the price of 400,000 men. He was now faced with the problem of capturing nearly four miles of ground, across which ran two strong defensive lines, for each of which the French asked the same price. He began by attempting to drive in towards the river against the Pepper Hill and Froide Terre defences. But this seems to have been only a demonstration, for the French army across the Meuse still clung to the slopes of Dead Man Hill and enfiladed any direct assault on the northern sector of Verdun.

Towards the end of June, General von Falkenhayn ordered demonstrations against General Pétain's forces in Champagne and General Foch's forces in Artois, while he

A STEEL-HELMETED FRENCH CAVALRY REGIMENT ON THE MARCH.
One heard little of cavalry in the long period between the Battles of the Marne and the Somme. Recurrence of mention of their employment after the great advance that began in July, 1916, was hailed as indicative of the turn of the tide in the Allies' favour.

was accumulating another great store of shells round Fort Souville for a fresh general attack on Verdun. By this time, however, the French Commander-in-Chief was completely in control of the entire situation on the western front. He had withdrawn his best force from the great Lorraine fortress and placed it under the command of another new general of the hurricane-fire school, General Fayolle, who with skilful secrecy was planning an offensive on the Somme River. In addition to the network of light railways winding everywhere into the French front, the French Staff had been enormously developing the quicker, more flexible, and disconcerting weapon of transport— the motor-lorry—which had saved Verdun. Round the Lorraine fortress hundreds of miles of new narrow-gauge railways had been built since February, 1916, and there was thus less strain upon the French motor organisation. Tens of thousands of lorries were now available for moving an army with great secrecy and expedition, the lorries being able to run almost into the lines. At night they discharged troops, ammunition, and the lighter weapons of war. The light railways, when relieved of much of the ordinary traffic at the busiest sector, became tracks for gigantic new howitzers that fired from the rails and moved up and down as occasion required. The general effect was that these new monster guns could come abruptly into action along the tracks where nothing unusual had been seen the day before by enemy aerial scouts.

All the chief elements of surprise were, **British offensive** therefore, in the hands of the Western **begun** Allies, while Falkenhayn was still doggedly and blindly reorganising a new battering attack on Verdun. In the last week in June a thing he had long expected happened. For ninety miles the British front flamed and thundered by night as well as by day, indicating that the untried new armies were about to make an attempt to attack. The Chief of the German Staff was not alarmed at this prospect, for it had all along been one of his objects to provoke a British offensive by continuing his pressure on Verdun. He considered that native British stubbornness might have served Great Britain well if her new recruits had fought on the defensive, and for this reason he had been averse to assailing her. On the other hand, he considered it impossible that her amateur artillerymen could work their new heavy guns with the minute precision and

PONTOON COMMUNICATION NEAR VERDUN.
Leading horses over a pontoon bridge connecting the east and west zones of fighting.

known from London that the British attack would come from Albert, and the Prussian Guard and other veteran corps were concentrated between Arras and Albert. In this matter, however, London gossip was somewhat misleading, and owing to the flexibility of the British feeding motor service, the main thrust was delivered, still with some surprise effect, to the south of the principal German concentration. In regard to the French offensive, the enemy was completely misled. He expected the blow to fall against his sector around Roye ; but the troops he massed at Roye had to be brought back in hasty confusion to Péronne. And this was only one of two great surprises

stop-watch exactness in timing which were necessary in a grand, modern offensive. He confidently expected that her hastily-trained new armies would display a rash, impetuous, and unorganised degree of courage which would result in such enormous casualties—at a comparatively slight loss in lives to veteran German defending troops—that her extraordinary military effort would prove to have been undertaken in vain.

It is not extravagant to say that Falkenhayn was cheered by the news that Sir Douglas Haig had opened a hurricane bombardment preliminary to the advance of large infantry forces. Not a single division at Verdun, brought from the general reserve at Cambrai, seems to have been hurried back towards the neighbourhood of the British front. The German corps already arrayed against the British were large, and included at least two divisions of the Prussian Guard. In Falkenhayn's view the quality of his choice veterans would outbalance the quantity of the half-trained British recruits.

Towards the middle of the week of the British bombardment the French guns from the Somme to the Aisne lengthened the line of thunder and flame until nearly one hundred and fifty miles of the German front was veiled in the smoke of heavy high-explosive shell. This might have been merely a strong artillery feint, intended to support the coming British thrust by inducing the Germans to scatter southward some of their materials and forces of defence. The enemy Staff, however, appears to have discovered by Secret Service work that France, though apparently exhausted by her tremendous efforts at Verdun, was still capable of undertaking an offensive movement in co-operation with Great Britain.

The German Secret Service, however, did not fully penetrate into the design of the Allies. Apparently, it was

156 miles of gun fire

TERRACES OF DUG-OUTS ON THE HILLSIDE BEFORE VERDUN.
High explosive was responsible for an extraordinary development of trench architecture and subterranean town-planning, brought to the highest point of perfection by the Germans, but practised by all the belligerents. Above is a remarkable photograph of the hillside dug-outs of the French army before Verdun.

which General Castelnau and his Staff prepared for the enemy in the last week of June. In the morning of June 30th, 1916, the local German command before Verdun made a violent effort to turn the flank of Hill 304 by a general attack all along the line to Avocourt. Terrific shell fire, storming masses of infantry, and liquid-flame attacks produced absolutely no impression upon the French lines, a small piece of ground on Hill 304 being recovered by the French counter-attack. But while this ferocious struggle was proceeding on the left bank of the Meuse, General Nivelle's men on Froide Terre and the height near Fleury advanced at ten o'clock in the morning, and by a magnificent piece of fighting recovered and held the fortified works of Thiaumont that barred the great ridge of Douaumont-Froide Terre. This extraordinary forward leap of the army of Verdun had great consequences, for the Thiaumont Works outflanked the German point of advance at Fleury, thus turning the stream of attack which the enemy was organising against Fort Souville.

It was essential to the Germans that they should immediately regain the Thiaumont Works. They battered the lost position with hundreds of guns and launched column after column of infantry in a pincer-like movement from the north and from the east. In the afternoon some Prussian troops again reached the works, but the French counter-attacked in the evening and once more won back all the ground. In the night the Germans renewed their storming attacks, which had to be delivered through a stupendous curtain fire of massed French parks of artillery. The French lost only some advanced positions on the slopes, the dominating position of Thiaumont remaining in their possession.

Recapture of Thiaumont Altogether the recovery of Thiaumont was the most successful of all the French recoils at Verdun. It showed indeed a degree of resiliency unparalleled in modern siege warfare. The fact was that General Nivelle had at last a definite object of high importance in making a leap forward. In his former swoop back to Douaumont Fort he was moved only by a consideration of local tactics and a vaguer policy of general strategy. His immediate object then had been merely to relieve the German pressure against Dead Man Hill on the opposite side of the river, by proving to the German commander that his line was perilously weak at Douaumont. In so doing he had also shown the German Staff that it must always take into consideration the potential offensive power of the army of Verdun. This had only been thrown out as an indefinite hint. But the fiercer and stronger leap back to Thiaumont, one day before the opening of the Franco-British offensive on the Somme River, was an act of downright intimidation.

The Germans had three thousand or more guns at Verdun, and an army of at least 600,000 men. More than a million Germans had been brought into action at Verdun on either side of the Meuse, nearly half of whom had been put out of action, the losses falling on the most useful arms—infantry, engineers, and artillery. General Pétain and General Nivelle had gradually built up around Verdun a French army equal in artillery power to the German, superior to it in engineering power, and balancing it in infantry power. As a matter of fact, the French infantry holding the heights around the Lorraine fortress was deliberately kept inferior in number to the German attacking infantry, with a view to opposing less men to heavy gun fire than the Germans exposed. But the French infantry made up in highly developed defensive engineering and very skilful cross-firing combinations of position for its wise weakness in mere numbers. Also, the French forces generally available for the defence were quite as large as the German attacking forces. The difference resided in the fact that each French division was kept fresh and full of spirit by being employed only in a short shift and then withdrawn for a rest. The famous Iron Division, for instance that had saved Verdun in February, soon recrossed the Meuse and stayed for some time available as a support, but then the men were allowed to return to their homes for a month's holiday. Coming back to depôt, the division was brought up to its establishment by fresh troops of a young class, and these were then trained in company with the refreshed veterans and solidly embedded in the fighting strength of the most glorious body of fighting men in the world. In other words, the great division was never worn down and changed in composition, in spite of the terrible heavy fighting continually thrown upon it. With its sister division forming the Twentieth Army Corps, the Iron Division emerged from Verdun stronger, if possible, than it had entered the most intense furnace of battle.

In the German Army, on the other hand, the divisions were kept in the terrible furnace of Verdun until they melted away. Seldom or never were they withdrawn after a sharp bout, when they could have absorbed and transformed the lads available to fill up their ranks. **Reckless use of divisions** Falkenhayn used his divisions as the Americans use their machinery. He kept them going until they were worn into scrap. It was only the broken remnant that was afterwards employed in building up another fresh force.

The German Staff had too mechanical a conception of infantry building. It had come almost to despise infantry and to rely chiefly upon guns and machine-gunners. These it was able to preserve in a fairly unbroken system of

MORE MEN TO HOLD THE FOE AT BAY: NEW TROOPS MOVE FORWARD AT THE CRITICAL HOUR.
Reinforcements for the French front before Verdun marching through a village to the strains of the national hymn. This illustration was secured just after the great blizzard which raged in the first days of the fearful struggle and helped to impede the German advance.

development, by a flow of half-trained drafts who were hammered into men of experience by more numerous veteran comrades and skilful commissioned and non-commissioned officers. For in artillery duels, even with thousands of guns on either side, counter-battery firing remained secondary in importance to high - explosive hurricane attacks upon entrenched hostile infantry and shrapnel storms against enemy troops advancing to attack or coming up as reinforcements. The general result was that casualties among German gunners were less in proportion than those among German infantrymen. As the German Staff no longer considered the infantry to be the queen of battles, they used up divisions of bayonets with little or no regard for the wealth of experience embodied in the rank and file. Very often a shattered division that retained the fighting strength of a brigade

False military economy was sent into action as a brigade the day after its defeat, simply because it was immediately available on the field of battle and Falkenhayn and his commanders wished at all costs to maintain an unremitting pressure.

It was the old Prussian mistake of endeavouring to rectify by a violent effort of will an error made in a matter of judgment. The Prussian had fought his way up, from the command of a couple of counties to the control of two great empires and a bid for the hegemony of the world, mainly by a remarkable driving force of character. The larger insight into human nature and affairs had never distinguished him, though he was careful and methodical, and often recognised the warlike value of intellectual power displayed by Teutons and Teutonic Jews of more flexible mind attracted to his service. He was incarnate will-power, in a degree surpassing that of the ancient Roman or the modern Anglo-Celt. The consequence was that, in the heat and fury of battle, when both commander and private were fighting on instinct and on the intuitions of instinct, the Prussian tried to conquer by sheer force of will. He held his wasting divisions to the work of incessant attack in a blind hope that the opposing French force might be nearing breaking-point and liable to give way if the assault were pushed to extreme desperation.

The French, on the other hand, fought with their fine intelligence sharpened to its keenest point. All that lucidity of intellect and quick reasoning power, which since the eleventh century have made France the directing mind of Christendom and the principal organiser of the entire range of European culture, were concentrated upon the task of Verdun with a general degree of intensity hitherto unknown in war. The will-power of France during this supreme clash of Gaul and Teuton was at least as vehement as that of Germany. The historic battle-cry " Ne passeront pas ! " expressed a force of national character as great as that of the Spartans who held the pass against the Persian

" Ne passeront pas ! " host, or—to give a parallel from French history—as great as that which the Franks showed at Roncesvalles. But the indomitable will of the French was animated and directed by an intellectual power both subtle and comprehensive.

The French gave ground continually in cases where the Germans would have vainly fought to the death. But seldom was the ground from which the French withdrew immediately lost to them. Their advance forces of infantry merely retired in order to facilitate the work of their artillery. And when the victorious Germans were shattered by a closing storm of heavy shell, the French infantry made a counter-attack, and in an epical hand-to-hand struggle showed their surprised enemy that there was a finer form of tactics than the blind, brutal, wasteful bull rush. Except in the first week of the Verdun campaign, when the weak forces of General Herr were half annihilated by parks of monster German siege-guns, the average losses of the French in the operations around the Lorraine fortress were much less than the losses of the Germans. For some

months every Frenchman that fell took with him two Germans, and the proportion of casualties was seldom less than that.

The consequence was that General Nivelle possessed an available force of French infantry superior in number to the wasted German forces. Had the general strategical situation of the Allies so required, he could at last have reversed the situation at Verdun and opened a prolonged driving attack against the Crown Prince's army. This design, however, was abandoned by the French Staff through lack of monster guns and shells. The best of General Nivelle's forces were withdrawn from his command when the victory of Verdun was definitely gained. No country could at the time carry on simultaneously two long hurricane-fire offensives. Even Germany had been compelled to leave the Russians and the British in comparative peace in order to maintain an attack against Verdun on a front seldom more than nine miles broad. All the cannon factories, high-explosive works, and heavy-shell plants of Germany could not do more than maintain the pressure alternately on the left and right bank of the Meuse at Verdun.

France, with most of her ironfields and coalmines in the hands of the enemy, could not do more than maintain an offensive along a front of about ten miles. In other words, she could not get sufficient guns and shells to attack on the Somme and on the Meuse. When, therefore, the Franco-British operation on the Somme opened, General von Falkenhayn began to withdraw men and guns from Verdun. He lightly reckoned that he would, henceforth, need on the Meuse only sufficient forces to maintain a defensive against a comparatively small French army. It was to check this German withdrawal that General Nivelle made his fierce and astonishingly suc- **Nivelle's clever** cessful return to the Thiaumont Works **counter-attacks** between Douaumont and Froide Terre. Thereby he distinctly showed that it was his intention to go on recovering at a comparatively slight cost the ground which Falkenhayn had spent half a million men in conquering.

Throughout the allied offensive on either side of the Somme the French army of Verdun exercised a persistent pressure against the German forces on either side of the Meuse. It was known to the French and British Staffs that German troops were being brought from Verdun to assist in the stand near the Somme. But General Nivelle saw to it that Verdun was not robbed of Germans in order to strengthen Péronne. He fought a long, persistent, detaining action. Naturally, he never launched a general offensive movement. His object was merely to intimidate the enemy and continually test him in small actions and counter-battery duels in order to see if he was growing weak at Verdun. So long as the German commander there retained his great arcs of guns and sufficient reserves of infantry to make counter-attacks after every small French advance General Nivelle was content. He pushed the enemy out of Fleury, and towards the middle of September, 1916, he recovered some of the woods above the Ravine of Death and established his forces near Vaux. By this time it was clear that the initiative in attack rested entirely with him, and that if the French High Command enabled him to accumulate a big store of shells, a great attacking force could quickly be thrown by light railway and motor transport into Verdun for a push towards the Lorraine ironfields. The German Staff, of course, was well acquainted with the main facts of the situation. Indeed, it was General Nivelle's principal task to keep it alert to the possibilities of the Verdun scene of operations, and though his local attacks were feints, any marked success could quickly be developed into a strong and alarming thrust. For all practical purposes, therefore, the French were masters of the field. They had won the greatest victory in defence known to history, and, with their Allies, they retained all the advantages of the terrific struggle.

Vice-Admiral Sir David Beatty, G.C.B., Commander-in-Chief of Battle-Cruiser Fleet.

[Russell.

Admiral Sir John Jellicoe, O.M., G.C.B., Commander-in-Chief of the Grand Fleet.

Rear=Admiral Sir Robert K. Arbuthnot, Bart., K.C.B., lost with his flagship the Defence.

[*Weston & Son.*]

Admiral Sir Cecil Burney, K.C.B., G.C.M.G., Second=in=Command of the Grand Fleet.

THE GLORIOUS BATTLE OF JUTLAND BANK. PART I.

How Germany Prepared for " The Day."

By H. W. Wilson and Edward Wright.

Supreme Ambition of the Kaiser to Obtain Command of the Sea and Become Lord of the World—Opposition of the Bismarckians and Intrigues of the General Staff to Overbear the German Naval Department—Pressure by France and Russia Compels Germany to Concentrate her Productive Energy on the Land War—Intensification of British Warship Construction and Augmentation of the Strength of the British Navy—Von Tirpitz Attempts to Redeem his Early Mistake of Producing Dreadnoughts Rather Than Submarines, and Contemplates Attrition of the British Capacity for Action by Submarine Piracy—Reasons for Von Tirpitz's Dismissal—Appointment of Reinhold von Scheer to the Command-in-Chief of the High Sea Fleet—Von Scheer and the "Nelson Touch"—Changed Conditions Since Nelson's Day—Adaptation of the Art of Making Preliminary Sacrifices in Order to Secure Superiority at the Crisis of the Battle—Rear-Admiral Hipper and his Battle-Cruiser Squadron—The Raids on the East Coast and " Tip-and-Run " Tactics—The German Submarine Flotilla near the Little Fisher Bank—The German High Sea Fleet Steams Out for Action, Wednesday, May 31st, 1916—Its Disposition and Use of Zeppelins—Blindness of Sir John Jellicoe's Fleet Owing to Lack of Long-range Rigid Airships—Approximate Strength of the Opposing Fleets—The Respective Odds as Calculated by the Law of the Numerical Square—Secondary Armaments and Relative Manœuvring Power of the Two Fleets—Choice of Time and Place in the German Favour—Why the British Command, with a Great Superiority in Force Available, Exposed Only a Fraction of the Grand Fleet to the Enemy's Concentrated Force—Sir John Jellicoe and his Plan for the Control of the North Sea—Admiral von Scheer and Sir John Jellicoe Playing the Same Game—Calculation of Time the Key to Victory.

N the afternoon of Wednesday, May 31st, 1916, William II. of Germany learnt what the supreme achievement of his reign was worth. Grandson of a Queen of Great Britain, he was the first Hohenzollern to appreciate the value of sea-power. Against the advice of his military leaders and against the judgment of his principal expert in foreign affairs, Holstein, the disciple and supplanter of Bismarck, the Emperor held steadily along the path of his ambition to become Admiral of the Atlantic. He saw that, with the command of the sea, he could become lord of the world.

In vain did his best men counsel him to concentrate on the conquest of the European Continent before openly setting out to build a stronger fleet than the British Empire possessed. Holstein, the principal force behind the passing figureheads of State Chancellors, resigned his work as Bismarck's successor, and died in a mood **Holstein's** of despair, because of the Emperor's **prophetic view** disastrous policy. He published his judgment that the premature rivalry in naval construction with Great Britain would end in Germany being crippled.

Bethmann-Hollweg, who nominally succeeded Bülow, but actually succeeded Holstein, adopted the idea of the dead Bismarckian. By intriguing with the General Staff, which was bent on attacking Russia, he deprived Grand-Admiral von Tirpitz of the funds needed for shipbuilding. The famous war levy of 1913 was spent on the Army. The Emperor William ceased his efforts to build a stronger fleet than the British, and strove only to keep this country

neutral in the great land war for the dominion of Europe. He was indeed convinced, from the faltering attitude of the Liberal-Radical Cabinet, that Great Britain was too cowardly to fight, and that in the end he could absorb the British Empire peacefully, as he was absorbing Austria-Hungary.

His men of the new school both flattered and restrained him by the theory that, in making Germany the second greatest naval Power in the world, he had safely insured against the British people taking **Germany's prelimin-** part in the coming struggle on the Con- **ary misconceptions** tinent. It was argued that the British race was selfish, timid, narrowly calculating. Rather than risk a terrific fleet action, in which, even if victorious, the losses would leave the British in a third or fourth rate position in regard to naval power, they would stand aside and see France bled to death and Russia reduced to vassalage. The world knows what happened. Over-confident in his undoubted but limited power over Great Britain, the German Emperor went too far. Listening only to his military advisers, he resolved to save the estimated loss of a hundred thousand men by avoiding the French fortress line and making an easier path through Belgium. Had he not invaded Belgium, the British Cabinet would have split over the question of entering the war, and the nation might have failed France, incurred immortal dishonour, and come eventually to a miserable end. Happily it was saved from the great temptation by the too arrogant foe, and when the British people manfully turned to work out its nobler destinies, it found that its strength at sea was equal to the strain.

As the notorious German naval expert, Count Reventlow, put it, there was no second greatest naval Power in the

COMMANDER-IN-CHIEF OF THE GERMAN HIGH SEA FLEET.
Admiral von Scheer, Commander-in-Chief of the German High Sea Fleet, avoided contact with Sir John Jellicoe. His services off Jutland, however, were rewarded with the Order " Pour le Mérite."

Department. The second-rate German Navy had largely to rest content with remaining secure under shelter of its coastal fortifications, while the first-rate German Army monopolised most of the steel-making plants. As Moltke and Falkenhayn no doubt pointed out, when Grand-Admiral von Tirpitz wanted monster naval guns and mountings from Krupp, the Fleet as it floated could at least avoid destruction, but the Army had to be given all available means of winning a decision — here on the Dunajec, there on the Narew, now on the Dwina, then by the Meuse — or the fortunes of Germany were lost.

In other words, the Armies of France and Russia exerted, in combination or alternately, such pressure on German armament resources that the common enemy of the Triple Entente had to abandon the attempt to remain as strong at sea as he was when the war opened. Had he been fighting against Great Britain alone, he might have equalled and, with his immense resources, overtaken her in ship-building. As it was, she alone threw her **Shipbuilder to the world** chief energies into naval construction. She was shipbuilder to the world, with a very remarkable number of yards for building merchantmen as well as fighting ships.

At some discomfort to the people from the enhanced cost of food, due to the lack of new cargo steamers, the British nation devoted all its yards to warship construction, and by augmenting the strength of its Fleet, which could also draw reinforcements from the Allies, placed it in a position to prevent any serious offensive by the enemy's Navy. In 1908, when the Germans were drawing very close in Dreadnought strength, their boast was an alarming menace. They then could truly say, as their Emperor had foretold, that Great Britain could only win a victory in the North Sea at the cost of falling in power below the United States. But in 1916 the Germans could no longer look forward in a fleet action to inflict crippling loss on the British Navy. In clear daylight, especially, its advantage in numbers had

world. There was one dominant Fleet, and another and quite a third-rate Fleet. By the most extraordinary paradox in history British sea-power became largely based upon the land-power of France and Russia. What Great Britain did herself in increasing her strength at sea between the declaration of war and the fleet action off Jutland was of secondary importance in comparison with the actual work done by the French and Russian Armies in augmenting her naval power.

For Germany was in a position in 1915 similar to that which she occupied in 1913, when she raised her battle resources by a war levy. Tremendous as was her industrial capacity of producing war material, that capacity was not adequate to all her needs. She could not devote all her steel-making plants and power tools to building thousands of heavy guns and turning out from a quarter to half a million military shells a day and at the same time rival Great Britain in warship con-**Germany diverted from sea-power** struction. By intense pressure on both the western and eastern fronts France and Russia compelled the enemy to concentrate his main productive energies upon the land war.

Great Britain therefore remained free to intensify her warship construction, and also to increase in an unparalleled manner the personnel of her Navy. She invented novel types of ships, such as the torpedo-proof heavy monitor, and brought out a squadron of fast battleships with monster guns. Ships of the Royal Sovereign class, mounting 15 in. guns, began to appear, while German ships, designed to carry guns of the same calibre, remained unfinished in the yards. Vast quantities of Krupp armour-plate, that would have gone into ships, were transferred to the German Army and used for protecting machine-gun redoubts and making casemates for quick-firers.

Mainly from necessity, and partly from its general tendency to take the military point of view, the General Staff of Germany was allowed to overbear the Navy

COMMANDER OF THE GERMAN SCOUTING SQUADRON.
Vice-Admiral Hipper, who commanded the German scouting squadron, was completely outmanœuvred by Sir David Beatty, but he received the Order " Pour le Mérite " from the Kaiser.

THE SINKING OF THE ARABIS OFF THE DOGGER BANK.
German disregard of the loss of life entailed by sinking enemy ships was infamous. One occasion when her sailors were alleged to have shown humanity was when two torpedo-boats sank the Arabis, February 10th, 1916. A Leipzig paper published this picture purporting to show survivors being picked up by the torpedo-boat.

become so great that it could expect to produce a concentrated fire, at the long range which suited it, which would destroy opponents without exposing it to very severe losses.

In the day of preparation Grand-Admiral von Tirpitz had mistakenly neglected to develop the one weapon that might have told against Great Britain—the submarine, and had spent most of his money on ships of the Dreadnought

Tirpitz and submarines

class, which he was afraid to risk when the great test came. For some months Tirpitz endeavoured to redeem his mistake by devoting a large part of his constructive power to the production of submarines. In the construction of large ships he seems to have completed by the spring of 1916 only the battle-cruisers Lützow and Hindenburg and the four battleships of the König class. He carried out only the ordinary programme of battleship construction and probably took over the German-built Salamis, which had been ordered by the Greek Government, and was designed, according to programme, to carry eight 14 in. guns. A considerable number of fast and powerful light cruisers were completed, apparently in the hope of getting some of them on to the Atlantic trade-routes. A small squadron of new German battleships, with guns of 15 in. calibre, was completing, but this new and important force was not in action in the Battle of Jutland.

The British Grand Fleet was perhaps weakened by the diversion of heavy guns and mountings from sea-going battleships in course of construction to slow coast service monitors. This was one mistake made, and it was revealed by Mr. Balfour, not very wisely. Another error alleged by Mr. Churchill to have been committed was negligence in pressing forward large ships. Still, with the new battleships mounting 15 in. guns, the new fast light cruisers with 6 in. guns, and with the increasing range and power of the British submarines—which kept at least level with the enemy's developments in underwater craft—the striking power of the Fleet was sufficient.

Yet it was in these circumstances that the German High Sea Fleet was brought to action. In the opening months of the war, when Germany was comparatively strong at sea, she avoided a fleet action. But when her relative naval power had declined, owing to British production of material and intensified training of naval reservists and recruits, she almost went out of her way to risk her Fleet. The reasons that led her to adopt this course are a matter of speculation. All the facts will not be known until long after the war is over. There are, however, indications that the change in policy was directly due to the retirement of Grand-Admiral von Tirpitz. The creator of the German High Sea Fleet was well aware of its growing weakness in the face of British constructive energy and Britain's ample opportunities for training men.

Discarding the plan on which he had built the German Fleet, Tirpitz resolved to keep his battleships safe in harbour, and to harass the British mercantile marine by submarine attack, with a view to reducing British sea-borne supplies to a point at which the British capacity for action would be decisively weakened. Then, with the squadron of heavily gunned German battleships due in the autumn of 1916, Tirpitz might have resumed operations against the British Navy. The German Grand-Admiral was so much convinced of the efficacy of his new form of underwater

The policy of piracy

piracy that he was willing to bring the United States into the field against the Central Empires rather than relinquish his system of attacking both belligerent and neutral merchant ships trading to the British Isles.

When the German Emperor and his Chancellor decided that Germany could not at the time afford to provoke the United States to side with the Allies, the Grand-Admiral had to be dismissed from the control of the Navy. Apparently in his view there was nothing of importance to be done at sea except to continue the submarine campaign against all shipping in the war zone around the British Isles. He could not see his way to risk the High Sea

Fleet until the new battleships with larger guns were completed, as he thought the odds had become overwhelming. But from the personal, and perhaps dynastic, point of view of the German Emperor something had immediately to be attempted with the Navy. The complete fiasco of the Verdun operations was beginning to tell on the spirit of the German people, and to aggravate the discomfort produced by the rigorous rationing of the nation due to the stoppage of Russian supplies and the partial blockade exercised by the British Fleet. The German High Command was well acquainted with the fact that Russia was quickly gathering new strength with the assistance of the munition factories of Great Britain and Japan. The transport of munitions past the northern coast of Norway to the new ice-free Russian port of Alexandrovsk would greatly increase when the ice in the White Sea broke and again opened the port of Archangel. It may be doubted whether the German Staff foresaw what renewed and augmented power Russia would display when the stream of sea-borne munitions was fully liberated by the breaking of the ice. But what they did see in the matter made them anxious, and Field-Marshal von Hindenburg, moreover, required a very considerable part of the German battleship and battle-cruiser strength for his proposed operations against Riga.

German Fleet and Riga

Political and military considerations, therefore, interfered with the purely naval strategy that had been established by Tirpitz. Had the Grand-Admiral been able to wait until the early autumn of 1916, his new fast battleships with 15 in. guns or 17 in. guns might have enabled him partially to balance the squadrons of the Queen Elizabeth and Royal Sovereign class. As it was, Tirpitz had to give way to the personal judgment of William II., who was influenced by Bethmann-Hollweg in matters of foreign and domestic policy and by the General Staff in regard to the overruling necessities of the German armies on both eastern and western fronts. In these circumstances the German Emperor needed a fighting admiral who was ready to take great risks in view of great results. The man was found in Vice-Admiral Reinhold von Scheer, who succeeded Pohl, the supplanter of Ingenohl, as Commander-in-Chief of the High Sea Fleet.

Before the war Scheer had been known as the leading German authority on Nelson. He had distinguished himself as a student of gunnery, tactics, and strategy; but above all this he was regarded as having penetrated the secret of the "Nelson touch" as Clausewitz had penetrated the secret of the Napoleonic method. In either case it is doubtful if the learned Germans bored their way by laborious researches into the ultimate secret of the British and French masters of war. It will be found

Modern men and master-militarists

that a modern French soldier, Captain Gilbert, discovered Napoleon's later and finer method and handed on his knowledge to General Foch and other French commanders now famous throughout the world.

The "Nelson touch" may be summed up as the art of bringing superior force to bear upon the enemy at the decisive point by a consummate use of judgment and seamanship. Like Rodney and other men of the older generation, Nelson was often ready to expose some of his leading ships to overwhelming enemy fire, with a view to winning such a position as would enable him to mass his inferior numbers against a fragment of the enemy's superior numbers. That is to say, he was ready to make a small preliminary sacrifice in order to break the enemy's line and destroy a considerable part of the enemy's ships. His method was essentially the same as that which Napoleon employed. Napoleon used to set a single division, such as that of Lannes, the task of withstanding a much superior part of a hostile force, in order to give the main French mass of manœuvre time to concentrate in overwhelming strength against a weak part of the enemy's line.

This seems to have been all that Vice-Admiral von Scheer acquired of direct value in his long studies of the Nelson method. Like all German admirals, he was at the beginning rather oppressed by the fact that he would have to fight against a Fleet of which both the matériel and the personnel were superior to the Fleet he commanded. None of the methods of the modern German school of military strategy was helpful to him. For since Moltke the German General Staff had merely relied upon the rapid, straightforward employment of the advantage of numbers and railway mobility. The manœuvre of envelopment, followed by a fierce thrust at the hostile centre when it had been weakened by the effort to strengthen its menaced flank, constituted the methods of German military strategy as developed by Moltke and his successors. The rest was mainly a matter of the technique of railway management, the technique of siege-gun transport, and the technique of a distinct and powerful machine-gun organisation.

In military matters the Germans were half blinded by the sense of their enormous strength; but with reference to the problems of naval warfare, the German admirals were compelled to devise a more subtle and economical employment of their forces. They stood in much the same position with regard to British admirals that French generals stood in with regard to German generals at the opening of the war. They had to seek for some method of bringing an inferior force to bear against a superior force, with such dispositions as would enable them to outnumber the more powerful enemy in the crisis of the battle. For, as Nelson said, "only numbers can annihilate." At Trafalgar his fleet was smaller than the combined Franco-Spanish fleet, and to obtain the numbers which annihilate he had to separate some of the hostile ships, concentrate his force around the separated squadrons, and then destroy them before Villeneuve could bring up the other enemy ships of the line.

New conditions of naval war

All the material conditions of naval warfare had greatly changed since Nelson's day. It had become difficult for a small fleet to engage a large fleet with any chance of cutting off part of the latter. Steam-power had made obsolete the factor of seamanship that told most in the days of sailing ships. If any advantage remained in seamanship, British flag-officers, by reason of their incomparable opportunities for gaining experience, ought to have possessed it. Practically all British seamen were long-service men, while the ordinary personnel of the German Fleet contained a considerable element of short-service, conscripted landsmen. Scheer had, therefore, to reckon that no study on his part would enable him to win by Nelson's main instrument of victory—unparalleled seamanship.

All that he could do was to adapt to modern conditions the art of making a preliminary sacrifice, which had been a tradition of the British Navy since the days of Rodney. The force designated for the preliminary sacrifice was the Battle-Cruiser Squadron under Rear-Admiral Hipper, which Sir David Beatty had hammered in the Dogger Bank Battle. This squadron had been strengthened, after the loss of the Blücher, by the addition of the new battle-cruiser the Lützow, a ship of 28,000 tons, eight 12 in. guns, twelve 6 in. guns, and a reputed speed of twenty-eight knots. The true speed seems to have been actually less than this. Then a later battle-cruiser, the Hindenburg, of 28,000 tons displacement, eight 15 in. and fourteen 6 in. guns, and a reputed speed of twenty-seven knots, was added to Hipper's squadron in the early spring of 1916.

For some reason at present unknown the Hindenburg does not seem to have been used in the action. It is possible that she developed defects during her gun trials in March, 1910. She does not appear to have been originally designed to carry 15 in. guns. Another battle-cruiser of the Hindenburg class, the Viktoria Luise, of 28,000 tons, eight 15 in. guns, and fourteen 6 in. guns, had been launched at Hamburg in 1914. But she does not seem to have taken part in the battle. No doubt the same reason that prevented the Hindenburg from appearing also affected her.

The absence of the Hindenburg left Hipper with five ships. He flew his flag in the Lützow, which was followed by a ship of a similar class, the Derfflinger, and the Seydlitz, of 24,600 tons, ten 11 in. guns, twelve 6 in. guns, and a reputed speed of 29·2 knots. Then there was the Moltke, of 22,600 tons, ten 11 in. guns, twelve 6 in. guns, and a reputed speed of 28·5 knots; while in the rear, in place of the vanished Blücher, was an unknown ship, which may have been the salved and repaired Von der Tann, of 18,700 tons, eight 11 in., and ten 6 in. guns, and a nominal speed of 27·6 knots.

The five ships under the command of Rear-Admiral Hipper were of almost decisive importance to the German Navy. In the absence of the 15 in. gun battle-cruisers, Hipper's squadron was the only manœuvring wing that Scheer possessed. But he was a man of sufficient courage and enterprise to fling out his sole available battle-cruiser force, and expose it to the fire of six British battle-cruisers, most of them armed with 13·5 in. guns, and reinforced by a fast British battleship squadron having 15 in. guns.

BRITISH PATROL BOAT STOPPING A SUSPECTED SHIP.
Every vessel that gave rise to the least suspicion was searched by the British patrol. Our illustration shows a vessel being stopped by a shot across her bows and held in the searchlights of the patrol in case more direct shooting should be required.

Such was Scheer's application of the Nelson method to the conditions of modern naval warfare. His total strength was barely more than half that of the British naval commander-in-chief's. Yet he was ready to imperil five of his Dreadnought capital ships, out **Scheer's bravery** of a total of twenty-one available Dread-**and enterprise** nought units, in a design to encompass the destruction of a part of the British Fleet. Had he won the victory he intended, it would not have been decisive, for the main British battle-squadrons would still have heavily outnumbered the German battle-squadrons. It is impossible to deny to Scheer praise for his boldness and sternness of conception.

In this respect we must remember that the German Navy is a modern child of the British Navy. During the reign of Queen Victoria, German naval officers came to this country to be trained, while a few British military officers went to Prussia for instruction. It was from British history that Vice-Admiral von Scheer and many other German admirals learnt to emulate the spirit of Nelson. When Great Britain was oppressed by the German-made mirage of an inevitable clash with Russia in Afghanistan, the British Government hoped that the German Navy in making would assist the British Fleet in the Baltic Sea. Until a few weeks before the outbreak of the war the old tradition of discipleship between the German and British Navies was maintained by German sailors. Captain von Müller, of the Emden, for example, used sometimes to take his holidays in England with British naval officers, and lightly talk over technical matters with them in a friendly way.

Had British naval officers been as simple as they seemed, their German disciples would have learnt a great deal from them. But British naval officers had more genius in all the arts of diplomacy than had most professed diplomatists. It may well be doubted if the Germans ever learnt anything of value in technique or construction from dining and holiday-making with them during the long period of tension following the passing of the famous German Navy Bill. All that the enemy discovered was that an inferior fleet was completely wasted if it remained upon the defensive. At all costs it had to strike, and in order to strike with effect it had first to fling out as a sacrifice its battle-cruiser wing.

What the Germans learnt

This, indeed, was what the former German naval commander-in-chief, Ingenohl, had attempted to do in those battleship raids against the East Coast that ended in the Dogger Bank Battle. The raids were designed to bring the British Battle-Cruiser Squadron under Sir David Beatty down from its base in pursuit of Hipper's squadron. About eighty miles away from the apparently fugitive ships of Hipper was the main German Battle Fleet, swinging up to envelop Sir David Beatty's squadron when the stern-chase was growing dangerous for Hipper. This plan of luring the Battle-Cruiser Squadron to destruction was not defeated by the Dogger Bank Battle. As we explained in a previous chapter of THE GREAT WAR, Sir David Beatty's second-in-command broke off the Dogger Bank action some time before the German Battle Fleet could close with him. Behind the battle-cruisers, and hurrying to their aid, was a British Battle Fleet under Sir John Jellicoe; but the situation was such that before the battleships could arrive the battle-cruisers would have received a severe hammering.

Sir David Beatty at the time was in the act of transferring his flag from the disabled Lion to an effective ship, with no power of control over the situation, or he would have maintained the action with Hipper's flaming and beaten ships in order to allow time for the British Battle Fleet in turn to envelop the German Battle Fleet. Had the Dogger Bank Battle been fought to a finish, it is thought it might have ended in all Hipper's ships being sunk, all the German battleships being sunk, and Sir John Jellicoe being left somewhat damaged, yet master of the seas. But, as the result of a chapter of accidents, nothing of a decisive character occurred

The German attack on Lowestoft was a perfect example of what Sir John Jellicoe described as the " tip-and-run " tactics of the German Fleet. At 4.30 a.m. of April 25th, 1916, five German battle-cruisers, accompanied by light cruisers and destroyers, appeared off Lowestoft. They were preceded and accompanied by Zeppelins. For twenty minutes Lowestoft was shelled, and a few projectiles were also fired by the enemy at Yarmouth. Some damage to property was done, though only four persons, all civilians, were killed. A British light-cruiser squadron appeared towards the close **German ships attack** of the bombardment, and with great **Lowestoft** gallantry attacked the enemy. It should have been blown out of the water, but it escaped with moderate loss and without a single ship disabled. In the same engagement the British submarine E22 was sunk, with the loss of all her crew except two. The Germans succeeded in effecting their retreat, having accomplished their purpose, which was to cause annoyance and loss. The Grand Fleet and Sir David Beatty's cruisers failed to catch them.

From a strategical point of view the policy of raiding

WITH THE GERMAN NAVY OFF THE SKAGER RACK.
An incident in the Jutland Battle. This illustration, reproduced from an enemy print, purports to show the scene aboard a German torpedo-boat at the moment of firing her torpedoes against British ships.

COALING A WARSHIP STEAMING AT TWELVE KNOTS AN HOUR.

A collier was towed astern, and sacks of coal were hoisted to a platform at the masthead, and sent by cable to the warship. Sixty tons of coal were thus transhipped within an hour. From the masthead to the collier's deck a net was suspended to shield the collier's hands from falling fragments.

the East Coast appears erroneous. The enemy gave the British Fleet too many chances of compassing his destruction. When progress in shipbuilding permitted Sir John Jellicoe to strengthen Sir David Beatty's cruising force by an additional squadron of fast battleships, certain new dispositions in regard to the positions of this battle-cruiser and battleship division upset the plan of the German admiral. He could not look forward even to a partial success, if his raiding squadrons were likely to be caught between the British battle-cruisers and the fast British battleships.

Hostile fleets manœuvre
There then came a period of quietude in the North Sea. The quiet was only the cover for an extraordinary amount of manœuvring between the opposing fleets. Hipper occasionally came out and ventured his single squadron within sighting distance of the British cruisers; but always the main battle force of the German High Sea Fleet was close behind the German battle-cruisers, and the British battle squadrons were also fairly close behind the fast British ships, and the Germans could do nothing.

On every occasion of this sort the enemy retired. It was not want of courage on his part, but a prudent strategy that made him refuse battle in such circumstances. The odds against him were so overwhelming that he could not hope even for the smallest partial success. In the great periodical sweeps through the North Sea, made with the entire forces of the British Fleet, no valid opportunity for successful manœuvre remained to the enemy. He could only withdraw to safety behind his mine-fields as soon as his Zeppelins and reconnoitring vessels warned him that the British battle squadrons were acting closely in concert with Sir David Beatty's cruising division.

In these excursions towards the Skager Rack the British cruisers used to pass near the fishing ground known as Little Fisher Bank. In this shallow the water was scarcely more than twenty fathoms deep, and towards the end of May the German admiral sent one of his submarine flotillas to lie in ambush among the Dutch fishing smacks

working over the shallows. No definite evidence is available that any Dutchmen engaged in the peaceful work of catching herrings for the German market acted in concert with the enemy underwater craft. Yet some of them showed remarkable phlegm in going on with their fishing while the flame and thunder of battle continued to rage for hours closely around them. It may seem rather extraordinary that the smacks should not have returned towards Ymuiden when the action opened and the opposing squadrons and divisions began to move forwards and backwards over the fishing grounds.

The submarines seem to have been in or near the bank when the German High Sea Fleet steamed out for action at dawn on Wednesday, May 31st, 1916. Behind a van of light cruisers and destroyers came Rear-Admiral Hipper's five powerful battle-cruisers. The squadron steamed towards the southern coast of Norway. Reaching a point west of Little Fisher Bank, it was over three hundred miles from the Firth of Forth, about two hundred miles from Heligoland, and nearly two hundred and thirty miles from Wilhelmshaven. In other words, Hipper came nearly half-way from his base to the nearest British base.

At Horn Reef, a hundred miles from Little Fisher Bank were the main German battle squadrons under Vice-Admiral von Scheer. They appear to have con-
sisted of sixteen modern battleships of the **German Fleet assembles** König, Kaiser, and other Dreadnought types, together with six older, slower, and feebler battleships of the pre-Dreadnought class. New and powerful light cruisers were with the battle fleet, and also some armed liners, brought up with the additional light cruisers apparently for the purpose of getting past the British Fleet at night to the trade-routes. A single Zeppelin was seen from the British Fleet early on June 1st, and Sir David Beatty in his despatch mentioned that it was possible that the enemy employed these fast aerial scouts in an effective manner. The Dutch trawler Henrietta reported seeing two Zeppelins moving with

extraordinary speed near the scene of action, between 5 and 6 p.m., flying south from the direction in which Admiral Jellicoe was advancing. As the enemy afterwards took the trouble to deny that either Zeppelins or submarines were employed, we have additional reason for supposing that he made full use of both these new instruments of attack and reconnaissance.

The weather was at first fairly favourable for Zeppelin work. The sea was calm, the air warm, and only a slight summer mist drifted in patches about the sea. Fire-control officers on either side could at first get a hit at a range of ten miles. Observing officers, placed in Zeppelins fitted with long-distance wireless telegraphy apparatus, and moving at a speed double that of the fastest light cruiser, were likely to be able to do valuable work in discovering first Sir David Beatty's three squadrons and then Sir John Jellicoe's Battle Fleet. On the other hand, the movements of Admiral von Scheer, about 6 p.m., when his light cruisers discovered the approach of the main British Fleet, suggest that he did not know it was so near. Had Zeppelins been reconnoitring, they must have discovered its exact whereabouts. Possibly the clouds were too low to permit of airships doing their work without risks which the enemy did not dare to take. They would have had to descend to search for the enemy, and might have been caught and shot down.

Value of Zeppelins

The British Staff unfortunately was without long range rigid airships for scouting. The neglect of such aircraft by the Admiralty in previous years hampered the British commanders at every turn, and placed them in a position of comparative blindness against an alert and all-seeing foe. The seaplane, in the state of development which it had reached in 1915-16, was not capable of prolonged expeditions. It had to be carried to the neighbourhood of the scene of action and then lowered from a ship. In rough weather this was a difficult business, nor was it always certain that the seaplane would rise from the water. On its return to the parent vessel it required to be reshipped, and the parent vessel was always exposed to submarine attack. Again, the seaplane, from its nature, was incapable of hovering, and it could not move slowly and steadily enough to permit the effective use of telescopes. Half a dozen Zeppelins attached to Sir John Jellicoe's fleet would have revealed to him the exact force and disposition of the enemy and the general direction of the German movements. They would also have shown him —in all probability—where the German submarines were placed. Nor is it at all probable that the weather would have prevented such observation, though the mist might have rendered it difficult and dangerous. We shall see later, as Sir John records, that on the following morning, June 1st, when the visibility was less than on May 31st (the day of battle), a Zeppelin at 4 a.m. was engaged by the British Fleet " for about five minutes,

Approximate British power

during which time it had ample opportunity to note and subsequently report the position and course of the British Fleet." What the German airship did on June 1st, British airships, had there been any, could have done on May 31st.

It is not permissible to state in detail the strength of the British Fleet. But if we take the British ships reported by the enemy as present in the action, and the German ships stated in Admiral Jellicoe's despatch to have been in line of battle, we obtain an approximate estimate of the opposing forces in this great fleet action.

BRITISH.
BATTLE-CRUISERS.

	13.5 in. guns.	12 in. guns.	6 in. guns.	4 in. guns.
1 Tiger	8	0	12	0
3 Lions	24	0	0	48
5 Invincibles	0	40	0	80
	32	40	12	128

FAST BATTLESHIPS.

		15 in. guns.	6 in. guns.
4 Queen Elizabeths		32	48

BATTLESHIPS.

	15 in. guns.	14 in. and 13.5 in. guns.	12 in. guns.	6 in. guns.	4 in. guns.
1 Royal Sovereign	8	0	0	36	0
12 Iron Dukes ..	0	120	0	48	128
1 Agincourt ..	0	0	14	20	0
10 Dreadnoughts ..	0	0	100	0	144
	8	120	114	104	272

GERMAN.
BATTLE-CRUISERS.

	12 in. guns.	11 in. guns.	6 in. guns.
2 Lützows	16	0	24
2 Seydlitzes	0	20	24
1 Von der Tann	0	8	10
	16	28	58

BATTLESHIPS (DREADNOUGHT CLASS).

	12 in. guns.	11 in. guns.	6 in. guns.
4 Königs	40	0	56
5 Kaisers	50	0	70
4 Helgolands	48	0	56
4 Nassaus	0	48	56
	138	48	238

BATTLESHIPS (PRE-DREADNOUGHTS).

	11 in. guns.	6.7 in. guns.
6 Pommerns	24	84

On the above figures the heavy-gun force of the two fleets would be somewhat as follows :

	GREAT BRITAIN.	GERMANY.
15 in. guns	40	0
13.5 in. and 14 in. ..	152	Some 14 in. In what ships doubtful.
12 in.	154	154
11 in.	0	100
6 in. and 6.7 in. ..	164	380

It is a curious fact that the following German battleships, which might have been expected to have been completed, do not seem to have been in line : Ersatz Wörth, T. and Ersatz Kaiser Friedrich III. They were reported to have been re-armed with 16 in. guns; as originally planned they were to have mounted eight 15 in. guns apiece, exactly the heavy battery of the Queen Elizabeth and Royal Sovereign classes. The largest enemy projectiles noted were 14 in. shells, which might have come from the battle-cruiser Salamis (building in Germany for the Greek Government when the war broke out, and certainly taken over by the German Government, as she was designed to mount eight American 14 in. guns), or from German battleships of the König class, supposing these to have been re-armed.

The heavy guns in action in the two fleets, and the weight of shell and speed (in feet per second) with which the shell leaves the muzzle of the gun, were as follows :

	BRITISH.		GERMAN.	
	Weight of Shell (lb.)	Feet per Sec.	Weight of Shell (lb.)	Feet per Sec.
15 in.	1,900	2,655	none	
14 in.	1,400	2,700	1,366	2,900
13.5 in. ..	1,250	2,700	none	
12 in.	850	2,800–3,000	860	3,080
11 in.	None		660	3,080

The higher the speed with which the shell left the muzzle of the gun, the greater was the force with which the target was struck. All the big guns had approximately the same rate of fire, which was two rounds a minute at

H.M.S. DREADNOUGHT IN DOCK.
Normal displacement, 17,900 tons; complement, 800 men; principal armament, ten 12 in. guns.

case under consideration. The Grand Fleet on paper was twice as strong in gun-power as the High Sea Fleet under Admiral von Scheer. So if the Grand Fleet were brought into action as a concentrated whole, it would have had four times the actual fighting strength of the enemy. Moreover, the mobility of its powerful fast battleship squadron of Queen Elizabeths would endow it with an additional manœuvring power, making it possible to increase its concentrated fire effect. It will, however, be found that the battle of May 31st did not altogether bear out this principle.

As against the British superiority in big guns and speed, the enemy carried a more formidable secondary armament and much heavier armour. Practically all his battle-cruisers, for instance, had 1 in. to

highest speed, though naturally this could not be maintained for many minutes at long ranges, where it was necessary to watch the fall of the shells and constantly alter the sights. At 15,000 yards and over the 15 in. gun was much more accurate than the 12 in. or 11 in. weapon. For in clear weather the 1,900 lb. shell made a tremendous splash, that could be seen ten miles away, thus enabling the range quickly to be found. The effect of the 15 in. shell was about five times as deadly as that of the 12 in., and eight times as deadly as that of the 11 in. projectile.

Allowing for the greater size and weight of a large proportion of British shells, the chances were two to one against the enemy in artillery; and an eminent French naval officer, Lieutenant Baudry, has argued that an important principle must be considered in calculating the odds in battle. It is that the square of the numerical strength of a fighting force represents its fighting **Problem of** strength. If, for example, two Dread- **numerical strength** nought battleships are fighting against one Dreadnought battleship of equal force, the actual fighting odds will not be two to one. They will be the square of 2 ($2 \times 2 = 4$) against the square of 1 ($1 \times 1 = 1$). The odds will be, in terms of actual fighting strength, four against one.

If three ships of one class concentrate against one ship of the same class, and the efficiency, the gunnery, and seamanship on each side are equal, the odds will be $3 \times 3 = 9$ against $1 \times 1 = 1$, or nine against one.

This law of the numerical square may be applied to the

THE FORWARD GUNS OF H.M.S. REVENGE.
Early in the morning on June 1st, 1916, Vice-Admiral Sir Cecil Burney transferred his flag from the slower Marlborough to the Revenge, and, partly owing to its position, the squadron he then commanded saw more of the enemy battle fleet than the other squadrons, and performed excellent work.

2 in. more armour on the gun-turrets than the British battle-cruisers. Where the British heavy-gun positions were protected by 9 in. armour, the German heavy-gun positions had 10 in. to 11 in. armour. In older ships of the same type, where British ships carried 7 in. armour, the enemy carried 8 in. armour. As for modern battleships, the Iron Duke, completed in 1914, may be compared with the König, completed in the same year. The Iron Duke—according to the German naval handbooks—carried an armour belt of 12 inches, with 10 in. armour on the heavy-gun positions, but the König had a 14 in. belt and 14 in. armour on her heavy guns. The superior armour placed by the enemy over his heavy guns added considerably to his power of resistance and reduced the odds against him.

In secondary armament the British ships were at some disadvantage. They had some hundreds of 4 in. guns in the battle-cruiser squadrons and the older battleships. During the first phase of construction of the Dreadnought fleet many naval critics lamented the fact that British designers were content to mount 4 in. guns as secondary armament when Germany was mounting 6 in. weapons. Only the latest British battle-cruiser, four of the Iron Duke squadron, the Queen Elizabeth, and the Royal Sovereigns carried a medium battery equal in calibre to that of the enemy. It was an undoubted defect that all the British Dreadnought ships with 12 in. guns, and many of the super-Dreadnoughts with 13·5 in. guns, should have been designed to carry only 4 in. guns as a secondary armament. Nevertheless, for an action at close range, the British strength in medium artillery was respectable. The British Dreadnoughts mounted one hundred and sixty-four 6 in. guns and four hundred and ten 4 in. guns, against three hundred and eighty 6 in. guns carried by the enemy's ships; but in judging the superb performance of the British destroyers in the battle, the fact that they had to attack vessels armed with an extremely powerful medium artillery must be taken into account. The German 6 in. guns would probably not play much part in the struggle between the big ships, but for meeting torpedo craft they were invaluable.

Value of 6 in. guns

When certain of Sir David Beatty's ships sighted Vice-Admiral Hipper's squadron at 2.20 in the afternoon of May 31st, 1916, the odds against the German battle-cruiser squadron were great. The British admiral had thirty-two 13·5 in. and sixteen 12 in. guns, with a total available secondary armament of twelve 6 in. guns and eighty 4 in. guns. The German admiral had sixteen 12 in. guns and twenty-eight 11 in. guns, with a secondary armament of fifty-eight 6 in. guns. Of the armaments of the light cruisers and destroyers on both sides no figures are available.

In regard to manœuvring power the German admiral seems to have been distinctly inferior, though the speed of his slowest battle-cruiser was nominally about twenty-seven and a half knots, and that of the slowest British battle-cruisers was only twenty-five knots; but if the British battle-cruisers as a squadron were faster, the four fast battleships forming part of Sir David Beatty's division were slower than the German battle-cruisers. The result was that the German admiral, during the first phase of the action, was able to engage Sir David Beatty's battle-cruisers, while keeping at such a distance from the 15 in. guns of the fast battleship squadron that the latter could not reach their targets. For nearly an hour the British battleships could give little help to the British battle-cruisers. This circumstance prevented an immediate and crushing defeat of the German admiral, who, as we shall see, won a very considerable advantage during the first battle-cruiser action. Figures on paper, such as we have given, may be greatly changed in the course of actual fighting. As a matter of fact, Sir David Beatty, in the first phase of the battle, engaged Vice-Admiral Hipper with an advantage of six ships to five, and of gun-power of five to three; but after he lost the Queen Mary and Indefatigable he was at a disadvantage of four ships to five. Despite the overwhelming superiority of the British Fleet, the most critical phase of the action was fought against an enemy in superior numbers.

Overwhelming British Fleet

One most important influence in the enemy's favour was that he was able to select the day and the place of battle. The British Navy had to be always on guard, always prepared to counter a German attack on the British coast or a German movement to convoy raiding cruisers through the blockading line. This necessity of constant vigilance prevented it from disposing of all its force at any given moment. Ships had from time to time to be docked and

refitted, otherwise they would have lost their speed and their fighting value. Moreover, at intervals they had to be detached for such work as testing their torpedoes and carrying out gunnery practice, which might not always be possible at the bases where they were normally stationed. From the published particulars we know that Sir David Beatty's force at full strength would have totalled fifteen large armoured ships - namely, five Queen Elizabeths and ten battle-cruisers. Of the Queen Elizabeths, the name-ship was not in the battle; of the battle-cruisers, the Australia was absent; while of the other nine battle-cruisers, three (the Invincible, Indomitable, and Inflexible) were not with Admiral Beatty when the battle began, and did not join him until some two hours after it had been in progress. Had he had all his battle-cruisers, he would have struck the enemy in the initial action with ten fast ships instead of six. Had he had all the Queen Elizabeths in the second stage of the battle, he would have had fifteen large armoured ships against the Germans, and in view of the immense amount of damage which he inflicted with only ten ships, it is possible that the battle might then have been the crushing and completely decisive victory which the British Navy sought.

Precisely the same conditions existed in the days of the old Navy. Nelson, on the eve of Trafalgar, was compelled to detach six ships of the line under Admiral Louis, to embark water and provisions, and these vessels were not with him when the battle was fought. It is a condition which every Staff has foreseen, and which necessitated the provision of a large margin of force on the British side, in the teeth of the British faction which complained of every addition to the British Fleet. The Germans could make all their arrangements, and choose the time and weather that suited them best. They could dock as many ships as they liked simultaneously, as there was little or no risk of a British attack on their perfectly fortified and well-mined coast. They could seize any opportunity of which their spy service provided them with information, and the incessant scouting of their Zeppelins weeks before the battle must have given them a tolerable idea of the British dispositions. If they happened to meet a weak British squadron they could concentrate on it. They could set submarine and mine traps, and could then fall back on them with the object of drawing the British into these snares, in the hope that the British naval predominance would be destroyed in a few hours. The torpedo and mine were complications with which Nelson had not to deal, and they hampered the British strategy and tactics seriously, and aided the inferior Navy, so long as it remained within narrow waters. Because these factors existed, the British admirals had to proceed with extreme wariness, and thus, though the submarine actually effected very little in the battle, it clogged the British operations and undoubtedly contributed to the escape of the German Fleet.

German naval advantages

The difficulties which Sir John Jellicoe and Sir David Beatty had to overcome were, then, most serious, and in following the British movements they must be constantly kept in view. The Germans were free from such anxieties, and, from their proximity to their bases, in the closing phases of the battle they would be able to employ a very large number of destroyers to cover the retreat of their fleet, if it encountered the British in force, or to attack damaged British vessels if the German heavy ships gained the upper hand.

Thus it was that the British command, with a great superiority in force available, exposed to the enemy's concentrated force in the initial fighting a fraction of the Grand Fleet. We have seen that it was the aim of Admiral von Scheer to bring about this result. Believing that only numbers could annihilate, he schemed to detach, envelop, and destroy a part of the British Fleet before the main British battle force could engage him. The German view of the Battle of Jutland was that Admiral von Scheer partly succeeded in his aim, and after inflicting great damage, skilfully broke off the action before he could in turn be shattered by Sir John Jellicoe. The Germans admitted they had sustained inevitable losses, but argued that they had largely achieved the end they had in view, and displayed strategy of the most brilliant kind in avoiding a decisive fleet action.

Before accepting this view of the battle, we have to consider the object of the commander of the British Grand Fleet. It is clear that the plan of bringing the British Fleet into action in several separate detachments was forced upon Sir John Jellicoe by differences in speed between his ships, and also by geographical conditions and the lack of suitable bases at the best strategic points. At the opening of the war, when the British Fleet sailed from Portland to its northern battle base, the fast battle-cruiser wing was detached from the main battle divisions. As a British Minister publicly stated, the new naval port at Rosyth in the Firth of Forth became the base of the Battle-Cruiser Squadron under Sir David Beatty. The Battle-Cruiser Squadron swept eastward and south-eastward as far as the Bight of Heligoland, acting as a far-advanced patrol for the British battle squadrons. A great distance separated this advanced British naval force under Sir David Beatty from the main naval force under Sir John Jellicoe.

In May, 1916, the advanced battle-cruiser force at Rosyth was strengthened by the 5th Battle Squadron, consisting of the Queen Elizabeth and her sister ships the Barham, Valiant, Warspite, and another, which last four fought in the Battle of Jutland under the command of Rear-Admiral Hugh Evan-Thomas. This additional force was placed under the general control of Sir David Beatty, who continued to fly his flag in the Lion, with Rear-Admiral W. C. Pakenham, in the New Zealand, and Rear-Admiral Osmond de B. Brock, in the Princess Royal, as subordinate flag-officers. The object of this change was greatly to increase the risks of the enemy's battle-cruisers if they attempted to raid the British East Coast towns. This fact was disclosed by Mr. Arthur Balfour, the First Lord of the Admiralty, in a letter to the mayors of Lowestoft and Yarmouth, after Admiral Hipper had sallied out and bombarded Lowestoft on April 25th, 1916. Mr. Balfour then stated that the Admiralty was bringing "important forces to the south."

In the absence of any official information to the contrary, it is to be presumed that the new disposition of the British forces was not made directly in answer to Hipper's revived threat against the East Coast. Mr. Balfour's letter evoked at the time some anxious criticism. It was against the settled British policy to scatter the Fleet for passive defence when the enemy had a great naval force concentrated and available. Concentration is the essence of ultimate success. In our last great Continental war the British coast was on rare occasions exposed to temporary attack, and French forces disembarked in Bantry Bay and at Fishguard. Such attempts to disturb the public spirit involve for the enemy the risk of wasting the forces available for the pitched battles on which depends the command of the sea. It has always been the British custom to look persistently to the grand decision, and to keep the British forces concentrated for the winning stroke.

Mr. Balfour's letter to Yarmouth

According to a British official commentator, the dispositions of the British Fleet on the eve of the battle were arranged with a view to bringing an unwilling enemy to battle. "The method," it is stated, "was drastic, and necessarily attended with risk, but for great ends great risks must be taken." Whenever the British command kept its forces closely together in its movements, the effect was to make the enemy avoid battle. The Grand Fleet might well have contained him, as it had done for twenty-two months, without risking any considerable part of its strength. But if it intended, for some reason, to induce him to stay and fight, there was one way only of doing this. It was to tempt the German commander, by giving him an apparent chance of catching the battle-cruisers separated from the main British force. Admiral von Scheer was ready to risk his battle-cruiser squadron in order to trap the British battle-cruisers. And it may be concluded that Sir John Jellicoe was also ready to let his forces come into action divided, in order to lure the High Sea Fleet into a pitched battle.

Divided forces as a lure

At the outbreak of hostilities Sir John Jellicoe was acting as Second Sea Lord, but he at once left his position

ROUGH WATER OFF THE GERMAN COAST.
German patrols leaving harbour for outpost duty in the North Sea.

at Whitehall to take the command of the Grand Fleet. He had long been designated for promotion in war to the supreme naval command, Lord Fisher having selected him for the position before 1909. In manœuvres Sir John had shown himself a fine tactician and remarkable strategist, and as a gunnery officer he had carried on the work begun by Sir Percy Scott, and contributed much to the development of scientific methods. Unlike most of the leaders of the German Navy, who were directed by a torpedo specialist, Sir John Jellicoe looked to gun fire to obtain a decision, and he contrived new ways of increasing the terrible effects of massed gun fire.

In the Commander-in-Chief we had a man of medium height, vigorous and alert ; one who combined the decision and energy of a man of action with the insight of a life-long student of war. His tranquil composure made him a tower of strength, and won the confidence of all. His was the calmness of a thinker who has profoundly studied his methods of action, and with a combination of unfretting patience and unrelaxing alertness awaits the opportunity

GERMAN U BOAT IN A NEUTRAL PORT.
The U35, which carried an autograph letter from the Kaiser to King Alfonso in June, 1916, at Cartagena, alongside an interned German steamer. In October the Allies issued a memorandum to certain neutral States giving reasons why submarines should be excluded from neutral harbours.

harbours in the North Sea area. Obviously a harbour of unusual size was required to accommodate the great force which Admiral Jellicoe commanded. As Mr. Arthur Balfour afterwards explained in the House of Commons, the British Government had built a fleet for the struggle in the North Sea, but had provided along the coast from which it had to operate no submarine-proof bases.

In these circumstances, which Sir John Jellicoe as a former Sea Lord had foreseen but had no power to alter, he removed the Grand Fleet into the northern mists. The deep water between Norway and the North of Scotland became his immediate cruising ground. His position enabled him to defeat any attempt by hostile cruisers to reach the British trade-routes. He could hold a raiding force northwards with his battle fleet, and envelop it southwards with his battle-cruisers. The periodical sweeps made through the North Sea by the Grand Fleet could not force the enemy to combat, yet each voyage strengthened the confidence of the British seamen, refreshed their fund of experience in the very varied circumstances of warfare in the North Sea, and helped to depress the spirits of the men in the retreating High Sea Fleet.

to strike. He was never hurried or unsteady. In the three qualities that give most edge to the gloriously common gift of courage—knowledge, intellectual energy, and presence of mind—Admiral Jellicoe stood out as a leader of men.

In the days before 1912, when there was no War Staff at the Admiralty, Sir John Jellicoe helped to work out, in manœuvres and in studies, the plan by which the British forces could control the North Sea. No doubt, if money had been available, the chief British naval strategist of the younger generation would have created suitable bases at the most favourable point on the East Coast; but under the Liberal Government funds for building immense submarine-proof harbours were lacking. When Sir John was a Sea Lord, the Board of Admiralty could not obtain from the Treasury the money needed for an adequate number of battle-cruisers, destroyers, and submarines. At the opening of the war the British Commander-in-Chief found himself with a superior fleet, but no large, secure

The Germans had to come well out if they were to snatch an opportunity of engaging the British battle-cruisers separated from the main British Fleet. Probably, in a general way, Admiral von Scheer understood the play of Admiral Jellicoe as well as the British commander understood his opponent's play. There seem to have been no great surprises on either side. Sir David Beatty knew that if he pursued Admiral Hipper he was likely to run into the High Sea Fleet. Admiral von Scheer should have known that if he pursued Sir David Beatty he was likely to run into the Grand Fleet. In both cases the chance of victory resided in a nice calculation of time.

GIANT DERRICKS IN PROCESS OF MANUFACTURE IN A SHIPBUILDING YARD.
The enormous increase in battleship building necessitated a vast increase in the preparation of plant. This official photograph, taken in one naval yard, shows huge derricks that are required for warships in course of construction.

Rear-Admiral The Hon. Horace L. A. Hood. C.B. M.V.O. D.S.O.

LOST WITH HIS FLAGSHIP THE INVINCIBLE, IN THE BATTLE OF JUTLAND

CHAPTER CXLI.

THE GLORIOUS BATTLE OF JUTLAND BANK. PART II.
Opening Phases : Cruiser Squadrons in Action.
By H. W. Wilson and Edward Wright.

Contact of the Fleets—Galatea and Another Cruiser of the 1st Light Cruiser Squadron Sight a German Destroyer and Engage Three Large Cruisers—Sir David Beatty Arrives to Force an Engagement—Disposition of the British Battle-Cruiser Squadron and the Grand Fleet—Admiral Hipper's Battle-Cruiser Squadron Turns Towards Horn Reef and the High Sea Fleet—Running Battle-Cruiser Action Opens at 18,500 Yards—Admiral Hipper Leads the British Fleet Towards his Submarine Ambush—Loss of the Indefatigable and the Queen Mary—Intervention of the Destroyer Forces on Both Sides—Gallantry of the 13th Flotilla, Led by the Nestor, Commander the Hon. Edward B. S. Bingham, who Wins the Victoria Cross on this Occasion—Rear-Admiral Evan-Thomas brings the 5th Battle Squadron Into Action at 20,000 Yards—Awe-inspiring Spectacle of the Battle—Sir David Beatty's Flagship the Lion Heavily Pounded—Admiral von Scheer Arrives with the High Sea Fleet—Composition and Armament of his Force—Sir David Beatty Manœuvres to Lead the High Sea Fleet Towards the Grand Fleet—Lieutenant J. C. Tovey's Daring Charge in the Onslow Against the German Battle-Cruisers—Paradoxical Change in the Situation at 5 p.m.—Rear-Admiral the Hon. Horace Hood brings the 3rd Battle-Cruiser Squadron Into Action—Sir David Beatty Endeavours to Cross the "T"—H.M.S. Invincible Blown Up—Complicated Conflicts and Manœuvres in the Mist—Rear-Admiral Sir Robert Arbuthnot brings his Cruiser Squadron into the Fight—End of H.M.S. Defence and Black Prince—The Warrior and the Warspite—Junction of the Battle-Cruiser Fleet with the Grand Fleet.

THE weather when the enemy was sighted was good. The sea was calm, and visibility was satisfactory. The lowness of the clouds indicated that mist would prevail in the evening. Captain Punt, of the Dutch trawler John Brown, stated that the atmosphere was hazy. He had noted that the German Fleet habitually came out in such weather, because then there was less likelihood of it being attacked by the British, and, if attacked, escape was easier. A misty night was probably part of Admiral von Scheer's calculation, to enable him to elude the forces under Sir John Jellicoe and get good cover for destroyer attacks.

Ominous movements took place that morning. Silent, unseen, the British Fleet was steaming to the scene of the encounter. No neutral sighted or reported it in the early hours of May 31st. Its multitude of grey ships passed across the North Sea bearing with them the salt of the nation, so soon to prove its faith and devotion and valour. Never has a force gone forth to battle with such spirit, and all those who were privileged to see the ships' crews before the engagement felt the most perfect confidence in their coolness and courage. Whatever blows of adversity might befall them, they would never falter. No suffering and no loss could daunt them. Nelson, in the grandest days of past British naval history, never commanded such a force. It was a fleet of ironclads manned by Ironsides, and as a new Revenge, built of steel and armed with 15 in. guns, sailed with that glorious array, so the indomitable heroism of Grenville animated its officers and men. As Theseus was said to have fought with the Athenians at Marathon, and as men believed they saw

Spirit and efficiency

St. George at Mons, so the spirits of Drake and Nelson should have been there to see how their children would uphold their renown.

During the previous forenoon neutral fishing craft south-west of the Little Fisher Bank observed German squadrons moving north-north-west. The first force was stated by Captain van Pel, of the trawler Josina, to have been over thirty ships strong. It detached a cruiser which overhauled the Josina. The second fleet was much larger, and numbered at least forty ships; it passed one hour later than the first force, and apparently kept in touch with the first force. The first fleet was undoubtedly Admiral Hipper with the German battle-cruisers, light cruisers, and some destroyers; the second force was Admiral von Scheer's battle squadrons and smaller craft. As the second force passed the Josina she heard the first shots fired on that tremendous day.

Prelude to battle

The fleets came into contact about ten minutes past two, when the Danish steamer Fiord was stopped by a German destroyer about one hundred and twenty miles west of the Danish coast, in the latitude of Aberdeen. A German officer approached her in a destroyer numbered "Hoch See Flotte 7," belonging to a squadron of fifteen destroyers and eighteen light and heavy cruisers. He asked the Danes if certain vessels which were just appearing on the horizon were British. The skipper said he did not know. The correct answer came in a tone of thunder. Two of Sir David Beatty's light cruisers, the Galatea and another, scouting in advance of his force, sighted the German destroyer. At 2.10 the Galatea hoisted the signal, "Prepare for immediate action," and followed it with "Enemy in sight." Speed was increased from twenty-two

SIR DAVID BEATTY'S BATTLE-CRUISERS IN ACTION WITH ADMIRAL HIPPER'S SQUADRON.
At 3.48 p.m. on May 31st, 1916, Sir David Beatty with his Battle-Cruisers engaged Admiral Hipper's Squadron at a range of 18,500 yards. A terrific running fight ensued in which Sir David completely outmanœuvred the enemy. This illustration is an impression of Admiral Beatty's battle-cruisers under the enemy's fire.

knots to the highest figure the engines could give. Both cruisers then opened fire at 2.23 p.m. The British 6 in. guns outranged the armament in the smaller German craft, but as the gunners of the Galatea were beginning to hammer the enemy three large German cruisers steamed up to help their destroyers.

The Galatea, flagship of the 1st Light Cruiser Squadron, under Commodore E. S. Alexander-Sinclair, poured a whole series of salvos (simultaneous discharge of a number of guns, usually but not always a complete broadside) into the enemy ships, which fired erratically and made no hits. A few minutes later they turned to port (left) to meet the larger British ships and supply them with information. Shells were now falling all round them but not hitting, and as they were drawing fast away from the enemy's large ships they decreased speed to about twenty-five knots, in order not to lose touch. Large shells began to rain about them as the range decreased. To fight heavy armoured ships was no part of their business, and they very properly once more increased speed, having manœuvred throughout this important period with consummate skill and coolness. The distance was once more opened out and the big shells came less often, but the enemy remained in distant view. It was at this point that other light cruisers of the same squadron came racing in and also opened fire. The "Cease fire," however, speedily sounded. The enemy was outside the range of the small cruisers' 6 in. guns, although his heavier 12 in. shells could still reach the British vessels. Commodore Alexander-Sinclair fell back on the big battle-cruisers of Admiral Beatty's fleet.

Sir David Beatty at 2.20 p.m. had received the first news from the 1st Light Cruiser Squadron that the enemy was at hand. He turned at once to the south-south-east, his object being to place his force between the Germans and their base and thus to cut them off. Five minutes later he received a second report, which informed him that the Germans were in strength and that he had to deal with something more than an isolated detachment of light cruisers. At 2.35 "a considerable amount of smoke was sighted to the eastward." Sir David had now placed

Salvo from the Galatea

the Germans in such a position that they could not get away without fighting him. The location of their smoke showed that he had cut them off. He therefore altered his course once more, turning first east and then north-east, directly towards them, to open battle.

The British dispositions at the moment when the enemy was sighted seem to have been as follows: The 1st and 3rd Light Cruiser Squadrons, with three destroyer flotillas, were scouting in advance, moving generally eastward. Behind them were Sir David Beatty's six battle-cruisers, and astern of them again the four fast battleships of the 5th Battle Squadron, under Rear-Admiral Evan-Thomas. Well away to the north-west was Admiral Jellicoe with the rest of the fleet and the main force of battleships. As soon as the enemy was sighted by the light cruisers, judicious dispositions were made by their commanders with splendid alertness and without waiting for orders. They extended and interposed a screen of ships between Admiral Beatty's main force and the enemy. Next, the 2nd Light Cruiser Squadron, under Commodore W. E. Goodenough, came in at high speed to take station ahead of the battle-cruisers. The British destroyer force present, consisting of the 1st, 9th, 10th and 13th Flotillas, conformed to the movements of the light cruisers.

Among the vessels in Sir David Beatty's fleet was the liner Engadine, fitted out as a seaplane-carrier, under the command of Lieutenant-Commander C. G. Robinson. At an order from the admiral, at 2.45 p.m. a seaplane was launched from her, with instructions to scout in a north-north-easterly direction. By 3.8 p.m. the machine was well under way, with Flight-Lieutenant F. J. Rutland as pilot, and Assistant-Paymaster G. S. Trewin as observer. At 3.30 p.m. their first reports were received by wireless in the Engadine. The British pilot had to descend to nine hundred feet above the sea, and approach within 2,000 yards of four German light cruisers, in order to identify them. The enemy fired every gun that would bear at the seaplane, without disturbing the clarity of the reports sent by the two flying seamen, whose achievement showed that seaplanes were of distinct value in such circumstances.

Ascent of a seaplane

Meanwhile, Sir David Beatty was moving at twenty-two knots with his six battle-cruisers and four fast battleships towards the Skager Rack in a north-easterly direction. He was feeling for Admiral Hipper's main force now he had cut it off. Seventy-one minutes passed between the reception of the first report of the enemy's presence, despatched from the Galatea, and the sighting of Admiral Hipper's flagship the Lützow. In this preliminary period the speed of the British Battle-Cruiser Fleet was comparatively slow and the course was slightly northward. The Grand Fleet, kept by wireless in touch with the direction and speed of Admiral Beatty's cruisers, drew somewhat nearer.

At 3.31 p.m. Sir David Beatty at last sighted the five German battle-cruisers, and the news was received with cheers by the crews of his ships. The moment the British came into view Admiral Hipper turned and steered towards the German battle squadrons and Horn Reef. Sir David Beatty had already, at 3.30, altered his course to east-south-east and increased speed to twenty-five knots, in instant pursuit, forming line of battle.

The British battle-cruisers and fast battleships were now approaching the High Sea Fleet at a speed of fifty miles an hour. The fast British ships were steaming nearly in a south-easterly direction at twenty-five knots, and the swift German battleships were running in a **Nearing the** north-westerly direction at nineteen to **battle area** twenty knots. Therefore the distance between the British battle-cruisers and the main enemy force was diminished by their combined speeds, while the distance between the Grand Fleet and the British cruisers was slowly increased by reason of the superior speed of the battle-cruisers.

If, in place of Sir David Beatty, the British Cruiser Fleet had been commanded by an admiral of cautious type there might have been neither a battle-cruiser action nor a fleet action. The cautious plan was to delay the pursuit of Admiral Hipper until the British fast battleship squadron was near enough to come into action simultaneously with the battle-cruisers, and until the Grand Fleet was within supporting distance. It is at least possible that if the Cruiser Fleet had waited for the co-operation of the Grand Fleet Admiral Hipper would have vanished. Nor was there seemingly time for Sir David Beatty to bring the four fast battleships closer in to him. At 3.48 p.m., when the action opened at a range of 18,500 yards, the Barham, Warspite, Valiant, and **Admiral Beatty's** another were 10,000 yards astern, to the **great risk** north-north-west. It would have taken only a quarter of an hour for the four fast battleships of the 5th Battle Squadron to combine with the six ships of the 1st and 2nd Battle-Cruiser Squadrons. But presumably Admiral Beatty calculated that if he lost this quarter of an hour he would lose all chance of striking the enemy now in sight and in inferior force.

Admiral Hipper at the opening of the action was favoured by fortune and by the great distance from the battle of the most powerful British ships, otherwise his five battle-cruisers should have been caught and sunk by the combined force of the British battle-cruisers and four supremely powerful British battleships. As it was, the German admiral left the fast British battleships sixteen miles away, and then began a furious running fight with Admiral Beatty's battle-cruisers. The action opened at twelve minutes to four at a range of about 18,500 yards (ten and a half land miles). Both forces opened fire simultaneously. The British gunners had the sun behind them; the wind was south-east and the air was clear. They were between the enemy and his base, and their guns were heavier and more numerous.

Before sighting the enemy Sir David Beatty's battle-cruisers had been steaming in line ahead—that is, with all ships exactly behind the flagship, and with four hundred yards of water between each vessel and the next. This order

THE WARRIOR'S SPLENDID FIGHT AGAINST FEARFUL ODDS.

The Warrior was one of Rear-Admiral Sir Robert Arbuthnot's 1st Cruiser Squadron, which gallantly sacrificed itself to break up the German screen of light craft round the head of the enemy's line. The heavy ships of the German Fleet concentrated their fire on the Warrior and disabled her. The Warspite came to her aid by engaging the enemy, and an effort was made to tow her to port, but she foundered.

is the most flexible for manœuvring purposes; but when fighting, if the enemy is ahead, only the leading ship has a clear field of vision and can bring its guns into action. To clear the smoke and enable all his ships to fire with effect, Sir David Beatty formed his six battle-cruisers in a line of bearing—*i.e.*, a diagonal line astern of the flagship. Forming ships on a line of bearing is a well-known disposition. It was in this order, in all probability, that Collingwood attacked at Trafalgar. In effect, five of the ships—Queen Mary, Tiger, Princess Royal, New Zealand, and Indefatigable—while preserving the prescribed distance of four hundred yards from each other, took station on a slanting line from the Lion. Each vessel then had a field of fire unobscured by the smoke from her forward neighbour.

Admiral Hipper's light cruisers and destroyers, which had formed his van when he was steaming westward, became his rearguard when his squadron turned south-east. The German light craft hung behind the rear German battle-cruiser, ready to dart between the two forces of big ships and defend and attack as directed.

Use of light craft The British squadrons of light cruisers and destroyer flotillas steamed in advance of the battle-cruisers, eagerly waiting to assail or repel the enemy. The general position was that, if either side attempted a torpedo attack, the menaced battle-cruisers would not waste heavy shell on the charging light craft, but kept their great guns hammering at the hostile capital ships, and used their auxiliary armament and their light craft to counter the threat of the torpedo vessels.

As the action opened, Sir David Beatty began to bear more to the east, and so reduce the space between the parallel curving course of the German and British battle-cruisers. In this way he gradually brought down the range from ten and a half to eight land miles. His chief object was probably to work across the head of the German squadron, and either compel it to turn away towards Admiral Jellicoe's fleet or rake it with concentrated fire. In closing, some advantage was sacrificed. The large British projectiles, as we have already seen, made a bigger splash than did the 11 in. and 12 in. German shells. This told for better spotting and hitting at a great distance. The German guns, however, were finely calibrated, and seem to have been fitted with sights of high quality; the German range-finding instruments were reported to have been equal to or even better than the British. The valuable scientific industry of optical glass-making, which Germany had established in the days of peace, served her magnificently in the days of war. She was able to keep her latest discoveries secret for the use of her Navy, and also to stop supplies of even ordinary optical glass to Great Britain. British men of science had to hunt for the formulæ of German optical glass, while the German Fleet was being **Value of German optical glass** equipped with such instruments as hurried and overtaxed scientific helpers in Great Britain could hardly be expected to improvise.

When the distance was lessened, Admiral Hipper's 11 in. and 12 in. guns were not hopelessly outranged by the British 12 in. and 13·5 in. ordnance. At eight miles the flatter trajectory of the bigger British guns did not tell much in the contest, and the difference in the shell splashes did not affect the marksmanship. The British ships retained, of course, the advantage of weight of metal and high explosive and delivered their blows with far more force. But the British superiority in metal seems to have been counter-balanced in some degree by the advantage in optical equipment and thicker armour possessed by the enemy. The British ships had heavier guns, but the enemy appears to have had better sighting and range-finding devices. His shooting was good. He had much improved since the Dogger Bank Battle.

Another factor may have entered into Admiral Hipper's calculations. He shaped his course so as to lead the British battle-cruisers towards a submarine ambush, which was apparently a matter of much importance in the enemy's general plan. The first German submarine seems to have been detected among the British light cruisers at 3.28 p.m. A U boat was then sighted, but she submerged before a gun could be trained upon her. Soon after four, Lieutenant-Commander F. E. H. G. Hobart, in the Landrail, one of the destroyers of the 9th Flotilla, sighted a German submarine near the Lion. The Landrail was trying at the time to take station ahead of the flagship, and was on the port beam (left side looking forward). She signalled another destroyer, the Lydiard, to assist in driving off the enemy submarines from the battle-cruiser squadrons.

The two destroyers had to remain on guard between the British big ships and the enemy's big ships, and their smoke caused considerable inconvenience to the gunners in Admiral Beatty's battle-cruisers; but as he acknowledged in his despatch, the two destroyers preserved his battle-cruisers from close submarine attack. The light cruiser Nottingham, which sighted a submarine on the starboard beam (right-hand side looking forward) also helped to defeat the enemy's first subtle plan of attack.

Admiral Hipper had succeeded in leading the British Cruiser Fleet into a living mine-field. Lying in ambush in the shallows of the Fisher Bank, the German submarine officers listened at their microphones for the sound of propellers. Distinguishing friend from foe, and important enemies from unimportant enemies, by means of the sensitive electric ear, the pilots of the submerged U boats moved beneath the waves at ten miles an hour towards the British battle-cruisers. To get a good shot with their torpedo-tubes the German officers had to lift their periscopes when they had come within sighting distance. It was then that they were observed and chased by the British light cruisers and destroyers. Only haphazard shots can be delivered from a submerged submarine, by judging the distance and course **Difficulties of U boats** of a big target, as revealed by the sound of approaching propellers. It may be that some U boats made chance shots of this sort, in the hope of sending torpedoes across the British line, in addition to trying shots with the aid of a hurried glimpse through the periscope.

No British ship of any class was struck. At least one German submarine was destroyed. Thus the submarine ambush failed of effect. It will be remembered that in the Battle of Heligoland Bight the enemy had launched submarines against the British battle-cruisers, but, after narrowly missing the Queen Mary, the U boats were defeated by the high speed of Sir David Beatty's squadron. Sir Percy Scott's prediction that the submarine would drive the super-Dreadnought from the seas was farther from fulfilment on May 31st, 1916, than it had been on August 28th, 1914.

While the British ships were passing through the submarine ambush the 1st and 2nd Battle-Cruiser Squadrons received two staggering, unexpected, deadly blows—apparently soon after 4 p.m., after only fifteen minutes of firing. At the time every material advantage seemingly rested with Sir David Beatty. There were six British ships in action against five German ships, with four additional and more powerful British ships approaching, but not yet within range. British broadsides of thirty-two 13·5 in. and sixteen 12 in. guns were engaging German broadsides of sixteen 12 in. and twenty-eight 11 in. guns. The weight of metal in each combined British salvo would be 53,600 lb., and in each German salvo 32,240 lb., so that in this matter the British had an advantage of five to three.

Despite the odds in Sir David Beatty's favour, the Germans won a series of preliminary successes, testifying to their luck and their marksmanship. The Indefatigable was the rear battle-cruiser in the British fleet, and the German gunners concentrated upon her and gave her a

H.M.S. WARSPITE ENGAGING SEVERAL GERMAN SHIPS IN THE JUTLAND BATTLE.
This powerful ship put up a great fight, although her steering-gear broke down at a critical moment. The Warspite alone sank and disabled several
of the enemy ships, eventually returning safely to port.

most terrific pounding. Part of her fire-control position
was observed from another ship to have been shot away,
and then she was struck by a series of salvos and sunk.
A British seaman in a light cruiser said that under
the enemy's massed fire the Indefatigable seemed to heel
over until her bilge keel could be seen. Then a salvo of
shells appeared to blow the bottom out of the ship. This
appears to have happened at five minutes past four, very
soon after the Germans got the range. In the Indefatigable
Captain Charles F. Sowerby and some seven hundred and
ninety officers and men went to their death. Two survivors
were picked up by German light craft after the British
Cruiser Fleet passed.

The New Zealand then became the rear ship in the line.
The fire-control officers in the German squadron singled
out the Queen Mary to be the next victim of the massed
fire of their guns. She had just knocked out her opposite
number in the German line, and her gunlayers had received
orders to shift target. As a gunlayer in the Tiger wrote :

Suddenly a most remarkable thing happened. Every shell that
the Germans fired seemed to strike the battle-cruiser at once. It
was as if a whirlwind was smashing a forest down. The Queen
Mary seemed to roll slowly to starboard, her mast and funnels gone
and a huge hole in her side. She listed again, the hole disappeared
in the water, which rushed into her and turned her completely over.

The Queen Mary, commanded by Captain Cecil I. Prowse,
with a complement of over a thousand
officers and men, was a most serious loss.
She was, with the Tiger, the latest of the
British battle-cruisers. She had a belt
of 9 in. armour, and 9 in. armour over her heavy-gun
positions, while the Indefatigable had only a 4 to 7 in. belt
and 7 in. armour over her heavy-gun positions. Yet the
newer and stronger ship was sunk by a few minutes'
concentrated fire as the older ship had been.

**Loss of
H.M.S. Queen Mary**

Two minutes before the Queen Mary sank the British
gunners set on fire the third battle-cruiser in Admiral
Hipper's squadron. This did not put her permanently

out of action. As was proved in the Dogger Bank
Battle, battering the side-armour did not speedily destroy
the ship, despite the fact that all the battle-cruisers carried
comparatively light armour and used guns of immense power.

The first phase of the Battle of Jutland seems to
emphasise certain facts First, in regard
to defensive power, the enemy's system of
armour in his battle-cruisers was sound.
Secondly, in regard to optical aids to
marksmanship, German technical science provided admirable instruments.

**Lessons of the
first phase**

When the Queen Mary sank the weather conditions
had changed to the advantage of the enemy. The British
vessels could be made out with comparative ease, but the
enemy ships to the north-eastward had entered a patch of
haze that rendered their outlines very indistinct. As soon
as the mist became troublesome the destroyer forces on
either side prepared to strike with the torpedo. Two
British flotillas were ordered to attack as opportunity
offered. At 4.15 p.m., when the air was growing hazy,
twelve British destroyers shot across the zone between the
big ships. They were :

13TH FLOTILLA.
Nestor (Commander the Hon. Edward B. S. Bingham),
Nomad (Lieutenant-Commander Paul Whitfield),
Nicator (Lieutenant Jack E. A. Mocatta),
Narborough (Lieutenant-Commander Geoffrey Corlett),
Pelican (Lieutenant-Commander Kenneth A. Beattie),
Petard (Lieutenant-Commander Evelyn C. O. Thomson),
Obdurate (Lieutenant Cecil H. H. Sams),
Nerissa (Lieutenant-Commander Montague C. B. Legge).

10TH FLOTILLA.
Moorsom (Commander John C. Hodgson),
Morris (Lieutenant-Commander Edward S. Graham).

9TH FLOTILLA.
Turbulent (Lieutenant-Commander Dudley Stuart),
Termagant (Lieutenant-Commander Cuthbert P. Blake).

The German flotilla which attacked simultaneously was
more powerful and more numerous than the British It

AN INFERNO IN THE RAGING SEA: GERMAN LIGHT CRUISER FIGHTS TO THE LAST.

Far into the night of May 31st-June 1st the British destroyers harried the retreating German ships. In their splendid pursuit they came across a number of German warships, some completely disabled, others partially battered, but still showing fight. This vivid illustration depicts a German light cruiser burning furiously amidships, illuminating the tragic sea and sky with her death-flames. Nevertheless, she continued to fight with her remaining guns until a British destroyer launched a torpedo into her, putting her finally out of action.

consisted of one light cruiser and fifteen destroyers. The German cruiser seems to have been of a new type, and armed with 6 in. guns. Such a vessel had an immense advantage over destroyers in her heavy battery, steady platform, and fire-control installation, but the British officers and men, by skill, manœuvring, good gunnery, and dauntless courage, did their best to atone for their lack of material advantages. In a brief, furious engagement at close quarters two German destroyers were sunk, and the light cruiser and thirteen remaining hostile destroyers were prevented from delivering their torpedo attack on the British battle-cruisers, and compelled to retire to the shelter of their own big ships.

The British destroyers sustained no loss in this dashing, victorious engagement, but as in the fight some of them had dropped astern, their torpedo attack on the enemy's battle-cruisers could not be delivered with decisive effect. The situation was that the British light craft had warded off the German onslaught on Admiral Beatty's battle-cruisers and inflicted severe punishment on the enemy; but, at the sacrifice of two destroyers, the Germans had taken much of the sting out of the British torpedo attack. Yet, gallantly led by Commander the Hon. Edward Bingham, the Nestor, Nomad, and Nicator, the destroyers nearest the German battle-cruisers, charged at top speed on the smoking line of big ships and each fired two torpedoes. The gunners in the German battle-cruisers, with their secondary armament of 6 in. guns, were a match for the three British destroyers. They could concentrate their fire on these three vessels, which alone of the twelve destroyers were able to push home. There were not enough destroyers to distract their aim and allow one or more of the British boats to close to such a range that its torpedoes could not miss. The Nomad was badly hit, and could be made out, stopped, between the British and German lines, where she was subsequently caught and sunk by the enemy. The Nestor and Nicator turned south-east, but ran into the midst of Admiral von Scheer's battleships. Through waters swept by a terrific fire Commander Bingham and Lieutenant Mocatta held steadily on. Reaching a favourable position, each fired a torpedo at the second ship in the enemy's line at a range of 3,000 yards. Before she could fire yet another torpedo the Nestor was badly hit and, swinging to starboard, almost collided with the Nicator. The Nicator **Great work of** altered course to avoid a collision, and was **destroyers** thereby prevented from firing her last torpedo. She escaped, with wonderful luck. But the Nestor was a wreck with engines stopped, and was caught by the enemy and sunk. Many survivors of the Nomad and Nestor were picked up by enemy craft, among them Commander Bingham, who for his magnificent conduct received the Victoria Cross, and Lieutenant-Commander Whitfield, who was promoted while prisoner of war to the rank of commander.

THE LAST SHOT OF THE GLORIOUS SHARK.
One of the outstanding incidents of heroism in the Battle of Jutland Bank was the splendid fight to a finish of the destroyer Shark. Pounded to scrap-iron by concentrated enemy fire, the Shark settled down with her brave and terribly wounded commander (Commander Loftus Jones) and a member of the crew firing a weapon almost from the level of the waves.

Commander Hodgson, in the Moorsom, of the 10th Flotilla, also carried out an attack on the enemy's battle fleet, and his boat escaped like the Nicator. Meanwhile, the Petard, Nerissa, Turbulent, and Termagant broke through the enemy's screen of destroyers and pressed their attack on the German battle-cruisers. Lieutenant-Commander Legge, in the Nerissa, states that one torpedo appeared to strike the unknown rear ship of Admiral Hipper's squadron. The Petard also fired all her **Equal losses in** **destroyers** torpedoes across the enemy's line. The destroyer losses on both sides up to this point were equal, the Nestor and Nomad being balanced by the sinking of two German destroyers.

The Germans profess that during this series of destroyer attacks Sir David Beatty " quickly steamed out of range on a north-western course." There is no trace whatever of such a movement in the British reports. The British admiral, with a sadly diminished force of four battle-cruisers, still gallantly maintained his position to the close of the first phase of the battle, which ended thus tragically. The second phase opened at 4.8, when Rear-Admiral Evan-Thomas with his four fast battleships came into action, but at a range of 20,000 yards, which in the haze and smoke was too great to permit his gunners to tear the German ships to scrap-iron with their 15 in. salvos. Already these battleships had fired at a German light cruiser, possibly the Rostock, and sunk her with astonishing speed. Their intervention in the fight gave the British once more the superiority in numbers. Admiral Beatty had now eight ships firing at the German five, two of which were showing evident signs of distress. From 4.15 to 4.43, says Sir David Beatty, "the conflict between the opposing battle-cruisers was of a very fierce and resolute character. The 5th Battle Squadron was engaging the enemy's rear ships, unfortunately at very long range. Our fire began to tell, the accuracy and rapidity of that of the enemy depreciating considerably. At 4.18 the third enemy ship was seen to be on fire." Possibly this was the ship which the Queen Mary had attacked with such vigour and success before disaster overtook her.

The scene at this point in the battle was the most awe-inspiring that the imagination of man can picture. The great grey ships tore through the water to the note of an unceasing, unearthly crashing, as the salvos beat like a rapid tattoo on the devil's drums. The water

Weird and wonderful scene rose in gigantic spouts, sometimes a hundred feet and sometimes two hundred feet high, as the falling shells lashed it like a monstrous hailstorm. Far away, dim forms could be indistinctly seen spurting scarlet flame in the mist, little more than dark dots on the horizon. They were the German ships, impalpable as ghosts, with dense smoke pouring from their funnels, and with the glow of fires in their hulls, caused by the British high-explosive shells. At moments the enemy passed altogether from view, though his fire always continued, and frequently the British gun-layers had no better target than the flashes of the German big guns in the growing obscurity. No man on either side could say for certain what was happening, so difficult was vision throughout the greater part of the fight and so disturbed was the atmosphere by the flame and smoke of the guns and the trembling heat-waves from the burning ships. In the air was an acrid smell of lyddite and burning wood, and the characteristic stench of cordite-wool that is being charred. In the sea floated everywhere wreckage and bodies from the vessels which had been sunk. And the battle had not yet reached its height.

The stokers in all the British ships worked like magicians to carry out Admiral Beatty's plans and get

Glory of the Black Squad ahead of the enemy. In the Dogger Bank action they had covered themselves with glory, but in the Battle of Jutland Bank they surpassed everything they had previously achieved. They may at times have caught the ring of splinters on the sides of the battle-cruisers as they toiled far below. It is said that the officers and men in the turrets sometimes thought that all their ship's secondary armament was busy repelling a torpedo attack, when, as a matter of fact, the noise was produced by German salvos exploding in the water.

Sir David Beatty's flagship the Lion did not escape injury in the storm of fire, and her signalling appliances were continually shot away; but Admiral Beatty's flag-lieutenant, Commander R. F. Seymour, managed to maintain communications, despite the hurricane of splinters and shells. The Lion received a heavy battering, but she gave more

than she got, and her crew were very proud of her. Admiral Beatty was on the topmost bridge, known as the "monkeys' island," directing operations, and, according to an eye-witness, was as eager, active, and cool amid the whirlwinds of death as in the safety of peace manœuvres.

By half-past four Admiral Beatty's ships had gained the upper hand against the German battle-cruisers by sheer coolness and hard fighting. Extraordinary as had been the marksmanship of the German gunners during the first half hour of the action, there are reasons to suppose it was based on superb equipment rather than on moral qualities. The German gunnery speedily deteriorated when the British shells began to strike home and shake the nerves of the opposing ships' companies. The enemy's shooting became uncertain, his shells often fell short, and his guns were served more slowly. The 5th Battle Squadron, unfortunately, was still firing at very long range, or Admiral Hipper's career might have ended then and there.

The brunt of the fighting was still borne by the four remaining British battle-cruisers, and such was the steadiness of Admiral Beatty's

officers and men, though one-third of their fighting force had been destroyed in so terrible a manner before their eyes, that they hammered Admiral Hipper's officers and men into a condition approaching impotency. One German ship was in flames. No doubt the slackening and irregularity of the enemy's salvos may have been partly due to the fact that his fire-control systems

CAPT. ARTHUR L. CAY,
H.M.S. Invincible, killed in action.

were disorganised by the British fire, and some of his turrets had almost certainly been put out of action.

Admiral Hipper, however, had now done his part. The third phase of the battle was opening. At 4.38 p.m. Sir David Beatty learnt from the light cruiser Southampton (Commodore Goodenough) that the German Battle Fleet was near at hand, ahead and to the south-east of him. He recalled the destroyers, and four minutes later the Lion sighted the dim grey shapes of the German battleships moving swiftly through the grey haze. For an encounter with these powerful, heavily-armoured ships his battle-cruisers had not been built, and the odds in gun-power would be enormously against him unless he promptly retreated. Moreover, a retreat would lead the enemy into Admiral Jellicoe's grip supposing the enemy pursued.

Admiral Beatty turned to starboard (or right), away from the enemy, reversing his course and steaming north.

CR. J. C. TOVEY,
H.M.S. Onslow.

CR. R. S. GOFF,
H.M.S. Garland.

LT.-CR. A. G. ONSLOW,
D.S.C., H.M.S. Onslaught,
killed in action.

LT.-CR. A. MARSDEN,
H.M.S. Ardent, commended.

LT.-CR. K. A. BEATTIE,
H.M.S. Pelican,
Commended.

(Photos by Russell & Sons, Lafayette, Vandyk.)

north-west instead of south-south-east, towards the British Battle Fleet. Admiral Evan-Thomas's four fast battle-ships had not yet turned, and were still steering the old course, so that they were moving in exactly the opposite direction, engaging the German battle-cruisers with all guns as these cruisers turned, which they did when the German battleships arrived on the scene; Admiral Hipper, thus heading the enemy's line, moved north-north-west.

The Southampton, with the 2nd Light Cruiser Squadron, continued meanwhile to hold on southward towards the High Sea Fleet. The British light cruisers steamed within 13,000 yards of the enemy battle fleet, and at this short range came under a " very heavy but ineffective fire," as Sir David Beatty reported. The German battleship gunners failed to hit the swiftly-moving Southampton and the ships of her squadron, whose task it was to ascertain the numbers of the German Dreadnoughts and super-Dreadnoughts and transmit information to Admiral Beatty, so that he might know the strength of the force that was attempting to compass the destruction of his cruisers.

COMMANDER H. E. DANNREUTHER, H.M.S. Invincible.

Admiral von Scheer's fleet was reported to consist of sixteen Dreadnought battle-ships and six pre-Dreadnought battle-ships. The German pre-Dreadnoughts do not seem to have taken any serious part in the running action which was now beginning, as their speed of eighteen and a half knots was too slow to enable them to close within range of the British battle-cruisers. Indeed, according to enemy reports, only eight battleships of the Kaiser and König classes were able to get within range of Admiral Beatty's vessels. These eight ships carried each ten 12 in. guns (or possibly 14 in. guns in some instances) and fourteen 6 in. guns, and had a speed of twenty-three knots. If this German statement is true—that only eight German battle-ships could fire—Admiral von Scheer had a total force of twelve large ships against the British eight. But if any British ship was crippled in the fight, it could not hope to escape as the Lion did when she was put out of action in the Dogger Bank Battle. Any such damaged vessel would be overtaken by Admiral Scheer's squadrons of slower Dreadnoughts and pre-Dreadnoughts. He had, in addition to his eight Königs and Kaisers, four Dreadnoughts of the Helgoland class, carrying each twelve 12 in. guns and fourteen 6 in. guns, and four earlier Dreadnoughts of the Nassau class, each with twelve 11 in. and twelve 6 in. guns. The speed of these two classes of ships was over

twenty knots. The six pre-Dreadnoughts carried each four 11 in. guns and fourteen 6·7 in. guns, with a speed of over eighteen knots.

There was, however, an important difference in fighting quality between the twenty-three-knot ships of the Kaiser and König classes and the twenty-knot ships of the Helgo-land and Nassau classes. The swifter ships could bring all their heavy guns to bear on the broadside, so that they delivered a combined salvo of eighty 12 in. shells every thirty seconds. The slower and older ships, on the other hand, could bring only eight heavy guns to bear on the broadside, though carrying each twelve guns. Their combined salvo was, therefore, only sixty-four shells every thirty seconds. All the British ships present could bring all their guns to bear on the broadside, except, of course, where turrets had been put out of action.

Reliance on speed

Admiral Beatty relied upon his speed. His four battle-cruisers were faster than the German battle-cruisers. The four fast British oil-fired battleships were able to keep close astern of the battle-cruisers. They had turned and fallen in behind Admiral Beatty's four big ships at 4.57, sustaining as they did so the fire of the leading German battleships. Admiral Beatty's situation was very far from being desperate. His eight ships formed an admirable, almost homogeneous manœuvring force, which possessed the advantage of superior speed. The British admiral could keep the enemy at long range if he wished to gain the full advantage from his heavier and more powerful 13·5 in and 15 in. guns. But his chief object was to lead the Germans within range of the British battle squadrons.

When Admiral Beatty turned northwards the weather conditions were as much against him as they had been against Sir Christopher Cradock off the coast of Chili. The German High Sea Fleet was half hidden in mist as it s'eamed up the Jutland Bank. All the British ships, farther out to sea, were moving through clear air, outlined against the bright western sky. This may have been a matter of luck for the Germans, or it may have been the result of careful calculation and planning on their part. By their superior speed, however, the British ships were able to reduce their disadvantage in the matter of weather conditions, and, as we shall afterwards see, Sir David Beatty entered on his northerly course with a great plan for turning even the weather conditions against the Germans, by working round them and forcing them out against the glow of the setting sun.

Beatty's great plan

The change of course from a south-easterly to a northerly direction was a ticklish matter. Admiral Hipper altered course soon after Admiral Beatty did. As the British ships turned in succession (*i.e.*, not simultaneously, but one after the other), they came under fire from both the German battle-cruisers and the leading German battleships. " Windy Corner " was the name the British sailors gave to the turning-point. The rear battle-cruiser in Admiral Beatty's squadron, the New Zealand, passed through waters lashed

CR. HON. EDWARD B. BINGHAM, V.C., H.M.S. Nestor.   LT.-CR. C. P. BLAKE, H.M.S. Termagant.   COMMODORE E. S. ALEXANDER-SINCLAIR, C.B., M.V.O., H.M.S. Galatea   CR. G. A. COLES, H.M.S. Ambuscade.   LT.-CR. CECIL CHARLES B. VACHER, D.S.O., H.M.S. Canterbury.

(Photos by Heath, Russell.)

THE FATAL STING OF THE "MOSQUITOES": BRITISH DESTROYERS SINK A GERMAN DREADNOUGHT ON ITS RETREAT TO KIEL.

The work of the destroyers in the Battle of Jutland Bank consisted of a series of brilliant actions from was further harried by the British "mosquitoes." This illustration, designed after a description by the earliest moments of the conflict till late into the night, when the fighting between the great battleships a naval officer who took part in the incident, shows a number of destroyers converging at top speed had actually been broken off. During its retreat to home waters the severely damaged German Fleet on a huge German Dreadnought, which was sunk by a well-placed torpedo.

by a furious hail of heavy projectiles, but escaped with only a trifling scratch. Behind the New Zealand the Barham, Warspite, Valiant, and another had now taken station, and were pounding the German battle-cruisers. Admiral Scheer's flagship and her sister ships of the König class had drawn close enough to fire salvos at the fast British battleships. But the latter, notwithstanding their speed, carried thick armour. According to the German accounts, they had 12 in. plating on their water-lines, and the same thickness over their heavy guns, and at the **British ships** range of 14,000 yards the German shells **shell-proof** did not penetrate. They stood the German fire admirably, and suffered little loss or damage. One hit received by the Barham dented her side six inches deep without breaking the surface of the plate.

About this time, towards five o'clock, the light cruiser Fearless, with the destroyers of the 1st Flotilla, arrived on the scene of battle and took station ahead of Admiral Beatty's ships. The light cruiser Champion, with the destroyers of the 13th Flotilla, took up a position covering the four fast battleships from torpedo attack, while the 1st and 3rd Light Cruiser Squadrons steamed to starboard (right), and the 2nd Light Cruiser Squadron to port (left) of Admiral Beatty's flagship

Admiral von Scheer was probably feeling very pleased with the position. He had concentrated a great force against the British Cruiser Fleet, and in the first part of the battle, when all the odds were against the five German battle-cruisers, they had sunk two out of the ten large British ships opposed to them. By two amazingly lucky strokes the outnumbered, outgunned, and somewhat slower German Battle-Cruiser Squadron had brought Admiral Beatty's battle-cruisers half-way to Horn Reef, and had destroyed one-third of the British Battle-Cruiser Fleet on the way. Admiral Hipper appears to have had one ship much damaged during the race to the south. Another German battle-cruiser had been badly hammered; but these German losses, to which one light cruiser and two destroyers must be added, were only modest when compared with the result achieved.

Though Admiral von Scheer had reason for being happy, his position was not, as the event proved, so strong as he supposed. For the game that Admiral Hipper had played against Admiral Beatty was exactly that which Admiral Beatty was playing on a larger scale against the German Commander-in-Chief. Admiral von Scheer had risked five large German ships against ten large British ships in order to lure the British Cruiser Fleet within range of the German Battle Fleet. And Admiral Beatty was now placing eight large British ships in a running fight against some nineteen German capital ships in order to lure the High Sea Fleet within range of the Grand Fleet. There was, of course, the very important difference that Admiral von Scheer accomplished his aim about five o'clock in the afternoon, when he could count on an hour of good daylight at least, while even if Admiral Beatty were successful he could not accomplish his aim, and make his junction with Admiral Jellicoe, until seventeen minutes past six in the evening, when the mist had gathered and thickened.

Admiral Beatty was forging steadily ahead of the leading German ships. When the great race began the British battle-cruisers were well in advance of Admiral Hipper's three remaining battle-cruisers, and the 5th Battle Squadron was well ahead of the 1st German Battle Squadron. The result was that the eight British ships could concentrate their broadsides upon Admiral Hipper's enfeebled and battered squadron. The Germans could not bring their rear ships into action because of the admirable tactics of the British Fleet. Admiral Beatty, as he worked ahead, closed somewhat on the enemy, to crush the head of the German line, altering his course to north (the Germans were steaming north-north-west), and shortening the range to 14,000 yards. Another German battle-cruiser quitted the line " in a considerably damaged condition." Before this occurred, the destroyers Onslow (Lieutenant-Commander J. C. Tovey), and Moresby (Lieutenant-Commander R. V. Alison), which had been detached to assist the seaplane-carrier Engadine, returned and took station on the engaged (starboard) bow of the Lion. At 5.10 the Moresby fired a torpedo, and eight minutes later she observed a hit in the sixth ship in the enemy line, which must have been a battleship. The British cruiser Fearless about this time reported seeing an enemy ship heavily on fire, and shortly afterwards a huge cloud of smoke and steam. As the same was seen when the Marlborough and Westfalen were hit, and both these ships undoubtedly escaped, it does not follow that the enemy vessel was sunk. But it was a fine feat to effect a hit with the torpedo at such extreme range.

At 5.35 Sir David Beatty turned north-north-east, heading the enemy off eastwards and enabling Admiral Jellicoe, who was now coming up to the north-north-west, to pass between the Germans and their North Sea bases if he were so disposed. If the enemy had not turned east under this pressure from the British cruisers and fast battleships, Admiral Beatty would have worked across the head of the German line and shattered the leading German ships. At 5.50 the first ships of Admiral Jellicoe's fleet came into sight. They were the three battle-cruisers, under Admiral Hood, of the 3rd Battle-Cruiser Squadron. Six minutes later the dim shapes of Admiral Jellicoe's battleships could be made out 10,000 yards north of the Lion. The crisis of the battle was past.

At 6.5 the Onslow, still on the engaged bow of the Lion, sighted a German light cruiser at a distance of 6,000 yards, which was apparently trying to torpedo Admiral Beatty's flagship. The British destroyer steamed out and engaged the cruiser, closing from 4,000 to 2,000 yards, and pouring into her some fifty-eight 4 in. shells. The German light cruiser was much more heavily armed, and possessed, by reason of her superior size, a far better fire-control system. None the less, she was hit again and again by the gunners of the Onslow. When she had been sufficiently hammered, Lieutenant-Commander Tovey swung his frail craft round and charged at the German battle-cruisers. He ordered all torpedoes to be fired. But just as he gave the order his boat was struck amidships by a heavy shell, and amid the confusion only one **The splendid** torpedo was released. Thinking that all **Onslow** his torpedoes were gone, Lieutenant-Commander Tovey, with his ship nearly broken in two, began to crawl away. But finding he had three torpedoes left, he again approached the light cruiser that he had already battered and torpedoed her. Then, turning on the German Battle Fleet, this most gallant British officer fired his two remaining torpedoes at the enemy's battleships, just as the steam failed in his damaged boilers. The action of the Onslow was observed by Rear-Admiral Napier, commanding the 3rd Light Cruiser Squadron. He said that after he passed close to the disabled and motionless

[*Lafayette.*
COMMANDER LOFTUS W. JONES,
H.M.S. Shark, went down with his ship working the sole remaining gun, though he had already had a leg blown off. He was posthumously commended for his services in the battle.

destroyer she was able to struggle ahead again, and made straight for the Derfflinger to attack her.

The Onslow was afterwards taken in tow by another damaged destroyer, the Defender (Lieutenant-Commander Lawrence R. Palmer). Having a shell in her foremost boiler, the Defender could only make ten knots; but at a quarter past seven in the evening, when German shells were falling round both boats, she closed with the Onslow and took her in tow. In the stormy night the tow parted twice, but was re-secured, and the two damaged boats struggled on together until the afternoon of June 1st, when the work of towing the Onslow was transferred to tugs.

Of all the deeds in the Jutland Battle, that of Lieutenant-Commander Tovey and his officers and men marked the highest point in skilled coolness. Torpedo work had been the speciality of the German Navy. Grand-Admiral von Tirpitz was a torpedo specialist. It was on his torpedo officers that he chiefly relied for the success of his policy of attrition. When "The Day" came the long-acclaimed and long-practised "hussar strokes" by German destroyer flotillas against the British battleships never took place. Up to the time when the Onslow's boilers stopped working only one German destroyer charge had been attempted, and it had failed at the outset before the British heavy ships needed to use their secondary armament. The British destroyers, on the other hand, claimed a hit on one German battle-cruiser early in the fight, and afterwards hit a German battleship. One German light cruiser and two destroyers had also been sunk by the British light craft. The comparatively light British losses in destroyers were caused entirely by close-range fire from big German ships, which when menaced with destruction discharged at them storms of shrapnel. The prince of torpedo officers was certainly Lieutenant-Commander Tovey, but he was only first among a large band of immortal heroes.

Zenith of pluck and skill

In this stage of the battle the British battle-cruisers had displayed surprising power of resistance. It had generally been expected that the lightly-armoured battle-cruiser, in the design of which protection had been sacrificed to speed, would be rapidly shot to pieces by the modern battleship. This was an article of faith in the United States Navy, as that able American gunnery expert, Captain William S. Sims, stated in a report on the battle which he drew up for the Secretary of the United States Navy. The German Commander-in-Chief, together with all the German naval authorities, had taken the same view of the weakness of battle-cruisers in a fleet action as United States officers had done. Admiral von Scheer appears to have regarded it as certain that he could destroy the four remaining British battle-cruisers in much less than the eighty minutes which the running fight northward lasted. The extraordinary resistance of the British battle-cruisers was, therefore, one of the greatest surprises of the action.

At a range of only eight miles, which was rather less than that at which the Queen Mary and the Indefatigable had been destroyed, the Lion, Tiger, Princess Royal and New Zealand, with all weather conditions against them, withstood the attack of all the ships that the German admiral could bring against them. Naturally, Admiral Beatty's battle-cruisers were considerably protected by the fire of the 5th Battle Squadron steaming close behind them. The German Dreadnoughts were too slow to close on them, though had they attempted to shorten the range they would have had to encounter a tornado of 15 in. shells from the thirty-two big guns of the fast British battleships; and the twenty-four 13·5 in. guns of the three leading battle-cruisers, with the eight 12 in. guns of the New Zealand, should have been exceedingly effective at the range of eight miles against even the heavily-armoured German capital ships.

Invulnerable at eight miles

The situation was paradoxical. At four o'clock in the afternoon, when Sir David Beatty had all the odds on his side and good weather conditions, an inferior enemy force inflicted tremendous losses upon him. At five o'clock, when the enemy had apparently very marked advantages in numbers and weather conditions, eight British ships outfought a much larger number of German ships. Between five and six o'clock Admiral von Scheer appears to have had at least two of his big ships put out of action, and two light cruisers sunk by gun fire. In this period no British ships were put out of action. It was perhaps then that Admiral Hipper lost his flagship the Lützow, and, like Admiral Beatty in the Dogger Bank action, had to embark in a destroyer and find a new flagship. He afterwards hoisted his flag in the Moltke; but at what hour he recovered control of his shattered squadron is not known. As the remnant of his squadron formed the head of the enemy's line, and was overreached by the speedier British battle-cruisers and also brought within range of the 5th Battle Squadron, it received a tremendous pounding. It was the chief aim of Admiral Beatty to maintain a massed fire against the continually weakening head of the enemy's line.

Reinforcements now began to reach Sir David Beatty. Rear-Admiral the Hon. Horace Hood, with the 3rd British Battle-Cruiser Squadron, consisting of the Invincible, Inflexible, and Indomitable, was coming up, steaming in advance of the Grand Fleet, and fast nearing the scene of action. At 5.30 Admiral Hood had observed the first indications of battle in gun-flashes and the sound of firing to the south-west. The haze was too thick to permit a clear view of what was happening, and he despatched the light cruiser Chester (Captain R. N. Lawson) to reconnoitre and enable him to effect his junction with Admiral Beatty. The Chester, pushing in, found herself cut off by a squadron of four German light cruisers, which had seemingly worked between her and Admiral Hood's battle-cruisers in the mist. She broke through the enemy after a fierce fight, which will be dealt with in detail later, and soon after six rejoined the 3rd Battle-Cruiser Squadron.

Trying to cross the "T"

Admiral Hood, as the result of this reconnaissance, turned north-west. Apparently he had steamed too far to the east in the haze and smoke. At 5.50 he was seen from Admiral Beatty's ships, and at 6.10 he sighted Admiral Beatty's battle-cruisers. He was then on the port bow of the Lion. As he came up he appears to have poured a heavy fire into a German light cruiser, probably one of the vessels which had engaged the Chester, and to have sunk it, for a great explosion was seen, which looked as though a shell from the Invincible had struck the enemy's magazine. There can be no doubt that the light German cruisers in their preliminary fight had noted Admiral Hood's approach and reported it by wireless to Admiral von Scheer, and the information may have been one of the factors that led the enemy to turn eastward about this time.

The design of the German commander was evidently to break off the action, and either pass into the Baltic or retire to his North Sea base under cover of the mist along the Danish coast. A sudden turn would have exposed him to disaster, and his only plan was to work east and so effect his escape. But Admiral Beatty had foreseen this move from the beginning of the running fight on the northerly course. It was the reason why he had worked well in front of the Germans, and had kept well in front of them during the fleet action. The aim of the British admiral was to cross the "T" at the moment of the grand crisis. Crossing the "T" is the commonest of all naval manœuvres in peace time, and the hardest to carry out in war. It consists in steaming at right angles across the head of the enemy's line and raking his leading ships as they are passed (in the position of the top stroke of the letter "T," the fleet "crossed" being in the position of the upright stroke), and crushing them with concentrated fire. Superior speed is the essence of the power to achieve such a manœuvre, and

VICE-ADMIRAL SIR CHARLES EDWARD MADDEN, K.C.B., K.C.M.G., C.V.O., CHIEF OF STAFF TO THE
COMMANDER-IN-CHIEF, GRAND FLEET.

REAR-ADMIRAL OSMOND DE BEAUVOIR BROCK.
C.B., C.M.G.

VICE-ADMIRAL SIR T. H. MARTYN JERRAM.
K.C.B., K.C.M.G.

VICE-ADMIRAL SIR F. C. DOVETON STURDEE, BART.,
K.C.B., K.C.M.G., C.V.O.

REAR-ADMIRAL HERBERT LEOPOLD HEATH.
C.B., M.V.O.

REAR-ADMIRAL ERNEST FREDERIC AUGUSTUS GAUNT.
C.B.. C.M.G.

REAR-ADMIRAL SIR WILLIAM CHRISTOPHER PAKENHAM
K.C.B. M.V.O.

REAR-ADMIRAL ALEXANDER LUDOVIC DUFF.
C.B.

REAR-ADMIRAL FRANCIS WILLIAM KENNEDY.
C.B

REAR-ADMIRAL MICHAEL
CULME-SEYMOUR, C.B., M.V.O.

REAR-ADMIRAL WILLIAM EDMUND
GOODENOUGH, C.B., M.V.O.

REAR-ADMIRAL SIR HUGH
EVAN-THOMAS, K.C.B., M.V.O.

REAR-ADMIRAL HON. HORACE HOOD,
K.C.B., M.V.O., D.S.O.

REAR-ADMIRAL TREVYLYAN DACRES WILLES NAPIER,
C.B., M.V.O. (in uniform of Captain).

REAR-ADMIRAL ARTHUR CAVENAGH LEVESON,
C.B. (in uniform of Commander).

all the principal navies of the world have vied for years in combining speed with gun-power and armour in their battleships, in order to give their fighting admirals the means of preventing their " T " from being crossed and, if possible, the means of crossing an enemy's " T." German naval constructors paid especial attention to the factor of speed, and in 1910 they had launched, in the Moltke, a battle-cruiser with a speed of 28·5 knots, capable of steaming round the older British battle-cruisers, whose nominal speed was only twenty-five knots. Fortunately, the German ships did not always maintain their trial speeds at sea, and fortunately the British engineers and stokers got far more out of their machinery than had been expected in battle.

As the race over the Dogger Bank and the Fisher Bank had shown, the German battle-cruisers had, as a squadron, sufficient speed and manœuvring skill to prevent the British battle-cruisers from " crossing " them. But in the northward turning movement Sir David Beatty had won so fine a start over Admiral Hipper, thanks largely to the excellent scouting of the Southampton, that the British admiral in the end was able to force the Germans either to turn once more or to have their line " crossed." His ships closed to a range of 12,000 yards as they threatened the head of the enemy's line, and increased speed to the utmost. Admiral Hood's squadron was now closing on the enemy's van. Its three additional battle-cruisers formed part of Sir David Beatty's command, and Admiral Beatty by wireless ordered Admiral Hood to take station at the head of his line of battle. Admiral Hood executed the order superbly, and brought his ships into action, as Sir David Beatty states, " in a most inspiring man-

Hood's brilliant seamanship   ner, worthy of his great naval ancestors." Admiral Hood's three ships as they entered the battle drew in exceedingly close to the enemy's line. About 6.21 they had reached their station in advance of Admiral Beatty, steering it would appear south-east, while the enemy was still on a generally eastward course, so that Hood, unless the Germans speedily turned, would be in a position to " cross their T." The Germans may have calculated that their fire was too terrific for his thinly armoured battle-cruisers to resist. For some seconds, or perhaps even minutes, they did not give way. The range shortened, first to 9,000 yards and then to 8,000 yards—extremely close for modern gunners and modern 12 in. guns. The fighting was of the most violent character. Sir David Beatty, noting the determination of his lieutenant, who might have cried like Troubridge at the Battle of St. Vincent, " let the weakest fend off," once more altered course, with the dash and alertness that marked his leadership, to give support, and at 6.25 turned east-south-east. Then " the weakest fended off." The German leading ship began to turn slightly, hauling round to south-south-east in that shell-smitten sea amidst the clouds of smoke and the unceasing roaring of the guns.

As she entered the battle with her heroic admiral, himself of a family which has given the British Navy some of its most glorious seamen, the Invincible opened a fearful fire upon an enemy battle-cruiser of the Derfflinger type, her match and more in guns, and greatly her superior in displacement, armour, and modernity. The German ship registered two or three hits, but her gunners were not as efficient as those of the Invincible. Commander Hubert E. Dannreuther, the gunnery officer, was several times congratulated on his shooting by Admiral Hood. The British gunlayers found their target with the first salvo. But while they were doing magnificent work and setting the enemy ship on fire the Invincible was sunk. Commander Dannreuther and the torpedo officer, Lieutenant C. S. Sandford, were among the six survivors. Commander Dannreuther, after being shot into the sea as from a catapult, went down twenty or thirty feet, and coming up found himself close to a floating target, and clambered on

it. First Range-finder Dundridge, flung from the control top, and Chief Petty-Officer Thompson were already on the raft. A few minutes afterwards a broad, smiling face, black with grease, soot, and oil, appeared at the side of the target. " That's Sandford," said Commander Dannreuther ; " an Irishman would be sure to smile after an experience like this." " You're right," replied Lieutenant Sandford, as he climbed on the target, from which half an hour later the survivors were rescued by the destroyer Badger. Another British ship, steaming into action much later in the battle, saw a number of men on a raft, who may or may not have been this party, and at first took them to be Germans. But as the ship passed, four of the survivors rose to their feet and cheered magnificently. They were true Invin-   **A cheer from the** cibles, this handful of half - drowned   **Invincibles** officers and men representing all that lived out of seven hundred and eighty Britons who went into action under Rear-Admiral Hood and Captain Arthur L. Cay. The spectacle of these men, fresh from the pit of hell, thinking only of their country's victory, was said by those who saw it to have been the most inspiring episode in the battle.

After the Invincible disappeared, the Indomitable and the Inflexible took up the contest with the German battle-cruiser of the Derfflinger class, and reported that a few minutes after the Invincible sank the German ship fell out of the enemy's line.

By this time there was risk of confusion between the various fleets now the German destroyers, light cruisers, battle-cruisers, and Dreadnoughts were wheeling slightly to avoid being crossed, and running eastward. In the first place, there was the continuing action of Sir David Beatty's reinforced battle-cruisers. They now consisted of six heavy ships, with their light-cruiser squadrons and destroyer flotillas. In the second place, the light cruisers and destroyers, including the Tipperary, Fortune, Dwarf, Sparrowhawk, Spitfire, and Contest, which had arrived close to the enemy, with Admiral Hood's 3rd Battle-Cruiser Squadron, were fighting with extreme intensity against the screen of light craft that Admiral Hipper and the officer commanding the leading German battleships had flung out to protect their wheel. In the third place, the 1st (Armoured) Cruiser Squadron, consisting of the Defence, Warrior, and Black Prince, under Rear-Admiral Sir Robert K. Arbuthnot, was now entering the fight. Admiral Arbuthnot's purpose was seemingly to join in the attack on the enemy's light-cruiser and destroyer screen, and so accelerate its destruction as to leave the German capital ships clear targets for attack by the British battle squadrons. In the fourth place, the four British fast battleships, under Admiral Evan-Thomas, though firing previously at the head of the German line and doing much of the work of crumpling it up, were unable to keep   **Manœuvres in the** up with the battle-cruisers, now hurrying   **mist** east at highest speed, and were trying to form ahead of the Grand Fleet and become the van of Admiral Jellicoe's squadrons. In the fifth place, the 1st Battle Squadron was opening fire on a battleship of the Kaiser class, and the 2nd and 4th British Battle Squadrons were finishing off a German light cruiser and deploying for the general fleet action, beginning with an attack on a battleship of the König class.

All these conflicts and manœuvres were taking place between 5.50 and 6.17 o'clock, on a sea shrouded in haze eastward, and dappled with large patches of mist northward and lighter drifts of mist westward. The German destroyers and light cruisers emitted great volumes of grey smoke to help in screening the movements of their defeated and fugitive battle-cruisers and battleships, and the smoke from the screen also thickened and darkened the patches of mist, so that the confusion and dimness increased.

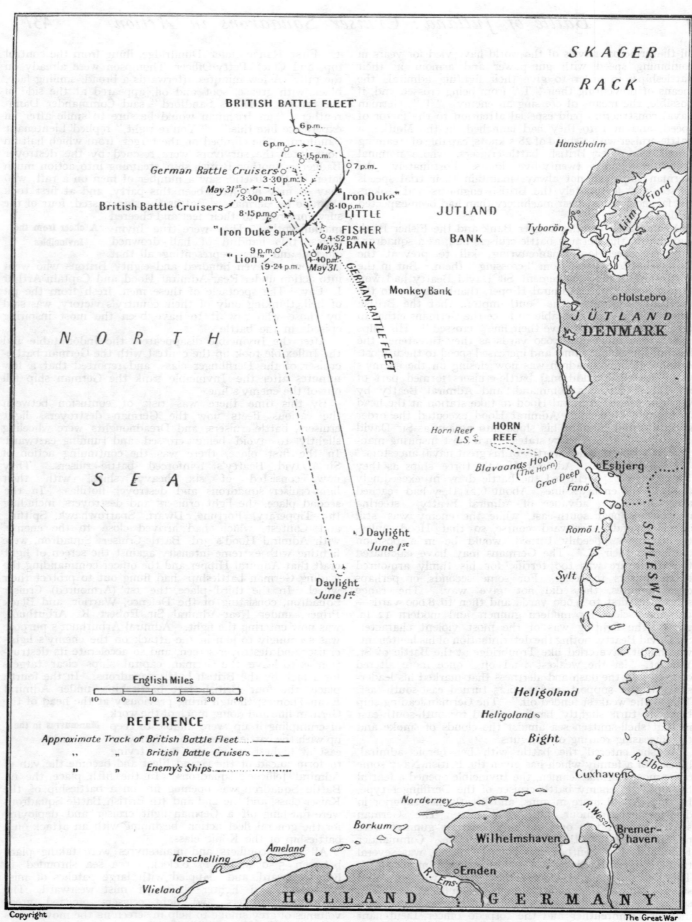

SKAGER
RACK

Hanstholm

Liim Fiord

Tyborön

JUTLAND
BANK

BRITISH BATTLE FLEET

6 p.m.

6 p.m.

6.15 p.m.

7 p.m.

German Battle Cruisers

3.30 p.m.

May 31st

3.30 p.m.

British Battle Cruisers

"Iron Duke"

8.10 p.m.

LITTLE
FISHER
BANK

8.15 p.m.

"Iron Duke" 9 p.m.

4.52 p.m.
May 31.

9 p.m.

"Lion"

4.40 p.m.
May 31.

9.24 p.m.
May 31.

Holstebro

JÜTLAND
DENMARK

Monkey Bank

N O R T H

GERMAN BATTLE FLEET

S E A

*Horn Reef
L.S.*

HORN
REEF

*Blavaands Hook
(The Horn)*

Eshjerg

Graa Deep

Fanö I.

Romö I.

SCHLESWIG

Sylt

Daylight
June 1st

Daylight
June 1st

English Miles

10   0   10   20   30   40

REFERENCE

Approximate Track of British Battle Fleet ————
"   "   British Battle Cruisers — — —
"   "   Enemy's Ships ·············

Heligoland

Heligoland

Bight

R. Elbe

Cuxhaven

Norderney

Borkum

Wilhelmshaven

Bremer-
haven

Ameland

Terschelling

R. Weser

Emden

R. Ems

Vlieland

HOLLAND   GERMANY

The Great War

THE MOST SKILFUL NAVAL MANŒUVRE IN HISTORY.

This chart must be taken only as a general indication of the courses of the opposing fleets. Sir David Beatty, with two squadrons of battle-cruisers and one squadron of fast battleships, first steamed southward and south-

eastward of the German Battle-Cruiser Squadron; then, sighting the German Battle Fleet, turned northward, afterwards bearing eastward and connecting with Sir John Jellicoe's Battle Squadrons.

About the time that Admiral Hood entered the battle, or perhaps a little earlier, Rear-Admiral Sir Robert Arbuthnot, with his 1st Cruiser Squadron, consisting of the armoured cruisers Defence (Captain S. V. Ellis), Warrior (Captain V. B. Molteno), and Black Prince (Captain J. P. Bonham), closed the head of the enemy's line. From the published evidence it would appear that when Hood turned to port, Sir Robert turned to starboard, the effect of which would be to bring him between the British Battle Fleet and the German line. The Germans had apparently flung out a squadron of light cruisers, with a flotilla of destroyers to attempt a torpedo attack on the British battle-cruisers, making use of dense patches of the mist, which about this time was so thick that from the Invincible the enemy could not be plainly seen till the German ships were only 8,000 yards away. The light craft may have been those which the Chester encountered and at which Admiral Hood fired. If not vigorously attacked they might have been able in the obscurity to get dangerously close to Sir David Beatty's ships, which were moving at high speed to head off the German battle-line. The British destroyer Onslow was at work engaging them when Sir Robert came into the fight.

Sir Robert Arbuthnot, in this last and greatest hour of his life, drove at the enemy light cruisers, one of which was swiftly disabled and perhaps sunk by salvos from the Defence and the Warrior, not far from the spot where the Onslow was at work. Sir Robert could see that the torpedo menace to Sir David Beatty's ships was extreme. As a matter of fact, the Defence and Warrior, while pursuing a German light cruiser, crossed the bows of some of Admiral Beatty's light cruisers. But as Sir Robert Arbuthnot pressed home his smashing attack, which broke up the German screen of light craft around the head of the German line, and cleared the way both for Admiral Hood's battle-cruiser squadron and for Admiral Jellicoe's battle divisions, a patch of mist lifted, revealing an amazing and terrible spectacle.

Arbuthnot's supreme sacrifice The weak armoured cruisers had done their work too well. Within a few thousand yards of them were three German battle-cruisers and the array of German battle-ships of the König and Kaiser class. The British cruisers were armed only with 9·2, 7·5, and 6 in. guns. The Defence was the strongest of the three, with four 9·2 in. and ten 7·5 in. guns, an armour belt from 4 to 6 in. thick, and 8 in. armour round the heavy turrets. The Warrior carried six 9·2 in. and four 7·5 in. guns, an armour belt of 3 to 6 in., and 6 in. armour round the turrets. The Black Prince carried similar armour, with six 9·2 in. and ten 6 in. guns. The age of the ships was from nine to twelve years; they had been rendered obsolete by the design of Dreadnought battle-cruisers in 1905, and their nominal speed was only twenty-three to twenty-three and a half knots.

Against the tempest of 11, 12, and 14 in. shells which swept them they were helpless. It is possible that, as Admiral Jellicoe suggests in his despatch, the three ships were lamed before they could withdraw. But it is also possible that Sir Robert Arbuthnot did not intend to retire. In his flagship he engaged the nearest German battle-cruiser for eight minutes. The Defence was repeatedly struck aft, and a terrific explosion occurred in the stern, but she still held on towards the enemy, firing with her remaining guns. Then she was hit forward, and in the smoke, steam, and flame of a great explosion one of the very finest of British fighting admirals vanished, with the Defence's captain, officers, and men. Captain Bonham, in the Black Prince, also held on steadily against the nine German battle-cruisers and battleships, and was crippled but not sunk, and his vessel disappeared from view to perish later in the evening.

Meanwhile, the Warrior was swept by salvos from the German battle-cruisers, which concentrated all their guns upon her when the Defence blew up. Almost the first salvo that struck the Warrior disabled her starboard engine-room and, wrecking her hydraulic pumps, compelled the turret crews to work their guns by hand. After the injury to her engine the Warrior began to slew round, and as the movement brought her port battery to bear upon the light cruiser which she and the Defence had set on fire, she hammered at her smaller enemy at short range. Then as the German battle-cruisers passed, making their turn southward, several German battleships came within range and battered at the crippled armoured cruiser with all their guns.

One shell wrecked the dynamo-room, extinguishing the electric light in the magazines and all the other compartments below, and cut off all the telephones. The deck was torn up and the engine-room badly holed. There were many casualties, and all the boats were smashed. The ship was in deadly peril when Admiral Evan-Thomas's squadron of fast battleships passed by. That admiral was then trying to form ahead of the Grand Fleet, but while preparing to execute this manœuvre either received orders or decided on his own initiative to form astern. As he was proceeding under heavy fire from **Warspite stands by the Warrior** the enemy's battle squadrons, the Warspite, under Captain Edward M. Phillpotts, the second ship in his line, seemed to all who watched in the British Fleet to turn to help the stricken Warrior. With her eight 15 in. guns the Warspite engaged several German battleships, which thereupon left the almost helpless Warrior in peace, and turned their guns on the Warspite. But with an armour-belt of 13 in. and 14 in. of armour over her monster guns, the sister of the Queen Elizabeth took her heavy punishment without wincing, giving her enemies blows of tremendous power, eight a minute.

This movement occurred through an accident which made the Germans think that the Warspite was their prey. The steering-gear broke down—perhaps injured by the enemy's fire—causing the helm to jam in such a position that the great battleship was carried straight towards the enemy into a hell of fire. Some six German battleships of the König and Kaiser class are said to have concentrated all their guns upon her. Despite this, Captain Phillpotts worked his ship round the Warrior, which slowly crept out of action, using her port engine. Scarcely was the Warrior out of range when her port engine-room became untenable, and the ship stopped dead. She would thus have lain helpless as a log under the fire of the German Fleet if the Warspite had not arrived in the nick of time. It was a wonderful sight to see the Warspite, when she herself was out of control, engaging an overpowering number of hostile battleships and keeping them all at bay with the big punch of her eight 15 in. guns. The shooting of the German battleships at this time must **Inferior German gunnery** have been poor, or she would not have escaped. Happily, as we have seen, the ship was worked round, and the engineers again got the steering-gear into action, with the result that the Warspite was brought under control and returned to her station, with only seventeen men lost out of her complement. No serious injury was done to the fast battleship, although the enemy sent destroyers after her, and then tried to reach her with submarines. The Warrior passed out of the battle.

It cannot be said that the fourteen hundred men in the Defence and Black Prince and the men killed in the Warrior went to their deaths in vain. The mist no doubt led Sir Robert Arbuthnot into a terrible ambush, but a gallant tactical idea can be traced in the sacrifice he made. He succeeded in taking the fire off the 1st and 2nd Battle-Cruiser Squadron and 5th Battle Squadron during a most critical period, when the Grand Fleet was deploying and when the full fire of the enemy fleet was concentrated upon Admiral Beatty's ships.

Sir Robert Arbuthnot was a fine, gentle, simple man, with the heroic temper of a Grenville and the devotion to duty of a Collingwood. The last time Collingwood went afloat he said to a friend : " My family are actually strangers to me. What a life of privation ours is—what an abandonment of everything to our professional duty ! And how little do the people of England know the sacrifices we make for them." So Sir Robert Arbuthnot never slept ashore after the war broke out.

When he went into the Defence, men reckoned that he went to death. His armoured cruiser was not fit to stand up to modern ships, yet she could not be **Against terrible** held back in battle by an admiral who **odds** intended to do the utmost he could for the Empire when the great chance offered. There was a period of twenty minutes' danger when Admiral Beatty's Cruiser Fleet shortened the range and five or six German battleships, close astern of the German battle-cruisers, were attempting to deliver a final concentrated fire on the British battle-cruisers, just before the battle squadrons of the Grand Fleet came into action. Then it was that Sir Robert Arbuthnot interposed his little weak squadron between the enemy fleet and the Battle-Cruiser Fleet and crushed the German torpedo onslaught. Admiral Arbuthnot's heroic and well-conceived movement of sacrifice was one of the finest deeds of an historic day.

Seeing that at least three German light cruisers in Admiral von Scheer's northern screen of light craft were put out of action about six o'clock by the British heavy cruisers and destroyers, and that first Sir Robert Arbuthnot and then Admiral Hood brushed the screen aside and came up with the hard-pressed Cruiser Fleet, the head of the enemy's line was in a thoroughly unfavourable position by the time Admiral Jellicoe's battle divisions came within range. The strength of Admiral Jellicoe's Fleet has properly been kept a secret, as the crumpled-up and fugitive enemy was scarcely in a position to discern, amid the drifting, smoky mist, the force that was being employed against him. All that was stated in Admiral Jellicoe's despatch was that the divisions of the Grand Fleet were led by the Commander-in-Chief, by Vice-Admiral Sir Cecil Burney, who was second in command, by Vice-Admiral Sir Martyn Jerram, by Vice-Admiral Sir Doveton Sturdee, the victor in the Battle off the Falkland Isles, by Rear-Admiral Alexander L. Duff, by Rear-Admiral Arthur C. Leveson,

and by Rear-Admiral Ernest F. A. Gaunt. In addition were at first the 3rd Battle-Cruiser Squadron, under Rear-Admiral the Hon. Horace Hood, the 1st (Armoured) Cruiser Squadron, under Rear-Admiral Sir Robert K. Arbuthnot, the 2nd (Armoured) Cruiser Squadron, under Rear-Admiral Herbert L. Heath, the 4th Light Cruiser Squadron, under Commodore C. E. Le Mesurier, with the 4th, 11th, and 12th Destroyer Flotillas. Admiral Jellicoe flew his flag in the Iron Duke, forming part of the 4th Battle Squadron. Sir Cecil Burney flew his flag in the Marlborough, forming part of the 1st Battle Squadron. Among the battleships present was the Revenge, similar to the Queen Elizabeth, but slower, of the Royal Sovereign class, with 15 in. guns.

Sir Cecil Burney was closest to the enemy fleet. At six o'clock, when Sir David Beatty was steering his Cruiser Fleet across the head of the enemy's line, the 1st Battle Squadron must have been only about twelve land miles north of the leading German ships. Had the air been clear, Sir Cecil would have been able to open fire upon the enemy, over the battle-cruisers. But in the confused mêlée and the thick weather extreme care was needed to prevent British ships from being mistaken for enemy vessels. It was difficult to see what was happening.

The shroud of smoke and the tongues and islands of mist made it impossible to distinguish the exact position of the enemy's fleet. The task of effecting the junction of the Grand Fleet with the Cruiser Fleet in such circumstances was a most complex and delicate operation, calculated to tax the powers of any admiral. It is a high distinction for Sir John Jellicoe that he overcame the great difficulties that faced him. To **Admiral Jellicoe's** the last moment he kept his fleet in **intervention** steaming order so as to preserve the utmost flexibility of deployment. But by what precise manœuvres the deployment was carried out must, as an official commentator states, be left in a mist as deep as that which hides the vital secrets of national defence. It is sufficient to say that the junction was effected with consummate judgment and dexterity, and so nicely was it timed that the deployment was almost completed when the 1st Battle Squadron came into action about seventeen minutes past six, and began the fifth phase of the battle.

GERMAN 12 IN. GUNS IN ACTION OFF JUTLAND.
Forward turret guns of a German battleship in full blast. The guns depicted are 30·5 cm., approximately 12 in. calibre, and their weight is in the neighbourhood of fifty tons. They fire an " all purposes " projectile, weighing about 1,000 lb., with a very considerable H.E. burster and a special fuse.

CHAPTER CXLII.

THE GLORIOUS BATTLE OF JUTLAND BANK. PART III.

The Grand Fleet Action and Minor Cruiser Engagements.

By H. W. Wilson and Edward Wright.

Sir John Jellicoe's Deployment Disconcerts Admiral von Scheer and Defeats his Plan to Release Auxiliaries on to the Trade Routes—Vice-Admiral Sir Cecil Burney, with the 1st Battle Squadron, Engages the Enemy at 10,000 Yards—Sir John Jellicoe, with the 4th Battle Squadron, Enters the Fight—Course of the Big-Ship Battle on Parallel Curves Similar to that at the Battle of Tsushima in 1905—General Deterioration of the Enemy's Nerve—Rear-Admiral Napier's 3rd Light Cruiser Squadron Attacks Battle-Cruisers and Battleships with Impunity—Sir David Beatty Punishes Admiral Hipper's Battle-Cruiser Squadron—Fine Fight of the Colossus—Superb Fighting of the Marlborough when Torpedoed—The 5th Battle Squadron's Experiences—Sir David Beatty Furiously Attacks the Enemy with Battle-Cruisers and Light Cruiser Squadrons—The Lion, Princess Royal, New Zealand, and Indomitable Punish Three German Battleships—A Great Ship, probably the Black Prince, Blown Up—General Conditions of the Fleet Action—Determined Destroyer Attack on the Enemy by the 11th Flotilla and the 4th Light Cruiser Squadron—H.M.S. Chester Runs the Gauntlet—Conspicuous Courage of First-Class Boy John Travers Cornwell, by which he Earned the Victoria Cross—Daring Achievements of the 12th Flotilla, the Shark, Commander Loftus Jones, Acasta, and the Christopher—Subsidiary Action of the 2nd British (Armoured) Cruiser Squadron under Admiral Heath—Brilliant Fighting and Manœuvring of the Hampshire—Use of Light Cruisers for Torpedo Work—Darkness and Fog Separate the Broken and Fugitive High Sea Fleet from the Grand Fleet.

THE British Commander-in-Chief kept his battleships in single line of battle, a formation which has rarely in naval history brought decisive results. It is obvious that he did this because in the mist it was the only formation which would prevent British ships from accidentally firing into one another. The line overlapped the enemy westward, while the advanced Cruiser Fleet threatened to overlap the enemy's head eastward. Admiral von Scheer must have been hard put to it to divine at what point the blow would fall. We know from Admiral Jellicoe's despatch that the order in which he finally deployed took Admiral Evan-Thomas by surprise, and upset the arrangements being made by the 5th Battle Squadron. It may therefore be supposed, since Admiral Evan-Thomas could not anticipate Admiral Jellicoe's dispositions, that Admiral von Scheer must have been disconcerted when a part of the Grand Fleet's line came into action against him a quarter of an hour before the other main British battle squadrons struck.

When the 1st Battle Squadron (under Sir Cecil Burney, who flew his flag in the Marlborough) **Admiral Jellicoe deploys** opened fire, the Marlborough was only six land miles distant from the enemy's 3rd Battle Squadron, and Sir John Jellicoe's manœuvres of deployment were nearing completion. Ahead of her to the east was a fast wing, formed of the 1st, 2nd, and 3rd Battle-Cruiser Squadrons, under Sir David Beatty, while the fast 5th Battle Squadron, which had constituted part of the Cruiser Fleet, was formed into a fast western wing of the armada.

The great British line of battle stretched for ten or twelve miles. The High Sea Fleet had with it armed auxiliaries and light cruisers, which, it appears, were to have escaped to the north-west during the confusion of battle, in order to swoop down on the trade-routes. The British dispositions defeated this scheme. A net was drawn round all the German naval forces present. Eastward they were cut off by Sir David Beatty from the Skager Rack, through which only a few battered German destroyers afterwards escaped in the mist. North and west the Grand Fleet was closing on them, and though nearly four hours had been spent in pursuing Admiral Hipper, and then luring Admiral von Scheer northward, at least two and a half hours more daylight remained. Only the mist frustrated the plan for the destruction of the enemy's forces which the British admirals had manœuvred to accomplish. **Mist saves the German fleet**

At the opening of the fleet action (6.17 p.m.) Sir Cecil Burney caught both enemy battle-cruisers and battleships at the close range of 10,000 yards. At this short distance the British 13·5 in guns told with terrible effect. First seven salvos were fired at a battleship of the Kaiser class. Of thirty-five rounds expended, ten were thought to have hit. Bright flames and dense clouds of grey smoke rose from the enemy, but she vanished in the mist and her fate could not be ascertained. Next a large four-funnelled ship, apparently a cruiser, was engaged, and afterwards another. About this time other battle squadrons of the Grand Fleet shelled an enemy light cruiser. At 6.30 Sir John Jellicoe in person entered the fight in the Iron Duke, with the 4th Battle Squadron, at a range of about 12,000 yards.

The general course of the big-ship battle in this phase was that the two lines, British and German, steamed on two generally parallel curves, the German Fleet inside the British curve. The position was almost identical with

441

that at Tsushima in 1905, where the battle very quickly settled down to a fight between the big Russian and Japanese ships, the Russians steaming on the inside curve and the Japanese on the outside. There were other close resemblances. Both battles were fought in May, and both in difficult conditions of visibility, so that at times Admiral Togo altogether lost sight of his enemy in the mist and smoke. The reason why the weaker fleet moved on the inside curve was this: It was in each case the slower fleet, and by turning inside the faster fleet it **Germans surrender the initiative** could avoid having its head "crossed," and could keep its guns bearing on the faster fleet steaming on the outside curve. It is a mathematical law that the inside curve is shorter. This law accounts for the fact that the German Fleet, with its pre-Dreadnoughts, capable of only eighteen or nineteen knots, was not hopelessly outmanœuvred and crushed by the British battleships, which could certainly steam at twenty and perhaps at twenty-one and a half knots. To keep on an inside curve, however, the Germans had in the closing hour of the battle to allow themselves to be driven away from their naval bases. They were forced to obey the British initiative; in a sense their movements were controlled by Admirals Jellicoe and Beatty.

The Iron Duke opened fire on a battleship of the König class, and began to hit her at the second salvo, only ceasing to hit when the target ship turned away. The other ships of the 4th Battle Squadron principally directed their fire at the series of appearing and disappearing targets formed of German battle-cruisers and cruisers which alternately started out of and vanished in the obscurity. Range-finding in these circumstances was an extremely difficult affair to accomplish accurately and quickly. Nevertheless, the British gunnery officers and gunners inflicted many hits. About the same time that the 4th

Battle Squadron closed with the head of the enemy line, consisting of Dreadnoughts of the König and Kaiser classes, with one or two battle-cruisers, the 2nd Battle Squadron, under Vice-Admiral Sir Martyn Jerram, came into action with the German Dreadnoughts and with a German battle-cruiser which had dropped back in the line owing, apparently, to severe damage.

During the course of the action the leading British battleships pressed close to the enemy, bearing in a south-westerly direction and diminishing the range to five miles. This was short range for Dreadnought and super-Dreadnought engagements, and when the 15, 13·5, and 12 in. shells got home the effect must have been dreadful. In many of the German ships the secondary gun-positions were covered with 6, 7, and 8 in. armour. The large British shells that missed the vital and heavy-gun turrets in the German Dreadnoughts would rend the armour over the German secondary guns into splinters of murderous power.

In the Grand Fleet the 1st Battle Squadron, under Sir Cecil Burney, sustained the heaviest answering fire from the fugitive and scattering German ships. But only the Colossus (Captain **The scattering foe** Alfred Pound) seems to have been hit, and her damage was of the most trifling description, though the range had fallen to five miles. She fired on a German light cruiser, probably one of those which had already been shattered by Admiral Arbuthnot. The vessel was seriously damaged, but it opened on the Colossus, and was given a dose of 12 in. shells, with which it vanished in the mist. Next a three-funnelled cruiser, perhaps the Kolberg, was made out, burning heavily; but she, too, fired and received a terrible answer from the Colossus, which left her ablaze from stem to stern, enveloped in smoke. Then out of the mist shot four destroyers, one of

ACTUAL PHOTOGRAPH OF ADMIRAL BEATTY'S BATTLE-CRUISER SQUADRON—
This remarkable impression was secured by an officer who actually took part in the great battle. Admiral Beatty's cruisers are racing towards

which was struck by 12 in. shells from the Colossus and vanished in clouds of dense blue smoke. All the four were put out of action. The experience of the other ships in the 1st Battle Squadron was similar — enemies suddenly appearing out of the mist and as suddenly vanishing. If the German marksmanship had fallen off, the Germans still fought bravely, and one example of their courage is noted by Sir J. Jellicoe in regard to a disabled German cruiser (one of the two mentioned above) that passed down the British line under a **German fire** heavy fire, which the crippled hostile light **deteriorates** craft gallantly returned with the only gun she had left in action. In a general way, however, the deterioration of the nerve of the German gunners, which Sir David Beatty had remarked when he pressed Admiral Hipper's squadron, was also observed in the German battle squadrons soon after the Grand Fleet closed them.

A remarkable proof of the manner in which the enemy's nerve had been shaken was given eight minutes after Sir Cecil Burney began to hammer the enemy's battleships. About 6.25 Sir David Beatty had turned south to get nearer the enemy's line, head the Germans off, and support the two remaining ships of Admiral Hood's squadron (the Inflexible and the Indomitable), which were only 8,000 yards from the leading German ship. This ship, one of the Derfflinger class which had sunk the Invincible, was beginning to turn as a blast of fire caught her. When the Lion drew more southwards the 3rd Light Cruiser Squadron, under Rear-Admiral Napier, who was steaming on Admiral Beatty's starboard bow, well ahead of the enemy, suddenly delivered an admirably timed torpedo attack. The Falmouth (Captain John D. Edwards) and the Yarmouth (Captain Thomas Pratt) fired torpedoes at the battle-cruiser of the Derfflinger class. One torpedo appeared to

hit, and a heavy underwater explosion was observed. Then all the 3rd Light Cruiser Squadron, being within the range at which their armament of eight 6 in. guns would tell, began to hammer German battle-cruisers and German battleships with gun fire.

None of the big 11, 12, and 14 in. guns of the enemy's heavy ships got home on the light cruisers, which had no armour protection. So much had the fighting efficiency of the enemy declined that the light cruisers were able to carry out their extraordinary attack with impunity to themselves. Admiral Napier deservedly won much praise for the determined assault he made upon apparently overpowering enemy forces. No doubt the high speed and manœuvring power of his comparatively small and frail craft enabled him to zigzag and thus disconcert the German fire-control officers. But the extraordinary impunity which attended the 3rd Light Cruiser Squadron immediately after the Defence blew up seems to show that Admiral Arbuthnot was within an ace of catching the Germans when they had been thoroughly shaken. The leading German ship of the Derfflinger class which fell out of line, after being attacked at short range by the Indomitable and the Inflexible and then torpedoed by the Falmouth and Yar- **Light cruisers'** mouth, was probably the severely **attack** damaged enemy battle-cruiser, which was again caught in the middle of the enemy's line with certain battleships of the Kaiser class by the 2nd Battle Squadron under Sir Martyn Jerram.

Vice-Admiral Sir David Beatty continued his east-south-east course apparently until ten minutes to seven. He then saw the leading battleships three miles from the Lion in a north-north-westerly direction. He reduced his speed to eighteen knots, and began to steer westwards, once more heading off the enemy. He ordered the Indomitable and

—ENGAGING THE GERMAN HIGH SEA FLEET OFF JUTLAND, MAY 31st, 1916.
the German ships firing all the guns that can be brought to bear on the foe. German shells are falling around the British battle-cruisers.

Inflexible, which had been ahead of him, to prolong the line astern. At seven o'clock the mist had gathered so thickly that no ship more than four miles off could be seen, and the German squadrons were for the time invisible. But it is interesting to note that for nearly an hour, between six and seven o'clock, when the British ships were steaming north of the enemy's line through the thickest part of the mist, their position was much more favoured by the thick weather than was the enemy's position. A curtain of haze veiled Admiral Beatty's three battle-cruiser squadrons, till only indistinct greyish outlines could be made out amid the grey mist, while the German ships in the clearer water southward and westward showed up against the sun at intervals, enabling Admiral Beatty to punish them very severely, and establish a definite superiority over them. The head of the enemy's line seems to have been completely broken up. Many German destroyers and German light cruisers had vanished. Nearly all the ships of Admiral Hipper's battle-cruiser squadron were on fire or temporarily crippled, and, as Sir David Beatty stated in his despatch, the majority of his battle-cruisers had as targets only German battleships. This was an amazing triumph for the British fighting seamen.

Beatty's decisive advantage

While the British battle-cruiser squadrons were pursuing the crumpled head of the enemy's line, which seems to have been reduced to two German battle-cruisers and one or two battleships of the König class, the British battle squadrons had proceeded eastward. Between the Battle-Cruiser Fleet and the Battle Fleet was the 2nd Cruiser Squadron, under Admiral Heath, to which the Duke of Edinburgh had been attached, though she belonged to Sir Robert Arbuthnot's squadron. This force had no opportunity of attacking the enemy's armoured ships.

The engagement between the 1st Battle Squadron, now preparing to turn south, and what remained of the enemy, was at its height. The Colossus, after all her adventures had a fresh encounter about this time. Suddenly a huge German ship came out of a patch of dense mist at no great distance and fired a salvo at the British ship. The salvo was ill-directed; perhaps the German gunners were flurried, as every projectile passed wide. Not such was the case with the Colossus' fire. She discharged two broadsides, hitting with every one of the twenty 850 lb. shells which they comprised. This was enough for the enemy. He turned and disappeared in the mist, with huge tongues of flame shooting high up from the neighbourhood of his conning-tower.

It was about this time that the Marlborough, leading the British van, was torpedoed. Probably the enemy mistook her for the Iron Duke; in any case, his light craft made desperate efforts to put her out of action. At 6.50 a light cruiser shot out of the mist, steaming at high speed towards her. The Marlborough's guns opened a terrific fire; the enemy was seen to have discharged six torpedoes, all of which ran, leaving white wakes, towards the flagship. Before they drew near her, her guns had ended the career of her assailant. At 4,000 yards the light cruiser was literally blown out of the water, a tangled mass of flame, steam, and smoke. A torpedo caught the Marlborough's starboard side.

Blown out of the water

A terrible column of water and smoke rose at 6.54 abaft her forward turrets. The great ship heeled over slowly to starboard, as the sea rushed into her torn side; then she slowly righted herself. A British light cruiser drew near to her, to be of use in case she went down; but the water-tight compartment system used in constructing modern battleships proved admirably efficient. The Marlborough, though listing to starboard, maintained a remarkable speed in the circumstances. The steadiness and discipline of her crew were superb. At 7.3, nine minutes after the mishap, she fired four salvos at a four-funnelled German cruiser, and at 7.13, immediately after-

wards, caught an enemy Dreadnought of the König class with fourteen rapid salvos, hitting the German frequently until the latter turned out of the line. Seeing that all the guns and gun-positions were no longer level, but slanting to starboard with the list of the ship, the manner in which the gunnery officers and gunlayers, under Captain John P. Ross, knocked out of the line this German Dreadnought, which carried 14 in. of armour on her belt and her turrets, was quite extraordinary. All the ship's company, and particularly the carpenters, engineers, and stokers, must have worked with steady, energetic skill in order to keep their torn, listing ship steaming at a good speed.

At half-past seven five German destroyers swung out between the lines, with the clear intention of finishing off the Marlborough. Seven of the British light craft intercepted the flotilla, and the Marlborough herself joined in the destroyer mêlée with her secondary armament of twelve 6 in. guns. Their fire was extremely effective at long range. The water around the five German destroyers was lashed with bursting projectiles, their attack was completely repulsed, and the destroyers were swallowed up by the mist or the sea. It is doubtful whether any of them returned. About ten minutes to eight the Marlborough was again attacked by two German Dreadnoughts, which opened fire at a range of about 12,000 yards. Their shooting, however, was not good. All the shells of their first five salvos fell short. The sixth and seventh salvo also missed. It was only at the eighth salvo that they hit one of the Marlborough's funnels. The Marlborough, on the other hand, is reported to have put her first salvo on the target as she opened fire on the leading German vessel. Soon the whole of the enemy's ship was enveloped in smoke and flame, as the Marlborough got shells home with every salvo. The crews of the British light cruisers and destroyers near at hand, watching the action, cheered their injured but grandly fighting big sister until the enemy vanished in an apparently hopeless condition. In one of the stokeholds of the Marlborough the men were working up to their middle in water. Many of the gunners were stripped to the waist in the fine old Trafalgar style.

Marlborough's great fight

The 4th Battle Squadron, in which Admiral Jellicoe's flagship the Iron Duke was placed, principally fought German battle-cruisers and cruisers as they appeared out of the mist, getting home effectively on several enemy ships. The 5th Squadron of fast battleships, under Admiral Evan-Thomas, which had taken station astern, seems to have been lucky in keeping the enemy almost continuously in sight, for the Barham is said to have been firing lyddite shells without intermission from 6.5 p.m. until a quarter to eight. The men then cooled their guns for twenty-six minutes, while the Grand Fleet took up the firing. At eleven minutes past eight the Barham reopened fire and continued for a few minutes, after which fire was ceased for the night.

In the long engagement of the 5th Battle Squadron, which had been Admiral Beatty's mainstay during all the critical period of the battle, several fires broke out in the Barham and her sisters, but all were quickly extinguished. The Barham had some officers and twenty-four men killed, the most touching death being that of the chaplain. He was struck by a splinter in the spine, and as he lay dying he prayed for victory for our Fleet, living just long enough to learn that the day was won.

Meanwhile, at six minutes past seven, Sir David Beatty, who was then steaming south-west, received a wireless signal from his Commander-in-Chief that the course of the Fleet was south. The Germans had completed a gradual turning movement near the Little Fisher Bank, and were being driven on a south-westerly course out to sea and away from their main naval base, which lay to the south-east. If Admiral von Scheer had been able to exercise any choice in the matter he would certainly have turned in a general southerly direction, in order to escape further punishment and get back to his mine-fields around Heligoland. But he had first been driven eastward by the manœuvre of the British Cruiser Fleet that threatened to cross the " T " of his line, and then he had been cut off from the Danish coast by the combined operations of Admiral Jellicoe and Admiral Beatty. And at last, when he tried to turn south, both the British Battle-Cruiser Squadrons and Battle Squadrons closed upon him in a southerly course, and in a race towards Heligoland pressed upon him sideways and forced him out to sea. The tactical reason for Admiral von Scheer's final turn westward was that he wished to escape from a position of disadvantage. British squadrons were firing on the bow of the enemy and endeavouring all the time to close, and the German commander headed westward in order to escape. He allowed the British Fleet to interpose between him and his bases rather than prolong the risks of a running fight at close range on a parallel course.

Forming the fast advanced force in front of the Battle Fleet, Sir David Beatty's six battle-cruisers constantly groped for the enemy as they hauled south-west **Enemy battleships** by south. At fourteen minutes past seven **sighted** two battle-cruisers and two battleships of the König class were again sighted at a range of 15,000 yards. The sun had now descended below the clouds, and for a very brief period the visibility greatly improved so far as the British were concerned. Their ships were on the misty eastern sky-line, and were hard to hit, while the four enemy targets were black against the lowering sun. Sir David Beatty increased his speed to twenty-two knots, opening fire at 7.17, and furiously engaged the enemy until 7.45. One German ship was set on fire and another dropped out of line right astern. The leading enemy ship, while keeping in a general westward direction, bore away rather to the north to escape, and avoid the unfavourable conditions in which it was shown

up against the eastern horizon. The German destroyers at the head of the line covered the retreat of their Dreadnoughts with a great cloud of grey smoke, and, veiled by this, they turned away and became invisible at a quarter to eight.

Thereupon Sir David Beatty ordered his 1st and 3rd Light Cruiser Squadrons to sweep to the westward and discover the head of the enemy's line, following himself in the same direction at 8.20 p.m., when **The Lion** the two German battle-cruisers and **roars** the battleships were again discovered, this time well to the north. In a terrific onslaught the Lion engaged the leading German ship at a range of less than six miles, set her on fire, the flames reaching up to the tops, and then tore open her port side, giving her a heavy list. The Princess Royal, with her 13·5 in. guns, set fire to a three-funnelled battleship (probably of the Helgoland class), while the New Zealand (Captain John F. E. Green) and Indomitable (Captain Francis W. Kennedy) made a combined attack with their sixteen 12 in. guns on the third German ship. They set her on fire and hit her so badly that she heeled over and hauled out of the line. If only the weather had continued clear, the British battle-cruisers should have sunk these three ships, which they had severely damaged in a contest lasting barely a quarter of an hour. A heavy mist came down once more from the sinking clouds and enveloped the broken head of Admiral von Scheer's fugitive fleet. The German ships were last seen by the Falmouth at thirty-eight minutes past eight, when they were steaming westward.

This was the close of the battle between the big armoured ships, and they were not again to come into contact. The British Fleet now lay to the south and east of the enemy's forces. At 8.40 Admiral Beatty's six battle-cruisers felt " a heavy shock as if struck by a mine or torpedo, or possibly by heavy wreckage." As, however, subsequent

TWILIGHT IN THE NORTH SEA: GERMAN BATTLESHIPS ON A RECONNOITRING TRIP.
Impression by a German marine painter, R. Schmidt-Hamburg, of the 2nd Squadron of the German High Sea Fleet going out into the North Sea in the twilight. In front is a patrol boat, lighting the way and assisting to disclose the general situation.

examination of the bottoms revealed no sign of such injury, he concluded that " it indicated the blowing up of a great ship." From German evidence the concussion was probably caused by the destruction of the hapless Black Prince. It has been stated that she was last seen from the British ships soon after 6 p.m., probably losing touch of the British Fleet through injury to her masts and wireless. A wireless signal was received from her after 8 p.m., but about the same time that the " heavy shock " took place the Germans state that an armoured cruiser of the Cressy class attacked them and was sunk in four minutes. The Black Prince

Mystery of the Black Prince

resembled the Cressy with her four funnels, and in the mist may have accidentally steered into the midst of the enemy's fleet. The speed with which it destroyed her—if the German report is true—suggests that the German Dreadnoughts were not completely demoralised. A second survivor of Admiral Arbuthnot's luckless squadron, the Warrior, was at 8.40 p.m. taken in tow by the seaplane-carrier Engadine and despatched forthwith to a British naval base.

In regard to the general conditions of the fleet action, the British Navy does not seem to have got more battleships into battle than the enemy had in line; indeed, according to Lord Sydenham, only eleven of Sir John Jellicoe's battleships were engaged. The enemy's tail-end of Dreadnoughts, doing 20 and 20.5 knots, were unable to keep up with the speedier ships of the Kaiser and König class during the preliminary race northward against the British Cruiser Fleet. The enemy had four of these rather slow Dreadnoughts, and, like the German pre-Dreadnoughts, they appear to have escaped severe gun fire, as by reason of their slowness they were at the rear of the German line. It was mainly between 6.17 p.m. and 7 p.m., when the mist was often light, and many enemy vessels showed up against the sun, that the leading British battle squadron struck its heaviest blows. These blows fell upon some three German battle-cruisers, three or four ships of the König class, and four or five ships of the Kaiser class. There is no mention in despatches of any of the enemy Dreadnoughts of the two earlier classes (Helgoland and Nassau types) being severely engaged during the first and deadlier phase of the general fleet action; but as the newer German ships were damaged and driven out of the line, the older German Dreadnoughts would be left, and might even have constituted the van of the High Sea Fleet when it began to steam westward in the evening. A three-funnelled German battleship, which is the Helgoland type, was certainly steaming at the head of the line with two German battle-cruisers at half-past eight, and was set on fire by the British Cruiser Fleet. When the German ships afterwards reassem-

Roll-call by wireless

bled in some sort of formation under cover of darkness as the result of wireless instruction, the units must have needed a considerable amount of sorting out.

Shortly before the close of the battle between the big ships, a determined destroyer attack was delivered on the German Fleet. At 8.18 the 11th British Destroyer Flotilla (Commodore J. R. P. Hawksley) received orders to attack. It formed the van of the Grand Fleet, and it was gallantly led into close action by Commodore Hawksley in the Castor. The 4th Light Cruiser Squadron, under Commodore Le Mesurier, was directed to support him. It had already brilliantly engaged and driven off a number of German destroyers which attempted to attack the British Fleet at 7.20 p.m. It now closed with the enemy's main fleet in the most dashing style, coming under a heavy fire from the German Dreadnoughts. The flagship Calliope was hit several times, but without sustaining serious damage, though she had several casualties. One German vessel was seemingly struck by a British torpedo, as an explosion in a ship of the Kaiser class was seen at 8.40, though this may have been caused by the gun fire of the Lion, which had, as we have seen, very severely injured

a German Dreadnought about 8.35. The 11th Flotilla seemingly could not find the enemy's heavy ships, but encountered and attacked a German destroyer flotilla, sinking one German destroyer at point-blank range.

Gun fire ruled the battle as the British school of naval tactics had foreseen. Even in misty daylight, with the scene of action clouded in smoke and evening coming on, the torpedo, on which the Germans largely relied, was seldom or never deadly in itself. Generally speaking, it was only when a ship was very severely damaged by heavy shell that the torpedo came decisively into play to deal the final blow. The British light craft did a considerable amount of daylight torpedoing—far more than the Germans accomplished by their combined submarine ambushes and light-cruiser and destroyer charges. This gave rise to a common idea in the British Fleet that a large number of enemy capital ships had been sunk. But, as was proved at the time in the Marlborough, and as the Germans had proved in the Moltke in the action of the Gulf of Riga, a modern ship of the Dreadnought type usually survived a torpedo explosion. Annihilation was mainly a matter of heavy gun fire, and clear weather was needed to enable the British 15 in., 13.5 in., and 12 in. guns to fire continuously from a quarter-past six to half-past eight. In itself this time was possibly sufficient to enable the Grand Fleet, which had deployed in a very favourable position, to accomplish the destruction of almost all of the High Sea Fleet. For the hitting power of the British Dreadnoughts was tremendous. For instance, one of the older British ships—said to be the Hercules—armed only with 12 in. guns, put her salvos in German battleship so accurately that the enemy vessel heeled right over under the blows and was put out of action. If ten 12 in. guns could produce this effect, the well-directed salvos of 15 in. and 13.5 in. guns should have been overpowering when maintained for two hours and more.

Power of 12 in. guns

That two large fleets should fire at one another with guns of the heaviest pattern—though the heavier weapons were almost uniformly in the British Fleet—and at ranges which were comparatively short, was certainly surprising to those who know what modern gunnery can do. The explanation is that men do not shoot quite so steadily in battle when there are guns shooting back; and that the art of directing guns so as to be sure of hitting moving targets has not yet been perfected. In the time which a shell takes to travel 10,000 yards a quarter of a minute will elapse, and the gunner, when he fires, has really to lay his gun on the point where the enemy will be fifteen seconds later. In that time the target may change its position sufficiently—should the enemy's course be altered — to escape a hit. Again, range-finding is a comparatively slow process in bad weather. In the case of the Iron Duke it is noted as a great feat that she put some of her shells at her second salvo on the target. Three or even four salvos may often be required before the range is found, and each salvo will occupy at least a minute if the fall of the projectiles has to be watched and the necessary corrections and adjustments made. A ship may then require anything from two to three or more minutes to find the range under favourable conditions; in bad weather the difficulties are greatly increased, as it may be hard to see the splash of projectiles at all. In the case of the British battle-cruisers after 7 p.m. on the 31st, the enemy was only visible from 7.14 to 7.45, and from 8.20 to 8.38. At 7.17 Sir David Beatty opened fire, and his ships may be supposed to have got the range about 7.20, after which they would have in most cases twenty-five minutes of uninterrupted firing. At 8.30 all the work of range-finding would have to be done over again.

Throughout the engagement between the heavy ships encounters between light craft were proceeding almost continuously, and the story of these forms an epic in itself. Certain of these encounters almost attained the dimensions of a great battle, as the destroyers fought to gain favourable vantage points for the attack on the large ships, and the light cruisers of either side strove to cover them, and the victors drove in on the opposing line of battle. It is a remarkable fact that the British almost uniformly gained the upper hand in these brief, fierce struggles, though from their proximity to their bases the Germans should have had a far larger force of destroyers on the scene.

One of the sharpest of these minor battles took place about 5.30 p.m. on May 31st, when, as we have seen, Admiral Hood, with his 3rd Battle-Cruiser Squadron, was approaching the main engagement, and sent the light cruiser Chester (Captain Lawson) in to reconnoitre. In a quarter of an hour the Chester met four enemy light cruisers and engaged against these heavy odds for twenty minutes. By fine tactics and skilful handling, Captain Lawson kept the fighting and steaming qualities of his ship unimpaired, in spite of the fact that the overwhelming gun fire of his four antagonists killed or injured many of his men. At 6.5 p.m. the Chester rejoined the 3rd Battle-Cruiser Squadron, and after the Invincible sank took station ahead of Admiral Beatty's squadrons.

British gains with light craft

They were the Shark (Commander Loftus W. Jones), the leading ship of the 12th Flotilla, the Acasta (Lieutenant-Commander John O. Barron), and Christopher (Lieutenant-Commander F. M. Kerr). They were steaming in front of the Grand Fleet, engaged, like the Chester, in seeing if the course was clear for Admiral Hood to swing his squadron down into Admiral Beatty's line. But the Germans had an exceedingly strong force of light craft acting northward as a screen and searching for the Grand Fleet. The result was that the Shark ran into a flotilla of enemy destroyers and light cruisers, and after firing a torpedo at the leading German ship, she was battered to pieces in less than ten minutes. One shell struck a propeller; another penetrated an oil-tank. Being out of control and in the centre of a very heavy fire, the maimed destroyer was reduced to a wreck, with dead and wounded strewn about the deck and most of her guns put out of action; but when the smoke cleared away, Commander Jones and two of his men could still be seen fighting with the only remaining gun. Then another German shell struck home, and a fragment of it hit Commander Jones on the leg and severed his limb. He remained at the gun until a torpedo struck the Shark, and then, swamped in her own oil, she went down by the stern, and all who

BRAVE MEN AT DIVINE SERVICE: MORNING PRAYERS ON BOARD H.M.S. SHARK.
The Shark, leading the destroyer flotilla, drew first blood in the Battle of Jutland, sinking two enemy destroyers before being torpedoed herself.

The Chester appears to have found the four German light cruisers between her and Admiral Beatty's ships. First she tried to get round the enemy's screen, but the Germans opened out, and forced her to run the gauntlet. Festoons of shrapnel, which the Germans in this battle seem to have employed against the smaller ships, burst about her, turning her funnels and bridge into the semblance of gigantic sugar-dredgers. But none of the German projectiles struck a vital spot. Early in the action John Travers Cornwell, a first-class boy working with a gun's crew at an exposed spot, was mortally wounded. Around him all the gun's crew were killed or injured; but the boy stood at his post, which was one of importance, until the end of the fight. Nothing then could save him. A little over sixteen years of age, John Travers Cornwell was a very young recruit to a Navy with ancient traditions of heroism. But his deed of splendour and self-sacrifice has become one of the great glories in our naval history, and has given him immortality here on earth. The Victoria Cross was awarded to him after death for his conduct in the hour of danger. Another boy of the Chester, E. T. Pearce, was serving at a dangerous post at one of the guns and was wounded very badly, but bore his agony in heroic cheerfulness, dying afterwards in hospital.

While the Chester was fighting her way through the gauntlet three British destroyers were surrounded by the advanced light craft of the German High Sea Fleet.

were left of the crew found themselves in the water. Sub-Lieutenant Vance, who had been working the gun on the forecastle with courageous skill, was killed with all his men early in the fight by a high-explosive shell. Only a handful of men were rescued by a Danish steamer after being five hours in the water. Some of those who had clung to a raft dropped off exhausted.

Behind the Shark was the Acasta, one of whose petty-officers reports that his company saw their leading destroyer fight her last gun and sink, and then took her place in the battle-line. The action between the British and German destroyers narrowed to a few hundred yards, both sides using all guns as fast as they could be loaded. The Acasta put on the utmost possible speed, and apparently drove through the enemy's screen and reached a point within easy torpedo range of the German battle-cruisers and battleships. At one of these a torpedo was discharged. According to Chief Petty-Officer A. D. Reid, the torpedo got home on a heavy German ship, and, as the Germans were then steaming southward, the victorious crew attended to their heavy casualties and set to work to save their boat. She was terribly battered, but they kept her afloat through the rough night, and on Thursday morning she was taken in tow and safely reached port. The Acasta and the Christopher would have suffered the same fate as the Shark had not one of the light cruisers

The Acasta's bull's-eye

of the 3rd Battle-Cruiser Squadron come to their help. The Germans had a powerful squadron of new light cruisers, acting northward with their destroyer flotilla, and it was the big shells from one of them that overwhelmed the British destroyers. But at six o'clock the Canterbury (Captain Percy Royds) steamed up to help the hard-pressed destroyer force. The Tipperary, with the smaller destroyers of her flotilla, including the Fortune, Sparrowhawk, and Spitfire, were in action near the Acasta, between the British battle squadron and the High Sea Fleet, but though the water around these light craft danced in geysers or swirled in whirlpools under the gigantic hail of heavy shells, no more British boats were sunk.

The 2nd British (Armoured) Cruiser Squadron (Rear-Admiral H. L. Heath) fought another of these subsidiary actions. Among its units was the Hamp-

The Hampshire's part shire, in which Lord Kitchener afterwards went down. Letters from officers and men in the Hampshire relate that the 2nd Cruiser Squadron arrived at the scene of battle between the battle-cruisers and battleships towards 6 p.m. A three-funnelled German cruiser steamed straight towards the Hampshire, apparently intending to make a torpedo attack. The Hampshire's first salvo missed, but the second caught the German and caused a great explosion. When the enemy ship drew off several more rounds were put into her, and she was so badly damaged when she faded into the mist that it did not look as though she could keep afloat. Afterwards the Hampshire ran into a nest of German submarines. Five were spotted. One of them disappeared after being fired on at very close range, and all the Hampshire officers and men in a position to see the affair felt sure that the U boat was sunk. A minute or two later the Hampshire, by brilliant manœuvring, sent her bows over another U boat. But neither the rammed submarine nor the shelled submarine was included by Admiral Jellicoe in the list of verified enemy losses, as there was no means of making sure that the two enemy vessels had been destroyed. According to Engineer-Commander E. Cossey, of the Hampshire, another British ship managed to sink a German submarine by gun fire on Friday morning; but this enemy loss was also omitted as unverifiable by Admiral Jellicoe.

It will be observed that both Admiral Jellicoe and Admiral Beatty at times employed their light cruisers for torpedo work. The reason seems to have been that these very fast vessels, originally designed for reconnaissance work and the support of destroyers, were magnificent though rather costly instruments for torpedo warfare by a chasing fleet against a retiring fleet. The speed of certain of the British light cruisers is said to have exceeded thirty knots. At this extraordinary pace they could often overtake the German battle squadrons, as the Falmouth and Yarmouth had done soon after the Invincible went down. When they got ahead of the German capital ships and were able to approach under cover of mist they enjoyed the same advantages

New and daring tactics as the flotillas guarding the rear of the German Fleet. That is to say, their torpedoes travelled towards the enemy battle squadrons, instead of travelling behind them and having to overtake them. It was new and exceedingly daring tactics to use a light-cruiser squadron to make daylight torpedo attacks. The Germans do not seem to have attempted anything of the kind, but they employed isolated light cruisers to support their destroyer flotillas, and they also used any single light cruiser that chanced to be near the huge British ships, in desperate attempts to relieve the pressure upon the head of their line when it became perilous. It is wonderful that the 4th Light Cruiser Squadron should have been able to operate under the enemy's guns in daylight at a range of 6,500 yards, and should have succeeded in crippling a modern German battleship supported by the fire of a heavy squadron.

The British light cruisers in the battle were vessels of considerable size and represented the highest pitch of light-cruiser construction. Each carried a complement of several hundred officers and men. The Calliope class was thus a most valuable force, and it was probably owing to the very favourable cover afforded by the mist that the audacious and successful course was taken of launching the squadron in a daylight torpedo attack. It was one thing to talk of " hussar strokes," as German torpedo officers had done ; it was another thing to discern, in the smoke, mist, and tension of battle, opportunities for delivering these " hussar strokes " with complete success. The British torpedo attacks were entirely magnificent. Had the Admiralty but built in the days of peace more ocean-going destroyers, Admiral Jellicoe would have been able to deal a decisive stroke towards winning peace for Christendom in the night of May 31st-June 1st, 1916.

At nine o'clock in the evening of May 31st the Grand Fleet and the Cruiser Fleet had completely driven the enemy westward and cut him off from his bases. Admiral von Scheer's battleships had been forced to execute very complicated manœuvres to escape from their pursuers. His broken van seems to have been in a latitude a little north of Dundee at 8.30 p.m. It was followed by the British Cruiser Fleet and 1st and 3rd Light Cruiser Squadrons, on a south-westerly course, until twenty-four minutes past nine. No enemy ships were then found to the south-west, and Admiral Beatty assumed that the Germans were still well to the north-west of him, so that the main British forces were established between Von Scheer and his base. The Cruiser Fleet, under Admiral Beatty, then began to move down in the darkness towards Heligoland, and on a parallel course, a little distance eastward, the battle squad- **Enemy driven** rons of the Grand Fleet also moved in the **westward** night towards Heligoland and the triangular stretch of water in the Bight in which the German bases lay. When day broke on June 1st, 1916, the British fleets were only eighty-five miles from Heligoland.

Admiral Jellicoe decided not to risk his flee in a close night action in these misty waters. Darkness and fog offered too many opportunities for destroyer and submarine attacks by the enemy. The British ships, with the waters before them illuminated only by blurred lanes of searchlight, would have been liable to blunder into minefields hastily laid by the enemy for the express purpose of snaring the British Fleet in the darkness. The British Commander-in-Chief had to be specially cautious, as his ships were the most vital element of force in the Grand Alliance—indeed its very soul. Most of his light cruisers and destroyers were needed to screen and guard his large vessels during the night.

The 2nd Light Cruiser Squadron, commanded by Commodore Goodenough, in the Southampton, had some extraordinary adventures in the night of May 31st. The Southampton, with the Dublin (Captain Albert C. Scott), and the Birmingham (Captain Arthur A. M. Duff), formed part of the force placed for the night in the rear of the battle fleet. Just at the fall of darkness, at 9 p.m., the ships of the 2nd Light Cruiser Squadron helped to repel a torpedo attack on the 5th Battle Squadron of fast battleships. Then at 10.20 p.m. a powerful German force, consisting of five heavy and light cruisers, came exceedingly close to the rear of the British Battle Fleet, and in the mist and darkness opened fire at short range for fifteen minutes, damaging the Southampton and the Dublin, happily without impairing the fighting and steaming qualities of the two ships. Their casualties, however, were severe, as the fire of the German squadron was very effective, and the Southampton seems to have been saved by the skill and resourcefulness with which Commander E. H. Rushton effected temporary repairs. At 11.30 p.m. two more large German ships, probably battleships, were sighted by the Birmingham, steering south.

CHAPTER CXLIII.

THE GLORIOUS BATTLE OF JUTLAND BANK. PART IV.
Night Attacks by the Destroyer Flotillas.
By H. W. Wilson and Edward Wright.

Deficiency of Fast Ocean-going Destroyers Robs Sir John Jellicoe of a Decisive Victory—Disposition of the British Flotillas to Protect the Grand Fleet and Provide for a Renewal of the Action at Daybreak—Captain Wintour, in the Tipperary, Leads the 4th Flotilla Into the Midst of the German Fleet—The Ardent, Garland, and Ambuscade Destroy a Battleship—The Spitfire Sinks a Cruiser—Glorious End of the Fortune—Captain Anselan Stirling Leads the 12th Flotilla in Another Charge Against Battleships and Light Cruisers and Blows Up the Third Ship in the German Line—The Mænad Torpedoes the Fourth Ship in the Line—Lieutenant-Commander Arthur Onslow Killed in the Onslaught after Torpedoing a Battleship of the Kaiser Class—High Sea Fleet Scatters and Makes for Wilhelmshaven—The 13th Flotilla In Action—Great Deeds of the Turbulent, Champion, Moresby, and Obdurate—Admiral von Scheer Escapes the British Encircling Movement—Vice-Admiral Sir Cecil Burney Transfers his Flag from the Marlborough to the Revenge—The Marlborough Reaches Port and Refits—Last Hours of the Warrior—Wounded and Crew Transferred to the Engadine—Flight-Lieutenant F. J. Rutland's Splendid Recovery of a Dying Man who Fell Between the Two Vessels—End of the Warrior.

THE ideal tactics were to search for the enemy with light craft and harry him continually in nocturnal torpedo attacks. Admiral Jellicoe did not possess sufficient destroyers to enable him to carry out this ordinary and even commonplace plan. The weather became rough in the night; the distance from the British bases was considerable, so that ocean-going destroyers were needed for serious work against the battered, scattered, and half-demoralised enemy forces. But it was part of the price of our pacifist ideals that on the night of the grand ordeal the weapons requisite to drive home the blow and complete the work achieved with so much agony and such sacrifice by the heroic British seamen were wanting. Some time before, Mr. Winston Churchill, then First Lord of the Admiralty, had declared that the days of the destroyer were numbered, and that all or most of their duties would be taken over by light cruisers and sub-

An infelicitous prophecy

marines. It seems very likely that his inaccurate judgment of the modern value of destroyers was a reflection of the opinion ruling at the Admiralty.

The need of small craft on this great day was absorbing. Destroyer convoys were required by the Marlborough and the Warrior. The security of the Grand Fleet and Cruiser Fleet, whose safety from nocturnal torpedo attack was vital to the interests of the Allies, engaged a very large number of light cruisers and destroyers. As Admiral Beatty remarks:

At 9 p.m. the enemy was entirely out of sight, and the threat of torpedo-boat destroyer attacks during the rapidly approaching darkness made it necessary for me to dispose of the fleet for the night with a view to its safety from such attacks, while providing for a renewal of action at daylight. I accordingly manœuvred to remain between the enemy and his bases, placing our flotillas in a position in which they could afford protection to the fleet from torpedo attack, and at the same time be favourably situated for attacking the enemy's heavy ships.

According to Sir David Beatty's despatch, his destroyers of the 13th Flotilla, under the command of Captain James U. Farie, in the light cruiser Champion, took station for the night astern of the Battle Fleet. The 2nd Light Cruiser Squadron was also placed in the rear of the battle-line during the night, having at 9 p.m. helped to repel the German destroyer assault on the 5th Battle Squadron. The general consequence was that the mightiest Fleet in the world, which was twice as strong as the Fleet ranking second in strength to it, could only spare three destroyer flotillas for nocturnal attacks against an enemy who had been badly battered by gun fire. The situation was altogether dissimilar from that which Admiral Togo developed at Tsushima, in the great battle with Admiral Rodjestvensky. In daylight the big Japanese ships sank, mainly by gun fire, four Russian battleships; but at night a host of Japanese torpedo-boats took up the work of destruction, sank four additional battleships or armoured cruisers, and drove into a hopeless trap the remnant of the Russian Fleet, which was captured or sunk next day. The Japanese gunners first wrought tremendous damage and shook the nerves of their opponents, and then the nocturnal torpedo attacks completed the destruction of Rodjestvensky's forces. The three available British destroyer flotillas were inadequate for the great and difficult task of destroying the High Sea Fleet. They consisted of the 4th Flotilla (Captain Charles J. Wintour), 11th Flotilla (Commodore James R. P. Hawksley), and 12th Flotilla (Captain Anselan J. B. Stirling). The magnificent work done by these small forces caused the enemy serious loss, but naturally failed to make the defeat a decisive one. They

Destroyer flotillas inadequate

showed, however, what might have been accomplished in the North Sea on the night of May 31st, 1916, if the Grand Fleet and Cruiser Fleet had possessed a much larger number of fast ocean-going destroyers.

The enemy had a large space of sea in which to evade attack. In particular there was a considerable breadth of water between the head of the British Fleet and the channels leading to the German bases. The British ships could not cover the southernmost line of approach to the ports behind Heligoland. German mine-fields and German submarines limited the area in which the British Fleet could wait to renew the action at daylight. Admiral Jellicoe had swept the Germans well to the west of Little Fisher Bank and far away from Wilhelmshaven. But when the enemy was lost sight of, nothing but the constant application of force could prevent him from making a wide sweep southward and then eastward, leaving the British line northward of him as he regained his harbours. He was only cut off from his bases while he remained northwest of the Grand Fleet. When he turned towards the south-east and began, in darkness, mist, and rough weather, to return to Wilhelmshaven, Admiral Jellicoe could only have held him back by a very strong force of light craft, over and above the light cruisers and destroyers required to screen his fleet. If he had had the additional light craft he would, no doubt, have kept in touch with the Germans

Enemy's advantage of sea area

thrown at once into disorder. The British destroyers found the position of the German ships by the flash of their guns or the loom of their shapes in the great lanes of light which the searchlights opened up in the darkness. The searchlights were switched on and off in all directions, their beams springing up and disappearing in a most confusing manner, while the British gunners aimed their 4 in. shells at the great reflectors. So the pitch-black night twinkled with flashes of intense radiance, calculated to dazzle the British crews, as the enemy searched for the attacking craft. The Tipperary seems to have been one of the first destroyers to be caught by the storm of bursting shells. She was hit by a heavy projectile, turned into a mass of raging flame, and quickly sunk. From German sources it seems to have been the Dreadnought Westfalen that hit the Tipperary with two salvos at a range of less than a mile. The smaller British destroyers, however, darting about the black sea like deadly dragon-flies in zigzag movements, designed to put the German gunners off their aim, broke right through the German screen of light craft, and found themselves between two lines of German battleships. They turned to steam up between these two lines in the very centre of the enemy's main forces. The position was absolutely extraordinary, such as young destroyer lieutenants imagined in their wildest dreams, but never soberly hoped to achieve against so cautious an enemy as the Teuton.

CR. C. W. E. TRELAWNY, H.M.S. Spitfire. Promoted.   MIDSHIPMAN M. W. B. HERVEY, H.M.S. Colossus.   ACTING-LT. H.R.H. PRINCE ALBERT, R.N. Commended.   CAPT. WILDE, R.M.A., H.M.S. Indefatigable. Killed in action.   LT. F. J. RUTLAND, R.N., Flight-Lieut. R.N.A.S. Awarded the D.S.C.

all night, and harried them continually with torpedo attacks. As it was, there seems only to have been sufficient matériel to make one nocturnal attack of importance.

The 4th and 12th Flotillas luckily found and attacked the enemy battle squadrons. Just at midnight Captain Wintour, leading in the Tipperary, with the Ardent, Fortune, Sparrowhawk, Spitfire, Garland, Ambuscade, and Contest behind him, shot into the midst of the German Fleet. All the boats of the 4th Flotilla were oil-fired, emitting neither smoke nor flame, and the Tipperary, the destroyer leader, was of 1,850 tons, twice the tonnage of an ordinary destroyer, 320 feet long, with a beam of 32½ feet, about one hundred and sixty officers and men, six 4 in. guns, and six torpedo-tubes. Built in 1914, she had a reputed speed of thirty-one knots. The boats she led were mainly of the 1913 class, of about 935 tons, 260 feet long, with a 28 feet beam, a reputed speed of about thirty knots, three 4 in. guns, four torpedo-tubes, and a complement of one hundred officers and men.

The 4th Flotilla had taken part in the opening of the fleet action, when two of its boats, the Shark and Acasta, had fought against great odds. But the odds were immeasurably greater in the final action which it fought so gloriously. Captain Wintour had brought his boats to a high pitch of perfection, and his great charge to the death was as noble as anything that can be found in British history. The enemy was severely shaken by the abruptness of the attack, and some of his ships seem to have been

The weight of metal and high-explosive brought against the mosquito craft was enormous. The range at times was almost point-blank, and the Germans occasionally tried to ram as well as shoot. On the other hand, from the German point of view, the situation was unnerving. The swift turns and dashes of the destroyers made them most difficult objects to hit between the switching off and on of the searchlights, and every flash of German gun fire indicated a target to the British torpedo men. It was a nightmare for the German battleships, and, according to their reports, there was at least one collision in which a German light cruiser was rammed by a German battleship.

The Ardent, commanded by Lieutenant-Commander Arthur Marsden, raced up to a German battleship that was going at a tremendous speed, and, steering into position, fired a torpedo that seemed to strike about amidships. The German leviathan lurched and heeled, and her crew could be seen rushing about the decks. Spinning round, the British destroyer marked another great enemy ship and dashed towards it, but was struck by a heavy shell, set on fire, and sunk. The Garland (Lieutenant-Commander Reginald S. Goff) and the Ambuscade (Lieutenant-Commander Gordon A. Coles) also released torpedoes against the battleship first attacked by the Ardent, and Admiral Jellicoe gave all three vessels credit for helping to destroy the enemy. The Spitfire (Lieutenant-Commander Clarence W. E. Trelawny) got home a torpedo in a very

A nightmare for the foe

CAPT. C. J. WINTOUR, H.M.S. Tipperary. Killed in action.

CAPT. E. M. PHILL-POTTS, C.B., H.M.S. Warspite.

CAPT. V. B. MOLTENO, H.M.S. Warrior. Commended.

CAPT. C. E. LE MESURIER, C.B., H.M.S. Cornwallis.

CAPT. R. N. LAWSON, H.M.S. Chester. Commended.

(Photographs by Russell and Heath.)

remarkable manner. A German cruiser tried to ram her, but the agile little craft turned and received only a glancing blow, and then at close quarters fired a torpedo at the enemy ship, which the British crew saw go down as they raced away. Lieutenant-Commander Trelawny was wounded and had a marvellous escape from death. As he stood on the bridge a shell passed across his chest, striking the buttons on his uniform, and carrying away the signalling gear and two of the men.

Fortune's splendid story The Fortune (Lieutenant-Commander Terry) sighted a big German ship as the British flotilla turned up the lane between the two lines of enemy vessels. She rushed at her big foe and launched two torpedoes, one of which was followed by the roar of an explosion. But dozens of guns were turned upon the Fortune, and she was blown to pieces. The first salvo smashed the forebridge, killing the commander and Sub-Lieutenant Paul and all other persons upon it. Then the foremost gun was knocked overboard with its crew; the gunlayer, who was aiming the gun at the moment it was struck, had the gunsight driven against his face, but went overboard with no injury except a black eye. The foremost boiler was smashed; the after-stokehold and engine-room were caught by a shell, and the amidship's gun was blown into the sea with its crew.

With both her engines torn out, the Fortune stopped dead and began to go down. The survivors of her hundred officers and men, as one of them, Chief Petty-Officer H. Hamnant—who tells the splendid story—relates, slammed away with their after-gun. When this was knocked out, they trained a torpedo-tube upon their nearest enemy. Just as the torpedo was fired the tube was struck by a shell, which lifted it in the air as the torpedo was leaving it, and completely finished the Fortune, setting her badly on fire forward; but as the survivors took to their two rafts they had the satisfaction of seeing their last torpedo running towards its mark. There were then thirty-five men alive of the Fortune's complement of a hundred.

They watched the battle flash around them, saw the fires die down in the Ardent and Tipperary, and observed, as they thought, a Dreadnought blaze up and glow like a gigantic cinder, and then go hissing to the bottom with one gun banging away at the British destroyers. As that terrible night wore on many of the men on the rafts began to die from exhaustion. It was a veritable sea of hell in which they floated—lighted with the sinister glare of the searchlights and the flashes of the guns, and incessantly lashed to spouts of foam with giant projectiles. One of the men went mad under the stress, and leaped into the sea. When daylight broke, no rescue could be attempted for some time, as enemy submarines were watching stealthily from their ambush, and tried to torpedo the first British destroyer that approached. When at last the destroyer Moresby arrived with a number of light cruisers and chased off the submarines, only seventeen men remained alive out of the thirty-five who had taken to the rafts when the Fortune sank. Only one of the British attacking boats seems to have come through unhurt, but the total loss of the Tipperary, Ardent, and Fortune must be regarded as very small in view of the extreme risks run and the terrible havoc reported to have been inflicted on the enemy. No charge of the Light Brigade or the Heavy Brigade in the Crimean War can compare with the attack of the 4th Flotilla for skilled heroism and inspired devotion.

The only achievement which challenges comparison with it was a similar charge made by the 12th Flotilla, under Captain Anselan J. B. Stirling. Six large enemy ships, some of them Dreadnoughts of the Kaiser class, **Charge of 12th Flotilla** with a number of light cruisers in addition, were taken even more completely by surprise by Captain Stirling than had been the division attacked by Captain Wintour. The gunners and searchlight men in the German ships were so unnerved by Captain Anselan Stirling's assault that they could not get a hit upon several of the mosquito craft. Many torpedoes were fired, especially at the second and third ships in the German line. The third ship was " observed to blow up "

CAPT. C. B. MILLER, C.B., H.M.S. Nottingham.

CAPT. T. D. PRATT, H.M.S. Yarmouth. Commended.

CR. J. P. CHAMPION, D.S.O., H.M.S. Mænad.

LT. JACK E. A. MOCATTA, D.S.O., H.M.S. Nicator.

CR. PAUL WHITFIELD, H.M.S. Nomad.

(Photographs by Russell, Heath, and Swaine.)

HONOURED FOR CONSPICUOUS GALLANTRY AND DISTINGUISHED SERVICE.
These four gallant recipients of Jutland Battle honours were shipmates. Left to right: Chief Sick-berth Steward A. E. Jones, C.G.M.; Officers' Cook (first class) H. F. Carter, D.S.M.; Chief Petty-Officer C. Hucklesby, Médaille Militaire; Leading Signalman W. J. Barrow, D.S.M.

in a roar of thunder, smoke, and flame, suggesting that the explosion of the torpedo had fired her magazine. Twenty minutes after this great feat one of the British destroyers of the "M" class, the Mænad (Commander John P. Champion), daringly returned to the attack, and though the enemy battleships were now perfectly on their guard, Commander Champion brought his swift new boat to a close range and put a torpedo into the fourth ship in the German line.

Lieutenant-Commander Arthur G. Onslow, in the Onslaught, another new destroyer, perished gloriously in his hour of victory. At a range of 1,000 yards he torpedoed a ship of the Kaiser class, and then moved swiftly off towards the rear of the enemy's line. The officers went on the bridge to congratulate him on his success; but in the rear of the German Fleet were the light cruisers that had failed to protect it from the 12th Flotilla. They swept the Onslaught with their salvos, and one shell struck the bridge, killing or disabling all the officers except Sub-Lieutenant Harry W. A. Kemmis and Midshipman Reginald G. Arnot, of the Royal Naval Reserve. Sub-Lieutenant Kemmis had only been promoted to acting sub-lieutenant since the outbreak of the war, and Midshipman Arnot was a still more recent recruit, but they manœuvred their battered boat successfully out of action and brought her safely to her home port.

The extraordinary feature of this glorious destroyer charge was that the Onslaught was the only vessel that received any material injuries. Save for the fact that **Onslaught brought** the 12th Flotilla had used nearly all its **to port** torpedoes, it was in a position to make a fresh attack. After having probably sunk one German battleship, holed another, and perhaps damaged a third, it was fit for action if it had had a reserve of torpedoes available. The superb successes achieved by the 4th and 12th Flotillas against the enemy's principal battle squadrons were not crushing because of the lack of yet more destroyers to follow and incessantly harry and annihilate the enemy. Demoralised he was in the fullest sense of the word, since he proved his inability to sink a single vessel of the 12th Flotilla which engaged him, sometimes at a range of a thousand yards. Admiral Jellicoe needed, in this critical phase of his operations, which should have gathered in the harvest of his victory,

not forty but a hundred or a hundred and fifty destroyers. The result was that no more direct torpedo attacks could be made. The British Command failed, from lack of vessels, to achieve its full purpose and cut Admiral von Scheer off from his base.

After the midnight attack the High Sea Fleet seems to have scattered and made for Wilhelmshaven in isolated units or in separate divisions, proceeding at the utmost speed. The British 13th Flotilla, stationed astern of the Battle Fleet, saw a German battleship steaming past with flaming funnels at half-past twelve. The nearest destroyers, the Petard and Turbulent, closed for an attack, but the German ship switched on her searchlights and, opening heavy fire, disabled the Turbulent and escaped. There must have been German small craft with her, and these must have escaped the notice of the British, for a number of survivors from the Turbulent were rescued by the enemy and taken prisoners.

At half-past three in the morning of June 1st the commander of the 13th Flotilla, Captain James U. Farie, in the new light cruiser Champion (armed with two 6 in. and eight 4 in. guns), sighted four German destroyers working round towards Heligoland, and engaged them for a few minutes. Another light cruiser in the rear of the British line, the Fearless, sighted a battleship of the Kaiser class steaming fast and entirely alone. The Fearless was not able to engage her, but believed she was attacked by the British destroyers and damaged in a short action that ended with a heavy explosion. This may have been the vessel that put the Tur-   **Loss of Pommern** bulent out of action. At 2.30 a.m. on   **admitted** June 1st Lieutenant-Commander Roger V. Alison, in the Moresby, and Lieutenant-Commander H. H. Sams, in the Obdurate, forming part of the 13th Flotilla, sighted four of the German pre-Dreadnoughts of the Deutschland class. The Moresby fired one torpedo at them. Two minutes later an explosion was felt, which may or may not have meant that the enemy battleship was sunk. The German pre-Dreadnoughts had not the remarkable system of watertight compartments which enabled practically all Dreadnoughts to survive any torpedo that did not explode their magazines. The German naval authorities afterwards admitted that they had lost the Pommern. This pre-Dreadnought of the Deutschland class had been torpedoed by a British submarine in the Baltic on July 2nd, 1915, but, according to reports published subsequently, was not sunk, as the torpedo caught her only on the bow. It was reported from an alleged German source that one of the latest German battleships had been named the Pommern, and that this ship was sunk in action as well as a Deutschland class pre-Dreadnought. There is, however, no authentic information available on this head, and the story is improbable.

It will be remarked that a Dreadnought of the Kaiser class, forming part of the squadron near the enemy's line, passed the British rear at 12.30 p.m., while four ships of the Deutschland class, originally forming part of the tail of the enemy's line, crossed the British rear at 2.35 a.m. on June 1st. Almost an hour afterwards four German destroyers passed within sight of the rear British destroyer flotilla, which may or may not have been the vessels that rescued the survivors of the Turbulent. From all this we may presume that the midnight charge of the 4th Destroyer Flotilla scattered the hostile fleet, breaking up its principal formations, and compelling Admiral von Scheer to make at once for Wilhelmshaven at any risk. Both Admiral Jellicoe and Admiral Beatty appear to have thought that the enemy would remain throughout the night cut off from his base and be compelled to renew action at daybreak in circumstances that meant annihilation. Sir David Beatty remarks in his report : " Our strategical position was such as to make it appear *certain* that we should locate the enemy at daylight under most favourable circumstances." Sir John Jellicoe states : " I manœuvred to remain between the enemy and his bases. . . . and at daybreak on June 1st the Battle Fleet, being then to the southward and the westward of the Horn Reef, turned to the northward in search of enemy vessels."

As nothing has been revealed regarding the dispositions of the Grand Fleet and Cruiser Fleet in the night of May 31st, and nothing definite is known of the dispositions of the High Sea Fleet at the time, it is impossible to trace the method by which Admiral von Scheer adroitly escaped the British enveloping movement. He seems to have owed a great deal to the fact that it was very foggy on the North Sea at dawn on June 1st, 1916. Nothing could be seen more than four miles away at the most, and three miles was often the limit of observation. Many British ships, however, noticed a Zeppelin sailing above them about four o'clock in the morning, and Sir John Jellicoe states that it " had ample opportunity to note and subsequently report the position and course of the British Fleet." In other words, it was able to tell the enemy how to elude the toils that were being spread for him. Sir John Jellicoe was as a blind man at this, the last moment when a complete victory was still possible, if only he had had the necessary instruments of reconnaissance and observation. Never did the Admiralty's and Government's lack of imagination and foresight cost the country more dearly.

Admiral Burney transfers his flag   During the night the speed of the torpedoed battleship Marlborough declined, till she had difficulty in keeping her station in the fleet. It was decided, in consequence, that Vice-Admiral Sir Cecil Burney should transfer his flag to the new battleship Revenge, which, according to the Germans, with two of her sisters mounting 15 in. guns, had taken part in the battle. The transfer was effected at 2.30 a.m. of June 1st, and the Marlborough was despatched to a British base. The enemy must have been watching her closely with his submarines, which no doubt had received orders to be in readiness to intercept any injured British ships. Such, however, were the skill and vigilance of the commanders of the British light craft, and so excellent was the moral of the ship's company, that the German submarines were beaten off. The Marlborough regained harbour quite safely, and some weeks later was again present in the British order of battle.

The Warrior, which, as we have seen, had been badly damaged early in the battle, was less fortunate. She was now in tow of the Engadine, and her hull was sinking lower and lower in the water. The sea was rising ; the waters in which the damaged vessel was being towed swarmed with enemy light craft and sub-

marines. There was little sleep for anyone on board her. The crew, who had lost heavily in battle, now covered themselves with honour by their conduct in this period of intense peril and effort. They " carried on," in the great phrase of the Navy, all night and when the grey dawn appeared, with no sign of anxiety or uneasiness. Early in the morning the Warrior developed a heavy list to port, and her last moments were clearly at hand. The wounded were brought up on deck, ready to be transferred, and as they lay there in the sloping ship the rising seas began to break over them. The order was given to abandon ship, and the Engadine, with brilliant seamanship, closed in on the sinking hulk—for the Warrior was now no more than this.

While the wounded were being moved one of them fell from the stretcher between the vessels. The position was   **A deed of valour** desperate, but Captain Molteno, of the Warrior, saw that several of his officers were preparing to leap in at the risk of almost certain death to their comrade's aid. He gave the order to them not to sacrifice themselves ; their country had far greater claim on their lives. But his order did not apply to Flight-Lieutenant F. J. Rutland, of the Engadine, who had already distinguished himself by his reconnoitring flight at the opening of the action. He jumped into the sea between the swaying ships and attempted to rescue the injured man. Unfortunately the man died from shock, injury, and exhaustion ; but this did not diminish the splendour of an act which shines among the many deeds of valour and love in that great agony of men. For this, Flight-Lieutenant Rutland received the Albert Medal of the 1st Class. Recommended also for honour in Sir John Jellicoe's dispatch, this gallant sailor-airman was further rewarded with the Distinguished Conduct Medal.

When all the crew had been transferred, and Captain Molteno, faithful to the great ritual of the Navy, had been the last to leave his ship, the Engadine dropped astern to get clear of the wreck and then steamed past it, while the Warrior's crew cheered the sinking hull for the last time, and sang one of their own pet variants of " Tipperary " : " It's a long, long way to the Warrior." Nothing more was seen of her. The waterlogged hull vanished astern in the mist, and subsequent search for it revealed no trace of it, so that it must have foundered during June 1st. It was abandoned seventy-five miles from the point where it had been taken in tow, at 7.15 on that morning.

GROUP OF CHIEF STOKERS OF H.M.S. QUEEN MARY.

All these gallant men were long-service men. Second on the left is Chief Petty-Officer Sparrow, who was within six months of completing his thirty-two years' service. He held the Long Service, Good Conduct, and South Africa Medals.

"I AM STANDING HERE TO-DAY AS YOUR SUPREME WAR-LORD, AND I THANK YOU FROM THE BOTTOM OF MY HEART."

Extract from the Kaiser's speech to officers and men who took part in the Jutland Battle. The vainglorious speech stated that British sea-power had been finally overthrown. This ceremony War-Lord addressed them from the deck of a flagship at Wilhelmshaven, and in the course of a took place on June 5th, no doubt before the exact results of the Battle had been ascertained.

[From an enemy painting.

THE GLORIOUS BATTLE OF JUTLAND BANK. PART V.

Summary of Gains and Losses, and Some Reports.

By H. W. Wilson and Edward Wright.

Victory but not Annihilation—Responsibility for the Failure to Destroy the German High Sea Fleet—Sir John Jellicoe's Tribute to Sir David Beatty—Sir John Jellicoe's Disappointment of the Crowning Triumph—Total Loss in Ships of the Grand Fleet—Sir John Jellicoe's Official Estimate of the Losses of the High Sea Fleet—Resistance of Dreadnought Battleships and Battle Cruisers the Surprise of the Action—Clumsily False Official Statements of the German Marine Office—Clumsily Foolish Report by the British Admiralty—The Effect of the Two Reports Abroad—The King's Message of Praise and Thanks to the Grand Fleet—Criticism of the General Situation by Captain Sims, of the United States Navy—Spirit and Efficiency of the Officers and Men of the British Navy—Appendix: Probable Composition of the Opposing Fleets.

E may sum up the concluding phase of the general fleet action by remarking that the British Fleet had the enemy at its mercy, with his ships scattered to westward, his crews seemingly demoralised, and his entire fleet cut off from its base. But it failed to destroy him at night because it could only spare three flotillas of searching and attacking destroyers from the task of screening the big ships. At dawn it failed to find and hold the enemy because it lacked large, swift, and powerful reconnoitring airships, while the enemy, who possessed such airships, discovered that the British Fleet was looking for him northward and made his escape southward. The authority at Whitehall concerned in the construction of large rigid airships and airshed stations on the East Coast, that decided in 1914 not to proceed with the construction of British Zeppelins and Zeppelin sheds, was largely responsible for the ultimate failure to annihilate an enemy who was beaten and almost enveloped. Equally responsible for the failure to win a victory in the Trafalgar style were the Admiralty experts, under Mr. Winston Churchill, who informed the then First Lord that the destroyer was an antiquated vessel, whose work would be better carried out by the light cruiser and the submarine. Nelson aimed at "not victory but annihilation," but then he had all the weapons he needed. If the Battle of Jutland was victory but not annihilation, want of essential equipment and material was the cause.

The British admirals did their work well. In regard to Sir David Beatty, we have the judgment of his superior officer, Sir John Jellicoe, that he showed

fine qualities of gallant leadership, firm determination, and correct strategic insight. He appreciated the situations at once on sighting first the enemy's lighter forces, then his battle-cruisers, and finally his battle fleet. I can fully sympathise with his feelings when the evening mist and fading light robbed the fleet of that complete victory for which he had manœuvred, and for which the vessels in company with him had striven so hard.

But who shall sympathise with Admiral Sir John Rushworth Jellicoe when, after waiting for twenty-two months and employing practically every kind of baiting manœuvre, he drew the High Sea Fleet into the grip of the Grand Fleet, cut the Germans off from their own coast, unnerved them with his tornadoes of heavy gun fire, and shepherded them north-westward on a line at least north of Dundee; but, because he had insufficient destroyers, and no first-rate airships whatever, had to let them slip through his hands? His torpedo-boat destroyers did not rejoin him until 9 a.m. on June 1st, 1916. He then remained near the line of approach to German ports for two hours, in spite of the danger incurred in waters adjacent to the enemy coast from submarines and torpedo craft. Reluctantly compelled to the conclusion that the High Sea Fleet had returned to its base, he searched the waters from Horn Reef to Little Fisher Bank, picked up some few survivors from the Ardent, Fortune, and Tipperary, rescued the crew of the Sparrowhawk, which had been rendered unseaworthy by a collision, sighted no enemy ships, and at 1.15 p.m. of June 1st shaped his course for home ports, which he reached on Friday, June 2nd.

Undoubtedly he had won an important victory. His total loss in ships was three fine battle-cruisers—Queen Mary, Indefatigable, and Invincible; three armoured cruisers—Defence, Black Prince, and Warrior; and eight torpedo-

[Russell.

MAJOR F. J. W. HARVEY, R.M.L.I.
Posthumously awarded V.C. for heroism in the Jutland Battle.

boat destroyers—Tipperary, Ardent, Fortune, Shark, Sparrowhawk, Nestor, Nomad, and Turbulent. The loss of such gallant and distinguished officers as Rear-Admiral Sir Robert Arbuthnot, Rear-Admiral the Hon. Horace Hood, Captain Charles F. Sowerby, Captain Cecil I. Prowse, Captain Arthur L. Cay, Captain Thomas P. Bonham, Captain Charles J. Wintour, and Captain Stanley V. Ellis, and those who perished with them, was an even more serious blow to the Navy and to the country. On the other hand, the enemy losses in ships and well-trained officers and men were judged by the British admirals to have been heavier.

The following is the official statement of German loss issued by Sir John Jellicoe, " after a most careful examination of the evidence of all officers who **Estimate of German losses** testified to seeing enemy vessels actually sink, and personal interviews with a large number of those officers. I am of opinion," Sir John adds, " that the list shown . . . gives the minimum in regard to numbers, though it is possibly not entirely accurate as regards the particular class of vessel, especially those which were sunk during the night attacks. In addition to the vessels sunk, it is unquestionable that many other ships were very seriously damaged by gun fire and by torpedo attack."

GERMAN BATTLESHIPS OR BATTLE-CRUISERS.

Seen to sink: 2 battleships, Dreadnought type; 1 battleship, Deutschland type.
Sunk (admitted by Germans): 1 battle-cruiser (Lützow).
Seen to be so severely damaged as to render it extremely doubtful if they could reach port: 1 battleship, Dreadnought type; 1 battle-cruiser.

LIGHT CRUISERS.

Seen to sink (one of them had the appearance of being of a larger type, and might have been a battleship): 5 light cruisers.

DESTROYERS.

Seen to sink: 6.
Seen to be so severely damaged as to render it extremely doubtful if they could reach port: 3.

SUBMARINE.

Sunk: 1.

When comparing the losses, it must be remembered that ships sunk can by no art of man be repaired, whereas experience shows that a warship, however damaged, so long as she remains above the water, can be reconstructed and put into fighting order. The Japanese proved this in 1905, when they repaired the Russian ships which had been left waterlogged wrecks in Port Arthur Harbour, some of which vessels, with the chivalry characteristic of their race, they restored to their old enemies when the latter became their allies.

It is not wise to attempt in any way to increase the estimate of German loss given by Admiral Jellicoe, for such a course would lead to under-estimating the enemy's strength in the next general fleet action. **Seaworthy, though damaged** On the other hand, there is no reason to suppose that all the British light cruiser and destroyer crews who felt certain that they got a torpedo home on a hostile capital ship were mistaken. If there was any mistake, it lay in thinking a Dreadnought torpedoed was a Dreadnought destroyed. This theory was disproved by the Marlborough; there the torpedo blew in the side of the great ship, yet left her fighting power almost unimpaired. The Marlborough was struck about 6.54 p.m. on May 31st, but she afterwards outfought a Dreadnought of the König class, and continued to serve Sir Cecil Burney as his flagship until 2.30 a.m. on June 1st. It is, therefore, extremely probable that several German battleships and battle-cruisers were torpedoed, and yet were able to return to their base, where they could be repaired in a month or two.

The capacity of resistance of both Dreadnought battleships and Dreadnought cruisers was the grand surprise of the action. The New Zealand went through the entire battle, including the fearful ordeal through which Admiral Beatty's battle-cruisers passed, almost without a scratch, her only injury being a blow on her armour which broke off a large splinter. One British ship was struck by fifty German heavy shells without being disabled, and lost less than ten per cent. of her crew. It may be, therefore, that the damage done by British gun fire to German ships was over-estimated. The British battle-cruisers and fast battleships, though subjected to continuous fire, with the exception of the three ships destroyed—it might almost be said by accident—were but little injured. On the other hand, it is probable that the British 15 in. shells wrought terrific havoc, while the 13'5 in. shells inflicted far more damage on the enemy than he was able to inflict with his 12 in. and 11 in. shells. In the case of the Lützow, the Germans some time after the battle admitted that she had been put out of action and abandoned by her crew in a sinking state when she had received only sixteen hits from heavy guns, which gives some measure of the destruction effected by the British shells. There were probably quite a number of British ships which were not much the worse for sixteen hits from the German heavy projectiles. The enemy seems throughout to have concentrated his fire on individual ships; but there is nothing in the British reports to indicate that the British followed this plan.

In general character, the battle resembled the naval engagements with the Dutch in the seventeenth century—engagements in which both sides claimed victory, and Great Britain usually enjoyed all the fruits of success. It rested with time to show if the enemy had received a staggering blow. It will be remembered that after the Battle of Dogger Bank, on January 24th, 1915, it was commonly thought that the German battle-cruisers would not again be seen; yet at least two of them, the Moltke and the Seydlitz, took part in the attack off the Gulf of Riga on August 19th, 1915. The Moltke was then torpedoed, but she appeared **Moltke twice " destroyed "** once more in the Jutland Bank action, after having been twice " destroyed."

On June 1st the German Marine Office stated that the only German ships lost in the action were the Pommern and the light cruiser Wiesbaden, while the Frauenlob was " missing," and " some destroyers " had not returned. A little later, survivors of the light cruiser Elbing arrived in Holland, with other survivors from the Frauenlob, when the German naval authorities officially stated that: " In order to prevent the spread of fantastic reports, it must be added to the statements already published that we were obliged to blow up the small cruiser Elbing, which was so heavily damaged by collision with another German warship that it was impossible to bring her back to port." Then on June 7th, 1916, the German Marine Office published the extraordinary statement that: " For military reasons we have refrained until now from making public the loss of the vessels Lützow and Rostock." Some days before this a statement of an unparalleled nature was issued. The " Wilhelmshaven Gazette " printed in large type a proclamation, signed by the Governor of Wilhelmshaven, informing the German public that the port was closed to ordinary traffic, and that permission for temporary visits to the town during the summer could only be granted in cases of extreme urgency, on condition that written applications were received by the police before the journey was made. It was reported about this time that a damaged German Dreadnought had sunk just outside Wilhelmshaven, in sheltered water.

The precautions the Germans took to veil their battered fleet from the eyes of their own public, and the belated attempt they made to explain to their people when correct news of the loss of the Lützow was spreading by oral report that the Marine Office had published lies " for military reasons," resulted in a moral victory for the Allies. The most pro-German of neutral States then began to see that there were definite limits to that " German truth " which had been so much acclaimed by German professors, and the neutral world, struck by this flagrant example of Teutonic veracity, lost faith in the mendacious reports issued from Berlin.

If, however, the German Marine Office was clumsily false in regard to its statements about the Jutland Battle, the civilian element in the British Admiralty was clumsily foolish. All news of the battle was withheld from the British public for nearly three days, while Northern Europe, Spain, and Greece were ringing with news of a great German naval victory. The school-children of Berlin were given the usual holidays; German Royalties sent telegrams of rhetorical tinsel to the German Emperor; Kaiser Wilhelm made a clamorous claim to something like a new Trafalgar in the North Sea, and a great German war loan was voted in the Reichstag on the full tide of exultation provoked by the tales of the German Naval Press Bureau and the German Emperor, and the silence of the British Admiralty. When the British naval authorities at last spoke of the greatest naval event since the Battle of Trafalgar, all they said was that the German Fleet, aided by low visibility, had avoided prolonged action with the British main forces, and the British Fleet had lost three battle-cruisers, three armoured cruisers, and five destroyers, while six other destroyers were not accounted for. At least one German battle-cruiser—the public was told—was **Dismal official** destroyed, and one severely damaged. **report** One German battleship was reported sunk during a night attack, and two German light cruisers were disabled and probably sunk.

Thus the only clear and definite claim officially made was that one German battle-cruiser was destroyed and one or two more German large ships severely damaged, against an admitted British loss of three battle-cruisers, three armoured cruisers, and possibly eleven destroyers. The solitary gleam of light in this dismal official report was the statement that " soon after our main forces appeared on the scene the enemy returned to port." All the naval experts on the Press who could have guided the public were officially prevented from commenting on the news.

As the result of these extraordinary measures, Saturday,

June 3rd, 1916, was a day of tragic apprehension in Great Britain. The officers and men of the Grand Fleet and Cruiser Fleet, after their fearful ordeal and their great deeds, were overcome with anger and amazement when they reached their bases, full of the emotion of a hard-won victory. For they met with commiseration rather than with congratulation.

Pure incompetence and lack of naval insight appear to have been the real explanation of the politicians' conduct in the matter. General feeling in the country, based entirely on the misleading **Its public** Admiralty report, was that the British **interpretation** Navy had met with a severe but not irremediable naval reverse. This interpretation of the official report was not singular. The Paris Press took the same view as the London Press, and tried to cheer up the British nation by pointing out that British naval strength was undiminished. In New York the Stock Market fell against the Grand Alliance, and there were some signs of a great break in French, British, and Russian securities. All down the coast of South America, through lands in which the Allies had most important interests, the braggart German claim to a great victory and the strangely diffident British report combined to create a general impression that the foundations of British sea-power had been shaken till they rocked under a daring and magnificent German attack.

When the report was drawn up in London, Admiral Jellicoe had returned to his base to refuel his fleet and replenish it with ammunition, and in the evening of June 2nd he announced himself ready for further action. The Admiralty was then in a position to issue a statement that the Cruiser Fleet, by a brilliant and daring manœuvre, had withstood the attack of the High Sea Fleet and drawn it northward to be attacked by the Grand Fleet, and that in spite of mist and darkness the Grand Fleet had cut the enemy from his base, inflicting upon him loss quite as heavy as that sustained by Admiral Beatty in the cruiser action, and had only missed him through fog on the morning of June 1st. Something like this was said by Mr. Winston Churchill, on being asked by Mr. Balfour's private

WHEN KING GEORGE ADDRESSED THE CREWS OF SHIPS THAT TOOK PART IN THE JUTLAND FIGHT.
An impressive ceremony at a naval dockyard. Alongside the quay is the Warspite, which engaged an overpowering number of German battleships in order to distract their fire from the disabled Warrior.

secretary, and then by Mr. Balfour in person, to draw up a statement likely to reassure neutral opinion in regard to the large results of the naval action.

The King, on June 3rd, in a message praised the splendid gallantry of the British officers and men, and commended their achievement, while regretting that the retirement of the Germans " robbed us of the opportunity of gaining a decisive victory." His Majesty once more put the true facts on record when he received the officers and men of the Grand Fleet after their return to port, and thanked the Commander-in-Chief and all his subordinates for doing all that was possible in the circumstances. " You drove the enemy into his harbours," he said, " and inflicted on him very severe losses, and you added another page to the glorious traditions of the British Navy. You could not do more, and for your splendid work I thank you."

Germany's Press victory The fact was that if the British Navy won a valuable naval victory, the Germans won a very important Press victory. The head of the German Naval Press Bureau was specially rewarded by the German Emperor, and he deserved his reward. Turning the British Admiralty communiqué adroitly to his own purpose, he made so jubilant an impression upon the German mind that the great new German war loan was voted with enthusiasm, and the effect of the Verdun defeat was almost blotted out of the memory of the German people, who for the time became absorbed in problems of sea-power.

Even the strange German admission that the loss of the Lützow and Rostock had been denied for military reasons does not seem to have undone the effect of the British blunder in reporting the battle. The German educated class may gradually have become doubtful whether the High Sea Fleet was quite so victorious as had been pretended, for the blockade continued unbroken ; but the German peasantry, the force on which the military caste chiefly relied, remained convinced that the huge sea power of Great Britain could be overthrown eventually by the same Prussian genius for war which was destined to overthrow the huge military power of Russia.

An impartial American critic, Captain W. S. Sims, whose authority stands deservedly high, contends that there was no need whatever to fight a battle. " The military situation," he says, " did not require the British Fleet to fight a decisive action or any action at all, because it already had practically as complete control of the sea as would have resulted from the defeat of the enemy fleet. Control of the sea is accomplished when the enemy is defeated or ' contained '—*i.e.*, watched by superior force in such a way that it can only fight against great odds— and the German Fleet had been ' contained ' since the beginning of the war, is now (in June, 1916) ' contained,' and doubtless will remain so."

He believed that there was nothing to prevent the British from concentrating by " very simple manœuvres," assembling their entire fighting force, and then with nine battle-cruisers, four fast battleships, and the entire strength of Admiral Jellicoe's Grand Fleet striking **An American critic's opinion** at the enemy. And he argued : " Considering the great superiority of the British both in numbers and power, one of two things must have happened : (1) Either the German Main Fleet would have been decisively defeated, or (2) it would have declined decisive action by retiring behind its defences, and even the latter (course) would have inflicted upon the Germans a humiliation impossible to conceal, much less to claim as a victory for the encouragement of their people. The latter (forcing the Germans to retreat before a concentrated superior force) could have been accomplished with little or no material loss, and if the Germans had elected to fight a decisive action there could be no doubt that both their proportionate and actual losses would have been vastly greater than the British. Also, in either case, the various types of vessels, including battle-cruisers,

would have been employed to the best advantage in the legitimate rôle for which they were designed."

Such criticism, coming as it does from a capable and thoughtful student of war, can only be answered when the full facts can be disclosed as to the plans of both sides. If, as has been reported, the German Staff had intended to employ the German Fleet during the summer in co-operating with Marshal Hindenburg for the reduction of Riga and an attack on Petrograd, the battle may have had far greater results than appear on the surface. Without naval aid Hindenburg could not expect to accomplish much—and, in fact, he did nothing. It may or may not be a mere coincidence that the great Russian offensive on the Austrian front, which was crowned with so wonderful success, began immediately after the battle. In any case the fact that most of the formidable ships in the German Navy were out of action—at all events for the time being— must have left the Russian commanders perfectly secure as to any menace against their northern and most vulnerable flank.

No unprejudiced person was likely to accept the German claims of a German victory. These were answered by the continuance of the blockade with undiminished vigour and by a curious fact which the German Staff was so simple as to report—that a weak British squadron of old ships during the afternoon of June 1st, when Admiral Jellicoe had vanished, cruised in the waters of Heligoland Bight. If the German Fleet had been victorious, here was an opportunity for it to strike a tremendous blow and annihilate the British force. The old battleships were not molested. They steamed to and fro, according to the German account, for some hours, and then they, too, vanished to their distant bases across the North Sea.

Something has already been said of the superb spirit of the British Fleet and the extraordinary efficiency shown by officers and men. **Our Fleet's efficiency** The tribute which Admiral Sir John Jellicoe, no mean judge, paid to those under his command will ever remain on record, a monument to the valour of the Grand Fleet :

The conduct of officers and men throughout the day and night actions was entirely beyond praise. No words of mine could do them justice. On all sides it is reported to me that the glorious traditions of the past were most worthily upheld. . . . Officers and men were cool, determined, with a cheeriness that would have carried them through anything. The heroism of the wounded was the admiration of all. I cannot adequately express the pride with which the spirit of the fleet filled me.

Sir David Beatty, one of the most gallant men who ever went to war, was just as emphatic in his testimony :

As was to be expected, the behaviour of the ships' companies under the terrible conditions of a modern sea battle was magnificent without exception. The strain on their moral was a severe test of discipline and training. Officers and men were imbued with one thought—the desire to defeat the enemy.

Every branch surpassed itself, every arm covered itself with glory. The engine-room department did magnificent work and maintained amazing speeds ; it showed, said Admiral Beatty, " the highest qualities of technical skill, discipline, and endurance." " Failures in material," said Admiral Jellicoe, " were conspicuous by their absence." Under the enemy's fire the control and drill of the British guns proceeded as though the German ships had been firing blank, and as though men were not falling and showers of deadly splinters flying at each successful German salvo. The medical department displayed special resourcefulness and devotion, while the chaplains, one and all, proved themselves heroes. One of the finest deeds of that day was that of the Rev. Anthony Pollen, in the 5th Battle Squadron, who plunged into a cordite fire which was burning with fearful violence to the rescue of two boys. He brought them out alive but himself was terribly burned. For this he received the Distinguished Service Cross.

Some days after the battle the Germans revealed the fact that they had rescued a certain number of men from the lost British ships, and paraded it as fresh evidence of

CAPT. HON. H. MEADE, D.S.O.

CAPT. J. M. CASE-MENT.

CAPT. H. B. PELLY, C.B., M.V.O.

CAPT. F. L. FIELD, C.B.

CAPT. M. WOOLLCOMBE, C.B.

CAPT. L. C. S. WOOLL-COMBE, M.V.O.

CAPT. PERCY ROYDS.

CAPT. R. W. BENTINCK, C.B.

CAPT. A. C. S. H. D'AETH, C.B.

CAPT. A. CHATFIELD.

CAPT. A. C. SCOTT.

CAPT. V. H. G. BERNARD.

CAPT. H. M. DOUGHTY.

CAPT. F. C. DREYER.

CAPT. A. W. CRAIG.

CAPT. C. D. ROPER.

CAPTAINS HONOURED AND COMMENDED FOR SERVICE IN THE JUTLAND BATTLE.

(Photos by Heath, Lafayette, and Russell & Son.)

their victory. The survivors were as follows: Queen Mary, one officer, two men; Indefatigable, two men; Tipperary, seven men; Nomad, four officers, sixty-eight men; Nestor, two officers, seventy-seven men; Turbulent, fourteen men. The first four ships were sunk shortly before the time when Admiral Beatty turned and retired before the Germans. The enemy's vessels would pass over the waters in which they had gone down, and the Germans would then naturally—if they showed any spark of humanity—rescue the men in the water. The Tipperary was sunk during the night attack in the midst of a great mass of German ships, so that there again there would be no difficulty in rescuing men from her. The rescue of men from the Turbulent is more curious, because the Germans were then in flight and the Turbulent was close to other British ships. No light on this matter is shed in any of the British or German reports. It is possible that the fourteen men were picked up by the four German destroyers which were seen late in the night steaming across the rear of the British line.

The battle has been compared with that of Quiberon Bay, when Hawke defeated Conflans in 1759. This comparison is not sound, for Conflans was seen no more at sea, whereas within three months of the Battle of Jutland, on August 19th, the German Fleet was

Germans rescue British sailors

out in a strength variously estimated by neutral captains at forty or sixty ships, of which at least twenty were Dreadnoughts, though, it is true, they manifested no eagerness to fight. Conflans' fleet, however, was of very different quality from Admiral von Scheer's. Under the basest of the Bourbons, Louis XV., the French Navy had lost its force and fire.

The Admiralty Board, in a despatch to Admiral Jellicoe some weeks after the battle, made some effort to undo the mischief caused by the timorous and half-hearted early reports. It declared that "the ships of every class were handled with skill and determination; their steaming under battle conditions afforded a splendid testimony to the zeal and efficiency of the engineering staff; while individual initiative and tactical subordination were equally conspicuous. The expectations of the country were high; they have been well fulfilled. My Lords desire . . . . to convey to you their full approval of your proceedings on this occasion."

There was a touch of unconscious humour in this last sentence, coming from a Board on which civilians—who knew nothing whatever of naval war—were so numerous.

No extravagant haste was shown in bestowing honours for the battle, and not until September 15th was the "London Gazette" published with the list of distinctions and promotions awarded. Sir John Jellicoe received the Order of Merit and Sir David Beatty the Grand Cross of the Bath. On the two admirals who had died so gloriously at the post of duty, Rear-Admiral Sir Robert Arbuthnot and Rear-Admiral Hood, posthumous K.C.B.'s were bestowed. Besides Boy Cornwell, to whom, as has already been stated, the Victoria Cross was granted posthumously, the same honour was given to Major Francis John William Harvey, R.M., who by an immortal deed, himself mortally wounded in a stricken turret, before he died ordered the magazine to be flooded and thus saved his ship. No man rendered nobler service on that great day; no name should be held by a grateful country in more affectionate remembrance. A third Victoria Cross was granted to Commander Bingham, who fortunately survived, though a prisoner, after leading the wildest and fiercest torpedo attack in history. No summary can do justice to the innumerable gallant deeds enshrined in that issue of the "Gazette"; it is a long record of heroism that transcends human praise and gratitude.

The Honours List

APPENDIX : THE COMPOSITION OF THE OPPOSING SQUADRONS.

The most probable composition of Admiral Hipper's Battle-Cruiser Squadron was :

	GUNS.	TONS.
Lützow	Eight 12 in., fourteen 6 in.	28,000
Derfflinger	Eight 12 in., fourteen 6 in.	28,000
Seydlitz	Ten 11 in., twelve 6 in.	24,600
Moltke	Eleven 11 in., twelve 6 in.	22,600
Von der Tann ..	Eight 11 in., ten 6 in.	18,700
or Salamis ..	Eight 14 in., twelve 6 in.	19,200

The highest speed would have been about twenty-five or twenty-six knots as a fleet.

The German Battle Fleet under Admiral von Scheer appears to have been composed somewhat as follows :

Grosser Kurfürst
Markgraf
König
} Each ten 12 in. (or 14 in.) guns, and fourteen 6 in. 26,500 tons. Twenty-three knots.

Kaiser
Friedrich der Grosse
Kaiserin
König Albert
Pr. Luitpold
} Each ten 12 in. and fourteen 6 in. guns. 24,300 tons. Twenty-one knots.

Helgoland
Thüringen
Ostfriesland
Oldenburg
} Each twelve 12 in. and fourteen 6 in. guns. 22,500 tons. Twenty-two knots.

Nassau
Westfalen
Rheinland
Posen
} Each twelve 11 in. and twelve 6 in. guns. 18,600 tons. Twenty and a half knots.

Deutschland
Pommern
Hannover
Schlesien
Schleswig-Holstein
Lothringen
} Pre-Dreadnoughts. Each four 11 in. and fourteen 6·7 in. guns. 13,000 tons. Eighteen and a half knots.

All the above ships have two funnels, except the six pre-Dreadnoughts and the four ships of the Helgoland class, which have three.

The British Fleet, so far as its force may be disclosed, was composed thus:

VICE-ADMIRAL SIR D. BEATTY'S BATTLE-CRUISERS.

	GUNS.	TONS.
Lion	Eight 13·5 in., sixteen 4 in.	26,000
Princess Royal	Eight 13·5 in., sixteen 4 in.	26,000
Queen Mary	Eight 13·5 in., sixteen 4 in.	27,000
Tiger	Eight 13·5 in., twelve 6 in.	28,000
Indefatigable	Eight 12 in., sixteen 4 in.	18,750
New Zealand	Eight 12 in., sixteen 4 in.	19,000

The highest speed as a fleet would be slightly in excess of twenty-six knots.

REAR-ADMIRAL HOOD'S 3RD BATTLE-CRUISER SQUADRON.

Invincible
Inflexible
Indomitable
} Each eight 12 in. and sixteen 4 in. guns. 17,600 tons. Twenty-five knots.

REAR-ADMIRAL EVAN-THOMAS'S 5TH BATTLE SQUADRON.

Barham
Valiant
Warspite
Another
} Each eight 15 in. and twelve 6 in. guns. 27,500 tons. Twenty-five knots.

CRUISER SQUADRONS.

1st.—Rear-Admiral Sir R. K. Arbuthnot.
2nd.—Rear-Admiral H. L. Heath.

LIGHT CRUISER SQUADRONS.

1st.—Commodore E. S. Alexander-Sinclair.
2nd.—Commodore W. E. Goodenough.
3rd.—Rear-Admiral T. D. W. Napier.
4th.—Commodore C. E. Le Mesurier.

The battle squadrons mentioned as present with Admiral Sir J. Jellicoe, the Commander-in-Chief, whose flag was hoisted in the Iron Duke, placed in the 4th Squadron, were :
1st.—Vice-Admiral Sir C. Burney.
2nd.—Vice-Admiral Sir M. Jerram.
4th.—Vice-Admiral Sir D. Sturdee.

The destroyer flotillas mentioned as present were :
1st.   11th.
4th.   12th.
9th.   13th.
10th.

First=Class Boy John Travers Cornwell, V.C., H.M.S. Chester.

Serbian cavalry equipped as infantry marching past at Salonika.

Italian troops on their way to camp after landing at Salonika.

General Sarrail inspecting Russian troops upon their landing at Salonika.

British military band playing the Russians ashore at Salonika.

Opening of the Allies' offensive in the Balkans: Russians advancing to the fighting-line from Salonika.

CHAPTER CXLV.

THE SALONIKA EXPEDITION AND THE INTERVENTION OF RUMANIA.

By Robert Machray.

Deceptive Beauty of Salonika—Geographical Importance of the City—How the Allies Went There in October, 1915—Inception of the Expedition—The Greek Invitation—Strength of the Forces of the Allies—Enemy Attack Fails to Materialise—Salonika Made Into a Great Entrenched Camp—Significant Precautions Taken—Islands Occupied Against the Submarine Menace—The Allies Move North Towards the Frontier—Marvellous Reconstitution of the Serbian Army—Problem of Transferring the Serbs to Salonika Solved—Unfriendly Action of Greece—Sinister Influences at Work—Small Beginnings of the Campaign—General Milne Succeeds General Mahon—Greece Surrenders Fort Rupel to the Bulgars—Indignation of the Majority of the Greeks—Venizelos Thunders—Action of the Allies—Pacific Blockade—Greece Yields—Advance of the Serbians—Entente Reinforcements—Vast Change in World-War—Bulgar Offensive—British Take Horse-shoe Hill—Serbs Lose Florina and Retire to Lake Ostrovo—Bulgar Advance Checked—Strange Doings of the Greek Government—Greek Macedonia Surrendered to Bulgars—Rage of the Pro-Ally Greeks—Christodoulos Makes a Stand—Revolution in Salonika—Fresh Action by the Allies—German Espionage Crushed—The New Factor in the War—Rumania Takes the Field—Her Reasons—The Oppressed Rumanians in Hungary—The Balkan Imbroglio—The Russian Victories—Rumania Strikes Hard—Invasion of Transylvania—Check in the Dobrudja—Greece Still Hesitating.

IN previous chapters we have explained something of the intrigues and counter-intrigues that have made the Balkan question the most difficult and complicated of all the international matters with which diplomacy and statesmanship have ever had to cope ; and the story has been told of the military events which resulted in the overrunning of Serbia by the Bulgarian hordes and the occupation of Montenegro by the Austrians. Now we come to deal with the inception and development of what is known as the Salonika Expedition, and the intervention of Rumania in the war on the side of the Allies.

Viewed from a ship out at sea, or from an aeroplane in mid-heaven, Salonika appeared a picturesque and even a romantic-looking city. With its white houses, domes, minarets, and battlemented walls, set off by the foliage of elm, cypress, and mulberry trees, it gradually rose from the shore, at the top of the bay of the same name, to the heights on which stood the Heptapygrion, or Castle of the Seven Towers,

and seemed to present a fascinating and beautiful spectacle. But never was there a better instance of the truth of the words that " distance lends enchantment." Apart from its ancient and splendid Byzantine churches and a few modern buildings of some size, the place as a whole was dirty, squalid, and mean, and as offensively odoriferous as any town in all the Orient. Like shabby neighbours, the old and the new jostled each other in its architecture, and made a medley of the people in its streets ; not, however, without contrasting notes of colour to intrigue the eye and give an interest to the scene.

For many centuries Salonika had been a city of great importance, coming next in fame only to Constantinople and Athens in the Near East. Founded several hundred years before the Christian era, it had seen many of the strange and stormy fluctuations incidental to such a lapse of time. Macedonians, Romans, Berbers, Normans, and Venetians had ruled over it. In more recent days the Turks had held it, and from it had sprung the Young Turk movement, which, though promising well at first, was

LEADERS IN THE LEVANT.

General Mahon, who commanded the 10th Division at Salonika (centre), with Lieut.-Colonel Cunliffe Owen, of the General Staff (on the left). In May, 1916, General Mahon was transferred to a command in Egypt.

GATHERING THEIR STORIES.
Serbian Staff officers explaining the fighting to British official correspondents.

way to Gevgeli and the southern Serbian front, to initiate what soon took on the aspect of being one of the most desperate enterprises of the whole war, but which in the long result turned out to be one of the best moves of the Allies.

At that time the British Government had not yet reached its decision that the allied troops should evacuate Gallipoli, though the subject was being considered seriously, for it had become perfectly certain that no success of high value could be anticipated any longer in the Dardanelles. Nor had it made up its mind what was to be done at or from Salonika. Misled by its false idea that Bulgaria was pro-Entente, it

destined to lead the Ottoman Empire to ruin. The Balkan Wars left it in possession of the Greeks, and one of the grimmest touches in its history was supplied by the murder in its streets of the Greek king under whom it had passed into their hands.

The reason why so many races fought for it lay in the special significance of its geographical position; it was the key of the Levant, as was explained in Chapter XCIX. A sure commercial instinct led the Sephardim Jews to settle there when, in the sixteenth century, they fled from Spain to escape religious persecution in that country. Under the Turks, these Jews and their descendants made Salonika a great and flourishing port, and it was they who did by far the most of its business, and were the most numerous element in its population at the outbreak of the war.

With October, 1915, there opened a fresh page in the long story of the vicissitudes of Salonika. On the first day of that month three or four British and French officers arrived in the city, and immediately conferred with the Greek

Conference with Greek officials

functionaries in charge of the port. And on the fifth day the bay was alive with a huge fleet of warships and transports of the Allies, from which, from eight o'clock in the morning, French and British troops disembarked. First came the 2nd French Division, brought in British vessels from Cape Helles in Gallipoli, and another French division from elsewhere, and then the 10th British Division from Suvla, also in Gallipoli, under Sir Bryan Mahon. This was the beginning of the Salonika Expedition, and crowds of wondering Greeks, Turks, Jews, and other nationals looked on and greeted the soldiers of the Entente Powers according to their varied predilections. A week later both General Sarrail, in command of the French, and General Mahon, in command of the British, were in Salonika. On October 17th about 14,000 French troops were on their

THE ENTENTE IN THE LAND OF DISCORD.
Group of allied officers, showing (in the foreground) General Howell conversing with General Gérome, of the French Army, on the Salonika front.

apparently failed to realise the vast strategic importance of Serbia, or that Salonika might very well be of hardly less cardinal significance in certain circumstances. Yet as far back as March or April, 1915, M. Briand, then not in power but afterwards, in the same year, Prime Minister of France, had urged that Salonika should be occupied by the Allies. On the British side the most distinguished advocate of this view, though that was months later, was Mr. Lloyd George. The fact of the matter would seem to be that from the beginning of the Dardanelles operations the British Government for a considerable period was completely obsessed by them, and that the Salonika Expedition, with its ultimate success, partook of the nature of a gigantic "fluke."

While the Entente Powers were still engaged in their negotiations with Bulgaria, they offered to her, about September 15th, a liberal readjustment of Balkan territory which, it was supposed, would satisfy her and bring her to the side of the Allies. As was shown in Chapter LXXXIV., Bulgaria was committed to Germany long before that date, but ignorant of this, the Entente went so far as to suggest —as a guarantee to her that she would really obtain that coveted territory after the war was over—that the Valley of the Vardar, in Macedonia, should meanwhile be occupied by troops of the Allies. These negotiations proved abortive, but in the suggestion was, perhaps, the first hint of the Salonika Expedition.

Then came the Bulgarian mobilisation, followed forthwith by that of Greece. Previous to the latter, M. Venizelos, then Prime Minister of Greece, had asked the French and British Governments, on the ground that Bulgaria had announced a policy of "armed neutrality," to despatch a force of 150,000 men to Salonika. The widespread belief among the Allies that Greece fully intended at this time to fulfil her treaty obligations to Serbia was greatly encouraged by a speech made by M. Venizelos in the Greek Parliament on September 29th, in which he said that the Greek nation was ready to resist every attempt on the part of any of the Balkan States to establish a predominance in the Balkans that would mean the end of the independence of the other States. But the Greek General Staff, backed by the pro-German elements in Greece, violently objected to the landing of the allied troops. In spite, however, of this opposition, M. Venizelos, under cover of a formal protest, gave in reality the sanction of the Greek Government to the expedition on October 2nd, and two days later, in the Greek Chamber, said that his country would " not take material measures to prevent the passage of Franco-British armies which were hastening to **Origin of the** the assistance of the Serbians, the allies **expedition** of Greece, who were threatened by the Bulgarians."

Such, then, was the origin of the Salonika Expedition. The same day which witnessed the beginning of the landing of the Allies at the port also saw the fall of M. Venizelos from power, owing to King Constantine's refusal to endorse his policy. Speaking in the House of Commons on April 18th, 1916, Viscount (then Sir Edward) Grey, in reply to a question whether any protest had been made by the Greek Government in connection with the recent occupation of Greek territory by the Allies, said that certain protests had been received from the Hellenic Government to the measures which the Entente Powers had been obliged to take in Greece or in Greek territorial waters. He added that the circumstances which had rendered these measures necessary were that the French and British Governments in the beginning decided to send troops to Salonika on the invitation of the then Greek Prime Minister, and though shortly afterwards there was a change of Government in Greece, accompanied by a **Change of Greek** change in her policy, the Allies could not **policy** then recede from the undertaking to which they had committed themselves. M. Venizelos had a majority in the Greek Parliament, and all the subsequent troubles of Greece arose from the determination of King Constantine to maintain what he called neutrality, in defiance of the Greek Constitution which placed him under it, and in disregard of the wishes of the great bulk of his people.

Instead of the 150,000 men for whom M. Venizelos had asked, only some 40,000 men were disembarked by the Allies in the first and second weeks of October, 1915. Of these two-thirds were French, the remainder being British. As late as October 26th, when Lord Lansdowne made an extremely discouraging statement on the matter in the House of Lords, the strength of the British force was no more than 13,000 men ; though a larger force was held in reserve. A third French and a second British division arrived in November. Large contingents coming in December and on into January brought up the total of the British in this area to five divisions. Even adding the three French divisions, the number which M. Venizelos had required was scarcely reached by the beginning of 1916. At no time prior to the Franco-British retreat from Serbia into Greece, of which an account was given in Chapter XCIX., would the combined force in the battle-line appear to have numbered much above 40,000 men, as against certainly quite five times that number of Bulgarians

GENERAL STAFF OF THE BRITISH ARMY ON ITS WAY TO FRENCH HEADQUARTERS AT SALONIKA.

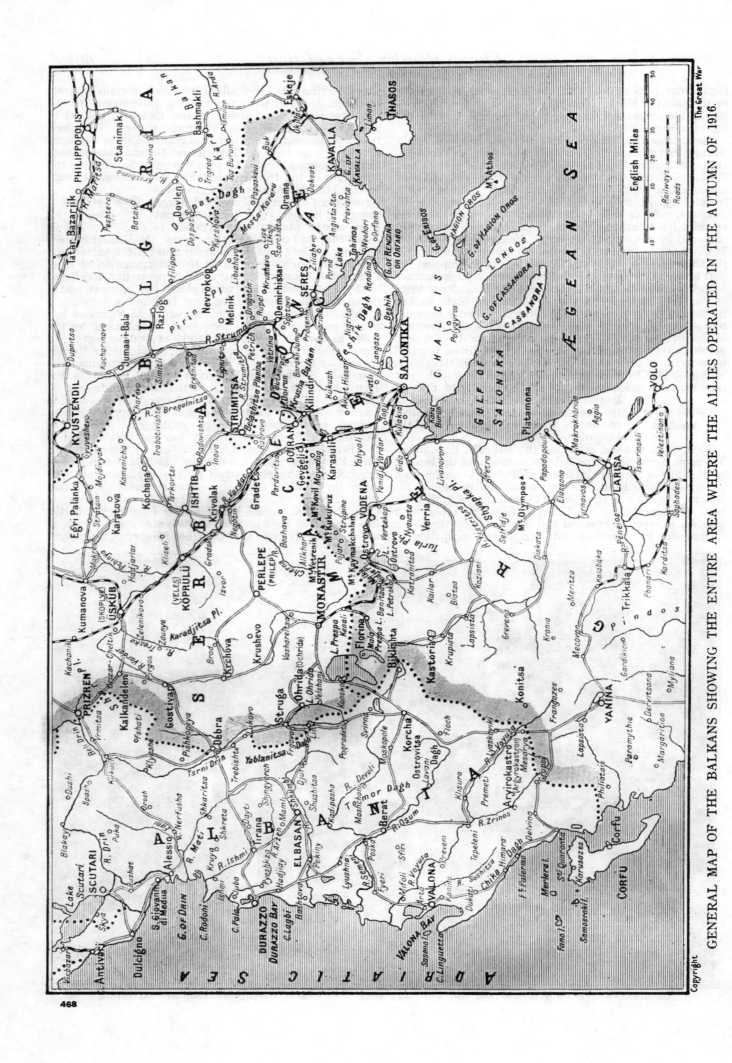

GENERAL MAP OF THE BALKANS SHOWING THE ENTIRE AREA WHERE THE ALLIES OPERATED IN THE AUTUMN OF 1916.

Copyright   The Great War

On April 10th, 1916, the British War Office issued a despatch, dated March 6th, from General Sir Charles Monro, covering the period from October 28th, 1915, to January 9th, 1916, during which that general was in command of the Eastern Mediterranean. In this General Monro furnished particulars of the Salonika Army, which was the official title accorded to the combined French and British troops in the district, related the circumstances that made necessary the retirement from Serbia, and mentioned the fact that the troops thus withdrawn were used as a protecting screen on positions forming a strong defensive line while the new British divisions were being disembarked at Salonika. This defensive line was about thirty miles from the port, and stretched from Karasuli, on the Vardar and the Salonika–Nish railway, to Kilindir, on the Salonika–Constantinople railway.

In the meantime the operation of disembarking was being carried out with all possible speed, which, however, was not very great. The Allies had been given the quay space reserved for Serbia, under an arrangement which had been agreed to between that country and Greece in May, 1914; and the accommodation thus provided was so limited that only about eight hundred tons of stores could be landed in a day. The organisation and resources of the allied Staffs on the spot were equal to the strain, and General Monro reported that it spoke highly for their capacity that they were able to shelter and feed the troops as they arrived. Further, in his despatch the general gave special prominence to the difficulties to which General Mahon had been exposed from the time of his landing at Salonika, and the ability that he displayed in overcoming them.

General Mahon's difficulties

At this time the impression among the Allies in general, and in Greece in particular, was that the Bulgarians, with German and Austrian supports, would press on across the Serbo-Greek frontier, attack the Franco-British force, march, if they could, to Salonika, and attempt to drive the soldiers of the Entente into the sea. It was in anticipation of this programme that the Karasuli–Kilindir line was selected and held. General Monro informed the Greek authorities, by Colonel Pallis, their representative from Athens, that it was the intention of the Allies to send up to this line the reinforcements which were being disembarked; and he stated in his despatch that this intimation was taken in good part by the Greek generals, who commenced to withdraw their troops farther to the east, where they did not hamper his plans, and that otherwise they showed a disposition to meet his demands in a reasonable and friendly spirit. Yet within a few weeks the British Fleet was compelled, by two significant demonstrations of its power, to bring the Greek Government and its master, the King, to their senses, and only then was full liberty of manœuvre accorded to the Allies within the region in which they were operating. King Constantine expressed his desire that the Allies should quit his country, and said that his Army would protect the re-embarkation of their troops; but by now the Entente Powers were wide awake to the genuinely great importance of Salonika, and resolved not to leave it.

TWO THOUSAND YEARS AFTER.
[French official photograph.
French machine-gunners athwart the remains of an old Roman bridge in the Macedonian marshes. French sailors are standing behind the gunners.

The fortification of the advanced defensive line and of Salonika itself was pushed forward by the Allies with feverish haste. For some weeks the impression persisted that the enemy, who, according to report, had handed over to Marshal Mackensen the chief command in this area, would advance in force across the border; but it was erroneous. Germany, having got control of the trunk railway through Serbia to Constantinople, seemed to be satisfied with this result of the campaign. She transferred most of her troops northward; and perhaps she was afraid of Russia, at this time massing large forces close to the Rumanian frontier, who accordingly had to be watched in that region. It may be that Greece intimated to her, as was alleged — though subsequent events hardly bore out the statement—that the Greek Army would fight the Bulgarians if they invaded Greek Macedonia, and therefore the Kaiser forbade a forward movement.

Whatever was the reason, the attack expected by the Allies did not materialise; and Teodoroff with his Bulgarians and Mackensen with his Austro-Germans remained on the north side of the boundary. In her arrogance Germany made a tremendous mistake, for if she had exerted her strength at once she probably would have been able to take Salonika. Her vainglorious overconfidence found ludicrous expression in the historic meeting at Nish on January 19th, 1916, of her Kaiser and the Bulgarian Tsar. The former greedily accepted the flattering phrases addressed to him in quaint Latin by the latter, which hailed him as Cæsar and *Imperator gloriosus*. But all the while there lay on their southern front the Salonika Army and its ever-growing menace.

Kaiser as Imperator gloriosus

It was to Salonika rather than the advanced defensive positions that the Allies turned their attention. Salonika had to be made secure, and their first effort was to see that enough territory was included within the fortified zone to prevent any enveloping movement on the flanks and keep hostile guns at a sufficient distance away. Nature, it might be said, had already come to their assistance. On the west of the city a swampy terrain extended to the Vardar, there a deep river, and the sea. On the north the

[Official photograph

MAN-POWER AND GUN-POWER.
Hauling a field-piece up a Macedonian incline. Officers and men are seen putting their shoulders to the wheel with truly workmanlike effect.

[Official photograph.

EXPERT OPINION.
General Zimbrakakis, of the Greek Army, admiring the quality of British ordnance at Salonika.

place was shut in by ranges of hills, with a valley to the east which contained Lake Langaza and Lake Beshik, and on the south sloped down to the Gulf of Redena (or Orfano). From this gulf to the mouth of the Vardar the whole allied line was about sixty miles long, and it took in a hinterland in the shape of the fork-like peninsula of Chalcis, the entire area forming a large and powerful sea base. While the fear of attack was still strong, trenches and other works were rapidly constructed and developed, numerous Serbian and other refugees adding their labour to those of the soldiers; and heavy guns, many of them naval, were emplaced at selected points. The French held the line on the west along the Vardar and on the north to the track of the Salonika–Constantinople **General Castelnau's** railway, whence the British carried it on **arrival** through the hills to the lakes, and past them southward to the sea.

Favoured by fine weather, the fortifying of Salonika was nearly completed by the end of December. On the 20th of that month the city had an unexpected visitor in the person of General Castelnau, who, only a fortnight before, had been promoted by General Joffre to be the Chief of the French General Staff, and whose opinion therefore carried great weight. Both in Paris and London deep anxiety was felt regarding the fate of Salonika and the Salonika Army, and Castelnau had come to see how matters really stood. After long conferences with General Sarrail and General Mahon, he made a full inspection of the place during the next few days, and pronounced him-

self thoroughly satisfied with what he saw. He told the two commanders that he approved of the dispositions they had made, and also of the general plan of defence. He wired to the French Government that he considered that the Salonika Army was perfectly safe, and doubtless the news was communicated to the British Government. On the other hand, the German Press boastfully announced that Salonika would be taken from the Allies by January 15th; but this prediction, like many another from the same source, was falsified. General Castelnau, after paying a call on King Constantine at Athens, quietly and confidently returned to headquarters in France.

No precaution was neglected by the Allies at Salonika. They had to provide against the attacks of enemy submarines in Greek territorial waters near the port, and take measures with regard to the hardly less dangerous activities of the spies with which the town, like all Greece, was infested. How the enemy con- **Precautions against** suls and vice-consuls—German, Austrian, **espionage** Turkish, and Bulgarian—were rounded up and sent off on a warship was recorded in Chapter XCIX. These men were the centre of the spy-system, and a great many other spies were got rid of at the same time. The submarine problem was tackled with determination and success. Early in the morning of January 28th an allied naval squadron appeared before the fortress of Kara Burun, fifteen miles south of Salonika, on the east side of the bay, and landed French troops, who quickly took possession of the place. By the evening it was held by detachments of British and French soldiers, as well as by landing-parties from British, French, Russian, and Italian ships—the presence of nationals drawn from every member of the Quadruple Alliance thus demonstrating the solidarity of the Allies. General Moschopoulos, the commander of the Greek forces in Salonika, had been apprised of the intended occupation, and his troops promptly evacuated the fortress a few minutes before those of the Entente appeared. This military measure the Allies justified on the ground that some day; previously a German submarine had torpedoed a British transport in the channel giving access to the port; they stated that it was impossible any longer to allow hostile submarines to navigate with impunity within range of the Kara Burun batteries. The Greek Government made the customary protest.

The same reason governed the action of the Allies in the case of the island of Mitylene, whence they removed the German, Austrian, and Turkish consular officials at the beginning of January. A British contingent was landed in the island of Chios, lying west of the Gulf of Smyrna, and arrested the German and Austrian consuls in mid-February. A week earlier a French detachment occupied Othoni (or Fano), an island about a dozen miles north-west of Corfu, to which the Serbian troops were being transferred. Here again the submarine peril had to be faced and overcome.

The same cause in April led the British **French occupation** and French Ministers at Athens to inform **of Thasos** the Greek Prime Minister that a naval observation station at Argostoli Bay, Cephalonia, an island of the Ionian group, was urgently necessary, and that this would be established but that there would be no disembarkation of troops, and the island would not be occupied. Once more the Greek Government protested against a "violation of the neutrality and sovereignty of Greece." In June French soldiers took possession of the considerable island of Thasos, close to the port of Kavalla, and held it as an anti-submarine base. Greece did nothing to put down the submarine menace, either in the Ægean or in the Adriatic, and the Allies had to take it in hand themselves.

January of 1916 passed over Salonika without the appearance of the much-advertised offensive of the enemy,

though Mackensen was said to be holding inspections as near as Monastir, and getting ready. There were air-raids by both sides, but of no particular importance. On February 1st a Zeppelin bombarded the city, and killed or wounded many Greeks, including some soldiers. In the course of that month the French raided with aeroplanes Bulgarian camps at Strumitza and other places with considerable effect. Five days after the Zeppelin raid the first encounter with the troops of the enemy since the Allies had crossed the border was reported near Lake Doiran, but it was a trifling outpost affair, and that month also went by without a sign of the expected offensive. On the contrary, there were intimations that the Allies, and not the enemy, might attack, particularly as large reinforcements were constantly arriving.

[*Official photographs.*]

REPAIRING A BROKEN GUN AT A FIELD WORKSHOP NEAR THE SALONIKA BASE.
A remarkable feat of rapid gun-repairing was recorded from Salonika. A faulty fuse caused the shell to explode in the mouth of a field-gun. All the crew escaped injury, and, bracing the weapon to a tree, they pulled out the broken inner tube and replaced it. The smaller illustration was secured as the gun was being chained to the tree.

MARTIAL TOWN-PLANNING IN MACEDONIA: BUILDING A SANDBAG VILLA SOMEWHERE AMID THE BALKAN HILLS.

A Bulgarian communiqué, issued two months afterwards, noted that in March the Franco-British forces moved out from the entrenched camp of Salonika and approached the Bulgarian frontier. It went on to say that the principal Franco-British forces were disposed in the Vardar Valley, and extended eastward to the Struma Valley, and westward to Florina. Sarrail, indeed, had been making reconnaissances from Salonika as early as the second week of February, and about that time occupied the terrain on the west side of the Vardar to a depth of six miles, to ensure the city from any assault from the direction of Monastir. On March 16th a French detachment took possession of some Greek villages close to the frontier in the Gevgeli-Doiran sector, which had been roughly handled by Bulgarians, and an exchange of artillery fire occurred near Machukovo, on the boundary. The Allies had moved north.

Salonika was passing through a period of change, according to a telegram from Mr. G. Ward Price, the official correspondent at the British Headquarters, which were in the city. He mentioned that the Castle of the Seven Towers was being modernised, as its battlements were being used as a signal station by British sailors, who also had built a hen-run on the top, and laid out a flower-garden with earth carried up bucketful by bucketful. They had even installed a bath there, and " where tortured prisoners groaned the British bluejacket now nonchalantly took his tub." Electric light and water had been laid on inside the grim old castle, on the second story of which another British institution had been brought into existence—a museum of the archæological remains in which Salonika and the country round about were rich. The Allies had decided to take steps to preserve the relics that they discovered for the benefit of the Greek Government, to whom such treasure-trove naturally belonged, and they found a curator for this museum in a well-known English professor of archæology, who was serving as a lieutenant of the Royal Naval Volunteer Reserve with the British forces in Salonika. The Allies did an even greater amount of good to the place by attending to the sanitation of the city and its neighbourhood, and in making roads throughout the district that were something like roads, and not merely successions of dirty mud-holes, with rough, slippery stones in between, and the peasants thereafter got to market with their produce in such comfort as they had never dreamed could exist in the world.

Handy-men at work

Towards the end of March, Alexander, Crown Prince and Regent of Serbia, arrived in London, where he was warmly welcomed. He had previously spent a few days in Paris, where also he had been exceedingly well received. He had gone through the terrible retreat, and the story of the sufferings of the Serbians had endeared him to the peoples of the Allies. With him was M. Pasich, the veteran Prime Minister of Serbia. The courage and hope of neither were abated. They had dark tales to tell of the dreadful excesses perpetrated on their unhappy country by its cruel Bulgarian and Austrian conquerors; but they also declared that the Serbian Army, which was recruiting its strength and refitting in Corfu, was burning to avenge the wrongs of Serbia, and soon would be in a position to add reinforcements to the Salonika Army. They spoke of a contribution to the common cause of 130,000 men, practically all of whom were combatants. It was a considerable survival from the wreck of the Serbian armies, and no such survival, probably no survival at all, would have been possible but for the co-operation of the British, the French, and the Italians. Food was supplied jointly by the British and the French, while the Italians provided the greater part of the shipping which conveyed the Serbians to Corfu.

Serbia's fighting remnant

But without exaggeration it could be said that the Serbian Army would have perished if the British Adriatic

Mission, at the head of which was General F. P. S. Taylor, C.M.G., had not saved it, with the help of the French Mission, and that these Missions would have worked in vain without the generous and ungrudging assistance of Italy. At Durazzo, on the Voyusa River, and at Valona British and Italians worked together. The latter did a very fine thing for the starving Serbians on the Voyusa. No ordinary means of transport being available, the pick of the Italian forces carried boots and food from Valona to the river on their backs for the helpless, worn-out, and famished Serbian soldiers. In bringing the Serbians from the eastern shore of the Adriatic Italy employed two hundred and fifty

FRENCH OUTPOST ON THE ALERT.
A symbolical impression. Sturdy and alert, a French sentry is seen looking out for Bulgars or Austro-Germans.

RARE FIGHTERS IN A RUGGED ENVIRONMENT.
Scottish sentries on the watch for the enemy from behind rocks on the Macedonian front. The allied army at Salonika was the most heterogeneous host ever gathered together for one ideal.

steamers, under the escort of units of her Fleet and of warships of the other Allies, and in spite of attacks by enemy aeroplanes, torpedo-boats, and submarines did not lose a single Serbian soldier at sea, an altogether remarkable achievement, for which she scarcely got sufficient credit at the time.

There had long been a certain amount of friction between Italy and Serbia with respect to the coast of the Adriatic on the east, and the splendid services that Italy rendered the Serbian Army naturally led to a better understanding between them. While in Rome during March M. Pasich called on Admiral Corsi to thank the Italian Fleet for having evacuated the Serbian Army from Durazzo, and in a published interview, while in London, he recognised the legitimacy of Italy's aspirations to supremacy in the Adriatic, not doubting that Serbia would be accorded her place on its shores. Germany had striven with characteristic, tortuous diplomacy to foster the view that the interests of Italy and Serbia in the Adriatic were quite irreconcilable. The distinguished Italian statesman, Signor Barzilai, speaking at Genoa on the topic, maintained that there was no need for their respective interests

to clash, and that to a sincere policy of reciprocation there was no obstacle which goodwill on both sides would not remove.

Having solved the problem of transporting the reconstituted Serbian Army to Corfu, the Allies next had to solve the further problem of conveying it to Salonika, a much more difficult undertaking, as the far longer passage by sea gave the enemy submarines more scope. There was a chance, however, of curtailing the voyage. It was thought that Greece might be willing to help the Serbians, still regarded by many Greeks as their allies, by permitting them to use her railways, a proceeding which would have materially reduced the risks from U boats by cutting off several hundred miles of the sea route. Accordingly, the Entente Powers proposed to the Greek Government that it should allow the Serbian troops to disembark at Patras, or some other port on the west side of Greece, on the railway which went on to Athens and thence to Salonika, the two cities having just been connected by the completion of the line to the latter. But the Greek Government declined on the now familiar plea of neutrality, and though the Entente Ministers at the Greek capital persevered for some time in pressing the suggestion, they withdrew it in the end. The whole Serbian Army from Corfu was sent all the way by sea to Salonika. The first detachment of it arrived there about the middle of April, and towards the end of July it was holding the left flank of the Allies, over against its old southern Macedonian frontier, and fighting the Bulgarians. While it lay in Salonika its perfect military fitness and the fine physique of its personnel attracted general admiration.

Serbians again in action

Greek neutrality from the start had been a very dubious thing, and it continued to bear the same character. If Greece—or, rather, the Greek Government—showed no

[*Official photograph.*
SNIPING FROM THE TRENCHES.
British officers at ease while the rank and
file do a little sniping.

disposition to help the Allies in the matter of the railway transportation of the Serbian Army, its neutrality in at least two other arguable questions appeared to take on a distinctly pro-German complexion. One of these, of which there was very little doubt, was that it was permitting, or at any rate conniving at, the use of some of the smaller Greek islands as bases for German submarines. The other was that which developed into what came to be known as the "Sacks Crisis." Of the two, the former was the more important, but the latter was extremely significant.

Sinister influences were unmistakably at work in Greece. The country, speaking generally, was divided into two parties, the Neutralists and the Ententists, and in effect the Neutralists were anti-Ententists. They were headed by M. Skouloudis, who had succeeded M. Zaimis as Prime Minister in the preceding year, and M. Gounaris, and behind them were the King and the openly pro-German propagandists. The other party was led by M. Venizelos, who, after once more

Greek Neutralists withdrawing himself from political life, had returned to it again, and ceaselessly **versus Ententists** maintained a pro-Entente campaign. The Greek Parliament met in February, but as the Venizelists had nearly all abstained from going to the polls at the last General Election because it was unconstitutional, the composition of the Chamber was Skouloudist. Later, M. Venizelos felt that a mistake had been made, and his party became active in politics in March and April, he himself in May being elected for Mitylene, where a vacancy had occurred.

In April huge commotion was caused in Athens by the disclosure of an alleged Greek breach of neutrality by the sale to Bulgaria by Greece of some 40,000 sacks which belonged to Russia and were stored at Salonika. A transaction of the sort had undoubtedly taken place in the preceding November, and the Entente Legations at

Athens took the matter up. At first the Greek Government denied all knowledge of the business, but could no longer persist in this attitude when the "Patris," the organ of the Venizelists, reproduced in facsimile the original typewritten copy of the telegram, which had been seized by the Allies at the Bulgarian Consulate at Salonika, and which revealed the complicity of the Government. The subject was ventilated in the Greek Parliament, and M. Skouloudis admitted that Bulgaria had asked for the sacks, but said that the request had been refused. The Russian Consul-General in Salonika replied to M. **Mystery of the sacks** Skouloudis that, on the demand of the Greek authorities, the sacks had been taken by Greek agents, and had disappeared from the place. Never thoroughly cleared up, the affair left a bad impression on the Allies in general and in particular on the Venizelists, who in the interests of the Entente were at this time holding a series of public meetings, which, however, were broken up by the Skouloudists, with the consequent intervention of the Government (Skouloudist) police, who arrested several of the Venizelists. Nevertheless, these meetings abundantly testified that M. Venizelos was as popular as ever with the bulk of his countrymen.

At the beginning of April the forces of the Allies daily were in touch with the enemy on the frontier, artillery duels and skirmishes between outposts occurring constantly. Many of the Greek villages in the vicinity were abandoned by their inhabitants, while other villages were plundered by Bulgarian comitajis, and there was some desultory fighting between them and Greek soldiers. The Allies made frequent air-raids on Bulgarian camps, and in the fourth week Salonika was again bombed by enemy aeroplanes. Heavy rains and snowstorms in the Balkans interfered with operations, yet on April 30th the British were engaged for the first time, but only in patrol encounters.

[*Official photograph.*
BOMBS AND RIFLES ON THE SALONIKA FRONT.
A lull in the fighting. Above: An officer lobbing Mills grenades.

FORT DE LA MACEDOINE, WHICH WAS OCCUPIED BY THE ALLIES.
Natural stronghold further consolidated with baskets of sand. The entrance to the fort is seen in the centre of the illustration.

On May 2nd a detachment of French troops suddenly appeared at Florina, twenty-three miles south of Monastir, arrested an Austrian consular official and some Turkish spies, and occupied the town. At three o'clock in the morning of May 5th a Zeppelin approached the harbour of Salonika, was picked out by the searchlights of the Allies, heavily fired on by the fleet, and hit by a naval shell. The airship dropped into a morass, and what of her had not been burned and destroyed was wrecked by the fall. Of her crew four officers and eight men survived and were captured, among them being her commander, who said that his object had been to bomb not the city but the warships in the bay. The situation on both banks of the Vardar underwent no change during May; but to the north of Lake Doiran the Allies took possession of Dova Tepe, close to the Bulgarian boundary, which before the month closed was to be the scene of great excitement. Along the whole front the organisation of the Franco-British line went on systematically.

An alteration in the British command was notified by the War Office on May 20th. General Mahon **New Salonika** was transferred to Egypt, where he **command** assumed command of its western frontier, and his place at Salonika was filled by General George Francis Milne, C.B., D.S.O., who had served with the Nile Expedition in 1898 and in South Africa. In the Boer War he was mentioned in despatches, and more recently he had also been mentioned twice in despatches for his services in France, where he had acted as Chief Staff Officer at the headquarters of the Second Army. He was one of the younger British generals, being forty-nine years old when he went to Salonika. General Mahon, who

had been very popular both with military men and civilians in Greece, left the city on May 19th, General Sarrail and other high officers, including Serbians and Greeks, bidding him a cordial good-bye at the landing-stage. As a correspondent wrote, the period Mahon had spent at the head of the British forces was one rather of hard work than of glory. In all the arduous and incessant labour which had converted Salonika into a vast and powerful entrenched camp, and of which **Honour to General** not a trace was in existence in the previous **Mahon** October, he had taken a great share, laying, in connection with General Sarrail, the sure foundations of future victory for the Entente in the Balkans.

In the last week of May the political—and to some extent the military—situation in Greece took a turn for the worse, which led the Allies to take a stronger line with the Government of the country. On the 26th a large force of Bulgarians, estimated at 25,000 men, accompanied by German officers and a few German troops, advanced from Petrich, appeared before Fort Rupel, and summoned its garrison to surrender, giving it two hours in which to clear out. Rupel was one of a chain of forts which the Greeks had established after the Second Balkan War to guard their Macedonian frontier from Bulgarian attack. It dominated the Struma Valley and the region of Demirhissar and Seres. About fifty-two miles north-east of Salonika, it lay on the most direct route to Sofia, the Bulgarian capital, and was of high strategical importance. Greece had spent half a million on its works, and it was well fortified. The commander of the garrison opened fire on the enemy, but after a few rounds held a parley under a white flag with a German officer, and shortly

475

after surrendered the fort to the invaders. He had received orders from the Greek Government to hand it over. That they were most distasteful to his men was shown by the fact that many of them wept as they marched out. Rumour asserted that two other forts of only little less military value, in the same locality, had also been relinquished to the Bulgarians, but this was not the case at the time. It was also said that the enemy was about to cross the River Mesta, which formed the boundary of Greece on the east, and that he had designs on Kavalla.

The great majority of the Greek people, who regarded Bulgaria as their determined and implacable hereditary enemy, expressed the utmost alarm and consternation. At first the Greek Government tried to influence popular feeling by representing that the surrender of Fort Rupel had not been made to Bulgaria but to Germany, who had given satisfactory assurances with respect to the preservation of the sovereign rights of Greece and the return of the place after the war, with compensation for any damage that might be incurred. But this was too flimsy a plea, and a storm of indignation and anger swept over the land. Especially was this the case among the population of Greek Macedonia, the threatened territory, who had the most painful recollection of the horrible excesses the Bulgarians had perpetrated in this district during the Balkan Wars, and now saw it passing into the hands of their savage foes once more. Many of them fled in panic. In Salonika there was a great demonstration against the surrender of the frontier to the Bulgarians ; ten thousand citizens marched in procession through the streets, carrying Greek flags at half-mast and hung with crape. Athens, controlled by the Government police, took the matter more quietly ; but the Venizelist Press, which came out with black mourning borders, was extremely outspoken, and asked why the Greek Army was mobilised if its mobilisation was used only for Rupel evacuations ? " Who could have imagined," said M.

[*Official photograph.*]

INFORMATION BY FLASH AND FLAG.
British signalling party in communication with Headquarters at Salonika.

Venizelos himself, " a Greek Army witnessing the Bulgarian flag replacing that of Greece ? " The Greek Government replied by justifying its action on the double ground that resistance would have been useless, and that to offer it would have been inconsistent with its policy of neutrality. It professed to be putting the Central Powers on an even footing with the Entente, but it made a formal protest to Germany and Bulgaria. An official communiqué from Berlin announced that German and Bulgarian forces occupied the important Rupel Pass, on the Struma, as a safeguard against an obviously-intended surprise by **Bulgarian invasion** the Entente troops. It added that " Our **of Greece** superiority obliged the weak Greek forces to give way ; and, for the rest, the sovereign rights of Greece were respected." By the end of May the enemy had advanced to Demirhissar, murdering and plundering as he marched southward, and it was plain that it was his intention to make for Kavalla.

The Allies could not view these proceedings with indifference ; and M. Briand, the French Prime Minister, declared that France, in conjunction with Great Britain, would begin energetic measures as a result of the Bulgarian invasion of Greek territory. On the morning of June 3rd Sarrail took the first step by proclaiming a state of siege

in the whole zone held by the Salonika Army, and occupied the principal Government offices in the city, including the post and telegraph offices, the wireless station, the police headquarters, and the water, gas, and electricity works, as well as the custom-house. He also demanded that certain Greek officers openly hostile to the Allies should be recalled from Salonika by the Greek Government.

But the Allies did a great deal more than that. On Tuesday, June 6th, they began a blockade of the whole Greek coast, an action similar to that taken in the previous November. The blockade was of the nature which is known as " pacific," but that it was sufficiently powerful **Blockade of Greek ports** was demonstrated by a semi-official Greek statement which said that " this virtual blockade of Greek ports threatened the starvation of the entire population of the kingdom and the ruin of Greek commerce." The Greek Government pretended that it was unable to understand why such a measure should be thought necessary ; but on June 8th it ordered a partial demobilisation of the Army, stating that this was done so that the presence of Greek troops should not interfere with the operations of the belligerents, and to reduce the financial pressure on the country, whose Budget showed a revenue of less than ten millions and an expenditure of over twenty millions.

Disgraceful demonstrations against the Entente occurred at Athens on June 12th, and an employee of the British Legation was attacked by the secret police. Threats against Great Britain and the other Allies were openly made by Government supporters. M. Skouloudis appeared to be resolved on resisting the blockade to the utmost, and the Allies were compelled, after relaxing it somewhat, to enforce it with much greater rigour than before. Meanwhile the Entente Ministers, who had been preparing a Note to Greece, revised it, and made its terms more drastic. They presented it to the Greek Government on June 21st, and the crisis was brought to an end forthwith by the resignation of the Skouloudis Cabinet and the appointment of M. Zaimis to the Prime Ministership, with his acceptance, in the name of King Constantine, of all the demands of the Allies.

In this Note, which was signed by the representatives of France, Great Britain, and Russia, the Protecting Powers of Greece, it was stated that Greece was not asked to emerge from her neutrality, though there were numerous and legitimate grounds for suspicion against the Greek Government, whose attitude towards the Allies had not been in conformity with its repeated engagements, nor even with the principles of a loyal neutrality. The Note accused the Greek Government of permitting the activities of certain foreigners hostile to the Entente. It pointed out that the entrance of Bulgarian forces into Greece and the occupation of Fort Rupel and other strategic points, with the connivance of the Greek Government, constituted for the allied troops a new threat, which imposed on the three Protecting Powers the obligation of taking immediate measures. It next alluded to the unconstitutional character of the existing Greek Government, and declared it was the right and the duty of the three Powers to see that this should be done away with.

ROUTE-MARCHING AMONG THE HILLS OVERLOOKING SALONIKA.

[*Official photograph.*]

Highland battalion on the march during manœuvres at Salonika. During the long interval between their occupation of Salonika and the opening of hostilities in August, 1916, our troops were kept in hard training for the arduous work before them.

The note said the Greek Government was hostile to the Entente, and it therefore demanded : First, the real and complete demobilisation of the Greek Army, and its return to a peace footing; second, a business Government that should be genuinely neutral; third, the dissolution of the Chamber, to be followed by a General Election; and fourth, the dismissal of certain officials who were responsible for assaults on peaceable citizens, and for insults levied at the Allied Legations and their members. It concluded by announcing that while the Protecting Powers continued to be friendly towards Greece, and were determined on the application of the indispensable measures without discussion or delay, they left to the Greek Government entire responsibility for what might happen if their just demands were not immediately accepted.

France, Great Britain, and Russia had been careful in this Note to differentiate between the Greek Government of M. Skouloudis and Greece as a whole, and this made a profound impression throughout the country. The Government Press was bitterly resentful of the Entente's interference with the internal affairs of Greece; but most Greeks were well pleased. In an interview M. Venizelos said the Note solved a situation from which there was no other issue. He spoke of the just severity of its tone, and the sincerity of its motives. The Protecting Powers, he maintained, had acted only like parents reclaiming a son's birthright. Henceforth Greece would be able to take up her life anew, and face the future with unbandaged eyes. M. Zaimis declared that everything would be straightened out with the Allies, and that he

M. Venizelos and
M. Skouloudis

would continue in the same path to the end. In all Greece there was no meeting called to protest ; the general feeling was one of relief when it was known that the crisis was over. More than once the tension had been very acute. M. Skouloudis had advised King Constantine to resist, and it was said that the King really thought of doing so but was dissuaded only at the last moment by Prince Nicholas and M. Zaimis. Had he declined to accept the demands of the Allies, there were plenty of Entente warships with troops not far from Athens, and they had instructions how to act. A German Mission, under a Major von Schweinitz, with promises that meant nothing less than an offer of military assistance, arrived in Athens a day too late to influence events. A decree ordering the general demobilisation of the Greek Army took effect on July 1st, but a fresh element in the situation appeared in the formation of " Reservists' Leagues," which were hostile to the Allies, and sought to make mischief.

German Mission
too late

During July Greece gradually became more tranquil, under the guidance of M. Zaimis, though he retained as members of his Cabinet several Ministers who were not exactly in sympathy with the Allies. The Franco-British Fleet, with considerable contingents of troops, still remained cruising near the Greek capital, reminding its unstable elements of the iron hand under the velvet glove. On the frontier heavy artillery duels continued, with apparently little result, and only on one part of it was there an advance, which was made by a Serbian division in the Moglena (or Karadjova) district, some twenty miles north of Vodena, west of the Vardar and south-east of Monastir. The Serbian force attacked the Bulgarians in this sector on July 24th, and on that day and the two following days carried the heights held by the enemy to the north of Serbiana, Kovil, and the slopes of Strupino. The Bulgarians counter-attacked on the 27th, but were repulsed with appreciable loss. The Serbians were only too happy to be fighting their old foes again, and their assaults were characterised by both dash and determination. As a result of this offensive the allied front was pushed forward in this region to within a few hundred yards of the boundary. On July 31st the Crown Prince Alexander landed at Salonika, and assumed the chief command of all the Serbian troops in the country.

At the beginning of August the front of the Allies stretched from Lake Prespa on the west to the Struma on the east, a distance of about two hundred miles. Reinforcements were still coming forward. Russian **Enter Russia and Italy** and Italian troops had landed at Salonika in some strength to join the British, the French, and the Serbians in the prosecution of the campaign. The first detachment of the Russians disembarked on July 30th, and that of the Italians arrived on August 10th. As the Russians came ashore they were greeted with the solemn benedictions of the Orthodox Greek clergy. The Italian Press commented on the appearance of their countrymen by the side of the soldiers of the other Allies in Greece as a special proof of the solidarity of the Entente Powers against Germany, upon whom Italy had not yet declared war. The spectacle of the unity of the Allies and their action in common, as demonstrated by this junction of the forces of five of the allied nations, to which presently was to be added an Albanian representation, headed later by their chieftain, Essad Pasha, could not but create a deep impression on the rulers and peoples of the Balkans. And this the more particularly because the aspect of the

entire war had recently undergone a tremendous change, and one that was wholly favourable to the Entente, owing to the success of Brussiloff's magnificent offensive on the Russian southern front in Europe and of the Franco-British offensive on the Somme. In Greece many regretful searchings of heart found expression because of the opportunities which the nation had lost for an alliance with the Entente Powers. But the Skouloudists—or Gounarists, as they were sometimes called from M. Gounaris, another anti-Ententist ex-Minister—remained impenitent.

British troops were in contact with the Bulgarians in the first week of August near Lake Doiran, and under cover of a dark, rainy night they rushed into the village of Doljeli, a short distance west of Doiran town, drove the enemy out of it, and returned to their lines. On the 9th the French bombarded Doiran, which lay on the south-west shore of the lake, and about thirty-five miles north-north-west of Salonika. Columns of smoke were seen to arise from the town, and following up the artillery preparation French infantry advanced, captured Height 227, two miles to the south-east, and took the railway-station, thus gaining possession of the line from Salonika as far as Poroi.

On the 10th a change in the allied commands was announced, by which General Sarrail became Commander-in-Chief of all the Entente forces in the Balkans, his place at the head of the French divisions being taken by General Cordonnier, one of the French officers who had emerged from comparative obscurity and achieved high positions during the course of the war. Cordonnier had been a professor at the École Supérieure de Guerre, and had published a careful study of the Russo-Japanese War, which had attracted attention, but at the outbreak of hostilities he was merely in charge of a battalion. He had evinced, however, such consummate military skill at Verdun that his rapid pro- **General Cordonnier arrives** motion was a certainty. It was at General Sarrail's special request that this brilliant soldier was sent to Salonika, where he landed on August 10th.

In the middle of August the forces of the Allies were advancing northward, though gradually and slowly, and, on the 15th, Doljeli was occupied by the French without opposition. But this capture appeared to be the signal for the onset of a powerful Bulgarian offensive, which next day developed along the whole battle-line. At Doljeli the infantry of the enemy, marching out from their permanent entrenchments close to that village, attacked the French in superior numbers and expelled them from it. Having been reinforced, the French vigorously assaulted the place and retook it. But the Bulgarians counter-attacked with energy and success, and it changed hands several times amid fierce fighting, in which the British participated. On the night of the 17th a British battalion had its first experience of hand-to-hand work in an assault of Horse-shoe Hill, an eminence which commanded the village, and by the free use of bayonets and bombs it drove the enemy off it, subsequently repulsing all his efforts. General Sarrail, speaking of the capture of this hill, said it was a splendid operation, especially the final bayonet charge, and though the men were untried troops, they behaved with admirable dash and courage—which, however, was only, he added, to be expected of British soldiers. On the 22nd the Bulgarians attacked the allied positions west of Horse-shoe Hill, but were driven back by steady machine-gun and rifle fire.

While thus active in the centre, or the Gevgeli-Doiran sector, of the front of the Allies, the Bulgarians showed still more activity on its flanks. Over against the allied left wing, or western part of the line, the Bulgarians had concentrated large forces under General Bojadieff at Monastir and Kenali, on the Monastir-Salonika Railway, and on August 16th they suddenly sprang a strong offensive against the front from Lake Prespa to Lake Ostrovo, which

EARS IN THE WALL OF ROCK.
A British signal officer at a listening-post in a trench cut through the solid rock in a section of the Salonika front.

[*Official photograph.*

ONE OF THE GREAT TRIUMVIRATE OF GREECE.
General Zimbrakakis, Minister for War in the Provisional Government established by M. Venizelos, in conversation with Lord Granard at Salonika.

was held by the Serbians, but towards its western extremity in weak force. At Florina, a small town in Greek territory, sixteen miles south of Monastir, there were only some Serbian advanced guards, or "observation-posts," which, after an exchange of shots, withdrew as the Bulgarians came on in overwhelming numbers, and the enemy thereupon occupied the place and its railway-station. A Berlin communiqué pompously announced that after the fruitless attacks of the Entente Powers during the past few days, the allied (Bulgaro-German) troops proceeded to deliver a counter-offensive, and that Florina had been captured after a fight against the Serbian Danube Division. Debouching from Florina, the Bulgarians in the next two days entered Biklishta, south of Lake Prespa, and took Banitsa, a station some miles farther on upon the railway to Salonika, and close to Lake Ostrovo.

On the 18th of the month the enemy, six battalions strong, attacked the Serbians along the front to the east and north of the railway, starting from Moglena, in the Karadjova Mountains, and ending above the villages of Strupino and Pojar, the sector in which the Serbians had been victorious in July, and though he fought with the utmost fury, he was thrown back on his original position with a loss of over a thousand men. On the following day the Serbians in this district counter-attacked the Bulgarians, and drove them across the frontier at Kukuruz, occupying the spurs of that mountain as well as those of another, Kaymakchalan.

Farther to the west the enemy continued his advance from Banitsa along the railway in an attempt to gain Vodena, and so to get in rear of the Serbians, who, according to a German statement, belonged to the Drina Division, in the Moglena (or Karadjova) district. The Serbians, still outnumbered, held them up for a while on the Malka Nidje Planina, but, giving way before the vastly superior strength of the invaders, slowly retired to Lake Ostrovo, where very heavy fighting took place. They occupied a defensive position between that lake and the little lake called Petrsko, and from midnight to five o'clock in the morning of August 22nd they stoutly maintained themselves in it, notwithstanding repeated and violent Bulgarian onslaughts. The progress of the enemy, who lost over 10,000 men in this sector, was completely checked, while all the time the Serbians in the Karadjova district were storming one peak after another, and threatening a descent into the Valley of the Cherna (Tserna) which lay beyond.

Greeks give way to Bulgars

Kastoria, a town on the high-road from Florina, which eventually reached the Ægean through Larisa at Volo, was occupied by the Bulgarians on August 22nd, the Greek local authorities retiring and leaving it in the hands of the enemy, as they had done when he appeared at Florina. The Bulgarians tried to resume their advance at Lake Ostrovo, and their official communiqué announced various victorious encounters with the Serbian forces, but the latter strengthened their front by recapturing Hill 1,506, three miles north-west of the lake, which they had previously lost. By the 25th of the month the Serbians were counter-attacking in their turn in this region, and had pushed back the Bulgarians for a considerable distance. Rumours at Athens said that the enemy had overcome the resistance of the Serbians at Ostrovo, and was marching on to Vodena, but this news, like so much other news from the Greek capital, was entirely false.

The anti-Ententists spread these stories for the purpose of discrediting the Allies. As a matter of fact, reinforcements were constantly coming up for the Serbians, who in any case fought with admirable courage and tenacity; and though on August 27th the Bulgarians brought new heavy guns to bear on the Ostrovo sector, and under their cover made three violent assaults, they were successfully repulsed with great slaughter. On the other hand, the Serbians in the mountains to the north conquered fresh positions on the slopes of Vetrenik, west of Kukuruz.

[*Official photograph.*

GREEK PATRIOTS WHO DREW THE SWORD FOR THEIR COUNTRY'S HONOUR.
Colonel Christodoulos (in centre) arriving at Salonika with his men who, resenting the Bulgars' invasion of Greek territory, forcibly resisted their occupation of the fort at Seres. General Zimbrakakis is seen on the colonel's left hand.

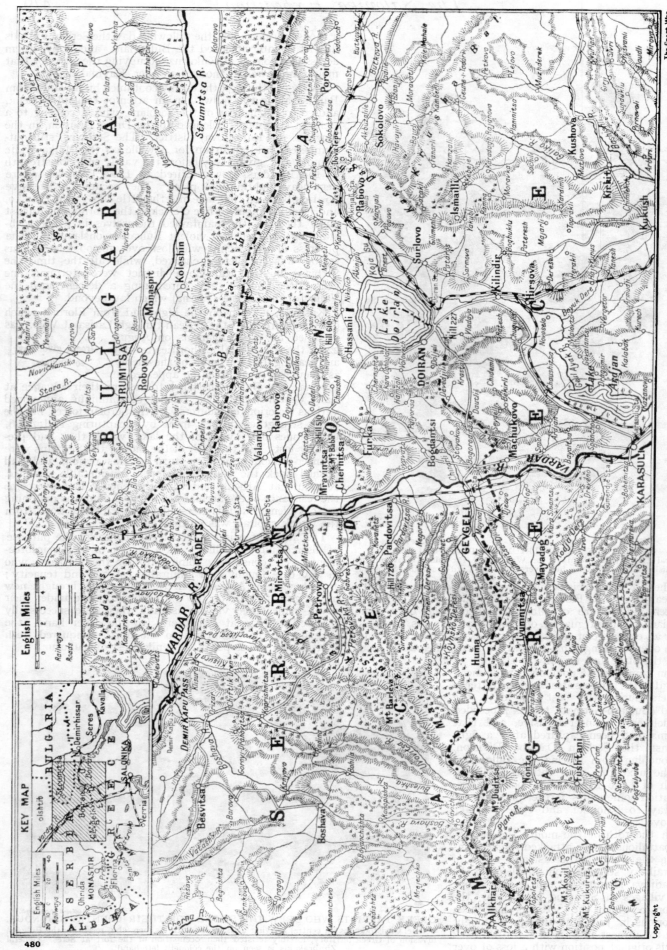

MAP OF THE VALLEY OF THE VARDAR: SCENE OF THE MAIN ACTIVITIES OF THE FRANCO-BRITISH FORCES.

The key map shows the proportion of the area taken in by the detailed map to the entire theatre of operations in the Balkans, exclusive of Rumania.

Copyright

The Great War

On the Allies' right, lying along the Struma, east of Salonika, the Bulgarian offensive was launched both from the north and the east. From the former direction the enemy advanced from Fort Rupel and Demirhissar on Seres, and along the roads farther east from Nevrokop, in South-Western Bulgaria, on Seres and Drama; and from the latter from across the Mesta River, also known as the Nestos and the Kara Su, towards Kavalla, which was only about twenty miles from the Ægean end of his eastern boundary. His first object was the occupation of the entire extent of Greek territory east of the Struma, a region which he knew was not held in any strength by the troops of the Entente Powers, and therefore could be easily seized —provided the Greeks made no resistance.

Greek collusion with the foe As soon as his march southward began it was evident that he was acting in collusion—or, at all events, in agreement —with the Greek Government. For at the outset the authorities at Athens ordered the withdrawal of the Greek forces which had stood in his path, and thus permitted him to descend into the plains of Seres and Drama without opposition. On August 17th-18th Krushevo, Starchista, and Lise—three fortified places immediately south of the frontier, east of Fort Rupel—were surrendered to him. Not a few of the Greek soldiers, indignant at this betrayal of the interests of their country, were very unwilling to quit these strategic points, and they offered some resistance at Krushevo and Starchista; but the Bulgarians got all three practically without an effort. The garrison of Fort Pheapetra, near Krushevo, fought more stoutly, but its action had no real influence. At the same time the enemy crossed the mouth of the Mesta, and sent forward patrols towards Kavalla, many of whose

BLACK LABOUR IN MACEDONIA.
African natives on the Macedonian front digging a shelter—extending many feet under the ground—from bombardment.

inhabitants straightway fled for refuge to the Island of Thasos, which had been in the hands of the Allies for some little time back.

The west bank of the Struma and Lake Tahinos, the expansion of that river towards the sea, formed the right flank of the Allies, and so far as the Salonika Army was concerned, the Bulgarians, if the Greeks had no objection, could have occupied the district east of it and marched to Kavalla long before August. On the east bank of the stream the Entente Powers had only scouting squadrons of cavalry, and these made no real attempt to stem the Bulgarian tide, but merely to watch and delay its advance. On August 19th and 20th French and British detachments were in touch with the enemy at various points from Barakli Juma, west of Demirhissar, to near Kavalla, and retiring according to **Bulgarian boasts of** instructions with very little fighting, **victory** though Bulgarian communiqués boastfully spoke of great victories, particularly over the French, in all this region. On the 20th a party of British Yeomanry destroyed the railway bridge at Angista Station, on the railway between Seres and Drama, to hinder the movement of supplies for the invaders. By the 22nd the Bulgarians were throwing up entrenchments on the east side of the Struma, between Lake Butkovi on the north and Lake Tahinos on the south, with their heavy artillery at Yenikeui; but an attack on French troops holding the Komarian bridge was repulsed, and north of Butkovi Franco-British forces easily defeated several assaults by which the enemy tried to recover positions he had lost. On August 23rd the British, in the face of a heavy fire, blew up three bridges at Neohori, where the Struma debouches into the sea. Special reference was made **by**

TOUCH AND GO: A GRENADE EXPLODES.
Instantaneous impression of a rifle-grenade bursting at the head of an entrenchment on the Balkan front.

General Sarrail to the excellence of the work performed by the British Yeomanry in the operations on the east side of the river.

On August 24th the Bulgarians were in Kavalla, and with one exception occupied all its forts, which were armed with many heavy guns, and with the other forts lost elsewhere had cost Greece more than four millions sterling.

On the 25th the place was bombarded by two British monitors and a cruiser. Though the enemy was now in possession of nearly the whole of Eastern Greek Macedonia, he had not gained it without encountering an increasing amount of opposition from certain portions of the Greek Army. According to a telegram to a Paris journal, the soldiers at Fort Stratila put up so determined a fight that the Bulgarians entered it only after Major Changas, its commandant, and all its garrison had been killed or wounded.

But it was at Seres that a part of the Greek forces made something of a stand. As the troops of the enemy had

[Official photograph.

PARADE BEFORE THE DOCTOR.
Indian mountain artillerymen on service at Salonika undergoing medical inspection.

closed in on the Greek guard at Demirhissar, one man, who slew a Bulgar to prevent his escape, succeeded in reaching Seres, and gave the alarm to Colonel Christodoulos, the temporary head of the demobilised 6th Division, which, about 5,000 strong, was stationed there. The general in command was absent on leave, and Christodoulos on his own responsibility immediately took up a defensive position outside the town, summoned the disbanded local reservists to rejoin him, and prepared to oppose the Bulgarians with all the energy that was possible in the circumstances.

When two regiments of the enemy approached him and demanded the surrender of the town, with its arms and munitions, he refused to comply. The Bulgarians began to shell the place, and a struggle ensued; but the odds were too great, and Christodoulos was com-

pelled to withdraw his men. However in the first week of September he arrived at Kavalla, where he drove the Bulgarians out of some of the forts which they had taken.

If the seizure by Bulgaria of Fort Rupel in May had created a very painful impression throughout Greece, the news of the further Bulgarian invasion of Greek Macedonia, east of the Struma, produced a much greater and more painful sensation among the Greek people. The Skouloudist (or Gounarist) Press, which was largely subsidised by the Germans, stood alone in expressing satisfaction with the situation, and many anti-Ententists condemned the action of the enemy in **Invasion of Greek Macedonia** quite as strong terms as did the Venizelists. At Athens the Government announced that it had received assurances from the Central Powers and Bulgaria that Greek sovereignty and the rights and liberties of the inhabitants would be respected in the occupied districts, and that the whole region would be evacuated after the war. But these promises were insufficient for true Greek patriots, and when it became known that Christodoulos and others were resisting the Bulgarians, the sympathies of the vast majority flowed out rather to these brave men than to the Government, which placed faith in the inveterate enemy of Greece. At Salonika a great meeting was convened to protest against any abandonment of national territory, and shortly afterwards recruiting commissions were formed who issued a proclamation calling on the disbanded reservists to enlist and fight the foe.

On August 27th a demonstration was made at Athens by fifty thousand Greeks, who called for M. Venizelos and begged his assistance to expel the Bulgarians. The appearance on his balcony of the statesman who had saved Greece before was acclaimed with tremendous cheering. In an intensely eloquent speech he thrilled an audience such as never had been seen previously in the capital. He told the people to send a deputation to King Constantine to say that he was the victim of military advisers obsessed by Germany, who had wrongly persuaded him that she was invincible. The anti-Ententists held a counter-demonstration, but it was not a success. That events in Greece were again coming to a crisis was shown by the retirement of General Dousmanis as Chief of Staff, and the appointment of General Moschopoulos in his place; as the latter had been on friendly terms with Sarrail at Salonika, it was thought that he would favour the Allies.

It was the city of Salonika itself that, on the last day of August, took a step, in the name of Greek Macedonia, that went much further in protest against the attitude of the Government than anything that had gone before, for it rose in rebellion, and formed a Committee of National Defence and a Provisional Government. At the head of this serious revolutionary development stood Colonel Zimbrakakis and Colonel Mazarakis, commanding the artillery brigade of the 11th Division of the Greek Army. They issued a two-page manifesto, one page being addressed to the Greek people and the other to the Army, which maintained that an unnatural state of affairs had lasted long enough, and urged the Greek soldiers to pay no attention to orders **Greek Provisional Government** from Athens, but to ally themselves with the Entente and drive the Bulgarians out of the country. It denounced the surrender of Greek forts and territory as an act of disloyalty and treason on the part of King Constantine and his Government, and declared that the time had arrived for Greece to take her stand by the side of the Allies.

The local police, who were well drilled, and equal in fighting quality to the men of the Army, supported the Committee of National Defence. They numbered over a thousand, but were not nearly so numerous as the three

German prisoners captured on the Balkan front on their way to prison camp at Salonika. Some of them wear labels inscribed with their names and regiments. [Official photograph.

Bulgarian prisoners interned at a Serbian camp near Monastir. Circle (official): Interrogating captured Bulgarian soldiers.

In their compound at Salonika: Types of German infantry photographed behind barbed-wire. These men were fighting, under Mackensen's command, in conjunction with the Bulgarians on the Balkan front.

BULGAR AND TEUTON PRISONERS AT MONASTIR AND SALONIKA.

KING FERDINAND OF RUMANIA.
His Majesty threw in his lot with the Allies on August 27th, 1916.

including the wireless system ; second, that enemy agents employed in corruption and espionage must immediately leave Greece, and not return till after the conclusion of hostilities ; and third, that the necessary measures must be taken against such Greek subjects as had rendered themselves guilty of complicity in that corruption and espionage.

Both of the Allies made a point of telling the Greek Government that the Note was not directed against Greece, but against Germany and the pro-Germans in Greece ; and on the 3rd their demands were formally accepted. Thereupon British police agents, wearing red armlets specially marked, proceeded to round up a number of persons known to have been engaged in espionage work, but later this hunting down of the Germans and their minions was handed over to the Greek Government. The notorious Baron von Schenck, who had been the head of the German intriguers, **Exit Von Schenck** and about fifty Germans and Austrians **and his spies** were secured, and on September 7th deported to Kavalla in a Greek steamer. A few days later the Allies had to make a new demand on Greece. It arose from a band of anti-Venizelists, belonging to the Reservists Leagues, bursting into the garden of the French Legation at Athens and firing several revolver shots. The Entente Ministers called for the suppression of these leagues, and the Government agreed to dissolve them.

But it was not only the distracted internal situation that was affecting at this time King Constantine, his Government, and the Greeks in general A new factor had appeared in the war which at once profoundly influenced them, the whole of the Balkans, and the entire aspect of the colossal conflict everywhere. This was the entrance into the struggle of Rumania, who declared war on Austria-Hungary on August 27th, and thereby definitely espoused the cause of the Entente Powers.

Greek regiments stationed in the town, and these declined to take part in the rebellion. In the afternoon the police, accompanied by hundreds of volunteers, paraded the streets, and Colonel Zimbrakakis led the column to the headquarters of the French, where he proffered the services of himself and his men to General Sarrail. During the night the revolutionaries attempted to coerce the soldiers at the barracks into joining them; bloodshed resulted, and Sarrail intervened to prevent further disturbances. The soldiers subsequently were disarmed and interned outside the town, the insurgents remaining in control, and sending deputations to Vodena and elsewhere for the purpose of encouraging the enrolment of volunteers.

Meanwhile the Allies had made a fresh move at Athens. On the morning of September 1st twenty-three of their warships, with seven transports filled with **Allies' new** troops, anchored four miles outside the **demands** Piræus, while other vessels of their Fleet lay in Salamis and Phaleron Bays. The most sensational reports instantly spread abroad, among them being a statement that King Constantine had abdicated, and that his son, the Crown Prince, had been appointed Regent, while another declared that Venizelos had formed a coalition with Zaimis, and that orders had been given for a general mobilisation of the Greek Army. None of these stories turned out to be true, but they were significant of the strain from which Greece was suffering. On September 2nd the allied warships landed parties who took possession of the wireless station at the arsenal, while several German vessels were seized, and their officers and crews arrested. France and Great Britain, on the evening of the same day, presented a Note to the Greek Government, in which they said—first, that having heard from a sure source that the enemy received information in divers ways, and notably by means of the Greek telegraphs, they demanded control of the posts and telegraphs,

CROWN PRINCE CAROL OF RUMANIA.
A portrait which shows the Rumanian heir in officer's uniform.

CHEERS FOR VENIZELOS: IMPRESSION OF THE GREEK PATRIOT AND HIS SUPPORTERS.
Greek public opinion was divided between the Germanophil King Constantine and the pro-Ally patriot Venizelos. Some idea of the popularity of this fearless statesman may be gathered from the dense crowd to whom he is responding from his automobile.

On the same date, by a significant coincidence, Italy, with whom Rumania was warmly sympathetic, declared war on Germany, after more than a year had passed since she had begun hostilities against the second of the Central Powers. During that month of August Italy had been doing splendid work for the Entente. North of her own territory she had won a magnificent victory by the storming and capture of the fortress of Gorizia on August 9th, and in the Balkans she had been harrying and pressing the enemy on the Voyusa River, north of Valona (or Avlona),

Italy's timely victories which town on the Adriatic had been seriously menaced by the Austrians in the preceding spring. Further, she was encouraging and assisting a revolt in Albania against the German Prince William of Wied, who had come again on the scene as the Mpret, or ruler, of that principality. She was also doing something to help the Montenegrins, who had risen in their mountains against their brutal conquerors.

Rumania had bided her time. For some weeks previous to her declaration of war report had been busy with regard to her probable action, and in Germany especially there had been a good deal of apprehension that at last, after two years of neutrality, she would come out against Austria, and, as that involved the allies of that empire, against the whole Germanic League. Hope had alternated with fear in the Dual Monarchy itself. But thinking that Rumania would continue in the same course as before, as she fancied there were some grounds for believing, the news fell upon her with a horribly jarring shock of surprise. When Germany, on August 28th, published her official notification of war on Rumania, she had the hardihood to allege that the latter country had "disgracefully broken" treaties concluded with Austria-Hungary and herself.

That this charge was false was sufficiently demonstrated by the policy, now one of entreaty and cajolement, and again one of threat and objurgation, which the Central Powers had maintained towards Rumania since the beginning of the war. They made offers to her which they trusted would purchase her support, and they said much

of the pains and penalties she would incur if she refused them. These would not have been necessary if she had been really bound to them by such obligations as were indicated by the Berlin communiqué. But whether flattered or contemned, she preserved throughout a sphinx-like silence, a perfect obduracy of composure. She was waiting on events, and governing herself accordingly. She knew as a certainty there was no chance of her realising her national aspirations through Austria, and while she was doubtful of the success of the Entente Powers she marked time. Perhaps the first definite signs of her preference for the Allies were shown by her acceptance of a loan from Great Britain in January, 1916, and the subsequent contract by which she sold to the British Government an enormous quantity of wheat.

Entente diplomacy had, of course, been active all the while in the interests of the Allies in Rumania, and it was widely known that many of her prominent statesmen, like M. Jonescu, and the bulk of her people were hostile to the Austro-Germans. But Rumania had before her eyes the tragic fate of Serbia, due to the inadequate help given that unfortunate land, and she was bound to see that she made no mistake which might entail upon her a like calamity. Her destinies were chiefly in the hands of M. Bratiano, her Prime Minister and Minister of War, and the leader of the Liberal Party in her Parliament. Able and far-seeing, but cautious and infinitely patient, he was not to be moved till he **Rumania's essential** was satisfied that the general situation in **caution** all the main theatres of the war clearly betokened the defeat of Germany as the ultimate result of the contest. By August it was plain that the Germans had failed at Verdun, that the Franco-British forces on the Somme were making good progress, and, what probably appealed to him most of all, that Brussiloff's armies had dealt Austria shattering, crushing blows in Volhynia and Galicia. The opportunity of joining up with those triumphant Russians on the frontiers of Hungary had come, and was far too good to be missed. Then there was the huge cosmopolitan army of the Allies at Salonika flanking Bulgaria. On every front of vital importance Bratiano saw that the enemy had lost the initiative, the principal thing in war, and had been reduced to the defensive. Rumania's day had arrived.

In the evening of August 27th the Rumanian Minister in Vienna called at the Austro-Hungarian Ministry for Foreign Affairs, and presented to the Dual Monarchy a Note, in which was set forth in considerable detail the case of Rumania against that empire, and which concluded with the declaration of war. The Note was a temperate,

Rumania takes the field true, yet dignified, statement of the position of Rumania with respect to Austria and Hungary, particularly the latter. The chief feature emphasised was the wretched condition of the Rumanes, as the Rumanian population of the Dual Monarchy was called, in Transylvania, a province of Hungary, who were kept ignorant and in a servile state by the Magyars. The Note candidly gave expression to the feeling of Rumania in this matter, which was the basis of her action, in the words: " Governed by the necessity of safeguarding her racial interest, Rumania sees herself forced to enter into line with those able to assure to her the realisation of the national unity." For her suffering kinsfolk in Hungary, groaning under Magyar oppression, the war was a war of deliverance, of emancipa-

FIGHTERS WITH A LATIN TRADITION.
Rumanian artillery. There is a marked similarity between the appearance of Rumanian soldiers and their Italian allies.

tion, of redemption. " For a period of over thirty years," as the Note averred, " the Rumanians of the Dual Monarchy not only never saw a reform introduced of a nature to give them even the semblance of satisfaction, but, on the contrary, they were treated as an inferior race." It was to free these poor people of her blood from their tyrants that Rumania primarily unsheathed her sword.

Anticipating the line that Germany would take, Rumania in this Note announced what were the real facts regarding the alliance between her and Germany and Austria. She admitted there had been a compact between her and what had been known as the Triple Alliance, which was composed of Germany, Austria, and Italy when the war broke out, but this agreement was essentially of a conservative and defensive character, its object being to guarantee the parties to it from any attack from outside. It contained no provision which constrained any of its subscribers to endorse or participate in aggressive action on the part of the rest or of any of them. So, at the very outset of the struggle, Italy, as well as Rumania, rightly viewing the belligerency of Germany and Austria as aggressive, emphatically declined to undertake hostilities with them against the Entente Powers. The Triple Alliance, however,

existed till 1915, when Italy, by declaring war on Austria, broke it up. Thereafter Rumania no longer considered herself bound by the alliance, which had in point of fact ceased to be, because of the withdrawal of Italy, and she was fully entitled to do what seemed to her to be best for herself as an independent State. And, further, she had looked on the treaty as securing peace to her. But with the power of Germany and Austria challenged by the Entente, of what value was it as a guarantee ? And still further, the alliance had wrought no improvement in the lot of the wretched Rumanes of Hungary, though she had hoped the opposite.

There was yet another important subject of solicitude for Rumania. Though she was not, properly speaking, one of the Balkan States, and the origin of by far the most of her population was entirely different from that of the races inhabiting the area known as the Balkans, her adjacent position had brought her well within the Balkan orbit, while the march of recent events had placed her at the head of the Balkan States. Her intervention in the Second Balkan War almost immediately resulted in the termination of that conflict, and at the same time gained for her a slice of territory from Bulgaria, who bitterly resented its loss, and was eager for an opportunity of getting it back—with interest.

Rumania wanted peace in the Balkans. But a new situation developed when Austria declared war on Serbia in July, 1914, and she could not see it without being seriously perturbed. She therefore asked Austria at the outset to say what were her intentions with respect to Serbia, and was told in reply that Austria was not inspired by the spirit of conquest, and sought absolutely no territorial acquisitions. Rumania witnessed what happened—Serbia overwhelmed in the end, notwithstanding the most glorious resistance, and her land apportioned between Austria and Bulgaria. The situation in the Balkans was changed much for the worse for Rumania, with Serbia gone, however temporarily, and the common enemy triumphant. Here was another reason for the entry of Rumania into the war.

When her day came Rumania struck at once and struck hard. Her king immediately placed himself at the head of her armies. Germany had found it difficult to believe that King Ferdinand, who was a prince of the House of Hohenzollern, and had been trained as a German officer, would ever appear in the field against her; but he was a constitutional sovereign, and, unlike King Constantine of Greece, was faithful to the oath he had taken on ascending the throne. He bowed to the will of his advisers and of his people, and **King Ferdinand's fidelity** cordially accepted their mandate. He had convoked the Crown Council which pronounced the momentous decision, and showed that he was a Rumanian before everything else, as he had announced on his accession. His consort, moreover, was a British princess, being a daughter of the deceased Duke of Edinburgh, and thus first cousin to King George. He issued a stirring proclamation to his people, in which he told them that the war had brought them the day that had been awaited for centuries by the national conscience, by the founders of the Rumanian State, by those who united the principalities of Moldavia and Wallachia in the War of Independence, and by those responsible for the national

Rumanian infantry, arrayed in full winter kit, on the march in the snow.

Rumanian lancers, dexterous fighters and expert horsemen, in training for the offensive against the Central Powers.

Stirring illustration of Rumanian cavalry charging. These photographs were taken by special permission of the Rumanian Government.

RUMANIA THROWS DOWN THE GAGE TO THE CENTRAL POWERS, AUGUST 27TH. 1916.

A NOBLE ALLY NOBLY HONOURED.
General Mahon, in command of the British troops at Salonika, investing General Sarrail, of the French Army, with the Order of St. Michael and St. George.

renaissance. " It is the day," he continued, " of the union of all the branches of our nation. To-day we are able to complete the task of our forefathers, and to establish for ever that which Michael the Brave was only able to establish for a moment—namely, a Rumanian union on both slopes of the Carpathians." In an Order of the Day he reminded his Army of its former victories, and said that the memory of its ancient leaders, Michael the Brave and Stephen the Great, whose remains lay in the earth it was going to set free, called to it to advance in triumph. " Show yourselves worthy of the glory of your ancestors," he concluded, " and in the centuries to come the whole race will bless you and sing your praises." King Ferdinand was at the front the day after war was declared, and within the next twenty-four hours his soldiers were in possession of every important pass leading into Transylvania.

Before the night of August 27th was over the Rumanians were marching into Hungary. An Austrian communiqué stated next day that on the " south-eastern and eastern frontier passes of Hungary our new enemy, Rumania, exchanged the first shots last night with our outposts in a treacherous surprise attack at the Roter Turm (Red Tower) Pass, and in the passes to the south-west and south of Brasso—or, giving it its German name, Kronstadt— advanced guards entered into combat on both sides early this morning, and the first Rumanian prisoners were taken." It observed a discreet reticence as to the number of prisoners the Rumanians had made. On the 29th Vienna issued a ludicrous message in which it said that, at all the crossings of the mountains along the three hun-
Vainglorious Austrian dred and fifty miles of the Hungarian-
communique Rumanian frontier, the Rumanians, wherever they met Austrian battalions, had to withdraw " with bleeding heads," but at the same time it admitted that the far-reaching encircling movement of the Rumanian armies had obliged an equally widespread Austrian retirement. Rumania took the offensive on the whole of her western frontier, from the neighbourhood of the Borgo Pass, on the borders of Bukovina, to the Iron Gates of the Danube at Orsova.

By the end of August she had driven the enemy back into his own territory for many miles, made striking gains along the strategic railways, captured Brasso as well as

Petroseny, an important commercial centre, besides several other towns and a score of villages, and was threatening Hermannstadt. In the beginning of September, after a desperate battle which lasted five days, she took Orsova, at the southern extremity of her western line, and forced the Austrians to retreat to the western bank of the Cerna, a tributary of the Danube, a few miles beyond the frontier. Meanwhile, a highly-significant telegram from Berlin had announced that in the Carpathians Austro-Germans were engaged with Russo-Rumanian troops. This meant that the Russians and the Rumanians had joined up in the north-west, and that the eastern front of the Allies, well over a thousand miles in length, now extended from the Dwina on the Baltic to the Danube, where it touched the north-eastern corner of Serbia.

From Orsova to the Black Sea the front of Rumania was approximately four hundred miles long, making with her other front a total length of nearly seven hundred and fifty miles— a tremendous line, to cover which her own forces, though nearly a million strong, were hardly sufficient. She had looked for Russian support, nor was she disappointed. As August closed thousands of Russian soldiers, under General Zaionchkovsky, formerly head of a Siberian division, were marching into the Dobrudja to the assistance of Rumania, as less than forty   **Russia joins**
years before thousands of other Russians   **Rumania**
had advanced through the same region
for the deliverance of Bulgaria, since turned a renegade and a traitress. Russian warships arrived at Constanza for the defence of the Rumanian coast. The southern part of the Dobrudja, the name given to the district in Rumania lying between the Danube and the Black Sea, and north of Bulgaria, had no strong defensive positions, and an attack was comparatively easy from that side.

After Rumania declared war there was some uncertainty as to what attitude Bulgaria would take up, but this was dispelled when the latter, on September 1st, declared war on the former in a Note, in which she reminded the other of what she called the " robbery " of a piece of Bulgarian territory after the Second Balkan War, the tract of land, in fact, that formed the boundary of the Dobrudja on the south. Next day Bulgarian and German troops, under the leadership of Marshal Mackensen, crossed this frontier, the Rumanian guards withdrawing before them, and on the 4th Russian mounted detachments came into collision with Bulgarian cavalry in this area. On the same day the enemy captured Dobric (Dobritch), and on the 6th took Tutrakan, also called Turtukai, inflicting on the Rumanians considerable losses. Silistria fell to the Bulgaro-Germans on the 10th, but the tide of invasion was stemmed at Dobric by Russo-Rumanian forces. And while this was going on in the Dobrudja the Rumanians were making steady progress with their advance into Hungary.

As a matter of course, Greece was deeply affected, and most of her people declared that she also must cast all hesitation and doubt aside, and stand in with the Allies. But in the middle of September, 1916, when this chapter was written, the old anti-Entente influences were still sufficiently powerful to prevent her from taking that course, M. Zaimis had resigned, and confusion worse confounded reigned in Athens.

General Cordonnier, appointed to command the French Balkan forces August, 1916.

KKK. 429

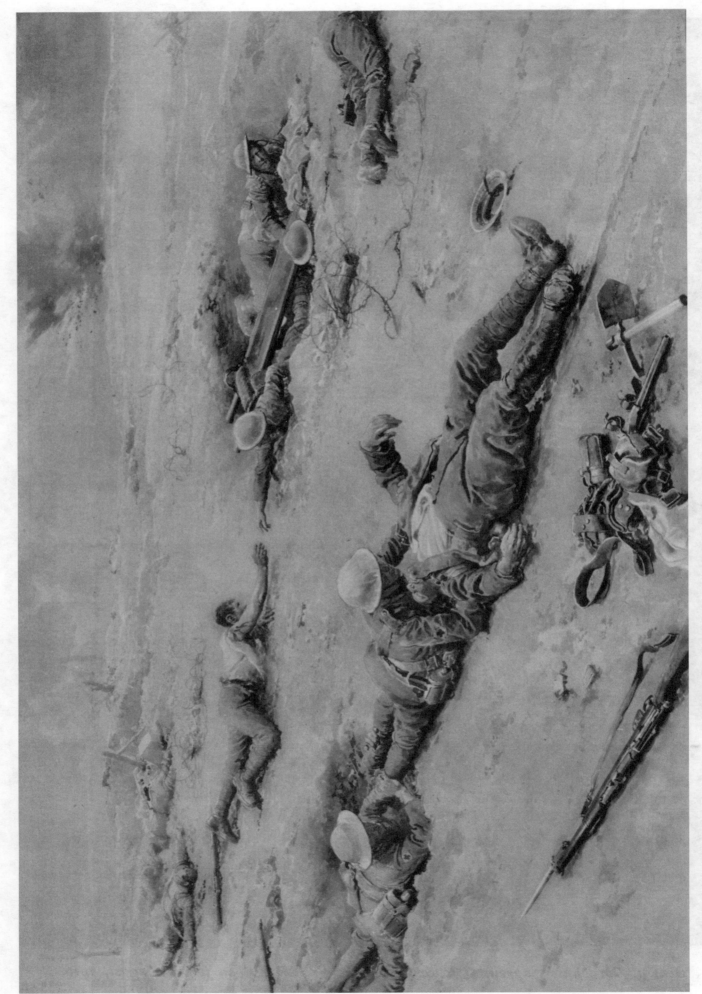

The first stage homewards: Regimental stretcher-bearers bringing wounded in from the battlefield to the collecting posts.

490

The second stage homewards : R.A.M.C. men conveying wounded from the collecting posts to the advanced dressing station.

Carrying in the wounded under fire: This man brought in twenty of his comrades.

CHAPTER CXLVI.

"FOR VALOUR": HEROES OF THE VICTORIA CROSS IN THE SECOND YEAR OF THE WAR.

By E. C. Buley, Author of "Glorious Deeds of Australasians."

Analysis of the List of Victoria Crosses Awarded in the Second Year of the War—Eight Crosses to the Navy, Six of them in Connection with the Landing on V Beach, Gallipoli. One at Cape Helles, and One at Kut-el-Amara—Four Crosses Awarded to Airmen : Captain Liddell, Captain Hawker, Sec.-Lieut. Insall, and Squadron-Commander Bell Davis, D.S.O.—Sixty-six Crosses Awarded to the Army, Thirty-one to Officers and Thirty-five to N.C.O.'s and Men—The Lancashire Fusiliers Elect Three Recipients of the Cross —Nine Crosses Won by Anzacs on Gallipoli in the One Month of August—Other Gallipoli V.C.'s—Captain Butler Wins the Cross in West Africa and Lieut. Dartnell in East Africa—Two Crosses Won in Mesopotamia—Three Indian V.C.'s—Two Crosses Won at Ypres—Lieut. Campbell Wins the Cross for Canada—The Rev. E. N. Mellish Wins the First Cross Awarded to a Chaplain in the War—V.C.'s Won at Loos, Hill 70, the Hohenzollern Redoubt, Hulluch, La Houssoie, Hooge, Vermelles, and Le Rutoire— Double Deeds of Heroism of Acting-Sergt. Raynes, R.F.A., and Lance-Corpl. Wyatt, Coldstream Guards—Crosses Won at Cuinchy and La Brique—Corporal Meekosha on the Yser—Sec.-Lieut. A. V. Smith—Captain Swinton, of the Indian Medical Service— Amazing Endurance of Lance-Corpl. Cotter, of the East Kents—Some Other Peers of Peerless Men.

BETWEEN August 4th, 1915, and August 4th, 1916, seventy-eight officers and men were gazetted as having been awarded the Victoria Cross. Thus fewer V.C.'s were awarded during the second year of the Great War than in the first year, when the total reached the number of eighty-three. When it is considered that the number of men on active service was far greater, this slight decrease might be held as evidence that the supreme reward for valour was more sparingly bestowed as the war progressed. The figures are deceptive, however, for during the first month of the "great push," which began in the month of July, 1916, a great number of V.C.'s were won, though the actual date of award takes them into the third year of the war.

A first analysis of the list shows that eight V.C.'s went to the Navy in the second year of the war, as compared with four in 1914-15. The Air Service also doubled its total of V.C.'s, earning four in the second year of the war as against two in the first twelve months. Of the sixty-six crosses which went to soldiers, twenty were won in Gallipoli, and of these nine fell to Anzac soldiers and one to a Gurkha. Crosses were won in Mesopotamia and in East and West Africa, and the remaining forty-two fell to soldiers fighting on the western front.

The magnificent services rendered by the Navy in the landing operations upon Gallipoli on April 25th, 1915, were rewarded by six crosses on August 16th. Five of these were won at the landing on V Beach, when a collier, the River Clyde, was crammed with troops and run

aground in order to provide cover for the soldiers until the actual stepping ashore. The ship had been specially prepared for the purpose by Commander Edward Unwin, R.N., who had seen that large portholes were cut in the sides of the vessel, through which the men were to pass down gangways to lighters, from which it would be easy to step ashore.

Unfortunately, when the River Clyde was beached, and when the lighters were run out, they failed to reach their proper place, and a gap was left between two lighters, over which the men could not pass. Some of them jumped into the water and waded ashore, but this method was too slow and costly. A heavy fire from machine-guns and rifles soon littered the first lighter with dead and wounded, and the men were ordered back into the River Clyde again.

Commander Unwin set about getting the lighters into their proper places, and in order to do so he exposed himself to the heavy fire, and, standing up to his waist in the water, directed the operations of a number of men as devoted as himself. Unprotected from the murderous fire, Commander Unwin worked on until the effects of the immersion became intolerable, and he returned to the ship, where he was wrapped in blankets until his vitality was restored.

He then returned to his dangerous post in defiance of the doctor's order, and saw the work finished. He was treated on his return for abrasions caused by three bullets, after which he entered a lifeboat and went ashore to the rescue of some wounded men. His magnificent efforts only ended when sheer exhaustion came upon him. For his services he was awarded the Victoria Cross.

CORPL. C. R. G. BASSETT, V.C.
New Zealand Divisional Signal Company.

493

Two midshipmen associated with him in this work were similarly honoured. The first was Midshipman George L. Drewry, R.N.R. He, too, stood under the hail of bullets in the numbing water, and worked oblivious of the danger in which he stood. Twice he tried to swim with a line from one lighter to the other, though he was wounded in the head and suffering from loss of blood.

After his double attempt to pass a line from one lighter to the other had failed, another gallant lad, Midshipman Wilfred St. A. Malleson, R.N., attempted the task, and succeeded in reaching the second lighter with the line. Unfortunately it broke, and he had to make the attempt again. Twice more he tried, being taken out of the water each time in a state of extreme exhaustion.

Only once before has the V.C. been won by a midshipman—at Tientsin in 1900.

Two able seamen of H.M.S. Hussar also won the V.C. during these difficult and dangerous operations. One of them, Able-Seaman W. C. Williams, exposed himself breast-deep in water for an hour under the heavy fire, holding a line. In the end the gallant fellow was killed. Seaman George McK. Samson, R.N.R., also of the Hussar, worked all day under fire in one of the

LCE.-SERGT. O. BROOKS, V.C., 3rd Coldstream Guards. Loos.

CORPL. ALFRED A. BURT, V.C., 1st Herts. Cuinchy.

ceased trying to find out, if we could, who and where the unknown hero was."

Before he was identified as the hero of this daring, Sub-Lieutenant Tisdall was killed, leading his men into action on May 6th. Poet, scholar, and athlete, he was the first "Chancellor's Medallist" of Cambridge to gain the V.C.

The seventh naval V.C. of the year was earned by Commander Eric G. Robinson, R.N., who was in command of a party put ashore from the fleet at Cape Helles on February 6th, 1915, their mission being to destroy the guns of Fort Seddul Bahr. The men were dressed in white, and so made a good mark for the snipers concealed in the rough ground behind the fort. For this reason Commander Robinson would not let them advance, but undertook the work of destruction single-handed. Under heavy fire he advanced alone to the guns, not knowing whether a force had not been left there to protect them. He blew up one 4 in. gun, and returned for another charge of explosive. With this he succeeded in blowing up the second gun and returned without losing a man.

Commander Robinson, who was awarded the V.C., had previously taken part in four

PTE. JOHN CAFFREY, V.C., 2nd York and Lanc. La Brique.

PTE. HARRY CHRISTIAN, V.C., 2nd R. Lanc. Western front.

LT.-COMMANDER E. C. COOKSON, V.C., D.S.O., R.N. Kut-el-Amara. (Killed.)

CORPL. W. COSGROVE, V.C., 1st R. Munster Fus. Gallipoli.

LCE.-CORPL. W. R. COTTER, V.C., 6th East Kents. Western front.

lighters, tending the wounded and hauling on the lines. Eventually he was dangerously wounded by a machine-gun bullet. Apart from these two men, there is only one instance of a seaman winning the V.C., and that happened in Japan as long ago as 1865.

Nearly a year after his death, the V.C. honour came to the name of one more naval hero of V Beach, whose glorious bravery was described at the time, but whose identity was not traced until long after his death. Sub-Lieutenant Arthur Waldene St. Clair Tisdall, R.N.V.R., heard wounded men calling for help from the beach, while the attempts were being made to effect the landing from the River Clyde. He jumped into the water, and pushing a boat before him as cover, went to the rescue of the men on the beach.

Four or five times he made the journey, assisted by Chief-Petty-Officer Perring and Leading-Seamen Malia, Curtiss, and Parkinson. "Time after time," wrote an eyewitness, "they visited that awful beach, and brought back wounded officers and men. Darkness came on, and the officer was nowhere to be found. All the petty-officer and bluejackets could say was, 'He's one of those Naval Division gents.' Days and weeks passed away, and I and others never

Lafayette. LIEUT. WILBUR DARTNELL, V.C., 25th Royal Fus. East Africa. (Killed.)

CORPL. J. L. DAWSON, V.C., 187th Coy. R.E., Hohenzollern Redoubt.

attacks on the mine-fields in the Dardanelles, always under heavy fire.

The scene of the exploit which won the eighth naval V.C. for the year was laid at Kut-el-Amara, and its hero was Lieut.-Commander Edgar Christopher Cookson, D.S.O., R.N. The Turks had placed an obstruction in the river, to the great disadvantage of the relieving force, and on September 28th, 1915, Lieut.-Commander Cookson took the river-gunboat Comet, with other river-gunboats and similar craft, to examine the obstruction, and to destroy it if possible.

The enemy was in ambush, waiting for them, and as they approached the obstruction the little flotilla came under heavy fire. It was found that a number of dhows had been fastened by wire ropes in the centre of the stream, completely closing the fairway. An attempt to sink the central dhow, which was the pivot of the barrier of boats, was made with gun fire; but it proved unsuccessful. Then Lieut.-Commander Cookson ordered the Comet to be taken alongside this dhow, and with an axe in his hand he jumped aboard her and tried to sever the wire ropes which bound her to the other vessels. While at this work he was struck by several bullets and killed.

Airmen are only awarded the V.C. under most exceptional circumstances, as the exploits of the airmen V.C.'s of the second year of the war will prove. The first was Captain John Aidan Liddell, of the 3rd Battalion (Princess Louise's) Argyll and Sutherland Highlanders and R.F.C. On July 31st he was engaged upon a long-flight reconnaissance over Ostend-Bruges-Ghent. While flying at a great height he was wounded by anti-aircraft artillery, a piece of shell breaking his right thigh. The pain and shock of the wound rendered him unconscious, and his observer found the machine dropping with an ever-increasing velocity, while he was quite powerless to avert the imminent catastrophe.

Captain Liddell recovered partial control after a drop of 3,000 feet, and by a great effort righted the 'plane. He was continually fired at, but stuck grimly on, though in a state of collapse. His magnificent grit was rewarded by his bringing the aeroplane back to the British lines, after half an hour of indescribable effort and agony. When examined, it was found that the control wheel and throttle control of the machine were smashed, as well as one of the under-carriage struts; so that the feat the officer accom-

CORPL. A. DRAKE, V.C.,
8th Rifle Brigade.
(Killed.)

MID. G. L. DREWRY, V.C.,
R.N. Reserve. Dardanelles.

made a great dive, which brought it so close to the German that as the gunner was able to fire a drum of cartridges into the enemy machine at close range.

This had the effect of stopping the German's engine, driving him to the desperate remedy of diving through a cloud, with the British machine hot in pursuit. Again the English mechanic got a chance, and this time brought the German down. The two occupants of the fallen machine scrambled out, and Lieutenant Insall made another great swoop of five hundred feet, permitting his gunner once more to get into effective range. The two men were driven away, one obviously wounded, and then the lieutenant completed his work by dropping a bomb upon the fallen machine, which was last seen wrapped in smoke.

The two airmen had then to run the gauntlet of the German trenches at an elevation of only 2,000 feet, and they passed this barrier, the lieutenant driving his machine and the gunner working cheerfully away at the machine-gun. Their adventures were not yet at an end, for their last exploit had been rewarded with a damaged petrol tank, which caused them to descend to the cover of a wood five hundred yards inside the British

PTE. R. DUNSIRE,
V.C.,
13th R. Scots.
"Hill 70."

LT. W. T. FORSHAW,
V.C.,
1/9th Manchester.
Gallipoli.

[*Vandyk.*]

BREV.-MAJ. FOSS, V.C.,
D.S.O.,
2nd Bedfords.
Neuve Chapelle.

SEC.-LT. B. H. GEARY,
V.C.,
4th East Surreys.
"Hill 60."

TEMP. SEC.-LT. R. P.
HALLOWES, V.C.,
4th Middlesex.
Hooge.

plished was one well-nigh impossible, even to a man in full possession of his strength and faculties.

A few days before, on July 25th, Temp.-Major Lance George Hawker, D.S.O., of the Royal Engineers and R.F.C., put up a remarkable fight against three German aeroplanes which engaged him at the same time. Each enemy plane had machine-guns, pilot, and observer; but Major Hawker met them single-handed in the air and routed them utterly.

One machine he tackled at a height of 10,000 feet and drove it to the ground in the British lines, both pilot and observer being captured. The second was badly damaged and compelled to descend, and the third then took to flight. For this exploit Major Hawker, who will be remembered as a famous sea-flyer in pre-war times, was awarded the V.C.

The third airman V.C. of the year was Second-Lieutenant Gilbert S. M. Insall, No. 11 Squadron R.F.C. With an observer, First-Class Air-Mechanic T. H. Donald, he was patrolling the German lines on November 7th, 1915, in a Vickers' battle-plane, when a German machine was sighted. Lieutenant Insall gave pursuit, and the German led him over a rocket battery, the only effect of the manœuvre being that the Vickers' machine

[*Elliott & Fry.*]

TEMP.-LT.-COL. DOUGLAS-
HAMILTON, V.C.
6th Cameron Highlanders.
"Hill 70." (Killed.)

[*Lafayette.*]

CAPT. P. H. HANSEN, V.C.,
6th Lincs Regt. Gallipoli.

lines. Here they had to submit to a bombardment, quite one hundred and fifty shells being fired at them. Under this fire they worked all night at repairing the damage, and at dawn flew the machine home.

A naval airman won the fourth and last airman's V.C. for the year. This was Squadron-Commander Richard Bell Davis, D.S.O., R.N. He took part in an aerial attack upon Ferrijik Junction, in company with Flight-Sub-Lieutenant Wyllie. The latter officer had his machine brought down, and in order to prevent it falling into the hands of the enemy he set fire to it. While he was at his work, Commander Davis swooped down and, in spite of the near approach of the enemy, picked him up, and reached the aerodrome in safety with him.

The soldiers who won the Victoria Cross number sixty-six, of whom thirty-one were officers, and thirty-five non-commissioned officers and men. The officers include two majors and nine captains, as well as one chaplain. Seven lieutenants and twelve second-lieutenants complete the total of thirty-one.

Included among the non-commissioned officers and men were seven sergeants, nine corporals, three lance-corporals, and twelve privates. A piper, a Gurkha rifleman, an

HONOURED GUESTS OF THE ANZAC CLUB IN WESTMINSTER.
Four of the Anzac V.C.'s who attended an "At-home" given in their honour by the Anzac Club and Buffet, Westminster. Left to right : Lieut. W. J. Symons, V.C. (7th Aust. I.F.), Capt. F. H. Tubb, V.C. (7th Aust. I.F.), Lieut. H. V. H. Throssell, V.C. (10th Aust. L.H.), Private J. Hamilton, V.C. (1st Aust. I.F.).

Indian lancer, and a sepoy made the list complete. Forty-one of these sixty-six Army V.C.'s were won by line regiments, and three more by Guardsmen, making a total of forty-four for the regular infantry. The remaining twenty-two included nine Anzac soldiers, one among them being a light horseman, five members of the Indian Army, one Canadian, two engineers, one yeoman, one chaplain, one officer from the R.A.M.C., one from the Indian Medical Service, and an artilleryman.

The honours were widely distributed, but the outstanding feature of the awards, next to the Anzac record of nine V.C.'s in a month, was the number won by Lancashire regiments. The Lancashire Fusiliers took three crosses, the East Lancashire Regiment two, the York and Lancaster Regiment two, the Manchester Regiment two, the Royal Lancasters one, and the Loyal North Lancashires one.

Other regiments with two V.C.'s were the Coldstream Guards, the Cameron Highlanders, the Royal Inniskilling Fusiliers, and the King's Royal Rifles.

The V.C. awards to the Navy for the miraculous landings on Gallipoli on April 25th, 1915, have already been detailed. A number of Army awards were also made, and notable among these were the V.C.'s awarded by the process of election. Three companies of the Lancashire Fusiliers were concerned in the exploit for which the three crosses in question were given. On landing, these companies were met by a deadly fire from hidden machine-guns, causing extremely heavy casualties.

Chosen trio of heroes

The uninjured men charged boldly up the face of a steep cliff, being checked in their advance by thick wire entanglements, which they cut. In the face of a murderous fire they gained the summit of the cliff and seized a position which made it possible for their comrades to land more safely.

Where all had shown such dash and bravery, the selection of the three men for special honour was left to the soldiers themselves. Their choice fell upon Captain Richard

Raymond Willis, Sergeant Alfred Richards, and Lance-Corporal William Keneally. The lance-corporal, who was picked up badly wounded, died shortly afterwards in a Malta hospital.

On the day following the landing, April 26th, Corporal William Cosgrove, 1st Battalion Royal Munster Fusiliers, took part in an attack on the Turkish positions east of Cape Helles. He led his section into action from the beach with great dash, and on the way encountered a high entanglement of barbed-wire. He approached it single-handed and under heavy fire, and actually pulled down the posts which supported the wire. This fine example of resource and courage was effective in making a way through this formidable obstacle, and contributed so much to the successful clearing of the heights that Cosgrove was awarded the V.C. The whole Gallipoli campaign was resplendent with single-handed feats performed in extreme emergency and against overwhelming odds. Of this character was the conduct by which Lieutenant Herbert James, of the 4th Battalion Worcestershire Regiment, won the V.C. Two gallant feats stood to the credit of this young officer. On June 28th, when an attack was being made in the southern zone of Gallipoli, a portion of a regiment near him had been checked in its advance, owing to all its officers having been put out of action.

Critical situations saved

Lieutenant James, acting on his own initiative, gathered some men together and advanced under heavy fire. Leaving these new-comers to collect the checked soldiers, he went back for another party, whom he also brought up, with the result that fresh life was instilled into the attack on this section of the line.

Later, in the night of July 3rd, he led a party of bomb-throwers up a Turkish communication-trench, and in the fight that followed lost all his men. Single-handed, he kept the head of the trench under a heavy fire and showers of bombs until a barrier had been built behind him and the position made secure.

A similar feat was performed by Captain Gerald Robert O'Sullivan, 1st Battalion Royal Inniskilling Fusiliers, on the night of July 1st-2nd, at Krithia. An important section of trench had been lost, and although Captain O'Sullivan did not belong to the troops detailed for its recapture, he volunteered to lead a bombing-party for the purpose. They had to advance across the open, under heavy fire, and having reached their objective, to bomb the Turks out of the captured position.

In order to see where his bombs were falling, this officer climbed upon the parapet, and from this exposed position directed the assault. He was wounded, but had stimulated his men to the recapture of the trench. Captain O'Sullivan, who had previously saved a critical situation on the night of June 18th-19th by his splendid courage, was awarded the V.C. for the two feats.

Another Inniskilling Fusilier, Sergeant James Somers, also of the 1st Battalion, remained alone in a sap which the Turks were attacking, waiting for bombs to be brought up for the defence. When they came, he climbed over to the Turkish trench and made a spirited attack upon its occupants. Later, he crossed the open under heavy fire, in order to bomb the Turkish flank, and several times ran back under fire for fresh supplies of bombs. Thus he played an important part in the recapture, on the night of July 1st-2nd, of a section of lost trench, and was awarded the V.C. for the service.

The first important military operation by the British forces in the second year of the war was the ill-fated landing at Suvla Bay. This operation was covered by a number of gallant demonstrations executed by the Anzacs, who already held the beaches nearer Fort Gaba Tepe; and among these assaults the capture of Lone Pine Plateau stands out by itself. The overwhelming charge of the 1st Brigade of Australian Infantry which carried the Turkish positions, and the stubborn defence during the ensuing four days, in which the 2nd Brigade of Australian Infantry also participated, will rank among the most glorious of all the brave deeds of the Anzacs.

Seven V.C.'s in four days In those four days no fewer than seven V.C.'s were won, three by officers, and the others by men who had not then attained to commissioned rank. Captain Alfred John Shout, of the 1st Battalion, had won the Military Cross when the Anzacs landed on Gallipoli and was the hero of a dozen dazzling exploits in subsequent affrays. On August 8th, 1915, he was attached to the headquarters of the 1st Brigade on Lone Pine Plateau, when a large body of Turks came down a long communication-trench which led from their position across the plateau. They came into sight around the last traverse, within fifty yards of headquarters, under the astonished eyes of Brig.-General Smythe himself.

They were checked, and then Captain Shout and his friend, Captain Sass, resolved to drive them back by the way they had come. Captain Shout went first, with a liberal supply of bombs, and his fellow-officer supplemented his efforts with a rifle. They drove the Turks back, bit by bit, inflicting loss upon them at each traverse. When a satisfactory spot was reached, they decided that a barricade should be erected, and in order to drive the Turks effectively away during the execution of this work, Captain Shout endeavoured to throw three bombs, which he lit at the same time. The third exploded in his hands, inflicting mortal injuries. A memorial monument to him has been erected in Darlington, New South Wales, the town from which he came.

Captain Frederick Tubb, of the 7th Battalion, was in charge of a small band of men belonging to that battalion in the morning of August 9th. They were holding a newly-captured section of trench at Lone Pine, the preservation of which was of vital importance to the whole position. The Turks persisted for some hours in their attempts to capture it, renewing their bomb attacks from time to time with fanatical bravery. Three times they succeeded in blowing down the barricade behind which the Anzacs sheltered, and as often Captain Tubb led his men forward, drove them back, and rebuilt the shelter. He was wounded twice, and almost every man of his small company shared the same fate. But they retained the position through the crucial hours, and handed it over to a strong party finally sent to relieve them.

For this work Captain Tubb was awarded the V.C., as were two of his non-commissioned officers, Sergeant William Dunstan and Corporal Alexander Stuart Burton. Burton paid for the honour with his life, and Dunstan was seriously wounded. He returned to Australia, where his native city of Ballarat had promoted a subscription to mark the appreciation his fellow-citizens felt of his gallantry. The sum already gathered was a substantial one when Dunstan heard of it; but he at once telegraphed his wish that he should not be presented with money merely for performing his duty.

During the night of August 8th-9th, Lieutenant William John Symons, also of the 7th Battalion, was in charge of

A "SPLENDID SCRUM" AT BAZENTIN-LE-PETIT.
An officer present at the trench fighting at Bazentin-le-Petit on July 14th, 1916, described it as "a splendid scrum." One section commander picked up a German and flung him bodily over the parapet into the remains of his own wire.

PTE. SAMUEL HARVEY.
V.C.
1st York and Lanc. " Big
Willie " Trench.

TEMP.-MAJ. L. G. HAWKER,
V.C., D.S.O.,
R.E. and R.F.C. Western front.

PTE. CHARLES HULL, V.C.,
21st Lancers. Mesopotamia.

another section of trench not far from that so bravely held by Captain Tubb. The fury of the Turkish attack was divided between the two places. All night the enemy kept up their bomb attacks, but always they were driven off. Early in the morning the lieutenant was called to a sap-head, where six officers had been killed or wounded in succession, and where a portion of the sap had been captured by the enemy.

Revolver in hand, he led a charge which drove the Turks out of the sap. He then superintended the construction of a barricade across the sap, holding up a wooden screen to shelter his men from the Turkish rifle fire. The Turks came close to this screen, and managed to set it on fire, but the lieutenant extinguished the flames without allowing the work to be interrupted. He held the position until relief came, and was awarded the V.C. for his great services.

Lance-Corporal Leonard Keysor, of the 1st Battalion, was awarded a V.C. for continuous work in the south-eastern corner of Lone Pine Plateau, extending without intermission from August 7th to August 9th. Keysor was one of the best bomb-throwers in the Anzac ranks, and in this engagement he threw and fielded live bombs for fifty hours without rest. The bombs used by the Turks were furnished with a ten-second fuze, and Keysor caught many of these as they landed, and returned them among the enemy, where they exploded.

Keysor was wounded and marked for hospital, but he declined to go. Later he was again wounded, and ordered back to the dressing-station ; but on his way there he

encountered a company which had lost all its bomb-throwers and volunteered for service with them. He continued fighting until a very difficult situation was eased, and won the admiration and regard of all who fought with him.

Dare-devil bravery of a different kind was shown by Private John Hamilton, of the 1st Battalion, who won the V.C. at Lone Pine on August 9th. He was stationed in a section of trench from which a view of the main Turkish communication-trench could be obtained by taking extreme risks. Hamilton climbed up on to the parapet, exposing himself fully, and from this post gave warning of the approach of each party of Turks which passed along the communication-trench.

His comrades attempted to build a sand-bag shelter around him, but could only succeed in covering the lower part of his body. Hamilton stuck to his self-imposed task, shooting at the Turks whenever any came in sight, and risking his life every minute he stayed there. He marvellously escaped wounds for five hours, during which time he rendered the most signal service to his side.

While the Australian Infantry were holding Lone Pine, the New Zealanders made an irresistible assault on the hill mass of Chunuk Bair, from a point nearer to Suvla Bay. In this attack, which began on August 7th, Corporal Cyril Royston Guyton Bassett, of the New Zealand Divisional Signal Company, won the V.C. for the most conspicuous bravery. Bassett's name had been a synonym for devotion to duty ever since the New Zealanders first landed on Gallipoli, and the deed of August 7th is but one among many with which he is credited.

A splendid New Zealander

The New Zealand Infantry had taken the ridge, and the work of establishing telephonic communication was undertaken by Bassett, among others. In broad daylight, and under a heavy and continuous fire, he succeeded in laying a line to the advanced position, and was awarded the only V.C. which fell to New Zealand during the first two years of the war.

The last Anzac to win the V.C. on Gallipoli was Second-Lieutenant Hugo Vivian Hope Throssell, of the 10th Australian Light Horse. His chance came in what was practically the last British offensive operation on the Peninsula—the capture of Hill 60 on August 29th-30th. A section of trench at the foot of the hill was taken by a charge of the Light Horse, in which Captain Fry, the leader, was killed. Lieutenant Throssell then assumed command of this important section of trench, and defended it against repeated attacks delivered by the Turks in overwhelmingly greater numbers than the defenders.

The attacks were maintained all through the night of August 29th, and well into the morning of August 30th. The young officer lost most of his best men, and was himself wounded twice. His good spirits never flagged, and by his unfailing courage and resource he encouraged the handful of men under his orders to maintain the defence

SEC.-LT. G. S. M. INSALL,
V.C.,
No. 11 Squadron R.F.C. Achiet.

[Elliott & Fry.
LT. HERBERT JAMES,
V.C.,
4th Worcs. Regt. Gallipoli.

TEMP.-SEC.-LT. F. H.
JOHNSON, V.C.,
73rd Field Coy. R.E.
" Hill 70."

LCE.-CORPL. W.
KENEALLY, V.C.,
1st Lancashire Fus.
Gallipoli.

PTE. HENRY KENNY, V.C.,
1st Loyal North Lancs.
Western front.

until the last. He succeeded in holding out until relief came, when he went away to have his wounds dressed. After that had been done, he returned to the trench to see that all was right there before going away to the beach.

Thus nine V.C.'s were won by Anzacs on Gallipoli in the month of August, 1915, a remarkable number when it is considered that the whole force at Anzac, at full strength, numbered no more than 30,000 rifles.

Of the Suvla Bay contingent, Captain Percy Howard Hansen, adjutant, 6th (Service) Battalion Lincolnshire Regiment, won the V.C. for remarkable bravery at Yilghin Burnu on August 9th, 1915. The advance of the regiment was checked by scrub fire, and eventually it had to retire, leaving some seriously wounded men behind it. Captain Hansen, gathering a few volunteers, dashed back through the scrub, and under a terrible fire crossed from two hundred to four hundred yards of open to the assistance of the men. He did this, not once, but several times, and saved from certain death, by burning, no fewer than six men.

Private Frederick William Owen Potts, of the 1st Berkshire Yeomanry (T.F.), won renown and the V.C. by dragging a wounded comrade to safety a distance of six hundred yards on a shovel. The incident took place at Hill 70, Gallipoli, on August 21st. Potts was himself severely wounded in the thigh, but he stayed with **Devotion to a** his comrade, who was unable to move, for **comrade** two days under the very parapet of the Turkish trenches. He was fired at by the Turks when he started in the dark for our own lines with his comrade on his novel sledge, but escaped further hurt, and arrived in camp about 9.30 p.m. on August 23rd.

Another Gallipoli V.C. was Lieutenant William Forshaw, 1/9th Battalion Manchester Regiment (T.F.), who maintained an unequal fight against overwhelming numbers of Turks through the days August 7th-9th, in the north-west corner of the position known as the "Vineyard." Three separate trenches converged at this point, and the Turks attacked by all three trenches at once. Lieutenant Forshaw was the soul of the defence, directing his men to great advantage, and all the time throwing bombs with fine effect. For forty-one hours he was throwing bombs incessantly, so that he could not move his stiffened arm when he was finally relieved.

After the first twenty-four hours of this work, the detachment to which he belonged was relieved, but he volunteered to stay on. A crucial point of the defence was a sand-bag barricade, and over this the Turks managed to climb on August 8th. The officer led a charge against them, shot three with his revolver, and recaptured the position.

West African fighting yielded one V.C. during the year; but though gazetted on September 2nd, 1915, the feat by which Captain John Fitzhardinge Paul Butler, King's R.R.C., West African Frontier Force, earned it was actually

performed on November 17th, 1914. With a party of thirteen men he went into the thick bush of Cameroon, and attacked an enemy force of one hundred, including several Europeans. His little band gained a victory and succeeded in capturing a machine-gun and a large quantity of ammunition.

Later, on December 27th, 1914, he made a reconnaissance under fire, by swimming the Ekam River with a few men. Having completed his observation, he swam back again, the total cost of the valuable knowledge he had gained being two men wounded while swimming the river.

East Africa provided an actor-hero in the person of Lieutenant Wilbur Dartnell, who left the stage to join the Royal Fusiliers (City of London Regiment). In an engagement at Maktau, East Africa, on September 3rd, 1915, it was necessary to retire, leaving several wounded men in a dangerous place. Lieutenant Dartnell knew that the black soldiers against whom we were fighting invariably murdered our wounded, and though himself wounded in the leg, remained behind in the hope of protecting them. He gave his own life in this gallant attempt to save others.

Among gallant deeds performed in Mesopotamia, that of Major George Godfrey Massey Wheeler, late 7th Hariana Lancers, Indian Army, was rewarded with a V.C. He took out his squadron at Shaiba, Mesopotamia, on April 12th, 1915, in an attempt to capture a flag which was the rallying-point of the enemy. The sortie was a gallant one, in which the enemy suffered heavily, and on Major Wheeler's retirement they came out of

PTE. THOMAS KENNY, V.C., 13th Durham L.I. La Houssoie.

LCE.-CPL. L. KEYSOR, V.C., 1st Australian I.F. Gallipoli.

TEMP.-LT. E. A. McNAIR, V.C., 9th R. Sussex. Western front.

PIPER DANIEL LAIDLAW, V.C., 7th K.O.S.B. Loos.   CAPT. J. A. LIDDELL, V.C., 3rd A. & S.H. and R.F.C.   MID. W. St. A. MALLESON, V.C., R.N. Dardanelles.   TEMP.-LT. G. A. MALING, V.C., M.B., R.A.M.C. Fauquissart.   CORPL. S. MEEKOSHA, V.C., 1/6th W. Yorks. Yser.

RIFLEMAN KULBIR THAPA, V.C., QUEEN ALEXANDRA'S OWN GURKHA RIFLES.
Himself wounded, this gallant Gurkha carried a wounded Englishman to comparative safety and stayed with him all night.   Next morning he went back twice to the German lines for wounded comrades, and then carried the Englishman in under heavy fire.

little Indian hillmen come under discussion. He was himself wounded, and behind the first German line. Making his way back, he found a soldier of the 2nd Leicestershire Regiment badly wounded and helpless. The British soldier urged him to save himself, but the brave Gurkha preferred to remain with him, which he did throughout that day and night.

Taking advantage of a patch of mist in the early morning, he carried him on his back to a place of comparative safety. Leaving the Englishman there, he went back twice into the German lines for two of his own wounded comrades. It was now broad daylight, but he finished his work by carrying the wounded Briton in on his back, under the enemy's fire.

Two other brave Indian soldiers were awarded the V.C. for similar devotion to wounded Britons. Sepoy Chatta Singh, 9th Bhopal Infantry, Indian Army, saw his commanding officer lying wounded and exposed, and left his safe cover to render assistance to him. First binding up the officer's wound, he afterwards stood up under heavy fire to dig cover with his entrenching tool for the wounded man. From early afternoon till dusk fell, a vigil of five hours, he lay beside his officer, and between him and the enemy, thus sheltering him with his own body from the danger of further wounds. When the friendly dark came at last, he went back for help, and returned to assist in bringing his officer back to safety.

Lance-Naik Lala, 41st Dogras, Indian Army, rivalled this courageous and devoted conduct. Finding a British officer lying near the enemy lines, he dragged him into a comparatively safe place, where were already lying four wounded men whom he had rescued and bandaged. From this shelter he heard the calls of the adjutant of his own regiment, lying wounded and helpless within a hundred yards of the Germans.

Facing almost certain death, Lance-Naik Lala crawled out to the officer, **Indian rifleman's heroism** and wished to crawl back, with the wounded man on his back. As this could not be done, he remained by him, and actually divested himself of the major part of his clothing to keep his charge warm. When dark fell he made his way back to his shelter, carried the wounded officer he had first tended to safety, and then returned with a stretcher to rescue his adjutant.

Two V.C.'s won at Ypres were gazetted during the year, the first going to Sec.-Lieutenant B. H. Geary, 4th Battalion East Surreys. He held the left crater at Hill 60 on April 21st, 1915, with his own platoon and some men of the Bedfordshire Regiment, and had to submit to a night-long bombardment which broke down the defences. Furious bomb attacks followed, till the crater was choked

cover to retaliate, forming an excellent mark for the Royal Horse Artillery's guns.

On the following day, April 13th, Major Wheeler was killed in leading an attack upon a position known as North Mound. When last seen he was spurring his horse against the enemy, far in advance of his squadron.

Another hero of Mesopotamia was Private (Shoeing-smith) Charles Hull, of the 21st (Empress of India's) Lancers. Captain Learoyd, the adjutant of the regiment, had his horse killed in a very hot engagement, and though the enemy was but a few yards away, Hull checked his own mount under heavy fire and took up the dismounted officer. This gallant act, which saved the captain's life, was performed entirely upon the initiative of the private soldier.

Rifleman Kulbir Thapa, 2nd Battalion 3rd Queen Alexandra's Own Gurkha Rifles, won his V.C. on September 25th by bravery and self-sacrifice that will ever be remembered when the splendid fighting qualities of the gallant

REV. EDWARD NOEL
MELLISH, V.C.,
British chaplain. St. Eloi.

CORPL. J. D. POLLOCK, V.C.,
5th Cameron Highlanders.
Hohenzollern Redoubt.

with dead and wounded men. The officer was the life and soul of a spirited defence. At times he used a rifle, again he could be seen hurling bombs at the enemy or mounting the parapet to scan the approaches in order to detect any Germans who might be coming to the attack. In these operations he continually risked his life, and eventually was wounded. He found time to arrange for fresh ammunition supplies, and to send reinforcements ; and in every way proved himself a capable as well as a gallant officer.

Five days later, on April 26th, Acting-Corporal Issy Smith, 1st Battalion Manchester Regiment, also won the V.C. at Ypres. Leaving safe cover on his own initiative, he went out a long way toward the enemy lines to assist a severely wounded man. He had to face heavy machine-gun and rifle fire, and on his return journey with the wounded man this risk was intensified ; but Smith brought him in safely. Later he displayed splendid bravery in bringing in many more wounded under fire, and in attending to them under fire at his own great, personal risk.

Among the last of the Neuve Chapelle V.C.'s to be gazetted was Captain Charles Calveley Foss, D.S.O., 2nd Battalion Bedfordshire Regiment. Captain Foss led a handful of eight men in a gallant counter-attack upon a section of trench which the Germans had captured from us. His attack was delivered with so much dash that the position was taken again, and the fifty-two Germans who held it were made prisoners. The position was a most important one, and its recapture with so few men was as serviceable as it was courageous.

The V.C. which fell to Canada was won at Givenchy on June 15th by Lieutenant Frederick William Campbell, 1st Canadian Battalion. Lieutenant Campbell took a machine-gun over the parapet to the German first line, and under heavy fire and bombing maintained the position he had taken up until every man with him had fallen. Finding himself single-handed, he advanced with his machine-gun, and occupied a higher and still more exposed position, from which he fired 1,000 rounds with

PTE. G. PEACHMENT, V.C.,
2nd K.R.R. Corps. Hulluch.
(Killed.)

PTE. F. W. O. POTTS, V.C.,
1/1st Berkshire Yeomanry.
Gallipoli.

excellent effect. To him is largely due the credit of holding back a counter-attack delivered by the Germans. In a subsequent engagement Lieutenant Campbell was so seriously wounded that he died of his injuries.

The second year of the war also saw the first V.C. allotted to a British chaplain. The Rev. Edward Noel Mellish, temporary chaplain, was formerly curate of St. Paul's Church, Deptford. At St. Eloi he displayed a marvellous devotion throughout three days of terrible fighting, and brought in single-handed no less than twenty-two wounded men, besides taking part as a volunteer in many concerted movements for rendering succour to the wounded. On the first day he passed continually from our original trenches to those we had captured, always under heavy fire. On this day he brought in ten men ; and some idea of the risk he ran may be gathered from the fact that three of them were killed before him, when he was in the very act of dressing their wounds.

On the second day he brought in twelve more men under similar circumstances, while on the night of the third day he headed a party of volunteers who performed similar dangerous but merciful work.

The magnificent bravery displayed in the September and October fightng at Loos, Hill 70, and the Hohenzollern Redoubt was productive of a large number of V.C.'s, the first to be gazetted being Lance-Sergeant Oliver Brooks, 3rd Battalion Coldstream Guards. Brooks had to meet and stem a desperate rush of German bombers on the night of October 8th near Loos. They had captured two hundred yards of trench, when the Coldstream, acting on his own initiative, led a counter-attack of bombers, and drove the enemy out of the trenches. " His bravery, in the midst of a hail of bombs from the Germans," says the official record, " was of the very first order, and the complete success attained in a very dangerous undertaking was entirely due to his fearlessness, presence of mind, and promptitude."

The award to Brooks was followed by a batch of eighteen other V.C.'s, won at Loos and in the neighbourhood.

ACT.-SERGT. J. C.
RAYNES, V.C.,
71st Brigade R.F.A. Bethune.

CAPT. A. MOUTRAY
READ, V.C. (Killed),
1st Northants. Hulluch.

SERGT. A. RICHARDS,
V.C.,
1st Lancs. Fus. Gallipoli.

[Lafayette.
LIEUT. G. A. BOYD-
ROCHFORT, V.C.
Scots Guards. Cambrin.

[Russell.
COM. ERIC G. ROBINSON,
V.C., R.N.
Dardanelles.

SEAMAN G. McK. SAMSON, V.C., R.N. Reserve. Dardanelles.　SERGT. A. F. SAUNDERS, V.C., 9th Suffolk.　TEMP.-SEC.-LT. A. J. T. FLEMING-SANDES, V.C., 2nd East Surrey.

Temp.-Lieutenant Colonel Angus F. Douglas-Hamilton, commanding 6th Cameron Highlanders, was killed at the head of his men on September 26th at Hill 70. The troops on either side of him having fallen back, he led his own battalion to the charge four times. At the fourth charge he had only fifty men left, and in this gallant charge he fell. It was no useless sacrifice he made, for owing to his efforts the advance of the enemy at this point was checked.

Another V.C. hero of Hill 70 was Second-Lieutenant Frederick H. Johnson, 73rd Field Coy., R.E. Though severely wounded, he led several charges against the German position, and that under very heavy fire. His example was contagious, and was instrumental in saving the position which had been taken. He remained at his post until relieved.

At Hill 70 Private Robert Dunsire, 13th Battalion Royal Scots, went out under heavy fire on the night of September 26th and rescued a wounded man from No Man's Land. Later on the same night he heard a wounded man close to the German lines calling for help. He crawled amid the hail of bullets across the open and brought in that man also.

Hulluch also supplied its quota of V.C.'s, foremost among whom was Captain Anketell M. Read, 1st Battalion Northamptonshire Regiment, who paid with his life the price of the valuable services he rendered. When the first attack was made on September 25th, 1915, he was partially gassed. None the less he struggled out to rally disorganised and retiring units. Several times he led such parties back to the firing-line, and there, under a heavy fire, moved about among them, inspiring them with fresh confidence. In this brave work he met his death.

Private George Peachment, 2nd Battalion King's Royal Rifle Corps, lost his life and won the V.C. at the same place on the same night. Peachment died in trying to save his company commander, Captain Dubs. The captain was lying wounded in the open, and Peachment crawled out to him under heavy fire. He knelt there in the open, indifferent to his great danger, attempting to render aid to his wounded officer. There was a shell-hole close at hand, in which a number of men had taken cover, but this brave fellow had no thought for himself. He was wounded by a bomb on this errand of mercy, and later met his death from a rifle bullet.

ACT.-CORPL. ISSY SMITH, V.C., 1st Manchester. Ypres.

SEC.-LT. A. V. SMITH, V.C., 1/5th East Lancs. (Killed).

Private Arthur Vickers, 2nd Battalion Royal Warwickshire Regiment, displayed most serviceable heroism at Hulluch in this attack. Finding that the advance of his battalion was held up by the German wire, he went out upon his own initiative, under very heavy shell, machine-gun, and rifle fire, and cut the wires. It was broad daylight at the time, and his escape from what appeared certain death is miraculous. He had the satisfaction of knowing that he had largely contributed to the success of the assault by this action, for which he was awarded the V.C.

At Hohenzollern Redoubt many brave deeds were performed, and for one notable act Second-Lieutenant Arthur J. T. Fleming-Sandes, 2nd Battalion East Surrey Regiment, was awarded the cross. He had to take over a company which had run short of bombs, and had been much tried by continuous bombing and heavy machine-gun fire. Their own store of bombs was nearly exhausted, while they could see the men on their right retiring.

The lieutenant at once grasped the critical nature of the situation, and collecting as many bombs as he could gather, sprang on the parapet and hurled them at the Germans. The enemy was only twenty yards distant and the officer was fully exposed. He was soon wounded by a bomb, and it is remarkable that he was not killed.

But he disregarded the wound and continued his bomb-throwing until he was wounded a second time, and put completely out of action. He had saved the situation, however, for his men gained new heart from his example and " stuck it out " splendidly.

At Hohenzollern Redoubt Second-Lieutenant Charles G. Vickers, 1/7th Battalion Sherwood Foresters (T.F.), also won his V.C. by a fine single-handed performance on October 14th. He had lost nearly all his men, and had to meet an attack from front and flank. There was only a barrier between him and the enemy and he had but two men to carry bombs for him. Yet he held the barrier single-handed for some hours.

In order to strengthen the precarious position, he further ordered that a second barrier should be built behind him, thus cutting off his only means of retreat if the first barrier should be captured. He held his barrier long enough to allow the second one to be finished ; and then he fell, dangerously wounded.

SERGT. J. SOMERS, V.C. 1st R. Inniskillings. Gallipoli.　SUB.-LT. A. W. ST. CLAIR TISDALL, V.C., R.N.V. Gallipoli.　SEC.-LT. A. B. TURNER, V.C., 3rd Berkshire. Vermelles.

[Canadian official photograph.
THE ULTIMATE EXPRESSION OF HUMAN COURAGE: CANADIANS ADVANCING UNDER SHELL FIRE.

One cannot contemplate troops advancing under heavy shell fire without marvelling at the nerve control which impels them forward. A squad of Canadians are moving along a communication-trench. The ominous smoke of bursting shells, the three shorn trees on the extreme right, which remind one of a distant Calvary, and the barren aspect of the entrench-mènt lend this illustration an intensely dramatic reality.

The bravery and initiative of Corporal J. L. Dawson, 187th Coy. R.E., saved a great many men from being gassed at Hohenzollern Redoubt on October 13th, 1915. The trenches were full of men at the time, and a heavy gas attack was in progress. Dawson, in order to get the infantry out of the trenches that were full of gas, walked up and down upon the parados in full view of the enemy, giving directions. He discovered three cylinders of gas that were leaking and rolled them away from the trench, where he fired bullets into them in order to let the gas escape. For his great and meritorious services he was awarded the V.C.

"Pluck, endurance, and devotion to duty beyond praise" won for Private T. Kenny, 13th (Service) Battalion Durham Light Infantry, the V.C. With his officer, Lieutenant Brown, Kenny was on patrol duty in a thick fog near La Houssoie on November 4th. They drew the fire of some Germans who were lying in front of their lines in a ditch, and the officer was shot through both thighs. Kenny hoisted him on his back and began to crawl about with him in the thick fog. **In "Little Willie" trench** Hard as he tried, he could not discover the path back to the British trenches. For more than an hour he crept about, disregarding the officer's repeated request that he should save himself. Eventually he sank down utterly exhausted, only to find himself lying in a ditch with which he was familiar. Leaving Lieutenant Brown there under cover, he went back for assistance, and the officer was brought in under heavy fire.

The coolness and bravery of Corporal James D. Pollock, 5th Battalion Cameron Highlanders, checked a German attack made on the Hohenzollern Redoubt by way of "Little Willie" trench. The enemy were working dangerously along the trench, when Pollock climbed out, and from the top of it threw bombs down upon them. He was exposed to heavy machine-gun fire, but he held them for an hour single-handed. In the end he was wounded, but he had checked the rush, and richly deserved his V.C.

In the same neighbourhood there was a heavy bombing attack made on September 29th by the Germans at "Big Willie" trench. Bombs were desperately needed to meet the attack, and Private Samuel Harvey, 1st Battalion York and Lancaster Regiment, volunteered to fetch **An exploit with bombs** them. The communication-trench was choked by wounded men and by the supports who were coming up to the fight; so Harvey had to run across the open under heavy fire. He made many such trips, and had carried thirty boxes of bombs to the front before he fell wounded in the head. The V.C. was awarded him with the remark that it was mainly due to his cool bravery that the enemy was driven back.

The devotion to duty shown by Lieutenant George Allan Maling, R.A.M.C., in the heavy fighting with which the Loos attack opened, was rewarded with the V.C. He worked in the open near Fauquissart, and during the twenty-four hours which began at 6 a.m., September 25th, 1915, treated more than three hundred cases under heavy shell fire.

Early in this trying experience he was knocked over and stunned by the bursting of a big high-explosive shell, which killed several of the men who were waiting for treatment. Another shell soon afterwards buried him and his instruments in debris; but he could not be deterred from his duty. His only assistant was wounded, yet he persevered with his work of mercy until he dropped from sheer exhaustion.

Hooge was the scene of the devoted action by which Second-Lieutenant Sidney Clayton Woodroffe, 8th Battalion Rifle Brigade (Prince Consort's Own), lost his life while winning the V.C. on July 30th, 1915. On that day the Germans used liquid fire, and drove back the British centre so far that Lieutenant Woodroffe found his position attacked from the flank and finally from the rear. In this emergency he showed the greatest skill in withdrawing his men. Then he organised a counter-attack under extremely heavy fire and was shot down while attempting to cut the German wire.

Wonderful courage at Hooge At Hooge, between September 25th and October 1st, Second - Lieutenant Rupert P. Hallowes, 4th Battalion Middlesex Regiment, behaved with unexampled bravery and energy throughout four heavy and protracted bombardments, heartening his men by his wonderful courage. On several occasions he climbed upon the parapet, oblivious of danger, in order to put fresh courage into the men. He is credited with a number of most daring reconnaissances of the German positions, and when bombs were needed he went back and brought them up under heavy shell fire. He did not live to know that his devotion had been rewarded with the honour of the Victoria Cross.

Piper Daniel Laidlaw, 7th Battalion King's Own Scottish Borderers, won the V.C. by one of those acts which will live for ever in history. His regiment was to open the attack between Loos and Hill 70, but while waiting for the signal, it was severely gassed. Noticing that the men were shaken by this experience, Laidlaw mounted the parapet and played his company into action, marching up and down on the edge of the trench.

The sound of the pipes acted like a charm, for the men dashed out of cover and went to the assault like inspired beings. Laidlaw continued to pipe from his exposed position until he was wounded.

"The bravest of the brave" was the epithet applied by his colonel to Second-Lieutenant Alexander B. Turner, 3rd Battalion Royal Berkshire Regiment, who was awarded the V.C. for services at Fosse 8, near Vermelles, which cost him his life, on September 28th, 1915. A great bomb fight was going on in Slag Alley, and it was only too apparent that the regimental bombers were held in check. Lieutenant Turner therefore volunteered to lead a fresh bombing-party.

He rushed down a communication-trench, almost unsupported, hurling bombs with such effect that the Germans were driven back one hundred and fifty yards. This gain not only allowed the reserves to advance without much opposition, but it covered the flank in a subsequent retirement, which otherwise would have cost some hundred men in its execution.

Posthumous honours were also paid to Sergeant Harry Wells, 2nd Sussex, who took command when his platoon officer had been killed in the advance of September 25th near Le Rutoire. He led them to within fifteen yards of

the German wire, losing men at every yard. When half the platoon had fallen the men were checked, but Sergeant Wells rallied them splendidly and led them on again. He fell while once more urging the scanty remnant of the platoon forward to the attack, leaving behind him an imperishable record of valour and determination.

A double deed of splendid courage and self-sacrifice is credited to Acting-Sergeant John C. Raynes, of A Battery, 71st Brigade R.F.A. On October 11th, at Fosse 7 de Bethune, he rushed forward forty yards under heavy fire to the assistance of Sergeant Ayres, who was badly wounded. He bandaged him, and returned to his gun, only to return when the "Cease fire" order was given With two gunners he carried Ayres in, when a gas-shell burst before the dug-out into which the wounded man had been carried. Raynes ran back for his smoke-helmet, which he put on the wounded man. Then, though badly gassed himself, he crept back to serve his gun again.

Next day, October 12th, Raynes was buried in the debris of a wrecked house in Quality Street. Eight men in all were buried, and Raynes was the first rescued. Though wounded in two places, he remained under heavy shell fire until all the men were extricated, and assisted in dressing them. His own injuries being dressed, he returned to his gun and reported himself for duty.

Another dogged Briton was Lance-Corporal George H. Wyatt, 3rd Battalion Coldstream Guards, who was awarded the V.C. for two separate acts of bravery. The first occurred at Landrecies on the night of August 25th-26th. The enemy had kindled some straw stacks in a farmyard by means of incendiary bombs, and Wyatt knew that if they continued to burn, the British position would become untenable. The enemy was but twenty-five yards away, but twice he rushed from the trench, daring the bullets that were poured at him, and extinguished the flames.

COMMANDER EDWARD UNWIN, V.C., R.N.
He was awarded the V.C. for his brilliant work at the Dardanelles in connection with the "Wooden Horse" ship River Clyde, of which he was commander.

Later, he was wounded in the head at Villa Cotterets, but continued to fight till the blood pouring into his eyes prevented his seeing. His wound was dressed, and he was ordered to the rear; but he preferred to return to the firing-line and continue the fight.

Corporal Alfred A. Burt, 1st Battalion Hertfordshire Regiment (T.F.), well deserved the V.C. for his promptness in tackling a huge trench-mortar bomb at Cuinchy on September 27th. The **Tackling a huge bomb** bomb fell in the front trench just when Burt's company was preparing to scale the parapet for a charge. He knew the great destruction its explosion would cause, and though he might have saved himself by taking cover behind a traverse, he disdained that course. He went forward to the fizzing bomb, placed his foot upon the fuse, and wrenched it out of the bomb, rendering it innocuous. The fuse he threw over the parapet.

Two V.C.'s were won in the fighting at La Brique in November, the first falling to Private John Caffrey, 2nd Battalion York and Lancaster Regiment. Caffrey first went out with Corporal Stirk to the assistance of a wounded man of the West Yorkshire Regiment, who was lying about three hundred yards from the enemy's lines.

The two men were turned back by heavy shrapnel, but were not content with the rebuff. They ventured again, and this time they reached their man, though they had to run the gauntlet of accurate sniping and machine-gun fire.

While Stirk was lifting the wounded man upon Caffrey's back he was himself wounded in the head. Caffrey put down his burden, bandaged Stirk, and helped him back to safety. He then went out alone to the wounded man, this making his third journey across the danger zone. This time he had the satisfaction of bringing the man in single-handed. A splendid exploit !

A private's splendid exploit

Similar devotion was shown at La Brique, on November 23rd, by Corporal Alfred Drake, 8th Battalion Rifle Brigade. With an officer and two men he was patrolling near the German lines when the party was discovered and fired upon. The officer and one man fell wounded. Drake devoted himself to the officer, while the remaining man carried in his wounded comrade. The last glimpse he had of Drake revealed him kneeling by the officer under heavy machine-gun fire, calmly bandaging his wounds and tending him. A rescue-party went out later and, crawling carefully close to the enemy lines, found the two men. The officer was unconscious but living, with his wounds carefully bandaged. By his side was the dead body of the brave corporal riddled with bullets.

Another November V.C. was that won by Corporal Samuel Meekosha, 1/6th Battalion West Yorkshire Regiment, in an isolated trench near the Yser on the 19th of the month. The trench was held by a platoon of twenty men, of whom six were killed and seven wounded by a heavy bombardment. Then came a shell and buried all the sound men remaining, with the sole exception of Meekosha. The corporal managed to obtain a runner, by whom he sent a message for assistance. He himself set about the work of digging out the buried men. Big shells were falling all about him, something like a dozen landing within twenty yards of the spot where, in full view of the enemy and at close range, he was stolidly digging for his comrades. At least four men owed their lives to his courage, justly described in the official record as magnificent.

One of the noblest sacrifices of the war—an act neither dated nor placed in the official notice—was that by which Second-Lieutenant Alfred Victor Smith, 1/5th East Lancashire Regiment (T.F.), lost his life and won the V.C. When in the act of throwing a grenade he slipped, with the result that the live bomb fell in his own trench near a group of officers and men. He shouted a quick warning and was able to get into cover. But as soon as he was safe he realised that the others could not find cover in time. Without a moment's hesitation he left his place of safety and threw himself upon the grenade in the moment of its explosion, paying with his own life for those of others whom he saved.

Lancashire man's self-sacrifice

The feat of the private who tore the fuse from a large minnenwerfer bomb was excelled by the conduct of Second-

WORK OF HIGH EXPLOSIVES: ENORMOUS CRATER IN THE SOMME AREA.
Mine-crater in High Wood. Its proportions can be gauged by comparison with the size of the figures in its deepest part and half-way up the side. Such craters, many of which were made along the French and Flemish fronts, tended to impede advances, particularly during the winter months.

Lieutenant George Arthur Boyd-Rochfort, Special Reserve, 1st Battalion Scots Guards. While in the trenches between Cambrin and La Bassée, at 2 a.m. on August 3rd, 1915, a huge bomb from a German trench-mortar landed on the parapet near a working-party. The lieutenant could easily have taken cover, but he rushed forward with a warning shout and seized the big thing in his hands. One great cast sent it spinning clear of the parapet, where it forthwith exploded. Had it been allowed to remain where it fell, many lives would undoubtedly have been lost. This V.C. hero had the experience of being medically rejected before he was accepted for the Army in April, 1915.

Returning a German bomb

Another act of supreme devotion, performed amid the explosions of the large bombs cast by the minnenwerfer, won the V.C. for Private Harry Christian, 2nd Battalion Royal Lancaster Regiment. With half a dozen comrades he was holding a crater in front of our trenches when the men were driven back by a heavy bombardment from the German trenches. Christian found, after retiring, that three men had not come away from the crater; he therefore returned alone to the place and found them buried. Under showers of bombs he dug them out one by one and carried them back to safety.

Repeated acts of bravery and devotion to duty resulted in the award of the V.C. to Captain John Alexander Sinton, M.B., Indian Medical Service. Though shot through both arms and in the side, he worked under very heavy fire, dressing the wounded, and refusing to go into hospital while there was light to work. Many previous instances of great bravery had been credited to this fine officer.

Even the records of the Great War hold few parallels to the endurance of Lance-Corporal William Richard Cotter, 6th East Kent Regiment. His right leg had been blown off at the knee and he was wounded in both arms, yet he made his way unaided to a crater fifty yards distant, where his men were in a critical position. A fresh counter-attack of the enemy was imminent, and Cotter made a new disposition of the men in order to meet it.

For two hours he directed the defence by word of mouth, and only when the attack had quieted down did he allow rough dressing to be applied to his wounds. It was fourteen hours later before he was moved back to a dressing-

PTE. A. VICKERS, V.C.,   TEMP.-CAPT. C. G. VICKERS, V.C.,
2nd Royal Warwick.   1/7th Notts and Derby.

station, yet in his great agony he maintained a cheerful demeanour, which had the most encouraging effect on all around him.

Another splendid soldier, who continued to fight when his foot had been blown off, was Captain Arthur Forbes Gordon Kilby, 2nd South Staffordshire Regiment.

By his own request he was selected to lead a forlorn hope against a strong enemy redoubt, his well-known courage **Gallant leader of forlorn hope** marking him out for this dangerous service. He ran at the head of his company along a narrow tow-path, under heavy machine-gun fire and a shower of bombs, and brought his men to the enemy's wire. Here he was shot down, and his foot was blown off by a bomb; but he continued to fire a rifle and cheer his men on by word of mouth. He never returned from the attack, and it is presumed that he died at the post of duty and extreme danger. He was awarded the V.C.

Severe and painful wounds did not deter Private William Young, 8th East Lancashire Regiment, from going to the rescue of his sergeant, who was lying wounded under heavy fire in No Man's Land. As soon as he left the trench, Young had both jaws shattered by a bullet, but persisted until, with the help of another man, he had brought the sergeant in. When he got to the dressing-station it was found that he had also been wounded severely in the chest by a bullet, and an official pronouncement that " his great fortitude could hardly be surpassed" was added to the "Gazette" notice in which the exploit which won him the V.C. was detailed.

Another Lancashire hero was Private Henry Kenny, 1st Battalion Loyal North Lancashire Regiment. Six times in one day he went out into the open under heavy fire, and every time he returned with a wounded man. As he was handing the sixth man over the parapet he fell wounded in the neck by a rifle bullet.

Sergeant Arthur Frederick Saunders, 9th Suffolk Regiment, earned the V.C. by magnificent work with machine-guns. When his officer was wounded, the sergeant took charge, and supported four charges of another battalion.

After being hoisted in the air with his men, by the explosion of a mine, Lieutenant Eric Archibald McNair, 9th Royal Sussex Regiment, was still capable of leading them with such great gallantry and skill as to be awarded the V.C.

MAJ. G. G. M. WHEELER, V.C., Hariana Lancers.   CAPT. R. R. WILLIS, V.C., 1st Lancs Fusiliers.   SEC.-LT. S. C. WOODROFFE, V.C., 8th Rifle Brigade.   LCE.-CPL. G. H. WYATT, V.C., 3rd Coldstream Guards.   PTE. W. YOUNG, V.C., 8th East Lancs.

CHAPTER CXLVII.

RUMANIA: FIRST PHASES OF HER STRUGGLE WITH THE CENTRAL EMPIRES.

By Robert Machray.

Vital Importance of Rumania in the War—Glance at her History—Past and Recent Glories of her Army—Remarkable Interview with King Ferdinand—His Condemnation of Germany—Strategical Significance of Rumania—Threat to German Dreams of Eastern Empire—How Germany Sought to Meet It—Other Reasons for German Action—A Big Source of Supply—The Rumanian Army—Its Great Reserves—Avarescu its Finest General—Difficulty of Rumania's Two Long Fronts—Invasion of Transylvania—Bulgarian Treachery—Dobruja Front Not Sufficiently Protected—The Forcing of the Passes by Avarescu—Russian Forces March Into the Dobruja—Brilliant Rumanian Victory at Orsova—Deep Concern of Germany at Rumanian Successes—Outcry in Hungary—Mackensen's Offensive in the Dobruja—Its Success at First—Rumanians Advancing in Transylvania—Mackensen's Defeat—Increasing German Pressure under Falkenhayn in the North—Heavy Fighting for the Vulkan Pass—Rumanians Lose the Roter Turm Pass—They Begin to Withdraw in the North—Loss of Brasso—Views in Bukarest—Bitter Struggles in the Passes—Germans Gain Ground—Apprehension in the West—Allies Take Steps to Help Rumania—Mackensen's Renewed Offensive—His Capture of the Constantsa-Cerna Voda Railway—Ominous Situation.

I N Chapter CXLV., which was a general review of the situation in the Balkans, with particular reference to the Salonika Expedition from its inception up to the beginning of September, 1916, mention was made of the intervention of Rumania on the side of the Entente Powers, and a statement was presented of the reasons which led her to take that fateful step. A brief account was also given of the preliminary operations of the Rumanians and of the enemy.

The struggle, as it proceeded, was marked by sharp fluctuations of fortune, which universally attracted special attention to this new theatre of the world-war, and emphasised its extraordinary importance. In the west, and indeed outside the country itself and its immediate neighbours, little was really known of Rumania, and, as a rule, no adequate conception had been formed in the popular mind of the vital significance that was attached to her place and part in the ever-unfolding drama of the whole colossal conflict.

Rumania, as Rumania, had been in existence, comparatively

THE KING AND HIS COUNSELLOR.
King Ferdinand of Rumania in conversation with his Prime Minister, M. Ion Bratiano.

regarded, for only a very short time. Many people were still alive who could remember when that name was conferred on the State which arose from the union of the principalities of Wallachia and Moldavia, for its public proclamation at Bukarest dated no further back than December 23rd, 1861.

Previous to that time both Wallachia and Moldavia had been provinces of the Turkish Empire, nor was it until sixteen years afterwards that the political connection of Rumania with Turkey definitely came to an end.

On May 21st, 1877, representatives of the Rumanian nation, drawn from all quarters of the land, met in the capital, and solemnly declared its independence, which was confirmed by the Congress of Berlin, July 13th, 1878. Three years later Rumania became a kingdom, and Carol I., the reigning prince, its king. In the Russo-Turkish War of 1877 the Rumanians effectively co-operated with the Russians against their former rulers, and their soldiers brilliantly distinguished themselves in the fierce fighting around Plevna, which would hardly have fallen when it did had it not been

507

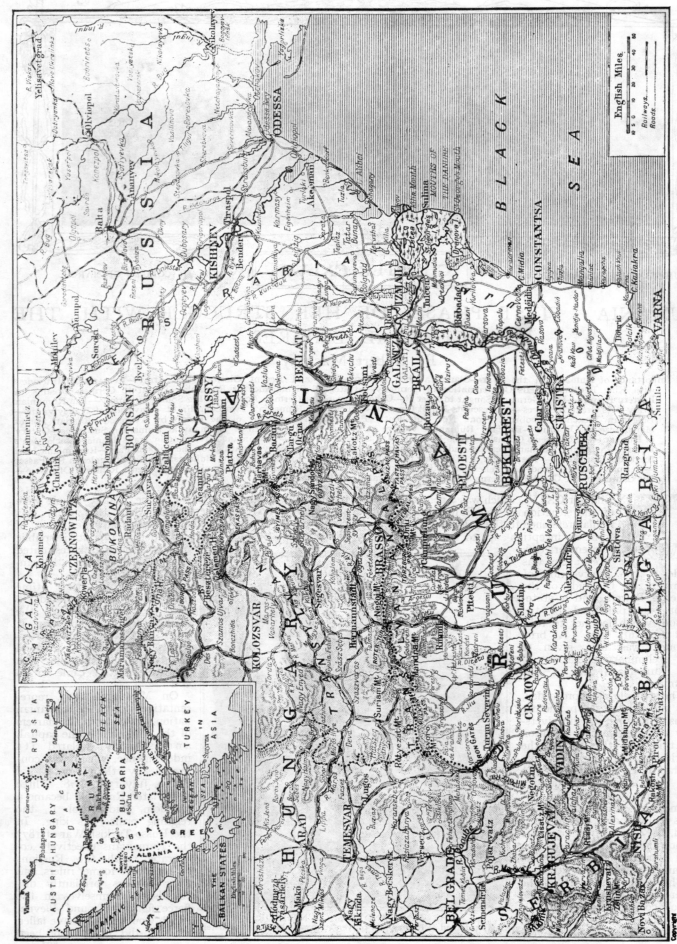

508

MAP OF RUMANIA INDICATING FRONTIER LINES AND PASSES.

The exceptional length of frontier lines from the Dobruja to Cernovitz will be noted. The Rumanian armies had to withstand Austro-German onslaughts from the north under General von Falkenhayn and Bulgarian and Turkish efforts from the south under General Mackensen.

for their courage and endurance. As one of the results of that successful war, Rumania received a large part of the Dobruja, the territory lying south of the delta of the Danube, and in 1913, after the Second Balkan War, was further aggrandised by obtaining from Bulgaria the cession of another portion immediately below it. (Chapter LXXXIV.)

In the Russo-Turkish War the Rumanian Army exhibited the highest military qualities under tests that were extremely severe. But the Rumanians had always been a notably fine fighting race. For many centuries the history of both Wallachia and Moldavia was a record of almost continuous and bitter contests, now with one enemy and now with another. On the declaration of war on Austria-Hungary, King Ferdinand, in the stirring Order of the Day which he addressed to his troops, was using no mere rhetorical expressions when he spoke of the victories of former times, but was appealing with unerring and tremendous effect to memories and traditions that glowed warm and bright in the soul of every one of his subjects.

A nation of fighters

King Ferdinand's allusion to the " Voivodes (Generals) Michael the Brave and Stephen the Great " recalled the most heroic figures of the deathless past—Michael, who for a while realised the national ideal of a Rumanian union on both slopes of the Carpathians by his bravery and skill in the field, and Stephen, victorious in forty-three battles, and the conqueror of Mohammed II. at Rasova in 1475. Though the Rumanians—or, to give them their ancient appellation, the Moldo-Vlachs— were finally beaten by the Turks, their martial spirit, as well as political address, was strong enough to keep them from being reduced to the condition of abject slavery which was the common lot of Serbian, Bulgarian, and Greek under the old Ottoman tyranny.

Yet Rumania was never a great State, either in territory or population. Dacia, the Roman province from whose colonists the modern Rumanians trace their descent, covered a more extensive area than any which could have been specifically described at a later period as Rumania. When the war broke out in 1914 its area was 53,689 square

miles; or about a few thousand square miles less than the combined area of England and Wales, and its population was only a little over seven and a half millions. There was, however, a Greater Rumania, for just across her boundaries were between four and five million people of her own blood, thus making the number of Rumanians in the world upwards of twelve millions.

These outer Rumanians were found in Hungary, in Bukovina, in Bessarabia, and in scattered communities in the Balkans, but the vast majority of them were in Hungary, in the province of Transylvania, on the other side of the northern and north-western mountain ranges, and there the Magyars, the ruling nationality, treated them like serfs. Primarily, it was to emancipate these oppressed men and women of her own blood that Rumania took up arms against the Dual Monarchy.

Under Magyar tyranny

In a remarkable interview, accorded at Bukarest to Mr. Stanley Washburn, the famous special correspondent of the " Times," and published by that journal on October 13th, 1916, King Ferdinand said that it was right that the world, in view of the enemy's malicious misrepresentations, should know what Rumania stood for in the great conflict, and what were the sacrifices and dangers she was called on to face when entering the " maelstrom where the giants themselves were clutched in a life-and-death struggle." He continued:

Rumania has not been moved by a policy of mere expediency, nor has her determination to enter this war been the outcome of any cynical material policy, or of bad faith to the Central Powers, but it has been based on the biggest principles of nationality and of national ideas. In every nation there are elemental public opinions which are instinctive rather than political. In Rumania, as in Russia, the tie of race and blood underlies all other considerations, and the appeal of our purest Rumanian blood that lies beyond the Transylvanian Alps has ever been the strongest influence in the public opinion of all Rumania from the throne to the lowest peasant. Inasmuch as Hungary was the master that held millions of our blood in perpetual political bondage, Hungary has been our traditional enemy. The Bulgar, with his efficient and unquestionably courageous Army on a frontier difficult to defend, has, logically, become our southern menace, and as a latent threat has been accepted secondarily as a potential enemy.

IN MODERN BUKAREST.
The Ministry of Foreign Affairs at Bukarest, a structure in Western European style with here and there a distinct Byzantine touch.

ROYAL PALACE AT BUKAREST.
The city itself has been called the Paris of the East, and is strongly influenced by French tradition.

KING FERDINAND'S THRONE-ROOM.
Interior scene in the Royal Palace at Bukarest, a salon not incomparable in style to that at Versailles.

VETERAN RUMANIAN PATRIOTS RECEIVED BY CROWN PRINCE CAROL.
An interesting ceremony reminiscent of other days when Russia and Rumania were allied against the Ottoman Empire. This photograph, taken after Rumania's intervention against the Central Powers, shows Prince Carol receiving veterans who fought under King Carol in 1877.

King Ferdinand went on to say that at the beginning of the war Rumania did not sympathise with Germany, but was not instantly hostile to her ; indeed, Germany had helped in the past to develop Rumanian industries and increase the prosperity of the country, and therefore Rumania had been friendly to her rather than otherwise. But after a time there appeared a moral issue which Rumania could not but appreciate. " As the war developed," the King observed, " the enemy's theory of frightfulness and lawlessness, which he had attempted to write into international law as a legitimate method of conducting war, came to affect opinion deeply." The principles that might is right, and that the end justifies the means, did not commend themselves to the Rumanians. These ideas were repulsive to them, but as they did not in their application touch the national life, the Rumanians stood outside the struggle.

" But with the progress of the war," the King added significantly, " Rumania began to feel the subtle force of enemy intrigue endeavouring in every way to force us into the war against our own real interests, using every argument to make the worse appear the better cause." Perhaps no more pointed condemnation of Germany was ever pronounced than that contained in these sentences, which fell from the lips of a prince of the House of Hohenzollern, a German by birth, and a German **A Hohenzollern** soldier by training, but a sovereign who **loyal to liberty** put the interests of his kingdom of Rumania first, last, and all the time.

German pressure on Rumania was very severe during the whole of 1915. The general situation in that period did not look well for the Allies. It spoke eloquently of the stability and worth of Rumanian character, that with Russia apparently beaten, with Britain and France at a standstill, and with Austria, Turkey, and Bulgaria, backed by German battalions, operating successfully in the Balkans, the Rumanians remained true to their better instincts,

and would not permit themselves to be seduced from their neutrality. They were neither to be bought with bribes nor intimidated by threats, to both of which they were frequently subjected, according to circumstances, by Germany. On the other hand, there was some disposition among the Allies, and even among certain of the Rumanians, to criticise Rumania for her inactivity on behalf of the Entente Powers during that period.

Commenting on this, King Ferdinand stated the position of his country—" A small Power with a small Army, surrounded by giants." **Rumania's critical** And he maintained that with a western **position** frontier in length greater than the British and French fronts combined, with a Bulgarian frontier almost undefended near her capital, stretching for hundreds of miles in the south, and with Russia in retreat, Rumania would have suffered swift annihilation if she had taken action at that time. Having regard to the dark fate of Serbia then, and considering the fluctuations that took place after Rumania began her campaign—at a juncture, too, when the outlook for the Allies was much more auspicious than ever before—the King must be judged to have gauged the position with accuracy. Rumania waited for the day when she could join in the war with a reasonable assurance of protecting herself and of receiving effective help from France, Great Britain, and—most of all —Russia.

Geographically, Rumania occupied a vitally important position with respect to the war and its strategy. On the north she had Russia, her ally, and Austria-Hungary, her bitter enemy, on the frontier. A peculiarity of her configuration in this direction was that her province of Moldavia was thrust up like a huge horn between Russian Bessarabia on the east and Austrian Bukovina and Hungarian Transylvania on the west. She was fronted on her western boundary by Hungary, Serbia, and Bulgaria, all practically German ground in 1916.

On the south, along the Danube and below her area of the Dobruja, lay Bulgaria. On the east was the Black Sea, for the defence of whose littoral she could rely to some extent on the Russian Black Sea Fleet, her own Navy being so inconsiderable as to be nearly negligible. On by far the greater portion of her frontiers she was encompassed by enemies when she opened hostilities. As against that, these frontiers were very strong by nature, except on the Dobruja line.

Nearly surrounded by enemies From near Mamornitsa on the Pruth, where that river flows in from Bukovina to form the boundary between Rumania and Russia in that quarter, to Orsova on the Danube near the Iron Gates there stretched long chains of mountains, chiefly the Eastern Carpathians and the Transylvanian Alps, forming a continuous and formidable rampart, only negotiable here and there by passes, some of which were easier than others, but all capable of effective defence. From Orsova eastward the Danube protected Rumania on the south till the Dobruja was reached. For a defensive campaign she was thus not ill-provided on the whole by the topographical features of the country.

Strategically, all Rumania, with the exception of the Moldavian horn, formed a big salient jutting out into the line of the Central Powers, and might become in strong hands a menace of the most formidable kind to the whole eastern front of the enemy. It was this that made Rumania's geographical situation of such enormous significance. The subjugation of Serbia—for the Entente one of the most unfortunate episodes in the war—had given Germany a broad passage from the north to the south and, what was even more valuable in her eyes, to the east. Germany and Austria were united with Bulgaria and Turkey, and the great trunk railway from Hamburg, through Berlin, Vienna, Belgrade, and Sofia to Constantinople and on into Asia Minor was to the enemy a visible sign of the probably complete realisation of

Germany's ambitious scheme for an empire from the North Sea to the Persian Gulf. The problem of the Allies was to break that union, to cut that railway, and so bring to naught the grandiose plan. If this salient of Rumania could be extended westward sufficiently the problem would be solved.

Immediately on hearing of Rumania's declaration of war on Austria, Germany declared war on the former, and at once set about in her arrogant way to organise a " punitive expedition " for the chastisement of the small State which had defied her ; but she had something far deeper in her mind, and that was to destroy this salient with its threat to her dearest dreams. Once having succeeded in this effort, she not only would have consolidated her whole eastern front, and rendered any change in it to her disadvantage extremely difficult, if not impossible, but she also would have gained a flanking position with respect to Russia. So far as Russia was immediately concerned, the Rumanian frontier became to all intents and purposes an enormous extension of her own front from the moment that Rumania began hostilities. The new front in Transylvania formed the southern flank of the whole allied line from the Dwina to the Danube.

There was another reason why Germany was anxious, and in fact determined, to get into and occupy Rumania, and it was economic. Previous to the intervention of Rumania, both she and Austria had drawn from the Danubian kingdom large **Rumania a valuable granary** supplies of wheat, maize, and petroleum. The blockade of the German coast maintained by the British Navy was for a long time much less rigorous than it might and should have been, yet it produced a considerable effect, which was rendered all the greater by poor crops in Germany, with the result that "bread-tickets" and other devices for husbanding the resources of that empire had to be resorted to. But had it not been for the food and oil that Germany was able to procure

OFF TO THE WAR: RUMANIA'S CROWN PRINCE SPEEDING TROOPS UPON THEIR WAY.
A Rumanian infantry regiment starting for the front in presence of Prince Carol. War was declared August 27th, 1916, and Rumania struck hard and at once against Austria-Hungary in Transylvania, occupying all the mountain passes.

THE NORTHERN PASSES OF RUMANIA.
Map showing the northern passes, from the Bukovina down to Brasso, where the Carpathian Mountains link up with the Transylvanian Alps.

from Rumania, her plight would have been far worse. For her size, Rumania was a rich country agriculturally. All Rumania north of the Danube sloped down from the mountains to that great river; farming began on the lower foot-hills, and continued wherever practicable almost down to the water's edge. The great bulk of the population was engaged on the land; the nobles had their estates cultivated by peasants, while thousands of other peasants tilled their own holdings, usually of from ten to twenty acres.

Rumania had always exported wheat and maize, but for some years past the working of the petroleum wells had been the chief industry, nearly twenty millions sterling having been invested in it, and her output of the oil was not far short of two million tons annually. The principal centres of the business were at Prahova, Dambovitsa, Bacau, and Buzau. In 1915 Germany obtained about 150,000 tons, and Austria over **German imports** 250,000 tons of petroleum from Rumania. **from Rumania** The Central Powers needed the oil; one of their main sources of supply had been cut off by the destruction of the wells in Galicia by the Russians, and with Rumania at war with them another channel was closed.

But there was more than this at stake. German finance and financiers had got such a grip on the commerce of the country that in that field Rumania was almost a dependency of Germany. The State had borrowed from the Germans nearly eighty millions sterling, and nearly half as much again had been invested by them in Rumanian banks and businesses. About ninety per cent. of the imports of Rumania were of Austro-German manufacture, nearly all her trade was in German or Austrian hands, and, in a word, practically the whole economic life of the nation had been directed and governed by Germans and Austrians. Germany, therefore, could desire nothing less than to see this rich little country slip out of her clutches;

on the contrary, it was her intention to gain through the war entire possession of it. One of the first measures taken by Rumania after war was declared was the sequestration of all enemy businesses within her borders. Political as well as economic and military considerations urged Germany on. Just as Rumania knew that she could never hope to realise her national aspirations through the Central Powers because of Austria, so did Germany know that a victorious Rumania meant such loss to Austria-Hungary, especially when coupled with the restoration of Serbia and the creation of a big southern Slav State under Serbia's leadership, that Austria would be seriously crippled and be of vastly reduced value to her as a political asset. And there was the further point, springing out of the defeat of the Dual Monarchy if it came to pass, that the disintegration of Austria would lay Germany open to the attack of the Allies from the south, and would eventually lead to the defeat of Germany herself.

It thus was certain that the enemy would do his utmost to crush Rumania, but it was equally certain that the Entente Powers were bound to do their utmost to prevent such a catastrophe.

In the interview quoted above, King Ferdinand said that Rumania waited to declare war until she was reasonably sure of being able to protect herself and of the support of the Allies. During previous years the Rumanian Army had been greatly augmented. In the Russo-Turkish War Rumania had two army corps, practically all her available strength, fighting the Turks. Each of these army corps consisted of two divisions, and both together comprised about 60,000 men Shortly after that war the Army was increased to four army corps, and as time went on and the State grew in wealth and population, it was made still stronger by various **Men and machines** legislative and other measures. In 1914 **of war** Rumania could have put into the field a force of upwards of 250,000 rifles, 18,000 sabres, 800 guns of various calibre, including 600 modern cannon, and 300 machine-guns. But these figures by no means really represented the full fighting strength of the country, as there were in existence very large reserves.

In Rumania military service was universal and compulsory. The system pursued was that young men aged nineteen to twenty-one received a certain amount of preliminary training at their homes; at the age of twenty-one they joined the Colours, serving two years in the infantry and three years in the cavalry, artillery, and engineers; thereafter these soldiers were placed in the reserve of the first line, where they remained for from four to five years; next they passed to the reserve of the second line; at the age of thirty-eight they joined the Territorial Force, in which they were classed till they attained forty-two years of age. Thus their total service lasted for twenty-one years. Such men as were not required for the annual contingent, as postulated by the laws governing conscription, or were exempted for any other reason, were placed in the supplementary reserve. The effect of the military system of Rumania was to accumulate very considerable reserves of trained soldiers.

In 1916 the Field Army of Rumania consisted of five army corps, known respectively as the Craiova, Bukarest, Galatz, Jassy, and Constantsa Army Corps, the names corresponding to the headquarters of the districts in which these corps were stationed. Each army corps comprised two divisions and a first-line reserve division of infantry, with a cavalry brigade of two regiments, and each infantry division had two brigades of two regiments, each of three battalions. And with each division went a battalion of chasseurs, an artillery brigade of two regiments

THREE GALLANT RUMANIANS SAVING THE REGIMENTAL COLOURS AT TUTRUKAN.

On September 6th, 1916, when things were going badly for the Rumanians, three soldiers of the 36th Regiment of Infantry swam the Danube, here a quarter of a mile wide and very rapid, in order to save the colours. Sec.-Lieut. Dimitrie Manu, who could not swim, bestrode a tree-trunk, holding the colours, and Sec.-Lieut. Aurel Mihnilescu and Sergt.-Major Constantine Sava swam, pushing the trunk with its precious load before them. The enemy were raining bullets on all who tried to escape across the river, but the dauntless courage of these heroes was crowned with success.

EFFECTIVE RUMANIAN ANTI-AIRCRAFT GUNS.
Bukarest was bombarded by enemy aircraft the very day after Rumania declared war, and subsequently suffered much from persistent raids by enemy Zeppelins and aeroplanes.

military supplies in very considerable quantities.

France was particularly active, as also in a less degree was Great Britain, in munitioning Rumania, but everything they despatched to her had to go for a long distance by sea, subject to the attacks of enemy submarines, and then by rail across Russia, from north to south, for several thousand miles, the time taken in effecting delivery being from four to six weeks. Russia had her own great and incessant needs; Brussiloff's magnificently successful offensive had increased them by adding another hundred miles to Russia's already lengthy front, but she at once did all that she could for Rumania, as indeed she

AIRSHIPS AND MEN OF RUMANIA'S FLYING CORPS.
Rumania was not ill-equipped with airships and with splendidly-trained pilots. The whole "machinery" of her Army was, indeed, remarkably good when she joined the Alliance.

with six batteries apiece, three squadrons of cavalry, and a company of engineers. The Regular Army, in addition to the five army corps, had two divisions of cavalry, each of two brigades, both having two regiments; with each cavalry division went two batteries of horse artillery.

In all there were one hundred and twenty battalions, nine rifle battalions, twenty cavalry regiments, twenty regiments of field artillery with six batteries (four guns) apiece, five howitzer divisions, three horse-artillery batteries, twenty-two companies of fortress artillery, and eight engineering battalions, including a railway battalion. The Army on a peace footing was officially put at about only 130,000 officers and men in 1914, but a few months after the war started Rumania commenced the mobilisation of her first-line reserves and, during the winter of 1915-16, of some of the reserves of her second line. It was estimated by good authorities that on August 27th, 1916, when she took the field, she had nearly 600,000 men under arms, either on her frontiers or at the depots, and that a number nearly equal could be called up in case of need from her still untouched reserves, her artillery being reckoned at about 1,500 guns.

Shortage of powerful guns

It was a well-trained Army, but lacked experience of actual campaigning. Not since Plevna, almost forty years back, had it been engaged in war, for its invasion of Bulgaria in 1913 was very little more than a military promenade. And while its artillery and other "machinery" were perfectly adequate for the Army on a peace footing and for a good deal more than that, they were not sufficient for a force of the size eventually mobilised. There was a marked shortage of really powerful guns. The horse and field artillery were armed with Krupp quick-firers of 3 in. calibre, and the heavy and mountain guns had come from the Creusot Works in France. The infantry was armed for the most part with Mannlicher rifles, but Rumania possessed hardly enough for 600,000 men, much less for the million soldiers and more she could summon to her standards. There was reason, however, to believe that for months prior to her declaration of war she had been acquiring large stocks of munitions of all kinds by way of Russia; and her Allies, as soon as she definitely ranged herself alongside them, began sending to her guns, particularly heavy weapons. machine-guns, rifles, and other

was bound to do, not only for the sake of Rumania but for her own interest.

At the head of the Rumanian Army stood the King, whose early training, as of all German princes, was that of a soldier. M. Bratiano, the Prime Minister, was himself Minister of War. By profession an engineer, he first was connected with the Rumanian State Railways, but soon gave his whole attention to politics, joining the Liberal Party, which had so long been led by his father, the eminent statesman—called, like his son, Ion Bratiano—who induced King Carol to join forces with Russia against Turkey in 1877. M. Bratiano had held the rank of captain in the Rumanian Army which invaded Bulgaria in 1913, and therefore had some experience of war conditions. Shortly after the commencement of hostilities he resigned the portfolio of war, and was succeeded by his brother, Vintila Bratiano.

General Zottu was Chief of the General Staff, with, as his Deputy-Chief, General Iliescu, who formerly had been Secretary of the War Office. The five army corps were commanded respectively by Generals Avarescu, Cotescu; Aslan, Presan, and Georgescu, but the most famous of them was General Avarescu. He belonged to the cavalry branch, and all the four others were artillery officers. As the campaign proceeded through its early stages, changes were made in the various high commands, but the name of Avarescu stood out ever prominent.

Like Sir William Robertson, Chief of the British Imperial General Staff, Avarescu had risen from the ranks. After serving in the Army as a private and becoming a subaltern he went to study at the military school at Turin He took part as a trooper in a cavalry regiment in the Russo-Turkish War, and gradually passing through all grades of rank was Chief of Staff in 1913, while the Second Balkan War was going on, and it was he who was responsible for the plan of the Rumanian operations which brought it to a close. He also had a wide experience of the political and diplomatic world. Speaking Russian fluently, he was sent on several missions to Petrograd. For a time he was Military Attaché at the Rumanian Legation in Berlin. He was in command of the troops in the peasant insurrection in the winter of 1907-8, and in the latter year became Minister of War. A man of great strength of

was successful in driving the enemy back for several miles. From the military point of view, Rumania's two long fronts—one facing Austria-Hungary and the other Bulgaria—constituted a serious and difficult problem. Rumania elected to attack from the former, while holding the latter, but, as it turned out, in insufficient strength. It was extremely natural for her to throw her main forces into the invasion of Transylvania, as from it came the call of the blood. No other action could so have commended itself to her people, burning to avenge the wrongs of their kinsmen and eager to regain their historic territory.

In the Order of the Day already mentioned, King Ferdinand said to his Army, "I have summoned you to carry your standards beyond the frontier, where our brothers are waiting for you impatiently and with hearts full of hope." It was an enterprise, however, for which the Rumanians required no urging, and further, they **Austrian atrocities begin** confidently reckoned on receiving sympathetic help as well as the warmest of welcome from these people of theirs on the other side of the mountains. That they were not disappointed was demonstrated in the most pitiful and tragic manner when the Austrians, after the Rumanian wave had receded, hanged hundreds of unfortunate Rumanes who had assisted or even greeted the Rumanian soldiers. The enemy here pursued a course precisely similar to that which he took in Galicia and Bukovina when, after the Russian retreat in 1915, he reoccupied these provinces.

With respect to the Rumanian advance into Transylvania, it is only fair to add that it looked for support on the right wing from the operations of the Russians under Lechitsky in Galicia and especially in Bukovina, where the two allied armies could effect a junction and undertake combined movements which would have a promising prospect of outflanking the enemy in that quarter. Inside of a few hours after the declaration of war the Rumanians had forced the passes all along the frontier, and for several days their campaign went with a rush, town after town and village after village passing into their hands with almost incredible swiftness.

But while they were making this rapid progress in the north, things were very different with them in the south,

RUMANIAN ARTILLERY.
Rumania took the field in 1916 with twenty batteries of field artillery and seven batteries of horse artillery.

character, with an extensive knowledge of international as well as local affairs, he had always been in favour of the Entente, and had never hesitated to say so. The Army had the utmost confidence in him ; and just fifty-seven years of age when his country entered the lists, he was, comparatively speaking, a young general—several years younger than most of the other leaders who held the highest commands whether of the allied or the enemy armies. When Rumania commenced the invasion of Transylvania he was at the head of the Second Army fighting at Orsova and in the mountains east of that town, but within a fortnight was transferred to the Dobruja front as Commander of the Army of the Danube, and

MODERN APPARATUS OF THE RUMANIAN ARMY MEDICAL SERVICE.
The Rumanian Army medical service was excellent, up to date in equipment and admirably served. In this photograph a modern disinfecting apparatus is seen passing before King Ferdinand's pavilion at a general review of all arms of the service held by his Majesty.

AVARESCU: RUMANIA'S MOST TRUSTED GENERAL.
General Avarescu (on the left) rose from the ranks to the pre-eminent position of Rumania's foremost general, charged with the most difficult task of holding the Transylvanian passes, and subsequently with the work of holding back Mackensen in the Dobruja.

and it soon unfortunately was evident that their plan of operations suffered from a defect of a grave character. This was that they had made a serious miscalculation with respect to the attitude of Bulgaria, and hence had not concentrated forces sufficient to protect their Dobruja frontier, much less to take the offensive from that direction. It was easy, as usual, to be wise after the event—to say that Rumania was wrong, and state that she should have declared war on Bulgaria and attacked her at once, even in preference to invading Transylvania. But the truth was that Rumania was misled by Bulgaria of deliberate purpose; though with the experience of the treachery of that country which she knew to be fresh in the Allies' mind, it was strange that she was so blind to the perils inherent in the situation. Everything was done to deceive her. She was assured that the Bulgarians sympathised with her efforts to set free the Rumanians of Transylvania from the Magyar yoke. Bulgaria did not immediately declare war upon her; for two or three days all seemed to be well, and doubt was everywhere expressed whether, in view of the great cosmopolitan army of the Entente Powers at Salonika, Bulgaria would dare to do anything against Rumania. One British expert took the view that Bulgaria, thanks to the menace of Sarrail, would be only too glad to remain neutral. Germany, who in reality knew perfectly what was going on, pretended not to be sure, and frantically besought her to be loyal and stand by her friends.

Bulgaria's two-fold treachery

Bulgaria revealed her true attitude by declaring war on Rumania on September 1st, but she tried in a characteristic fashion to keep the news from the latter as long as possible.

On that day M. Radoslovoff, the Prime Minister, addressed a Note to the Rumanian Minister in Sofia, containing a string of allegations regarding injurious "incidents" on the Rumanian-Bulgarian frontier, which he maintained had occurred during the previous months, and all of which he declared were caused or provoked by Rumania. The document concluded with the announcement of the existence of a state of war between the two countries. The Rumanian Minister duly received the Note, but he was not allowed to communicate it by telegram to Bukarest, nor otherwise to acquaint his Government with what had taken place till a week had elapsed. Before then, as a matter of course, the information had reached Rumania through other channels, but Bulgarian duplicity and bad faith were apparent in the entire trasanction. And all the while Bulgaria had been quietly but effectively accumulating troops for an attack on Rumania's Dobruja front, and besides concentrating a considerable army of her own, had brought up strong contingents of Turks, the whole under German direction and supported by German soldiers.

Forcing the mountain passes

No suspicion of the treacherous part Bulgaria was playing was entertained when the main forces of Rumania were set, essayed, and succeeded in the task of forcing the passes of the Carpathians and of the Transylvanian Alps on the night of August 27th, 1916. The mountains, which locally have distinct names besides those by which the giant ranges are generally known, rise from 3,000 to 9,000 feet above sea-level, and the passes across them are of varying degrees of importance. Those over the Carpathians, from north to south, are in their order the Tolgyes, Bekas, Gyimes, and Oitoz Passes, the third being the best of them, as it had railway communication from Targu Ocna in Rumania to Csikszereda in Transylvania, the line there linking up with the circular strategic railway running from Brasso (Kronstadt) north to Toplicza and then south-westward down the valley of the River Maros.

The passes over the Transylvanian Alps are from east to west the Buzau, the Bratocea, the Predelus, the Predeal, the Tomos, the Törzburg (or Pasul Bran), the Roter Turm, the Vulkan, and the Varciorova. By the six mentioned first, roads led to Brasso, and the Predeal had a railway from Bukarest to the former centre, while at the foot of the Törzburg on the Rumanian side a line came up from Bukarest, the terminus being Campu Lung. The Roter Turm, along the valley of the Oltu, had a railway from Piatra in Rumania to Hermannstadt and thence on to Budapest in Hungary. The Vulkan was not crossed by a railway, but had railway termini on both sides of it within fairly easy distance; the chief towns on the Transylvanian side were Petroseny and Hatszeg. The Varciorova gave entrance to Orsova on the Danube. Of all the passes, the Predeal was nearest Bukarest.

An Austrian communiqué, dated August 18th, gave the earliest news of the Rumanian offensive by announcing that during the preceding night the Roter Turm Pass and the passes leading to Brasso had been suddenly attacked by the Rumanians. Next day Vienna stated that Austro-Hungarian troops were engaged at all the crossings of the mountains on the whole frontier; that the Rumanians everywhere had been repulsed, their losses being heaviest near Orsova, in the Roter Turm, and in the passes south of Brasso; but that the far-reaching enveloping movements of strong Rumanian forces had necessitated the withdrawal of all the Austrian advanced detachments to a position prepared in the rear, according to plans which had been made long beforehand in view of such an eventuality. The enemy had been taken by surprise. A Rumanian communiqué, issued very early in the morning of the same day, gave a long list of places captured by King Ferdinand's soldiers, and mentioned that the Fourth Army Corps had made prisoner over seven hundred and forty men.

King Ferdinand of Rumania: A portrait taken in June, 1916.

GENERAL CHRISTESCU,
ASSISTANT CHIEF, GENERAL STAFF.

GENERAL I. CULCER,
COMMANDING THE FIRST ARMY.

GENERAL COANDA,
DEPUTY-INSPECTOR-GENERAL OF THE ARMY.

RUMANIAN CAVALRY SC

Distinguished Rumanian generals attached to the General Staff a

GENERAL ILIESCU,
SECRETARY-GENERAL TO THE WAR OFFICE.

GENERAL ZOTTU,
CHIEF OF THE GENERAL STAFF.

RTING OUT ON PATROL.

GENERAL CRAINICIANU,
COMMANDING THE SECOND ARMY.

anding armies in the Transylvania and Dobruja Campaigns, 1916.

Rumania's Red Hussars: Maxim section at driving practice.

By the last day of the month the Rumanians under Avarescu had progressed so rapidly with their invasion that they were in possession of Petroseny, north of the Vulkan Pass, and of Brasso, beyond the Predeal ; their troops were pouring through the Tolgyes and Bekas Passes in the far north, and were threatening Maros Vasarhely, one of the principal towns of Central Transylvania and a military base ; while their victorious advance by way of the Gyimes had compelled the enemy to retreat to the heights east of Csikszereda, a town situated about twenty-three miles within the frontier. At the same time a sharp struggle, with fortune turning to the Rumanians, was going on for the Varciorova Pass on the Danube.

As the month closed, Bukarest chronicled the significant fact that Russian troops had crossed the Danube into the

Arrival of the Russians

Dobruja, where they were enthusiastically welcomed by the population, and that units of the Russian Black Sea Fleet had arrived at Constantsa to help to defend the Rumanian littoral. On August 31st, General Zaionchovsky, commanding the Russian forces in this area, and his Staff were in the Rumanian capital, and were received by the King. Everywhere the Russians, against whom there had been some prejudice in the past because of their occupation of Bessarabia after the war with Turkey in 1877, were greeted with the utmost cordiality, the Rumanians showering flowers upon the troops of the Tsar as they marched through the streets of the towns on their way to the front. General Zaionchovsky issued an Order, in which he spoke of the Russian expedition's purpose and aims, and exhorted his men to win the good opinion of the Rumanians by showing that their conduct was above reproach. Serbians, who had succeeded in escaping from the clutches of the Bulgarians in 1915, had been formed into a brigade, which was incorporated with the Russian force. But in the north-western area the Russians already stood by the side of the Rumanians. On August 29th a Berlin official message announced that Austro-German forces had had encounters with Russo-Rumanian advanced detachments in the Carpathians.

Apart from the fighting in and beyond the passes, nothing of very special moment took place till September. Austrian monitors shelled Varciorova, Turnu Severin, and Giurgevo on the Danube, and captured some small craft at Zimnita, while the Rumanians were reported to have bombarded Ruschuk, the chief Bulgarian port on the river. On the night of August 28th Bukarest had its first experience of an air raid, a Zeppelin and an aeroplane dropping several bombs on the city. Other raids of a most formidable character took place daily during the following month.

September opened well for Rumania. Her advance into Hungary still continued, with much the same extraordinary rapidity, the enemy retiring with some precipitancy, and nowhere offering a really serious resistance. On the first of the month the Rumanians won a striking victory in the taking of Orsova, after a bitter struggle which had gone on without cessation for five days. For the first day or two of the battle the Austrians claimed that they were entirely successful, and alleged that their opponents had been completely repulsed ; but the event proved that their statements were fallacious. The Rumanians persisted in their assaults on the strong Austrian positions with the most desperate bravery, took two heights, the Allion and the Drenek, each over a thousand feet, respectively east and north of the town, and finally drove the defeated enemy across the River Cserna, a northern tributary of the Danube. The way seemed to lie open for that offensive movement of the Allies across the south of Hungary which should cut the railway from Vienna to Sofia and separate Germany and Austria from Bulgaria and Turkey. In the Entente countries the most sanguine expectations were aroused, but the chief enemy was fully alive to his danger, and had taken steps to obviate it.

PRECAUTIONS AGAINST INFECTION.
Rumania, so alert in other branches of progress, was equally to the fore in the care bestowed on her soldiers before they were sent to the front, as evidenced by the above photograph of a scene at an inoculation station.

Hungary was calling loudly on Germany for help, and at the same time was spurred on to renewed efforts. Brussiloff's great campaign in Galicia and Bukovina, in which many Hungarian regiments had suffered most heavily, had depressed her spirit, and there had been much talk of the probability of her making a separate peace with the Allies ; but the Rumanian invasion, which filled the Magyars with furious rage, put new life into her. Profiting by Rumania's illusions with respect to Bulgaria, Germany was ready to strike in the quarter where a blow had been least anticipated, and on September 2nd the strong composite force of Bulgars, Turks, and Germans, which had been quietly concentrated behind the Bulgarian frontier, crossed the Dobruja line, and, driving on the weak Rumanian guards, achieved instant success. Presently it appeared that this army was commanded by the redoubtable Marshal Mackensen.

Lying to the east of the Danube, and between it and the Black Sea, the Dobruja formed a four-sided tract, about a hundred miles long by sixty broad, and comprised an area of about 6,000 square miles. A considerable portion of it consisted of lagoon, marsh, and sandy plains, **German drive into Dobruja** the central part being similar to the Russian steppes. Its most important feature was the delta of the Danube on the north—an immense triangular, reed-covered flat, with many lakelets and morasses, through which flowed the three streams into which the great river divided as it neared the sea. Only one of these branches, that known as the Sulina, was easily navigable. Roads were not numerous, and few were good in the Dobruja ; but here were two railways, one from Bukarest to Constantsa, and another running from this line, south of Medgidia to Dobric, and then into Bulgaria. The former line was of great importance, as it gave access to Rumania's chief port. The Dobrujan part of it had been constructed by a British company in 1860, but was purchased by the

Rumanian Government in 1882. The line crossed the Danube by a bridge over eleven miles in length, its western end being at Fetesti and its eastern at Cerna Voda.

Costing a million and a half sterling, the bridge was a wonderful engineering achievement; the only other bridge across the Danube for many hundreds of miles was at Belgrade, and that was much smaller. The Rumanian bridge consisted first of a bridge of three spans, five hundred yards in length, then of a viaduct eight miles long, on piers built on islands, and finally of a bridge eight hundred and fifty yards in length, of five spans, over the main channel of the river, which reached a depth there of a hundred feet. At its highest point

QUEENLY SOLICITUDE FOR RUMANIAN SOLDIERS.
Another illustration of Queen Marie, taken during a visit to a Red Cross hospital. She was accompanied by Prince Nicholas, in the uniform of a Boy Scout.

A ROYAL RED CROSS NURSE.
Queen Marie of Rumania devoted herself to tending the wounded from the beginning of Rumanian hostilities. Her Majesty is seen about to enter the hospital of the Armenian colony at Bukarest.

the Cerna Voda Bridge was a hundred and twenty feet above the low-water level of the Danube. It was to gain possession of the railway, and capture the bridge-head if possible, that Mackensen directed his offensive.

Without any natural line of defence, and having no fortified positions to guard it, the Dobruja frontier was easily penetrated. On September 3rd a Rumanian despatch announced that the enemy had attacked along its whole front south of Dobric, but had been repulsed. Next day, however, it was clear that the enemy was still advancing, as he had reached by then a point eight miles north-west of Dobric, and everywhere was some distance within the frontier. On the 4th the Bulgarians captured the town just named, and German and Bulgarian forces stormed the

fortified advanced positions of the Rumanians at the bridge-head of Tutrakan (Turtukai) on the Danube. Severe fighting developed at both of these places. Reinforced by the Russians, the Rumanians held up the Bulgarians for some time in the neighbourhood of Dobric, but eventually were pushed back, though without much loss, while at Tutrakan they suffered a serious defeat. The enemy was in greatly superior strength both in men and artillery at Tutrakan, and his heavy guns battered to pieces its fortifications. Ten times did the Rumanians repel his assaults with the most heroic courage, but in the issue were unable to achieve victory, and the place fell into Mackensen's hands on September 6th.

An attempt at assistance by the garrison at Silistra failed. Both the German and the Bulgarian communiqués spoke boastfully of the fall of Tutrakan, and claimed the capture of upwards of 20,000 Rumanians, but the figure was grossly exaggerated. Yet the Rumanian loss was heavy, being not far short of 20,000 men, half of whom perished in the struggle, the number of dead demonstrating how strenuous had been the defence. Consequent on the fall of Tutrakan the allied forces, which were commanded by General Aslan, retired northward, evacuating Silistra on September 8th. **Bukarest remains** The news of these reverses and of the **calm** withdrawal was received with calm in Bukarest, where it was declared that the capture of Orsova from the Austrians completely offset it, and it was pointed out that meanwhile the invasion of Transylvania was pursuing its victorious course.

On the northern frontier the Rumanians made farther advances in the face of increasing opposition in the early part of September. They entirely occupied Czekely, in the Haromszek, the district lying north-east of Brasso, captured Sepsiszentgyorgy, a town thirty miles within the Transylvanian south-eastern frontier, forced the Austrians to retreat west of Csikszereda, and on the eighth were in possession, according to their communiqué of that date, of Toplicza, San Milai, Delne, and Gyergyoszentmiklos. They were pressing the Austrians heavily in the Petroseny-Hatszeg sector. They had taken over 4,000 prisoners, some guns, and a great quantity of miscellaneous booty, including railway rolling-stock, cattle, and large convoys of provisions. But while they were meeting with a growing resistance, it still was not very energetic, as the Austrians were in weak force. The policy of the latter was to withdraw, under cover of rearguard actions, in the general direction of the Maros and Oltu valleys. They announced that they expected to return shortly, when expected reinforcements would appear on the scene, and it certainly was the case that they destroyed hardly anything in the shape of railways, bridges, tunnels, or roads.

Hungarian refugees at Budapest On the other hand, the Hungarian Szeklers, panic stricken, burned their homes, killed their cattle and pigs, and fled from the country they themselves had devastated to Budapest, which soon was filled with thousands of refugees. The Rumanians continued to progress in all sectors, especially towards Hermannstadt, capturing several places on the way, among them being Schellenberg, where Michael the Brave defeated a Hungarian army in 1599. But now the reinforcements for which the Austrians had looked began to arrive. On September 13th Berlin announced that German troops were in contact with the Rumanians south-east of Hatszeg, near Hermannstadt. Within a few days the contest in the whole area north of the passes began to undergo fluctuations, the advantage continuing generally with the Rumanians for some time longer.

In the meantime a bitter struggle had been proceeding in the Dobruja. On September 12th the Bulgarians attacked Lipnitsa, fifteen miles east of Silistra, but were vigorously counter-attacked, and after an engagement lasting all night were heavily defeated by the Rumanians, who captured eight German guns. Fighting went on on this whole front on the line to which the allied troops had retired, but it was regarded as unimportant, though the Bulgarians, whose veracity was not above suspicion, said they were advancing triumphantly. Then, suddenly, the world was astonished by hearing it officially stated that the German Kaiser had sent a telegram to his consort, in which he said that Mackensen had informed him that the Bulgarian, Turkish, and German forces had won a decisive victory in the Dobruja. The victory turned out to be by no means as decisive as the Emperor had hoped, but it led to a further withdrawal northward of the allied line. According to a German journal, it had been gained by a series of strategic moves, which threw the Rumanian division operating on the Danube upon the Russians in the centre of the front, while at the same time the Rumanian left wing was also driven in on the Russians, the result being a disorderly retreat attended with heavy losses.

Kaiser's premature jubilation

All such reports were discounted by the peoples of the Allies at the time, because it was strongly suspected that inflated accounts of enemy successes were being published with a view to influencing subscriptions to a new German loan which was then being floated. But there could no longer be any doubt of the advance of Mackensen when Bukarest announced on September 17th that the Russo-Rumanian troops had fallen back to strong positions on the line Rasova, ten miles south of Cerna Voda, to Tuzla

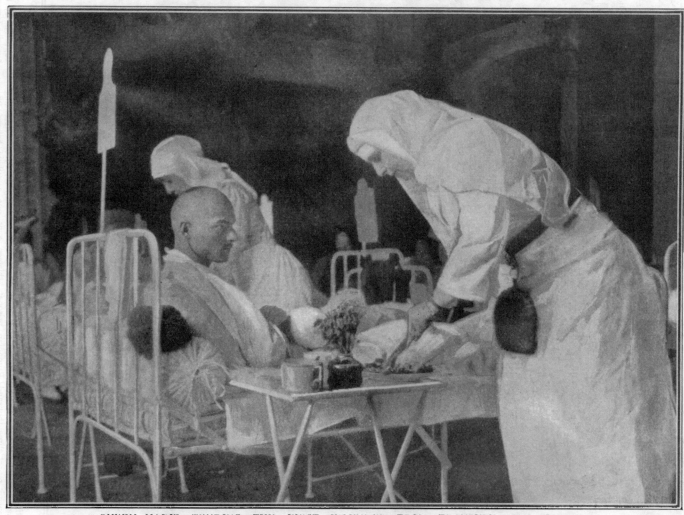

QUEEN MARIE TENDING THE FIRST WOUNDED FROM TRANSYLVANIAN FIELDS.
The Royal Palace at Bukarest was converted into a military hospital, and Queen Marie, together with her two beautiful daughters, Princess Marie and Princess Elisabeth, tended her wounded soldier-subjects. This charming illustration shows her Majesty in the act of cutting up the dinner of a Rumanian soldier whose wounds prevented him from using his hands.

AFTER THE BATTLE OF HERMANNSTADT: AN ENEMY'S IMPRESSION OF THE RUMANIAN RETREAT.

Illustration, reproduced from a Leipzig journal, purporting to depict the retreat of Rumanian forces after their defeat by General von Falkenhayn at Hermannstadt on September 30th, 1916. According to the enemy report three thousand Rumanian prisoners, thirteen guns, one aeroplane hangar, two aeroplanes, ten locomotives, and about seven hundred waggons of munitions and equipment were captured by the Austro-Hungarian troops. The Rumanians admitted their retirement before greatly superior forces, but two days later they were winning ground again in this region.

twelve miles south of Constantsa. As the last-named was not fortified, the menace to it appeared to be serious.

Some days earlier the situation in the Dobruja had seemed sufficiently grave for Rumania to transfer General Avarescu from the Transylvanian theatre, where he had been conducting highly successful operations, to this threatened area. He arrived at this front on September 16th, and made a thorough review of the position. Rumanian forces had been brought from the north-west, and further Russian reinforcements had come marching from across the Danube into this district. On the very same day a great battle began between the rival armies. Large numbers of Bulgarians, Turks, and Germans, supported by powerful artillery, made the most desperate efforts to break through the allied line, but it stood firm, and all the violent assaults of the enemy were foiled. His attack was most persistent and determined on the right near Rasova, on the Danube, his intention, no doubt, being to pierce the line in this sector and capture Cerna Voda, thereby cutting the allied communications with the rest of Rumania. On the 18th the issue of the battle was still uncertain, but next

that area. The Germans admitted the tenacity of the Rumanian resistance, but disguised their defeat. Mackensen retreated for some miles, organised a strong line of defence from the Danube about Oltina to a point south west of Toprosari and thence to the Black Sea, south of Tuzla.

As a natural outcome of their success, the Rumanians were in much better heart and more confident with regard to the military position in the **Dobruja situation** Dobruja. They also set to work with **improved** energy to strengthen their front, and made it so powerful that they believed it could resist any attack; but in this, unhappily, they were destined to be undeceived.

Interest now passed again from the Dobruja to Transylvania, where the struggle was beginning to assume an appearance that was less exclusively favourable to the invaders. In the third week of September the Rumanians continued to progress westward, occupying, after brief engagements, Homorod Almas, south-east of Szekelyudvarhely, Köhalom, north-east of Fogaras, and Fogaras itself, a town of some note situated midway between Brasso and Hermannstadt. In these affairs the enemy

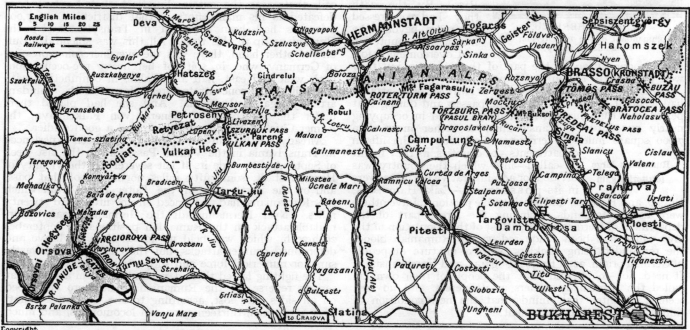

GATES OF RUMANIA : STERNLY-DEFENDED PASSES IN THE TRANSYLVANIAN ALPS.

Map showing the positions of the Transylvanian passes, whence the Germans under General von Falkenhayn sought to invade Rumanian territory. The most important passes are the Predeal and Roter Turm, the former carrying the railway from Kronstadt to Bukarest, the latter carrying a return line from the capital to Hermannstadt.

day Avarescu received fresh reinforcements, and then being in a position to take the offensive, succeeded in driving the hostile forces back in confusion and with heavy losses. Severe fighting raged through the night, but developed into a complete triumph for the Allies. In the morning Mackensen began a general retreat, his troops setting fire to all the villages en route, and wreaking their spite and rage on their unfortunate inhabitants if Rumanian.

It had been a heavy ordeal for the un-
A splendid seasoned Rumanian soldiers, who were
victory opposed by picked enemy battalions, but
they passed through it with the utmost credit, proving themselves to be first-class fighting men. An official message from Bukarest noted that this splendid victory was "due to the supreme courage and devotion of both officers and men," and that several Rumanian and Serbian colonels fell at the head of their regiments. Another official bulletin said that General Sarrail's strong offensive in the south of the Balkans at this critical time had exercised a beneficial effect on the situation in the Dobruja by distracting Mackensen's attention and holding up Bulgarians, who otherwise might have been rushed up to

lost over nine hundred prisoners. At Barot, an important strategic point dominating the railway from Brasso to Foeldvar, the Rumanians registered on the 16th the farthest reach of their advance in that district up to that date—they were thirty miles across the frontier.

Germany, however, had now come in some force to the assistance of the Austro-Hungarians; her soldiers were fighting fiercely in the valley of the Streiu near Hatszeg, and the Rumanians were holding the conquered ground only with difficulty. On the 14th and 15th a two-days' battle took place in the defile of Merisor with Hungarian forces, which, after bitter fighting, were defeated. Merisor, from which the defile got its name, was a little town about a dozen miles west of Petroseny, in the same region as Hatszeg, all being north of the Vulkan Pass. On the 18th, German troops, under General von Staabs, thrust back the Rumanians in the Hatszeg sector after a very stubborn resistance, while in the north, in the Gyergyoi Havasok and Kelemen Hegyseg ranges of the Carpathians, enemy forces, predominantly German, commenced to oppose the invaders with much more resolution than before.

GENERAL HERESCU.
Commandant of the 1st Division of
Rumanian Cavalry.

An Austrian communiqué of the 20th announced the complete repulse of the Rumanians south of Hatszeg, and the reoccupation of Petroseny, while a Berlin telegram of the following day stated that both sides of the Vulkan Pass had been carried. But on the 22nd the Rumanians renewed the contest for this pass, and by a successful encircling movement forced the enemy three days later to evacuate it and the contiguous Szurduk Pass. By the 28th they had progressed ten miles beyond the frontier, encountering and overcoming a formidable opposition on the part of the Germans, but they were not able to regain Petroseny.

A month had elapsed since their swift surprise attacks had resulted in the capture of the passes, and during that period the Rumanian Army had succeeded in occupying nearly one-third of Transylvania, or rather more than 7,000 square miles of territory. Four out of the fifteen departments—or counties, as they might **Rumania's large** be called—into which the country was **territorial gain** divided for administrative purposes, were in its possession—Czik, Haromszek, Brasso, and Fogaras, and considerable portions of five others were also in its hands, including the larger part of the department of Hermannstadt. Most of the population of the area which had been conquered was of Rumanian blood, the remainder being Szeklers, with a mixture of people of German origin, as in Brasso, Fogaras, and Hermannstadt. It need not to be said that the people of their own kin hailed the Rumanian soldiers as deliverers, and no idea seemed to enter their minds that the new condition of things might not be permanent.

The " Transylvanian Gazette," the organ of the Rumanes, issued at Brasso, published an article, shortly after the occupation of the town, in which it said : " Awake, Rumanians ! The glorious Army of the great King Ferdinand is among us. Our brothers, our liberators, have arrived, for the hour has struck. You carry on the points of your bayonets the future of Rumania from the Theiss to the Black Sea." There was much to encourage such glowing and confident language—but the near future held deep disappointment. On the one hand, the territory occupied by the Rumanian Army stretched from Orsova north-easterly to a little south of Hermannstadt, went on a few miles to the north of Fogaras, thence passed west of Szekelyudvarhely, which had been captured on September 16th, and then ran on north in the Kelemen Hegyseg Mountains, and up **Germany's heavy** towards Dorna Watra to join the Russian **pressure** line in that neighbourhood. It was an impressive extent of territory won from the hated oppressors of the land, and though there was an offset in the Dobruja, where the enemy was still in possession of Rumanian soil, there was the outstanding fact that he had been defeated in his main effort in that district. Over 7,000 prisoners had been captured in Transylvania by the Rumanians up to this time. All this was splendid. But, on the other hand, there was the ever-increasing pressure of Germany, who, in spite of her heavy pre-occupations both west and east, had been able, in conjunction with her allies, to concentrate great forces with abundant artillery against Rumania. And she had placed them under the leadership of General von Falkenhayn, the former Chief of her General Staff, and a good soldier.

Already this pressure by Germany had been experienced in Transylvania in the Vulkan Pass, and in the last week of September it made itself felt severely in the vicinity of Hermannstadt, some fifty miles north-east of that pass, and on the north side of the Roter Turm, from which the Rumanians had advanced from fifteen to twenty miles. Near Hermannstadt the Germans began a formidable attack on the Rumanian positions on September 26th-27th, which was held up for a while by brave and determined counter-attacks, but the enemy was in vastly superior numerical force and supported by heavier guns.

The fighting lasted three days, and ended in a somewhat serious reverse for the Rumanians, who were enveloped on all sides, and lost, according to the German account, over 3,000 men, thirteen guns, ten locomotives, and much

GENERAL AVARESCU.
In command of the First Rumanian Army
Corps.

GENERAL COTTESCU.
In command of the Second Rumanian
Army Corps.

GENERAL PRESAN.
In command of the 7th Division, Fourth Army
Corps.

RUMANIAN GENERALS IN THE FIELD.

other material. Their retreat through the Roter Turm had been cut off by a column of Bavarian Alpine troops, who had made a daring march across the mountain heights and occupied the pass well in their rear. The surrounded Rumanians defended themselves with desperate courage, and tried to break through the ring that encircled them, but only a comparatively small number succeeded in escaping towards Fogaras, from which town another force of their own had tried to make a diversion. This battle, called by the Germans the Battle of Hermannstadt, resulted in the re-occupation of the Roter Turm by the enemy, and on October 1st he was at-

Battle of Hermannstadt tacking a Rumanian force south of it near Caineni, thus having for the second time got a foothold within Rumania.

As October came in the struggle was renewed in the Dobruja, a Turkish and Bulgarian division being repulsed near Toprosari, south of Tuzla, by Russo-Rumanian troops. The Allies made an assault on the whole of the line to which Mackensen had retreated after his defeat of September 16th-20th, but though they inflicted heavy losses on him and captured thirteen of his guns, they did not succeed in causing him to retire farther. It was probably to assist this offensive movement that a Rumanian force, several battalions strong, crossed the Danube, and landed at Rjahovo on October 2nd, a village on the south side of the river about midway between Ruschuk and Tutrakan, and in rear of Mackensen's defences. A pontoon bridge of boats had been cleverly got into position under cover of night, and the landing was made without any trouble, as the Bulgarian guards on the bank were taken completely by surprise and killed or captured. The Rumanians seized the neighbouring villages, but on October 3rd retired across the river again. A Bukarest communiqué announced that the demonstration had accomplished its purpose. The Bulgarians magnified this withdrawal into a great victory for them, asserting that soldiers of theirs from Ruschuk and Tutrakan assaulted and defeated the Rumanians, who had the utmost difficulty in escaping to the other side of the river, as the pontoon bridge had been destroyed by the fire of Austrian monitors, and that the " battlefield was covered with Rumanian dead."

The Rumanians did not admit any such loss as this statement alleged, and in any case their crossing of the river was in itself a remarkable feat. In recent times the two historic crossings of the Danube under hostile conditions were those of the Russians in 1811 and

1877, the Turks being the enemy on both occasions. The Rumanians demonstrated, at all events, what they could achieve in this direction.

While this indecisive fighting was continuing on the southern front of the Rumanian Army, Falkenhayn's offensive on the northern showed augmenting power and momentum. It was now extending farther east in Transylvania, his chief objective being Brasso and the passes leading south from it into Rumania; but it also pressed with increasing severity on the

GENERAL POPOVICI.
Inspector-General of Rumanian Cavalry.

Rumanian forces in the whole north-west of the country. In the district of Brasso, the most distinctively Rumanian town in all Transylvania, which the Austrians had evacuated and the Rumanians had occupied in the first days of the campaign, the German concentration in superior strength had the same effect as at Hermannstadt. Whereas Falkenhayn had gathered together a large army, probably of from twelve to fourteen divisions—or about a quarter of a million of men—for his offensive, the Rumanians had reduced the number of their effectives in all this area in order to counter Mackensen in the Dobruja.

Stubborn fight at Sinka

Their mobilisation was still incomplete, they were fighting hard at this time in and about the Vulkan and Roter Turm Passes, in which they were regaining some of the ground they had lost, and also were meeting fresh attacks farther north in the mountains. Unable to offer a successful resistance to Falkenhayn's main movement, they put up a stubborn fight in the sector of Sinka, north-west of Brasso; but he was too strong for them, and forced them to withdraw from their trenches. Driven back on both wings, the main body retreated through the Geister Wald, and Brasso fell to the enemy on October 8th. There was

GENERAL GEORGESCU.
Attached to Staff of British Army.

GENERAL IANCOVESCU.
Secretary to the Ministry of War.

GENERAL LUPESCU.
Of the Rumanian Army.

MORE LEADERS OF RUMANIA'S ARMY

no question of the fine military stuff of the Rumanian soldiers ; it was simply that the odds were far too heavy.

On October 7th a semi-official statement, issued in Bukarest, thus described the situation which had been brought about by the German general's advance : " In the

Well-organised retirement.

valley of the Oltu, in the Transylvanian plain, and in the region of Hermannstadt-Fogaras - Brasso the Rumanian troops, faced by much superior enemy forces, mostly Germans, have been skilfully withdrawn to strategic positions on the Carpathian (Transylvanian Alps) frontier in order to ensure a strong defence of the four passes from Brasso into Rumania." It added that the Austro-Germans were plainly endeavouring to strike a desperate blow, and were bringing up troops from all the other fronts for this purpose. The retirement of the Rumanians in this district had been well organised, as was evidenced by the fact that the enemy claimed the capture of not more than a few hundred prisoners, in addition to over a thousand taken at Brasso, while it was the fact that he himself had lost six hundred prisoners at Henndorf, fifty miles from Brasso, and eight hundred at another point. Fogaras, between Brasso and Hermannstadt, had been evacuated on October 6th. North and east of Brasso the Rumanians also were in retreat, Szekelyudvarhely being abandoned on the 8th, when it was occupied by Hungarian Landsturm hussars. On the same day Berlin announced that the Rumanians were withdrawing " on the entire eastern front."

They were in truth retiring everywhere in Central Transylvania, but in the valley of the Maros still held their positions for some time longer. Besides being in superior force, Falkenhayn enjoyed a distinct advantage over the Rumanians in having a lateral railway close to the frontier, for by means of it he was enabled to transfer troops very rapidly from point to point, and to send reinforcements where most required. By October 11th the retirement of the Rumanians from all their advanced lines in the country was general. Next day Falkenhayn was making a strong bid for the passes, the heaviest fighting going on in the Törzburg, Predeal, and Busau Passes. At last the Rumanians had to withdraw towards Crasna, a customs station on the frontier. The situation was now becoming dangerous, and falling back on her greatest soldier, Rumania sent General Avarescu from the Dobruja, where he had done so magnificently, to the north, to take command of the Second Army, which was defending the passes after its withdrawal from Brasso.

It was an anxious time. Bukarest, usually a city of pleasure, had become serious, but its citizens were full of hope. Events had taken on an unpleasant appearance, but they trusted that their trials would not last long. One thing did really give them great concern. From the beginning of the campaign they had suffered much from air raids, in the course of which many hundreds of innocent people, mostly women and children, had been killed and injured. The frequency and persistence of these attacks by Zeppelins and aeroplanes excited

feelings in them of intense hostility to Germany, who was the chief author of them, but this was further heightened by sensational discoveries of disease germs and explosives made in the garden of the German Legation. The question was asked for whom and what these were intended, and the answer was easy. Another example of characteristic German " frightfulness " was seen in the throwing of packets of poisoned sweetmeats from the aircraft that swept over the city and the surrounding country. Bukarest —all Rumania—was roused to furious indignation by these horrible instances of German Kultur.

Bukarest was hopeful about the campaign, although the enemy progressed in the northern area, and was known to be increasing his strength in the southern area by bringing up large contingents of Bulgarian and Turkish troops. The situation was not really such as to make

for cheerfulness. By the middle of the second week of October, Falkenhayn's offensive, which had dislodged the Rumanians from nearly the whole of the ground they had occupied in Transylvania except in the north-east, was becoming more and more formidable. In the main it was directed on two areas—the region of the passes leading south from Brasso to Bukarest, and the region of the Gyimes Pass in the north-east. In the latter district the Rumanians, about October 11th, had withdrawn from Csikszcreda and adjacent positions, as well as those higher up on the circular strategic railway in the valley of the Maros, because they were threatened with envelopment in all this quarter.

Near the Oitoz Pass there was fighting of an intense kind in which the Rumanians barely held their own, and this reflected on the stability of the defence higher up at the Gyimes. Falkenhayn's weight fell most heavily on the vital passes from Brasso to Bukarest, and that it was telling was evident from an official Rumanian communiqué of October 12th, which stated that " from Mount Buksoi as far as Bran," or the entire frontier crossed by the four chief roads, several enemy attacks had been repulsed— the mention of Bran implying that Falkenhayn had carried Mocciu, the point in the Bran or Törzburg Pass that he had been assaulting on the previous day.

GENERAL BELAYEFF : AVARESCU'S RUSSIAN COLLEAGUE.

General Belayeff commanded the Russian army which co-operated with the Rumanian forces under General Avarescu in resisting the first onslaught of the Central Empires.

Avarescu and the Second Rumanian Army fought with desperate valour to hold Falkenhayn, and on October 13th their magnificent efforts were crowned with success at the Buzau and the Predeal Passes, the Germans being checked and thrown back. The victory of the Rumanians in the Predeal was important, as this pass was nearest to Bukarest, had a railway and a good road, crossing the mountains almost due south of Brasso at a height of a little over 3,000 feet. But on the following day the Rumanians

Victory in the Predeal

were driven out of the Törzburg Pass and had to withdraw to Rucaru, a small town six or seven miles within their own territory. It was against this pass that Falkenhayn had first flung his forces after the capture of Brasso, and after a bitter struggle had gained an entrance to it a week before. At Rucaru he was in the foot-hills, well below the top of the Törzburg.

Rumanian infantrymen helping one another to fasten their knapsacks at Bukarest railway station while waiting to entrain for the front.

[Photographs taken by special permission of the Rumanian Government.

King Ferdinand's ardent warriors undergoing preliminary training before being sent to the area of hostilities.

MOBILISATION SCENES AT BUKAREST AFTER THE RUMANIAN DECLARATION OF WAR.

From Rucaru the road went over high, rolling ground to Campu Lung, ten miles farther south, where was the terminus of a railway running south-eastward to Bukarest, some ninety miles away. On the other passes he made no advance that day, and was defeated on his flanks, on his left in the Oitoz Pass, and on his right in the Vulkan Pass. The fight for the passes raged all through the 15th and 16th, **Violent struggle at Rucaru** the struggle being most violent and obstinate at Rucaru, while about the same time the Russians in the Dorna Watra district, where the troops of the two Allies met, began a strong offensive, with a view to taking off the pressure on the Rumanians lower down, but were countered by "great forces," as the Petrograd official message stated. On the 17th Falkenhayn forced his way across the Gyimes Pass, and reached Agas, seven miles beyond the frontier. On that day no change was noted in the region of the passes south of Brasso, but fresh fighting was reported near the Roter Turm.

On the whole Carpathian and Transylvanian Alps frontier the enemy was attacking with great determination, and it had become still plainer that Germany was resolved to deliver with all her strength that desperate blow which Bukarest earlier had announced was impending. The success, so far, of Falkenhayn had created anxiety and apprehension in the west. In the House of Commons, Mr. John Dillon, an Irish Nationalist member, introduced the subject, and asked the Government to give an assurance to Rumania that the utmost resources of the British Empire would be used to rescue her from the danger of sharing the fate of Belgium and Serbia. Mr. Lloyd George, as Minister of War, said in reply that the Government had not the least doubt that Germany had concentrated her strength with a view to attempting to crush Rumania, being urged thereto not only by her own interests, but from a spirit of resentment and hatred because the brave people of that country had dared to challenge her power near her own home. But, he

WHERE THE RUMANIANS FOUGHT A COMBINED GERMAN, BULGARIAN, AND TURKISH ARMY:
In the foreground is seen the Feteshti Bridge, carrying the line from Bukarest across the marshes of Baltu Island, over the Cerna Voda Bridge and along the stretch of upland to Babadagh. On the extreme left, in the background, is seen the

continued, the Allies were fully alive to the situation, and would make every effort to protect the Rumanian Army. About a fortnight later, when the whole position in Rumania had become worse on account of the success of Mackensen's renewed offensive in the Dobruja, he made a similar statement in Parliament.

In order to assist and counsel the Rumanians, France sent a Military Mission, headed by General Berthelot, and it arrived in Bukarest in the third week of October. It was known that France was sending huge quantities of munitions, that Britain also was doing a great deal in the same way, and that Russia was strongly supporting Rumania. And as the Rumanians under Avarescu continued to resist with persistence Falkenhayn's attacks, even inflicting heavy defeats on him in some of the passes, confidence in the ability of the Rumanian Army to hold him off was to some extent restored. On October 18th, in the Gyimes Pass, the Rumanians won a victory that cost him nine hundred prisoners and twelve guns, and

at Agas, in the Oitoz region, surprised one of his detachments, capturing three hundred prisoners and some machine-guns, while their strenuous opposition in the Brasso passes prevented him from advancing. Yet the general situation on the northern front was still very serious ; nor was it rendered less serious by Mackensen's fresh offensive in the Dobruja, which started on October 19th and within a few days resulted in grave loss to the Allies.

As has been seen, the Russo-Rumanian forces in the Dobruja, now commanded **Indecisive Dobruja** by General Christescu—who had been **fighting** Avarescu's Chief of Staff before that general's transference to the northern front—had been unable to make any real impression on the line to which Mackensen had retreated after his defeat on September 20th. During the second and part of the third week of October there were encounters between the respective combatants, and an artillery duel was maintained most of the time, but nothing of vital importance happened. Judging, perhaps,

THE MARSHY UPLANDS OF DOBRUJA, LOOKING ACROSS THE DANUBE TOWARDS THE BLACK SEA.
the Dobruja to Constantsa, which was evacuated by the Rumanians on October 22nd, 1916, after its oil stores had been fired, our ally retreating position of the River Pruth, which marks the political boundary between Rumania and Russia.

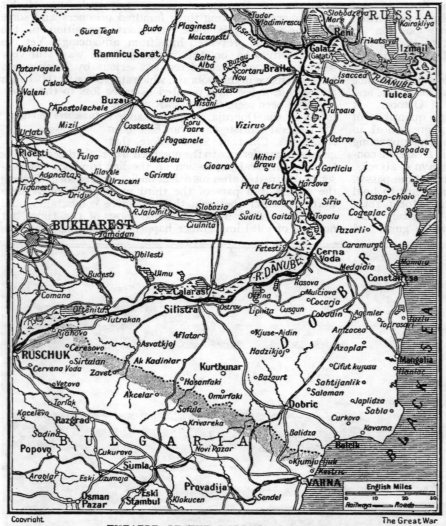

THEATRE OF THE DOBRUJA CAMPAIGN.
Map of the Dobruja front from the Danube to the Black Sea, showing the principal battlefields along the river line from Ruschuk to Cerna Voda.

that the enemy's menace in this quarter had passed away, or if renewed could be thwarted, the Rumanian High Command probably had sent Rumanian regiments across the Danube to the assistance of Avarescu in the fight for the passes; but whether this were so or not, Mackensen undoubtedly had taken advantage of the opportunity to accumulate an army much more powerful than that with which he had opened his campaign in the beginning of September, and was merely biding his time to resume it.

According to one report, the Russo-Rumanian army began an offensive against Mackensen about October 17th.

Mackensen's main objective

A great battle was joined two days later, and the German commander launched his superior forces in waves of assault on the allied positions, after an intense artillery preparation which destroyed the Russo-Rumanian lines of trenches at several points from south of Rasova on the Danube, through Agemler, near the Bulgaro-Rumanian railway, south of Cobadin, to Tuzla on the Black Sea. On October 21st it was announced from Bukarest that the allied troops had been compelled to retire in the centre and on the right wing, and a Russian official telegram of the same date stated that the enemy had taken Cokarja, a village lying north-west of Cobadin. The Germans

claimed to have captured, after stubborn fighting, Tuzla and the heights north-west of Toprosari and west of the former, as well as the heights near Mulciova, south-east of Rasova, and declared that they had taken many prisoners, including 3,000 Russians, and some machine-guns, but no mention was made of artillery gains. This success of Mackensen now threatened in a very direct manner the railway from Cerna Voda to Constantsa.

This railway had been Mackensen's objective from the outset, but his first attempt to seize it had failed; that he was succeeding was clear on October 23rd, when it was announced from the Rumanian headquarters that the Allies had retired immediately to the south of the track. Having taken Toprosari and Cobadin, the Bulgarians pushed on to attack Constantsa, which fell into their hands on October 22nd after a fierce struggle. Under cover of rearguard actions and the fire of the Russian Black Sea Fleet, the authorities of the town contrived to get away most of the stores, burning what they were unable to remove. The Russian ships did not leave the port until everything that might have been of use to the enemy was destroyed or in flames. By far the greater part of the population made good their escape; the Bulgarians found that the place had been very thoroughly evacuated and that no booty worth speaking of was to be got. The allied troops retired in good order to Caramurat.

On October 23rd Mackensen stormed Medgidia, on the railway about twenty-five miles west of Constantsa, and also captured Rasova, in spite of the bravest efforts of the Russo-Rumanians to hold them. The German report affirmed that in these and other operations on this line the Allies lost 7,000 men in prisoners, besides twelve guns, and the capture of Constantsa was in itself a heavy blow to them. The Rumanians made a splendid attempt to hold the eastern end of the railway at Cerna Voda, where the great bridge crossed the Danube; but the **The fall of Constantsa** pressure of Mackensen was too overwhelming, and early in the morning of the 25th they had to abandon the bridgehead and withdraw by the bridge, which they afterwards blew up. The railway was in the possession of the enemy, who thereby achieved an uncommonly important success.

Mackensen had taken the railway, but he was still on the wrong side of the Danube, and its crossing had to be made if he was to co-operate effectively with the Germans in their efforts to penetrate into Rumania from the north. In that theatre the position fluctuated from hour to hour. The north-eastern passes showed some improvement for the Rumanians, but in the northern passes—from Hatszeg, Hermannstadt, and Brasso—where the fiercest fighting continued and the enemy struck with far heavier weight, he was able to report progress, capturing the Vulkan Pass on October 25th, and advancing farther south by the exits of the Roter Turm, the Törzburg, and the Predeal Passes. The situation had an ominous look for the Rumanians, but they faced it with undiminished courage and resolution.

CHAPTER CXLVIII.

HOW THE ALLIES PREPARED FOR THEIR GREAT OFFENSIVE ON THE SOMME.

By Edward Wright.

New German Battle Tactics at Verdun Adapted by the Allies for Use on the Somme and the Ancre—The Enemy's Positions on the Somme : Bapaume, Péronne, and Chaulnes—Vast Preparation for the Offensive Movement—General Fayolle's " Workshop "—French Naval Ordnance in Land Warfare—Allies Secure the Mastery of the Air—Simultaneous Co-operation of Guns and Infantry Essential to Success—Problem of Reversing the Comparative Losses of Attacking and Defending Troops—Infantry Airmen the Supreme Weapon of the French Offensive—The Somme Valley the Crux of the Allies' Position—General Foch's Subtle Design upon the Promontory of Santerre—Enfeeblement of the Forces of the German Empire the Primary Design of the Allied Staffs—Successes of the Bretons and French Colonials—General Fayolle's New Method of Deploying Troops—Achievements of the Foreign Legion, the French Colonials, and the Moroccan Division—Biaches Fort Captured by French Bluff—French Colonials Carry La Maisonette—Defeat of all German Counter-Attacks—End of the First Phase of the Battle of the Somme.

N preparing the Somme offensive the French and British Staffs profited by all the lessons of Verdun. The Germans, throughout the war, had done the chief work in inventing new methods of attack and also of defence. Their position of advantage was largely due to the superiority they enjoyed in regard to heavy weapons. At Ypres, in October, 1914, they originated the intensive system of attack on a narrow front, owing to the chance that the siege-guns, which they had employed in the Siege of Antwerp, were then close to their hand for battering-ram operations against our shallow, hastily-made trenches. At that time the French lines near Verdun offered the enemy most opportunity for a decisive thrust, as the younger Moltke pointed out. But Falkenhayn, the new Chief of Staff, thought it would be better to use the great German and Austrian siege train against the British sector to which the monster guns could quickly be hauled. And so our little Regular Army, which was equipped only for mobile warfare and relied upon the French Army to carry out siege operations, found itself overwhelmed by monster artillery to which it had no means of replying. Later, at Neuve Chapelle, we improvised a siege train out of heavy naval guns manned by

FRENCH LEADERS ON THE SOMME.
General Fayolle (left), who was mainly responsible for the preparations for the great French offensive, in conversation with General Berdoullat.

our superb Marines. But our naval shells, available for army use, were mainly shrapnel and common shell ; our armament firms and our official high-explosive works produced altogether only a few thousand high-explosive shells a day, and even after months of attempted speeding-up, our average daily production of the kind of shell needed in the new trench warfare remained terribly inadequate to the needs of our troops.

At Neuve Chapelle our Staff showed a remarkable power of invention, but it was the enemy who profited by our fine scheme of attack. Falkenhayn and his Staff merely substituted high-explosive shell for the shrapnel we had been using, and, by means of an arc of heavy guns, they accomplished at Gorlice against Radko Dimitrieff's army the work they had vainly attempted the previous autumn against our Expeditionary Force. Then at Loos the British Staff once more tried to improve upon the lesson it had learnt in its victorious stand at Ypres. We improved the method of a rush attack, heralded by the hurricane fire of parks of artillery all connected to a controlling telephone exchange. But the German Staff had worked out a magnificent system of defence against heavy-gun fire. It constructed shelter chambers beyond the reach of the heaviest shell, connected its lines with tunnels

INCOMPARABLE FRENCH ORDNANCE IN ACTION.
French 4·8 in. gun in a battery. Technically heavy artillery, these were like toys in comparison with much of the ordnance employed.

PICKED GUN-CREW WORKING A HOWITZER.
General Fayolle's concentration of artillery for the offensive of July, 1916, was unprecedented and—as the event proved—irresistible.

to enable reinforcing troops to escape our curtains of shrapnel fire, and excavated mazes of well-organised machine-gun redoubts that enabled a hundred tenacious men to check the advance of ten thousand charging infantry. We failed to shatter the improved German defences because of our continued lack of high-explosive shell and heavy howitzers.

In the meantime our French comrades, who possessed a fine high-explosive shell and the plant needed for making the delicate fuses, did not fare much better than ourselves, in spite of the advantages they enjoyed as a nation equipped for warfare on the Continental scale. Large though their private and public armament works were, they were utterly inadequate to the needs of the new system of trench warfare. The French Staff had called to the Colours tens of thousands of men used to machine-tool work and ordinary steel-making. The feeling of the military

professional class throughout Europe had been against allowing valuable mechanics to go on with the work of war for which they were best fitted. Even company and battalion commanders in the spring of 1915 were averse to allowing the mechanics in their ranks who had become experienced veteran soldiers to withdraw into munition factories. Few officers cared to see their company or battalion weakened by untried recruits, and it was not until the clamour caused by our crisis in munitions rang through the world that France became generally convinced that men who could use a machine-tool skilfully were of more use in a factory than in a trench. In Champagne and in Artois brilliant French commanders had, in the spring and autumn of 1915, tried to break through the German lines by the same swift battering-ram attack as the British Staff had employed. In fact, our Chief of Staff, Sir William Robertson, and the French assistant to General Joffre, General Castelnau, had shared each other's ideas and arrived at approximately the same methods of attack.

Franco-British co-ordination

Then these methods were again employed, with various improvements, by Field-Marshal von Haeseler in the attack on Verdun in February, 1916. Haeseler still aimed to break through the French lines by swift attack lasting only three or four days. His design was to place his heaviest and longest-ranged guns close enough to dominate the first, second, and third lines of defence. Having carried the high ground near the French second line, he brought a considerable part of his lighter artillery near it, to assist with close-range fire a great infantry thrust which was designed to break right through the French front. This advance, however, was defeated at Douaumont by the famous Iron Division, and after trying to advance again by means of a hundred thousand troops the German Staff worked out another new form of siege warfare.

It no longer attempted to make an abrupt and decisive break. It increased the number of guns on both sides of the Meuse and began a slow, terrible, see-sawing, grinding movement against Dead Man Hill on the

left and the Vaux promontory on the right. German official statements explained to the world that a new form of battle tactics was in operation, and though the Allies' Press tended to ridicule the enemy's proclamation, there was an uncommon amount of truth in it. The Germans, after their great defeat on April 9th, 1916, had invented another and a more formidable form of attack, which aimed only indirectly at winning the ruins of the sixteenth-century fortress of Verdun. The grand object of the new kind of attack was to wear out the French Army by a continuous system of small, intense, alternating assaults on selected points of the thirty-mile front around Verdun. It may be contended that the new method employed by the Germans was imposed upon them by the remark-
German methods adapted able victory won by General Pétain. True enough. Nevertheless, the method which the enemy was compelled to adopt was both sound and novel. The French Staff studied it with admiring care, and tested it by their magnificent defence until they discovered all its possibilities. Then they worked out certain improvements which the enemy had not foreseen, and, in collaboration with the British Staff, planned a great offensive in the new style on the Somme and Ancre Rivers.

The principal idea in this new form of operations had been fairly stated by the German Staff. It was necessary for an attacking army to begin with no attempt to make an abrupt break-through. There was to be neither a Neuve Chapelle nor a Gorlice, but only a slow and patient movement of artillery and infantry against the enemy's

line. The attacking army was to be supplied with thousands of guns and millions of shells as for an old-fashioned, whirlwind operation. But the larger part of this enormous strength was to be held in reserve and only brought forward gradually as the guns were hauled forward. This meant that the Germans would always be allowed time to construct new lines in their rear. Thus the piercing of their front was scarcely contemplated. When the attack was being planned by the French and British Staffs the enemy's lines by the Somme extended backward in three main zones for a depth of about six miles. He had a comparatively small number of light guns between his first and second lines, and a considerable number of moderately heavy guns

French official photographs.

GIANT FRENCH GUNS THAT PULVERISED THE GERMAN POSITIONS ON THE SOMME.
A 16 in. gun in position. In circle: Another piece of heavy ordnance. The construction of hundreds of miles of railway enabled the French to use heavy naval ordnance and monster army howitzers of a new pattern in their Somme offensive, moving them rapidly to any point.

RE-ENTRY OF CAVALRY INTO THE WAR.
The expulsion of the enemy from the positions he had occupied for nearly two years enabled the superb French cavalry to resume their proper duty as horsemen.

pastoral region near the allied base of Albert that, when our troops extended southward in order to assist the French, our force on the Somme was given the nickname of the " Deathless Army." Hard-fighting brigades, withdrawn from the ghastly fenland around Ypres, regarded a turn in the Somme district as a comparative h o l i d a y. Only around the German salient by the slopes of Fricourt did any continuous activity occur. This activity was mainly confined to incessant mining that churned the woods into a desert of leprous, tumbled earth and chalk, on the acid-stained surface of which scarcely a tree-trunk was visible.

The French forces south of the Somme had a similar point of un-progressive local mining activity

between his second and third lines, while most of his heavy and long-range batteries were placed among the hills in the rear of his third line. Three rail-heads fed his positions with men, munitions, and food. On the north was the station of Bapaume, in the centre by the bend of the Somme was the railway town of Péronne, and in the south was the railway town of Chaulnes. Of these three towns Péronne was in many respects the most important, for about eight miles eastward of it was the railway junction of Roisel, the capture of which would cut the line through St. Quentin, which fed a vital sector of the German front.

Enemy's underground preparations   None of these towns in the German rear was, however, easy of attack, and none of them had any great economic or political significance, such as Lille and the coalfields near Lille had. A very difficult country of chalk heights extended for miles from the German fire-trenches to the German rail-heads. The undulations of chalk, which were easy to excavate, had been transformed by the industrious German sappers into deep and intricate earthworks that seemed impregnable. All the old farmhouses were provided with an extraordinary system of cellarage, dating from the sixteenth century, when German troops used to sweep on this part of France from the Netherlands and force the people to go underground for shelter until the French king could bring up forces to retrieve his northern dominions. The Virgin of Péronne, who saved her country in one of these invasions, was almost as famous in France as Joan of Arc, and her town is still known as Péronne the Virgin. An allied offensive movement on Péronne was therefore calculated to stir the historic memories of the French troops and the French people; but, unfortunately, the well-known underground refuges of this former frontier province of France were of great use to the enemy. By tunnels and communication saps he had transformed every hamlet into a profound subterranean fortress, and in many places he had constructed steel-domed works, screened with trees and containing quick-firers.

Since the fierce conflicts during the race to the sea, in which the armies of General Castelnau and General Maud'huy held back the heavier gun forces of General von Einem, there had been no action of importance in the Somme area. So comparatively quiet was the lovely

FRENCH CAVALRY ON PATROL.
Romantic impression of the chivalry of France mounted once more and patrolling the bushy slopes of a valley in Picardy.

near Lihons. But, generally speaking, the Germans were allowed an unusual stretch of repose amid their fortified heights north and south of the Somme. It seems, indeed, to have been a matter of subtle policy on the part of General Joffre, General Castelnau, and General Foch to allow the enemy to think that his Somme defences were too strong to be assailed.

The result was that he was lulled into a false sense of security when in the last week of June signs of an impending movement in force were violently visible along the north-western front. First of all the British front flamed and thundered for ninety miles from the north of Ypres to the south of Albert. Day and night our terrific bombardment continued, and then the French guns from the Somme to the Aisne lengthened the hurricane of fire, until it extended at times to a distance of nearly a hundred and eighty miles along the German lines.   **180 miles of flame**

The German Staff clearly foresaw that a great British attack was preparing. For amid our day and night bombardment parties of our men raided the enemy trenches with astonishing vigour in order to test the strength of the forces holding the first hostile zone. The French bombardment, on the other hand, seemed to be only a feint, intended to divert German forces from the sectors which Sir Douglas Haig had planned to attack, though the great line of flaming thunder was sometimes

GALLOPING THE GUNS INTO ACTION ON THE CREST OF THE MOOR.

Rushing up the "75's" during the Somme advance. Their wonderful mobility was one of the most valuable qualities of these famous guns. General Fayolle, indeed, regarded them almost as machine-guns and used them in incredible numbers.

EXHILARATING CHARGE OF CAVALRY DOWN THE HILL AND THROUGH THE STREAM.

French cavalry in full gallop saddle-deep through a stream. The camera is seldom so successful in conveying the sense of exhilaration which fires the actors in a thrilling situation as in this animated and picturesque impression from the Somme front.

A KNIGHT OF FRANCE.

[French official photograph.

French dragoon in the new uniform evolved to suit the new conditions of active service, though lance and helmet recall the Middle Ages.

extended by the French almost to Rheims. General von Falkenhayn and his Staff did not think that the French Army was in the position to make a grand and prolonged attack. By overestimating the French losses in the long and arduous Verdun battles the German Staff had arrived at the mistaken conclusion that the French reserves were so thoroughly wasted that France could do little more than make a demonstration to help the British attack. A French attack was expected, but it was supposed it would not last long, and would only be employed to assist the British operation.

Subtle French strategy　　This enemy view of the practical impotence of France was exactly that which General Joffre and General Castelnau had been trying to establish. The chief difficulty of the French commanders during the ordeal of Verdun had been that they did not want to cheer their people at the price of fully informing the enemy that the striking force of France was unimpaired. They had to let the German Staff think that Verdun had almost bled France white, and at the same time keep their own nation from growing too despondent over the apparent growing enfeeblement of France and the apparent weakness of the new British armies. The moral atmosphere was in some respects rather similar to that obtaining before the victory

of the Marne, and the French people must have suffered from deep anxiety while General Joffre and General Castelnau played their masterly trick of deluding the German by his own weapon of over-confidence.

As a matter of fact, preparations for a long and great French offensive on the Somme had begun in March, 1916. Veiled by the increasing activity of the French airmen, hosts of working troops gradually transformed the countryside. There had only been one poor branch railway line feeding the front after the German guns had destroyed the fragment of main track running to Albert. But the French troops increased the ten miles of railway running from Bray to Rosières to hundreds of miles of track. At the same time the British troops doubled the lines running to their bases and created numerous branch lines until more than six hundred and ten miles of new lines were constructed, with more than a hundred new stations.

Just before the battle the work was pushed on with extraordinary intensity. One railway-station, with first-rate platforms for handling heavy shells, was built by French soldiers in five days—by French infantry troops, not by the engineering corps. Another station, formed where the regular railway joined the narrow-gauge lines, extended over a square mile of what had been wheat-fields. General Fayolle, commanding on the Somme under General Foch, remarked that he no longer controlled an army but a workshop. " Before the infantry-man," he said, " comes the shell ; before the shell comes the gun, and before the gun comes the wheelbarrow. A trainload of wheelbarrows is a glorious reinforcement. And next in value to a ton of shells is a ton of wood."

Our Staff culled expert lumbermen from the Dominion forces and set them working in speed competitions with French axemen among the woods near the Somme to get timber for the great offen-　**Lumbermen's** sive movement. Huge quarries were　**great part** blasted in the nearest hard rock to obtain macadam for new motor roads and stone for the new railway lines. Great new waterworks were constructed as for a city of millions of inhabitants. For every army corps needed 15,000 gallons of water a day. The French had thousands of motor-lorries, liberated from Verdun by the completion of General Pétain's large light - railway system. Our army also had an enormous fleet of motor-vehicles, and the Allies used their new and old roads for bringing up troops and light material in order to relieve the pressure upon their six or seven hundred miles of railways.

This relief was especially necessary towards June 26th, 1916, when General Foch began to join in our extraordinary bombardment of the German lines. Sir Douglas Haig opened his hurricane fire a week before his troops advanced, and instead of massing his guns and storing most of his shell on the Somme sector, he first concentrated his fire around Arras and around Lille. An extremely flexible and smoothly working system of shell transport and gun transport was needed in order to deceive and perplex the enemy by continually shifting the terrible stress of heavy-gun fire. But both the British and the French had constructed, in their huge new railways of ordinary and narrow gauge and in their maze of new motor roads, the means of quickly changing their points of terrific gun fire. General Foch seems to have thrown his greatest weight of metal on the Chaulnes and Roye sectors, leaving the Somme front comparatively quiet. On June 29th the Sixth German Army made a strong raid between Chaulnes and Roye in an endeavour to test the French strength there, but its attacking infantry was broken by gun fire before it reached the opposite trenches. The German commander, who is said to have been General von Einem, was completely misled by the tremendous force of General Foch's artillery demonstration in the south, and removed regiments from the neighbourhood of Péronne towards Chaulnes. While the Germans were marching away from the real point of attack many of the great French guns came back to the Somme and started firing in an appalling manner.

General Foch did not regard the famous French 3 in. quick-firer as a piece of artillery. He called it a machine-gun, and used it practically as such. His main weapon of attack was the heavy piece of very large calibre. In addtion to the big howitzers employed in the Champagne offensive in the autumn of 1915, several still more powerful types of siege-guns had been transformed into mobile artillery. Most of the great pieces mounted along the coasts of France had been taken out of the forts for use in the Army. Before the war the French Navy had 13·6 in. guns and numerous 11 in. and 12 in. guns, some employed in coast batteries and some stored in larger number for replacing the worn-out guns of the Battle Fleet. The actual mastery of the seas exercised by the British, French, and Italian Fleets permitted the French Navy to hand to the French Army a very large and powerful armament, including some 15 in. guns, throwing a shell nearly a ton in weight. In this connection it may be remarked that the British Fleet repaid the debt it owed to the French Army. As we have pointed out in a previous chapter, the French Army, which had always held from two-thirds to three-quarters of the entire military forces of Germany, compelled the German steel-makers and steel-workers to devote most of their energies to military weapons, with the result that German naval construction fell far behind British naval construction. But now we see that the mighty striking power thus developed in our Fleet enabled the French to weaken their great system of coastal fortification and turn over heavy guns by the hundred for service in the French Army during the most important

British Navy helps French Army

of allied offensive movements. We regard this matter as an illuminating and inspiring example of the alternations of strength gained by the Allies through generous and far-reaching co-operation.

The huge pieces of French naval ordnance were adapted to the needs of land warfare, and built into a kind of land gunboat running on rails, capable of rapid transport, facile gun-laying, and progress behind every strong infantry advance. Some special new army howitzers of 16 in. calibre were mounted in the same manner. Some of the pieces had a range of twenty miles, which, when their massed fire was directed by aeroplane, caused terrible disturbance to the enemy's centres of communication. The 16 in. guns, rolling on eight-wheeled bogies, looked like gigantic telescopes as they lifted their barrels above the arch of their steel bridges. Each piece, with its mounting and waggon, weighed a hundred and seventy tons, yet two men, turning a crank like that of an ordinary garden-pump, could move the gigantic tube easily, while another man squatting on the breech sufficed to tip it up. A little crane worked by one man lifted up from an armoured tender a monster shell and placed it in a set of guides from which the projectile travelled automatically into the breech.

Adapting naval guns

Such is the description given by a French writer, and it will be seen that all the mechanism was practically that of a 15 in. gun-turret of a battleship. The new French and British mobile howitzers and cannon of very large calibre were turned into mobile pieces owing to the skilled experience of naval engineers. Our naval engineers, having special practical experience of the successful mounting of 15 in. guns, were able to help their brilliant French

[French official photograph

BUILDING AN OFFICER'S POST OF SAND-BAGS IN A QUARRY.

Trench architecture attained extraordinary developments in the prolonged period of trench warfare that ensued after the Battle of the Aisne. This photograph shows a commander's post in process of construction in the extreme northern lines of the French front.

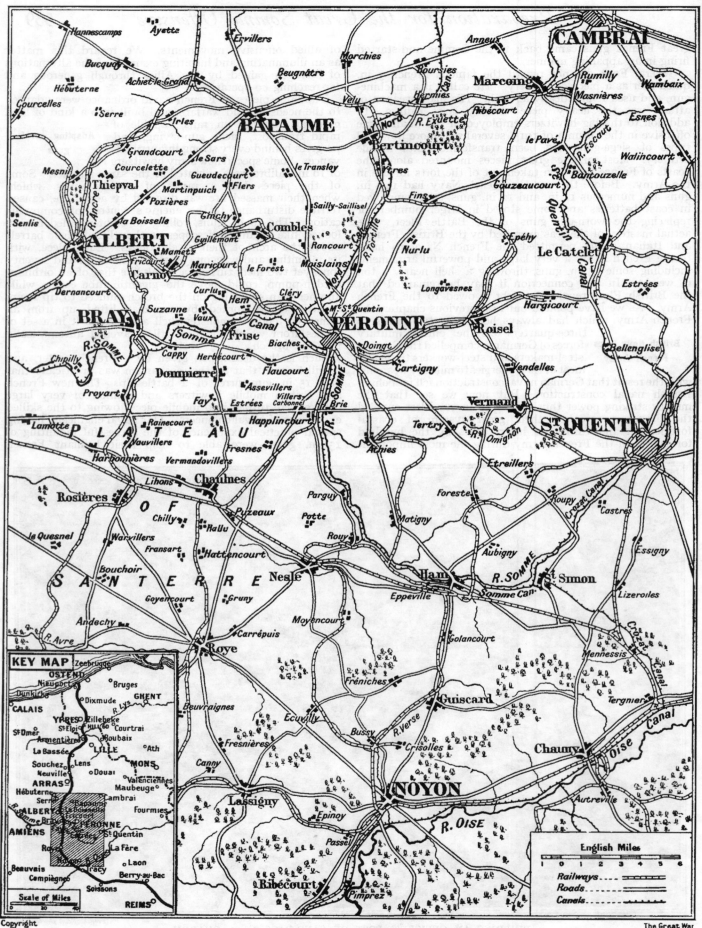

AREA OF THE FRANCO-BRITISH OFFENSIVE BEGUN JULY 1ST, 1916.

That part of the allied line in the west which was the scene of the bitterest fighting in 1916 extended from Hébuterne to Noyon. The Allies joined hands approximately at the Somme River. From July 1st a general offensive was kept up with occasional interruptions, principally due to weather conditions. Towards the end of November the British were threatening Bapaume and the French were within striking distance of Péronne.

The Great War

comrades. On June 28th parks of these monster guns steamed suddenly into action along the Somme, and tremendously reinforced the large ordinary mass of fixed heavy howitzers which were pounding the German lines from their concealed gun-pits. When the railway artillery arrived and each piece went to the place marked out for it, the reason for the construction of hundreds of new railway-stations became apparent to every infantryman. The infantry, that for four months had dug and built and carted, had a final intense spell of navvy work imposed upon it. The troops had to help the gunners in transporting the lighter kind of shell from rail and motor trucks to the underground storing places in the hillside. They had to collect their own stores of hand-grenades, aerial torpedoes, and other ammunition close to the front, for transport into the enemy's lines when these were captured; and when all the immense and varied work of porterage was going on the face of the countryside had to be changed at once. Every object of a destructible character which had served or had seemed to serve the enemy as a ranging mark for his guns was destroyed throughout the area in which the Eleventh French Army was operating. Big tree-trunks, ruined houses, and other noticeable small features were removed with unexpected suddenness, so that German forward observing officers and German aerial observers would find their firing maps almost useless in the morning. They could no longer tell their gunners to train a few points away from some small object that had marked the landscape since the beginning of trench warfare. New and emptier firing maps had to be made by the enemy, but he was given no time in which to make them.

Blinding enemy observers

When morning came and his kite-balloons ascended in the rear of his lines for their usual work of gunnery control, squadrons of allied aviators soared up and over the front. Then above these squadrons circled the flower of French Fokker fighters and the picked fighting pilots of the British Flying Corps. General Foch had collected the best airmen from Verdun and Champagne, and led by Lieutenant Guynemer, with his long list of victories, and by a young British officer from Nottingham—who surpassed even the famous Frenchman in the number of German machines he had brought down—the struggle for the mastery of the air began.

On this struggle depended everything. If the Allies could not blind the German guns their own artillery would have to work at a disadvantage, and the movements of troops and supplies would be seriously impeded. But the mastery of the air was won with surprising rapidity. The lower attacking squadrons swooped upon the German kite-balloons through a tempest of shrapnel from enemy anti-aircraft batteries. Each pilot planed down in a steep curve and fired into the envelope of the German balloon a special missile, causing the gas to explode in a sheet of flame. All that the Germans could do, with the air dominated for thirteen thousand feet above them by layers of allied machines, was to haul down their balloons in frenzied haste. One French airman made his usual swoop on a balloon, but, as he was about to fire, his right thumb was broken by a shrapnel bullet, and the pain caused him to shoot wide and miss. Usually, after making the

SOUL-STIRRING SCENE JUST BEHIND THE LINE.
French Colonial soldiers on their way to billets after a spell of duty in the first line. The cherished standard is carried at the head of the regiment, and each seasoned warrior bears an expression of determination to do his utmost for the cause of France.

downward swoop and loosing his explosive missile, a pilot turns his machine upward to avoid the attentions of "Archibald," the anti-aircraft gun. The wounded French pilot was climbing up quickly when he saw that he had failed. He looped over and made for the balloon again as it was being hauled down, and at a distance of only a hundred yards from the earth he swept through a hail of fire, was wounded again in the thigh, but held on, exploded the balloon, and managed to get back to his aerodrome. In all, fifteen German observing balloons were brought down by the new missile, which seems to have been the invention of a French naval officer, and first used at Verdun two months before. Although the Germans at times sent one of their remaining balloons up for a few minutes and hauled it down quickly before an allied pilot could approach, the German guns and the German Staff were practically blinded. Their machines could not attempt to cross the allied lines, singly or in fighting squadrons, without being assailed by a superior number of French and British machines of remarkable power, handled by men of consummate skill. The weather was bright and sunny, but the sky was dark from the enemy's point of view.

General Fayolle had an entire fleet of photographic machines operating all day over the enemy's lines. Each piece of destruction wrought by the French guns was photographed immediately afterwards, and in a short time the photograph was developed and fixed, and being closely studied by French Staff officers. If the picture was not entirely satisfactory the observing machines again went up, followed by photographic machines. The gunners fired some ranging shots, and received messages from the observing machines, under whose direction they again poured an intense fire on the half-destroyed works, when more photographs were taken for the use of the Staff.

Work of aerial camera-men

There seems to have been little counter-battery firing from the German side. Especially in and around the ravined plateau of Santerre, looped by the Somme and overlooking Péronne, did the German artillery seem very weak. It was indeed reported that the enemy began withdrawing his heavy guns from Santerre when the enormous increase of French fire showed the German commander he had been mistaken by General Foch's demonstration at Chaulnes and Roye. But he could

PPP.

WAR-TIME WAITERS ON THEIR WAY TO THE SOMME FRONT WITH THE FIRST COURSE.
Staff of a field-kitchen carrying soup to their comrades in the trenches. Cheery scene on any French road in the vicinity of the battle-line.

not retire many guns, and he could not withdraw or reinforce his troops, for when the huge French parks of artillery were definitely set to their work their action was like that of a titanic and ineluctable piece of mechanism. The longest ranged cannon kept up their fire on the distant German rail-heads; other batteries of naval guns maintained an incessant tempest of explosive shell and shrapnel on the roads and railway tracks along which munitions, supplies and men were usually moved towards the communication-trenches. Then these trenches, often beginning six miles in the rear of the enemy's fire-trench, were incessantly battered by high-explosive shell. The German front line was destroyed by great aerial torpedoes, of a new model, launched from new mortars of an improved quick-firing kind. The destruction of the enemy's barbed-wire was undertaken by the "75's." All this went on in daylight and darkness, with the effect that the German infantry, artillery, engineers and army service corps, who occupied three zones of defensive lines, were cut off. Meanwhile, upon every trench, every system of works, and every sap there rained the great shells from the French "heavies" and mortars. General Fayolle blasted a way for his troops with deadly precision and appalling scope. He was on the retired list when the war opened, but having obtained the command of a regiment when General Joffre reorganised the officering of the armies, he won distinction under General Foch during the underground battles in Artois, and then rose, like General Pétain, to an army command during the arduous autumn struggle in the German lines in Champagne. In fact, Fayolle and Pétain emerged from the slippery, muddy slopes of Champagne as the proved leaders in the next French offensive movement. General Foch welcomed his old comrade back to Picardy, and with him planned in minutest detail all the new technique necessary in a slow, progressive advance. The later methods used by the Germans at Verdun were

German front line destroyed

carefully studied, as we have already pointed out, but General Fayolle had many important new matters of organisation to introduce into the general scheme.

In particular, his experiences in Champagne, where by a rapid thrust he had almost broken right through the German lines, convinced him that success critically depended upon a closer, simultaneous co-operation of guns and infantry. The problem was to connect an advanced victorious wave of troops a mile or more in the enemy's lines with the motionless heavy batteries four, five, or six miles behind them, so that the distant monster guns should act continually with the infantry like a row of giant machine-guns. Every ordinary means of signalling was developed by long practice. The infantry carried small white flags with which they marked each position they conquered, and in each position they also lighted Bengal fires and signalled with rockets. Likewise they flag-signalled, as the British armies had done from the beginning; they helio-graphed; they used telephones, rapidly laid behind them by observing artillery parties, and also portable wireless instruments. But all this expansion of ordinary means of communication did not content General Fayolle. His grand aim was to kill Germans without losing Frenchmen. He intended to work almost entirely with his guns, and use his infantry chiefly to occupy and consolidate the positions that had been won by his artillery. In order that France might emerge from the Great War not only victorious, but with her stock of virile strength large enough to engender and maintain a strong, great, new generation, it was necessary to save the men from disablement and death.

General Fayolle looks ahead

In other words, the French commander and his Staff had to discover means of reversing the comparative losses of attacking and defending troops. All that the Germans had accomplished in defence, by combining machine-gun fire and curtains of shell fire with deep bomb-proof shelters and sunken zones of barbed-wire, had to be answered by some new and efficient method of pushing an attack. The fine genius of the French nation was equal to the occasion, and under the fostering care of General Fayolle and General Foch an idea that General Pétain had adumbrated at Verdun was worked out into an eventful, permanent addition to modern methods of warfare.

During the month of preparation the personnel and the matériel of the French Flying Corps were greatly increased. Instead of relying on officer pilots, as did the British Army with its class traditions, the French Flying Corps recruited its personnel largely from young non-commissioned officers of proved merit. The young men of the new school were encouraged in a frank, democratic way by official bulletins that gave the names and the list of victories of the best fighters, so that the sporting spirit of the French public was largely concentrated upon the achievements of men like Guynemer. This system of competitive publicity, which the Germans also used in rather a braggart way, seems to have been regarded as vulgar by the **French Flying Corps** directors of the British Flying Corps. But **increased** the thoughtful French commanders, who adopted the method of advertising their crack pilots so that they could be listed like English batsmen according to the number of their wins, had a very serious purpose in thus popularising military aviation. They needed emulous, spirited, capable young flyers by the thousand instead of by the hundred. It was, indeed, likely that they would at last require a very large and

continuous stream of flying recruits, which meant that they would need a very much larger number of candidates for testing in the aviation school.

For the supreme weapon of the French offensive, on which General Fayolle depended to save his troops, was the formation of a large corps of infantry airmen. It was the special work of these men to scout in advance of each French attacking force, **Triumph of** and watch from an altitude of one to three **infantry airmen** hundred feet the progress the men made and the obstacles they encountered. It was expected that the loss in pilots and machines among the new infantry aviation squadrons would be very considerable, for they would have to move very low down in a much restricted area, expose themselves while watching their own troops and the enemy's machine-gun positions, and be further occupied in wirelessing to their batteries and to their headquarters. They were also trained to bring their machine-guns and Lewis guns into action by swooping on enemy forces. Happily, the Germans were entirely taken by surprise by this well-organised system of aerial direction in the attack.

The fire of the French and British guns increased in fury on June 29th, which was the date that seems first to have been fixed for the assault. But no order was given to the troops, either because the bombardment was not thought to be sufficient, or more probably because the rumour as to the date of the movement had been deliberately allowed to reach the enemy and induce him

A MOMENTARY HALT IN THE STEADY VICTORIOUS ADVANCE.
Rifles stacked and heavy packs laid down, these dogged French soldiers were resting in the grateful shade of one more orchard-surrounded, old-timbered homestead saved for France.

[French official photograph.

A MESSENGER OF MARS CROSSING NO MAN'S LAND.
French "runner" carrying a brigade message across a Somme battlefield, every foot of which was ranged by German artillery and snipers.

to pack his reserve trenches. During the last two days of the bombardment these reserve trenches were subjected to an especially terrific fire, and several zones of shrapnel were maintained over all the enemy's routes of supply and reinforcement. According to a German statement, every place within ten miles of the firing-line was smitten with heavy shell and incendiary projectiles. Then in the morning of Saturday, July 1st, 1916, the British and French infantry forces climbed out of their trenches and advanced into the German lines.

General Fayolle's army connected with the British Army north of the Somme at the village of Maricourt. Here, General Balfourier, the army corps commander of the Twentieth Corps, had his troops of the 29th Division—the incomparable Iron Division—stretched down to the river at Vaux. Then by the canal-locks in the river valley, at Eclusier, another famous French African force, the Colonial Division, with which General Pétain had conquered the Hand of Massiges in Champagne, extended southward towards Fontaine-les-Cappy, where a fine Breton force was arrayed against the enemy.

The crux of the position was the dividing line of the Somme Valley, separating the Ironsides from the Colonials. The small split stream of the Somme ran through marshes from one to two miles broad, the marshes being cut by a canal as well as by the river. Above the wide, winding zone of the marshes rose on either side a rampart of chalk. The river cliffs were in turn dominated by ridges, from three hundred to four hundred and fifty feet high, occupied by the

Somme ridges and marshes Germans north-west and south. All the hamlets, woods, and fields in the large southern angle of the Somme running to Péronne were dominated by the main German heavy batteries on the slopes of Mont St. Quentin north of Péronne; and at Villers Carbonnel, four miles south of the town, there was another important mass of long-range German siege-guns. The consequence was that, although Péronne was only about six miles from the trenches of the French Colonial Division, there was no chance of storming into the town by a direct frontal attack. For the great, curving, marshy river valley turned sharply south by the old, grey, lovely walled city, and if the French troops

had there crossed the stream, canal, and marsh they would have had to work through a large stretch of low ground westward, which was surrounded by an amphitheatre of downs, on the farther slopes of which the Germans had placed guns by the hundred. In other words, the wedge of lowish, seamed tableland extending from the southern French sector to the enemy's railhead at Péronne, was a great natural trap. Troops who stormed into it from the west would be held up by the river and exposed to a cross-fire of artillery. This was no doubt the reason why General von Einem thought that the allied bombardment on the southern side of the Somme was merely a distracting demonstration, and that General Foch and his able Staff intended to launch their real assault at Roye and Chaulnes.

General Foch, however, had worked out a brilliant and subtle method of turning the marsh-moated and hill-ringed wedge of chalk south of the Somme into the main leverage point of the allied advance. About four miles north of the river was the town of Combles, around which ran a branch railway which the enemy had enlarged and connected with a network of field railways. This railway, nicknamed the "Tortillard," or "Wriggler," by the allied troops, twisted down ravines screened from direct fire. **Value of** But General Foch calculated that if **Santerre Plateau** the wedge of the Santerre plateau, south of the river, could be won, tunnelled, and excavated, it would become a superb base for heavy howitzer fire against all the German positions northward around Combles. The fact that the southern wedge of chalk was a hundred and fifty feet or more lower than the northern main German artillery positions did not militate against howitzer fire effects so long as the Allies held the mastery of the air and possessed a stronger force of monster mobile siege-guns. General von Einem and his Staff were relying upon ideas about hill positions which had been rendered obsolete by the rapid progress of airmanship and by the transformation of even 3 in. field-guns into semi-howitzers.

So the principal operation of General Fayolle's army consisted in making a rapid seizure of the low river promontory of Santerre, on a six-mile front from the village of Curlu on the northern bank to the hamlet of Fay in the south. It was known that the fighting would be hardest among the northern downs and ravines around Combles, and that when the enemy was thoroughly alarmed and able to concentrate men by the half million against the Allies he would strike his hardest blows by the river, at the delicate junction-point of the French and British Armies. It was for this reason that the Iron Division was placed north of the river, alongside veteran British regiments commanded by our great thruster, Sir Henry Rawlinson. For practical purposes the men of the Iron Division and their comrades of the Twentieth Army Corps formed part of the British Army. They worked slowly forward with our troops in a slow, half-circling, and very wide sweep directed through Bapaume and Combles, towards the rear of Péronne. The task of capturing Péronne, after grinding down the larger part of the entire forces of the German Empire, was to be performed by the British Army and the French corps connecting with it.

Bayonet charge of French infantry over shell=swept open ground.

Uninvited guests: Frenchmen taking cover in a captured German ammunition depot.

French heavy howitzer in action with plentiful ammunition in reserve.

French artillery observation post in a tree among the hills.

But this apparently very round-about and gradual operation pivoted upon General Fayolle's remarkable plan for conquering quickly and at little cost the low promontory of Santerre south of the river. As we shall afterwards see, the French and British Staffs had only a remote interest in the capture of Péronne. They chiefly designed to bring about a tremendous, long conflict with the main forces of the German Empire, and wear those forces gradually down until all the fronts held by German troops were permanently enfeebled. When the work of enfeeblement begun at Verdun was completed on the Somme the general allied offensive would take place. In other words, the Battle of the Somme was not—to use the new, expressive, cant phrase—the "great push." It was only the western factor in the combined allied movements of great pressure which the army of General Brussiloff in the east, the Rumanian Army, the army of Salonika in the south-east, and the army of General Cadorna in the south of Europe were planning to conduct against the Central Empires and Bulgaria.

EAGER HANDS AND EFFICIENT MACHINE.
Some idea of the size and power to which French ordnance attained in the third year of the war may be gauged from this illustration showing four Frenchmen charging a heavy howitzer.

At half-past nine on Saturday morning the French Colonial and Breton troops advanced to the attack. The Bretons were middle-aged reservists, who had distinguished themselves in some fine defensive work at Quennevières alongside the Zouaves. Quiet, settled, steady married men, they had borne themselves calmly under bombardments and rush attacks in the sedentary life of the trenches, but only their own commander seems to have been strongly convinced that they would show great driving power in attack. Nearly all the other attacking French and Colonial regiments were led by battalions of fresh young troops, directed by old, experienced officers and supported by battalions of the finest veterans. The extraordinary reservists of Brittany, however, equalled the best active troops in endurance, skill and charging power.

Marvellous Breton reservists

Kinsmen of the Welsh who emigrated from Britain in the days of King Arthur, these middle-aged Celts were transformed by the fury of battle. Half an hour before the advance they asked permission to sing, and, chanting the "Marseillaise," they went forward in platoons with their lines straighter and steadier than they would have been at manœuvres in peace time. They captured the hamlet of Fay, and, between Fay and Soyécourt, they advanced to the outskirts of Estrées, which was a vast subterranean fortress the approaches of which were drenched with shells by a park of heavy German guns at Villers Carbonnel, four miles directly in front of Estrées. Villers Carbonnel, south of Péronne, and Mont St. Quentin north of the town, were the two grand artillery positions of the enemy, each comprising hundreds of siege-guns that swept all the Santerre promontory. Months had to pass before Villers Carbonnel was even remotely threatened by the French troops. It was the main rallying-point for all the German forces south of the Somme, and though seldom mentioned in communiqués, was one of the most important places in the European War. Many of its guns were destroyed by the terrible plunging shells from the new monster French artillery. But the Germans managed to transport new howitzers at night across the river valley and maintain the strength of the position. The gallant Bretons dug themselves in near Estrées and swung their northern wing forward towards Belloy and Assevillers Behind them were some regiments of the famous Foreign Legion, who afterwards relieved them when they had gallantly won and held the most difficult and most critical position in the allied line of advance.

Meanwhile, the Colonial Division, with its coloured troops, renowned for their terrific ardour in attack, enjoyed itself in an amazing fashion. On this point of the front, between Frise and Dompierre, the Germans had not expected to be attacked, and were completely taken by surprise. This was the chief reason why the French Colonial Division, forming the centre of General Fayolle's army, had an astonishingly easy task in the morning of July 1st.

Neglecting the village of Frise, in a marshy loop of the river on their right, the Colonial troops marched into the ruins of Dompierre and Becquincourt, which formed together a large mass of shattered buildings the size of a town. The cellars in the chalk plateau were originally deep, and for nearly two years the Germans had burrowed deeper and linked up their caverns with tunnels until the two connected villages were transformed into a subterranean Gibraltar. But the new French monster siege-guns had smashed in many of the thick vaults, choked the entrances, broken the armour that had protected machine-guns and artillery, and destroyed practically every wall above ground. Among the French gunners were men picked from other sectors because they were natives of **How Becquincourt was won** the places on which their guns were trained. In particular, there was one young farmer of Becquincourt who took a savage pleasure in destroying his own fine old farm buildings and getting his huge shells well down into his own cellars. When the village was won, and he contemplated the unrecognisable heap of stones representing the house of his birth, he said, with the professional pride of an artilleryman, "What splendid shooting!" After so extraordinarily devastating a bombardment as this there was no infantry battle, but merely a walk-over. The remnant of the garrison of Dompierre, consisting of two hundred men and

EFFECT OF FRENCH ARTILLERY FIRE ON A GERMAN POSITION IN CHAMPAGNE.
[French official photograph.]
The original trench was blown out of recognition, dug-outs were obliterated, and great mounds of earth were piled high on the parapet, through which the stakes supporting the barbed-wire defences are protruding.

officers, was captured by the French Colonials at the cost of only one man killed on their side. The hamlet of Bussus, south of Dompierre, was also carried with little loss. The casualties of the entire Colonial Division numbered only six hundred and forty, after breaking through the entire system of the first German zone of defences and reaching the second zone, between Herbécourt and Assevillers, in the evening of July 1st.

Great gains at Yet the hostile organisations were
small cost extremely elaborate. At Dompierre, for instance, the attacking troops had to cross in the first place the German fire-trench; in the second place two twin trenches, a hundred yards behind, protected by fields of barbed-wire; in the third place the Wolff trench, with another zone of wire entanglements a hundred yards farther; and in the fourth place the village itself and the connected ruins of Becquincourt, with their underground maze of fortified works. One large cavern, west of Dompierre, was equipped with two great vats for the manufacture of poison gas. From the vats pipes ran into the fire-trenches. But the heavy French shells had broken the gas system before a favourable wind could be used by the enemy. It was creditably reported that the two Colonial regiments engaged in surrounding all this German system of works had five men killed and sixteen wounded while working through the first four rows of trenches, losing afterwards, as we have already stated, one man in Dompierre itself.

At Estrées, farther south, the Breton reservists avoided a frontal attack, and rapidly working round the village on both sides, enveloped it and stormed it from the rear. Their casualties, though somewhat larger than those of the skilled attackers of the Colonial Division, yet remained

exceedingly small when compared with the former allied average of losses in conquering intensively fortified trench systems. The miraculously insignificant number of casualties among the French south of the Somme was not entirely due to the fact that the enemy in this sector was taken unawares. His routine system of artillery defences was very formidable. After the terrific bombardment he was still able to bring into action hundreds of guns which he had kept silent and concealed during the hurricane French fire.

There were batteries in the Bois de Mereaucourt, north-east of Dompierre, batteries in the folds of ground behind the village, and a mighty collection of guns south-east of the village. And when the French gunners lifted on the German rear, indicating that their infantry was about to advance, hundreds of German guns put a great curtain of shrapnel over the French fire-trenches and the neutral zone between the opposing hedges of barbed-wire. At the same time the French communication-trenches were also shelled and shrapnelled, with a view to stopping supports and reinforcements and supplies. In the ordinary way, therefore, shrapnel wounds should have been inflicted in severe proportion upon the charging French forces.

But among other things, such as aerial **French advance**
infantry, General Fayolle had thought **in single file**
out during his experiences in Champagne a new method of deploying troops. Each assaulting regiment advanced in single file through the zone of hostile shell fire. The target they thus presented was scarcely more than three feet wide. Near the enemy's fire-trench the thin stream of blue-clad figures changed formation, and went forward in slow, long waves of attack in very open order. If any machine-gun that had escaped destruction then opened fire upon them, all the men fell down and

sought for cover in the shell-holes. Their officers would not allow them to charge, and often prevented them from trying to creep cautiously round an active centre of resistance. There was, indeed, some trouble at first, especially with some of the French Colonial troops, accustomed to swift, fierce, hand-to-hand bomb and bayonet conflicts in former offensive movements. But the strangely loud drone of propellers at once confirmed the orders violently shouted by the French officers, and the troops understood why they had to tumble into cover at the slightest sign of hostile resistance. The novel aerial infantry of France was operating just in advance of each attacking wave, at a height varying from three hundred to a hundred feet. Some of the pilots came low and shot down, from the rear of the enemy machine-gun positions, the German crews, and then signalled their own infantry to advance. Other pilots, who could not bring their guns to bear on some deadly knot of resisting Germans, dropped smoke-bombs upon them, or wirelessed their position to the French artillery.

Vanguard of aircraft

Then above the heads of the sheltering attacking troops screamed a shower of well-aimed shells, which blasted away all opposition. The troops then arose and walked onward, preceded by their aerial scouts, enskied machine-gunners and celestial bomb-throwers. Naturally, the French Staff work was of almost superhuman perfection, for each regimental brigade, divisional army corps, and Headquarters Staff had alert and finely-trained eyes aloft and in advance of its troops, and wireless messages told the chiefs in the rear more about the state of affairs in the breaking German line than was known to the men who were actually breaking the line.

There is only one criticism that can be passed upon General Fayolle's and General Foch's handling of the situation south of the Somme on July 1st. This criticism was made by the military expert of the "Temps," himself an officer of high rank. He pointed out that the attack between Dompierre and Estrées was so perfectly conceived and executed that the relatively small number of German troops in front of Péronne was completely surprised and overpowered. It would have been quite easy for General Fayolle to have smashed right through the hostile organisations and won all the promontory in the great angle of the Somme Valley. This rushing conquest might have been completed in twenty-four hours. As it was, the Colonials and the Bretons only occupied the centre of the German first line on Saturday. Then on Sunday the Colonial Division drove into Bois de Mereaucourt behind Frise, bombed two battalions of Germans out of their shelters, which had been dug to a depth of sixty feet, and a French infantry division, working along the river, then enveloped Frise and its reed-grown peninsula of marsh. At the same time the main fortresses in the German second zone of defence from the river bank to Assevillers were crumbled into a wilderness of broken, yellowed chalk, powdered brick, and splintered wood by the incessant fire of the French heavy guns. The rails on which these guns moved were extended into the German line, so that the steaming monsters of battle obtained a wide dominion over the German system of defence. By the evening of Sunday, July 2nd, Assevillers was reached and all Herbécourt taken, and many heavy German siege-guns captured.

The next morning the Foreign Legion, that ranks in

French expert criticism

SHATTERED BY A SHELL CYCLONE: GERMAN TRENCHES BEFORE DOMPIERRE.
Utterly barren appearance of the war landscape before Dompierre, on the French front. The country for miles around was comparable to some tropical desert, the broken barbed-wire and scorched shrubs looking from a distance like cactus undergrowth. On the horizon is the shattered village.

fury of driving power and tenacity of hold with the Iron Division, was deployed between Estrées and Assevillers. It will be remembered that the Foreign Legion had been badly shattered near Vimy Ridge in the spring of 1915, and practically destroyed in a terrible yet victorious charge in Champagne the following autumn. But sufficient officers survived to transmit the great spirit of the Legion to the thousands of new foreign recruits, attracted to the service of the most glorious torch-bearers of democracy.

Foreign Legion's fine work　France was unique in her radiant power of alluring to her banner the fine fighting men of neutral Europe. Reborn from its triumphant grave in Champagne, the Foreign Legion charged again on the German works by Estrées which the Bretons had been unable to conquer, captured five hundred prisoners, and then swept onward, by their left, to Belloy, a hamlet beyond the second German line. Belloy was stormed on July 4th, with the ravine west of Assevillers. As Belloy was scarcely two miles west of the grand German artillery centre of Villers Carbonnel, the work of the Foreign Legion was carried out in circumstances of extreme difficulty. The German commander brought

RUSSIA IN THE WESTERN CONFLICT.
[French official photograph.
Russia, despite her great obligations on the eastern and Caucasian fronts, was able to send several thousand sturdy fighting men to operate in Champagne. This illustration shows Russian soldiers digging communication-trenches.

back the troops he had vainly sent to Chaulnes and Roye, and collected reinforcements from the Aisne front and poured them continually against the Estrées-Belloy sector. That is to say, he tried to stop the French advance south of the Somme by taking it in the right flank. He seems to have possessed new railway communications running towards Villers Carbonnel, enabling him to keep a stream of munitions flowing to that point, while his fresh troops struggled forward on the shell-swept roads and the shrapnel-drenched communication-trenches.

The Foreign Legion, like its predecessors of the Breton Division, was soon forced to stand on the defensive, and search for cover in ground that the French guns had already rendered untenable. The Legion thus succeeded to the most desperate job on all the allied line of advance. Elsewhere troops could withdraw a few hundred yards without seriously upsetting the design of the great progressive attack. But the point held by the Legion was the supreme pivot on which all the French and British troops northward were slowly wheeling. The Legionaries had to hold fast, and fast they held, until by a gigantic

artillery duel the massed French siege-guns beat down the German ordnance at Villers, and made it necessary for the enemy to reconstruct the lines of traffic in his rear. Thereupon, there was a pause, during which the forces on each side slaved at navvy work and stupendous engineering operations.

Meanwhile, the Colonial Division and the Moroccan Division, reinforced by young French infantry, continued their promenade along the southern cliffs of the Somme, that rose in places two hundred feet above the canal, stream, and marsh. In the morning of July 3rd the village of Feuilleres was conquered, together with Bois du Chapitre, more than two miles behind the first enemy line. In the afternoon the third zone of German defences was penetrated by the canal at Buscourt, and pierced again two and a half miles southward at the village of Flaucourt. At Flaucourt the magnificent fighting men from French Africa were more than three miles inside the hostile front, after only fifty-five hours of fairly light combat and remarkably small losses. A force of about 20,000 German troops had been put out of action—nearly a third of it had been captured, more than a third of it had been killed, and the larger part of the remainder seriously disabled. Then a force of Guards and divisions formed of a medley of battalions, had been caught by shell fire as they marched up to strengthen the breaking lines. When, greatly reduced in number, they came into action in the valleys and stripped woods, ruined farmhouses and obliterated hamlets, they were hammered into impotence by the heavy French howitzers.

After the Colonial troops had captured Flaucourt, which with its caverned ways was the principal rallying-point for all the German forces in front of Péronne, the division was informed it was to be sent to rest quarters. The men were much offended. They had only been fighting night and day for fifty-five hours, going on short rations, and suffering from thirst on the sun-smitten plateau. "Why should we hand over our victories to other men?" they said. "We are not tired. We took Flaucourt, and we want to keep it." This deplorable example of lack of discipline in the coloured contingent of a military democracy was telephoned to General Fayolle, who smiled, and allowed the Colonials to have their own way. On the left wing by the river a French infantry brigade, on the night of July 4th, captured the farm buildings of Sormont, and the Moroccan Division and the Colonial troops pushed onward from the French centre, while on the right wing a great leap forward was made towards the village of Barleux. Barleux was scarcely more than a mile north of the mass of German guns at Villers Carbonnel.

The German commander answered this **Spirit of French** move by a violent bombardment of **Colonials** the exposed French flank at Estrées and Belloy. It was costly work for the German gunners to fire in the darkness, against which every tongue of flame from their pieces could be seen, either by direct observation from the French lines or by aerial observers in kite-balloons and night-flying aeroplanes. The long-range railway batteries in the rear of the French forces fired at the targets of flame and wrought great havoc. Nevertheless, the enemy gunners stood to their dangerous work, as it

PIONEERS LAYING NEW LINES OF COMMUNICATION.

French pioneers worked incessantly to establish complete lines of communication throughout the entire length and breadth of the western front. Many of the lines they laid were of sufficiently solid construction to remain permanent after their immediate purpose should have been fulfilled.

CARRYING ROADS FOR HEAVY TRAFFIC OVER THE SWAMPY GROUND.

French engineers making a road for the passage of troops and heavy artillery over swampy ground. The foundation of these roads was made with trunks of trees, and for this purpose whole forests were cleared of all their timber.

was absolutely necessary for the grand counter-attack their commander had at last prepared.

Among the troops collected for the answering German thrust was a Bavarian division, which displayed a fine gallantry. Some companies of the Foreign Legion were hard pressed in Estrées, and the eastern part of Belloy was captured. But the Legionaries and their comrades had only retired in accordance with the disconcerting tactics of the men who handled the 3 in. quick-

Estrées and Belloy captured

firers. A storm of little melinite shells fell on the lost portions of the two villages; a brief message along the telephone wires brought a tornado of bigger shells from the French rear. Then abruptly both the light and heavy pieces lifted, and the resilient French troops returned with bombs and recovered all the villages. Having thus staggered the enemy, they attacked him on both flanks along the system of trenches running between Estrées and Belloy, which were entirely captured by July 5th, completing the conquest of all the second German positions south of the Somme on a front of six miles.

The tireless Colonial Division advanced from Flaucourt to Hill 63 on the road to the village of Barleux. The German commander again launched a furious flank attack on the Estrées-Belloy line, but the Foreign Legion had organised its quick-firing batteries and shattered every wave of assault well before their trenches were reached. This defeat exhausted the hastily gathered German reinforcements on the Péronne sector. According to an officer of the Prussian Guard captured in front of Péronne, the reinforcements had been sent up without direction, without connecting Staff work, and entirely wasted in a criminally ineffective manner. There was another pause

during which the French extended their railways, enabling their heavy mobile guns to steam close to the enemy. On July 8th the left wing of French infantry operating by the river seized some of the farm buildings of Bazincourt —a victory which brought the French line at this point five miles into the enemy lines. Then the enormous parks of heavy French guns that had been brought up behind the French infantry division and the Colonial Division swept the end of the Santerre plateau with a tornado of shells quite as terrific as the bombardment of June 30th.

Under the arc of roaring projectiles the French infantry advanced on the fortified village of Biaches, which was a German divisional headquarters, while a Colonial regiment moved out more to the south towards the dominating point of the Santerre plateau, known as La Maisonette. The eminence by the chateau of La Maisonette was known as Hill 97 (318 feet high), and surrounded with woods, affording magnificent cover. The height was only a mile away from Péronne, with the canal and river gleaming at its foot and miles of lower country stretching eastward. Across these low tracts ran the main German railway line of communication to Roisel,

nine miles distant, and Cambrai, Mons, and Cologne. Then, in the same low exposed country, a second important

Strategic value of La Maisonette

railway line of communication ran south-eastward towards Ham and Noyon, while a third line ran south to Chaulnes and Roye. The hill of La Maisonette was, therefore, a position of extreme strategic importance. In the Franco-Prussian War, when a French army under Faidherbe held Péronne, and a German army under Manteuffel attacked from the west across the Somme as the army of General Fayolle was doing, the fight for the dominating point of La

[French official photograph.

THE ENDLESS CHAIN OF AMMUNITION SUPPLY IN FRANCE.

French artillery batteries on the way to the front passing through a village on the Somme. The convoy coming in the opposite direction consisted of ammunition-waggons returning empty after lodging their delivery at various batteries during the night.

Maisonette decided the day, and the victorious Germans captured the town of Péronne and swept on towards Laon.

The Germans were therefore precisely aware of the strategical value of La Maisonette, upon which their Staff officers had published many studies in connection with the war of 1870. Modern artillery had greatly increased the importance of La Maisonette, especially in the conditions of the new trench warfafe. In 1870 Manteuffel could not rely entirely upon a direct driving thrust from La Maisonette into Péronne, and he combined this thrust with a turning movement through Bapaume, exactly as Sir Douglas Haig and General Foch were

WATER RESERVOIRS ON THE FRENCH FRONT.
In some places reservoirs of water were established for the use of men in the front trenches; the water was filtered for drinking.

SOUP TRAINS IN THE TRENCHES.
Soup was taken up to the first-line trench in tanks, and run on a little railway laid along the communication-trenches.

doing. There was a height across the river about a mile north of the town, the famous Mont St. Quentin, which was forty-two feet higher than La Maisonette and also backed by downs of much greater altitude. The enveloping movement by Bapaume was therefore more necessary, under modern artillery conditions which favour the defence, than it had been in Faidherbe's and Manteuffel's days.

On the other hand, the extraordinary range, the enormous fighting power, and rapid rate of fire of the latest type of heavy pieces of ordnance gave La Maisonette a curious, independent value of its own. No infantry advance could be made from it across the river **Great communications** valley into the wide stretch of low country **threatened** beyond, because the German guns on Mont St. Quentin and the greater northern height near Bouchavesnes would have annihilated the attack ng troops in the great hollow around Péronne. But, though any infantry movement was impracticable from La Maisonette, a gigantic artillery operation against three railway lines of communication at Péronne was easy. Railways, roads, and the Somme Canal, with its valuable barge transport of munitions and supplies, could be permanently cut by the French from La Maisonette.

There was another great strategical advantage attaching to the hill which we will discuss later.

It will be seen that, even from a local point of view, the German commander had made a serious miscalculation in thinking that his Péronne sector in the last week of June, 1916, was an unimportant one, from which defending troops could safely be drawn to strengthen Chaulnes and Roye. In the first week of July he had made a further blunder, by flinging most of his reinforcements away in vain counter-attacks on the strong French left flank at Estrées, near which General **German commander's** Fayolle had for months been siting an **blunders** overwhelming number of heavy howitzers. La Maisonette, with its connections at the village of Biaches, was the supreme object of all General Fayolle's operations south of the Somme, and the German commander was retired in disgrace by Falkenhayn and replaced by another army chief. Several of the army corps and divisional generals on the Péronne front were also retired in disgrace.

In the morning of July 9th a reconnoitring line of French grenadiers investigated the north-west, western, and south-western trenches of Biaches. Then in the afternoon, with the bombardment working up to its supreme intensity, the main French forces of infantry walked forward, with their advanced supports of the new aerial French infantry. The battalion commanders led the way, armed with rifle and bayonet like their men, and inspiring these with their own superb determination. It took only a few minutes to capture the system of trenches, and, while the cleaning-up companies stayed and completed their work, the first and second waves of assault rolled into the village. In the underground defences by the shattered houses the struggle was fierce but short, and at six o'clock in the evening only a few houses in the south-eastern corner still enclosed some living enemies. In the heart of the position the conquering troops discovered a dining cavern with a table laden with fine food, wine, and boxes of cigars, prepared for the divisional German Staff, but looking like a delicate attention to meet the needs of the victors.

When the trenches had been reached and passed and the village taken, there occurred one of those checks in the assault which are frequent in the modern war

ONE OF THE HEAVY GUNS USED BY THE ALLIES IN ITS MASSIVE SCREENED POSITION ON THE SOMME.

Heavy naval ordnance and other monster howitzers of 15 in. and 16 in. calibre were freely employed positions to point on specially constructed railways, along in the tremendous artillery bombardments that preceded the Allies' advances and reduced the enemy which also the great weight of the necessary ammunition was conveyed easily and rapidly.

of position. Despite the greatly improved method of aerial reconnoitring, a strong hostile work had been left unsubdued in the rear of the new French line. Near the road to Herbécourt was an old position known as the Fort of Biaches, which formed part of the bridge-head of Péronne, and had been flanked first to the right and then to the left without being enveloped. Unseen wire entanglements hidden in the grass held up two charges. The German machine-guns continued to fire, and seriously interfered with the French operations. The French brigadier-general tried at first to destroy the redoubt by the massed fire of trench-mortars. But their shells had not sufficient penetration. So the engineers were asked to push a sap into the work and blow it up; and it was found it would take at least six days to mine the fortified caverns.

It looked as though the entire infantry operations around Biaches would have to be postponed in order to allow the heavy guns to make precise measurements of

[*French official photograph.*

TENDING THE WOUNDS OF AN ENEMY.
French Red Cross doctor applying his skill to a German prisoner's wounded leg. On the right, three generations of French women regard the operation with interest not unmixed with sympathy.

the little island of resistance from which the victorious troops were held up only thirty yards away. A few trial shots from the French monster guns might have blown up the French infantry instead of breaking into the German shelters. Then a French captain of infantry said: "I can surprise the work." And by one of those strokes of audacity that seem incredible the gallant captain succeeded. He had learnt the exact position of the trench leading to the fortress, and going ahead of his party of eight volunteers he worked at first alone into the position and found it empty. All the Germans were under shelter, as the volunteers behind the captain were throwing hand-grenades. The captain shouted, "Come out!" A group of grey figures appeared; then another group emerged with a sergeant, who seemed to be the leading spirit of the defence, for the officers continued to remain underground. The astonished Germans stared at the French captain, and then made a movement of fight. But the captain shot the first man down with his revolver, crying "Forward!" His own eight supporting men arrived, and the two German groups surrendered. Searching in the shelters, the Frenchmen found two officers and many more men, and returned at last down the communication-trench with a hundred and fourteen prisoners— all that remained of a company. For twenty-four hours the Germans in Biaches Fort had stopped every assault made upon them, only to be captured at last by a magnificent bluff.

While the attack on the Biaches positions was thus drawing to a successful close, a regiment of the Colonial Division advanced on La Maisonette. Here the first defences were carried in one fierce leap, and on the left the triangular wood south-east of Biaches was conquered as far as the cemetery. Then an orchard on the right, where machine-guns had been concealed between the trees, was swept by a terrible bayonet charge. The two flanking forces closed around the chateau on the hill, and after suffering in an ambush formed by a party of Germans who pretended to surrender and fusilladed the men who came forward to receive them, the Colonial regiment took La Maisonette. The German commanding

Biaches Fort surprised

officer, a colonel, was found in his shelter with six other officers, and two hundred survivors of the garrison were made prisoners. The number would have been larger but for the infamous trick played upon the Colonials. These were men from Northern Africa and Senegal, representing the famous "Black Force" of France which, owing to its superb framework of officers, won an uncommonly high place in the European War. An amazing frenzy of attack, like that of a Dervish or Ghazi charge to the death, had been the chief characteristic of the Colonial troops, who often worked side by side with a Moorish division. But in the Somme operations the African troops acquired a cautious patience equal to anything shown by the best white troops. And as their long periods of waiting under terrific shell fire in the shattered hostile positions they conquered did not in any way lessen their lightning violence in attack, they were the terror of the Teutons. "The black friends of France," Erich von Falkenhayn sneeringly called them in an official communication. What was intended as a jibe became a fine compliment. True friends of France, the coloured troops were repaying her for her civilising, educative work in Africa. They fought for ten days from Dompierre to Biaches, and won the chief honours in the first phase of the Battle of the Somme.

The Colonials took only seventy-five minutes to conquer La Maisonette. They gave General Fayolle, at Hill 97, the culminating point of the battlefield, with an observation-post overlooking the German lines on the right bank of the river from Mont St. Quentin to Mons-en-Chaussée. The Germans had organised the position with great care, especially in the northern tract of woodland, Bois de Bias. Caverns thirty feet below the ground were connected by tunnelling with the positions in the valley near the canal, and in the marshes hidden batteries of machine-guns were trained on the northern slopes. It was difficult to attack the Germans in the marshes, and General Fayolle made no attempt to do so. He was very well content with his extraordinary conquest of all the northern and north-eastern part of the plateau of Santerre.

He did not want Péronne. The general situation was

Colonials conquer La Maisonette

such that Péronne was for the time more useful to the Allies as an enemy position than it would have been if captured by the Colonials. At this stage it is necessary to refer to the map of the theatre of all the Somme operations in order to understand that point in the strategy of General Foch which the German commander had overlooked. It will be seen that the French infantry division and the French Colonial Division had, by July 9th, done more than interrupt the railway, road, and canal communications of Péronne. They enfiladed the German positions north of the river from Guillemont and Ginchy to Combles and Rancourt. All the main defensive positions of the enemy in the vital sector where the army of General Balfourier and the army of Sir Henry Rawlinson were co-operating in attack became subjected to a terrible cross-fire of heavy shells from French guns placed in the large wedge of newly-won territory south of the river. Cléry, Feuillaucourt, and Mont St. Quentin in the first line; Hardecourt, Maurepas, and Bouchavesnes in the second line; Guillemont and Ginchy, Combles and Morval, Rancourt and Saillisel in the third line—all these main northern hostile positions of decisive importance were outflanked by the southern French advance into La Maisonette. Around Bray and around Albert were some thousands of British and French guns firing straight against the German front north of the River Somme, and it was more than the German gunners on this sector could do to reply to this frontal artillery attack. But a day or two after La Maisonette was won a considerable part of the French artillery south of the Somme was brought up and concealed in the woods and ravines in front of Péronne, and the muzzles were swung northward towards Bapaume.

Hostile positions outflanked In the circumstances, it did not much matter that the southern heights from Feuilleres and Dompierre to Biaches and La Maisonette were considerably lower than the northern heights occupied by the Germans. Howitzers never aim directly at a target. They fling their shells miles into the sky, in such a way that they can pitch on distant, unexposed slopes and invisible ravines. There was no need to place a howitzer on a hill, and, in fact, the best position for such a piece is a lower slope or a valley that enemy guns cannot reach by direct fire, and enemy observers cannot see except from kite-balloons or aeroplanes. As the Allies held the complete mastery of the air the Germans could not discover the positions of the French howitzers on the Santerre plateau.

All that the German commander could do was to endeavour to mass guns on the southern line of the new French wedge south of the river, and especially to increase his artillery at Villers Carbonnel. But here again General Fayolle had a marked advantage in cross-fire against his opponent. In the first place he could continue to concentrate heavy artillery from Estrées to Soyécourt, directly in front of Villers Carbonnel. In the second place he could abruptly turn all his guns in the La Maisonette wedge southward against Villers Carbonnel, while he also hammered this position with frontal fire.

New German commanders

From the German point of view, therefore, the loss of La Maisonette was exceedingly alarming. No point won by the Allies, from Neuve Chapelle to Loos and from the attack on the Labyrinth to the storming of Tahure, was so critically important as La Maisonette. The new German commanders, General von Gallwitz, who had

been one of the principal assistants of Hindenburg on the eastern front, with General von Stein, a former Minister of War and assistant Chief of Staff, came to Péronne and Combles with new armies to retrieve the endangered situation. In addition to these new army chiefs, some of the most brilliant of German army corps generals of the new school were sent to the Somme.

General von Falkenhayn was nearing the end of his extraordinary reign. He retained sufficient power to rob Hindenburg of his best remaining man—Gallwitz, who had forced the Narew, capturing Warsaw and its great neighbouring fortress when Leopold of Bavaria was unable

ENEMY FIRST LINE TROOPS IN CAPTIVITY.
Types of German prisoners, who came through the terrible ordeal of the Franco-British bombardment on the Somme front. The men were temporarily confined in barbed-wire compounds.

to effect anything. There was further a rumour that Falkenhayn also brought to the Somme another leading man of Hindenburg's school—General von Below, the conqueror of Lithuania and Courland. Mackensen, who emerged into fame under Hindenburg in the Kutno battle, was removed to Bulgaria, after having been vainly proposed to the German people as a better popular idol than the old Field-Marshal. Ludendorff had resigned, and his chief—with a disorganised Staff and army commanders of commonplace ability and a record of failures, such as Linsingen and Bothmer—was struggling to check General Brussiloff's advance in Galicia and prevent Rumania from entering the field.

GERMANS CAPTURED AT MAISON ROUGE.
An entire company of Germans, with their officers and equipment, captured by the French at Maison Rouge, July 20th, 1916.

SEARCHING THE GERMAN PRISONERS OF WAR.
On July 20th the French captured 2,900 Germans, including many officers, with three guns, thirty machine-guns, and much material.

Men of the stamp of Gallwitz were desperately required on the eastern front. Gallwitz was experienced only in meeting the former conditions of Russian warfare, where his guns and shell supply had always enormously preponderated over the small, starved Russian artillery. Under the new and disconcerting conditions of the western front, where for the first time he was faced by an organisation of heavy artillery, shell supply, air power, and rail and motor traffic superior to that which he hastily took over, Gallwitz was ineffective. He did not know the country; he did not know the character of the allied troops; he could not safely make the slightest guess at the play of mind of men of such genius as General Foch and General Fayolle. It is hard to see why such a man as Gallwitz was brought west by General von Falkenhayn, except as a final and vain act of spite against Hindenburg. If Gallwitz was a man of any intrinsic value that value was wasted at Péronne.

The failure of Gallwitz

All that the new German commander could do was to launch, under cover of heavy mist in the evening of July 15th, a strong infantry attack on Biaches and La

Maisonette. The French troops in the village and around the hill acted in their usual manner, which should have contained no surprise for a German tactician accustomed to their ways. When the hostile batteries on Mont St. Quentin and around Villers Carbonnel opened a hurricane fire the French infantry retired by underground ways, leaving only a few machine-gunners to impede the coming advance. Meanwhile, the French batteries divided their work; some guns put a curtain over the approaches by which an assault could be made; other guns went in for counter-battery firing, and wrought great damage among the flame-tongued pieces of ordnance that were drenching Biaches and La Maisonette with shell.

Enemy trapped and shattered

At heavy cost the German infantry entered the village and stormed the hill. The French infantry retired before its losses were severe, and calmly waited until the apparent victors were massed on the edge of the plateau. Then the stupendous weight of every French gun within range fell upon Biaches and La Maisonette, and upon the main German artillery positions and communications. When the French gunners lifted from the hill and the village the French infantry charged, and the enemy was broken and trapped. Fierce, terrible hand-to-hand fighting went on amid the woods in the darkness, and in the morning the ground was again firmly in the possession of our magnificent allies.

Up to this date the loss of La Maisonette had not been admitted by the German Staff, and the attack launched in great force across the river was designed to recapture the hill and make it appear as though it had not been in French possession. According to a statement issued in Berlin, the Kaiser came to the Somme to watch the fighting. But the Nero of Germany had ever been the herald of defeat when he came to any hotly-contested field in the west. After the anxious Emperor had his anxieties increased and his belief in Falkenhayn finally destroyed by witnessing the first vain and costly counter-attack across the river, the new German commander on July 18th made another prolonged and violent attempt to recover La Maisonette. But each wave of assault was smashed by French fire. General Fayolle's master-gunners had got hundreds of additional guns into position during the nine days since the Colonial troops stormed the hill. On the left at Biaches some small German parties managed to creep along the canal into a few houses, but they were bombed out of the ruins in a few hours.

For all practical purposes La Maisonette had become impregnable. The time which the French had won enabled them to tunnel, excavate, build, and fortify, so that light railways, new roads, and railway-stations were constructed in the rear of La Maisonette, together with great underground storing-places, dormitories, and dining-places.

The definite consolidation of the great French conquest of La Maisonette marks the end of the first phase of the allied operations on the Somme. The flanking fire from numerous heavy howitzers, which the French were able to train for a radius of many miles over the Bapaume sector, was largely responsible for the succeeding victories of the French and British troops north of the river. In the second phase of the allied operations the main interest shifts across the Somme to the army of General Balfourier and the armies of Sir Douglas Haig. General Fayolle's main forces then stood fast at La Maisonette, and formed the handle of a great and terrible sickle that quickly cut down half a million Germans. The southern army, however, did not remain entirely on the defensive in regard to infantry actions, while its mighty guns were striking

But in turn General Foch suddenly extended his line of attack southward, and by storming into Vermandovillers, he compelled Gallwitz again to move guns and troops back to Chaulnes and relieve the pressure on General Fayolle's forces in the southern angle of the Somme. During August, 1916, there was a tremendous artillery duel around Chaulnes, and in the first week of September General Micheler launched his series of magnificent attacks, All the first zone of German positions from Barleux to Chilly, south of Chaulnes, was stormed and occupied. The communications of Chaulnes were cut, so that General von Gallwitz and the new German Chief of Staff, Hindenburg, had another very critical and imperilled sector, needing continually troops by the hundred thousand, guns by hundreds, and shells by the half-million.

The direct, immediate, and local effect of this stroke was to lighten the labour and free the striking power of the French forces in the angle of the Somme. The Germans had to weaken their artillery concentrations around Villers Carbonnel and Mont St. Quentin in order to make a stand about Chaulnes. But by weakening their artillery around Péronne, Gallwitz and his Staff brought more trouble on their heads. The French guns

NOVEL USE FOR DONKEYS IN WAR TIME.
[French official photograph.
On the Somme front the ancient and much ridiculed quadruped was used to convey food to the first-line trenches. Their small proportions enabled them to pass through narrow communication trenches and tunnels.

the enemy sideways and cutting his Péronne communications. The infantry, including the African troops and many French regiments, moved across the river to join the British forces, and a new French battering-ram, the Tenth Army under General Micheler, came into action on a new, long northern front. On Thursday afternoon, July 20th, all the first German zone of defences from Estrées southward to the hill of Vermandovillers, two miles north of Chaulnes, was stormed and held, and a strong German counter-attack easily broken with machine-gun fire and shell fire.

In the war of positions Chaulnes was linked with Cologne and Metz and transformed into one of the vital points of the great German salient. The German commander had long been anxious about Chaulnes, and it will be recollected that he drew troops away from the Somme in order to prepare against a blow that General Foch did not deliver. When, however, the Colonial troops stormed La Maisonette, General von Gallwitz reversed the policy of his predecessor and weakened his lines around Chaulnes in order to strengthen the artillery and infantry south of Péronne.

in the southern angle of the Somme again turned north towards the Combles and Bapaume area, and there co-operated in another terrific day and night cross-fire with the French and British guns north of the river. So far as could be seen at the time, General Foch and Sir Douglas Haig possessed a series of extraordinary advantages over the enemy, which they were developing with terrible mathematical precision to a gradual close. And because the movement was gradual it was extraordinarily deadly.

South of the Somme the Germans were half enveloped and disastrously enfiladed. From the middle of July their sound and saving course was clearly to retreat to the next strong line beyond Péronne, and thus avoid the great and draining waste of life and expense of munitions. But no withdrawal took place. Did Hindenburg find that Falkenhayn had left things in such disorder on both sides of the Somme that the local German commanders could not extricate their troops? We may find some light on this problem in the story of the Franco-British operations north of the river.

END OF VOLUME 7.

THE GREAT WAR

VOLUME 8

Painted by C.M.PADDAY.

"The Biter Bit:" Liner's successful defence from Submarine attack.

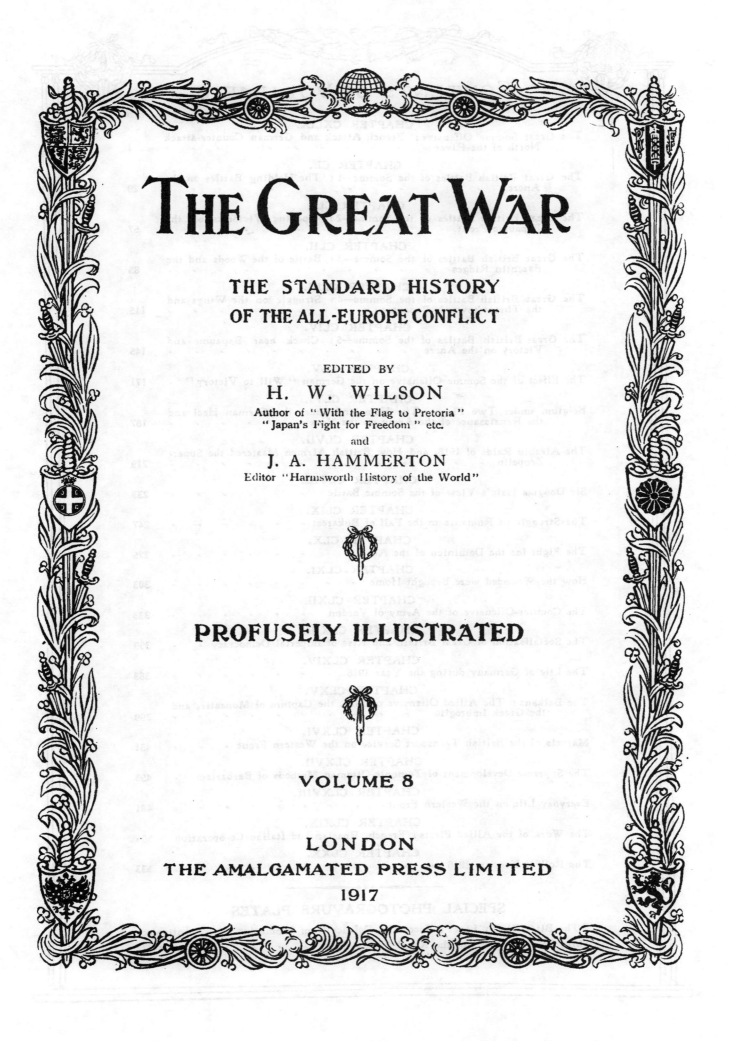

THE GREAT WAR

THE STANDARD HISTORY
OF THE ALL-EUROPE CONFLICT

EDITED BY

H. W. WILSON

Author of "With the Flag to Pretoria"
"Japan's Fight for Freedom" etc.

and

J. A. HAMMERTON

Editor "Harmsworth History of the World"

PROFUSELY ILLUSTRATED

VOLUME 8

LONDON
THE AMALGAMATED PRESS LIMITED
1917

CONTENTS OF VOLUME 8

SPECIAL PHOTOGRAVURE PLATES

THE GREAT WAR

THE STANDARD HISTORY OF THE ALL-EUROPE CONFLICT

VOLUME 8

CHAPTER CXLIX.

THE GREAT SOMME OFFENSIVE: FRENCH ATTACK AND GERMAN COUNTER-ATTACK NORTH OF THE RIVER.

By Edward Wright.

Difficult Junction-Point of French and British Armies—General Fayolle Crosses the River with the Iron Division—Grim Character of the Ironsides of France—Young Men for the Charge and Veterans for the Counter-Defence—Cigarette Promenade and the Gendarme's Hat—Fighting in the Churchyard of Curlu—French Pause until British Come into Line—Storming of Spahn and Eulenberg Quarries—Hem and the Perfection of French Staff Work—Consternation of German Troops under Unexpected Heavy Fire—First Complete Prussian Defeat Since 1815—Vast German Concentration Against the Allies—Alternate Hammer Blows by French and British—General Foch's System of Echelon Formation—Terrible Ravine Fighting near Hem—Glorious Work by a Young French Battalion—General Fayolle Makes another Spring Forward—The Epic of Maurepas—Prince Eitel and the Demoralisation of his Guardsmen—General Micheler's Army Surprises the Enemy—France Takes Over Two-thirds of the Battle Front—The Breaking of the Prussian Guard and the Capture of Le Forest—Diary of a Prussian Guardsman at Rancourt—How the Fighting Nobles of Prussia Failed their Men.

IT will be remembered that early in 1916 a Silesian regiment made a surprise attack on the southernmost point of the British front at Carnoy and on the linking French position across the Somme at Frise. The British troops repulsed the enemy from Carnoy, but the French troops which had held Frise lost the trenches and made no attempt to recover them. The French pointed out that this village in the marshes of the Somme was a point not worth holding by either side, and that they willingly surrendered it to the enemy.

It was generally thought at the time that this statement was merely a palliation of weakness on the part of General Foch. But later events proved that the report he had sent to French Headquarters was matter-of-fact truth. Frise, lying in a mass of reeds, looped by the lagoons and branching waters of the Somme and dominated on either side by the cliffs of the high chalk plateau, was a death-trap to the army that held it. The French **German thrust at Frise** were glad to let the Germans occupy it, and it was an expensive piece of window-dressing on the part of the German commander when he advanced his lines slightly and threw forward a large garrison of Silesian troops, who remained at the mercy of the French guns, in a watery soil, which made the casualties from frost-bite and rheumatism far more numerous than the losses from shell fire.

The German thrust at Frise, however, incited Sir Douglas Haig and General Foch to consider together the natural difficulties of the geographical and tactical situation on the Somme. The junction-point of two large armies, speaking a different language, drawing their supplies from different bases, and working on different methods of attack and defence, was undoubtedly a point of great weakness. The large Valley of the Somme, with its marshes, streams, and canal, had seemed to be a natural division between the allied hosts.

Sir Douglas Haig and General Foch, however, found that the valley accentuated the inconveniences of their point of junction. It allowed the enemy too many opportunities of massing and striking against one ally, before a combined artillery and infantry counter-attack could be improvised. So against natural appearances, **Allies rearrange fronts** the delicate junction-point of the two armies was shifted northward, and the French Army took over both banks of the Somme, and afterwards relinquished its front in Artois, enabling Sir Douglas Haig to organise without a break one long British line from the north of Ypres to the south of Albert.

General Foch, however, still remained somewhat at a disadvantage in possessing merely some three miles of lines north of the Somme, from Maricourt to Eclusier. Owing to the small area of the ground, he could deploy only a small French force north of the river, and this force was at a disadvantage in being cut off from its main army by two and a half miles of swamp and water, and in having a foreign army on its left, formed of new recruits with strange weapons, ammunition of uninterchangeable character, and entirely different methods of fighting. For example,

British troops when on the defensive relied greatly upon their Lee-Enfield magazine rifles, with which they could fire fifteen rounds in thirty seconds, while French troops relied mainly upon their fast and flexible 3 in. quick-firing field-gun, which enabled them to withdraw from their trenches and then recover them by a surprising and lightly purchased recoil. The gunners of the field-artillery of the new British army could not work the miracles which the long experienced artillerymen of France could accomplish with facile adroitness.

Contrasts in Anglo-French tactics

On the other hand, the French infantry-man with his obsolescent Lebel rifle, having an inferior magazine capacity, could not achieve the extraordinary results of the "mad minute" of rapid musketry fire by which again and again the British line had held fast against tremendous odds.

From the days of Napoleon and Sir John Moore this curious difference between French and British tactics had obtained, Napoleon relying upon massed artillery fire and Moore upon the intensive training of his infantry in musketry fire. One might almost go back to Agincourt, with its example of combined shock tactics on the part of the French and of highly trained individual marksmanship on the part of the English bowmen, in tracing this instinctive difference between the methods of fighting of the two allied nations.

The French generally were always more scientific than the Englishman or the Anglo-Celt, while the British were strangely individualistic, with the happy though somewhat chance power that comes from highly-strung individual effort. Quite a generation before Napoleon, the French were our superiors on land in finely developed artillery concentration, and except in the Franco-Prussian War, when Marshal Lebœuf crippled the artillery of his country by giving it defective fuses, French field-

artillery in action had been in advance of all others since the eighteenth century.

For twenty years French gunners had been broken to the service of their quick-firer, and even the French reservists knew how to serve the "75." When the Italians adopted a gun of the "75" type, French experts reckoned it would take Italy ten years to impart into both her active Army and reserve such experience in artillery work as France had patiently and gradually attained. France was a nation of artillerymen of exceptional skill, whereas Great Britain had only a small professional class of veteran gunners, whose quick-firing gun, moreover, was inferior in quality to the French. In methods of attack there was not much difference between the two co-operating armies. Indeed, as the war went on the French and British closely approximated in their weapons of advance. They had the same kind of quick-firing trench-mortar for discharging heavy aerial torpedoes upon the German first line. They both used their light artillery to break his wire entanglements, and their heavy siege-artillery was similar in calibre and in mounting, and obtained from the same steel-makers.

ALLIES MEET ON THE SOMME.
French infantry returning from the trenches meeting a British battery.

In defensive operations, however, the old difference which had caused difficulties at Ypres in the autumn of 1914 still obtained along the Somme. The French gave ground when they could not keep the enemy back by curtain fire from their heavy artillery, and returned when their guns had annihilated the stormers of their lost position. This was a method of defence of a terribly deadly scientific character, requiring an extreme precision in co-operation between the infantry and the artillery. The British, on the other hand, still prided themselves on never budging from a trench, and as all their recruits were trained towards the old standard of the "mad minute" of rifle fire, they could often shatter an enemy charge with the

FRENCH TROOPS BUILDING SHELTERS AGAINST ARTILLERY FIRE.
Shelters against heavy artillery fire had, of course, to be of the strongest possible construction, and were made of enormously stout timbers roofed over with corrugated iron on which sand-bags were stacked.

help of machine-guns, without asking from their artillery more than a shrapnel curtain over the German line.

Both the French and the British methods of breaking up an attack were effective, and by means of them some of the greatest actions in the war were won; but it can be seen that, at the critical junction-point of the two armies, the French could not continue to hold their advanced positions lightly, while the British on their left held on in strength and perhaps were turned. In these circumstances, General Foch did the British Army the honour of placing by its side at Bray the Iron Division of France. Behind the Iron Division were the other regiments of the

FOUNTAIN ON THE SOMME.
French soldiers drinking at a fountain in the vicinity of the Somme.

COLONIAL WARRIORS IN THE SERVICE OF FRANCE.
French Senegalese going up to the first line on the Somme. They were employed in opening the attack south of the river.

Twentieth Corps (which was in the French Army what the Tenth Legion was in Cæsar's forces) directed by General Balfourier, who had saved Verdun before General Pétain took control.

The Twentieth Corps had been peculiarly reorganised for the great offensive. The veteran troops, who had first shown their tremendous power of resistance on the heights around Nancy, where they shattered the combined efforts of the army of Bavaria under Prince Rupert and the army of Metz under Heeringen, were brigaded with battalions of the youngest French recruits. The older men, annealed in every great furnace of battle on the western front, and as famous as the Old Guard of Napoleon, had come to take a check or a success with equal mind. On each occasion they did all that men could do, and whether it were done victoriously or in vain, the Ironsides were neither elated nor cast down. The swing and resilience of their march lent a grace to the grim strength of their movements, and their uniforms of horizon blue and their finely-modelled casques of steel gave them a touch of warlike beauty; but there was a Puritanic strength in their quiet and determined faces.

All that has slumbered in the complex French character since Henry of Navarre bought Paris by going to Mass, was not only revived but wrought to an incomparable pitch and scope by the ordeal of this war. The gay volatility of France—largely derived in the seventeenth, eighteenth, and nineteenth centuries from a decadent aristocracy lacking the reality of power and having little to do but to amuse itself—vanished. A dour type of Frenchman emerged from the working middle-class, the industrial class, and the small-holding peasantry, and led by the fighting remnant of the old nobility that produced officers of the stamp of Castelnau, became a great and fructifying world force, as had been the case temporarily and with a much lower degree of discipline during the revolutionary wars. An extraordinary hardness of intellect was now combined with the better known flexibility of the French mind, and the result was such a keen, steady, wide-eyed grimness of character as astonished every friendly foreigner acquainted with French life.

Generally speaking, the French peasant was in the fighting-line and the French mechanic in the war factory, railway, and the motor service. The Iron Division was largely recruited from Paris, **Power of** and its calm, sombre fighting men formed **French peasantry** a type of a strangely new Parisian. But the army on the whole was provincial In other words, France was seen inside out. Her wage-earning city class—adventurous, humorous, and touched of old with social gaiety like all floating, hazarding city classes—was removed into the background. The more settled, less expressive, harder-minded, and more resolute tillers of the rich, fertile soil of France became the protagonists in the tragedy of Europe. Though after Sedan they had refused to follow Napoleon III. and even Gambetta, they were now ready

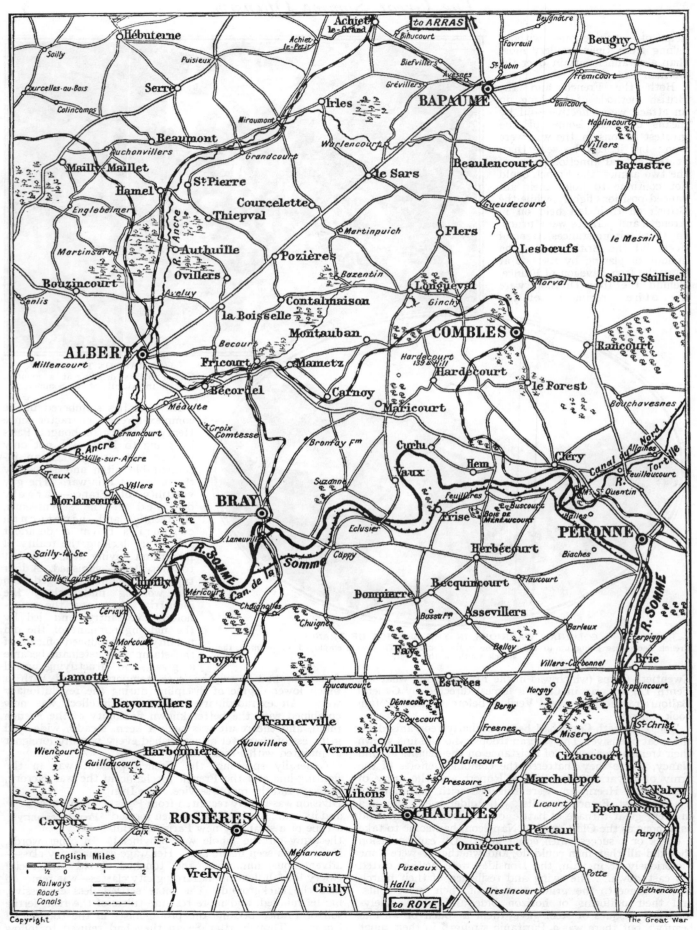

THE AREA OF THE GREAT ALLIED OFFENSIVE NORTH AND SOUTH OF THE SOMME.

Copyright

The Great War

4

to follow Joffre in a manner that recalled the days of Joan of Arc. And whereas Joan of Arc had many Frenchmen against her, including the large realm of the Burgundians, Joffre had all France with him, and he also had a great Colonial Empire, upon which to draw for fighting planters and superb native troops. But through all the sombre, brooding, quiet temper of the Ironsides of the Twentieth Corps ruled the French spirit. The French were the Roundheads and the British the Cavaliers of the combined forces

Most of the qualities usually attributed of old to French soldiers were to be found in the British camp. The French had dash, but little of the strange, radiant humour which men long fronting death sometimes use to cover their intensity of feeling. The French Staff, however, neither expected nor desired these veteran troops to go forward with excessive speed. It wanted them to be slow, grim, cautious, and tenacious. But with that **Youth in the Iron** subtlety and minute care in planning, **Division** which gradually made the French genius for organisation more formidable than the trained German talent, the youngest class of French soldiers was brigaded with the old troops. Thousands of youths of twenty and twenty-one years of age were formed into battalions and attached to the Iron Division. The officers and non-commissioned officers were the most experienced in the world. The youths themselves were naturally proud beyond expression at being incorporated into the Iron Division, and all their training in the new tactics could not dull the ardour of their temperament. They wished

to show they were worthy of the honour of being placed with the Ironsides, and it was practically certain that with the good leading they had they would accomplish all that the impetuosity of youth and the valour of inspired patriotism could achieve.

The scheme of the commander of the Twentieth Corps was plain and simple. He intended to use his young battalions in capturing the German positions and his veteran troops to hold and consolidate the conquered ground. Then by the time the first German counter-attack in force had been met and broken, the **How black and white** young battalions would have sufficient **combined** experience to fight regularly alongside the veterans of Verdun. It will be remembered that the French coloured troops south of the Somme had been employed to open the attack there, because of their racial impetuosity of temperament, while the greatly enduring and tenacious metropolitan infantry had been kept back for use as a holding force. In both cases the idea was first to exploit as much as possible the effect of surprise when the enemy was attacked in a position which he had weakened himself, and then to bring up the hardest-tempered French fighting forces when Falkenhayn and Hindenburg were making their supreme efforts to retrieve the situation.

The Iron Division seems to have come into the first line on June 24th, 1916, after having spent four days in support. The British troops near Carnoy connected with it by the village of Maricourt, and from this village the line stretched southward for three miles to the loop of the Somme at Eclusier. In front of the Frenchmen was a

[*British official photograph.*

HISTORIC PHOTOGRAPH OF LEADERS OF THE ALLIES IN FRANCE.
This famous photograph was taken during one of the King's visits to the western front in the course of 1916. The figures in the group are—from left to right—General Joffre, President Poincaré, the King, General Foch, and Sir Douglas Haig.

difficult hill country, with wooded slopes and chalk, through which the line of the Péronne-Bapaume road could be traced by its straight row of little trees. At the end of August, 1914, when Kluck was driving the British Expeditionary Force before him, a battle had been fought in the forest heights around Combles. A French Territorial division, without artillery, tried to arrest the march of a German army corps which was outflanking the retiring British force. The Germans, however,

Changes since were not delayed for an hour. They won **Germans took Combles** the battle at a marching pace under the cover of their artillery fire, and, in an astounding stride, took Combles and the neighbouring heights, and then turned south-eastward for another attempt to envelop the 3rd British Division.

The changes since the first battle at Combles had been immense, especially in regard to the artillery force employed on either side. All the last week of June, 1916, the French siege ordnance north of the Somme co-operated with the British heavy artillery and crashed with earthquake effect on the enemy lines. At first the German fire-trenches were spared, and only the second and third zones of defence were attacked. This was only done in view of the amazing

precise French gun fire, the young Ironsides were able to deploy in the open with very little loss.

In front of them was a steep cliff known from its shape as the Gendarme's Hat, which the enemy had spent twenty-two months in converting into a formidable fortress. There was a line of trenches at the foot, a second line running midway across the face of the great rock, while a third line was hewn along the crest, all the lines being connected with underground burrows and zigzags of deep, open cuts. The French siege-guns, however, in collaboration with the trench-mortars, had broken up everything—firing-lines, machine-gun positions, shelters, and saps. The young battalions heading the charge had scarcely any fighting to do, and they captured the cliff, on a front of a mile and a half, with their rifles on their shoulders, a pipe or a cigarette in their hand, and singing the "Marseillaise."

One blue wave went straight up and over the cliff, another swept round the low hills on the left, and a third advanced near the river. In half an hour the three forces met victoriously on the summit. Then, continuing their extraordinary promenade, the battalions went on to the village of Curlu. By the river, however, it was a crawl rather than a promenade, because German machine-gun ambushes were expected in the wide expanse of islanded marshes and the hundred little split, meandering streams of the Somme. General Fayolle's plan was to envelop the wide marshes on July 2nd, when he had broken the German front on the high ground each side of the river. He did not want to have men entangled and lost amid the bush-grown islets in the river valley. He therefore left the enemy forces there in peace, while he worked on both sides of the river towards their rear. On the high ground beyond the Gendarme's Hat the second German line was occupied without resistance, the garrisons having either fled in panic or been withdrawn—panic being the more likely explanation.

At five o'clock in the afternoon two French companies entered Curlu, and after a sharp bout of house-to-house fighting forced the Germans almost out of the village. One of the prisoners they took told them there were six German companies in reserve in Spahn Quarry close by. The man was not believed, but it was soon

A CORNER OF A FRENCH FIELD ARMY KITCHEN.
Never before were armies so well fed as in the Great War, but the conditions under which the men's needs were supplied were by no means uniformly so comfortable as those represented in the above picture.

increase of power of the new trench-mortars employed by the Allies. In the closing scene the quick-firing mortars poured aerial torpedoes in extraordinary quantities into the German fire-trenches, blowing them in and choking the entrances to the deeper dug-outs. At the same time the light French field-guns destroyed the German wire entanglements, and then, on the three-mile front from Maricourt to Fargny Mill, the men of the Iron Division advanced to attack about seven o'clock on the morning of July 1st, 1916.

Infantry, Zouaves, and Chasseurs, forming the successive waves of the assault, had been packed overnight in departure saps dug in front of the firing-trenches during the great bombardment. These parallels of assault, as the new advance saps were called, were designed to save the customary loss of life incurred in climbing over the parapets of the first line under a storm of shrapnel and machine-gun bullets from the alert and desperate enemy. Owing partly to this precaution, but mainly to the terrific and

discovered that he was telling the truth, out of a feeling of disgust for his own officers. The Germans at the time were holding an underground position beneath the cemetery of the ancient church, the vaults of which they had prolonged into Maxim-gun shelters amid the tombstones.

The six German reserve companies from the Spahn Quarry reinforced the garrison in the vaults of the church and began an overlapping counter-attack upon the two French companies. No reinforcements could reach the little French force, as the **Peril at the** German guns were then flinging a terrific **Gendarme's Hat** curtain of shrapnel over the ground between the village and the Gendarme's Hat. The French captain was killed and his men extremely hard pressed, when one of the machines of the new aerial artillery swooped through the rain of hostile shrapnel, studied the position swiftly and accurately, and by dropping a smoke-shell on the ruined church rectified the fire of the French guns.

The two advanced companies fell back to a line of shell-holes outside the village, made by their heavy guns, and waited according to orders. The victorious counter-attacking Germans at the time were only six yards away from the diminished French advance force. But a few seconds after the aerial infantryman had made his signal the French guns concentrated on the ruins of the village. The vaulted underground fortress was penetrated by huge projectiles, and the curtain fire from the hostile batteries was w e a k e n e d by counter-firing, enabling French reinforcements to arrive.

For half an hour the new tornado of shell poured upon the village, and also upon the quarry, and at half-past six in the afternoon the younger Ironsides again went forward and burst right t h r o u g h Curlu. What subterranean forts the heavy French shells had not destroyed they had choked, closing the entrance, blowing earth down the stairways and imprisoning the enemy machine-gun sections. The veterans of the division then came forward with machine-gun companies, and rapidly improvised a temporary system of defence. This was a work for which their experiences at Verdun fitted them, and though they only arrived at midnight they dug themselves in strongly at the end of two hours.

French occupy Curlu
All this time the distant German howitzers were bombarding the village their troops had lost; but the Frenchmen found certain vaults still uninjured beneath the church, cleared the entrances, installed their battalion commander beneath the sacristy of the vanished thirteenth-century Gothic building, and by means of patrols marked the ranges of the slopes leading to Rouge Farm.

The veterans knew what was coming, and were prepared to meet it. At two o'clock in the morning of July 2nd a strong column of Bavarian Landwehr, which had collected at Hardecourt, swept down by the plateau on which stood the Rouge Farm. But all the tableland was abruptly illuminated by French star-shells and swept by a terrible curtain fire. Those Bavarians who got through the barrier were caught at short range by the machine-guns of the Ironsides, and though the German commander continued to push his men forward, every wave of attack was broken.

But after holding on to the village the Iron Division found itself unable to advance farther when day broke. As will be seen from the map on page 4, any advance eastward from Curlu was swept by frontal gun fire from Mont St. Quentin, and enfiladed northward from Hardecourt and the batteries around Combles. On the southern side of the river, Frise and Feuilleres, with numerous

A JUGGERNAUT ON RAILS.
Giant machine of destruction on rails, covered with a hangar which was disguised by paint in such a way as to be rendered invisible to hostile aviators.

RAIL SPEED AND GUN POWER.
The proportions of the huge weapon can be gathered from this illustration.

SOMBRE MASS OF CLANKING STEEL.
A casual glance reveals what appear to be a succession of harmless cattle-trucks. The gun revolved on a pivot, thereby having a range of many miles on all points of the compass.

GUARDING AGAINST COUNTER-ATTACK.
Preparing a cheval-de-frise, an effective if primitive way of rapidly consolidating a captured trench on the Somme line.

and the crack troops of France, after taking Curlu in a rush, made no further move for three days. They burrowed in the ruins of the village, and with pick and shovel again excavated the ground, deepened the old German works, and bombed their way north-east, so as to extend their trenches on Rouge Farm plateau, and south-east, where they made parallels of assault towards Hem. The fortified chalk quarries, which the Germans had named Spahn Quarry and Eulenberg Quarry,

MORE EFFECTIVE THAN SOLID BARRICADES.
How the barbed-wire was wound round the three stakes from a coil French soldiers completing a cheval-de-frise.

machine-gun positions in the marshes, remained in the hands of the enemy, and enabled him to take in flank any French force advancing eastward. And there was another and larger disadvantage.

The original French line at Fargny Mill, by Curlu, had been more than five miles east of the British line at Fricourt. This was not due to any fault or weakness on the part of the British troops. They had merely taken over the position as the French had left it during the race to the sea, at which period the Germans, by reason of their stronger artillery, gained a wide dominating hilly salient between Albert and Arras. The great salient extended beyond the French position on the Somme, leaving only a small square of land by the river in the possession of the Allies.

This square of land was about five miles long, consequently the German guns could sweep it from both the east and from the north; and having conquered Curlu, the Iron Division had to endure a furious double bombardment from the east and from the north; it had to wait until the thrust of the British forces, which was made directly northward, relieved the pressure. In this connection, it must be remembered that the main burden of the attack fell upon the British army, which had to take about thirty square miles of fortress country before it could get into line with the French force north of the Somme.

Indeed, the French forces both north and south of the Somme formed the pivot of the allied attack, and had, therefore, to wheel through a smaller extent of country than had the British army. Of the two French forces, the work of the Iron Division was more arduous than the work of the Colonial division across the river. On the Péronne front the Germans were not only taken completely by surprise, but their position in the great loop of the river was naturally weak, as the wide, marshy valley around them made their communications difficult and hazardous.

North of the Somme, on the other hand, the Germans had a firm, manifold, and well-sheltered network of communications, backed by an intricate railway system and numerous well-placed and well-dug-in parks of artillery. Had the Iron Division attempted a swift thrust forward, such as the Colonial Division successfully made in the Péronne sector, the consequence would have been similar to that which befell certain British divisions at Serre and Thiepval. Caution was the essence of success north of the Somme,

Burden of attack on British

were also approached by tunnel and sap. The period of waiting was filled in by a continual and intense artillery action, in which the French guns dominated all the hostile batteries and wrecked the German positions and communications. Counter-battery firing was developed with particular fury, with a view to beating down the German guns and lessening the storm of shell on the French infantry. By the evening of July 4th the French artillery north and south of the river had been brought well forward and again dominated the Péronne and Combles area. In the night the heavy French guns lighted the darkness, pounding the second German line into shapelessness, lashing at the third German line to prevent supports moving, and sweeping every road and railway track within ten miles of the front. The British guns were carrying out the same work of destruction in the Bapaume area, so that the position of the enemy from Bapaume to Chaulnes was one of deep and perilous suspense. At three o'clock in the morning the young battalions of the Iron Division were again ready to attack. They waited in their saps while the great shells cleared the ground before them, levelled the houses, and pierced the caverns.

At seven o'clock the morning mist lifted and the attack was launched. There was no struggle, and at half-past eight the enemy's new first line was quietly occupied. The principal conquests of the advance were at first estimated to be the great quarries of Spahn and Eulenberg. These immense holes in the chalk plateau, with their sheer sides, caverns, and underground communications, easily sheltered

Work in the Bapaume area

Great Britain had done little or nothing to increase food production. Thenceforward the real danger which Germany had to fear was the failure of cotton, leather, rubber, wool, vegetable oils, alcohol (for explosives), fats, and nitrates, rather than an insurmountable shortage of food.

In the matter of food production, as in other directions, the Germans had made far-seeing preparations, recognising that wars are won in advance by taking care and thought, and always intending to attack their neighbours. In spite of the rapid increase of urban population and manufactures in the twenty years before the war, they had enormously increased the annual production of corn and potatoes from

A LOST HARVEST.
This fishing steamer, sent to the bottom by German pirates, was said to have a cargo of herrings aboard worth about £50,000.

HER LAST—AND VAIN—APPEAL FOR HELP FROM SHORE.
Torpedoed within sight of shore, a sinking steamer shrilly blew her siren in appeal for succour for the crew, but in vain. Aboard the waiting submarine her callous destroyers remained listening to her swan-song until she went down, meanwhile taking this photograph during her last moments.

15,000,000 tons of corn to 27,000,000, and they had at the same time raised the number of live stock from 50,000,000 to 56,000,000. They grew at home in 1913 all the rye they required, 67·7 per cent. of the wheat consumed, 97 per cent. of the oats, and 98·6 per cent. of the potatoes. They exported sugar largely. They had a sufficient supply of potatoes not only to feed human beings and animals, but also to provide raw material for starch and spirit manufacture. While good land in improvident Great Britain was lying derelict, waste land in Germany was being eagerly reclaimed. A sturdy population was maintained, at the cost of great sacrifice, on the soil to form the backbone of the German armies; whereas in Great Britain, at every turn, the interests of agriculture were neglected. The immense agricultural strength of Germany was one of the factors which enabled her to withstand the pressure of the blockade.

The blockade did not exhaust Germany's food supply with the rapidity that many expected. It also did not affect her finances so seriously as might have been anticipated. She had seized the richest mineral areas in Belgium

and France, and had obtained in them assets of incalculable value which she utilised with an entire disregard for the rights of property. The rich Belgian and French coal and iron fields were exploited, so as to give the largest possible yield, with forced labour, and with no care for the future of the mines. The heart was picked out of them, and the coal and iron ore thus secured were worked up in French or Belgian or German factories and foundries, again with forced labour, into products of which neighbouring neutrals stood most sorely in need. Switzerland, Holland, and Sweden were supplied with a certain quantity of coal, iron, and steel, on condition that they paid for it in gold or food, and complied with Germany's diplomatic demands. Thus these products not only strengthened German finances and enabled Germany to carry on a very valuable trade, but they also served as counters in the diplomatic game. The Allies were bled while Germany drank up their blood. Without the iron ore of the Briey district of France, east of Verdun, the German output of munitions could not have been maintained. The ore fields there were of extraordinary richness, and their loss was an immense catastrophe for the Allies and a prodigious success for Germany.

German industrial organisation

In time of peace and several years before the war the German industrial organisation had been equipped on a scale equal to the supply of all Europe, especially in such machine-tools as the big lathes used for big-gun production. Warning had been given of this in 1908 to the British Government, which treated it with ridicule. Hence Germany had no need to transform herself, at incalculable expense, for the manufacture of munitions when she began the war. Everything was ready to hand, and she had not to make the machinery to make rifles and guns, or to

B

TRENCH TORPEDOES BEING CARRIED UP TO THE
FIRING-LINE.

impudence to proclaim that it was inhuman for the Allies to employ heavier artillery than the Teuton had in position. " Le bombardement, ce n'est pas la guerre," as a French satirist translated the German complaint.

The French in these attacks noticed some signs of a decline in moral in the German troops. Subordinate battalion officers were quite as much affected as the men. The old non-commissioned officers showed most pluck and endurance. The company officers of the professional military class were also good, but there were not many of them. Those who survived the terrible process of attrition of the past two years had been promoted, and their place was supplied by the former one-year volunteers from the well-to-do middle classes, and these it was who did not resist successfully the strain of the first complete and co-ordinated allied offensive in the west since the Battle of the Marne.

The French Army was in much the same condition of cadres as the German Army. The personnel of the active corps had wasted away in the long war. Most of the veterans of the rank and file **Marne and Somme** had arrived as reservists and drafts. **contrasted** Young officers on the active list had been killed or disabled in very large proportions, owing to the French custom by which all officers, including brigadier, divisional, and army corps generals, charge at the head of their men, and are among the first to be brought down by hostile machine-guns and curtain fire. Democratic France, however, had maintained a strong and experienced framework of officers by promoting distinguished privates and men of non-commissioned rank. The French Army offered a career open to talent and character, as in the wars of the Revolution. In addition to the losses in battle, a large number of generals had been retired on a charge of incompetence, enabling colonels, majors, and captains of genius to rise even quicker than Napoleon's marshals had done.

The campaign on the Somme imposed a more severe test on the German proletariat than their tremendous sacrifices at Verdun. For the first time since the Battle of Ligny, in 1815, the Prussians were robbed of all initiative, compelled to stand in passive defence and beaten. The difference between the Battle of the Marne and the Battle of the Somme was of a telling character. On the Marne the Germans suffered a check like that at Verdun. The initiative of the attack had been theirs, but when their advance was checked they ably withdrew from a weak position and renewed their attack in a terrific running fight to the Yser. This brought them a large new gain of territory, and, despite their losses, the spirit of their troops remained high.

We have, therefore, to go far back to Ligny, in 1815, to find a parallel to the Franco-British successes north and south of the Somme. For the first time in its short but marvellous history the mighty modern military State created by the Prussians had lost its power of attack, had been thrown on the defensive, and had been unable to hold its intricate and magnificent system of fortification. The armies of Great Britain in the first weeks of July do not appear to have noticed any important signs of the failure of the German spirit. It may be that the presence of two divisions of the Prussian Guard in the sector attacked by British troops, and the checks to the British advance from Gommecourt to Thiepval, served to sustain the moral of the troops facing the British. But the German army farther to the south had no local successes in defence to balance or palliate its grave and general defeat. The German Staff had to reorganise it completely to check the sign of demoralisation.

General Fayolle was at first opposed by only four divisions, but at the end of ten weeks' fighting the Germans had at various times brought up against him nearly thirty-five divisions. Yet these thirty-five divisions—nominally over 500,000 infantrymen strong—were division after division overborne, outfought, and compelled to surrender their vast systems of fortification.

Verdun. The weary Belgian troops on the Yser had probably been the first to feel the full weight of modern monster siege ordnance brought against field defences. From October, 1914, to July, 1916, the German armies had always employed heavier high-explosive shell and larger quantities of this heavy shell than their opponents. The allied troops had withstood the stunning shock of hurricane high-explosive fire with superhuman endurance. After the first racking effect of surprise had passed they finally had almost come to think that the struggle against the German war-machine was to be an ordeal in which there would be no relief from the enemy's overwhelming artillery power.

Apparently the German troops were of the same opinion. Even at Verdun their 16·5 in., 12 in. and 11 in. howitzers, and 15 in. guns had permanently domin- **German infantry** ated the battlefield, and the French, **tested** with guns of smaller calibre, had resisted by a skilful employment of their light field-guns and light machine-guns. They had never been able to make a counter-attack in grand style with a dominating force of heavy artillery. They had snatched small positions from the Germans instead of winning them by superior fire. On the Somme, for the first time in their military career, the German infantrymen were tested by the same ordeal as their gunners had imposed upon the allied infantry, and, although the Germans had abundance of native courage which was to serve them well when they had recovered from their consternation, they were disheartened by the terrible strokes delivered against them. Some German newspapers had indeed the childish

Over the top with the bayonet to win a few more yards of sacred France. Remarkable illustration taken at the moment of a charge.

Gallant handful of Poilus gallantly led by their officer towards the German lines. A photograph secured at great risk to the operator.

THE SPIRIT OF FRANCE AFTER THIRTY MONTHS OF ENDURANCE: A VIGOROUS CHARGE UNDER HEAVY FIRE.

GERMAN "PIGEONS" BAGGED BY THE FRENCH.
Small wing-bombs taken from the Germans during the Somme fighting.
These bombs are called "pigeons" by the Poilus.

the line bends curiously back to the rear of Hardecourt and the neighbourhood of Maurepas, and again turns by Hem to Cléry-sur-Somme and Péronne. This railway was named the Tortillard, or Twister, by the Allies. It ran in a series of wild zigzags, twisting oddly by the flank of hills and through woods, and each of its stations was a battle site. The Albert-Combles section of line, with stations at Bois de Bornefay and Guillemont, whence a branch line ran to Waterlot Farm, was a line of terrific attacks and counter-attacks. The section from Combles to Péronne, that fed the guns and machine-guns, mortars and hand-grenade depôts at Falfemont Farm, Hardecourt, Maurepas, and Cléry, formed the objective of the Iron Division. In the second week of July it cut the line between Hardecourt and Maurepas and also broke it near the river at Monacu Farm.

There was a long and misleading lull in the operations on the Somme, which was eagerly misrepresented by the Press agents of the German Government as a definite defeat of the Franco-British forces. On July 8th the Iron Division, which had remained almost motionless on its left at Maricourt, made a leap forward and got in line with the British army by storming the village of Hardecourt. The French brigade at Maricourt had stood upon the defensive for a week, while the advance proceeded on either side of it, because it had been expected that the first great enemy counter-attack would be launched at the connecting-point of the allied armies. This, no doubt, would have been done if the brigade at Maricourt had swung forward on July 1st with the rest of the allied forces of attack. But by holding back until the British troops neared Bois de Favière, and the French troops consolidated themselves in Curlu and Hem, the force at Maricourt, which had gradually extended over Rouge Farm plateau, was able to leap forward without imperilling the strength of the juncture of the allied armies.

The storming of Hardecourt French guns had been brought on Rouge Farm plateau to take Hardecourt on the southern flank, while the heavy French ordnance around Maricourt hammered the village from the east. With this terrific cross-fire to cover them, the light-blue soldiers bombed their way through Favière Wood alongside the khaki-clad fighting men of Great Britain, took five hundred prisoners, and then charged into the ruins of Hardecourt, and in a fierce little subterranean conflict occupied all the caverns and tunnels.

The storming of Hardecourt completed the first phase of the French operations north of the river. All the first zone of enemy works for a depth of a mile to a mile and a half was carried. But the second zone of defences was more formidable than the first, and needed enormous preparations in order to attack it with success and economy of life. It will be observed on the maps on pages 4 and 20 that a branch railway runs from Albert by Fricourt, Carnoy, Trônes Wood, and Guillemont to Combles. From Combles

BOMBS AND GRENADES CAPTURED ON THE SOMME.
Vast quantities of German munitions of all kinds fell into the hands of the
Allies during the advance that began in July, 1916.

Then for some time the French remained fairly quiet. They were waiting for their heavy guns to advance south of the river towards La Maisonnette and Biaches, and take the enemy forces around Combles in the flank. Canal monitors for operation against the German positions near the Somme Valley were also being launched and tested, and the effect of their sudden attack on the enemy's machine-gun positions in the marshes and his gun positions from Cléry to Mont St. Quentin was likely to be very valuable. But the main reason for the long delay in the French operations north of the river was to be found in the British position. The British army had, as we have seen, much the harder and more important task. It had to carry the high ridges rolling towards Bapaume before the shorter pivot line of the smaller co-operating French force could securely move forward. The enemy had collected the enormous force of sixty-nine new divisions against the armies of General Fayolle and Sir Douglas Haig.

The German commander on the western front had

On the Somme: French grenadiers bombing the enemy trenches near Maurepas.

Giant German periscope captured on the Somme. Inset: The instrument packed for transport.

Hoisting a 16 in. shell to the breech of a powerful French gun.

Fierce hand-to-hand fighting at Rancourt, the fall of which contributed to the Franco-British capture of Combles.

altogether one hundred and twenty-four divisions, deployed from the Belgian coast to the Swiss frontier. These divisions he continually shuffled from one sector to another, and in weeks when the conflict on the Somme was extremely furious he was known to have had the extraordinary number of twenty-six divisions moving from one position to another. Falkenhayn at the time was creating new formations for a possible campaign in Transylvania against the Rumanians, or a new offensive against Russia or France. German divisions were in some cases being reduced from twelve thousand bayonets to nine thousand bayonets, and new artillery and material were being collected for service with the new army. Battalion commanders in all those parts of the western front that were **German strength on** not liable to violent attack were often **the Somme** robbed of hundreds of their best men to provide the framework of some new formation. But before this new formation was equipped and organised a Franco-British movement on the Somme often caused the German troops to be diverted there.

The general effect was that rather more than half the entire German forces in Belgium, France, Lorraine and Alsace was successively massed between Bapaume and Chaulnes on a winding front of little more than thirty miles. The Germans concentrated their guns in this small sector even as they concentrated their troops. The consequence was that the French and British commanders had always to be extremely careful not to advance beyond their immediately available strength. If they formed a weak salient at any point, the enemy would drive upon it in huge strength from two directions.

The small French force north of the river was particularly cautious, because it served as the joint in the allied operations. For nearly two weeks it merely worked at gradually clearing the ground in front of it, while the British forces were widening the line near Guillemont. Then, on July 20th, when the enemy had massed against the British forces in the Longueval salient, General Fayolle swung all his armies forward on both sides of the river, taking nearly 3,000 prisoners, sixty machine-guns, and three pieces of ordnance. The immediate aim of this move was to teach the enemy that he could not safely concentrate only against Sir Douglas Haig's forces.

The Germans, in fact, released their hold on Longueval and Delville Wood (Bois de Delville), whence they sent reinforcements to Maurepas and the vicinity of Hardecourt. But the northern French force still fought forward with surprising rapidity, and in three hours it accomplished the work for which an entire day had been allowed. It carried the positions between Hardecourt Hill and the Tortillard railway line, and annexed a considerable stretch of the enemy's position southward towards Cléry. The prisoners taken between Hardecourt and the Somme were more numerous than the total casualties, slight and severe, of the regiment that led the attack.

It might have cost but few men to have pushed through the German reinforcements hastily brought from Longueval, and to have reached the outskirts of Maurepas. The French commander, however, was satisfied with cutting the railway and with relieving the situation of the British forces northward. His new line already formed a slight salient, which the Germans outflanked from their Guillemont position. He therefore stood firm on his new line of approach to Combles, and waited for another ten days until Sir Douglas Haig had secured the whole of Delville Wood and Longueval. Then, on July 30th, the French again drove in along a four-mile line, running from Maurepas to Monacu Farm by the river. They penetrated the second German zone of fortification to a depth of half a mile in places, and reached the outskirts of Maurepas. Thereupon, the Germans swung a large fresh force against the new French line, recaptured Monacu Farm, again lost it, and fell back without making any change in the situation.

The general effect of these operations was that of all

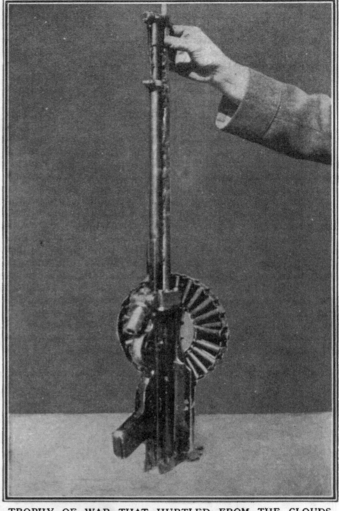

TROPHY OF WAR THAT HURTLED FROM THE CLOUDS.
German mitrailleuse which fell from an aeroplane into the French lines—presumptive evidence that the enemy aircraft was damaged.

alternate hammer-blows by the French and British. At first glance it would seem as though the result could have been obtained more quickly if the two blows had been delivered simultaneously. So it would, had there been any intention of rapidly breaking the enemy's front. But as this design had been abandoned from the start, and a gradual scientific process of grinding down the enemy's strength elaborated, the alternate hammer-strokes were strangely disconcerting to the enemy. He countered each blow at the outset by bringing up fresh divisions and keeping them in line until they were used up, and the ground they had recovered was lost.

By this time the allied force engaged **Method of alternate** in the attack was almost as exhausted **blows** as the German forces it had conquered, and time was needed to relieve or reinforce it and bring up more munitions and improve the defences.

But only a couple of miles away from this scene of temporary inaction and balanced thrust and counter-thrust a fresh and fully-organised French force abruptly delivered another smashing hammer-stroke, which compelled the German commander to divert all reinforcements southward. Then, when these reinforcements had exhausted themselves in vain counter-attacks, and stood badly in need of fresh troops and fresh supplies, the re-organised British forces a couple of miles northward again struck and broke the enemy's positions, thereby relieving the French at Maurepas and Hem from further counter-attack, and creating more anxieties for the German Staff.

The alternate hammer-stroke was thus the more distracting and wearing method from the German point of view. All that Prince Rupert of Bavaria could do to relieve Stein or Below by counter-attacking on the British left flank and the British Bapaume front was more than balanced by General Foch's southward thrusts from Barleux to Chaulnes. On both flanks of the Franco-British advancing salient there was a balance of forces with a residue of advantage on the side of the Allies. Nothing, therefore, could lighten the German position at Combles, at which the Franco-British hammered distractingly.

Advantage with the Allies

At the point of junction between the allied forces there was, moreover, a fine element of rivalry working in both the French and British troops. They were a mutual admiration society, and their admiration took the noble form of endeavouring to rise each to the height of the other's skill and heroism. New French army corps, coming for their spell of driving work through Bray towards Maurepas, after months of passive defensive toil at Verdun, were strangely cheered to find that they were at last deploying in a great advance alongside the home and oversea troops of the British Empire. All that the French peasant had been told he only half believed, but all that he saw with his own eyes became an imperishable memory in French life. The sight of cheering khaki lines going into action on the Frenchman's left flank roused him to his highest pitch of skill and steadiness. He wanted the "Englishman" to see with what masterly keenness the

veterans and youngsters of France were working towards a decisive victory. When relieved, he sometimes shared the sports of the British troops and, as a worthy comrade of Carpentier, succeeded at times in beating the Briton at his own games. All this made for a superb efficiency of combination in the attacks delivered from that junction-point of the two allied armies which might have been their principal point of comparative weakness.

As was explained in the previous chapter, General Fayolle's main force was at first employed south of the Somme in clearing the Péronne front and in pressing against the flank of the enemy from Barleux to Estrées. North of the Somme the French commander, with his chief, General Foch, had only a comparatively small force, that served as the pivot of the great British thrust towards Bapaume. The pivoting force could not with any security work forward beyond the line gained by the British army.

In the technical military phrase, the Franco-British operations on either side of the Somme were conducted in échelons. An échelon, in ordinary language, means the round of a ladder or a stepping-stone, but as a technical term it stands for a series of formations like the squares on the diagonal line of a chess-board. That is to say, the various armies or forces are not exactly behind each other but are placed diagonally in a succession of retreating sharp angles.

Operations in echelons

General Foch, the most brilliant of modern strategists, revived the use of échelon formations (which Frederick the

[*French official photograph.*

DEVASTATION WROUGHT BY THE GUNS IN INVADED FRANCE.
View of a Somme village after the troops had gathered the ruins together. All the bricks from these shattered villages were taken to make and repair roads, and only the broken woodwork remained to mark the site of former happiness.

FRENCH CANAL MONITOR MOVING AGAINST THE ENEMY.
Canal monitors were very effective in bombarding the German machine-gun positions in the marshes and his gun positions from Cléry to Mont St. Quentin.

BUSY TOW-PATH SCENE ALONG THE SOMME CANAL.
The network of canals in the Somme Valley was fully utilised by the French for both transport barges and armed monitors.

Great had employed) in the Franco-British operations on the Somme, where he generally directed and co-ordinated the work of Sir Douglas Haig and General Fayolle. His advanced échelon extended south of the river to La Maisonnette, and outflanked, with its monster siege-guns, the German positions around Combles. Across the river was another French échelon, forming an acute angle with the La Maisonnette force, and thus exposing the Germans in the angle to attack on both sides.

Sir Douglas Haig had a small but powerful échelon running from a point near Maurepas northward towards Delville Wood. Above, on the Bazentin Ridge, he had his most advanced force placed so that it faced Delville on one side and Pozières on the other. Then **Facing Delville and** westward, from a point near Pozières to **Pozieres** Thiepval, ran another British échelon, which completed the principal Franco-British battle formations. Every angle was precisely adjusted to the general scheme. No échelon moved forward until the Allied Staff had worked out the general result and had arranged and harmonised the adjustments that were to follow all along the line. Each angle was the scene of continual desperate fighting.

There were recessive angles, such as the French angle at Hem, in which the Germans occupied a narrow salient and desperately threw in division after division under conditions of disadvantage that led to the rapid wasting of their reserves. General Foch used the great moat of the Somme Valley in a masterly way to protect his most advanced échelons at La Maisonette and render the enemy there almost impotent. On the other hand, the two main British angles of attack were not recessive but projecting. The enemy, therefore, could attack them in persistent and enormous force on both sides, the British troops being in each of these places in a narrow salient, with each base of the salient cut by a hostile curtain fire, making reinforcement and munitioning very difficult.

Thus the brunt of the fighting fell upon the British troops, yet until they straightened out their angle at Delville Wood and Guillemont the French échelon below them could not be advanced without making another and most perilous

angle right at the delicate junction-point of the French and British armies. The interplay of the attacking échelons was affected by numerous local factors, arising from the varying nature of the terrain, and particularly from the amount of dead ground which either side enjoyed. Ravines, for instance, were of priceless value, as the French had taught the Germans at Verdun. A deep and meandering ravine, with steep sides, was a position of the highest known strength if it were subtly and curiously fortified.

The first French échelon north of the Somme was immobilised for nearly two weeks by a ravine near Hem. On August 3rd the French infantry took the red buildings of Monacu Farm by the river east of Hem, was thrown out of the farm by a fierce counter-attack, and returned and reconquered the shapeless ruins. The French heavy guns on the high ground south of the valley made Monacu a death-trap to the Germans. **Death-trap at** But the hostile ravine running north of **Monacu** Hem and linking with the important enemy position on Hill 109 south of Maurepas was a grave obstacle. It ran through Hem Wood, and at the bottom of the gully was a well-made hollow road screened by almost sheer sides from sixty to seventy feet high. Northward, the Germans held a fortified chalk quarry, and on the western edge of the wood were steep slopes dotted with clumps of wood, and in these clumps were bomb-proof machine-gun posts. Two valleys—the Valley of the Ravine and the Valley of Riez—extended beyond the position and afforded further stretches of dead ground, in

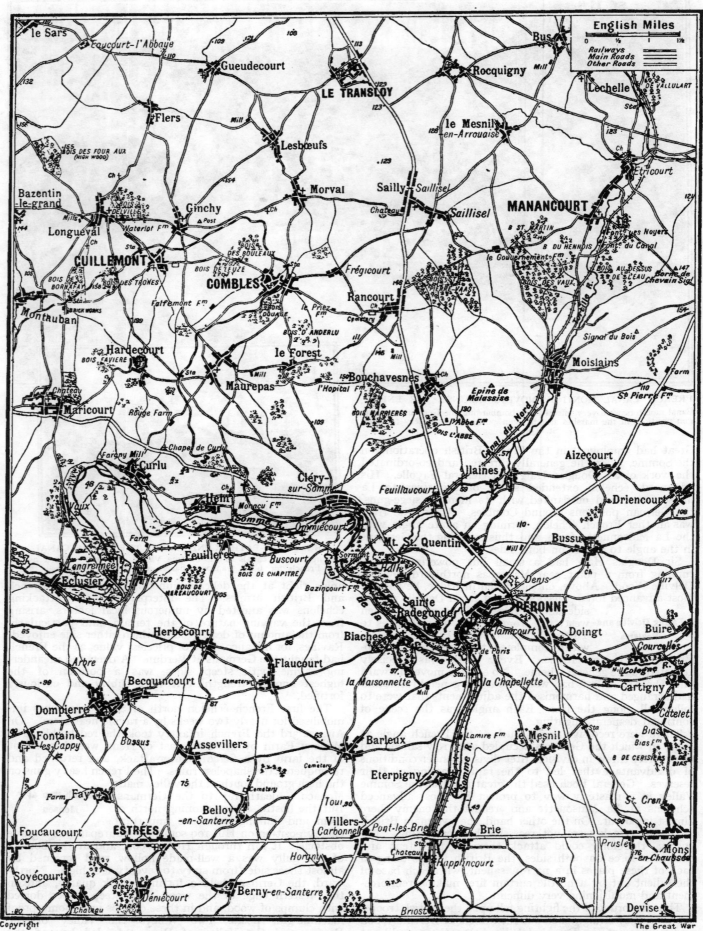

LARGE-SCALE MAP OF THE FRENCH FRONT IN THE SOMME SECTOR.

AT BEAUMONT-HAMEL.
House at the level-crossing at Beaumont-Hamel protected by barbed-wire.

through the wood into the railway line on the way to Cléry. It was all done by sprinting, but sprinting of a highly disciplined and co-ordinated sort. When the battalion broke through the wood its work was finished, and it was due to retire so that a fresh battalion could continue the advance with the same surprising impetuosity. But the victorious young recruits had lost so lightly and were so confident that they received permission to go on. Advancing in the night by little rushes, they approached another wood, near the road running from Maurepas to Cléry. In the wood the Germans had a strong trench, with another series of western outworks, commanding the outlet from the Valley of the Ravine and the entrance to Riez Valley.

The French heavy artillery was directed by telephone to fire hundreds of big shells on the slopes leading to the inaccessible dead ground that could not be bombarded. The shells were so directed that they excavated a complete system of defensive craters in front of the two companies deployed for the attack. The companies then charged the German machine-gunners and the great trench in the wood. The light-blue figures covered the ground with the utmost rapidity, trying to get within grenade range of the German gunners before the latter could mow them down. The French on the left wing were caught by a rain of bullets and tumbled into their prepared shell-holes, a hundred and fifty yards from their objective, and began to dig forward. But the right wing was either luckier or quicker, and in a great bound it reached the face of the German fieldwork and pitched hand-bombs into it.

The French employed a type of hand-bomb which made

Charging the machine guns

which the Germans built modern barbicans in the form of machine-gun redoubts.

The dead ground could not be reached by any French shell. It was so screened by steep natural ramparts that no howitzer could pitch a shell that would fall plumb on the enemy's positions. In these circumstances the French commander was practically stalemated. His vast and elaborate machinery of war was useless, and, like the German commander at Verdun when General Pétain organised the ravines there, he had either to admit defeat or fall back upon primitive methods of attack by massed infantry against machine-guns and curtain fire.

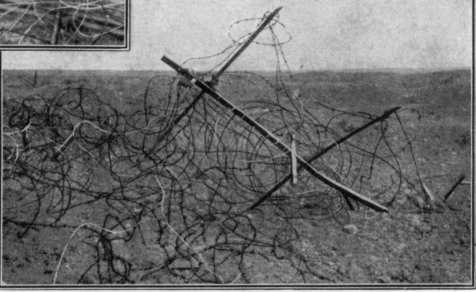

EFFECT OF SHELL FIRE ON WIRE ENTANGLEMENTS.
German barbed-wire defences uprooted, broken, and twisted by the high-explosive shells poured on them prior to the advance of the French infantry on the Somme.

This method was adopted. But instead of trying to choke the German guns by a rush attack with a division or an army corps, the French general brought up, on August 9th, a single battalion of untried youngsters of the 1916 class. For two days there were skirmishing reconnaissances between patrols, during which the famous force of Chasseurs Alpins got into position on the tableland north of the great ravine. Then on August 11th the young battalion of the line west of the gully made a splendid charge into the quarry, captured the redoubts in the clumps of trees, descended the ravine from the north, taking the German positions there in the rear, and stormed

scarcely any noise when it exploded and threw no deadly fragments of steel. But it was most effective in clearing trenches and dug-outs, as it contained a gas which made any place in which it exploded uninhabitable. The contest lasted from the afternoon of August 12th until late in the night of August 13th. There were many glorious little episodes. Ten Frenchmen and a subaltern fought for twenty-four hours at a distance of six yards from a strong enemy post and, with practically no shelter themselves, kept the Germans helpless in their "funk-holes," where they were at last captured. Another young French officer, with more ardour than experience, leaped on the

FRENCH TROOPS IN ACTION ARRIVING AT VERMANDOVILLERS, AS SEEN FROM ABOVE BY A FRENCH AIRMAN.

This photograph was taken by a French airman flying at a low altitude. It shows the French troops passing through the trenches in the course of their successful attack on Vermandovillers, September 17th, 1916. General Fayolle had an entire fleet of photographic machines operating continually over the enemy's lines. Each piece of destruction wrought by the French guns was photographed immediately, and the developed photograph was closely studied by Staff officers. If the picture was not satisfactory the observing machines went up again, followed by photographic machines. The gunners fired ranging shots and received messages from the observers, under whose direction they poured a fresh intense fire on the points, when more photographs were taken for the use of the Staff.

parapet of an unconquered trench, was caught by a bullet that inflicted a scalp wound, and was thereby so angered that he snatched a rifle with fixed bayonet from his nearest man, leaped into the trench and, with his men blindly following him, cleared it out. As the attacking battalion was soon curtained off by heavy hostile shell fire it ran the danger of exhausting its ammunition. But with its reserves sapping through the lines of shell-holes, communications were established and more grenades brought up, and in the night of August 13th the entire position was conquered by this single battalion.

At Verdun the Germans, on occasion, wasted several divisions in a vain attempt to conquer by rush attacks a key-position in dead ground such as **German waste and** these thousand French recruits stormed at **French economy** comparatively very light sacrifice of life. One of the chief reasons for our allies' successes of this kind was that their men advanced in very open order and with great rapidity, and yet remained not only steadfast and undaunted but in perfect control.

After the advance beyond the ravine and Riez Wood, and the sweep of the Chasseurs Alpins farther north, the way was cleared for an attack in force on the German line. The weather had been very hazy, making artillery observation difficult and checking the operations. But having used the mist to cover his infantry charges in the hand-to-hand fight with bombs above Hem, General Fayolle, when the air cleared, brought a terrific cross-fire from his heavy guns to bear upon the German front from Maurepas to the river. Along a line of four miles the French infantry went forward against the picked German troops that had been brought up to save the Bapaume-Combles front. A division of the Prussian Guard was arrayed against the junction-point of the allied armies, and the Brandenburg regiments were marshalled against the British force in the Guillemont angle, while well-tried Bavarian forces held the southern plateau of Maurepas and Hill 109.

A most desperate struggle was expected against the Prussian Guard in the village, and the French infantry-men at this point were timed to reach their goal in a slow movement lasting twelve hours. They did their work, however, in thirty-five minutes, capturing the cemetery and the church, and beating back a succession of fierce counter-attacks delivered from the underground ways in the village. On the plateau south of Maurepas the

fighting was extremely fierce, as the Germans held on with fine valour and brought up fresh troops. The attacking regiment, however, had fewer than three hundred men killed and wounded during the conquest of four systems of trenches, all strengthened by redoubts and underground communications. Hill 109, with its terraced works, held by a Bavarian battalion, was stormed quickly and with little loss, as the heavy French guns had destroyed the main block-house and put out of action the larger part of the garrison. All the four-mile enemy front, with its difficult ravines and elaborated defences, was carried, to an average depth of half a mile, in eighty minutes.

The German commander vainly tried to recover Hill 109, which dominated all the French positions south of the river, by a violent counter-thrust from Cléry. His troops, hurriedly flung forward without proper preparation, were entirely wasted, being caught in a tremendous outburst of gun fire on the southern and western arcs of French guns. This badly-managed affair temporarily exhausted the enemy's means of reaction, and the victorious French force consolidated its new positions on Monday, August 14th. The next day the Colonial Corps, which had finished its work south of the river, where the Tenth French Army, under General Micheler, had taken over the line from Barleux to Estrées, came into action on the northern sector where the Ironsides and their comrades were entering on the hardest part of their work.

On August 15th the French guns again delivered an intense preparatory bombardment, lasting until the afternoon of August 16th. Then, in conjunction with the British attack on Guillemont, the French infantry of the line and the Colonial **Allied gain towards** Corps again broke into the German **Maurepas** front. The left wing of the advance did not make much progress, as the Prussian Guard fought desperately around Guillemont and Maurepas against the Allies. But the Guillemont-Maurepas road was reached at several points, bringing the French troops within a mile and a half of Combles. The right wing swung forward more rapidly, and penetrated, for a third of a mile, all the new German fieldworks between Maurepas and Cléry.

Maurepas itself was still not entirely conquered, as the Germans held two block-houses in the northern corner of the village, from which they had a line of communication with their new main position at Le Forest, which could not be reached by the French guns. Two-thirds of Maurepas

GENERAL BALFOURIER AND OTHER IMPORTANT FRENCH OFFICERS WATCHING THE PROGRESS OF ONE OF THE GREAT BATTLES IN THE SOMME SECTOR.

OFF ON THEIR HEROIC MISSION: THE RED CROSS MOVING FORWARD TO THE FRONT LINE.
Members of the French Red Cross drawing wheeled stretchers in the rear of an attack. Everywhere are signs of the all-destroying shell.

had been carried in the first assault, and only three French companies, under a major now famous throughout the Army, were sent forward to complete the conquest of the village. The enemy was entrenched in the cellars in the northern corner, and provided with machine-guns that had escaped the allied gun fire. The small French force dug itself in on a line fifty yards from the enemy, linking up the shell-holes that ran by the ruins of the houses. Soon the German guns began to rain down shells on the conquered part of the village, where the French troops only managed to construct one shallow trench after an hour and a half's work. The major saw that all his men would be wiped out by the hostile curtain fire if more cover was not at once obtained.

So he advanced his company another thirty yards towards the two uninjured German underground fortresses —an achievement that had to be accomplished under machine-gun fire and showers of grenades from the enemy. When the lines were thus approached the German gunners tried to shatter the new French position with shell fire, and drew their curtain of shrapnel and high explosive a little backward for the purpose. Happily, the Allies mastery of the air was absolute in this area, and the hostile artillery, having no aerial observation, had to work only by the map. The result was that their own troops in the northern part of Maurepas began to send up green rockets, indicating that they were endangered by their own artillery.

The major and his men thus obtained protection from the German guns, and worked forward until at one place there was only a wall between the opposing forces, who lobbed grenades over the broken brick-work on each other's heads. The French **Grenade work at** found, however, that no decision could be **close range** won in this way, as the enemy was able to bring up constant reinforcements from Le Forest. In co-operation with their heavy artillery the major and his men suddenly fell back to a telephone-post, just short of the zone of the German curtain fire.

The heavy French artillery hammered in a terrific manner the German corner of Maurepas. But though the storm of huge projectiles lasted some hours, no injury of importance was done to the German block-houses. They were on dead ground, which could only be reached, as in the former case of the ravine in the Hem sector, by a series of very large howitzer shells falling almost sheer from the sky. Expert as the French gunners were, not one of their shells directly penetrated the underground system of works held by the enemy.

When the major sent out his patrols the Germans hoisted their uninjured machine-guns from the deep caverns and opened fire in undiminished strength The hostile riflemen could be seen standing, visible to the waist, in a trench on the left and assisting the machine-gunners to sweep the ground. The situation was extremely difficult for the major, for he had arranged with his head-quarters that as soon as the preparatory bombardment ceased a fresh French force was to close on the enemy from the left to assist the frontal charge.

He saw that if his men did not immediately charge against the machine-guns the fresh force of French troops co-operating on the wing would be surprised by a murderous flanking fire. "It is always better to be killed oneself than to cause the death of one's comrades," said the major afterwards. "So we went forward and drew the enemy's fire." The heroic company ran from shell-hole to shell-hole, incurring heavy losses in saving their comrades on the wing. Arriving close to the German position they crouched in holes near the loopholed wall from which the enemy gunners were firing and waited there until nightfall. The darkness brought no opportunity for a rush attack, as the Germans maintained unceasingly a barrier of fire on the bare slope in front of their block-houses.

Nevertheless, the major was not brought to a standstill. Unperceived by the enemy, he withdrew all his men from the shell holes, and massed them on the left wing with the fresh troops, and then made an unexpected flank attack over ground where the Germans were not maintaining a curtain fire. The attacking troops went forward to the northernmost houses of Maurepas, yet here again they were brought up by a German machine-gun placed in a great iron tank that formed the water reservoir of the village. The tank seemed impregnable and its iron sides were proof against bullets. The major, however, had foreseen possible difficulties and had brought up a small ·37 in. gun, and four of its little shells, fired at point-blank range, penetrated the iron reservoir, quickly putting the machine-gun section out of action, and enabled the major to surround the village and kill or capture all its garrison.

The struggle in Maurepas did not end until August 24th, and while it was going on General Fayolle assisted his troops in the village and the British and French forces around Guillemont by throwing fresh forces between Maurepas and Guillemont. They stormed a wood south of the latter village and captured eight guns there on August 21st. Southward by the river another French force entered the outskirts of Cléry, after breaking a great counter-attack by the Prussian Guard and the Bavarian and Saxon Corps working with the Guardsmen. On August 24th, when the conquest of Maurepas was completed by the surprise attack from the north, the main French force advanced to Hill 121, south-east of the village on the line of advance towards Le Forest. Again the Germans violently reacted, and on August 25th, made a furious attempt to recover Hill 121 and re-enter Maurepas. But the Prussian Guardsmen were shattered by the French machine-guns and hemmed in on their rear by the barrier fire of heavy French howitzers. Thousands of them could neither retire nor attack, and after vain forward rushes and futile attempts at retreat a remnant of some six hundred dropped their rifles, lifted their hands and surrendered. This incident was a terrible example of the science underlying the slow progress of the Sixth French Army. When that army occupied an important enemy position such as Hill 121, the Germans were left no opportunity of successfully counter-attacking in force. All the approaches were dominated by the French guns some days before the French infantry went forward. Here **Allies' dominating gun fire** and there a ravine or tunnel allowed the enemy to make a struggle for a trench with bombs and machine-guns. But no main operations could be conducted with success against the two great advancing arcs of allied artillery.

There was a pause of ten days by General Fayolle's army after the conquest of the Maurepas line. The British army was also strangely quiescent during this period, beating off counter-attacks by the enemy and making small improvements in its front by means of bomb attacks. German newspapers reported that the Allies had been fought to a standstill. As a matter of fact, the apparent stagnation on the Somme veiled an unparalleled amount of preparation. The French losses in life, wear in armament, and expenditure of shell since July 1st had been less than was anticipated.

A BREAKAGE IN THE GERMAN LINE.
French official photograph.
General Fayolle inspecting with soldierly satisfaction the destruction of German trenches on the Somme, the work of efficient artillery concentration.

Instead of France being enfeebled by her magnificent part in the offensive, she was bringing into action another army as large as that of General Fayolle, and supported by as many heavy guns and as great quantities of shell as the Sixth French Army was using. French munition supply was increasing like that of the British, so that another great French attacking force, the Tenth Army under General Micheler, was able to come into action from the south of the Somme to Roye.

This was the reason for the phase **Foch's far-reaching** of inaction north of the river. General **strategy** Foch's design was that Sir Douglas Haig and General Fayolle should renew their combined advance between Cléry and Pozières and press it fiercely for a day or two, in order to attract all the floating German reserves on the western front. These reserves were known to be at the time small and fluctuating, consisting of detachments collected from quiet sectors of the front. And as General von Falkenhayn was creating new formations by reducing his divisions, and was extremely sparing of the new guns needed to replace worn-out weapons, the prospects of the new French army seemed favourable.

The design of the French and British Staffs was to compel Falkenhayn and his successor to spend more men, more guns, and more shell north and south of the Somme, and thus facilitate the work of the Russian armies and the action which Rumania was preparing. But the German forces in the western theatre of war had first to be extended almost to breaking point in order to interfere with Falkenhayn's creations of new formations and complicate all the problems he had left to Hindenburg.

On Sunday, September 3rd, 1916, General Micheler was ready to strike. General Fayolle and Sir Douglas Haig, whose guns had been thundering uninterruptedly for days, opened the second phase of the allied offensive on a front of about thirty miles, from Thiepval in the north to Chilly in the south. Of this longer line the British forces, which had hitherto carried the main burden of the attack, were responsible for a short third. The other two-thirds were entrusted to two of the incomparable French armies which had endured the long and terrible conflict at Verdun.

Extraordinary method was the secret of France's disconcerting vitality. She was employing in attack more skill in saving the lives of her men than she had shown in her superb defence of Verdun. And as her officers had had three months of experience in the new tactics of economical assault, General Foch was able, by reason of the acceleration in French and British munition making, to engage another great French army **General Foch preserves his men** in the vast offensive movement, with the assured confidence that he would waste the enemy's man-power and submit him to continually increasing strain without nearing the point of exhaustion of French manhood.

In conjunction with the British attack on Guillemont and Ginchy the French forces north of the Somme advanced the whole of their line from Le Forest to Cléry. North of Le Forest the enemy's positions were stormed to the outskirts of Combles. The village of Le Forest, lying on a hill five hundred feet high, was a very important artillery position, and some fourteen German guns were captured about it. Here one French subaltern with a platoon went too far in advance and was surrounded by about five hundred Germans. The young officer charged with his handful of men, and the Germans, shaken by the terrific bombardment, fled and left forty prisoners and the most important position on the Somme. Through the unexpected gap thus opened the Sixth French Army advanced nearly a mile beyond Le Forest and half-way to Rancourt.

The German commander hurried up more men on Sunday evening and launched a heavy counter-attack against his lost position south of Le Forest. Again the French siege-guns, directed by airmen and officers on the ground with wireless instruments and telephones, caught the counter-attacking force in a great blanket of shrapnel and high-explosive, and left the French infantry scarcely any work to do, except to go on with the work of building up cover in the shattered German lines.

All Sunday night the struggle went on, and while the Germans were trying to batter in the new British northern salient at Ginchy the men of the Sixth French Army did all they could to relieve the pressure upon their British comrades by furiously pressing the advantage they had won between Le Forest and Rancourt. The French gunners watered the ground immediately in front of their infantry with a broad and intense band of mingled shrapnel and high explosive, and when Hospital Farm and the redoubts west of Marrières Wood were reduced to chaos by the monster French shells the French patrols advanced and signalled to their main forces that no resistance was to be expected. In this cautious and overwhelming way the extraordinary progress of the Sixth French Army continued until September 6th, when the edge of Andernu Wood, all Rainette Wood, and part of Marrières Wood were added to the list of French conquests.

More than three thousand prisoners were taken and a total of thirty-two guns, including twenty-four of heavy calibre. Large stocks of 6 in. shells, numerous machine-guns, and some trench-mortars were amongst the booty, together with an observation balloon employed by the Germans in the rear of their lines, where they had fancied they were secure. The speed and vehemence of the accelerated French movement had, it was clear, taken the enemy commander completely by surprise. The victory of Le Forest was especially significant in that it was won against the finest division of the Prussian Guard, with the German Emperor's son, Prince Eitel Friedrich, at its head, these Guardsmen being supported by picked divisions of other German troops.

At Maurepas the French soldiers had met Prince Eitel's Guardsmen in fine style. The Prussians were out-manœuvred and defeated, but though their noble officers did not display any **Decline of the** striking skill, the men fought with indo- **Prussian Guard** mitable stubbornness, and not until they were disabled or killed did the victorious French battalion make any progress. Scarcely any prisoners, except wounded men, were taken at Maurepas. Every Prussian there seems to have sworn to fight to the death, and fulfilled his oath, The French battalion that obliterated a regiment of Prince

[French official photograph.

FRENCH ARTILLERY CONCENTRATING IN READINESS FOR A BOMBARDMENT OF THE GERMAN POSITIONS ON THE SOMME.
Under cover of a wood, some miles behind the line, batteries of artillery are about to take up new positions. The excellent condition of the horses, which were mainly used to transport these light weapons, will be noted.

CANNON CAPTURED FROM THE GERMANS DURING A BIG BATTLE IN PICARDY.

In the summer and autumn of 1916 the German losses in guns were so heavy that special Army Orders were issued deploring negligence on the part of soldiers. and warning them that a great supply of metal could no longer be guaranteed by the Government.

Eitel's division in these circumstances did splendid work. Despite this defeat at Maurepas the best division of the Prussian Guard saved its honour in the struggle.

But it was otherwise in the struggle about Le Forest some twelve days later. In the course of the war the Prussian Guard had several times been defeated and broken, but it had never been dishonoured. At the Marne and at Ypres it charged to its doom, as steadily as it did at St. Privat, in 1870. Some of its divisions had been re-made, owing to its great losses, but the old traditions of intrepidity had survived. We can, however, trace the decline of these traditions in the battle that raged in the first week of September, 1916, in the woods and farmsteads between Le Forest and Rancourt. Definite evidence of some demoralisation in the Prussian Guard is found in the following diary discovered on the field of battle :

Nesle, August 22nd, 1916.

To-day at two o'clock in the morning we were relieved in our new position by the 30th Regiment of Infantry. We had been immediately told, at the moment we occupied it, that we should not remain long in this position. We remained there exactly fourteen days. All the division was relieved. Marching for three hours, we have arrived a mile and a half in the rear of Nesle. We put up our tents in a wheat field, and got a hot meal and slept under canvas. How long will our rest last? The devil alone knows. Where shall we be sent to next? Who can tell ? But we must hope that the war will not last for eternity. God ! If only all this beastliness would come to a quick end. But it is easier to get sense into an ass than into mankind. As for myself I am going to do my best to get safe and

From a diary of discontent

sound out of all this madness. Our condition of mind is actually the following, though our leaders don't suspect it : Every man is planning and seeking some way of getting out of the mess. Every possible means is considered. We are led like a flock of sheep, and treated either like children or like criminals. Oh, how I hate it all ! Words fail me to describe what I feel. We have not had much rest to-day. Polishing ourselves up and other foolery of the same kind. We got some preserved beans and a bottle of mineral water, which we had no right to take.

August 23rd, 1916.

Yesterday night I laid down in the open,. but I could not sleep until midnight. The vermin and the flies kept me awake. When I got up this morning at eight o'clock I felt absolutely done up.

Ah, God, when shall I be able to sleep in a bed ? But, after all, everything is indifferent to us except peace. If only all those whose mouths are always filled with talk about victory could lead this fight for life for a fortnight, peace would soon be made. For there's nothing more convincing than solid facts. Decidedly this war will not end. It is enough to drive a man mad. Everybody wants to get wounded, just enough to allow him to go home. Nobody wants to distinguish himself. That is the real truth of the matter. All the newspaper wordiness is only humbug. We " heroes " are men who act under constraint and force, and in sheer despair, because we cannot do anything else. Maybe what leads us on most is the hope of getting out of it with a slight wound. Yet that is no good, for we are obliged to come back.

Acting under constraint

At the present moment the food is decent. We call it "offensive fodder." The only thing that makes me keep up is that there are so many men with children among us, and they have far more cares than I have.

Lieremont, August 28th.

I have been again in the infirmary. The heat has increased. Would to God I could become really ill and get out of this beastliness ! We are little more than six miles north-east of Péronne. We have just done eight hours' work. In the evening a French airman dropped a proclamation in German. " German soldiers ! Rumania, the ally of the Central Empires, has just declared war on Austria-Hungary." If this is true it will hasten the end of the war.

August 31st.

This evening we left Lieremont in full kit, and made our way to the reserve position at Rancourt. We arrived completely done up after forty-five and a half hours' marching. Several times we took the wrong road. The fact is, our officers are regular donkeys. We left several men on the way, who only rejoined us this morning.

Rancourt, September 1st.

We are in a cellar ; nineteen of us in so narrow a space that we cannot stretch our legs. And it is full of flies. To-night we have to eat from the field kitchen, and somewhere on the road, and we shall have three days' rations to live on until we are relieved. By day we must not show ourselves because of the airmen. I forgot to say that on August 30th Communion services were held for men of both religions. My comrade and myself did not go. I have lost my faith in this mass butchery. I cannot see the thing otherwise. Any man who retains all his faculties is compelled to lose his faith in such an age as ours where the happiness of millions of men is delivered over to the devil. It is absolutely inconceivable.

Rancourt, September 2nd.

The news is confirmed that Rumania has declared war upon us. Ah, God, if a man could only find some way out of this chaos ! No one knows for what reason and for what aim we have made war. How much longer will this terror last? I get giddy when I think of it. And you, my dear parents, you must be dying of worry and anguish! Oh, my poor mother, if only I could hold you in my arms!

Rancourt, September 4th.

Yesterday, Sunday, all our 1st Battalion, with the commander and all the officers and men—the complete battalion—was captured by the French in front of Maurepas. It seems the French have advanced a mile and a half. A hair's-breadth more and I should have been captured with them. Our proud 1st Franz Battalion has knocked under. I give up trying to describe **Hopeless conditions** the impression it made upon us. All my friends, all my comrades, are lost to me, and more than ever I have the feeling of being abandoned to my fate. My comrade has had a good wound. The lucky devil has gone back to Germany. The lucky devil! Our company actually consists of one lieutenant, two sergeants, two corporals, and thirty-four men instead of one hundred and ninety-eight it had before. All four companies of the battalion are in the same condition. Everything is done for. For the moment we are in a wood under canvas.

Rancourt, September 6th.

We slept at night in the rain. Very hard. At midnight we set out, and we were as dirty as pigs when we reached this nest of vermin and flies—Rancourt. In the cellars it was just a dunghill that we had for quarters. We have neither time nor means of cleaning ourselves. It is an utter dog's life, and I am astonished we can remain alive in such conditions. If you only knew what I feel. Disgust is nothing to it. We envy the lucky beggars who have been taken prisoners, or have been slightly wounded and so got out of it.

September 7th.

Yesterday at eleven o'clock, we left for this place, the rest of the 1st Battalion, to take up the position. On reaching the third-line trench we lost our way. I was not alone this time. Two groups of ten men were in the same case. As by magic our officers disappeared from the surface of the earth. So again we were left alone. We wandered for some hours in this labyrinth, stumbling from one shell-hole into another, and at last we decided to return to Rancourt. We went back there and got into the cellar we had occupied before and slept till the next day. At ten o'clock we got up, ate and drank all we carried, and set out to find the regimental Staff."

Here the diary ends, as the Zouaves of France came up with bomb and bayonet. It will be seen that it was the crack 1st Battalion that suddenly surrendered. Then a remnant of it, having been abandoned by its officers, ran away from the position it had been ordered to hold, with the result that two regiments of Zouaves drove for some miles through the German lines and reached Boucha-

vesnes. Since the days of Frederick the Great the Prussian Guard had been the model of all soldiers of the world. At worst, as in that great catchword of the days of Napoleon, it had known how to die. Now it was not only beaten, which is an accident that may happen to any corps through the fault of the higher command, but it was reduced to despair.

Battered by the new British armies at Contalmaison, outfought by the Australians at Pozières, and hammered by the French infantry of the line and Zouaves at Le Forest and Rancourt, the remnants of the three divisions of the Prussian Guard had to be withdrawn from the field. Their officers, picked from the best fighting men of the old Prussian nobility, hid in dug-outs, and left their men to do whatever they liked, which was either to break and fly for shelter to the rear or to give themselves up at the first opportunity.

The mechanism of the German war-machine was still very strong after the Franco-British offensive had proceeded with grim irregularity on the Somme for three months. Krupps were accelerating their output by getting their large new works in Bavaria into productive order. The German Flying Corps, which had shown such marked inferiority throughout the campaign, was being provided with a large number of improved machines. The amount of heavy shell fired by the enemy was increasing, and the task before the Allies still remained arduous and long. But there were clear and manifold signs that the spirit of the best Prussian troops—Guardsmen, Brandenburgers, and others — was no **German** longer what it had been. Some Bavarians **demoralisation** had begun to revolt at Verdun, when the process of mass butchery, to which the diarist Guardsman refers, was only in its opening stage. At Verdun the Prussian troops had held on loyally and stubbornly, had surrounded the mutinous Bavarians, and had been not merely ready but eager to shoot them down. But now the finest of the Prussians were losing faith in their leaders and hope in the future. Unfortunately, events in the East were to restore German confidence and undo much of the work done so painfully on the Somme.

FRENCH GUNNERS HOLDING THEIR EARS AGAINST THE BARK OF A HUGE NAVAL GUN.

CHAPTER CL.

THE GREAT BRITISH BATTLES OF THE SOMME.

I.—The Holding Battles on the Ancre.

By Edward Wright.

Somme Operations Resemble Siege of Sebastopol—United States Army Takes Four Years to Travel Eight Miles to Richmond—Gigantic Trial of Strength Upon a Fortified Line—Superior Franco-British Man-Power Balanced by Germany's Production of Steel—Convict Machine-Gunners Work their Sentences Out in the Field—Why the Germans were Confident they Could Resist—Their Unparalleled System of Fortification and Improved Machine-Gun Defence—British Difficulties in Handling Siege Ordnance—New Armies Go Into Battle to Learn How to Fight—Germans Break Canadian Line at Ypres to Prevent Allied Offensive—Fine Recovery by Canadians Saves the Situation—Great British Bombardment on Ninety-Mile Front—Sir Douglas Haig Misleads the Enemy and Induces him to Weaken his Somme Defences—Extraordinary Gallantry of Midlanders at Gommecourt—London Territorials Break into Enemy's Line but are Cut Off by the German Guns—Heroic Charge of British Troops at Serre—German Gunners Annihilate their Own Infantry—Not One Straggler in the British Army—Terrific Struggle around Beaumont-Hamel—Immortal Achievement by Ulster Division—Glorious Tragedy of the Ancre Brook—Englishmen and Newfoundlanders Charge to the Death—Thiepval Rushed and Lost.

E have seen in the previous chapter that General Foch and Sir Douglas Haig planned their combined operations on the Somme according to old-fashioned methods of siege warfare. That is to say, instead of attempting in an abrupt, decisive way to pierce the enemy lines, they intended gradually to master one by one the zones of hostile works. We must, therefore, remember when reading the story of the Somme that the allied operations more closely resemble the Franco-British campaign against Sebastopol than any modern battle except Verdun.

When the French and British armies laid siege to Sebastopol they were for a long time unable to envelop the great arsenal on the Black Sea. The defending Russian forces remained in complete communication with the interior of Russia, and were able to bring up troops for the defence outnumbering the troops that were attacking. Hence the progress of the Allies seemed exceedingly slow, and for nearly a year the ground gained at heavy cost of life could be measured on the ordinary map only with a microscope. Pessimistic Frenchmen and Britons were able

to calculate that, at the rate of time occupied in winning the Mamelon, centuries would elapse before the Franco-British forces reached Moscow.

But, in fact, the struggle in the Crimea was not an ordinary siege. It was a prolonged trial of strength between the Russian Empire and the French and British Empires. And when at last the sustained pressure of the Allies forced the Russians out of a few miles of powerfully-fortified lines, the Tsar asked for terms of peace, though he had scarcely lost any territory. Vast as were his resources in man-power, he found that the great siege operations had decided the ultimate issue.

Therefore, we must not measure the Franco-British advance between the Ancre and the Somme on a large map. In addition to the parallel of the Crimean War we might bear in mind also one of the opening incidents of the American Civil War, when the United States Army moved upon the Confederate capital of Richmond. The Federal troops reached a signpost reading, "Eight miles to Richmond." A satirical Confederate had altered the legend to "Only eight miles to Richmond." It took the

THE BRITISH COMMANDER-IN-CHIEF.
Wherever Sir Douglas Haig was seen during the Somme battles his air of cheerful confidence was noted.

PICTURING THE WAR.
[Canadian official photograph.
Canadian official photographers collecting film records while artillery observers are watching the fall of shells on the German trenches.

Federal armies of over a million men nearly four years to travel those eight miles. There were times when it seemed that Richmond would never be reached by a victorious Federal army. But when the break at last occurred, it was as decisive as the sudden movement of violence which a winning Japanese wrestler makes, after being engaged for hours in an apparently motionless struggle with an opponent. When the Confederate lines broke, more than the eight miles of fortified ground in front of Richmond were lost. The man-
American Civil War hood of the Southern States was destroyed
precedent or disabled, and all the treasure, food, and power in those States exhausted.
The campaign on the Ancre and the Somme was a gigantic trial of strength, upon a fortified line, between the British Empire and France and her colonies on the one side, and some two-thirds of the military and warlike industrial forces of Germany on the other side. Except for a comparatively small diversion of the French strength to Salonika, and some more serious distractions of effort on the part of the British Empire in Egypt, Salonika, Mesopotamia, and East Africa, the entire military forces of France and her colonies and the British Empire, with troops from Belgium, were arrayed against a large part of the land forces of Germany. For, from Riga to the Bukovina, Russia not only held the Germans on the German sectors of the eastern front, but inflicted such defeats on the main Austro-Hungarian armies as compelled the Germans to reinforce heavily their tottering allies.

In these circumstances the combined French and British man-power was considerably superior to the available German man-power. But this superiority in men did not of itself promise victory. Germany was still ahead of the Allies in the production of steel. The incomparable achievements of the German steel-makers rank among the dominating features of the war. With some help from the Austrians they had to work against Great Britain, France, Russia, Canada, Japan, and the United States. Yet, despite this enormous rivalry, the Teutonic steel-makers succeeded in producing more steel than their military and naval authorities wanted. German steel was so superabundant during the crisis of the war that it was used on railways for sleepers, in order to save that wealth in German forests with which German merchants intended

to monopolise various important timber industries when peace was made.

After siting 2,000 howitzers and cannon around Verdun in May, 1916, the German Chief of Staff still possessed more artillery than he could use with his formations. When the Battle of the Somme opened he was engaged in reducing each division to two-thirds of its strength in infantry, and using the other third to form new divisions, for each of which some two hundred new guns, with practised artillerymen, were waiting. Only about half of the young German recruits of the 1916 class appear to have been brought into action by the beginning of July,

FOLLOWING A MEMORABLE FIGHT.
[Crown copyright.
Three Staff officers watching the progress of the Battle of Pozières. One of them has been putting the finishing touches to a field chart.

1916. General von Falkenhayn was, with admirable statesmanship, trying to save the German lads of twenty-one, twenty, and nineteen years of age, keeping them as much as possible in depôts and training camps, and employing older men of the Landsturm class as a kind of stucco work to fill the gaps of little importance between his machine-gun redoubts and sunken parks of artillery.

He produced a new type of machine-gunner by taking out of prison thousands of able-bodied convicts and allowing them to redeem their sentences by desperate service in the field. Some of these men were chained to the machine-guns they had **German convict** been trained to use, in order to make sure **machine-gunners** that they would fight to the end. Others were closely watched in battle by non-commissioned officers with revolvers. The use of chains, however, seems to have been exceptional, as many of the worst criminals of Germany seem to have fought quite as ferociously as the average virtuous conscript.

The machine-gun was the supreme weapon of defence of the Teutons. In 1913 the plant for making machine-guns had been secretly extended in a very large way to provide for the enormous increase of German machine-guns which took all French, Russian, and British generals by surprise in 1914. Then, in the magnificent organisation of German munition works in the winter of 1914, tens of thousands of machine-tools normally employed in ordinary work were put on to machine-gun making, and in a few months the German machine-gun was produced in such extraordinary numbers as to balance the hundred thousand new riflemen Great Britain brought to the front. Possessing a superabundance of steel, and as many machine-tools as she could find hands to work, Germany continued to increase her machine-guns until the marksmen she had originally employed as sharpshooters were armed with weapons firing six hundred rounds a minute. When the history of the war is made clear we shall probably find that the main reason why the British organisation of snipers won, by the spring of 1916, a definite superiority over the Jägers of Germany was that most of the Jägers had been withdrawn from the shell-holes in No Man's Land into machine-gun redoubts behind the barbed-wire.

British snipers versus Jagers For at the end of two years of terrific warfare Germany was in the extraordinary position of having more weapons than she could use. In a very general way it might be said that the German infantry, with all its best marksmen removed into the machine-gun organisation, became merely the sentinel force that apprised machine-gunners and artillerymen of the position of an attacking enemy, and discovered, by means of bombing raids, the position of an enemy standing on the defensive.

The German Staff did not waste the lives of its troops, even when it flung them against Verdun by the hundred thousand. The enemy always strove to accomplish his ends by mechanical power, so as to economise the manhood of his nation. When he failed in this aim, as he did at Verdun, it was not for want of hard study in the science of slaughter, but for lack of as inventive a mind as the best French generals possessed. To arrive at a clear and just estimate of the achievement of the British armies between the Ancre and the Somme we must revise some of our ideas about Neuve Chapelle, Rouges Bancs, Festubert, and Loos, and allow that the probable result **Teuton power of defence** of these actions was that the British losses were not less and possibly were more than the German losses. The Germans, therefore, were not entirely without grounds for regarding Loos, Festubert, Rouges Bancs, and Neuve Chapelle in the same light as the British regarded the First and Second Battles of Ypres. In plain language, the enemy had maintained a victorious defence in four great battles, and these successes of his at least offset the two great defensive victories at Ypres—possibly outweighed these.

Moreover, the larger part of the Regular British Army and a considerable part of the British Reserve and Territorial forces had been exhausted in vain attempts to break the enemy line. At Loos the first hundred thousand men of the new national army had come into action, and had been seriously depleted in strength. The German Staff, therefore, considered that the small force of well-trained British troops had been worn down, and that the vaster body of fresh men could be repulsed with comparatively

ROLL-CALL OF THE SEAFORTHS AFTER THE FIRST DAY'S BATTLE ON THE SOMME.
The great allied offensive began at half-past seven in the morning of July 1st, 1916, and was delivered with the utmost gallantry. Our casualties were necessarily heavy, but a large proportion were comparatively slight wounds from shrapnel and machine-gun fire.

INDIAN CAVALRY ASSEMBLED READY TO ADVANCE INTO ACTION ON FRANCE'S DAY, JULY 14TH, 1916.

The second stage of the Battle of the Somme began on July 14th, 1916—France's day—with an attack on the main German second lines between Pozières and Longueval. The most dramatic incident was a splendid and successful charge of Dragoon Guards and Deccan Horse through the cornfields, the first time our cavalry had been in action for a period of eighteen months.

small effort. It expected that the German veteran artillerymen and veteran machine-gunners would work among the charging masses of British recruits more havoc than the veterans of the Regular British Army at Ypres in October, 1914, had worked among the charging masses of hastily-trained German recruits.

The German Staff had two important grounds for their confidence in German power of resistance. In the first place, its system of field fortification was of incomparable strength. Nothing approaching it had been seen since the days when the Chinese Wall and the Roman Wall were constructed. On some sectors, twenty miles in length, there were from three to four hundred miles of connected earthworks, caverns, and tunnels, where barbed-wire was used in a way that showed the superabundance of German iron. One-ton shells could not penetrate the principal subterranean fortress centres. The forts of Liège, Namur, Antwerp, and Paris were of small strength when compared with the gigantic German system of defence. All that the Germans had learnt when using their monster siege-guns against Belgian, French, and Russian works of armoured concrete had been skilfully employed in making their own lines impregnable.

After the Battle of Loos they perfected their system of defence by a new method of machine-gun fire. Instead of bringing the gun on to the parapet to repel a hostile charge, they constructed, in the redoubts, loopholes almost on ground-level, from which their gunners in bomb-proof chambers could rake the ankles, waist, and breast of attacking infantry. Below the bomb-proof chambers, which resisted all but the heaviest shell, was a lower cavern that no shell could penetrate. In important positions hoists were installed, by means of which the machine-guns could be lowered into the cavern during a hostile bombardment, and almost instantaneously raised to the loophole when hostile infantry appeared. Large stores of hand-grenades, small-arms ammunition, and shells were accumulated in caverns in the lines against the British and French movement. At every point there was more ammunition to hand than any charging British force could bring with it or procure afterwards. This elaborate organisation was the first reason for the confidence of the German Staff.

In the second place, the German Staff reckoned that an attacking British army would be inept in heavy artillery work and Staff work. In the British Navy it takes many years to make a first-rate gunlayer capable of handling the 12, 13·5, and 15 in. guns with exact skill. Howitzers of similar calibre had become the most important of military weapons, though thousands of 6 in. and 9·2 in. pieces of ordnance constituted the only possible means of shattering the new, deeply-excavated systems of field fortification. Great Britain had never foreseen the need of such large pieces in land warfare. Her small original force of Royal Garrison Artillery, trained in the use of heavy guns, had only a few 9·2 in. weapons and a scanty number of 6 in. howitzers. The consequence was that when the Royal Garrison Artillery had to be expanded into a very great body of men and officers, the recruits had to wait a long time before they could be provided with even a few

German Staff confidence

REPLENISHING THE BATTERY BY THE ROADSIDE. [*British official photograph.*]
Reserve of munitions just arrived at a British battery. R.F.A. men were discharging their load of shells while the guns hidden among the brushwood continued to shell the enemy lines.

guns for training purposes. At the front, Royal Marines with naval guns at first did what they could to supply the place of a military siege train. But the guns that could be spared from the Navy were relatively few in number and absolutely inadequate in character. For it was not guns that were most needed for penetrating enemy subterranean fortresses, but heavy howitzers, employed with a special and delicate technique. When the British Ministry of Munitions began to supply heavy howitzers in increasingly large calibre there was a tendency among the British public to regard the problem in armament as solved.

But, in point of fact, the national army was only at the beginning of its greatest difficulty. A large supply of siege-guns and high-explosive shell was only the material and secondary factor in the matter. The primary and intellectual factor was that of the men behind the guns. How were the new recruits to find, in a few months, the means of becoming expert in their arduous and intricately-scientific work ? All the mighty contending Continental armies, maintained by a system of conscription in days of peace, had ready hundreds of thousands of trained gunners, who were worked up, by nearly two years of incessant battle experience, into artillerymen of a magnificent class. The German heavy artillerymen, for instance, after blasting their way into Antwerp, went down to the Belgian coast and there outfought all the battleships and monitors that Great Britain could spare against them, drove off the squadrons of Admiral Hood and Admiral Bacon, and made Zeebrugge for a time a German war port strongly secured against a bombardment by the highly-trained gunlayers of the British Fleet.

Problem of trained gunners

It was against such men as these victorious German artillerymen, with an experience varying from the Dunajec to the Verdun hurricane-fire operations, that the new bodies of inexperienced, hastily-trained Royal Garrison Artillery had to contend. There were, of course, British artillery officers surviving from the small Regular Army to direct some of the batteries. But most of these officers had been promoted from the field-artillery, where they handled little guns. The technique of the new big howitzers, with the new system of aerial control from kite-balloons and aeroplanes, was a perplexing matter even for a field-artillery officer of experience. It was as if the British Army, mainly accustomed to 3·3 in. guns, were suddenly to be provided with as large ordnance as the British Navy, and set to fire against British gun-layers and British gunnery lieutenants who had been practising for ten years with their gigantic pieces.

Germany's new magazine-rifle

The training of the new British infantry was good. Indeed, it was miraculously good, and in one branch of attack—bomb-throwing—its skill seems to have been at least equal to all that which the troops of Germany had acquired in a year of trench warfare. The musketry of the infantry, though far from equalling that of the incomparable riflemen at Mons and Ypres, appears to have been almost as effective as that which the French conscripts attained with their inferior Lebel rifle. The Germans had a new magazine rifle, holding twenty rounds, but did not use it as well as the new British soldier used his Lee-Enfield. And even in bayonet work the new British soldier was not at much disadvantage when charging an average German force. The British machine-gunner was also good, having been promoted by reason of his special marksmanship from the multitude of the new infantry.

The new British field-artillery seems to have been of fair quality. Before the war the French used to say it took ten years to make a first-class man for their 3 in. gun. Naturally, British civilians who entered the Army in 1914 and 1915 were not transformed by the summer of 1916 into the peers of the field-gunners of France. But their native alertness of mind and the fine system of accelerated training designed for them, together with the opportunities for battle practice they received on first going to the front, transformed them into men of a useful sort. They needed an abundance of shell, though with this abundance they did not always breach the hostile zones of wire entanglement; still less could they sweep with unexpected gusts difficult bits of land as French gunners could. But having regard to the extraordinary circumstances, their work was most praiseworthy. All this the German Staff allowed in its study of the situation on the western front. Having achieved most of its great successes east and west by means of siege-guns, worked by the most highly trained body of expert gunners outside the British Navy, the German High Command concluded that the British attack would be wrecked through inefficient handling of the British heavy artillery.

What the enemy expected

The enemy expected that there would be no close and precise co-operation between the advancing waves of British infantry and the battering-ram of British heavy shell fire. Sir Douglas Haig divined what the enemy thought in the matter, and frankly recognised the factors of weakness in his own vast but improvised forces. In the first grand clash of Briton and Teuton he took all possible steps to remedy the inexperience of his troops.

[*British official photograph.*

THE STRUGGLE FOR THE SPUR: SHELLS BURSTING NEAR THIEPVAL.
Thiepval was won by the British, September 27th, 1916, after terrific fighting, and with its capture—and that of Combles by the French and British in co-operation—the whole Bapaume Valley was dominated.

[Canadian official photograph.
CLOSE VIEW OF GERMAN GAS SHELLS EXPLODING NEAR THE PARAPET OF THE CANADIAN TRENCHES.
This remarkable impression was secured by the Canadian official photographer actually installed with his apparatus in the trenches, which had been the constant target of enemy shells judging by the pock-marked condition of the terrain in front of the parapet.

At the opening of the campaign of the Ancre and the Somme the machinery of Staff control in the new national British Army was still imperfectly tested. Sufficient officers of experience survived the wreck of the regular forces to make the material work of British organisation in France and Flanders a monument to the genius of their race. Railway and motor transport, food and water supplies, and all the business side of warfare were conducted with foresight and high energy. But, on the other hand, the enormously enlarged corps of British Staff officers contained many men who had never helped to manœuvre masses of troops on a modern battlefield against concealed machine-guns and shell curtains of heavy projectiles. For some of the best of them were men who had distinguished themselves in South Africa, and tended instinctively to rely more upon their fund of former experience than upon the lectures they received from officers who came from the front to teach them the new lessons of warfare.

Enemy brigade, divisional, and army corps Staff officers had been tested year after year in grand manœuvres, and finally brought as near as possible to **Differences in** general perfection by twenty-three months **Staff control** of warfare under changing conditions. Standing on the defence, these enemy Staff officers, working by telephone in underground chambers, with regimental officers whose temperaments they had continually tested in the heat of conflict, had a fairly easy mechanical task of a kind to which they were well accustomed. But the new British Staff officers had to help to work brigades and divisions in the open and in a most disconcerting fog of battle, with field-telephone lines breaking under hostile shell fire, platoons and companies continually getting disconnected, and confusion prevailing at those critical points in the line of advance where the controlling mind of the commander was most needed.

All this was foreseen and yet inevitable. The new armies had practically to go into battle to learn how to fight. The German Staff was almost arrogantly confident of its power to cripple permanently the new forces of the British Empire before these forces could learn how to win a siege battle. Sir Douglas Haig and his **Third attack** Staff were quietly confident that, in spite **on Ypres** of the terrible disadvantages under which the new armies laboured, these armies would quickly learn as they went forward, and become in a few months masters of the field. The British public were too optimistic and the French public too pessimistic of the unsounded capacity of these new British levies. Sir Douglas Haig and his army generals did not look forward to any striking success at the start. The increase in munitions was outbalanced by the lack of men with long training. But the British commander reckoned on the native strength of character in his new troops to enable them to win through the terrible period of experiment while they were being moulded in the furnace of battle and there transformed into quickly-made veterans.

By June, 1916, the enemy knew what was coming, and he tried to distract Sir Douglas Haig by starting a third attack on Ypres. After a long and savage bombardment, masses of hostile infantry on June 2nd broke the Canadian line from Hooge to Hill 60, captured Major-General Mercer and Brigadier-General Williams, and threw the Canadians a thousand yards behind their original line. But the next morning the Canadians counter-attacked and regained nearly two-thirds of their lost ground, and on June 13th

"KAMERADEN" FROM MONTAUBAN.

After an advance at Montauban, German soldiers who took refuge in the cellars from the intense bombardment came up and surrendered to passing British infantry. Many of them had been imprisoned in their funk-holes for days, cut off from the communication-trenches by an effective artillery barrage.

assisted a series of ten raiding-parties, who broke into the enemy's fire-trenches and took some prisoners.

When day broke, the bombardment was resumed on a front of ninety miles and the German batteries became curiously silent. The new Royal Garrison Artillery were still only practising and getting an exact knowledge of their weapons and of the science of co-operating with their aerial observers. Heavy explosions of ammunition dumps in the enemy's rear and violent attacks on his gun-pits, resting-places, and lines of communication made this practice fire resemble the real thing. By night all the sky was lighted with the unceasing flash of the guns, and at Amiens and other westerly French towns people began to climb to their roofs in the darkness and watch with grim joy the roaring rim of radiance on the horizon. Nearly a quarter of a million of shells a day were being spent in this enormous registering fire.

Sir Douglas Haig used his parks of new artillery in much the same way as a fencer employs his rapier. Possessing, in his huge fleets of motor-lorries and his network of light and ordinary railways, a rapid means of supplying every sector, the British commander continually shifted the direction of the main head of shell that was pouring from the British war factories. On June 27th he selected the region between the Ancre and the Somme as his chief demonstrating point, and with his great rail-mounted guns steaming into action he pounded the enemy's lines between Gommecourt and Mametz, and then launched a series of raids at this point. At the same time a strong demonstration was made against the important German position at Angres, well to the north of Arras, where the Highland Light Infantry inflicted heavy loss on the Germans and took a considerable number of prisoners.

Gas attacks were used all along the front further to annoy and distract the enemy and induce him to prepare in the wrong place for the coming offensive movement. On June 28th the registering fire ceased and the veritable bombardment opened. Rumours ran, in both France **Opening of bombardment** and Great Britain, that the attack would be made on this day, and that Albert was the principal centre of operations. There may have been some indiscretion on the part of British officers and their relatives that afforded material for the club gossip concerning Albert. On the other hand, the enemy seems to have been misled to a considerable extent by the changing point of intensity of the British fire and by the rumours that his secret agents collected. He expected the attack to occur between Arras and Albert, and his principal artillery and best and most numerous troops were rapidly collected on this line. The troops in the

they again went forward and recovered the ridge between Hooge and Hill 60, and thus made the Ypres salient as secure as possible.

Meanwhile, vast preparations for the grand offensive were proceeding without interruption from the enemy. His swoop against the Canadians was met by the troops of the Dominion, with a little help from the Anzacs on their right and the British troops on their left. Though the Germans employed ten thousand troops to create a diversion, these were fought down by local effort, without producing the least change in the allied scheme. The new heavy artillery began to practise up and down the enemy's line, and the new trench-mortars, which had a special part to play in the coming operations, also battered the enemy's trenches in an apparently aimless way. On June 25th the trial registering of the new British siege-guns was undertaken, with such increasing intensity that the fire resembled the grand bombardment. Armed with a new missile against balloons and airships, the British aviators astonished the enemy by suddenly destroying six of his kite-balloons. In the night the extraordinary heavy gun fire continued and reserve trenches must have suffered rather heavily during the period of the great bombardment. But with stern and effective reticence the army commanders under Prince Rupert of Bavaria refrained from replying to the extraordinary hostile fire. For one of the chief aims of the British gunners, from June 28th to July 1st, was to discover the enemy batteries, which had been reorganised and strengthened in view of the coming attack. In a great artillery duel these batteries could have been destroyed or weakened by fierce counter-firing, and the **Silence of** task of the British infantry would then **enemy batteries** have been much facilitated. The Germans had always begun their great offensives by provoking an artillery duel. But when their aim was to stand upon the defensive they showed resolute wisdom in keeping their guns silent and hidden, and letting their infantry in the trenches endure to the uttermost.

The British guns thus appeared entirely to dominate the battlefield, and when they were joined by the artillery of all the French armies from the Somme to the Aisne, the scene by day and night was one of infernal splendour and fury. Amid the deafening tumult and acrid smoke the work of the infantry was almost as heavy as that of the gunners. In the toil of feeding the guns the crews were not sufficient, and the infantry had to help to transport the shells from the lorries and trucks in order to keep the gunners employed in firing and prevent their ammunition dumps from growing too small afterwards, when prolonged and costly shell curtains would be required to help the infantry movements.

Towards the end of June the raids and the gas attacks augmented in number and violence. At Neuve Chapelle, on June 30th the German position was penetrated deeply to the second line, making it appear that a veritable offensive was contemplated at this point. The Staff of the Crown Prince of Bavaria became anxious and, as some German newspapers afterwards admitted, at last expected a veritable grand attack from Lille to Bapaume. They looked upon the French bombardment, as has already been explained, merely as a demonstration, and thought that Arras would be the centre of conflict, with perhaps Lille on the north and Bapaume on the south as the wings of the terrific struggle. The Vimy Ridge, south of Loos, which had been the scene of an early demonstration by some fine Lancashire troops, was the principal point of concern of the enemy commander, and it was from this ridge to the height of Gommecourt that he arrayed his main forces with new guns and the support of the Prussian Guard. But when the hundreds of British guns were suddenly augmented by hundreds of quick-

firing mortars, at dawn on July 1st, 1916, the Germans found they had been outplayed. Only a small section of the front where they were thoroughly prepared was assailed. This small sector ran from Gommecourt to Thiepval, and here the Prussian Guard, with hundreds of concealed guns, was ready for any event. But south of Thiepval, in the sectors of La Boisselle, Fricourt, Mametz, and Montauban and a dozen more villages to the south, which were attacked by the British and the French, the enemy was taken at a disadvantage.

This was a triumphant success for the munition workers of the Western Allies. At an expense of millions of shells, and the life of the tubing of hundreds of guns, such a stress of fire had been maintained for four days and four nights around Lille, the Vimy Ridge, and Arras that the enemy expected an attempt would be made to thrust through towards Douai and Cambrai. It was, indeed, rumoured that he massed at last nearly twenty-four divisions in the

CLEARING LURKING GERMANS OUT OF THE CELLARS UNDERNEATH MONTAUBAN.
Montauban was captured in the early days of the great advance. The maze of underground cellars had been used as store-houses and living quarters, connected by long galleries, and all these had to be cleared of lurking enemies by armed parties carrying electric-torches.

E

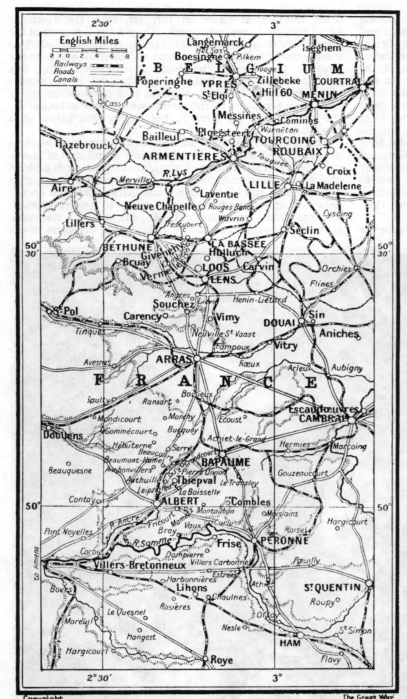

GENERAL MAP OF THE BRITISH FRONT FROM YPRES TO PÉRONNE.

which Sir Douglas Haig made with his heavy guns. But as the most gigantic of these guns fired from rails, it could rapidly be moved along the network of light lines to the empty chalk downland by the Somme River. This was a country of difficult and intricate undulations that offered no immediate prize to the attacking Allies.

To General Foch falls the honour and the responsibility for selecting the apparently uninviting region of the Somme as the point of attack. He was able, with the help of Sir Douglas Haig, to convince his chief that a pure military operation on the Somme, where the British had excellent means of communication and the French possessed also a magnificent railway service, was the best available means of answering the increasing German menace to Verdun. It was necessary, in the interests of all the Allies, that the untried British levies should prove themselves in battle as soon as possible. And nothing was more favourable than that the chief striking forces of France should make use of the main line from Amiens to Paris to come strongly into action by the side of their new comrades-in-arms.

If only the millions of citizen soldiers of the British Empire, with their gigantic new material, could be transformed into experienced fighting men of the scientific school, without being crippled in the process of winning experience, the cause for which France, Russia, Italy, Belgium, and Serbia were fighting would be enormously promoted. Rumania was hesitating because she thought that the great new British Army, with its great new guns and its great new shell supplies, was a mere lath-and-plaster façade, without the solid strength of a military State possessing millions of well-trained conscripts.

Everything depended on the quality of the new British troops. At Verdun, Germany, the most powerful military State in the world, had lost men at the rate of a hundred thousand a month, without in the end making any very important gain of ground. A counter-attack lasting a few hours was ere long to rob her of her most expensive gains. Great Britain, a new-comer among modern military States, was destined to grind forward, incurring losses proportionately serious. But her recruits were about to show that they could hold what they won with a tenacity surpassing that of the veteran corps of the enemy. For about two and a half months a terrible struggle raged between the Ancre and the Somme, until something like a miracle occurred, and by painful and laborious ways the Briton won the mastery. He seemed to improve in every direction, and by astonishing skill as well as downright pluck he outfought the enemy and stormed the main crest of the Bapaume ridges.

In spite of heavy losses, which must have been at least as large as those which the Germans incurred in their sheltered defences, the outcome was inspiriting to all the Allies and disheartening to the Central Empires. It meant that the new armies had trained themselves in action into one of the most efficient fighting forces in the world. All that the British nation and Mr. Lloyd George had accomplished, in raising and arming millions of men with a speed hitherto unknown in history, was perfected by the achievement of Sir Douglas Haig and his army commanders and Staff, in transforming with utterly amazing rapidity an extraordinary multitude of untried recruits into practised fighting men of fine quality. Thus a new factor of great moment appeared in Europe, and it became a question of increasing the output of munitions

New factor in the war

sectors fed from his great rail-head at Cambrai. One of the reasons why he was expectant of an attack on his northern wing was that this wing covered most of the coal-mines of North-Western France. The coal-field had been the chief and immediate objective of the earlier Franco-British attacks. With an abundance of native coal that could be transported cheaply by canal to her munition centres, France would have been able to wage the war with increased strength, and neither the German General Staff nor the Staff of Prince Rupert thought that the great Franco-British movement would be designed without any direct regard for the lost French coal-field. In the German operations at Verdun, as we have seen, the vital iron basin of Briev had entered largely into the German commander's choice of the sector he attacked. All this went greatly to increase the weight of the mighty and expensive feint northward

Supports moving up on the morning of September 25th, 1916, the day when our troops, attacking everywhere with success, captured the two militarily important villages of Morval and Lesbœufs, and thereby practically severed the enemy's communications with Combles.

British troops advancing on the crest of the hill. Morval stood on a height north of Combles, and, with its subterranean quarries, system of trenches, and wire entanglements, constituted a formidable fortress.

[*British official photographs.*

Germans after being taken prisoners were employed to carry back our wounded from Morval. The number of prisoners taken on the 25th was large, and in comparison with the results achieved the British losses were comparatively small.

SCENES IN THE SUCCESSFUL ADVANCE UPON MORVAL, SEPTEMBER 25TH, 1916.

[Canadian official photograph.

THE PICK FOLLOWS THE BAYONET.
Types of Canada's finest manhood, men from the Far West used to life in the open air, and thus some of the most formidable fighters among the Empire's armies. This illustration shows them proceeding to consolidate new gains on the Somme front.

and maintaining the strength of the new armies to ensure victory. Great Britain at last had men able to handle all the gigantic machinery of war with precision and thorough technique, so that the increase in new machinery at last promised to be decisive.

All this we must bear in mind when studying the first phase of the operations. For in this first phase there are many episodes which seem disheartening unless we clearly understand that they were only incidents in a long and eventually successful apprenticeship in warfare waged by half-trained and untried men.

The attack was conducted by the Fourth British Army, numbering some 144,000 infantrymen, arranged in six army corps. Near Gommecourt was the Seventh Army Corps, under Lieutenant - General Sir T. D'Oyly Snow; then came the Eight Army Corps, under Lieutenant-General Sir A. Hunter-Weston; the Tenth Army Corps, under Lieutenant-General Sir T. Morland; the Third Army Corps, under Lieutenant-General Sir W. P. Pulteney; the Fifteenth Army Corps, under Lieutenant-General H. S. Horne, and the Thirteenth Army Corps, under Lieutenant-General W. N. Congreve. The leader of the Immortal Division at Ypres in 1914, General Sir Henry Rawlinson, promoted chief of the Fourth Army, was in command; Sir Douglas Haig, as Commander-in-Chief, exercised general control, with Lieutenant-General Sir L. E. Kiggell as his Chief of General Staff. The opposing commanders were General von Marschall, on the Gommecourt-Serre front, and General von Below, with General Sixt von Armin as one of his army corps commanders, on the Somme front.

The opposing army leaders

When the British guns lifted at half-past one in the morning of July 1st, 1916, all the attacking forces from Gommecourt to Thiepval rushed into an inferno. The opposing fronts faced each other on gentle slopes, with the narrow bottom of the Ancre brook making a level in the southern part. The Germans held a series of high points of great natural strength, each of which had been turned into an underground Gibraltar, interlocking with each other and commanding each other. The northern height of Gommecourt was the westernmost German salient in France, and it had therefore been fortified with extreme industry and skill and garrisoned by the Prussian Guard. The German artillery was densely massed in the rear of the seamed and ravined plateau. There were hundreds of new 6 in. guns firing shrapnel and maintaining two or more wide and distinct curtains of death over the ground where the British troops charged.

The enemy knew the great movement was coming. Before the quick-firing mortars ceased to pound the enemy's fire-trench, and before the field-artillery finished shooting down the wire entanglements and the heavy guns lifted on the hostile rear, German gunners were back in their bomb-proof shelters and traversing the ground between the front with their terrible cross-fires of streams of bullets. All along the British line dense smoke-screens were projected over the enemy's trenches to blind his gunners and his observation officers. But this device did not have full effect, as the hostile machine-guns and artillery had all their ranges carefully marked, and maintained a regular mechanical sweep of fire over No Man's Land and the British trenches. It was as though a gigantic single machine-gun was levelled at the British lines, worked by some mighty engine. There were, however, some curious differences in the manner in which the heroic charging divisions went to their death.

North of Gommecourt a division of Midland troops had the most difficult task of all. They were on the extreme northern edge of the attacking line, and had to open the battle by making a thrust along the northern side of the high-wooded enemy salient at Gommecourt. The **Heroic Midlanders at Gommecourt** height itself was not assailed, as it was impregnable to a frontal attack, but an attempt was made to envelop it by Midland troops on the north side and London troops on the south side. The Germans were well prepared on this sector, being in very strong force with many new guns, and with their positions not seriously injured by the great British bombardment. There was a very wide gap between the opposing lines, and though one of the Midland battalions, in a splendid effort, drove a trench the previous night towards the enemy's parapet and thus reduced the charging distance, the assault failed.

For when the troops came out steadily and coolly, they were swept by machine-gun fire on their flank from the peak of Gommecourt, raked in front by streams of bullets, and further crushed by a shell curtain between the wire entanglements. So numerous were the German guns that they were able to maintain another barrage over the British trenches. The Midlanders showed extraordinary gallantry by marching through this enveloping storm of death. But they were brought down in such numbers that only a remnant reached the German line, and the reserves, with the shell curtains falling behind them and before them, were unable to strike home with any effect. The courage of the troops was glorious, but the enemy's machinery of slaughter was too powerful and precise to be overcome. The heroic remnants, that had attempted to make a long thrust below the peak, were at last recalled after reaching the point they had been set to attain.

> Now all is done that men can do,
> And all is done in vain.

So it must have seemed to the broken and withdrawing Midlanders. But, like all the apparently beaten British

Sir Douglas Haig (right) with Sir Henry Rawlinson, commander of an army on the Somme.

Wiring party off to consolidate newly=won terrain on the western front.

Infantry leaving the trenches to take part in the battle before Morval.

Reserves and stretcher=bearers moving up on the morning of September 25th, 1916.

Bombing party setting out for the German trenches in single file.

While waiting for the order to advance: A young Canadian officer giving some final instructions to his men.

troops on the northern sector of attack, they were accomplishing the heaviest work of victory on the glorious July 1st, though they did not know at the time that they were in any way successful. We have seen that the enemy had a large number of new guns, a vast store of shell, and two divisions of the Guards Corps as a local strategic reserve—all ready to strengthen any weak part of his line. This great mass of men and guns was partly misplaced, through being stretched above Arras; and at any cost it had to be prevented from moving quickly down to the Somme, where it was urgently and vitally needed.

Splendid London Territorials

The Midland Division was the first British force to engage in the great northern holding action, which made the British and French northern successes permanent and less costly at the critical junction-point of the Franco-British forces.

Then to the south of the Gommecourt wooded height the splendid London Territorial Division succeeded in making a complete thrust along the great German salient. In charging, the men had to cover a very broad stretch of ground four hundred yards deep in some places. Yet they almost completely escaped the front and flank machine-gun fire which shattered the strength of the Midland charge. Their good fortune was probably due to the fact that the wind was in their favour. Blowing from the south-west, it rolled the black clouds of screen smoke in blinding, choking masses over all the hostile gun positions, whereas the Midlanders, being on the northern side of the high German wedge, could not get the wind to carry their smoke-screens against the enemy. All along the changing angles of the fighting front this deadly difference in the action of the smoke-screen was found. As the wind was south-west, only hostile trenches lying on a northerly or north-easterly line were liable to be smothered in the black smoke discharged from cylinders by the British troops. All trenches in the German angles running south of the attacking force were saved from the smoke-screen, and the German machine-gunners in the southern positions had a clear field of fire.

The enemy tried to crush the charge at the outset by an enormous barrage of high-explosive shell. The great bursts of explosion opened the ground under the racing feet of the men, destroyed some of them so that they could not be traced, and caught many others with flying fragments of steel. Those who survived dared not look back, for fear of weakening themselves by the sight of their stricken friends. Half walking and half running they reached the ruin of the German first-line trenches, which was a sea of tumbled earth, timber wreckage, and strewn sand-bags. But many of the dug-outs, going thirty feet down, had remained intact. As the line had been strongly held, they were full of Germans, who dauntlessly came forth with bombs and machine-guns to contest the position. The high-nerved and alert Londoners, however, remained masters of the situation. A number of them swirled into the strong underground system on the left, and with their hand-bombs knocked out machine-guns and machine-gun crews. On the right another battalion, with equal quickness, stormed a formidable redoubt in a very nasty piece of ground. Then, secure at the wings, the centre

went forward, part staying to clear the caverns while others bombed their way down the shattered German communications. Some four hundred prisoners were taken with remarkable ease and still more remarkable celerity. Apparently it was a notable victory, for everything that London had been asked to win had been won.

It was one of the quickest pieces of work that had been done in the war. But when the armed guards tried to escort the first batch of prisoners to the British lines an obstacle was met. The enemy's wall of fire had become impassable. Some two hundred prisoners were rushed through it, but many more perished with their guards. The German gunners must have seen their own grey-clad men going back, but they sternly killed them by the hundred with a continually increasing shower of shell rather than allow any British soldiers to come forward.

For some hours the Londoners held on to the first zone of captured works containing three lines of trenches and to various strongholds and redoubts in front of the second zone of defences. Meanwhile, the other British troops on either side of the London Division had been

LOOKING TOWARDS A VALUABLE PRIZE. *[British official photograph.*
Within a hundred yards of Thiepval two vigilant Britons were keeping watch on the enemy, awaiting a favourable moment when they and their comrades could go forward and capture this important position at the bayonet's point.

beaten back, leaving the metropolitan troops in a salient of the enemy's lines. Thereupon, the Germans, having held their ground successfully on the northern and southern sectors near Gommecourt, massed their guns on the Londoners. In addition to intensifying the curtain of high explosive and shrapnel over No Man's Land, that prevented supplies of reinforcements from arriving, the phalanxes of German artillery smashed the British trenches and communications.

Numerous as was the British artillery, which had apparently dominated all the field to a depth of ten miles for a week, it could not cope with the unexpected number of hidden German guns. The command of the air won by British aviators was not of much immediate use, **Hidden German gun-trap** as an extraordinary quickness and precision in discovering the hostile gun positions and registering upon them would have been needed to wage a successful artillery duel.

It will be remembered that in the same operation the French troops at Curlu were caught in a similar trap, but were rescued by their aerial artillery, who so controlled the fire that the hostile counter-attacking force was

TAKING COVER.
Motor machine-guns taking cover in a sunken road.

LIMBERED UP AND AWAY AT FULL SPEED.
Motor machine-gun battery leaving camp in answer to a signalled summons from a hotly-pressed part of the front.

[*British official photographs.*

obliterated. The Londoners, however, do not seem to have been assisted in this way, as it was only later that the British Staff fully adopted the French method of aerial control for infantry attacks. The trapped London battalions were assailed by numerous parties of bomb-throwers, who had abundant ammunition and maintained a furious combat until the small supply of bombs of the Britons was exhausted. Desperate efforts were made by the Territorial reserves to get new bomb supplies through the walls of shell fire. A party of sixty men set out; three came back. All the carrying parties failed, with terrible casualties, and many single men perished in vain attempts to get through with bombs. The British guns tried to maintain a similar impassable barrage over the German communications, but the German bomb-throwers, men of high courage and audacity, not only got through the shell curtain, but crossed in small groups on the top of the trenches and flung their missiles down upon the Londoners.

Londoners' terrible ordeal

Late in the afternoon the battalion on the left of the salient were enfiladed by heavy machine-gun fire, and the supply of bombs was practically exhausted. For some time the heroic Londoners went about collecting German bombs, but this curious method of getting supplies was soon worked out. At last, surrounded by increasing numbers of hostile bomb-throwers, hammered by shell fire, swept by streams of bullets from machine-guns, and with most of their leading men picked off by snipers, the Londoners left a series of heroic rearguards, and, carrying their wounded, retreated—a tragically diminished force—through the barrages of their own lines A very fine stand was made on the left of the salient by an officer

and seven of his men. All ammunition was finished; the bombers had empty hands and only a few cartridges remained. The officer collected the cartridges, and with his seven men held the barricade until it was blown away and five of the defenders killed. The two remaining men and the officer held the enemy back alone, and by a miracle of luck managed to get into our own lines with nothing but a few slight wounds.

South of the London Territorials at Gommecourt was a quiet gap in the battle such as occurred at intervals all along the fighting-line. Sir Henry Rawlinson left unattacked nearly all the high German strongholds on the downs. Instead of wasting men in a general frontal attack, the British general attempted a series of pincer movements between the hills.

From the British position at Hebuterne a strong British force made a turning movement around the high plateau of Serre in conjunction with another attacking force that set out from Auchonvillers towards Beaumont-Hamel. This was an operation of grand importance, designed to carry the great broken slab of chalk, from which the vital German railway junction of Achiet-le-Grand could be dominated. One of the railway lines from Achiet-le-Grand ran along the Ancre brook and fed the fortress

46

system immediately in front of Bapaume. Another railway line from the junction ran into Bapaume itself, and thence connected by means of light railways with the strongholds around Combles. It had been foreseen by Sir Douglas Haig and his army commanders that the thrust by the Midlanders and Londoners against Gommecourt might only succeed in holding up the enemy's mass of men and guns in the north. But it was hoped that a firm footing would be obtained on the Serre plateau, enabling siege-guns to be brought up against the Achiet rail-head.

Weather favours the Germans A magnificent body of troops from regiments with great traditions engaged in the struggle for the plateau. In front of Hébuterne, however, Prince Rupert of Bavaria had begun his mighty, concealed line of preparations that stretched northward past Arras to Souchez near Lens. The weather, though dry, became overcast and dull, making artillery observation work very difficult. This condition of the air greatly favoured the enemy, as it enabled his numerous new batteries, which had remained silent and hidden during the long British bombardment, to carry out their mechanical work of maintaining curtain fire at marked ranges, with but little serious interruption from the counter-fire of the British guns. And the British gunners, despite their enormous wealth of munitions, could hardly have been expected to prove as expert as the enemy. Especially in regard to indirect firing at sheltered enemy positions in hollows did their preliminary work at times show a lack of precision. Many. of the artillerymen, recruited since the outbreak of war and left to wait for many months till guns could be spared for training purposes, were new to heavy-howitzer work.

The best controlling officers with most experience seem to have been placed against the Fricourt and Montauban sectors, where a permanently successful British advance was an absolute necessity, in order to save the French

from being outflanked and thrown back. And here the British artillery work was such as to excite the admiration of the French, the hostile trenches being pitted with shell-holes as regularly and as closely as a machine punctures the division between postage-stamps. But on the northern sector there were some wire entanglements by the first German fire-trenches which were intact after a bombardment lasting a week. In places the foremost German parapet, though exposed to the fire of British trench-mortars, field-guns, and 6 in., 9·2 in., 12 in., and 15 in. siege ordnance, remained sufficiently uninjured to enable German gunners to hoist their machine-guns on the breast-work and shoot down the charging infantry in the open.

Yet, despite the natural inexpertness of some of the artillery preparation and counter-battery firing, the attack on the Serre plateau was conducted with extraordinary intrepidity. In open order at four yards interval, with a good distance between each wave of assault, the men advanced at a quick marching pace from their assembly trenches around Hébuterne. The enemy's lines ran at all angles, on ground that sometimes sloped up and sometimes sloped down. Thus, although the general attack was made in an easterly direction, some of the assaulting waves rolled north-eastward with a south-westerly wind behind them driving their **British use of** smoke-screen well upon the enemy, while **smoke-screens** other attacking forces, such as that which moved along the valley up to Beaumont-Hamel, advanced in a southerly course and could not use a smoke-screen, as it would have been blown back in their faces.

In one of these clear spaces, where the wind was against the British troops, the enemy displayed an unusual amount of courage. Amid the closing bombardment by quick-firing trench-mortars some of the Prussian Guard hoisted their machine-guns on unbroken parts of the parapet, came out into No Man's Land, and delivered an immediate counter-attack against the charging lines of British troops.

INDIAN CAVALRYMEN ROUND-UP FUGITIVE GERMANS IN "DEVIL'S WOOD."

Delville, or "Devil's" Wood, as it was appropriately nicknamed, will go down to posterity as one of the hottest centres of Armageddon. The bitterest fighting took place here in the early days of the Somme offensive. On one occasion a number of Germans were trapped by a tempest of shells and endeavoured to reach a safer part of their line. At that moment a troop of Indian cavalry dashed in upon them. The enemy surrendered to the Indians, and one of the Germans, who spoke English, asked for mercy on behalf of his comrades.

A DESERTED STRONGHOLD.
[Canadian official photographs.

Once heavily fortified German entrenchments as they appeared after a British bombardment. Equipment scattered about with, on the right, a bayonet stuck into the soil, suggests a precipitate retreat on the part of the occupants of the trench.

German guns and German mortars opened a terrific fire as soon as the British guns lifted, so that the fury and precision of the counter-movement were of a staggering nature. Having regard to the fact that the troops concerned were mainly new levies, whose confidence had been greatly excited by the power of their own guns, and who were caught unexpectedly before their attack had developed, the conduct of the men was beyond praise and beyond comparison.

In no armies is the courage of the men trusted entirely. It has been found in every severe attack and in every arduous defence that a considerable proportion of troops lose heart and, pretending illness or wounds, creep out of the battle-line. This matter was minutely studied by the Germans after the war of 1870, and they found that some of the most successful of their divisions showed in great battles an alarming proportion of malingerers. To guard against this weakening of the line a strong cordon of military police always followed the attacking troops and drove back the irresolute into the firing-line. Only when the fugitives break away in such numbers that the military police cannot cope with them, even by shooting some of them down, does a modern line give way. This is how it becomes possible for tyrannical military States, such as Germany and Austria, to compel races they oppress— like the Poles, Bohemians, and Serbs—to fight for them against their will. The Teutonic military police are armed with machine-guns as well as revolvers, and connected by telephone with the batteries. They annihilate any Polish or other troops of oppressed nationality who refuse to stand in the firing-line. Napoleon employed a similar system when he compelled the Prussians to fight for him against the Russians, and all modern armies exercise varying degrees of pressure in the immediate rear of the troops they deploy. This is one of the sombre factors in a modern battle.

But it can now be clearly explained to British readers. For against all precedents and all expectation there was

New Army's splendid spirit

no work for the military police of the British armies on July 1st, 1916. Here there were no stragglers. The New Army at once created for itself the finest tradition in the world. It was composed of troops of such quality as the old Duke of Wellington used fondly to imagine he might have obtained if he could have drawn upon all the manhood of his country—troops such as he sadly confessed he never possessed in any of his wars.

Shells and streams of machine-gun bullets made gaps in the thin lines of khaki figures, but the depleted lines continued to surge forward into the caverned strongholds of the enemy, where relief was obtained from the fire of the German guns at the cost of a ghastly hand-to-hand struggle with bomb and bayonet. The German organisation and resource

A CAPTURED "FUNK-HOLE."

Entrance to a German officer's dug-out. Many of these shelters remained intact in spite of the terrific bombardments.

as displayed in the northern sector were marvellous, but when it came to a sheer test of manhood on fairly equal terms the German veteran was not a match for the British recruit. The Briton's advantage resided largely in his athletic habit of body and his sportsmanlike spirit. A friendly French military critic, indeed, said that the Briton entered the campaign on the Somme as a sporting athlete and emerged from it a cautious professional soldier. In this connection it must be borne in mind that pure pluck and gameness were the only available qualities of race that could have carried the new levies through their fearful ordeal. The punishment they received, to use the word in a sporting sense that offends the Germans, was indescribable. But the men who survived went steadily on. Among them were the Middlesex—the bravest of the brave—the Devons, the Lancashires, South Wales Borderers, the Dublins, Inniskillings, and the Border Regiment. The Royal Irish Fusiliers, York and Lancasters, Seaforth Highlanders,

Captured German howitzer on the battlefield near Mametz Wood.   Right : A machine-gun found in the German front line.   The operator was lying dead in the trench.   Only one British soldier was wounded in front of this gun.

A German gun, half of whose shield had been destroyed by a direct hit.
Right :   Canadians testing a captured machine-gun.

[Official photographs.

A few of the German guns captured by the British.   Between July 1st and November 1st, 1916, the Allies captured 130 heavy guns, 173 field-guns, 981 machine-guns, and 215 trench-mortars—and, in addition, 73,000 officers and men.

SOME OF THE GERMAN GUNS CAPTURED BY THE ALLIES

BRITISH SOLDIERS HURRIEDLY ENTRENCHING BEHIND A COVER OF SMOKE IN FRANCE.
Smoke, an obvious but effective form of cover, was utilised both for offensive and defensive movements. In the former case it was produced by specially thrown smoke-grenades.

Hampshires, Somersets, and Essex also nobly distinguished themselves. The East Lancashires and York and Lancasters were among those who suffered for their heroism. Not one battalion was missing at the end of the action, though many were at times enveloped by hostile infantry and cut off by shell curtains.

In the fierce confusion of hand-to-hand fighting, amid the maze of German trenches, redoubts, tunnels, and entanglements on the Serre plateau, regiment after regiment drove into their first objective, and then vehemently tried to penetrate the enemy's second zone of defences. Sometimes the advance over the great down was undertaken with more spirit than science. The signalling between the foremost infantry and the protecting heavy artillery miles in the rear does not appear to have been conducted with the general precision of the French operations. Like the French, the British used Bengal fires and rockets to indicate their successes. But this rough method could not convey to the observation officers any detailed information about affairs in the distance ; and the military critic of the leading newspaper of France, "Le Temps," even remarked that some of the Staff work in the northern sector was wanting in efficiency, with the result that the efforts of various successful battalions were not rapidly co-ordinated and strongly supported.

It certainly would be only reasonable to suppose that many of the members of the brigade and divisional Staffs were, like the troops they handled, going through their apprenticeship and winning experience as they went along, and the difficulties they had to contend against were greater than those on the French sector. The two gigantic shell curtains, which the massed German guns maintained by means of new shrapnel and high explosive, were calculated

Staff work in northern sector

to upset all Staff work, even the most experienced. Telephone lines lasted scarcely a minute, and the men who tried to lay new ones fell before they could do so. Messengers and liaison officers perished when attempting to get through the barrages, and in the dull atmosphere of the afternoon both heliographic work and ordinary aerial observation are said to have been impeded. Only by the use of a very large force of aerial infantry, which would have been much more exposed to gun fire than was the French aerial infantry, could the British Staffs have maintained a close control of all the troops fighting in front of the German zones of incessant shell fire.

On the other hand, the German Staff work was also interrupted and partially disorganised by the British barrages over the enemy's rear position. An historic instance of this condition of things was seen in the heart of the great plateau, where the village of Serre lay in ruins far behind the battle-front. By a magnificent feat of fighting and endurance a small party of British troops burst right through the German lines and, in a dashing advance of a mile, stormed and carried part of Serre village. In some respects this impetuous little break-through was the most sportsmanlike thing in the whole battle. But it was scarcely an operation of a modern scientific sort, as it was not supported by strong forces on either flank.

Audacious entry into Serre

The village, though in ruins, contained in its underground works a large mass of Germans armed with machine-guns and bombs, and the enemy army corps commander had a cross-fire of heavy batteries directed on this key position. On arriving in the village and meeting with strong opposition, the small party of British troops somewhat hastily signalled their partial success by means of rockets. The German gunners saw the signals, and, although their Staff must have been in telephonic communication with the large German garrison, the hostile batteries opened an annihilating fire on Serre and killed, wounded, and suffocated their own men who occupied nearly all the position. It seems clear that somebody in a position of authority on the German side either lost his head or acted on the British signal, without waiting for confirmation from his own officers in Serre. Friend and foe were overwhelmed by the tornado of shell, and with a blind, brutal sacrifice of a large body of defending troops the small and audacious attacking party was defeated.

About two miles south-west of Serre the hostile stronghold of Beaumont-Hamel was the scene of a struggle of awful intensity. Rising to a height of about two hundred feet above the valley of the Ancre, and connecting with the neighbouring hamlet of Beaucourt, lying on the plateau directly above the ravine of the brook, Beaumont-Hamel was the most formidable of all the German fortresses. Its underground system, elaborated in the easily-worked chalk, was superior in strength to that of Thiepval on the other side of the Ancre ravine. Wave after wave of the finest flower of British valour broke against the burrowed rampart above the Ancre brook.

Epic of Ancre brook The Germans on the height brought their trench-mortars into action as soon as the British guns lifted, showing that no vital damage had been done by the long and heavy bombardment. Then through the German barrage and the rake of machine-gun fire the Inniskillings, with the Irish Fusiliers, Irish Rifles, and other battalions of the Ulster Division, English troops, and the Newfoundland Regiment made an immortal attempt to achieve a great victory against all odds. The Inniskillings, advancing with great dash, went over the ridge, south of Beaumont-Hamel and flanking the Ancre brook. On their right a battalion of·Fusiliers heading the main Ulster force stormed into the hollow where the trickle of water of the Ancre flows down to join the Somme. The Inniskillings won the ridge and vanished into the smoking furnace of the valley, and there they were joined by the long-jawed and stern-eyed Covenanters, who had swept over two lines of enemy trenches and were charging deeper into the hostile works.

What made the charge of the Ulstermen especially memorable were the circumstances in which it was undertaken. In the first place, the British bombardment in the Ancre section had not been completely effectual. Much of the barbed-wire and other entanglements **Overwhelming enemy fire** had been blown away, but awkward patches still remained, and even the parapet of the enemy fire-trench had not been battered down, but only holed, and the holes formed a kind of battlement which the Germans used as machine-gun emplacements. All this was only the beginning of the Ulstermen's difficulties. The massed German artillery was of arrogant strength about the Ancre brook, where the Ulster Division was formed up in a wood for attack. Long before the hour of assault, when the British guns were still maintaining the general bombardment, the German gunners opened an overwhelming shell fire upon the packed trenches in the woodland. The enemy clearly knew the exact position of the Ulstermen's parallels of assault and, in a rapid and intense fire, they turned the top half of the wood into a slope of shattered stumps and white chalk holes, in which it seemed impossible that anything could remain alive.

Some of the leading battalions suffered heavily, yet when these untried Irishmen emerged from the shattered wood and began to walk slowly over No Man's Land, they went as steadily and as coolly as though they were on the training-ground. The enemy's gun fire continued to rake

|Official photograph.

AN OBJECT-LESSON IN MINING WARFARE ON THE WESTERN FRONT.
Lieutenant-General Sir Herbert Plumer and a group of officers on the edge of a mine-crater which had been exploded for instructional purposes. The lecturer can be seen by Lieutenant-General Plumer's side, speaking through a megaphone.

UNDER LOCK AND KEY: GERMAN PRISONERS CAPTURED DURING A SOMME ADVANCE.

[*Official photograph.*]

Seated, standing, or sprawling on the ground of their camp, from 1,500 to 2,000 German prisoners are of the officer class—were truculent and confident. The sight of so many captives apparently gave enduring the first hours of captivity, having just been rounded up on a Somme battlefield. Many of considerable satisfaction to the large number of British soldiers who are seen congregated in the them did not disguise their pleasure at being out of the war. A few were morose, others—particularly background of this illustration.

them from the left, the enemy's machine-guns enfiladed them from a village on their right. Nevertheless, battalion after battalion walked out of the wood of death and then, going forward at the double with the Ulster battle-cries of " No surrender ! " and " Remember the Boyne ! " made one of the most glorious charges to the death in history.

The front line of German trenches was stormed by the Fusiliers, and on their flanks their comrades thrust and bombed the Germans from a series of redoubts. A large number of prisoners were taken, and they refused to cross their own shell barrages, and begged to be allowed to lie down and wait. But the dauntless Ulstermen shepherded them across the zone of death, and continued to work forward and upward, while the fire increased in raking power from both sides of the Ancre hollow. The German second line was taken through a ring of shrapnel and machine-guns,

A PAYMASTER'S OFFICE ON THE SOMME.   *[British official photograph.*
British soldiers lining up for their pay at an improvised office in a shell-hole.

and then, with the enemy's fire pursuing them in greater intensity, as more enfilading redoubts were approached, the brown waves burst over the third and fourth German lines until only the fifth line remained to be conquered.

Officers in neighbouring corps and divisions fighting on the heights around the great salient the Ulstermen had made were amazed at the terrific drive of the division. But they pointed out that the last and fifth line could not be carried until the flanks of the victorious force were cleared. The Ulstermen had produced a long, narrow salient, like a knife-thrust, running through the enemy's lines on either side of the Ancre. It was necessary to widen the conquered position in order to get more elbow-room, and to destroy various enfilading hostile posts, before the final thrust could be delivered. In several places desperately brave German machine-gunners had retired during the charge of the Ulstermen into caverns running beyond the main underground chamber. The attacking troops had thrown bombs by the half dozen into the principal caverns and had seemed to clear them. But in many cases the Germans had sheltered in the outrunning chambers, and when the bombs had all exploded they cautiously crept up and peered through periscopes. Then, finding no British garrison at hand, they emerged and resumed the struggle. Thereupon the Irishmen were raked from the rear, where the enemy's shrapnel was also falling upon them, and their thinning lines began to waste away at a deadly rate.

The order was given for the heroic division to stay in the captured enemy's fourth line, until both flanks were cleared and the " resurrected " Germans in the rear were cleared off. But it was the anniversary of the Boyne, and the original order to the division appears to have directed them to press onward as far as they could hold. Very probably the second order, countermanding the final attack, did not get through the enemy's shell curtains and streams of flanking machine-gun fire. However this may be, the Ulstermen continued their incomparable charge. The German gunners swept them with shrapnel as they worked forward in rushes from the fourth line. Yet, by a miracle, small parties of brown figures could be seen through field-glasses from the British lines struggling forward into the last German trench system. The fifth line was won, but the heroic remnants that won it were so small and so

Charge of the Ulstermen

closely hemmed in on either side by the enemy that they could not get sufficient hand-bombs up to establish themselves strongly. Both corps on the right and left of the Ulster Division had been unable to advance far enough to give support.

Then occurred a splendid tragedy of deathless heroism. Some of the Ulstermen would not retire. Directly in front of them they could see a beaten and retreating enemy, and they were not in a position to appreciate their danger on their long flanks. No veteran troops would have done what they did, and, except as an example of vehement spirit, their action was vain. Instead of withdrawing, some of the parties in the fifth German line stayed and fought until they died ; then, with their supplies of bombs and other ammunition running out, the remnant of the division tried to hold the fourth line while reinforcements came through the dreadful valley of death.

The Ulstermen at this time still held in their grasp the promise of a great and far-reaching victory. Half shattered as were the descendants of the terrible Ironsides that Cromwell planted in North Ireland, they remained defiant and full of menace. Blood told. Chiefly to the men of Ulster, England in the eighteenth century owed the loss of her New England colonies, and they it was who afterwards did more than the Catholic Irishmen to attempt to make Ireland independent with the help of Republican France. Always they had been the most persistent fighting race in Western Europe, and in a century of peace they had maintained their extraordinary fury of character by provoking annual street fights with the Catholic Irishmen. Small in number but strangely strong in soul, they constituted, in all attempts at settling the Irish question from the days of Pitt to the days of Asquith, the hardest political problem of the British Empire. Just before the outbreak of war they were ready to fight the Nationalists, and their threat was intended in sombre, deadly earnest. And in the valley of death by the Ancre the amazing race of Ulstermen, with their curious combination of Puritanic grimness and Celtic perfervidness, displayed to their Catholic countrymen on their left flank, who were themselves among the finest fighters in the field, the sheer, dreadful, driving power with which they went to war. Not since the Irish Brigade broke the British column at Fontenoy was there seen so mighty an explosion of Irish valour.

Promise of a great victory

PACK-HORSES OF THE SOMME.
How ammunition was conveyed to the Somme batteries when the weather was so inclement as to turn many of the roads into quagmires such as this illustration forcefully depicts.

With half the men out of action, and the advanced fifth line driven in, the Ulstermen still held Thiepval Wood on the southern heights of the Ancre, while across the brook they maintained connection with the forces fighting around the Serre plateau. Some six thousand Ulstermen, closely wedged all round by the enemy, but thrust well into the hostile lines, constituted the central pivot for both the attacking British wings. If their principal gains could have been maintained, the pressure on the German front would have been doubled, and the combined thrust towards Bapaume and Achiet could have been driven home with unusual speed. Reinforcements were, therefore, sent up to the hard-pressed Ulstermen, but the enemy machine-gunners and snipers who had arisen from their caves and dug-outs made things very difficult in the narrow angle of advance. The first strong supports seemed to reach their objective through the valley, and sent up signals of success. Then a second support of English battalions went forward, with much hard fighting and fearful losses. Later in the day the Newfoundland Regiment charged over the hill on the north-western slope with the aim of clearing the flank of the Ulstermen.

Charge of Newfoundlanders

The Germans were increasing in strength and cutting off patrols and groups and bits of battalions between Serre and Beaumont-Hamel and the Ancre brook. When the Newfoundlanders appeared on the ridge, in an air from which the smoke had cleared, they encountered a converging machine-gun fire through which they could not pass. There was especially a south-easterly slope firmly held by the Germans and packed with guns that raked every foot of land on the northern slope across which the Newfoundlanders marched. This slope had been reconnoitred the night before by British patrols and found to be weakly held. But it had been greatly strengthened by the German commander on Saturday morning. Clearly he knew what was coming. The enemy's fire was like a driving rain across a Scottish moor, but never a Newfoundlander wavered. Wounded men crawled for shelter into shell-holes, while German bullets swept the top of the grass above them with the effect of a heavy wind. The noble regiment wasted away in tragic heroism on an impossible task, and few returned at night to the British lines. By a miracle some men managed to reach the German line on

the height, and there found that the hostile wire entanglement was practically intact. One private, who got nearest to the German trench, had all his comrades shot down on either side of him, and fell himself into a shell-hole full of dead. For four days he remained there, with shells and bullets falling about him, and fed on the rations of the dead, and then falling back, met a British patrol.

Getting no assistance on their flanks, the Ulstermen in their advanced positions were subjected to a series of vicious attacks with hand-grenades. Yet they not only withstood the Germans, but drove them back with heavy losses. But at nightfall they ran out of bombs, and

[*British official photographs.*
GETTING MUNITIONS OVER MUD.
Two old retainers which had experienced the gloom and peril of the winter battlefield. The horses were carrying shells over rough country.

after continuously and desperately struggling for fourteen hours, and capturing a large number of prisoners, of whom only five hundred got through the German shell curtain, the Ulstermen began to fall back to the two first German lines. There they made another great stand through the night and following day, until a relieving force, organised of men who had been fighting for thirty-six hours, carried ammunition and water to the gallant garrison. The old Ulster Volunteer Force, originally designed for the event of civil war, sacrificed itself for the Empire and the cause of humanity. Fearful as were the losses of the division, and vain as seemed the sacrifice of thousands of Irishmen, Englishmen, and Newfoundlanders, it was on the pivot of the Ancre that the southern British wing won forward to victory. But before the field of success was reached there was another scene of disaster. **Terrible fighting around Thiepval**

Between the valley of the Ancre and the southern ridge of Bazentin was the village of Thiepval, backed by a down rising two hundred and ninety feet above the brook. Here raged one of the longest and most furious battles on the Somme. The hamlet of Grandcourt on the north-east, the hamlet of St. Pierre Divion on the north-west, with Thiepval, Leipzig Redoubt, and Mouquet Farm on the southern slopes, formed the four sides of the great chalk

Where top-boots were an advantage. Crossing a muddy road:

British billets at "Mud Terrace," as it was humorously and appropriately called, and some soldiers coming through the rain in macintoshes.

[*British official photographs.*

Hauling a big gun into position, an operation which was greatly impeded by inclement weather. The upper illustration gives an idea of the depth of mud in parts of the Somme area. A horse has actually sunk up to his haunches in the mire.

CAMPAIGNING IN THE MUD: FORETASTE OF WINTER CONDITIONS ON THE SOMME.

stronghold. The British attack was made in a series of thrusts from the north and the south and in the centre. Early in the day the village of Thiepval, where two valuable roads crossed, seemed to have been won by a series of furious springs. But the men advanced too confidently through the village, and the Germans, who had been hiding in deep caverns, came out into the streets and with machine-guns, rifles, mortar-bombs, and hand-bombs, assailed the victors in the rear with surprising effectiveness. The tactics of the French armies on the Somme were different. Each French attacking force was carefully trained and controlled to divide on a captured line, first into a strong bombing and clearing party that penetrated into the entire system of caverns and firmly held it, and secondly into a lighter and reconnoitring party that went cautiously forward under the eyes of its aerial infantry to prepare the way for a farther advance.

Nevertheless, a considerable degree of success was at first won around Thiepval from the drive of the Ulstermen on the north and the thrust of the Borderers and

cauldron of seething green, black, and white fumes. From a quarter to four to a quarter past five, when the struggle was at its fiercest, Thiepval, seen from the high ground in the British lines, was a sight of volcanic horror. Here the main concentration of British artillery overlapped the misplaced line of the principal German batteries, and from both sides shells and mortar-bombs poured in an incessant flood upon the down, ruins, copses, and river valley. All the night the contending lines and groups swayed over the slope, till the German commander, having countered **End of the first phase** the attack on the Gommecourt and Serre sectors, brought reinforcements down to Thiepval and retook some of the ground south of the village.

At the end of the first phase of the struggle on the Ancre sectors the British gains were limited to small reaches cut out of the German front line and united to the British fire-trenches. The men would have done better had they not gone so far. The advance had been too quick and hasty. All that was actually accomplished after the rushes into

THE MEASURED TREAD TO THE FIRST LINE.
Dogged determination suggested by every line of their heavily-encumbered figures, these men were on their way to take their turn in the trenches.
[British official photograph

Serre and Thiepval, and the partial envelopment of Beaumont-Hamel, was a great and costly holding action on a winding front of more than ten miles. It facilitated the main advance towards Bapaume, and in this measure served a purpose. But clearly the movement was not designed merely to hold the enemy, it was intended to break the first zone of German defences across the Ancre brook, and speed, by a northerly turning movement, the Franco-British advance on Bapaume, Combles, and Péronne. This indecisive result of the Ancre attacks most seriously interfered with Sir Douglas Haig's and General Foch's plan of the offensive. It left the British army on the La Boisselle and Montauban line with scarcely any elbow-room in which to work forward. The enemy retained a tremendous flanking fire over the small new British salient, together with rampart after rampart of high downs overlooking the comparatively low ridges around Albert from which British observation officers directed their guns. Months had to pass before some of the high ground round Thiepval

Manchesters and other battalions working from Authuille towards the copse known as Blighty Wood. All the Thiepval woods were covered by the main mass of the new German guns which Rupert of Bavaria had sited with a view to breaking the British offensive at a single blow. As the British troops advanced among the trees they were caught in an intense barrage by shells of many colours— the small green 4·2 in. universal shell that **Advance through the woods** combined a high-explosive effect with a rain of bullets; the black new 6 in. shrapnel with its increased propellent power, and shattering high-explosive shells of all sizes. "They threw everything at us except half-croons!" said a Scotsman. In Blighty Wood the Germans accurately marked all the ranges before their retirement, and with machine-guns, mortars, and artillery maintained a sweep of fire over the huddled heaps of their own dead that had been slain by British guns and aerial torpedoes.

By the time that all the front trenches had been secured and Thiepval won and lost, the little town became a devil's

was won, giving room and observation to the British forces. Thus the Battle of the Ancre on July 1st, 1916, ranks with the Battle of the Lille Ridges on May 9th, 1915, as failing to achieve its main objective. At Rouges Bancs and Aubers, Sir John French had lacked heavy guns and high-explosive shell. This grand deficiency in the machinery of war had been made good when the Battle of the Ancre opened, but the issue of the battle was practically identical. Something more was needed than thousands of guns and millions of shells. And this something the new British armies laboriously and terribly acquired, sifting out new leaders of talent and Staff officers of ability and general experience as it crawled forward from trench to trench and from shell-hole to shell-hole. Bulldog courage was at first the only really effectual virtue of the citizen army of the British Empire. Strangely like a bulldog fighting a quick and clever retriever in woolly armour, the slow-minded but stubborn Briton got at first a small and unimportant hold, and then worked up his grip until it became dangerous to his foe.

THE GREAT BRITISH BATTLES OF THE SOMME.
II.—Opening Victories on the Bapaume Front.
By Edward Wright.

Apparent Strength and Real Weakness of German Position North of the Somme—A Two-Mile Slope Directly Exposed to British Shell Fire—Extraordinary Phalanxes of Allied Artillery on Four-Mile Front—Perfection of Lancashires' Team-work at Montauban—The Navvy Labour that Won the Battle—Footballing East Surreys and the Fight around the Warren—Great German Counter-Attack Broken by Lancashires—Gordons, Devons, and South Staffs at Mametz—How the Yorkshires Took the Crucifix Trench—Terrific Conflict at Fricourt—Heroism of German Machine-Gunners at La Boisselle—The Clash of the Children of Odin—Tynesiders, Royal Scots, and Suffolks Thrust Towards Contalmaison—Immortal Display of Tragic Valour—Terrific Struggle around Ovillers—Ditch and Cave Warfare on the Great Slope—Sir Douglas Haig Feints below Lille and Springs Again Towards Contalmaison—Great General Battle between Reinforced Germans and the Toiling Fourth Army—Yorkshiremen Reach Contalmaison Only to Draw Back—Large Balance of Gains Won by the British—Opposing German General's Praise of the New British Troops—Enemy Confesses He Had Not Foreseen and Prepared Against the Somme Operations.

THE British front near the Somme River was apparently weak, but really strong. It ran for the most part along a hollow, threaded by two small water-courses and undulating between them. In the lowest levels the British fire-trenches were some three hundred and fifty feet below the topmost ridge occupied by the enemy The German works seemed unassailable. The first hostile line, composed in places of seven systems of earth-works, was a maze of connecting communications, and rose in terraces to the ridge of Montauban, which was about two hundred feet above the British trenches near Fricourt. Beyond the Montauban ridge there was a fall into a tortuous ravine, along which wound a stream. Then the land again rose in long slopes for nearly two miles to the second and higher ridge at High Wood, Martinpuich, and the Pozières Windmill. It was about three and a half miles from the British line in the hollow to the principal German observation-posts on the main Pozières-High Wood ridge.

Before the development of heavy-artillery tactics the

THE FINAL ORDER BEFORE THE ASSAULT.
Lancashire Fusiliers fixing bayonets just before charging, July 1st, 1916. They were one of the half-dozen regiments singled out for praise in the first accounts of the British offensive.

broad rolling slopes held by the enemy and fortified by him with mole-like industry would have been regarded as practically impregnable to attack. Indeed, the ground had been carefully selected by the Germans in August, 1914, and rapidly organised by their engineers in October, 1914, after having been carefully surveyed by their Staff officers and General von Kluck in person some years before the outbreak of hostilities. As we have before remarked, the slopes between Combles and Bapaume had been the theatre of a notable battle between General Faidherbe and General Manteuffel in 1870, and since that date thousands of German officers had studied this classic field of war. The Germans displayed all their foresight, all their patience, all their attention to minute precaution in their lines immediately north of the Somme River.

This was why the enemy was confident that no serious attack would be made upon him around Fricourt. He thought that the two-mile slope of intricately fortified ground, garrisoned by good troops sheltered in deep underground chambers, and swept by the fire of hundreds of concealed guns, was perfectly

[*Canadian War Records*
NOVEL AMBULANCE.
Bringing wounded men from the field on a light railway truck drawn by a horse.

secure. He would, in fact, have welcomed a grand attack there, so assured was he of his natural advantages of ground. But he reckoned that commanders of such talent and experience as General Foch and Sir Douglas Haig would not waste men in vainly attempting to win the great slopes. So he placed his reserves, new guns, and main ammunition dumps farther north.

In Champagne and at Verdun, however, some of the best French generals had discovered that a long slope overlooking lower but undulating ground was a weak position. By arraying hundreds of long-range howitzers and cannon against a long gradual slope it could be made uninhabitable. All that was necessary was that the heavy artillery of the attacking force should be more powerful than the batteries of the defending force. Given anything like an equality of munitioning between the opposing armies, it was fairly easy for the attacking commander to make a sudden concentration of heavy ordnance against a long slope held by the enemy with only a normal number of pieces. Ridges with long slopes had lost their value, causing such a revolution in tactics as overthrew all the traditions of warfare that had grown up since the Stone Age. Any force on an exposed hillside and summit could be slaughtered by massed siege-guns and driven away without an infantry charge. The ravines between two heights or ridges were, however, difficult to attack, even with the indirect fire of howitzers. The strength of the German position around Fricourt lay in the ravine winding from Fricourt behind Montauban towards Guillemont and Bazentin. The rest of the battlefield for the most part consisted of exposed slopes, giving little shelter until the ravine behind Thiepval was reached.

Defect of German position

This view of the matter had been explained by the famous French divisional commander, General Marchand, who forced a similar slope in Champagne in the autumn of 1915, and came in the autumn of 1916, when his wounds

were healed, to lead his men again in the Somme battle. The ideas of General Marchand were those of the French Staff, but no British writer explained them to the British public, perhaps because it was thought unwise to enlighten the world and the enemy in July, August, and September, 1916, as to the grand defect in the German position. The German commanders engaged in meeting the British attack, including General von Below, General von Stein, and General Sixt von Arnim, appear to have held to the exploded notion of the defensive value of long slopes. Rather than retire for three or four miles to the tangle of downs in front of Bapaume, the German commanders deployed hundreds of thousands of men, who wasted away in the terrific furnace of British artillery fire. Naturally, the enemy deserved to be encouraged when he was defending the indefensible.

It was not until the battle had lasted some three months and the great slope had been won that General Marchand hinted to his own countrymen the secret of the British offensive. When the slope was won and the contending forces began to fight over the long, undulating reverse incline going down to Bapaume, the advantage of ground was altered. It fell in turn to the Germans, who had then greatly increased their heavy artillery and rained millions of shells upon the British trenches, exposed from Flers and Eaucourt l'Abbaye to Courcelette and the ground near Grandcourt. This, as we may as well explain in advance, was one of the reasons why the British movement slackened when it won the main ridge and began to descend the long incline to the strategically important little town of Bapaume, where it was directly exposed both to the cannon and howitzers of General von Below's army.

FIRST STEPS TOWARDS HOME.
[*British official photograph.*
How wounded came down to the clearing station. Light railway commandeered by the R.A.M.C.

[*British official photograph.*
BACK FROM BAZENTIN.
Wounded soldiers arriving at a dressing-station in the R.A.M.C. train. Doctors and orderlies are seen giving first-aid.

It is now clear that Sir Douglas Haig enjoyed a great advantage of ground on that part of the front he skilfully selected for his main attack. As we have seen, he completely misled the enemy by his stupendous artillery demonstration in the last week of June, 1916. By one of the most brilliant feints in the history of warfare he induced the Germans to waste most of their strength around Arras. Then, while General Micheler further misled the enemy well to the south, at Roye, Sir Douglas Haig struck unexpectedly at the defensive German positions by the Somme, in conjunction with General Fayolle's similar surprise attack.

The southern British line of battle stretched from the hill of Ovillers, four hundred and twenty-six feet above sea-level and separated by a wide slight hollow from the somewhat lower southern hill on which the village of La Boisselle rose. Then came another valley, nicknamed Sausage Valley, above which the ground rose nearly a hundred feet to Fricourt Down. South of this down the village of Fricourt tumbled in utter ruin at the mouth of the ravine which wound behind Mametz and Montauban. These two villages rose on a long mass of rounded chalk four hundred and twenty-six feet above sea-level, with the few main bosses jutting two hundred and thirty feet above some of the British fire-trenches around Carnoy. The Mametz and Montauban Down, forming the grand bulwark of the German system of fortification on the Bapaume sector, was particularly strong

TAKING UP SHELLS TO THE GUNS. [*British official photograph.*]
British soldiers pulling a trolly laden with heavy shells along a light railway to the guns, a duty in which they delighted.

[*Official photograph.*]
RAILWAY SPINNING.
Taking rails along a light railway for its own extension.

east, while the guns on the Bazentin ridge swept it from the north, and batteries at Pozières shelled it from a westerly direction. Exposure to this intricate and threefold cross-fire of artillery constituted the main disadvantage under which the British troops laboured. As explained in a previous chapter, the southern British army and the connecting French force

It broadened and rose eastward, where three high woods, Favière Wood, Bornafay Wood, and Trônes Wood, with Delville Wood above them, afforded cover and dominating observation points for many German guns. These guns could sweep the Montauban ridge from the

occupied the low-lying salient of some four square miles by the Somme River. And as the British were north of the French, they alone came fully under the enemy's cross-fire.

The attack on the Montauban ridge was, therefore, an affair of peculiar difficulty. On July 1st the French wing at Maricourt only advanced towards Favière Wood, penetrating the enemy's lines to a depth of less than half a mile. This left full scope for all the enfilading hostile batteries in front of Guillemont to bombard the flank of the British advance at Montauban.

The delicate junction-point of the allied armies had to move forward with extreme caution for fear of a great counter-attack

Crowded four-mile salient

against the linking units of the Franco-British armies There was a further difficulty in regard to the very restricted space between Fricourt and the marshes of the Somme, which was available for massing the British and French parks of artillery. The enemy on the heights had a large arc of great depth, on which he could station his field-guns and heavy ordnance, while the Allies, being closed in a narrow salient, had a line of only four miles from Fricourt to the river along which to concentrate, row behind row, the guns of both Sir Henry Rawlinson's and General Fayolle's armies. The result was such packed phalanxes of British and French guns as made everything that Mackensen, Hindenburg, and Haeseler had organised seem insignificant. There was a very grave disadvantage in the extraordinary closeness with which the British and French guns were packed together on the four-mile front. The target they offered to the enemy was such as gunners had never dreamt of. A German shell, fired at hazard between

[*Canadian War Records.*]
LOADING AN AMMUNITION TRAIN.
Loading ammunition cases on a light railroad motor-train behind the firing-line. The distribution scheme was perfect for an infinite supply from all the munition works.

WORCESTERS RETURNING FROM THE TRENCHES THROUGH HEAVY RAIN.
Conditions of trench life in wet weather steadily improved after the first winter, but at their best they remained a tremendous test of the spirit and physical endurance of the men—a test which was triumphantly withstood.

Fricourt and Curlu, might always strike some gun-pit, ammunition depot, supply train, or infantry communication. Between the close-set array and long wedge of batteries of all calibres, many of them working in the open, there had to be maintained routes of movement and supply and munitioning for the attacking infantry. The perfect organisation by means of which the two great British and French forces, crowded into a salient four miles broad, preserved a long-sustained energy of movement until victory was obtained, forms one of the most remarkable pieces of Higher Staff work in the history of the war. Clearly the Staff officers of the High Command of Great Britain contained men of genius. The brain of the British Army was excellent, and only its latest and improvised and untested extended nervous system, represented by the Staffs of new divisions and brigades, showed occasionally any deficiency in function.

Brilliant British Staff work

Special care was taken in all the details of Staff work of the southern British army. The team work of battalions, brigades, and divisions around the Montauban ridge showed what the old professional British Staff officer could have done had there been time to amalgamate the Regular Army with the Citizen Army. When the British Staff College training was combined with two years' experience of Continental warfare, the gentlemen with the red tabs were superior to the similar directing class of the German Army. The checks on the Ancre front arose from the fact that Great Britain, in July, 1916, had not sufficient Staff officers remaining from the original Expeditionary Force to control every detailed movement of the great new national armies. Happily, the best of those that remained worked well in the vital sector.

At Montauban all went magnificently. The Prussian regiment holding the village was annihilated by the preliminary bombardment, and replaced, by July 1st, by 3,000 men of the 6th Bavarian Reserve. All these 3,000 Bavarians were eventually killed or captured by the British

infantry. The attack was entrusted to two Lancashire brigades, largely composed of Manchester men, on the left of whom were the East Surrey, Kent, Essex, Bedford, and Norfolk Regiments. The Manchesters, who led the charge, were composed of the worst material in the world from the German point of view. For they were town lads of a highly industrialised breed—clerks, warehousemen, and cotton operatives drawn from the smokiest city in the world. But factory life had not sapped them of vitality and spirit. They broke through the large-boned peasantry of Bavaria with all the ancient courage of the strange, romantic Iberian race that Lancashire has sheltered for thousands of years in her hills.

The charge of the Manchester battalions was conducted with Napoleonic perfection. The artillery preparation was superb, and greatly facilitated their onset. The six or seven hostile trench systems, with five or more zones of wire entanglement, had been blasted into chaos by heavy shells and aerial torpedoes. The defences rose on a slope, forming a sort of great spider-web of parapets, communications, and frontal and flanking redoubts—all directly exposed to the plunging fire of British mortars and siege-guns. A large part of the new Bavarian garrison was put out of action a few hours after it arrived in the trenches by the stupendous volcanic eruption of high explosive from the British artillery phalanx. When the guns lifted, about half-past seven on the morning of July 1st, and the quick-firing trench-mortars sent their last torpedoes travelling visibly into the German fire-trench, the enemy batteries northward and eastward were unable to help their infantry, for they were in turn assailed by an indescribable tornado of heavy shell. Scarcely any new German guns had been sited in this part of the front, which was under the control of General Sixt von Arnim. The fact that he replaced the shattered Prussian regiment, on the morning of July 1st, by the 6th Bavarian Reserve shows he expected an attack, but he did not foresee the strength of it.

General Arnim misled

Most of his guns were placed in orthodox fashion on the reverse slope of shelves and ridges, where they were searched out by the British artillery.

Amid a Niagara of sound from their guns and from some assistant 3 in. French quick-firers, the two Lancashire brigades charged up the height, in a good wind that carried their smoke-screen blindingly upon the enemy. One German section in a vital spot was completely blanketed by the thick smoke, and the leading officers of the Lancashires appreciating the situation, hurried their men forward and then collected them from wide groups of sixes into closely working companies that broke into Montauban village. Many Bavarians, though absolutely fresh troops, were completely cowed by shell fire and at once surrendered, and three of their field-guns were taken. But the ubiquitous and heroic German machine-gunner gave some trouble. Amid the terrific bombardment, some of these admirable and imperturbable men hastily constructed rough brick emplacements behind the ruined walls and fought to the death. One Manchester sergeant, turning a corner in Montauban, was caught in the ankle by a stream of machine-gun bullets that also hit him over the heart. He thought he was dying, but in spite of

Dogged German machine-gunners

his broken ankle he stumbled on and bayoneted the machine-gunner, and then sitting down to die found that the two bullets that had thumped over his heart had been turned aside by a shaving-mirror and a novel he had taken to read in the German trenches.

Joyful to find he had only a broken ankle, the sergeant got along a bit farther with his men, and disarmed another German gunner on a platform high in some trees, and shot him down before he could do much mischief. Meanwhile, the cellars of the village were thoroughly cleared by bombing parties, and the magnificent soldierly qualities of the Lancashire lads were displayed by the quickness and

THE MAGIC OF THE PIPES: TWO TYPICAL INCIDENTS WHERE THE BATTLE ROLLS.

[British official photographs

Black Watch celebrating the capture of Longueval with pipe and drum. On the left three officers are seen seated at a table, while other members of the audience are looking on from trench parapets. Above: Five splendid Scots swinging back to billets to the skirl of the bagpipe, which doubtless went through the ordeal of battle with its owner; a delightful photograph with the appeal of many a more ambitious work of art.

CAVALRY ON THE MOVE: EQUESTRIAN ACTIVITY IN FRANCE WITH THE FIRST FLUSH OF DAWN

After nearly two years of comparative inaction, British cavalry—Dragoon Guards and Deccan Horse—took part in a minor though significant affair near the Bois de Foureaux, during July, 1916. The sight of a strong patrol of horsemen going forth further heartened British infantrymen already elated by a foretaste of victory. Mr. A. C. Michael expresses the scene with his usual skill and dramatic effect.

skill with which they rebuilt the defences of Montauban. It is hardly too much to say that they were equal to the veteran Iron Division of France in the speed and efficacy with which they fortified the ground they had won. This businesslike navvy work of theirs was soon to prove the decisive factor in the first phase of the British action by the Somme.

Meanwhile, an unexpected piece of good luck enabled the more easterly Lancashire brigade to strengthen itself greatly on its right. Between Montauban and Bornafay Wood there was a large brickfield, lying on the dominating slope beyond the village. Airmen's photographs had shown that this flanking work was a nest of machine-guns and trench-mortars, and it was feared it would prove a terrible obstacle in the drive up to Montauban. Therefore, in the original plan of attack, it was arranged to pass by this stronghold and make no direct attempt to take it, but leave it to be gradually encircled. Only a small force was detached to reconnoitre the brickfield, but instead of reconnoitring it they captured it and made prisoners of

East Surreys at the Warren the survivors of the company that garrisoned it. The position was a ghastly monument to the destructive power of British guns. The sheltering brick-stacks had been scattered on the machine-gun sections concealed behind them ; the dug-outs were caved in, and the deeper caverns choked. Since the attack on the brickfield near La Bassée the British Army had obtained guns throwing a shell of immense weight, with the result that the brick-stacks exploded into innumerable and deadly fragments.

On the left of the Lancashire brigades the Bavarian machine-gunners were not blanketed so well by the British smoke-screen. In particular, there was a very strong redoubt known as the Warren, which by reason of the curious twist in the wind as it flowed up the slope was not screened from the attacking infantry. Here some of the Home County battalions were caught by a scythe of bullets, and compelled to shelter in shell-holes and wait for relief. But the hostile gunners were mastered by the spirited East Surreys, who went forward with a great rush, playing footballs into the German line through the enemy's curtain of shrapnel fire like the London Irish at Loos. They broke far into the network of defences, cleared the ground, and then directed other battalions round the worst clump of German machine-guns. By steady fighting and good team-work, the great danger spot was overlapped by English bomb-throwers, and then the supporting troops, who had got somewhat too far to the right of their original line, went over to the left and captured the long German position running westward from Montauban, towards and through an orchard. By this means the Warren was completely enveloped and ferreted out, and some eight hundred prisoners taken.

With Montauban carried on one flood of invasion, and the flanking brickfield on one side and the Warren on the other wrested from the enemy, his position became perilous. For the British advance at this point was much the deepest along the whole front, a depth of a mile and a half of intricately fortified ground being occupied by the victorious division. The German commander hastily prepared a grand counter-attack, and at three o'clock on Sunday morning the 12th Reserve Division and the 16th Bavarian Regiment—15,000 men in all—tried in turn to inundate Montauban. On the north side of the village, overlooking the valley of the Fricourt stream, the Germans retained a long position that wound from the rear of Bornafay Wood to within a few yards of the new line made by the Lancashire men. Eastward of the village, also, the German positions were very close to the British. In these circumstances the enemy commander reverted to the method of a mass attack, and launched his men in dense grey waves upon the fatigued Britons. The strength and massive character of the German attack were a surprise, but the Lancashires and their comrades had also a surprise for the enemy.

[Canadian War Records.
CANADIANS COLLECTING KIT AFTER A BATTLE.
Advancing men naturally discard as much as possible of their impedimenta. After an action much of this is collected, as well as arms and cartridges left by the wounded and dead.

Since Le Cateau and Ypres the marksmen of the Regular British Army had fallen, or had gone into the machine-gun organisations ; but they had left behind them the technique of the intensely rapid fire that had saved Western Europe on at least two occasions. The trainers of the New Army did not only attempt what was possible in regard to rifle fire, but, carried away by enthusiasm, owing to the glorious tradition of the " mad minute," took in hand the millions of new recruits and achieved the seemingly impossible. They reduced the minute to a mad thirty seconds, in which twenty rounds were discharged by the Lee-Enfield. No doubt the marksmanship of the Citizen Army was inferior to that of the old long-service Regular soldier. On the other hand, quick accuracy of vision seems to have been a native quality of the **A surprise** British race, and this quality, educated **for the enemy** by the finest musketry instructors in the world, employing disappearing targets and a system of platoon competitions, administered to General von Arnim and the German Staff a severe and disconcerting shock.

German masses had gathered in the woods in the darkness, but as they came out on the open slopes flickering search-lights caught them and star-shells illuminated them, and though they charged with high personal bravery they went the way of the first new German formations at Ypres. Onward they surged, wave after wave, the living storming over the fallen and arriving, by reason of the density of their masses, within point-blank range of the defenders of the village. They were badly caught by the raking fire of the British machine-guns that had been hastily emplaced around the ruins, but this the German commander had allowed for when he formed his dense columns. Then, however, came the great surprise of the new British infantry.

IN THE ENEMY'S QUARTERS.
Staff work in an underground stronghold captured from the Germans.
A telephone exchange is seen affixed to the wall, while the dug-out boasts
the convenience of electric light.

Between the spouts of flame from each Vickers gun and
Lewis gun there was an unbroken line of smaller flames
from thousands of rifles, into which clips of cartridges were
being fed with mechanical regularity. A score or two out
of 15,000 German troops got into a British trench known
as the Staubwasser trench, and were killed there. Nearly
six thousand fell on the slopes around Montauban village,
where the wayside image of the Virgin Mary rose above
the indistinguishable ruins of the houses. The rest of the
broken German brigade fell back to the second zone of
defences running from Longueval to Bazentin-le-Grand,
under a terrific fire from the British artillery. The German
divisional commander flung out every man he had without
making the least impression upon the British line. He
was afterwards retired from his command, apparently on
the charge of having arranged his great counter-attack
with too much haste. But the failure was not his fault.

Triumph of the citizen soldier Every officer in the German Army had
underestimated the fire power of the new
British citizen soldier. German newspapers rang with praise of the old British
regular private, who was justly said to have used his rifle
as if it were a machine-gun. But all this hostile praise was
intended to reflect upon the steadiness and marksmanship
of the new British soldier, who the enemy thought could
be easily staggered and swamped by the brutal method of
the mass attack. At Montauban, at 3 a.m. on Sunday,
July 2nd, 1916, the new British soldier violently conquered
the respect of his veteran enemy.

On the left of the victorious Lancashires, East Surreys,
and other Home County battalions, the land dropped in a
steep slope south-eastward to Mametz village. Here there
was a closer tangle of German defences, rising above the
British front line at Carnoy, and falling to the north into
the narrow valley of the Fricourt stream. The caverned
fortresses were not entirely choked by the British artillery,
and by reason of the lie of the ground the screening smoke
clouds did not veil some of the most important hostile
redoubts. North-countrymen and South-countrymen of
Great Britain at first advanced easily up the down with

s'oped arms, among them being
the Gordons, Devons, and South
Staffordshires. Connecting with
the Manchester troops, the South
Staffords crossed the enemy's
first line in a promenade. No
machine-guns worried them, the
enemy's artillery fire scarcely
troubled them, and stalking
among the dug-outs they gathered
groups of disheartened grey figures
who surrendered easily. But near
the end of Mametz village a
strong position, known as Danzig
Alley, remained uninjured by
British siege-guns, and full of the
fresh troops General von Arnim
had sent forward. At this place
the Gordons seemed about to
capture a village without a
struggle when they were caught
at a range of a hundred and
twenty yards by a machine-gun
blast. "Suddenly," wrote an officer

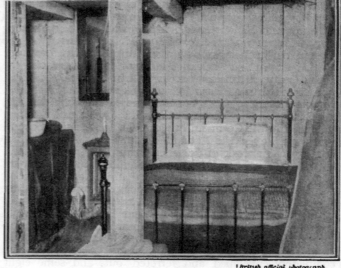

SUBTERRANEAN BED-SITTING-ROOM.
Some of the German shelters in Picardy actually contained beds and
bedding, as well as mirrors, one being seen suspended on the wall over the
small table.

of the Gordons, "a machine-gun opened upon us point-
blank, and caught us in the face. I shouted to my men to
advance at the double, and we ran forward through a
perfect stream of shattering bullets. Many of my poor boys
dropped, and then I fell and knew nothing more for a while.
But afterwards I heard that we had taken Mametz, and held
it still. My Gordons were fine, but we had bad luck."

The battalions sent up to reinforce the Gordons were
caught in a sudden barrage of German shrapnel. The
German guns beyond the Bazentin ridge had lost their
observation-balloons, while their directing airmen had
been chased from the sky, and as they were also subjected
themselves to a severe battering they did not get the
exact range when first the British smoke-screens were
loosened. Yet as soon as the leading battalions of attack
got through, the German gunners worked by the map
over the British front and over their own lost line, and
catching in a furious fire the supporting troops of the attack,

made the struggle around Mametz a desperate affair. The Devons had also had to charge like the Gordons through a tornado of machine-gun bullets, and in the turmoil of these two checks some of the supporting battalions, harassed by the enemy's curtain fire, lost their direction and confused the Staff work. Nevertheless, the magnificent heroism of the Highlanders and the lads of Devon was not wasted. The remnant of these battalions continued the great charge, bombed the German gunners to death and held the line. Then, reinforced, they swung up the valley of the Fricourt stream and, taking the Germans in an enveloping movement, mastered Mametz and all the reverse slope of the down facing Mametz Wood. This turning movement between Mametz and Fricourt was of double importance. Fricourt village, lying near the lowest hollow in the British line, was an extraordinarily strong position. The German engineers had achieved their masterpiece of subterranean fortress work in this apparently weak part of their lines. A great wedge of downland rose steeply above the village, and with its tunnelled communications, caverned machine-gun redoubts and large hidden garrison made a frontal attack impossible. No artillery could reach the main force of defenders, and their machine-gun emplacements remained intact. At the opening of the British movement, when smoke-screens were useless against the Fricourt promontory, the attacking troops on both sides were compelled to swerve more than their commander had intended. But the formidable stronghold, which constituted the enemy's key position to the Bazentin ridge, was slowly enveloped, and then, as it weakened, stormed by a second frontal attack.

Mametz gained at the double

While English and Scottish troops worked down from Mametz to the western side of the promontory fortress, a magnificent body of North-countrymen — Yorkshiremen, Northumberland Fusiliers and others—with the Somersets in support, made a drive of heroic tenacity across the high ground north of Fricourt. The charge of the Yorkshires was one of the most superb examples of intrepid suffering in the war, ranking with the advance of the Ulstermen and the London Territorials at Gommecourt. There was an open slope, a hundred and fifty yards broad, between the British assembly trenches and the enemy's fire-trench. Some of the German redoubts remained uninjured by the British artillery, and the German machine-gunners sat thirty feet down, with their guns ready to be hoisted up, and looking through long periscopes, through which they could see the first wave of attack. Before the order came through their telephones the grey machine-gunners were upstairs with their guns and mowing down the khaki line. With every gun team there was a picked rifleman, whose orders were to kill every British officer. Few of the leading lieutenants escaped, and in one battalion only two officers who were dressed as privates remained to direct the men.

With nearly all their officers gone and their ranks horribly thinned by the swathes that the machine-guns cut, the lads of the North Country held to their task, every man playing up to the others as well as he could. To many the charge was just a dreadful blank. " I went mad," said one Yorkshireman, " and all I can remember is finding myself in a trench with the Germans lying dead around me, and myself throwing bombs at a clump of men in grey uniforms." But there was one Yorkshire sergeant who retained his presence of mind and found a way of escape. He and his men were lying down to avoid the stream of machine-gun bullets, but he noticed that the enemy gunners were traversing only ankle high, and thereby killing his crouching men. He saw it would be better to be hit in the ankle than in the head. He sprang up and led a charge, surprised the enemy, and captured the machine-guns without receiving a scratch.

Canny Yorkshire sergeant

All this was done in a heavy curtain fire from the German

THE FORBIDDING ASPECT OF THE NEUTRAL ZONE : IMPRESSIVE FRENCH OFFICIAL PHOTOGRAPH.
Some faint idea of the horror and desolation of No Man's Land may be gleaned from this picture. It winds, a strip of bare earth, between the opposing trenches only a few yards apart, dotted with still figures that cannot be brought in. Beyond it shells are bursting continually.

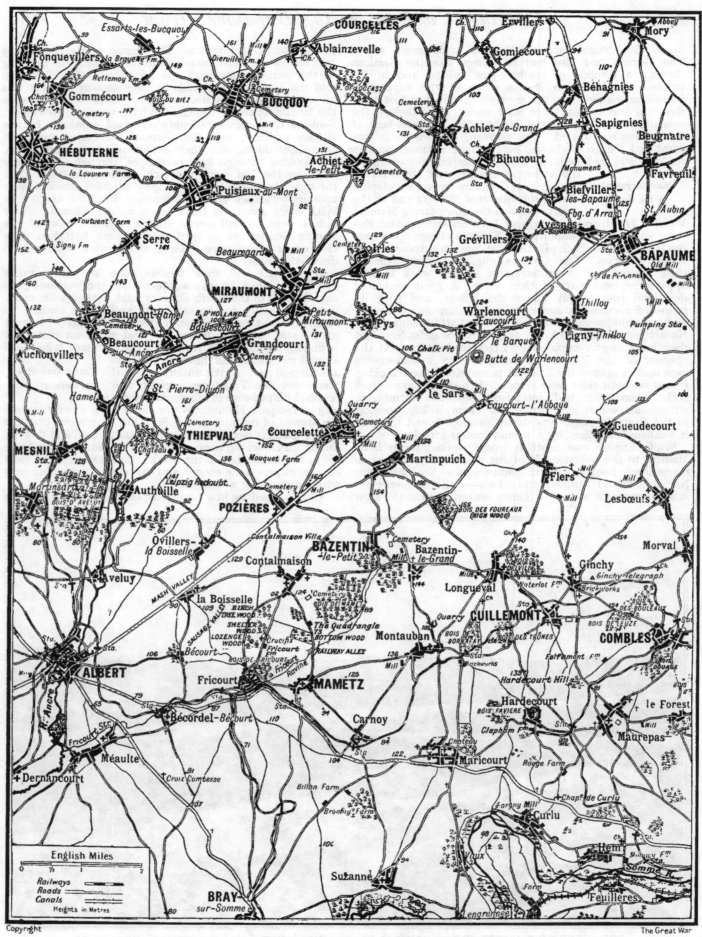

AREA OF THE BRITISH OFFENSIVE NORTH OF THE SOMME.

This map shows the points of fiercest fighting during the course of the British advance across the rectangle of ground contained by a line drawn from Albert through Hébuterne, Achiet-le-Grand, Gueudecourt, Combles, and Mametz.

artillery. But when the West Yorkshires and their comrades broke into the enemy's trench system and bombed their way through caverns and winding, narrow ditches six feet deep, the bombing parties had some relief from shells, and fighting with great fury forced their way up the ridge to Crucifix Trench. Stumbling over shell-holes and dead and mangled bodies, they reached the trench of the Crucifix and found it full of Germans. Their work, however, had been carried out ahead of the Staff time-table, and all the approaches to the Crucifix were being violently hammered by British guns. But the Yorkshiremen, lashed to absolute recklessness by their heavy losses, would not stay until their messengers dashed through the enemy's curtains. Charging through the British gun fire they

A HAUL OF UNWOUNDED MEN.
German prisoners in a trench waiting to be sent to a compound behind the lines.

[*British official photographs.*

THE HUN LOOKING MORE OR LESS PLEASANT.
Smiling types of enemy captives photographed before being sent to the rear. They do not seem to be any the worse for their experiences. Or is it that they were glad to get out of the inferno?

the ruined Crucifix position. Another small Yorkshire party pushed still farther into the German lines and tried to capture Birch Tree Wood. It was under an intense fire from the British guns, and no Germans were visible; but hundreds of them were concealed beneath the ground, watching all that happened through long periscopes. The handful of Yorkshiremen escaped death by a miracle; but one man was cut off and yet was not attacked, with a tornado of British shells around him and enemy snipers watching beneath the ground for a safe chance of shooting him. He saw a German come crawling along, bleeding as he crawled. Then by the wounded German came a wounded Yorkshireman. The German shot him with a revolver, and the uninjured English spectator in turn shot the murderer, and then got back to a German dug-out in which were three dead Germans, with whom he remained for eight hours until the British bombardment ceased.

During these eight hours the nine hundred survivors of the first British assault, who had reached the Crucifix position, were sub- **A night in Crucifix** jected to the massed fire of the German **Trench** guns. All the night of July 1st the Germans bombarded the Crucifix, while the British bombarded Shelter Wood and Birch Tree Wood. The design, of course, was to keep the infantry on both sides down by an unending blast of shell, and thus to enable bomb throwers to work forward. The North-countrymen were in the worst situation, as the trenches they held had already been completely wrecked by their own guns, and they could not find proper cover

jumped into the sunken road and into the main trench, took all the Germans that remained prisoners, and began to bethink themselves of their own position. Their captain was struck down with a bullet in his ribs, and suffering great pain, but he sent up a red rocket, and at the signal the British guns lifted and crashed beyond into Shelter Wood.

The rocket, however, was seen from the Bazentin ridge, and the German gunners there at once shortened their range and began to register around the Crucifix. The wounded Yorkshire captain sought for cover, and with ten men dragged himself towards Shelter Wood. Finding that a thousand or more Germans garrisoned the wood, he slowly crawled back and directed the consolidation of from the enemy's intense heavy fire. But the granite character of the Yorkshiremen enabled them to endure the night of indescribable horror, and when morning broke and found the gallant nine hundred tragically diminished in number, with their fighting spirit raised to still wilder frenzy, they again advanced and, in fierce bombing sprints, tore more ground from the enemy and tightened the neck of the net around Fricourt.

From the line of trees that fringed the slope where the famous Crucifix rose the Durham Light Infantry, who fought a great fight alongside the York-

Victory at Fricourt

shiremen and Northumberland men, made sallies into the copses where German machine-guns were concealed, and enlarged the British grip on the Fricourt promontory. All Sunday the struggle went on behind and through Fricourt, where the victorious North-countrymen were surrounded on three sides, as the division on the left had only advanced in small groups that were unable to make good the ground they had carried in their first rush. Gradually, Sir Henry Rawlinson and his southern army corps commanders, by violent counter-battery firing and continual bombardment of enemy infantry positions on the heights, diminished the strength of the German barrier fire and strengthened the

[*British official photograph.*

LIGHT REFRESHMENTS FOR SLIGHTLY-WOUNDED MEN.
Great as our casualties inevitably were in the Somme advance, it was established that the proportion of slightly-wounded men to the total was unusually high. Refreshment stalls were pitched immediately behind the fields of battle for the use of the walking wounded.

division on the right of the North-countrymen. On Sunday afternoon Fricourt fell.

North of Fricourt, in another high angle of downland, was the hill village of La Boisselle, lying between Mash Valley and Sausage Valley, and forming the mighty outwork of Contalmaison. Like Fricourt promontory, La Boisselle seemed too strong to be carried by a frontal attack. The downland village, however, was a point of decisive importance, as it rested on the highway from Bapaume to Albert, and was barely two miles from Albert. Its great hill completely dominated the little town, and the German batteries, firing at close range, reduced the place to as wild a ruin as Ypres. Only the Virgin of Albert strangely survived the wreck. Above the red ruin of the shattered cathedral the image of the Mother of Christ leaned from the wreck of the tower, and though the bright statue seemed ever about to fall, as shell after shell roared by it, it remained bowed as in benediction over the rubble of the old city.

La Boisselle, with its volcano of batteries and observation-posts and shell-pitted high road, was the grand menace to the British and French forces on the Somme. A strong and sudden German advance from La Boisselle would

have cut the allied communications in the four-mile Somme salient. Special attention was therefore devoted to La Boisselle by the British troops around Albert. Mining operations on a gigantic scale were undertaken some weeks before the offensive, and on the morning of July 1st the advance was heralded by three tremendous explosions that destroyed an important stretch of enemy redoubts. Then, as the works went up in smoke and dust, the Lincolns charged over the craters and invaded the village. But the German machine-gunners in their burrows beneath the houses fought with admirable fearlessness and, supported by three regiments of Baden troops, checked the frontal assault. One Baden gunner, who maintained his deadly work until Monday afternoon, excited the admiration of the men who at last captured him. He was badly wounded in nine places, yet he worked his gun for nearly sixty hours with only a few short intervals for sleep.

The German was on the whole a great fighting man. The position to which he had lifted his Empire quickly by war after war was a solid testimony to his strength of character, and this strength of character had not weakened since 1870, but greatly increased An Englishman of genius who knew more about Germany than any of his countrymen, Professor Cramb, prophesied just before his death in 1913 that the clash of the children of Odin—Teutons and Englishmen and Lowland Scots— would result in an unparalleled display of spirit on both sides. For fifteen hundred years the two great streams of Northerners had flowed apart without conflict. The Germans had won and lost a great European empire in the Middle Ages, had depopulated their own country in wars of religion, and only slowly recovered unity and population. Then, mixed with a large Slav element— the original Prussian and Wend —the Continental Teuton at last made a bid for the empire of the world against the island Teutons who had mixed in England, Scotland, Wales, and Ireland with Celt and Norseman. From Charlemagne to Bismarck there had been an almost uninterrupted peace between the two chief races of Northern adventurers. Great Britain had fought Bavaria and beaten her in the days of Marlborough, and before those days Queen Elizabeth broke the power of the Hansa towns. But never had there been a main struggle between the German and the Briton until the New British Army charged into the enemy lines in July, 1916.

The Anglo-Celt was more adventurous—the Slavic-Teuton was more patient. In hardness of character they were alike. But the Anglo-Celt represented the spirit of liberty, while the over-organised German, with his curious strain of Slavic submis-

Anglo-Celt v. Slavic-Teuton

siveness, stood for little more than the virtue of almost perfect discipline. Nearly all the strong points of the German line were garrisoned by hundreds of men who had volunteered to fight to the death. Some of them were cowed into surrender by the overwhelming power of the British artillery. But, generally speaking, the German showed himself a man of heroic mould, and the extraordinary virtue he displayed is the best and the fairest evidence of the quality of the untried British troops who mastered him. Had the Germans been a free race and the Britons a modern feudalised race, the issue of the battle would probably have been different.

Heavy gun in action at long range from a rail emplacement.

[*Official photographs.*

Impression of the smoke-cloud emitted by one of our big guns when firing.

Gunners and horses hauling a heavy weapon into position on the Somme.

Convoy of motor=transports passing a column of New Zealanders on the march.

Artillery officers using a captured German gun against the enemy.

Canadians fix bayonets in readiness for a charge on the Somme.

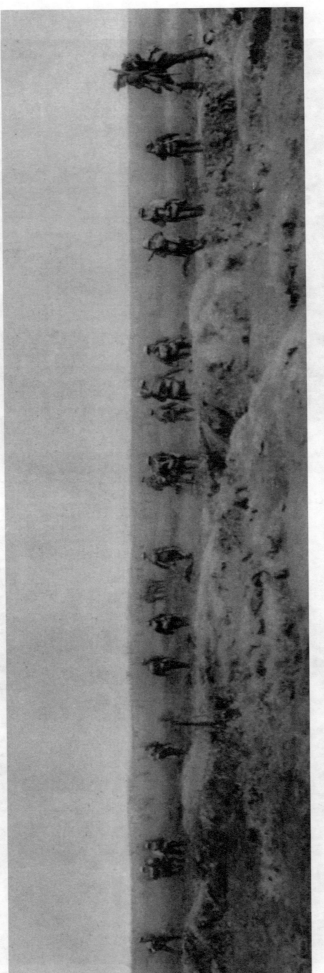

British troops advancing in open order through shell and gun smoke.

Supports and reserves armed cap-à-pie moving up to the Somme line.

Fine as was the democracy of France, it could not have saved itself by its own effort. Even with the help of the backwood peasant communities of Russia and the inefficient system of Imperial bureaucracy of those village communities, the French democracy, with its tendency to race suicide, could not have survived against the better organised Teuton. On the sea power, financial power, shipping power, and manufacturing power of the Anglo-Celt the strength of the Allies rested, and it was not until Great Britain improvised a vast army that hope of victory could be entertained. And such was the warlike genius of the Teuton that the ultimate issue seemed still to incline to a stalemate, even when Great Britain struck her first blow in full force.

At La Boisselle, where Sir Henry Rawlinson's Staff had done their utmost to achieve success, the operations were brought to a standstill by the German machine-gunners. A report came through of the capture of the village on Saturday morning, and Sir Douglas Haig believed he had won the position when he issued his bulletin at 1.15 p.m., July 1st, 1916. But the German troops there continued to fight strongly until the afternoon of Monday, July 3rd. They retired into their caverns during the first hasty, sweeping charge of the British troops, then emerged with their machine-guns, and by desperate attacks in front and rear and on both flanks defeated the troops in both the first assault and the supporting movement. Only the remnant of a German battalion was in La Boisselle, running short of food and quite without water ; but the store of bombs was large, and though the attacking forces drew away at intervals to allow the massed British siege-guns to pound the chaos that had been a village into something like a lunar desert, the encircled Germans fought on heroically amid the blasts of heavy shell-fire, and were conquered only by slow bombing advances.

Heroic struggle for La Boisselle

Many acts of cruelty were committed by the Germans on July 1st. For instance, they captured a wounded British officer, and after deliberating the most ghastly means of putting him to death, bound his suffering body on the parapet telling him he should there learn what it was to stand the fire of his own guns. By a strange chance the exposed, wounded, and manacled man survived the gun fire and was rescued by British troops after his torturers had been killed in fair fight. But though the German was often a vile brute, he was also a great fighting man. Weeks of incessant warfare had to pass before he generally showed signs of failing confidence in himself.

Around La Boisselle some of the deeds of the British troops appeared at first more adventurous than scientific. The advance past La Boisselle to Contalmaison was a splendid and memorable thing, like the charge of the Light Brigade. But it does not seem to have been a perfect example of siege-battle technique. Many of the men who took part in it were Tynesiders, with Irish blood in them, who went forward cheering while their pipers played them on. Royal Scots and the Suffolks took part in the long, terrific charge that broke clean through the enemy's first zone of defences and reached his second

ENTENTE IN MEN AND MACHINES. *[British official photograph* British gunners bringing a French howitzer into position.

zone at Contalmaison. The German guns put out a heavy curtain of shrapnel, through which the waves of khaki surged steadily forward, the men going at parade step with imperturbable courage. Then at the second German trench the defending machine-guns came into action with devastating effect. The Tynesiders and their comrades were enfiladed from the high ground at La Boisselle, the bullets coming pattering down in showers, so that when they hit men in the shoulder they came out at the wrist.

"It seemed to me," said a Lincoln man, "as though there was a machine-gun to every five men." Handled with deadly skill by the gunners, the unnumbered Maxims about La Boisselle brought down Irishmen, Scotsmen, and Englishmen by the thousand. Yet the extraordinary brigade held on its course and, passing La Boisselle, entered the scene of a more terrible ordeal. Every machine of death the Germans had was turned upon the head and flanks of the shattered but undaunted Britons. Trench-mortars ploughed the ground and blew men asunder ; high-explosive shells roared down in heavy salvos, while shrapnel and machine-gun fire played continually all along the route of advance, back to the British trenches. Amid this whirlwind of death a force of German troops appeared unexpectedly, under the covering fire of their guns, to stay the advance. But the sight of resistance in human form was a relief rather than an extreme menace to the suffering Britons. The Royal Scots went forward at the double with the bayonet, and killed or captured all the Germans. The other battalions also changed step into the double, and in a long, furious spurt killed, captured, or routed all the Germans in the woods and works before Contalmaison. Then as the leading troops settled to consolidate the ground won, the battalions that had been behind them came forward and fought towards Contalmaison, which was reached by the Suffolks.

Ordeal of Contalmaison

The position bore mute testimony to the valour of the new British soldier. The three high entrenched downs in front of Contalmaison—Ovillers, La Boisselle, and Fricourt—were strongly held by the enemy, and days had to pass before they were conquered. But by a feat of incomparable vehemence and tenacity the division to which the Suffolks were attached had thrust itself far into the rear of the enemy's line. What was then needed, while this brigade was being reinforced in great strength, was a directing squadron of aerial infantry to carry Staff orders to the victorious brigade to clear its flanks and enable it to advance southwards against the rear of the enemy lines. But at the hour in which the wonderful charge was driven home to Contalmaison, some of the brigadiers and divisional generals who were attacking La Boisselle and Fricourt appear to have thought that they were in a position to master the villages, advance over the downs, and connect near Contalmaison.

All down the line, during the first rush into the hill villages, there was an almost general misapprehension of the strength of the enemy forces concealed underground. These concealed forces were not always attacked in overwhelming strength, owing to the fact that, as they were invisible, an immediate farther advance

Enemy's under-
ground defences

seemed to be the obviously correct tactics. To seize as much ground as possible before the enemy recovered from the stunning effect of the bombardment appeared good tactics. From the marvellous thrusts made by the Manchesters at Montauban, the Gordons at Mametz, the Suffolks at Contalmaison, the Ulstermen in the Ancre sector, and the North-countrymen at Serre, we may fairly conclude that this series of long swift thrusts was designed by the General Staff because the long bombardment was expected to crush the enemy's first line. The unparalleled strength of the enemy's underground defences may thus have been underestimated, and the destructive power of the new heavy British artillery rather overestimated.

The troops who reached Contalmaison were in much

[*British official photograph.*

HIGH SPIRITS AND HIGH COURAGE MARCHING TOGETHER.
The East Yorks marching up to the trenches the night before an attack, their boyish spirits an essential part of the splendid fighting quality they consistently displayed from the very beginning of the advance.

the same position as the troops that had got into Serre. There was no other British force in the neighbourhood to which they could link up, as the other thrusts had been checked. So Contalmaison had to be abandoned, and the Suffolks and their comrades drew back towards the vicinity of La Boisselle, under an indescribable combination of shell fire, machine-gun fire, and front and flank bomb attacks, such as made the awful conditions under which the charge had been driven home seem light compared with the conditions of a retreat. The charge of the Light Brigade in the Crimea, undertaken by long-service men going at a gallop against slow, muzzle-loading guns and slow, short-range rifle fire, does not bear comparison with the charges which the new British infantry made at a walking pace, down valleys two miles long, against machine-guns firing six hundred rounds a minute, quick-firers throwing twenty shells a minute, and scores of siege-guns and trench-mortars. Wordsworth said of his countrymen in the Napoleonic era : "In everything we are sprung of earth's first blood." And he founded this claim upon the fact that Great Britain had produced Shakespeare and Milton, But without derogating from the genius of these poets, every man and woman who had children or kinsmen in the national army feels that something greater even than the greatest poetry had been achieved by the average young Anglo-Celt of the present time. The dead increased in number, but that which upheld them did not die, and either quickly or slowly it will turn this blood-stained planet into a fairer training-place for the pilgrim soul of man.

The toll of sacrifice on the tragic and glorious First of July was as heavy around Ovillers, between La Boisselle and Thiepval, as it was north of the Ancre. Ovillers, rising on a large, high down behind Pozières, and flanking the highway to Bapaume, was a position of terrible strength. Its zones of barbed-wire defences were in places more than a hundred feet deep, and the galleried caverns running through the chalk were so profound that the thunder of exploding shells on the ground above could scarcely be heard through the steel doors. But the light British artillery and the British trench-mortars had been excellently handled on some sectors around Ovillers, where the Dorsets, the Manchesters, the Highland Light Infantry, and Borderers swept over the enemy's front line with comparative ease. In

A WELCOME HALT BY THE WAYSIDE.   [*British official photograph.*
Worcesters resting on their forward way have a cheery greeting for the official photographer. They were among the regiments that had much heavy pounding, but always gave more than they got.

CHEERS FROM THE WILTSHIREMEN. *[British official photograph.*
Spirited scene as a number of gallant Wiltshiremen passed by the official photographer on their way to the Somme front.

the second line, however, a large body of Germans emerged full of fight from their burrows, and a battle of bombs opened. The Englishmen and Scotsmen rushed the line with the bayonet, and the German bomb-throwers would not face the cold steel at close quarters, and surrendered. Their water-pipes had been smashed early in the bombardment.

After the first successful drive around Ovillers a wall of shell on the British trenches and the ground between the Germans' lost line shut off the victorious brigades from their supports. The enemy arose from his subterranean retreats and, with bombs and machine-guns, trench-mortars, and skilfully placed snipers, battered the head of the advance, while the barrage fire almost severed its neck. The struggle rose to supreme intensity on Saturday afternoon, when the British wave that had swept over Thiepval in the morning and over La Boisselle began to recede, and Ovillers, lying between these two main strongholds, was strengthened by the enemy and retained. The British troops held to the ground they had won on either side of the village. Also in the elbow between Ovillers and Thiepval a formidable work known as the Leipzig Trench, guarding the southern approach to Thiepval, was at last carried after a long and violent struggle. But at nightfall on July 1st all the line south of the Ancre from St. Pierre Divion to Fricourt was practically unconquered.

Each great bastion of tunnelled chalk held out against the gallant and battered British divisions clinging to the lower slopes. Only at Mametz and Montauban was there a decisive break in the enemy's first zone of defences. Little more than three miles of connected works had been carried to a depth of a mile and a quarter by the six British army corps under Sir Henry Rawlinson, which had gone into action on a front of sixteen miles. The general situation at nightfall resembled that of General Castelnau's forces in the Champagne offensive in the autumn of 1915. The British left wing, led by two newly promoted generals—Lieut.-General H. S. Horne and Lieut.-General W. N. Congreve—had forced the enemy's line as the troops under General Pétain had done at Massiges. But the main movement had not produced the designed effect.

There was, however, a profound difference in the spirit of the two offensives. Sir Henry Rawlinson,

who had made his name as the leader of the Immortal Division at Ypres, where he had been reinforced by Sir Douglas Haig's two divisions, was fully prepared for a slow, long, grinding movement. Unlike General Castelnau in Champagne, he had not expected to storm through all the enemy's lines. The utmost he had attempted was to master the first zone of German defences, and though he had not fully achieved this end, he had at least driven a three-mile wedge through the hostile fortress system. And by means of the wedge at Montauban and Mametz he began to disrupt the principal German positions south of the Ancre.

There was a rapid reconcentration of British artillery on the Somme sectors, and the great head of shell was all turned south. Although this move was answered by the shifting of German guns from Prince Rupert's front to the Somme sector, the complete massing of the British artillery was carried out more quickly. From Thiepval to Fricourt the German hill fortresses incessantly flamed and smoked with exploding British shells. Trench after trench, already menaced by British soldiers lying in shell-holes and gutted, broken ditches, was blasted by the Royal Garrison Artillery, who were learning their work with astonishing quickness. Continually, amid the thunder and counter-thunder of the British and German guns,

Capture of Fricourt

the bomb-throwers of the New Army worked forward and behind Fricourt, La Boisselle, and Ovillers. Fricourt fell first—at two o'clock on Sunday afternoon. Its capture enabled Sir Henry Rawlinson to increase the pressure on La Boisselle, which became the scene of fighting of tremendous severity on Sunday night. There the British troops made small but constant progress, hammering at the garrison on one side and stalling off counter-attacks by fresh German troops that poured forward from the east. The struggle in the Hohenzollern Redoubt in the autumn of 1915 had seemed at the time to be the summit

THE SLEEP OF THE BRAVE. *[British official photograph.*
Royal Fusiliers resting after an action. Most of them have shed part of their equipment, the better to rest after their strenuous work. A party is playing cards.

CAPTIVE AIRCRAFT ABOUT TO ASCEND.
Observation-balloon being inflated somewhere behind the British lines.
The first photograph shows men of the R.F.C. bringing up the " nurse "
balloon.

NEARING THE NECESSARY PRESSURE.
The observation-balloon rising from the ground as the gas is being pumped into it. It is being held in
position by members of the Royal Flying Corps.

[*British official photographs.*

of human endurance. But the ditch and cave warfare that went on south of the Ancre in July, 1916, exceeded in ghastly ferocity and strain the fight in the Hohenzollern. The area of mole warfare was much larger, and, instead of a brigade carrying on the fight, army corps were fed through the shell curtains into the pitted, ditched, and parapeted slopes, which seemed to the casual eye a vacant stretch of lumpy, undulating ground.

Two invisible forces pounded the empty waste of chalk and gravel into white scars, spurts of white dust, flames, and windy funnels of green, black, and white smoke. Sometimes the red breath of a gun could be seen, but this was unusual, as it provoked counter-battery firing. The guns were hidden against reverse slopes or amid trees, and trench-mortars, that also produced terrific explosions, crawled unseen, like toads, at the bottom of the trenches. All that was plain to see was the long line of British and French kite-balloons squatting on their air-bags near their heavy hidden guns, while convoys of allied flying machines scouted over the enemy's lines, with perhaps one German observation-balloon timidly ascending for a brief glance at the British motor-lorries conveying the infantry to and from the field of battle.

Now and then a faint stir of movement appeared on the bright surface of shell-ploughed chalk. Brown figures, lying apparently dead in the holes, would rise and converge upon some long white scar that suddenly became tipped with flame. It was a British bombing-party charging a German machine-gun redoubt. And if they won the redoubt, the invisible German guns would strangely turn on it, in answer to some red signal fire or telephone message telling that the position had been lost. Such was the spectacle of modern scientific warfare, to which the thunder of guns, the racking shell explosions, the roaring travel of shells, the whistle of bullets, and rattle of machine-guns made an infernal accompaniment. Poison gas from high-explosive shell, chlorine shell, and bromide shell drifted about the slopes and made yellow stains upon the freshly turned soil. To add to the horror of the empty, flaming, screaming, rocking scene, the German machine-gunners and riflemen employed in large proportion explosive bullets, which are properly used only to strike the ground and measure the range. Yet in this daylight nightmare and nocturnal inferno the apprentice soldiers of Great Britain stuck to their work as nobly as the practised veterans of France, and by the pure virtue of their manhood and the native gift of leadership of their officers, ground the enemy down, forced him to surrender La Boisselle on Monday afternoon, and in the night broke a great counter-attacking force that came up in massed columns.

Surrender of La Boisselle

The nest: A canvas hangar at the front in France, with one of its mono-plane occupants just being brought in.

Taking wing: A flight-commander starting off upon a raid over the enemy lines in a biplane.

Anti-aircraft gun ensconced among the sheaves of corn, and (inset) an aeroplane out on reconnaissance passing over a mill—two pictures full of a curious and suggestive poetry.

[British official photographs.

Group of British airmen in front of a machine. Germany produced a few airmen of genius, but as a body her airmen did not prove comparable to their British and French competitors, who definitely secured supremacy in the air towards the end of 1916.

MEN AND MACHINES OF THE ROYAL FLYING CORPS IN FRANCE.

LIEUT.-GEN. SIR T. MORLAND, D.S.O.
Commanding the Tenth Army Corps of the
Fourth British Army on the Somme.
[Langfier.

LIEUT.-GEN. W. N. CONGREVE, V.C.
Commanding the Thirteenth Army Corps of
the Fourth British Army on the Somme.

A few hundred of the Germans managed to retake one of the small defences south of the village, but in another conflict that lasted twenty-four hours the fatigued but indomitable Britons in La Boisselle recovered all the village. Then, holding off the increasing multitudes of German troops coming south from Prince Rupert's army, the British forces near the Bapaume road pressed upwards against Ovillers.

The capture of La Boisselle was a decisive factor on the Somme front. It gave the army under Sir Henry Rawlinson the room it needed for an advance up the Bazentin slopes to the German second zone of defence. But later, it appeared that the German High Command and the Staff of Prince Rupert of Bavaria thought that Sir Douglas Haig was dissatisfied with the progress of his Fourth Army, and intended to attempt another break farther north. This led to a telling piece of feinting by the British commander. He divined the misjudgment of his opponents, and skilfully played upon it by resuming his demonstrations against the Prince of Bavaria. There was an abrupt renewal of British activity around the French mining districts south of Lille. On July 6th the enemy's front at La Bassée and Hulluch was furiously bombarded, then swept with a flood of poison gas, and afterwards blanketed in black smoke-screens. Behind the smoke-screens the Royal Welsh Fusiliers and the Highland Light Infantry raided the enemy's trenches, killing hundreds of men and capturing material and troops.

All this seemed to indicate that Sir Douglas Haig was testing the enemy's line on the old battlefield, with a view to a multiple offensive. The German commander behind the Royal figurehead, Prince Rupert, was confirmed in his idea of the general situation, and led to keep a large force of guns in the north when they were vitally needed upon the Somme. In the art of reading the enemy's mind Sir Douglas Haig at times approached the Duke of Wellington, and though the skill with which he played on the enemy's fears was somewhat veiled by the stable conditions of war on

Scots and Welsh at Hulluch

entrenched fronts, the success of the great Scotsman served considerably to help his fighting army commander, Sir Henry Rawlinson. At present it is only from unconscious hints in German accounts of the operations that we can trace the effect of Sir Douglas Haig's demonstrations before and during the Ancre and Somme operations. Naturally, no German admits or is allowed to admit that artillery and shells were retained on the Lille and Arras front which might have stopped the progress of the British Fourth Army on the Bazentin slopes. This, however, is what seems to have happened, owing to the fact that Sir Douglas Haig was a better general than any German facing him. The day after the feint below Lille the British garrison in La Boisselle made a tiger leap towards Contalmaison, and captured a maze of German trenches over a space of nearly ten thousand square yards. At the same time a brigade on the left drove into Ovillers, while another brigade on the right linked up with the La Boisselle force and captured two of the woods above Fricourt.

Lancashires at Bornafay Wood

During the struggle immediately south of the Ancre the victorious British corps around Montauban, Mametz, and Fricourt pressed against the enemy continually. On the right wing the large wedge of ground won by the Lancashires was extended on July 3rd by a storming advance into Bornafay Wood between Montauban and Longuval. The Germans had trenches on the southern and northern edges of the wood, with a row of entrenched redoubts down the middle. But in the first assault the Lancashire men broke into the sloping mass of shattered trees, and then by twenty-four hours of bomb and bayonet work entirely captured the wood on July 4th. They thus obtained command of all the valley of the Fricourt stream fronting the main slopes of the Bazentin ridges. The capture of the Bornafay Wood assured our hold on the Montauban heights, endangered the flanking German position in Trônes Wood, compelled the enemy to withdraw most of his guns around Guillemont, for fear they should be taken in a sudden assault, and relieved

GENERAL MARCHAND AND GENERAL MICHELER.
General Marchand (on the right), the famous French divisional commander, was badly wounded in 1915 when commanding in Champagne. In the autumn of 1916, his wounds being healed, he was given a command on the Somme. General Micheler had also been previously wounded.

the pressure on the Franco-British junction-point near Hardecourt.

Meanwhile, the British position on the left of the Mont-auban-Mametz ground was not so satisfactory. The enemy still retained a large wedge of wooded slopes and sheltering hollows in front of Contalmaison, and the reduction of this intricate system of fortified copses and trench undulations went on rapidly after the conquest of Fricourt. On July 2nd a fresh brigade replaced the gallant troops that had carried Fricourt, and charged into the high wood above the village. Swept at point-blank range by machine-gun and rifle fire and torn by shrapnel the leading battalions held on, and the heroic survivors got through the wire entanglements, and by slow, savage fighting captured the whole of Fricourt Wood by nightfall. All the night the diminished but undaunted brigade, which had had no sleep since July 1st, endured a heavy, smashing bombardment. When day broke, the men again charged the blunted top of the enemy wedge that ran from Bottom Wood, behind Mametz, through Railway Alley to Lozenge Wood and Shelter Wood near La Boisselle.

Vigorous frontal attack

A great stretch of wire entanglement protected the front of the enemy's works. A sharp, fierce storm of shells from the British guns swept away the wire with-out, however, damaging the sunken earthworks. And against these strongly held and intact works the gallant brigade made a vigorous frontal attack. The first wave of khaki surged out and withered away in the terrific German fire. A second wave speeding up, drew closer, but also ebbed away in death and agony. But the third wave broke over the German parapet, swiftly followed by a fourth and a fifth; several hundred prisoners were taken, and only a remnant of grey figures escaped into Shelter Wood. The British soldiers raced them across the slope, and before the original garrison of Shelter Wood could form up with the fugitives all were overwhelmed, and another four hundred prisoners were taken.

This frontal attack appears to have been made in misapprehension. The British brigadier, at the opening of the action, sent a company against the enemy's flank at Bottom Wood, which was quickly taken, and the con-querors began to bomb their way back towards Railway Alley.

Another company broke into the enemy's system on the other side, and also began to work back to Railway Alley.

Thereupon some of the Germans in the central Railway works lost heart, and, break-ing from all control, fled up the bare slope towards the great quadrangle of trenches which lay in front of

the village of Contalmaison and Mametz Wood. The sight of these enemy fugitives led to the belief that all the Railway system had been abandoned by the enemy, owing to the pressure on his flanks. It was in these circumstances that the frontal attack was undertaken, and the superb steadiness of the troops enabled them to win a larger victory than would have been possible had the German garrison been able to retreat in order into Shelter Wood. Lonely Copse and the works in Lozenge Wood were also stormed by the brigade, who took another hundred and fifty prisoners on the heights between La Boisselle and Fricourt, and enabled all the ground between these villages to be consolidated in preparation for the advance on Contalmaison and the great Quadrangle works that linked Contalmaison with Mametz Wood.

The Quadrangle, a mile in length and half a mile wide, connecting with Bazentin and Contalmaison, was a position of deceiving strength. It ran down a long slope into a hollow, and was protected by the Montauban and Fricourt ridges from the direct fire of the British artillery. It was diffi-cult to place howitzer shells, at long range, exactly on the yard's **Fall of the great Quadrangle** breadth of the great works, and the light British field-guns had to fire practically in the open, under the eyes of German observation gunnery officers on the Bazentin ridge, in order to break down the wire entanglements around the Quadrangle. There was more than a quarter of a mile of bare slope between the British valley position at Bottom Wood, and the German machine-gunners, working through loop-holes in their dug-outs thirty-five feet above the charging British infantry, poured a deadly plunging fire down the long incline. Three frontal attacks on the Quadrangle failed, and it was only captured, after five days' operations, by a flank and rear attack from Mametz Wood and Contalmaison.

Before the fall of the Quadrangle, General von Below on the morning of July 7th fought a grand pitched battle with Sir Henry Rawlinson. The German commander on the Somme front, with General von Arnim as his local subordinate in the Bapaume sector, employed all the avail-able strength of Ger-many against the Fourth British Army.

He borrowed the best troops of General von Marschall from the Arras front, collected divisions, brigades, and even battalions from the Aisne and Cham-pagne sectors, greatly increased the number of guns around Ba-paume, and made a supreme attempt to obtain a decision. The British offensive had then been proceeding day and night for a week, and the German commander reckoned

GENERAL VON STEIN.
Commander of an army corps in General von Below's army.

GENERAL SIXT VON ARNIM.
Commander of the Fourth Army Corps in General von Below's army.

GENERAL VON BELOW.
Commander of the German army upon the Somme front.

HANDFUL OF ROYAL WEST KENTS COVER THEMSELVES WITH GLORY IN DEFENDING TRÔNES WOOD.

One of the outstanding incidents of heroism in the early days of the Somme advance was the stand made by a handful of West Kents, almost surrounded by an overwhelming number of the enemy, in Trônes Wood. The men had become separated from the main attack, which was unsuccessful. A stronghold was organised, and with unlimited ammunition and two Lewis guns the enemy was kept at bay till dawn, when relief arrived.

that the survivors of the infantry in the battered British Fourth and Third Armies, and all the gunners and sappers who had been working for these armies, would have been tired out. The German High Command had had seven days in which to collect a mighty army of fresh troops, which was écheloned for many miles behind the Somme front. Headed by the Prussian Guard, fresh divisions were flung against the British army with a design to wear it down and bring it to a standstill. All that the Britons had won by months of concealed preparation, vast artillery demonstrations, and disconcerting raids had now to be held against a strengthened and desperate foe who had had time to mass his machinery in fairly equal force. All guns fired as fast as they could be served, in a mutual bombardment to which the preliminary artillery preparation of the British offered no parallel.

With the heavens roaring above them and the earth breaking beneath them, the main forces of Germany and the main forces of Great Britain met on equal terms. On July 7th, 1916, when the British brigades were sweeping upward from La Boisselle, Fricourt, and Montauban in a heavy rain that flooded trench and shell-hole and reduced what little cover there was, 5,000 men of the 3rd Division of the Prussian Guard tried to reinforce the garrison of Contalmaison, which was yielding, and advanced in close formation between the village and Mametz Wood. They were caught by the British guns and thrown back. Behind the shell curtain that caught the Guards came the slipping and lumbering, widely-spaced and heavily-laden Yorkshire infantrymen, and, as the Prussians reeled, the khaki figures loomed out amidst the splintered trees of Mametz Wood and closed the Prussians, killing, capturing, or dispersing all of them. Then the Yorkshires, with other North-countrymen, dashed into Contalmaison, cleared the cellars and fragments of wall with bombs, and released some British prisoners. By noon the village was completely stormed and occupied. But the rest of the Prussian Guard Division returned to the attack with magnificent intrepidity, and, coming down through the barrier fire of British shells, recovered Contalmaison. The Yorkshiremen, however,

Below's gigantic effort

held on near by in Mametz Wood, and the large number of captives they had taken from the finest force in Prussia, before storming Contalmaison, were disgusted to find they had fallen to the new British levies. They thought the British Guards alone could have put up so terrific a fight.

All the afternoon the battle swayed with indescribable intensity from the Ancre to Trônes Wood. British airmen began to act as aerial infantry, and swooped down on German battalions, raked them with machine-gun fire, and then directed long-range guns upon them.

Aerial infantry in action

The Bavarian regiment that had been driven from Montauban and taken shelter in a hollow near the top of the Bazentin ridge was observed by low-flying British air scouts and swept with shrapnel. When night fell both sides had captured hundreds of prisoners, but the British had won more ground and inflicted very severe punishment on the enemy. Some thirty yards of trench around Thiepval was all that the Germans had gained since daybreak. The British troops had advanced in Ovillers, and had progressed on a front of nearly two miles around Contalmaison.

The lie of the ground was against the enemy, as he had to fight on a wide-exposed slope upon which a great mass of British guns had been skilfully posted by months of organising work. The enemy had not prepared water reservoirs for the million men he gradually brought into battle in the narrow front between Combles and Thiepval. He used shells sometimes at the rate of a million a week on a front of little more than six miles. But as he had been struck unexpectedly on the Somme, he had not prepared platforms for unloading his trucks and stacking his shells where they could not be exploded by the long-range British artillery. His troops that detrained at Bapaume were continually caught by British naval guns, and the roads by which they marched to the communication-trenches were roads of death.

The crown of the Germans' misfortunes was their defeat in the air. After much delay Fokker had at last been temporarily conquered by Mr. Sopwith and other British and French aeroplane builders, and the aerial motor of the

German Mercédès Company had been rivalled, if not excelled, by British motor engineers, who had once had to work under the drag of the Royal Aircraft Factory. The traditions of the Mons era, when Messrs. Vickers, Mr. Roe, and other British aeroplane makers gave Sir John French's army fighting machines superior to those the Germans possessed, were revived and gloriously developed owing to the agitation initiated by "the Northcliffe P ess" that followed the Fokker successes. The British pilot, who had made himself the peer of the British seaman, was again provided with material means of meeting the enemy on equal terms.

Fokker finds his peer

The result was that the German disappeared for a time from the sky in almost the same measure as he disappeared from the North Sea. He could not direct his guns or observe the preparations for British infantry movements. All his railway centres from the Yser to the Aisne were subject to aerial bombardment. At times his troop trains were wrecked by bombing airmen, and when the troops fled from the carriages the British airmen descended and lashed them with machine-gun fire. These consequences of the loss of the mastery of the air told heavily upon the spirit of the German infantry. In many of the letters taken from prisoners the death-dealing exploits of French and British airmen and the refusal of battle by German airmen were chief causes of complaint, distrust, and war weariness.

The second week of the British offensive opened with the garrison at Ovillers still holding out in a mass of ruined ditches, unrecognisable rubble, and shell-holes deep enough to drown a man, and full of mud. The main work of the British army consisted of navvy labour, making new positions, new roads, and ammunition store caverns, to enable the guns to move forward towards the conquered ground. There was also heavy labour in improving the positions won on the slopes of the downs, and in making new communications to hollows that the German artillery could not easily reach. The rain impeded all this new labour of organisation. The chalk became as slippery as asphalt, and the horses and mules that worked behind the old railway lines took long to bring up the building material and stores. Like Mackensen in Galicia, Sir Henry Rawlinson worked onward only as fast as he could prolong his railway system. His motor-lorries moved the troops with perfect flexibility, but when the big guns went forward new railway-stations had to be built at the end of the three thousand miles of track that served to feed the batteries with millions of shells.

While the labour of extending the range of the artillery was proceeding, the British troops on the right flank on July 8th stormed into Trônes Wood, capturing a hundred and thirty prisoners and several machine-guns. As at Contalmaison, the enemy at once reacted and launched a great mass of men down the bare slope leading to the lost wood. But the Iron Division of France, that linked with the British army near this point, had brought forward some of its quick fi ers and worked them upon the slopes around Trônes Wood. Also some British batteries of 18-pounders were trained on the western approaches to the climbing woodland, and from the combined allied batteries there poured such a dense storm of high-explosive and shrapnel shell that the enemy masses were shattered before they could strike.

Iron Division strikes hard

All that the British troops suffered on July 1st between Gommecourt and Fricourt was well balanced by the ghastly punishment inflicted on the enemy in his large and ill-prepared counter-attacks such as this. On July 1st

CONCLUSION TO A VAIN GERMAN EFFORT: ATTACKING ENEMY ARRIVE AS PRISONERS.

German prisoners coming into the British lines after a futile counter-attack on Trônes Wood, following upon a particularly heavy bombardment. Although the first wave of infantry managed to get through the British barrage, it fell foul of some unbroken barbed-wire entanglement, and was held up, having no alternative but to surrender and cross the British trenches as captives. This convincing illustration shows the Germans, with hands above their heads, being shepherded through the unbroken obstruction by a businesslike-looking guard.

possibility of achieving a success. Thus did the native strain of brutality in the feudal caste of Germany, which made them devils in the hour of victory, weaken their military efficiency in the hour of defeat. Instead of saving their men for intelligently designed counter-strokes they wasted their forces prematurely in a series of brutal and ineffectual convulsions. Animating the bulldog courage of the British and the incomparable resilience of the French there was a quality of directive intelligence, which the German, for all his stubborn ferocity, did not display. He was a master of the routine of warfare, and industrious in preparation of a mechanical kind, but when manœuvring in difficulty, after being shaken by

[*British official photographs.*
RESPITE BEFORE ACTION.
Royal Welsh Fusiliers in bivouac behind the lines.

the British troops in the Ancre sector did at least break and hold considerable parts of the enemy's defences. But great bodies of German troops were smashed before they could attack, owing to the lack of skill of German commanders and German Staff officers. The enemy's artillery preparation was often futile, as he merely hurled shells on the British infantry positions and left the supporting British artillery practically undamaged by counter-battery firing. This in turn was due to the enemy's absolute defeat in the aerial struggle. An officer

Nemesis of German brutality of the Royal Flying Corps has stated that during the first phase of the Somme battle fourteen German reconnoitring machines crossed the British lines during a period in which three thousand British and French machines crossed the German lines.

Under these conditions the tragic lack of preparation shown in the German counter-attacks can be explained. On the other hand, a long and confidential report upon the situation, written by General von Arnim, was captured by the British, and in this technical and careful judgment of the German operations Arnim clearly indicates that some of his leading officers lost their presence of mind and wildly flung their troops out to die when there was no

NEAR TRÔNES WOOD.
Units busy laying the foundations of an advanced dressing-station.

a great reverse, he did not display the intellectual grasp that Frenchmen and Britons had shown during their great recoveries from serious checks and disasters. Such at least seems to be the verdict of Arnim upon his own officers.

With some illuminating extracts from the memorandum of General Sixt von Arnim we may well conclude this chapter:

The British infantry has undoubtedly learnt much since the autumn offensive. It shows great dash in the attack, a factor to which immense confidence in its artillery greatly contributes. The Briton also has his training and his physique in his favour. I must acknowledge the skill with which the British rapidly consolidated their captured positions. The British infantry showed great tenacity in defence. This was especially noticeable in the case of small parties, which were very difficult to drive out when once established in the corner of a wood or a group of houses.

Particularly noticeable was the large proportion of medium and heavy guns in the British artillery, which, apart from this, was far superior in number to ours. The British ammunition seems to have improved considerably. All our important tactical positions, and all our known infantry and battery positions, **Arnim's tribute to British** were methodically bombarded by the British guns. Extremely heavy fire was continually directed on to the villages immediately behind the firing-line, and on all natural cover afforded by the ground. Well-organised aerial observers assisted in registration and fire-control, and at night our villages were frequently bombed by aeroplanes.

The German general then goes on to deal with the general defects of his own organisation. He says that the German method of making trenches was wrong, and contends that the British system should be adopted.

ROYAL WARWICKS RESTING IN RESERVE.
Everyday scene on the Somme during the great British offensive.

The German trenches were too narrow, and needed to be widened to prevent the troops being buried by British shells. The German telephone system and signalling system proved totally inadequate, and required to be developed on the British model. German airmen were condemned for their lack of courage, and told to take a lesson from " British airmen who are often able to fire successfully on our troops with machine-guns by descending to a height of a few hundred yards." The British method of keeping rifles from being clogged with dirt was also recommended, and the heavy German machine-gun was condemned. But this is the most remarkable passage in General von Arnim's report :

Arnim on counter-attacks

Insufficiently prepared attacks and counter-attacks nearly always fail from being too hurried. If counter-attacks which, on account of the situation, ought to be methodically prepared are hurried, they cost much blood, and cause the troops to lose their trust in their leaders if they fail, which nearly always happens in such a case.

His last complaint of importance forms a striking testimony to the strategic genius of Sir Douglas Haig :

The supply of artillery ammunition of all kinds during the first days of the battle did not equal the great expenditure. Reserve supplies were only available in very small quantities. From July 15th onwards the supply of ammunition was better, but the supply was never sufficiently ample to make good the expenditure in the event of the railway being blocked for one or two days. The lack of gun ammunition was always felt, and large reserves were never available.

General von Arnim then goes on to explain how, in the first days of the battle, ammunition had to be borrowed from the northern army group, and brought up at night under very difficult conditions. All this signifies that Sir Douglas Haig's great demonstrations on the Lille and Arras sectors were successful in attaining their aim. The Germans had millions of shells in reserve, but these

THE VIRGIN AT ALBERT.

When the Germans shelled the Church Tower at Albert the statue of the Virgin on the summit was bent over at right angles, and there remained as if blessing the town.

reserves were dumped too far away from the Somme, and fifteen days elapsed before General von Below's army corps commanders obtained a considerable part of the ammunition they needed. All the preparatory organisation work, carried on for months by the British and French forces on the Somme, had passed unperceived by the enemy. For General von Arnim states he had no proper organisation for transporting large quantities of munitions and supplies from his ordinary railway-stations to the battle-front. His maps of his own ground were insufficient, not only in number but in execution. His gunners had not the proper ranges of the lost German positions, and could not work with precision from the new gun-sites to which they had to withdraw.

In fine, the German army at Bapaume was caught unawares by the British offensive that had been openly in preparation for months. Towards the close of his memorandum General von Arnim has a curious sentence. He tells his officers to arrange that all infantry preparing for an assault should use puttees like British troops. Why puttees and lace boots should add more power to an attacking force the general does not explain. It seems as if he wanted his troops to look as much as possible like Britons, to veil the fact that they had not " the training and physique " of the once-despised amateur soldiers of the island race.

German confession of inferiority

THE MADONNA OF MONTAUBAN.

Montauban was the target for some of the most terrific shell fire ever rained on one spot. When we took the place this statue, and the German shell at its feet were the only things found whole.

THRILLING INCIDENT OF THE GREAT SOMME ADVANCE: THE CAPTURE OF FALFEMONT FARM.

British troops, streaming up from the corner of Wedge Wood in the left middle distance and along that formerly was Falfemont Farm. The farm buildings stood where the white heap is at the the chalk trench in the foreground, are entering the left-hand corner of the rectangular bit of ground right-hand corner of this site. On the extreme right the Germans are fleeing towards Morval Church.

THE GREAT BRITISH BATTLES OF THE SOMME.
III.—Battle of the Woods and the Bazentin Ridges.
By Edward Wright.

Battalion Reorganisation in the Fourth Army—General Jacob Reinforces the Somme Attack—Defeat of Prussian Guard at Contalmaison—Great Welsh Victory in Mametz Wood—Swaying Conflict in Trônes Wood—Heroic Stand by West Kents—Sussex Victory Relieves Kent—How Sir Douglas Haig Celebrated France's Day—Storming of Bazentin Wood—Adventurous Advance into High Wood—Battle of Bazentin-le-Grand—Unexpected Cavalry Charge into Enemy's Third Line—Highland Pipers at Longueval—Terrible Struggle Beneath the Village—South Africans Capture Delville Wood—German Commanders' Ghastly Method of Attrition—South Africans' and Highlanders' Marvellous Defence—Prussian Guardsmen in Ovillers Defeated by Thirst—Extraordinary Exploit of Lancashires—Anzacs and Territorials at Pozières—Conquest of Main Ridge—Twenty-four Square Miles of Somme Fortifications Won in a Month.

THE Englishman learns slowly from books, but quickly from experience. When he is mixed in proper proportion with his kinsman the Lowland Scot and his fellow-islanders the Gael and the Welshman, the combination does not lack intellectual quickness. The lesson all the Britons had received in the Ancre sector from General von Marschall and General von Buchs had been a hard one, but it was rapidly turned to profit. Sir Douglas Haig and General Kiggell came down to the Somme, and with Sir Henry Rawlinson and his brilliant lieutenants improved the organisation of the armies. By the end of the first week of July, 1916, the German trick of hiding hundreds of men in underground caverns during the hostile charge and bringing them up to attack the rear of the advancing troops had been countered. Battalion organisation was conducted on the new French model. Charging troops had to travel light without their packs, and were divided into three orders. First came the fighting troops whose work it was to carry positions with bomb and bayonet, with a few machine-

gun teams and Lewis gun teams in support. Second came searching parties whose duty it was to take over each captured position, work through the underground cellars and tunnels, and thus prevent any surprise in the rear of the fighting troops. Third came the consolidating parties for sapper work and assistance to the first and second orders. All three orders travelled light, and relied upon following battalions to get through the enemy's fire curtains and bring them food and supplies.

The artillery, which was daily improving in marksmanship, needed little reorganisation. The German gunners were for the time thoroughly beaten in front of Bapaume, and the British artillerymen were able to work in the open air. Tens of thousands of Britons, pallid as miners through living in gun-pits, began to redden and brown under the summer sun and wax in health and self-confidence. They could see that the enemy was at the time defeated in gun-power. The British guns stood close together on the fields, blazing at the hostile slopes and pitching into the hostile hollows without being strongly countered. For General von Arnim could

AFTER A WAR COUNCIL.
General Joffre, Sir Douglas Haig, and (right) General Foch leaving head quarters at the conclusion of a conference.

[British official photograph.

PREPARING PROPS FOR HEAVY-GUN EMPLACEMENTS. [British official photograph.
In the vast preparation for the Allies' advance on the Somme, General Fayolle said that a ton of wood came next in value to a ton of shells.
Much of the wood, felled by battalions of lumbermen, was wanted for props for gun-positions, and some of these are here shown being cut.

scarcely get enough ammunition to maintain barrages over the ground where the British infantry was working. He could not spare shell for much counter-battery firing, and had, indeed, more than he could do to keep his gun-positions hidden. He was fighting desperately for time to procure more shell and more guns, and though in the end he won the time for which he fought, his period of weakness in turn enabled the British command to put the British troops fully through their period of apprenticeship and make them veterans in the art of war.

The famous report by General von Arnim **Arnim's valuable** contained, in addition to the extracts **criticisms** given in the previous chapter, certain technical criticisms on the way in which the British troops had fought. These criticisms have not at present been published, but they were more valuable to the British Staff than the praise that Arnim bestowed upon his enemies.

Meanwhile, Sir Henry Rawlinson's army, after being checked by the heavy rain at the end of the first week in July, was reinforced by the Second Army Corps under Lieutenant-General C. W. Jacob, and continued to move forward all along the line towards the enemy's second zone of defences on the Bazentin ridges. There were four main obstacles to the British advance. On the left was Contalmaison, which the Prussian Guard had recovered. In front of this village was the great Quadrangle Work, which was connected by a German light railway with the large obscure fortress of Mametz Wood. Then about two and a quarter miles east of the great wood was the German bulwark of Trônes Wood stretching in front of Guillemont.

Contalmaison was the chief key position, as it was the support to the frontal downland village of Ovillers. In Ovillers the German garrison was still strongly holding out, and it could not be taken in the rear until a way of approach was secured from Contalmaison. But the first two drives into Contalmaison had failed, owing to the

enemy's strength in the Quadrangle and Mametz Wood. Therefore, instead of attempting any further single operations, Sir Henry Rawlinson arranged, on July 10th, a general attack against the Contalmaison-Quadrangle-Mametz line. The German garrisons had been served with an emergency ration of seven days' food, and given the order "To the last man." But though they were the finest troops in the German Empire, and included a large force of the Prussian Guard, they were not equal to the task assigned to them. The preliminary British bombardment was of unparalleled intensity and part of the garrison of Contalmaison lost heart under it, and, fleeing in the open, were caught by the British shrapnel barrage and also mowed down by the machine-guns of their enemy's supporting forces. Amid the partial confusion caused by this flight the north-eastern corner of Contalmaison was stormed by two companies of British troops. This was an extraordinary achievement. For the Prussian Guard in and around Contalmaison were ten times as numerous as the victors. The enemy was taken completely by surprise. He had expected an attack from the south, where there was an open space of twelve hundred yards, swept by his machine-guns and his artillery fire. But a small British force had worked the day before towards Horse-shoe Trench, on the flank of Contalmaison. The Horse-shoe position **Horse-shoe position** was carried by a British officer, accom- **stormed** panied by one man. He stormed across the intervening space with a load of bombs, killed the enemy gun crew and bombed out the other occupants of the trench. This fine feat opened the way to Bailiff Wood, and in the afternoon of July 10th, when the forces of Contalmaison were massed southward where the main British attack was preparing, the five hundred men from Bailiff Wood rushed the north of the village and began to bomb their way southward.

At the same time another and a larger British force of two thousand men advanced on Contalmaison in short, swift rushes covered by artillery fire. Taken on two sides, the Prussians fought variously. About two hundred of them were as brave as men could be, and struggled until they died. But by far the greater part broke when the British bayonet lifted over their parapet. But, again as they fled, the British artillery caught them, and their bodies were afterwards found in masses of four hundreds beyond the village. The Germans furiously counter-attacked, but in vain. The guns of Great Britain had moved forward and covered all the approaches to the village.

An American observer, Mr. D. Thomas Curtin, saw the return of the Prussian Guard from Contalmaison when they arrived in hospital trains at **Broken Guards return** Potsdam. The German public was ex-**to Potsdam** cluded from the station, and the wreck of the Guard was secretly removed to hospital by innumerable furniture vans. The blow delivered by the new British soldier had been so heavy that the German authorities were afraid to let their people see what had happened.

Contalmaison, however, was only the left flank of the battle-line of July 10th. South of the village was the great Quadrangle Work, which was connected by a German light railway with Mametz Wood, Bazentin, and Martinpuich. We have seen in the previous chapter that the Quadrangle, with its line of plunging fire, wire entanglements, and redoubts, resisted the first frontal attack. But on succeeding days most of the work was gradually mastered by bomb fighting of a most ferocious kind. Quadrangle Trench, Quadrangle Alley, and Wood Trench, all held in great strength, were conquered by the evening of June 10th. There then remained only one formidable position

south of Contalmaison, consisting of Quadrangle Trench and Acid Drop Copse, which was a great machine-gun position leading to Pearl Alley.

The Quadrangle support was the western bulwark of Mametz Wood as well as the southern outwork of Contalmaison. But when most of the Quadrangle had been reduced by the afternoon of July 10th, Mametz Wood became exposed to attack on three sides. The wood was a masterpiece of defensive strength. In the autumn of 1914 it had consisted of two hundred and twenty acres of finely cultivated saplings, which were being gradually thinned to produce good timber. The enemy allowed the wood to run wild for two years, until it became a tangled jungle of young trees and brambles, through which a man

[British official photographs.

IN THE FIRST-LINE TRENCHES: FAR FROM THE PACIFIC SHORES.
New Zealanders, having consolidated a switch trench, enjoy a short spell of rest, and incidentally some slices of bread and jam. The smaller photograph shows a group of the same regiment in a shell-hole on the Somme front.

had to twist his body in order to get forward. In this impenetrable growth the enemy cut drives to facilitate the movement of his troops, built a light railway, concealed batteries of guns, most of which he afterwards removed, constructed machine-gun redoubts, and thickened the southern end of the wood with lines of barbed-wire.

Mametz Wood was so strong that the British general operating from Montauban decided at first to leave the great wood for siege operations, and work round on either side of it until it was enveloped. His patrols had begun to penetrate the southern edge on July 6th, and they caught the Germans asleep there, killed fifty of them, and found two field-guns put out of action by British shell fire. After this brilliant dash the attacking troops consolidated themselves in a small patch of trees known as Marlborough Wood, lying between Montauban and Bazentin, and flanking the eastern skirts of Mametz Wood. From this eastern position the British general prepared his main attack upon the jungle forest. The enemy on the Bazentin ridge saw what was coming, and in the afternoon of the general British attack the German guns opened a terrific barrage fire over the bare valley between Marl-borough Wood and Mametz Wood. But **Victory at** the British attack on this side never **Mametz Wood** developed. All the preparations had been a ruse. For while the German guns were barricading the eastern valley a strong British force stormed into the southern side of the wood, and preceded by a moving zone of terrific artillery fire that overwhelmed the garrison and levelled the trees, the attackers went through the tangled growth like a forest fire.

[British official photograph.

TRAVELLING WATER-BUTTS ON THE WEST FRONT.
Highlanders quenching their thirst at travelling water-butts. Above:
Hauling an electric engine for condensing water to a Somme position.

There was three-quarters of a mile of broken woodland seamed with open drives, along which machine-guns played, and full of caverns, gun-pits, and unexpected entanglements. The fighting was of a wild, rough-and-ready kind, for the clumps of unbroken thicket round which the men worked prevented close co-operation. It was a true soldiers' battle, and revealed both the virtue and the defect of the new British levies. Their driving power, singly or in groups, was magnificent; to it the victory was due. But the leading men were at last carried away by the pure lust of battle. At the northern edge of the wood, when the entire position was practically conquered, the British artillery, working by the watch, were maintaining a heavy shell fire over the fugitive enemy. By this time the infantry had got well ahead of their time-table, and being more impatient than regular soldiers or veteran conscripts would have been in the same circumstances, the vehement young Britons advanced through their

A POPULAR POINT IN THE ADVANCE.   *[British official photograph.*
Thirsty soldiers who took part in the Somme offensive drawing water from a well on one of the main roads leading up to the battle-line.

own shell curtain, in order to deal a quick and vital blow at the enemy.

This was an example of courage in the wrong place. The head of the British force was badly battered by its own guns, and then counter-attacked by the German reserves and compelled to fall back to the middle of the wood. In the night the Germans lashed the trees with a heavy bombardment, and then launched a strong counter-attack from the north-eastern and northern sides of the woodland. This counter-attack completely failed, owing to the fine musketry, machine-guns, and bombing skill of the new British soldiers. In the morning of July 11th five Welsh battalions again advanced through the northern stretch of the broken tangle of trees. Most of the ground was won, but there was a strip of fifty yards on the northern edge which the Germans made impassable. In their line of works there they had trench-mortars as well as machine-guns and rifles, and they checked every Welsh charge by means of big bombs and streams of bullets.

The Cymric troops retired from the zone of death, and for half an hour their artillery pounded the edge of the wood. Then another advance was attempted, but the bombardment had not put all the German machine-guns out of action, and the newly-fallen timber made barricades against the attack. Nevertheless, the wasting Britons once more resumed their heroic work, and in a final effort of indomitable pluck they carried the enemy's lines in the afternoon. Among the spoils were four light or heavy guns, several trench-mortars, many machine-guns, and some four thousand prisoners, all captured by one British army corps. The prisoners came from the 3rd Reserve Division of the Prussian Guard, the 16th Bavarian Regiment, and the 122nd Würtemberg Regiment, with units from the 77th and 184th Regiments. These prisoners were exclusive of those taken at Contalmaison and beyond, and their numbers and diversity proved that the victorious army corps that captured Mametz Wood had at least beaten a German army corps and practically destroyed it. The British gunners engaged in the Mametz operations were also highly distinguished by their quickness and scientific precision. Prisoners by the thousand testified to the fury of their fire, and remarked that it was far worse than anything they had endured at Verdun, and Sir Henry Rawlinson especially congratulated the gunners for their work in Mametz Wood. Here, at nightfall on July 11th, the new British line was within three hundred yards of the second zone of German defences on the Bazentin ridges.

While the battle was going on in Contalmaison and Mametz

Brilliant work of the Welsh

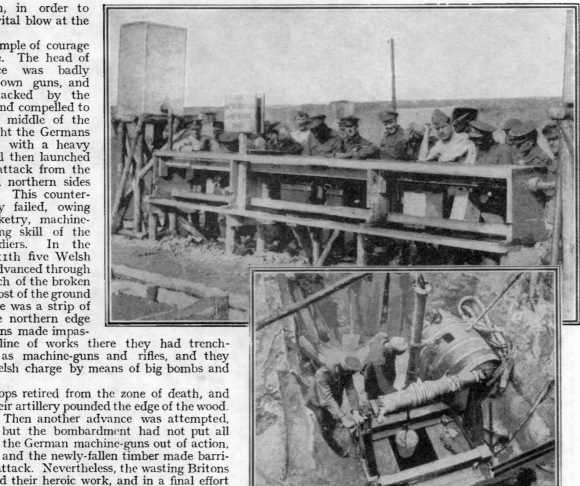

MINING OPERATIONS IN AN ENEMY TRENCH.
German soldiers engaged at a mine-shaft on the Somme front. Above: British water depot where bottles and dixie-tins could be filled.

THE PUMP IN PICARDY.
At a pump alongside a light railway. Soldiers filling flasks and tins with water. A network of such railways laid down behind the first line greatly accelerated operations.

SAVAGE HAND-TO-HAND FIGHTING WITH BOMB AND BAYONET IN DELVILLE WOOD.

In Delville Wood, called "the Devil's Wood," the South Africans in particular had some savage fighting. "The ghastliness of the place has left its mark upon the minds of many men who are not troubled much by the sights of battle," wrote Mr. Philip Gibbs. "Those slashed trees, naked trenches, and smoking shell-holes build up a nightmare that men will dream again."

Wood the German commander tried to redress the losses on his left by a furious drive from his right into Trônes Wood. This wood was some two and a half miles from Mametz Wood, stretching across the top of the narrow valley along which a stream ran to Fricourt. It lay about a mile east of Montauban. The enemy had two railway lines running through it and connecting it with Guillemont and Combles. Trenches extended through the middle of the wood and along the northern and southern sides, while wire entanglements with machine-guns behind them protected the western edge from assault. The Lancashire troops that captured Montauban quickly extended their hold to the large intervening woodland of Bornafay Wood.

Fighting in Trônes Wood

Then, on July 8th, a lodgment was gained in Trônes Wood by fighting of a most violent character, in which the British infantry, assisted by French gunners with "75" quick-firers from the famous Twentieth Corps, rapidly developed their partial grip into an advance of a thousand yards through the dense green tract.

Trônes Wood then became a long, wide wedge, fourteen hundred yards from north to south and four hundred yards along its base, driven against the enemy's second line at Guillemont and Longueval. But there was a serious disadvantage in the new British salient. It was swept on three sides by heavy German gun fire, and also enveloped on these three sides by German infantry. General von Arnim, therefore, exerted all his available strength in men and shell to cut off this long wedge of hostile woodland. After a bombardment of guns of all calibres, the German infantry attacked in the evening of July 8th, and was shattered by French and British guns. Again, in the afternoon of July 9th, the Germans charged in great force, were broken by gun fire, re-formed, charged once more and were completely broken by the fire of the French and British guns.

Then, while the battle was raging at Contalmaison and Mametz Wood, General von Arnim spent his men's lives in tens of thousands in an effort to recover Trônes Wood. With 6 in., 8 in., and 12 in. howitzers he sought out the light French and British artillery that had broken his former charges. He hammered the wood from end to end with high explosive and shrapnel, and then, by enveloping assaults, he strove to recover the last bulwark of Guillemont and Longueval.

A strong attack from the east was completely repulsed, but as it ebbed away another grey mass stormed into the southern end of the wood, and as the leading battalions reached the last German trench there, their supports were caught by gun fire and they themselves were smashed by hand-bombs, bullets, and bayonets.

The position then resembled that at Montauban after the Manchesters had broken a grand counter-attack. But the German commander was being supplied with new troops, collected by the hundred thousand from all other fronts. Unperturbed by his tremendous losses, he flung out two more divisions at night to repeat the enveloping assault. For the fifth time his men completely failed under a hurricane of shell fire from British guns west of Trônes Wood and French guns near Hardecourt. But in the afternoon of July 10th a sixth desperate attack enabled the Germans to regain the greater part of the wood. Successful as the enemy's tactics seemed then to be, the British Fourth Army had by far the larger balance of human gains. The slaughter among the Germans was comparable with that which had occurred at Ypres in the autumn of 1914, and in spite of their ghastly sacrifice their hold upon the wood was not strong.

The guns of France dominated the wood from the region of Hardecourt, and the guns of Great Britain enfiladed it entirely from the region of Montauban. The British infantry had two routes of approach, one from Bornafay Wood and the other from the entrenched high ground

southward. And at this critical period the general superiority of the allied artillery told widely upon the enemy. All German troops in the firing-line, in the supporting villages, and on the roads from the rail-head were exposed to unceasing gun fire. As it is reckoned there were then thirty German divisions congregated in front of Bapaume against the British front alone, their density exposed them to unusual punishment. For above the British guns were the keen-eyed, audacious British airmen, exercising for the time the supreme mastery of the air. Under these conditions a conflict of savage attrition amid the shattered holes, shell-craters, and wrecked trenches of Trônes Wood tended to the advantage of the British army.

In the morning of July 11th the wood was again swept by the allied artillery with shells ranging down from seven hundred pounds to eighteen pounds. After some hours of a general ploughing fire the guns massed in a single gigantic machine effect, and punctured the ground in regular holes as the British infantry again advanced. The men went on slowly from shell-hole to shell-hole behind the line of black-red wavering funnels that marked each explosion of high-explosive shell. As

[*British official photograph.*

A HELPING HAND FROM THE ENEMY.
German prisoner, captured during the early days of the Somme advance, holding a motor-cycle steady while the despatch-rider starts the machine.

the funnels of smoke rose from the earth a streak of little clouds of smoke appeared in the sky. This was the shrapnel curtain that forced the enemy garrison to remain in its dug-outs. The German gunners in turn threw a hurricane of shrapnel over the approaches to the wood, and this operation was also answered on the British side by counter-battery firing directed by scouting aeroplanes. In the event the British artillery prevailed, enabling the British infantry once more to sweep the blasted wood as far as the northern trench connected with Longueval. On July 12th the enemy again counter-attacked and recovered a considerable part of the wood. The next day the famous West Kent Regiment entered the salient that the British soldiers had begun to call Hell Hole Wood, but after a fierce, swaying, hand-to-hand conflict, amid the thunder of British, French, and German artillery, the West Kents had to give ground.

Terrible see-saw conflict

By an enveloping operation the German commander cut off a hundred of the West Kents in the upper part of the

AFTER GALLIPOLI: AN ANZAC CORNER IN THE WESTERN BATTLE-LINE.
At a field-kitchen within the Australian lines. Scene in a Colonial corner of Picardy where some of the Anzacs were enjoying afternoon tea.
Beneath the ridge are seen the dug-outs, whose entrances were neatly consolidated with sandbags and corrugated iron.

[British official photograph.]

wood and broke into the battalion headquarters of the regiment on the southern side. The temporary headquarters was badly battered by the enemy's heavy shell fire, and as officers and men were driven to seek cover, the gun fire lifted and the German infantry charged forward in the darkness. " Stand to arms!" cried an officer who saw them coming. With a dozen orderlies and signallers, hastily arming themselves with bombs and rifles, he beat off the counter-attack. Meanwhile, the hundred men and their captain in the middle of the wood saw the Germans stream by them, but collected some Lewis guns and ammunition abandoned by other troops in an earlier struggle and constructed a ring position by one of the enemy's original roads through the woodland.

Heroic stand by West Kents

For twenty-four hours the Germans attacked the little band of heroes on all sides. They tried to rush the Lewis gun positions by bomb attacks, delivered under the covering fire of massed machine-guns. They attempted to creep in the darkness from shell-hole to shell-hole and wear the West Kents out by lobbing grenades at them. But the British captain had arranged such lines of fire with his Lewis guns and rifles that every attack was broken. Thirty-five Germans were made prisoners during the vain rush attacks, and as these men had been well provided with food and water, their capture helped the defence. But the situation was one of indescribable strain. For Sir Henry Rawlinson, thinking that the wood had been entirely lost, was subjecting all of it to a bombardment of unparalleled intensity. The British general was preparing to storm the enemy's Bazentin line. For this purpose he had massed on the narrow Somme sector all the guns, unneeded for local defence, that had been employed in the first ninety-mile bombardment. On the rest of the British line there was only artillery for protection and demonstration effect. Every available British gun, with many French guns, was trained on Trônes Wood and on the surrounding villages and ridges. On July 1st the gun fire had been too much dispersed, owing to the fact that the army still had not all the artillery and shell required for action on a wide front. On July 14th the guns and head of shell were concentrated with incomparable intensity on a very small segment of the hostile line. Part of this bombardment fell on the West

Kents. But they were a regiment with a reputation second to none—the regiment that never lost a trench and made generals out of its colonels. They grimly endured the British hurricane of shell, which had its helpful side, as it interfered with the movements of the enemy. Despairing of carrying by infantry attack the position held by the little English band, the Germans parleyed and asked the West Kents to surrender to avoid destruction by artillery. No surrender being offered, the enemy began to place field-guns in position. Meanwhile the tornado blasts from the massed British guns rose to an extreme intensity on the morning of July 14th, and behind the moving barrage of shell came the Sussex and other English county regiments. Trônes Wood was slowly but decisively conquered in a terrific infantry action conducted under a stupendous double crash of shell from British and German arcs of artillery. All the ground wrecked by British gunners to help their troops was again ploughed by German gunners to check the British advance. Amid these contending storms of thunderbolts the Sussex heard the cry, " Hallo, boys !" It came from the glorious party of West Kents who were thus rescued, after achieving one of the finest exploits in the war.

July 14th was the anniversary of the storming of the Bastille, and the great festival day of the French Republic. In Paris and London remarkable preparations had been made for the civic celebration of the day on which the new spirit of Continental democracy in Europe was born, and France succeeded the United States as the torch-bearer of liberty. Sir Douglas Haig, being a prac-tical-minded Scotsman, went his own way to celebrate the festival of France. He brought down men from the Ypres salient, hardened to every form of trench warfare, and five divisions that had won their first honours around Loos, and formed these into a new spear-head of attack. For a week the Staff officers worked day and night, snatching little sleep and little food at odd hours, while they linked the new forces with those that had won the first battle and arranged more guns and more shell against the strongly reinforced enemy batteries. On July 11th the new bombardment began in a manner that made the first great bombardment of July 1st seem an ordinary operation. The sky, ridges of ground,

How July 14 was celebrated

earthworks, and woods about Bazentin blazed with bursting shell. A blinding light leaped about like an infernal will-o'-the-wisp. The sight and the sound were such as to make even the waiting troops of the attack sweat with fear, and always the nerve-racking tumult increased as more British batteries of monster guns steamed into action.

The night of war on July 13th was of volcanic grandeur. Great clusters of shell burst all along the German second line, tearing open the ground and making **Night of volcanic** fountains of flame. In the British line **grandeur** the black undulations seemed everywhere reddened with the short stabs of fire coming from the assaulting guns. At three o'clock the moon wore below the sky-line, and the smoke of the explosions veiled the stars. Soon the first faint grey edge of early summer dawn glimmered over Bapaume, and, strangely amid the immense thunder of battle, a lark rose amid the whir of the great shells and miraculously made her song heard.

For as though at a signal from the angel of the dawn, the guns suddenly hushed. But the silence was still more deadly than the tumult. It was the moment of the great infantry attack, and as the gunners ceased firing to change their range, tens of thousands of dim figures sprang from their assembly trenches and went out and up the pitted slopes where the ruins of the villages of Bazentin-le-Grand and Bazentin-le-Petit, Longueval, and Guillemont glimmered on the great ridge. Everything was exactly timed.

While the lark was still singing the dawn broadened, enabling the Britons, who had got safely out in the open in the darkness, to see their way, discern each other, and keep formation. Then the dawn song of the lark was overwhelmed. All the British guns crashed on their new targets. A rattle of machine-guns came from the enemy's line, and as white, red, and green rockets soared beyond Contalmaison above the large wood in front of Bazentin-le-Petit hundreds of German guns joined in the indescribable tumult.

Additional German gunners had come from Gommecourt and other northern sectors to inflict, by their terrific barrage, another decisive defeat upon the attacking British infantry. But conditions were different from those at Gommecourt. Five minutes after the German curtain of shrapnel and high explosive fell on and in front of Mametz Wood an aeroplane **British airmen** hummed over the thin lines of khaki **intervene** figures. It was scarcely more than five hundred feet high, and the heroic pilot went right through the shrapnel curtain. Other machines swiftly followed him, until the entire scene of enemy activity was being studied by the new British aerial infantry. Some of them were spotters, who eyed the red tongues of the hostile barraging guns and at once brought down upon them salvo after salvo of heavy British shell. Others were veritable infantry of the air who swooped with machine-gun fire upon German troops

[*British official photograph.*

LONGUEVAL AFTER THE BRITISH HAD RECOVERED IT FOR FRANCE.
July 14th, 1916, saw the beginning of the second stage of the great Battle of the Somme, and on that day the British troops penetrated into the German second line, capturing Longueval, Bazentin-le-Grand, and Bazentin-le-Petit in their stride.

HOW AN AVALANCHE OF IRISHMEN OVERWHELMED A GERMAN TRENCH AT GUILLEMONT.
Irish troops particularly distinguished themselves at Guillemont. At one spot the advance was held up by a machine-gun, but a company of Irish rushed the gun, bayoneted the gunners, and captured the trench after a fight in which bayonet, butt, and fists were freely used.

and even attacked field-artillery gunners and anti-aircraft gunners who were visible from above. At the same time as this direct aerial pressure was exerted against the enemy, the successes and difficulties of the leading British troops were observed by aerial guardian angels and signalled to the patrolling Staffs.

At four o'clock one of the enemy's main positions, Longueval, was set on fire by one of the monster British guns, and the ruins burned like a great torch high on the slope against the background of Delville Wood. Meanwhile, the attacking British divisions were carrying position after position with clockwork precision. On the **Longueval position in flames** left they had a long series of woods and copses through which to fight. Each clump or tract of trees was organised by the enemy in the manner of Mametz and Trônes Woods. There were barbed-wire between the stems, snipers in rows behind the barbed-wire, machine-guns behind the snipers, and trench-mortars and field and heavy artillery in the rear, with underground shelters for each garrison. Nearly everywhere steep slopes rose from the British departure trenches to the German works, so that the defending troops had a sweeping, plunging fire of bombs and bullets against the attacking troops.

But the wonderfully rapid artillery preparations of the British army robbed the German garrisons of their natural advantages of ground and of their scientific advantages of fortification. At a little distance in front of the soldiers of the New Army there was a cloud of bursting shell. Beneath this cloud the Germans could not stand and live ; a hail of shrapnel beat upon them, mingled with the hammer-blows of high explosive that wrecked their parapets. They therefore retreated into their dug-outs, and then, at the moment nicely arranged by the synchronised watches of infantry and artillery officers, the guns suddenly lifted and the infantry went forward, catching the Germans before they could leave their shelters. Here and there an enemy machine-gunner arose in time to work his gun, and had to be desperately attacked by some heroic bomber or enveloped when the line had gone forward on either side of him. But, generally speaking, the speed of the infantry assault, combined with the precise march of the hammering line of British shell fire, defeated all the work of the German engineers.

Every Briton knew it was France's Day, and his cries of "La belle France !" and "Vivent les Français !" heartened him in his terrible and noble work. The troops that advanced against Bazentin-le-Petit, on the highest part of the ridge, were already veterans in the Somme battle. They had carried the angle in the German first line from Mametz to Fricourt, and stormed beyond to Danzig Alley and Bottom Wood. Many of them had been fighting since July 4th, and had done splendidly at Contalmaison. The new front they had to attack consisted of a zigzag line, with two sharp wedges south of Bazentin-le-Grand Wood. They had first to get through a wide zone of barbed-wire entanglements, then capture a long work, and afterwards break through another wire entanglement, storm a second fortified line, wage a bomb fight all through the wood, make a final charge over a slope, and bomb the village garrison out of their cellars.

There the British artillery was magnificent. Practically all the wire was cut, enabling the attacking troops to strike the trenches almost without a check, and get into the wood under favouring circumstances before the sky brightened. This saved them from the worst of the enemy's shell curtain, and, working forward with skilled dash, they won the wood in about an hour and a half. In addition to hidden machine-gunners and concealed parties of bombers, the troops in the wood had to contend against an heroic type of German who **Storming of** sniped from the tree-tops. These snipers **Bazentin-le-Petit** had had to endure the terrific and overwhelming bombardment, and the courage with which they stuck to their exposed position showed that the great British success was not obtained against a race of weaklings.

While the attack on the great wood was proceeding, other battalions on the left went in short rushes up the open incline to the village, and in less than half an hour blasted and stabbed their way into the ruins. This underground fortress was held almost entirely by machine-gunners, but the British movement had been so quick that it was not clear day when the bomb-throwers began to work beneath the jumble of brickwork and splintered stone on the crowning ridge. One sergeant, wounded at the opening of the cellar fighting, got first-aid from an orderly, and helped to dress three injured men of another battalion.

Then the four wounded men and the orderly crawled on the prowl, and spied a party of twelve Germans working a machine-gun from a cellar and taking a British force on the flank. A couple of bombs put the machine-gun out of action, and then five more Germans ran from another spot into the underground retreat. " Hands up ! " cried the sergeant. All except a German non-commissioned officer offered to yield. The wounded sergeant leaped upon the man who wanted to fight to the death, and all the party then surrendered. At half-past five both the wood and the village were won. In every enemy trench or knot of caverns the cleaning-up troops were preventing the attacking troops from being assailed in the rear, and collecting prisoners by the hundred and preparing the way for the consolidating parties.

Irish intrepidity at High Wood

The enemy forces that had retired on Martinpuich made a hasty violent counter-attack in the morning, and threw back the men who had won the village. But a signal brought the heavy British guns down on their old mark, and behind the tornado of shells Irishman and Briton again advanced and retook all the ruins. A second counter-attack was attempted, but it did not trouble the victors. A signal was sufficient to put a storm of shell over Martinpuich and the intervening ground, and under this mechanical rain of death the large hostile force was shattered and dispersed.

It was bad tactics on the part of the local German commander to use up his available troops in this manner. For he still held a large patch of woodland, three-quarters of a mile from the village, from which he could dominate all his lost position. This dominating point of the Bazentin ridge was the famous Foureaux Wood, called High Wood by the British soldier. High Wood was strongly connected by a maze of trenches with Martinpuich and Flers, and

was further flanked eastward by an intricate series of works of which Cork Alley was the first. Southward and lower down the slope High Wood was protected by German guns around Delville Wood on the one side and Pozières on the other side. Thus from four sides the Germans could defend High Wood. But the brilliant British brigadier-general, who had won Bazentin-le-Petit and extended his gains into the ravine east of the village, looked at High Wood and thought it would be worth winning. When the second and larger German counter-attack staggered and broke under the fire of the British guns, the Irishmen and their comrades advanced up the open slope, and in spite of the German machine-guns firing down from the corners of the wood, the positions were stormed with superb intrepidity and telling skill. Then, in a fierce, sharp struggle, all the wood was carried as far as the concealed northern line of works, to which the enemy was able to hang by pouring forces in from either side at Martinpuich and Flers. The operation seemed to be hazardous and unsound. Indeed, the enemy must have thought that this amazing leap on to the crowning tangle of foliage overlooking all his undulating positions running down to Bapaume was an error that balanced his two hasty and vain counter-attacks.

The strategy of sacrifice

At the time of writing, Sir Douglas Haig's judgment on the affair had not been published, but on the information then available it would seem that the extraordinary first swoop into High Wood was a fine example of the strategy of sacrifice that enables victories to be completed. It was a disconcerting menace to the enemy's third zone of defences. For if the dominating observation-point could have been permanently secured, the superior fire of the British artillery could have been constantly directed with precision against nearly everything visible between

CAPTURE OF A GERMAN HEAVY GUN NEAR HIGH WOOD.
Near High Wood a battalion of the New Army came on a heavy gun which had been caught by a shell as the gunners were limbering up to get away before our barrage passed them. They captured the gun and accounted for the remaining gunners, who were hiding in dug-outs close by.

[*British official photograph.*

SEAFORTHS HOLDING A FRONT-LINE TRENCH FACING MARTINPUICH.
The Seaforths distinguished themselves nobly in the advance, and notably in the assault upon the Serre plateau. The German organisation and resource displayed hereabouts were marvellous, but the sheer pluck and gameness of the British were invincible.

High Wood and Bapaume. The German commander, therefore, had to concentrate his principal forces on the task of making High Wood uninhabitable by the spear-head of the British army. He turned hundreds of guns upon the southern part of the woodland, and upon the hollow between the wood and the Bazentin villages, and at the same time he fed troops through Martinpuich and Flers into the network of works around the wood.

And in spite of these great efforts of the enemy the comparatively small British force in High Wood maintained

South Africans at Delville Wood

its ground all the night of July 14th and the day and night of July 15th. Only in the morning of July 16th did the advanced troops quietly withdraw to the new British main line in the Bazentin villages. The enemy had suffered so heavily in the surrounding works that he allowed the British to retire down the ravine without molesting them. The general result was that while the enemy had vainly been endeavouring, from the evening of July 14th to the early morn of July 16th, to recover High Wood by storm, and exposing his troops by divisions to incessant bombardment by a superior mass of British guns, all the conquered second zone of German defences was firmly consolidated and linked to the first zone of German defences. No grand counter-attack disturbed the British engineer and his assistants.

Had High Wood been left unoccupied, a large part of the German army of a quarter of a million men would have been thrown against the improvised British positions in the Bazentin villages, the enemy would have had a central wood in which to mass, and his position in the wood would not have been known. He would also have had the ravine between the two Bazentins and High Wood as partial cover from the British guns. But, owing to the brilliant strategy of the British commanding officer at Bazentin-le-Petit, the principal weight of the German counter-attacks was misdirected against High Wood, and there worn down to temporary exhaustion, while the new British line was being built up impregnably at the centre. It is scarcely too much to say that all the permanent successes on the new main line were secured, at comparatively small cost in the menacing circumstances, by the rapid and disconcerting thrust far forward into the

enemy's third zone of defences at High Wood.

There was another and somewhat similar leap forward at the most critical point of the right attacking line between Bazentin-le-Grand and Guillemont. Here Delville Wood was stormed and held with magnificent courage by the South African brigade, while the new main line behind them was consolidated. In the first assault along this part of the line there was a check at the hill village of Bazentin-le-Grand, defended by two parallel lines of trenches, rising a hundred and thirty feet above the river valley, from which the British troops advanced. Some of the barbed cables on the topmost slope had resisted all the shells poured upon them and were almost intact. Charging up the long slopes in the darkness before dawn the Britons on either side of the village crawled under the entanglements or blanketed them with greatcoats and climbed over and fought down the enemy machine-gunners with bombs.

Then, while some of the Yorkshiremen in the centre were being held in shell-holes by uncut wire and machine-guns, near the sunken road running from Bazentin-le-Grand to High Wood, a Scottish battalion came up in support on the right, leaped into the trenches leading towards the village, and, bombing along, silencing all the hostile machine-guns, captured the remnant of the hostile garrison, thus enabling the British centre to go forward into the village.

Bazentin-le-Grand, an historic place in modern science, where Lamarck, the forerunner and rival of Darwin, was born in 1744, had been dubiously studied by Sir Douglas Haig's Staff. It was a natural hill fortress. By reason of its old-fashioned system of deep, vast cellars, and its sheltered position in a northern hollow behind the Bazentin-Longueval ridge, its underground works and machine-gun emplacements seemed secure against direct, frontal gun fire. A long, violent infantry conflict was, therefore, anticipated in the village. But the British chief gunnery officer had worked better even than he knew. Enfilading Bazentin across the long valley of the Fricourt stream and assailing it frontally by howitzer fire from the direction of Montauban, he had pulverised the picturesque old village. It is estimated that in the last twenty minutes of the preliminary bombardment more than two thousand heavy shells were pitched exactly on to Bazentin-le-Grand. A single 15 in. shell striking stone causes a violent shock over a wide area, and in that area will kill by concussion. And a 12 in. shell has a shock action of considerable extent.

Fall of Bazentin-le-Grand

For two days shells of large calibre had been falling into the village, and when the final delivery of two thousand shells occurred, the remnant of the garrison, though saved from splinters in their great caverns, had little fight left in them. When, therefore, the Scottish battalion knocked out the six machine-guns in front of the village, and released for action the central Yorkshire forces, Bazentin fell practically without a serious struggle. Yet there was one huge cellar under a farm in the village capable of holding fifteen hundred soldiers. Only by a direct hit with a 15 in. shell could the vast underground retreat possibly have been penetrated, and no direct hit had been made.

On the Somme: Highland regiment moving up to the first line.

Steel casques and kilts: London Scottish swing forward to the trenches.

Cruising over broken ground: British "tank" lumbering into action.

German prisoners coming into the British lines after a "tank" attack.

Land cruiser astride a large shell=hole on the Somme front.

Front view of a "tank" crossing the neutral zone between the lines.

Australians ramming a shell into the breech of a heavy howitzer.

London Riflemen in reserve awaiting the signal to go over the top.

The Germans at the time were using it as a shelter for their wounded. These were brought in large numbers to the British lines, together with five hundred and fifty unwounded rank and file, and twenty-three officers and a commandant. Some heavy howitzers were also taken around the village, and the casualties of the British attacking force were only a fraction of the losses they inflicted on the enemy. In technique as well as in material results the victory at Bazentin-le-Grand was splendid evidence of the qualities of the new British soldier.

When Bazentin-le-Grand was taken, and connection made at the cross-roads northward with the force that had taken Bazentin-le-Petit, three more en-**British cavalry** trenched works were carried in the valley **in action** between Longueval and High Wood. Then, while the advance on Longueval and Delville Wood was progressing in a fierce and stern fight, there occurred a most unusual and picturesque incident. For the first time since the autumn of 1914, British cavalry took part in a battle in France. Between High Wood and Longueval was a long slope of ripening corn, from which a German force of riflemen and machine-gunners were enfilading the advancing British wing. The enemy was concealed in the long green stalks, with a line of hidden sharpshooters protecting his machine-guns. No infantry rush attack was practicable in the circumstances; but, to the consternation of the Germans, a squadron of British horsemen and a squadron of dark, turbanned Indians abruptly appeared in the forefront of the British army. They were the Dragoon Guards and the Deccan Horse, and they went in a swift line through the cornfields, doing terrible work with lance and sabre, until the Germans flung themselves down and screamed for mercy. The fields were cleared as far as the machine-gun positions, and the cavalry then sent their horses back and dug trenches to hold the ground for the infantry. This extraordinary charge seems to have been carried out at little cost, owing to the fine manner in which the horsemen were directed

[*British official photograph.*
UNDER THE RED CROSS.
Striking photograph of an advanced dressing-station right up against the battle-line on the western front. The Red Cross emblem was fixed on a shell-shattered tree.

by an airman. Some horses were lost by machine-gun fire, but the unexpected speed of the attack saved the horsemen.

After the cavalry charge and the advance from the left into High Wood, the main stress of the battle fell upon the South African troops and their Scottish comrades who were fighting around Longueval and advancing into Delville Wood. The great knot of German fortresses around Longueval and Trônes Wood was to make one of the supreme furnaces of the Somme battles. The German positions composed of Longueval, Delville Wood, Ginchy, Guillemont, and Trônes Wood, formed a rough rectangle with a frontage of nearly two miles. Two high ridges, with a third neighbouring ridge northward, ran through the rectangle, affording dominating observation-points for enemy gunners, and providing two partly wooded hollows in which reserves could shelter from direct fire. About two miles east of Guillemont was the great hollow of Combles, where the enemy had immense stores of munitions with railway communication to Guillemont. Beyond Combles a northern valley ran to the high road from Bapaume, from which another light railway had been constructed by the Germans in the rear of the High Wood ridge. Owing to the situation, the enemy commander could quickly throw huge **Storming of** forces against two sides of the British **Waterlot Farm** salient, and even threaten the rear of the British from the railway line south of Combles. It was not until the French army worked forward and upward from Hardecourt that the British salient was partly relieved from pressure. There were from four to five blasting cross-fires from German batteries of all calibres playing for weeks on the British salient about Longueval. Yet Sir Douglas Haig maintained the conflict for reasons of strategy.

In the first operations on July 14th a remarkable amount of success was obtained. Trônes Wood was, as we have seen, entirely recovered by the Sussex Regiment and their comrades. Above the Englishmen, and working

[*British official photograph.*
NOVEL SIGNPOSTS ON THE SOMME.
Obsolete rifles affixed to tree-trunks and manipulated by wires to point the direction of an advance. In the background are the ruins of a village in No Man's Land.

along the Guillemont trench and upward along the "Tortillard" railway towards Guillemont railway-station, a brilliant and adventurous body of Scotsmen broke through the wire entanglements and through the double row of works in front of Ginchy, stormed Waterlot Farm, and got a footing in Guillemont. And before this success was fully achieved another fine Scottish force, acting in front of the South Africans, ascended in the darkness the long hill rising in front of Bornafay Wood to Longueval. The

Kilties enter Longueval

Germans had a line of works on the high ridge, from which they swept the mile's breadth of gradual incline down to the railway and stream in the hollow and the low northern edge of Bornafay Wood. In the ordinary way the great bare slope to Longueval was impracticable for charging troops. No dense or wide formation could climb the long gradient against machine-guns and massed artillery. Death could be dealt quicker than men could move. But the great superiority of the British artillery rendered possible an operation that avoided nearly all the disadvantages of the slope. While the guns were still pounding all the German lines for a depth of seven miles, the Scottish force went out in the darkness and, in careful touch, gradually moved upward. Had all the German guns available then swept the slopes with shrapnel the Scotsmen would have been destroyed. But the enemy did not expect an advance until daylight, and the stealthy attackers, with reconnoitring patrols searching their path on either side of the sunken road leading to Longueval, neared the first hostile line of works when a huge British shell set the hill village on fire and lighted the figures climbing the jut of downland. As soon as the British movement was seen the German guns threw out a shrapnel curtain, and also ploughed the incline with high explosive, and veiled the field

with smoke-bombs. Men began to fall in large numbers. But with their pipers playing them on, the Highlanders swept up the ridge, and finding a gap in the wire, went in waves into and over the first hostile fire-trench. Every attacker carried a supply of bombs, most murderous weapons in close combat, for one of them can kill a group of men sooner than a bayonet can kill a single man. The Germans fought well, but were rapidly overpowered by the grim Scotsmen, who knocked out all the machine-gunners, and, leaving their cleaning-up parties behind, rushed the second line of trenches.

Here the dug-outs had been badly made, being probably a hasty improvisation after the battle of July 1st. Many were hardly bomb-proof, and had suffered badly in the bombardment. From one dug-out came a German officer carrying a large axe, who said in English : " I surrender ! " " Drop that axe first ! " said a Highland sergeant. In reply the axe was flung at the sergeant's head, but he dodged and used his bayonet. Still onward went the kilties into the charred ruins of Longueval, where the great fire had died into a smoulder. In spite of the fire the Germans were still holding the broken walls and gaping

DELICATE OPERATIONS.
Men of the R.G.A. setting fuses to shells. A pile of completed projectiles is seen on the right.

and roofless buildings. German courage and German discipline certainly bred some great examples of heroism. The bombardment had been as heavy and as prolonged as that of Bazentin-le-Grand, but some officers at Longueval were of the tiger kind that fights to the edge of doom.

In one important redoubt six machine-guns swept the ground and the tumble of earth that had been a road. But if the German was a man of iron, the Scotsman was a man of steel. In spite of the half dozen machine-guns the redoubt was rushed and bombed. Then followed a ghastly struggle in the numerous cellars, where a desperate remnant of the German garrison waited like

A TROPHY FROM THE FIELD OF VICTORY.
Type of heavy cannon used by the Germans against the Allies on the Somme. The weapon was abandoned by the enemy and was hauled to the British rear.

[*British official photographs.*]

wolves in the darkness, and flung bombs at the sound of an approaching footstep. It was cave warfare, with all its primitive horrors intensified by high explosive weapons. Men crept about with cat-like stealthiness, saw of each other at times only the glint of the eyes, and closed in the gloom in a death-struggle. But the Highland battalions had lost many men that day; and when the Highlander has comrades to avenge, and is fighting man-to-man in dark caverns, the extreme of German desperation will not daunt him, but only sharpens the edge of his mind. Longueval was quickly conquered underground as well as above ground.

The surface fighting was also peculiar. For Longueval was not a village so much as an inhabited wood. It was part of Delville Wood, and the forest trees, thinned and stripped by tens of thousands of British shells, still partly concealed the roofs of farmsteads and cottages with their branching foliage. And, as in other wooded places on this day of main conflict between two great empires, the Germans were perched in the trees with machine-guns and magazine rifles. Some fifty hours of incessant bombardment with shells of all calibre had not broken the nerve of the picked Teutonic sharpshooters. Men in fire-control stations in the Jutland Battle had not to stand such a shelling as the German snipers endured in their forest eyries in the second week of July, 1916. Many of them drew blood from the Scotsmen whom they took by surprise, but each of them was in turn revealed by the sound of his weapon and shot.

As the Scotsmen settled savagely to their work of clearing the woodland village the South African brigade advanced beyond into the inferno of Delville Wood. The South Africans were good men and famous, for many of them had already made the strangest Odyssey of the war. Some had fought in the farmlands and wastes of South Africa against the rebel commandos of Beyers and De Wet. After the closing drives upon their misdirected fellow-countrymen they had followed General Botha into German South-West Africa, where by arduous desert-fighting and terrible rides they had enveloped the enemy. Next they appeared in Egypt as troopers training into infantry, and under General Lukin they swept westward into the Libyan wastes, and there conquered the fanatic Senussiyeh. And now, after many journeyings and many battles, they had achieved their heart's desire and were fighting in the main theatre of war alongside the national armies of England, Scotland, and Wales. and the generous volunteer forces of Ireland. They would have gathered in much greater force in France had not their aid been

The inferno of Delville Wood

[*British official photograph.*

BRINGING IN THE WOUNDED ACROSS NO MAN'S LAND.
Dramatic impression of wounded being brought in across the neutral zone. Four German prisoners are carrying a wounded soldier on a stretcher, while behind them R.A.M.C. workers are tending another victim under a cloud of mine-smoke which hangs ominously in the air.

required also for the campaign in German East Africa. If ever men were strung up to the highest pitch of human endeavour the South Africans were. Veterans of fame in desert warfare, they had met for the first time the awful weight of modern Continental artillery in Bornafay Wood, where the first large number of their graves was dug. On the morning of July 14th they advanced from the wood and up the opposite long slope under very heavy fire from the German guns, and then began to extend the new British Bazentin-Longueval line by fierce and most wearing forest fighting in Delville Wood.

There were open glades in the park-like pleasaunce where the German machine-gunners had a sweeping line of fire. But, heralded by a terrific hail of British shells, with their scouts pushed out near the zone of shrapnel and high-explosive, the South Africans stormed through the wood. Caught on their left by machine-gunners and sharpshooters hidden in a thick undergrowth fringing the glades, and enfiladed on their right by a field-gun at close range, the South Africans not only stuck to their task, but carried it out quickly in an exultant rage. Their losses were heavy, including two commanding officers, who fell in Longueval. But Colonel Tanner, who controlled the forces in the wood, prepared to hold it at any cost. The enemy forces at Flers and Ginchy had a great network of trenches surrounding the wood on three sides, with more than a dozen parallels of assault leading towards the wood.

Five days' awful ordeal

The situation was desperate. But, as in the similar case of High Wood, this thrust towards the enemy's third zone of defences had to be maintained to enable the work of consolidation to go on in Bazentin-le-Grand, Longueval, and Trônes Wood. These places were completely wrecked by British and German shell fire, and days were needed for the sappers to build new works and shelters, and make secure communications with the Montauban line. The South Africans in Delville Wood and the Scotsmen in

OFF THE BEATEN TRACK.
[British official photograph.
Familiar steam-roller in difficulties on one of the uncertain roads leading to the Somme front. Two Scottish soldiers are lending a hand to right the cumbersome Invicta.

Longueval and the Waterlot Farm line had to draw the strongest part of the enemy's gun fire and attract the main force of his counter-attacking infantry in order to enable the British army to consolidate its great central gains.

So for five days the wasting but indomitable brigade of South Africans held the wood they called Hell's Wood against all the mechanical and human forces the German commander could bring against them. The disadvantage of Delville Wood was that the larger part of it sloped down into the Bazentin valley, and was directly and closely dominated by a maze of German trenches on two high downs near Flers. The Germans had a pitch of sixty-five feet to the left and the right and the rear of the South Africans in Delville Wood. The wood was within range of a plunging machine-gun fire as well as direct gun fire. The South Africans had attacked through the concentrated curtain fire of hundreds of German guns, and all the while they held the wood these guns not only maintained their fire but, reinforced by numerous batteries, constantly intensified the bombardment. At intervals the smoke and the poisoned fumes and the blaze of German shrapnel,

high-explosive, poison gas, and blinding gas liquid flame shells, lifted from the South Africans' front and deepened on their rear. Then under cover of machine-gun fire from the northern ridges the German infantry advanced.

In the afternoon of July 18th came the enemy's first violent reaction against the British offensive on the Somme. For eighteen days the hostile counter-blows had been merely of a defensive kind. The German had struck back simply to win time for strengthening himself on the ground to which he had retreated. But on July 18th the German army commander on the Somme front considered that he had the entire situation well in hand, and made a well-considered and long-prepared attempt to wrest the initiative from Sir Douglas Haig. As the British line had been withdrawn from High Wood he did not assail the Bazentin front. This had become a strongly-entrenched line, open only to direct frontal attack. The German commander showed his common-sense in selecting the right corner of the new British ground, from Delville Wood to Trônes Wood, and the point at which the British and French lines met. This opened the critical ordeal, foreseen by the allied commanders at the time when the Iron Division came across the Somme. The unusual slowness with which the German had prepared only indicated the might in which he had gathered for the grand trial of strength.

It is about two and a half miles from the northern part of Delville Wood to the southern slope of Trônes Wood. On this front, according to the German official report, merely two Prussian regiments, numbering six thousand men, were deployed for attack. But, according to French military experts, six German divisions were at first arrayed in écheloned columns and poured continuously against two and a half miles of British trenches. The assault opened, after a long, intense, and terribly heavy artillery fire, at half-past five in the evening and went on all night. As the leading German battalions fell, supports came forward. Sometimes there was a pause for more artillery work at points where the British line was impenetrable, but the principal design was to keep the British troops extended in violent defence, and feed forward fresh attacks until the South Africans, Scotsmen, and Sussex men were physically exhausted.

On the Trônes Wood front, where the enemy had generally to make a direct frontal attack, all his efforts were broken. Above the wood, in the angle of Waterlot Farm, three assaults were shattered by artillery barrages and Vickers and Lewis gun fire. But in the extreme salient of Delville Wood, which the Germans attacked from three sides, the South Africans had to give ground and fall back to a trench midway in the park. At the same time the Scotsmen in Longueval had to retire from the low-lying northern edge of the village. All night the fight went on, and all the next day and the next night. On a front of two thousand yards at Delville Wood, on July 18th, the enemy deployed four out of his six divisions, and of the four divisions thirteen battalions could be traced from prisoners left in our hands. By July 21st, when the Delville Wood battle was still raging, many more German

A grand trial of strength

Some of the prisoners taken by the British during the Somme advance on July 1st, 1916.

British troops watching German prisoners passing down to the "cages" after the taking of Guillemont. Above: Prisoners coming into La Boisselle. When they began to recover from the nerve-shattering effect of our bombardment and assault most of the men showed genuine relief at being safely out of a terrible business.

VIEWS OF THE GERMAN EXODUS FROM GUILLEMONT AND LA BOISSELLE.

AT THE SIGN OF THE RED TRIANGLE.

[British official photograph

The work of the Y.M.C.A. during the war was beyond praise, its organisation perfect and its personnel devoted. The trench shop shown here was stationed right forward in the firing-zone.

a hail of shot falling about him from enemy snipers and machine-gunners. But nothing hit him ; and after stopping every German attack on his section, and getting his weapon jammed and coolly adjusting it, he carried on until his ammunition was exhausted, and then fell back to cover bearing his gun. Colonel Tanner was w o u n d e d, and Colonel Thackeray took command of the forces in the wood, while General Lukin continually moved from the wood to the village, studying the situation and directing his officers.

When the South Africans were broken by the enemy's terrific, searching gun fire and his incessant waves of infantry attack, the fragments of battalions, scraps of companies, and shreds of platoons rallied beside the Scotsmen in a reserve trench in the rear. Then, a mere handful, the South Africans and Highlanders counter-attacked, and by a miracle of fighting drove back the hostile grey masses and saved the situation. The reserve trench, on which they rallied, was an improvised affair already wrecked by shell fire. It could have stood no assault ; every man

troops had been pushed forward into the furnace. Yet on this day there were South Africans yet to be found fighting in the woodland. For seven days and nights they had scarcely slept at all, except while standing. Even when falling asleep as they stood, they awakened quickly enough to eject the masses of grey figures charging over the stumps of the vanished trees. When the brigade was relieved, after a hundred and twenty hours' fighting, some of the men who had borne the brunt of the conflict asked to be allowed to continue the battle.

Gallant gunner saves the line A drawn, wild-eyed set they at last looked —men with fagged brains and outworn bodies. Yet they fought on, when they might have been relieved. In the darkness and confusion of one mass German attack a hundred of the South Africans suffered a fate similar to that of the West Kents. The trench they were holding ran north and south through the wood. In the retirement of the main body, touch was lost, and the small advanced force enveloped. The enemy could be heard approaching from east and west, for as the Germans advanced they pitched bombs before them at a venture, hoping to provoke the fire of any chance opponents in their path.

The South Africans made no movement until the figures of the Germans were close and distinct. Then with bomb and rifle fire they brought the first enveloping force down, and turned about in their trench and held off the Germans on the other side. When the Germans re-formed and made a simultaneous attack eastward and westward, half the South Africans in the trench faced one way and half the other way. At last, breaking the ring, a little victorious remnant came forth, joined hands with other troops, and with them renewed the attack. There was another gallant incident in connection with a Lewis gun team, which saved the line at a most perilous moment by playing on the enemy while exposed itself to an overwhelming counter-fire. Soon only one gunner was left to turn the drum of the remarkable Lewis gun, invented by an American, much to the benefit of the British soldier and British airman. The single Lewis gunner continued to fire, with

in it would have been killed or taken, and the corner-stone of the Franco-British front lost. The desperate counter-charge staggered the enemy, and by its miraculous success made him apprehensive of the presence of a strong British reserve. He drew back cautiously to avoid a trap that did not exist, and gave the heroic remnant time to improve their position. The Highlanders had a series of four strong points, hastily but well made, and with the help of some South Africans with Lewis guns they broke the enemy. The South Africans inside the edge of the woodland had in an open drive, named Buchanan Street, a shallow trench that still held, and there in the close of the Germans' first operation they held out against all assaults and won. Ten battalions of Germans failed completely to penetrate the weak and scantily manned British line.

When, on July 20th, the remnant of South Africans was relieved, leaving the flower of their force in the terrible wood, and the splendid Highland Division on the Longueval-Trônes Wood line went into rest quarters, the enemy attacks continued with unintermittent violence. In effect, the German commander formed an army of nearly a hundred thousand men into an illimitable column, less than a mile and a quarter wide, and fed the edge of this column against the **German method of** British human emery-wheel in the **attrition** lower part of Delville Wood and Longueval. It was attrition on a colossal scale and yet of narrow intensity—a gigantic knife formation driven against the most delicate point in the allied front.

The design of it seemed to have been due directly to the German High Command, who selected General von Stein to control the operation. Stein was a man of the Falkenhayn class—a combination of military politician and Great Staff strategist. Above him on the Somme were two of Hindenburg's best men, Gallwitz and Below, who had shown themselves in Russia to be masters of swarm attacks when they possessed a high superiority in gun-power. This superiority they did not possess on the Somme. For some weeks they did not even attain an

A Somme ridge alive with soldiers. How our men were protected against the enemy fire when away from the front line.

[British official photographs.

Two veterans contemplating the effect of British artillery fire on the German trenches at Ovillers, which had been originally constructed with all the skill and thoroughness of the Teuton mind.

BRITISH SHELTERS AND SOME SHATTERED GERMAN DUG-OUTS.

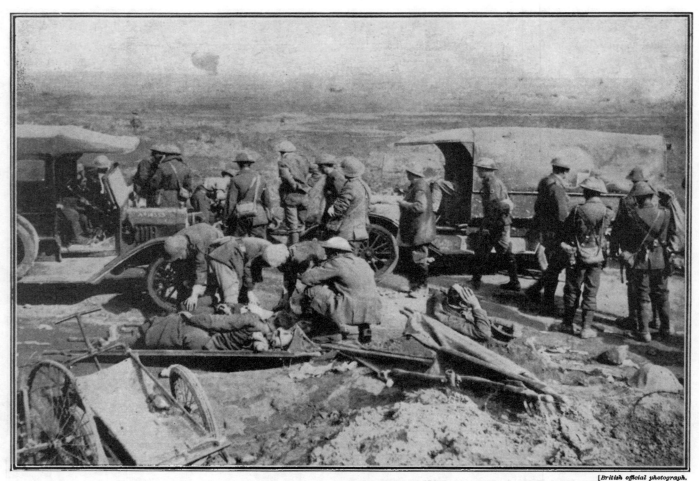

FIRST-AID ON THE BATTLE-FIELD: A CAMERA IMPRESSION ON THE SOMME FRONT.
Wounded soldiers undergoing quick but expert treatment at an advanced dressing-station. As soon as their immediate needs were satisfied the motor-ambulance conveyed them to the base hospital. On the horizon the smoke of a bursting shell can be distinctly seen.

equality with the Allies in heavy-fire power. So they sacrificed men by the ten thousand in attempts to achieve a practical decision by forcing back the British line. Their larger underlying intention was to shake the nerve of the British people, and prepare the way for a negotiated peace, by proving at what a fearful common loss Germany was ready to achieve a great defensive victory.

Much of the heaviest fighting occurred in the long, narrow valley running from Flers to the Bazentin villages, and passing through the lower and northern parts of Delville Wood and Longueval. The outskirts of Longueval became the Hougomont Farm of the main new British front on the Bazentin height. By attracting and distracting much of the enemy's chief force the village facilitated the defence of the ridge. The Germans had to come down the northern slope of the valley, cross the ravine, and climb up the southern slope. All the ground they covered in order to get within bomb-throw of the British works was heavily curtained by the British artillery. Trees or undergrowth no longer gave any screening shelter, for the ground was bared and broken by incessant shell fire alternating from either side, according to the swaying of the infantry lines. The shell-holes were **Another Hougomont** likewise of little use, as machine-gunners **Farm** and snipers on the ridges could fire down into the craters.

All this told against the Germans, who were the attacking force. They worked forward by means of strong lines of machine-guns under cover of storms of 6 in. shell. The British troops appear to have relied mainly upon the light and handy Lewis gun, with its spurts of fire from a revolving drum. The weight and cumbersomeness of the German weapon formed a serious disadvantage when the teams had to speed up behind a line of bomb-throwers. The Briton used his guns up in considerable quantities, and

abandoned them when they had paid for themselves and a rapid retirement was inevitable. This was really a tribute to the productiveness of the British munition factories, enabling lives to be saved at a little expense in machinery. And though the German communiqués at times boasted about the scores of Lewis guns captured, practically every gun had done terrible work before it was left in the wood.

After the main body of South Africans were relieved, the brunt of the fighting fell upon the splendid Scottish regiments who had made a great fight around Waterlot Farm and Guillemont, **Scots encounter** and upon the English battalions who **Brandenburgers** moved up in support. The Prussians, who made considerable gains on July 18th, were pressed back into the valley on July 19th and July 20th. A fresh Brandenburg division advanced up the village street and up the gradient of the wood, only to be countered by the Highlanders. Then, on July 20th, Sir Douglas Haig threw a new and unexpected weight into the main battle-front, and enabled Sir Henry Rawlinson to make a sudden spring from the Bazentin ridge to High Wood.

This general resumption of the offensive was based upon an important success on the left flank of the British line. Here the downland fortress of Ovillers, which had been stormed and lost on July 1st, had barred for more than a fortnight the use of the wide slopes rising by Contalmaison Wood to the high dominant point of Pozières. A force of Prussian Guards held the deep caverns in the chalk height and manned the concrete emplacements in which there were slits for working machine-guns. The Prussians were men of an indomitable character. Although all the buildings above them were obliterated by unceasing heavy gun fire, they continued to fight for every yard of ground. Early in the struggle a force of fresh British troops rushed the underground fortress from the western side and, linking up with the original attackers, cut the ruined village in half and emptied the southern part of prisoners, leaving the enemy isolated on the higher ground northward.

All that then remained to do was to clear out the Guardsmen. But the underground city of Ovillers was not easily cleared out, being held by an heroic band, led by officers who clearly understood the large, strategical value of every day's resistance. The system of caverns afforded lodging for more than two thousand men, and the roof of earth was so thick that a tornado of exploding 8 in. shells sounded beneath like the buzzing of bees in the thatch of a cottage. Electric dynamos and engines lighted the whole of the subterranean city, from which shafts like chimneys ran to concrete emplacements. In the shafts were pulleys for hoisting machine-guns and ladders by which the teams ascended. More than twenty of these chimneys were concealed in the upper earthworks, enabling the garrison to make surprise escapes and surprise appearances. Bombs thrown down the staircases of the upper dug-outs did no injury to the men listening in the lower caverns and peering through long periscopes in the vicinity. For some time the enemy was fed with supplies coming from the north and east, and when he was entirely enveloped he had a large store of food, enabling him to stand a siege.

Underground city of Ovillers

For seventeen days handfuls of English and Irish soldiers fought the Germans above ground and underground, in broken traverses, shell-craters, ditches, corridors, and caves. The Irishmen tried to carry a redoubt by storm, but were caught in streams of machine-gun fire. The Cheshires went forward in small parties with hand-grenades, and sapped down to the underground city and mined the roof of it. Neither side bombarded the upper ruins, where not a fragment of wall remained two feet high.

The gunners were afraid of hitting their own men, and merely maintained a terrific barrage over the hostile communications. But eventually it was the British shell curtain that completed the conquest of the place. The original large force of Prussians was reduced to a hundred and forty men, and many of the cellars were foul with the bodies of the dead. For days no water reached them, and their stock of mineral drinks was exhausted. Worn out by seventeen days' fighting, and with their blood poisoned for want of water, the remnant of the Guard surrendered— two officers and a hundred and twenty-four men—and were received with the honours of war by the British. Gallant Sir Douglas Haig went out of his way in his daily report to speak of the bravery of the remnant of Guardsmen who had so seriously checked the development of the British offensive.

Honour to a brave foe

But while the siege of Ovillers was still proceeding, some of the Lancashire men engaged in cave warfare on the right of the underground fortress prepared the way for an important movement that was to follow the fall of the frontal down. Some young officers were asked to send out a patrol northward. A detachment went forward in the darkness, led by a young machine-gun officer, who took sixteen machine-guns with him. With his little but well-armed company he struck up an old bit of communication-trench leading to Pozières. Thousands of Germans were entrenched on the mile-and-a-half slope leading to the main ridge, but for some reason the vital communication-trench was neither garrisoned nor watched. The Lancashire detachment worked upwards for a mile to a strong redoubt containing four machine-guns, their teams, and a bombing detachment. Certain measures were taken in regard to the redoubt which need not be detailed, but which resulted in the redoubt being made harmless, and the adventurers then went nearer to Pozières and, by another

[*Canadian official photograph.*

TENDING THE WOUNDED UNDER FIRE AT AN ADVANCED DRESSING-STATION IN THE SOMME SECTOR.
The peril of the wounded as well as the R.A.M.C. is demonstrated by this illustration, showing an enormous shell bursting near an advanced dressing-station. The camera has caught the anxious movements on the part of the doctor and one of the wounded men in the foreground.

HIGHLAND BRIGADE MARCHING BACK AFTER TAKING MARTINPUICH.
[British official photograph.
Martinpuich was strongly fortified and held. The ruins of the village bristled with machine-guns, and our men fought forward until the whole place was in their hands, and they dug themselves in on the farther side

successful trick of war, captured four machine-guns. When day broke, the Lancashires had consolidated themselves in an impossible little British fortress in the heart of the German lines, and close to Pozières. They saw many things which they afterwards reported to Headquarters, and which the Staff found extremely useful in supplementing the results of aerial reconnaissance. Having seen all that could be seen, the Lancashires did not retire or hide themselves, but opened fire down the great slope on all bodies of German infantry moving beneath them against the British trenches. At first the enemy thought that some well-placed shrapnel was doing the damage, but the noise of twenty strange machine-guns in action near Pozières became too startling a thing to pass unnoticed.

An infantry attack was made from the hill village, and broken up by the machine-guns. The enemy then trained his artillery on the British position, and started a wide enveloping movement with his infantry. While the ground was being ploughed up with high explosive, the Lancashires retired, carrying all their own machine-guns and the four captured German guns, and leaving an officer and six men as a rearguard. Those who came back unwounded numbered at first only one officer and one man. But thirty-six hours afterwards a sergeant came in carrying a wounded Irishman. The two were friends, and the sergeant had remained by Pozières, with heavy shells falling on all sides of him, and the wounded man in a delirium and shouting threats to the Germans. After bringing back his comrade and getting a drink of water, the sergeant again went out to search for another wounded man.

This remarkable piece of reconnaissance was of great service during the enemy's incessant attack on the Delville Wood salient. It cleared the way for a great balancing movement against the opposite enemy salient of Pozières, which had become fully exposed to assault after the fall of Ovillers. In the battle of the Bazentin ridges no attempt had been made to extend the action towards Pozières. The farthest point gained by the British about Bazentin-le-Petit was a little over a mile east of Pozières. A considerable part of the intervening space was conquered in the early morn of July 16th, when a fine body of English county troops, with whom were some Irish, broke into the trench system around Pozières to a considerable

Briton and Irishman at Pozières

depth. At the same time other attacking troops worked towards Martinpuich, thus exposing more of the eastern flank of Pozières to attack, and increasing the length of the enemy salient.

This operation was covered by a general advance of the Bazentin line, during which the ravine running to Longueval was crossed and a considerable part of High Wood snatched once more from the enemy. The drive into High Wood, which the troops again entirely stormed in their first rush, deeply disconcerted the German commander. He slackened his operation in Delville Wood and Longueval, according to the wish of the British commander, and turned his main forces to the task of recovering the supreme observation-point that overlooked all his centre to Bapaume. In a series of smashing and costly attacks he recovered the northern trench in High Wood, and then in a long, set fight of exceeding bitterness he strove to recover High Wood.

Every enemy attack was countered with mighty gun-power and violent infantry action by the British commander, who had brought Devons, Suffolks, Cornish men, and Edinburgh men forward from the Bazentin ridge against the High Wood ridge, while the men in Longueval swept back towards the northern end of Delville Wood. On July 23rd all Longueval was won and part of the northern slope beyond carried. This savage thrust once more provoked the enemy commander, who launched more of his men in masses around the Delville ridge salient, which was at last forced by the Brandenburg division, whose prowess Kaiser William had proclaimed to the world in the first capture of Douaumont Fort at Verdun. But a considerable part of this terrific movement of the British centre appears to have been only in the nature of a demonstration by Sir Douglas Haig. High Wood was still but a pawn in the game he was playing, and though he needed it to safeguard the western flank of his Delville Wood salient, in view of a combined Franco-British movement towards Combles, this allied movement on the grand scale was not yet ripe for execution. Sir Douglas Haig was threatening his opponent in the direction of Combles, but he was making this threat in order to obtain more elbow-room around Thiepval.

Brandenburgers at Delville

He needed a longer front of attack in the direction of Bapaume, because behind this extended main front he would have more room for deploying troops and siting guns. Beyond Pozières there was a windmill on the highest part of the downland, quite as valuable for observation purposes as High Wood in regard to the Bapaume front, with the additional attraction of a large outlook across the Ancre sector. It was against Pozières that Sir Douglas Haig was preparing his main attack while he provoked the enemy commander at High Wood. Before the fall of Ovillers the Royal Fusiliers and other London troops began a strong advance along the highway from La Boisselle to Bapaume. Men recruited from the Stock Exchange, Lloyd's, the Baltic, and Corn Exchanges had a leading part in the uphill fighting from La Boisselle. The enemy on the Pozières slopes swept the Londoners with machine-gun fire and hammered them with shell. But in ten days of continuous fighting the Royal Fusiliers and their comrades made ground steadily, and skilfully

Column of German prisoners, captured during the first battles of the Somme, about to travel from Southampton Station to internment.

Types of German prisoners of varying ages, some wounded and many of them without their caps, passing through Southampton under guard.

Men of the Prussian Guard marching through the streets of Southampton, whence they experienced the pleasure of travelling first-class to the North

More types of German man-power in the third year of the war. It was noted that these prisoners were shorter in stature and less developed.

PRISONERS FROM THE SOMME ON THEIR WAY TO INTERNMENT IN GREAT BRITAIN.

consolidated their gains until these formed another direct way of approach for the critical attack on Pozières. Then, after the fall of Ovillers, a London Territorial division profited by the great reconnoitring achievement of the Lancashires and ascended the slope north of the Bapaume Road towards the enemy's intricate system of works west of Pozières.

There were then three British spear-heads moving against the three sides of the Pozières salient. But Sir Douglas Haig was not content with these preparations of attack. From two to four zones of barbed-wire surrounded the supreme hill village, which also had a network of trenches running entirely round it, a gridiron of trenches crossing it, and a subterranean fortress beneath it. German batteries covered Pozières and its long bare slopes from the Ancre sector on the right flank, from the Bapaume sector in front, and from Martinpuich, Eaucourt l'Abbaye, and Flers on the left flank. In view of all these difficulties, the most famous thrusters of the British Empire—the Anzacs—were brought from Armentières to Contalmaison Villa for the closing drive against the height. The Australians and New Zealanders had not been long in France, but during the Somme operations some of them had finely distinguished themselves near Armentières, on July 19th, by making a great raid on a three-thousand-yard front against the Bavarian troops.

Anzacs raid Bavarians They there carried the whole of the first zone of defences against machine-gun fire and a shell curtain, and though the Germans flooded their lost works, the Australians remained all night waist-high in water, and, after digging communication-trenches back to their own lines, returned with two hundred prisoners. The enemy's extraordinary trick in inundating his lost trenches and then bombarding all night the shelterless, swimming victors was a severe test of the mettle and resource of the Australians, many of whom were new recruits to Anzac.

Under the direction of their leader of genius, General Birdwood, the First Australian and New Zealand Army Corps prepared to advance from the tongue of land on which Contalmaison Villa once stood. The direction of the attack ran below the ridge line where the English county regiments had worked towards Martinpuich. In conjunction with the main Anzac attack against the south-eastern side of the enemy salient, another main attack was planned against the south-western side of Pozières by a fine English Territorial force. On Saturday, July 22nd, the British guns broke in a storm of fire upon the eight-mile arc of German positions from Thiepval to Guillemont. As the day wore on the gun fire increased, until every battery and its aerial observer and forward observation officer were working at the utmost pressure.

Move on Thiepval and Guillemont

The German commander divined what was about to happen on his centre and Delville Wood flank, and his gunners tried in turn to disable the waiting British infantry by means of tear-shells and gas-shells. The mutual bombardment went on at nightfall, when counter-battery firing was facilitated by the darkness. The British artillery being the more powerful, then overcame the hostile batteries, and the sweating, deafened, toiling, victorious gunners worked in a fierce burst of energy until midnight, and then lifted all their fire beyond the Pozières-High Wood ridge.

Thereupon, the British infantry line went forward over the old battlegrounds of Guillemont, Longueval, Delville Wood, High Wood, and the rearward works of Pozières. The men crept out in the darkness, as in the battle of the Bazentin ridge, and by reason of their long practice in nocturnal raiding kept formation in the gloom with the skill of veterans. The enemy system was broken beyond Waterlot Farm by a magnificent rush, and Guillemont was entered and the German forces there engaged, while the conquered works were being consolidated. The Bantams were in this great holding action, and, tough and wiry, proved themselves fighting men of the first order.

[*British official photograph.*]

BRITISH HEAVY HOWITZER IN ACTION ON THE SOMME FRONT.

TROOPS MARCHING OVER A SAND-BAG BRIDGE ACROSS A TRENCH IN FRANCE.
[*British official photograph.*]
Where roads intersected the line of trenches they were carried across it over bridges constructed of sand-bags, the appearance of which recalled the walls built of unmortared slabs of stone that are characteristic of English moors and fells.

The first batch of the Derby groups was also remarkable for some good work. The British line was carefully pushed forward from Waterlot Farm, partly through Delville Wood and High Wood, with some extension towards Martinpuich. But on this section the men were deployed as economically as possible, with a view rather to provoking a great counter-attack in circumstances adverse to the enemy than to winning any considerable ground.

Meanwhile, the Australians and the Territorials leaped upon Pozières. The Anzacs had to cross a wide, grassy flat under a hail of German shrapnel, and **Anzac valour at Pozières** they covered this ground swiftly and with few casualties, as the German trench beyond was entirely destroyed by the British guns. Not one hostile machine-gunner remained active in the first line, and the few German troops who survived were cowed and caught. But the enemy's second trench, running just beyond the old tramway to Bapaume, under the fringe of the village, was tongued with fire from machine-guns that played on the slope up which the Australians advanced. With shrapnel falling about them like rain, and cascades of bullets making gaps in their line, the Australians tenaciously held on and reached the second trench.

In many parts the Germans were numerous and full of fight, but in a very sharp action they were mostly bayoneted or captured. This second trench was deep and well-built, and though so smashed in some places by heavy shell that some Australians passed it without knowing it was a trench at all, it afforded abundant good cover for the conquerors. The Anzacs knew how to dig, and what digging meant in a modern battle. Rapidly they repaired the damage done by British guns, and after this short interval of consolidating work their supports arrived. Then, with an obscure multitude of sappers behind them labouring furiously to link the slope and the flat to the British system at Contalmaison Villa, the charging forces

of the division stormed forward again into the small woods at the back of the village street. There, against the glare of the shells, they saw two large mounds defended by riflemen. They knew what the mounds were, and with their blood quickening at the sight of their first great prize, they bayoneted the Germans and captured the two guns. Then sweeping past the gun-pits they stabbed and bombed their way into the heart of the village. At the same time the British troops on the Bazentin front carried part of the enemy's new switch-line that had been improvised to connect the south-eastern corner of Pozières with Martinpuich and Flers. But the Martinpuich forces strongly counter-attacked, recovered the switch-line, and with bombs tried to harry the Australians. A small party of the Anzacs vigorously maintained the struggle in the switch, while their leading battalions closed with the village garrison, and spent a wild night driving through shrapnel, shell, and machine-gun fire, fighting round difficult angles, over ruined walls, and in underground ways.

The Anzacs had no ground of complaint against the German High Command, for they were opposed by the best regiments of the Prussian Guard, in addition to some sturdy Bavarians. The Guardsmen it is said by men in a position to judge, were **Peers of the** not such fine bayonet fighters as the **Prussian Guard** Turks in Gallipoli, but in hand-bomb and machine-gun warfare, and disappearing and reappearing subterranean movements, they maintained the great standard of resistance their comrades had reached at Ovillers. But the tall, lithe Australian, with his touch of an Italianate temperament laid upon his hard Northern qualities, was a match for the finest of the Guardsmen. In particular, his capacity for discipline and being controlled amid the confusion of nocturnal warfare in a chaos of ruins and a maze of subterranean retreats made him the peer of the finest trained private in Germany. When morning broke, the High Street of the village had been cleared and the ruins of the western side were firmly held by the conquerors. On the opposite side of the village the London Territorials worked forward towards the cemetery, lying in a hollow north of Pozières. The design was to get the British machine-guns trained on the enemy's rear, so that when he broke under the Australian attack he would be brought under a terrific enfilading fire during his flight. On the night of July 22nd the Territorials charged up the slopes from Ovillers against the gridiron system of trenches which the Lancashire reconnoitring party had explored. Strongly fortified machine-gun posts dotted the large system of German trenches, and the funnel of valley ground running up to the cemetery was commanded by enemy fire from both sides—from the high ground above Thiepval on the left and the high ground around Pozières on the right. Admirably handled, the Territorials fought up the valley with discreet skill combined with vehement valour.

On the first night, when they had the advantage of surprise, they captured a great deal of ground without serious loss to themselves. Every hour the next day they stubbornly pushed forward, now working around a redoubt and capturing it, and now rushing a bit of trench

and bombing along it. For three days and nights the Territorials pressed the enemy back, and at nightfall on July 25th they achieved their task. The main German line, just below the cemetery of Pozières, was penetrated, and junction made with the Australians at the top of the village. Spreading at once to the left and the right along the German main line, the Territorials worked down on one side to the Bapaume road, and on the other side fought upward with the Australians towards the Windmill position, which was the crown of all the Somme ridges.

In the meantime, the Australian forces in Pozières, after being subjected to a racking bombardment, in which the enemy used a new flame-shell that emitted a jet of liquid fire as it fell, waged a terrific kind of in-fighting with the Pozières garrison, whom they at last drove northward from the top of the village towards the Windmill. Then the machine-guns of the enveloping Territorial troops swept the fugitives and the conquest of Pozières was completed, bringing to a close the second phase of the Battle of the Somme. Delville Wood was also finally conquered on July 27th.

Enemy's new flame-shell

Since July 1st the British forces had gained an area of twenty-four square miles of the most strongly fortressed hill country in history. In addition to the enormous amount of engineering work with which the enemy had laboured to make the downland impregnable, all his best army corps had been employed in constant defence and counter-attack. Artillery was accumulated by him in rapid, regular effort, and in the Pozières battle 9 in. German shells were fired at comparatively short range. Nevertheless, the new British machinery of war continued to overpower all that the enemy could bring to bear after a generation of preparatory work and two years of war experience. The mill on the Somme was grinding slowly, but grinding small. Germany had two hundred divisions in the field, and at least three-quarters of this gigantic force had to pass through the mill.

THE DUKE OF CONNAUGHT AMONG THE IRISH TROOPS IN FRANCE.   [*British official photographs.*

One of the first things the Duke of Connaught did when he returned from Canada in the autumn of 1916 was to visit the western front. He is shown here inspecting some of the Irish troops, and (above) watching an Irish battalion march past.

THE GREAT BRITISH BATTLES OF THE SOMME.
IV.—Struggle on the Wings and the Thrust towards Bapaume.
By Edward Wright.

The Summer Lull on the Somme—Was Sir Douglas Haig Short of Men?—The Problem of the Reverse Slope—Kent, Sussex, and Surrey at Mouquet Farm—Checks at Guillemont—Whirlwind Assault on Wonder-Work—Second Check at Beaumont-Hamel—Anzacs on Mouquet Ridge—Irishmen and Englishmen in Combination—Magnificent Victory at Guillemont—Irish Forward and English Half-Backs in the Sunken Road Battle—Epic of Ginchy—Leuze Wood Skirmishes—West Countrymen on the Falfemont Ridge—Mass Attacks by Prussian Guard—The Falfemont Pawn and the Leuze Wood Winning Piece—Subtle British Strategy—Success in Farm and Wood Advances—Arrival of Hindenburg and Preparations for Great Allied Movement—Wiltshires' and Gloucesters' Successful Attack on the Wonder-Work—First Appearance of the "Tanks" in Action—Wonderful Gunnery of the Royal Garrison Artillery—Intervention of the "Tanks" in the Fight for the Sugar Factory—Canadians Capture Courcelette—Rout of the Bavarians and Capture of Martinpuich—Londoners and Territorials Annihilate the German Garrison in High Wood—New Zealanders Capture Flers—Glorious Charge of the Guards—Lieut.-Colonel J. V. Campbell Wins the Victoria Cross—The Fight for the Quadrilateral—Practical and Moral Effect of the "Tanks"—Far-reaching Importance of the British Victory.

AFTER the capture of Pozières village and the final conquest of the Longueval-Delville Wood salient in the last week of July, 1916, there was an apparent lull on the British front for the extraordinary period of five weeks. It was the height of favourable summer weather, with dry ground and clear air, yet no forward movement of importance occurred. Only small gains of ground were made at heavy cost, and it seemed at times as though the enemy had accomplished his main design and fought the new British armies to a practical standstill. Statements were published in the English newspapers revealing the fact that new recruits of the Derby group class from Kent, Surrey, and Sussex were thrown into battle alongside the Australians at Pozières. Most of the men who came under the Derby scheme could not handle a rifle or throw a bomb at the beginning of the year. Experience of trench warfare they had none, and though they fought with such vehemence that they were nicknamed "The Derby Devils," their appearance in the forefront

LIEUT.-GENERAL CLAUD WILLIAM JACOB, C.B.
[Elliott & Fry.
Commander of the Second Army Corps in Sir Henry Rawlinson's army on the Somme in the great advance in 1916.

of the fiercest part of the battle-line seemed to indicate that Mr. Asquith's Coalition Cabinet had not properly provided in advance the number of men which Sir William Robertson and the Army Council needed to maintain Sir Douglas Haig's forces in full and persistently offensive strength.

But though the delay in establishing a system of national service may have partly conduced to the apparent great lull in the British operations through the month of August, 1916, there is another factor in the situation that may have been of supreme importance. We have already touched on it in the opening chapter of the British operations on the Somme, in connection with General Marchand's view of the geography of the battle. On arriving at Pozières and the middle of High Wood and the northern edge of Delville Wood on July 27th, 1916, the British army had almost topped the highest ridge in the Bapaume sector. Had all the ridge been then at once carried in a rush, and a new line of works built on the reverse slope, the troops in these new works would have been caught at a very heavy disadvantage. Many of the hostile batteries would have had a direct fire against the faces of the reverse northern slopes, while British cannon would have been almost useless, and only British howitzers, which could pitch their shells over any ridge, would have been serviceable.

The great event in the eastern theatre of war did not tell upon conditions on the Somme front. The German High Command was undisturbed by the entrance of Rumania on the side of the Allies. This had been foreseen for quite a year and, indeed, in August, 1915, General von Falkenhayn had been on the point of invading Rumania, and was only turned from his purpose by the Hungarians' and Austrians' savage desire first to overthrow Serbia. Rumania, with her Krupp guns and Krupp ammunition of very limited quantity, was regarded as a rich and easy prey that could be taken with small forces by an artillery

struggle. The artillery and shell had long been provided for the capture of the Rumanian corn-fields and oil-fields, and in view of the possible intervention of Rumania Germany had reduced the infantry in her divisions from twelve thousand to nine thousand bayonets, maintaining the number of guns, with a consequent expansion in the proportion of artillery to bayonets by one-third.

Both Hindenburg and Falkenhayn were content with the situation on the Somme in the first week of August, 1916. They had placed there an immense force, with a million men in and about the lines, and large reserves available at a few days' notice from the quieter sectors of the western front. The German artillery and the German shell supply began greatly to increase after the period of intense strain on the front passed in the middle of July. In the battle of the Bazentin ridges the British army had almost achieved a break-through, owing to General von Arnim's lack of shell. But this lack of shell had been due merely to lack of transport, which in turn was due to want of light railways and general preparation for a grand offensive. The fundamental lack of preparation was remedied by frenzied labour on the sectors fed by the Cambrai and St.

Rumania and the Somme

[*Canadian War Records.*

CANADIANS GOING "OVER THE TOP" DURING THE BATTLE OF THE SOMME.
These two dramatic photographs, taken at the critical moment of the order to go "over the top," show the last man scrambling up the steep and slippery parapet of a trench, and (above) some of his comrades getting well away on their terrible rush across the open ground.

Quentin railway centres. Then with the vast munition factories of Germany fully linked to the battle-front, and with guns moved from Verdun to the Somme, the enemy High Command looked with confidence to a great defensive victory that should balance the Verdun defeat.

Had Sir Douglas Haig been as bent on winning all the crowning heights of the Somme as the German commander at Verdun was bent on winning the Mort Homme and the Froide Terre ridge, the expectation of the enemy High Command might have been fulfilled. But the British commander knew all there was to be known about the geographical factors of modern war. At Mons he had fought on the Wellington tradition and left the ridge to the enemy, and shot him down when he stood against

[Canadian War Records.
CANADIAN BRIGADIER AND HIS STAFF.
Brig.-General A. H. Macdonell, C.M.G., D.S.O., is the fourth figure from the left.

CHEERING CANADIANS COMING BACK AFTER CAPTURING COURCELETTE.
September 15th, 1916, was the Canadians' day of glory. The capture of Courcelette had not been planned for that day, but "having eaten up everything that was set before them, the Canadians were hungry for more," and in two hours they rushed and secured the very formidable German positions at that place.

the skyline. Then, as artillery developed and high observation posts were needed for heavy-howitzer fire tactics, Sir Douglas Haig held the low hills around Ypres because of their great value in trench warfare. But, as we have seen, he came down to the Somme with a new idea in regard to hill positions with long slopes. And when he had entrenched around Pozières, High Wood, and Delville Wood against practically half the entire forces of Germany, exasperated by a succession of heavy defeats and ardent to recover the ground they had lost, the wary and subtle Scotsman no longer offered battle, but rather accepted it. He had everything he wanted in view of a pitched battle. His men were sheltered from direct fire behind a great slope, and close behind them were the Bazentin ravine and the Montauban ravine, that afforded considerable shelter from howitzer fire. The organisation of the transport to the

batteries in the firing-line was practically as perfect as it could be in the circumstances. Except, perhaps, to a small extent on Hill 150 at Ginchy and about Thiepval, the enemy retained no secure point of observation from which he could bring his guns directly to bear over the British lines. Moreover, as his means of aerial fire-control had been severely restricted, his artillery had to work for the most part by the map. British and French gunners, on the other hand, had forward observation officers in many good positions, a stable line of observation balloons, and hundreds of aeroplanes constantly exploring the hostile front and rear.

The German losses had been very heavy. Members of the French and British Staffs estimated that the enemy had used in the Battle of the Somme in two months as many German divisions as had been employed in fighting at Verdun in five months. This, of course, included the troops used against **Heavy German losses** both the British and the French, but it was probable that, owing to the superiority of the Allies in guns, and the constant shock of their artillery attacks, the German troops rapidly became shaken, and had to be withdrawn with a smaller proportion of actual casualties than they had suffered, without losing their moral, in offensive operations such as that at Verdun. On the other hand, the use of large drafts of Derby recruits in various British regiments was some indication of losses in the attacking army. And it might be argued that a decision would have been obtained on the Somme line by the winter

CANADA'S DAY AT COURCELETTE : FURIOUS HAND-TO-HAND FIGHTING IN A SUGAR-REFINERY.

Among the brilliant feats of the Somme battles Canada's prowess and heroism shone at Courcelette, where men from the Dominion drove the enemy out of the sugar-refinery, the adjacent trenches, and finally from the whole village. This spirited illustration shows the furious hand-to-hand conflict for possession of the ruins of the sugar factory.

if universal compulsion had been established in Great Britain after the Battle of Loos, thus enabling the harvest sown by the constant British artillery pressure on the Somme in August and September, 1916, to have been fully reaped by intense and constant infantry action.

As it was, Sir Douglas Haig had to maintain for some weeks a kind of offensive-defensive on the Pozières-Guillemont line, and wear down the enemy there by a little war, while slowly preparing for another movement on the grand scale. On August 4th the wedge of downland between Thiepval and Pozières was attacked. It was a position of immense strength, defended by four lines of works and more than seven communication-trenches, with a great stronghold northward at Mouquet Farm, which was linked by a tunnel-way to Thiepval and to the village of Courcelette, lying in a hollow and showing only its tall chimneys above the main ridge.

Attack on Mouquet Farm

A force of Kent, Sussex, and Surrey men, brought up to strength by Derby drafts, made the attack on a front of a mile and a quarter. The battle opened just as the summer twilight was falling, at nine o'clock in the evening, and this unusual time seems to have found the enemy unprepared. German sappers had come out to repair their wire entanglements when the Kents surged against the works defending Mouquet Farm. Helped by the gathering twilight, the Kents avoided most of the enemy's machine-gun fire. Then, to the cry of a young lieutenant : " Now boys, give them Kentish fire ! " they leaped into the enemy's works and bombed their way towards the farm. Here, however, they were checked by concentrated machine-gun fire and by the enemy's local reserve arriving, no doubt, through the tunnel. The enemy's main trench was taken, together with a number of support-trenches, and in addition to a large body of enemy wounded, more than a hundred men of the favourite soldiers of the Kaiser —the Eleventh Prussian Corps—were taken prisoners.

At the same time the Sussex Regiment, with the Australians on their right and the Surreys on their left, " went over the top," and took another large section of the enemy's main work and two hundred prisoners. There were several acts of gallantry on the part of the men of Sussex. One lance-corporal, in the midst of a furious hand-to-hand fight, leaped on a parapet with a Lewis gun and, firing over the heads of his own bombers, smashed the enemy's rear and shattered a counter-attack. In another case a corporal, who was a very small man, climbed the parapet during a bomb fight, jumped on the head of the big leading German, took him and eight more Germans captive, and brought the nine prisoners into the British lines. A good many of the Derby men had their first experience of a modern battle in the Sussex Regiment, and their officers, who had been somewhat apprehensive of the quality of these half-trained new men, became loud in their praise. " Their discipline was fine, and they are dashed fine chaps," said one of their officers.

As for the Australians, having fought until they fell asleep as they stood, and borne for a fortnight the burden of the battle, the men born under the Southern Cross did not know when they had enough fighting. Some of them in the trenches alongside the Sussex had not been informed about the attack, as it was intended they should rest for a time while the Englishmen cleared the down on their left and prepared for the assault on Mouquet Farm, which was one of the key positions to Thiepval. But when the Sussex swarmed over the parapet the Australians shouted : " Say, boys ! Where the h—l are you going ? " " Over there," said the men from one of the fairest of English counties, pointing to the German trenches on the great down. " By God, we come with you ! " said the Anzacs. " We're going to get our own back."

So the slouch hats went over with the flat-cap brigade, though little difference between them could be seen at the

Onset of Anzacs and Sussex

time, as all wore pudding-dish shrapnel helmets, with monstrous gas-masks that make a charging line of modern infantry look like figures in a nightmare. The onrush of Anzac and Sussex demoralised most of the Germans in the trenches, and they fled into shell-craters and dug-outs from which they were ferreted like rabbits.

In the centre of the line between Mouquet Farm and Pozières Windmill the Surreys were as successful as their comrades, and, when day broke, the line around Pozières had been extended for more than a mile to a depth of from four hundred to six hundred yards. This provoked a strong German counter-attack, which was arranged for August 5th, but countermanded and finally delivered on August 6th and 7th. The delay was due to the anxiety of the German commander to make certain that his force was strong enough to regain the lost ground. He collected some four thousand troops belonging to the two divisions of the Ninth Reserve Corps, but used them at first in a wild manner. On August 6th a single German battalion attacked the trenches won by the Sussex and, using flame-projectors, took a part of the position but quickly lost it. The following day the main counter-attack was carried out by three thousand men, who advanced over eight hundred yards of open ground, wheeling to the right as they came on.

Liquid flame in counter-attack The manœuvre under fire showed fine discipline. For as the attackers wheeled they were caught by a terrific artillery fire, and then raked with Lewis guns and rifles. The men with the flame-projectors again cleared small pieces of trench in a few places with their jets of fire. But when the German bombers entered the trench they were taken on both sides by the infuriated men of Sussex, Kent, and Surrey, who smashed them with high explosive. About four-fifths of the attacking German force were killed or taken without effecting anything. The use of liquid flame seems to have been designed to frighten the men of the Derby class; but it had the opposite effect.

The flame looked like a big gas-jet as it came towards one, and the natural instinct was to jump back and get out of the way, for even a man who was getting used to shell and bullet did not like the prospect of being roasted alive. But the devilish weapon was not effective. Its range was very limited, and the men who manipulated it were usually shot or bombed. Around Pozières the actual cases of burning were very few, while the fury of battle that the use of liquid fire aroused was largely responsible for the amazing punishment that the three Kent, Sussex, and Surrey battalions inflicted upon a fresh and superior force. **Enemy use of phosphorus shells**

It was about this time that the enemy began largely to employ another form of frightfulness. For some time he had been using liquid-fire shells as well as liquid-flame projectors in the battle of the ridge, and when he lost most of the down fronting Courcelette he added phosphorus shells to his armoury of scientific barbarism. Months before, he had tried shrapnel bullets buried in phosphorus powder, with the intention of causing horrible poisonous wounds. Now he employed phosphorus as a direct weapon in itself, throwing phosphorus shells mingled with a large number of gas shells around the Bapaume road. Amid this strange hail of bullets, shell fragments, stinking gases, blinding gases, phosphorus balls, liquid flames, and high explosive, all blended with clouds of smoke and dust, the troops of the British Empire struggled onward through the greatest fortress system man had ever made.

The conditions of the advance were terrifying, especially around the bare plateau above Pozières, where the enemy maintained an equilibrium of forces. Troops at times had to stand a week's shelling and counter-attacking, merely as a preparation for the advance they were designed to make. Some of the Sussex men are said to have fallen asleep in No Man's Land while engaged in rushing an enemy trench. They fell down as if they had been shot, and could not be roused because they had had no sleep

GLORIOUS CHARGE OF THE COLDSTREAM, GRENADIER, AND IRISH GUARDS.
September 15th, 1916, when the British took Martinpuich and Courcelette, was marked by a superb charge of the Guards. Three battalions of the Coldstream Guards charged in line, followed by Grenadiers and Irish Guards. They all advanced into the enemy's positions until they were two thousand yards ahead of their starting-point.

for a week. A commanding officer is reported to have remained alert and in victorious control of his men after getting one and a half hour's sleep in a hundred and sixty-eight hours of gas attacks, heavy bombardments, and bomb attacks. Until the Anzacs, Londoners, and South-Eastern county regiments broke into the zone of German defences in front of Courcelette, the enemy had sixty batteries of light guns in and about this part of his line. The Anzacs saw the gunners limbering up and retreating over the plateau in one of the early British movements ; another mass of German field-guns about

Checks at Guillemont Thiepval swept the Pozières plateau at close range, and as the distance from Pozières to Thiepval was only about three thousand yards, much of the slightly tilted face of the plateau was under fire from the enemy's machine-guns.

The British and Australian troops had to work forward from saps. From these they rushed out and bombed some German strong point, or broke into a trench and then

[*British official photograph.*

TOWARDS THE GOAL : THE EAGER OUTLOOK OF BRITAIN'S ARDENT INFANTRYMEN.

Awaiting the signal to attack, two British soldiers are looking towards the enemy lines on the Somme. The attitude of the man nearest to the parapet is characteristic. His figure suggests strength and confidence, while his gaze is that of a man accustomed to look on death without fear.

fought desperately along it, while the Germans dodged in and out of dug-outs that had each two or more underground exits. No shred of honour, no remnant of humane feeling stayed the German from winning a temporary advantage. One of his most common tricks was to peer from the depths of a dug-out and appeal to the British bomber not to throw a bomb down as the cavern was being used for wounded men. If the bomber foolishly descended to look at the wounded and arrange for them to be taken to the hospital, he was attacked by a gang of German scoundrels as he stood outlined against the light of the entrance. If the bomber did not descend, the Germans, none of whom was wounded, had time to escape by their underground ways to another subterranean retreat.

Around Pozières the enemy forces became more numerous than the British, and though this circumstance

hindered the advance it enabled the British artillery to do murderous work upon the plateau. At Guillemont, on the other flank of the enemy's arc of hills, the density of his troops was still more remarkable. According to the calculations of the British Staff, he had eleven thousand men garrisoning two thousand yards of trench around the village. This amazing concentration of effort against the British advance was evidence of the Teuton's military industry, but it failed to give his troops the spirit of attack, and allowed the British guns to inflict casualties which were on occasion fifty per cent. heavier than the enemy's losses in previous bombardments.

On the other hand, the enemy by massing troops around Guillemont, close to the point of union between the French and British armies, succeeded in checking the Allies' advance at this point. Since July 15th, when the High-landers took Waterlot Farm, the ruins of Guillemont had been partly entered during the swaying of the battle-line between Delville Wood and Trônes Wood. On July 30th both the French and British attempted an advance on Guillemont, but found the position too strong to be carried. The German system of works stretched southward for a mile to Falfemont Farm, on a down above Maurepas, and extended eastward for another mile to Leuze Wood and northward for another mile to Ginchy.

The enemy thus had three high bases for the defence of Guillemont, which was a mass of ruins lying right at the head of the Fricourt valley, with high ground sheltering it southward from direct fire. On August 8th another attempt was made by Sir Douglas Haig to capture Guillemont. After the usual long and furious bombardment, the British troops advanced in the darkness before dawn and broke into the village. But in the confusion and varying successes of a large nocturnal operation some of the attacking forces lost touch. On the extreme right the troops did very well, and in a rapid movement conquered the high ridge south of Guillemont and gained an important stretch of ground at small cost.

The forces on the left, however, were checked in the gloom by machine-gun fire in front of the village. This was the ordinary hazard of every trench battle, where some redoubts in the hostile line have always to be enveloped. Immediately alongside the checked force another fine body of troops enjoyed better fortune and, meeting with little resistance in the enemy's battered lines of works, drove right into the village, inflicting heavy losses on the Germans. Then occurred a stroke of bad luck. The victorious troops, who were still fighting amid the ruins in darkness, lost touch with the battalions held up on their left. Instead of holding on to the important part of Guillemont they had won, some of the men venturously worked through the whole chaos of brick and tumbled earth until they reached the extreme south-eastern corner of the village. They were but a mere island in a hostile sea, with the depth of the village between them and their friends and the enemy all about them.

When the sun came up and lighted the scene it was too late to rectify the lines of the operation. The German gunners swept the ground with an incessant curtain fire, and German bombing-parties continually attacked the little island of khaki. In **Caught in a sea of fire** reply the British gunners drew their curtain of fire round the village and, after a long wait to give the enveloped men a chance of fighting their way out, swept all the ruins with heavy fire. In the evening some of the adventurers returned through two zones of death ; the following day more came back, and in the second night and the third day others returned. Small were the numbers that fell into the hands of the enemy, though he claimed a large capture in his official report.

After the failure of this operation the French and British troops again combined in an attack around Guillemont in the middle of August. But again, though ground was

Reinforcements moving towards Flers to consolidate this part of the German first line, captured on September 15th, 1916. The men are carrying picks and shovels, all-important implements in siege warfare.

British cavalry keeping in form, ready for any emergency on the Somme front. Horsemen frequently took part as infantrymen, but opportunity was afforded for cavalry manœuvres behind the lines.

Wave of infantry advancing in open order under heavy fire. A large German shell is seen exploding a few yards to the rear of this gallant handful of our citizen soldiers making history.

FORWARD SABRES, RIFLES, AND PICKS: BRITISH MOVEMENTS IN THE SOMME SECTOR.

AFTER GUILLEMONT: PILGRIMS OF PATRIOTISM.
Covered with a blanket each casualty was laid carefully by the roadside to await the motor-ambulance. On the occasion above illustrated a passing armoured car had apparently volunteered to assist in the work.

FIRST-AID IN THE FIRST LINE.
Tending the wounded in the trenches. One soldier had just had his leg bandaged, while another, wounded in the arm, was being given some nourishment.

gained about the western outskirts of the village and in the direction of Ginchy, the main position at Guillemont remained unconquered.

The rest of the month of August was spent in local fighting around Thiepval, Mouquet Farm, High Wood, and Guillemont, which provoked the enemy to make great counter-attacks. For example, on August 17th, six lines of enemy infantry advanced against the Anzac and British troops on the Pozières front, but were caught by howitzer fire on the northern slope, swept by field-guns when they topped the ridge, and then completely broken by machine-guns, rifles and bombs when they neared the trenches. On August 20th the enemy turned the point of his counter-attacking forces against High Wood, but failed. Then on August 24th he made an assault on the grand scale on the new British line between the quarry

at Guillemont and the wreck of the railway-station there. The attack was opened in the twilight and pressed with extraordinary resoluteness. The only result was that the great determination of the Germans was measured by their great losses. All the British line stood firm, and with shrapnel showers and streams of bullets reaped a terrible harvest of death. Two days afterwards a strong force of the Prussian Guard endeavoured to recover the ground about the Leipzig salient at Thiepval which the Wiltshires and the Gloucesters had won. But again the British line was unbroken, and a remnant of Prussian Guardsmen fled from the trenches held by the English county regiments. We shall never know how much the old glories of each county regiment told in the war. Every recruit knew what standard he was expected to attain, and in many cases he astonished the most confident of his officers by a superhuman capacity for endurance of the most gallant kind.

German Wonder-Work at Thiepval

In the intervals between the great German counter-attacks the British army slowly worked forward against all the main points of the German defences, by means of whirlwind bombardments followed by rushing bomb attacks. Thiepval was approached within a thousand yards, close to the elaborate maze of trenches, dug-outs, and machine-gun works which the Germans had gloriously named their Wonder-Work. From the Wonder-Work the Prussian Guardsmen who garrisoned it swept all the ground to Skyline Trench and Mouquet Farm. Around Mouquet Farm the Anzacs pressed just outside the defences and along the road leading to Miraumont. East of the deadly and mysterious farm the British troops gradually sapped and bombed their way, a hundred yards at a time, towards Martinpuich. But in all this local British action there was little more than an equilibrium of forces, in which the balance usually inclined to the side that was standing on the defensive. The main advantage of the British was that they still left the enemy on part of the slope of the great ridge, and there hammered him by means of an unparalleled mass of artillery that ranged to his rail-head and over all his communications.

But after the extraordinary pause of five weeks, from the last week in July to the first week in September, Sir Douglas Haig managed to obtain more infantry, and brought to the Somme front some fine brigades of Irish soldiers, with West Countrymen and English Riflemen. In the meantime the vast machine of British artillery had been again strengthened, and the main ammunition dumps had increased in size, despite the daily lavish expenditure of shell. The army under General Fayolle north of the Somme had enlarged its line of action and augmented its effectives, with the result that more pressure could be exerted against the great block of German works between Combles and Péronne. Everything was ready for a great new offensive movement by the Allies on a front of some nineteen miles. The opposing enemy commanders, General Baron von Marschall, General von Stein, and General Kirchbach, anticipated the attack, and filled the shell-holes in No Man's Land with snipers and manned the machine-gun posts with picked and desperate teams who vowed to fight to the death. For eight hours the British guns bombarded all the German positions from Beaumont-Hamel and Guillemont. Then on the night of September 3rd, in the darkness before the rising of the moon, a large force of British and Australian troops approached the enemy, and just before dawn advanced into the open.

The German line on either side of the Ancre brook was penetrated with comparative ease below Beaumont and Thiepval, the hostile line of machine-gun fire being beaten down by a bombardment of great accuracy and intensity.

Holding General Marschall's forces

But after two systems of works had been stormed and the men were organising the ground they had won, the German guns opened on a great arc above the Ancre and prevented the lost trenches from being repaired. Amid this storm of shell the hostile infantry counter-attacked and, though they were checked and punished, the British troops were forced to withdraw to their own line. For the second time the Ancre positions had proved impregnable. This northern action, however, was designed from the beginning as a subsidiary affair to hold General von Marschall's forces and prevent them from swinging round to the assistance of General Kirchbach. Sir Douglas Haig did not want guns removed from the Beaumont-Hamel area

[British official photographs.

THE VIA DOLOROSA AFTER VICTORY: WOUNDED BY THE WAYSIDE IN FRANCE.

Wounded men collected from the field awaiting the ambulance to take them to the base. Doctors and orderlies are tending them. The helpless attitudes of men who, a few minutes previously, were the finest examples of soldierly physique, provided one of the most moving spectacles behind the battle line. In circle: Assisting a soldier injured in the leg over a trench. Some ammunition-cases were improvised as stepping-stones.

MEN WHO FOUGHT TO A FINISH.
German dead in the enemy's first-line trenches amid the débris of a few hand-grenades, broken rifles, and steel helmets. The disposition of the grenades suggests a deadly hand-to-hand encounter.

Faced with shell fire and raked with machine-guns, the Irishmen swept so quickly on to their main objective, the sunken road, that they passed over some knots of Germans in the quarry north of the road. When the Germans emerged with machine-guns to take the Irishmen in the rear, according to their old tactics, some English Riflemen, led by a quick-eyed colonel, extended into the quarry and cleaned it out. Thereupon, a German officer, caught in the act of playing dead dog, tried to buy his life by offering the English officer his gold watch. When the watch was refused, he pressed it upon a corporal. There are some extraordinary qualities in the Germans—a mixture of the basest and the highest.

While the Riflemen surrounded the south-west of the village the Irishmen went onward like an avalanche of footballers. Their forwards cleared the village in a rush, went over the slope **On the road** beyond into the valley, and apparently **to Ginchy—** reached Leuze Wood. Machine-guns swept them on either flank and even caught them in the back. But the men followed their pipers and broke the spine of the German defence, and as the ground was methodically cleared behind them by the more cautious English Rifles, the charge was a fine combination of rush tactics and scientific consolidation.

The important sunken road was transformed into the main British line, leaving Leuze Wood reconnoitred as the next objective. But besides driving thus far into the enemy's position immediately around Combles, the dashing Irishmen on the left, after breaking clean through the north of Guillemont, continued along the road to Ginchy. Here they were stopped by machine-gun fire from the cellars and underground works, but they hauled forward trench-mortars, levelled all the works with aerial torpedoes, and conquered in another fierce rush the High Street and most of the houses. Then, assailed by converging columns of fresh German toops, the Munsters, Dublins, and Irish Rifles drew back from the northern part of Ginchy, but clung to its southern outskirts. They were battered incessantly by cross-fires of German artillery of all calibres, lashed with machine-gun squalls, and cut off from supplies and supports by terrific barrages of shell. But they hung on with amazing courage while General von Kirchbach brought two fresh divisions forward.

For five days and nights the Irishmen lay in shell-craters south and east of Ginchy, scantily fed, heavily shelled, and with little sleep. On the third night they dug towards each other from their craters, and formed the shell-holes into a connected shallow trench. In spite of the strain and misery of lying in the open under a heavy fire, the men were so keen on conquering Ginchy that those who had been lightly wounded would not go to the field hospital, and pleaded to be allowed to stay. Irish orderlies vanished from Headquarters and were discovered in the firing-line. "I missed Guillemont," said one of them, "and I must be in at Ginchy. If I'm all right, I'll come back when it is over. I am very sorry."

On September 8th the German commander threw his new troops into the village, with a great store of food, and the fresh Prussians and Bavarians were ready for a fierce tussle. At least one German sniper tied himself to a tree-top to make sure his courage would not give way, and most of the Bavarian machine-gunners were resolute to fight to the death. But when the Irishmen made their closing charge, in the afternoon of September 9th, they covered six hundred yards in eight minutes of furious battle, reaching again the High Street in the heart of the village. As the yelling Dublins advanced, two hundred Germans surrendered from a trench running from the western line to the centre of Ginchy. On the other hand, some furious Bavarians left their cellars and fought madly in the open until they were bayoneted or bombed. Fighting then continued in the village around nests of machine-guns, which were silenced by trench-mortars, and along a road

to the Bapaume sector, because he had another and larger operation in view in the middle of September. He had, therefore, to make General von Marschall apprehensive, and partly to this end the fierce demonstration on the Ancre was arranged, while the Australians violently pressed the enemy at Thiepval by a drive into Mouquet Farm and the ridge beyond and above it.

While the northern point of the German line was thus being threatened, the main British attack was delivered with victorious skill against the southern point of the hostile arc of works at Ginchy and Guillemont. Again the enemy divined what was about to happen, and as the attacking troops were waiting in their assembly trenches they were hammered with some ten thousand **Irish pipes** poison-gas shells. But the bursts of gas **at Guillemont** did not seriously impair the vigour of the massed Irish and English troops. There were men of Connaught, Leinster, and Munster waiting in the rainy night in front of Guillemont, with English Riflemen alongside them. The Riflemen had already had a long and trying ordeal in the trenches, and the Irish regiments were brought up to the battered position to add fresh energy to the attack. The heavy German bombardment continued upon the new Irish divisions, and became so intense that it seemed impossible for men to live under it, much less advance. The Irishmen, who were mostly Roman Catholics, knelt down under the terrific gun fire and received absolution from a devoted chaplain. Then to a tune on the Irish pipes they went forward with headlong impetuosity, and with the English Riflemen on their right broke right through the ruins of Guillemont and reached the sunken road leading south-west from the village.

Lieut.=General Sir Thomas D'Oyly Snow, K.C.B., commanding the Seventh Army Corps.

British troops who took part in the capture and occupation of Lesbœufs.

Moving a British heavy gun up to the front by man=power.

After Lesbœufs: Troops swing along to the strains of fife and drum.

Tractor hauling a heavy howitzer to a new part of the front.

Between our barrage (left) and German shells (right) British infantry storm the Schwaben Redoubt.

where the enemy had another line of machine-guns that shattered a fine Irish battalion in a few minutes. But again the useful trench-mortar was brought forward and the enemy gunners were shelled out, while a sergeant, two corporals, and a private of the Munsters recaptured three hundred feet of trench from which their comrades had been driven, and then held the wide gap unaided for several hours.

As the first Irish regiment poured into the village on one side, fresh English troops poured into it from the other and cleaned up the ground. But when the Irishmen drove through the northern end of Ginchy it was found that a junction could not be made with the troops on the north-west, so that the left flank, composed of a detachment of Dublins and Royal Engineers, was left "in the air." But

—and the triumphant return the gallant party began trench-digging in a fierce and sustained spasm of labour, and when long afterwards reliefs came up, there were fourteen hundred yards of new, good trenchwork protecting the north-western part of the captured village. Meanwhile, the battalions that had led the charge delivered their thrust so rapidly that an hour after they left their shell-holes they had patrols working a quarter of a mile beyond the village up the slope leading to the Ginchy Telegraph.

When the Irish brigades marched back towards camp in the afternoon of September 10th, the worn, shrunken battalions, mechanically keeping step with a piper at their head, were a sight to stir anybody with Irish blood in them. For more than a week the men had been fighting, and little sleep had they had. Their eyes were bloodshot and ringed with shadows, their seamed faces were grey with dust. The mud was caked on them, and their bodies huddled forward in the weakness of utter fatigue. Yet a spirit of triumph shone from them. They had made Ginchy and Guillemont monuments to the valour of their race.

And Leuze Wood was largely theirs also. While the struggle had been raging east of Guillemont and around Ginchy, other British troops had advanced alongside the French above Maurepas towards the ridge crowned by a cluster of trees sheltering Falfemont Farm. From this farm a line of German works ran north-westward through Wedge Wood to Guillemont. Another series of works and connected shell-holes extended north-eastward from Falfemont Farm along a spur of downland leading into Leuze Wood. Leuze Wood was a great stronghold, containing three lines of fortifications backed by another five lines of works running down to Combles. English troops, including a splendid force of West Countrymen, under a famous general who had broken the Prussian Guard at Ypres two years before, met the Prussian Guard at Falfemont Farm, which soon became the Hougomont of the Guillemont battle-line. To strengthen the resemblance with the field of Waterloo there was, behind the enemy's line, the sunken road running from Wedge Wood to Guillemont. Part of it had been captured by the Irishmen in their first long lunge through Guillemont into Leuze Wood. And while the English Riflemen who followed the Irishmen were consolidating the northern end of the sunken road a surprise rush up the slopes to Falfemont Farm had been made. But this gallant attempt to snatch another important position at the close of a day's great conquests was defeated by a force of the Prussian Guard who charged with the bayonet from the trees about the farmstead and recovered all the ground to Wedge Wood.

The next day Falfemont became a gambit pawn in the terrible play of war. The West Country battalions approached the hill farm on the southern and western slopes with the intention of storming it. The design was that their attack should draw German reinforcements along the spur from Leuze Wood. Then the main British forces, gathering in the northern part of the sunken road from Guillemont, were to make a sustained rush into the

[*Canadian War Records.*

STOIC COURAGE UNDER PAIN.
Tending Canadian wounded who took part in the victory of Courcelette. In the foreground a soldier of the Dominion was having a nasty hand wound dressed, and he bore his pain with stoic courage.

western side of Leuze Wood. Leuze Wood was half a mile in the rear of Falfemont Farm, so that if the main British attack succeeded, the garrison of the Prussian Guard on the southern spur would be enveloped.

About three o'clock in the afternoon of a ghastly Sabbath, in rolling, open, shell-shattered country, as desolate and as cratered as the mountains of the moon, thin lines of khaki figures poured from the sunken road on one side and up the southern slopes of the Falfemont spur on the other side. There was scarcely any artillery fire, as the lines of conflict were too close. The British guns were pounding the enemy's reserve positions and communications, while the German guns were shelling Guillemont. In the scene of the fighting there was only the rattle of machine-gun fire. The British troops were

in very wide order, to escape the scything **Wedge Wood and** streams of bullets, and every time they **Falfemont Farm** crouched for cover in shell-holes their own

machine-guns played on the enemy's hostile posts and thus screened the advance. On the north Wedge Wood was taken after a bombing scrimmage, and out of the middle of it came a group of grey figures—enemy prisoners. Meanwhile, the southern waves of attack on Falfemont Farm had a very long slope to climb, but they broke into the German triangle of trenches on the spur going down to Leuze Wood, and then encircled the farm westward and northward.

Thereupon, a curious thing occurred. All the Germans seemed to be in wild confusion. Some ran from Falfemont Farm towards Leuze Wood like panic-stricken fugitives, while larger masses came from Leuze Wood towards the farm, and after running a little way scuttled back. The

TRUE TO ITS PLACARD: A "TANK" WINNING ITS WAY ALONG A SOMME VILLAGE STREET.

So well kept was the secret of the "tank" that its advent into the arena of the west front completely staggered the enemy. As the swaying leviathan rolled up the High Street of a Somme village the Germans in the vicinity threw up their hands and surrendered to the oncoming British infantry. The "tank" acted as a veritable guide to victory, forging its way through obstacles, defying bullets, bombs, and shells, explanation was that the main British attack on Leuze Wood was developing furiously, and the German commander was hesitating whether to abandon the Falfemont position and concentrate around Combles or endeavour to hold the entire line. While he hesitated the West Countrymen topped the southern edge of the spur and worked forward through the thistles and among the bare poles that had once been trees.

This decided the line of action of General Kirchbach. He sent a battalion of the Prussian Guard forward from Leuze Wood along the spur. The Guards advanced shoulder to shoulder in a disastrously obsolete formation, intending no doubt to repeat the bayonet attack of the previous day. Scarcely a British shell touched them, but when they neared the British line they fell in a compact mass under machine-gun and rifle fire Twenty minutes later another German counter-attack was organised in exactly the same way, and again nearly all the men taking part in it fell face forward. Somebody on the German side was badly blundering, and apparently he was removed, for a third counter-attack was launched from Leuze Wood, and on this occasion the Guardsmen, with scraps of other corps, worked forward in a scientific way in open order, taking cover in the shell-holes in the chalky ridge, and managed to hold the farm. But the West Countrymen clung to the northern spur, to the southern slope, and to the western way of approach from Wedge Wood, and at night in a deluge of rain they worked forward in a wild soldiers' battle. By dawn the farm was almost surrounded, and in a final daylight rush from three sides all the garrison was slain or captured.

Capture of Leuze Wood

Meanwhile, the main attack on Leuze Wood succeeded, owing to the enemy's distracted efforts to hold on to the Falfemont spur. By Sunday night a footing was won in the western part of the wood, and afterwards, in the drenching rain and darkness, with the battle raging all along the line to Ginchy, High Wood, and Mouquet Farm, the thrust into Leuze Wood was stubbornly pressed against tremendous resistance. Leuze Wood was at the time the most vital point in the enemy's system of defences north of the Somme. What was taking place was the Battle of Combles, with the French forces thrusting on one side of the hill rampart at Le Forest and the British forces thrusting against the other side at Leuze Wood. The wood crowned a hill higher than all others round the large, long valley of Combles, and so was an all-important observation centre. When it was won, British artillery officers sitting at the end of a telephone wire could place shells by the thousand exactly upon every position in and around Combles. So long as Leuze Wood was not won, the enemy, who had large military stores in Combles, could maintain strong reserves of troops in the valley and feed them against the French and British armies on either side. The German commander, therefore, fought with extreme tenacity to retain the wood on the dominating hill. But such was the sustained fury of attack of the British and Irish troops that, in four days' and nights' persistent action against all available enemy divisions, the whole line was slowly advanced a mile east of Guillemont, and all Leuze Wood was conquered in the night of September 6th.

[*British official photograph.*
WEAVING A SHELL CURTAIN ON THE WEST FRONT.
Putting over a heavy barrage. Gunners at work during the early days of the allied offensive. A pile of empty shell-cases and a lack of tunics and shirts indicate the measure of their enthusiasm.

The enemy, however, still retained two lines of works on the slopes going down to Combles and two communication-trenches running up to his lost wood. All this system of hostile works on the reverse slope was covered by hundreds of German guns on the Rancourt down across the Combles valley. A British advance into Combles was, therefore, impracticable until the French forces had worked round to Rancourt; and, moreover, an immediate advance was not necessary, seeing that the British gunnery directors could look down from their newly-won position on all the enemy's positions as far as Morval, and shatter them with incessant howitzer fire. There was no reason in using infantry to slay the enemy when artillery could do the work with mathematical deadliness. The next move lay with General Kirchbach, and under cover of darkness before dawn on September 8th he made a terrific essay to recover Leuze Wood and save Combles, only to have his troops driven back after ferocious hand-to-hand fighting. Two days afterwards, as already related, the whole of Ginchy village was captured. At the same time a general British advance was made from High Wood to Leuze Wood, and ground won for another offensive movement on the grand scale, for which mighty preparations had been in progress during the Battle of Combles.

Hindenburg had come to the western front to converse with Gallwitz, Below, and Stein concerning the British Army. What he saw and what he learned in the middle of September directly led to the later colossal German effort to levy the entire Teutonic population for the purpose of producing more munitions and getting every possible fit man who could be spared from war work into the Army. On September 11th the enemy tried to storm back into Ginchy, but was repulsed with heavy loss. He returned to the attack on September 12th and was again severely defeated. He re-formed his battered troops and reinforced them, and made a third great counter-attack; but what men of his entered the British trenches alive became prisoners. The next day the German official report admitted for the first time the loss of Ginchy. The delay of four days in the acknowledgment of defeat served to indicate with what large forces of effectives the vain counter-attacks had been made. The

Hindenburg's visit of inspection

PART OF THE IRISH BRIGADE COMES BACK WITH LAURELS FROM GUILLEMONT.

The Irish Brigade added to their sheaf of laurels by their brilliant capture of Guillemont and Ginchy. Under a terribly destructive fire, men from Connaught, Munster, and Leinster went forward to the attack at Guillemont with a headlong impetuosity which carried them right through the village towards Leuze Wood.

design had been to recover the village at any cost, and then pretend it had never been wholly lost. For, as Hindenburg was officially stated to be on the western front in the second week of September, the loss of such key positions as Ginchy and Leuze Wood was calculated to shake the faith of the German public in their dictator. The loss of Leuze Wood was not admitted.

But this veil of pretence was rent and blown away while Hindenburg was still on the Somme. On September 14th the Wiltshires and the Gloucesters, who had been clinging to the southern slopes of Thiepval, made **Famous " Wonder-** a night attack upon the famous Wonder- **Work " stormed** Work and stormed the maze of earthworks and caverns in a rush that completely demoralised the garrison, composed of detachments of the Reserve of the Prussian Guard. Here and there a sturdy Guardsman stood out and fought with bayonet and bomb, but along most of the line the crack troops of Prussia bolted across the open, and ran blindly into the British artillery barrage. One Guardsman excused his fugitive comrades by saying that our men " charged like the wind," and gave no time to the defenders to get their weapons between the preliminary bombardment and the artillery rush. The Wonder-Work was built on a spur that overlooked all the left of the British advance along the Pozières ridge to Mouquet Farm and Courcelette.

And the next day, after two German attacks on the Wonder-Work had been beaten back, one of the greatest movements in the war abruptly opened. Hindenburg and his generals were hoping that, after two and a half months of continual fighting, the offensive energy of the British Army was permanently diminished. Thirty German divisions had been shattered and withdrawn from the British front. It did not seem possible to the enemy that the British army, which was being filled out with drafts of the Derby class in July, 1916, could persist in attacking at its pristine pace in the middle of September, 1916. The German High Command expected only some persistent but small movements, such as that proceeding against the remnant of their second zone of defences about Combles. But behind Combles and in front of Bapaume the Germans had a third zone of defences on the Flers line, which had

been enormously strengthened by constant digging since the opening of the Somme battles. Stein had largely extended the machine-gun organisation, and Below, in his search for artillery to overbalance the British guns, had seriously weakened the German lines around Verdun. The ruling German opinion was that the British would go on losing a hundred thousand men a month against the German machine-gun positions without making any further large gains of ground in the autumn, except that Combles might fall to them.

But after much delay, due largely to official lack of judgment, the genius of the British race had produced a new engine of war in the form of a land monitor. From the armoured motor-cars used by the Royal Naval Air Service in support of aeroplanes there had developed the plan of a modern war-chariot for attacking entrenchments and machine-gun redoubts. The increase in heavy artillery, leading to the employment of combined parks of two thousand guns shelling No Man's Land from either side, at first led some generals to think that a moving fort would be useless over ground holed with heavy shell and ramparted with earthworks, ruined houses, and stumps of forest trees. In spite of almost general discouragement the naval men continued to work at their idea, in which Mr. Winston Churchill became interested, and Mr. D'Eyncourt, the Director of Naval Construction, undertook the design of a landship capable of carrying out an attack against entrenched positions. Soldiers played a great part in developing the new instrument of war, and Colonel Swinton was particularly **Entry of the** prominent in this work, though, according **" tank "** to a statement made by the Financial Secretary to the Admiralty, officers of the Royal Naval Air Service, with the Director of Naval Construction and the Assistant-Constructor, Mr. F. Skeens, were chiefly concerned in the preliminary work of design. The practical work of construction, which called for high and ingenious talent, was carried out by Mr. W. A. Tritton, managing director of Messrs. Wm. Foster & Co., who built the cars.

They were known as " tanks " while being transported and stored at the front, in order to avoid exciting general curiosity among the troops and the German spies in North

Western France and the nook of Flanders. But when the covering of the "tanks" was removed and the cars brought out to be tested, the British soldier completely exhausted his great gift of the language of imagination in trying to describe the huge steel monsters. They looked somewhat like giant toads of the nightmare age of the dragons of the slime. They were painted in brown, green, and yellow, to harmonise with the landscape of the Somme. As they moved forward with their big blunt snouts thrust in the air, and bodies wheelless and limbless, yet with a smooth, deliberate motion like that of a footless reptile, the British army broke into Homeric laughter—the monsters were such a mixture of horrible strength and fantastic appearance. They could climb a shell-crater or straddle over it ; they could rise up against a wall and push it with the weight of many tons until it fell down ; they could flatten out earthworks ; bullets and hand-grenades made no impression upon them ; and with an armament of machine-guns firing in all directions

Weird dragons of the slime and directed by periscopes they could annihilate battalions of infantry. Only artillery fire could penetrate their armour.

In one of his scientific fantasies Mr. H. G. Wells had described the landship, and it is possible that his brilliant piece of scientific fiction inspired the men who first worked out the design.

The humour and the strange strength of the "tanks" helped to increase the confidence of the British, Canadian, and Anzac forces that were arrayed for battle on the front of six miles from the ridge of Pozières to the northern edge of Leuze Wood. At dawn the massed guns began firing steadily, but not with any remarkable volume of fire. As the sun lifted and drew the moisture out of the earth, a dense white mist rose from the valleys and blotted out the ridges, and through the mist brigade after brigade of infantry went over the parapet against the fortified villages of Courcelette, Martinpuich, and Flers, and the trench systems running down to Bouleaux Wood at Combles.

In front of Courcelette the enemy was fully prepared to make an ordinary grand attack himself. He had massed troops in his front and reserve lines, and thrown **Advance on Courcelette** out advanced patrols and bombing-parties between the opposing parapets along the Pozières ridge. There can be little doubt that General von Below had arranged a main attack on the British line from Pozières to High Wood as an answer to the Guillemont-Ginchy and Leuze Wood operations. On the Guillemont and Leuze Wood front his forces were also massed in very considerable numbers, but apparently more for a subsidiary action than for a complete offensive against the entire British line. The principal German concentration was on the Bapaume sector, in front of Courcelette, Martinpuich, and Flers. The Second Bavarian Corps was very closely packed about Courcelette, so that in some stretches of trench one man per yard was killed solely by British gun fire. Clearly the enemy commander did not anticipate that his army would be caught before it could strike, and be compelled to stand

REINFORCEMENTS GOING FORWARD ON THE SOMME FRONT.   [*British official photograph.*

Under the lee of a shell-marked wood. A column of men is seen marching up to the front, followed by an officer, whose beautiful charger is a feature of this illustration. In the background the remnants of a large country-house still dominated the French highway.

GUARDS AT RESPIRATOR DRILL.
The hideous masks enhanced the formidable
appearance of these fearless fighters.

on the defensive. For, in view of a defensive battle, the troops would have been more widely spaced to avoid shell fire, and would have been largely saved for counter-attacks after their own artillery had done all it could to shatter the hostile offensive. In all probability there was a race between Sir Douglas Haig and General von Below to open a strong offensive, and the race was won by the British commander because he still held the mastery of the air and, observing the hostile preparations, outspeeded them.

Very close was the struggle for the initiative. The British commander seems only to have won by some minutes. At night the Canadians were densely assembled on the Pozières ridge, from a point near Mouquet Farm to a point above the village and windmill captured by the Australians. They were bombarded with blinding shell and gas shell, and then taken by surprise in a rush attack of the Bavarians. Elbow-room was needed in order to engage a charging mass of bomb-throwers with machine-gun supports, and the Canadians had no elbow-room. But they somehow managed to master the raiders and resume their own order of advance. Not a Bavarian escaped. A Lewis gunner killed those who came over the parapet, and an officer with a party of twelve bombers dealt with the other assailants. Then at twenty past six in the morning of September 15th, 1916, men from Toronto, London, and Kingston, and men from Winnipeg, Regina, Vancouver, and Eastern Canada, led the first assault, while behind them came clearing-up forces of French Canadians, Halifax and Montreal men, and a light infantry regiment that formed the van of attack in the second operation. On this occasion there was no long and intense preliminary bombardment of the enemy's lines to herald and advertise the infantry movement. In order to take the Germans

Close struggle for initiative

by surprise the troops advanced soon after their gun fire opened and walked behind a moving zone of shell and shrapnel. The new Royal Garrison Artillery had become in six weeks a corps of master-gunners. They were able to execute perfectly new ideas of their leading commanders, such as the long-practised artillerymen of Germany either never dreamed of or thought too intricate in execution to attempt.

The design of surprise underlay all the British tactics in artillery, infantry, and aerial work. And it was by staggering and dismaying the enemy by surprise upon surprise that the greatest of modern British victories was gained. The Germans were relatively as strong on the Bapaume

OUT TO SAVE LIFE, NOT TO TAKE IT.
Regimental stretcher-bearers on their way out to bring in wounded. This photograph was taken near
Ginchy, where the Irish regiments distinguished themselves so brilliantly.

front as they had been on July 1st on the Ancre front. They had more than a thousand guns in action against the British troops, and considerably more than ten thousand machine-guns, while their troops were massed in extraordinary density. The difference in the issue arose from the fact that the attacking forces were not only more practised and more alertly intelligent. but were remarkably inventive. They had done much more than learn from experience—they had discovered for themselves new ways and means of warfare.

Their artillery method was an expansion of the whirlwind bombardment, in which magnificence of scope was combined with minute intricacy of detail. Every battery commander and officer had a list of time-tabled targets corresponding with the prearranged steps of the infantry movement. This was apparently the usual thing ; but there was much more in it than the ordinary covering fire of an advance. For as the hostile works had not been shattered beforehand, the moving line of thunderbolts had to effect all that days of bombardment might have done. A week's artillery work of destruction had to be crowded into

British artillery miracle

less than half an hour, and yet performed with extreme precision. And the heavy gunners and the field gunners firing in front of them accomplished the task set them. All the circumstances cannot yet be explained. We cannot state how long many of the new men and officers of the Royal Garrison Artillery marched and drilled and practised with the rifle before they had heavy ordnance to learn to handle. But it may be fairly said that their achievement was in the nature of a miracle—a miracle of intellectual quickness and capability. When the Briton does hustle, under masterful and brilliant direction, he sometimes accelerates with avalanche effect.

The German gunners, however, had a kite-balloon watching the Pozières ridge, and when the Canadians came out behind their smoking, flaming line of pounding shells they were in turn assailed by a heavy and continuous artillery fire. The leading battalions had many men put out of action—killed, blown up, or **" Crême de Menthe "** buried. But the men went steadily on**at sugar factory** ward, keeping exceedingly close to their artillery barrage, and thus came with disconcerting suddenness upon the Bavarians sheltering in dug-outs. German machine-guns and many snipers, nevertheless, assailed them. For the enemy had thrown advance parties forward into shell-holes beyond his own earthworks. Most of these were rushed and slain, and the waves of assault rapidly spread down the long slope, a mile in depth, to the hollow where Courcelette lifted her ruined chimneys. The ground was open and terribly exposed, and the enemy had a great trench running at an angle to the line of advance, so that as each company reached it they came under a flanking fire from the unassailed part of the works. Almost parallel with this long diagonal trench was a similar long work, covering the other side of the village, and between the two long protecting arms was a series of half a dozen small works, the most important of which connected with the sugar factory near the Bapaume road.

In a succession of splendid bursts the Canadians secured their left flank by extending towards the Thiepval front, and in frenzied fighting broke rapidly through all the enemy positions as far as the sugar factory. Here they were desperately engaging a row of machine-guns when at a ponderous pace "Crême de Menthe," the leading landship, arrived. She and her fellow monster "Cordon Rouge" had been outpaced by the furious Canadians, but slowly and surely the new engines of war crawled into the forefront of the battle. "Crême de Menthe" sparkled with blue fire as the German machine-gunners whipped her vainly with bullets. Rising in weird toad-like fashion, she prowled about the sand-bagged and concrete redoubt, with her guns sweeping every grey figure in sight. The garrison was beaten down in front and enfiladed sideways, and by the afternoon the factory fortress was won. At the same time the trenches known as Candy Trench and Sugar Trench, on either flank, were stormed by most heroic assaults, wave following wave until the enemy was rushed. Then

WASTE AND REPAIR OF MAN-POWER ON THE BATTLE-FRONT.
[British and French official photographs.
British troops going aboard motor-lorries to be taken to the advanced front. Above: View of the battlefield near Courcelette, with Red Cross waggons waiting to take back wounded. Despite the waste of life, the Allies' man-power steadily waxed as that of the Germans waned.

Wounded brought to the roadside near Guillemont to be taken away in ambulances. An eye-witness said there was not one of the wounded whose eyes were not alight with the fire of triumph. Never was the British Army in better spirits, more elated and confident than on this memorable day when the most shattering blow was dealt to the enemy that he had yet received.

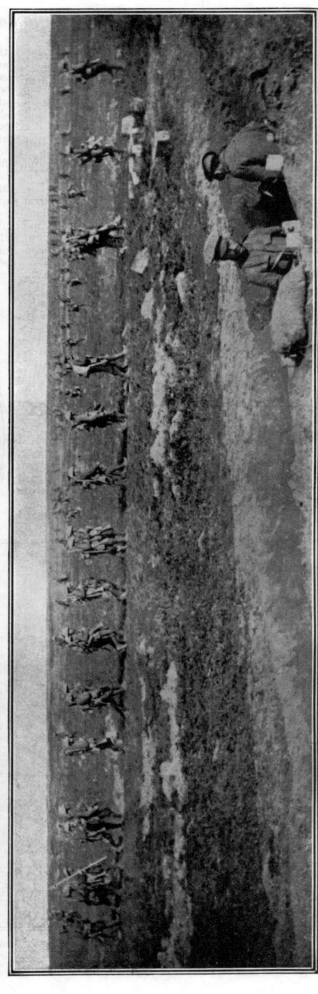

Infantry reinforcements moving up to the front during the battle. Authorities agreed that September 15th was, perhaps, the greatest day since the Battle of the Somme began. Three villages, Courcelette, Martinpuich, and Flers, were occupied, and the British troops advanced over most of the front to a depth of nearly two miles, taking more than twenty miles of German trenches in that area.

[*British official photograph.*

THINGS SEEN IN FRANCE, SEPTEMBER 15TH, 1916, ONE OF THE MOST MEMORABLE DAYS OF THE GREAT ADVANCE

Sir Julian Byng, the corps commander, was informed by one of the new aerial Staff messengers hovering over the conquered sugar-works that the entire objective of the Canadians had been secured and patrols pushed forward towards the village and the gun-pit to the south-east.

Like all good cavalrymen, General Byng was a born thruster, and by his grasp of initiative had constantly risen during the war. Courcelette, an unexpected prize of the highest value, was offered to him by the eager Canadians, and he rapidly planned the great extra operation. The enemy's second long system of trenches, running from the north-western edge of the village towards Mouquet Farm and linking Courcelette directly with the Ancre positions, was designed for attack. It was carried in a skilful and dashing manner by a veteran light infantry regiment of Canada and a Montreal battalion, who established a strong position covering Courcelette from counter-attack from the Ancre side. Simultaneously, the fine French-Canadian force who had been clearing up dug-outs under heavy fire in the early part of the day moved against the village, with a Halifax battalion co-operating on its left.

Canadians' revenge at Courcelette

Just at the edge of the tangle of streets, trenches, and battered buildings the French-Canadians were held up until their own shell fire lifted. Then with wild cries they poured inundatingly into Courcelette, were caught on the right by machine-guns, rushed the guns, and bombed their way northward. The larger part of the garrison of 2,000 Germans had no zest for battle. Some knelt with raised hands in the streets imploring mercy ; others crept out of dug-outs eager to surrender ; and though it was not the task of the charging battalion to take prisoners—the captives properly falling to the clearing-up parties—the French-Canadians angrily saddled themselves with more than three hundred unwounded Germans by the time they reached the quarry and made a line northward and eastward of it. Then the Halifax men closed round while the remnant of the hostile garrison fled over the crest, throwing away rifles and equipment as they ran. Thus within a little more than twelve hours the Canadians took all enemy positions on a wide front to a depth in places of 2,000 yards.

The important victory at Courcelette was not won lightly, but it thrilled Canada. The fighting men of the Dominion had long stood on the defensive, and had endured many grievous things. Against them the enemy had employed his first clouds of poison gas, and they had saved Ypres. Against them he had made, still at Ypres, his last important offensive movement, killing two of the best-loved Canadian commanders and rousing the men to extreme fury. In these circumstances the Canadians came to the Somme in berserker mood. And when the day was won, their extraordinary gain of ground and tale of prisoners and war material did not greatly interest them. "Vaches !" screamed the French-Canadians when the Bavarians held up hands. They despised their prisoners, for they wanted to meet only Germans ready to fight to the death. And on the whole the Second Bavarian Corps in the early part of the day gave them what they wanted, as was seen from the thousands of grey forms in trench, dug-out, and shell-hole. And in the night of September 15th the Canadians consummated their revenge for all they had suffered in the northern salient. Seven times the enemy counter-attacked and was not only completely repulsed, but was pushed back farther by fresh assaults.

Alongside the Canadians a fine force of British troops broke the enemy's lines in front of Martinpuich in a swift assault of twenty minutes, but were held up before the main fortress by a Bavarian division that had distinguished itself in the defence of the Hohenzollern Redoubt in the Battle of Loos. The struggle amid the dug-outs and underground ways of the village might have been as severe as the Hohenzollern conflict. For the buildings had not

ENTRANCE TO A CAPTURED GERMAN DUG-OUT.
German thoroughness brought subterranean architecture to an amazing point of elaboration which, incidentally, suggested some doubt on their part of speedy victory in the war.

been levelled as in the first Somme actions, but only rent, gutted, and unroofed by the sharp whirlwind bombardment. Numerous walls and large fragments of brickwork remained for machine-gun shelters, and the eastern and western outskirts of Martinpuich were labyrinths of fortification. Eastward, especially, with three communications connecting with High Wood, there was an astonishing lacework of redoubts, ditches, and caves, with cross-fires of many machine-guns. A frontal attack was attempted by the British troops, but was met by a counter-attack, with forces gathering from the sides, and the assailants were driven back. But the "tanks" turned the course of conflict from a combination of rush approach and prolonged siege operations like Ginchy into a swift and overwhelming victory like Courcelette. The Bavarian peasantry were frightened by the new war chariots when the monstrous things reared up against the works and spat death around, like the flaming dragons of fairy-tales. In one case a hundred Bavarians surrendered to a "tank," and two of the crew emerged and stood guard over the captives until the infantry arrived. Another car, on its journey through the village, came upon a dug-out and sat upon it. The cave was the regimental headquarters. The colonel stepped forward to see what was the matter, put up his hand at the nightmare spectacle, was taken into the car and carried about, an interned alien, during further operations.

Flaming dragons at Martinpuich

Owing to the nature of the easterly trenches at Martinpuich the action about this central downland village was linked with a terrible battle that raged for hours in High Wood. Stormed first in the middle of July and afterwards continuously hammered by heavy guns, and continually swept by infantry attacks of the fiercest kind from both sides, High Wood remained to a considerable extent in the enemy's possession in the middle of September. As a theatre of ghastly destruction it surpassed in horror and chaotic aspect Delville Wood and all other scenes of human endurance and chemical annihilation. The amount of high explosive, splintered steel, and leaden rain that had been poured on what had been a wooded peak was incalculable.

A force of gallant London troops made a direct attack upon the German works in High Wood, which had been strengthened with iron girders and concrete blocks and an enormous amount of barbed-wire. The day and the night before the attack German guns played intensely on the Londoners' positions in the wood, and when they went over their parapets the number of the enemy machine-guns was so great that their noise drowned that of the artillery. The fighting was savage beyond description, and when the London battalions seemed to be absolutely at the end of their resources some "tanks" moved into the wood. But even their marvellous powers of breaking down obstacles and climbing up and down the tumult of earth did not enable them to make a path for the infantry. Naked human courage had to carry out that which the powerful engines of war could not accomplish, and at last, after three bounds towards the end of the wood, the valiant city men gave their artillery the signal for a closing whirlwind bombardment. This completely broke the nerve of the High Wood garrison. Three hundred ran out and surrendered, and a few minutes later another large body fled towards Martinpuich, but were caught by English Territorials working on the left of the Londoners, and annihilated with mortars, bombs, rifles, and machine-guns.

Londoners' ordeal in High Wood

Not one German was seen to escape. Meanwhile, the hard core of the defending force still held their ground in positions where one desperate man with a machine-gun was stronger than a hundred riflemen. But at one o'clock in the afternoon the last German gunner was put out of action, and the Londoners went forward beyond the wood to Prue Trench, and could not find an enemy. No counter-attack was made, and for some days no Germans were seen. After this terrific conflict Martinpuich was encircled in the evening, and carried with comparatively slight losses by a combination of "tanks" and infantry, which took more than a thousand prisoners.

Victory at Martinpuich

London again took an important part in the greatest tactical success of the day—the drive from the Delville Wood line into the enemy's third zone of defences at Flers. Labyrinth after labyrinth of works, entanglements, and underground ways was forced with wonderful speed by London and North-country recruits and the superb fighting men of New Zealand, with a squadron of "tanks" acting sometimes as supports and sometimes as an advance guard. Before the main operations started at dawn a detachment set out in the dark for the extreme eastern angle of Delville Wood, where the enemy retained a foothold in a spot known as Mystery Corner. The men got among the Germans before the latter could work their machine-guns, and in a short burst of fighting with bomb and bayonet the mystery was cleared up, and found to consist of a hairpin wedge of trenches, connecting with the hostile main line. Fifty prisoners were taken and several machine-guns, while two "tanks" loomed in the first glimmer of dawn against each side of Mystery Corner, and squatted upon the German trenches and found them to be already heaped with dead—

ONCE A RAILWAY STATION.
Guillemont Railway Station as it was when the British finally recaptured it from the Germans.

slain in the first burst of British whirlwind gun fire.

Meanwhile, the New Zealand troops moved out. On their right they were supported by battalions largely recruited from London. Their left flank, however, was dangerously exposed, because the Londoners who had been launched upon High Wood were held up by the enemy there. But the New Zealanders did not trouble about danger from Martinpuich. Men from Auckland, Canterbury, Otago, and Wellington, tried in the mountain battles of Gallipoli, put their trust in the bayonet, and rushed with scarcely a check all the ground for five hundred yards to the enemy's Switch Trench in front of the Flers zone of defences. Splashed with shrapnel and raked with machine-guns, they reached

STRETCHER-BEARERS AND DRESSING-STATION AT GUILLEMONT.
Guillemont was captured on September 2nd, 1916, after a stubborn resistance. Our casualties were naturally heavy, but they bore small proportion to the heaps of German dead over whose bodies the position was won. The desperate nature of the fighting may be gauged by the appearance of the ground in the above photograph.

BRITISH 18-POUNDER GUN IN ACTION IN A GLADE.

[British official photograph.

General consent awarded the palm to the French " 75 " for effectiveness in the war, but French artillerymen were enthusiastic in their praise of the British 18-pounder guns and of the high efficiency of the gunners who worked them.

the Switch Trench and there had a bitter fight to the death with a force of Germans of high courage. Only four Germans remained alive after the savage hand-to-hand clash, and the wave of New Zealanders was thinner when it came out on the other side, where the ground stretched for eight hundred yards towards the heavily-wired and deeply-dug Flers line.

Here the New Zealand Rifles went down a long slope in very wide order and quick rushes against a tempest of lead. Fine as was the work of the Royal

Bitter fight to the death

Garrison Artillery, they had not been able, in rapid direct firing, to destroy either the wire entanglements or the earthworks of the Flers zone of strong fortifications. An infantry assault would have been terribly costly and probably vain, as there was another deep system of German works close behind the first wired line. But two " tanks " that had fallen behind the New Zealanders, owing to the number of shell-craters and pits in their path, slowly crawled forward, sometimes with their tails above their heads and sometimes with their heads above their tails. They sidled along the barbed-wire and buried it in the earth ; then poking their monstrous noses over the hostile parapets, they hauled themselves over, firing all the time from both sides of their painted bodies at the German machine-gun teams and bombers.

Having saved the New Zealanders' lives and time and trouble by facilitating the capture of the Flers line, one of the " tanks " lumbered after them across a sunken road,

with steep banks and very deep dug-outs, from which the Germans fled without a fight. The New Zealanders, flushed with victory, made another great leap. They covered seven hundred yards to a line running westward to the top of Flers, while a German battery fifteen hundred yards away shelled the Anzac " tank " but missed it repeatedly, and was put out of action by the British artillery.

But all this time the New Zealand left flank remained " in the air," as the Londoners held in High Wood could not connect. Nevertheless, the thin and unsupported wedge of New Zealanders swung out to the left, and made a fighting flank up the front of the valley running north-west of Flers, far beyond the village. This hazardous position they held until ordered **New Zealanders** to draw back to a line running straight **at Flers** westward from the top of Flers village, looking down upon Eaucourt l'Abbaye and the tumulus of Warlencourt, with the chimneys of Bapaume immediately behind.

Far along the flank of the New Zealanders German troops held out in shell-craters, with the way open behind them so that supports might come down and drive a wedge between the New Zealanders and the London men north of High Wood. There followed a long and swaying battle between the Anzac wedge and the fresh troops that the German commander poured on their flank, from the afternoon of September 15th to the evening of September 21st.

The New Zealanders reached their extreme point beyond Flers in six hours' fighting by noon. At four o'clock the first 4,000 Germans were thrown upon them. Not only was the attack beaten off, but the Wellingtons went forward and took the trench from which the counter-attack had been launched. Then followed five days and five nights of continuous attack and counter-attack, in rapid successions of the fiercest bomb and bayonet fighting. Canterbury, Otago, Wellington, and Auckland covered themselves with glory, and chief among them was a captain of the Canterburys, who led many of the most desperate struggles and came through them all unhurt. In one general attack the London troops on the left were compelled to give ground. But as they retired, the New Zealanders went forward and cut across the German line half-way towards Eaucourt l'Abbaye. Then, in a magnificent resurgence of energy, the Londoners recovered the ground they had lost, and, breaking right through the German line on a front of a mile, filled out all the interspace between Flers and Martinpuich and formed an even, solid front between the two villages.

Amid the ruins of Flers on the right of the New Zealanders were the metropolitan troops, with other **Episode of Mystery Corner** Englishmen, who had started operations in Mystery Corner of Delville Wood. As the first wave of their attack went out at dawn the small band of conquerors of Mystery Corner, who were resting on the line appointed them, rose and joined in the Flers attack, and, keeping abreast of the foremost wave, acted as a connecting link between the Flers attack and the force that advanced from Ginchy. From the Delville Wood side Flers was a double maze composed of four main lines of defence, with enfilading positions driven out at right angles like teeth on a rake, and innumerable minor posts and organised shell-holes. Apparently it was impossible ground for troops to take in a rush. But the new terrors that crawled by day, in advance of the infantry wave, towards all difficult places, made the operation miraculously rapid.

EARTH'S AGONY UNDER THE HORROR OF MODERN HIGH-EXPLOSIVES.
British official photograph of a yawning crater wrought by a mine explosion, as seen after the British troops had broken the last German resistance and captured the position. Above: Canadian official photograph of one of the enormous shell-holes in the line of the advance.

COMBLES : THE TOWN IN PICARDY WHERE THREE ARMIES MET.   [French official photograph.

Combles was retaken on September 26th, 1916, by the French and British in co-operation, both entering the town simultaneously. The town was deemed of such importance by the Kaiser that when it was captured in 1914 he had a medal struck to commemorate the triumph as an incomparable feat of arms. The Germans had held it in force, and enormous accumulations of munitions were captured by the Allies.

Flers was captured in about three and a half hours. The men had not seen much fighting before going into the furnace of the Somme, but the general who had trained them was sure of them, as he had taught each man to carry out his task even if all the officers fell. They had a depth of 2,500 yards of highly-fortified ground to cover on the way to Flers, and they went forward, keen and alert, to the first German line which, like others on the enemy's front, was full of enemy dead, caught by the gun fire that mowed the way for the British troops.

The two first waves stayed in the trench to clean it up ; a third and fourth wave swept onward over shell-craters, against machine-gun positions and continual squalls of shrapnel fire, until they came upon a hidden trench protected by unbroken wire. The "tank" rolled forward, sat on the wire and on the earthworks ; the troops passed and resumed their fighting forward movement. Meanwhile, another "tank" went on ahead alone and, like a huge pachyderm strayed from some **"Tank" in Flers** extraordinary menagerie, sauntered up **High Street** the High Street of Flers. From the ruins German machine-gunners and riflemen played on it with scarcely more effect than boys with pea-shooters, while the cheering, laughing troops who saw the sight could scarcely go on fighting for the moment, being overcome with the wild humour of it all. There were sixteen guns about the village that might have put "tank" after "tank" out of action, but they were captured by the foster-children of the "tank," together with a thousand prisoners.

When all the village was won the victors went forward to the Lesbœufs Road and stormed it, and formed a strong line well to the north of the main fortress in the Germans' last zone of defences. Then, after beating off an enemy counter-attack, the troops eastward, who had been holding little more than a series of shell-holes with a wavering connecting link, climbed out of their holes in the evening of September 16th, and, rushing through open country, where the air was thick with machine-gun bullets, stormed a well-made German trench, and there strongly consolidated on a good line of advance for a further break into the German line. Meanwhile, a solitary "tank" slithered on an exploring expedition from Flers to Gueudecourt, and reached the latter **Towards the** village, practically piercing the entire **Combles valley** German front. But after some exciting adventures it was struck by a shell and crippled, and its skipper, after making it useless to the enemy, left it lying a landmark to the men on either side, and the crew returned to Flers and worked among the wounded. The wrecked "tank" seems afterwards to have been recovered.

From the Flers and Lesbœufs line northward to the Leuze Wood and Combles valley line southward there was a long, deep, rolling space to be conquered under conditions of extreme difficulty. Except in the northern sector, where the deep Flers zone of works began, there were but a few old and well-marked trenches seaming the bare slopes and open hollows. The enemy had merely constructed wavering lines of shell-holes, lightly strung together, strengthened by unexpected nests of machine-guns and garrisoned by the Prussian Guard and other troops of the first quality. In some places there was half a mile of untrenched ground between the Scottish, Irish, and English troops who worked east of Ginchy

DRILL BEHIND THE FIRING-LINE.
The King (second figure from the left) watching men at drill immediately behind the firing-line on the occasion of the Royal visit to the west front shortly after the beginning of the Somme offensive.

towards the Combles valley. The distant Prussians maintained an incessant and sweeping rain of bullets from positions that could not be spotted and pounded by British gunners. Uncommon skill and high daring were required in working through the rain of lead, in order to close at last upon the Guardsmen. Even when the hand-to-hand tussle came the Prussians stood firm with bomb and bayonet and machine-gun, and only after a ferocious bout of in-fighting was the first line taken. The second fell more easily, and the third was quickly stormed.

The British Guards had a most arduous task, as befitted men of their reputation. They moved from the crest of the ridge, and could see nothing beyond and knew little of what was there. It was supposed they had some open ground before them ere they arrived at the first main trench they were told to take. But so soon as they topped the crest the right of their line found itself against trenches, with uncut wire, of which nothing had been known. Two short trenches they were, held by seven companies of a famous German regiment. Moreover, the troops on the right of the Guards were held up by a great work known as the Quadrilateral, which was a position humanly impossible to take at that stage of the operations. But the Guards never faltered, and they charged onward for nearly a mile with their right totally exposed and swept by machine-gun fire that caused most of the casualties they suffered.

Fine advance of the Guards

Early in the fight the Guards learnt that the troops in front of them were old enemies, whom they had met before in the Second Battle of Ypres and held when all the odds were on the German side. Now that there was something like an equality in a long, raging hand-to-hand battle, the Guardsmen stormed out for a deadly return match. The seven companies behind barbed-wire in the surprise trenches were reached in a tearing struggle, and clubbed with rifle-butt or caught on the sharper end. Every man was either killed or captured. Meanwhile, the left of the Guards' line went over the first trench, and wheeled against a diagonal trench and beyond into the famous Switch Trench. But in this manœuvre over hopeless ground, with no landmark to map it out, the right and left hand troops lost touch, and though they went abreast over the

Switch they left some Germans in a gap, who raked them flank and rear until some of the Guards turned back and dealt with them.

The next trench the Guards tried to bomb, but they found that bombing was slow work, and formed up again with the bayonet and went over the position like lightning. Then amid a chaos of earth like a frozen sea, where no man could see much more than the immediate bank or hole in front of him, the Guards worked forward for five hours, always with machine-gun fire pouring on their exposed right flank. At last some battalion commanders held a conference in a shell-hole, and endeavoured to find out at what spot on the map they had arrived.

THE KING ON THE BATTLEFIELD.
Sir Henry Rawlinson, commanding the Fourth Army on the Somme, pointing out to the King positions marked on a map which General W. N. Congreve, V.C., commanding the Thirteenth Army Corps, is seen holding.

They were about a mile in the enemy's country, and as their flank was still exposed they dug between some shell-holes and rested after one of the finest movements in the annals of the Guards. All four races shared fully in the glory—Scots and Irish, Welsh, Coldstreams and Grenadiers —and none wanted more credit than the other.

A quaint and picturesque incident made the Coldstreams remarkable, and won the Victoria Cross for their leader. Two waves of the 3rd Battalion had broken against the German machine-guns, and Lieutenant-Colonel John Vaughan Campbell took command of the third line, which was also broken and scattered in shell-holes by the enemy's streams of fire. The colonel went into battle with his revolver in one hand and his huntsman's horn in the other. He sounded the horn, which had been given to him by his non-commissioned officers and men, and as the clear ringing notes pierced the rattle of the enemy's guns the Guards came running up from their cover and, forming in line under their colonel, took the trench with the bayonet, while the Irish Guards came up in support, and the Grenadiers also swung forward. Two "tanks" seem also to have worked with the Guards and eased the situation in another place where they were held up by unbroken wire in a trench lined with machine-guns.

The shallow ravine running out before the hamlet of Morval was one check to the advance through the wilderness beyond Ginchy. But the most serious obstacle on the glorious fifteenth of September was a quadrangle of trenches between Ginchy and Leuze Wood. The redoubt was on the Ginchy-Morval road at the point where the road bent under a sheltering clump of trees. A large four-sided work extended about the redoubt, from which all forces advancing eastward from Ginchy were enfiladed. At the same time their right flank was swept from a strong point north of Bouleaux Wood and from other places beyond.

In spite of the heroic sacrifices made by the British troops they could not get within rushing distance of the Quadrilateral. All day they were scattered in shell-holes before this formidable work, or driven back in their lines. An advance on the front being impossible, some men pushed up on the left on an exploring expedition, and finding their right flank "in the air," turned and attacked one of the auxiliary trenches, and bombed down it, fighting along both sides south-eastward towards the redoubt. When night fell

HONOUR FOR THE BRAVE.
King George decorating heroes of the Royal Naval Air Service somewhere in Flanders.

the troops thought that they had won the Quadrilateral, but they had gained only an unsuspected trench protecting its southern and western face. The ground between them and the machine-gun fort was covered with wire entanglements, and they had to fall back once more to allow a field of play for the heavy artillery.

All the next day the guns crashed on the position, and in the evening the men who had made the first attack from the north and west resumed the struggle with extreme energy. For they were determined the position should fall to them. While the defenders were fighting stubbornly with both bomb and bayonet another attack was delivered from the

south which surprised the distracted garrison, who lost a hundred and seventy unwounded prisoners and nine machine-guns. Still the Quadrilateral was not entirely conquered. A resisting force remained in a sunken road, lined with numerous dug-outs, and here hard fighting went on for a long time. Most of the Germans refused to surrender, coming out into the open and fighting and falling to the bayonet or being bombed in their caverns. They were Bavarians of the 7th and 21st Regiments, and when their superb resistance was broken on September 18th the line was extended a thousand yards behind the Quadrilateral.

During the first check at the Quadrilateral an advance was made from Leuze Wood to Bouleaux Wood, where a "tank" went across the Combles valley to Morval, expecting the infantry to follow. But the infantry had been held up by a German work, and the mothering monster toddled back to search for her lost flock, and, bucking over the hostile trench, crushed the garrison. This gymnastic feat led to a downfall. Unexpectedly the "tank" encountered a deep crater, and before her machinery could be adjusted for a slide down and a crawl up she toppled over and became an armoured barricade between British and German bombers. The skipper and crew safely emerged, and under heavy fire tried to hoist their monster out of the pit, but finally the "tank" had to be abandoned until the line was pushed forward to Morval.

Bavarians' superb resistance

The regiments that distinguished themselves in this mighty battle were so many and heroism so common that no authority has yet attempted to gather material for regimental histories. But by universal consent—hostile, neutral, and allied—his Majesty's Land Navy on making its first appearance won the supreme honours of the day.

Major Shrapnel was second only to the Duke of Wellington on the field of Waterloo by reason of the new shell he gave to British gunners, and we may say that the inventors of the "tank" were second only to Sir Douglas Haig in the victory of the main Bapaume ridge by reason of the new weapon in trench attack they gave to the British infantry. The "tank" seriously disturbed Germany, not merely by what it accomplished, but by the power of high invention it revealed in the men behind the new British armies. All that Count Zeppelin had accomplished in many years of experiment with a new weapon of war was surpassed in utility by Britons in months.

[*British official photographs.*]

ROYAL OBSERVATION-POST ON THE SOMME.
Observers and signallers at work on a sand-bag embankment whence the King watched the progress of a battle on the occasion of his Majesty's visit to the Somme front during the summer of 1916.

LIFTING THE BRITISH BARRAGE TO LET THE INFANTRY LOOSE IN THE ALLIED ATTACK UPON COMBLES.

At the pre-arranged moment an officer leaped on to a battery earthwork, megaphone in hand, and blew a shrill whistle, the signal for the barrage fire to lift. At once the heavy guns massed behind and the field-guns forward lifted, and the infantry went "over the top," in extended order, or threaded their way along the trenches with rifles, bombs, and Lewis guns, against the enemy's position at Combles.

THE GREAT BRITISH BATTLES OF THE SOMME.

V.—Check near Bapaume and Victory on the Ancre.

By Edward Wright.

Problems of the Great Ridge—Four Phases of the Mighty Battle of Bapaume—The Mystery of Mouquet Farm—Genius of German Engineers—Final Conquest of Thiepval—The " Tank " at the Chateau—Epic of Schwaben, Stuff, and Regina Works—Germany's Desperate Fight for Time—Great British Movement on Bapaume—Bouleaux Wood Device and the Discomfiture of the Enemy—Battles of Morval and Lesbœufs—Glorious Adventures of Private Jones—Conflict Between a " Tank " and Five Hundred Germans—Nocturnal Franco-British Advance into Combles—Ludendorff's Apology for Defeat—New Enemy Tactics to Avoid Infantry Fighting—Remarkable Battle of Eaucourt l'Abbaye—German Line Broken at Le Sars—Shell-hole Warfare and Autumnal Rains—Germans Left to Drown on Bapaume Line—Magnificent Scottish Victory in Beaumont-Hamel—Terrible Contest in Y Ravine—Naval Division Storms the Ancre Valley—Extraordinary Achievement of Colonel Freyberg—English and Irish Troops Capture St. Pierre Divion—The Great Tunnel and the Resurrection of the " Tank."

THE great British thrust in the middle of September, 1916, almost completed the operations on the Somme. The enemy's front there was heavily dented. On the fortified line of his own choosing the German commander was severely defeated and thrown back. Not only were all his original zones of defences taken, but the new works he began to construct on July 2nd, 1916, after the loss of Mametz and Montauban were penetrated between Flers and Le Sars. Only by a miracle of skill and heroism on the part of his thinned line of machine-gunners and sharpshooters, between Gueudecourt, Lesbœufs, and Morval, did he save one of his main masses of artillery from capture between September 16th and September 21st, 1916. As it was, that artillery was severely hammered and damaged by the British siege ordnance, which was being reinforced by new large pieces.

By the evening of September 15th all the summit ridge between Bapaume and Albert was won by Sir Douglas Haig, with the exception of the Thiepval peak and the Morval spur at either end. British forward observation officers around Mouquet Farm, Pozières Windmill, High Wood, and Ginchy overlooked the enemy's movements for miles beyond Bapaume, and brought their parks of howitzers crashing down upon the hostile forces they spied through their glasses. All that our northern army had suffered for two years around the Lille ridges, where the enemy had observation over them to direct his heavy artillery, was at last balanced by the advantages gained by our southern army. The ground won was the main watershed of the entire jumble of downland stretching from the Somme valley to the flats of Douay. Except for the footholds he was soon to lose about Thiepval and Lesbœufs, the enemy had on the Bapaume sector no outlook more than five hundred feet above the sea. His highest positions were a hundred feet lower, and beyond Bapaume the

IN THE ENEMY'S CAPTURED LINE.
[British official photograph.
Six hours before this photograph was taken—on the glorious September 15th, 1916—the shattered, half-filled trench from which an officer is seen making observations was the German front line.

undulations gradually sank to two hundred and fifty feet above sea-level.

On the other hand, there were some grave disadvantages attaching to the winning of the dominating summit ridge by the British. Direct cannon fire against the Germans became difficult. There was at first little room between Courcelette, Martinpuich, and Flers and the great backing ridge, and the advancing infantry forces, with their machine-gunners, trench-mortar parties and "tanks," occupied the strips of favourable ground. Then came, just after the victory, a great downpour of rain that seriously retarded the forward movement of artillery, as the slopes were transformed into slides of mud. Even when the British army extended its conquest of the lower ground facing Bapaume the action of its cannon remained restricted. The enemy sheltered in all the folds of land, and his cannon had a direct fire upon the reverse faces of the main watershed, while his howitzers pitched shells everywhere.

Bapaume's four phases

In short, between July and September, the geographical conditions of the British and German armies were reversed. By hard fighting the British continually approached within

MAP ILLUSTRATING THE SECOND PHASE OF THE BATTLE OF BAPAUME.
Large-scale map of the area of Sir Douglas Haig's operations in combining with the French army in a decisive enveloping movement against the German base at Combles.

two miles of Bapaume, but they could not capture the city because, among other things, their position along the Thiepval-Martinpuich-Ginchy ridge exposed them incessantly to a smashing direct fire from hostile guns in the northern hollows, similar to the fire they had poured on the enemy when he was on the watershed and they were in the southern hollows. Then, heavily aggravating this disadvantage of the attacking British forces as they descended from the great ridge, there was an immense mass of hostile artillery and infantry across the Ancre, which maintained a long and terrific flanking attack upon the western side of the thrusting Franco-British armies.

From the middle of September to the middle of December, 1916, there were four important phases of the mighty Battle of Bapaume which followed upon the great victories of the Somme. In the first place, Sir Douglas Haig countered the menace to his left flank by exerting a most violent counter-balancing pressure against the German Ancre position from Thiepval to Grandcourt. In the second place, the British commander cleared his right flank by combining with the French army in a decisive movement of envelopment against the German base at Combles. In the third place, after clearing his flanks, Sir Douglas Haig attempted a direct forthright thrust against Bapaume. Checked on

this sector, he opened the fourth phase of the struggle by a very brilliant movement of surprise across the Ancre, in which Beaumont-Hamel, St. Pierre Divion, and Beaucourt were stormed. This brought the British army up to the Serre plateau, with larger elbow-room for operations against Bapaume, and effected an improvement of promising importance in the general operations of the Western Allies.

The first three phases often occurred in couples or all at the same time. For the Ancre line, the Bapaume line, and the Combles line were continually assailed simultaneously. But for the sake of clarity of idea we must separately relate the story of each phase.

After the advance of the Australians and Territorials to the Pozières ridge all attempts to extend westward along the heights towards the neck of high land between Courcelette and Thiepval were persistently checked. It will be remembered that the Kents, Sussex, and Surreys at last took the down that dominated Courcelette. But, though gallantly helped by the Anzacs, they could not hold the western slope on which were scattered the ruins of Mouquet Farm. Then, on September 3rd, when the Irish brigades were storming Guillemont, the Australians made another effort of sustained violence against Mouquet Farm. Not until the farm was secured, with its opportunities for flanking machine-guns against the German works south of Thiepval, could the great caverned down of Thiepval be fully subjected to siege operations. Mouquet Farm was thus a key position, and the skilled men of Australia did all they could to acquire the key. At dawn, after a hurricane bombardment, answered by a tempest of curtaining shell from General von Stein's artillery, the Tasmanians and Queenslanders stormed the neck of high ridge, while the Western Australians, with more Tasmanians, broke into the farm below and dug a good line among the shell-craters two hundred yards beyond the Mouquet ruins. This looked like an act of permanent conquest, for the Anzac is a master of the art of defensive digging. But owing, as it seemed at the time, to some confusion in fortifying the conquered farm, the Germans got through a gap between the Tasmanians and Western Australians, and after a prolonged battle of intense fierceness lasting two days and two nights recovered the farm ruins.

Then, in the afternoon of September 15th, the Canadians, flushed with their victory at Courcelette, resumed the attack upon the extraordinary farm and captured it by a strong rush attack, as the Anzacs had done. It was well known that the Germans had two large caverns beneath the almost indistinguishable site of the buildings, and both the Australians and the Canadians secured these subterranean halls of refuge. But after the Canadians had deeply entrenched beyond the farm, as their comrades of the Southern Cross had done, their line was also driven in by a German counter-attack which, in the ordinary way, should have failed at Mouquet Farm as it did around Courcelette.

Mouquet Farm taken and retaken

Standing originally a four-square block of picturesque buildings at the cross-roads midway between Thiepval and Pozières, Mouquet Farm became the greatest mystery of the war. Months after the loopholed walls had vanished, and shell after shell had penetrated the cellars beneath, the

Germans there broke all advances upon Thiepval. Their caverns were cleared with bombs and occupied; the connecting tunnel was held, and a trench dug a furlong in front of the wreckage. Still the enemy returned and recovered all the position.

In the latter part of September, when a nocturnal attack gave the British back part of the farm, the troops found themselves harassed in an uncanny fashion. One morning an officer, talking to a sentry, saw two Germans by a slag-heap behind him, and thinking they were deserters ready to surrender, approached them and was shot dead. The sentry ran forward, and no Germans could be found. A tunnel was discovered and blocked while strengthening a trench; but still the British line continued to be assailed from the rear when it was being attacked furiously in front. The enemy had constructed underground corridors from the Thiepval region, and the exits from these corridors did not run openly into the caverns beneath the farm, but

A LIGHT-HEARTED COMPANY.
Happy veterans from the Island Continent. Australians on their way up to the line on the Somme.

into inconspicuous corners of ground where a covering of rubble and earth protected the subways from notice. In the night, during counter-attacks, German sharp-shooters and machine-gunners would raise the protective coverings and emerge and go forward and break the Anzac, Canadian, or British line by a drive from the rear. But the success with which the exits were concealed for months from the keenest-eyed fighting men of the British Empire, after continual defeat had made them intensely alert and suspicious, is high testimony to the genius of some Teutonic sapper officer.

The mystery of Mouquet Farm was not cleared up until the entire fortress system around Thiepval was penetrated in a grand storming operation on September 26th, 1916. It was

then necessary that an enveloping movement around the down should pass by Mouquet Farm, in order to consummate the main operation of attack. The troops were ordered to swing past the farm ruins and let the hidden garrison do its worst behind their back. So the waves of infantry surged over the position and past the trench that marked the reach of the early Anzac advance. As they crashed upon the neck of the Thiepval system, grey groups of machine-gunners and sharpshooters emerged from the Mouquet slope. But a party of pioneers, headed by a young officer, saw the Germans emerge, and took them captive without a fight. Then, going down into the chambers and tunnels, more pioneers fell upon the rest of the enemy and, after a battle of six hours beneath the earth, solved part of the mystery. The last secret of the farm was unwillingly revealed by a German officer taken prisoner in the middle of November. He asked how many of our men had been blown up in the final conquest of the Mouquet position. He was surprised to learn no volcanic explosion had occurred there. A vast amount of explosive had been buried below the lowest cellars, but the electric firing wire had been cut.

Mouquet Farm's last secret

Meanwhile, by the last evasive rush over the uncanny and tragic farmstead, there was successfully reopened the struggle on the long Thiepval spur of the main watershed, which the heroic Ulster Division had gallantly tried to carry in one rush on July 1st. Only at this point in our history can we fully appreciate the magnificent drive made by the Ulstermen when they lacked support on either flank. For it will now be seen that what

[*British official photographs.*]

COLLECTING BOOTY AT ST. PIERRE DIVION.
Participants in the victorious attack in the region of Beaumont-Hamel on November 14th, 1916, collecting rifles abandoned by the enemy when evacuating the position. Though the Germans relied mainly on machine-guns, there was no dearth of rifles.

a single division of Northern Irishmen came near to accomplishing in a few hours, afterwards required the most desperate efforts of a powerful army to achieve very gradually in the course of weeks. Undoubtedly the enemy had strengthened his positions between Thiepval down and the Ancre between July 1st and September 26th, 1916. But the original fortress with its original garrison still constituted the knot of resistance.

Three thousand Würtembergers of the 180th Regiment of the Line, mostly veterans who had fought down the Meuse to the Marne and back to the Aisne and Somme, formed the garrison of Thiepval. They had asked, as a matter of the honour of their regiment, to be allowed to defend Thiepval to the end of the war. For two years they

[British official photograph.
CYCLISTS ON THE MARCH.
Notwithstanding the enormous number of motor-cycles, the humbler "push-bike" remained in constant use in France.

ORIENTAL SOLDIERS AND THEIR OCCIDENTAL "MOUNTS."
Indian cyclists on active service in France during the great advance on the western front. Fit and well turned out, these smart soldiers, headed by their sturdy sergeant, were pleased at being made a subject for the exercise of the official photographer's art.

[British official photograph.

chateau, and along the road to Mouquet Farm. Through the storms of lead, nevertheless, the lines of attack moved onward and upward, behind their heavy screen of shell and shrapnel and bursts of bullets from their Lewis guns. Within an hour the surface of the larger part of Thiepval village was overrun, and the dreadful work of cave fighting was opened in dug-out systems and tunnel entrances. But the chateau held out, for no infantry could storm through its machine-gun streams of bullets. British troops crouched in shell-holes in front of the red walls, waiting for nightfall for a possible opportunity to emerge. But the *deus ex machina* solved all difficulties —or, rather, he remained in the

had at their own desire remained in the fortress, which they had promised should never be lost. They had fortified themselves in Mouquet Farm fashion, hollowing out in the chalk cavern below cavern, with connecting tunnels and numerous emergency shafts and machine-gun redoubts. But they also had many slightly covered exits running beyond works they might lose, enabling them to make rear surprise counter-attacks in the Mouquet manner. Only after Courcelette, Martinpuich, and Flers fell did the Würtembergers contemplate eventual defeat, and even then they were resolved to put up a good fight.

The main British attack was made from the south, from the captured outer line known as the Wonder-Work to Mouquet Farm. There was about five hundred yards of open space to be crossed, and as soon as the waves of khaki appeared on the slopes hostile machine-gunners and snipers rose from shell-holes and tunnel shafts in the apple orchard, south of the village, around the red ruins of the

machine with his attendant spirits—and as the skipper of a "tank" charged ponderously head-on at the chateau, broke through the mound of earth and brick, with all available guns playing upon the startled Würtembergers. These held up their hands, while the British infantry were cheering their "tank," and the German battalion commander came forth and surrendered.

Night fighting at Thiepval

At nightfall all the German batteries situated between Gommecourt and Grandcourt tried to blast the British forces out of the conquered village by a tempest of high-explosive shell. But the victors retired to the caverns of Thiepval and strengthened their clearing-up detachments in the long and terrible struggle that was still raging in the underground city. In the horrible strife in darkness the attackers at last ran short of ammunition, but found large stores of German egg-bombs that enabled them to intensify their assaults. Bomb, knife, and bayonet were used, yet even when all the hostile positions seemed to be secured, parties of Germans would emerge in the rear from secret bolt-holes and sweep the apparent victors with machine-gun fire. Thiepval fortress was like an iceberg—nine-tenths of the bulk of it was hidden below the surface. All night subterranean warfare went furiously on, but in the morning, after more than half the effectives of their three battalions had been killed or wounded in battle, and another third taken prisoners, the veterans of Würtemberg broke, and the entire village was carried.

Naturally, so strange and confused a conflict was distinguished by many examples of heroic skill. One British private was in a trench held partly by the enemy. A German bombing-party approached, and instead of retreating he attacked, first with his own revolver, then with the rifle of one of the Germans he had slain, and afterwards with another captured rifle. He killed two officers and twenty-two men, and took captive the last member of the bombing-party. Having **Examples of** been wounded in the knee in the combat, **heroic skill** he had his leg dressed and went back and fought with his battalion until it was relieved A Canadian, who had walked and rowed five hundred miles to reach a recruiting office, and had since risen from the ranks, silenced single-handed a machine-gun that was holding up his men, and died the moment he had killed all the enemy gunners. Another hostile gun-team was slain by a lance-corporal, who was killed while shouldering the German gun. Three Australians—two wounded and one unhurt—were rescued in German territory about Mouquet Farm, where, since the Anzac attack, they had lived in a shell-crater on the food and water which the unwounded man obtained each night by crawling out and searching the bodies of German dead.

The ferocious fighting in and under Thiepval was only preliminary to the long main struggle for the Thiepval spur. The Würtembergers played an effective part in the battle by their stubborn defence of the village. For high above the village rose the dominating ridge, where a tangle of fortified positions, famous as **Tangle of** the Schwaben Redoubt, extended for a **fortified positions** third of a mile from a point near the Crucifix where the Ulstermen fell after their thrust across the Ancre ravine. In the strength of at least a brigade the Germans held the Schwaben Redoubt, the Crucifix Trenches, and the cemetery farther south. Most of the large slab of land they held was some thirty feet or more above the slope on which Thiepval spread in vague brick-dust. But this advantage in altitude did not assist the enemy; it merely exposed him more severely to British gun fire. What did help him was the fact that his long systems of works connecting Thiepval spur with Grandcourt and Miraumont— the Schwaben Redoubt, the Stuff Redoubt, the Hessian Trench, and Regina Redoubt—ran along the edge of the Ancre ravine. Whenever the British troops in a successful attack reached the ravine edge all the downward slope towards the Ancre was swept by machine-gun and shell fire from the opposing face of the river valley between Beaumont-Hamel and Miraumont.

The conditions on this sector were thus a vivid illustration of the revolution produced by recent developments of heavy artillery. A great deal of the extraordinary defensive

GERMAN PRISONERS FROM THIEPVAL ON THE MARCH TO THE "CAGES."

Thiepval, the twentieth village recovered from the enemy after the beginning of the Battle of the Somme, was carried September 26th, 1916. It had been garrisoned since September, 1914, by the 180th Würtembergers, veteran troops of the finest quality. A thousand of them, and more than three thousand other Germans, were captured during the struggle for the fortress, and a vast quantity of war material was taken.

s

power of the Germans was derived from their low sheltered positions in and about the Ancre ravine. Much of the difficulty of the British attacking movement was due to the high exposed slopes on which their infantry operated. So long as the German ordnance around the Serre plateau and Miraumont could mass on a vast arc against a small number of British cannon sited on the higher Thiepval and Martinpuich spurs the British infantry worked forward against serious odds. The British army could bring to bear upon the enemy only the indirect fire of howitzers, while the Germans had the direct fire of a

thousand cannon and howitzers and tens of thousands of machine-guns.

There were other factors in the situation. For example, the British commander could throw a very heavy cross-fire of howitzer shell upon the German positions along the Ancre by concentrating the artillery on the Gomme-court-Beaumont-Hamel front. And although the enemy could answer this bombardment by cross-firing from his Bapaume front against the flanking British lines along the Ancre from Thiepval to Grandcourt, he had also to meet the British and French guns on this front. The British salient from Thiepval to Combles produced a German salient from the Ancre to Gommecourt, and both salients were, naturally, subject to cross- **Stuff and Schwaben** fires. Superiority was a question of **Redoubts taken** numbers of guns, and here the British army, by the calibre and quantity of its artillery and the speed of its munitioning, retained the advantage.

But, owing to the nature of the ground about the Ancre, the enemy for a considerable period launched successful counter-attacks against every important British advance. The Stuff Redoubt, on the east of Thiepval, was captured on September 27th by a whirlwind bombardment of heavy shell, followed by a series of leaps by the British infantry. The next day the Schwaben Redoubt was assailed in the same manner and carried. But the moment the position was lost the German guns in turn churned up the undulating lines of chalk to prevent the victors from consolidating the works. Then in the night the counter-attacks began,

[British official photographs.

JETSAM LEFT ON THE SHORE BY THE RECEDING TIDE OF INVASION.
View of Beaumont-Hamel after the British recaptured it in November, 1916. The village was once a collection of pleasant houses with well-timbered gardens dotted about the slopes, and a population of some seven hundred people. When the Germans were driven out nothing was left but stark stumps, discoloured earth, and a litter of broken bricks. Above : A British soldier cleaning his stock of hand-grenades.

THE BROKEN ROAD FROM FLERS, CAPTURED ON SEPTEMBER 15TH, 1916. [British official photograph.
Indian cavalry despatch-riders on their way back from Flers. The route was lined with the débris of houses and shell-shorn trees. On each side British soldiers were clearing up the wreckage in view of further military movements. Before and after the bayonet and rifle, the most important tools were pick and spade.

and continued until September 30th from the Schwaben lines on the Thiepval spur to the Hessian lines near Grandcourt. The struggle in places was of a savage persistency. Parts of the Hessian Trench held by the Canadians changed hands four times by September 30th, and though most of the Hessian work and all the Stuff work remained then in possession of the British and Canadian forces, the Germans recovered half the Schwaben line, thus recovering their footing on the high part of the Thiepval ridge.

It was not open field fighting. Between Thiepval and Grandcourt the Germans had a chain of forts, oval redoubts, and circular redoubts dug above the Ancre valley, and buttressed with stones and timber, with cement emplacements for machine-guns, and a skilful, intricate network of communications threading the sunken roads, gullies, and fields. Most of this elaborate fortification had been constructed after the opening of the Franco-British offensive, and the mark of the Teuton genius who had improvised the mysterious defences of Mouquet Farm was evident in the southern works of the Ancre. He was one of the greatest military engineers of his period—possibly greater than any engineer in the British, French, or Russian Armies. It must be remembered that we were fighting against a European nation in the full flower of its genius. Its architects showed more original talent than those of any other nation, and had begun to experiment with the new material of armoured concrete in the creation of that sound new style which the commercialised American genius was too decadent to accomplish and the British and French genius too somnolent even to attempt.

Its discovery of the X-ray had opened a new, vast field of physics ; its doctrine of the " quanta," in regard to the mystery of electronic forces, promised an extraordinary, abnormal revolution in **Mark of the Teuton genius** mathematical concepts. It was a race at the supreme moment of its renaissance, brimming over with vitality and creative imagination.

Great was the energy of mind Germany had shown in the arts of peace ; great was the energy of mind she displayed in the arts of war. Stronger she was in fighting against defeat than in fighting for victory. For, when disaster shook her modernised feudal system of leadership, her numerous men of native talent emerged from the middle classes and imparted new and higher force into the campaign of resistance. Hindenburg's triumph over the Kaiser and the Great Staff was significant of a national change. In the incessant strain of battle, avenues were opening to all talent, and though the great landowners and industrial and financial magnates strove to preserve their system of Imperial oligarchy, tools began to fall into the hands of men who best could use them. Hindenburg's order that munition-workers should be especially well fed, at the expense of the rest of the working classes, was indicative of a formidable new energising stress of thought in the strongest military race in the world. Far from repenting their criminal blunder of engineering a war for the eventual **Germany's desperate** dominion of the earth, the German **fight for time** people as a whole were still confident they could attain the end they had in view, by more gradual means than they had first supposed.

Meanwhile, Germany continued to fight for time on the Somme, at the cost of three-quarters of a million casualties. She inflicted equal losses upon the British and French armies, the British having half a million men put out of action, and the French possibly half that number. As the two Allies divided the terrible cost of attrition, their sacrifices would not have weighed so heavily upon them as the enemy's sacrifices did upon him, but for certain circumstances. The British Army was still hampered by the delay to organise and train the entire man-power which should have been put in the field to prevent defeat. The French Army was in such a condition that it had already to be economical of man-power, and its directors were beginning to look to Great Britain and Italy for additional infantry. From the point of view of the enemy High Command, the prevention of a break-through in the Bapaume sector was the only matter of supreme concern. If the front were held through the winter the effect of the mass levy then under consideration would, it was expected, alter the tragic complexion of affairs.

From the last week of September to the second week in November, 1916, a struggle of incessant violence went on by the ravine of the Ancre above Thiepval to the area of Miraucourt. Neither side made any decisive gain of ground, yet the forces of guns and men employed were large. The rain of shell was continuous, and at intervals it increased to a terrific tempest, behind which the infantry crawled from crater to crater through mud, water, and dead. Among the more remarkable assaults was that of October 14th, when the British resumed their hold on Stuff Redoubt, capturing three times more prisoners than their casualties. Then on October 17th the Bavarians were pushed farther from Schwaben and Stuff works. They returned in

THE RULING PASSION TO RELIEVE MONOTONY AT THE FRONT.
[British official photograph.
Card party happy in their game amidst a heap of munitions, a veritable scientific volcano. Most of the known card games and doubtless new ones were in great favour, and chess, draughts, and dominoes were equally popular between the shell storms.

great force on October 21st, and in a hand-to-hand combat all along the Ancre front regained part of their old positions. But the British and Canadian troops had also been preparing that day to attack, and they broke furiously upon the weakened Bavarians, and along a three-mile line of battle recovered Stuff Trench and the posts about Schwaben Redoubt, together with the Regina Trench, originally named after a Canadian force. Some twelve hundred prisoners were taken. Then on November 11th the eastern portion of the Regina Trench was also recovered.

This, however, only restored the line held by the British army at the close of September. For six weeks there had been an intense, grinding balance of forces along the Ancre, but as the line formed the exposed flank of the large British wedge driven towards Bapaume, it may fairly be concluded that the violent and prolonged fighting on this sector was on the whole a defensive victory for the British army. No attempt was made by Sir Douglas Haig to break across the Ancre valley by a main offensive movement and get in the rear of the Serre and Beaumont-Hamel front. His continuous local pressure was intended to anticipate and exhaust the forces which General von Marschall would, if left alone, have used in a grand assault on the British flank.

But while thus holding up and wearing down a strong hostile army on their left flank, the British forces found considerable difficulty in making progress on their front towards Bapaume. Here there occurred a forward sweep, similar to the sweep over the Thiepval down, but it was followed by a grinding equilibrium of opposing armies also similar to that obtaining in the Thiepval-Ancre sector. Yet at first, with the French breaking westward at Bouchavesnes and the British army striking out north-westward at Lesbœufs and northward at Le Sars and Warlencourt, there was the promise of a victory of liberation greater than that of the Marne. A German army order of September 21st, for example, insisted on the importance of Lesbœufs as " the last protection of the artillery, which must in no circumstances be lost."

Just before this a heavy fall of rain that went on for twenty-four hours gave a saving breathing space to the

Promise of a greater Marne

enemy, as it made the chalk slopes of the High Wood watershed so slippery that the advance of the British artillery and supply train was retarded. But this sudden turn of wet weather served to increase the discomfort of the beaten German troops, who had retired into shell-holes in and around the partly broken last German line—between Le Sars and Gueudecourt and Lesbœufs A highly important stretch of ground on the Le Sars and Gueudecourt sector was won without a struggle by a British patrol that pushed out and found that a German battalion had fled because it had not been relieved. The British force behind its patrol had prepared for a violent conflict, but discovered no enemy to fight. In the same sector, at a point near Eaucourt l'Abbaye, a similar abandonment of a position by weary, disheartened and angry Germans occurred.

So extraordinary was the weakness of parts of the Bapaume front that the British commander could not get his patrols to work forward quickly enough to keep touch with the enemy. British cavalry forces had to ride out and reconnoitre the ground to find where the Germans were in strength, and where progress could be made merely with the shovel, instead of with bomb, bayonet, and heavy shell fire. The cavalry patrols advanced to the neighbourhood of Pys, meeting with no resistance except from scattered snipers in shell-holes and a few resolute machine-gunners sheltering in the sunken roads that wound through the folds of chalk.

In these circumstances the leading British army corps commanders prepared, as rapidly as the weather allowed, another great blow against the Bapaume front, and on September 25th, 1916, victory again crowned the efforts of the tired but enthusiastic army of the Somme. It was the anniversary of the Battle of Loos, and the memory of that early and partial success of the first new national force was celebrated by such a display of the growing strength of the British Empire as shook the entire fabric of the Teutonic Empire.

Bouleaux Wood menace avoided

The pivot of the attack was Bouleaux Wood, just above Combles. From the western edge of the wood all the British forces on the right flank were to swing forward against Morval, Lesbœufs, and Gueudecourt, while the forces in the British centre also moved forward so as to close about Gueudecourt from the northern side. As at the same time the French army was pressing up from Fregicourt, on the western ridge above the Combles valley, Combles was immediately menaced by the Allies' movement. The British offensive extended far beyond Combles, and employed the instant threat to this enemy base, as a means of weakening the German line near Bapaume. Thus there was subtlety as well as strength in the British attack.

The German commander could see what was impending, and with strategic insight he packed Bouleaux Wood with an extraordinary number of machine-gunners and strong trench-mortar detachments. He thought to break the attack by disposing his forces in a sharp wedge at the point on which the assaulting line pivoted, so that his resisting wedge would shear through the charging waves of infantry. But by a tactical stroke more brilliant than the skilful disposition of the enemy, the menace at Bouleaux

The Big Cranes

Gigantic cranes for lifting big guns.

The above illustration and those on the three succeeding pages are representative of the magnificent series of drawings by Mr. Joseph Pennell depicting work at the munition factories in Great Britain. These drawings are the result of personal visits made by the artist, with the direct sanction of the Ministry of Munitions, to our mighty centres of labour in 1916.

Welding a shell at Vulcan's forge: Colossal hammer at work on the white=hot steel.

154

Big gate of the big shop: Unique scene of British war=time industrialism.

Building a big=gun turret for one of Britain's super=Dreadnoughts.

Wood was entirely avoided. In the morning of the great battle several British battalions that had been fighting heavily in the ridge campaign and had suffered many losses, rallied with a fine spirit and set to work to secure the point on which success depended. They advanced against Bouleaux Wood, and in five minutes of fierce combat stormed two lines of trenches on the western edge of the long, narrow copse. The masses of Germans hidden among the shattered trees waited for the khaki line to swing out again for the decisive forest battle.

They waited in vain. A British pioneer battalion was furiously labouring in the captured new outer trenches, and transforming these into a wall that shut the picked German force out of the great battle. The Germans had either to advance into the open and attack, or remain idle while the fortune of the day was going against them for miles along the more northerly position. " You didn't play the game in Bouleaux Wood," complained an enemy officer. " You ought to have attacked us." Instead of so doing, the entrenched

Morval and Lesbœufs stormed Britons worked along an embankment running at right angles from their line and, after a savage bomb fight in a warren of dug-outs, outflanked the hostile garrison of the wood and gained an easy way of approach to Combles.

But long before Combles fell, positions of more importance had been conquered north of the town. At noon on September 25th the British artillery was firing in a desultory way about twenty shots a minute. Abruptly, a thousand shells hurtled upon the German lines and continued to fall at the fiercest speed with which the gunners could feed their pieces. This stupendous tempest of death lasted only ten minutes; then it slackened as the British infantry poured out on the wilderness of chalk and assailed the lines that the guns had hammered. Again all the infernal fury of the artillery filled the sky and smote the earth. The second bound of attack was coming, and the German artillery across the Combles valley and along the Péronne road answered with a rain of shrapnel, through which the British troops worked forward from the cover of holes and lumps of earth.

All the line about Morval was soon a single continuous bank of smoke and flame. Yet in their third bound the Britons reached the hill village lying on the low western spur of the High Wood watershed. It was a knot of caverned ruins and redoubts, all framed by an unusual number of country roads worn deep into the chalk by the traffic of a thousand years. These sunken roads were the strongest positions held by the enemy. His artificial lines of firing-trenches and support-trenches were carried with remarkable ease, as their narrow, shallow openings gave little protection against heavy high-explosive shell. But the wider and steeper hollows of the sunken road, lined often with dug-outs and manned by many machine-gun teams, survived the whirlwind artillery fire and checked the waves of assault.

In material the contest was on fairly equal terms. The enemy had at last so increased his masses of artillery that almost for the first time in the Somme battles he was able to undertake serious counter-battery firing, while maintaining an enormous curtain of shrapnel and high-explosive over the lines of infantry attack.

But the spirit of the Britons was far stronger than the

STEEL HELMS AND BAYONETS. *[British official photograph.*
Fully equipped for battle, British infantry filing into a newly-constructed trench. They were apparently pleased with their new quarters.

spirit of the Germans. They went steadily through the hostile barrage, running after their own zone of shell fire. Checked at first south of Morval, they broke across the machine-gun positions on the north, and then in a furious hand-to-hand fight in the ruins they gradually drove the Prussian garrison into a corner of cellars and loopholed works. In less than three hours all the village was taken, except for an island of machine-gunners that gallantly held out until the supporting batteries of field-guns behind them retired to escape capture.

At the hamlet of Lesbœufs, on the northern slope of the western spur of the watershed, the defenders displayed less stamina, in spite of the fact that they had been informed by a special army order that their position was of supreme importance. Around the broken farmsteads and white-walled manor-house, fortified sunken roads rayed like the tentacles of an octopus. But the attackers reached the roads ahead of their time-table. They found then only a remnant of dismayed grey figures crouching amid shattered machine-guns and collapsed dug-outs. A few hundred feet away was Lesbœufs, with scattered fire coming from its wreckage. So the conquerors went forward; some fought up the High Street, bombing out the gunners and snipers; others enveloped the village, and the garrison surrendered.

Pure science in attack did not tell entirely in these victorious operations. The force of character of the British private was a grand factor of success. Private Tom Jones, of the Cheshires, was one of the heroes of the day. After the village was captured and the men were digging themselves in, the enemy maintained a most distressing fire over the position. Jones turned to his officer and said: " Let's get at them, or there will be trouble." **Adventures of Private Jones** But the officer thought a charge would only result in disaster, and that it would be better to hold the ground that had been won. The shower of bullets continued, and the man next to Jones was hit. " If I'm to be killed, I'll be killed fighting, and not digging ! " said Jones. Grabbing his rifle and loaded with bombs he rushed towards the German trenches. Four bullets flicked his body, but only pierced his clothes. Onward he went and disappeared.

Then two of his friends said: " He's gone, and we're going, too." They charged forward, and other comrades followed. But when they reached the big hollow, which the Germans were holding, an amazing scene awaited them. Jones had taken a hundred and two prisoners, including

A COLLECTING STATION.
A few of the thousands of prisoners captured at Beaumont-Hamel detained in a collecting station until it was convenient to remove them for internment.

COUNTING THE PRISONERS CAPTURED AT BEAUMONT-HAMEL.
Sir Douglas Haig reported that after the terrific fighting at and near Beaumont-Hamel, which resulted in the British capturing that great fortress position in the third week of November, 1916, more than seven thousand prisoners were counted.

a Staff officer. He had jumped into the hollow and bombed three men who first showed themselves at the entrance of a dug-out. Then he ordered the garrison to come out, holding up their hands, to avoid more bombs. One by one they came forth and lined up, until more than a hundred stood with raised hands before the Englishman. When his comrades arrived Jones was wondering how to march his prisoners out, without allowing those farthest from him to escape or attack him. But when help came every German was shepherded towards the prisoners' "cage," and Private Jones was recommended for the Victoria Cross by eleven officers.

Between Lesbœufs and Gueudecourt was a long double system of works known as Grid Trench and Grid Support, that extended northwards in a curve some five miles long. Wire entanglements strengthened the Grid, from which outworks also ran at intervals. But the extraordinary whirlwind fire of the British guns rapidly broke a path through the Grid, and in gradual, stubborn spurts the infantry worked through and over the enemy's work into

the northern part of Gueudecourt village. At the southern edge a detachment of German machine-gunners, crouching in a redoubt at the junction of two sunken roads, checked the advance on that side and prevented the village from falling at the same time as Morval and Lesbœufs. All the night the enemy garrison held out, but when day broke the encircling movement was continued, with the assistance of a "tank."

This monstrous "toad," with armour-plated hide, had a soul like that of Jones, of the Cheshires. It was brimming over with initiative. In a businesslike way it carried out the task assigned to it and broke into the southern redoubt, helped to take three hundred and fifty prisoners there, and then assisted the infantry in clearing the cavern of the village, from which three hundred more Germans were extracted. When the surface fighting was over the "tank" explored the slopes beyond, like Alexander, seeking new worlds to conquer. It came upon another trench containing a large force of Germans, and a British pilot flying overhead saw the frightened enemy force come forth, waving white handkerchiefs and other emblems of surrender.

"Tank's" extraordinary capture

It was an extraordinary capture. The Germans numbered at least five hundred. But the "tank" had no room for them. It turned, in more than elephantine majesty, to escort its captives to Gueudecourt, when its machinery went wrong and brought it to a standstill. Thereupon the Germans, gathering courage, assailed their crippled captor. They bombed its armoured skin, shot at the slits from which its guns fired, and at last climbed upon its back and head, seeking for holes large enough in which to drop egg-bombs or shoot bullets. The "tank" fought stolidly, as its crew had to wait until the grey figures came in the fixed line of fire of its guns. While it was ringed round like an elephant against a pack of red wild dogs, the British infantry streamed up from Gueudecourt to the rescue. There was a furious battle around the "tank," and when the Germans fled they left nearly three hundred dead or wounded around the modern chariot of war. Behemoth himself was not seriously hurt; the bombs only scarred him, and when the trouble in his interior was put right his fighting powers were as good as ever.

At the time the historic conflict between the land monitor and the German infantry opened, an event of a memorable kind was occurring four miles southward along the line of battle. For the first time in two years of trench warfare on the western front the Allies were recovering a town from the enemy. Hamlets and villages had been won in various advances, but Combles was the first town in Western Europe to be wrenched from the slave-raiders of the new Assyria.

The operation was made practicable by the British conquest of Morval, a mile and a half due north of Combles, and the French advance into Frégicourt, half a mile west of the town in the great hollow. By meeting each other half-way across the hollow the Allies could envelop Combles and capture the large amount of war material the enemy had stored there to supply his large forces lately deployed on the eastern heights. The enveloping movement began in the evening of September 25th, when the British troops that had held the pivoting trench in Bouleaux Wood sent out patrols to explore the slope

Historic meeting in Combles to the hollow. All the night the British artillery flung a heavy barrage across the neck of Combles valley to prevent the enemy from removing material from the town. This was effected. Four thousand 6 in. shells were afterwards captured, and the cellars were full of rifles and ammunition. The heights above blazed with the fires of war against the autumnal starlit sky; but in and over Combles there was a sombre quietness. The British patrols, however, found some German patrols in the town, and after a sharp exchange of shots killed ten opponents and captured thirty. Then cautiously the streets were explored by tired, grim men who had been fighting desperately all day. They feared a

trap, and the silence and gloom made them only more careful. Their machine-guns covered every movement made by the advanced scouts. At a quarter-past three in the morning of September 26th a patrol reached the railway-station and saw a group of figures emerge from the shadows on the other side. "It's the blooming French!" "Ces sont les Anglais!" are said to have been the historic words at this glorious meeting of khaki and horizon-blue which set the crown upon the greatest victory of the Western Allies since the Marne.

When the sun rose and the day wore on, the last definite zone of hostile works immediately in front of Bapaume was captured—from Gueudecourt to Combles. The allied forces, which for three months had gradually diverged towards different objectives on either side the great downland valley, stood united above the valley at Lesbœufs on the site of their greatest victories. Then there was afforded a striking instance of the observation value of the dominating ridge that had been won. In the afternoon three famous Prussian regiments were launched on a great counter-attack in a supreme endeavour to resume the defences of the Gueudecourt line. They appeared on the rising slope near Le Transloy and were ranged by forward observing officers, who brought battery after battery upon them. Good fighting men these Prussians had proved themselves in clash after clash with the British. But the incessant wear of desperate battle had unstrung them and robbed them of their native courage. Though they were veterans of many fierce encounters, they broke like an untrained mob and at the first shock bolted, flinging away their weapons to speed their flight to shelter. The field was littered with their rifles and equipment.

Prussian flight at Le Transloy

With certain exceptions the German forces south of Bapaume were generally in the same condition as the Prussians at Le Transloy, or tending to that condition. Among the exceptions were some heroic knots of machine-gunners, backed by regimental officers of the fine, stern school, and some fresh forces newly blooded to British siege warfare, such as the German naval brigades hastily railed from the Nieuport area to fill the gaps in the line against the Canadians near Grandcourt and Le Sars. A Bavarian force, renowned for its conquest of Fort Vaux at Verdun, also came, after a rest, refreshed into the furnace of

KIT INSPECTION BEHIND THE SOMME LINE: AN IMPORTANT ITEM OF ACTIVE SERVICE ROUTINE.

"THREE MUSKETEERS" OF 1916 IN AN EPIC HAND-TO-HAND ENCOUNTER AT COMBLES.

Combles fell to the Franco-British forces to the accompaniment of bitter hand-to-hand fighting. During a night assault three irresistible Frenchmen came upon six of the enemy. Risking the odds the Poilus charged, two armed with rifles and bayonets, the third with bombs. The Germans endeavoured to resist, but were no match for their quick-witted adversaries. One Frenchman threw away his rifle and grappled the nearest German, the second hurled bombs from a bag which he carried in his left hand, while the third got to work with the bayonet. Those Germans who survived took to their heels.

Bapaume, and distinguished itself by its energy of resistance. But taking, as representatives of its two races, the general body of German forces and the general body of British forces, which had alike sustained the effort of conflict from the middle to the end of September, the German was patently beaten by the Briton.

In a very remarkable communiqué issued from Berlin on September 26th, 1916, General von Ludendorff, the lieutenant of Hindenburg, frankly admitted defeat, but alleged that the Franco-British forces had won the victory by superior machinery. "Our heroic troops," he stated, "had to face the massed employment of materials prepared after many months of labour by the warlike industries of the whole world." But this again showed that the German was patently beaten by the Briton. The "whole world," as seen by the Dictator of the Central Empire and his assistant, consisted of those munition factories of the United States, which were not, like most of the munition factories of Japan, concerned only in supplying the Russian and Rumanian front with guns, shell, rifles, and other means of war. If great neutral industrial nations like the United States were able to follow the old example of the Germans and Austrians, and provide belligerents with munitions, their trade in military supplies in the present case was governed entirely by the British Fleet. Owing to the scope of British sea-power no important neutral industrial State, except Sweden, could supply Germany with material of war in any considerable quantity. The Allies' sea-borne traffic in munitions, in despite of the activity of German submarines, was one result of Great Britain's practical mastery of the seas. Another result was the facility with which she transported troops and guns to Flanders, France, Greece, and Egypt.

Effect of British sea-power

Ludendorff's reference to the superiority of the Franco-British material of war was the consequence of the industrial organisation which Mr. Lloyd George, as founder and director of the Ministry of Munitions, had perfected in the face of great difficulties. In 1909 Germany had energetically begun to prepare new instruments for a great war of aggression. Then, when her preliminary organisation of all means of destruction proved ineffective, in the autumn of 1914, she alertly made a more tremendous effort, and won another long lead against all the Allies. It was not until the summer of 1915 that Great Britain was moved, by a tragic revelation in the "Times," to organise her industries fully for war. Even then a considerable period had to elapse before the work of the new Ministry of Munitions told on the fortunes of the field of battle. In September, 1915, the northern British thrust above the Loos sector failed because the provision of guns and high-explosive remained inadequate to the needs of the Army. Thus if, as General von Ludendorff admitted, Great Britain, by a miraculous effort of improvisation, succeeded in surpassing by September, 1916, the enormous output of German guns and shell available on the western front, this was evidence that in all fields of conflict the Briton had —for the time at least—beaten the German.

[*British official photograph.*

EXAMINING GERMAN MACHINE-GUNS CAPTURED AT BEAUCOURT.
To the Royal Naval Division fell the distinction of taking Beaucourt, rushing on the way a hidden redoubt whence machine-guns poured a stream of lead upon them. They captured about 2,000 prisoners and many of the machine-guns that had harassed them.

Hindenburg indeed admitted in the most practical fashion that he was worsted. For though it was not publicly known at the time, before the end of September, 1916, he opened negotiations for an armistice. This, of course, was done, through the Imperial Chancellor of Germany, with a view to arriving at a settlement. No doubt there was a secondary strategic ruse underlying the primary significance of the request for an armistice. The Teuton used a double-barrelled gun. He intended by his confession of weakness to make Rumania and Russia slacken in their vital work of strictly co-ordinating their forces and strategy, so that he might strike at the Rumanian frontiers with unforeseen swiftness and strength. But while thus preparing to hit with one barrel, if he missed with the other, Hindenburg seemed to be in earnest in his suggestion of an armistice. Not until it was rejected did he undertake his supreme efforts in munition production and recruiting—the impressment of all able Russian Poles and Lithuanians as "cannon-fodder," the general deportation of labour from Belgian and French territory, and the mass levy in the Central Empires.

The most brilliant and daring of German publicists, Maximilian Harden, conveyed the lesson of Bapaume to his countrymen in the form of an historic parable. He suggested that a certain nation, which had opened a great war under the assumption that it was, as the **Parable of Rome and Carthage** modern Rome, mistress of the world, was likely to prove only the modern Carthage. Ancient Carthage, he pointed out, would have done well to avoid utter destruction by accepting the position of junior partner of the Roman Empire.

Harden might have gone on to remark that if Rome at the height of grandeur had been leagued with the Athens of Pericles, and with a Macedonia possessing large, undeveloped resources—Carthage and the dependencies of Carthage would have been unwise to emulate the atrocious savageries of the Assyrians.

On the battlefield in front of Bapaume, meanwhile,

IN THE NEW ZEALAND LINES.
Sir Joseph Ward, Finance Minister of New Zealand, emerging from a captured German dug-out on the occasion of his visit to the lines in Picardy.

This was the reason why, for a week or more after the rupture of the Grid line, British cavalry patrols continued to be able to scout an uncommon distance ahead of the infantry before coming upon any powerful trap or defensive work. The governing idea was to leave an extraordinarily broad glacis between the German fire-trenches and British assembly trenches. In some places there were a thousand yards of exposed, torn, difficult slope left for the attacking infantry to cover before bomb and bayonet could be used. This much enlarged the defensive power of the German artillery. Then, to restrict the striking power of the British artillery, the fire-trench was manned mainly by machine-gunners well spaced out.

some German of genius seems to have emerged and saved the situation by a superb display of tactical skill. Had Sir Douglas Haig possessed in the last week of September, 1916, a good reserve of capably-trained conscripts, there can be no doubt that the German front would have been pierced. A grand decision hung in the balance. Owing, however, to the delay in establishing a system of national service in England, Wales, and Scotland, there appear to have been insufficient troops in the field to deliver with overwhelming force the final, disruptive thrust.

Germany, distracted by her new Rumanian campaign, threw her naval divisions into the western field as her ultimate resource. Great Britain then **New enemy** brought her naval brigades to the Ancre, **tactics** and they at the time were all she could afford. The struggle became as close as that at Ypres in 1914, when one fresh division on either side might at last have turned the tide of war. General von Below used his men in a mercilessly effective mass. Nearly every division was employed until its fighting strength was spent. Often it was then withdrawn, filled out with drafts, rested for a few weeks, and sent forth again to be worn down. On some occasions this terrible process was thrice repeated, with the result, already seen, that apparently veteran brigades broke at the first new shock. Nearly three-fifths of the entire field forces of Germany were ground in the mill of the Somme, and between them they suffered nearly 700,000 casualties. Germany was thus very close to the end of her immediately available resources, considering the immense fronts she had to garrison in the western and eastern theatres of trench warfare.

With conditions thus set, some unknown German genius of war arranged his country's remaining pawns in such an effective new disposition that a decisive defeat was evaded. His problem was first to reduce the deadliness of the British artillery and limit the effect of the higher power of observation due to the Franco-British position on the ridge and superiority in the air. Next was the task of preserving the German infantry from the terrible wastage of persistent close conflict with British infantry. Both these ends were attained by one means— the German infantry forces were withdrawn to a slight extent and dispersed.

[*British official photographs.*]

AN OFFICIAL CONFERENCE AT THE FRONT.
General Sir Douglas Haig settling a point of detail with Mr. Lloyd George in the presence of General Joffre and M. Albert Thomas, the French Minister of Munitions.

To protect the gunners from raids the ordinary infantry was largely dispersed in an organised system of shell-holes across the wide slopes. Whirlwind shrapnel bombardments, so finely developed by British gunners, did not seriously disorganise the new shell-hole battalions.

Enormous was the amount of shell necessary for the intensive searching of ground in which a score of sharp-shooters were taking cover in craters. To a considerable extent shell-hole warfare, with its extraordinary scattering of forces **Shell-hole warfare** according to the lie of the land, dis- **and Hazy Trench** placed deep trench and cavern warfare.

The sunken roads and valleys that seamed the long low undulations of chalk became the backbone of the new hostile defensive system, but this backbone would have been shattered by intensive artillery attack if the roads and valleys had not been lightly held and a considerable force of the holding infantry scattered widely in the fore-front, in linked systems of shell-holes and many separate craters. The character of important examples of the advanced shell-hole system is depicted in the name of

Hazy Trench, lying beyond the Grid line. Stormed by the British in the first advance from the Grid, it was abandoned by them because of its weakness and feeble trace. Resumed by the enemy and transformed by him into a source of annoyance, it was at last subjected to serious attack. The British artillery hammered it as if it had been a real trench, with the result that when the charging waves of infantry reached their objective they had the disappointment of not being able to find it. There was nothing to take and hold. Whether the Germans had been buried or had crawled to other shell-holes was a matter of speculation which remained undetermined.

For about a fortnight, from

[*British official photograph.*]
NEW ZEALAND'S PREMIER IN A GERMAN TRENCH.
The Hon. F. W. Massey, Prime Minister of New Zealand, paid a visit to the western front during 1916. This photograph shows him on a visit to captured German trenches.

[*British official photograph.*]
FIRST LORD OF THE ADMIRALTY AT THE FRONT.
The Right Hon. A. J. Balfour, at the time of this visit to France still First Lord of the Admiralty, inspecting dug-outs and shelters on the western front.

September 28th to October 12th, a cumulative series of small advances was made on the Bapaume front from Le Sars to Lesbœufs. Often positions of high tactical value were won at astonishing slight loss. Such an action was the progress towards the ruined monastic edifice of Eaucourt l'Abbaye, where the British line was moved forward eight hundred yards, with total casualties amounting only to twice the number of prisoners taken. In other places, such as the low hills near the Péronne-Bapaume road, the quality of the defending forces was high, and the British movement, therefore, slow and difficult. This patchwork character of the enemy's arc of deployed troops, by turns ragged and firm, was no doubt related to the length of time the men had been fighting between the Somme and the Ancre. When at last fresh and rested troops could be found to hold the entire arc, the British offensive there came to a practical standstill.

On September 30th Destremont Farm, south-west of Le Sars village, was taken. On October 2nd the vaulted ruins of Eaucourt l'Abbaye were occupied, then partly

Advance at Eaucourt l'Abbaye

recovered by the enemy, and finally securely conquered by the British two days afterwards. October 8th was another red-letter day in the annals of the New Army. It marked the capture of the cellars and shattered farmsteads of Le Sars, forming the strong point at the north-western end of the old long Gird system of works. It was the twenty-second village captured by the home and overseas troops. The actions at Eaucourt l'Abbaye and Le Sars were one long connected battle against an unusually intense concentration of German forces, consisting of a Bavarian division and an Ersatz division arrayed upon a front of only 3,000 yards. The line also was unusually strong; the first part of it had been the last zone of the original hostile works, and the second part had been constructed at the beginning of July, 1916.

Assault against Le Sars

On October 1st a general assault was delivered against Le Sars and Eaucourt l'Abbaye, with the object of taking the first line of German trenches. All the trenches were taken except a short stretch fronting the abbey. But on the east of the abbey a more fortunate body of the attackers broke through the entire German works and, extending north of the ruins, held on there. Then the "tanks" came to the help of the checked British centre and conquered the main trench and advanced into the abbey ruins. One monster that could not move farther operated as a stationary fort, the wounded skipper lying with two of his men in a shell-hole for two days. Meanwhile, the Germans remained in a gap on the west, and both attackers and attacked were ignorant of the general situation. A German detachment crossed the open ground on the north to reinforce the conquerors there, and the men in it were shot or captured. The prisoners complained that their comrades on the northern side must have bolted without giving any warning, as the detachment had moved forward as a relief. Then a larger enemy force came to the new eastern British line to take over the position, and was also tragically surprised.

By this time the German commander, a mile away, grasped the situation. He launched a strong counter-attack through the western gap, and recovered the front trench. The British still commanded the communication from the abbey eastward and northward at nightfall. A day was

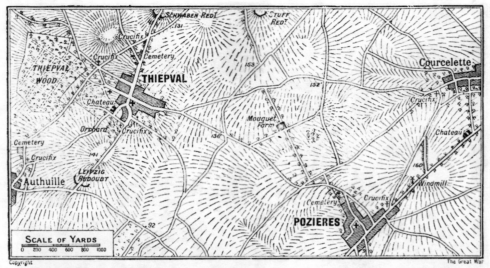

AREA OF THE FIGHTING FOR POSSESSION OF THE THIEPVAL RIDGE.
Mouquet Farm was a key position to Thiepval. It was connected with the Thiepval region by underground corridors, whence the enemy had assailed the British line from the rear.

spent in strengthening the captured positions and bombing the enemy farther back. Then on October 4th the abbey was furiously shelled and the entire place carried by British infantry, crawling through deep, grey, slime puddles and by waterpools that had once been shell-craters. Nearly a battalion of Bavarians made a fierce stand in the huge abbey vaults; they hid in dark corners, waiting with bomb and rifle, but they were cleared out. The British soldier was a supreme expert in the art of subterranean warfare; his experience in the matter was large and varied.

When the vanishing abbey was reconsolidated by the conquerors, who found the vaults a paradise after nights and days spent under continual rain, the operations against the neighbouring fortress of Le Sars were resumed in greater force. The Reserve division there was known to be one of the most demoralised. British machine-gunners had fought down German machine-gunners in order to protect from German fire the groups of grey figures that openly left their trenches and walked in surrender to the attacking line.

Halt at the Butte of Warlencourt The capture of Le Sars was not a struggle but a rounding up, complicated by knots of resistent machine-gunners and a number of desperate sharpshooters, including officers of the old school. In the first rush a sunken road running through the middle of the wreckage was taken; in the second rush the troops were out on the farther side, along the Bapaume road. A thousand prisoners, mainly the Reserve division, were taken. East of Le Sars the Bavarian troops fought hard and well, but after a fierce tussle their line was broken and half the ground covered towards a prehistoric tumulus known as the Butte of Warlencourt, where the great British offensive gradually came to a standstill.

The tumulus stood about fifty feet above the level of the land, and the Germans had dug into this burial-place of some chieftain of immemorial days and transformed his monument into a bomb-proof shelter for a strong machine-gun force, which enfiladed all British infantry movements from the Le Sars and Eaucourt l'Abbaye line.

The butte was bombarded with monster shells, and the battered heap of earth which they left was

carried by the British, recovered by the Germans, stormed again by the British, and again recovered. After a month's fighting, between October 9th and November 6th, in which Anzac forces were engaged, most of the ground about the butte remained in the enemy's possession. It seemed as though the Germans at last had fought their opponents to a standstill, and as if the butte would be the monument of the close of the Battle of Bapaume as the Hohenzollern Redoubt was the monument of the close of the Battle of Loos.

The master factor in the situation was the weather. The autumnal country song of the Somme downlands should run to Shakespeare's refrain, "The rain it raineth every day." And it also rained nearly every night. Night frosts set in early. Chalk usually permits rain to drain off rapidly; in this respect it is superior to gravel, for gravel is often thin and patchy, while chalk is solid and deep. General Castelnau opened the first great French offensive in Champagne in February, 1915, because the chalk there had absorbed the winter rains quicker than the soil on other western sectors. But the bosses, ridges, and rolls of chalk between the Somme and the Ancre in

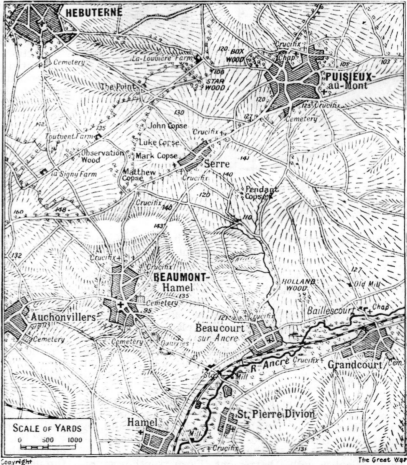

THE BATTLEGROUND BETWEEN THE ANCRE AND THE SERRE PLATEAU.
Failing in his thrust against Bapaume, Sir Douglas Haig effected a surprise movement across the Ancre, in which Beaumont-Hamel, St. Pierre Division, and Beaucourt were stormed.

TRACTOR TAKING A BRITISH HEAVY GUN TO A FRESH POSITION IN THE ADVANCE.

the late autumn of 1916 were of a peculiar nature. On Sussex downs, from the Stone Age, men have been wont to make dew-ponds in the chalk. On the downs and slopes south of Bapaume the labours of a million or more munition workers of Great Britain, France, Germany, and the United States resulted in the creation of a million or more shell-craters. And for months the rain kept the craters full of water. In the excavation works of the big shells there was sufficient depth of water for men to drown. They drowned singly, by scores, and then by hundreds, and finally by thousands. It was the result of the new method of shell-hole warfare that the enemy had developed.

It was not while charging that men were caught in these deadly pools. The end came usually in the darkness, through utter exhaustion, when the sharpshooters moved about laboriously in the gloom, their boots sticking in the deep slime as they were relieved or came out on duty. Many of them had to work all day in the water of the holes or the mud of the shallow linking trenches. It grew very bleak and chilly at night. What the Germans suffered we can only guess from a consideration of the geographical position and the weather conditions. They were in low-lying land, channelled with valleys and pitted with innumerable earthen cisterns in the form of shell-craters. Immediately above them was a high, long watershed, down the northern sides of which the rains soaked and streamed towards the Bapaume area. All their old works on the dry uplands were places of winter comfort and protection for their enemies. Most of us know what the British army endured in the winter of 1914, when it stood frost-bitten in the marshes around Ypres and Lille, while the German army sat in comparative ease on the eastern hills and ridges. It was long before the German public knew what its main army suffered in the watery craters, frozen puddles, and solidifying slime about Bapaume in the winter of 1916. There are more ways than one of killing—disease is as enfeebling and deadly as poison gas or phosphorus shell. The brilliant German commander who invented shell-hole warfare did not foresee all the results of this manner of holding a front.

Clearly Sir Douglas Haig, at the beginning of November, 1916, was well content with the position of affairs on the Bapaume front, for Bapaume was his to take. He had but to give the order, and his reinforcements of fresh troops of superb quality, including the Naval Division that had proved itself on the Gallipoli Peninsula, would have fulfilled his command. But for good reasons the Germans were allowed fully to enjoy the benefits of their geographical situation.

The British commander and his Chief of Staff, General Kiggell, and our southern army commanders had been studying the advantage of another lowland area. This consisted of the wedge of the Ancre valley, with its rising slopes between Beaumont-Hamel and St. Pierre Divion. Its conquest would free the British left flank on the Thiepval spur from all annoyance around the Schwaben Redoubt, and transform the lee of all the Thiepval upland into a shelter from the enemy's enfilading fire from the Serre plateau. Farther along the Ancre front near Grandcourt the British troops were on a low slope and exposed to close-range observation across the hollow. The strength of the enemy during the soaking, freezing winter was likely to be improved by operations down the Ancre. For months the heavy British artillery north of the brook had been pouring an intense enfilading fire upon the enemy batteries that faced Thiepval, Courcelette, and Le Sars. There was therefore nothing unusual when the British guns from the Gommecourt to the St. Pierre Divion sectors began to exhibit a fierce activity. It seemed merely to indicate that the forces on the Thiepval-Le Sars line thought of working from the Schwaben, Stuff, and Regina Trenches. But in the darkness before dawn on Monday, November 13th, 1916, the main mass of British artillery smote the German Ancre position from Gommecourt to St. Pierre Divion with a might then unparalleled. As the British munition factories increased their output, until the help of the United States could be dispensed with, so the terrific striking power of Sir Douglas Haig overreached the enemy's efforts to increase the German production of shells. About six o'clock, when a thick winter fog shrouded the marshes of the Ancre and kept back the glimmer of daybreak, the guns divided for their special tasks.

One great mass lifted, and created with its shells an appalling "stationary" barrage on the enemy's communication-trenches and reserve position. Another mass operated in front of the waves of infantry attack and formed the "creeping" barrage that kept down enemy machine gunners and cleared the last obstacle of the advance. Both the near mobile wall of steel and the distant stationary hurricane of shrapnel and heavy high explosive were operated with tremendous violence. Surprise was the essence of the action. And the Germans were entirely surprised. At some of the most important points they were in their dug-outs, waiting for the "creeping" barrage to move, when the bombers rushed the trench. The German artillery was taken still more unawares than the infantry. Over half the front of advance it did not curtain the lost ground, and the victorious troops strolled about in the open smoking cigarettes. The enemy gunners were too busy getting their pieces removed beyond the risk of capture to drench the lost fortress with shell and hinder it being reconsolidated.

The success was the finest achievement in technique of the British army. In classic method it surpassed the victory of Thiepval and ranked with the French recovery of Douaumont. Practically perfect aerial reconnaissance and forward observation work resulted in swift and exact

165

STORMING THE SCHWABEN REDOUBT: SURRENDER OF THE GERMAN FRONT LINE AS THE BRITISH SWEPT OVER THE SUMMIT.

Schwaben Redoubt was one of the strongest German front-line positions, occupying the crest north of Thiepval and representing the summit of the spur, with a full view over the northern valley of the Ancre.

This illustration shows our barrage working ahead of our infantry, who are sweeping over the tangle of trenches, shooting, bombing, and bayoneting, while Germans frantic to surrender wave white flags in the redoubt.

166

execution. The infantry movement was made on a front of about five miles from Gommecourt to St. Pierre Division, with the marshes and stream of the Ancre dividing the front into two sectors. The action about Gommecourt was of a holding nature, designed to prevent the troops about the Serre plateau from moving to the assistance of the garrison of Beaumont-Hamel. The northern demonstration also had the foreseen effect of distracting some of the weight of the enemy's shell fire, and thus lightening the real task on either side of the Ancre. The vanished village of Beaumont-Hamel was the main objective. It was reckoned to be the strongest fortress in the German line. The French had vainly assailed it when they held the Somme front. The British had failed there with heavy loss on July 1st, and had again attacked in vain in the early autumn. The houses had disappeared, but beneath their ruins was an underground town. Two cemeteries, two quarries, and a chalk-pit were worked into the defensive system, together with a long Y-shaped ravine sheltered from gun fire. Single dug-outs were of such a size they could hold four hundred men, and beyond the subterranean corridors were underground lanes running to Puisieux. Five lines of trenches with wire entanglements formed the mere approach to the village, which rested in a hollow on a slope rising to the Serre plateau.

Bitter conflict of Y ravine

Simultaneously with the fine holding advance against the northern side of the Serre plateau that sternly continued throughout the day, a representative force of Scotsmen went forward in bounds behind a creeping barrage. Two days of dry weather had partly dried the porous ground, so that the mud on the slopes was not a deadly impediment. Only at one spot was there a considerable remnant of the elaborate wire entanglement. All the rest of it, not only before the fire-trench, but before each successive line beyond, had been swept away. The trenches and position were so battered that a week afterwards the British sappers were still searching for the mouths of buried dug-outs. Scarcely any resistance was at first encountered, except before the prongs of the Y ravine. The ravine was full of sheltered machine-guns that no howitzer shell had reached, and the gunners maintained continuous streams of bullets at the entrance. Shelled at this point, the Scotsmen flowed round either edge of the great gash, which ran thirty feet deep and twenty-five hundred feet long, above the Ancre marshes. The Germans, in two years of labour, had burrowed into the steep banks of the gully, and there made caves capable of containing 1,500 men. From the ravine a tunnel ran to the fourth line of trenches in the rear.

Swerving on either flank of the flame-rimmed mouth of the ravine, the attackers worked in the darkness up either side of the gully, passing over two obliterated trench systems with scarcely any struggle. The difficulty of keeping touch in the gloomy fog was fully offset by the cover afforded by the darkness and by the surprise effect produced on the enemy infantry. But the third trench system, flanking the Y, was strongly held by men aroused by the battle, and the Scotsmen had a furious hand-to-hand conflict. They left the two sections of trench full of dead, and then with bayonet and bomb they turned behind the prongs of the Y, and tumbling down the steep banks assailed the garrison in the heart of their central fortress. Bitter beyond description was the conflict, and while the body-to-body grapple was at its height the British commander skilfully made another frontal attack. The Germans then were trapped. When they swung forward to hold the mouth of the ravine, the attackers in the middle of the gully pressed their rear. When they swung backwards to strengthen their rear, the forces against their front advanced. Meanwhile, towards the end of the Y, other troops broke down upon the enemy. There was a period of murderous confusion, but the Teuton saw it did not last long. First singly, then in groups, he surrendered, and in the afternoon all the ravine was won. One Scots private was remarkably canny. A German officer surrendered to him. Instead of sending his prisoner to the British lines, the Caledonian led him to a suspected dug-

MAP OF THE BAPAUME FRONT: THE LE SARS-GUEUDECOURT SECTOR.
In late September, 1916, the last German line on the Bapaume front was already partly broken, the enemy being so disheartened that he abandoned more than one position without a struggle.

out and told him to order the men to come out. The officer put in his head and shouted the order, and there meekly emerged fifty Germans.

While the combat in the ravine was increasing in fury, other Scottish troops swarmed over the dip of the hill into Beaumont-Hamel, and more or less captured the village. There was really no village to capture, but the attackers took all the surface positions in sight, bombed some of the entrances to the hidden town below the ground, and stood guard over all suspected spots. This may sound businesslike to the civilian, but it was a wildly romantic affair, marked by great adventures. Mr. H. G. Wells, in one of his mingled moods of Dickensian humour and technical insight, could tell the tale of the Scotsman and the giant periscope had he but been bred north of the Tweed, and there are scores of other fine stories which, we trust, the land of Sir Walter Scott will some day commemorate in literature. Sir Douglas Haig was mindful of the land of

The victory of Beaumont-Hamel

his birth when he gave to a Scottish force the hardest and most glorious task in all the Somme operations. This kind of intensive patriotism is likely to prove the soundest and perennial source of energy in the flexible yet firm Anglo-Celtic federation that loosely calls itself an empire.

Yet great as were the Scotsmen, they did not win the highest personal honour of this memorable day. Fame fell most brightly upon a New Zealand officer with a Germanic surname, to remind some of the perfervid British Chauvinists that, in addition to King Albert and Queen Elizabeth of Belgium, there are in the world many men of Teutonic blood who are as stubbornly averse to Prussianism as is any Frenchman or Englishman. Lieutenant-Colonel B. C. Freyberg before the war was a long-distance swimmer, born in New Zealand, and at the opening of the Gallipoli campaign he swam to the shore of the Saros Gulf and there lighted flares to induce the Turks to mass in the wrong spot to repel a landing. In the Ancre battle Colonel Freyberg commanded a battalion of the Naval Division that advanced on the right of the Scottish force and stormed the river valley to the hamlet of Beaucourt.

The enemy regarded the valley as a masterpiece in fortification. So it was. But in spite of the network of entrenched lines, with machine-guns working on sliding platforms or beds of concrete on a broad field of fire, the position was not, as the builders fancied, impregnable. In the foggy darkness the naval men followed their barrage through a wire barrier forty feet wide and eight feet high, which was mown down **Colonel Freyberg's** like grass by the shells. Behind the first **achievement** two rows of trenches loomed the riverside redoubt, against which English and Newfoundland troops had heroically broken on July 1st, while the Ulstermen clung to the high ground by Thiepval Crucifix. The fortress was in a hummock, swelling like a whale's back above the water. Four hundred Germans rose from their caves in the hump of earth and with their machine-guns swept the battalions on the left and held them up. But though the wave of the attack broke against this rock, fragments of naval men got by the post on the right by pressing in the shelter of its steepest face, where no machine-gun could be brought to bear. Then it was that Colonel Freyberg began to work towards a fine victory against heavy odds. He led his own wasting battalion a thousand yards beyond the fort and the checked left wing of the Naval Division, and by grim fighting and brilliant handling maintained the advance for fourteen hours, until the scattered advanced units were lying just outside the hamlet of Beaucourt with three machine-guns to strengthen their lines. Colonel Freyberg had been wounded in going over the parapet, and struck three times more by shell splinters and bullets. But wrapped in bandages he led his men on till nightfall. Then at 8 p.m. he resolved to take the position. He combined a large fragment of two hundred and fifty men of one battalion with one hundred and fifteen men of another, fifteen of a third,

and fifty fine adventurers from the impeded brigade on the left. The night was spent in making preparations for the assault. As day broke, giving just enough glimmer to see the crumble of small ruins, Colonel Freyberg and his little scratch force moved out and captured Beaumont in ten minutes' bombing, bayoneting, and punching.

While the garrison at Beaumont was surrendering to the liveliest casualty in any army, the garrison of the riverside redoubt was being interviewed by a "tank." The Germans attempted no **Capture of** resistance, but thrust up from one of **St. Pierre Divion** their shelters a long pole with a streamer of white cloth dangling from it. The terror of the "tank" was upon them, as they afterwards confessed. A threat had been sufficient, coming from the toad-like thing of which all Teutons had fearful rumour.

Another "tank" played a terrible jest with some of the German forces holding the third great Somme fortress captured on the day of victories. South of the Ancre the enemy had retained since the charge of the Ulstermen all the slope of downland between Thiepval Wood and the riverside. Close to the water a church stood about a cluster of houses known as St. Pierre Divion. The buildings had vanished, but the enemy continued to dwell in the cellars. By the hillside, at the water's edge, he made openings that led into the great T-tunnel, running for five hundred yards through the hill. At the end of the right working was a cross tunnel forming the top of the T, and extending for two hundred yards on either side. Offshoot workings from the tunnel led into innumerable rooms and suites of rooms. Then, from the top of the tunnel, shafts ran to the surface of the lower slope of Thiepval down, below the famous Schwaben Redoubt and above the riverside hamlet. Thus any frontal attack on St. Pierre Divion could be met by the garrison climbing through the holes in the tunnel to the hill trench and pouring a deadly fire upon the attackers below. A sheltered communication-trench known as the Hansa Trench connected the troops in the hamlet with the general Ancre front opposite Beaumont-Hamel.

English and Irish troops were employed in an enveloping movement against the St. Pierre Divion position. A flanking force moved northward to the Ancre, near Beaucourt, from Schwaben Redoubt and Stuff Trench, while a frontal force moved in an eastwardly direction against the tunnelled face of the hill, where the waters of the Ancre swerved down towards the Somme. In the flanking movement from Thiepval the left of the attacking line swung over the hill-top, while the right formed the pivot of the sweep. The enemy had four entrenched systems, with various connecting works on a large boss of chalk, one hundred and sixty feet above the river valley. He could retreat down his shafts to the T-tunnel, where there was a huge store of ammunition. But the enveloping attack caught him, in the fog and darkness of early morning disastrously, by surprise.

A SOMME SILHOUETTE.
[British official photograph.
Striking impression of a cavalry patrol on the watch from an elevated point of the battle-zone.

VIEW OF THE VALLEY OF THE ANCRE WHEN THE FLOODS WERE OUT.

[British official photograph.]

Weather conditions in the Valley of the Ancre in December, 1916, brought a period of forced inaction, which was exceedingly trying for our troops. When the ground was at its worst many of them were in shallow, undrained trenches, and their chief consolation was that the enemy's sufferings were even worse.

A great relief was taking place along the Ancre valley. The 38th Division was being relieved by one of Ludendorff's new formations, the 223rd Division. The Duke of Albany was waiting at the Somme Headquarters to review his regiment, which had been ordered to move out down the shrouded ravine. Neither division was properly armed. The 38th was laying aside its armament and smartening up its appearance for a happy rest in billets. The 223rd was marching down the riverside, confident of the cover of fog and gloom and unprovided with machine-guns, when the terrific barrages of British artillery roared down from the west and from the south, in an absolutely overwhelming cross-fire of shells ranging down from one ton in weight. Such rapid mechanical slaughter ensued, amid the confused and half-disarmed force of an army corps, as moved even the writer of the official German communiqué to state next day that "important losses" had occurred.

Then it was that the whirlwind method of intensive bombardment, against positions measured almost to an inch by months of aerial study and hill observation, gave wings of victory to the charging infantry. The relieving division in the valley reeled back, broken and demoralised, so that Colonel Freyberg, with a handful of unorganised scraps of naval men, was able to take Beaumont. The division that was being relieved could not get back properly to fighting trim before the British troops on the Thiepval line fell upon them. Chiefly using hand-grenades in large quantities upon the crowded and dismayed trenches, the attackers had a miraculously small amount of machine-gun fire to encounter, as the confusion of relief work and the fog made many gun-teams almost powerless. Hands went up by the thousand, and after all the slope had been won down to the river, a still more extraordinary event occurred. The German artillery did not fire. The victors sat out on the parapets smoking cigarettes and watching the conflict across the valley. Panic had struck the enemy Staff. The German guns did not fire because they were being moved back in frenzied haste to avoid capture.

The frontal attack across the Ancre marsh and river, against the low eastern sector of St. Pierre Divion, did not prosper with such

A BRAVE AND BRILLIANT LEADER.

Capt. (Temp. Lieut.-Col.) Bernard Cyril Freyberg, V.C., D.S.O., R.W. Surrey Regt. and R.N.D. He organised the attack on Beaucourt and Beaumont in Nov., 1916, and by his personality, valour, and utter contempt of danger secured the capture of the fortress-villages and 500 prisoners.

driving speed. Charge after charge was made against the village and the hillside; but the enemy's principal line of works remained unbroken. Thereupon, one of the life-savers of the British army crawled over the Ancre meadows and lifted up its steel snout. But at the critical moment something went wrong, apparently with the gear of the "tank." The crew closed the firing-holes and sat tight, and the Germans, as in the affair beyond Gueudecourt, gradually gathered courage to assail the fabulous machine of which they had hitherto heard much and seen nothing. An oldish, energetic colonel was the leading spirit in the affray. He was bent

upon distinguishing himself as the first man to capture in fight the last creation of the hated "Englishmen." Under his orders the "tank" was assailed in every likely manner. Men crawled under it to see if it could be blown up; men crowded around it, just outside the range of their own bomb splinters, and tried to crack its armour with high explosive. Very patiently the skipper of the "tank" waited, watching everything through his periscope. Not until the Germans were close about him in large force did he give his crew the command they eagerly awaited. Then the dead monster came to life, and with every gun firing a stream of bullets destroyed the throng of attackers. The sheltered enemy machine-gunners were next assailed by the lumbering terror, and early in the afternoon the infantry were in the village and beginning with electric torches to explore the great tunnel.

Dead "tank" comes to life

The result of the swift and crashing victory of the Ancre was something that could not be measured at the time. It staggered Germany, and led to Bethmann-Hollweg's open proposal for peace negotiations the following month. No doubt this futile proposal was in the nature of a double-barrelled gun, like the private proposal that was made soon after the Somme Battle in September.

The primary significance was patent. The new British and overseas armies had put the fear of death into the hearts of the ruling classes of the German Empire. Between the Somme and the Ancre the common opinion was: "We have them beaten."

[British official photographs.]

WASTE AND DEVASTATION ON THE COMELY FIELDS OF FRANCE.
Section of a captured German trench after bombardment by the British artillery, shattered into heaps of debris and reduced to unrecognisable and useless chaos. Above: British wiring-party going up to the front after heavy rain.

THE EFFECT OF THE SOMME OFFENSIVE ON THE GERMAN "WILL TO VICTORY."

By Basil Clarke.

EDITORIAL NOTE.—In the preceding five chapters of THE GREAT WAR our readers have been shown very clearly, and in great detail, the progress of the whole Somme Offensive of 1916; and they have seen how the British Army, starting at the beginning of July with certain initial shortcomings, had, before the end of November, but not without heavy sacrifice, established an unmistakable ascendancy over the enemy. In the following chapter Mr. Basil Clarke, well known as special correspondent of the "Daily Mail" in various theatres of the war, who was one of the Press correspondents present on the western front towards the end of November and the early part of December, 1916, illustrates, by means of quotations from numerous captured documents and interviews with prisoners taken during the later phases of the Somme Offensive, how the whole fabric of German military confidence was crumbling under the increasing pressure of the Allies, and particularly how the improvement in British heavy artillery had brought to the minds of the Germans along the western front their first real fear of doom impending.

Yes. Those damned British have certainly the devil in them. They are determined to pay our beautiful country a visit and to get there by force.—Extract from letter from his home at Algenrodt, found in the pocket of a German soldier captured during the Somme Offensive.

[British official photograph.

KING NICHOLAS ON THE WESTERN FRONT.
The much-tried monarch of the Black Mountain (Montenegro) and victim of the Austrian offensive in January, 1916, photographed with General Sir E. H. H. Allenby.

A S a result of the British Army's offensive on the Somme from July 1st onwards the Germans, as has been shown in preceding chapters, lost heavily in ground and in men; they lost specially-chosen positions on the fortification of which months of labour and all their experience of modern siege warfare had been expended, positions which they had regarded as impregnable and invincible. They lost men at a casualty rate never equalled by their armies in the whole history of the war. They lost also stores and many munitions of war. But in addition to all these losses they suffered yet further losses—losses which if less material, less easy to see and to assess, were not the less important and far-reaching in their results. These were losses in confidence, in hope, in keenness and enthusiasm for the fight, in pertinacity and doggedness of purpose—in all those valuable abstract qualities, in fact, which, fagoted together, make up the one comprehensive military word "moral."

The moral of the German army on the Somme and the moral of the German nation behind the Somme—both alike suffered a heavy depreciation as the result of the work done by our army during July, 1916, and later. In fact, there were competent critics of war who went so far as to assert that the blow to German military and national moral inflicted by our advances along the Somme and the Ancre in this phase of the war under review was the most conspicuous item in all the long list of benefits that accrued to the Allies as a result of that offensive.

This seems a sweeping claim, but it is far from being without basis. After personal investigation on the battlefields, after talks with German prisoners newly captured, after seeing what they had gone through and reading their own accounts of what they had felt and suffered, there remained for me personally no doubt that as a result of the Somme offensive the Germans had arrived at a new conception of what they were

171

RETURNING FROM MORVAL.
Some of our wounded, helpless but happy, being brought back from the front at Morval. Their general cheerfulness was in striking contrast to the dejection of the German prisoners employed as stretcher-bearers.

AFTER GUILLEMONT.
Another example of the way in which German prisoners were enlisted in the service of humanity. Four Teutons are here seen carrying one of our wounded to a dressing-station after the taking of Guillemont.

WAITING FOR THE AMBULANCE.
British and German wounded, made as comfortable as field conditions permitted by the first-aid care of the R.A.M.C., awaiting the arrival of the ambulance to convey them to the nearest dressing-station.

"up against." Their own oral testimony after capture and their own written testimony before capture (or before the idea of capture ever confronted them) leave no doubt of this. Captured German letters and documents show clearly that as week after week of the Somme push went by the German troops came gradually to a fearful realisation of what war and unsuccessful war might be, of what the British soldier, even the much-scorned "newly-made" British soldier, might be ; of what immense military resources those British soldiers had become possessed. And these German writings show further that as week **Decline of German** followed week there came to the German **confidence** soldier's mind the first vision of impending defeat ; after that a steady decline in confidence, till the border-line was crossed at last and hope gave way to despair and the certainty of defeat.

By means of German writings and documents captured during the offensive I will try to illustrate this gradual falling-off in German moral. First to show something of the battle conditions on the Somme as they appeared to German eyes, and something of the confusion and disorganisation caused by our relentless attacks. Here are a few days' entries from the diary of a man of the 14th Bavarian Infantry Regiment :

10-9-16.—At 11.30 p.m. our 3rd Battalion attacked at the same time as the 19th Infantry Regiment. But they fought against each other, as there is little difference at night between the steel helmets. Every one of the 3rd Battalion officers was wounded and some were taken prisoner. The ranks were very depleted.

11-9-16.—To-day we were relieved by the 7th Infantry Regiment. Also our attacking party is ready, as they have just come. Relieved at 4 p.m. and guided from our second line to our 3rd Company. Trenches quite fallen in ; plenty of dead and buried. Shrapnel and artillery continuously active. Now you see men running like cattle, but when they go into position no one is visible. On the way to the 6th Company we lost our way and arrived at our 3rd Battalion, which was attached to the 19th Infantry Regiment in support. Dead and half buried were to be seen in masses, both in and out of the trenches. Heads were sticking out in the middle of the trenches. Six or eight men were lying near me, piled one on top of the other. On the way to our 6th Company, which we finally found after a search of two and a half hours, there were just as many men and corpses buried by shell and men who had not been properly buried. We saw some hideous sights. However, we arrived safely. Half an hour later we went through communication-trenches Floss and Leiter to the third position.

12-9-16.—At 10 p.m. relief for the first and second line. We had some men wounded by shrapnel in going. After being relieved, the enemy's artillery fire became more intense and lasted so until morning. Lively artillery activity all day, also great enemy aerial activity. British aviators and artillery greatly to be feared. One often thinks their gunners get no food or pay unless they shoot continuously. Owing to their shrapnel fire, fires broke out. Every night our patrols had to go to the 4th Company, which is 550 yards more to the right, and also men from the 4th Company had to go to the 3rd Company. At 2 a.m. one man from each group is appointed to fetch food. This man is exposed to every danger from 2 to 8 o'clock. And what have we to eat for it all—1½ ounce cheese, ¾ ounce butter, coffee in service bottles not fit to drink, water would have been better. The day before last we had tinned meat which stank so much it made one sick. In the evening the artillery fire became less.

14-9-16.—From morning till night very heavy artillery fire of the heaviest calibre. Our position always under fire. Enfiladed on our right. We may thank our God if we come through this.

15-9-16, 1.30 a.m.—Our artillery is lively. The British artillery naturally replies. Every moment one thinks they will attack. Gas shells come. During the hour the 4th Company has had many casualties; we, on the other hand, fairly few. At daybreak, 7 a.m., the heavy British artillery begins with one hundred shots as one shot. One also hears shrapnel and small-calibre shell whizzing over our trenches. We ought to be relieved to-night. The 2nd Battalion had a very bad time in the second line, mostly from heavy-calibre shells.

15/16-9-16.—Apparently as soon as the British get a fresh waggon-load of ammunition they fire it off at us immediately. Their captive balloons look straight into our trenches. Aviators are busy guiding the enemy's artillery fire.

In the above striking document one can see something of the gradual appreciation by the mind of the writer that he and his comrades were confronted with a new and more difficult set of war circumstances than they had been accustomed to. He begins, unconsciously

Self-revealed enemy nervousness no doubt, with instances of the short-comings of his own army, then goes on to deal with the persistence of the enemy, then with the enemy's superiority in certain respects. As days go by there is an increase in the note of nervousness in his writing, and had that diary only been written up to a later date one might have been able to follow in the case of one man the gradual losing of hope and the coming of despair into the German ranks. Unfortunately for this purpose the capture of the writer put an end to his daily record of impressions.

The diary of a man of the 1st Company of the 66th Infantry regiment (52nd Division), however, may be of use in helping one a little further. Writing about a week later than the previous writer, and from much the same neighbourhood, he says:

[British official photograph.

GOOD WORK UNDER COMPULSION.

An incident behind the lines at Thiepval. British soldier bringing in two German prisoners, one of whom is seen carrying a wounded comrade of his captor. The other is a member of the German Red Cross.

[British official photographs.

WOUNDED GERMANS CAPTURED AND "CAGED."

German wounded under guard enjoying a brief halt by the roadside on their way to the "cages" after the taking of Guillemont, captors and captured finding solace in the cigarette. In circle: On arrival at one of the "cages" set apart for their temporary accommodation the wounded Teutons had their injuries attended to by surgeons of the Royal Army Medical Corps, after which they were removed to an internment camp.

For almost a week this most awful heavy artillery has been bombarding our lines, back and front. With an interval from nine till midnight the British have been sending over the heaviest shells day and night without pause. The dug-out shakes, creaks, and trembles. Now the entrance has again been destroyed. Always this nerve-racking feeling of anxiety that next moment one is going to be buried under the wreck of the dug-out. Up to now it has been all right, but "How long?" is the ever-anxious question. The 3rd Company to the right of us have had again two dug-outs destroyed. Several dead, etc. One is prostrated by this terrible suspense waiting for this awful fire to cease. In this way one becomes a nervous wreck.

British air superiority Letters written near the end of the same month (September) show a still greater German anxiety and the first dawning fear of defeat. An officer of the 170th Regiment, writing on the 27th to a brother-officer farther south, says:

You are still in Champagne and no longer in the witches' cauldron, on the edge of which we here are sitting, always waiting to fall into it from one side or the other. Just now it is very rough here again. In the past few days the air has been alive with aviators, and still more so with heavy shells, which have again been flying about our heads and behind our backs upon our poor comrades below us on our flank in Thiepval and on to our batteries. Yesterday at noon

BEHIND THE LINES ON THE SOMME.
[*British official photograph.*]
During the "great push" of 1916, when large numbers of German prisoners were being taken, such scenes as this were frequent behind the lines of the victorious advance. The British soldiers form a happy frame to a varied study in German facial expression.

there was an intense bombardment frightfully near us at Beaumont, and an attack which is said to have been repulsed. We shall not learn details until we see the official communiqué. You will readily understand if you study the map that we are following developments down there with strained attention. The number of guns—and of the heaviest calibre, too—which the British now possess is uncanny, and the amount of ammunition they fire off is quite fabulous. And what makes it so bad, their airmen are constantly over our lines discovering our batteries so that they may be peppered. They are always attacking our captive balloons, too, which is the same thing as putting our eyes out. Meanwhile, the sky is black with enemy balloons while our German airmen . . . . But of that I must say nothing. It would merely be pouring water into the Rhine. Solely the British artillery, the British Flying Corps, and their balloon observation have given them the successes they have obtained in their offensive. That they have gained no more is due to our German infantry. But we could save many thousands of lives if we had the British airmen and gunners. It makes one despair to think of it all.

From the rank and file of the German army about this time (September 30th) came letters that put even more forcibly the horrors through which they were passing and the effect which their sufferings had on their taste for fighting and their hopes of victory.

A man of the 66th Infantry Regiment wrote:

Dear Wilhelm,—I send you greetings from my grave in the earth. We shall soon become mad in this awful artillery fire. Day and night it goes on without ceasing. Never has it been so bad as this before. We sit all day deep down in the earth with neither light nor sunshine, but just waiting for death, which may reach us any moment. I ought not to write like this to you, dear Wilhelm, but I must. Again a big attack is coming on! Shall we ever meet again? God alone knows! This is awful!

A man of the same regiment wrote:

To-day I have changed my shirt for the first time for twenty-four days and washed myself. That is something. We have no rest from the enemy's artillery. It plasters us continually with guns of all calibres. The roar is tremendous. You, dear father, being a gunner, will know what guns of 9 in. to 11 in. mean and the sort of noise they make . . . Who thought this wretched war would last so long? People always thought it would be over this summer or autumn at latest, but one will soon have no more hopes. I think we shall have to spend another winter in the trenches. If only this fraud of a thing were over!

Letter in shorthand from a soldier:

Dear Friend,—At last the promised letter, but it will not be of the kind I had hoped at first. This is a terrible time for me, a time of great spiritual trouble. It is not a matter of my own welfare. That does not trouble me much. I have had for a time great doubts as to the result of the war, and for this I have had good reasons. You have read, no doubt, of Thiepval. But I can tell you that for us it was absolutely crushing. According to my idea, every German soldier from the highest general to the meanest private had the feeling that now Germany had lost the first great battle. I myself could not eat anything for eight days. And then the great submarine campaign! After that the friction with America! What disillusionment we had to suffer. For a soldier's heart every moment has become hellish torment.

A man of the 1st Musketeer Battalion, Fourteenth Army Corps, wrote:

In the past few days we have been having a very rough time indeed. The British attack us every day and have again penetrated into some of our positions. They constantly follow up their successes. We are in a fix here. If they go on doing the same for a few days more and we are not taken out the outlook is bad—for me. But we mustn't let our courage drop or we are lost. We must call on God to defend us and protect us so that we may come safely out of it again—for to-morrow we are going to be relieved.

The above writer gives incidentally a quaint illustration of the German egoist outlook. The Almighty is to be called upon for special protection till another German soldier comes along to take the writer's place in the threatened trench! The fate of the trench and of the new occupants seems not to enter into his calculations. His letter concludes with some apprehensions. "I hope the relief will go off all right, for we know nothing of our new platoon commander and nothing of the company."

Through the month of October the tone of the German troops, as revealed in their letters, became steadily more despondent. **All trenches destroyed** Writing on October 3rd, an officer of the 111th Regiment Infantry Reserve said:

We have now been sixteen days in the front lines and have built dug-outs. The British attack regularly every day. For the first few days we had to live without cover in the trenches till we made the needful holes for ourselves. It was highly precarious. We had losses again as heavy as those we had at Fricourt. From one single shell we had sixteen dead besides several wounded. I can tell you it is awful in the front line. Every day we get from one to two hours' intense bombardment and the fire from individual guns never ceases. You can imagine that the men go through frightful

High School and Church, and (centre) the Faidherbe Memorial, Bapaume. In 1870 a great battle was fought at Bapaume between the First German Army and the French Army of the North, commanded by the famous General Faidherbe. Right:} The Church Tower, Grandcourt.

General view of Beaumont-Hamel and (right) houses in that village wrecked by French artillery. After an unsuccessful attempt in June, the British recovered Beaumont-Hamel in November, 1916, the victors being the Royal Naval Division, led by Col. Freyberg, who was awarded the V.C.

The Town Hall and (right) the Place Faidherbe, Bapaume. The pictures on this page are reproductions of some of a series of photographs taken by officers and men of a German reserve corps stationed on the western front between Arras and Péronne. The series has a pathetic interest, because soon after the photographs were taken the great allied offensive began, and in the course of it many of the places included in the series were levelled to the dust.

CAMERA VIEWS OF BAPAUME, GRANDCOURT, AND BEAUMONT-HAMEL.

experiences. There is no longer a question of a dug-out for them. There is no longer even a trench, let alone a dug-out, in the first line. The trenches have been smashed up. The men lie in shell-holes. The dug-outs which we have made in order to get a bit of cover do not fare any better. Some were knocked out by shell fire even before they were ready. The trenches are constantly under fire. We are going slowly back.

A man of the 11th Company, 360th Regiment, wrote :

I must tell you that I am now on the Somme and things are going just wretchedly here. If I come back safe and sound I may indeed thank God. I could tell you much about things here, but I must not. We have had already six days in this dug-out. It is terrible here from morning till night. Our nerves will soon give way.

Diminishing German hopes

A man of the same company of the same regiment wrote, four days later :

Since October 1st we have been on the Somme. The horrors that go on here I will write and tell you if ever I come through this show. To put it shortly, it is frightful. Could one but get a light wound it would take one back to Germany. Every wounded man goes back. To-night we go into the first line, where the 1st and 2nd Battalions have had such heavy losses. But keep a stiff upper lip.

So far it will be noticed that the letters are those of soldiers who realised that they were in a very " tight place," but who had not completely given up hope or lost all their confidence. The extraordinary difficulties of the position seemed most to impress them, and it is worthy of notice in this matter that troops newly brought into the Somme battlefield seemed as deeply impressed with its awfulness as troops who had spent some time there. The 360th Regiment, for instance, did not go into the line till the

beginning of October, but after one week a member of it wrote about his nerves giving way.

But before very long hope vanished. The Somme came to be looked upon as one vast graveyard for German troops. Men even on coming into it gave up all hope of leaving it alive. Comrades already there warned comrades coming that they were going to their death. More than one letter spoke of the Somme battlefield as Germany's " blood-bath." Here are some characteristic letters, written in the second and third weeks of October, which speak for themselves.

From a man in the 111th Infantry Reserve Regiment :

Hans is dead. Fritz is dead. Wilhelm is dead. There are many others. I am now quite alone in the company. God grant we may soon be relieved. Our losses are dreadful. And now we have bad weather again, so that anyone who is not wounded falls ill. This is almost unendurable. If only peace would come !

From a man of the same regiment :

Dear Brother,—If only this war would end ! You know, it is far from jolly here in the Somme blood-bath. We have been now twelve days in filth. Day and night one has to be on one's feet. Our food is always cold. We are short of drink — only two mugs of coffee a day and perhaps a bottle of water that must be divided among three men. In part the trenches have quite caved in. We walk in mud up to our knees.

Growth of German pessimism

From a man in the Mörser Battalion :

Dear Nephew Alfred,—I was glad to get your letter last night. I should never have expected that you would be coming so near to me, for Cambrai is only about sixteen miles from here. I am convinced that we shall soon meet here, for your destination is most probably here also, and that is—to your death. Thousands lie dead already. It will not be so bad for you perhaps if you are not in the front-line trenches. But I must tell you at once that anything like what happens here has not happened before in this

[British official photograph.

ADVANCE, AUSTRALIA !—TO THE TRENCHES.

From their camp at the rear a typical body of men of the Australian Contingent are shown as they were setting forth to take their place in the firing-line on the western front. Many had exchanged the characteristic felt-hat for the less picturesque but more serviceable trench-helmet. They form a representative group of the Colonial troops who played such a conspicuous part in the epic battles of the Somme and the Ancre.

[*British official photograph.*

GRENADIERS AS ROAD-MENDERS.
Keeping the roads in order is a specially important feature of modern warfare, and the Grenadier Guards are here seen taking their share in this essential work.

war. But if it is your ill-luck to come here you will see for yourself. There is intense artillery bombardment every night which absolutely stuns us. Two weeks ago we were relieved, and our joy knew no bounds. But when we were twelve miles behind Cambrai we were fetched back by motor-cyclist!

From a man in the 110th Infantry Reserve Regiment:

We are here till Monday evening, the 16th. We have had dreadful losses again. I sha'n't get leave I suppose until we have left the Somme, but with our losses what they are, this cannot be long or there will not be a single man left in the regiment. I am glad to hear that Gustav is out of this filthy business. You can form no idea of what we suffer here. Perhaps you think the offensive is like the one in Champagne. Here the filth reaches over eighteen inches above one's boots. The British attack almost daily. The dead lie all around. But I won't go on telling of all this misery. Only one thing—if we are here for long I shall hardly see you again. Painful as it is for me to write you like this, it is my duty. Oh, if only this ghastly war would come to an end!

The following letter is an illustration of the utter abandonment of hope:

Dear Ewald,—You will wonder at this letter I am sending you to-day, and I cannot properly explain it myself. If after reading it you think it is nonsense you can burn it, of course. Perhaps it is due to a presentiment, perhaps to melancholy. You will think: Has he time to brood over things? But neither you nor anyone can understand unless you have been in the field here. Of those who are here—and on all our fronts—a very small number will ever see their homes again. And your class and year recruits will not be the last to fall victims to this murder, which was begun by a Higher Power. It is decreed by this Power that we shall be completely annihilated. The sooner we acquiesce the sooner will the end come, for the end will come after all. Since we shrink from confessing this it will be all the longer. And, after all, it has only been slow suicide.

Foreseeing the end.

The discomfort, depression, horror, and terror suffered by those German soldiers on the Somme were not without

their natural product — resentment. The soldiers resented the work that had brought about the war; they resented the methods by which the war was carried on. Officers and even the highest powers of the German State began to come in for burning criticism. Who was responsible for this deplorable state of affairs, for this wholesale slaughter, this appalling discomfort and all else? These questions clearly began to occupy the mind of the German rank and file, and letters curiously fearless and desperate, considering that any one of them might be read by censors and visited upon the heads of the writers, were written from the dank dug-outs and trenches of the Somme to friends and relatives away back

[*Canadian official photograph.*

SOLDIERS FROM CANADA ROAD-MAKING IN WESTERN FRANCE.
Men of the Western Dominion—accustomed, maybe, to paying taxes in the form of work on the making of public roads—found a comparatively congenial task on captured ground of the western front in France in preparing the way for further operations.

in Germany. And with this growing resentment there came also loss in moral. In men harbouring such ideas the fighting spirit could not remain at the old level. A curious attitude of "What is the use of it all?" crept into their letters; officers and Government were scoffed at, and even in writing there were confessions of a deliberate intention to shirk the fight and its duties and risks whenever occasion for doing so offered. Here is a characteristic letter, written during October, by a man of the 3rd Ersatz (Reserve) Regiment:

Dear Grete,—The war of 1914-16 is a low, scoundrelly affair, and the Prussian Government is just as guilty of it as any other Government. It is carried on with the object of murdering men so that the Government may keep the upper hand. The officers we have up to the rank of captain are mostly boys who have no idea of anything. They draw good pay and get good food and drink in abundance. We, on the other hand, live miserably, and don't even receive what we should. The German papers are always writing about other States, but the German Government is far worse. It deceives the people in a shameless way. One sees it now very clearly in this wholesale murder. One can hardly help being ashamed of being a German since we put up with all this. We should really turn our rifles round and destroy the whole

X

Government. If, dear Grete, I should happen not to return, remember what I have written to you about it all, and that " the gang " have caused us to be killed for mere sport. It is different with the enemy ; he has not nearly so many losses. If only one of us shows himself they let fly plenty of ammunition, but even though they may be working in hundreds without cover our guns do not fire. They are not allowed to do so, for there is a shortage of ammunition. Yet the newspapers write that it is the enemy who is short of ammunition—by which they mean that we ourselves are.

It is already quite clear that Germany is losing and is getting into a terrible state. For the upper ten thousand this may not be so bad, but for the poor people and the soldiers it is pitiful. In Germany the poorer people are just as grievously deceived as we are here. At first it grieved me very much to see what the officers squandered and the material they wasted. But now they cannot waste enough to please me. In fact, the thing to do is promptly to bury whatever material there is to carry when one is a member of a working-party—whether it is wood or nails or cement. For the sooner that the money is at an end the sooner this murder on a large scale will cease. We get lousy and completely ruined here. In the line the officers live in bomb-proof dug-outs ; we, on the other hand, have filthy, wet, tumble-down holes. And the pig of a feldwebel lieutenant says : . . . [very coarse]. That is what a German officer will say to men who are fathers of families ! Our officers are incapable of making war. I have heard it only too often from old soldiers that under proper leadership we should often have been able to do something without such heavy losses. If the young officers would not swagger so much, and would treat the men more like human beings, we should be more content and more would be accomplished. But we loathe our officers. We are bound to do. But the whole thing is nothing more than a swindle. In this wholesale murder we realise how completely we are under the knout. In a way, it is a piece of luck that all men are in this universal slaughter-yard, for all will be en-

Spirit of revolt lightened. Even the women in Germany must be getting to know how badly we Germans are cheated and deceived.

Here is another letter showing a similar intention to shirk all work and danger as much as possible :

Dear Jacob,—If only this terrible swindle would cease and let us get home . . . I can assure you that when I am in the trenches no work will be done. And, further, I shall not go in front of the trenches. What is the use ?

Were such letters as these the exception ? Without corroboration of some sort it would be hard to believe that this spirit of revolt and slackness was in any way common among the German troops who were bearing the

brunt of the repeated British attacks at this time. But there is ample corroboration from other sources that this fall in the moral of the Germany Army was very widespread, and, in fact, that some regiments were in a state not far removed from mutiny and refusal to fight. Desertions and surrenders became more common than ever before. Every Army, of course, has its " slackers," who will rather lay down their arms than fight, but the German Army, after the first few months of our offensive on the Somme, reached a state in which this spirit was dangerously prevalent. Malingering in all its forms was tried with a view to escape from service in the trenches ; and not by privates and non-commissioned officers alone, but even by commissioned officers. Several German soldiers' letters that came under my notice made sneering comments upon sprained ankles, neuralgia, chills, and other minor ailments " mysteriously contracted " by officers near the time when their turn to take duty in the line fell due. In the Bavarian regiments desertions became very common. Their men would cross the lines at night and come towards our trenches with uplifted hands, and with pleadings not to be shot at. A prisoner of the 393rd Regiment, taken at Courcelette, said that they had surrendered without firing a shot. The sentries had purposely refrained from giving the alarm when our men attacked, so that all might be captured without being forced to offer a resistance.

Readiness to surrender

Incidentally, the following German Order, captured at Courcelette, though referring to a slightly earlier period, throws some light on German discipline in that district :

IMMEDIATE.
   To the Camp Commandant, Courcelette.
   I request that in view of the relief of Infantry Reserve Regiment 121 by Infantry Reserve Regiment 99 taking place this evening, and in order to prevent drunkenness and excesses, all canteens in Courcelette should be immediately closed until the relief has been completed. There are a great many men belonging to different formations who are very drunk already this evening, which, considering that they are going into line to-night, is a serious matter.
                              (Signed) JOANNANT.

Prisoners of the 361st Infantry Regiment gave further striking testimony to the loss of moral among German troops. They stated that, after their regiment had lost 1,300 men in a fortnight, officers refused to lead their men to the front line, and that several companies on being ordered to march into the trenches refused to move.

Prisoners of the 74th Landwehr stated that one of their officers had told them, during a fearful preliminary bombardment by the British guns, that as soon as our men came over the trenches to attack they were to surrender.

In support of these amazing confessions—which, taken alone are perhaps not very sound evidence, seeing that they are the statements of prisoners, with whom it is always customary to put the best light on their actions and to make excuses for their conduct— there is the additional evidence of German " Orders of the Day " which made open reference to " many cases " of cowardice and refusal to obey orders. One " Regimental Order " read : " I must state with greatest regret that the regiment during its change of position had to take notice of the sad fact that the men of four companies, inspired by shameful cowardice, left their

[British official photograph.
ABANDONED BY THE GERMANS ON THE SOMME FRONT.
Part of a great heap of bombs, grenades, and miscellaneous stores which the Germans were forced to leave behind them when they were driven out of St. Pierre Divion during the great advance on the Somme. The abandonment of such materials indicates the rapidity of the " push."

companies on their own initiative and did not move into line." Another Order said: " Proofs are multiplying of men leaving their positions without permission and hiding at the rear. It is our duty —each officer at his post—to deal with this fact with energy and success."

Measures taken for dealing with this state of things were noteworthy more for their " energy " than for their " success." Executions for cowardice and for dereliction of duty became numerous. Prisoners state that a reign of terror was instituted in several regiments. Men were shot in batches. The choice confronting the reluctant fighters was that of being shot by the British if they went into the

[*French official photograph.*

GERMAN ARTILLERY FROM THE SOMME FRONT.
Many in number and varied in character were the specimens of artillery captured during the advance on the Somme front. These pieces, among those taken by the French, bear distinct evidence, in battered wheels and carriages and even broken muzzles, of the severity of the attack.

[*French official photograph.*
FROM " KULTUR'S " ARMOURY IN THE WEST.
Various forms of the weapons used by the Germans and captured by the French during the fighting on the Somme. In the foreground are two of the " flame-throwers " which the enemy, in defiance of civilised usage, introduced into warfare.

front trenches or by their own men if they loitered behind. Men had thus to be driven into the trenches. Undoubtedly many of them went forward with no other motive than that of deserting at the first opportunity. They waited their chance, and then made their way across the lines towards our trenches. Moonlight nights were especially favoured by them for this purpose. For then the British could see in good time the number of the men approaching the lines and their state as to being armed or not. In the moonlight nights of early December great numbers of the enemy came over in this way. More would probably have come but for the fact that our men were not always in the mood to treat them very graciously. That our men had a curious reluctance to taking deserters in this way was made clear to me more than once. One amusing objection was related to me in these words by a North-country soldier : " The blighters come over here in the night and eat up every bit of grub we've got in the trench."

When desertions and refusals of duty increased instead of diminishing, the German Command was reduced to the expedient—unprecedented, I think, in this war—of holding

up to German soldiers the example of the enemy, the hated British soldier and his fortitude and valour. Of this there is actual record in German Regimental Orders which were found in captured positions. One of them was in the following striking terms :

To the hesitating and faint-hearted in the regiment I (the commanding officer) would say these words : What the Briton can do the German can do also. But if, on the other hand, the Briton really is a better and superior being, he would be quite justified in his aim as regards this war—which is the extermination of the German.

There is a further point to be noted. This is the first time the regiment has been in the line on the Somme, and, what is more, we are here at a time when things are relatively calm. The British regiments opposing us have been in the firing-line for the second— and in some cases for even the third—time. Heads up, therefore, and play the man !

After this Order, which must have come as a last effort to spur on the German soldier, I will say no more on the fall in the moral of the German soldier than merely to record the fact that in December there were numerous desertions from even the Prussian Guard Division—a division which had hitherto **German divisions** stood for all that was most valiant in **wiped out** the German Army, and which had often given battles royal to some of our own finest troops.

The next point for consideration is this one : Admitting that German troops on the Somme suffered a serious set-back in moral as the result of our offensive, to what extent did this affect the German Army as a whole ?

Careful researches go to show that the average life of a German division in the Somme offensive was about three weeks, after which it had to be taken out to be reformed. Many of them were past re-formation, and were virtually wiped out. During the first ten weeks of the offensive fifty-three divisions were pitted against the British in this battlefield, and only fourteen of these fifty-three remained in the line at the end of that time.

By early December another sixty-seven divisions had known the horrors of that battlefield, making in all no fewer than one hundred and twenty divisions to pass through this awful ordeal. Many of those divisions, or, rather, the broken remnants of them, left the Somme to be scattered over the whole field of war, wherever Germany had troops. There would not be a theatre of war in which the dreadful tale of German losses and suffering on the Somme would not be the talk of every tent, billet, and mess. Each remaining soldier of those divisions would be as a missionary of " doubt "—doubt of Germany's chance of escape from her foes. And with that tale and its telling there would go into each listener's ear the true story of the New British Army—its men and its guns. Though the war was not yet finished, nor the Somme offensive yet over, a new respect and fear of British arms and doubt in his own would grip the German soldier's mind from that moment.

To what extent were the German people affected by the Somme defeats? Was the full sinister significance for Germany of these dreadful months ever allowed to reach the civil population of the country? The German soldiers' letters that have been quoted give ample illustration of what these writers would have told their friends and relatives if they could. But how could such letters ever have passed the German censors, who, as has been well established, kept a lynx eye over all correspondence going from the front to friends at home? Whether such dolorous letters would ever have reached their destination if they had not fallen into the hands of victorious British troops does not matter much, for if such letters did not reach home the writers of such letters reached home in their thousands—wounded and sick in mind and in body. The tale that they would pour out upon the bosoms of wives and mothers as they lay wounded and broken would be the very same tale as is told in those heart-broken letters from the trenches and dug-outs of the Somme. And that dreadful tale would now be told not in cold ink on cold paper but with living voice, in **Effect on German civilians** fullest detail, and with the glistening eyes and the shattered, shuddering frame of the speaker to illustrate the horrors of which he spoke. Undoubtedly the true tale of the Somme reached the homes of Germany quite safely.

Here are one or two letters written from Germany to men in the Somme trenches, showing how the news was percolating through in spite of all censorship.

Letter to a man of a Bavarian infantry regiment :

Things must be dreadful on the Somme. From what soldiers tell us who have been there it is hellish. But the papers only give the casualties of the enemy, while ours must be infinitely worse. —S. Kleintz.

A letter from Karlsruhe to the same man :

So you are fighting on the Somme! It seems terrible. We shall soon have had enough of it. It cannot go on much longer. At home here we have nothing more to eat. Last night we had an air-raid alarm and sat again in the cellars.

To a man of Infantry Regiment 153 :

Bitlorfeld.

Is not this world-conflagration ever to be extinguished? To-day men of 47 and 48 years went off. One's heart could bleed. Fresh soldiers again and again go off. Opitz's son is among the fallen on the Somme. Every day these dreadful sacrifices! What can come of it all?

To a man of Infantry Regiment 66 :

Brunkau.

So the British want to break through on the road to Bapaume? It is to be hoped they will not succeed. Also with the French on the Somme. Everywhere it is frightful. If only their superiority does not become too great! It seems hardly possible for you to withstand the assaults of your enemies.

To a man of Infantry Reserve Regiment 77 :

Luneberg.

I see from your letter that you have gone with your regiment to the Somme. May Heaven protect you in that dreadful place! I only wish that you may be made prisoner. I agree with you that those at home can form no idea of what you have to go through there. If some at home could do so, they would not fleece the mothers and wives and children of those who are fighting there, and suck their blood in the way they are doing now. One's blood freezes in one's veins when our shameful band of profit-snatchers shout out daily from their well-gorged throats : " Hold out ! '

To a man of an infantry battalion, Fourteenth Army Corps :

Every day whole trainfuls of wounded arrive here from the Somme. Do take care to get away from that dreadful place.

" That dreadful place "—so the Somme became known to German civilian and soldier alike, and on the Somme German military moral touched its lowest point since the beginning of the war.

Remembering the undoubted heroism of German troops at earlier periods of the war—their wonderful self-sacrifice, for instance, on the banks of the Yser, before Verdun, and elsewhere—one hesitates to believe that the horrors of **Deterioration of fighting spirit** unsuccessful warfare were alone responsible for this great lapse in fighting spirit. There were two further outstanding causes for it. In the first place the regiments that faced the British on the Somme and the Ancre in November and December were very different in make-up from the regiments that fought even in July. The men were less fine physically, and had had less military training. Some of them were well on in years while others were very young, the explanation being that all recent drafts into the regiments had been drafts of middle-aged men or of youngsters of the 1917 class. These latter were undoubtedly keen as fighters, but they had neither the strength nor the training of the older German soldiers. Of the best type of German soldier—the type that fought so resolutely, if so unsuccessfully, on the Yser—relatively few remained. Watching the prisoners coming into the " cages " after Beaumont-Hamel and the other fights of mid-November, many a British onlooker, myself among them, remarked upon the altered physique and bearing of the German troops. The finest type of German soldier was in the minority.

One of the German officers captured on that day, a member of a brigadier-general's Staff, was questioned about this falling-off in the appearance of the troops, and he made a frank admission. " The German soldiers of to-day," he said (as reported by a writer of the " Petit Parisien ") " are in no way comparable with the soldiers who fought under Von Kluck and Von Bülow two years ago. The finest troops of Germany, of which she was so proud, have melted away under the fire of the French and British guns. There now remain so few of them that they can only be used to stiffen regiments of young recruits and middle - aged men. The young ones go bravely into the fight and let themselves be killed, but they know nothing about warfare. The old ones, on the other hand, have no heart for war and fighting, and never lose an opportunity of surrendering. They are mere dummies, not fighters at all." This candid officer added that, if the Allies did pierce the lines on the Somme, Bapaume must fall.

[*British official photograph.*

A SOMME MESSAGE.

With a handy piece of chalk the British soldier often indulged his ever-ready humour in such a manner as this, the words roughly inscribed on the gun being the " compliments " that accompanied the shell upon its way into the lines of the enemy.

General Robert Nivelle, Commander=in=Chief of the Armies of the North and North=East.

Sand-bagged shelters and soldiers' graves in a shell-shattered avenu...

long the borders of the Yser Canal between Boesinghe and Lizerne.

Mitrailleuse section of the Belgian Army heading a march to the front.

New fleet of armoured cars built for the reconstituted Belgian Army

Without accepting all that this candid enemy had to say in criticism of his own troops, there was undoubtedly more than a grain of truth in what he said, as was borne out by the observations on the field of battle of myself and more expert military observers.

Before I leave this point concerning the physical quality and military training of the new drafts supplied to make good the great gaps made in German regiments which visited the Somme, let me quote one illuminating letter, written by a soldier whose battalion had left the Somme " for repairs," to a comrade still remaining there :

My Dear Wilhelm,—You do not know Strehlon, but one thing will certainly interest you. Since September 1st our battalion has received 600 recruits, but they are not the sort of people that can be any use in war, at any rate, though they may be some good for work on garrison duty. These people, who practically without exception have done no previous military service, are to be trained for only three weeks and then to be sent off to the areas behind the front. They relieve those men fit for active service who are still behind the front. I believe our Hindenburg is responsible for this idea. Certainly he intends to strike a decisive blow, and in order to bring the greatest possible force into action he is relieving the people behind the front. You can't imagine what " apparitions " there are among those passed as fit—garrison or working battalions. In spite of that, the medical officer has passed about 350 men out of 600 as fit for " active service." Yes, Wilhelm, you would be astonished and I am also. I, myself, am only fit for garrison duty. But I can't help it. My wound is still suppurating. So, recently we have had two more declarations of war, but after the rest this is nothing. What it means is that our front has been lengthened, and—owing to that—the war.

The second reason for the falling-off in the fighting spirit of the German troops opposing our men on the Somme—over and above the great fact that they were beaten—lay in the doleful news which **Despair in German** they were all this time receiving from **homes** home. Though the richer people of Germany may have been able at this time to get all the food they needed, it is clear that the poorer people —the wives and children and mothers of Germans fighting in the ranks—were suffering great hardship, and in some cases actual hunger. To their men-folk, themselves struggling in the trenches against a powerful and relentless enemy, these women wrote letters that would have taken the " fight " out of almost any man. Imagine the feelings of any soldier, himself in desperate danger and suffering acutest discomforts, upon receiving from his wife at home a letter such as one of the following :

Whenever you come home do try to bring a bit of meat or fat with you. We have nothing.—(Letter from Hamburg, 22-9-16.)

I wish I, too, were a soldier like you. One gets enough to eat then —(Letter from Mouschwitz, 19-10-16.)

It is a pity that you cannot come on leave. But what do the great care about the poor ? Everybody else may perish if only they may fill their bellies. But they cannot escape God's punishment.—(Letter from Meisdorf, 12-10-16.)

Erna went to Oberniebelsbach to-day to see if we cannot get a bit of fat or butter or eggs. You cannot get anything here, and the food from the war-kitchens (Kriegsküche) is uneatable.—(Letter from Karlsruhe, 8-10-16.)

It will soon come to this here—that we shall live on dry bread, potatoes, and salt. . . . Klegstoten has returned from England, having been released. He says there is plenty to eat there, and that anyone can buy enough **Sacrifice in** there, and that things are not nearly so dear as **vain** here.—(Letter from Goostenmunde, 11-10-16.)

If you have any old stockings, please do send them home. We get no wool at all.—(Letter from Dortingen, 8-9-16.)

We get half a pound of bread a day regularly, and a pound and a half of potatoes, and a quarter of a pound of meat weekly. On that we are to work hard ! We just cannot do it. But what are we to do ? It cannot be altered.—(Letter from Lothfold, Hanover, 18-9-16.)

I have by me further letters from German civilians which might be quoted to show gravest discontent with other war woes besides the food scarcity—with the work shortage, for instance, and poverty ; with the recruiting hardships ; with casualties, and the insatiable life-appetite of war. But enough has been done. From the documents already quoted in this chapter one sees German soldiers writhing under the continual hammer-blows of a relentless and superior enemy ; German soldiers reduced to sloth, and even to cowardice, by the dreadful nature of their sufferings. Behind these soldiers one sees also—in these documents—a nation fast becoming not only intolerant of their own hardships, but more and more convinced as week followed week that their sacrifices were vain, that their manhood was doomed.

Noting these things, so strikingly testified by German pens and lips, it seems not too extravagant a conclusion if one marked down in history the Somme offensive of 1916 as the starting-point of the end—of the great German collapse. Those " damned British," thanks to Germany's own handiwork, had certainly " the devil in them " and meant to pay their Fatherland a visit. Germany seemed, before 1916 was ended, to have realised this at last.

[*British official photograph.*

MUTE APPEAL FROM FRANCE FOR HELP AND SYMPATHY.
Vivid presentation of the havoc wrought by invasion in the remote recesses of pastoral France. The pitiful desolation of the scene seems to have caught and stirred the imagination of the British soldiers halted for a moment on the muddy road

DEFENDERS OF THE LAST UNVIOLATED STRIP OF THEIR HOMELAND.

Belgian troops on a road on the Yser passing as they marched to and from the trenches. The Belgian line ran from Nieuport to Neuve Eglise, less than thirty miles, and guarded the seven or eight miles in depth of Belgium that were left uninvaded.

RUSSIA COMMEMORATES HER PATRON SAINT'S DAY BY HONOURING BRAVE BELGIANS.

The Tsar of Russia took the occasion offered by St. Nicholas' Day—December 6th, 1916—to mark his appreciation of the bravery of Belgian soldiers, and through one of his generals conferred medals upon a number of officers and men at the Belgian Headquarters.

BELGIUM UNDER TWO FLAGS:

The Homeland Under the German Heel and the Renaissance of the Army on the Yser.

By F. A. McKenzie.

Position of Belgium in the Second Year of the War—Passionate Devotion of the People to their King and Queen—German Military Administration and Civil Government of the Country—Modification of Local Government—Press Censorship—" La Libre Belgique "—German Exaction of Indemnities, Fines, and Extraordinary Taxes—Persecution of Individuals—Patriotism of the Church—Cardinal Mercier and his Lenten Pastoral—Vain German Attempts by Bribes and Threats to Secure Belgian Labour—Registration and Deportation of All Able-Bodied Labour—Cardinal Mercier's Protest to the Civilised World against the Enslavement of the People—German Acquisition of the Material Wealth of the Country—Urgency of the Food Supply Question—The Commission for Relief in Belgium and Mr. Herbert Hoover's Model Organisation—Methods of Purchase, Transportation, and Distribution of Foodstuffs—Benevolent Work for the Destitute—Dr. Lucas's Report on the Health Conditions of the Population as a Result of the German Occupation—Some Main Facts of the Reconstruction of the Belgian Army—Work of the Belgian Army during 1915 and 1916—Vain German Attempts to Create Schism between Flemings and Walloons—Belgian Refugees in England—What Will the Future Be ?

THE position of Belgium in the second year of the war was one of extraordinary interest. Almost the whole of the kingdom was occupied and controlled by the enemy. The King and Government had been driven back on a little strip of their own territory, stretching from Nieuport to Neuve Eglise, a strip less than thirty miles long and seven or eight miles broad. During these weary months of waiting this was all that was left of their European country to King Albert and his faithful subjects.

Flanders and Hainault, Namur and the province of Luxemburg, Liège and Mons, the great cities of Antwerp, Brussels, and Ghent, and nearly all of the sea-coast had passed for the time into German hands. The strip left to the Belgian King was most of it nothing but a ruin, and all was under the fire of the enemy guns.

The little summer seaside resort of La Panne, so small that it does not find a place in many atlases, was the temporary Belgian capital. The quaint old town of Furnes, full of vivid memories of the days of the Inquisition, was the chief centre of population. Here and

THE LION OF FLANDERS.
Throughout the war King Albert (right) refused to leave the strip of kingdom left to him behind the Yser. He gave his whole time to his Army, and was a familiar figure in the front trenches.

there a village was left half whole. Loo, for example, still kept its houses intact on one side, although its beautiful old church to the east had been wantonly shattered by German shells. Ypres, the ancient manufacturing town of West Flanders, still in the hands of the Allies, was smashed to worse than nothingness, and most of its houses were piles of rubbish—the cathedral ruined, the Cloth Hall destroyed, and not a house whole in the place.

Yet from this strip of ruined land King Albert and his advisers started bravely on their work of reconstruction. The hearts of his people from Ostend to Arlon still beat true to him. Day by day men made their way through the German barriers of electrically-charged wire into Holland so that they might join their King and die for their country if needs be. The French Government provided Belgium with official quarters in Havre, with land on which munition factories could be built, with port accommodation at Gravelines, and with quay room at Calais. The Belgian Army, almost annihilated in its brave and successful efforts to keep the Germans back on the Yser, was reconstructed to meet the new conditions, and soon a powerful and well-armed

187

BELGIAN RECRUITS IN TRAINING IN FRANCE.
France provided camps for the man-power of Belgium that survived in freedom after the German onrush was stayed, and here every man underwent training to take his place in the reconstructed Belgian Army.

PRACTICE WITH LIVE BOMBS.
Bomb practice in a training camp for Belgians in France. In handling these most destructive weapons action had to be automatic, for the life of every man in a trench hung on the fraction of a second.

LEARNING HOW TO STALK THE LURKING FOE.
If sheer courage were needed to capture a trench, caution and cunning had to be superadded in clearing the enemy out of it. This part of the modern soldier's craft was an essential part of military training.

force arose from the heroic remnants of the old. Here was a King with his kingdom almost gone, and yet showing to his people and to the world at large a supreme example of courage and determination. "Punch" well expressed his position in a cartoon. The Kaiser was shown taunting King Albert. "You have lost all," he sneered. "Not my soul!" the King replied.

A large number of Belgian people, several hundred thousand, had escaped from the German rule in Belgium and made their homes in France, Holland, or England, or in the little bit of remaining Belgian dominion, but over seven million people still remained in the German occupied territories. These were made to feel to the full the iron heel of the Hun. The series of outrages which marked the German entry into Belgium, the destruction of villages and towns, the hangings and shootings at the will of drunken soldiers, and the nameless brutalities of August, 1914, came to an end. A system of callous exploitation was set afoot—fines raised on any and every excuse, heavy taxation, and the wholesale plunder of means of production. The country was "bled white." And then, to crown all, Germany, in defiance of all humanity and international law, began the wholesale deportation of the civilian population of the country to what was virtually slave labour.

Under the iron heel

Ruined towns and villages still bore witness to the early days of the German invasion. The most dreadful of these was Dinant, where 1,263 houses out of 1,375 had been completely destroyed, and where the people were weighed down with the unthinkable memories of the black days when the Germans shot unarmed leading citizens, turned their machine-guns on women and children in the caves by the river-bed, and slaughtered in a few days 800 people of all ages and both sexes. Then there was Louvain, where the heart of the city with the old university building and the wonderful library had gone, and 1,120 houses had been destroyed.

Termonde, a busy town close to Antwerp, had been completely wiped out at the will of the German general who, with his aides, had sat in a garden by the riverside drinking champagne and singing while the town was burning to the ground. Villages by the score and hundred told the same tale of wanton destruction, villages ranging from the Liège border to the outskirts of Ghent. In four of the nine provinces 18,207 houses and public buildings had been burned or otherwise destroyed.

Much more serious, however, than the destruction of the houses and the killing of people at the beginning of the war was the economic condition of the country. Manufacturing had almost totally ceased. The Belgian worker in iron would not produce war munitions for Germany, despite the utmost coercion, and little else was wanted.

Manufacturers could not obtain raw material from abroad and could not export their goods even if they made them, for Belgium was closely blockaded by the Allies. The country could not produce sufficient foodstuffs for itself, and had it not been for the generous aid from outside, aid which reached the country through the American Commission for Relief in Belgium, a large part of the population must have starved. As it was, by the autumn of 1916, one-third of the population depended for their food on charity.

The kingdom of Belgium still existed. That was a fact of the utmost political importance. King Albert ruled not over a State of 11,373 square miles as in the old days, but over two hundred square miles of largely ruined land in Belgium itself and a Colonial dominion in Central Africa. Yet he was still a King in being, recognised by other Great Powers as a reigning sovereign, having his Army, his Court, and his Ministers. His palace was a country house at La Panne.

The King and his devoted wife put on one side for the time the trappings of State. They sent their children to school in England, having them back with them for the holidays. The King gave his time to his Army. Day by day his car might be seen tearing along the roads behind the lines. It would stop, now at Dixmude, now at Elverdinghe, now at divisional or brigade headquarters, and the tall, slim, and singularly youthful figure of the monarch would emerge for a conference with his generals or a word with his soldiers. He would leave his car at the final point near the German lines to which cars could possibly go, and would set out on foot round the front trenches. What thoughts must have been his as he paced the shallow lines on the west bank of the Yser Canal and looked across at the fair country—his own land— on the other side now held by his foe!

Brave King and devoted Queen

The King was not always alone. The Belgian people in those days accepted one statement as unquestionably true. "Wherever the King is," they told you, "the Queen will be near." Queen Elizabeth was originally a German princess, for she was one of the Bavarian Royal Family. "But she has done her best to wipe out that fact," said the Belgians. Her time was largely devoted to works of mercy and charity, supervising the hospitals, cheering the wounded, and looking after the well-being of her husband, as any middle-class wife might have done. Sometimes she would get away from her wounded and her sick and set out with the King himself into the trenches.

[*French official photograph.*

LESSONS IN TRENCH WARFARE.
Another camera-impression of the newly-organised Belgian Army in training. This photograph shows a company lesson in trench warfare at one of the training centres.

[*French official photographs.*

CAVALRY OF THE NEW BELGIAN ARMY IN TRAINING.
Horses and men enjoying an exhilarating gallop down a vast stubble field near a cavalry instruction camp. Above: Up the bank and through the stubble again. The Belgian cavalry had ever been noted as splendid horsemen, and the squadrons that rode along behind the line in the waiting months of 1916 were as fine as any Belgium had ever seen.

USELESS DESTRUCTION BY A FOE ANGERED AT BEING BAULKED OF HIS DESIRE.

An enemy bombardment on the Belgian front. The Belgian Army held a section of the line from immediately north of Ypres to Nieuport by the sea. During 1915 and 1916 the Belgians were attacked by the Germans with sufficient frequency to keep them in touch with the realities of active war, but the fighting they experienced was little more than skirmishing in comparison with the tremendous battles that raged on the other fronts.

Every Belgian regiment had stories to tell of how the Queen had been among them, how she had never flinched when the shells whistled overhead, and how she had laughed contemptuously when a German bullet angrily spat by. The soldiers told how when the fighting had been hard and they were wearied, they found their young Queen there, cheering them, helping them, encouraging them. Quite early in the war Queen Elizabeth became almost a traditional and sacred figure to the Belgian Army. Men who had lost all faith in the Unseen, men to whom the ancient traditions of the Catholic Church, the Church to which their forefathers belonged, were nothing more than mockery, found a new saint to hold in veneration—their Queen.

Rule by martial law

Let us attempt to picture Belgium as it was in the second and at the beginning of the third years of the war. The country was at first entirely under military administration. The railways were solely available for the Army. Posts, telegraphs, and telephones could not be used. People were not permitted to leave the districts in which they lived, except after obtaining special military permits. Everything was done to discourage the inhabitants from going from place to place. Military governors ruled by martial law. There were constant hunts for spies and for escaped prisoners, and the punishment of those suspected of aiding the Allies was prompt and very heavy. The German troops at this time were, in some cases, guilty of many outrages; although in other districts it is only fair to say they behaved with restraint and moderation.

The first great development came with the establishment of civil government over a part of Belgium. The conquered country was split up into three divisions. There was first a limited area immediately behind the fighting-line, called the " operation zone"; this was purely a military area. Behind that was the " Étape zone," covering much of East and West Flanders, which was governed directly by the Army. The larger part of Belgium was, however, regarded as occupied territory, and was called the " occupation zone " with a joint civil and military general government over it. At the head was the German Governor-General, Baron von Bissing, who succeeded General von der Goltz, and his administrative offices were known as the Kommandantur. In the " occupation zone " the people were gradualy allowed more liberty of movement, and the use of railway and internal post was restored.

Throughout the whole of the country, with the exception of the " operation zone," the old system of local government was maintained, under German control, and with certain modifications imposed by the Germans. Thus the communes and municipalities had their mayors (or burgomasters); the provincial councils were maintained and were made to vote the money demanded by Germany; the civil courts still sat. In some cases, such as local disturbances due to lack of food, the German authorities refused to take action. " This," they said, " is the business of the Belgians themselves It has nothing to do with us." The population in the area of civil government numbered close on 6,000,000.

The Press was rigidly censored. Some of the leading Belgian papers, refusing from the beginning to submit themselves to German domination, had closed down their offices and transferred their headquarters to London. One of the most notable of these was the great Brussels daily, " L'Indépendance Belge," which, from almost immediately after the German occupation in Brussels, appeared in London. Another was "La Métropole," which also issued a London edition, after closing up its original offices. **Treatment of the Press** The papers that decided to continue publication in Belgium itself had a very precarious and difficult existence. They were suspended or suppressed at the will of the authorities.

The importation of foreign newspapers was strictly prohibited, and any person found with one of them was severely punished. But no punishment could restrain the Belgian people in their hunger for news. They disbelieved, and not without abundant reason, the German statements of the progress of the war. German placards pasted on the walls of the cities giving news of victories were torn down or pasted over. A new business arose—that of smuggling in English and French newspapers. Certain tobacco merchants were reported to be agents for this contraband trade. Runners made their way through the highly-electrified wires separating Belgium from Holland with their precious loads. As much as fifty francs was paid for a copy of the " Times."

When an English paper was smuggled in, girls set to work typing out sections of it, and these sections were passed round from hand to hand. Some of the newspaper agents were shot in making their way over the border; others were captured. German spies got to work, and a number of tradesmen accused of being distributing agents were arrested and severely punished. Even girls were not spared. Baron von der Goltz issued a special edict calling the attention of the population of Belgium to the fact that the sale and distribution of newspapers and of all news reproduced in any manner, which was not expressly authorised by the German censorship, was strictly prohibited.

A newspaper mystery " Every offender will be immediately arrested and punished by a long term of imprisonment." This threat was carried out. For example, one girl, Camille Pousseur, was sentenced to two months' imprisonment for buying foreign newsapers and copying them.

The German authorities were greatly disturbed by the secret publication of an exceedingly outspoken patriotic paper, " La Libre Belgique." It appeared irregularly, and the manner of its distribution was a mystery. Every prominent German in the country would one morning find a fresh issue delivered at his house. Sometimes it arrived by the revived post ; sometimes it had been slipped into his letter-box during the night. Its literary contents were witty and scathing. It made fun of the enemy in every possible way. It declared that it was issued by the Belgian Patriotic Propaganda and submitted to no censorship. Its price was " from zero to the infinite—purchasers are requested not to exceed this limit." It gave as its telegraphic address " Komman- **Defying the** dantur, Brussels." " Our general offices **censorship** are installed in an automobile cellar owing to the impossibility of having them in a stationary place." " Advertisements : Business being at a standstill under German domination, we have suppressed the advertisement page, and advise our supporters to save their money for better times."

Its favourite butt was Von Bissing, the Governor-General. On one occasion it declared that Von Bissing was the same man as the Lieutenant von Bissing mentioned by Sir William Russell, the famous " Times " correspondent, as one of the looters of treasures from the Chateau of St. Cloud during the Franco-Prussian War. On another occasion it appeared with a photo of General von Bissing showing him deeply immersed in reading " La Libre Belgique." Under-neath he was made to say, " How happy I am to be able at last to read a paper which is not under German censorship and to be able to learn the truth."

It had a dictionary of words beginning with the letter " K," a favourite letter with the Germans. Here are some of the definitions :

Kathedral.—Target for 17 in. guns.
Kamerad.—The word German troops use to signify their wish to surrender.
Katastrophe.—The finish of strategic movements planned by the Crown Prince on land, and on sea by Admiral von Tirpitz.

[Belgian official photograph.

NEW MEN, NEW METHODS, AND NEW MACHINES OF THE BELGIAN ARMY.
Quick-firing gun emplacement on the Belgian front, with a trench egress at the rear which enabled the men to leave their post without exposing themselves to enemy fire. The reconstituted Belgian Army was equipped so generously and so efficiently, especially in regard to its artillery, trench mortars, and machine-guns, that early in its history it was able to boast it had more machine-guns to a regiment than any other one of the Allies.

TRENCH-MORTAR PRACTICE.
Belgian recruits at trench-mortar practice
on a training ground in France.

The whole of the extensive German spy system in Belgium was put to work to discover the editors, printers, or supporters of this paper. A reward of several thousand pounds was offered to anyone disclosing the identity of the editors or publishers. Domiciliary searches were made in the homes of people supposed to be connected with it. At one time the Germans suspected that M. Lemonnier, the Acting-Burgomaster of Brussels, might have something to do with it. The Town Hall and M. Lemonnier's private house were searched in the most rigid manner, but nothing was found. On another occasion the Germans ransacked a convent from roof to cellar, believing that the paper was produced there. But equally in vain. After each search, out would come "La Libre Belgique" again, once more wittily flaying its foes.

The German lacks a sense of humour, and the sprightliness of the paper made the authorities more furious than ever. The number of arrests rapidly increased. A lady, Miss Schepens, was sentenced to five years' imprisonment for supposed connection with the hated sheet. A lawyer at Liège, M. Jean Davin, was sent to prison for three months on the charge of having contributed to it and having published some pamphlets without leave of the censor. Two Jesuit Fathers and a boy of sixteen, Jean Lenertz, of Louvain, son of a professor who was killed during the massacres in Louvain, were arrested, and one of the Jesuits, Dubar by name, was sentenced to twelve years' hard labour in July, 1916.

"La Libre Belgique"

It might have been thought that the Germans would have had statesmanship enough to attempt to conciliate the Belgian people and to endeavour to steal their allegiance from the Allies. No doubt they wished and intended to do this, but it soon became evident that the German administrators were not men great enough to accomplish

it. They treated Belgium as a conquered country that had to feel the heel of the conqueror.

One of the first things done was to exact an enormous indemnity from the country as a whole, an indemnity of £19,200,000 to be paid in monthly instalments. This was afterwards made a permanent monthly contribution of forty million francs (£1,600,000) during the war. An extraordinary tax was collected from the property of absentees, amounting to ten times the ordinary personal tax. Heavy fines were inflicted on towns and cities on various excuses, and humiliating punishments were imposed. Thus the Governor-General imposed a fine of £50,000 on Brussels because it celebrated the Belgian National

ABSORBED IN A TASK OF INTEREST TO ALL.
Practising the use of double grenades fired from trench-mortars at a training centre. All the very latest improvements of trench artillery were lavishly supplied to the Belgians in the course of the re-establishment of their Army in readiness for the carrying out of its heroic struggle

Fête Day. Although the fine was afterwards withdrawn, the fact that it had been imposed rankled. The townspeople of Malines were sentenced for the same offence to remain indoors between ten o'clock at night and five in the morning. The village of Hamont was fined £50, and all the people ordered to be in their houses by 7.30 every night for fifteen days, because the Germans disapproved of the conduct of one youth there. The military governor of the province of Antwerp fined that city £5,000 because allied airmen had made raids near to it.

Then the Germans tried to interfere with the ordinary life of the people. The names of railway-stations were altered from French to German. Towns were rechristened. The very time of day was changed to German time, and a process of Germanisation was attempted. The use of the French language in official transactions was forbidden. It was forbidden to use French in public notices, and French street names were abolished. These were little things which hardened the hearts of the people against alien rulers more than many great changes.

Next came a series of persecutions. People were arrested and punished on the mere suspicion of disliking the Germans.

This did not apply only to Belgians. One officer in the United States Army, Major Dutton, was fined £25 by the military tribunal in Brussels for disrespectful conduct towards a German officer. Had the Germans been able to collect fines from all Americans who spoke disrespectfully of their officers their problem of war finance would have been solved! A Brussels doctor was arrested for speaking his mind too freely in a tramcar. Numbers of men, some of them in eminent positions, were taken away without warning to prison at Charleroi or elsewhere, kept there for some time, and then released without apology or explanation.

In August, 1916, the German authorities arrested one hundred

ANCIENT BUILDINGS THAT ATTRACTED THE ATTENTION OF " KULTUR."
Ruins of a famous tower, once a landmark in an historic Belgian town. Much of the havoc in Belgium was wrought gratuitously, and was not incidental to necessary artillery action, material destruction being part of Germany's policy wherever her armies penetrated.

[French official photograph

HALL-MARK OF THE HUN.
Shattered villas, with graves in every front garden, showing how the Germans carried on their system of ruination in Flanders.

Jesuit Father was arrested in the Church of the Sacred Heart at Brussels for a sermon he preached.

MM. Timmermans and Walrand have been sentenced to six days' imprisonment for having insulted some Germans.

The assistant stationmaster of the Gare du Nord, Brussels, was arrested some time ago and imprisoned. No one knows what has become of him.

MM. Brilla and Benoy, of Antwerp, have been condemned to a month's imprisonment for refusing to make known to the German authorities the hiding-place of an old soldier.

Some time ago we reported the incident of a postman of Reckheim being arrested as he got out of the train along with his young wife and brother-in-law. The Germans have tortured the woman so that she has died.

M. Gerard Smeets, a contractor of Maaseyck, has been imprisoned for several weeks for having refused to work for the Germans. He has, however, been compelled to put his workmen, etc., at the disposition of the Germans,

and fifty persons at Brussels on suspicion of having taken part in the formation of a Belgian association designed to serve as an intermediary between soldiers on the Yser front and their relatives in the occupied portion of Belgium. A manufacturer in Antwerp was condemned to five years' penal servitude for corresponding with his sons at the front. He was not alone. In Brussels, in particular, many people were sentenced to several years' imprisonment on the same charge. In Ghent seventy women were arrested for having received letters from their husbands or sons in the Army. The boat which carried the letters had been betrayed by spies and seized. The number of people executed in Belgium for high treason against Germany was estimated by the summer of 1916 to have reached five hundred. This did not include those who had been summarily executed as francs-tireurs. The Belgian papers were full of items such as these:

Father Fallon, Jesuit, Prefect of the Old College of St. Michel at Brussels, has been condemned to three years' imprisonment and has been deported to the citadel of Rheinbach for having helped some young men to rejoin the Belgian Army.

Forty Jesuits have already been imprisoned. Recently a

and they have had to work night and day for the enemy.

Westwezel has been fined £40. Some days ago the Germans discovered an old pail hanging from the chains of the electric standards. Without taking the trouble to discover the culprit, they saw a means of getting money and demanded the fine. None of the inhabitants are allowed to leave their houses after seven in the evening.

The lawyer De Baer, after eighteen months' captivity, has escaped, and has arrived in England.

Five young men of Louvain have been condemned to three and six months' imprisonment for having sung in the streets of Louvain and Heverlé.

Scorn for the invader

The Governor of Namur district has punished the whole population of the town for having cheered an aviator.

All the inhabitants of the boulevards of Brussels have to be in their houses by 8.30 in the evening, and all lights to be extinguished at that hour. The reason for this is that the people cheered with frenzy an allied aviator who flew round the town.

Joseph Mahi, of Val-St.-Lambert, has been condemned to death, his wife and their daughter, aged ten, to two years' penal servitude. Reason unknown.

The people of Belgium treated the invaders with contemptuous scorn. The Germans had occupied their country; they were in possession of the machinery of

REVOLVING ANTI-AIRCRAFT GUNS IN BELGIUM.
Her geographical position made Belgium the theatre of great aerial
activity during the " waiting months," and her air service was energetically
developed, the Allies providing it with the best and latest material.

A "SOIXANTE-QUINZE" MOUNTED ON A PIVOT.
The French " 75 " proved a most effective anti-aircraft weapon. Mounted
on pivots, like this one used in Belgium, the " 75's " were mainly responsible for the fact that German flying men gave Paris a wide berth.

government ; they could punish with death if they wished.
All that was self-evident.   But these things did not prevent
the Belgians as a whole from regarding the Germans
with open contempt.   One of the favourite amusements
of the street boys in Brussels was to march behind the
German soldiers, mocking them by attempting a ridiculous
goose-step.   This was carried so far that the German
authorities had to punish a number of the boys to stop it.

When the people of Belgium were forbidden to keep
their national Fête Day, July 21st, as a holiday, and were
ordered to open their shops and conduct business as usual,
many of the shopkeepers multiplied the prices of their goods
that day fourfold and fivefold, while some
lads were around the street early in the
morning and emptied pots of paint in
front of the doors of certain pro-German
shops so that no one should be able to enter.   The tradesmen
dressed their windows for that day in extraordinary fashion.
One milliner had nothing but green hats and green ribbons
in her window.   The authorities were furious.   This
was treason !   The milliner was fined £500.   A fruit
merchant committed a yet worse offence.   He dressed his
window with red tomatoes, yellow citron, and black raisins,
thus making the Belgian colours.   He was fined the same
amount.   The Governor-General could do nothing but inflict
heavy fines on Brussels and the other cities, and childish
punishments, such as that people should remain within doors.

**Fines for window-
dressing**

194

The attitude of the Church cannot be passed over without record.   Belgium in the days before the war was
divided perhaps more sharply than any other country in
Europe into clerical and anti-clerical parties.   The clerical
party was opposed to conscription, and the Army held that
it was responsible for the delay in military preparations
which caused Belgium to be so ill-equipped when war
broke out.   The Army consequently felt very bitterly
towards the priesthood as a whole.   Yet in the dark
days of German occupation many of the priests set splendid
examples of patriotism.

In large numbers of churches throughout the country
the Belgian flag, tabooed elsewhere, was draped about the
altar, and the Belgian people joined in singing their own
national anthem each Sunday morning.
Time after time priests went so far in their
patriotic   sermons   that   the   German
authorities dared even the wrath of the
Church and arrested and punished them.   The Jesuits gave
particular offence.   By July, 1916, forty Jesuits had been
already imprisoned.   A celebrated Dominican, Father
Huygens, of Ghent, was condemned in the autumn of 1916
to ten years' penal servitude by a German court-martial
on account of a patriotic sermon which he had recently
preached.   Other priests were sent to long terms of imprisonment in fortresses for helping young men to rejoin the
Belgian Army.

**Heroes in the
Church**

The great figure that stood out above all other Church-
men was Cardinal Mercier, Archbishop of Malines.   He
openly opposed the German administration.   He refused
to be silent about the outrages which had marked the first
days of the German occupation of the country, and he
demanded that they should be independently investigated.
He appealed now to the Pope, now to the Cardinals,
Archbishops, and Bishops of Germany, Bavaria, and Austria-
Hungary, and now to the world at large to hear the truth.
He sent pastorals to his clergy, and he preached sermons
fired with the loftiest patriotism.

In Lent, 1916, after a visit to the Pope in a vain effort
to secure his intervention, he published a pastoral which
sent a thrill of fresh confidence throughout his people.
" The day will come when we shall weep no more, when
we shall be no longer scattered, when our families will
be reunited never to be parted again," he declared :

My conviction, both natural and supernatural, of our ultimate
victory is more firmly rooted in my soul than ever.   If, indeed,
it could have been shaken, the assurances given me by several
disinterested and careful observers of the general situation, notably
those belonging to the two Americas, would have sufficed to
consolidate it.

We shall triumph, do not doubt it, but we are not yet at the end of our sufferings.

France, Britain, and Russia have engaged not to conclude peace until the independence of Belgium is completely restored and an ample indemnity has been made to her. Italy, in her turn, has given her adhesion to the London compact.

Our future is not doubtful.

But we must prepare it.

We shall prepare it by cultivating the virtue of patience, and the spirit of self-sacrifice. " Be of good courage," says the Psalmist, " and He shall strengthen your heart, all ye that hope in the Lord." Viriliter agite et comfortetur cor vestrum, omnes qui speratis in Domino.

" There is no king saved by the multitude of an host," says the Psalmist ; " a horse is a vain thing for safety, neither shall he deliver any by his great strength . . . Our soul waiteth for the Lord ; He is our help and our shield."

He told the Belgian people that they had already won a moral triumph. Their sacrifice of goods, homes, sons, and husbands for their plighted troth had won the homage of the world. " The moral triumph of Belgium is a very memorable fact for history and civilisation. Your generation has made a glorious entrance into history." Brave words these from the chief priest of a stricken nation, when armed enemy guards watched the very entrances of the archiepiscopal palace through which the message was sent, and when enemy legions had bombarded the cathedral and burned large parts of the city in which the Archbishop lived. " You are conquerors ! " That was the spirit of Belgium even in the darkest days.

Cardinal Mercier's brave words

Yet, looking over the country there was much to discourage and much to depress. Almost every factory and mill was closed, unable to obtain supplies and having no market for its goods. The streets of Brussels, in ordinary time full of gay life, were strangely silent. No private motor-cars were running, for it was impossible to obtain petrol, and the tyres had been confiscated for their rubber. Every bicycle had gone, for the rubber of the bicycle wheels was wanted by the Germans

Crowds of people, workless and underfed, moved sombrely through the avenues. Shops dealing in articles of luxury were still open and still made a brave display, but they had very few purchasers save occasional German officers. Most shops supplying foodstuffs were closed. Banks throughout the country were ever under the fear that the Germans would finally deprive them of all their resources. Business men told how their best stocks had been taken to Germany.

Placards on the walls advertised alleged German

[Belgian official photograph.

GUNNERS AND GUNS THE GERMANS LEARNED TO FEAR.

Heavy howitzer, an 8·5 in., in position and about to fire. The Belgians concentrated on the improvement of their artillery, and with a strong force of new guns and a host of trained gunners they soon became noted among the Allies, and inspired the Germans with a most wholesome respect for their efficiency. Above : Soldiers of a regiment of Guides returning for a necessary spell of rest to billets during relief.

victories, but people paid little heed to these. They had heard too much of imagined German triumphs to believe them. The more flamboyant the notices were, the more the Belgians took heart. "Things are going well to-day," they said to one another. "The Germans have claimed another great success. We wonder where they have really been defeated!" Now and then rumours would spread over the city and over the countryside,

Winged messengers of hope　no one knew how, telling of coming relief. Often the guns would be heard on the coast, the guns of British ships bombarding the German positions around Ostend and Zeebrugge.

Sometimes the people would watch warily through the darkness as allied aeroplanes came along bombing German strong points. Sometimes a Belgian airman would pass over, greatly daring, and would sail even over Brussels itself, scattering proclamations telling of coming victory. Thus in September, 1916, a Belgian airman dropped over Brussels thousands of copies of a handbill headed "Proclamation to the Belgians."

Belgians! The end approaches! Before Verdun the heroic and sublime resistance of the French Army has broken the gigantic German offensive. Upon the Somme the victorious British and French Armies continue to progress.

In Volhynia and in Galicia the Austrian troops have been hurled back by the Russians, and their broken ranks, reinforced by corps of Germans and Turks, are impotent to bar the way against the continuous pressure of the Allies.

The Italians have thrown back the invaders.

Your unbreakable courage, your dignified pride, and your unflinching energy are the admiration of the entire world.

The monotony of life was only relieved by some fresh proclamation from the Government announcing a new offence or fresh punishment. Here is one:

Whoever within the territory governed by the Governor-General, is found guilty of suspected incendiarism, causing an inundation, attacks on or resistance to the representatives of German civilian or military authorities, will be punished by death, or, if extenuating circumstances are proved, by ten or twenty years' penal servitude. Whoever spreads false rumours in regard to the German Army or of so-called victories by the Allies, or stirs up a rebellion or instigates soldiers to act contrary to their military duties, will be punished by five years' imprisonment

The Germans desired to make use of the manhood of Belgium. They wanted the Belgian railwaymen to operate the lines. This in itself would have saved them an army corps. They wanted to employ the great ironworks of Belgium and the skill of the artificers of Liège in making weapons. But here they found themselves met by the stubborn resistance of the entire nation. The Belgian people refused absolutely to work for the enemy. They were threatened, punished, almost starved, to compel them to give way. All was in vain. Here is an example given by Director Bicknell, of the American National Red Cross:

[*Belgian official photograph.*

AMPHIBIAN WARFARE.
A front-line trench in the inundated region of Belgium.

Malines is the site of extensive railway repair shops, and as the operation of the railways by the Germans was steadily reducing the rolling-stock through accidents and natural wear, the German Government decided that Belgian workmen formerly employed in the repair shops should be forced back into them. An order was issued that no more food be distributed by the relief committee until the men returned to the shops. Farmers and gardeners were forbidden to bring in their produce. No inhabitant was permitted to leave the city. Sentries were posted about the outskirts, and a barbed-wire barrier erected round the city.

The people of Malines, however, would not give way; and, finally, in deference to a protest from the Red Cross, the Germans gave up the attempt.

One method adopted by the Germans was to offer very high wages. At one place they offered as much as £2 a day to special men.

[*Belgian official photograph.*

PRIMEVAL MARSH IN THE ESTUARY OF THE YSER.
An immense watery expanse stretched before the Belgian front, strewn with decomposing bodies of men and beasts. In the rear the accumulated floods from the heavy rain, having no outlet, covered again large areas once wrested from the sea. The whole estuary reverted to primeval marsh.

M. Hulzebusch, the Secretary-General in Brussels of the Imperial German Railways, declared that they would compel the people to serve by starvation. At Luttre the German authorities summoned workmen to the central shops, ordered them to resume their work, and promised increased wages.

The ordinary workmen were offered five, six, and seven shillings a day, while machinists were offered a pound a day. The workmen promptly and indignantly refused, whereupon the Germans shut them up in railway-carriages and declared that they would not be allowed to leave until they had consented to do as required. Day by day they threatened them with deportation to Germany, where they would be

PAST THE POLLARD WILLOWS.
Belgian troops on the march back to billets through the mud.

Following this, on May 10th the Germans arrested M. Kesseler, the director of the central workshops at Luttre. He was taken to prison at Charleroi and put in a cell with nothing for his bed save a straw mattress. From here after a time he was taken back to Luttre, where a number of workmen had already been punished by the Germans. A written notice had now been distributed among the men that they would be sent to prison-camps in Germany if they still refused to work.

Asked by the German authorities to attempt to persuade his men, M. Kesseler replied that he had sworn loyalty to his King, and that he did not mean to perjure himself. He was then asked to persuade the men to work on the

"CORDUROY" PATH ALONG A BELGIAN TRENCH.
Not the least of the difficulties that confronted the Belgian Government was that of housing and finding accommodation for troops in a damp and sparsely populated region wholly unsuitable for maintaining armies through a winter campaign.

compelled to work without any pay at all. They told their families what was happening to their husbands and fathers, in the hope that they would persuade them to give way.

Finally a time limit was fixed. If they did not start to work by a certain day they would be taken away. On the morning announced for their departure the people of Luttre crowded around the station, and as the train steamed out the prisoners stood at the windows responding to loud shouts from the crowds, "Long live Belgium!" The departure was a bluff on the part of the authorities, for when the train reached Namur it stopped, and the workmen were liberated.

Some days later a fresh attempt was made. A number of workmen were taken up by force to the shops, and there a German officer ordered them to return to work. They stood still, making no move and saying no word. The officer then turned, and shouted bullyingly at them, "You need not think you are going to escape like the other fellows did!" Thereupon the workmen cheered, and shouted "Long live Belgium! Long live our soldiers!" What was to be done with such obstinate fellows?

locomotives on the promise that they should only be used for commercial, not military work. He told them what the Germans had said, and declared that he left it to each man to do as his conscience dictated. The men promptly intimated that they did not believe the German pledge.

M. Kesseler and some other officials were again sent back to the prison at Charleroi. One hundred and sixty-six workmen were deported to Germany. About sixty other men were also arrested shortly afterwards.

Much the same thing happened at Sweveghem, where there was an important wire-drawing mill. Here the Germans ordered a quantity of barbed-wire for their trenches. The three hundred and sixty workmen immediately refused to continue work. The burgomaster of the village, the communal secretary, and the senator of the district were thereupon arrested by the Germans and sent to Courtrai, the burgomaster being released the same evening.

Sweveghem was at once surrounded by a cordon of troops, and no one was allowed to enter or leave it. All

BELGIANS TAKING 3 IN. MORTARS UP TO THEIR POSITION.

When the new Belgian Army at length came into being its equipment was admirable, lacking nothing. The artillery especially was excellent, and in the short front before the Belgian Army the Germans were often quiet lest the Belgian guns and trench-mortars should open out on them and deal them severe punishment. Here a number of the soldiers are seen dragging these small guns to their front.

supplies of provisions were cut off. All vehicles of every kind were stopped. A few days afterwards it was announced in the village that if the work was not begun within the next twenty-four hours severe penalties would be incurred. All the inhabitants of the place from fifteen to forty-five years old were ordered to present themselves at the Public Hall. Some of the workmen were dragged by force to their establishments. The troops attempted by all kinds of brutalities to compel them to give way. Sixty-one of the men were sent to prison. Here their wives were taken to see them, and the Belgians declared that the women were odiously maltreated on the journey to the prison. The burgomaster was forced to issue a notice asking the men to go on with their work. They ignored the notice.

In studying these incidents, it is well to remember that The Hague Convention, in rules of war to which Germany among other countries gave adhesion, formally forbade any Power occupying conquered territory to compel the people to do work or to perform services of a kind which imposed on them the obligation of assisting operations of war against their own country.

The system of deporting able-bodied labour into Germany was extended as time went on, and in the summer and autumn of 1916 large numbers, not only of men but also of married women and girls, were forcibly taken from their homes in Belgium and sent to Germany ; some of them to work in the harvest-fields, some to work in factories. Homes were broken up and the greatest hardships inflicted. Many of the women and girls were allowed to return when the harvest was over, but many others, men particularly, were kept in a state of semi-slavery in Germany. Germany was developing to the full the art of **Deportations to slavery** attempting to subdue and break the spirit of a brave people by systematic, purposeful, and merciless brutality. The hardships under which the Belgian people suffered were not of the thrilling and dramatic nature that some of the people experienced early in the war, but they were of a kind to test the courage and temper of a nation to the full.

In October, 1916, the German authorities in Belgium began the wholesale deportations of Belgian able-bodied men. This virtually meant the reduction of Belgian manhood to a state of slavery, with the added bitterness that the slave was torn away from wife, children, and home. It was disguised at first as a plan for helping the Belgian unemployed, and with an hypocrisy already too familiar in the actions of the enemy in King Albert's country, the Germans even plumed themselves on their benevolence and kindness.

On October 3rd a decree was issued from the German General Headquarters subjecting to forced labour all able-bodied Belgians who, through lack of employment or for any other cause, were dependent on others. This decree was quickly put into effect. The unemployed were required to register, and the local officials were forced to hand in lists of them. Those who refused were penalised Thus the members of the Municipal Council of Brussels were arrested because they would not supply lists. Uhlans would ride into towns, call all the men together, and hurry them off to waiting trucks. At first only real unemployed were **Real aim of the enemy** taken. Then every able-bodied man in some districts, even though a man of means, was seized. Soon in other districts every fit man between eighteen and thirty years of age was registered or deported.

It became apparent that the real aim of the Germans was to supply the lacking man-power in their own land from the population of Belgium. The numbers of the enslaved soon rose from thousands to tens of thousands, then scores of thousands. In the city of Ghent alone it was estimated that by mid-October no fewer than five thousand men had been taken. The scenes on their departure, scenes repeated all over the land, were moving in the extreme. Women and children, mothers with babies in their arms, others with infants barely able to walk clinging to their knees, stood around weeping and lamenting. In Ghent itself there was the greatest excitement. A fever of indignation spread through all classes. Crowds assembled in the streets, singing patriotic songs and shouting satirical remarks at every German they met. This gave the enemy opportunity to apply further punitive measures.

An official notice was posted on the city walls explaining what had happened. The German authorities declared that a situation had been created which was impossible. Large numbers of men had continued out of work for two years, with inadequate relief. The long spell of idleness was doing them great harm. Hence the decision to make them work. They would not be made into soldiers. They would be fed and housed, given free medical aid, and paid a minimum wage of threepence-halfpenny a day for each day of actual work. Specially diligent men would earn more, and foremen would receive sixpence a day. Each man could receive a postcard weekly from his family, and send one card. People who circulated wicked rumours about the men's treatment were severely censured.

Explanations such as this did little to calm the popular excitement. From all parts came tales of more frequent raids. At place after place the men were paraded, examined like cattle, and the strongest ordered off. Where the local authorities imposed difficulties, or refused to aid the Germans, the towns were fined and the officials removed. Thus Bruges was fined £5,000 a day for each day's delay in assembling the men, and the burgomaster, an old man of eighty, was deposed from his office because he refused to be complaisant.

Then tales came from the borders and from Germany itself, telling of the hardships of the men en route. Dreadful narratives were received of their condition during the journey when, packed in cattle-trucks, hungry and thirsty, they were carted off like beasts to market. One correspondent of a Dutch paper told how, standing near the frontier, he had seen the slave-trains arrive. The men looked as though they had been snatched straight from work, an odd commentary on the German explanation that only the unemployed had been taken.

Cardinal Mercier's protest Thus a butcher boy was still in his white apron, farm labourers were still in mud-covered clogs, fresh from the fields, and mechanics bore on them clear marks of toil. Other accounts told how as the trucks passed through some districts pitiful people pressed up trying to throw anything they could to the hungry men in them.

Once in Germany, they were made to feel the full force of their slavery. They were put to any work the enemy pleased, mining, digging trenches, making barbed-wire, working in furnaces. No scruple, no thought of international law counted now.

Cardinal Mercier once more came to the front with bold protests against the illegality and brutality of the business. In an open letter to the civilised world, sent on behalf of the Belgian bishops, he told how he had already protested to General von Bissing. Then only men actually out of work were affected. Now, he added, "all sound men are taken away without distinction. They are packed into goods trucks and carried off we know not whither, like a gang of slaves." The Cardinal went on to show how Germany had broken repeated promises and solemn undertakings. Then he added:

The naked truth is this : Every workman taken from Belgium means one soldier more for the German Army. He is intended to take the place of a German workman, out of whom a soldier is to be made. So that the situation which we now lay before the civilised world comes to this. Four hundred thousand workmen have fallen victims to unemployment against their will, and, for the most part, as the result of the German régime of occupation.

Troops of soldiers force their way into these poor homes, tear the young men from their parents, husband from his wife, father from his children. They guard with bayonets the doors through which wives and mothers desire to run and bid a last farewell to those taken from them. Soldiers separate the prisoners into groups of forty or fifty, and load them by force into goods trucks. The engine stands under steam, and when the train is full the superior officer gives the signal for departure, and once more a thousand Belgians are carried off into slavery and, without formalities, are condemned to the hardest punishment known to punitive legislation—namely, deportation. They know neither where they are going nor for how long. All they know is that their work is to profit the enemy alone.

IN FLOODED FLANDERS.
Flooded land along the Belgian front proved a fatal barrier to the German advance. At its edge here it will be seen that the water rose up to the horse's girth.

The news of the slave-raids was received by the neutral world with horror. In the United States the Government showed its feeling by ordering the American representative at Berlin to inform the German Foreign Office that the deportations could not but have a most unfortunate effect upon neutral opinion, particularly in the United States, which had the interest of the Belgian civilian population so much at heart. American indignation was strengthened by reports from American citizens in Belgium, which emphasised and added detail to the brief Belgian accounts received. Washington's protest was echoed

WATERY BARRIER ALONG THE BELGIAN FRONT.
By releasing the pent-up waters of canals and dikes the Belgians interposed between themselves and their ruthless foes an effective No Man's Land. Over the flooded polders the Belgian soldier looked with grim satisfaction at the friendly element in which large numbers of his enemies had been swept away.

in other neutral capitals. In the British House of Commons Lord Robert Cecil told the nation that mere words of protest against a policy of atrocities like this were of little avail. The only action that could finally solve this problem was to wage the war with all our power.

The Germans continued semi-officially to paint their policy as one of philanthropy. "All in all," declared one such statement, "the measures have had a thoroughly good success, and one doubtless can expect that the Belgians themselves will gradually realise the utility of these regulations."

Slow and gnawing torture

What said the Belgians? M. Emile Cammaerts eloquently expressed the feelings of his fellow-countrymen in a statement printed at the time in the "Observer," November 19th, 1916:

If things are allowed to go on at this rate we shall witness the wholesale deportation of an entire people reduced to slavery. All the country's best blood will be used up in the German workshops and mines, or, worse still, in the trenches which the enemy is

PROUD MOMENT OF A BELGIAN OFFICER'S LIFE.
It was indeed a proud moment for the soldier when, in the presence of the officers with whom he would henceforth rank, he took the oath. Standing by the well-loved "drapeau Belge," held by a veritable giant of a standard-bearer, he swore fidelity to King and Flag.

building behind the front in Flanders and Northern France. Our preachers have frequently chosen recently as a text the well-known Psalm: "By the waters of Babylon we sat down . . ." Did they guess that Belgium should not only suffer from exile and oppression, but that her sons should be carried away captive in the land of her conquerors?

This is, indeed, worse than the disaster of the invasion, worse than the retreat from Antwerp, worse than the wholesale massacres of Louvain, Tamines, Andenne, and Dinant; worse even than the ceaseless persecutions to which the nation has been subjected during the last two years. Any military defeat may be avenged by a glorious victory, destroyed towns may be rebuilt, dead martyrs may be worshipped, persecutions may be endured. But what will Belgium's answer be to this new crime? What will she be able to say if no one is left at home to speak? Up to now she had merely suffered in her body; she had been wounded, bullied, and starved, but her indomitable spirit remained free. To-day her soul is stricken. Every one of these captives will have to choose between death and dishonour; his spirit will be broken by a slow and gnawing torture endured in complete isolation.

The steady absorption of the wealth of the country went on all the time.

Two illustrations of the German plans for acquiring the

material wealth of the country may be given. The German Commissioner at Brussels demanded a forced loan of £40,000, three-fifths of the amount to be furnished by the Belgian National Bank and two-fifths by other banks. The directors of the National Bank were told that if the money was not forthcoming they would be arrested. When they declined to pay, one of their leading members, M. Carlier, was taken as a prisoner to Aix-la-Chapelle, where, according to a Belgian official statement, he was treated with brutality and forced to carry a heavy wooden fetter.

It was reported shortly afterwards that the Germans had also arrested M. Carlier's daughter in order to bring pressure upon her father. Having arrested the banker, the Germans naturally sought some excuse for their action, and so they spread reports abroad that he was one of the most bitter of Germany's enemies. One German newspaper declared that during the Siege of Antwerp he led the anti-German movement among the people there. "It is with great delight that we see the end of this pernicious worker, one of the most dangerous agitators in Belgium." And all because he refused to sanction a plan which would have given him and his fellow-directors a mass of German paper of doubtful value in place of their own good money. However, on threats of seizing all the properties of these private banks, the Germans obtained the coveted money.

In the autumn of 1916 the German Government seized two hundred locomotives, five thousand vehicles, and several hundred miles of rails belonging to the Belgian light railways known as the Chemins de Fer Vicinaux. These light railways were the great rural means for the transport of goods, and the result of the seizure of the line, coming as it did just before the beet harvest, was to arrest the internal traffic of a large part of the country. Food could not be conveyed into the districts and the beet supplies could not be sent out.

If the Belgians offended against the Germans, they were punished with great severity. Men were sentenced to heavy fines and imprisonments for breathing a whisper against the invaders. Germans of good position, on the other hand, could commit atrocious crimes and go almost unpunished. The most notorious example of this was the murder of Baron d'Udekem d'Acoz, a well-known Belgian noble. The baron was living on his estate, and several German officers came to his house, he being forced to receive them and house them. It was suggested that, as was only natural, he felt none too friendly towards these enforced **Murder of a Belgian noble** enemy guests, and did not take particular pains to conceal his distaste of their presence. He disappeared, and three months afterwards his body was discovered by a gamekeeper in a wood on the estate. An examination of the body showed that the baron had been killed by a shot from a revolver in the back.

It was said at the beginning that the German officers might possibly know something about the baron's disappearance. The German police arrested the baron's wife and kept her in prison for some time, treating her

BELGIAN NATIONAL SPIRIT MAINTAINED ON ITS NATIVE SOIL. [*Belgian official photograph.*

Proudly holding on to what was left of their own land, the Belgian troops were still able to celebrate their national fetes on national soil unsullied by the Hun. On the plage of that short stretch, for so long all they had of enemy-free coast, the troops that took part in such celebrations showed by their soldierly bearing something of that sturdy confidence in the future for which they were ready to strike with effective force.

NEW BELGIAN ARMY IN THE MAKING. [*French official photograph.*

Whatever Belgium lost when her fair land was overrun by ruthless German hordes, as it was finely said, she kept her soul. This was illustrated by the heroic tenacity with which the last strip of Belgian territory was held by the remnant of her troops, and by the readiness with which her manhood responded to the need for building up a new Army. Part of that new Army is here shown during its training in a coastal town of France.

KEEPING THE MACHINE-GUNS WELL FED.
Carrying supplies of munitions to advanced machine-gun sections was an hazardous undertaking, calling for the greatest care. It will be observed that the men had to crawl along and take advantage of the slightest inequality of the ground in getting to their comrades' position.

with the utmost severity. Soon after the body was discovered, a chauffeur in the service of Prince Stolberg, one of the officers who had lived with the baron, denounced his master as the murderer, and accused another officer, a Count Gagern, of being his accomplice.

The accusation was so specific and detailed that the German authorities could not pass it over. The two officers were arrested and tried by court-martial. Their arrest caused a great sensation, for the prince belonged to one of the oldest sovereign houses of the German Empire.

Guilt condoned by the Kaiser

Both prisoners were found guilty. The prince was sentenced to death, and the count to ten years' hard labour. Now comes the amazing sequel. Shortly afterwards, the Kaiser remitted the sentences on both the prince and the count—the same Kaiser who could find no mercy in his heart for Miss Cavell.

The case of Miss Cavell has been so fully treated elsewhere in this work that it is unnecessary to do more than refer to it here. It was a striking example of the work of the German spies maintained all over Belgium. There were spies everywhere—in cafés, in street cars, in shops, in every crowd. The German spy system was in many ways the most odious and repulsive part of the German rule in Belgium.

Food supplies soon became a question of very great urgency.

In the autumn of 1914, when the opposing armies formed the long trench line in Belgium and in Northern France, which was to fix their position for two years and more ahead, it soon became evident that unless some extraordinary measures were taken to feed the Belgian people, large numbers of them must die of starvation. Belgium in normal times imported the greater part of its food supplies. Seventy-eight per cent. of the wheat consumed in the country came from abroad. The proportion of other staple articles imported was also very high. Now many of the crops had been destroyed. In many districts it had been impossible to harvest them because the men had been called up to war just as the grain was ripening.

Germany could not or would not help the conquered country. She wanted all the food she could secure for herself, and was only too ready to steal from the Belgians the little

they had. The big stocks of grain and other foodstuffs in the country when the Germans came were commandeered by them. Importation in the ordinary way was impossible. The allied fleets barred the seas. The Allies could not and would not permit the general importation of food supplies. Had they done so, Belgium would simply have become a channel for the conveyance of food to Germany, and the allied blockade would at once have been rendered vain.

Yet something had to be done. To permit a population—including the inhabitants of Northern France in the occupation of Germany—of 9,500,000 people to starve was unthinkable. Here was a case where neutrals might

BOMB-THROWER TAKEN BY THE BELGIAN ARMY.
That formidable examples of the bomb-thrower were employed against the Belgian line is well shown by this photograph of one of those very powerful weapons, which was captured from the Germans at Ramscappelle.

act, and the United States rose splendidly to the occasion. An organisation was formed, the Commission for Relief in Belgium, which undertook nothing less than the work of purchasing, conveying, and distributing sufficient essential foods for the whole population in the allied territory occupied by Germany to the west. President Wilson, with the friendly co-operation of other neutral countries, appointed a committee of picked business men, who flung themselves into the work of raising money by millions of pounds, purchasing foodstuffs in millions of tons, and distributing it throughout the conquered territories.

Splendid neutral relief work

To describe the work of the Commission for Relief in Belgium as the greatest philanthropic effort of any age is inadequate. The conception was grandiose; the execution of the scheme was admirable. The Commission was fortunate in its leader. Mr. Herbert Hoover, who became chairman and active director of the entire undertaking, was one of the newest types of great American business organisers.

A young Californian with a distinguished university career, and a trustee of his *Alma Mater*, the Leland Stanford Junior University, Mr. Hoover had for nearly twenty years since his graduation been engaged in big works of organisation. A mining engineer by profession, he began his wider career by taking over the management of a group of mines in Western Australia. From there he went to China as head of the newly-created Government Department of Mines; later on he came to London, where at the time war broke out he was the controlling head of undertakings employing 125,000 men.

The Director of Relief When the American authorities appealed to him to guide the work of the new Commission he probably had little idea that he was setting his hand to a task that would take not a few weeks, or a few months, but years at the very prime of his manhood.

He quickly gathered around him a group of young Americans—engineers, university professors, Rhodes scholars from Oxford, men of real business experience. They were full of enthusiasm, and one and all gave their services freely. They set themselves to their task as they

BELGIAN HILL-TOP GUN-PIT.
With their gun-pit masked by gorse bushes, such as this, the men of the machine-gun sections were able to give a good account of themselves against the enemy.

would have gone into any vast business undertaking. They laid their plans carefully and exactly. They divided the work into sections, put responsible men in charge of each, gave them a free hand, and established from the beginning a system of inspection and reports which kept those at the head in complete touch with all that was happening.

The work of the Commission naturally divided itself into three or four main sections. There was the diplomatic side. The goodwill of both the allied and the German Governments must be maintained. If the Allies did not approve of what the Commission was doing they could prevent its importation of foodstuffs. If the

Germans, on the other hand, suspected that the Americans were working in a way unfriendly to them, they could have closed down the entire operations of the Commission in an hour. The Commission had one work and one work alone—to feed the people—and its members were rigid in their determination to maintain neutrality.

Next to the diplomatic work came the procuring of funds. The heart of the world had to be touched by a knowledge of the needs of Belgium. Money had to be raised on a scale never previously dreamed of in the history of philanthropy. Soon the Commission was spending considerably over £1,000,000 a month. All this amount was not raised by public gifts, although the public in the allied countries and in every neutral nation—notably the United States—did splendidly. By far the greater part was paid to the Commission by Great Britain and France, and even by the Belgian Government on the loans granted to it by the allied Governments. The different Governments quickly became convinced of the admirable disinterestedness of the Commission's organisers.

It is obvious that in the purchasing of food by the million of tons a very little skill may make a very great difference in the total prices paid. The Commission had first to make up its mind what were the essential food-stuffs it would buy, and then it had to procure them at as low a rate as possible. It early decided that its staple importation must be wheat **Million a month in** and flour for bread. After this came **philanthropy** maize, and it was in time realised that one of the best foods was rice. Beans and peas, bacon, lard, and potatoes were also bought in large quantities. In the first month the total food purchased came to 26,000 tons, there then being considerable quantities of foodstuffs remaining in the country. As these supplies failed, the importations increased within a year to close on 120,000 tons a month. The Commission was made the sole importer of wheat from overseas into Belgium. It had to procure not only food to be distributed among the destitute but also to be sold to all classes.

In purchasing it went to the fountain-head. Thus it bought most of its wheat in the Chicago wheat-pit and its rice in Rangoon. The Chicago Board of Trade became its purchasing agent, an honorary purchasing agent that watched the market more closely than the keenest broker.

WELL-GUARDED ENTRANCE TO A BELGIAN TRENCH.
Such important positions as those at the trench-endings frequently formed the most effective points for machine-gun emplacements. In the Belgian, as in the other lines, these machine-guns played a vital part in the operations, forming one of the most effective means of stopping or holding up an attack.

During the first year of its existence the Commission paid from 5 to 10 per cent. less for its high-grade wheat than any other large purchaser. It secured special freight rates for the carriage of its foodstuffs to the seaports, partly on account of the enormous size of its transactions and partly from the goodwill of all for its work. The Commission had the same success in Rangoon. It waited until the markets were exceedingly low and then flooded them with an order for 40,000 tons of rice. Next day the price of rice rose 20 per cent., but the Commission had its orders already accepted at the lowest price of the year.

A record for Rotterdam Then came the work of transportation. The Commission had to hire its own ships, on long charter or short, and soon it had no less than seventy-five steamers in its employ. Here, as in other operations, exact office work told. Things were so planned that when a steamer reached a port there was a cargo waiting for it. There were no delays and no lost time. When the steamers reached their port of destination, Rotterdam, all was ready for the discharge of their cargo. And so the ships were kept moving all the time. The speed in discharging the cargo steamers and the cheapness per ton made a record for Rotterdam.

The cargoes were all landed at Rotterdam, and from there placed in barges and distributed to various central points in Belgium. The canal system which connects Rotterdam up with practically the whole of Belgium and a considerable part of Northern France, including Lille and Cambrai, was made the main means of conveying the food over the country.

In the work of distributing the food supplies of Belgium the Commission worked through a system of provincial and local committees, which were directed by the Belgian National Committee at Brussels. These local organisations were operated by no less than 37,000 voluntary workers, all people of responsibility. Thus the National Committee at the top consisted of a group of prominent Belgians working in conjunction with several representatives of the Commission for Relief. Each communal committee usually had the burgomaster at the head of it.

Watching over the work of these different committees, helping, acting as intermediaries when difficulties arose with the Germans, preventing abuse, and keeping a general check on things, were the American workers, young, keen, active volunteers, who were ever on the move from end to end of the land.

The work of distributing the foodstuffs was kept quite apart from the work of charity. Each communal committee was able to order within certain fixed limits what it required. It paid for this in cash to the provincial committee, and the provincial committee paid in cash to the central organisation. The wheat—to take the main article imported as an example of what happened with other goods—was distributed on an arranged plan to certain mills throughout the country, the millers being paid for their work of grinding it into flour.

Experience proved that the utmost nourishment was obtained by an 82 per cent. milling. At first it was the general practice to mill 90 per cent. of the wheat into flour, and to use the remaining 10 per cent. of bran for fodder. In ordinary milling for white bread only about 65 or 70 per cent. of the flour is used. By using 82 per cent. as a standard, the maximum of nourishment was obtained, and although numbers of Belgian people would have greatly preferred a finer white bread, their wishes had to give way to the essential requirements of the situation.

From the mills the flour was issued to the communal committees, and they in turn served it out to the bakers. Each baker had his old list of customers, and he was allowed to bake according to the number of these. **Distribution of flour and bread** The most satisfactory plan was eventually found to be to pay the baker so much per loaf, the baker being under contract to produce 4 lb. of good bread from each 3 lb. of flour allowed to him.

The baker did not himself do the distributing of the bread. When baked it was handed in by him to a central shop, the communal warehouse, from which the purchaser obtained it.

The bread was issued to the purchasers by tickets, the general allowance being 330 grammes (about three-quarters

QUEEN ELIZABETH SHOWING SYMPATHY WITH HER WAR-SHATTERED COUNTRY BY PERSONAL VISIT TO THE FRONT.
From the first unjustifiable attack by Germany on Belgium's neutrality the bravery of King Albert and his Queen commanded widest admiration. The King and Queen remained ever in close touch with their heroic troops who held on to so much of their land as had not come under the iron heel of the Hun. Here her Majesty is seen as she visited one of the ruined districts immediately behind the firing-line in Flanders.

of a pound) of bread per head daily. The purchasers were given cards showing the number of persons in their houses and the amount allowed to them. They were required to obtain their bread as a rule from the nearest distributing depot and to take it away themselves, each family going for their supply three times a week. Every baker's bread was kept separately, and the customer who desired could change from one baker to another. By this means the bakers had the best of all stimulus to keep up the quality of their wares.

The price of bread was fixed by periodic agreement. It was found in practice that this system of direct purchasing and whole-sale distribution worked out very advantageously to the buyer. There was a saving of 10 per cent. on the cost of wheat up to the time it reached the mill in Belgium, but the greatest saving of all was in the cost of general distribution. "If the Commission saved 10 per cent. on the price of the wheat from the Chicago pit to the Belgian mill," wrote Mr. Robinson Smith, one of its active organisers, "it saved from 30 to 40 per cent. from the mill to the mouths of the people. This can be very easily demonstrated. In normal times the most the Belgian farmer gets for his wheat from the miller is 16 francs for 100 kilos (13s. 4d. for 220 lb.), and the normal price of bread in Belgium is 30 centimes a kilo (3d. for 2 lb. 3 oz.). The average cost to the miller (acting for the provincial committee) of the Commission wheat during the first year was 32 francs 7 centimes per 100 kilos (£1 6s. 8¾d. for 220 lb.), yet the average price of bread during the same period was only 38 centimes per kilo (3¾d. for 2 lb. 3 oz.).

"In other words, the miller had to pay more than double for his wheat because it was war time, but the people had to pay only 27 per cent. more for their bread."

KING ALBERT'S DAY IN HUN-FREE FLANDERS.
It was still possible to celebrate King Albert's Day in one of his country's churches, though all that was left to him was but a strip of Western Flanders. On the occasion represented the Duke of Teck was among those present at the celebration. The lines of helmeted soldiers are eloquent of the conditions in which the service was held.

A comparison of figures month by month from the beginning of 1915 showed that during most months the people in Brussels were paying less for bread of **Brussels bread** the same quality than the people of **cheaper than London** London, and this notwithstanding the very high extra transportation costs into Belgium. The Commission had not only a monopoly for the importation of flour, but it also purchased the entire crops of the farmers in Belgium itself.

The larger part of this saving was due to the reduction in the cost of distribution. Competitive shopkeeping was practically abolished, and a striking example was given of the fact that eventually it is the consumer who pays for competition. One shop did the work of distribution which was done by forty shops in the old days. The communal store did not confine itself to the sale of bread. It supplied all the goods provided by the Commission, and it was encouraged to extend its field as largely as possible, for the more it sold the more widely distributed were its overhead charges.

It was not enough, however, to import food into the country and to distribute it at the cheapest possible rate. There were large numbers of people who could not afford to pay even the minimum price. For them there must be charity. It was to purchase food for them that the allied Governments and the charitable public of the world had subscribed so freely. Destitution was mainly felt among the industrial population; the farmers were most of them better off than ever, because of the high prices to be had for their products.

The number of Belgians without means increased as the war went on, until by the autumn of 1916 it amounted to

A A

BELGIAN GUNNERS TESTING THEIR NEW WEAPONS.
Fine work was done by the Belgian artillery in the stubborn defence by which they held the enemy after his onrush had been stopped. Here a gun-detachment are to be seen as they carefully learned to sight their weapon preparatory to going forward to their service in the front line.

assistance to artists, to foreigners, to doctors, and to the dispossessed. Some were for the clergy, some for the destitute young mothers, and so on. Large amounts of new and second-hand clothing were received from all over the world, and were badly needed. This clothing was distributed only to the destitute, and without charge. Gift shiploads of food sent to Belgium were of temporary assistance. But it was soon realised that the need was too big for occasional gift cargoes to be more than a drop in the bucket in meeting it.

The Commission aimed at obtaining as its main resource gifts of money, which could be fairly distributed and used directly in purchasing food which had been distributed over the country by the Provisional Department of the Commission. A great deal of help was also given in providing fresh homes for the large number of people whose houses had been destroyed during invasion. Considerable numbers of Belgians were at the beginning forced into the open fields or cow-sheds, overcrowded in the remainder of the undestroyed villages, or driven into the slums of near-by towns. Householders were given loans or supplies of material to help them to rebuild.

about one out of three in the population, or close on two and a half millions. But for outside aid the greater number of these must undoubtedly have died of sheer hunger. Germany did very little indeed. One or two show places were maintained in Brussels and elsewhere to which neutral journalists were carefully conducted that they might see the benevolence of the Prussian to his foe. But the entire field of German benevolent activity covered at the most a few hundred people.

The Commission for Relief in Belgium worked on its benevolent side in close co-operation with the Belgian organisation, the Comité National de Secours et d'Alimentation. The main basis of the financial resources for this work came from monthly grants of £1,000,000 from the allied Governments, of which Great Britain contributed half to the Belgian Government for the service of the Commission. In addition to this, the Commission obtained aid from 4,000 committees established in many neutral and allied countries.

The main work of feeding was done by giving regular rations of food to millions of people each week. In each district the voluntary committees of local workers sought out the really needy. Any person whose income did not amount to 4s. 2d. a week was entitled to assistance. Nothing could be more eloquent of the terrible conditions existing in Belgium than that over two million people qualified for relief under this condition. There were various precautions to prevent the relief being abused.

Seeking out the really needy

The Government subsidy was spent largely on semi-official relief, such as allowances to families whose bread-winners had been lost owing to the war, supplementary allowances to the destitute, advances to families of officers and non-commissioned officers, assistance to communal organisations, and advances to building and loan societies, charitable institutions, and educational institutions. The money coming from charity largely went on direct feeding and clothing the destitute, and providing temporary shelters, and on the establishment of special committees.

One of these committees started to obtain work for lace-workers, some gave special

APPROACH TO A CRITICAL CORNER BY BELGIAN SCOUTS.
Very special training was required for those who undertook the hazardous and vitally important work of scouting. Crossing an emergency bridge this small party of Belgian Scouts, in their new khaki uniforms, were advancing as though beyond the reeds they might come in touch with the enemy.

GERMAN MARINES ON THE BELGIAN SAND DUNES.

Denied that service afloat for which they had been trained by the fact of their ships being kept securely in harbour, the German Marines were marched off to fill places along the depleted line of the western front.

The companies of them shown here were wending their way along the Flemish dunes during the German occupation. The wire entanglements were for the defence of the shore against landing parties.

The scale of help varied according to the conditions of the person. Let us take as a typical example the case of an unemployed labourer or artisan with a housekeeper or wife and a family. He himself would be allowed 2s. 6d. per week, 1s. 3d. would be allowed for the wife, 5d. for each child under sixteen, and 2s. 6d. for children over sixteen, formerly employed or at school. Thus a man and wife with three young children would receive five shillings a week. This would not be given in money. It would be delivered in "bons"—that is, orders for rations to that value at the communal provisional committee, or to accredited tradesmen for native supplies. This assistance was not, however, all. The communal committees were encouraged to devise methods for helping special classes, particularly nursing mothers and children.

Health of the populace

The aim of the Commission was to maintain the people of Belgium in a state of health. How far did it succeed in its aim? A very interesting report by an American medical man, Dr. Lucas, was published in August, 1916. Dr. Lucas, in response to an invitation from Mr. Hoover, spent some months in Belgium examining the health conditions of the population. He found that the amount of food being supplied through the work of the Commission, the utmost food that it could give, was barely enough. "Even with these supplies," he wrote, "the population has existed upon the narrowest margin of dietary necessaries. . . . In a general way there can be no doubt that the vitality and resistance of the majority of these classes (the industrial and minor commercial classes) have been lowered." He found an increase in tuberculosis due to under-nutrition.

Dr. Lucas gave a number of facts showing the alarming growth of consumption among the working-class population, directly attributable to the great shortage of fats in their foods. The lack of meat, the growing failure of milk supply, the diminution in the native supply of vegetables and fruit, all had evil results. From Brussels came the news of a considerable increase in the number of cases of tuberculosis, and a large number of relapses among old, arrested cases that had been supposed to be cured.

The Antwerp conditions were told in reports for the first seventeen weeks in each year. In 1913 the mortality from tuberculosis during that time was 7·1 per cent; in 1914, 9 per cent.; in 1915, 9·5 per cent.; in 1916, 13·2 per cent. In Namur the deaths from tubercular causes had almost doubled. The doctors further found evidence of the lowered vitality of the people in the fact that, according to the current opinion of employers and others able to judge, the labouring man was not able to do the amount of work he formerly did. "His energy and power of production are considerably less, and he becomes much more easily fatigued than usual."

The reports from maternity hospitals showed that the weights of babies born in 1916 were less than the average of infants born before the war. There was a great diminution in the birth-rate compared with the average of some years before the war. The birth-rate had fallen in 1916: In Brussels, 48 per cent.; in Antwerp, 41 per cent.; in Louvain, 41 per cent.; in Namur, 42 per cent.; in Liège, 41 per cent. "The lowered vitality of the women due to under-nutrition may be accepted as the chief factor." The one bright fact was that the infant mortality had fallen since the beginning of the war. Dr. Lucas's report well showed in the cold language of science the disastrous effects of war and enemy rule on the Belgian people.

"If it had not been for you, we should have starved to death," was a common phrase, said thousands upon thousands of times by the Belgians to the American workers. Mr. Hoover and his band of enthusiastic assistants did a work that will go down in the history of the world as a model for all times. Its magnitude, its efficiency, its application of the most modern methods of business to charity, and its practical qualities were almost beyond praise. One fact alone may serve to show the business skill behind the Commission. The costs of administration for the year 1914-15 amounted to £101,994 14s. 10d., or three-fourths of 1 per cent. on the total value of the supplies handled.

Business skill of the Commission

The Commission, however, took shrewd advantage of variations in the rate of exchange, in handling the large sums remitted between the different branches, and it actually earned a profit in exchange—in excess of the average bankers' rates — of £106,189. In other words, its profits on exchange more than covered the whole cost of administration. The extent of its work can be judged from the fact that from November, 1914, to October, 1915, it purchased provisions to the value of over twelve and a

GENERAL DE WITTE. [*French official photograph.*]
The distinguished cavalry commander of the Belgian Army in Flanders.

half million pounds, and its operations in all amounted to £17,257,591.

In endeavouring to obtain a complete idea of the food situation in Belgium, it is necessary, however, to go beyond the work of the Commission, although this body became more and more, as time went on, the feeding agent of the Belgian people. At first it imported about one-third of the food necessary for the whole nation. By the autumn of 1916 it was sending about four-fifths of the total supplies, and about six million people were receiving food on the carte de ménage. What of the supplies produced in Belgium itself? The townspeople complained very bitterly of the conduct of the peasants and small farmers who forced prices up to the utmost limit. "They demand our last halfpenny," cried the people of Louvain. In July it was said in Brussels that there were houses in which people had not potatoes even for six weeks.

Increasing cost of commodities Butter fetched 7s. 6d. a pound; veal, mutton, or pork 4s. 2d. a pound. Coffee was 5s. per pound, eggs cost 3d. each. In many places no coffee was to be had, and the real bean was replaced by a substitute, Kneipp Malt, which sold for about 5d. per lb.

Butter and fats were extremely rare. Meat was only issued in many places as a ration of three and a half ounces for each adult a week. Sugar was very scarce. Powdered sugar fetched one shilling and sixpence a pound. Soap sold at nearly half a crown a pound. St. Nicolas reported that the chief misery was among the middle class, who actually suffered more than the working people, for the latter received relief from committees. Clothing was at almost impossible prices. Ordinary shoes cost from 28s. to 30s., while the best quality of shoes cost as much as £2 8s. to £3.

In Liège, where there were large numbers of unemployed, many demonstrations were organised against the high cost of living. The demonstrators were particularly furious with the farmers and the milkmen. Guards waited at the various entrances to the city, seized the milkmen as they came in and compelled them to sign an undertaking to sell their milk at a reasonable price. A butter merchant who refused to sell butter to the people found himself the centre of very unpleasant demonstrations, and was burnt in effigy. In the few shops where milk was sold policemen had to be stationed to control the crowds of people who flocked to them. On July 15th it was announced, "There is no more milk."

In September and October, 1916, the condition of affairs, so far from getting better, was worse than ever. "Life is insupportable for the middle classes," was the common complaint. "The countrymen enrich themselves by exploiting the people of moderate means who are unable to go to the relief committees," was another complaint. **Belgian Army's renaissance** Butter was generally unobtainable except in small contraband supplies, which fetched from three shillings to four shillings per pound; although, in some communal stores, small quantities were to be had at two shillings and twopence per pound. Meat varied in price. In some parts, like Bruges, it was as low as from three shillings to three shillings and sixpence per pound; at Charleroi it was priced at four shillings and sixpence to five shillings; in one other part the price was given as high as five shillings and sixpence per pound. Potatoes in many towns were as high as fourpence a pound. Tea and coffee were eleven shillings per pound. There were no more haricot beans in many places, either white or brown.

In some towns like Ghent a weekly ration of potatoes was given of two pounds per head. "The very dog is transformed into sausages," one writer complained, "and then we have to pay three shillings per pound for him."

At Louvain it was reported that the number of sick was very great. At Antwerp there was a procession of women and children carrying black flags to the Town Hall, to protest against the insufficient ration of bread and against abuses in the distribution of soup. The price of clothing and shoes grew higher and higher. Generally they were treble their old price.

The renaissance of the Belgian Army has been described in some detail in an earlier chapter. Yet one may be pardoned for recalling here some of the main facts. After the great Battle of the Yser, in which forty-eight thousand wearied Belgian infantrymen, fresh from the terrible experiences of the Siege of Antwerp, made their last despairing stand against the hitherto triumphant German divisions, men realised that the old Belgian Army had virtually done its work. It had fought from August, 1914, until November, 1914, against the greatest military Power in Europe. It had fought almost alone, because its Allies had been unable to help it in many a stricken field.

Many Belgian soldiers and officers heard Mr. Winston Churchill at Antwerp promise that if the Belgians would hold on, adequate British aid would come to them. "You must hold on to Antwerp," he told them. "We are sending help." And the Belgians saw the help that came— the boys of the Naval Brigade, untrained sailors many of them, lads brave to the point of rashness, but some of them scarcely able to handle a gun. They counted their numbers—quite inadequate for the task.

The promise of the British statesman had caused them greater loss than they otherwise would have suffered. They recalled, too, how the strong French forces that were to have reached Namur never came at the critical moment, and how the French divisions, badly led, had broken and abandoned their naturally strong positions on the Meuse heights under the German attack.

The Belgians recalled these things without bitterness, but it would be a mistake in attempting to estimate their

New Northern Lights wherewith the Navy sought the enemy that flew by night.

Skeleton of the Zeppelin brought down on the Essex coast, September 24th, 1916.

Gondolas and propellers of the Zeppelin destroyed in South Essex, September 24th, 1916.

The broken Titan lay outstretched across two fields and over an Essex by-road.

After the crash: Smashed framework and twisted lattice of heat-corroded aluminium.

The crowning mercy, Cuffley, September 3rd, 1916: All that was left at dawn of the night-raiding Zeppelin.

attitude to believe that they forgot them. They remembered as well how one gallant British division had advanced beyond Ghent to aid them, and how the French people later on had done much to atone for the failure at the beginning. If the result of it all had been that the Belgian Army had been smashed in its attempt to keep back the German flood and in its final effort which ended in the holding up of the Germans on the banks of the Yser, the cruellest punishments of all had been suffered.

The Belgian generals and statesmen surveyed the field in the days immediately after the Battle of the Yser. They frankly recognised that they themselves had been none too well prepared for their task. The reorganisation of their Army had been delayed too long. Essential measures for defence had been emasculated, because Parliament at one stage had refused to vote the necessary supplies. The arms and equipment of the Army were out of date, the uniforms were many of them Napoleonic. The organisation needed recasting. What Belgium must have, if she was to help to recover her own territory, was a modern force, trained, drilled, dressed, equipped as were the Armies of its Allies. And so the great work of military reconstruction began.

Beginning the great work

The Belgians were fortunate in having a very solid substratum to build upon. A number of officers still survived, officers who were veterans in experience of actual warfare. Their numbers were sadly diminished. Out of 3,000 officers at the beginning of the war, four hundred and thirteen had fallen in August, 1914, and four hundred and thirty-nine in September, without counting the wounded and a very large number killed in October on the Yser. The effective Army had been reduced to 32,000 men, and even this pitifully small group was largely composed of men who had been worn out in the months of fierce fighting—many of them wounded, many of them ill. A new army had to arise.

The Belgians concentrated on the improvements of their artillery. Their old guns were of very varying type, many quite unsuited for modern warfare. Now they began to accumulate a strong force of new guns, and to train an army of artillerymen. The guns of the Belgians soon became noted among the Allies, and in the short front of the Belgian Army the Germans were often quiet lest the big guns, the "soixante-quinze," and the trench-mortars of the Belgians should open out on them and deal cruel punishment.

It was determined that the new Army should be as far as possible of young men. Here came one great difficulty in recruiting. The vast majority of the young men of Belgium were in territory occupied by the Germans, who naturally did not intend to let them out to fight them. There were considerable numbers of Belgians in England and in France. These, with the soldiers of the old Army, formed a nucleus, and thousands of young men broke through the frontier barriers between Belgium and Holland, and from Holland made their way to England to serve their King. Fresh conscription laws were passed, but for large numbers of the Belgians no conscription was necessary. The man who allowed his sons to remain in safety in neutral lands when Belgium was calling for them was looked upon by his fellows as little better than an outcast.

One well-to-do Belgian visited a general at the front, an old friend of his, whom he had not seen for many years, to ask his help in securing permission to see his two sons. "Certainly," the general replied. "Tell me which regiment they are in, and I will see that you get through to them at once." The man stammered, hesitated, and blushed. "They are not in the Army," he murmured. "I wanted permission from the authorities to go to Switzerland, where they are, to see them." The general's eyes flamed with sudden wrath. He rose to his feet, stretched out his hand threateningly. "Get out of here!" he shouted. "Don't pollute this office by remaining in it! I give you

BELGIAN MARINES IN THE TRENCHES.
Belgium has no navy, and her Marines, like those of Holland and Austria, are a military organisation of infantry and artillery used chiefly in garrison work and not as complements of sea-going ships.

one minute to leave, and if you don't quit you will be thrown out! The Belgian whose sons are resting in Switzerland has no place here. Go!"

And so the new Belgian Army came into being with the glorious traditions of the old and with the methods of the new. It adopted the familiar khaki uniform, with certain little decorations which the Belgians love. Its equipment was in every way admirable; from the most efficient form of gas-helmet to machine-guns nothing was lacking. It was the boast of the Belgians that they had more machine-guns to a regiment than any other part of the Allies. Their cavalry still retained its ancient fire.

The Belgian cavalry have ever been noted as splendid horsemen, and the squadrons that rode along behind the lines in the waiting days of 1916 were as fine as any Belgium had ever seen. In the earlier days of the war the Belgians had done well with their armoured-car corps. They still retained their armoured-car companies; they even sent a corps of them to help the Russians. Many of the officers who had done good work in the earlier fighting were still at the head of them, and they were looking forward for the moment when they might advance on to the foe.

Improvement on the medical side

One of the greatest improvements made by the Belgians in their new organisation was on the medical side. In the early fighting of 1914 the Belgian Medical Department had been overwhelmed. A considerable amount of help, notably from England, and especially from the British field hospital at Furnes, had been afforded, but it was inadequate to meet the needs. There were hospitals without supplies, hospitals with doctors who had no real surgical experience, hospitals insufficient to hold one-tenth

[*Belgian official photograph.*

TYPE OF BELGIAN ARMOURED-MOTOR GUN.
Armoured motor-cars were used effectively by the Belgian troops and the British naval force in Belgium in the early stages of the war. The service was greatly developed in the reconstructed Army.

and October, did not keep out the slimy mud of the polders, mud so tenacious that, in order to reduce cartage to a minimum, the farms of the neighbourhood are built in the centre of the fields which are under cultivation.

Good drinking water was lacking, the wells were contaminated, and the cisterns did not hold enough.

The number of sick admitted to the hospital increased considerably. In December, 1914, the proportion reached 1·78 per cent. of the effective troops, in January, 1915, 2·55 per cent.

It was a dreadful time. But the authorities acted energetically.

Out of five hundred and fifty doctors in the service, fifteen had been killed and fifty-five wounded.

A series of fresh hospitals was erected, sanitary conditions were revolutionised, a whole system of hospitals in the rear was planned to which the wounded could be

of the wounded that were sent to them. The Belgians lost in the early days 11,685 officers and men killed. In three days alone, in October, 1914, 9,050 wounded men were taken back to temporary hospitals. The suffering among the troops at that time was fearful, and much of it might have been avoided had there been an adequate medical service.

Sufferings of the soldiers With the memories of these ghastly days fresh in their minds, the Belgians began to transform their service. What was their position at the start? One Belgian official account may well be quoted :

In October, 1914, at the front, there stretched an immense watery expanse, in which could be seen floating about the decomposing bodies of men and animals. In the rear the accumulated floods from the heavy rains, having no other way to escape, again covered the ground in many places which had been formerly wrested from the sea with much painful toil. The estuary of the Yser thus became again the marsh of the epoch of the Menapians.

The position of the Army lay thus between the drier and more healthy regions which were occupied by the Allies, with the dunes of the coast on the one side and the undulating country of Poperinghe on the other.

The inevitable depression of spirit which comes after days of violent action, the exigencies of the service which required the same work, the same duties in the same regiment from men of different ages and of considerably different physical capacity (our military reorganisation was not then complete, and its rapid mobilisation had somewhat rushed things) ; the innumerable difficulties of housing, provisioning, and accommodation in a part of the country which was not suitable for maintaining armies through a winter campaign ; the special mentality of the soldier who had not yet had much discipline in the direction of the preventive treatment of contagious diseases ; the prolonged stay in the damp trenches, often filled with the water of the Yser ; the rain, the wind, the cold at the beginning of December ; all these conditions together were more than enough to ensure an outbreak of winter complaints, or of epidemic diseases.

The Battle of the Yser ended just at the beginning of the winter season. Nothing had been prepared for a stay in this inhospitable region.

The soldiers had but little shelter from the rain and the mud. They had only a very small number of separate tents, each made of a piece of impermeable canvas, over a yard square. The normal population of the region was less than 30,000 ; it was now more than quadrupled, first by the Army and then by the influx of the inhabitants who had fled before the invasion.

If the provision of food and ammunition was satisfactory, the replacing of equipment gave rise to many vexations. A change of linen was often wanting in the months of November and December, 1914. The shoes, worn out by the incessant marching of September

[*Belgian official photograph.*

TWO OF BELGIUM'S NEW IRONCLAD LANDSHIPS.
Another type of armoured car, with a fleet of which the Belgians were provided. The flat plains of Flanders, when free from inundation, were admirably adapted for the use of these engines.

sent quickly, the ambulance service was reorganised, and a number of ambulances sent from England and elsewhere were employed. Thus, under the new system, there came a series of fixed hospitals at the front. The Belgian field hospital at Furnes had 100 beds ; a large hospital at La Panne was opened in November, 1914, with 800 beds ; a third hospital near Adinkerke, known as the Hospitale Cabour, was opened at the end of April, 1915. It was of special interest to the outside world because the Radiograph Department was under the control of Madame Curie, the famous French woman scientist. A fourth hospital was opened four months afterwards at Bourbourg. These hospitals, one and all, were equipped in the most modern and efficient way. **Modern hospitals** They were staffed, in part, by famous **and ambulances** specialists from all parts of the world, who had volunteered their services. They not only carried on the work of healing, but also maintained research laboratories.

Twenty-eight ambulances were actively engaged in conveying the wounded as soon as possible from the hospitals at the front to the base at Calais, where various special hospitals had been organised. Experience had shown that it was not wise, however, to centralise the wounded too much around Calais, and so a large hospital

RUSSIAN STAFF OFFICERS' VISIT TO THE BELGIAN FLYING CORPS.
The officers inspecting various kinds of air-bombs are from left to right: Captain Prefviano, Russian Attaché to the Belgian Headquarters Staff; Colonel Koudatcheff, General Romanowsky, Major van Crombrugghe, Chief of the Belgian Flying Corps; Colonel Loganoff, Flight-Captain d'Heudecourt, Flight-Lieutenant Coomans, and Commander de Haon, of the Belgian Headquarters Staff.

district was created at Rennes, in France, with thirty-one hospitals and 5,000 beds. Here also a series of hospitals for convalescents, for the mentally affected, for nervous breakdowns, and for the tuberculous were established, with a total of over 2,000 beds. Several hospital trains were built for conveying the men there.

A number of Belgian doctors arrived in England in November, 1914, to arrange for the housing of the wounded here. They went first to the Salvation **Task of the New Army**, which was of the greatest ser-**Army** vice to them at the beginning. Then Belgian general hospitals, three in number, were created, under the general name of King Albert Hospitals. The chief of these was at Staffordshire House, Store Street, Tottenham Court Road, which the Belgians obtained, thanks to the generosity of Messrs. Bourne & Hollingsworth, the well-known drapers.

The Belgian Army, as re-created, did not immediately attempt a great offensive against the Germans. There was abundant reason for this. It was in the highest degree desirable that the Belgians should have an effective military force ready to hand when the moment came for the reoccupation of their own territory. Had they attempted to take a leading place in the fighting of 1915-16 their little Army would have been virtually wiped out. They had created, it is true, an effective force more than equal to their original Army at the outbreak of the war, but that would have counted for comparatively little in battles where the men on either side were numbered by the million.

It must not be imagined, however, that the Belgian Army during the months of waiting did nothing. It held one section of the allied line from immediately

north of Ypres to Nieuport by the sea. During 1915 and 1916 it was frequently attacked by the Germans, and it made counter-attacks in response. Such fighting was never much more than skirmishing, but it was enough to keep in touch with the realities of war, and the Belgian Army looked forward eagerly, passionately, to the hour for revenge. Every officer, nearly every soldier, had tragic and bitter memories of the horrors of the early days. They could tell tales of brutal outrages, often to their own kith and kin, that would have seemed incredible to the outsider. Numbers of them had never seen their wives and children for two years and more, for wives and children were still in Belgium, under German rule, and any attempt to write to them was made a crime by the Germans, a crime bringing quick punishment on the women in their power.

In the days before the war the Germans had quietly and secretly attempted to promote hostility between the two great branches of the Belgian people—the Flemings and the Walloons. The Flemings had certain racial attributes in common with the Germans. German writers claimed that they were of Low German race, and could adapt themselves readily to the German nature. To the disappointment of the Germans, however, the Flemings were as fierce against them when the war broke out as were the rest of their countrymen. The greatest insult that could be inflicted on a Fleming was to suggest that he had any likeness to a German.

After the occupation of the country the Germans,

BEER CELLAR OF A TRENCH CANTEEN NEAR THE YSER.
Quite apart from any other justification for the supply of beer to the Belgian troops as part of their provisioning, good drinking water was lacking in Belgium, for the wells were contaminated and the cisterns did not hold enough.

[*Belgian official photograph.*

FIELD-TELEPHONE OPERATOR AT WORK.
Portable telephones played an inestimable part in the Great War. They were indispensable, indeed, for their only possible supplanter — portable wireless transmitting and receiving apparatus—had not been brought to practicable perfection.

however, renewed their Flemish campaign. In the prison camps in Germany the Flemish prisoners were separated from the others and treated differently. A mysterious propaganda arose, and numerous pamphlets were issued attempting to split the nation. The Flemings were offered privileges. Towns were renamed in Flemish. Public notices in various parts had to be written in German or Flemish, and not in French; and, finally, as a crowning bribe, it was announced that a Flemish university was about to be founded at Ghent. For years the Flemings had desired this, and had striven to secure its establishment. And now they were offered it as a free gift from Germany. Leading Flemings were approached with splendid offers of professorships. Every possible inducement **was** offered to the Flemish families to send their sons. Men who had made themselves prominent in opposing the scheme were summarily punished, and two noted Belgian scholars, Professor Pirenne and Professor Frederieff, were sentenced to a long term of penal servitude for their unfriendly attitude. But the bribe failed. Only a few men of second and third rate standing consented to serve as teachers. The Flemings, as a whole, would have nothing to do with the university To them Belgium was one.

Attempt to bribe the Flemings

Between August and November, 1914, many Belgian people fled from the advancing Germans and found refuge in England. Their numbers were probably not less than 250,000. Certain towns, such as Folkestone, were for the moment almost flooded with the Belgians. These people, many of them formerly in easy circumstances, arrived usually with nothing but what they stood up in, and even the clothes they wore were often the first garments that had been snatched up as they hastily rose to escape from the German troops. Organisations were quickly improvised in England to deal with the Belgians, and large numbers of British families offered hospitality.

At first the British Government proposed that these Belgians should be treated as the guests of the nation. It

was feared that we ourselves were in for a period of considerable unemployment, and it was not deemed wise to allow friendly aliens to rob our own people of work that was wanted. So numerous regulations were passed the real purpose of which was to prevent the Belgians from obtaining employment here. We should feed them, house them, clothe them, and do our best to provide comfortably for them, but they must not undersell our own people or undercut them in the labour market.

Before many months it was realised that this line of policy was a very great mistake. It was bad for the Belgians and bad for ourselves. No people can live for months in unaccustomed idleness without some deterioration, and the Belgians were no exception to the rule. Many of the refugees did not settle down easily in British families; their ways of life were different, and there came, with the best of will on both sides, a clashing of customs. In the distribution of the refugees among families some mistakes were inevitable. There were cases where Belgian peasants were sent as guests to wealthy homes, and found themselves suddenly surrounded by luxuries, and expected to observe social conventions totally alien from their lives.

The refugees in England

ARMY SIGNALLER AT WORK IN FLANDERS.
The enormous development of field-telephone and telegraph systems naturally largely replaced the method of visual army signalling by means of flags or semaphores, but for distances up to four miles the flagging method remained in constant use.

The Belgian woman, used to regard fresh air as little better than poison, found herself in the home of some fresh-air enthusiast who regarded windows as parts of the house made only to be left open. Some of the Belgians came here with bitterness in their heart for the Allies, who they thought had betrayed them—bitterness which they did not hesitate to reveal. They might well have been pardoned when it was remembered that they had lost homes and often their dearest ones in the great retreat.

It was found further that so far from Britain experiencing a growth of unemployment because of the war, there was a great scarcity of labour, thanks to the enormous demands for war supplies. Now the Belgian labour was wanted. King Albert urgently appealed to Britain not to pauperise his people by supplying their wants without letting them work. The result of all this was to bring us to the second stage of the Belgian influx, when every effort was made to find work for the Belgians, and to enable them to maintain homes of their own in England where they could live as they had been accustomed to. Large numbers of them quickly found employment in armament works, in mines, and on the land. Others were absorbed in the motor trade and in the woollen industry.

Belgian women were employed in very large numbers in munition factories, earning wages in many cases far beyond what they had ever dreamed **Following Huguenot** possible. There were still a certain **example** number of people utterly unsuitable for work here. For them provision had to be made. There was also a certain group of undesirables whose presence caused much perplexity both to the British and the Belgian authorities.

Just as in the seventeenth century the Huguenots, driven from France, founded their colonies here, colonies which left their distinctive mark on England for centuries to come, so did the Belgians of the early twentieth century. The Huguenots arrived to settle permanently among us. The Belgians came with the intention of returning as soon as possible to their own land. But as the months passed on and extended into years they found their hold on life in England growing closer and closer. With their own Press, their own amusements, and their own life, they soon became recognised as a distinctive part of London. Belgian pastry-cooks in Oxford Street and Piccadilly and elsewhere soon became noted. Belgian cafés arose by the dozen in the little streets around Tottenham Court Road, the Liègoise, the Belgique Libre, and the like. Apparently these cafés had few English customers; they were the little meeting-places of the Belgians themselves. Belgian dress-makers, after a time, modified what Englishwomen at first thought their somewhat extreme modes to British requirements, and obtained a comfortable clientèle.

The Belgians cannot be said to have introduced many new industries as the Huguenots did. One somewhat curious feature of their coming was the establishment over London of various houses for the sale of horse-flesh. To the Englishman the display of horse-flesh as a food seems repulsive. The Belgian has no such feeling. One firm alone had by the autumn of 1916 seven shops in and around West London for the vending of such luxuries as "Les filets d'Anvers," "Les Saucissons de Boulogne," "Les Saucissons de Ménage," etc. English people, truth to tell, looked somewhat askance at the bright and clean shops where the sausages and neatly rolled ribs and clean-cut fillets of horse were displayed.

What was to be the future of Belgium? That was anxiously asked by many of the Belgians themselves. What would happen when the allied armies succeeded in advancing and the Germans were driven back from point to point in Belgium itself? Was the field of Waterloo once more to be the battleground on which the fate of Europe should be decided, and were the Germans to wreak their vengeance in the hour of defeat on the Belgian people? Was it likely that they would, as they retired, leave nothing but ruins behind them, and that the fall of Germany should be preceded by the burning of Brussels, the destruction of Ghent, and the obliteration of Bruges? These were questions to which no answer could be given. Everyone recognised that Belgium had not yet reached the end of her era of suffering. There was yet a long and painful road over which the martyred nation of Europe must travel.

Among the people of Britain one feeling predominated. Britain realised that Belgium by her splendid response in the early days of the war had saved the Continent of Europe

from German domination. The feeling of the nation was well expressed by Mr. Asquith when he said "Belgium has deserved well of the world. She has placed us under an obligation which as a nation we shall not forget. We assure her to-day in the name of this United Kingdom and of the whole Empire that she may count to the end on our whole-hearted and unfailing support."

Lord Curzon expressed our sentiments still more eloquently:

Belgium by her conduct, and still more by her example, has rendered a priceless service to humanity, for she has once more taught the world the sublime truth that national honour is preferable to national security; and that, though the body may be destroyed, the spirit is immortal. For the moment a crown of thorns has been pressed down upon her temples, but Europe—nay the civilised world—will see to it that she is healed of her grievous wounds; and some day, let us hope before long, she will live again in the recovered prosperity of her people and the admiring gratitude of mankind.

Amid the varying fortunes of the war the British people never forgot their debt of gratitude. "We shall never sheathe the sword," said Mr. Asquith, "until Belgium recovers in full measure more than all that she has sacrificed." In the summer of 1916 the German Government tried indirectly to induce the Belgian King and the Belgian Government to cease their hostility. It was intimated to them that much would be done to conciliate them. Germany would withdraw her armies from Belgian soil as soon as military conditions permitted, and she would even compensate Belgium liberally as an ally for the damage that Germany had done to her territory as a foe. Belgium might even remain a separate unit in the German world-State.

German diplomacy attempted to hold before the King's eyes the glittering vision of himself back again at Brussels, in his palace, enthroned afresh in the hearts of his people, the man who brought them relief from the horrors of war and freedom from military rule. The tempting bait was offered in vain. The Belgian people had tasted to the full the harshness and inhumanity of German methods. It knew too well the value of German promises. It had pledged its troth to the Allies. Its sons had fought side by side with the Allies as comrades, and were fighting side by side still. Between them and Germany lay a great and impassable barrier of ruined homes, of murdered old men and women and children, and of endless agony Thousands of Belgians in German prisons were alone a barrier against improved relations. What Germany had done was not to be forgiven. No bribes could atone.

And as Belgian statesmen looked forward to the future they realised that the prospect was not altogether black. When Germany was defeated Belgium was to be restored. The rebuilding of her ruined houses and the restoration of her stolen treasures would alone ensure for her a period of great industrial prosperity in the years immediately following the war. Belgium still **Looking to the** retained the mass of her manhood **future** uninjured. The losses in the early fighting, heavy as they seemed at the time, had been small compared with the losses other nations incurred.

Belgium, with a compact community of between seven and eight million people, occupying one of the best geographical sites in Europe, knit by ties of blood and sympathy to her fellow-conquerors, might well start out on a long period of sustained well-being. The bitter memories of the early years of the war could never be effaced. But even bitter memories would be softened as time went on, and would be illuminated by the unforgettable tale of the brave men and women who had shed on Belgium's record an imperishable glory.

MR. HERBERT HOOVER
Chairman and active Managing Director of
the Commission for Relief in Belgium.

Immediately the searchlights found her, shells burst near the Zeppelin, and soon afterwards her outline became visible in a white glow.

When she was aglow from end to end she tilted, gradually became perpendicular, and began her awful plunge down to the earth.

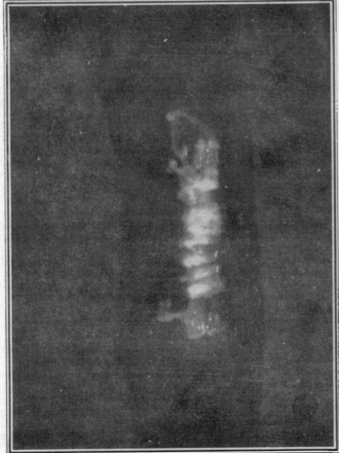

During her fall a large section of the airship seemed to break away, and fell almost vertically, still burning fiercely.

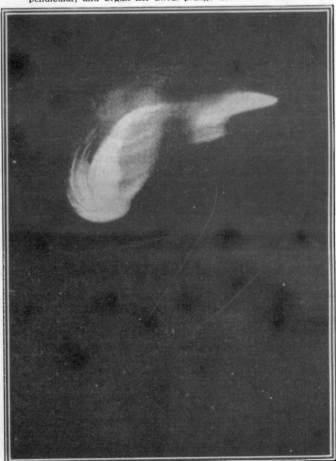

The flaming gold-and-ruby mass came down swiftly with a roar, shooting out showers of sparks as it fell.

THE END OF THE RAIDER: POTTER'S BAR, OCTOBER 1ST, 1916.

THE AIRSHIP RAIDS OF 1916 AND HOW BRITISH AIRMEN MASTERED THE SUPER-ZEPPELIN.

By H. W. Wilson.

Construction of Super-Zeppelins in 1916 Specifically for the Destruction of London—Systematisation and Organisation of Defence—Forced Landing of L33 in Essex, September 24th—Details of Construction of its Hull, Gondolas, and Machinery—Size and Horse-power of the Earlier Naval Zeppelins—L15 Brought Down near the Mouth of the Thames, March 31st—L20 Grounded on the Norwegian Coast, and Destroyed by the Norwegian Government, May 3rd—L7 Destroyed by British Submarine E31, May 4th—LZ85 Destroyed by British Battleship near Salonika, May 5th—L11 Damaged, August 2nd—Military Zeppelin Destroyed by Lieut. W. L. Robinson, at Cuffley, September 2nd—L32 Destroyed by Lieuts. Sowrey and Brandon, and L33 by its Own Crew when Forced to Land, September 23rd—German Chagrin and Fury—L31 Destroyed by Lieut. Tempest, October 1st—Super-Zeppelin Destroyed by Lieut. Pyott off the Durham Coast, and Another by Lieut. Cadbury and Sub-Lieuts. Pulling and Fane off the Norfolk Coast, November 27th-28th—Ruin of the Prestige of the German Zeppelin Fleet—Tables of Airship Raids and German Airship Losses in 1916.

TOWARDS the close of the spring of 1916 reports began to appear in the German and the Swiss Press of a new type of Zeppelin surpassing in size and power everything that up to that date had been constructed. The new airships, it was said, were being specially built, from Count Zeppelin's designs, for the destruction of London. They were to carry an increased armament of guns and a heavier cargo of bombs. Their peculiar virtue lay in a far larger displacement, which enabled them to reach and hold much higher altitudes in the air, and in a greatly enhanced speed. There were tales that their gondolas would be armoured and would be so built as to serve as boats if they should by any chance have to descend at sea. As for their range of action it was to be such as to bring the whole area of the British Isles within their power of attack, and even to enable them in fine weather or with a favourable wind to cross the Atlantic.

These great engines actually existed, and were no mere figment of the imagination. Their capacity for mischief was immense had the British anti-aircraft

THE MEN WHO HIT LZ85.

Control officer and gunlayer who sighted and laid the British battleship's anti-aircraft gun that brought down the LZ85 in the marshes of the Vardar, near Salonika, May 5th, 1916.

service remained sunk in the torpor and indolence of "darkness and composure" which had been the air defence policy in 1915. Fortunately, throughout the spring the British military authorities—who had now been put in complete control of the arrangements for meeting Zeppelin attack inland—were working, too, though they talked very little indeed. The organisation which they were creating was not perfected for many months. The problem of defeating Zeppelin attack was now studied seriously for the first time, new devices were tested, and the methods were thought out which were ultimately to be successful, and which, had they only been applied in early 1915 might have saved hundreds of British lives and grave loss of prestige. It was a close race. To obtain satisfactory means of combating the Zeppelins and keeping them off the great British munition-making centres was indispensable for the success of British arms, and there were moments in early 1916 when it almost seemed as if the enemy aircraft had the game in their hands.

The special methods introduced by Lord French and the Royal Flying Corps were necessarily kept secret if only because they

219

promised a plentiful harvest of blazing airships did the Zeppelins persist in continuing their raids. This much could safely be said at the end of 1916 : The arrangements for defence were systematised and organised. The enemy gradually began to feel that he was under the constant observation of an invisible eye, such as that with which the Mormon " destroying angels " followed their victims. He might be in mist or hovering over remote fenland districts, almost out of touch with man, and yet this uncanny surveillance followed him. Where there was surveillance there was always the unnerving possibility of attack by the British defence forces. The bombing of British women and children had been an enjoyable enough pastime in 1915—with the sole interlude of Lieutenant Warneford's heroic and successful attack upon a returning Zeppelin. In 1916 it began to grow risky, and towards the close of the year it had become infinitely perilous to the assassins of the air. It was a distinct triumph of British skill and ingenuity that means were found to conquer the super-Zeppelin and to rob it entirely of its menace. The elimination of the Zeppelins was a correspondingly severe blow to the Germans, who placed the most extravagant hopes in these ships.

From time to time the new airships were seen exercising over Lake Constance, carrying out trial trips from Count Zeppelin's yard at Friedrichshafen on that lake. Neutral observers noted

THE MEN WHO HIT LZ77.
Adjutant Gramling, who directed the fire, and (left) Private Pennetier, who laid and fired the shot that brought down the military airship LZ77 near Revigny, February 21st, 1916.

their immense size, the large number of gondolas, the extraordinary speed with which they moved. It was not till the autumn of 1916, when one of these mysterious giants, intact but for its outer covering and the material of its gasbags, fell into the hands of the British forces, that the exact details of its construction could be ascertained. They will be of intense interest to posterity which may never see a Zeppelin. The airship in question, L33, was one of the very largest type built by the enemy. It was compelled by the British artillery fire to make a forced landing in Essex, where the crew, after setting it alight, surrendered, and where its hull, gondolas, and machinery could be studied at leisure, and were examined by the writer.

The super-Zeppelin was of immense bulk, little inferior in size to a Lusitania. It displaced fifty tons weight of air and contained 2,000,000 cubic feet of gas. Its outer surface was not of gold-beaters' skin, which in the past was commonly employed for airships, but of finely-woven Manchester cotton. On this cotton delicate wavy lines were printed in black or darkblue. The colour effect of the envelope seen from a distance was grey ; closely examined it looked like newspaper covered with very fine print of a microscopic fount. This material was perhaps adopted to render the airship less visible, though it is also possible that the lines may have been printed to make the fabric resemble

DAMAGE DONE IN PARIS BY AN ELUSIVE AND SHY NIGHT-RAIDER.
A Zeppelin raid was made on Paris, January 29th, 1916, resulting in fifty-seven casualties, of whom twenty-six were killed. No military purpose was achieved but some material damage was done, as shown in these two photographs. Another raid was made the following night, but thereafter the air defences of Paris were so well developed that the French capital was left unassailed by Zeppelins.

shirting and enable it to pass the blockade. It was not varnished or treated in any way, except, it may be, by a solution for rendering it non-inflammable. It played in the airship the same part as the thin outer steel plating of a seafaring vessel. It was tough and very hard to tear, while it would offer no resistance to artillery projectiles unless these had extremely sensitive fuses.

As the outer steel plating of a sea-going vessel is carried on frames, so was this cotton covering of the airship. But whereas the frames in a sea-going vessel are of steel and are ponderous, in the airship they were of the lightest metal available, an alloy of aluminium, and of lattice-work design, with an air of extraordinary

INTERESTING EXHIBIT AT FINSBURY.
In the course of one of the air raids over East Anglia a Zeppelin jettisoned, or lost, her observation-car, which was found, with some hundreds of yards of the connecting wire, by a farmer next morning.

LONDON'S LORD MAYOR VIEWS LONDON'S ENEMY.
The remains of the Zeppelin which was brought down at Cuffley by Lieut. Robinson, V.C., September 2nd, 1916, were placed on exhibition at the Honourable Artillery Company's Headquarters, Finsbury. Sir Charles Wakefield opening the exhibition.

fragility about them that made them seem almost fantastic. Besides these frames there were similar longitudinal girders running the length of the ship. The enormous skeleton of metal, six hundred and eighty feet long and seventy-two feet in beam, covered over an acre of ground and looked as large as a fairy-like but shattered Crystal Palace. In shape the hull was stream-lined, which means that the forward end was comparatively blunt and was larger

Form of the Super-Zeppelin in diameter than the amidships portion. Astern it tapered down and terminated in a fine point at the tail. The general shape of the hull was that of a huge cigar with twenty-five sides. In this respect it differed markedly from the earlier Zeppelins, which were not stream-lined, but had the bow shaped similar to the stern, and had only seventeen or eighteen sides. The super-Zeppelin's hull was far more favourable to a high speed. It seems possible that she may have attained eighty miles an hour in fine weather conditions, though her average speed would not be more than fifty miles an hour.

Within the great cigar-shaped hull were twenty-four gasbags made of a silk fabric, coated with indiarubber varnish, and gas-proof. Each bag was shaped like a Cheddar cheese, and probably each was fitted with two valves, one of which was hand-operated and opened at the top of the airship, while the other, an automatic valve for releasing the gas when the pressure rose dangerously, was placed at the side of the hull. Passing through the gasbags by a gas-tight valve, **Use of the** and running from end to end of the hull, **central cable** was a great wire hawser. From this radial wires were carried to each aluminium transverse frame, as the spokes of a cycle-wheel run from the hub to the rim of the wheel. These radial wires kept the gasbags apart, and when the great central cable was tightened —for which a very simple device was fitted—the tension on them was tautened, too, and the whole framework of the ship was braced, exactly as the masts of a sailing ship are braced at sea by tightening the stays and rigging. The great cable, the existence of which no one in this country had suspected, thus served to keep the hull of the ship together and to relieve the strain on it when it was exposed to gun fire or to wind.

On the top of the hull forward was a small platform on which two 5 in. guns, firing a little shell of nearly a pound weight, were mounted, entirely isolated from the rest of the crew. Right astern, not far from the apex of the tail, was another station for a single 5 in. gun, in a yet lonelier and more dangerous position. These were the weapons to which the designers of the super-Zeppelin trusted for repelling aeroplane attack. These remote stations in the great rustling hull were reached by a ladder or by climbing the aluminium lattice-work girders from the "cat-walk," which ran along the keel. This walk gave a means of passing from end to end of the hull, but it was so perilously narrow that to use it must have severely strained any but the steadiest nerves. The width of the gangway was only nine inches of the thinnest three-ply wood, laid directly on the girder framing. If a man missed his footing he would shoot through the flimsy cotton cover and fall to certain death, though there was a handhold, in the form of a rope, to enable him to grope his way in the darkness of the ship's interior.

The earlier naval Zeppelins were of one-third the size and horse-power, with screws at the side and engines of rather under 500 h.p. The petrol tanks of the super-Zeppelin carried 2,000 gallons, and were all placed in or near the "cat-walk," so as to keep them well away from the engines. There were many ingenious contrivances, among them an apparatus for releasing the mooring-ropes by the pressure of a button. The exhaust from the engines appeared to be carried up through the hull of the airship so as to keep the gas warm when cruising in the frightful cold of the upper air. A smoke-producing apparatus was fitted. Like other Zeppelins, this airship was probably equipped with a small observation car capable of containing one man, which could be lowered 1,000 yards, and was connected with the airship by a telephone cable. One of these cars was jettisoned by the enemy in East Anglia, and if none was found in L33 it was perhaps because she had thrown her car overboard at sea before she grounded.

The report that the gondolas were armoured was explained by the appearance of the aluminium of which they were made, and which looked like burnished steel. The metal was a very tough sheeting, about a fifth of an

LUCKY SURVIVORS OF L20.
The crew of the Zeppelin, fortunate in having escaped with their lives, were brought ashore by Norwegian officers.

In this dim alley-way, abaft the forward gondola, was the bomb-chamber, where were hooks for sixty bombs, which may have weighed one and a half tons or more. The hooks were operated electrically by sixty buttons on the murder-keyboard, which was placed in the forward gondola. In form the buttons resembled electric bell-pushes. When the button was pressed the hook released the bomb; a lever was previously moved which opened a sliding shutter, allowing the bomb to fall. This device was the crudest possible, and it made accurate aiming out of the question. Anyone who examined it would understand why Zeppelins never hit their target. A lavatory was also placed in the "cat-walk," but there were no arrangements for cooking.

Arrangement of the gondolas
The gondolas were four in number. Two of these were like large boats, about fifty feet long, placed forward and astern in the centre line. The two others were much smaller, and were placed abreast on either side of the hull, nearer the centre of the ship. The forward one contained the captain's cabin, with wheels controlling the two rudders for vertical and horizontal movement, and other controls for the petrol tanks and the water ballast. The gondolas were covered in with fabric but had non-inflammable celluloid windows. Abaft the captain's cabin was the wireless-room, which was little more than a cupboard, six feet by four feet, and abaft that again was a 240 h.p. Mercédes-Maybach engine with a dynamo and two machine-guns. The engine drove a propeller immediately behind the gondola and underneath the hull. The two small amidships gondolas each contained a similar engine driving a similar propeller, with a dynamo and a machine-gun. The large gondola astern carried three engines, two of which drove propellers at the side of the airship by bevel gearing, and the third a propeller astern of the gondola and underneath the hull. Each engine was fitted with a dynamo, and in the gondola there were two machine-guns. Thus there were six engines each of 240 h.p., totalling 1,440 h.p. in all, six dynamos, six propellers (four under the airship and two at its sides), and six machine-guns, besides the three 5 in. weapons at the bow and stern.

RUINED CAR OF L20 IN CUSTODY OF SOLDIERS.
On the night of May 2nd, 1916, the L20, returning from a raid on Scotland, in the course of which she had almost certainly been crippled by shell fire, fell into the sea near Stavanger. The wreckage was seized by the Norwegian Government and placed under military guard.

inch thick, and was strongly stayed. The gondolas appeared watertight, and would probably have floated but for the heavy weights which they contained.

The crew numbered twenty-three, men of all sizes and not chosen for their lightness. They wore very heavy and warm clothing, and many of them had a special knowledge of East Anglia—indeed, one had worked in Colchester.

The engines were fitted with silencers outside the gondolas, but, notwithstanding these, the noise which they made was very great and was noticed all over the district where the airship landed. Such were these super-Zeppelins, of which the first seems to have been completed in June. L33 on her tanks bore the mark "H 14 7 16," which probably stood for "Herbst (summer) 14th day, 7th month (July), 1916."

German hopes of these ships ran high, and were not daunted by a series of misadventures to the old type of Zeppelin in the spring. On March 31st five Zeppelins raided the Eastern Counties, and one of the five, L15, was hit by the British anti- **Some intercepted** aircraft guns and was finally compelled to **raiders** descend near the mouth of the Thames, where it was attacked by three British patrol vessels. The men on board were rescued, but not before they had set fire to the gas and destroyed the ship. Little more than a month later, on May 3rd, L20, which was probably returning from a raid on the Scottish coast, was caught by a storm and swept towards Stavanger, in Norway. Her petrol ran out, and owing to the failure of her engines she could not be kept under control. She struck the Norwegian coast with great violence, and was badly damaged, though nearly all her crew escaped with their lives. As she became a danger to navigation and there was risk of the Germans carrying off the hull, the Norwegian Government ordered her destruction. On the following day a number of British light cruisers in the Bight of Heligoland sighted L7, which was apparently watching their movements, and at once attacked her. They hit her with gun fire and damaged her badly. She hovered low down near the water, not far from the enemy coast, in an area within which it was perilous for British surface ships to venture. At this juncture a British submarine, E31, suddenly rose from the sea, fired several rounds into the airship's wreck, setting it on fire and completing its destruction, and took off seven of the crew. The others presumably perished.

On the following day, May 5th, at the other end of the battle-front, near Salonika, yet another Zeppelin was destroyed. This craft,

Beginning of the raids

LZ85, was a military airship of the very latest design, but was much smaller than the German naval Zeppelins. She had for some weeks been stationed on the eastern front, and used to raid the allied lines and depots at Salonika. On this particular date she ventured too close, within range of the allied warships. They opened a sharp fire on her and struck her several times, the first hit being claimed by a British battleship. She dropped, disabled, in the marshes near Salonika, where her crew set her on fire. Most of them were captured, but one or two succeeded in making their way to the Bulgarian lines. After this affair enemy airships gave Salonika a wide berth. LZ85, when examined, proved to be almost identical with LZ77, which the French had shot down in flames on February 20th-21st near Verdun, after three hits with their incendiary shell. She had two gondolas, five propellers driven by five engines, and bombs of three sizes, weighing 220 lb., 175 lb., and 110 lb.

In July the new super-Zeppelins began their flights over England. Between May

UNGAINLY WRECKAGE OF THE WONDER SHIP.
After the L20 got away from the English coast she seems to have gone adrift in a storm until, depleted of gas, she dropped into the sea, where she broke in half.

2nd and July 28th there was a long interval during which the enemy airships attempted no raids, possibly because the shortness of the nights, in view of the growing efficiency of the British anti-aircraft artillery, made the Germans chary of taking risks. On the night of July 28th, however, in very warm and fine weather, three airships crossed the coast and travelled over Yorkshire and Lincolnshire. These three may have been L31, L32, and L33, all of the super-Zeppelin type. They did no damage, and the object of their visit was a little difficult at the time to understand. What was taken for a raid may have been only a trial run.

On the 31st six or seven Zeppelins crossed the coast at various points and cruised over no fewer than seven of the Eastern Counties. They flew at enormous heights and dropped bombs at random in the oddest places. But again they did no damage beyond burning a haystack. On August 2nd they reappeared, when eight Zeppelins, two of which, according to the enemy, were of super-Zeppelin type, dropped bombs in the Eastern Counties, again causing only trifling damage and injuring no human being. They were heavily fired at, and after this raid L11 was seen steering in very damaged condition over Dutch territory, where she ought to have been shot down. She was attacked with musketry by the Dutch, but was not hit. The enemy had now adopted a practice of regularly crossing Dutch territory, but although his callous breach of neutrality was resented he was very rarely effectively attacked during these acts of trespass. On August 9th there was another raid by a large number of airships, in which South-Eastern Scotland was visited and twenty-seven casualties were inflicted. On August 23rd a solitary airship, probably reconnoitring, crossed the coast, but, though she dropped many bombs, she did no damage whatever.

THE DOOMED LEVIATHAN WRITHING ON THE WAVES.
Another view of the broken-backed leviathan, its hinder half almost submerged. Above: Having got quite close to shore the Zeppelin was visited by many people, who rowed out to see the wreckage before it was finally destroyed by the Norwegian authorities.

In May, 1916, the German Admiralty reported that one of a party of raiding airships had failed to return. This was why.

L7 had been hit by gun fire from H.M. cruisers Phæton and Galatea and finally brought down by a British submarine.

While her broken, blazing hull was disappearing in the waves, her crew swam to the submarine which had dealt the knock-out blow.

They were hauled aboard the submarine and, thankful to be alive, insisted on shaking hands warmly with their humane captors.

DESTRUCTION OF L7 NEAR HORN REEF IN MAY, 1916.

The Germans, in fact, now fought shy of points where they knew anti-aircraft artillery was mounted, while they found it increasingly difficult to discover their own whereabouts. The darkening of all lights had been so effectively enforced, after long and inexcusable delay, that the largest city might be quite invisible from above. In the early raids they could steer straight for the glare of London, which shone before them like a beacon. Now that glare had disappeared. And as they groped and felt their way they must have often heard the humming of British aeroplanes and known that they were being watched and followed by the invisible eye.

An effort to attack, however, was made on August 24th, when some six Zeppelins raided the East and South-East Counties.

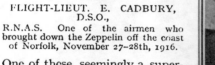

FLIGHT-LIEUT. E. CADBURY, D.S.O., R.N.A.S. One of the airmen who brought down the Zeppelin off the coast of Norfolk, November 27–28th, 1916.

One of these, seemingly a super-Zeppelin, reached outer London, and there dropped incendiary and explosive bombs, damaging an engineering works and a power station, the latter very slightly. Forty-four persons were killed and injured, and the raiders escaped unhurt. This apparent failure on the part of the defence forces was severely criticised, and defects were removed. From this date the raids began to be increasingly disastrous to the enemy.

On September 2nd the greatest raid yet planned was made. All Germany was agog with anticipation. Three super-Zeppelins, at least seven other Zeppelins of the naval pattern, and three military rigid airships took part in this invasion, which was to lay London in ruins and attack most of the great manufacturing centres of the Midlands. It ended in the most grotesque failure. In the Eastern and South-Eastern Counties the airships wandered about, lost in the upper air, evidently quite uncertain of their position, and dropped a large number of bombs at random, with so little result that only fifteen casualties were reported.

Two of the airships were hit by the British artillery, but were not, unluckily, set on fire. One of them threw overboard many objects, including an observation car and portions of her machinery and armament. On the following

THREE HEROES OF THE R.F.C.
From left to right : Lieut. W. L. Robinson, V.C., Lieut. W. J. Tempest, D.S.O., Sec.-Lieut. F. Sowrey, D.S.O.

SUB-LIEUT. E. L. PULLING, D.S.O., R.N.A.S. Who assisted in the destruction of the Zeppelin off the coast of Norfolk, November 27–28th, 1916.

day this airship was seen by the Dutch passing their coast and going very slowly, while her crew could be discerned jettisoning various objects to get away.

The squadron of military airships was less fortunate. Two of the three were driven off London by the fire of the anti-aircraft guns. The third airship attempted to attack by the east. About 2.20 a.m. of the 3rd, which was a very clear starlit night, though with cloudy patches here and there, the enemy was plainly seen by spectators over a vast area near London. Pencils of light swept across the

LIEUT. I. V. PYOTT, D.S.O., R.F.C. Who brought down the Zeppelin off the coast of Durham, November 27th, 1916.

LIEUT. A. DE B. BRANDON, D.S.O., R.F.C. Who brought down the Zeppelin L32 in Essex, September 24th, 1916.

SUB-LIEUT. G. W. R. FANE, D.S.O., R.N.A.S. Who assisted in the destruction of the Zeppelin off the coast of Norfolk, November 27–28th, 1916.

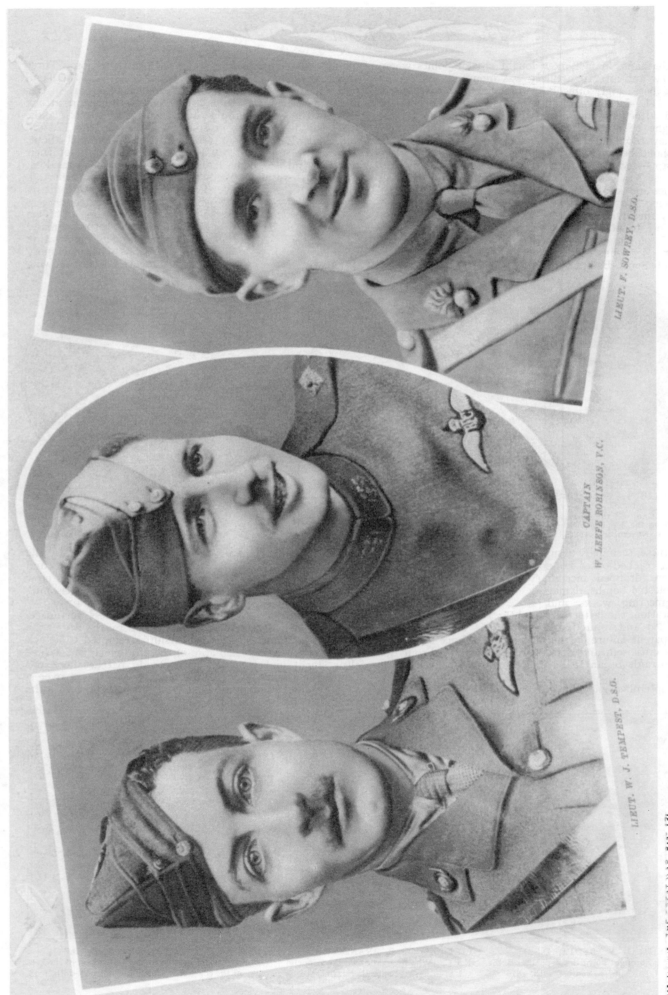

LIEUT. F. SOWREY, D.S.O.

CAPTAIN
W. LEEFE ROBINSON, V.C.

LIEUT. W. J. TEMPEST, D.S.O.

Three Famous Heroes of the Royal Flying Corps

was calm and starlit, with patches of cloud. Two of the airships actually reached London and dropped many bombs there, in the southern and south-east district, killing twenty-eight persons and injuring ninety-nine. Though several small houses were demolished and a few fires were caused, no military damage was inflicted and no munition works were hit. It is possible that these raiders escaped. In the country there were fifteen casualties, while a railway-station in one Midland town was injured. Against this the enemy suffered very serious loss. One of the super-Zeppelins, L32, was attacked east of London by two British fighting aeroplanes, brilliantly piloted by Lieutenants Sowrey and Brandon, both of the Royal Flying Corps.

Again enormous crowds over a vast area witnessed a thrilling combat in mid-air. Again they suddenly saw a glow like that of a red-hot cigar appear at one end of the Zeppelin. For a few seconds the vast mass of the airship remained aflame at a height of about 8,000 feet; then, as in the case of the vessel destroyed by Lieutenant Robinson, it plunged swiftly to the ground, lighting up the whole sky with a crimson glare. Again all on board perished. Some of the crew were flung out, probably the men manning the guns on the platforms on the top of the hull and at its tail; others remained in her to the end and perished by the most appalling of deaths in the blaze which swept them to earth.

Earlier in the night British anti-aircraft guns struck another Zeppelin of the giant type, L33, attempting to reach London. She seems to have been hit on her petrol tanks, some of which showed dents when she was captured, and also on the bevel gearing of one of her wing propellers, which was shot off. She was seen at many points in Essex travelling low down and in evident difficulties. Eluding the British aeroplanes which hunted her furiously to complete her destruction, she passed over the Essex coast, steering to sea. It was noticed that her

Fate of the L33 engines made an unusually loud noise and seemed to be running very badly; moreover, she was flying so low that she was evidently all but helpless.

The airship proceeded about a couple of miles out to sea when her crew, presumably realising that the fate of the men in L19 awaited them if they persisted in any attempt to cross the North Sea, returned shoreward with the engines thundering like those of a dozen goods trains running up-hill. The great vessel came gliding in at low speed, almost touching the surface of the water, and took the land safely not far from the coast. As it came down it cut a deep furrow, and finally came to rest

PLACED ON THE PINNACLE AND VERY THRONE OF PERIL.

On the top of the hull of the super-Zeppelins was a small platform, nine feet square, fenced in with a light wire railing, on which were two ·5 in. guns, firing a one-pound shell, for repelling aeroplane attacks. Imagination cannot conceive a more perilous post for any gunners to occupy.

twenty yards from a wooden cottage The Germans on board, who numbered twenty-two, shouted a warning to the people in this cottage, who were frightened out of their wits by the sudden apparition of this grey, colossal monster at their very doors, and perhaps imagined that the nightmare of an invasion by airship was at last being realised. After the warning the Germans set fire to the airship. It burnt with four sharp puffs of flame, emitting such heat that the paint on the cottage was badly scorched. No bombs, of the explosive kind appear to have been on board when L33 came down, but there were incendiary bombs, which were used to injure the structure and render the vessel incapable of repair.

The little body of Germans, one of whom had been slightly injured when the ship grounded, collected, seemingly in great terror of attack by the people, who certainly had no cause to be merciful to these offenders against the laws of war. They marched off on the road to Colchester, which one of them knew well. They threw

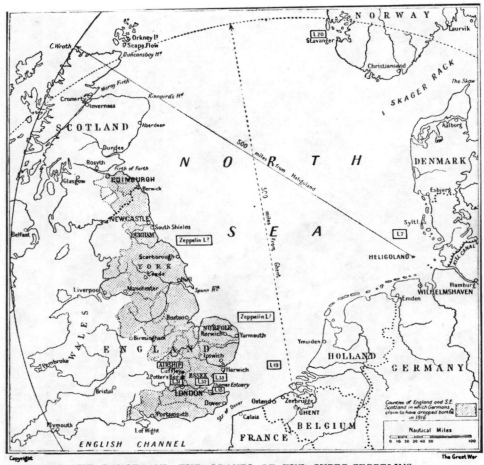

THE RANGE AND THE GRAVES OF THE SUPER-ZEPPELINS.
Chart showing the five-hundred-mile radius of operation of Zeppelins over the British Isles, and the approximate points at which Zeppelins were brought down during the course of 1916; five in the North Sea, one in the Thames estuary, and four on the land. The centres of the five-hundred-mile radius taken are Heligoland and Ghent respectively, and the distance is calculated in nautical miles.

assiduously preached "hate" against Great Britain. They had created a passion for aimless outrage and wanton murder, and had convinced the German nation that Zeppelins were perfect instruments for this campaign of terror and cruelty. And now Germans generally demanded that the raids should continue, and indeed blamed the airship crews because they were not sufficiently active or sufficiently merciless. To abandon the raids altogether would be to admit that the large capital and immense amount of labour sunk in the Zeppelin had been wasted. British estimates, after a study of L33, gave the cost of such a vessel at something between £250,000 and £500,000, and the time required to build her at six months. And there was not only the actual structure of the airship to be taken into account, there were the enormous sheds needed for sheltering it and the hydrogen factories for supplying it with gas.

It was true that the Zeppelin had proved of the highest value for naval scouting, which was its proper sphere of action, within which it was most serviceable so long as it was not resolutely attacked by aeroplanes from aeroplane-carrying ships. But in view of Germany's position, not more than a dozen large airships were needed for this special business. The others represented so much material wasted, and Germany was now beginning to run short of material.

German opinion was summed up by the Munich "Neueste Nachrichten," which wrote: "The glorious German aerial engines of war penetrate to England's heart, and London trembles before their attacks, which it is hoped will be more frequent in future." And on September 25th the airships were ordered once more to attack. On this occasion seven Zeppelins crossed the coast (the dwindling number showed that Germany had not anything like the force available which she was commonly supposed to possess). They attacked the South Coast, East Coast, North-East Coast, and North Midlands. No damage was done to factories or works, but several small cottages and houses were wrecked, and thirty-six persons were wantonly killed and twenty-seven injured. The enemy falsely claimed to have bombed Leeds, Lincoln, Derby, Portsmouth, and York. On this occasion, perhaps owing to mist, no airship was brought down. The attacks were made on residential districts where working-class people lived.

Renewed raiding activity

On October 1st ten Zeppelins crossed the British coast, striking at London, the Eastern Counties, and Lincolnshire. It was a very clear, dark night, and quite early in its course the London anti-aircraft defences came into action. A further great advance had been made since the raid of September 23rd, and this time two large Zeppelins which endeavoured to reach London found every attempt to penetrate the line of defences frustrated by the guns and searchlights. While they were engaged in endeavours to break through, one of them was attacked by an aeroplane

away their weapons, and presently meeting a special constable made their formal surrender to him.

Both the airmen concerned in the destruction of L32 received honours and rewards for their splendid work. They were awarded the D.S.O., apparently because the British authorities were of opinion that, with the better methods which had been introduced, the destruction of Zeppelins was a relatively simple business. Yet some idea of the strain to which they were exposed may be gathered from the fact that Lieutenant Sowrey fainted from exhaustion and cold when he made his landing.

The loss of these two magnificent airships caused intense chagrin and dismay in Germany, so much so indeed that it offset the really important successes which the German armies were gaining against the Rumanians. The official report spoke of the "extraordinarily heavy fire with incendiary shells" which had destroyed the two airships. Yet a third Zeppelin sustained some damage. It was seen off the Danish coast, heavily down by the stern, with German destroyers accompanying it, and, according to fishermen's statements, which may or may not have been true, it sank in the Bight of Heligoland. In any case, the loss of this vessel was not acknowledged by the enemy.

Germany's fantastic tales

The German Government was now in a most difficult position. It had led the German people to suppose that British towns could be attacked and laid in ruins by German airships. The false and fantastic tales which it had published of the airships' exploits had given a totally misleading impression of the effect produced by haphazard bomb-dropping. The German authorities had also

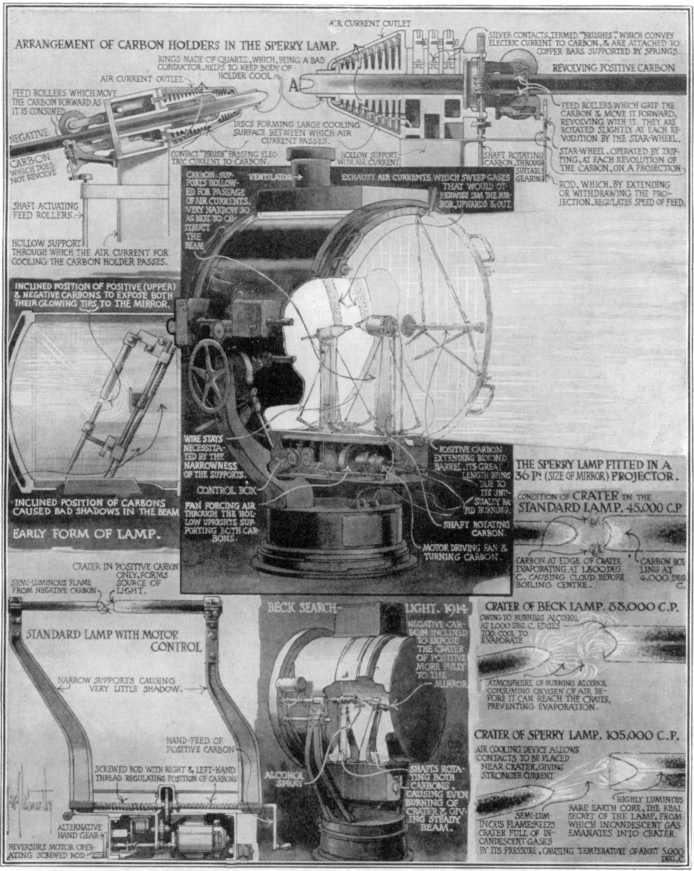

SUPER-SEARCHLIGHT USED AGAINST SUPER-ZEPPELINS.

Exchanging new lamps for old is an enterprise in which some of the wizards of science are ever engaged, and during the sporadic attempts of the Germans to rouse civilian alarm in Britain by indiscriminate "frightfulness" from the air, steady attempts were made at improvements in the searchlights employed for finding the whereabouts of high-flying raiders. These graphic diagrams give details of the Sperry lamp, an American invention, and compare them with the details of other lamps. The Sperry, it was claimed, was greatly superior in effectiveness and brilliancy to all earlier lights. In the country of its origin it was stated that the highest brilliancy of the crater of the positive carbon of the Sperry lamp was about two-thirds of that of the sun. Although necessarily somewhat technical, the descriptions given serve to indicate some of the important ways in which this light differed from those that it was designed to supplement or supersede. The light from the crater of the positive carbon thrown on to the mirror at the back of the projector and thence reflected in the intense beam of light not only enabled the watchers of the skies to pick out the aircraft sailing high overhead at night-time, but also served to confuse those navigating the raider.

GONDOLA OF A WRECKED RAIDER.
Although it had turned turtle amid the wreckage, both the size and shape of the gondola of a Zeppelin are well shown in this photograph.

piloted by Lieutenant Tempest, of the Royal Flying Corps. The crowds below now knew what to expect, and watched eagerly. A little before midnight a bright glow was seen on the tip of one Zeppelin, cruising at an enormous height ; the airship capsized with the glowing tip pointing downwards, righted itself, then, with the glow spreading, broke into two flaming balls, which were probably the two ends with the two heavy gondolas, held together by the cable, and finally fell as one big pear-shaped mass of crimson fire to the ground at Potter's Bar, where it lay, a blazing heap of metal, cotton, and wood of the size of a large house. A cordon of troops swiftly encircled it.

This Zeppelin was speedily identified from the wreckage as L31, the first of the super-Zeppelins, and the third of that type destroyed by the British forces in this country. For its destruction Lieutenant Tempest received the D.S.O. He was injured, but not seriously, in making his landing after putting the airship out of action. All the crew of L31 perished. Her captain was the ablest and most experienced airship officer in the German Navy, Lieutenant-Commander Mathy. He had escaped death in the first

German officer's mythical narrative

two German naval airships, L1 and L2, which were destroyed by accident previous to the war, by the curious chance that in each case he happened to be ill, though he had been told off to take part in the trials. He commanded the airship which bombed London in September and October, 1915, on each occasion killing and wounding a large number of non-combatants, with no military aim. He was apparently so much pleased with his exploits that he gave a largely mythical account of the September raid to an American correspondent, which has this historic value that it affords some idea of what an airship crew feel and observe during an attack.

"London," he said, "is darkened, but sufficiently lighted to enable me to see its reflected glow in the sky nearly forty miles away." (This applies to September, 1915, and was afterwards entirely changed.) "A large city, seen at night from a great height, is a fairylike picture. There is no sign of life, except in the distance a moving light, probably from a railway train. As in the twinkling of an eye all this changes. A sudden flash and a narrow beam of brilliant light reaches out from below and begins to feel around the sky. A second, third, fourth, and fifth come out, and soon there are more than a score of criss-crossing ribbons—tentacles seeking to drag us to destruction. Now from below comes an ominous sound that penetrates the noise of the engines. There are little red flashes and short bursts of fire. Above the Bank of England I shouted through the speaking-tube connecting me with my lieutenant at the firing apparatus, ' Fire

slowly ! ' Mingling with the dim thunder from the guns below came the explosions and bursting flames of our bombs. Over Holborn Viaduct, in the vicinity of Holborn Station, we dropped several bombs. From the Bank of England to the Tower—a short distance—I tried to hit the bridge, and believe I was successful. Arriving directly over Liverpool Street Station, I shouted ' Rapid fire ! ' and bombs rained down. I could see that I hit well, and apparently did great damage.

" I am not afraid of aeroplanes, and think I could make it interesting for them, unless, perhaps, there was a regular swarm. It takes some time for an aeroplane to climb as high as a Zeppelin, and by the time it gets there the airship would be gone. Then, too, it is most difficult for an aeroplane to land at night, while a Zeppelin can stay up all night."

In the raid in which the super-Zeppelin was destroyed at Potter's Bar very trifling damage was done, and only two casualties were inflicted. The airship crews seem to have been unnerved by the losses they had suffered, and except in the case of the two ships which tried to reach London were careful to keep out of reach of the British defences. Though many bombs were dropped, only four houses were damaged, in addition to some greenhouses. The Germans professed that the raid had been successful, and that London and the mouth of the Humber had been bombed.

Airship crews unnerved

For some weeks after this the weather remained very unfavourable, and no raids were possible. On the night of November 27th the Zeppelin crews were again driven out to attack the British coast. The number of airships engaged is not officially stated, but seems to have been about five, for the total of effective vessels which the Germans had available was steadily falling. Four of these appear to have attacked the North-East Coast and dropped bombs in Durham and Yorkshire, doing very little damage beyond hurting a few innocent women and children. One of them was engaged by an aeroplane, piloted by Lieutenant I. V. Pyott, of the Royal Flying Corps, off the Durham coast. The airship, after a short engagement, took fire, and the flames spread along her till she began to fall. Her end was witnessed by large crowds over a great area. It came in the same fashion as with the other Zeppelins, except that the blazing mass fell into the sea. Boats put off from the shore, but when day broke there was nothing to be seen on the water but a thick, oily scum. The number of this airship has not been published.

While this was happening in the North, another large airship had crossed the East Coast and pushed inland towards the North Midlands, where she dropped various bombs at random. So far she had not been attacked, but

EXAMINING A ZEPPELIN ENGINE.
Men of the Royal Flying Corps showed considerable interest in all that remained of the engines of the airships that were brought down.

on her return journey she began to feel the bite of the strengthened British defences. Aeroplanes chased her ; guns opened on her. It seems certain that she sustained some damage, as she travelled very slowly, and may, indeed, have stopped for some time not far from the Norfolk coast, where she evidently succeeded in making temporary repairs. Day was at hand when she was seen, now at a great height and travelling fast, voyaging towards the sea. She passed through a zone of gun fire, where the gunners claim to have inflicted on her at least one hit, and then stood out to sea not alone, however, but followed by a number of aeroplanes, piloted by officers of the Royal Naval Air Service, who stuck to her in the most determined fashion, and showed that they were resolved not to let her go. In the grey light her gunners must have seen her assailants plainly, but were unable to beat them off. The people on the coast watched the thrilling battle in the sky at a height of 8,000 feet. Four aeroplanes were in action, supported by an armed trawler. The aeroplanes again had the upper hand. Lieutenant Egbert Cadbury and Sub-Lieutenants E. L. Pulling and G. W. R. Fane drew closest to her and hit her repeatedly, till the flames swept along her side, and she, too, plunged a hissing mass into the sea.

The officers concerned in the destruction of these two Zeppelins received the D.S.O., which they had so gloriously earned. The name of the second Zeppelin has not been published ; her destruction was important, as this was the first occasion on which a Zeppelin on its homeward way was caught by the British forces and brought down. The feat, moreover, was accomplished by the R.N.A.S., which had previously shown great courage in attacking enemy airships, but for want of proper armament and organisation had not been able to bring them down. The record of the two flying branches for 1916 now stood at four destroyed by Army airmen and one by Navy airmen. The British casualties in this raid were seventeen, the German would be at least forty-four, as twenty-two officers and men formed the crew of a Zeppelin.

Thrilling battle in the sky Later in the morning on which the Norfolk Zeppelin had been destroyed (November 28th) a German aeroplane made a pointless attack on London. It appeared over the capital about noon, and dropped six bombs from a height so great that the occupants of the machine could not have taken any proper aim. This wanton piece of mischief caused only the slightest damage, but inflicted injury on nine persons, one of whom was seriously hurt. The aeroplane, on its return journey, was brought down by the French at Dunkirk, when it proved to be manned by two

DIAGRAM OF THE STRUCTURE OF A SUPER-ZEPPELIN.
This diagram, by Mr. S. W. Clatsworthy, illustrates the notable features of a super-Zeppelin, as described in this chapter by Mr. H. W. Wilson, after his examination of the L33, brought down in Essex. The type appears to have been standardised, and it included all the best points of airship construction which German ingenuity had devised up to the end of 1916.

naval lieutenants. This affair, though in itself of the extremest insignificance, was important as indicating the real danger which threatened Britain from the air—that of aeroplane attack on the great cities. The sole effective protection against this was the certainty that such attacks would be followed by British reprisals, as neither machines nor guns could prevent enemy aeroplanes, which fly very high at 10,000 or even 15,000 feet from reaching towns and dropping bombs on them.

The close of the year saw the effective German Zeppelin fleet reduced to somewhere about twenty airships, and entirely shorn of its prestige. It could no longer frighten women and children in isolated villages and remote little towns ; in the last five raids it had suffered far more damage than it inflicted. It had tried every stratagem attacks in mass, attacks isolated, attacks on London simultaneously delivered from several directions, attacks avoiding London and the growing power of the metropolitan defences. All had failed. The prime instrument of "frightfulness" was useless on land; the dream of laying London in ruins by Zeppelin bombs had for ever vanished. There remained the motives, which were set forth by Captain Persius in the "Berliner Tageblatt":

> The measures of (air) defence taken in England demand a considerable personnel and much matériel. Numberless defence stations have been created which require the attention of many thousands of officers and men, including the crews needed for handling the guns and manipulating the searchlights. These need very careful and highly-trained men. Guns, munitions, searchlights, aeroplanes, have all to be provided for this special purpose. There are other consequences. When the alarm of an attack is raised, everything has to be darkened, causing not inconsiderable disturbance and delay of railway and harbour traffic.

So far as these were sound arguments they amounted to an indictment of the Asquith Coalition Government for failing to take reprisals, and thus permitting Germany to immobilise a large force of men and guns in this country, while leaving the enemy free to send every man and gun to the two fronts for the attack on the Allies.

AIRSHIP RAIDS ON GREAT BRITAIN IN 1916.

No.	1916.	Area Attacked.	Number of Airships.	Number of Airships Destroyed by British in these Raids.	Killed.	Injured.	Barometer and Weather Conditions in London.*
1	Jan. 31	Norfolk, Suffolk, Lincs, Leicestershire, Staffs, Derbyshire	6 or 7	0	67	117	30.2 ; slight rain and fog. L19 wrecked on return
2	Mar. 5	Yorks, Lincs, Rutland, Huntingdon, Cambridgeshire, Norfolk, Essex, Kent	3	0	18	52	29.7 ; snow in north, squally
3	Mar. 31	E. and N.E. Counties . . .	5	1	43	66	30.2 ; dull
4	Apr. 1	N.E. Coast	?	0	16	100	30.1 ; clear
5	Apr. 2	S.E. Counties of Scotland ; N. and S.E. Counties of England	?	0	11	11	29.9 ; clear
6	Apr. 5	N.E. Coast	3	0	1	8	29.8 ; clear
7	Apr. 24	Norfolk and Suffolk . . .	4	0	0	1	30.0 ; moon rose 2.5 a.m., sky overcast. Enemy reconnoitring for German battle-cruisers
8	Apr. 25	Essex and Kent	?	0	0	0	30.1 ; clear, moon rose 2.27 a.m.
9	Apr. 26	E. Kent	3	0	0	0	30.3 ; misty, moon rose 2.43 a.m.
10	May 3	N.E. Coast England and E. Coast Scotland	5	0	9	27	29.9 ; gusty, uncertain weather L20 wrecked on return
11	July 29	Yorks and Lincs . . .	3	0	0	0	30.3 ; very fine and warm
12	July 31	Kent, Essex, Suffolk, Norfolk, Lincs, Cambridge, Hunts	7	0	0	0	30.2 ; very fine and warm
13	Aug. 3	Norfolk, Suffolk, Essex, Kent .	8	0	0	0	30.3 ; fine
14	Aug. 9	E. Coast England ; S.E. Coast Scotland	7 to 10	0	8	36	30.3 ; clear and warm
15	Aug. 23	E. Coast	1	0	0	0	29.9 ; windy
16	Aug. 25	E. and S.E. Coasts ; outskirts of London	6	0	8	21	29.8 ; stiff wind S.W.
17	Sept. 2	E. Counties and outskirts of London	13	1	3	12	30.0 ; overcast
18	Sept. 23	London, S.E., E., E. Midlands, and Lincs	12	2	38	125	30.0 ; clear, with ground mist
19	Sept. 25	N. Midlands, E., N.E., and S. Coast	7	0	36	27	30.0 ; clear, with ground mist
20	Oct. 1	London, E. Counties, Lincs . .	10	1	1	1	30.1 ; very clear, dark night
21	Nov. 27-8	N.E. and E. Coast . . .	?	2	4	37	30.2 ; clear, frosty ; fog later
			Over 103	7	263	641	
	Add in 1915 . . .		. . .	. . .	171	454	
	Total Casualties 1915-16		. . .	. . .	434	1,095	

* No moon, and wind light or calm unless otherwise stated.

GERMAN AIRSHIP LOSSES IN 1916.

German rigid airships positively known to have been destroyed by the Allies or wrecked in 1916, and the loss of which was acknowledged by the enemy. [These were in addition to other losses which were not reported.]

No.	Date.	Name of Airship	By what Nation Destroyed.	How Destroyed.	Where Destroyed.	Fate of Crew.
1	Feb. 2	L19 . .	—	Wrecked, after being hit by Dutch fire	North Sea . .	Killed
2	Feb. 21	*LZ77 . .	French	Gun fire	Révigny . .	Burnt to death
3	Mar. 31	L15 . .	British	Gun fire	Thames . .	Most taken prisoners
4	May 3	L20 . .	—	Wrecked	Norwegian Coast	Saved
5	May 4	L7 . .	British	Gun fire of fleet	North Sea . .	A few taken prisoners
6	May 5	*LZ85 . .	Allies	Gun fire of fleet	Salonika . .	Prisoners
7	Sept. 3	*Rigid Airship	British	Aeroplane	Cuffley . . .	Burnt to death
8	Sept. 24	L32 . .	British	Aeroplane	Essex . . .	Burnt to death
9	Sept. 24	L33 . .	British	Gun fire	Essex . . .	Prisoners
10	Oct. 1	L31 . .	British	Aeroplane	Potter's Bar .	Burnt to death
11	Nov. 27	Zeppelin L ?	British	Aeroplane	N.E. Coast . .	Burnt to death
12	Nov. 28	Zeppelin L ?	British	Aeroplane	E. Coast . .	Burnt to death

* Army Airships.

CHAPTER CLVIII.

SIR DOUGLAS HAIG'S VIEWS OF THE SOMME BATTLE.

EDITORIAL NOTE.—Without unduly swelling the bulk of this history, it is impossible to reprint within its pages the historic documents published by the various Governments, much as the Editors would have liked to include them. Readers, however, can find such documents easily available in other cheap forms, and have the advantage of knowing that the essence of them all is introduced with care by the writers of THE GREAT WAR into their orderly and more pithy narratives. The most important of the British despatches published up to the end of 1916 was the long and convincing document which Sir Douglas Haig had finished under date December 23rd, and which the alertness of the new Government issued at the psychological moment when the German peace bluff was still occupying the minds of neutrals. This despatch came as an inspiration to further effort, as a message of good cheer to the Allies, and readers of THE GREAT WAR who take the pains to re-peruse the series of brilliant chapters on the Battles of the Somme, by Mr. Edward Wright, may be surprised to notice how closely his deductions tally with the statements of Sir Douglas Haig. The historic importance of the despatch, however, has made it desirable to add a chapter to THE GREAT WAR in which the whole is analysed in about one-third the space of the original, and presented to the reader in a manner probably calling for less study of detail, without losing anything vital which the British Commander-in-Chief had thought fit to communicate to his Government for publication.

N the middle of December, 1916, Hindenburg's lieutenant, General von Ludendorff, began to support Bethmann-Hollweg's intrigue for a German peace by a great Press campaign throughout the Central Empires and all neutral States. He asserted that the Somme campaign had been a German victory, and public opinion in some neutral countries inclined to the German view of the great battle, owing to the fact that operations had been brought to a temporary standstill by the wet winter weather. A large body of American opinion appeared to be strongly influenced by the claims set before the public in the United States by German agencies of many kinds, so that there was danger of the most powerful neutral State adopting the view that the war had been fought to a stalemate, and that a negotiated peace was inevitable.

The new Government of Great Britain was too alert to allow the enemy to win a military Press campaign in regard to the Somme, similar to the naval Press campaign he had won in regard to the Jutland Bank action. The British Commander-in-Chief, Sir Douglas Haig, wrote out his despatch on December 23rd, 1916, and its rapid publication, under the new Secretary of State for War, at once defeated the enemy's design to regain with the pen the prestige he had lost with the sword.

Throughout the war Great Britain had been the only belligerent that regularly published despatches from her Commanders-in-Chief after every important campaign. Even the details of the disasters in the Gallipoli Peninsula and the Kut-el-Amara region had been related in British official despatches, while the German Staff kept back the official history of the first campaign on the Sambre and Marne. The continual contrast between the frankness of British military authorities and the reticence of German military authorities served to inspire confidence in Great Britain, more particularly as the despatches of Viscount French and Sir John Jellicoe were written in clear and telling language, enabling all the world to understand and judge the evidence set before them. A despatch from a British Commander-in-Chief tended

British official photograph.

DAWN OF THE DAY OF BATTLE, JULY 1ST, 1916.
A British general officer with his Staff on the morning of the first attack. On July 1st, at 7.30 a.m., after a final hour of exceptionally heavy bombardment, our infantry assault was launched along the Somme.

GIVE-AND-TAKE IN TRENCH WARFARE.
Bomb section of the Seaforth Highlanders firing a trench-mortar, the bomb clearly visible in its flight. The range of these mortars varied considerably, but they all proved immensely effective in the trench warfare.

to inspire, in neutrals as well as in Allies, trust in its veracity. Thus, Sir Douglas Haig inherited a splendid fund of prestige when he sat down to describe the character and result of the Somme Battle, and defeat thereby one of the most subtle German intrigues for the establishment, through the pressure of American opinion, of an enemy peace.

In sober, professional, lucid diction the great Scotsman draws an outline sketch of the greatest battle in the history of the world ; and though, by reason of the millions of men engaged, he cannot follow the example of Viscount French of Ypres and give particulars of the deeds of British units, his long despatch is in many ways the most interesting document of the war. He reveals the fact that Marshal Joffre in person and himself first discussed all possible alternatives of action on the western front, and came to a complete agreement as to the most promising enemy sectors for a combined British and French offensive. There was a serious British difficulty in that a large proportion of officers and men of the New Army were far from being fully trained, and every week they could be held back for further training increased their numbers and enabled them to obtain a larger supply of munitions. But as the Germans continued to press their attacks at Verdun, and the Austrian offensive made ground in the Trentino, the common interests of all the Allies compelled Sir Douglas Haig to move before he had gathered his full strength.

Deciding on the great push

As the strain on Verdun continued to increase, Sir Douglas Haig agreed with Marshal Joffre to launch an offensive by the end of June, 1916. Three objects were aimed at by the British commander. He intended first to relieve the pressure on Verdun ; second, to assist the Italians and the Russians, by stopping all transfer of German troops from the western front ; and third, to wear down the enemy forces opposed to him. No attempt to break through was therefore designed. But, within the limits of the British commander's plan, great successes were gained in three directions, in any one of which success would have justified the operations. Verdun was relieved. The main German forces were held on the western front,

and a great campaign against Russia prevented. Finally, the enemy strength was weakened in a very serious manner. Four-fifths of the total number of German divisions in the principal theatre of war were thrown one after another into the Somme Battle. Some of these forces were used up twice ; some of them were used up thrice, and the outcome was such, Sir Douglas Haig suggests, that if the weather had not broken at the end of the campaign and interrupted the operations, a grand decision would have been obtained. "There is sufficient evidence to place it beyond doubt that the enemy's losses in men and material have been very considerably higher than those of the Allies, while morally the advantage on our side is still greater."

Sir Douglas Haig goes on to point out that these results were largely obtained against veteran enemy forces by British troops mainly raised during the war. Many Britons counted their service by months, and gained in the Somme Battle their first experience of warfare. We were compelled to use untrained officers and men, or else to defer the offensive until we had trained them. If this had been the case, we should have failed our Allies, says the British commander, and he proudly remarks that the achievement of his troops, under such conditions, against an Army and nation whose chief concern for years had been to prepare for war, constitutes a feat without parallel in history.

Beginning of the battle

After describing the difficult downland country and the great strength of the enemy fortifications, Sir Douglas Haig distinguishes three phases in the operations. The first phase opened with the attack of July 1st, the force of which surprised the enemy and threw him into considerable confusion. The Fourth British Army, consisting of five army corps, under the command of General Sir Henry Rawlinson, attacked on the line from Maricourt to

A ROLAND FOR AN OLIVER.
In reply to the message of death and defiance sent as shown in the photograph in the left-hand column, the Germans fired a shell which burst immediately in front of the gallant Seaforths' trench.

[British official photograph.
A HALT FOR HOT COFFEE.
Behind the lines on the western front were roadside
places where passing soldiers could always get hot coffee
and biscuits to cheer them on their way.

IN THE GRIP OF WINTER BEHIND THE WESTERN FRONT.
Peaceful scene at a railway supply depot in France, where varied transport vehicles gathered
to get hay and straw for conveyance for use at the front. The state of the snowy roads
may be gauged by the clogged wheels of the familiar van on the left.

Serre. Then troops from another army, commanded by General Sir E. H. H. Allenby, attacked at Gommecourt as part of a subsidiary operation. Sir Douglas Haig states that he expected no results of importance in the actions above the Ancre, from Gommecourt to Beaumont-Hamel. The aim in this sector was to hold up the enemy's reserves and occupy his artillery while his line was being broken south of the Ancre.

The British troops advanced to the attack with perfect steadiness, and, in spite of a very heavy barrage from the enemy's guns, met with immediate success on their right. They carried Montauban, and, forcing their way over open ground into Mametz, pressed the enemy on three sides at Fricourt and reached their objective in the valley. Farther north, the villages of La Boisselle and Ovillers were prepared for capture by the achievements of British troops, who drove deeply into the German lines on the flanks of these strongholds. But at Thiepval, and along the valley of the Ancre, and on the Serre plateau, there was a series of striking early successes that could not be developed. British troops penetrated into the defences of Grandcourt and fought into Thiepval and Serre. The enemy's resistance at Beaumont-Hamel and Thiepval made it impossible to forward reinforcements and ammunition, so that the gallant attackers were compelled to retire at night to their own lines. The troops that assailed Gommecourt also forced their way into enemy positions and, having fulfilled the object of their subsidiary attack, drew back.

At the close of the day Sir Douglas Haig decided to follow up his great successes south of the Ancre, while holding the enemy north of the river. A brilliant New Army commander, General Sir Hubert de la Poer Gough, came forward with the Fifth British Army, to which the two northern corps from the Fourth Army were attached. General Gough was placed in charge of the operations from Serre to La Boisselle, with orders to maintain a steady pressure on the German front, and act as a pivot for the swinging line of the Fourth Army under General Rawlinson. Meanwhile, the Fourth Army continued its advance and captured Fricourt and Fricourt Wood, and then in four days' fighting, on a front of over six miles, swept over the enemy's first and strongest system of defences, drove him back for more than a mile, and stormed four of his great village strongholds.

It became necessary on the sixth day to relieve the fatigued troops and bring forward both the light and the heavy artillery to prepare the way for another successful

235

WELL EQUIPPED FOR BAD-WEATHER WORK.
Typical working-party on the Western Front. They set out with waders for the wet places, waterproof sheets for body covering against the heavy rain, and trench-helmets against shrapnel. The mud on the shovels shows the kind of ground in which they had to work.

Bazentin-le-Grand were gained, and higher up the ridge Bazentin-le-Petit and its wood were taken. Then it was that the German soldiers began to break without waiting to be attacked, and General Rawlinson, who had foreseen this event and brought up cavalry to profit by it, threw out horsemen and infantry and cleared nearly the whole of High Wood. This was the great testing day of the new national forces of Great Britain, and they triumphed over their veteran enemy in a manner that marked a new era in the history of Continental Europe.

Thus ended the first phase of the Somme Battle. The enemy's second main system of defences had been captured on a front of over three miles. He had been forced back another mile, and had lost 6,000 yards of the main ridge and four more of his village strongholds. At one point his third system of defences had been penetrated. The skill, daring, persistence, and determination of the new British soldier had been shown in a magnificent manner, and Sir Henry Rawlinson clearly emerged as a commander of genius. Despite the shaken condition of the German troops, the great strength and depth **Second phase of** of their defences enabled them to **the battle** win time to bring up mighty reserves.

There then opened the second phase of the Battle of the Somme This phase lasted many weeks. Having found his strongest defences unavailing, and being fully alive to his danger, the German commander put forth all his efforts to maintain his hold upon the main ridge. The result was a prolonged struggle between the contending armies, in which by slow and difficult progress the British troops won, in the words of Sir Douglas Haig, "a fighting superiority that left its mark on the enemy." Their conquest of the ridge became the visible symbol of the moral fact that they were proving themselves the better men.

assault. Local actions were continued meanwhile, and the ground cleared towards the enemy's second line of defences. At dawn on July 14th the Fourth Army made its second great leap forward, after the most extraordinary nocturnal manœuvre of any modern army. The story of this manœuvre forms one of the revelations of the historic despatch. In the darkness the troops moved out over open country, for a distance of nearly a mile, and lined up near the enemy's trenches without being observed by any hostile patrols. The mechanical perfection of this uncontested advance was attained, as Sir Douglas Haig emphatically repeats, by an army the bulk of which was raised after the beginning of the war. In both magnitude and precision the operation was a classic example of Staff work, and its success was largely due to the fact that many battalion, brigade, and divisional commanders went out themselves to study the ground over which they intended noiselessly to work their troops in the darkness.

Just as the dawn began to glimmer over the crest, enabling the men to distinguish friend from foe at a short range, the assault was delivered, with crashing surprise effect along a front of three miles, from Longueval to Bazentin le-Petit Wood. As a result of the amazing nocturnal advance General Rawlinson's army had reduced the distances between it and the enemy from 1,300 and 1,900 yards to 300 and 500 yards. It transformed conditions of annihilation into conditions of victory. The enemy's first trenches were rapidly stormed, and some of his troops thrown into a state of demoralisation. Trônes Wood was taken early in the morning, and nearly all the defences of Longueval were overrun by the afternoon. In the centre the village and wood of

PRIMITIVE BRIDGE ACROSS THE ANCRE.
Where one of the bare boles which represented what had been a wood had fallen across a narrow part of the river, soldiers found a convenient means of crossing. The shell which had felled the tree had built a bridge.

[Gale & Polden.

Lieut.=General Sir Hubert de la Poer Gough, K.C.B.
Commander of the Fifth Army on the Somme.

Flight of Germans before a gas attack on the Somme as seen from the air.

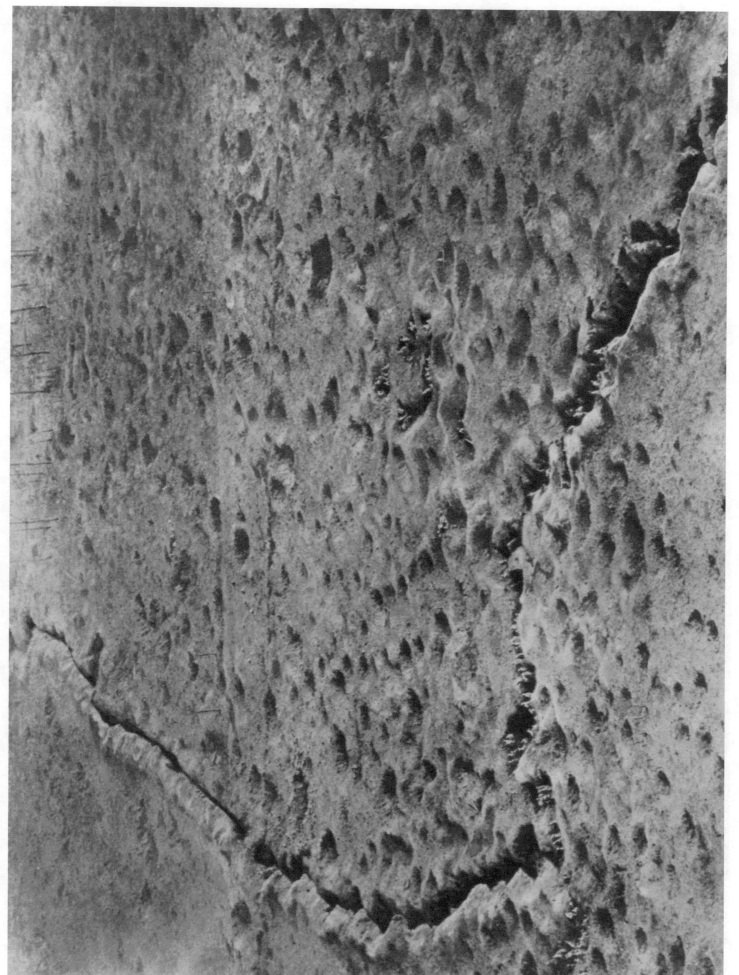

Airman's view of the advance of French infantry after a bombardment on the Somme.

Lieut.-General the Hon. Sir Julian Byng, K.C.B., K.C.M.G., M.V.O.
Commander of the Canadian Army Corps on the Somme.

In this decisive trial of moral strength, that lasted from July 17th to September 9th, Sir Douglas Haig remarks that unfavourable weather increased the difficulties of Sir Henry Rawlinson. Direct observation of our artillery fire was limited by the nature of the ground, and we greatly depended upon observation from the air. But though the British pilots were masters of the air, they could not for several weeks get the clear atmosphere they needed. Rain fell in unusual quantities in July and August, and when there was no rain there was an almost constant haze with frequent low clouds. Although the weather thus helped the enemy by mitigating his defeat in the air and his lack of artillery concentration, the Fifth British Army maintained its methodical step-by-step advance around Pozières and Thiepval. Along the right flank, held by the Fourth Army, where the British lines formed the sharp salient at Delville Wood and Longueval, Sir Douglas Haig judged that the situation called for stronger measures. The enemy was able to bring a concentric artillery fire to bear upon the salient and upon the narrow space

WINTRY AMENITIES ON THE SOMME. *[British official photograph.*
Companions in difficulties. A typical example of the cold and slushy ways that led from the rear to the flooded trenches. Through a morass of snow and mud, an Army Service man, with the aid of a patient pony, is seen conveying a supply of much-needed waders to his comrades, who were holding their own in even worse conditions in the front line.

behind it, where great numbers of British and French guns, ammunition heaps, and supplies were crowded together. Sir Douglas Haig admits that the position of things in and around the salient was such as should

Critical salient recovered

have made any commander very anxious. For if the enemy had been able to drive in the salient, and so gain direct observation on the ground behind, he could have thrust a knife into the junction of the British and French armies.

Sir Douglas Haig says that he had "good grounds for confidence that the enemy was not able to drive from this position troops who had shown that they were able to wrest it from him." So he ordered the Fourth Army to hang on to the salient while he was arranging to swing his right flank into line with his centre. In order to do this he had to capture first the Guillemont line, and secondly the Ginchy line, and the enemy recognised the importance of retaining these two lines. They were naturally very st ong, and had been elaborately fortified. But the German commander was not content with them. He had lost trust in his defences, and after digging and wiring many new trenches both before and behind his original lines, he brought up fresh troops for another great test of strength.

After a short pause to enable his tired troops to be relieved and his guns moved forward, Sir Douglas Haig prepared for his swing against Guillemont. But before he could strike there came the expected German counter-attack against Delville Wood and Longueval. By sheer weight of numbers the Germans forced their way through a large part of the wood and into the northern part of the village. The British commander retaliated by ordering his Fourth Army, on July 23rd, to thrust forward on a wide front from Guillemont to Pozières. At the same time the Fifth Army, under General Gough, moved directly against Pozières, and by the morning of July 25th the whole of the village was carried.

The entrance of the Fifth Army into violent battle greatly relieved the Fourth Army, and by the end of July

all the critical salient of Delville Wood and Longueval was recovered, after incessant, desperate fighting. This served not only to achieve the immediate object, but to shake once more the enemy's nerve. Then, after a fortnight of terrible wearing-down attack and counter-attack, Sir Douglas Haig's original design of swinging his right flank up in line with his centre was undertaken by slow but stubborn pressure. On July 30th the village of Guillemont and the ridge of Falfemont Farm were vainly assailed. One attacking battalion drove through Guillemont, but was obliged to fall back, as the battalions on either flank were checked. On August 7th the British troops again entered Guillemont, and were again compelled to retire owing to checks on their flanks. Sir Douglas Haig states that he then came to the conclusion that Guillemont could not be captured by local attack, except with very heavy loss. He therefore arranged with the French army on his right for a series of combined assaults, delivered in progressive stages, from Maurepas to Ginchy.

The Allies' first attempt to carry out this scheme was made on August 16th, and met with only partial success. Two days later a larger combined attack was undertaken, in which very valuable progress was made, Guillemont railway-station and the outskirts of Guillemont village being occupied. During this period, when the Fourth Army was battering furiously on the right wing, the Fifth

Ability of the New Armies

Army bombed its way over the crest of the main ridge to Pozières Windmill, and there secured artillery observation over the enemy's lines in front of Bapaume. The way was thereby opened for a large general attack by both British armies, and after laborious preparations lasting for a fortnight a third grand assault was delivered at noon on September 3rd, from the Ancre to Falfemont Farm On the front attacked by Sir Hubert Gough's army the battle led to no gain of ground of importance. But the enemy was held and badly punished, and prevented from assisting in the defence of his eastern flank. Against this flank Sir Henry Rawlinson's army drove with victorious

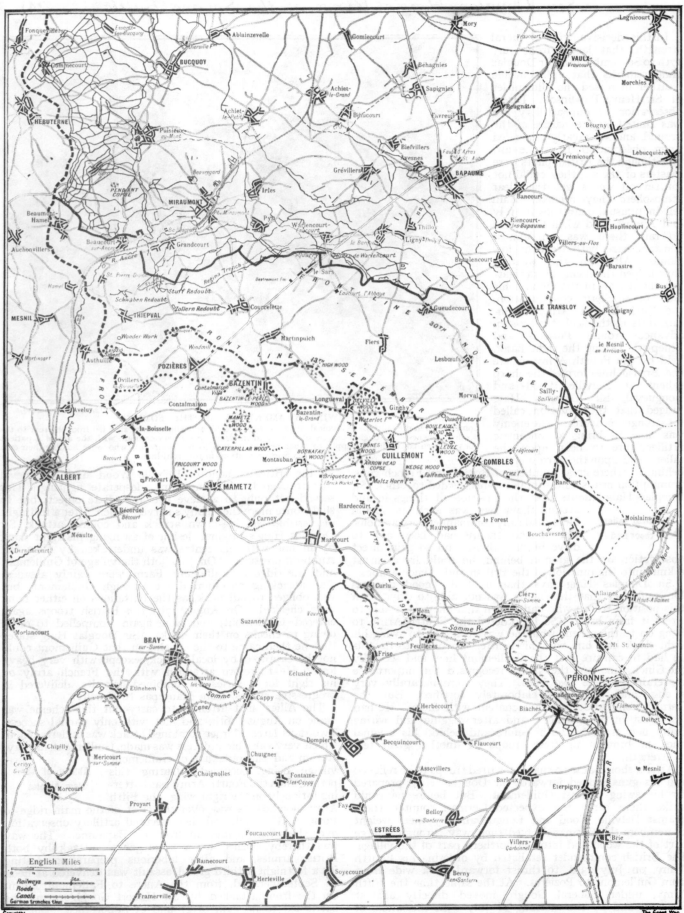

AREA OF OPERATIONS COVERED BY SIR DOUGLAS HAIG'S DESPATCH, DECEMBER 23RD, 1916.

The district of the Somme from Hébuterne southward to Eclusier and Estrées, showing the position of the Allies' line at dates between July 1st and November 30th, 1916, particularised by Sir Douglas Haig, and also the network of German trenches which then lay to the east of the new advanced line of the Allies.

skill and ardour. Guillemont was stormed and the line around Ginchy broken, and ground was won in Delville Wood and High Wood. Falfemont Farm, after being gained and lost on September 3rd, was occupied piece by piece on the morning of September 5th, and the important position of Leuze Wood was cleared of the enemy on the following day. The barrier which the enemy had maintained for seven weeks was broken. The right of the British line was advanced on a front of about two miles to an average depth of about one mile, and with the fall of Ginchy, September 9th, all the objectives of the assault were permanently attained. In this connection Sir Douglas Haig remarks :

[*British official photograph.*
TRENCH MEN AS TRENCHERMEN.
Feeding the armies on the western-front was a triumph of organisation. This shows reserve trench men welcoming the arrival of the bearer of their dinner dixey.

STRETCHER-PARTY READY FOR THEIR WORK ON THE SOMME.   [*French official photograph.*
British ambulance and stretcher parties were frequently bivouacked in the battered French villages and farmsteads behind the Somme front.   From such a bivouac this stretcher-party is shown starting for the firing-line to succour the wounded.

The weak salient in the allied line had disappeared, and we had gained the front required for further operations. Still more importance, however, lay in the proof afforded of the ability of our New Armies not only to rush the enemy's strongest defences, as had been accomplished on July 1st and 14th, but also to wear down and break his power of resistance, as they had done during the weeks of this fierce and protracted struggle. The great depth of his system of fortification gave him time to reorganise his defeated troops, and to hurry up numerous fresh divisions and more guns. Yet, in spite of this, he was still pushed back, steadily and continuously. The enemy, it is true, had delayed our advance considerably, but the effort had cost him dear ; and the comparative collapse of his resistance in the last few days of the struggle justified the belief that, in the long run, decisive victory would lie with our troops, who had displayed such fine fighting qualities and such indomitable endurance and resolution.

The third phase of the battle opened in the second week of September in an atmosphere of victory. The centre of the British line was excellently placed. Practically all the forward crest of the main ridge had been captured by General Rawlinson's and General Gough's armies. On a line of 9,000 yards, from Delville Wood to Mouquet Farm, the British and overseas troops overlooked the lower slopes held by the enemy, and brought their artillery to bear

upon him. Then, for a farther 3,000 yards, the Fourth British Army was firmly established on the ridge above the Combles valley, while the French army was advancing victoriously on the other side of the valley. But though the British centre was tremendously strong, there was still much difficult ground to be won on the flanks.

On the left flank General Gough's army had hard work before it. It had still, on the main ridge above Thiepval and in the village itself, to carry defences that Sir Douglas Haig describes as being " as nearly impregnable as Nature, art, and the unstinted labour of nearly two years could make them." On the right flank General Rawlinson's army had almost as difficult work before it in the direction of Morval. This hamlet rose on the end of a long spur beyond Ginchy and Leuze Wood. The enemy's guns, sited around it, commanded a great field of view and fire in every direction. The nearest British force was at Leuze Wood, 2,000 yards distant, and separated by a broad, deep branch of the Combles valley. Across the valley eastward was   **Cordial feeling between Allies**
the high ground of Sallisel and Sailly-Sallisel, which were to form the objectives of the French attack. The enemy's fire from these eastern heights swept the British way of advance to Morval, and as the guns at Morval also commanded this way of approach, the conditions of the advance were exceedingly difficult. But the advance had to be made, for the British Commander-in-Chief observed that he could not safely swing out from his centre unless the Morval spur were occupied. Otherwise his central thrust down the lower slopes of the main ridge would have been battered from the rear by the hostile guns around Morval.

It was a situation in which unity of command appeared to be essential. A subsidiary sacrificing movement was

WHERE BRIEF PERIODS OF REST WERE PASSED. [British official photograph.

After a spell in the firing-line the troops were relieved, and returned to the rest trenches behind the front ; but the rest was rather one from the actual strain of fighting than cessation of work. Though this picture was evidently taken at a quiet moment, the great heap of trenching implements in the background may be taken as indication of the strenuous duties which frequently accompanied the " resting " spells of the soldiers.

required. But, instead of unity, there was a national division between the British and French attacking forces. It was most necessary for the French to co-operate in the British attack by advancing towards Sailly-Sallisel. In order to do this they had to work forward along a narrow corridor between the vast woodland fortress of St. Pierre Vaast and the branching Combles valley. Yet the cordial good feeling between the allied armies and their earnest desire to assist each other, says Sir Douglas Haig, proved as effective as unity of command. All difficulties were removed by the French commander arranging to divert the enemy and work along the corridor, in support of the British offensive.

Opening of the third phase

The third phase of the Somme Battle was then opened by the Fourth Army swinging up before Morval and descending down the main ridge towards Bapaume. Sir Douglas Haig arranged that if the Morval line was reached by General Rawlinson's men, the Fifth Army under General Gough should use the victory on the right flank as cover for a sudden descent upon the villages of Martinpuich and Courcelette, near the Ancre line. Early in the morning of September 15th General Rawlinson's army swept out and won immediate success on almost all the front it attacked. The new, heavily-armoured British cars, known as " tanks," were brought into action for the first time, and coming as a great surprise to the enemy rank and file, gave valuable help in breaking down his resistance. Two hours and twenty minutes after the assault opened some " tanks " entered the village of Flers and penetrated the enemy's last line of fortification. The troops that followed the " tanks " quickly cleared the village and occupied the enemy's trenches some distance beyond it. High Wood was carried after many hours of very strenuous fighting, and, what was of most importance, the British right flank was advanced against the enemy's strong line of defence from Morval to Gueudecourt, so that preparations for assaulting this line could be carefully and yet speedily organised. This series of remarkable successes by General Rawlinson's army enabled the battle plan to be modified, and in the afternoon of the same day the waiting Fifth Army under General Gough, which had been cautiously advancing across the northern slopes of the Thiepval ridge, leaped out upon Martinpuich and Courcelette and stormed both villages with extraordinary ease.

Sir Douglas Haig gives it as his judgment that the British victories of the middle of September were of larger scope than any success obtained since the beginning of the campaign. In one day's fighting the troops broke through two of the enemy's main systems of defence and advanced on a front of more than six miles to an average depth of a mile. Three large villages, each powerfully organised for prolonged resistance, were taken, and all this was accomplished with small losses in comparison with the large forces employed.

Owing to the demoralisation of the enemy the Fourth Army was able rapidly to break the Morval-Gueudecourt line and combine with the French Army in capturing in inexpensive fashion the highly important town of Combles. Sir Douglas Haig then remarks that the successes of the Fourth Army were so considerable that he was able to prevent the enemy from recovering from the blow he had received by throwing the Fifth Army forward in fresh vigour against the Thiepval ridge and village. Staggering already from the strokes delivered by General Rawlinson's men, the Germans were in no condition to resist the untired and highly confident forces of General Gough. The enemy's positions on the left were stormed with remarkable ease, and though he resisted in the strong works north of Thiepval and in the secret recesses of Mouquet Farm, he was completely overcome by September 27th. On the same day the Fourth Army captured nearly all the ground in front of Le Sars by walking forward on a front of nearly two miles to a depth of five hundred to six hundred yards. On this sector the main body of German troops fled before the intended action opened. Two days afterwards a

Demoralisation of the enemy

single company carried the key position of Destremont Farm, thus opening the way to the capture of the last portion of the enemy's original defences at Le Sars and Eaucourt l'Abbaye. Three days of incessant rain gave the stricken and disheartened Germans temporary relief. But, in spite of the weather, the British guns were brought forward, and on October 7th the conquest of the last defences on the western flank of Bapaume was completed.

Thereupon, Sir Douglas Haig says, he deliberately stayed the British advance along the southern side of the Ancre toward Bapaume.

I was quite confident of the ability of our troops to clear the enemy entirely from his last positions whenever it should suit my plans to do so. I was therefore well content with the situation on this flank. Along the centre of our line from Gueudecourt to the west of Le Sars similar considerations applied. As we were already well down the forward slopes of the ridge on this front, it was for the time being inadvisable to make any serious advance.

But on the eastern front of Bapaume, where the enemy had a strong system of trenches and was digging fresh works in feverish haste, Sir Douglas Haig remarked a great opportunity.

In this direction we had at last reached a stage at which a successful attack might reasonably be expected to yield much greater results than anything we had yet attained. The resistance of the troops opposed to us had seriously **Weather** weakened in the course of our operations, and **compels a halt** there was no reason to suppose that the effort required would not be within our powers.

The British commander states his view of the situation in very modest language. Bapaume was his to take, and in taking it he thought he could easily make a downright rupture of the German front around the village of Le Transloy. But he goes on to say that, unfortunately, very unfavourable weather set in, and continued with scarcely a break until the early part of November. Poor visibility interfered with the observation work of artillery, and constant rain turned the hastily dug trenches into channels

of deep mud. The ground became almost impassable, making the supply of food stores and ammunition so difficult that Sir Henry Rawlinson found it impossible to exploit the situation with the rapidity necessary to enable him to reap the full benefits of the advantages he had gained.

For these reasons alone the Germans, in their period of extreme weakness, were saved from a decisive defeat that would have thrown them out of a large part of the French and Belgian territory they held. When the weather improved in the second week of November, turning to a dry, cold, misty season that still **Great decision** hindered gunnery action and left the **postponed** ground very bad in places, Sir Douglas Haig abandoned the idea of fighting for a great decision. He does not in his despatch repeat his reasons, but we can conclude from the suggestions he makes in previous paragraphs that he correctly foresaw the period of dry weather would be short, and that his guns and supply trains would again be bogged before he could drive the enemy into open country and engage in the great battles of field manœuvre. Had rain set in when all the German trench-line was ruptured, the enemy would have withdrawn close to his rail-heads, and possessed firm roads and firm ground around and behind his new front. The British armies, on the other hand, would have had to get across the deep stretch of mud on the old battlefield, and as there was not a good road across this sea of mud, the movement of men and animals, motor-vehicles and heavy guns, would have been fatiguing and disastrously slow.

"It was necessary," said Sir Douglas Haig, "to limit the operations to what would be reasonably possible to consolidate under the conditions." Therefore, only the command of the Ancre valley was made the object of the last important operation of the British armies in the winter of 1916. On November 13th, on a gloomy morning dense with fog, part of the Fifth Army under Sir Hubert

PACK-HORSE CAVALCADE CARRYING RATIONS THROUGH A RUINED VILLAGE. [*British official photograph.*

Although the modern method of motor transport was largely employed along the western front, there was also here and there reversion to a more primitive manner of conveying rations and other stores to the troops.

Here the amused looks upon the faces of the road-mending squad seem to show that the men saw matter for mirth in the employment of the old-fashioned pack-horse train for bringing up their stores.

Gough attacked the enemy's strongholds on both sides of the Ancre River. The last spur of the Thiepval ridge was captured by an action remarkable for rapidity of execution and lightness of loss. The number of prisoners was greater than that of the attackers. Then the village of St. Pierre Divion was taken by a British division that suffered less than six hundred casualties and made 1,400 prisoners. At Beaumont-Hamel the struggle was more severe, but the great stronghold fell, and the following morning the spur of the Serre plateau was carried and the hamlet of Beaucourt occupied. Serre itself, in the opinion of Sir Douglas Haig, was saved from capture only through the ground there being so muddy that the rain which fell during the attack interrupted the supply of ammunition when the troops had won the enemy's trenches.

Thus ended the third phase of the Battle of the Somme, in which the British Commander-in-Chief completely attained his three main objects, besides bringing Germany desperately close to a defeat that would **Three main objects** have probably been a rout. When the **attained** struggle closed in November the strength of the enemy forces in the western theatre of war was greater than that strength had been in July. His abandonment of the offensive against Verdun had not released forces for action on the Russian front, but had only provided insufficient reinforcements for the Somme front. So worn down was the enemy's strength

that he had to keep in the autumn more men on the Somme front than he had concentrated in the summer battles. Yet the increased number of men and guns he employed could not prevent the British armies from advancing at any point where the ground was not impassable.

The conclusion of Sir Douglas Haig's despatch is prophetic:

The enemy's power has not yet been broken, nor is it yet possible to form an estimate of the time the war may last before the objects for which the Allies are fighting have been attained. But the Somme Battle has placed beyond doubt the ability of the Allies to gain those objects. The German Army is the mainstay of the Central Powers, and a full half of that Army, despite all the advantages of the defensive, supported by the strongest fortifications, suffered defeat on the Somme this year. Neither the victors nor the vanquished will forget this; and though bad weather has given the enemy a respite, there will undoubtedly be many thousands in his ranks who will begin the new campaign with little confidence in their ability to resist our assaults or to overcome our defence. Our New Armies entered the battle with the determination to win and with confidence in their power to do so. They have proved to themselves, to the enemy, and to the world that this confidence was justified, and in the fierce struggle they have been through they have learned many valuable lessons which will help them in the future.

A prophetic conclusion

Such was the great answer the new Prime Minister of the United Kingdom made, by the medium of his leading commander, to the intrigues for a German peace, engineered by Bethmann-Hollweg and Hindenburg and their agents and dupes in neutral or pro-German States.

WINTER'S WHITE AND PEACEFUL WEAR: FIRST SNOWFALL IN FLANDERS.

With its covering of freshly-fallen snow this stretch of Flemish fields scarcely suggests that it was near the battleground of the western front, in that small tract of the Belgian kingdom that was kept free from the ruthless invader. The scene, with its ditch-side rows of pollarded willows, it distant farm buildings, and its cultivated ground showing through the thin covering of snow, suggests rather a typically peaceful countryside.

CHAPTER CLIX.

THE STRUGGLE IN RUMANIA TO THE FALL OF BUKAREST.
By Robert Machray.

Rumania Hopeful—Circumstances against Her—Two Grave Miscalculations—German Aims—Great Struggle for the Passes—Position at the End of October, 1916—Fine Rumanian Defence—The First Battle of Targu Jiu—Magnificent Rumanian Victory—Bavarians Flee in Disorder—Wounding and Death of the Victorious General—Continued Desperate German Assaults on the Passes—Hindenburg's Plan—Slight German Gains in the North—Fierce Fighting on the Upper Alt—Falkenhayn Strikes Along the Valley of the Jiu—Rumanian Retreat—Germans Win the Second Battle of Targu Jiu—Serious Situation Rapidly Develops for Rumania—Enemy Out of the Mountains Into the Plain—Fall of Craiova—Successes of the Allies in the Dobruja—But Mackensen Crosses the Danube—Situation Growing Worse—Line of the Alt Turned from the South—Retreat of the Rumanians—Orsova Army Cut Off and Captured—Combined German Advance in Wallachia—Heavy Fighting on the Alt—Germans Pressing On—Bukarest in Danger—Capital Transferred to Jassy, in Moldavia—Great Russian Offensive in the Carpathians—Too Late—Battle of the Argesul—Rumanians Overwhelmed after Brave Resistance—Retreat Eastward—Allied Efforts in the Dobruja—British Armoured Cars' Fine Work—Bukarest Doomed—Evacuation and Surrender—Rumania Resolved to Carry On.

AS part of a general review of the position of affairs in the Balkans from January to September, 1916, Chapter CXLV. recorded the intervention of Rumania on behalf of the Entente, and at the time it was written great expectations were entertained among the Allies of the high importance of the rôle that gallant little country was to play in the stupendous drama of the world-war. The narrative presented in Chapter CXLVII. of the first phases of Rumania's struggle with the Central Empires showed how these expectations, which at the outset seemed destined to be speedily realised, became dulled and clouded as the whole situation gradually assumed an ominous aspect.

Rumania herself had by no means lost hope, and she confronted her perilous position with wonderful courage and resolution. Determined to offer the utmost resistance within her power, and supported by the prospect of receiving adequate help from her Allies, she continued to make an heroic stand against heavy and ever-increasing odds. But the battles in which she had been worsted by the Germans under Falkenhayn in the region of the northern passes, particularly those in the neighbourhood

of Brasso (Kronstadt), had unmistakably demonstrated that she was severely handicapped by being opposed to artillery much superior to her own. The unfortunate issue of her two months' conflict with Mackensen in the Dobruja bore further witness to the same serious deficiency in guns.

Her Army was good, and its spirit was excellent. Her peasant soldiers were brave, and fought with all their heart and soul for their native land, to which they were devoted, but they were hardly a match for veterans. The vast majority of Rumania's officers and men had had no actual experience of war, whereas the forces of the enemy were composed of picked troops inured to campaigning, and from knowledge acquired in the varying conditions of warfare ready to take full advantage of every opportunity. The contest was one between the skilled soldier and the unskilled soldier, with the scales in any case sharply weighted down against the latter by the better " machinery " of the former. Thus the b e n e f i t s derived by R u m a n i a from her strong natural defences were more than offset by the preponderant power developed in the German offensive, the success of which was another example of the virtue of " big

KING FERDINAND OF RUMANIA AND HIS HEIR.
Throughout the fighting in Rumania, King Ferdinand, who enjoyed the absolute devotion of his people, was constantly at the front. He is here seen motoring with the Crown Prince Carol.

battalions " — on twentieth - century lines. Assistance was sent to her by her Allies, but the turn of events, which was little short of tragic, proved it to be insufficient to protect her from disaster. Nor was Russia, from whom alone of the Entente Powers she could anticipate strong immediate support, especially in men, able to place at her disposal in time the large forces, backed by heavy guns, which were necessary in the circumstances. Some people were inclined to suspect the Russians of lukewarmness towards Rumania, and there were whisperings, probably of pro-German origin, even in Bukarest to that effect; but such was not the fact.

M. Jonescu's tribute to Russia. M. Take Jonescu, the eminent Rumanian statesman and patriot, rendered a distinguished service to the common cause when he announced in the most emphatic language, in reply to this calumny, that Russia not only had performed all that had been expected of her by his country, but had done ever so much more.

Prior to her declaration of war Rumania had long been courted both by the Entente Powers and the Central Powers, and when it was known that she had decided to take the field against Austria-Hungary there had been enthusiastic rejoicing, and apparently with good reason, in all the lands of the Allies. In the statement of her case against the Dual Monarchy, which she published to the world on entering on hostilities, Rumania had expressed her belief that her action would shorten the conflict and hasten the overthrow of the enemy. And, outside enemy countries, that was the universal opinion. As the campaign proceeded, however, what occurred plainly indicated that this confident forecast was entirely erroneous, and consequently there was deep disappointment on the one side and corresponding jubilation on the other.

As the days and weeks wore on through November and the first part of December the struggle went more and more deplorably against Rumania, and it was manifest that her plan of campaign had been vitiated from the very start by grave miscalculations. These were twofold.

First, her conception of the strategy of the campaign was faulty, as the progress of events showed only too clearly. Her invasion of Transylvania, coupled with the neglect of the Dobruja, proved a gigantic mistake that had the most serious consequences. Her Allies had urged her to secure herself on the north by occupying and fortifying the passes into Transylvania, and at the same time to attack Bulgaria with all her strength on the south. But, swayed by political rather than military considerations and hoodwinked by the wily, guileful pretences of Bulgaria, she did not accept and act on this counsel. The Bulgarians were not attacked, and the Dobruja was practically left unprotected against a strong assault, a blunder well-nigh as fatal as that which kept the Serbians from attacking the Bulgarians in the early part of October, 1915 (Chapter XCIII.). The result was that Rumania suffered her first serious check in the loss of Tutrakan (Turtukai) in the second week of the campaign, and that reverse led in its turn to the withdrawal of considerable forces together with her best general, Avarescu, from the north to the south, thus weakening the assault on Austria-Hungary and throwing all her operations out of gear.

With Bulgaria against her, Rumania's strength was greatly beneath what was essential for her long frontiers. She had bargained with Russia to be given two divisions of infantry and a cavalry division in the Dobruja, but this reinforcement, large as it was, was not nearly sufficient to balance the account, far less to turn the whole position to her distinct advantage and ensure success. In other words, Rumania had overestimated her military resources. Further, she had under- **Rumania's grave miscalculations** estimated those of the enemy. This was the second of her grave miscalculations.

On her behalf it had to be admitted that in making this huge mistake Rumania did not stand alone among the Allies. Constant reports, which had all the semblance of authority, pictured Germany and her chief supporter, Austria-Hungary, as " exhausted " by reason of the Franco-British, Russian, and Italian victories during the summer on the Somme, in Volhynia and Galicia, and in the Trentino. There was little doubt that Rumania joined in the war just when she did because of these great triumphs of the Entente Powers. The tremendous losses which the Dual Monarchy had sustained under General

CONSTANTSA, THE CHIEF PORT OF RUMANIA, CAPTURED BY THE GERMANS, OCTOBER 22ND, 1916.
Constantsa, looking westward from the Black Sea, with the residential quarters on the north, and the harbour, granaries, and oil-tanks on the south (the left of the picture). The loss of the town involved the loss of much grain and oil, and also the cutting of a short line of communication between Bukarest and Odessa by the Black Sea.

Brussiloff's marvellous offensive had had a very direct bearing in bringing about the intervention of Rumania, who was led to believe that Austria-Hungary could do but little against her, and Germany not much more. She was soon undeceived.

By transferring regiments from various parts of her fronts and remaking up divisions, and by utilising Austro-Hungarians, Bulgarians, and Turks, Germany had put into the field against Rumania by the end of September armies approximating to three hundred thousand men, with an abundance of powerful artillery, and this large figure as regards troops was something like doubled by the beginning of November. To a certain extent Germany paid for this accumulation of forces elsewhere, but doubtless she considered that what she achieved thereby in Rumania was bought at a comparatively low price, for the results that she gained by this effort, though not all that she had hoped, were, it had to be acknowledged by the Allies, of very considerable importance.

In Chapter CXLVII. it was observed that Germany had three aims or ends in view in her offensive against Rumania, in addition to her determination to " punish" that small country for what she absurdly termed its " disloyalty and treachery " to the Germanic League. The first of these was military in its character, the second political, and the third economic.

As for the first, Western Rumania, or Wallachia, formed a salient jutting out into territories all of which were in the hands of Germany and menacing her whole eastern front ; but more particularly it was dangerous to the success of her grand

DISAPPOINTING THE INVADERS' HOPES.
Mackensen's force pushed through the Dobruja, hoping to seize much-needed oil at Constantsa. That the Russians and Rumanians before retiring carefully destroyed the extensive oil-tanks the pillar of smoke from the burning oil effectively shows.

OIL-FIELDS—BUT NO OIL FOR THE HUNS.
That the Austro-German sweep into Rumania was partly inspired by the desire to capture oil and corn in bulk was well understood. Fortunately, however, the rich oil-fields were so badly damaged before abandonment that they could not be immediately utilised.

Berlin-Bagdad Railway scheme. By the end of the first week in December she had, in effect, cut off and occupied that salient, and had made her eastern position by that much more secure, thus realising her immediate aim or objective. And with the realisation of this went that of her two other aims, which were to improve the political value of Austria-Hungary, and to obtain new supplies or sources of supply for her own

people. Her defeat of Rumania gave the Dual Monarchy fresh stability, and at the same time put herself in possession of such stores of wheat and petroleum as the retreating Rumanians were unable to remove or destroy, as well as of much potential wealth in the shape of farm and oil-producing lands.

It could not be denied that these results were of very considerable importance, and must lead to the prolongation of the war. On the other hand, in what must have been the enemy's chief aim of all — the destruction or capture of the Rumanian Army—Germany had not succeeded. The safe withdrawal of the main Rumanian forces after the fortune of war on the Argesul had compelled the evacuation of Bukarest, was made possible by the extraordinarily gallant and effective defence by the Rumanians and the Russians of the passes east of Brasso and on the Moldavian frontier — on most of which the Germans, in spite of the most persevering endeavours, were unable to make any serious impression, but, on the contrary, were checked and even thrown back. It was probable enough that these German efforts on the north-west of Rumania represented a determined attempt to cut across Moldavia, and in that way to pen in the bulk of the Rumanian Army and separate it

Where Germany failed

from the remainder with its chief Russian supports. But if that was the case, it was completely defeated. In this region Russian assistance was most effective.

Military operations of an offensive nature were far more difficult on the Moldavian frontier, with its lofty mountains and general lack of roads, than on the Wallachian frontier, with its comparatively easy passes and highways, and it was in the latter area that the Germans under Falkenhayn delivered their heaviest blows. Mr. Hamilton Fyfe, the well-known and well-informed special

Weakness in the High Command correspondent of the " Daily Mail," in a despatch from Bukarest, dated November 20th, and published by that journal on December 13th, 1916, stated that at the opening of the campaign the hope was very widespread in Rumania that her Army would be able to occupy Transylvania without vigorous opposition, and that, as the invasion met at first with no forcible opposition, the hope grew. Then came Falkenhayn's thrust, forces for which everyone had come to know had been assembling in Hungary. "The Rumanian Headquarters Staff," added Mr. Fyfe, "was not prepared for it, and too much was left to generals on the spot."

TURKISH PRISONERS TAKEN IN THE PREDEAL PASS.
Much stubborn fighting took place in the passes between Hungary and Rumania, and there the heavy pressure of the enemy was long withstood. Before being compelled to retire the Rumanians captured large numbers of prisoners, including many of the Turkish allies of the invading Austro-Germans.

This weakness in the High Command was in itself calamitous. Changes were made in the chief commands, but with no very marked improvement in the field as a whole. Taking everything into account, it unhappily became only too certain that Rumania was inadequately equipped for the tremendous task which she had undertaken. And what was equally apparent was that the Governments of her Allies must also have misjudged the situation, otherwise they would hardly have permitted her to enter the lists when she did. Rumania and the Allies suffered accordingly. Soon it looked as if Rumania—or at least, the larger and richer part of it—would have to endure the dark fate of Serbia, the prodigious victories of the Entente Powers in other areas of the war having been insufficient to ameliorate her position. Even the capture of Monastir by the Allies had no appreciably favourable effect.

The narrative of the campaign given in Chapter CXLVII. concluded with the events which occurred in the closing days of October, 1916. Mackensen had taken, after heavy fighting, the Constantsa-Cerna Voda railway in the Dobruja, and the Russo-Rumanian forces were retreating towards the northern part of that province. In

Moldavia the Rumanians generally were holding, and in some cases improving, their positions ; but in Wallachia, in the passes south of Hatszeg, Hermannstadt, and Brasso, where the enemy struck most fiercely, they were losing ground, notwithstanding their most valorous struggles to retain it. Whatever had been the want of prevision at Bukarest, whatever were the defects in the equipment of the Rumanian Army, the Rumanian soldiers fought with stubborn courage—as the enemy more than once testified.

From about October 10th, when the Rumanians were compelled to withdraw in Transylvania towards the passes, Falkenhayn had continued to press them back. In the middle of the month he had succeeded in driving them out of the Törzburg and Gyimes Passes, and on the 25th had captured the Vulkan Pass, beginning that advance along the valley of the Jiu which, though encountering defeat at first, was to have such a strangely decisive influence on the fortunes of his whole offensive, of the entire campaign, and of Rumania. Next the Germans took the Predeal Pass and the little town of Predeal. At that time they had a firm foothold on Rumanian soil also at Rucaru and Dragoslavele, the latter just south of the former place, on the south side of the Törzburg, on the road to Campu Lung, as well as at Caineni, at the southern exit of the Roter Turm, which they had taken as far back as the beginning of the month. Orsova and the Varciorova Pass were still in the possession of Rumania.

Falkenhayn was trying to break the determined and, for a while, not altogether ineffective resistance of the Rumanian forces by one or more of the passes, or the exits from them, along the vast mountainous frontier. He was really feeling for the weakest sector in this long front, and the scouting aeroplanes with which he was well supplied incessantly brought him information as to the positions and movements of the Rumanian troops, and enabled him to make good use of his guns. The Army of Rumania had a serious shortage in aircraft, as in wire-entanglement nippers, field telephones, and other munitions, but both France and Great Britain did something towards making up the deficiency. A wireless message from Bukarest reported the arrival there of four British aeroplanes from Imbros on October 24th ; more British machines came later from Tenedos, and a hundred and twenty French aeroplanes had previously reached the country from General Sarrail at Salonika, or from elsewhere.

In the Carpathians Falkenhayn continued to meet with little or no success, but in the Transylvanian Alps he made progress by violent assaults, backed by his superior artillery, south of Predeal and in the vicinity of Dragoslavele at the foot of the Törzburg, **Enemy stubbornly** along the two roads which offered the **opposed** most direct access to Bukarest. The hardy Rumanians clung to their poor entrenchments most tenaciously, and inflicted repeated repulses on him, but they had to yield slightly under the severe pressure which he put upon them. By the 27th the Germans, however, had got no farther south of Predeal than Azuga, five miles nearer the capital, while in the valley of Pravatz, in the Törzburg district, they suffered a decided reverse, the terrain, according to the Rumanian communiqué, being covered with enemy corpses.

OVER THE HILLS TOWARDS THE LONGED-FOR PRIZE.

Between their country and Hungary the frontier which the Rumanians had to defend was mainly mountainous, and in parts densely wooded. This striking photograph shows a detachment of troops on the march towards the Transylvanian frontier, impelled by the fervour of their desire to gain freedom for their compatriots under alien rule.

RUMANIANS FIGHTING IN THE TRANSYLVANIAN ALPS.

During the early advance of the Rumanians into Hungarian territory the fighting formed a great contrast with the trench warfare that was being carried on in other parts of Europe. Here among the wooded hills the soldiers had abundance of natural cover as they advanced against the enemy in that brief triumphant forward movement following their entry into the war.

AWKWARD CORNER ON A RUMANIAN HILLSIDE.
In taking the batteries of artillery into the hills, the strong Rumanian ponies proved capable workers, despite the roughly-made tracks, laid "corduroy" fashion with wood, along which the guns had to be dragged.

WRECKED BRIDGE AND ROUGH SUBSTITUTE.
When compelled to fall back before the enemy's overwhelming advance, the Rumanians were careful to harass the pursuing enemy by blowing up bridges. On the left is an iron bridge, which they destroyed during their retreat in Transylvania, and on the right the temporary structure which took its place.

The Germans paid a high price for such small gains as they made. The Rumanian withdrawal was slow, and soon stopped. The Russian official statement announced that on the northern frontier of Wallachia the Rumanians had arrested the enemy's offensive and were consolidating their positions. How splendid was the defence of the peasant soldiers of the little kingdom, led in this quarter of it by General Avarescu, and forming part of the Second Rumanian Army, was shown by the fact that it was not till weeks later that the Germans could report something more substantial than trifling, inconsiderable advances on either of these two roads to Bukarest.

South of the Roter Turm, the next great pass west of the Törzburg and the Predeal, Falkenhayn also launched on the Rumanians many desperate assaults, which official telegrams usually described as taking place in the valley or neighbourhood of the Alt (Oltu, or Aluta). This river flowed from Transylvania, past Fogaras, into Rumania, crossing the country from north to south till it reached the Danube, and almost bisecting Wallachia, the western

half being called Oltenia, the eastern Muntenia. In the summer this stream was not a great river, but when swollen by the late autumn and early winter rains and snows it attained such depth and width that it came next in importance to the Danube, the Pruth, and the Sereth in Rumania.

By this time the weather had broken. Heavy rains had swept the plains and much snow had fallen in the mountains; the Alt was becoming a formidable obstacle in the military sense. The storms impeded operations, whether of friend or foe, but did not cause them to cease. East of the river the Germans attacked continuously for several days, and after some checks captured the villages of Rakovitsa and Titesti, both about eleven miles south of the frontier. The Rumanians were afterwards withdrawn a little farther into the interior, and as October closed were holding up the invaders.

Meanwhile, more to the west, the struggle in the Jiu valley, south of the Vulkan Pass, had been maintained, and as it proceeded it developed unexpected and sensational features. In this region Falkenhayn attacked first with the 11th Bavarian Division, composed of hardy highlanders used to life in the mountains under all conditions. **First Battle of Targu Jiu**

On October 24th the Rumanians, who in this sector belonged to the First Rumanian Army, began to retire before it, and continued their withdrawal during the following day. This retirement signified a hostile advance of twenty miles into the country, and the enemy was in sight of Targu Jiu, a town of some ten thousand inhabitants, lying on a high tableland picturesquely surrounded with wooded hills. Many of its people fled, and the military authorities, fearing the worst, gave orders for the evacuation of the rest of the civil population. The Rumanian soldiers, however, held the place, and now occurred one of the most glorious episodes on their side in the entire campaign.

Considered one of the best divisions of the German Army, the 11th Bavarian Division, to which had been added four cavalry regiments and some howitzer batteries, was commanded by General Knesler, and never anticipated anything approaching a defeat. Indeed, only a few days before the Rumanians turned and counter-attacked, General Knesler had received a flattering communication from the German Kaiser, who congratulated his "gallant troops on their success," and the Bavarian leader was so certain of victory that some cavalry of his, who were near Targu Jiu, had orders to take possession of that town on "October 27th at 2 o'clock in the afternoon." Little did the Germans imagine what was about to happen.

General Dragalina's victory

In this region the Rumanians were led by General Dragalina, who very shortly before had been placed in command. A fine officer, his rise had been rapid. Only eleven months previously he had been a colonel. When the campaign began he was at the head of a division, soon was given an army corps, and almost immediately afterwards an army. His forces at Targu, wearied by incessant fighting, were inferior to those of the Germans, and his situation was desperate, but having received some much-needed reinforcements he resolved to counter-attack on a bold plan and roll back the tide of invasion. Splitting up his little army into three parts, and regardless of the fact that his projected course of action left the rear on his right exposed, he pushed forward and fell with great impetuosity on the flank of the enemy, who was completely surprised and broke up in panic. This occurred on October 26th, and the Rumanians pressed home their advantage next day.

An official Bukarest message, dated October 28th, announced the beginning of this brilliant victory in the words: "In the valley of the Jiu the enemy, who had advanced to the west, was vigorously attacked by us and completely vanquished." The communiqué went on to state that four hundred and fifty prisoners, three guns, and sixteen machine-guns with their equipment had been captured, while a thousand Bavarians lay dead on the field. But the Rumanian victory developed into something far bigger, for as their offensive continued they made further important gains. Bukarest reported on the 29th that the Rumanians were progressing and pursuing the enemy, who was retreating into the mountains. The despatch added: "We have captured an additional ten officers and two hundred and fifty Bavarian soldiers. Reserve Sub-Lieutenant Patrascoiu, with the unit under his command, took two howitzer batteries of 105 mm. (4 in.) calibre, belonging to the 21st Regiment of Bavarian Artillery. The guns were immediately put into action against the enemy, and rendered us great service. We have also captured four more machine-guns and many limbers."

Rout of the Bavarians

Day after day the Rumanians drove on the defeated Bavarians, taking from them many hundreds of additional prisoners and much booty as they fled up the river towards the Vulkan Pass. According to one report, the victory

RUMANIANS RECROSSING THE BOUNDARY RIVER AFTER THEIR INCURSION INTO TRANSYLVANIA.
The invasion of Transylvania by the Rumanians at the outset of their campaign was a strategical blunder that had serious consequences. The invasion amounted to little more than a raid quite ineffectual to bring emancipation to their compatriots under Austrian rule.

FF

of the Rumanians was partially due to the use of a ruse which had been employed as far back as the thirteenth century—trees were cut down on the hillsides and hurled into the valley to stem, or at least to hinder, the German retreat, thus increasing the enemy's difficulties and consequently swelling his losses. As a result of the battle—the Battle of Targu Jiu—the Germans lost 2,000 prisoners, an equal number in killed, and thousands of wounded, besides many guns of various types and large quantities of ammunition. And the invaders had been beaten back from the railway, for Targu Jiu was the terminus of the line from Craiova, where it connected with other lines running east and west. All Rumania breathed more freely for this victory.

A striking but sad illustration of the mischances of war

was given in this battle by the wounding and death shortly afterwards of the general who had planned and started this magnificent counter-attack. Four hours from the commencement of the offensive General Dragalina was hit in the shoulder and the arm. While inspecting the positions he had gone too near the German lines, and at three hundred yards range his motor-car came under the fire of a hostile machine-gun. His arm had to be amputated, and this, coupled with his other injuries, so aggravated a disease from which he had suffered for some time that his condition soon was hopeless, and he died in the midst of victory—a great loss to his country. He was succeeded in the command of the First Rumanian Army by General Culcer.

At the opening of November the feelings of apprehension among the Allies and in Rumania itself with respect to the situation had been considerably decreased by the success of the Rumanians Falkenhayn concentrates his efforts in the Jiu valley, and by the stoutness of their resistance at other points on the Wallachian mountain front. On the Moldavian frontier and as far as the Predeal the position remained much the same; since a repulse of the Germans from the Gyimes it had been favourable on the whole for Rumania. But the thrusts of the enemy still were delivered with great force from the Predeal to the Roter Turm; first, in the valley of the Prahova, south of the Predeal, second, in the district round Dragoslavele, south of the Törzburg, and third, in the valley of the Alt, at the exit from the Roter Turm.

In the first sector Falkenhayn, having failed to penetrate to the plain by the lower defiles, was concentrating his efforts to break through in the mountains near Azuga. But the Rumanians put up a great fight, and repeatedly counter-attacked him. A German communiqué of November 2nd claimed that these counter-attacks had

RETREAT IN GOOD ORDER BY STREAM AND MOUNTAIN PASS.

Rumanians leaving their position in a defile during their retreat before Falkenhayn and Mackensen. Aided by the Russians they retreated in good order, and early in January, 1917, were on the line of the River Sereth. In circle: Cunningly concealed positions for the defence of the Predeal Pass which, however, was captured at the end of October, 1916, by Falkenhayn, who thus became master of all Wallachia.

AUSTRIAN PRISONERS EN ROUTE FOR INTERNMENT.
In the early stages of their brave struggle the Rumanians captured goodly numbers of prisoners from among the various nationalities concentrated against them. Here Austrian soldiers are seen being marched as captives into the country which they had come to conquer.

failed with sanguinary losses to their opponents, but did not mention any advance of their troops. The same despatch announced, however, some gain of ground in the second sector. But it was in the Alt valley that Falkenhayn with large bodies of troops was attacking incessantly and most heavily.

It was by no means sure that he would succeed anywhere in debouching into the plain, notwithstanding all his tremendous endeavours, but these continued night and day. Bukarest apparently was confident that he would fail, and general opinion in that capital took the view that the mountains, with their defence in good hands, would remain an impenetrable barrier. Furthermore, Russian troops had arrived in the country. North of the Danube they were commanded by General Belaieff, a distinguished Russian general. On November 1st General Sakharoff, the victor of Brody, was in Bukarest, whence soon afterwards he proceeded to take the leadership of the Russo-Rumanian forces in the Dobruja.

The presence of these two eminent soldiers also tended to hearten the Rumanians and to cause **Arrival of Russian** them to take an optimistic view of affairs. **troops** Another circumstance that contributed to their cheerfulness was the weakening of the pressure of Mackensen in the Dobruja, where only encounters between outposts and patrols were now recorded, and General Christescu, the Rumanian commander, was establishing himself on a line some thirty miles north of the lost Constantsa-Cerna Voda Railway. Greatly encouraged, too, by the splendid success of the French at Verdun on October 24th, and by that of the Italians on the Carso on November 1st, they looked for fresh relief from some new offensive of the Allies in the west or on some other front.

What the country thought about the campaign as late as the second week of November was expressed by its semi-official journals in a review of the results of Rumania's two months of war. This stated that by maintaining her defensive towards the north Rumania had fully justified the

RED CROSS HELP IN T. E FIRING-LINE.
In the Rumanian campaign, as in the west, the Red Cross services were gallantly to the fore. Above is pictured a dramatic little incident just behind the firing-line on the edge of a wood, a wounded Rumanian soldier receiving prompt first-aid from a Red Cross comrade.

correctness of the political considerations which had decided the declaration of war against Austria-Hungary, and at the same time had paid due regard to the military considerations imposed, the considerable extent of Rumania's frontier, and the geographical configuration of the land.

It took the view that the Germano-Bulgarian success in the Dobruja had enabled General Sarrail to defeat the Bulgarians at Florina, while the Rumanian offensive against the Carpathians and Transylvanian Alps had drawn off large numbers of troops from the other fronts, thus facilitating the French victory at Verdun and the Italian victory on the Carso. It maintained that the advantages to the common cause of the intervention of Rumania, even with the enormous sacrifices it had involved, had been clearly demonstrated. It evidently considered that, while it could not be said that all was well, the worst was past, and that brighter and better days were

RACIAL BROTHERS UNITED ON THE BATTLEFIELD.
Conference between French and Rumanian officers. The Rumanians, as their name indicates, are of Roman (Latin) origin. Racially and temperamentally they have much in common with the French, whose allies they became against the combination of Germanic peoples with whom their King was connected by ties of blood.

Constantinople railway as his only means of communication with Bulgaria and Turkey. What actually occurred proved that he had made no mistake in his calculations. Up to the end of the first week of November it was impossible to say where the German pressure was most severe along the roads leading south from the Predeal, the Törzburg, and the Roter Turm Passes. Obscured by the violent fighting that was going on in these sectors, what was taking place south of the Vulkan passed almost out of sight, and what happened there a week or so later came as a great and intensely painful surprise, not only to the Allies in general but also to the great majority of the Rumanians themselves. Preoccupied, as Hindenburg intended, by the defence of the roads from the central passes, the Rumanian High Command had not a sufficiently strong force to meet his attack from the Vulkan Pass. Hence came swift and irremediable disaster.

in store. Hardly had that second week of the month gone by when the situation, which had suddenly undergone a terrible change, proved how mistaken all this hopefulness was.

Hindenburg, in absolute command of all the Germanic armies, saw no chance of a successful offensive on any other front, and being well informed, no doubt, of the military deficiencies of Rumania, thought he perceived his opportunity in that country. By November he had got together large forces in and about the mountains on the north and in the Dobruja. Competent authorities placed the troops at his disposition in these areas as high as thirty divisions, and though this estimate perhaps was excessive, it was not much above the truth. Of these divisions at least twelve were German. According to report, he summoned Mackensen and Falkenhayn to meet him in Belgrade at the beginning of the month, and when he had heard their views gave them his final instructions. His plan was for Falkenhayn to strike deeply into Western Wallachia, or Oltenia, by the Vulkan Pass route, while that general was maintaining overwhelming pressure farther east in Wallachia and holding his front in Moldavia. Mackensen, meanwhile, was to get ready, behind his line in the Dobruja, to force the crossing of the Danube, and join up with Falkenhayn when the passage was effected.

These operations, if successfully carried out, would shorten his front, provide an excellent base for the invasion of the rest of the country, and give him besides the mastery of the Danube, which the Rumanians by their capture of Orsova in the first days of their campaign had taken from him, leaving the Belgrade-Sofia-

South of the Predeal Pass the River Prahova flowed down from the mountains through the rich oil-bearing district to which it gave its name, and farther south joined the Jalomita, one of the tributaries of the Danube. A beautiful country of hills and streams and sylvan glades, much frequented by the Rumanian aristocracy in the summer, it was a region with a railway and good roads. A fine highway passed from the frontier village of Predeal through Sinaia—where King Ferdinand had a residence—Campina, and Ploesti to Bukarest.

In the early days of November the upper valley of the Prahova was the scene of the most furious contests. The Rumanians successfully withstood numerous assaults and repulsed others in the defiles, but on November 5th a

GENERAL AVARESCU: RUMANIA'S MOST TRUSTED GENERAL.
General Avarescu, Commander-in-Chief, under the King, of the Rumanian Army. He received his baptism of fire as a cavalry lieutenant in the Russo-Turkish War of 1877, and was Chief of Staff in the Balkan War of 1913. Afterwards Inspector of Cavalry, he was appointed Commander-in-Chief in August, 1916.

Berlin communiqué announced that previous German successes south of the Predeal had been completed by the storming of the Globucetu position, which had been specially prepared and was defended with stubbornness. An Austrian telegram added that the Germans, with whom were Austro-Hungarian troops, had vigorously followed up their success by capturing the second Rumanian line of entrenchments beyond. On the 6th the enemy took Mount Omu, 4,356 feet high, six miles south-east of Predeal. Then for the next two or three days there followed a tremendous bombardment by heavy guns of the Rumanian lines, succeeded by continuous, fierce assaults on the Rumanian left wing. The Rumanians replied by sharp counter-attacks on both sides of the road from the pass, but the Germans made progress west of Azuga on the 10th, after sanguinary encounters in which they had heavy losses. On the following day Vienna stated that west of Predeal the Germans stormed six successive positions, which they held against two desperate counter-attacks. Two days later the Rumanians repulsed two enemy assaults in the direction of the Cerburai vale, north-west of Busteni, seven and a half miles south of Predeal, and the starting point of the oil-fields in the district. On the 15th there was comparative calm in this region, the Rumanians maintaining themselves on the ground to which they had withdrawn. Aeroplanes bombed Sinaia on the same day. Up to this date the enemy had not gained much south of the Predeal from the Second Rumanian Army, whose work there was directed by General Avarescu in person.

During these two weeks of November the story of the struggle in the sector south of the Törzburg was less favourable to the Rumanians. There the Germans were already established in the vicinity of Dragoslavele, in the valley of the Rucar, and there was heavy fighting about November 5th in the hilly uplands between the Argesul and Targu valleys north-east of Campu Lung, the enemy claiming gains of ground and the loss to the Rumanians of a thousand killed. In this region Falkenhayn was well supplied with guns, and he battered down the trenches of his opponents. He progressed slowly, however, as he was constantly counter-attacked in difficult country which lent itself to assaults on his flanks. On the 11th he lost some of his trenches, but on the 13th he captured Candesti, a small town close to Campu Lung, and seventeen miles south of the frontier—on that date the farthest point he had reached in the interior of Rumania.

The enemy gains ground

On the 15th Bukarest announced that in "the region of Dragoslavele the enemy has attacked on several occasions,

MASCOT OF THE RUMANIAN REGIMENT OF THE WHITE BULL.
Adorned with the national colours—yellow, blue, and red—this magnificent white bull was led at the head of the regiment to which it gave its name. Sent to the army with a herd for conversion into provisions it took the fancy of some infantry officers who bought it for a regimental pet or mascot.

assisted by heavy artillery, but has everywhere been repulsed, our troops maintaining their positions." That day, according to the German account, saw only slight fighting on the whole Transylvanian front; but the Germans had meanwhile made a decided advance, and closely menaced Campu Lung, with its railway to Pitesti and thence south-east to Bukarest and south-west to Slatina and Craiova. Yet a fortnight passed before they were in Campu Lung.

However heavily Falkenhayn struck from the Predeal and the Törzburg, he struck still more heavily from the Roter Turm along the valley of the Alt. There his forces were led by General Kraft von Dellmensingen, the Bavarian commander who was credited with having conducted the successful encircling movement which resulted in the defeat of the Rumanians in the Battle of Hermannstadt. Under him were Bavarian and other German troops, as well as Austro-Hungarians, forming in all an army of considerable strength.

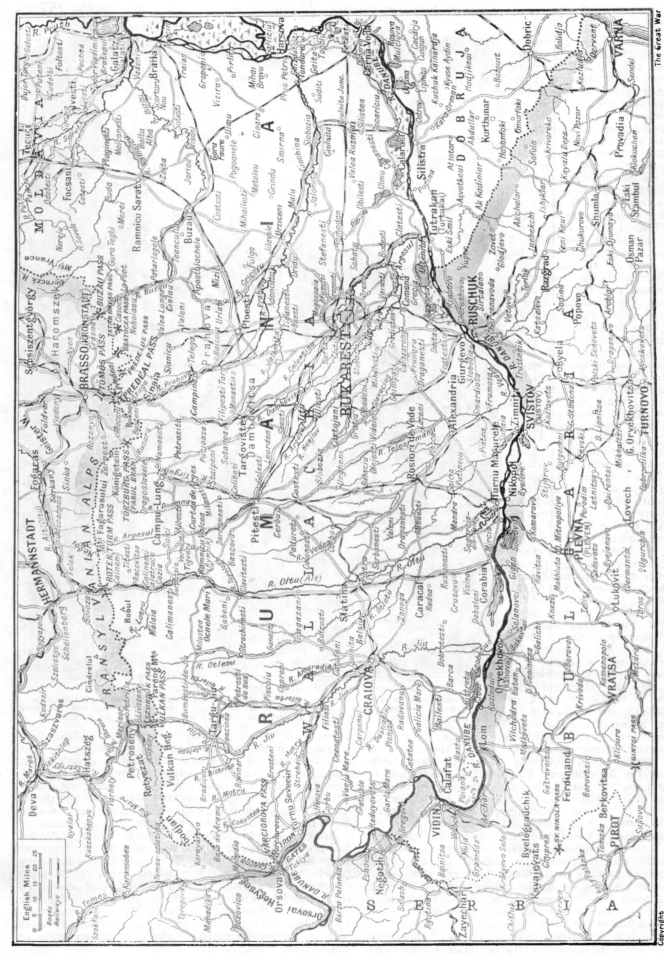

The Great War

Copyright

MAP OF RUMANIA SHOWING THE AREA CAPTURED BY THE GERMANIC POWERS UP TO THE END OF 1916.

Rumania formed a huge salient jutting out into the territories in German hands, and thus was exposed to attack by the Austrians on her Transylvanian frontier and on the line of the Danube by the Bulgarians. Disregarding the advice of the Allies she made an incursion into Transylvania, but her plans were thrown out of gear by the enemy's capture of Tutrakan. Mackensen swept from the west and south and Falkenhayn from the Transylvanian Passes, with the result that by the end of 1916 all Rumania was in their hands from the Iron Gates to the River Sereth, comprising notably the rich grain lands round Craiova.

On November 5th and 6th he made violent attacks on the right bank of the river near Racovitsa-Titesti, some eleven miles south of the frontier ; and on the 7th, near Spinu, fourteen miles from the head of the pass, drove the Rumanians back with a loss to them, according to the official German message, of over a thousand prisoners. His immediate objective on the east side of the Alt appeared to be Curtea de Arges, with its rail-head, and he had set in motion a formidable body in that direction along the road from Caineni. Two days later he reported that he had crossed the Baiesti sector, fifteen miles south of the frontier, and had captured Sardoiu, sixteen miles south, with the positions on the adjoining heights on both sides, having defeated fierce Rumanian counter-attacks. On the 10th he made a farther advance by " successful fighting in which," it was said, " Bavarian infantry, Austro-Hungarian mountain troops, as well as German Landsturm forces, especially distinguished themselves."

The Rumanians resisted doggedly, and on the 11th were able to state they had made progress on the left bank of the river, recapturing Mount Fruntsi, and had arrested the enemy's march on the right bank at Saracinesti, ten miles from the frontier. But they were not able to hold the Germans, and their communiqué of November 14th admitted that the enemy, by using fresh and superior forces, had driven them back after repeated assaults, in the course of which positions changed hands several times. On the 15th Dellmensingen was close to Salatruc, on the east bank of the Alt, twenty-one miles within the frontier, and near Brezoiu, on the west side of the river, fifteen miles into the interior. The German communiqué of the 16th acknowledged the fine resistance of the Rumanians in this quarter by stating that the peasant soldiers were " stubbornly defending their native soil." In this region the enemy had now deployed on a wide front on both sides of the Alt, thanks to superior numbers and heavier guns.

Beginning of the catastrophe — That fortnight's struggle along the roads south of these three central passes of Wallachia ended in loss of ground, but there had been no great victory on the one hand and no grave disaster on the other. The Germans spoke of the taking of large numbers of prisoners, but the previous experience of the Allies had thrown suspicion on all such assertions. The enemy did not dwell on the capture of many guns. His own losses unquestionably were considerable, but he made these good by bringing up fresh forces in strength. He seemed to have no lack of men. The situation had an unpromising appearance for Rumania, but could not be called desperate. It was what took place in the same short period in the region of the Vulkan Pass that precipitated the catastrophe.

On November 6th the Rumanian official telegram announced that the enemy had received reinforcements in the valley of the Jiu, and that the division which had beaten the Bavarians and driven them with great losses back into the Vulkan Pass had discontinued its pursuit. In this sector the Rumanians had only this single division, and after some slight fighting on the 7th the Germans began a new offensive against it on the next day ; but they did not develop their attack in great strength till about the 11th of the month. For this effort the Germans outnumbered the Rumanians by more than two to one. The remains of the 11th Bavarian Division, which had been so roughly handled in the first Battle of Targu Jiu, had been withdrawn, and its place had been taken by the 41st Prussian Division. There was besides another German division, with additional troops, mainly cavalry regiments, and extra artillery. The total amounted to about 50,000 men, who were commanded by General Schmidt von Knobelsdorff, an officer of experience, whose name had last been heard of in connection with operations on the Russian front west of Lutsk early in the preceding October.

A correspondent declared that in an Order of the Day

the Kaiser had said to the Prussian division, " We must destroy the enemy." The defeat of the Bavarians, which had enraged him as much as it had encouraged the Rumanians, had to be avenged, and care was taken that there should be no mistake about it. Foreseeing the difficulty, if not impossibility, of coping with such forces, the commander on the Jiu of the division of the First Rumanian Army asked the High Command for substantial reinforcements, but did not receive them. Some battalions indeed were sent to him, but they arrived too late, and in any case were inadequate in the circumstances.

On November 10th the Bukarest official despatch referred to the position in the valley as unchanged, but after mentioning fighting next day on the Moldevis Hill, east of the river, and about five miles south of the frontier, the communiqué of the 12th said that a violent German attack had compelled the Rumanians to retire slightly to the

"SCRAPS OF PAPER" THAT REMOVED BARRIERS.
Representatives of the foreign Press who wished to accompany the Rumanian Army when it took the field had to be well furnished with " scraps of paper " in the shape of credentials. These were closely scrutinised at the barriers before their holders were allowed to pass through.

south. Under the pressure of Knobelsdorff, which was augmenting hourly, this withdrawal continued, and by the 14th the Rumanian division, already reduced in numbers, was driven south of Bumbesti, a village thirteen miles within the interior. It then fell back on Targu Jiu, whence roads ran east to the Alt and west to Orsova, which town the left wing of the First Rumanian Army still held. For some time little news had come through with respect to the situation at this important town on the Danube, but on November 12th Berlin spoke of German advanced troops pressing forward there, and on the following day of unsuccessful Rumanian counter-attacks with strong forces to the north of the town. Falkenhayn's strategy was keeping this part of the First Rumanian Army—the part which later was known as the Orsova Army—far too busy for it to send any help to the fiercely assaulted centre in the valley of the Jiu.

Beginning on November 14th the second Battle of Targu

Jiu lasted for three days, and its issue, in a complete victory for the Germans, practically decided the fate of Rumania. There was a tremendous struggle, but the enemy was superior in everything except courage, and their courage, which was never in question, did not avail the Rumanians, who, w i l d l y shouting "Hurrah ! Hurrah ! " threw themselves on the German ranks with the utmost contempt of death, but were beaten back or mowed down by the overwhelming fire of the enemy's artillery and numerous machine-guns. It was a thoroughly unequal contest, and from the outset of the battle the result was certain.

The first intimation of the Rumanian defeat was contained in a message from Bukarest

AN ENEMY FOOD CONVOY.
Part of a team of laden donkeys whose services were requisitioned by the Austro-Hungarian Army in the task of provisioning their posts in the snow-capped heights of Wallachia.

HALT FOR REFRESHMENT IN THE TRANSYLVANIAN ALPS.
With the advent of winter the task of provisioning the Austro-Hungarian mountain posts became one of exceeding difficulty. Pony and donkey teams had to wend their way up the snow-covered mountain sides. Our photograph shows one such team making a halt for much needed refreshment in the bleak but picturesque surroundings of snow-covered mountain slopes.

communiqués of November 19th. At first some doubt was cast on their truthfulness, but they were accurate enough. Berlin, after announcing in its characteristic-ally complacent manner that the German operations o n t h e Southern Transylvanian front since the end of October had progressed as intended, declared that the German and Austro-Hungarian troops had forced a way out of the mountain passes into the Wallachian Plain. "In the Battle of Targu Jiu," it said, "we have broken through the stubborn resistance of the Ruma-nians between the Jiu and the Gilort, strong enemy forces being defeated with unusually high casualties. Enemy attempts to encircle us from the east with fresh forces failed. Our troops are in full pursuit of the enemy, and have reached the rail-way from Orsova to Craiova." It affirmed that the total booty of the Ninth Army, the Germanic force operating in Wallachia, between November 1st and 18th, amounted to 189 officers and 19,338 men, 26 guns, and 72 machine-guns, besides 17 munition cars.

Enemy in the Wallachian Plain

Vienna's official telegram gave some additional details. It stated that the southern wing of the forces of the Arch-duke Charles—who soon afterwards became Emperor of Austria and King of Hungary on the death of the Kaiser Francis Joseph—had met with complete success. As previously mentioned in Chapter CXXXVII., the command of a small part of Germany's eastern front had been entrusted nominally to Austria, on the rearrangement of commands which took place because of General Brussiloff's triumphant offensive during the summer in Volhynia and Galicia, and the Archduke Charles occupied this post. But he was a mere shadow, as Hindenburg was in reality

dated November 16th, which, after admitting the retirement on the Alt, that had brought the Germans in that quarter twenty-three miles south of the frontier by that date, said: "In the region of the Jiu our troops have also retired in the direction of Copaciosa (south-east of Targu Jiu), and of Carbesti (south of Targu Jiu)," the former twenty-three and the latter twenty-five miles from the Rumanian border in the Vulkan Pass. A telegram of the next day's date gave particulars of a further retreat of five miles to Stafanesti, but suggested that all was not yet lost by stating that the enemy was being attacked on his flanks with heavy losses to him. The reinforcing battalions had come up, and they checked the tide partially, but could not roll it back. The Rumanian front was broken. A Reuter message put it down to the continual fresh troops the Germans were able to fling into the battle-line, and, above all, to their far better guns.

How disastrous was the defeat of the Rumanians was not understood, and then not fully, among the Allies in the west till the publication of the German and Austrian

dictator of all the operations of the Central Powers and their Turkish and Bulgarian friends. This Vienna communiqué said :

"Falkenhayn's army during the last few days in the Battle of Targu Jiu forced an outlet from the mountains, and a column advancing in the valley of the Motra (or Motru, a western tributary of the Jiu, joining the latter near Filiasi) reached the railway from Varciorova (near Orsova) to Craiova. The Rumanian resistance was of the fiercest nature in many places, finding **Loss of Targu Jiu** expression in bitter counter-attacks east **and Craiova** and south-east of Targu Jiu which were in vain."

Knobelsdorff was pushing forward quickly with his cavalry and light guns on a wide front, which extended from the Motru on the west to the Gilort, an eastern affluent of the Jiu. With all possible speed he was making for the Orsova-Craiova-Bukarest railway at several points, this being the line of communication with their eastern forces of the Rumanians who were fighting at Orsova and on the Cerna, the stream close to that place, and now in great danger of being isolated, as in fact they soon were. News from Bukarest at this critical time was scanty, and what accounts reached London of all that was happening so unfortunately for the Entente cause came belatedly from Petrograd, which announced the loss of Targu Jiu and the retreat of the Rumanians to Filiasi. Knobelsdorff was not altogether unopposed, for fighting in rearguard actions was reported on his whole way southward, but the Rumanian strength was exhausted, and his progress was very rapid.

Passing through Filiasi, where began the Wallachian Plain, the Germans were in possession of Craiova by noon on November 21st, having marched from Targu Jiu, some sixty miles away, in about four days. There was a short fight in front of the town. According to the German communiqué of the 22nd, this was what occurred : " Quickly breaking the resistance of the defeated enemy by bayonet attacks and assaults, the West and East Prussian Infantry from the north, and squadrons of the Queen's Cuirassier Regiment from the west, were the first German troops to penetrate into Craiova."

The capital of Oltenia, and the most important Rumanian town west of Bukarest, from which it was distant one hundred and twenty miles, Craiova was a thriving place, with a population of over fifty thousand. Besides being the headquarters of the First Rumanian Army, it was a busy trading centre, with much business in corn and cattle, as it stood in the midst of a rich agricultural district. Its capture by the Germans had some economic significance for them, as, in addition to the stores of supplies in the place, the farmers in the neighbourhood still had on hand considerable stocks of wheat and maize. But its occupation from the military point of view was of even greater importance to the enemy, as it was well in the rear of the Orsova Army, lying seventy-five miles to the west, whose safety was very directly involved.

Two or three days before this army—sometimes known as the Army of the Cerna—had been stated to have made a " slight retirement, but nothing of importance," and from this it was apparent that it had not begun to evacuate its chief positions. This was confirmed by a Berlin telegram of November 22nd, which reported German progress at Orsova. As the railway from Filiasi to Craiova was in the hands of the enemy, the retirement of this force could only take place by the roads in the country between Craiova and the Danube, a somewhat narrow corridor. In Britain it was hoped that the Rumanians in this area would get away, **Fate of Army** and for some time there was uncertainty **of the Cerna** as to their fate, but in the end they fell a prey to the Germans. Meanwhile, the remnants of the gallant division which had fought so stoutly, though unsuccessfully, in the Jiu valley, retired east of Craiova in the direction of the Alt.

During these eventful weeks of November events had not exactly stood still in the Dobruja. Indeed, in that area it looked for a while as if the achievements of the Russo-Rumanian troops might be considered as an offset to some extent to Falkenhayn's advance from the

RUSSIAN CAVALRY AND TRANSPORT CAMP IN THE DOBRUJA.

With the force that Russia sent to assist the Rumanians in their too long delayed attempt to repel the strong Germano-Bulgarian invasion of the Dobruja, there was a goodly body of capable cavalry. The enemy had been given too long a period in which to consolidate his offensive, and the fighting proved a series of delaying actions. Above is a graphic impression of one of the horse and mule lines in the Dobruja.

TICKLISH OUTPOST WORK IN THE TRANSYLVANIAN ALPS.
A vivid idea of the arduous character of warfare on a mountainous frontier may be gathered from this view of a position which the Rumanians held near the Predeal Pass. Men who had been relieved are to be seen scrambling down from their observation post ; the precipitous nature of the descent being shown by the different methods adopted by the men negotiating it.

hamlets which they were forced to abandon.

With the assistance of the Danube Squadron, Harsova was reoccupied on the 9th At this place, where was one of the few good possible crossings of the Danube, as the left bank of the river was free from those broad marshy tracts which made military movements exceedingly difficult elsewhere on that side, Sakharoff was about twenty-five miles from Cerna Voda. Berlin, in a curious telegram of that date, said that on the front of the army group of Field-Marshal von Mackensen, in the Northern Dobruja, advanced reconnoitring detachments, in accordance with their instructions, " avoided all engagements with the enemy infantry." It was exactly a fortnight before this that Mackensen's forces had reached the Harsova-Casapkioi line.

On November 10th appeared indications of an important new move. Petrograd reported on that day that Russian cavalry and infantry had occupied Dunarea, the Danube station, two miles west of Cerna Voda, and were fighting for possession of the famous bridge, after an engagement in which over two hundred of the enemy had been killed and a number of prisoners, together with a machine-gun, were taken. Two days later the advance of the allied forces had progressed from Harsova to Topalu and Ghisdaresti, on the right bank of the Danube, about twelve miles from the bridge. On the 13th Cerna Voda was shelled from the left bank of the Danube. An attempt was being made on Mackensen's flank, but according to the German account it was unsuccessful from the first. Three days later a Russian communiqué spoke of allied progress south of Topalu in the direction of the bridge, and then there came a calm on this front. Mackensen had fallen back to a line, which he had strongly fortified, covering the Cerna Voda-Constantsa railway, and no very determined effort was made to dislodge him from his well-prepared positions.

On the 21st Cerna Voda was once more bombarded, but by that time it was plain that the Russo-Rumanians were not in sufficient force to drive Mackensen from **Germans across the Danube** it. Though his army had been depleted of some troops for the relief of the Bulgarians at Monastir (which General Sarrail captured on November 18th), it had been reinforced by Turkish and other contingents, and was more powerful than ever before. On the 24th the Allies made a slight impression on his centre and left in the Dobruja, but that date was really remarkable for quite another and much more important event, which at once attracted the keenest attention throughout the world. That day Berlin announced that the Danube had been crossed at several

Transylvanian passes. In the beginning of the month the Russian Black Sea Fleet more than once bombarded Constantsa and Mangalia, its guns doing great work on the former place, which was set in flames. But these naval operations could have little influence on the campaign in the Dobruja itself. The allied operations in the field in that area were now directed by General Sakharoff, who, in taking command of the combined Russo-Rumanian forces, issued a stirring address in which he exhorted his men always to advance and never retreat. In the early part of this month large Russian reinforcements arrived on this front, and the influence of the new commander was quickly felt. On the 7th and 8th progress was reported along the whole of the allied line, and it was noted that as the Bulgarians retreated under Sakharoff's offensive they systematically set fire to and destroyed the various Rumanian villages and points, and this startling news unfortunately was true. Now was explained the curious German telegram referring to Mackensen's retirement in the Northern Dobruja according to plan. It had been a voluntary, a calculated withdrawal—a screen, as it were—behind which he was concentrating his men and maturing his schemes for forcing the passage of the great river, the formidable natural obstacle that protected the south of Wallachia from him. Perhaps an indication of what was coming was contained in a Bulgarian communiqué, published a fortnight earlier, which reported on November 9th that two German companies, supported by a group of Austrian monitors, had carried out a small raid on the left bank of the Danube above Zimnita, opposite the eastern outlet of the Belen Canal, and had forced the Rumanian guards to beat a retreat—whereupon the raiders took some loot, did a certain amount of damage, and then returned without molestation to their own side of the river.

It was from Sistov, opposite Zimnita, that, helped by a thick fog, a large body of Mackensen's troops crossed, and established themselves at the latter town, the point at which the Russians and Rumanians, going the other way, had crossed the river in 1877 on their march to Plevna. Other of the Field-Marshal's forces gained a passage at Islaz, a few miles farther up the stream. A Berlin message asserted that the "Danube army chosen for operations in Western Rumania" made the crossing to the left bank **Exultant German** "in the actual presence of Field-Marshal **communiqué** von Mackensen." A subsequent despatch suggested that a rising of the Danube, owing to a thaw which had set in, had had no effect on the success of the operations. The Rumanians offered a gallant resistance, but they were far outnumbered and outgunned.

The German communiqué, in an exultant tone, declared that in fighting their way across, Mackensen's troops "co-operated excellently," and that "in addition to our brave pioneers, assistance was given by the Imperial Motor Boat Corps, the Austro-Hungarian Danube Flotilla, under the command of Captain Lucich, and the Austro-

Hungarian pioneer detachments of Major-General Gaugl." The passage of the river was preceded by an intense bombardment, which was maintained until the Germans had secured a firm footing on the left bank at the selected points. The mention of the help rendered by the Austrian river craft showed that the enemy was now in control of the river from Orsova downwards. Sofia, in a belated despatch, stated that Bulgarian detachments took part in the capture of Zimnita.

At Islaz, Mackensen was close to the mouth of the Alt, while at Zimnita he was some miles east of it—in other words, he had turned the Alt on the south, and the line of this river was that **Mackensen before** on which the Rumanians in Wallachia **Alexandria** were at the moment making a stand. A Bukarest telegram said that the invaders were being held at both Zimnita and Islaz, but the Rumanian opposition was soon overborne. Marching rapidly from the former town, Mackensen struck up along the River Vedea towards the capital, and on November 26th he was standing before Alexandria, about fifty miles south-west of it. Another column of his, composed mainly of cavalry, pushed up north along the valley of the Alt, and got into touch with the German forces in that area. The crossing of the Danube by Mackensen had made the whole position of the Rumanian Army much worse, and particularly of that portion of it which had retreated east after the fall of Craiova. The outlook for Rumania became gloomy, but she still gamely struggled on.

After Knobelsdorff's troops took Craiova on November 21st, what remained of the division which had been driven out of the valley of the Jiu had, after crossing the Altetsu, retired to the Alt, on the line of which their comrades, taking every advantage of the natural features of their country, continued to offer a strenuous resistance in the face of the heaviest odds. Most of the guns had been got away from Craiova, as well as their ammunition, and the Rumanians made a great stand in this area.

General Berthelot, the head of the French Military Mission, and a soldier who knew what he was talking about

MUNITION TRUCKS SHELL-WRECKED—YET REMAINING ON THE RAILS.

Extraordinary results of explosions were frequently observed, as in this scene, where parts of a Rumanian munition train still kept the rails though shattered to little more than framework, while the neighbouring coach was blown right over. The force of the explosion may be gauged by the quantity of wreckage which the soldiers were engaged in clearing away from the vicinity of the railway line.

paid a fine tribute to the fighting qualities of the peasant troops. "I myself," he said, "have seen infantrymen and artillerymen who after fifteen days of continual fighting were as fit as on the first day. A regiment of artillery fought in the Prahova valley day and night for about three weeks." But mere courage and endurance could not prevent the Germans, with their larger and fresher forces, backed by superior technical means, from advancing, and towards the end of November the whole line of the Alt was in their possession.

During the third week of that month General von Dellmensingen had kept up the severest pressure in the northern sectors of the Alt. After a prolonged bombardment of the Rumanian positions there, he attacked fiercely at Albesti, five miles north of the rail-head of Curtea de Arges, at Vernesti and Surpatsi, the one three and the other ten miles west of Albesti, at Monastire, and at Cozia, on the west bank of the river. Here, as late as November 22nd,

RUSSO-RUMANIAN RAILWAY COMMUNICATIONS.
Deficiency of railway communication with Russia had much to do with the Rumanian disaster. After Constantsa was lost only the Czernovitz-Galatz and Odessa-Reni lines remained for transport. All the other lines connecting with Bukarest were in enemy hands.

Bukarest stated that the Rumanians maintained themselves, but being forced southward next day they put up a strong fight at Rymnik, meeting all enemy attacks most tenaciously. But further German forces, under Falkenhayn's general direction, were advancing in strength lower down against the Alt, as Berlin announced on the 24th, by which date their vanguards were actually approaching the river. Rymnik was captured on the 26th, but on the hills north of Curtea de Arges the Rumanians still held on, and fought most stubbornly.

The German official report of that date announced that, in the region of the Lower Alt, German cavalry, under the leadership of Lieut.-General Count von Schmettow, overthrew a Rumanian cavalry division which offered

resistance, and pressed on victoriously. It added that the roads from the river eastwards were encumbered with fleeing supply columns, and that the route of flight was marked by burning villages. The fact was that the line of the Alt, as a strong defensive barrier against the invaders, had lost its value when it was turned by Mackensen on the south from Zimnita, and the Rumanians could not hold it. There would not appear to have been one big Battle of the Alt, but a series of desperate struggles on the north, and in the centre around Slatina, all of which eventually went against the Rumanians. The line of the river had to be abandoned, and this meant that the enemy had already gained possession of territory a hundred miles in width from the extreme western frontier of the little land.

Before this it had become unpleasantly certain that the Rumanian force known as the Orsova (or Cerna) Army had been definitely cut off. An Austrian communiqué of November 23rd said that on the army front of the Archduke Joseph, who had succeeded the new Austrian Emperor in the chief command, the Austro-Germans on the Lower Cerna had set foot on the left bank of the river, and a message of next day's date made it plain that Orsova itself had been captured, as it announced that German and Austro-Hungarian troops had repulsed the Rumanians east of it. On the same day Turnu Severin, on the Danube below the Iron Gates, fell into the enemy's hands The fate of the Orsova Army was still obscure, but it presently was ascertained from a Berlin telegram that some of its battalions were stubbornly defending themselves in the wooded hills lying north of Turnu Severin.

It was learned from a Russian source that in the meantime these brave soldiers, who must have realised that they were in a hopeless case, turned on some enemy detachments which had been sent to round them up, routed them, and captured two guns. On **Capture of** November 27th they were less successful **Orsova** in an engagement south-east of Turnu Severin, the Germans claiming to have taken from them guns and 1,200 men. Four days later a Berlin message said "they were striking about in all directions, but could not escape from their inevitable fate." Continually followed up by encircling movements, the Orsova Army succeeded in retreating as far east as the Alt, but there it was forced into a decisive action, and obliged to capitulate with 8,000 men. That took place on December 6th, and was the end of an heroic story, little of which came to light, but which could readily be imagined.

Among the results of the capture of Orsova, Turnu Severin, and the reaches of the Danube east of them as far as Ruschuk, was a gain to the Germans or Bulgarians, who had co-operated in the taking of Turnu Severin, of six steamers and eighty barges, "mostly loaded," according to the Berlin account, "with valuable cargo." Besides, the control of the river gave the enemy specially fine facilities for the transport of munitions and all manner of supplies.

With its left flank turned by Mackensen's advance from the Danube, as was narrated above, the Rumanian Army had been unable to make that stand on the Alt which had been anticipated, and it withdrew eastward, across the foot-hills in the north and the plain lying south of them, in the general direction of Bukarest, which was now more or less directly menaced. The forces of the Germans in Wallachia were henceforward divided into two groups; one was the "Ninth Army" under Falkenhayn, and the other was the Danube Army under Mackensen, who shortly afterwards assumed command of both groups.

Following his usual tactical methods, the enemy struck hard at the Rumanian wings. On the north General Dellmensingen drove back the Rumanians behind the sector of the River Topologu, and advanced ten miles east of Rymnik. Some details of the fighting involved

Sighting an enemy airman: French anti=aircraft gun in action.

Russian forces on the way to join hands with the hard=pressed Rumanian

...lumn of troops accompanied by artillery passing through a Rumanian town.

Airman returning at sunset after a successful journey over the enemy lines.

were given in the Berlin telegram of November 27th, which said : " East of Tigveni (on the Topologu) the Saxon Infantry Regiment No. 182, admirably supported by the Neumark Artillery Regiment No. 54, which, for the purpose of more rapid intervention, advanced close to the enemy, broke through his lines, and took from him ten officers, four hundred men, and seven machine-guns." The numbers given showed, however, that this was merely a local success. On the south, Mackensen's Danube Army on November 27th took Alexandria, a town of 14,000 inhabitants, on the Vedea, with a considerable trade in grain,
and it also occupied Rosiori and Valeni,

Fall of Alexandria and Giurgevo
higher up the same river. According to a despatch from Sofia it was the Bulgarians who captured Alexandria, and their booty was said to include a locomotive, one hundred and forty railway waggons, and a " large quantity of provisions."

Petrograd supplied further information with respect to the events of November 27th. After alluding to the retirement to the east of the Rumanians in Western Wallachia, under the unrelenting pressure of the enemy, this communiqué defined the line which the Germans had reached. It ran from Darmanesti, south of Campu Lung, and about eighty miles north-west of Bukarest, to Prunaru, thirty miles south-west of the capital, and thence to Slobodia, a little east of Giurgevo, on the Danube.

The Russian statement added the ominous words that the Germans had advanced along the turnpike road to Calugareni, which was only seventeen miles distant from Bukarest. But this account, bad as it was, did not state the whole truth, which had not reached Petrograd when the communiqué was issued, with respect to the situation on the Danube, for also on November 27th Giurgevo itself was in the hands of the enemy. This well-known river port, which had been bombarded several times, lay about forty miles south of the capital.

A Sofia despatch, while reporting that the Danube Army of Mackensen continued to advance without interruption, gave some news regarding the capture of this town. After mentioning various crossings of the Danube, from Rahova to Bechetu, and from Lom Palanka, and Widin to spots on the Rumanian shore, it stated : " Our troops, advancing on the left bank of the Danube, attacked Giurgevo, supported by Austro-Hungarian and Bulgarian monitors. After a sanguinary fight, lasting from eleven o'clock in the morning to five o'clock in the afternoon, the town was conquered. The Rumanian troops and population were seized with panic and fled towards Bukarest." Farther down the river strong artillery attacks were made on Oltenitsa, over against Tutrakan, and only some thirty miles from Bukarest. Thus on the south the threat to the Rumanian capital was growing more and more direct hour by hour.

On the north and west, in Great Wallachia—or Muntenia, as the region east of the Alt was called—the menace to Bukarest came nearer and nearer. On the 28th Dellmensingen, continuing his progress from Rymnik, took Curtea de Arges, in the region of the head-waters of the River Argesul, and the rail-head of a line running through Pitesti to the capital. The place was stubbornly defended to the last, but the enemy's big guns prevailed, and forced the Rumanians to retire. In this sector Falkenhayn was

able to make use of the railway from Hermannstadt across the Roter Turm, and bring up fresh forces, which he threw against the trenches of the peasant soldiers, who were worn out with the incessant strain of many weeks of hard fighting, and who had no available reserves.

The German official message of November 29th announced that the Ninth Army, with which the Danube Army was in contact, was pressing forward victoriously on the whole of the Wallachian front, and on the evening of that day Pitesti, an important centre from which radiated several railways, was said to be in the possession of the enemy, bringing him on the north-west to within about sixty-five miles of Bukarest. Another German column captured Campu Lung on the same date, taking 1,200 prisoners, seven guns, and a " large quantity of baggage." Around Dragoslavele and Campu Lung the Rumanians had long and successfully defended the exits from the Törzburg Pass, but now were compelled to abandon them. Berlin also announced on that day the capture of another Rumanian force of 1,200 men, with ten guns, and a number of machine-guns, near Ciolanesti, this achievement, it was asserted, being accomplished by a squadron of cavalry belonging to a cuirassier regiment.

A passing gleam of sunshine lit up the fast darkening

WITH THE ENEMY LOOKING TOWARDS WALLACHIA.
When the concentration of the enemy on their front began to press back the gallant Rumanians, enemy progress through some parts of the mountainous frontier country was fairly rapid. The enemy gun in this photograph was laid on one of the hill-sides facing the Wallachian Plain.

sky of Rumania. Her troops, as November closed, made progress in the valleys of the Prahova and the Buzau, in the oil-bearing districts, but their success in these sectors had no influence on the general situation, which increasingly and unmistakably indicated the peril in which Bukarest stood. A short time previously the Rumanian authorities in the capital had realised the greatness and imminence of the danger, and as a measure of precaution had transferred the seat of Government to Jassy, the chief city and capital of Moldavia. Thither went the Ministers of the Allies and of neutrals with their Staffs. An old-world, sleepy university town, Jassy suddenly was transformed into a busy city, as, in **Government moves** addition to the Government and the **to Jassy** Legations, thousands of the better class of the population in the invaded areas fled there for refuge.

Among the Allies in Western Europe it was anticipated that the Rumanian Army would fight a great battle somewhere in front of Bukarest, probably on the line of the River Argesul, and in the event of defeat would fall back to defend the capital, its fortifications then forming the pivot of a new defensive position. It was understood that the city was a fortress of the first class, having thirty-

TYPICAL FIELD-KITCHEN NEAR PLOESTI.
Behind the lines, with their very neat and serviceable portable stoves, the Rumanian soldier-cooks prepared the meals for their fellows who were engaged in keeping back the enemy long enough to allow of the oil-wells in the district being so destroyed as to be of little value to the invader.

gains. The country operated in was one of the most difficult in the world, and the weather experienced was of the severest winter type. In any case, if the Russian movement in force in this area was intended for the relief of Bukarest, it came too late.

The expectation that the Rumanians would make a stand on the Argesul was realised. On November 30th, the eve of the Battle of the Argesul, the German line formed a concave curve, a sort of half-moon, beginning on the north at Predeal, passing south-west through Campu Lung, then going almost due south to the west of Tirgovistea, whence it went along the valley of the River Glavaciog, and finally bent south-eastward to Calugareni,

WELL-MASKED RUSSIAN BATTERY IN RUMANIA.
Although the men and munitions it poured into the struggle were not sufficient to stop the torrent of invasion, Russia's aid proved of immense value in holding up the enemy on the re-formed Ser-th lines. Its efficient artillery was of special service to its harassed ally.

six powerfully armed and armoured forts, disposed in a ring at an average distance of four miles from the suburbs. It was true that these forts were in existence, but there was much doubt as to their value. They had been constructed by General Brialmont, the Belgian engineer who had built the fortresses of Liège and Namur.

The story of the fate of those two places did not promise well for a successful defence of Bukarest. Verdun, a French fortress, had held out against the German siege trains and infantry attacks of the most intense kind, but Liège and Namur had succumbed with what appeared astonishing quickness. Yet it was widely believed in the west that the Rumanians would try to hold the city—the city which expressed Rumania better than any other place in it. As the Germanic forces drew closer and closer to Bukarest, Berlin and Vienna newspapers had much to say of the formidable strength of the fortress, in spite of the fact that the German authorities, who controlled their Press and told it what to state, must have known the exact condition of the place from the military standpoint, as they had their spies everywhere, and were extremely well informed with respect to everything going on in Rumania. Germany wished to make out that, if Bukarest fell into her hands, she had taken it by assault —not that it had been evacuated.

Shadows gather round Bukarest

While the shadows were gathering round Bukarest, General Belaieff, who commanded the Russians on the Moldavian front, attempted a diversion by beginning an offensive on a considerable scale on the north-western frontier. This movement started on November 28th, and met with some success, which, however, was powerless to avert the fate of the capital. The Russians, after extraordinarily bitter fighting, captured a series of heights. On the 29th Berlin said that " in the wooded Carpathians, on the frontier range of Moldavia, the Russians pursued their attacks without achieving important results," and that at the cost of heavy sacrifices they " had to be content with small local advantages." For some days the Russian offensive was maintained, but without any substantial

Comana, and the Danube. The Russians had reported that the villages of Comana and Gostinari, less than twenty miles south-south-east of Bukarest, had been occupied by the enemy, but on the other hand they stated that on several of the roads in that corridor between the Danube and Bukarest, Mackensen's forces had been repulsed.

The Ninth Army of the Germans was disposed in three parts. One part, which had marched from Craiova, was now commanded by Lieut.-General Kuhne, and it formed the right centre of the enemy's attack on the line of the Argesul. Immediately above him was that part which, led by Dellmensingen, had advanced along the Argesul from its sources in the mountains, after severe fighting, by way of Curtea and Pitesti, and it formed the left centre. On Dellmensingen's flank, and stretching eastward, was that part which had advanced through Campu Lung, under the leadership of Lieut.-General von Morgen. The German right wing consisted of the Danube Army of Mackensen, the portion of it which had crossed the river at Zimnita, having as its leader General Kosch, and that which had made the passage at Islaz, having its units strung along north of the river till they touched hands with Kuhne's troops on the right centre. The Ninth Army was predominantly German, with a large percentage of Austro-Hungarians. The Danube Army was a composite force of Germans, Austro-Hungarians, Bulgarians, and Turks. In all probability, the total strength of the two armies was well over 400,000 men.

Opposed to these great Germanic forces were the First and Second Rumanian Armies, with part of the Third Rumanian Army and some Russian divisions, all under the chief command of General Avarescu. The Rumanian Army, though battered and war-worn was

"FRIGHTFULNESS" IN BUKAREST.
Corner of the house of the British attaché in Bukarest, photographed after one of the periodical bomb-dropping expeditions over the Rumanian capital by Teutonic airmen in pursuit of their policy of "frightfulness."

SURVEYING THE DAMAGE.
Sir George Barclay, the British Ambassador to Rumania, with Colonel Thompson (his military attaché), and Captain Watford, inspecting the effects caused by the Zeppelin bomb which struck Colonel Thompson's house in Bukarest.

full of fight. It was still intact, as a wireless message from Bukarest, dated November 30th, made perfectly clear. This said that if it was true that the German Chief Command had obtained considerable strategic advantages, it also was true that it had failed in its essential task, which was the destruction of the principal Rumanian forces. The Rumanians, it stated, had refused to allow themselves to be encircled, and had retired from position to position, taking with them their heavy guns and field-artillery. The enemy likewise, it noted, had failed to envelop the Rumanian force on the Danube, notwithstanding his immense superiority in artillery, and in spite of Bulgarian and Ottoman assistance.

It was to this quarter of the Danube front, from which Bukarest was most closely threatened, that the Russians had rushed up large reinforcements—amounting, according to one despatch, to three divisions, one being composed of Cossacks. If a statement of the enemy could be credited, Avarescu's plan was to execute a turning movement with the combined Russo-Rumanian troops in the south against the Danube Army, while he held the German Ninth Army in the centre and the north. And it certainly was the

case that a great effort—not unattended without a distinct if in the end ineffectual victory—was made by the Allies in the area immediately west and south of Bukarest. But the attempt, which undoubtedly was made with determination, to check and hold the Ninth Army in the centre and the north proved abortive, and this was fatal. The allied operations then going on in the Dobruja with some gains had no more beneficial effect on the situation in Wallachia than the Russian offensive had in the mountains of Moldavia.

Battle was joined along the whole line on December 1st, the bitter struggle reaching its greatest intensity on the 2nd and 3rd. On their left the Germans attacked violently from the direction of Campu Lung, and forced the Rumanians back into the valley of the River Dambovitsa towards Meulosani on the first day, and pressing on compelled a further retirement on the second. In this sector the conflict proceeded among the wooded hills on both sides of the river, and the German progress was not rapid, yet the enemy continued to gain ground. But the scene of the fiercest fighting was farther south, in the region surrounding Pitesti—the German left centre.

Fierce fighting near Pitesti

In the Dambovitsa valley there were no good roads, and movement was necessarily restricted, but from Pitesti there were both a railway and a fine highway making for Bukarest, and it was along these that the enemy drove with all his might. On December 1st desperate encounters took place near Golesti, four miles south of Pitesti, and, on the 2nd, Bukarest announced that th Rumanians had been obliged to retire slightly. The Berlin communiqué of the latter date, after stating that the conflict on the Argesul was growing into a great battle, said that the Germans and Austro-Hungarians south-east of Pitesti had defeated and broken through the Rumanian army which had accepted battle there.

Going into details this telegram stated that the Bavarian Reserve Regiment No. 18, which had "repeatedly distinguished itself, penetrated to one divisional headquarters, and took from it orders of the General Staff, from which it appeared that the position we pierced was to be held by the First Rumanian Army to the last man." This telegram went on to add insult to injury by remarking that "the army commander, doubtless conscious of the low moral value of his troops, informed them, in Rumanian phraseology, that he expected them to ' persevere and fight unto death against the cruel barbarians,' threatening cowards in his army with immediate death." Such comment came strangely from German lips, as if the German commanders never threatened their men with death if they retreated, and never chained their men to machine-guns to prevent them from running away!

A subsequent communiqué announced that in the Argesul valley "two battalions of the West Prussian Reserve Regiment No. 21, with artillery under the command of the wounded Major von Richter, of the Neumark Field Artillery Regiment No. 54, advanced as far as Gaesti " (forty-two miles north-east of Bukarest), on the evening of December 2nd, and captured six howitzers. A Vienna message, which gave the name of the commander of the Rumanians in this district as General Stzatilescu, declared that a Bavarian regiment advanced " far beyond the enemy lines."

Farther south, in the region of the River Glavaciog and of the River Neajlov, both western tributaries of the Argesul, violent fighting occurred, which eventuated unfavourably for the Rumanians. On December 1st they **Growing menace** met with a slight success, taking several **to Bukarest** hundred prisoners and ten machine-guns, as well as war material. Next day the struggle had become more intense, the Rumanians fighting with the utmost resolution, but the onward sweep of the Germans could not be stopped. The battle in this sector, which lacked roads, was not, however, of decisive importance, and was, in fact, subsidiary to that part of it going on from Pitesti, and also to that taking place at the same time still farther south on the Glavaciog and the Neajlov almost due west of Bukarest, and in the area south of the capital.

On the southern front—that forming the right wing of the Germans and the left of the Rumanians—the pressure of the enemy was most severe. Before December 1st the Danube Army had occupied positions only from nineteen to twenty miles from Bukarest, and the menace to that city appeared far stronger there than from the north and west, but the rapid advance of the Ninth Army had put a somewhat different yet still more threatening edge on the situation. The Danube Army, however, pushed on. On the first of the month it forced a passage far down across the Neajlov valley, and was approaching the lower course of the Argesul, which was only three or four miles from the ring of forts surrounding the capital. The villages of Comana and Gostinari were already in the enemy's possession, and the peril of Bukarest was pronounced. But at that moment there came relief, thanks to the Russians, though the **Rumanians between** relief was only of a temporary nature. **two fires**

On December 2nd a Turkish division was defeated at Draganesti, and the Germano-Bulgar forces in the region of Ghimpati and Mihalesti, the latter being but six miles from the forts, were driven some miles to the south. The enemy also was forced out of Comana and Gostinari, losing many prisoners and no fewer than twenty-six guns. Berlin had nothing to say about this defeat, but maintained that later Russian attacks had been repulsed, while a body of Rumanian troops, which had pushed forward south-west of Bukarest over the Argesul and the Neajlov, was outflanked and thrown across the Neajlov to the north-east, with many casualties. In the upshot the counter-offensive of the Russians and Rumanians did not achieve permanent success in this area, and meanwhile the Rumanians higher up on the Argesul were heavily defeated.

On December 3rd the Battle of the Argesul passed into its last phase, and came to an unfortunate conclusion for Rumania and the Allies. It was the continued progress of the left centre of the Austro-Germans along the Pitesti-Bukarest railway and road, in spite of the most gallant efforts to arrest it, that practically settled the matter. The enemy's left wing under Morgen, in the northern area, took Targoviste, a former capital of Wallachia, and a commercial centre situated on the edge of the oil-fields. Dellmensingen, marching on triumphantly from Gaesti. again attacked the First Rumanian Army, overthrew it, and, according to Berlin, drove its remnants beyond Titu, a town where the railways from Pitesti and Targoviste joined, en route for Bukarest, thirty miles distant. This communiqué went on to state that these remnants were driven "into the arms of the oft-tried 41st Infantry Division, under the leadership of Lieut.-General Schmidt von Knobelsdorff." This force was part of the German right centre, the troops of which had advanced across the Walla-chian plain from Craiova.

The Austrian official report of December 4th told how " this group advanced yesterday as far as Titu and caught up there the Rumanian army, which was defeated to the south-east of Pitesti," and it added that strong Rumanian detachments were destroyed. The Rumanians were between two fires and were over-whelmed. This decided the whole battle, particularly as farther south the enemy was successful on the left bank of the Argesul, north-west and west of Bukarest, and still farther south the Russians and Rumanians were unable to make headway, but, on the contrary, were repulsed and had to retire some miles eastward. It was a defeat for Rumania on the

FIELD-MARSHAL VON MACKENSEN AT THE GREAT DANUBE BRIDGE.
Having gained control of the great bridge linking Rumania with the Dobruja, Field-Marshal von Mackensen and his Staff contemplated their advance with self-satisfaction. They realised later that their overrunning of the Rumanian territory on both sides of the mighty river was not to provide them with that rich booty in corn and oil for which they had hoped.

TYPES OF RUMANIA'S FIGHTING-MEN.
Rumanian soldiers passing along a communication-trench.
They proved sturdy fighters, though after their initial
triumphant advance against Hungary they were unable to
withstand the weight brought against them by the foe.

whole line. Germany reported: " December 3rd
brought with it the decision of the Battle of
the Argesul. It was won.'' Joy-bells rang in
Berlin.

According to German official accounts, the
Rumanian Army suffered in this battle
exceedingly heavy and sanguinary losses. As
many as 12,500 prisoners were claimed for
the operations on the 3rd alone, and it was
averred that the booty in " field materials and
war materials was immeasurable.'' At Titu
thirteen locomotives were taken ; the Danube
Army captured thirty-five cannon. No doubt
the spoil that fell into the clutches of the
enemy was very considerable. But his estimates usually were excessive, and the great
fact remained that, with all his success, he
had not been able even yet to roll up and
destroy the Rumanian Army, as was his intention and
desire.

While the Battle of the Argesul was being fought the
Russians and Rumanians were attacking the enemy with
great vigour in the Dobruja. On December 2nd Bukarest
reported violent assaults on the hostile
positions in this area, and announced that
the fighting had been carried up to and in
some cases past the wire entanglements on
this front. A message from Petrograd of the same date said
that the Allies had gained possession of the western part
of the Cerna Voda bridge, and in the region of Kalakeui-
Satiskeui, about twelve miles north of the Cerna Voda
railway, had compelled a retirement of the foe from several
heights. Next day the Russians continued their desperate
attacks on the Bulgarian left wing close to the Danube.
Counting the assaults made on the 2nd, they delivered

**British aid in
the Dobruja**

RUMANIAN PADRE IN THE FIRING-LINE.
Priests attended the Rumanian soldiers even into the firing-line. Here one of them is seen
in the foreground with soldiers moving forward through long grass. The hills are characteristic of the scenery of Rumania where it approaches the Hungarian frontier by
the Danube.

seven attacks in all in this sector, each more fierce than
that which had preceded it. The well-tried and trusted
Siberians of Russia made progress, but in the result were
held up. The Sofia communiqué, which gave some information of this conflict, but not of a specially accurate kind,
alleged that the Turkish troops captured an armoured car,
from which they made prisoner two British officers and
six men. It also asserted that of three armoured cars that
were engaged two were destroyed and the third driven off.

Two squadrons of British armoured cars had co-operated
with the Russians in the latter's campaign in Eastern
Armenia during the summer, and these were the cars which
had been transferred to Rumania. After a month's journey
from the east they made a sudden and dramatic appearance
in the Dobruja. Under heavy fire and at great risk they
forced a passage through the enemy's lines and succeeded
in cutting off a considerable force. Contrary to the

273

statement of Sofia, all the cars got back safely, but this was not accomplished without some loss in personnel, one officer and six men, who had left the cars in order to save them by a ruse, being taken prisoners by the Turks. It was reported from Petrograd that Commander Locker-Lampson, in command of the cars, had been wounded, but this happily proved incorrect, as almost immediately afterwards it was known that the gallant commander had arrived in England fit and well. By December 4th the fighting in the Dobruja died down, the allied forces retiring to their trenches. They had been unable to give any real help to the hard-pressed Rumanian Army on the other side of the Danube.

After the Battle of the Argesul the Rumanians retreated eastward, fighting continuously, and occasionally delivering fierce counter-attacks. On December 4th and 5th there were incessant rearguard actions on all the roads from Targoviste to Ploesti, and from Titu to Bukarest. The Germans, throwing forward their cavalry, marched on

existed for its defence, and there was neither governor nor commandant. In other words, Mackensen was free to occupy it. On the morning of the 6th, soon after he had received this reply, the Germans began moving into the city. First, some of their cavalry took possession of a fort on the north side; next, infantry pushed forward and held most of the forts on the west. According to the official German account of the occupation, "the enemy infantry offered resistance, which was quickly broken." From the south the Bulgarian troops of the Danube Army entered the city without opposition. Bukarest, in fact, was not taken—it was surrendered. If there was any fighting, it was either in ignorance of or contrary to the orders of the Rumanian authorities. The communiqué quoted above said that the enemy troops entering Bukarest were "received enthusiastically, and decorated with flowers."

How Rumania took the blow

While the loss of Bukarest had in the circumstances no very extraordinary military importance, yet as the capital of the country, its passing into the rapacious hands of Germany could not but have a decided influence politically. Furthermore, its capture, with the seizure of the greater part of Wallachia, could not but go a long way to encourage the Germans both in the field and at home, and make up to some extent for their own serious economic position. Along with the news of the fall of the Rumanian capital came that of the taking of Ploesti, in the heart of the oil-fields, and the cutting off, according to the German plan, of the Rumanians retiring from the Predeal Pass— all heavy blows, though the tragic course of the campaign after the second Battle of Targu

GERMANY'S DREAM: THE "BREMEN-BERLIN-BOSPHORUS-BAGDAD-BAHN."
Germany's most gigantic project was a transcontinental railway from the North Sea to the Persian Gulf. This map traces the line, which the Kaiser alliteratively termed the Bremen-Berlin-Bosphorus-Bagdad-Bahn, and shows how vital to it was the Germanisation of Serbia and Rumania, both of which menaced it between Belgrade and Sofia.

without halting in both directions. In the former region they were making straight for the valley of the Prahova and the rich oil-fields. Moreover, the Prahova valley was the line of retreat of that part of the Rumanian Army which had so bravely and successfully withstood for a couple of months all the determined efforts of the Germans to emerge from the Predeal Pass, and the enemy aimed at cutting off this force.

The march from Titu south-east had Bukarest itself as its objective, but the force employed in this operation was not the first body of enemy troops to reach the city. On December 5th Mackensen crossed the Argesul in the immediate neighbourhood of Bukarest. Early next morning Bulgarian troops of the Danube Army cleared the places on the southern bank of the river of such Rumanians as had till then maintained themselves there, and then they advanced on the capital, to find that it had already been evacuated, a step which had been rendered imperative by the result of the Battle of the Argesul, if indeed it had not been determined on and proceeded with some time before, as there was every reason to believe.

Germans enter the capital

On the previous day Mackensen had sent a parlementaire with a letter into Bukarest demanding the surrender of the fortress. When the parlementaire returned to Mackensen next morning the Field-Marshal was informed that the Commander-in-Chief of the Rumanian Army of the Danube refused to accede to his demand, inasmuch as Bukarest was not a fortress, but an open town. No forts or troops

Jiu had prepared the Allies for them to some extent, but they were none the less grievous. As Mr. Lloyd George said, in the memorable speech of December 19th which marked his first appearance in the House of Commons as Prime Minister, the cause of the Entente had suffered a real setback.

General sympathy flowed out to the Rumanians, who had fought so well and had made such sacrifices. Rumania herself was determined to carry on. King Ferdinand and his Queen did not leave Bukarest till December 2nd, and then they motored to Jassy, whither M. Bratiano and the other members of the Government had already gone. The first Royal act at Jassy was the issue of a decree calling a meeting of the Rumanian Parliament for the furtherance of the war.

CHAPTER CLX.

THE FIGHT FOR THE DOMINION OF THE AIR.

By Edward Wright.

Inferiority of British Machines—Germany's New Achievement in Aerial Equipment—All the Allies Temporarily at a Disadvantage—General Pétain Speeds-Up French Aircraft Production—Lord Kitchener Reorganises British Material—Arrival of New Fighting Machines and End of the Fokker Crisis—Brilliant Exploits of British Pilots—Captain Albert Ball's Great Record—Defeat and Death of Immelmann—Fine Work by Photographing Airmen—British Aerial Spotters Trick the Enemy Gunners—Wild Adventures of Bombing Aviators—Extraordinary Scene at Libercourt Junction—Testimony of a German Soldier to Terror Caused by British Airmen—Destruction Wrought by Daylight Over the Enemy Lines by Allied Aeroplanes—Achievements of the Contact Patrols—Surrender of a German Trench Garrison to a British Airman—Some Distinguished British Aerial Gunners—Destruction of Enemy Observation Balloons by Nieuport Scouts—Doom of the Zeppelin as a Military Engine—Competition Between British and German Inventors—Work of the Burbidge Committe e and of the Bailhache Committee into Production of Aircraft and Administration of the Flying Service—Establishment of an Air Ministry—The Naval Side of Aerial Warfare—Activity of the Royal Naval Air Service on the Coast, in the Mediterranean, Mesopotamia and Eastern France—The Battle of Jutland and its Lessons with Regard to Aeronautics.

I N Chapter CXII. we brought down the history of the aerial services of Great Britain to the end of March, 1916. The serious losses of the Royal Flying Corps on the western front from October, 1915, to March, 1916, seemed to show that all was not well in regard to the production of British machines. On the Mesopotamian front the machines of the Royal Flying Corps and the Royal Naval Air Service, engaged in the attempt to relieve the garrison of Kut, were. also inferior (Sir Percy Lake stated) to the new aeroplanes with which the Germans supplied the Turks. The Allies generally seemed to be in a condition of inferiority in regard to aerial equipment. At the opening of the Battle of Verdun the French Army had been blinded by the onset of Fokkers, Aviatiks, Rolands, L.V.G.'s, and other German machines of an improved kind. On the Russian front the anti-aircraft defences were so weak that the Germans were able to employ Zeppelins on daylight reconnaissances to a distance of a hundred miles

into Russian territory. In aeroplane work the Russians were also at a serious disadvantage, owing to the fact that their number of highly skilled aircraft mechanics was very small, and insufficient not merely for productive purposes but for field repairs.

The fact was that in the autumn and winter of 1915 the Teutons had repeated in aerial material their achievement in shell production of the winter of 1914. By speeding-up the production of improved types of machines and engines they won a very important material gain over the Allies. Only the Italians, with their rapid production of small-crew airships and double-engined bomb-dropping machines of the Caproni type, maintained something like an equality with the Austrians. The Italians appear to have had to borrow fast aeroplanes of the Nieuport class from France in order to maintain some hold upon the air. And this hold was not altogether strong and alert ; for the Austrian offensive in the Trentino in 1916 opened with such unusual force as to take the Italian commander by surprise.

British official photograph.

"MARK OVER ": AWAITING THE TAUBE.
British anti-aircraft gun-crew watching the approach of a Taube over Salonika, and awaiting the precise moment to fire. A number of Serbian Staff officers were intensely interested spectators of the incident.

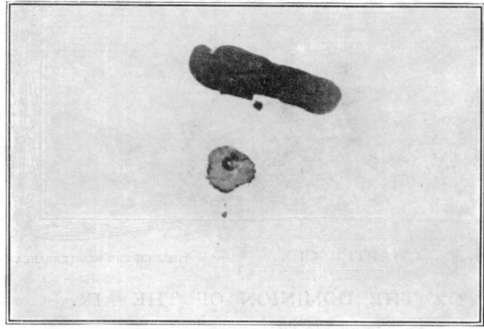

CRITICAL MOMENT IN AN AIRMAN'S LIFE.
A German long-range shell struck a French kite-balloon that had gone up on observation work over the Somme. The observer immediately released his parachute and dropped from the balloon. The camera caught the incident before the parachute had had time fully to expand.

numbers before the improved official F.E. machine arrived. The new Martinsyde machine, the fighting Maurice, and the new Sopwith—the last of which had been waiting for official recognition since June, 1915—were placed at the service of the Royal Flying Corps pilots.

In place of the problematic 200 h.p. engine of Royal Aircraft Factory design, the Rolls-Royce Company, after refusing to work on this engine, produced a splendid 250 h.p. aero-motor of an original kind. The fate of one of the new Rolls-Royce engines was not happy. It was fitted into a Government machine, and entrusted to a pilot who had never flown to France. Being ordered to fly to the front, he lost his way, strayed over Lille, was attacked by German guns, and coming down presented the enemy with a valuable and early example of the new aero-motor on which Great Britain was largely relying to regain her dominion of the air. But this misfortune, which occurred at the end of May, 1916, happened too late to enable the Germans to profit by it. The enemy, on his part, may have had machines to equal the Rolls-Royce aero-motor, for the Mercédès, Benz, and other German engines had been developed soundly and progressively throughout the war. There was nothing strikingly new in their design, but they were certainly efficient. The enemy engine-builders may have found the Rolls-Royce worth copying, but time was not allowed them to adopt it.

The old Royal Aircraft Factory production, the B.E.2c machine, designed by one of the few fine private designers temporarily attached to the Government works, had become antiquated owing to the progress made by German, British, and French manufacturers. British air losses had been partly due to the B.E.2c being sent out alone on reconnoitring or bombing work, and becoming "Fokker fodder" when the German falcons swooped from their towering pitch. Hundreds of British machines of an obsolescent or inefficient type had been manufactured to the order of the Government by firms new to the art of aeroplane construction. Some of these firms had been delayed in production by late alterations in the drawings they had received from the Royal Aircraft Factory authorities, and by downright errors in official drawings. Moreover, the official designs were reported to have a lack of simplicity that further delayed production.

But serious as were the defects in the War Office organisation for providing the British Army with the means of holding the command of the air, General Trenchard, the active chief of the Royal Flying Crops, devised a brilliant method of operation as soon as he obtained from private British firms a few battle-planes capable of assisting the Bristol "Bullet" pilots and Vicker "gun-'bus" pilots, and manœuvring against the new Fokker. The old, slow machines were sent out in flocks from six to twelve. High above the weak flock of workers circled two or three of the battle-planes, ready to engage any Fokker that swooped into the field. By the first week in May, 1916, duels in the air began to grow infrequent. Combats took place between squadrons of fast fighting machines, whirling against each other with their machine-guns flashing, while far below them there was often a flight of almost defenceless working planes—usually British—waiting the issue of the battle

Brilliant use of new machines

In France General Pétain and General Nivelle took instant steps to obtain machines with the speed and powerful climb of the victorious Fokker. It was essential to General Pétain's system of artillery defence that his army should enjoy a considerable command over the air. Under the stress of his fierce organising genius the brake of French officialism was loosened, and a large number of enterprising private aeroplane-making firms of France found a freer field of development. The result was that the tale of French air victories began rapidly to increase, and a considerable number of fighting French pilots competed with each other in public records of their successes.

At the same time, as was reported in the French Press, a naval lieutenant invented an effective method of setting on fire the row of German kite-balloons that stretched in two long wings on either side of the Meuse, and formed the eyes of the two thousand German guns that bombarded the defences of Verdun. By means of his new missile used against the balloons and his fast new aeroplanes employed against the Fokker and Aviatik, General Pétain restored the eyes of his army, and though he did not succeed in blinding the German gunners, he seriously interrupted their powers of aerial observation, and enabled his own inferior artillery to withstand the greatest striking power the enemy could bring into the field.

Thus characteristically France solved her problem of air power by her genius for improvisation, without any public scandal over her former official negligence. The soldiers supplied the lack of prevision in the politician and the bureaucrat. In Great Britain Lord Kitchener also proceeded by energetic action to repair the defects in Army material which had arisen under the rule of the Royal Aircraft Factory and the military authorities who relied upon this factory. General Brancker, an artillery officer with flying experience, was made Director of Air Organisation, with as assistants two capable officers from the front—General Salmond and Colonel Charlton. The best available material from private and foreign sources was ordered in considerable quantities, and the personnel of the Royal Flying Corps was quickly and largely expanded. A private British machine, the De Havilland, began to be used on active service in large

Lord Kitchener's reforms

BELGIAN'S PARACHUTE ESCAPE FROM A BURNING BALLOON.

Parachutes attached to observation kite-balloons are the observer's sole means of escape if his balloon is brought down. In the case depicted here a Belgian kite-balloon, or "sausage," caught fire, and the observer, getting his parachute free without a hitch, came gently and safely to earth, preceded in his descent by his ruined balloon, from the burning envelope of which smoke is seen rising on the extreme right of the picture.

CAPTIVE AIRCRAFT USED BY FRENCH OBSERVERS.
One of the " tailed " observation balloons—familiarly known as "sausages "—employed over the French lines. Its strange shape and the ballonets threaded on the anchoring rope were designed to maintain while it was aloft the steadiness necessary to accurate observation by the man in the car.

Certain losses continued to be inevitable. At times the British Staff suspected the enemy was concentrating at an important point. Where this was being done the Germans had taken measures to mask their activity from hostile aerial observations. Their anti-aircraft guns were numerously disposed about the point, and an unusual number of their fighting planes were constantly watching there. But British pilots in a new fast Scout, in which armament was sacrificed to speed, went out in formation to investigate. Occasionally some of these scouts were brought down by the enemy, but part of the formation returned with news perhaps likely to save the lives of hundreds or thousands of British infantrymen. Such sacrifices of a part of the whole were especially required in the spring of 1916, when there were still insufficient of the new fighting planes strongly to convoy every working squadron on the British front.

As summer wore on, and the number of fighting planes increased and the finest Fokker pilots went down one after the other to death, the perils of the British scouts, spotters, and bombers were diminished. For in the end Great Britain and France held for a time a practical dominion of the heavens. Meanwhile, some remarkable battle practice went on behind the British front in the late spring and early summer of the year. From aerial photographs a good reproduction of the German system of fortifications was constructed on the practice field, and over the lacework of trenches the British infantry manœuvred in attack, in conjunction with low-flying, directing airmen known as " contact " patrols. Signor Marconi had recently invented an apparatus whereby aeroplanes could receive as well as transmit wireless messages. It is not stated whether his new instrument was generally employed in the Somme Battle. Communication between the infantry and the contact patrols was usually maintained by flares, mirror signals, and other ordinary devices, such as General Nivelle had developed in his efforts to return to Douaumont Fort at Verdun. As we have before stated, the French attribute the invention of contact airmen or aerial infantry to certain of their younger generals. But we understand from British officers back from the Somme front that the idea is also claimed to be of British origin.

A British origin has also been claimed for the invention of the first effective missile for the destruction of kite-balloons and airships by airmen in aeroplanes

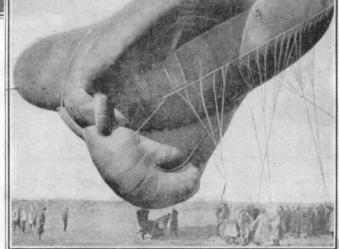

IMPROVED TYPE OF FRENCH " SAUSAGE."
Ingenuity successfully working on the results of experience evolved this queer-looking observation balloon, which was so constructed that the observer was able to remain steady at a height and so carry on his work even when a goodly gale was blowing.

or seaplanes, which we have attributed, on French authority, to a French naval lieutenant. Perhaps there was a coincident stir of invention in both allied countries, leading to results that were almost identical. The stimulus and the sustained work of preliminary creation in regard to the most novel and effective of war machines came from the Royal Naval Air Wing that operated in France and Flanders with the Expeditionary Force. The Admiralty, moved by officers of the Royal Naval Air Service, claims to have presented the Army with the "tank." The British kite-balloon was also developed by the Royal Naval Air Service and transferred to the Royal Flying Corps. Altogether there seems to have been an unusual energy of mind in the British Air Services, and, according to report, some officers produced designs for new aero-motors of considerable merit.

Organising talent was displayed in the field in a thorough rearrangement of the Royal Flying Corps under General Trenchard. Six distinct orders of machines were developed. Above all were the fighting planes, divided into two classes, one of which operated over the British lines in a defensive manner while the other swept out over the German lines and attacked Fokker pilots, and at the same time protected British working machines. The working machines were usually arranged in scouting groups, artillery observation groups, aerial photography groups, bombing raid groups, and infantry contact groups. All this sub-

CIRCLING THE FLEET IN THE MEDITERRANEAN.
British airship flying round the fleet in the Mediterranean. As new "eyes" for the Navy, aircraft came to be recognised as an auxiliary as important to the sea services as they were to those of the land.

division of labour tended to produce specialised kinds of aviators, so that an expert in photographing the German trenches could not always be regarded as a deadly marksman for bomb-dropping expeditions.

By reason of the nature of things the fighting pilots in the warplane order came most brightly into the limelight of fame. Chief among them was the young son of a former Mayor of Nottingham, Captain Albert Ball, who ranked in the summer of 1916 above all French and German fighting pilots in regard to his record of kills. He was only nineteen years of age, and as reported, he had taken part in one hundred air combats, and had brought down thirty enemy aeroplanes. He won the D.S.O. for attacking six German machines in one flight, forcing two down and driving the others off. Then in an attack on the enemy's kite-balloons he used all his bombs and failed to hit, returned for a fresh supply, flew back, and brought a balloon down in flames.

[*British official photograph.*]

RETURN FROM A LONG RECONNAISSANCE.
Naval airship arriving at its accustomed landing-place after a lengthy flight. The eager men beneath were hurrying to help in making the airship snug on her reaching the ground.

On another occasion Captain Ball observed a formation of seven enemy machines, drove at it, shot one German down at fifteen yards range, and forced the other enemy pilots to retire. A few minutes afterwards he saw another formation of five hostile machines, and, in an attack delivered at a range of ten yards, sent one down flaming to the earth. Attacking another machine of the same formation that was vainly firing at him, he tumbled it into a village, causing it to break up on the roof of a house. This exhausted all Captain Ball's ammunition, and his machine was considerably damaged. But on reaching his aerodrome he obtained more cartridges and, returning to the fray, assailed three more German machines and compelled them to dive away. By this time shortage of petrol compelled Captain Ball to end his day of amazing exploits.

Afterwards, when on escort duty in a bombing raid, Captain Ball saw four German machines in formation, and swooping on them, shot down the nearest one, scattered the others and then descended near the ground to make certain he had wrecked the machine that first came under his fire. Later, this prince of British pilots espied twelve German machines in fighting order, and, driving right in among them, with the fire of one drum of his Lewis gun tumbled one machine to earth. Three other enemies

Captain Ball's great exploits then closed around him, and he gave them a drum of cartridges each, with the result that another German plane crashed down. By this time Captain Ball's aeroplane was badly damaged ; but, limping along at a low altitude, he landed safely in his own lines. During his hundred fights Captain Ball had six machines so damaged that he was forced to make a quick landing, but he escaped without serious personal injury, and by the end of the year he was awarded two bars to his Distinguished Service Order.

Almost equal in renown for a single special feat was Sec.-Lieutenant George R. McCubbin, who came from South Africa and served as a mechanic before he was promoted pilot. While still an apprentice as a fighting airman he went out with Lieutenant Savage and saw his comrade brought down by the king of the Fokker fighters, Lieutenant Immelmann. A few days afterwards, on June 18th, 1916, Lieutenant McCubbin, with his observer handling a machine-gun, engaged Immelmann and sent his machine crashing to the ground, Immelmann being killed. Captain R. N. Adams, who attacked six enemy machines over the enemy's lines, set one on fire and drove off the others, was another noted pilot. Lieutenant Dirk Cloete first acted as observer to Captain Adams, and shooting an enemy machine made it turn upside down. Then promoted pilot, he saw his former chief, Captain Adams, engaged with six enemy machines, and diving into the affray, sent one enemy crashing to the earth, and helped to fight the other five away, another of which was brought down by Captain Adams. Captain R. Balcombe-Brown was remarkable for his improvisation of skill. One day at dawn he began to learn how to handle a new machine, and yet by the evening with this new machine he brought down a German kite-balloon.

One machine against ten

Captain W. A. Summers, as pilot, and Lieutenant W. O. T. Tudor-Hart, as observer, appear almost to have topped the list in the fight against odds. With their single machine, when quite unsupported, they attacked over the German lines a formation of ten enemy aeroplanes. Under constant heavy fire from as many as four hostile machines at one time, they broke up the formation in a fight ranging many miles over the enemy's territory, and though their own machine was badly damaged they continued their extraordinary struggle until all their ammunition was expended. Captain A. W. Vaucour also attacked ten hostile planes and broke their formation, and on other occasions shot down German after German.

FRENCH ARTILLERY BOMBARDMENT AS SEEN FROM A FRENCH OBSERVING AEROPLANE.
Circling over the battlefield like a hawk, a French aviator secured this wonderful picture of the French shells bursting over the enemy lines. More than any amount of verbal explanation does a photograph like this enable the layman to realise how the development of aeronautics affected the accuracy of artillery fire and, consequently, the issue of battles.

CUTTING THE ENEMY LINES OF COMMUNICATION ON THE MEDITERRANEAN FRONT.

[British official photograph.

Direct hit from the air. A naval airman poised in an aeroplane at a height of a thousand feet destroyed the centre span of this railway bridge in the Mediterranean theatre of the war by a well-aimed bomb, and a flying photographer obtained the striking evidence of the effective damage done. That the river was one of very considerable breadth is indicated by the many arches of the road bridge nearer the foreground.

Captain W. A. G. Bellew, formerly of the Connaught Rangers, was another great fighting pilot. First, with three other machines, he attacked eight German planes and forced one to the ground; next, in his single machine, he attacked four Fokkers, sent one crashing to death, and forced a second low down. Afterwards he escorted a bombing expedition, when two of the working machines lagged behind, owing to the low clouds, and were attacked by three Fokkers. Turning back to help his comrades, Captain Bellew attacked the three Fokkers, drove two off, and shot one down. Lieutenant D. K. Paris, when far within hostile territory, noticed that a British machine had been brought down by German gun fire, and with the help of his pilot, Captain Grant Dalton, he landed, destroyed the machine, rescued the British pilot, and brought him back ninety miles to the British lines. Lieutenant J. D. Latta was a famous kite-balloon destroyer and a deadly Fokker fighter. Major L. W. Brabazon Rees equalled, if not excelled, the record against odds of Lieutenant Tudor-Hart. While on flying duties Major Brabazon Rees sighted what seemed to be a party of British bombers returning home. Flying up to escort them he discovered that the covey consisted of ten enemy machines. One came out to attack him, and he damaged it in a fierce, short fight, **Major Brabazon** and forced it down in the German lines. **Rees' achievement** Five other machines then closed upon him, but he sent two more down badly damaged and dispersed the other three. Seeing another two going westward he chased and attacked them, but on getting to close quarters he was wounded in the thigh. His injured limb prevented him from managing his machine, but he soon recovered control and, closing with the enemy within a few yards, he continued to fire until all his ammunition was spent. Thereupon, he brought his machine safely into the British lines. Lieutenant C. M. B. Chapman was a successful

Fokker fighter against heavy odds. On one occasion he assailed three L.V.G.'s and a Fokker, and shot the last down. Sec.-Lieutenant H. Cope Evans brought down four enemy machines in a fortnight, and Lieutenant W. E. Harper forced two down in one combat, and destroyed several more in other contests.

Captain Dixon-Spain, with Lieutenant Reid as pilot, became a master fighter. On one day they attacked and drove off a hostile machine, and a few minutes later four more German planes **Long list of air** were sighted, three of which were attacked **heroes** one after the other and driven back, while the fourth machine was tackled by another British patrol. On another occasion Captain Dixon-Spain and Lieutenant Reid swooped on to two German machines, forced one down and drove the other off. Two days later another German couple were dealt with in the same manner, one machine being shot down and the other being pursued to its aerodrome. A Canadian pilot, Lieutenant E. R. Hicks, won distinction by assailing a German flight, bringing down two of the machines and driving the other three over the enemy lines. In bombing work he was equally deadly. Working first at 800 feet and then at 300 feet, he wrecked enemy trains in movement and bombarded a railway-station.

The list of British fighting pilots of public distinction is too long to set out in detail. By the end of the Somme offensive their exploits required a volume to relate. Captain W. D. S. Sanday, who led more than thirty-five patrols in gallant fashion, destroyed at least four enemy machines. Captain A. M. Wilkinson shot down five machines by the end of August, 1916, and then went on destroying more. Captain L. P. Aizlewood got between five enemy machines and their lines, and driving on them held his fire till he was only twenty yards off. The machine he hit and ruined

RETURNING OVER NO MAN'S LAND.
French aeroplane as it neared home after a reconnoitring excursion. The scene shows the devastation caused by shells between the opposing trenches.

Similar in businesslike quality was the labour of the "spotters," or aerial artillery observers. They were the mobile advanced guard of the officers in the long line of kite-balloons in the British rear, who continually studied through glasses all signs of activity on the hostile front, and communicated their views to their siege-guns near by. The observers in the circling machines did not appear to be thoroughly proficient during the first phase of the great preliminary bombardment in the last week of June, 1916.

Scarcely a German battery was damaged by the guns they were directing. But in the closing and most violent phase of British gun fire the hurricane of shells searched nearly every hostile battery position, for these positions had been carefully studied and yet left unassailed until the last hour lest the enemy gunners should become anxious and change to new sites **Artillery observers'** in the night. As it was, the Germans **fine work** suspected nothing, and thought they had escaped notice, and only when the British infantry was preparing to advance were their positions smothered in an extraordinary storm of heavy shell. Afterwards, when the weather grew unfavourable, and low-hanging clouds and mist interfered with the task of the British aerial artillery observers, the pilots operated under desperate risks in order to serve their guns. Captain Leoline Jenkins was conspicuously skilful and brave, flying for a long time at a very low height under continual gun fire and machine-gun attack while finding targets for his howitzers. Captain J. U. Kelly was accustomed to come down very low to obtain information. He descended through clouds to 500 feet, and flying over the German positions was wounded

collided with his plane as it fell, breaking his propeller. Though barely controllable, the British machine was landed on British ground by the brilliant pilot. Captain J. O. Andrews was a fine leader of fighting patrols, and shot down four enemy machines. Captain I. H. D. Henderson was a most versatile airman. He destroyed a kite-balloon, and acted as contact pilot to infantry in several actions, in one of which he attacked the retiring German artillery. Then, in a more powerful machine, he had an adventurous week as a high-altitude fighter. He first shot down a German machine, went out and dispersed a formation of six hostile planes, and afterwards attacked and brought down a biplane, and, when fighting in formation, drove down an enemy that had wounded his leader. Captain K. N. Pearson, Lieutenant H. H. Turk, Lieutenant S. E. Cowan, and Captain G. M. Moore were brilliant fighters.

The work of the photographic group of machines, although less spectacular than that of the fighting pilots, required equal coolness and skill. Captain M. McB. Bell-Irving, for instance, was seriously wounded in the head when taking photographs of the German positions. An anti-aircraft gun caught him with shrapnel, and half blinded by blood he steered for the nearest aerodrome. Wounded so seriously that he could not last out, he yet managed to land in the British lines, where, after giving orders for the safe delivery of his photographs, he collapsed.

ONE NIEUPORT CHASER PHOTOGRAPHED FROM ANOTHER.
At a height of between six and seven thousand feet an aviator-photographer on a Nieuport chaser biplane was able to get—neatly framed as it were in the stays of his own machine—this effective picture of one of his companions in the sky.

and almost blinded, yet returned to his own lines with his machine and much useful knowledge of the enemy's activities. Captain J. L. Chalmers specialised in counter-battery work. He flew very low under heavy fire, watching for flames from German guns, and directing his own artillery exactly upon the hostile batteries. His machine was badly damaged by shell fire, but he brought it back, and in another flight discovered and put out of action four German batteries. Captain H. J. F. Hunter was a "spotter" of equal skill and coolness. When such men were busy at work the German artillery often remained inactive in fear of destruction, and the British troops had their task greatly lightened.

Wild adventures befell many of the bombing flights of British machines. They came fully into action in the latter part of June, 1916, when the new fighting planes had lessened the power and scope of the Fokkers, Rolands and L.V.G.'s. Under the protection of their own battle-planes the raiding bombers delivered a continual succession of masterly strokes that maimed the German army. The enemy's lines of communication were severed in the critical days of the Somme campaign, and generally menaced throughout the struggle when the weather was not extraordinarily adverse. Sec.-Lieutenant P. Huskinson was conspicuous for his bombing skill. Single-handed, he attacked an important railway-station through which a German train was passing. Under continuous fire he descended close to the station and train, released upon them

Bombing from low altitudes
his store of high explosive and then, with his damaged machine working low over the hostile country, like a wounded duck about to fall, he crossed the German lines, again under heavy fire, and made a safe landing.

Sec.-Lieutenant A. S. C. MacLaren was another bomber of great daring. While sweeping over a German aerodrome he saw a hostile machine on the ground preparing to start. Pilot and observer were in their seats, and mechanics were clinging to the wings. Mr. MacLaren swooped within a hundred feet of the ground, and, dropping a bomb into the machine, blew it up, killing pilot, observer and mechanics. Then swerving, he released another bomb on a Fokker machine in a hangar, destroyed both, and soared away before the enemy recovered from the surprise. Captain E. J. Tyson was a train-wrecker and raider of high distinction, and with Lieutenant J. R. Philpott carried out a series of great actions.

SQUADRON OF BELGIAN BIPLANES.
Flying ground behind the Belgian front, taken from an aeroplane flying above. A squadron of machines as they were ready to take the air against the enemy.

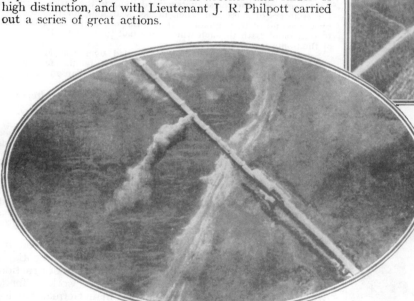

GERMAN AVIATORS BOMBING THE CERNA VODA BRIDGE.
Sometimes airmen were able to obtain conclusive evidence of the effect of an attack. Having dropped bombs on the long railway bridge linking Rumania with the Dobruja, some German aviators secured this photograph showing that they had scored a hit.

On July 1st the British bombing raiders worked with tremendous energy. A large German ammunition dump was set on fire; railway centres were wrecked, and troop and supply trains hit and stopped. One British pilot, attacking a station, was impeded by engine trouble, and while vainly trying to release his bombs on the target was attacked by two German battle-planes. Yet circling three times over his objective and beating off his attackers, the pilot cut the railway completely, and also destroyed a neighbouring building. Towards the end of the month of July the sky had been so cleared of Fokkers, Rolands and L.V.G.'s that four British bombing machines made an extraordinary raid practically unmolested by hostile machines. There was an important German railway centre where large quantities of ammunition had been stored. It was attacked in the afternoon of July 27th, when packed with trucks, carriages, and locomotives. The rolling-stock was struck and set on fire and the ammunition sheds were hit. The enemy, being taken by surprise, used neither anti-aircraft guns nor battle-planes against the low-flying raiders.

On a later occasion the vital junction of Libercourt, south of Lille, was the scene of a remarkable bomb attack. Around the junction, at distances of a few miles, were three German aerodromes so arranged as to protect the knot of railways between Lille and Douai. At one o'clock in the day, when the German pilots were slackening off for lunch, a shower of bombs crashed into the air-sheds. Most of the bombs caused no explosion, but transformed each aerodrome into a blinding, choking cauldron of smoke. Above the thick screen of fumes the attacking planes continued to circle, dropping high explosive into the volcanoes of smoke they had made. At least two of the aerodromes were set on fire. While the operation was proceeding, a train left the junction running southward and another train approached along the branch line. Thereupon two British squadrons swooped down from the sky low upon the trains. The engine of the first train was hit and thrown from the rails, and the leading carriages telescoped. It was a troop train, and the men poured from the wreckage and raced for cover towards a large wood. But the British pilots came still lower, and their observers played with machine-guns upon the Germans, who had massed together in panic, and killed and wounded many of them between the track and the wood. The wrecked train blocked the line and compelled the second train to come to a standstill. The locomotive was destroyed by twenty-pound bombs, and several of the carriages blown up. Again the troops poured out, seeking shelter, but as they ran the attacking pilot came close to the earth, enabling the observers to route the fugitives with machine-gun fire.

Meanwhile, Libercourt Station, with its buildings, sidings, and rolling-stock jammed into the yards, received a cargo of heavier bombs, some of which weighed a hundredweight. The force of the explosions hurled the carriages across the rails, and the station was a spectacle of wild ruin when the British squadrons left it. The fighting planes that guarded

CAPTAIN ALBERT BALL, D.S.O., M.C., HERO OF THE R.F.C.

When only nineteen years of age he had taken part in a hundred air combats and destroyed thirty enemy aeroplanes. Awarded the D.S.O. and bar in September, 1916, for gallantry and devotion in the field.

the bombing squadrons, circling high in the air above the German aerodromes, had practically no work o do. Only one German machine appeared, and it bolted when threatened, and every British plane got home without mishap.

This was not an isolated incident, but a representative affair. Every week bombing raids of equal intensity occurred behind the German front, from the Yser to the Somme and from the Somme to the Aisne. Bapaume Station, Achiet Junction, Cambrai Station, and Douai Station were incessantly assailed. The full catalogue of German sidings, railway works, aerodromes, and ammunition sheds that were damaged would be a very long one. British raiders from the Royal Flying Corps and Royal Naval Air Service reached to Mons, Brussels, and Namur by the middle of August, 1916, paying special attention to the Zeppelin sheds at Maubeuge on their way, and

timing their most important attacks so as to find the Belgian railway centres full of rolling-stock, troops, and munitions.

A reign of terror was imposed upon the Teuton soldiery. Letters taken from dead and wounded foes, while the great wedge was being driven between the Ancre and the Somme, told of the panic caused by the British raiders, of heavy loss of life inflicted upon the hostile forces, and of confusion and weakness due to the interruption of the movement of troops by railway.

From the diary of a German private of the 18th Reserve Division we obtain a telling description of the effect on the enemy of the combined work of British aerial directors of long-range guns, aerial raiders of railway centres, and aerial machine-gunners :

Many times, long before a German battalion arrived near the trenches, it was but a collection of nerve-broken men, bemoaning losses already suffered far behind the lines and filled with hideous apprehension. For British long-range guns were hurling high-explosives into distant villages, barraging cross-roads, reaching out to rail-heads and ammunition dumps, while British airmen were on bombing flights over railway-stations and rest billets, and high roads down which the German troops came marching at Cambrai, Bapaume, in the valley between Irles and Warlencourt, at Ligny-Thilloy, Busigny, and many other places on the lines of route.

Troops arriving at Cambrai by train found themselves under the fire of a single aeroplane which flew very low and dropped bombs. These exploded with heavy crashes, and one bomb hit the first carriage behind the engine, killing and wounding several men. A second bomb hit the station buildings, and there was a great clatter of broken glass, the rending of wood, and the fall of bricks. All lights went out, and the soldiers groped about in the darkness amidst the splinters of glass and fallen bricks, searching for the wounded by the sound of their groans. It was but one scene along the way to that blood-bath through which they had to wade to the trenches of the Somme.

Squadrons of British aeroplanes circled over the villages on the way. At Grevilliers, in August, eleven bombs fell in the market-square, so that the centre of the village collapsed in a state of ruin, burying soldiers billeted there. Every day the British airmen paid these visits, meeting the Germans far up the roads on their way to the Somme and swooping over them like a flying Death. Even on the march **Evidence from a German diary.** in open country the German soldiers tramping silently along—not singing, in spite of orders—were bombed and shot at by these British airmen, who flew down very low, pouring out streams of machine-gun bullets. The Germans lost their nerve at such times, and scattered into the ditches, falling over each other, struck and cursed by their non-coms., and leaving their dead and wounded in the roadway.

As the roads went nearer to the battlefields they were choked with the traffic of war, with artillery and transport waggons and horse-ambulances, and always thousands of grey men marching up to the lines, or back from them, exhausted and broken after many days in the fires of hell up there.

From a military point of view the damage done by raiding Zeppelins over England and Southern Scotland was quite insignificant in comparison with the destruction wrought in daylight by British aeroplanes working for a distance of a hundred miles behind the main German battle-front. By the end of the year it was estimated that the Allies had carried out a total of seven hundred and fifty bombardments. The French claimed two hundred and fifty bombardments, and estimated that the British had made a hundred and eighty between Ypres and the Somme. The two Allies also conducted most of the hundred and seventy-four bombardments in the Balkans. The number of enemy aeroplanes brought down was estimated at nine hundred, four hundred and fifty being claimed by the French and two hundred and fifty being brought down by the British. Eighty-one hostile observation balloons are reported to have been destroyed, forty are said to have been struck by French airmen, and twenty-seven by British airmen.

The achievements of the new contact patrols were usually less picturesque than the feats of the fighting and raiding flights. But the work accomplished by the slowest and lowest order of machines told on the event of the battle in many remarkable ways. The small losses of the French Army, for instance, were directly attributed to the fact that the troops generally advanced two hundred yards

SEC.-LIEUTENANT G. R. McCUBBIN, D.S.O.
While still an apprentice as a fighting airman he, on June 18th, 1916, brought down Immelmann, "the king of the Fokker fighters."

[*Swaine.*

MAJOR BRABAZON REES, V.C., M.C.
Attacked ten enemy machines; three he sent down and, though wounded, fought the rest until his ammunition gave out.

[*Chancellor.*

SEC.-LIEUTENANT S. E. COWAN, M.C.
Awarded the M.C. in May, 1916, and later a bar to it, for fine work in aerial combats, having shot down four enemy machines.

behind their own shell curtain, while contact patrols above them studied their movements and continually reported to their gunners. Any check or any enemy preparation for counter-attack was communicated by the patrols to the gunners, so that the French infantry could immediately be helped. In the British Army a similar system was practised beforehand, and developed on the battlefield. At the opening of the Somme offensive some of General Horne's troops were held up before Dingle Trench by German bombers. In the ordinary way the attack might have been checked at this point, necessitating long delay in preparing an enveloping movement which would have weakened the general operations. But a British contact patrol on a French machine observed what had happened. Swooping down to three hundred feet, he dropped a large bomb on Dingle Trench with such marksmanship that the hostile garrison was annihilated, and General Horne's troops were able to work forward in an action of decisive importance. We have already marked a similar feat by a French contact patrol in the chapter dealing with the capture of Curlu. In this case the patrol signalled the French infantry to withdraw. When they were out of the danger zone, he called in a large force of heavy French artillery, hammered the village with shell, and again signalled his infantry to make the charge upon the stricken foe.

Both British and French contact patrols took to using machine-guns as well as bombs upon the hostile infantry.

Heroic work of contact patrols

The airmen continually grew more audacious in their attacks upon entrenched German troops. They descended at last so low that their position seemed to be one of prolonged extreme peril. But, as a matter of fact, the contact patrols felt comparatively happy when they came from 8,000 feet down to 500 feet and lower. The idea of setting frail flying structures operating just above the heads of the hostile infantry was not only daring, but subtly clever. For when the machines were at an altitude of only a few hundred feet they were too low for German anti-aircraft guns to attack them. "Archibald," as the German anti-aircraft gun was nicknamed, was designed to fire almost straight into the air, and he was usually placed high upon the main Somme watershed, screened from the direct fire of the allied artillery. His gunners, therefore, had considerable difficulty in suddenly training him low upon the western slopes, and over these slopes his shrapnel shells would have burst over the heads of his own infantry.

The result was that the contact patrols were often exposed only to machine-gun fire and musketry fire from the hostile trenches over which they operated while their own infantry was advancing to the attack. There were some casualties from machine-gun and rifle bullets, but the loss was nothing in comparison with the high value of the work of the contact patrols in helping the infantry, directing the British artillery fire, and swooping down on the enemy with machine-guns. Until the "tanks" appeared in the middle of September, 1916, and put a

Swooping down on the enemy

CAPTAIN A. M. MILLER, D.S.O.
Brilliant pilot who engaged enemy gun positions at the Bazentins, and cleared the way for the cavalry.

[*Elliott & Fry.*

CAPTAIN W. SANDAY, M.C.
Led over thirty-five patrols in gallant fashion and destroyed at least four enemy machines.

CAPTAIN W. BELLEW, M.C.
On three occasions attacked numbers of Fokkers and other enemy machines and destroyed several.

CAPT. M. McB. BELL-IRVING, D.S.O., M.C.
Wounded on air - photographic work. Awarded M.C. July, 1916.

new terror into the German troops, the enemy's apprehension centred upon the British and French contact patrols. Hundreds of letters taken from dead, wounded, or captured Germans spoke in bitter tones of the apparent cowardice of their own airmen, and of the terrifying swoops by allied contact squadrons using bombs and machine-guns. The crack battalion of one of the Prussian Guard Divisions at last broke and fled, and allowed Bouchavesnes to be taken by the Zouaves, owing to the fact that both officers and men were demoralised by machine-gun fire from French aeroplanes.

"The Englishmen come so low you have to take care the propeller does not hit your head," said a German soldier writing home. "We cannot move by day, as they see us and fire upon us with machine-guns. Perhaps one of these days they will come and haul us **Airman captures an** out of the trenches by the scruff of the **enemy trench** neck." "Our airmen," wrote another German infantryman, "sit in the best restaurants plastered with medals, and grow fat, but, as for flying work, they never think of going near Mr. Englishman."

One British airman at last practically fulfilled the prophecy of the German who said he expected to be taken from a trench by an airman by the scruff of his neck. When the British infantry was finally pushing beyond the great ridge, a contact patrol, operating in advance of his infantry, flew down on a German position, three hundred feet long, intending to sweep it with his machine-gun. But as he whirred above the parapet the German garrison waved to him with everything white they possessed. Thereupon he signalled to his own infantry, and they came up and organised the surrender. Having regard to all the circumstances, this

exploit may fairly be accounted the most remarkable incident in the war. Before it happened the Germans had begun to surrender to the new wheelless mobile British forts, but although this was a strange and picturesque incident, it was something that could be foreseen. But that the garrison of a long German trench should surrender without firing a shot to a British aeroplane, that could not operate along the ground or penetrate the hostile dug-outs, was extraordinary evidence of the condition of unthinking demoralisation into which the Germans had been hammered by aerial gun fire.

Captain A. M. Miller was in some ways the most distinguished of aerial gunners. He was known as a deadly troop-train bomber, and as a pilot who single-handed had attacked five German machines. But his exploit of singular quality was that carried out as contact patrol in the first action near High Wood in the middle of September, 1916. The reader will remember that Sir Henry Rawlinson felt the enemy near to breaking-point at the Bazentins, and abruptly flung out cavalry in advance of his infantry. The Dragoons and Deccan Horse charged forward, guided by Captain Miller. But this brilliant pilot espied a line of German machine-gunners in a field ; they would have caught the British and Indian squadrons at a disadvantage. Captain Miller swooped and flew low along the front of the enemy gun positions, lashing them with his Lewis gun and drawing their fire. Then the cavalry charged home,

[*Canadian War Records.*

STRAINING AT THE LEASH.
Observation balloon about to ascend. The stern was held down by men of the Flying Corps, while the bow strained at the rope as it was gradually and carefully paid out from the motor.

and made a dashing success of the action at remarkably slight loss. Captain J. G. Swart and Captain H. E. F. Wyncoll were also fine contact patrols.

Captain K. R. Binning was distinguished by two contact patrol flights over the German trenches, in which, while his machine was repeatedly caught by machine-gun and rifle fire, he coolly noted the position of both German and British troops, and brought his artillery to act with decisive precision. Captain C. C. Miles also showed great dash and keenness of judgment in sweeping low over hostile positions, being at last badly wounded ; and Sec.-Lieutenant F. E. S. Phillips, after much fine contact patrol work, carried on when his machine was damaged by hostile fire, discovered the development of a German counter-attack, and put the guns he directed so exactly on the gathering foes that they were broken before they could make their charge. Lieutenant R. Johnstone displayed remarkable initiative and courage, turning his artillery on to columns of German infantry, and fighting German gunners, in counter-battery duels, when low clouds and

[*Canadian War Records.*

MENDING PUNCTURES IN A BALLOON'S SKIN.
Repairing a kite-balloon which was slightly damaged during a gusty day. The utmost care had to be taken to prevent the ladder on which the operator stood from coming in contact with the delicate envelope.

mist veiled his view and compelled him to circle close above the enemy, under heavy fire.

In the destruction of German observation balloons, which was a matter of high importance at the opening of the Somme offensive, the new Nieuport Scouts were very effective. They were fat, little slug-like things, presenting scarcely any target, as they combined terrific speed with perfect ease of manœuvre. Each pilot is said to have carried eight incendiary rockets, so fixed for firing that they could be loosened by pressing a button: simple tactics adopted at the time when the Germans were unsuspicious. The pilot climbed over the German lines at a height of about 8,000 feet, attracted the attention of " Archibald," the enemy anti-aircraft gun, dodged and outspeeded his gunners, and finally dived some 3,000 feet for the sausage-shaped balloon, the Army name of which was Rupert. As the balloon came in sight of the pilot the hostile mechanics on the ground, seeing that something dangerous was threatening, worked away at their winches to bring the balloon quickly and safely to earth. As the gasbag swayed from side to side the attacking machine almost reached it, and appeared about to make a ripping collision. But at the critical moment the pilot made a vertical " bank," causing his machine to veer away. As it veered he pressed the button, and eight fiery rockets shot out in fan formation upon the doomed gasbag. If but one rocket hit, a ribbon of flame appeared upon the balloon and spread into a great flash, giving the German

Canadian War Records.

AN EASY AND A SAFE DESCENT.
A kite-balloon descending behind the Canadian lines. Two officers usually went up with the standard British balloon, one to attend to its management, the other to make observations.

Canadian War Records.

GROUNDED FOR OVERHAULING AND REPAIRS.
Another view of the balloon which is shown on the opposite page undergoing repairs. The war balloons utilised by the British forces were usually made of goldbeater's skin, and were of comparatively small cubic capacity.

observing officers no time to seize a parachute and try a leap for safety. The huge envelope was destroyed with dreadful rapidity. Many officers of the Royal Flying Corps were sorry for opponents they killed in this way. But war is war, and it was not the Allies who first sent hundreds of men up in enormous gasbags to rain death down upon women, children, and peaceful men in the starlit gloom of moonless nights.

Long had it taken the inventive minds of France and Great Britain to arm the aeroplane and seaplane with a decisive instrument for attacking both stationary and dirigible balloons. Nearly twenty-three months of war passed before proper appliances were abundantly provided for pilots practised to use them. The small, quick, heavier machine definitely triumphed over the colossal and slower airship, upon which the Germans had for years built their hope of becoming lords of the earth. All that afterwards happened at night-time at Cuffley,

Potter's Bar, and elsewhere in England, was but the inevitable sequel to the rapid series of events occurring on either side the Somme River. The Zeppelin, the Schütte-Lanz, and the Parseval were clearly destined to go the way of the German kite-balloons that the Parseval firm had invented. All that remained to do, as the Nieuport firm had shown in Lieutenant Marshal's flight from France to Poland, was further to develop the engine power and petrol-carrying capacity of the flying machine. But the range of the Zeppelin enabled it to retain an important advantage in the work of naval reconnaissance in favourable weather.

Even in this respect the position of the Zeppelin was not secure against the genius of the British inventor. Indeed it was commonly foreseen that the production of a special type of seaplane-carrier, with a speed of forty knots, might result in the British Navy acquiring the air dominion of the North Sea. There was a time when German sailors gladly volunteered for Zeppelin work, but drew back when called upon to go down in submarines against the anti-submarine weapons of the British Fleet. Teutonic seamen, it is said, used to be enticed into submarine duty by the offer of subsequent Zeppelin work. But the wholesale destruction of German balloons on the Somme in the summer and autumn of 1916 was an event pregnant with menace to all Teutons used to floating in the air on bags of gas. The enemy had boasted that his chemists could compound a mixture of gases, light enough to keep a Zeppelin afloat at 10,000 feet or more, and yet incapable of being set on fire. This, however, was practically a

Wholesale balloon destruction

MUTUAL RESPECT AND COURTESY OF GALLANT MEN.
British airmen, outmanœuvring the German occupants of a monoplane, beat them down to earth. On landing, the victors approached the vanquished and saluted and shook hands with them with genuine respect.

scientific impossibility. Gases of a non-combustible nature were too heavy to lift a bag and a great mass of metal high in the air. It was the principle of the lighter-than-air dirigible that was smitten by fire above the Somme, leaving the field of aerial warfare entirely open to the accelerated development of the flying machine invented by the Wright Brothers—scions of the race that built the steam-engine and the locomotive, discovered the electrical dynamo, and constructed the telegraph, the power-loom, the machine-tool, the steamship, and the turbine. Nearly every instrument of high power in modern civilisation that the Anglo-Celt had not invented was mainly contributed to the common stock of mankind by the French-man and the Italian. The Teuton was able to improve, in a commercially successful way, the inventions of other races, as Count Zeppelin improved upon
German new-type the airship of Santos Dumont. But he
machines was not equal in originating energy of mind to the peoples of Western and Southern Europe arrayed against him. Such, at least, seemed to be the heartening lesson of the aerial campaign on the Somme.

All that the fighting pilots of the British Empire and the French Republic needed was material equal to the production of the enemy. The German seemed at the time to rely almost entirely upon the thorough organising talent of his race. He laid his plans far in advance, and laboriously increased the horse-power of his machines by known and sound methods. After creating the 200 h.p. Fokker he went on to develop two new types, after-wards famous as the Albatros-Spad, and the Halberstadt. The Halberstadt Works were of British origin, having been founded before the war by Sir George White, of the Bristol

Works, at a time when private British aeroplane-makers received little encouragement from the War Office and the Royal Aircraft Factory, and had to extend into Germany in order to keep their men and plant going. This was the reason why the old Bristol "Bullet," which did good work on the British side in the early campaigns, became the foundation of some of the best machines made by the Halberstadt Works.

In their latest machine the Halberstadt makers were reported to have taken the Morane as a model, and used a Benz engine of great power. The new Spad, made by the Albatros firm, was another imitation of a French model. The original Spad came from the Société Pour les Appareils Deperdussin, and the **Getting above the** initials of the firm formed the name of **Fokkers** the machine. The Germans, as usual, employed a very powerful engine, and produced an aero-plane with remarkable climbing power and a speed of one hundred and twenty miles an hour.

In the autumn of 1915, when the Fokker crisis arose, the British pilots often operated scarcely higher than 8,000 feet, mainly in obsolescent machines of the Royal Aircraft Factory design. In their new Fokkers, with engines of 200 h.p., Immelmann, Bœlcke, Wintgen, and other German pilots, used to wait at an altitude of 12,000 feet and dive down on the B.E. machines. In the end Immelmann was killed, largely by his machine being excelled by a British private production—the new Martin-syde—while another British private production—the De Havilland fighter—cleared the sky of Fokkers to a consider-able extent before the Royal Aircraft Factory brought out its new fighting machine, an improved F.E. with a Rolls-Royce engine.

From the end of March to the middle of October, 1916, the new British machines enabled the officers of the Royal Flying Corps to meet the enemy on terms of equality in equipment. The result was the greatest allied victory since the Battle of the Marne. German gunners and German Staffs were reduced to a condition of purblind-ness. On some sectors their power of vision only extended a few hundred yards beyond their fire-trenches, while the aerial eyes of the British and French Armies ranged hundreds of miles over the scenes of German activities. By two of the new Sopwith aeroplanes the Krupp Works at Essen were at last bombarded. The feat was accomplished by two French airmen, Captain de Beauchamp and Lieu-tenant Daucourt, on September 22nd, 1916. The Sopwith enabled them to make a flight of 500 miles with a cargo of bombs. On November 17th Captain de Beauchamp took another cargo of bombs in his Sopwith biplane, passed over Friedrichshafen (one of the centres of Zeppelin con-struction), turned northwards to Munich, and bombed the Bavarian capital, then veered southwards, crossed the Alps, and landed in Italy. And the machine that did this was ready for use at Kingston-on-Thames in either May or June, 1915—nearly six months before the new Fokker appeared.

When the Fokker was at last beaten, the Royal Aircraft Factory, with Colonel Mervyn O'Gorman as superintendent and Sir David Henderson as military chief, does not seem to have prepared alertly against the arrival of enemy machines of greater capacity. In the first week of October, 1916, the new Halberstadt, with a 240 h.p. engine, and the German Spad, of similar power, soared above the British fighting planes. Possessing terrific speed and extraordinary power of climb, the Halberstadt and the Spad enabled the new school of German pilots to excel the records of operating altitude of Immelmann, Bœlcke, and Wintgen. At the amazing working height of 20,000 feet sometimes reduced to 17,000 feet, the German officers were able to swoop upon all British battle-planes that could not cruise at more than 12,000 or 15,000 feet.

Casualty lists began to show that the Royal Flying Corps was again losing heavily. Sir Douglas Haig, in his

Lieut. Nungesser starting off in pursuit of enemy aeroplanes. He and Lieut. Guynemer won an international reputation surpassing that of Immelmann and Bölcke, both of whom they survived.

Two photographs of Lieut. Guynemer flying in France. This intrepid flying man headed the list of successful French airmen up to the end of January, 1917, having thirty victims to his credit and a record for "braces" exceeding that achieved by Bölcke.

Lieut. Nungesser photographed on his return from the flight in which he brought down his twelfth victim. By the end of November, 1916, he had raised his "score" to eighteen, being second to Guynemer, and followed by Adjutant Dorme with sixteen.

LIEUTENANTS GUYNEMER AND NUNGESSER, THE CHAMPION FIGHTING AIRMEN OF FRANCE.

communiqués, admitted day after day serious losses in machines; and war correspondents at the front, some of whom had never seen for months a German aeroplane over the British lines, observed that the enemy was becoming more venturesome. Then, in his historic despatch, written in the last week of December, 1916, the British Commander-in-Chief pointedly remarked: "I desire to point out that the maintenance of the mastery of the air, which is essential, entails a constant and most liberal supply of the most up-to-date machines, without which the most skilful pilots cannot succeed."

Long before these words of warning from the highest authority were published, efforts were made to reform British aeroplane construction. At the beginning of August, 1916, an investigating committee—composed of a business man, Sir Richard Burbidge, a great inventor, Sir Charles A. Parsons, and Sir H. F. W. Donaldson, of Woolwich Arsenal—reported on the condition of affairs at the Royal Aircraft Factory at Farnborough. It was found that the 3,000 hands in the factory had produced since the war began only fifty ordinary machines and small quantities of spare parts to very numerous orders. Bad organisation was shown in sending out to private firms engaged in making Government machines drawings of an incorrect kind. In addition to these gross mistakes, firms engaged in making machines to the designs of the Royal Aircraft Factory had **Reform of Royal** often to submit to numerous altera- **Aircraft Factory** tions in the design made after the issue of manufacturing drawings. The combination of absolute errors and continual changes in drawings issued to the trade was regarded by the committee as being the reason for "a considerable amount of criticism passed on the Royal Aircraft administration."

The committee proceeded to remark that the factory efficiency in experimental work and in finished productions could be increased, on existing wages cost, by reorganising the works and managing them on a businesslike and engineering basis. Several departments of a non-productive nature were found to be full of men who were not doing their proper amount of work, and, in spite of the

[*Canadian War Records.*]

AERIAL OBSERVER AND THE SCENE ABOVE WHICH HE FLOATED.

When observation or kite balloons had ascended, the crews on whom fell the duty of looking after them were duly marched back to their stations. A Canadian observer took the notable photograph of the scene from which he had just risen. Above: The balloon seen from below, with the observer in the small car, from which he was able to see far across the enemy lines. Aeroplanes served as effective guardians of the tethered balloons.

ample financial resources of the factory, production had been delayed owing to want of a large stock of material. Labour-saving devices were not employed in a scientific way, although the Royal Aircraft Factory was connected with the National Physical Laboratory, and presumed to be royally equipped with all that scientific genius could devise. The success of the Fokker pilots was attributed to " some lack of foresight—whether on the part of the Royal Aircraft Factory or the War Office is not clear—as to the size of the engines required to meet war conditions." In conclusion, a plan of thorough reorganisation was proposed.

This plan was carried out, and in September, 1916, a new superintendent was appointed in the person of the chief engineer of the Midland Railway, Mr. Henry Fowler. Closer and more friendly relations were instituted between the Royal Aircraft Factory and the many inventive minds in private British aeroplane works and aero-motor works. The 200 h.p. R.A.F. engine, designed under the old régime, was severely criticised in the House of Commons, and alleged to be, in the opinion of a leading engineering firm engaged to manufacture it, impracticable.

About the time when the Burbidge Committee began investigating the organisation and production of the Royal Aircraft Factory, another committee was appointed, with Mr. Justice Bailhache as chairman, to report on the administration of the Royal Flying Corps. The final report of this committee was issued on December 20th, 1916, a few days before Sir Douglas Haig stated in his despatch that better machines were still needed. The Bailhache Committee found that the military authorities had on occasions greatly delayed to order available high-powered engines. For example, there was twelve months' delay in supplying the Royal Flying Corps with machines fitted with the 110 h.p. Le Rhône. On the other hand, a high-powered engine, designed by the Royal Aircraft Factory, and offered for construction to the Rolls-Royce Company and refused by them, was ordered in large quantities by drawings from other private firms before the engine had been proved. The Rolls-Royce Company went on with their own 250 h.p. aero-motor, which proved successful. But the committee found that Sir David Henderson relied on the unproved R.A.F. engine because it was of R.A.F. design.

In the opinion of the committee, the position of Sir David Henderson was an impossible one so long as he remained responsible both for the Royal Flying Corps as a fighting force and its equipment and for the Royal Aircraft Factory. It was said that the feelings of the

Bailhache Committee's Report

FRENCH BIPLANE IN PURSUIT OF FLYING ENEMY MACHINE.
Flying at a lower altitude, a French photographic airman succeeded in getting this fine camera record of a stern chase far above him, where a compatriot was in pursuit of a German A.E.G. biplane. The photograph well illustrates contrasting types of aeroplanes.

private manufacturers against the Royal Aircraft Factory were strong and bitter, but as most of the leading manufacturers seemed afraid of losing Government work if they came forward as witnesses, little evidence of charges against Royal Aircraft Factory officials was obtained. Yet the committee considered that the feeling of the private manufacturers that their designs did not receive fair treatment and their finished products fair tests, in comparison with those of the R.A.F., could not be removed under the existing conditions. The lack of judgment of some of the subordinate officials had been deplorable, and private manufacturers who came in contact with them had, so Sir David Henderson himself admitted, genuine cause of complaint. The lack of tact might have been answerable, in the Committee's opinion, for much of the dissatisfaction which the trade was alleged to feel. But the most important sentence of the Committee was that " the later productions of the Royal Aircraft Factory are not, on the whole, so good as some of the machines now produced by some of the private manufacturers."

In regard to the fighting organisation of the Royal Flying Corps the committee found some serious deficiencies. The war had been proceeding for over a year before an aerodrome was fitted up for aerial musketry. No school for air fighting was constructed until September, 1915, and the small one then set up at Hythe was insufficient. No reason was given to the committee why the school for musketry was not opened sooner.

Fighting organisation of the R.F.C. There were many cases of pilots having to fight in the air without a sufficient knowledge of their weapons. Moreover, the frequency with which machine-guns jammed in the early aerial combats was, the committee suggested, a sign of lack of careful training in aerial musketry.

In regard to the Fokker crisis, the Bailhache Committee found that the loss of the mastery of the air for some six months from October, 1915, to March, 1916, was due to the fact that the old Royal Aircraft wholesale product B.E.2c was not so fast or so handy as the Fokker. There

BIPLANE THAT NOSE-DIVED BEHIND THE ENEMY LINES.
German photograph, said to be of a British biplane that descended near Lille. The fight for air supremacy was marked by occasional notification that a machine had fallen behind the enemy lines, or had "failed to return." This photograph records one such episode.

were some machines at the front capable of dealing with the Fokker on equal terms, but they were not available in sufficient numbers. Which, being interpreted, means that they were machines of private design, the makers of which had not been favoured with large orders. In conclusion, the committee recommended that the position which Sir David Henderson occupied should be split up into a fighting command and an equipment directorship. A single equipment department should supply both the Army and Navy Flying Services. The continued existence of the Royal Aircraft Factory was recommended, not as a manufacturing establishment, but as a research and experiment centre and drawing office, the full time of the hands being occupied, when not needed on experimental work, in the making of spare parts and repairs.

All this investigation and advice, with the consequent reorganisation of the War Office works and an establishment of an efficient Air Ministry, came too late in the year. The Spad and the Halberstadt, with their climb of 20,000 feet, were first in the air. And although Sir David

Henderson and his subordinates had not shown any lack of foresight, according to the judgment of the Bailhache Committee, the position of things at the front after nearly thirty months of war was such as to make Sir Douglas Haig patently anxious. Meanwhile, a new source of trouble arose in a quarrel over common sources of equipment between the Royal Flying Corps and the Royal Naval Air Service. Mr. A. J. Balfour, as First Lord of the Admiralty, was apparently in a strong position. His technical advisers in aerial affairs had relied upon private British makers long before the opening of the war, and had given orders that saved some of the best of them from bankruptcy at a time when the Royal Aircraft Factory seemed to discourage private enterprise. Owing to the difference between the deplorable ways of some military officials and the kindly, helpful courtesy of naval officials, the Navy obtained in advance equipment that the Army afterwards found it wanted. The quarrel shook the foundations of the new Air Board, which had been formed in May, 1916, as a breakwater against the strong current of agitated popular feeling in the matter of the Air Services.

A capable man, Lord Curzon, was appointed chairman of the Board, but he was unable to impose agreement upon the representatives of the Naval and Military Wings.

The fall of the last Asquith Cabinet and the creation of the great new War Ministry under Mr. Lloyd George called Lord Curzon away from the Air Board, much, no doubt, to his relief. He was succeeded as chairman by Lord Sydenham, a man of great experience in military material. But the abrupt resignation of Lord Sydenham, on December 30th, 1916, indicated that the tension in the Air Board had been increased rather than diminished by the publication of Sir Douglas Haig's request for better machines in larger numbers. Thereupon, the new War Ministry made a determined effort at a thorough and reorganising development of the Air Board into a great Air Ministry. The most successful of British engineers, Lord Cowdray, was made Air Minister, and given the Hotel Cecil as his office. Admiral Vaughan-Lee, the Chief of the Naval Air Service, was succeeded by one of the most expert of flyers, Commodore G. M. Paine, for whom a remarkable new position was created as Air Lord of the Admiralty.

This innovation was made under the new régime of Admiral Jellicoe, who had learnt from experience how important a part aircraft played in naval actions and patrol work. Lieutenant-General Sir David Henderson remained Director-General of Aeronautics, and occupied on the Army Council a position similar to that which Commodore Paine filled on the Board of Admiralty. The Ministry of Munitions **Lord Cowdray made** took over the control of the production **Air Minister** of aircraft for both Services, in order to put an end to the competition between the Navy and Army. Mr. Percy Martin, managing director of the Birmingham Small Arms Company, and Mr. William Weir, a well-known pump-maker of Glasgow, were appointed as representatives of the Ministry of Munitions on the new Air Board.

The idea of the new scheme appeared to be that the Air Board should design machines and that the Ministry of Munitions should make them. Strong objections were raised against this scheme, and how it would work remained to be seen. The chief requisite in organisation was to keep the leading designers in close touch with the fighting

On the battlefield: French soldier carrying in his wounded officer under fire.

Regimental stretcher-bearers bringing in a casualty from the battlefield.

R.A.M.C. men attending to the wounded at a dressing-station.

How the wounded were brought home. Stations of the Red Cross

With the R.A.M.C.: Evacuating a dressing=station under heavy shell fire.

Casualties arriving at a clearing hospital for operation and full attention.

Placing the wounded in a hospital train for transport to a base hospital.

From battlefield to dressing=station, clearing hospital, and base hospital.

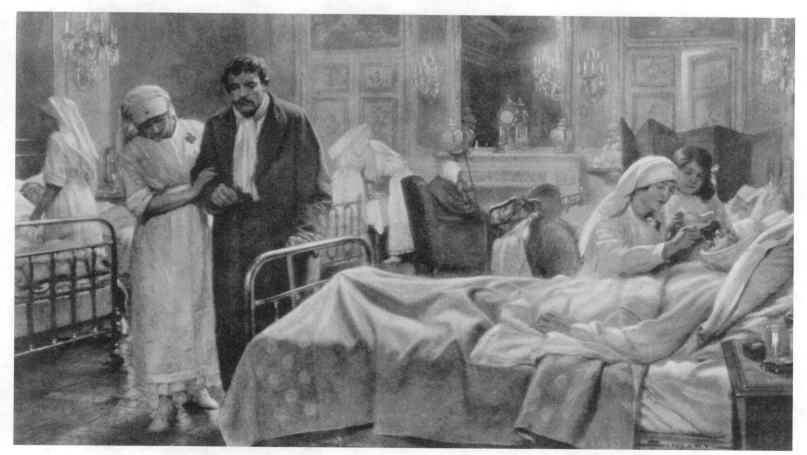

Ladies of France nursing wounded in the salon of a great mansion.

From war vessel to hospital ship : Transhipment of sick and wounded at sea.

forces, so that constant foresight in the development of machines and engines might govern the productive work of the munition factories.

The Spad and Halberstadt crisis of the autumn and early winter of 1916 was not so serious as the Fokker crisis of the previous year ; for, mainly as the direct result of public agitation, the inventive and organising genius of Great Britain was aroused to progressive activity. Accidents, however, continued to happen in extraordinary sequence. The first De Havilland fighter, answering the

Three untoward incidents Fokker, was shot down by the enemy in the spring of 1916, the day after it arrived at the front. Then the first new Government machine, with the first 250 h.p. Rolls-Royce engine, was landed in the enemy territory. And on January 3rd, 1917, the first British machine of superior power to the Spad and Halberstadt was likewise given to the Germans. It was a Handley-Page " super-aeroplane," with two Rolls-Royce engines, giving together 500 h.p., and the R.N.A.S. pilot lost his way in the mist and landed within the enemy's lines

The loss of the Handley Page warned the enemy of what he would soon have to encounter, and showed that the Admiralty, like the War Office, was wrong in sending single examples of new types to operate in an experimental way on the front, instead of reserving each machine for trial flights at home until a large formation could be sprung with surprise effect upon the foe. Nevertheless, this last untoward incident, like the first, was indicative of the rapidly developing power of British aircraft. Engine power had not directly increased between May, 1916, and January, 1917, but British aeroplane design, as the lost Handley-Page machine proved, was progressing in a masterly manner.

On the naval side of aerial warfare, during the period under review, there were some stirring incidents, considerable progressive work under difficulties, and some dull, stagnant conditions. The Royal Naval Air Service seemed to lack something—something the Royal Flying Corps possessed. No doubt incessant fighting on a large and ever-increasing scale made for efficiency in the Military Wing. Naval patrols in small airships and seaplanes had constant and arduous work, watching coastwise and channel traffic, in searching for and hunting submarines, and occasionally pursuing a Zeppelin. The Naval Wing in Flanders, attached to the Dover Patrol, was a splendid school of diverse experience. Its officers spotted for the British bombarding squadron, during attacks on the enemy batteries along the Belgian coast ; they attacked and destroyed hostile submarines, Zeppelins, and Zeppelin sheds ; kept under regular observation all enemy movements in Western Flanders, in co-operation with the Belgian Air Service, and made numerous bombing raids. Excellent work was also done by the Thames Patrol, and various coast patrols had a history of exciting achievements in the anti-submarine campaign. One naval aeroplane, for example, is reported to have swooped on a U boat and driven it on a mud-bank, where it was afterwards captured by a patrol ship.

Owing, however, to want of high-powered engines and machines of superior petrol and bomb carrying power, the Naval Wing failed to develop its early plan of raiding enemy home bases. No raids of naval importance were made after the futile expedition to Zeppelin centres in Schleswig-Holstein on March 25th, 1915. Apparently the policy of Mr. Arthur Balfour and Admiral Jackson differed in the matter of naval air development from that of Mr. Winston Churchill, Prince Louis of Battenberg, and Lord Fisher. Not until Sir John Jellicoe became First Sea Lord was there any definite evidence that the problem of winning the command of the air over the North Sea was being solved energetically by the Board of Admiralty.

Meanwhile, a certain aerial activity was maintained in the Eastern Mediterranean, by means of obsolete, slow seaplane-carriers and machines of inadequate capacity and engine power. On April 14th, 1916, Constantinople was bombed by three naval pilots, who made a round journey of three hundred miles, and another naval pilot raided Adrianople and attacked the enemy's vital railway communications between Germany and Turkey. Had the machines been powerfully engined and capable of carrying each two hundredweights of bombs, this operation against the Berlin-Bagdad line would have been well worth continuing with great energy, in aid of the Russians on the

BRINGING ORDER AND BEAUTY INTO WILDERNESS AND WASTE.
Anti-aircraft guns were stationed at several spots in London where improvements had not proceeded beyond demolition of houses formerly occupying the site. The men at one such station occupied their leisure in making a rock-garden from what was only a waste heap of rubble and broken masonry.

Erzerum front and the British on the Kut-el-Amara front. But after April nothing more was done in the matter for eight months. Only in December, 1916, was the enemy's vital link line again attacked by the Naval Wing, and a bridge below Adrianople, crossing the Maritza River, bombed so that one of the arches was destroyed. Clearly some wing-commander or squadron-commander in the Eastern Mediterranean saw how General Townshend and his division might have been saved, by im-

Aircraft in the South-East peding south of Adrianople the flow of German and Austrian munitions into Asiatic Turkey. But the material available on the spot was not of the highly developed quality needed for maintaining a heavy aerial bombardment on the Berlin-Bagdad line.

In the stand of General Townshend's division at Kut-el-Amara, and in the efforts made to raise the siege by Sir Percy Lake and General Aylmer, pilots of the Royal Naval Air Service played a picturesque and romantic part.

SEAPLANE STARTING FROM ITS PARENT SHIP.
In the Battle of Jutland, Flight-Lieutenant Rutland proved the utility of seaplane work in naval fighting, he being enabled to send clear reports from a range of 3,000 yards.

Their machines, like those of the Royal Flying Corps pilots in Mesopotamia, were of an inferior type. Two German airmen on modern Fokkers inflicted considerable losses on the British flyers, whose machines lacked speed and climbing power. But despite these disadvantages, which were similar to those under which British aviators in France and Flanders laboured, the airmen in Mesopotamia made a gallant attempt to supply and feed the besieged garrison of Kut. Seaplanes rising from the Tigris and aeroplanes flying over the sand dropped fishing-nets, tools, and technical instruments into the Kut camp. Then, when the garrison began to run seriously short of food, the naval and military pilots dropped, in the course of one hundred and seventy journeys, eight tons of flour, salt, tea, and other supplies into the hungry and encircled river fortress. In this operation the Fokkers only destroyed two British machines, though Sir Percy Lake remarked that the German machines were " of superior speed and fighting capacity." It was not until August, 1916, that British pilots on the Tigris obtained machines enabling them to cope with the Fokker airmen.

Seaplanes in Palestine

Months after Kut had fallen and the advance of the Russian Army of the Caucasus had been stayed, attempts were made by British naval airmen to damage the Turkish lines of communication in another direction. Between August 25th and 29th a series of attacks and reconnaissances upon enemy railways in Palestine was carried out by a seaplane squadron. But the machines

PREPARING A GERMAN SEAPLANE FOR FLIGHT.
During 1916, German seaplanes raided England on eleven occasions, once even penetrating as far as London. No damage of military importance was however effected by these raids.

used had such small climbing power that the low Palestine mountains were found difficult to surmount. Nevertheless, damage was wrought on the track and rolling-stock of an important junction, and the railway-station at Homs, north of Damascus, was reached and bombarded. In the same month British naval aircraft assailed the Bulgar lines above Kavalla, broke down a railway bridge, smashed trucks and carriages, and set on fire the headquarters of the 10th Bulgar Division. Along the Seres-Drama line a dramatic situation was produced. The Bulgar troops were bombed out of their billets, and scattered in such panic that the camp was abandoned. All these expeditions, however, only worried the Turk, the Bulgar, and the Teuton transport officer. No decisive military effect was produced.

Farther reaching, though less spectacular, was the work performed in Eastern France by the Third Wing of the

SALVAGE OF A DAMAGED RUSSIAN SEAPLANE.
Comparatively little was heard of the Russian Air Service, but it was known nevertheless to have done good work. In August, 1916, Russian seaplanes bombarded Varna with considerable effect.

TRANSPORT OF AN AEROPLANE IN FLANDERS.
Aircraft was not overlooked when the Belgian Army was reconstituted behind the lines in Flanders, and under Major van Crombrugghe the Belgian Flying Corps became highly efficient.

R.N.A.S. This was the largest British naval aerial unit in existence, and in July, 1916, it was sent in answer to a request for assistance from the military authorities of France. The French commander had wisely determined to strike hard and persistently at the main source of all the enemy's strength—at the blast furnaces and steel-making works of Lorraine, from which much of the steel used by German naval and military forces was obtained. On July 30th a small force of naval planes co-operated with the French squadron in bombing the German benzine stores at Mülheim, on the Rhine. On August 10th the wing in Flanders sent five machines against a Zeppelin

GERMAN FLYING MACHINES THAT PASSED UNINJURED INTO FRENCH POSSESSION

Aeroplane brought down intact by Sergeant Flachaire near the German lines. It was immediately covered with brushwood to hide it from the enemy's observers, who would have turned their artillery on to it, the

Germans having strict orders to destroy, if possible, all machines brought down uninjured. Right: A Fokker, brought down in the French lines, packed up for removal to the rear.

shed near Brussels, and at a height of only two hundred feet the shed was hit eight times and set on fire. The Flanders Wing was apparently still undermanned and undermachined for the raiding work it had been carrying out for nearly two years; for the day after the Brussels raid the Royal Flying Corps took up the task of long-distance raiding, and with sixty-eight machines reached Namur, Mons, and Busigny, as well as the Zeppelin sheds at Brussels.

Another little naval raid on Namur was at last followed, on October 13th, 1916, by more strenuous action by the Third Naval Wing in Eastern France. In co-operation with French and American airmen, the British pilots and bomb-droppers crossed the Rhine and ascended the Neckar to the town of Oberndorf, where the Mauser rifle factory was established. According to foreign report, the squadron

set out from the recovered part of Alsace, and after a flight of nearly one hundred miles loosed a hundred and thirty hundredweights of high-explosive bombs upon the Mauser Works. The great main building was considerably shattered and set on fire, the damage done being estimated at some hundreds of thousands of pounds. On the return journey the squadrons had to fight a series of hard battles, in which the Germans lost eight machines, the French five, and the British three.

In November, 1916, the Third Naval Wing, still co-operating with powerful French bombarding squadrons, made a series of important nocturnal raids on the blast furnaces and shell-making works in the Sarre area of Lorraine. In particular there was one foundry distinguished for producing special steel for German naval guns. When the British naval airmen finished their work of

PROOFS OF THE SKILL AND INTREPIDITY OF THE ALLIED FLYING CORPS.

British soldiers examining a German aeroplane captured, almost uninjured, in Artois; the officers were taken prisoner. Right: Many war trophies were placed on exhibition in the courtyard of the Hotel des Invalides in

Paris, with a view to stimulating the patriotic pride of the public in the achievements of the Army. They included one of the German Fokkers which had been brought down by French airmen.

unloading a ton of high explosive, there were only two chimneys more or less intact in the great hostile establishment, and it was reckoned that months would elapse before steel could again be made in considerable quantity in that corner of the Sarre valley. The French, however, were at this time using upon the blast furnaces around Metz bombing machines that carried each one-sixth of a ton of high-explosive missiles, and though British naval pilots also did some notably good work, they do not appear to have been provided with planes of such capacity as the alert French authorities had obtained.

Ocean-going seaplanes　　Yet the British Naval Wing at home, which absorbed seventy-five per cent. of the personnel of the flying section of the Navy, was then progressing in a remarkable manner in the development of its instruments. Along the British coast were patrol stations, commanded by officers of inventive mind. These officers had been working for a long time on the problem of the ocean-going seaplane—a machine capable of crossing the Atlantic, and therefore capable of long endurance in any combat with Zeppelins for mastery of the air over the North Sea and the Baltic. Towards the end of 1916 it was reported that the ocean-going British seaplane was in existence.

Undoubtedly this pregnant stir of research, experiment, and invention in the once despised and neglected Naval Air Service was accelerated if not directly produced, by the circumstances in which the Battle of Jutland Bank was fought in May, 1916.

The natural consequence of a disturbing succession of disasters to the enemy Zeppelin fleet in May, 1916, was that German airship pilots became a great deal more apprehensive of British naval gun fire.

The production of a super-Zeppelin of greater lifting power and speed was hastened at Leipzig and Friedrichshafen, in order to obtain an instrument of long-distance naval reconnaissance that would not be seriously endangered by the guns of British warships. Having in the meantime taught the enemy caution in his reconnoitring and patrolling flights over the critical theatre of naval operations, the British admirals planned the great sweep to Jutland that led to the first fleet engagement between Great Britain and Germany.

By design, perhaps, Sir John Jellicoe and Sir David Beatty selected for their operation a day of clear weather but low-hanging cloud. The visibility was good enough for gunners to hit at a range of ten miles, but the roof of cloud came so very low over the sea that any Zeppelin attempting to reconnoitre had to descend to within easy range of destruction.

On the other hand, the lowness of the clouds did not interfere with the action of the instrument of aerial reconnaissance that the British Navy was slowly developing. There was still scope for seaplane flights from a carrier-ship, and during the preliminary skirmish in the afternoon of May 31st, 1916, between the British and German light advanced forces, the captain of the Engadine sent up Flight-Lieutenant Rutland and an observer, and by bold and skilful manœuvring within close range of the fire of

four hostile light cruisers the pilot discovered the enemy's position and part of his strength, and by wireless message sent the information to the admiral commanding the Cruiser Fleet. Unfortunately, the British seaplanes and their carrier then seem to have disappeared from the front of the conflict. This event, which may have largely contributed to the indecisiveness of the later general engagement, was due to the fact that the authorities responsible for the construction of the seaplane-carriers lacked strategical foresight.

What was needed was a number of seaplane-carriers with a speed at least as high as that of the best British light cruiser and destroyer leader. The carriers should have been always in the van of the battle-cruisers and battleships, and they should have existed in such numbers as would have enabled one or more seaplanes to keep within sight of the enemy battle-cruiser squadron, and search for the enemy battleship divisions. The quality of machines available in Great Britain was adequate to this task, but there does not seem to have been a carrier-ship of modern type. All that the old, slow Engadine could do was to show what far-reaching possibilities of aerial reconnaissance and guidance existed, and then to drop far behind destroyers, cruisers, battle-cruisers, and battleships—a straggler from the glorious battle-line.

There are grounds for supposing that the enemy admiral had half a dozen Zeppelins flung out over the North Sea, on reconnaissance work and on piloting duties for the German submarines that waited in ambush by Little Fisher Bank. But the thick blanket of cloud between sky and sea prevented the German airships from carrying out the highly important work for which they had always been designed.

The day thus closed, from the aerial point of view, with a slight undeveloped advantage on the British side. The heavier-than-air seaplane had proved its worth under conditions in which the lighter-than-air airship was discomfited. But in the following night and the following

LORD COWDRAY, THE FIRST AIR MINISTER.
[Elliott & Fry.]
When the Air Board was reorganised into a great Air Ministry at the beginning of 1917, Lord Cowdray, the most successful of British engineers, was appointed the first British Air Minister.

morning the Zeppelin squadrons in turn proved their worth, and unlike the solitary British seaplane on a slow carrier-ship, developed their advantage in a manner that told upon the general course of the battle. While Admiral Scheer's hammered and scattered squadrons were endeavouring to find a path of safe return to port, and incurring heavy losses as they blindly ventured within the field of action of British destroyer flotillas, the Zeppelins discovered, soon after daybreak, the exact　**Zeppelins as** position of the British Grand Fleet and the　**"eyes"** British Cruiser Fleet. Guided by wireless messages from his aerial pilots, Scheer drew southward round the flank of the British line of battle, and reached the protection of his mined waters without any further attack from the battle squadrons of Great Britain. There can be little doubt that on June 1st, 1916, the possession of either Zeppelins or of ocean-going seaplanes in very fast carrier-ships would have enabled Sir John Jellicoe to accomplish practically the entire destruction of the enemy force. As it was, the enemy escaped, and the damage done to him, though severe, was so inconclusive that in about three months time he was ready for action again, and more adventurous than ever he had been. In clear weather, on August 19th, 1916, the German High Sea Fleet steamed towards the British shore. It was not a battle-cruiser raid, as on former occasions, but a fleet movement in force, directed apparently against the British Cruiser Fleet under Sir David Beatty. The design was to provoke Sir David to accept battle or allow the British coast to be insulted, before the British battle divisions under Sir John Jellicoe could again close upon the German battle divisions. The master instrument of this great manœuvre was a squadron of Zeppelins, disposed so as to command an immense field of vision over all the waters in which British forces could collect. The Zeppelins' pilots, just as the preliminary skirmish of light cruisers opened, were thus able to perceive the Grand Fleet approaching to co-operate with the Cruiser Fleet. Thereupon Admiral Scheer broke off the action and, with ample time for withdrawal, returned to his far-distant base.

Ministry of Munitions intervenes   Twice had the naval airships of Germany saved the High Sea Fleet from destruction. It was patent, therefore, that the British Fleet would also manœuvre at a continually serious disadvantage unless it obtained—and obtained quickly—instruments of long-distance aerial reconnaissance equal to those possessed by the enemy. Sir John Jellicoe moved strongly in the matter, and the urgency and scope of his aerial requirements formed possibly the reason of the great dispute over the sharing of available aero-motors and other material between the representatives of the Military and Naval Wings on the Air Board. The awakened Navy wanted everything it had ordered in advance or had any right to acquire, while the equally awakened Army, fighting for a grand decision on the Somme, instantly required everything within reach that the Royal Aircraft Factory had neglected to prepare for it in the winter of 1915.

The upshot of this rather stubborn struggle between the Air Services was not unhappy, though it led to the intervention of the Ministry of Munitions as umpire and universal provider to both wings. In January, 1917, after thirty months of war, Great Britain became fully roused to the supreme task of winning the permanent command of the air over both land and sea. Her large engineering and manufacturing resources, her fund of designing genius, and her inexhaustible material resources, domestic and imported, were at last placed fully at the disposal of men capable of constructing super-Zeppelins and ocean-going seaplanes. The prospect was already full of promise when Sir John Jellicoe left the Grand Fleet in order to become First Sea Lord. And into his new task he threw himself with all the energy and lucidity of his vigorous mind. What development of the Naval Wing he promoted, with the help of his new Air Lord, Commodore Paine, will be discussed in a later chapter on aerial matters.

WITH BRITISH SEAPLANES IN ASIA AND AFRICA.

In the stand of General Townshend's division at Kut-el-Amara, and in the efforts made to raise the siege by Sir Percy Lake and General Aylmer, pilots of the Royal Naval Air Service played a serviceable part. The low sandy shore seen here formed a capital base for the seaplanes, to which the shallow draught monitors afforded necessary protection. Above: Seaplane, sent to observe the effect of the shell fire from the monitors Severn and Mersey on the German cruiser Königsberg, concealed up the Rufiji River in Africa, " taxi-ing " back to its parent ship.

[*Bassano*

Open ward at a Birmingham hospital for soldiers—1st Southern General Hospital—where the men could receive the full curative benefit of the air.

[*Bassano.*

Where wounded soldiers recuperated.   Summer scene on the terrace of one of the great London hospitals.   Above : Major-General Lord Lovat, at the East Suffolk Ipswich Hospital, presenting the Military Medal to Private Green for heroic work at Arras.

WHERE WOUNDED SOLDIERS WERE NURSED BACK TO HEALTH.

CHAPTER CLXI.

HOW THE WOUNDED WERE BROUGHT HOME.

By Basil Clarke.

EDITORIAL NOTE.—The magnitude attained by the British Army in France was such that the treatment of the casualties became a matter of passionately intimate concern to almost every house and cottage in the Empire. It is characteristic of men of our race to be as silent about their sufferings as about their deeds, and the result was that the endurance of the wounded and the devotion of those who tended them seemed likely to remain generally unknown. The Editors of THE GREAT WAR, recognising that the treatment of the wounded was an integral subject of their history, resolved to secure an authentic record of the work from one of their war correspondents, and thus Mr. Basil Clarke, provided with proper credentials and assisted by the cordial co-operation of the military authorities, went to an advanced trench on the Western Front, and, following the regimental stretcher-bearers to the first case to which they were called, he accompanied a casualty through every stage of the journey from the battlefield to the quayside in England. This chapter contains his story, the narrative method adopted giving it a valuable actuality. The Editors wish it to be understood that every incident is true and that the story is an essential part of the history of the war.

"S tretcher - bearers! STRETCHER - BEARERS! STRETCHER-BEARERS!"

The call came faintly at first from somewhere down the trench, far away to the right of us; but other voices took it up and passed it along. Nearer and nearer it came, from voice to voice, some high, some low, till you could see the soldier that shouted it last—a lusty fellow whose ruddy face and green "tin hat" peeped above the rim of the next shell-hole. There, with face towards us and a yellow, muddy hand encircling his mouth for a megaphone, he passed on the words in a deep bass bray; for just as all men in a village community will stop what they are doing to give a hand in putting out a fire, so will men in a trench help, as a point of honour, to pass on the word for the ambulance men. It is one of the unwritten laws—and who knows but that it may be his own turn to need them next!

The company stretcher-bearers were at tea at the moment in a trench dug-out near me. A corporal pulled aside the sheet of flapping, mud-stained flannel which served the double purpose of door and "gas-stop" to the dug-out, and shouted in the words "Bearers—right!" Tea was forgotten. One man alone lingered to lift a petrol-can of boiling water from a crackling fire of box-wood, and then he, too, scrambled up the steps of the dug-out. The first man up had seized one of the light stretchers of wooden poles and canvas that stood upright near the dug-out door. "Stretcher-bearers—right!" he shouted, and away to the right they went, six of them, splashing along the trench.

HONOURABLE DISTINCTION FOR GALLANT MEN.

Great Britain was later than her allies in granting a distinctive badge to disabled soldiers who returned to civil life. In 1916 this badge was issued to men who had been discharged disabled.

"Trench" is perhaps something of an overstatement. It had been a trench when the Germans made it—and a very good one, too. But only four days earlier it had been taken from them after weeks of consistent shelling, and now, what with rain and with shell damage, it was a long series of mud-holes joined together, sometimes by hummocks of earth, sometimes by short lengths of trench, indifferently clear. The part from which we started had been put to rights again—or "consolidated," as the official communiqués express it.

The walls had been rebuilt and trued, a parapet had been superimposed upon the enemy's old parados; there were even duck-boards underfoot to walk upon—and duck-boards are the last word in trench comfort. But before the stretcher-bearers had gone very far—with me plodding slowly behind—the trench reverted once more to its old damaged state as when captured, and to get along it became as hard travelling as any I have known. In places you splashed through a foot of water, otter-hunting fashion; in other places you had to scale hummocks of slimy clay; in others you went through quicksands of viscous, treacle-like fluid that sucked the very boots from one's feet. Many a soldier has come out of one of those mud-pools minus boots, stockings, and puttees.

I myself, who had nightly a battle royal with my top boots to get them off, found them sucked off by that mud as easily as though they had been gripped in the finest bootjack ever invented. The trouble with these holes was to get past them and yet to retain one's foot-wear. But to stand still was to be lost, stuck fast, perhaps

[British official photograph.

HOMEWARD-BOUND : "GOOD LUCK! GOOD-BYE!"
Warm friendships were made in the military hospitals abroad, and there were great leave-takings when the fortunate wounded, passed for home, left their less badly wounded comrades and started homewards.

[British official photograph.

INDIANS CARRYING THEIR WOUNDED OFFICER.
The devotion of our Indian soldiers to their officers in France was touching; partly, perhaps, because they alone among all those around were familiar with their language and their customs.

even to die, as more than one poor lad has done up on those bleak, muddy slopes of the Somme.

The hundred and fifty yards we went seemed to me one hundred and fifty miles. I arrived a very bad last—as the racing reports might express it—and only just in time to see the six stretcher-bearers putting the finishing touches to the " first-aid " dressing which they had been applying to one Private John Chatterton Hollinwood Oldham, of the Cottonopolis Regiment. The corporal was talking as he bound up the wounded limb—quietly " strafing " the injured one. " Why the divvle you fellows won't keep your field-dressin' in its right place fair beats me. You have a special pocket made in your tunic linin' for it ; you have a nice clean dressin' served out to you in a waterproof bag, and all that's asked of you is that you should keep it in that special pocket, and s'elp me if there's one of you as 'll keep it there ! Is yer 'ed comfy, mate ? Take a pull outen my bottle an' a bit of a breather 'fore we starts to yank yer down to the aid post."

Oldham used his interval of rest to tell us how a sniper had caught him. " Copped me fair, 'e did," he said. " My

own fault, too. Ah see'd the blighter earlier this morning, workin' out on 'is belly along the brow of th' hill, and had a pop at 'im with my rifle. Missed 'is bloomin' 'ead by about a foot. Saw the spit of my bullet aside his left ear. 'E 'opped it quick. But arter that Ah forgets all about 'im, never thinkin' as 'e'd crawl out for another go at me. As Ah were crossin' that bit o' open ground about five minutes back 'e pops me one over, fair in the thigh. Ah reckon summut's bust from th' feel on it. Do you think as it's a ' Blighty ' one, corp'ral ? "

" Shouldn't be surprised," said the corporal, pretending to be cross. " Beats me why some o' you lads comes 'ere without your mothers. Didn't ye see the notice along that open patch, tellin' **First stage of the** you to ' 'ware snipers ' ? Ah put it up **journey** mysen on that very place an hour after Gummy' Arrison were 'it in th' back on t' same bit o' land. Well, time to be off. Lie easy, mate, an' we'll 'ave you down in a couple o' shakes. Ready, lads ! "

The bearers, who had been sitting on their haunches on the side of a low hummock of clay, slid down it on their heels. One of them had lit a cigarette during the rest. He now took it from his mouth, and without a word stuck it in the mouth of the patient, which opened for it as readily as that of a young chick for food. " Thanks, matey," he said simply. " Ready ? Lift ! " Two men held the stretcher-handles. Two men walked at the sides with hands on the stretcher-bars, steadying it and taking the weight whenever one of the carriers stumbled—a frequent event. One man walked in front, picking out the best of the track—or, rather, the least difficult of the track. The other walked behind.

How those men ever got that stretcher and its heavy load over the places they did is to this day beyond me. With no further load than a gas-mask and a walking-stick, I had trouble enough myself. At times we came to places where all six men had to give a hand. The poor lad on the stretcher was bemoaning the trouble he was giving. " Can't Ah get out an' walk a bit ? " he asked plaintively. " One o' you gimme a hand an' Ah'll hobble a bit ! " " You howd yer 'ush, my lad ! " was all the corporal answered him ; and he held it. For his leg was paining badly. I could see him opening and shutting his eyes every now and again with pain. Once he seemed to lose consciousness ; then he opened his eyes again, but only for an instant. It was to say : " That sniper feller Fritz 'ad a round fat face an' spectacles. You'll 'appen to know 'im if ever you sees 'im messin' about again on the ridge." He was quiet for a minute, then he added : " If you do, ony o' you chaps, you might let 'im know as Ah'm not 'arf done for yet." Then he was quiet, his eyes remaining shut.

We came at last to a bit of quaggy road, which one man, by making a dash as over thin ice, might possibly have got through ; for six men and a stretcher this was impossible. The corporal called a halt, and himself tried the place. " It's no go, lads," he said, scrambling back out of the bog. " We'll have to go outside. But bide a bit, boys ; Ah'll make a bit of a look round." He walked on and shouted warily to a solitary figure with a rifle who was standing thirty yards farther on, upon an island of clay built up in a little sea of water and mud. " All quiet, mate ? " he asked.

Held up by snipers

" Nowt but a few shells going," came the answer. " A few snipers were out earlier, but they've 'opped it."

" Think we'll be all right to take this fellow outside ? He's pretty bad."

" You *might*," said the other, rather grudgingly, as he looked up at the sky. " Light's beginning to get yeller, and it's agen the snipers. You *might* be all right."

The corporal stood in thought for a moment. " Ah'll just 'op out of the trench an' 'ave a look round." And with that the cool fellow climbed up the side of the trench remains and, pivoting round on his stomach at the top, lay with his gaze towards the enemy trenches. Pulling his iron helmet low down over his eyes, he looked intently from under the rim. He had been there perhaps a minute, when he suddenly slid headfirst down the trench side— which, among its many other imperfections, sloped at this point instead of falling perpendicularly. And at that very moment there was a whistle of bullets just over the trench parapet and shots rang out from the German trenches, less

than a hundred yards to the east. The corporal struggled to his feet, muddy but unhurt.

He plodded back to his comrades. " Can't be done yet, boys," he said coolly. " We'll have to wait. Sorry, sonny," he added, turning to the man on the stretcher. " Fritz has not drawn off yet. We'll have to keep you 'ere till it's a bit darker." He eased the patient's position on the stretcher, saying : " Can'st stick it a bit ? Art a all reet ? " 'The lad shivered. " Ay, tha't cold." And with that the corporal took off his own greatcoat and spread it over the boy on the stretcher.

There, in the cold light of the ebbing day, we waited. The sun sank grudgingly and yellowly behind us, throwing a cold, brassy sheen on to the yellow clay that encompassed us all about. The colder wind of evening came. You could hear the faint swish of it over the trench-tops, and fitful gusts came along the trench—strong enough to make

"BLIGHTY JUNCTION." A RED CROSS TRAIN LEAVING FOR THE COAST. *[British official photograph.*

Walking cases arriving at a hospital train and (above) British wounded in a Red Cross train in France. Casualty clearing stations were usually established near a railway so that the more serious cases, as soon as they were in a condition to be moved, could be transferred easily to hospital trains for conveyance to hospitals of a more permanent nature where they could receive the fullest attention.

BACKWATERS OF WAR: RECEIVING PATIENTS ON A RED CROSS BARGE. *[British official photograph.*

The wonderful system of waterways in France proved of incalculable utility in the war, and that not only for the transport of munitions and attacking enemy positions in low-lying districts such as those below

Péronne. On many of them hospital barges were placed where wounded were received and moved to the rear with a minimum of discomfort from vibration on the painful journey to hospital rest.

little frills and ruffles on the surface of the water and mud. The patient and his stretcher had been laid on a strip of ledge on the western wall of the trench—a bit of the old German fire-step that had somehow escaped destruction. His eyes were shut. Once his lips moved. His mind was evidently wandering back to his native Lancashire, and to his work on the cotton. "It's bloomin' cold i' this 'ere mill!" he said dreamily

The sun sank between two stunted and shell-shattered trees. I watched it through a gap in the back of the

Under cover of twilight

trenches. Yellows and reds smeared the sky-line in a gradually lessening patch, which at last faded out. The stunted trees went with them. I was chattering with cold. My feet seemed frozen—as painful as if they had been squashed under a cart-wheel. Without warning, a German shell whined through the air over our heads and dropped somewhere in the village behind us. It was the first of many. "That's Fritz beginning his evening 'strafe'!" said the corporal. "Come on, lads. Time to get a move on!"

The patient was silent and motionless on his stretcher. The corporal scrambled again up the side of the trench, and again lay on his stomach on the top. Two minutes or so he waited, and then he stood upright. A bullet might have pinked him at any moment. But none came. Instead another shell wailed through the air and on to the village below. We heard the solemn "crump" of it as it exploded. "Now, boys," he said, "'ave yer gas-masks ready. We don't want to be messed up fiddlin' for them things when a 'stinker' comes over." Then he looked over his men, and said: "Stuffy, you come along by me up 'ere, and the other lads will heave the stretcher up to us."

"Stuffy," without a word, scrambled up the trench wall

and stood by the corporal. The other four between them lifted the stretcher from its ledge and high above their heads. The corporal and "Stuffy" took the handles from their uplifted hands and bore the weight of the stretcher till two of the lifters had scrambled up. "You others had best go by the trench," said the corporal. "No use a whole harmy corps walkin' about in the open. Meet you at the 'aid post.'" And with that the four of them and their burden moved on over open ground in full view of the enemy, relying on their luck and the twilight to preserve them. Every day and every night those plucky regimental stretcher-bearers do the like.

The trench opened at length on to a narrow road cut through a hill, and called the Waggon Road. By this road you reached the village below—the newly-captured village of Beaumont-Hamel. It was a village no longer. Every building had been razed flat by shell fire, and such habitations as remained were old German dug-outs underground. At the entrance to one of these was a rough signboard which, in white letters on a black ground, proclaimed the name, "MannheimVillas." A pennant, which in daylight showed its colours red and white, fluttered above the signboard as the mark of an ambulance-station.

Regimental aid post

This was the "regimental aid post." Every regiment has one or more just behind the line at some spot which is "sheltered." Sheltered is largely a figure of speech, however, for though the regimental aid post is, perhaps, out of the line of direct rifle fire from the enemy trenches, it is in the way of all the shells that are going. Shells were dropping now about Mannheim Villas, and dropping so unpleasantly close that I, for one, was only too glad to leave the upper earth for the cover of a dug-out.

You entered Mannheim Villas by a flight of wooden steps.

(twenty or so), sloping downwards steeply from Waggon Road towards the hill out of which the road was cut. The dug-out ran under the hill parallel to the road, and at intervals there were stairs and flue-holes leading upwards from it to the road, and meeting it at right angles. The main passage of the dug-out must have been nearly fifty yards long, but it was not all on one level, and one ascended and descended stairs in most perplexing fashion.

Our patient was lying in the " dressing-room " at the foot of the first flight of steps from the road. The four stretcher-bearers were sitting on the floor breathing heavily. Here the dug-out was about ten feet wide and seven feet high, and lined throughout with stout planks. Vertical beams supported the roof, as in a coal-pit. A lamp and several extra candles, lit as soon as the patient had arrived, shed a not too bright light over the curious scene. To the right, at the foot of the steps, was the dressers' table, covered with a spotless white cloth, on which lay dressings and lotions, basins, swabs, scissors, and all the rest of a surgeon's simpler accessories. In a canvas sling in the roof overhead were splints of all shapes —crooked splints for arms, straight splints for legs, splints in all sorts of fantastic shapes to suit any injury, and all ready to the dresser's hand. Warmth came from the fire under a great cooking-copper built in with cement.

In the "dressing-room"

A crowd of muddy R.A.M.C. men and regimental stretcher-bearers looked on as the dressing was done, for beyond this room were their quarters, and, with the shells flying outside, everyone who had no work out of doors was underground. The landing of the shells sent a curious, shivering shock through the dug-out, but, thanks to its depth and solidity, they did no great harm. Shrapnel and flying shell fragments could find no way down here unless they came down the stairway, and that would need a specially unlucky shot.

No one took the slightest notice of the shells. I watched the faces, thrown into fierce lights and shadows by the flickering illuminants, and as " crump " followed " crump " outside not an eyelid flicked. I doubt whether the men were even conscious of the noise. Night after night of shelling had made them disregard it.

Trench-made "pals"

The patient's dressing was now finished, and his stretcher was put near the stove so that he might get warm before going off on the next stage of his journey. As he lay there, a young mud-stained soldier came running in a great hurry down the steps of the dug-out. He did not notice the stretcher in the shadows near the boiler. " Has Private Oldham gone off yet ? " he gasped. And, without waiting for an answer, he added breathlessly : " Is 'e bad ? Where's he going to ? What's his——" Seeing several eyes upon him, looking as though for an explanation of his eagerness, he explained as follows : " Oh, there's nowt amiss, but I'm 'is pal, you see, an' I thowt I might 'appen to see 'im afore 'e left." He paused for breath, and went on : " Th' lieutenant let me come down. Sent me with a message to the colonel, 'e did, so as I might drop in at the aid post 'ere on my way." Another pause, an then : " You see, I didna know as he were wounded till quarter of an hour ago. Th' chaps told me, an' I went to th' lieutenant right away " Another pause. " You see, I'm 'is pal ! "

The lad could not have been more than twenty, and he

READY AND WAITING TO ASSIST THE WOUNDED AT A BASE IN FRANCE.
Squadron of British Army Red Cross motor-ambulance cars at a well-sheltered French base waiting for their complements of wounded passengers to take them a stage farther on the road to " Blighty." The devotion to duty, the untiring keenness in their work shown by the motor-drivers and the men in attendance on the ambulance cars called forth much commendation from all those who came in contact with them.

stood there in all his mud, with the lamp-light glinting into his bright eyes, coming ever back to that simple soldier formula, "I'm 'is pal!" as though in those mystic words lay explanation enough for any queer thing a soldier lad might do concerning another. And in those simple words lies, as every soldier knows, explanation enough for many a risk, many a kindness, many a sacrifice, many a heroism between one soldier and another. There is no truer, cleaner thing in all life than these "palships" of the trenches.

The lad could see that his explanation satisfied everybody—for all of them were soldiers, and knew—and he began his questions again. "Was 'e bad? 'Ow long's 'e been gone? Where's 'e gone to?" The men grinned. The boy looked round to try to see where the joke lay. A voice came at that moment from the shadows near the boiler—a voice singularly sturdy and strong. "'E ain't gone nowheres, 'Arry Droilesden," it said. "'E's 'ere!"

The voice was too well known. The boy went along the dug-out in a few quick strides. Having reached his chum's stretcher, he looked at it and his friend stolidly for a moment, and then came the following conversation:

"'Ello, Jack!"

"'Ello, 'Arry!" (Long pause).

"You been and cotched one?"

"Ay! Ah cotched one all reet."

"You 'ave an' all? Is it a bad 'un?"

"Oh, just tidy like."

That was all. From that moment John Oldham might have been to Harry Droilesden the least interesting person or thing in all the Somme battlefield. They did not talk; they did not even look at one another. After standing for some time idly looking round the dug-out, Harry sat down on the ground near John's stretcher. Now they will talk, thought I. But no. Harry had merely sat, it seemed, the better to scrape mud from his puttees with the jackknife which he now produced for that purpose. Possibly they spoke later. I don't know. For an R.A.M.C. captain took me away at that moment to be shown over the dug-out. I would rather have stood in my corner keeping a quiet eye on the strange meeting of Harry and John.

We went down another flight of steps and thus into the main tunnel of the dug-out. Here, as "upstairs," the walls were solid timber-lined. There were lamps at intervals. Men were lying on the ground, some of them writing, some card-playing, some reading. We stepped over outstretched legs as we walked along. Then the tunnel ascended by ten or twelve steps and became rather wider. Here were a number of men lying and standing in the neighbourhood of a big brazier filled with glowing coals. The smoke, or rather some of it, left the dug-out up a long sloping shaft to the right, which in the dug-out's German days had been an extra entrance. But a shell had upset the wooden staircase, and the passage had been remade into a chimney and ventilating shaft. Farther along the tunnel in a little cubicle on the left no bigger than a good-sized packing-case were three officers, two of whom were playing piquet while the third looked

In the surgeons' dug-out

on. A candle stuck on the lid of a cigarette-tin was their only lighting. These were "regimental surgeons," off duty. The Royal Army Medical Corps supplies one or more surgeons to each battalion to be "attached" to that battalion. These officers in turn pick out a number of men from their battalion and train them in first-aid, stretcher drill, and the care of wounded. These bearers go into trenches with their battalions and follow them into action. They have all the risks of war and few of the joys of fighting, their duty being merely to collect the wounded from the trench or the battlefield as the case may be, and to get them as far as the regimental aid post. The stretcher is the most usual means of transport if the patient cannot walk, but many a wounded man is brought to the regimental aid post on the back of a stretcher-bearer or a regimental pal.

From trench to hospital

I noticed at the aid post that some of the bearers were of the R.A.M.C., while others wore regimental badges. It was explained to me that the aid post is the point at which the R.A.M.C. and the regiments in the line link up, for at the aid post the wounded pass definitely from their regiment—which knows them no more until they are cured—into the hands of the R.A.M.C., who are responsible for all future treatment. In calm times the R.A.M.C. do not go nearer the line than the aid post, but when any fighting is going on they go forward to help the regimental medical workers. Thus, at all stormy times, the R.A.M.C. are sharers in whatever risk is going at the moment, and the number of men of this valiant corps who have lost their lives is testimony enough to what these risks may be.

The officers are no safer than the privates. For though it is an order that medical officers must expose themselves as little as possible, they may be called up into the line at any moment to deal with an urgent case that cannot be moved without surgical treatment.

ON THE ROAD TO RECOVERY.
Indians who were wounded at the front being conveyed in a Canadian Women's Motor Ambulance to the Convalescent Home at New Milton, in the health-giving neighbourhood of Christchurch, Hampshire.

Every one of the surgeons in that aid post was well acquainted with the trenches at their worst, and, for that matter, the aid post itself was anything but a haven of safety. The hurtling shells outside reminded one of that.

We arrived back at the dressing-room of the dug-out and found John Oldham ready for moving. A runner had been sent to the "motor-car station" to tell them to send a car forward to the motor control, and the patient was to be carried down to the control to meet it. For it was impossible to bring a motor-car so far forward as the aid post. The road from it was no more than a rough path, made with bricks and planks across a wilderness of shell-holes and hummocks. The battered houses of the village had yielded the materials.

We set off, and I noticed with misgivings new shell-holes right alongside the track on which we were to walk. They had not been there half an hour earlier when we passed along the track—of that I was certain. It was dark now—pitch dark save when star-shells rose slowly into the sky from the German lines behind us, throwing for a few seconds a pale, sickly whiteness over a great circle of earth.

An eerie thing it was to walk here in the dark, picking your way by tapping with your stick the broken bricks of which the road was made ; then, suddenly, to find the whole world lit up as with a ghostly moonlight. Each light stayed only long enough to reveal the grim signs of war immediately about you. It might **Meeting the** be only the stretcher-bearers whom you **ambulance** noticed in their queer iron helmets—making still queerer shadows—all marching in step, with their stretcher and its silent burden, rocking rhythmically up and down to each step they were taking. Or a flare might disclose to you the barren countryside, all shell-heaps and shell-holes, with here and there a tree disfigured by shell till its few remaining branches, broken short, stood out hideously, like gnarled, rheumatic fingers clawing greedily at an unreachable sky. Once a flare revealed to me what I thought at first were figures of men sleeping out in the open. But their poses were not those of sleep. Legs, top-booted, stretched out sprawlingly from under stiff-looking greatcoats ; arms reached out unnaturally to clasp distant clouts of clay ; and a sleeper's head might lie in a pool of water and trouble him not at all. For they would never wake up, those sleepers. The little round caps they wore showed them to be Germans.

After going about half a mile along that road I saw, some twenty yards off, the red glow of a cigarette upon a face behind it. A man was leaning, smoking, against a motor-ambulance which was hiding under a bank, without lights. This was the nearest point to which a motor could approach the trenches. The driver stood by while the R.A.M.C. men opened its back canvas flaps and lifted the stretcher into the dark body of the vehicle. "Will you ride in the van or do you care for a walk ? " asked my guide, an R.A.M.C. captain. I was anxious not to lose touch with the patient, but on being assured that I should overtake him at the next stopping-place I agreed to walk. One man got in the waggon with the patient, the others stood by to see him start away. "Good-bye, Jack," said one of them to him as the engine began to turn. "Hope it's one that will take you back to 'Blighty.'" The speaker was Harry Droilesden. With this good wish—the best wish you can wish any wounded British Tommy—he drew off and turned once more with the stretcher-bearers towards Beaumont-Hamel—Beaumont-Hamel with its mud and its shell-holes and its star-shells and its dead. For myself **Still within** I was glad to be leaving that war- **shell-range** worn spot and all its dangers behind me.

I said something of the sort to the captain, adding that adventures and dangers and risks were the pleasantest things in the world—when they were well behind you and you were through them. I even found myself stepping out with vigour, under the stimulus of this idea of danger faced and at last successfully passed.

EMBARKING BRITISH WOUNDED ON A HOSPITAL SHIP IN MESOPOTAMIA.
Various causes, chiefly climatic, contributed to aggravate the discomfort of the wounded in Mesopotamia. The Tigris, however, provided a smooth passage for their removal in hospital ships to the base. After General Townshend was forced by starvation to surrender Kut-el-Amara, the Turks, by general consent chivalrous foes, allowed him to send all his wounded by this means to the British lines lower down the river.

MM

SIR ALFRED KEOGH, G.C.B.
Reappointed Director-General of the A.M.S. after the outbreak of the war. He occupied the same position from 1904 to 1910.

"Depends on what your idea of danger is," he replied. "You are not likely to be sniped here or mined or blown to bits with a hand-bomb as you were in Beaumont-Hamel. That's true enough, but there are enough dirty roads to death to be ound in this area to suit my appetite any day. In fact, about this time of day I would feel safer in the trenches than where we are at the moment."

He looked at his watch, the luminous figures of which showed with a faint pale-green light in the darkness. "Yes," he went on. "They usually begin shelling for working-parties about this time, and you never know quite which district they'll pick upon."

He explained that both sides did most of their work in the trenches—such as trench-digging and repairing, dug-out making, wire-laying and so on—at night, and that working-parties were sent up from villages and camps behind the lines to do it. At night, therefore, the Germans began to shell these villages and the roads leading from them in the hope of hitting working-parties while they were assembling or were moving up to the lines along the roads. "They might begin any minute to drop them on this road," he concluded.

I pulled my shrapnel helmet till it hung more protectingly over the nape of my neck, and walked on with my enthusiasm distinctly modified. Five minutes later, as we plodded along that dark, uneven road, the shelling began sure enough. But the spot which the enemy had chosen that evening was not our own immediate neighbourhood but the village to which we were walking and to which John Oldham and his motor-ambulance had gone on. This was the village of Mailly Maillet. It lay a few miles before us, and the German shells on their way to it passed over our heads. We could hear each of them, first behind us, a thin piercing whine which gradually rose in pitch and grew louder as the shell passed overhead, then grew faint again. A second or two later we heard the boom of the shell's explosion in the neighbourhood of Mailly Maillet. Some shells, we noticed, passed over without being followed by any "crump" from the village. We heard the explanation later, which was that a number of them were "duds," having failed to "go off."

Motor control post

I am afraid I loitered just a little on the road to Mailly. One excellent excuse I found for doing so was to turn aside to see the motor control post. It was a ruined homestead by the roadside, the roof of which had been patched up with tarpaulin sheets and the walls with sand-bags. Thus repaired, it made a quite presentable shelter in spite of all the German shells had done. A man with a rifle and a lantern bawled: "Who goes there?" as we approached in the darkness.

An R.A.M.C. sergeant was in command of the place, and with one or two helpers he arranged for a regular service of ambulance-cars between Beaumont-Hamel collecting post and Mailly Maillet behind, and for any extra cars that might be summoned by runner. In a little book which he showed us by lamp-light he had the time of the "runner's" arrival and the time the car was despatched.

Retaliation by six to one

Apparently the most advanced posts of the field ambulance organisation had not attained to the luxury of a telephone service yet. But seeing that even the gunners had all their work cut out to maintain telephone lines over these shell-swept areas, a telephone corps for the R.A.M.C. was probably too much to ask for.

We came out into the darkness of the Mailly road again to find that the British guns had taken up the challenge of the enemy's "strafe" and were replying with rather more energy than the enemy was showing. I gathered, in fact, that the British policy of retaliation at this period of the war was grossly generous, the general idea, both in battery and in trench, being to send back six times the quantity of whatever the Germans "sent over." Thus, if any German infantryman in a playful moment pitched up a hand-grenade to drop into your trench, the scheme of things was promptly to throw six back. Should a German gunnery officer, to gratify a whim or a visitor—as I myself have been gratified by gunnery officers, who as a genus just love to say: "This is how she does it," and then to fire off their biggest gun, much to the shock of that visitor's ears and system

SIR W. A. LANE, BART., C.B.
Distinguished surgeon who was awarded the C.B. for his valuable services to the R.A.M.C. during the war.

SIR B. G. MOYNIHAN, C.B.
Mentioned in despatches for his services in the war, Lieut.-Col. Sir Berkeley Moynihan, of the R.A.M.C. was awarded the C.B. early in 1917.

—well, should a German gunner give way to such a weakness, the British gunner felt in all politeness bound promptly to fire off six shells as big or bigger; and if he felt particularly active that night he would not stop at six times. Another little disinterestedness about the British gunners that struck me was this—that none of them seemed inclined to throw work on "the other fellow." Thus, if six shots

LT.-COL. HENRY DAVY, C.B.
Consulting physician to the Southern Command, who was given the C.B. early in 1917 for his work in the R.A.M.C.

or so were needed to keep up the fair proportion of six shots for one shot sent over by some chance German battery, every single battery that heard the shot seemed to think the task of answering was its own especial prerogative and not that of "the other battery" round the corner.

It is only in this way that I can explain the extraordinary response given to those score or so of German shells that flew over our heads on the Mailly road that night. Every British battery for miles around seemed to have awakened **Advanced dressing-** from its slumbers by those shots, and to **station** be working now like a railway breakdown gang for vigour. Batteries to the right of us, batteries to the left and in front of us, all were barking away in wonderful fashion. The white-blue flashes of field-guns and long guns, the pink flashes of "hows"—as howitzers are called—lit up the earth. To add to the sky effects the Germans, becoming nervous of an attack, perhaps, began to send up star-shells and flares in great quantities.

To stand thus, in a quiet country lane, hearing the amazing barks of many different guns and the whine of many different shells, and to see gnarled and shattered trees jump out at you, black and still and horrible against momentary backgrounds of livid flame, struck me as the most unreal thing I had ever experienced. But for one's ever-conscious knowledge of its full horror and deadly reality, one would have thought it all a product of stage-craft rather than of war.

. . . . . .

From among the mud and ruins of Mailly Maillet—which had suffered from the gun fire of British, French, and German alike in its day—my guide picked out a little house with whitewashed walls, standing alone in a ruined garden. Every window of the house was broken, and curtains of felt or flannel, fastened only at the top, had been hung inside to cover up the wooden window-frames. If you watched these curtains closely you would notice that they flapped with every gun that was fired in the neighbourhood, and with every German shell that arrived in the village. The house had escaped major damage. A chimney-pot or two had been hit, and there were jagged chunks out of the wall in one or two places; but little else. The one great German shell that would have "done for" that place and demolished it entirely had repented at the last moment and failed to explode. It lay on the little back lawn for all eyes to see by day and for all shins to hit by night—a "dud." You fell over it when you walked into the back garden at nights. It was the usual thing, in fact, for your host in that house to say, if you spoke of going out of doors for a breath of air at nights: "Don't fall over the shell."

That house was an "Advanced Dressing-Station," an important link in the medical scheme of things out at the war. Its commanding officer was the captain who had kindly acted as my guide to Beaumont-Hamel, an excellent soul from far New Zealand. "Now, this advanced dressing-station," he had begun, when we entered, "receives wounded from its regimental aid posts at Beaumont and —— But I won't tell you another word till you've had some tea, so you can put that notebook away for a spell and—Wait!"—this last word in a shout. I thought he was joking still, but a rosy-cheeked orderly

put his head inside the door and said, "Yes, sir?" Tea was ordered, and I made the discovery that the orderly's name was Wait.

"Your patient, Oldham, is all safe and sound in the cellars," the captain added, "and will not be going farther for an hour or so, so you can put your mind at rest. He won't escape you."

"Why in the cellars?" I asked.

"Because," he answered, "whenever the village is being shelled, as it was when we came in, all the patients we may have in here at the time are carried down into the cellars. They'll come up again when it's over. Get some tea!"

The captain had poured me out a tin mug of tea from a tin teapot. Toast had come in on a tin plate, and butter lay near at hand in a tin can.

"Milk, orderly!" sang out the captain.

"I'll have to get some more out, sir," said the orderly, "and the—er—the gentleman there is sitting on it."

The upturned wooden case which served me for a chair was rummaged in, and from it was produced a tin labelled "Milk." The orderly jabbed the spike of his jack-knife

WOUNDED SLUNG ABOARD A RED CROSS SHIP IN A BOX-STRETCHER.
Box-stretchers were among the ingenious contrivances utilised for getting the wounded men aboard the hospital ships in a way that should minimise their discomfort. These box-stretchers, it will be observed, were sufficiently large to take two men who were not too badly wounded to be able to sit up.

cleverly through the lid in two places, one on each side, and when he upturned the tin over my tea mug there flowed milk from the lower hole, excellent stuff of the density of cream, while through the upper hole of the tin lid went in air to take the place of the milk that came out. The day of thick and sticky canned milk was over.

Over tea and toast and jam I had time to take stock of the queer room in which we sat. It was the captain's bed-room, sitting-room, dining-room, reception-room, and office all in one. The walls were of plain, whitewashed plaster, and the windows—or rather the window-holes—were covered with sacking, which **An officer's** flapped listlessly in the wind and heavily **quarters** at every gun shot or shell fall outside. The one lamp of the place stood in the middle of our tea-table. Its glass mantle had been broken and repaired —very dexterously, I thought—with surgical sticking-plaster. Its flame threw firm, black shadows of you on to the whitewashed wall behind. Some busy soul had occupied himself in tracing out these shadows of men as they sat at the table, and the wall was covered with charcoal silhouettes. One aquiline portrait was labelled "McMurtrie," another was labelled "Torrance"—former occupants, no doubt, of this primitive little billet. The captain's camp bed lay in a far corner among some boxes of tinned milk, petrol-cans, and other stores. A bright fire of wood flickered in a rusty little grate, sharing about equally with the plastered lamp the duty of lighting the room.

After tea I found John Oldham again. He was in a cellar, with low-arched roof, lying on his back on a stretcher under a blanket, just above the edge of **Good-humour of** which appeared the glowing tip of a **the wounded** cigarette and his face.

"How goes it now?" I asked him. He grinned, and said, in a voice full of mock woefulness: "Well, Ah'm just about as well as can be expected, thank ye, sir."

Other patients lying on their backs on the cellar-flags near him all laughed at this, and I gathered from a friendly corporal that this was the recognised reply of Tommies who, while feeling in pretty good spirits, were anxious not to be regarded as well enough to be sent back to the trenches. For a little hospital treatment, even in the dark cellar of a shelled villa, came like a spell of paradise to lads who had been weeks in the dreadful trenches of the Somme. Not that Oldham, with his thigh wound, ever stood any risk of being sent back. Still, it pleased him and his sense of mischief, as active in him as in all good soldiers, to pretend that he was shirking going back. It was one of the forms of humour at the front to pretend to be "funking" or shirking. As they lay helpless I could hear them joking one to another about their illnesses and wounds. I remember one big fellow, whose face had been half blown away by a shell, and who, when he thought no officer was about, said, in a mock, pathetic voice, for his fellows to hear: "I think I could just take a little gruel now, doctor." And then he himself and all his pals laughed as at a joke of priceless merit —the truth being, of course, that if he did manage to eat

even a little gruel that would be all that he could manage. But that same spirit of fun-making seemed to hang about some of our British wounded even to the end; they died mocking their wounds.

As soon as the shelling stopped the patients were carried to more airy quarters upstairs. The change was, no doubt, welcome enough, for the fire which had been lit in the cellar to take the chill and dankness off the place was behaving badly and sending more of its smoke into the cellar than up the chimney. The orderlies were coughing heartily enough, but the patients seemed not to notice it. The Somme had, apparently, made any other conditions seem comfortable. The stone steps leading to the basement had been covered with a smooth plank, and up this inclined plane the patients' stretchers were slid with greater ease and steadiness than would have been possible if they had had to be carried. "It's as good as th' toboggan at Blackpool," said one voice; and from the voice and the accent—which made "pool" rhyme with the word "foal," as a Piccadilly "johnny" might pronounce it—I recognised friend Oldham, of Lancashire.

WOUNDED MEN CROSSING THE CHANNEL.
"Walking cases"—that is to say, wounded men who were able to move about by themselves—could enjoy the sea-breezes on deck during the Channel crossing en route for hospitals at home.

From the cellar the patients, who numbered perhaps a dozen, were carried to more airy quarters in the attics. Here they lay anxiously speculating as to their fate. Would they be kept here for a day or two and then sent back to the trenches, or would they be passed on to a base hospital or to "Blighty"? This last was what every man hoped for; but, of course, for all of them it was impossible. Slight cases of injury or sickness would lie here perhaps for a day or two and then go back to duty. Others might go only a little way down the lines of communication, there to lie up till better. Others might get as far as the sea-coast of France to one or other of the base hospitals. Every type and condition of hospital, in fact, between the trenches and home would sift out some patients for treatment, and only the lucky few would ever achieve their dream of being sent home to "Blighty" and seeing their friends once more. Once when I went upstairs to have another look at the patients a discussion was going on between two or three of them as to their respective chances of being sent home. They were lying on their stretchers, some smoking and talking, others asleep. A solitary lamp shed a faint, flickering light over their recumbent forms. "Ay," said one voice, as though in disputation over some point a neighbour had raised, "it's true enough that I've only a bullet wound in the arm, as you say, but I've got a touch o' bronchitis an' all! Heard the orderly say so when he heard me wheezin'!"

"That's all very well," said another voice, "but did he write it down on yer ticket? You could have 'hydrophobie' also, an' it wouldn't help you two-penn'orth if th' doc. didn't write it down on yer ticket!" (The ticket to which he referred was the little label—white for non-dangerous cases, red and white for dangerous cases— which was tied to the jacket of every patient at the regimental aid post, and which, with any necessary emendations or additions made at intermediate dressing-stations, went with the patient from first to last as the medical summary of his case and symptoms.)

"Can't say as it's on my ticket, as I knows on." Here the voice was raised to call to the orderly, who was not far away: "Hi, matey, you might read us out what's written on my ticket!"

"Wait till daylight, and get to sleep, my lad," said the orderly not unkindly. "It's latish. You ought all on yer to be getting a bit o' **Patients and their** sleep instead of chattering away there **"tickets"** like a girls' school. Be good lads an' get to sleep." He reminded me of a mother. There was silence for a while in the little whitewashed attic, and then the voice went on in a whisper: "Yer bronchitis will be a good help if it's on yer ticket. We'll read it in the mornin'. My chance is pretty all right, I think. I've got a 'temperachure,' besides my wound. 'Undred it were when it were last took. Pretty good that! They think a lot about temperachures. Orderly told me so. Very particklar about temperachures." So they talked, on their stretchers, in that dimly-lighted attic. Oldham, I noticed, was asleep.

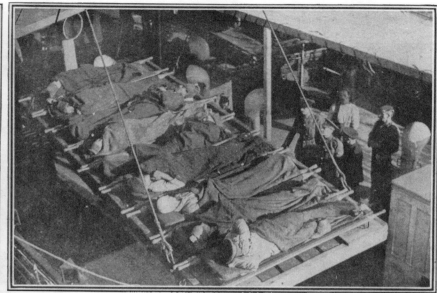

Hoisting cot-cases on shore by crane from the hospital ship for transference to the train alongside the quay.   Left : Interior of a corridor ward in the hospital train.

Right : Stretcher cases arranged on the platform ready to be placed in the train.   Left : Ambulance men lined up at the station waiting to disembark the wounded.

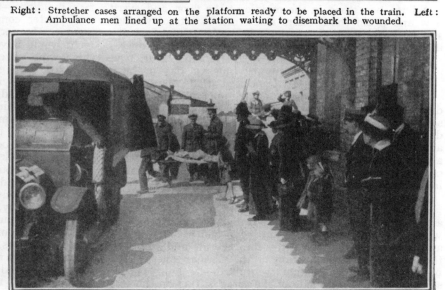

" Special " cases coming ashore from the hospital ship.   Right : The end of the journey. Carrying the patients from the station to the ambulances waiting to convey them to the hospital where, if within the competence of man, their cure would be completed.

SCENES ON THE HIGHWAY OF SUFFERING: FROM PAIN TO HOME AND HEALTH.

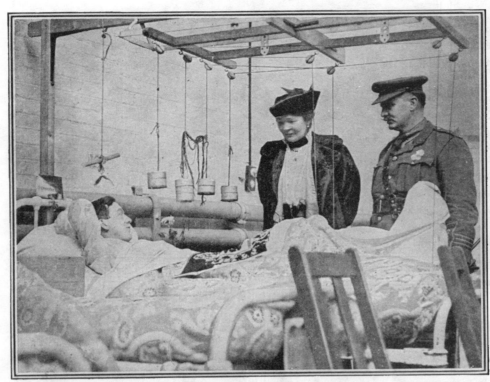

THE DUCHESS OF CONNAUGHT AT THE CANADIANS' HOSPITAL, TAPLOW.
Mrs. Astor opened a hospital for wounded Canadians near Taplow, and the first task the Duchess of Connaught performed when she returned to England in 1916, after the Duke retired from the Governor-Generalship of the Dominion, was to visit the Canadians under treatment there.

I went downstairs again, and into the room opposite the doctor's. This was the receiving-room and dressing-room. A big Primus stove sent up a dull droning from a point near the empty fireplace. By lamp-light a surgeon was dressing a dark-red gash in a man's back. Another patient waited near, sitting on a form. Very interested he seemed in all that was being done to his colleague. He caught an orderly's eye, and, speaking with difficulty through a swollen mouth, he explained his case. " Small tube blew out of our gun. Got me fair in the teeth it did, and laid out a tidy few of them on the floor. Guess I'll have to have a nice new set of top ones from the dentist when I get home. Fancy me wi' a nice set o' false teeth ! Won't I be a swank ! " And he laughed at the prospect.

A huge box stood in the middle of the floor, and every now and again the dressers threw into it bits of wound-stained lint. With these grim tokens of war and casualty it was full. " We empty it once a day in slack times," said an orderly, " and three, four, five,

Anti-tetanus injection

or even twenty times a day in busy times." I noticed that one of the treatments meted out to all wounded dressed at this station was a hypodermic injection of some white-coloured fluid. This was to guard against the deadly disease tetanus, or lockjaw, the germs of which live and thrive in the yellow mud of the Somme. As it was almost impossible that any wound incurred in this district could have escaped contact with mud, the anti-tetanus injection was given in every case.

⋅   ⋅   ⋅   ⋅   ⋅   ⋅   ⋅

John Oldham was sent farther down the line that night, and I went in the same motor-ambulance with him. It was moonlight now, and the gun fire had ceased, though an occasional star-shell soared into the air and whitened the sky over in the direction of the German lines. The roads were quiet. At first we talked—he lying on his stretcher on the right side of the car, I sitting on the seat on the other side. He told me he was a spinner by trade, and that he and many other spinners had joined up at the beginning of the war in a Pals' battalion recruited in the

neighbouring city of Manchester. He went on to tell me of his pals, and what had happened to them, and of the places they had been in on the line. But, sitting there in the darkness of the ambulance-waggon, rocked by the lurches of the car on the uneven road, he seemed to tire. His voice became more of a monotone, and I ceased to answer any of his remarks ; and, sure enough, before many minutes he was asleep again. I turned aside the back flap of the car and looked out. The moon, though hidden now, was sending a soft luminousness over things Now and again we passed a soldier in an iron helmet plodding along the road. In one ruined home-stead, without roof, was a tiny fire, round which three or four soldiers were sitting. The earth round about was strewn with barrel-shaped coils. The spot was a barbed-wire " dump." Once we passed a little train of supply-waggons, empty and halted by the roadside. A lantern glowed under each tarpaulin roof, showing that each was in use as a tent or shelter. From one waggon, in passing, I saw the faint, blue light of a Primus stove. Between the two sides of the waggon were frames of wood with sacking stretched tightly across them to serve as beds.

Sentries and military police with lanterns were posted along the roads at intervals, but they did not trouble us much. Our driver and his car—which did this particular run many times a day—were too well known for them to need to stop us. And so, in good time, we arrived at the next halting-place for wounded from this particular part of the Somme front. It **Main** was a " main dressing-station," and it **dressing-station** was in the village of Bertrandcourt.

Switching sharply to the right, our car passed under a brick archway and into a big open square. It had been the yard of a farm, and was flanked on all four sides by low farm buildings—those curious buildings of bricks and beams and plaster common to all the farming villages of the Somme. In normal times that farmyard at this time of night would have been dark and quiet, save, perhaps, for the lowing of cattle in the byres. But now dim lights twinkled from every side of the square, and uniformed men, some carrying lanterns, were moving busily about.

A little squad of R.A.M.C. orderlies came at a trot to meet our incoming car, and as we came to a standstill they formed up in line at our back without question or word, each man ready to make things easier for any poor wounded lad that might be inside. As the canvas flap of the waggon was pulled aside I stood up and leapt out, but before I reached the ground stout arms caught me suddenly under the armpits and lowered me to the ground as gently as though my twelve-stone weight had been twelve pounds. " Take it gently, sir," said a reproving voice, " you might 'appen to do yourself harm if you don't go gently." In the dark they had mistaken me for a wounded officer—as was natural, perhaps, seeing that I was riding in an ambulance-motor and that my uniform was that of an officer. I may mention now that on all my journey from the front to home R.A.M.C. men of all grades showed the same inclination to treat me as an invalid. I had to explain to them that I was neither wounded nor ill, but even then they would sometimes look me over carefully for a casualty card, or " field medical card " as it is called. Some of them seemed disappointed that they could do nothing for me ; and the way they leapt away to help any wounded Tommy or officer was evidence enough of their real keenness.

The commanding officer of this main dressing-station—an R.A.M.C. colonel—had himself come out to see what cases our ambulance-car and others behind it had brought along I made myself known to him, and presented my credentials. He took me with him while he

Feeding the wounded

saw to the disposal of the cases, and then said I must have something to eat before I looked over the station in more detail.

Along a muddy lane we plodded to a little white cottage, by the door of which were painted the words, "Officers' Mess. Field Ambulance. No.——" In a plain kitchen some half-dozen officers were sitting round a rusty fire-grate before a fire which shed a thin fog of smoke into the room. A lamp-light shone upon the remains of dinner—for dinner, late in this busy camp, was just over. I made there the acquaintance of officers some of whom (as I learned later) had given up medical practices and positions at home to come out and " do their bit," and it was no rare thing to see streaks of silver in the hair of an officer wearing the modest two stars of a lieutenant. An orderly of size and venerable age found me some mutton and cabbage on a tin plate, and, in a confidential whisper, asked me whether I would like whisky-and-water or tea. I have noticed before, in Canada and elsewhere, how hard work in primitive conditions conduces to the tea habit. When I remarked something of the sort to the colonel he mentioned that almost the only drink and the only thing asked for by the wounded men and sick who came up from the trenches was tea. " They are offered cocoa or coffee or soup, or a hot meat-drink of some kind, but almost all of them," he said, " ask for tea."

" It's a curious thing, too," added the colonel, as we walked down the lane again to the station later, " that they won't eat meat. At first, when they come in, muddy and tired and weak, they don't seem to want anything much, but a mug of hot tea brightens them up, and then they feel they can eat. And what do you think they like best ? Bread-and-jam ! Wounded Tommies who will not look at sandwiches or meat-stew or anything else will eat ravenously of bread-and-jam. My own belief is that you can't do better for a wounded man, especially walking wounded, than feed them up, and I have watched a good deal to see the thing that they like best. Bread-and-jam comes an easy first."

By this time we were in the receiving-room of the dressing-station. A barn had been provided with a canvas roof and partitions, and also with a big waterproof ground-sheet for a

flooring. Acetylene lamps gave quite a good working light, and the chamber was kept at a pleasant warmth by a circular stove, the flue-pipe of which passed through a tin panel let into the canvas sides of the chamber. This tin-plate—it was no more than a petrol-tin cut up and flattened out—struck me as an ingenious way of overcoming the risk of a fire in the canvas wall due to a too hot flue-pipe.

The first thing that happened to every wounded man who entered that reception chamber was to have details taken of his name, regiment, wound, and conditions as shown on his little field medical card, and after that to be fed, washed, and tidied up, and given new garments if necessary. Most wounded were able to walk, and they were told to pass over to the refreshment buffet, which, with a bright light of its own, stood in a separate partition under the presidency of a cheery-faced orderly in shirt-sleeves and a white apron. Before him was a counter filled with eatables. His opening question to each man was this : " Now, my lad, tea, coffee, cocoa, soup, or

PRINCESS PATRICIA OF CONNAUGHT VISITING WOUNDED CANADIANS.
Wounded soldiers readily relieved the tedium of convalescence with unaccustomed tasks, and many and wonderful were the things which many of them learned to make. Princess Patricia, whose name will ever be linked with that of one of the many brave regiments from the Western Dominion, interested herself in this soldiers' special form of art needlework. Men of Princess Patricia's Canadian Light Infantry were among the earliest of overseas troops to take part in the war on the Western front.

stew?" It might have been all one word and one dish by the businesslike way he rattled it off. But the Tommies understood all right, and one and all chose tea. As he filled mug after mug it struck me that he did it more by his sense of touch and weight than by sight, for his eyes were roaming about all over the wounded, and his lips were repeating again and again the cheerful invitation: "It's all right, my boys, pick up anything you fancy. It's all yours, and it's there to be eaten." And with his eyes and a nod of the head he would beckon to any soldier who seemed to be hanging back and press him to choose something from among the great platefuls of sandwiches, bread-and-butter, bread-and-jam, cake, and so on which filled the counter. The artillery man with the damaged mouth mumbled, on being pressed to eat, that he could not eat anything because of his sore jaws, whereupon the attendant

WOUNDED BRITISH OFFICERS AT CHATEAU D'OEX.
Comrades in misfortune who spent eighteen months in a German prison before they were transferred to Chateau D'Oex, in Switzerland. Seated (right), Lieut.-Col. Maxwell Earle, D.S.O., Grenadier Guards, and (left) Capt. Henderson, London Scottish. Standing (right), Major R. A. Birley, R.F.A., and (left) Lieut. T. Dobson, R.N.D.

said: "Oh, I'll soon fix you." He busied himself behind the counter for a minute and then presented the artillery-man with a basin of hot bread-and-milk.

The stretcher cases lying in another canvas partition were feeding or being fed by orderlies when I went in to see how friend Oldham was getting along. "Just had a cup o' real good tea," he said cheerily, "and now I am going to slip my face round this." And he held up for my inspection a big slice of bread-and-jam. "Makes you hungry motorin'," he added quite seriously. My mind went back to that solemn and jolting night ride of ours in the darkness of the motor-ambulance car, and I thought I had never heard the word "motoring" more curiously applied.

There was to be no transport of wounded that night to stations farther down the line, and when I left the main

dressing-station for the officers' mess again the patients had been "bedded down" for the night. The colonel had taken me round various dark canvas wards, with an electric pocket torch to light us, promising me a more detailed "look round" in the morning, and I walked up the lane with him to the mess with curious memory pictures going through my mind of recumbent figures of wounded men in all positions—pictures of men with placid faces, calmly sleeping, of men with faces furrowed by pain, of men lying with bodies bent and limbs awkwardly extended—and all these pictures were cut out in circles from surrounding blackness by the white glow of a pocket torch. It was as though I had been in a dark room, watching lantern slides on a screen; circular slides showing poor wounded, bandaged, and "splinted" humanity in vivid lantern pictures.

. . . .

I slept that night on a camp bed in a cottage in the village. There had been some discussion in the mess earlier as to where I should be billeted, and someone had said: "In the padre's billet." The padre was away on leave, it seemed, so I was given his bed. They took me along a muddy lane, then through a gate in a wall and up a garden path to a white, low-roofed cottage. In a ground-floor room, littered with ornaments and furniture and luggage, were two soldiers' beds. By the light of my candle I could see that a man was already asleep in one of them. Upon the other, a few inches above the wooden floor, were some blankets and an officer's greatcoat. Three stars on a black ground on the shoulders told me that it was the padre's. May I thank him now for the comfort of his greatcoat that night. For it was bitter cold.

I did not feel like sleep. For a time I lay awake with the candle on the floor near my face, watching the flickering shadows it threw upon the whitewashed ceiling. Everything was quiet save for the ticking of a watch somewhere in my neighbour's clothes and **Halted for the** the quiet moaning of the wind in the wide **night** chimney of the cottage. Then he began to breathe heavily, and in a minute a loud voice came to me from his bed, saying: "Look here, you'll have to get those waggons into better shelter than this, and quick, too."

"Sorry, what's that you say?" I replied. He did not answer. He was asleep. I learnt next day that he was an officer of motor transport. His cares were evidently following him in his dreams.

At length I seized my boot, and with the heel of it knocked out the candle, trying then to sleep. But after perhaps ten minutes the solemn "crump" of a shell somewhere in the neighbourhood made me wide awake once more. I listened for another. It came along, and though it was well distant the cottage and my bed gave a little shiver. There came another, and I felt certain I heard the fall of a "dud" shell in the near neighbourhood of the cottage. I felt for the candle and found it, but there were no matches I got up and searched, but could find none. The room was inky dark. Feeling my way I found the door, went out into the passage and opened the front door. A cold wind rushed in. Here in my pyjamas I stood watching the restless swaying of the bushes in the garden and the white flashes of guns and star-shells in the sky away to the east. There was not a sound in the village of Bertrandcourt; not a light. The moon, behind banks of clouds, cast a filmy pale-blue light on the white walls of the cottage. If shells were causing those dull, flat thuds that I could hear every now and again, certainly no one was taking any notice. I went back and crept in among the blankets and the great-coat once more, and was half asleep when sounds, as of a fierce quarrel—in French—and moans came from the neighbouring room of the cottage. For two or three minutes it went on in most amazing and unnatural fashion—all in one voice, till I guessed that here again was some-one talking in his sleep—some old Frenchman apparently infirm and short of breath, for he gasped as he talked and scolded.

An orderly standing at my bedside with a candle woke me next morning. Then he flung back the heavy wooden shutters and let the morning sunshine into the room.

As I stood washing, the door of the further room opened, and out came the queerest old man. He was dressed in some quaint dressing-gown and a little black skull cap, from under the sides of which protruded fuzzy tufts of silvery hair. His head, under the skull cap, seemed to taper almost to a point. He had a round, clean-shaven face, ruddy as an apple; heavy white eyebrows, and beneath them little twinkling eyes of extraordinary brilliance. As I did not know him from Adam I was not a little surprised when he trotted up to me playfully, and with many smiles patted me on the bare back.

A HAVEN OF REST.
Chateau d'Oex, Switzerland, where British sick and wounded, released from Germany, were sent for internment.

GUESTS OF THE POLYTECHNIC AT LUCERNE.
A number of French and British prisoners of war interned in Switzerland were sent to the hospital at Lucerne, which was specially arranged for operations rendered necessary by faulty treatment by German surgeons. Mr. and Mrs. Robert Mitchell entertained this party at the Polytechnic Chalets, Lucerne.

He cocked his old head on one side. Then he turned, and. repeating:

"Very bon, very bon, very bon," he trotted back to his own room.

I learned later that the old gentleman was the village curé—very old indeed, though growing younger in manner every day. It was his cottage in which I had slept. The war had upset his mind very much, and he was very, very old; so I felt glad I had not chased him out the bedroom with my shaving-brush as I had once thought of doing.

The main dressing-station at Bertrandcourt, seen by daylight, looked much bigger than it had done the night before; one saw that in addition to all its farm buildings, made habitable and usable by canvas roofs, floors, and partitions, it had also many canvas

"You Engleeshman? Yes? Very bon," he said, all in one breath. "Germans—Allemands—no bon, no bon." He shook his head fiercely, then he calmly looked me over as I stood there in my pyjama trousers. He stroked my bare arms, and went on: "You soldier? Engleesh soldier? Very bon, very bon." He never waited for an answer to anything, but went on: "You marrié? You got pretty wife, very bon, yes?" I could not help grinning, and he continued: "Bon, very bon." He passed his hand over my chest and back, then hit me on the chest with his fist.

"You fort, yes? Very strong, very bon, yes?" I replied in French to the effect that I was very well, thank you.

marquees, stretching out into the orchard behind. Here, too, was a dug-out for "shelly" days, as my guide expressed it, capable of sheltering a hundred patients if need be. This was one of the best specimens of British-made dug-outs I saw on the Somme, and it disposed effectually of the statements one often heard that only the Germans could build dug-outs.

Equipment of dressing station

The equipment of the main dressing-station was considerably more extensive than that of either the advance dressing-station or the aid post. Quite extensive medical work could be done here if necessary. One interesting feature was the oxygen tent, in which stood an oxygen cylinder with a cunning little contrivance (made from

N N

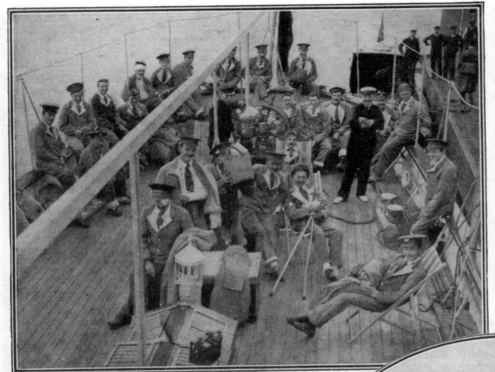

OFF FOR A TRIP ON THE THAMES.
Grateful London overlooked nothing that could contribute to the pleasure of the convalescent wounded. Thames steamers, which had long lain idle at their moorings, were recommissioned to take them on trips up and down the river.

held open for him by the sergeant in charge of the camp "pack store." The sergeant explained to me that every article found on a wounded man had to be accounted for on every stage of the journey from trench downwards. Every wounded man's pocket possessions and luggage were entered on printed forms, item for item—knife, watch, rings — even down to simple, valueless things such as "a key-ring without keys," which item I saw figuring solemnly on the list of personal possessions of my friend Oldham. The driver of any car receiving a patient had to give a receipt for any kit and personal possessions of the patients he received. When he delivered his patient to the next medical post he took a receipt from the keeper of that station's pack store, into which they were put

a petrol-can, a tin bath of water, and some tubing), with which oxygen could be administered to half a dozen patients at once from the one cylinder. An incinerator was busily at work in one corner of the grounds, making a merry smoke of its own. In another corner were good-sized kitchens with cooks busily at work. As I walked round with the colonel, men were busy improving the pathways between the various tents or wards by laying "duck-boards" upon them. Duck-boards laid on wet and slippery mud make perhaps the most slippery pathway possible—a pathway most dangerous and difficult for a wounded man or for a stretcher-party. But this path can be made "non-skid" by the simple device of laying wire-netting such as is used for chicken-runs over the surface of the wood. This plan had been followed at Bertrandcourt, and the paths were quite safe and comfortable under foot.

Oldham had passed a fair night in one of the canvas wards of the dressing-station, and it was decided to send him on that day to the next medical post on the long journey home—a casualty clearing-station. He heard the news secretly from me with a pleased grin, for it was not always an easy thing for a wounded man to learn whether he was to be moved and what his destination was. In fact, he could be kept at any of these medical posts on the line, if his case was capable of treatment there—and if there was room to spare—and eventually he would be sent back to his regiment without ever getting nearer to the one great place he hoped to go to—"Blighty." Every move farther down, therefore, was regarded as a "score." The parties of wounded leaving any medical post for the one lower down were all smiles and good-humour. They would be that much nearer "Blighty."

One point interested me as the big "Bulldog" motor-ambulance car was being loaded up with its freight of wounded. The driver was signing his name in a book

Wounded men's possessions

LEAVING THE TEMPLE PIER.
A party of wounded soldiers embarked at Temple Pier on board the Port of London Authority's steamer Conservator for a day on the Thames.

pending the wounded man's recovery or removal to another post. In the case of officers all luggage, as well as equipment, had to be signed and accounted for in the same way. The list of a man's belongings had at the first opportunity to be signed by the man himself as being correct. In the case of an officer his servant's signature was regarded as sufficient. If a man were too ill to sign, then one of his officers had to sign. Money and jewellery and other small valuables were put in a little bag and tied upon the patient.

Our carload for the journey to the next post consisted of five patients and myself as inside passengers. There were only two stretcher cases—Oldham and a young Scottish soldier, who, though suffering from a most painful shell wound, lay quietly on his back smoking cigarettes. The other passengers were "sitters," as walking wounded or sick were called for purposes of transport. Among them was a young officer suffering very badly from bronchitis. He spent much of the journey apologising to me—and himself I think—for having left the trenches. He was ill and so weak that he only just failed to be a stretcher case. He seemed terribly depressed—not so much by his illness as at having to "throw up the sponge," as he termed it, and leave his work. "Stuck it as long as I could," he told me. Then there was silence in the car for perhaps five minutes. I was thinking of something else when he turned to me again and said: "Wouldn't have cared if I could have stuck it till we were relieved." Another pause for coughing, and then: "We'd only another day to go." He made more remarks of like nature before the journey was finished. His failure was on his mind, it was clear.

It became cold as the sun sank, and one could see that the patients tired. The men sat or lay with closed eyes. There was no talking for the last half-hour of our journey. When at last we ran into the casualty clearing-station, beyond Puchevillers, it was dusk. A gang of German prisoners, who had been doing some path-making about the camp, were forming up under their escort ready for the march home to their barbed-wire camp across the fields. Our car was unloaded by orderlies, whose first care was to get the patients to the receiving-shed, where their names and particulars were taken, and then on to the refreshment buffet. For the first step towards curing a wounded man at this medical post, as at all previous

Casualty clearing-station

posts, seemed to be to feed him—very sound treatment, too, so the wounded appeared to think. Within half an hour sick and wounded alike were snug under blankets.

．　．　．　．　．　．　．

A casualty clearing-station was the nearest medical post to the battle-front that had something of the permanence and the resources of a real hospital. This casualty clearing-station covered several acres of ground. Its buildings were all huts or canvas marquees, it is true, but in them was to be found the most complete surgical and medical equipment, even to X-ray department, pathological department, and the rest. Here also, for the first time on the Via Dolorosa which the wounded man followed to get from the front to his home, were to be found women—British nursing Sisters. It was one of the greatest moments of that journey for the wounded Tommy—that moment when he met a British woman once more, perhaps for the first time after weeks and weeks in the trenches with not a soul within miles, either friend or enemy, but men.

WOUNDED MEN WHO ENJOYED A DAY AT THE ZOO.
Australians from the Dardanelles at the Zoological Gardens. Many people arranged to give outings to the convalescent wounded soldiers, and the Zoo—with rides on the baby elephant for the youngsters—proved unfailingly attractive to a large number of them.

The effect which this presence of their countrywomen had on the wounded struck me as remarkable. I watched friend Oldham being carried into his ward. He was tired and inert. As the men orderlies attended to him he lay listless and irresponsive even to pain when they moved him. The lamps were just being lit. He took no notice of anything. Then a Sister came quietly into the ward. At the voice of a woman speaking English, Oldham's eyes opened wide at once; he raised his head from his bed to see who had spoken. Other eyes than his opened, too. Of the new patients in that ward there was not one save those already asleep who did not become agog

[Bassano.

HAPPY HOURS IN THE GROUNDS OF ONE OF THE LONDON MILITARY HOSPITALS.
It was a pleasant time for the wounded men and their families when visiting day came round, and more especially when convalescence and climatic conditions enabled the reunions to take place in the open air. In this large hospital at Bethnal Green a concert-theatre was erected in the grounds, and the wounded men and their visitors were able to enjoy the music provided for them by a goodly band of performers.

with interest at the sound of an Englishwoman's voice. They followed her about the ward with their eyes. She stood still when her work was done and spoke to the soldier in the bed nearest her. They chatted for three or four minutes, and one could see the interest of the wounded man in his steadfast gaze upon her. There was a pause in the talk, but he still looked at her. Then, feeling perhaps that some little apology for this was due from him, he said: "Do you know,

Women nurses and the wounded Sister, you're the first Englishwoman I've seen or heard speak for over forty weeks."

I had a word or two with her later. She was a comely, motherly woman of thirty-five or so. "The Tommies seem interested to find their countrywomen here, Sister," I said.

"Yes," she replied, "it's funny, isn't it? I don't think there are many new patients come along here from the front who don't pass some remark to the Sisters to show that they are glad to see us. They will watch you all round the ward, and some of them, if you don't happen to speak to them, will speak to you, just asking you some little question or other. They like to keep us talking."

MAGIC WHEEL TO "MASSAGE" NERVES.
Revolving wheels, which brought a constant succession of different colours before the eye, were tried in treating men with nerves shattered by shell-shock, the idea being that the optical effect "massaged" the nerves.

We've all noticed it. Poor fellows, they tell us sometimes that it does them more good than medicine to see an Englishwoman again, and I am sure it's not just soldier's 'blarney,' you know, because they are so serious and polite to us, and tell us about their homes and their wives and mothers and sweethearts. Perhaps it is that the sight of women again makes them think of home and makes them forget for a time the dreadful things they have been seeing and feeling out yonder." She nodded her head in the direction of the German lines, whence the sound of gun fire came now faint and distant.

When Sister had left the ward I walked over to Oldham's bed. I had noticed his interested eye on Sister and me as we had stood talking. "It looks a bit more like civilisation to see an Englishwoman again, doesn't it?" I said, being anxious to know what he thought of it. "By gum, it does that there!" he said warmly. "Makes you kind of feel," he said, with pent brows that showed something of his effort to express his thoughts—"makes you kind of feel——" He stopped. He was very weak and

worn. His nether lip trembled for a second like that of a little boy and tears rolled down his cheeks. Poor lad!

An orderly came bustling along with an extra blanket, and without looking at the patient's face, he went through several bustling manoeuvres—with especial vigour, I thought. "Now you're more in parade order, my son," he said, as he finished. "Give us a shout if you want anything!" I was standing at the foot of the cot looking about the canvas ward, so as not to seem to see the patient's little lapse. The orderly stood by me, and with his back to Oldham said in a low voice: "I seen him upset 'isself, sir. They very often breaks down for a minute just when they arrives. I never lets on I sees 'em, but just finds a bit o' somethink to do about their beds, breezy-like, you know, sir, and you talks a bit to 'em, breezy-like, and they pick up in a second. When his wounds is redressed, you won't hear so much as a ' mew ' from 'im, no matter how we hurts him. I expect, sir, it's just the bit of 'omesickness breakin' out of them when they're weak-like!"

The point, apart from its greater size and better equipment, that distinguished a casualty clearing-station from earlier medical posts on the road home was that it was, generally speaking, on a railway. It was intended for the surgical treatment and the safe housing of wounded until such time as they were fit for sending back to their units, or for transport to some hospital of a more permanent nature. A railway ran alongside the casualty clearing-station of Puchevillers, and, as I walked round that side of the camp with the commanding officer, an ambulance train shunted slowly into position in the nearest siding, ready to take down to the coast a new load of wounded. It was a train of great length—seventeen long coaches in all—and they were coloured a pale khaki brown and a deep brown, almost black, with red crosses on a white ground coming at frequent intervals on their sides. The train seemed empty, but my guide climbed up to the door of a coach on which were painted the letters " C.O." (commanding officer), and along the narrow corridor inside the coach we met that officer himself coming out to meet us. He wore the three stars of a captain, as did also his assistant, a young man perhaps half his age. The older officer had been a lecturer and examiner in medicine at one of the leading universities of Scotland, and now, after twenty odd years spent in turning out medical men and officers for the R.A.M.C., he had left this work to come out and " do his bit " as an officer himself. One of the many oddities of his position was that men whom he himself had trained were now in the Service high above him. Some of them had to give him orders—for which in some cases they apologised profusely—still calling him " Sir," as in their old student days.

Learning that I wished to travel in a train down to a " base " with a load of wounded, the train commandant pressed me very warmly to make my quarters with him until such time as the train should start, an offer of which I thankfully took advantage. I spent three days with that train as my home—most comfortable and most interesting days, too.

In an ambulance train

The train officers' coach was an English railway coach of the ordinary corridor type, but divided in the middle of the corridor by a door. At each end of the coach was a little sitting-room, and towards the centre were separate compartments, used as private bed-sitting-rooms by officers of the staff. The captain and his helper and I had one end of the coach up to the dividing door; the other half was occupied by the three nursing Sisters attached to the train staff. The forty or fifty male orderlies, nurses, cooks, etc., who constituted the remainder of the train staff were housed at the other end of the train. In the middle of the train were the kitchens and administration coaches. All the other coaches were " wards " for wounded and sick. The last coach of the train—that is to say, the one immediately behind ours—was the isolation ward for infectious

General Mangin, who commanded the troops that recaptured Douaumont, October 24th, 1916.

French soldiers in the sleeping-cabin of a bomb-proof casemate in recaptured Vaux Fort.

Verdun in 1916: Its streets sand-bagged, shell-shattered, but still French.

Verdun, heroic city of France, viewed after the siege of 1916 from the spire of the Église du Collège.

cases, should there be any. Thus the medical men of the train and the Sisters could visit from their coach either the wounded wards or the isolation ward, whereas all the patients and orderlies were cut off from the isolation ward, unless they visited it by passing through the officers' and Sisters' quarters.

In these small but cosy quarters that night I dined excellently, chatted with the commandant, and slept. Sitting there on a bleak siding in that tiny cabin, with the wind playing shrill little tunes through our ventilators, reminded me very much of being quartered in a yacht lying in some harbour or quiet waterway. Just before turning in that night I did look out of the window, half expecting to see water about us; but the moonlight shone only on the quiet siding and the casualty clearing-station round about us, upon the wet canvas tents of which it threw a faintly glimmering sheen like that of shot silk. Once in the night a train passed us, from which came the murmur of innumerable voices and a most curious stamping noise, like the clumsy beating of many wooden drums. I leaned up on my elbow to see what made it. The train was full of soldiers. They were stamping their feet on the carriage floors to keep warm.

City of tents and wood huts

On the following day, after a breakfast of " ration " bacon—which struck me as the best bacon I had tasted since the war made good bacon impossible for civilians—I looked more closely into that little city of tents and wood huts that formed the casualty clearing-station of Puchevillers. This was one of the normal casualty clearing-stations of our Somme front. There were special clearing-stations elsewhere for special types of casualty. For instance, stomach wounds all went direct from the advanced dressing-station or main dressing-station to a casualty clearing-station specially set apart for stomach cases; head wounds all went to another casualty clearing-station direct. Other cases came to a clearing-station of the type of Puchevillers. The size of the place was considerable. It covered many acres of ground, and had its roads and cinder-paths laid out with all the trimness and permanency of a home hospital. There was a wooden pavilion, too, with a piano and a concert-room, from which, as I passed it, came the sound of a woman's singing. " Practising for the camp concert to-morrow," my guide explained.

I looked in at the camp officers' mess that morning, and was not sorry I had taken up quarters in the ambulance train ; for the officers' mess-room was a tent—into which the cutting wind found innumerable entrances—warmed by one small stove. Lunch was just over, and four or five medical men were huddled round the stove having a smoke before going back to their duties. Of what those duties consisted I could form some idea later in the afternoon, when the commandant took me into the operating-theatre, a big marquee lit by a blaze of artificial light. Here three operations were being done at once. There were operating-tables for twice as many. The place reeked of chloroform. Three supine figures, partly naked, lay inert on tables. Sitting by the head of each was an anæsthetist, patiently dropping chloroform on to the mask that covered each gently moaning mouth. White-coated surgeons with bare arms and dark rubber gloves were cutting and probing and cleansing away the corruption caused by bullet and shell and bomb ; white-robed nursing Sisters stood by with bowl and swab and other appurtenances of this craft ready for handing to the surgeon at even a nod from him.

I walked back from the operating-theatre to my quarters in the ambulance train with my respect—and distaste—for a surgeon's handiwork both enhanced. Poor Oldham was to go through something of the same sort later on ; but my resistance to chloroform fumes had not been sufficiently cultivated as yet to enable me to stop and see him through, as I had intended. Rather did I feel that yearning for a cup of tea such as the sick and wounded Tommies felt, and I climbed from the siding into our

MRS. ST. CLAIR STOBART.

Mrs. Stobart was one of the British nurse-heroines of Serbia during the period of that gallant kingdom's most terrible trial. Her field hospital did invaluable work, and she was devoted in her attention to the poor Serbian refugees as well as to the wounded. Mrs. Stobart received the Serbian Order of St. Sava and the Order of St. John of Jerusalem.

railway carriage full of hope, for I had caught the passing glance of an orderly carrying a teapot. Alas ! it was going to the Sisters' sitting-room in that *terra incognita* at the other end of the coach. But I was in luck that day, for on entering the commandant's cabin he informed me that I had been invited to take tea with the Sisters that afternoon. He himself took me along and presented me to them— Sister Paul, Sister Mahoney, and Sister Thompson.

Very shyly and very kindly they gave me tea from their excellent brew. This with their Garibaldi biscuits and Scottish shortbread proved an excellent antidote to chloroform fumes and surgical sights, and I found my joy in life slowly returning under their cheery stimulus.

Good, jolly women were those nursing Sisters, practical, natural and friendly as are most British women who have seen life and done things and faced the world. As I sat chatting with them it dawned upon me that, with the brief exception already noted, I had not spoken to an Englishwoman for five weeks, and I realised faintly some of that queer satisfaction which the Tommies showed when they came, after weeks of men and war, to set eyes on a country-woman once more.

Preparing the hospital train

The day of the train's departure came at last. A medical transport officer mounted to the footboard of our carriage and announced the news through the window. " We'll make you half a cargo here," he said, " and then you can back up to Varennes for the rest of your load. You'll have something over four hundred in all ' liers and sitters.' "

ribbon and on others a strip of white. I little thought that I was watching the distribution of pleasure and pain such as only a wounded Tommy can know. But the glittering, glad eyes of the lads who received a red ribbon and the smothered groans of those who were given a white showed me that the distinction was of great moment to these men. One poor lad who had been leaning up in bed watching with feverish eyes the orderly with his ribbons and his written lists, fell back with a groan on seeing a white ribbon tied to the handle of his stretcher.

"Oh, heavens!" he exclaimed, and then shutting his eyes he took no more interest in the proceedings. The red ribbon was **Colours of pleasure and pain** the distinguishing mark for patients who were to go on the outgoing train to the coast, perhaps even to "Blighty." The white was to mark those who were to stay behind. The soldier's only recompense for being wounded is to be sent home. To get the white ribbon, therefore, was hard.

Orderlies came into the tents in couples and carried out the stretchers bearing the red ribbons. There were great leave-takings. Some of the men had been as long as a fortnight at the clearing-station, and a fortnight in a sick-tent is the equivalent of months of ordinary life, especially so far as the making of friendships goes. "So long, old pal; better luck to you with the next train down. If I get 'ome I'll go and see your folks as I promised. So long,

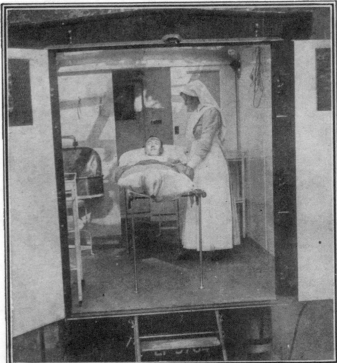

MOTOR HOSPITAL.
Operating-theatres on wheels, which proved of great value to surgeons in the field, were simply and efficiently designed and arranged for emergency work.

Everyone in the train seemed glad at the news, for pleasant idleness in a siding did not seem to appeal to them at all. "Oh, yes," said one of the Sisters to me, "we'd sooner be running with a load of patients than be standing doing nothing." People who are in love with their work can talk like that. Soon both the camp and the train were all activity. A big Belgian locomotive, in control of an English driver, backed slowly down on to us from somewhere and coupled up. Before long a new and pleasing warmth was creeping through the train from the steam-pipes in every coach. Big double doors in the centre of each ward-coach were thrown open. Train orderlies with masses of blankets, pillows, hot-water bottles, and cushions were scurrying along the train leaving little "dumps" of these things at the end of each coach. Other orderlies seized them and began the making up of beds on the iron-frame bedsteads that stood three by three, one above another, ship fashion, along the sides of the coaches. The **Lunch for four hundred** kitchen coach was a pleasing litter of peeled potatoes and food tins, steaming coppers and roaring fires, with half a dozen men galvanised into double activity by sudden orders for "lunch for four hundred" in two hours' time. Such an order would tax a shore hotel on the fringe of a Covent Garden, let alone an ambulance train tucked away in a remote French siding where not even a loaf could be bought.

In the camp "ashore" things were just as active. I followed round one canvas ward-tent an orderly who was tying upon some patients' stretchers a little strip of red

REMOVING THE PATIENT AFTER SURGICAL ATTENTION.
Testing the field operating-theatre, which was presented to Italy by the Wounded Allies' Relief Committee before it left London. Everything was arranged for maintaining perfect steadiness while the theatre was in use for the great purpose for which it was designed.

old lad." And a hand from a bed in the dimness of the tent waved to another hand that was waving from a stretcher being carried out towards daylight and the train, and perhaps "Blighty." Glad were the eyes of the men on those moving stretchers, but they left heavy, weary eyes in the tents behind them.

No sooner had the last "red" stretcher been borne on its way than from the other end of the tent, casually, and as though by accident, strolled "Sister." She went round the beds doing little tasks and talking to the patients as she worked. It was by no accident that she came. I accused her later of a motive in coming. "Yes," she admitted with a smile. "I knew the last patient had gone, and I came along just to have a look at those who were left. Train time is one of their bad times, you see, when they are not going." Then she began to busy herself again with the patients. I don't know just how much or how important work those British nursing Sisters did at Puchevillers, but whether that work was much or little, important or trivial, their mere presence and womanly good sense and kindness were a tremendous help to the curative resources of the station. Let me say here, too, that right through our hospitals in France—and in Britain for that matter—good womanly nursing and sympathy, so far as I saw it, had everywhere a curative value that vied with that of any medicine. It was whispered to me in the base hospitals nearer the coast that Sisters and nurses were expected to be more "distant and dignified," that they were kept under a much stricter discipline, and that the reason of this was the number of distinguished visitors—women among them—who came to these places with a sort of policeman's eye for everybody and everything, especially for their fellow-women, the nurses and Sisters. If this accusation was true the Army and the nation suffered a loss.

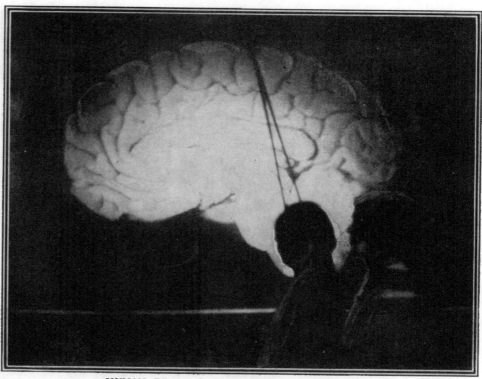

HUMAN BRAIN SHOWN BY THE EPIDIASCOPE.
By means of the epidiascope opaque objects can be projected on a screen in natural colours, microscopic subjects being highly magnified. The light used is 10,000 c.p. electric arcs playing on a series of mirrors. This photograph was taken at Bedford College for Women.

Outside the tent-wards orderlies were lifting the stretchers on to pair-wheeled, rubber-tyred ambulances. Upon one of these each patient was wheeled by an orderly along the smooth cinder-paths of the camp to the train siding. Friend Oldham was there, all smiles and good spirits. Morning mist was on the ground, and it was cold and cheerless enough, but there was not a man who did not look happy. And when they caught sight for the first time of the name of that simple railway siding, posted in white letters on a black signboard, more than one hand went up from under a stretcher coverlet and more than one throat raised a little shout of pleasure, for the name of that siding was—"Blighty Junction."

At "Blighty Junction"

The joke may strike one as simple enough, but to those poor lads it was priceless. "Blighty Junction!" they chuckled. "Very good, that is; very good!" And they continued to smile at the happy memory of it. Or was it perhaps at the happy memories and prospects it evoked?

There were some handshakings, much shouting of "Good-bye!" and "Good luck!" Patients had to shake hands with orderlies who had tended them, and there were one or two surgeons I noticed who had friends among the patients. "I want to thank you for all you've done for me, sir," I heard one lad saying to an R.A.M.C. officer, who before he donned the King's khaki was a specialist of some repute. "Oh, that's all right; don't speak of that," said the surgeon cheerily as he took the hand that reached out from under the coverlet and shook it. "Good luck to you, lad, and let me know how that leg of yours goes on." The boy was lifted into the train, and as his orderly tucked him into his bed the patient was saying: "What he done for me would have cost any 'civvy' (civilian) a hundred guineas—no less. He never operates for less than that. Took my leg off for nothink, 'e did—for nothink. I meant shakin' 'ands wiv 'im afore I left."

The train was slowly on the move by this time. The steam of the engine added its whiteness to that of the mist, and the casualty clearing-station of Puchevillers was blurred out for us tent by tent as it were. The last figure I made out was an orderly with his wheeled ambulance empty going back towards camp. He turned to wave us another good-bye.

The casualty clearing-station at Varennes, which emerged suddenly from the mist, after an hour or two of slow running and stopping, was very like Puchevillers, but here they brought down the wounded men's stretchers to the train either by hand or loaded upon trucks on a hand railway. Three on a truck, laid crossways upon it, the wounded were rolled along rails made of wood, which left the camp by three paths, meeting the ambulance train at right angles. From here they were lifted into the train. To learn what the task of carrying the wounded is like I was allowed to take one stretcher along the little platform beside the train. Its occupant was a thirteen-stone Irish soldier. After going some fifty yards with him I realised better—and with aching arms—the work done in the trenches, where men might have to carry a wounded comrade for a thousand yards or more, and over rough ground and slippery mud instead of on a smooth plank platform, before they could put down their burden—to go back for another.

Before getting back into our carriage the train commandant and I had a word with the engine-driver, whom it was odd to see pull himself smartly to attention. Before the war he had been a driver on a Midland Railway engine at Leicester and Derby, and when volunteer drivers were called for he had responded. He wore dark blue overalls and a peaked blue cap on which were the crown and the "R.E." of the Royal Engineers Corps. He dabbed a handful of oily cotton-waste into his pocket, I noticed, ere he saluted the commandant.

Out of sound of war

We steamed slowly away from Varennes in the half-light of a wintry afternoon. The guns up at the line were booming a dull and distant note, and as we crawled farther away they grew feebler and feebler, and finally faded out. Thus did we leave the war behind us at last—and even to me, unwounded, its absence was a relief. For five weeks I had lived ever within sound of the guns and their rumbling drone, near or distant, and though one becomes used to

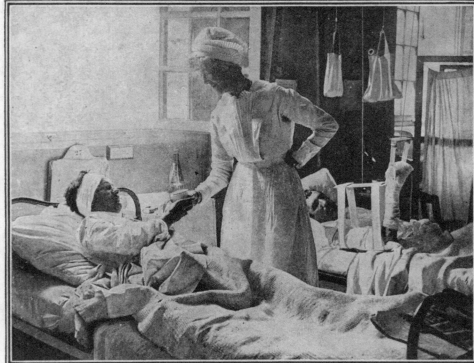

AN AMERICAN BENEFACTRESS.
Mrs. W. K. Vanderbilt in the American Hospital at Neuilly, near Paris, of which she was one of the founders.

their sound, the absence of it comes as a relief. To wounded men it is an especial relief. Medical officers at aid posts, advance dressing-stations, main dressing-stations and casualty clearing-stations alike, had assured me that of all the things a wounded Tommy resents most about these places is the fact that the guns and the din of battle can still be heard from them. Often, of course, the wounded lying in these places had to be carried down into cellars and dugouts to avoid shell fire, and in their weak and helpless state this, I was told, annoyed them beyond measure.

The next coach forward from ours was the wounded officers' coach. Half of it had been converted into a little saloon for use as a mess by "walking" cases, or "sitters," as they are called on the train. I looked in in the course of the afternoon, and found half a dozen or more officers pretty comfortable, reading, or sleeping in easy-chairs. One party were playing bridge.

Patients on the train Farther along this coach were officers' stretcher cases. Among them I found a young Flying Corps lieutenant, whose machine I had seen hit by a German "Archie" gun one day when I went into the trenches beyond Beaumont-Hamel. The engine of the machine had been carried away, and the machine had half floated, half fallen to earth. The airman was not hurt by the fall, which occurred, fortunately, just inside our lines, but a shrapnel fragment had hit him in the back. He was very cheery, and we had an interesting chat. He could have

been hardly more than twenty. I passed through the kitchens on my way forward in the train, and the quartermaster, a genial Irishman, once retired but now returned to the Colours, invited me to sample some broth that was just being served out to the patients. It was made from tinned "Maconochie," with added water, seasoning, and beef-juice—and excellent fare it was.

As I stood taking my broth a bright little orderly caught sight of me as he dashed through the coach with a tier of mugs, and, pulling himself smartly to attention, asked: "Can you speak German, sir?" If so, would I help him with some sick German prisoners who were in his ward. He was anxious not to give them the wrong kind of food, he said, but to continue the diet they had been having in the casualty

GROWING HEALTH WHERE ORCHIDS ONCE WERE GROWN.
Highbury, the beautiful Birmingham home of the late Joseph Chamberlain, was converted into a V.A.D. hospital. Billiard and bagatelle tables were placed for the amusement of convalescent soldiers in the house once devoted to the famous orchids with which Mr. Chamberlain was associated in the public mind.

clearing-station. I went along with him and asked the Germans, of whom there were eleven, what each had been having to eat. There is, perhaps, no race which answers a question about food more readily than the German. Several robust-looking men among them said they had been having meat and chicken and bread and—as one man expressed it enthusiastically—" *Alles was gut ist* " (everything that is good). Another poor soul in spectacles said he had been given only rice-pudding and milk, "for eating gave him great 'belly pains,' " he added, dolorously. He was a poor, feeble little fellow and had worked as a chemist in Germany. The war, he said, had undermined him quite. He was not strong before, but now he was like a gnat ("*So wie eine Mücke*") He had been very kindly treated, he said, as a prisoner. Another of the Germans had been captured in Beaumont-Hamel. Our shell fire, he said, had been dreadful; but, as all the garrison were well underground, they thought to be able to hold the place. Their officers had said that the British were fools even to attack it, and had prophesied that we should have finally to leave off the direct assault and try some other means.

Cigarettes were being served out to the British soldiers by Sister Paul from a big tray. Before she came to the Germans I had handed them a few of my own, fearing that they would get none. The quartermaster passed at the time and said: "You needn't have done that, sir; we give them a smoke or two. All fare alike in this train, Germans and all. When a man's sick or knocked out of action that's excuse enough for treating him kindly."

Certainly the British Tommies, who fought the Germans — and

The give-and-take of war

whose view ought, therefore, to count for at least as much as those of people who didn't fight him—always treated the German prisoners and wounded in a friendly way. In that train, though they could not speak together, they were exchanging friendly signs and nods. Some exchanged small souvenirs. One German soldier had a British bullet that had been taken out of his lungs. A British Tommy, who had come from the same part of the line, asked to see it. As he weighed it in his hand, looking thoughtfully before him, he said to his nearest pal: "It would be a very funny thing if I had shot that bullet, wouldn't it? But who knows I didn't?" He looked at the German, who,

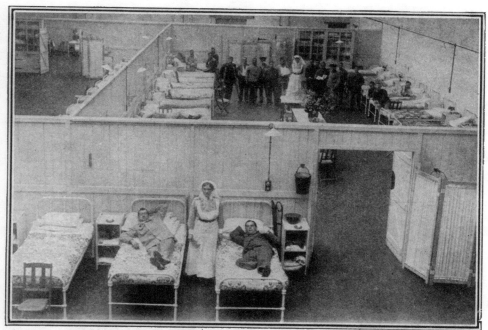

CLIVEDEN HOSPITAL: JUST BEFORE VISITING HOURS.
Visitors' Day, one of great expectancy in every hospital, was a day of especial interest for soldiers wounded in the war and for their friends. This photograph shows a ward in the Cliveden Hospital prepared for the admission of visitors.

of course, understood nothing. Then the speaker made a curious request to me: "Tell him what I have just said, sir." With some curiosity I translated for the German this odd speculation. He smiled and shrugged his shoulders, and replied calmly as he puffed at his cigarette: "That doesn't matter to me. Perhaps I shot him." Thus impartially and dispassionately was the give-and-take of war recognised by soldiers who had fought and suffered. It was something of a lesson, perhaps, for less tolerant people who have not fought.

Tea in the commandant's cabin that afternoon was a hurried affair for all save me. There was much work to be done, and I was left alone with my second cup. The lamps had been lit. Outside the weather was raw and dark, with some mist. The long, heavy train was rumbling rhythmically at a sober pace over the metals. The electric light in the white ceiling brightened and waned at slow, regular intervals. I sat back in the comfortable seat watching it, and with my mind wandering, dreamily perhaps, over the events of the day and that week, and earlier weeks. I had seen these young soldiers, or their kind, in the full vigour and rigour of war —war that admitted of no comfort, no softness, or even gentleness; grim, hard, unfeeling war, coldly callous and horrible. Now these among them had got their quietus—some for a time, some for a longer time, some for ever —for not all among that trainful of wounded men would pull through. You would have thought to find them much subdued. I had looked for traces of this, and had seen hardly one. Even as I sat there they began singing comic songs. I walked along to the first ward-coach. A chorus

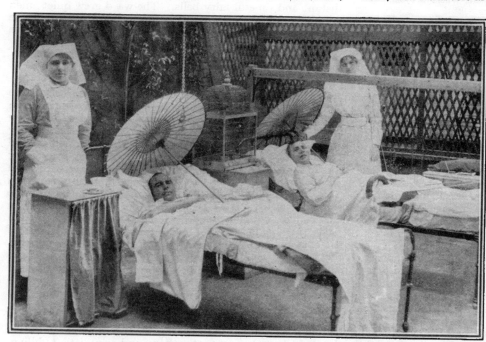

OPEN-AIR TREATMENT AT THE COULTER HOSPITAL. [*Bassano.*
Corner of the open-air ward at the Coulter Hospital, Grosvenor Square. Londoners became very familiar with the picturesque sight of these hospital wards set up on the leads and balconies of the great houses, where wounded men got full benefit of the air.

MOVABLE ICE-MAKING PLANT AND KITCHEN.

The equipment of the British Army Medical Service was as near perfection as human organisation can attain, and was the only matter in respect of which Germany frankly admitted British superiority and imitated British methods. This was one of the Red Cross vans containing ice-making plant and kitchen.

they were in a mood for music, the ward Sister disappeared, and in a few minutes an orderly appeared carrying a gramophone and some records. Some light music and songs were played, and the men listened from their beds with keen attention. And then it remained for that gramophone to reveal in them their real nature—a gentler, deeper nature than that shown in their songs laughing at death. The orderly put on a record of a little violin and piano piece. The Sister had said it was getting too late for more music ; it was bed-time. But in answer to several pleadings she had said they could play one more record if they chose a "quiet one" that would not disturb men who by now were ready for sleep. The piece opened with a haunting little melody, almost like a cradle-song. I jotted down the few bars of it which are given below.

The violin played the melody with its childish thirds and sixths, played it softly, wistfully, soothingly, naïvely (Fritz Kreisler, I think, was the player), and the piano accompaniment, coming faintly and with that strange

song was in full progress. The words of it struck me cold. They were singing this :

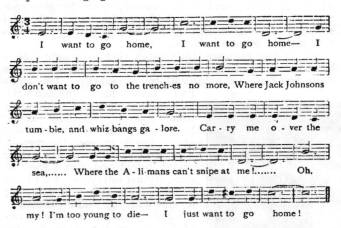

I want to go home, I want to go home— I don't want to go to the trench-es no more, Where Jack Johnsons tum - bie, and whiz bangs ga - lore. Car - ry me o - ver the sea,...... Where the A - li - mans can't snipe at me !...... Oh, my ! I'm too young to die— I just want to go home !

A not inappropriate song, you say, for wounded men to sing. True enough. But not as they sang it. They were singing it *as a comic song*, with laughing faces. I stood, almost in horror, watching one poor wreck of humanity, whose face peeping from a mass of bandages was almost whiter than his wrappings, as he sang " Oh, my ! I'm too young to die ! " actually with a happy grin, and with his one remaining hand beating time above his

Spirit of the wounded

remaining hand beating time above his stretcher. He wore the " dangerous case " ticket, red and white, and had death written all over him. One of the surgeons who saw my fascinated gaze halted for a second as he passed me to say, in a grim sotto voce, " He'll do well if he gets his wish." "Shouldn't they stop him ? " I asked. " Not a bit of it ! " he said cheerily. " That's the spirit that may help him dodge death after all. I like to hear them." From this song they turned to queer songs of their own making, sung to hymn tunes—songs that scoffed at duty and war and death, and many serious things—in fun. Finding that

elfin tinkle that the gramophone lends to the piano's tone, had about it a curious prettiness and sweetness like distant and tuneful fairy bells. The ward grew quiet ; men who half an hour before had been singing a lusty defiance to all the gentler moods of life, listened now with rapt eyes and with faces curiously relaxed, like those of sufferers suddenly released from pain.

Influence of music

The second movement of the piece was struggling and fretful music. The men fidgeted a little and some closed their eyes. But the opening refrain, in all its childishness, came back again before long, and again they listened—listened as a sleepy child to a mother's crooning. The piece finished. They did not speak. The instrument was picked up and carried away without one remonstrance. They did not even look ; they lay there with closed eyes as though to keep with them for the night the visions and the thought-pictures to which that plaintive child music had given rise. The lights were turned down. Soon there was not a sound save an occasional sigh and the rhythmical rumble of the train over the metals. And I caught myself tiptoeing out of that coach as I might have done out of a children's nursery. Poor lads ! Right through the livelong day they had been full of " go," " full of fight," full, even though wounded, of the healthy animal spirits which the British soldier, like every healthy child, knows. But with the evening, and dark, and the coming of weariness due to their weakness, the softer, gentler side of their nature shone through—shone through at the subtle crooning of a gentle bit of music. It might have been a mother song and they little toddling, sleepy tots again.

I asked the Sister later to show me the gramophone, for on it I had noticed a little brass plate and some printing.

The printing said: " From Members of the Dunhill Parish Church, Dumbartonshire, Rev. Dugald Clarke, October, 1916." I thought the givers of that gramophone and my unknown namesake the minister would like to know something of the pleasure they had given by their gift.

The train stopped during the night at the long, deserted platform of a deserted station, Abbéville, I think. The commandant jumped out and beckoned me to follow him. He walked to the front of the train before it had started again, boarded it and walked through, inspecting each ward and coach on his way. The patients were asleep. You could stand at the end of a ward-coach and count before you thirty-six beds, in threes, one above another as on board ship, and see in each bed some figure of pain. The dimness of the lighting seemed to make even more grotesque the strange and unnatural positions in which wounded men lie. Here and there an arm or leg extended from a bunk, and part way across the narrow passage between the beds. You had to walk carefully so as not to touch it and disturb the sleeper. You had to take care also not to tread on the men of the undermost bunks, some of whom preferred to hang limbs or shoulders half out of bed and on the floor. "They find the position that is most comfortable," said the captain, "and we try to let them lie as they like."

Once, I remember, a battered and bandaged hand suddenly reached out right in front of me as I passed along the narrow centre aisle and hung most pleadingly, and, so it seemed in the half-light, like that of a beggar in a Bible picture asking for alms. The captain had gone on in front. I thought the patient wanted someone to look at his hand, but a glance at his eyes showed me he was sound asleep. Involuntarily the paining limb had stretched out suppliantly, seeming to beg for itself for ease from its pain, to plead for itself while the owner slept. I took the hand and gently put it back across the patient's heaving chest and under the sling from which it had escaped. He sighed, but did not even open his eyes, then lay peacefully.

Reaching the coast

Unseen by me, the commandant had turned back to wait for me and had been watching me from the end of the coach. "We shall have to find you a job in the train's nursing crew," he said with a smile.

Near the door of the next coach Sister Mahoney was putting a hot-water bottle to a sleeping man's feet. The captain felt the man's pulse and asked her some questions. They spoke in whispers. On the corner of the man's bed hung the little red-and-white "danger" ticket. I recognised in the patient the singer of "I'm too young to die."

We reached the coast in the wee small hours. Motor-cars in scores it seemed, and bearers in dozens, were there. By the wan light of white arc lamps the stretchers were lifted out of the train; some of the patients did not wake, and were carried over the cobbled streets of the old French town to base hospitals, there to rest till cured or till ready for sending oversea to that longed-for haven of all wounded, "Old Blighty." One glimpse of the busy workers and motor-men and orderlies as friend Oldham was carried indoors at one of these hospitals, and I turned away. No need for me to describe a base hospital again. Oldham would be in safe keeping and would not be moved again for at least many hours. I should find him again. I walked back through the quiet streets. No bed was to be had, but I slept quite soundly that night on a wooden form in the railway transport office at the station, with a small heap of railway guides for a pillow. The corporal in charge of the office, formerly a clerk at the Railway Clearing House, London, made me a sandwich and a cup of tea. A deep rumble shook my form an hour later. It was my ambulance train going back to the front for another load of wounded.

"Blighty" at last

A big ship, painted a bright apple green and bearing on its side a mammoth Red Cross. w ited at the quayside not many days later. Again the string of motor-ambulances, again the careful carrying of maimed men on stretchers— Oldham among them, the lucky ones—again the filling of bed bunks one above another. And then the big green ship glided noiselessly away from the quayside of that old French port. She flew a red-and-white flag as the sign of her merciful calling, and when daylight ebbed at last and the sun sank into a mush of heavy brassy clouds away on the sky-line, she lighted up a girdle of green lamps about her waist—a girdle as of rich sparkling emeralds that enveloped her all about. Set among them on each side, as in rubies, were red lights in the form of the great Red Cross.

In the pallid light of an early morning a magic word went to and fro among the worn men who filled the cabins fore and aft of that apple-green ship. That word made lame men and sick men drag themselves up in bed on their elbows; it made men who could even hobble get out of bed to look out of the port-holes. And through those little brass-ringed circles of weather-smeared glass they gazed rapturously at the dark grey slabs of a dock wall, at the black-timbered walls and the wet, slate roof of some dock warehouse, at a dock crane with thin outstretched arm that reared backwards and upwards till lost to sight in the mist. The rain fell. Fog rose from the yellow-green water of the dock. An old man hobbled from under a shelter to a plump bollard near the dockside. He looked at the murky sky both to north and to south. Then into that dock he spat deliberately. That was what those worn soldiers gazed out upon through the little round brass-rimmed windows, and their eyes sparkled with moisture at the mere sight. Throats moved without words issuing forth, till at last pent-up feelings found vent in one hoarse murmur—"Blighty!"

WOUNDED SOLDIERS ENTERTAINED AT VOLUNTEER SPORTS.
Sports at North Ealing arranged for the entertainment of wounded men by the London Volunteer Rifles. The visitors were watching a ceremonial parade.

RUINS OF THE ARMOURED CONCRETE FORT DOUAUMONT ON THE OUTSKIRTS OF VERDUN.

Two views of Fort Douaumont, a focus of some of the fiercest fighting in the Battles of Verdun. Its proclamations that he ever issued. Retaken by the French and lost again, it was finally capture by the Germans on February 26th, 1916, provoked from the Kaiser one of the most flamboyant reaptured by them in their magnificently successful counter-offensive towards the close of the year.

CHAPTER CLXII.

THE COUNTER-OFFENSIVE OF THE ARMY OF VERDUN.
By Edward Wright.

Noyon and Falkenhayn's Miss—Nivelle Awaits His 16 in. and 20 in. Guns—Germans Vainly Attempt to Distract the French—Terrific Battle of Thiaumont—Knife-like Drive Against Souville Fort—New German Method of Infiltration—Crown Prince's Army Exhausted—Nivelle Wins Mastery of the Air—Brandenburg Troops Reproached for Cowardice—Hindenburg Prepares a French Victory—Remarkable Genius of General Nivelle—The Storming Return to Thiaumont—Enemy Provoked to Attack—Battle Around Souville Fort—The Deceptive Tactics of General Nivelle—Germans Move Half their Guns from Verdun—How the British Army Helped the Army of Verdun—Nivelle Uncovers His New Big Guns—Consternation of Enemy—30,000 Frenchmen against 63,000 Germans—Swift and Smashing Victory of Douaumont—Strange Adventure of a Zouave—The "Black Friends of France" and the Heroism of a Sahara Prince—Ironic German Staff Publication—Lardemelle's Division Advances on Vaux—Enemy Retires without Battle—Superb Engineering Feat by General Nivelle—New French Commander-in-Chief—Retirement of Crown Prince—Battle of Vacherauville—German Line Pierced on Pepper Hill—Great French Flanking Movement on Louvemont—Passaga's Division Storms into Bezonvaux—Extraordinary Gains and Small Losses—Significance of General Nivelle's New System of Attack.

WHEN, in the last week of June, 1916, the guns on either side the Somme thundered a message of relief to Verdun, the situation around the citadel of Lorraine was such as to cause anxiety. At a disastrous sacrifice of men and material General von Falkenhayn had penetrated to the inner ring of defence of the gateway of the Meuse. But it can now be frankly stated that Falkenhayn made a mistake in strategy in selecting Verdun for a concentration of two thousand guns and a million and a half men. The sector he should have attacked, in the judgment of French military authorities, was that between Lassigny and Soissons. At the point of this angle was the historic town of Noyon, held by the Germans, and only fifty miles from Paris. An overwhelming and sustained thrust from Noyon, if conducted with as much success as the preliminary drive at Verdun, might have alarmed the French people and provoked a premature reaction from the British Army. Noyon, it can now be admitted, was the real point of hazard in the view of the French Staff. Our allies did not fear the actual

[French official photograph.
FORT VAUX'S ONLY ENTRANCE AFTER THE BOMBARDMENT.
How effective had been the terrific bombardment by the French which caused the Germans to evacuate Fort Vaux is seen in this photograph of the only way that was left by which the French could enter when they finally retook the stronghold.

piercing of their line, but the spirit of the public might have been disturbed if a battle had opened with unparalleled violence only fifty miles from the capital.

As Falkenhayn aimed above all at a moral effect on French opinion, he failed in the aim which led him to concentrate against Verdun. It was his superior railway facilities in the Metz area and the desire to increase the prestige of the heir to the Hohenzollern throne that led him to select Verdun as his grand objective. Even had he taken Verdun he would not have seriously weakened the French front. For on the western bank of the Meuse the French held another line of fortified hills that would probably have cost the German Army another half a million casualties to capture. Behind the western heights of the Meuse the French had a third great line of defence in the upland Forest of Argonne, and again behind the Forest of Argonne, going towards Paris, was the long line of cliffs of High Champagne. Having regard to the superb condition of the French Army and the experienced skill of its chiefs, the attack on Verdun did not, from the beginning, promise any decisive break in the

AN OLD MONARCH OF WAR.
[French official photograph.
French monster mortar at Verdun. In ten days this old warrior hurled nearly a thousand shells, each of 1,100 lb., at the enemy. The French soldiers knew and liked its roar.

French line, such as the enemy produced in Galicia in 1915 and in Rumania in 1916.

It is said that Marshal Joffre was relieved when the expected thrust occurred at Verdun instead of at Noyon. The Noyon problem had been openly debated in the French Senate by that past-master in the art of upsetting Ministries, M. Georges Clemenceau. For political reasons the French Commander-in-Chief was glad that the blow fell where it did. It enabled him to give Sir Douglas Haig four more months to train the new British levies and accumulate munitions.

France also required time to produce in effective quantities her new 16 in. howitzer, which was a complete answer to the old 16·8 in. Krupp howitzer. By June, 1916, the speeding-up of French munitions of war was fairly complete. In fact, little more could be done without entirely new machinery in the way of peat furnaces to increase the native resources of France. She had lost most of her iron-fields around Verdun, and most of her coal-mines around Lille. To supply the place of black coal, she had developed her "white coal," and erected an extraordinary number of turbines and dynamos in the Alps and other centres of water-power.

Then, with help from British and American steel-makers and colliery owners, the captains of French industry enormously extended their output. In January, 1915, the total production of small French shells was only 65,000

a day. It was nearly double in six months, and later increased to a great figure which it is best not to state. But it was more than forty times the production of the French light shell in August, 1914. The rate of production of light field-artillery was increased thirty times; that of heavy artillery twenty-four times; while the manufacture of heavy shell was ninety times as great, and the manufacture of machine-guns one hundred and seventy times as great. The French 16 in. howitzer was ready for action on a large scale in July, 1916, and in an astonishingly short time it was succeeded by a masterpiece of appalling range and smashing force—the 20·8 in. Creusot.

It was the production of the 16 in. gun and the approaching completion of the 20·8 in. monster, with an abundance of shell of these calibres, that inspired the French commander with confidence in the issue of the Verdun campaign. There were not, however, immediately available sufficient guns and shell of the new type to enable a double offensive to be conducted on both the Somme and the Meuse. Neither France nor Great Britain, in the summer of 1916, had arrived at such a pitch of power in munition manufacture as would allow them to press the enemy to breaking point by hammering simultaneously from Verdun, from both sides of the Somme, and from Loos and Arras.

The army of Verdun under General Nivelle had still to stand on the defensive, for lack of heavy artillery and **Holding the gateway** heavy shell, in order to allow the armies of General Foch to co-operate with the British forces in further wearing down the enemy's strength. But the heroic defenders of the gateway of Lorraine knew that the first part of their work was completed, and that they would swing forth in a counter-offensive in the autumn. On June 12th, 1916, an Order of the Day arrived from General Joffre. He said:

The plan matured by the Councils of the Coalition is now being fully put into execution. Soldiers of Verdun! It is to your heroic resistance that this is due. Your defence was the indispensable condition for success. On that rest our victories, now close at hand; for that is what has created in the general theatre of war in Europe the situation, out of which will arise to-morrow the definite victory of our cause.

On June 23rd, General Nivelle issued the following order:

The hour is decisive. The Germans, feeling themselves hemmed in on all sides, are delivering furious and desperate attacks in the hope of reaching the doors of Verdun before they are themselves attacked by the united forces of the allied armies. Comrades, you will not let them pass! Your country calls for yet this supreme effort from you. The army of Verdun will not allow itself to be overawed by shells or by that German infantry whose efforts it has smashed for the past four months. The army of Verdun will know how to maintain its glory intact.

A STRONGHOLD OF FRANCE IN FRENCH KEEPING AGAIN.
Despite the terrific intensity of the many bombardments to which it was subjected, and the mass of metal hurled upon it, much of the interior of Fort Vaux was found intact when the French reoccupied it in November, 1916

ON THE WAY TO THE RELIEF OF THE GLORIOUS FRONT LINE NEAR VERDUN.
Behind all that was left of a shell-destroyed wood in the neighbourhood of Thiaumont—to the north of Verdun—the French Poilus had a brief rest on their journey to the relief of their comrades in the front line, and to taking their part in the driving back of the enemy.

On the day on which General Nivelle's order was issued the British guns opened their bombardment from Ypres to the Somme, and warned Falkenhayn of what was about to happen. The German Chief of Staff thereupon asked the commander who was in active control of the Crown Prince's army to make one more attempt to snatch a decision at Verdun. It will be remembered that General Nivelle had recovered, on June 23rd, the northern key position of Thiaumont Work, between Douaumont and the ridge of Froide Terre. The recovery of this fortified height left the enemy powerless to close upon the old inner Fort of Souville. Souville Fort had been constructed, with the neighbouring north-eastern Fort of Tavannes, after the war of 1870, and before the invention of the high-explosive shell in 1886. The two old forts were therefore of little direct, practical value against the enemy's gigantic array of heavy siege ordnance, ranging from 16·8 in. Berthas to the 8 in. howitzer which was the principal German weapon against Verdun. The 8 in. howitzer had a range of about six miles, and was employed in parks, and not in batteries, to produce an overwhelming hurricane of trench-smashing shell.

Struggle for Thiaumont

Towards the end of June the Germans turned hundreds of these 8 in. guns upon the Thiaumont Work and Souville and Tavannes Forts and Froide Terre. Then after days of bombardment, which the French guns answered with telling vigour, a terrific infantry battle raged in and around Thiaumont.

The French lost the work, but stormed back on the morning of June 30th, through a series of dreadful hostile curtain fires, and recovered the position. In the afternoon the Germans returned in dense columns, and were mowed down by gun fire and machine-gun fire. By persistent pressure of packed waves of attack the Germans at last re-entered the work at three o'clock in the afternoon,

but at half-past four they were again thrown out by strong storming columns of French infantry.

The next day the German commander made another succession of grand attacks on Thiaumont, and apparently, in his report to the Great Staff, claimed to have entered it, after a struggle of forty-eight hours. He attacked on a wide front from the Damloup Hill eastward to the height of Froide Terre northward, and while pressing the French on both these flanks, drove in at the centre, which was Thiaumont. But the Second French Army stood firm all along the line on the historic day when the Allies were breaking the German defences on either side of the Somme.

Premature German claims

The German eastern wing stormed up and into Damloup, rising south of Vaux Fort. The French surged back and recovered Damloup, were again driven out on July 3rd, and once more went back and re-established themselves on Damloup. Meanwhile, the awful struggle on the Thiaumont Hill went on with increasing fury, each side concentrating by telephone control the fire of all available heavy guns, over a wide arc, upon the few furlongs of the coveted key position.

The Crown Prince was in one of those desperate positions in which German Army commanders on the western front were frequently placed, owing to over-confidence. He had rashly claimed, in a public communiqué, to have re-conquered the Thiaumont Work.

He also claimed to have conquered and occupied the Damloup Hill. And though the French were in both positions, he brazened out his false claims, while using his men up by the forty thousand in order to palliate by ultimate success the mistaken reports he had made to his own General Headquarters. The Berlin communiqué of July 4th was written in an extraordinary style. It ran: " The reputed official French reports regarding the recapture of the Thiaumont Work and the Damloup battery are

335

invented fables." Somebody was very angry, but whether it was the Crown Prince and General von Mudra who were vexed with themselves, or Ludendorff and Hindenburg who were raging at the mistake of the younger Hohenzollern, is not clear. At an inordinate waste of life in the Fifth German Army under the Crown Prince, the Chief of Staff at last managed to cover up the early false claim in regard to Thiaumont Work by burying the hill in explosions of heavy shell and launching column after column of storming infantry, who regained the work for the fourth time. The French troops remained in immediate contact with the position, and at Damloup Hill, in spite of violent bombardments and continual infantry actions, they continued in possession.

The enemy's recovery of Thiaumont was an affair of importance. It again opened the way for an advance upon the old inner defences of Verdun, and enabled Falkenhayn to proceed with his plan of obtaining a success on the Meuse that would divert French forces and munitions from the Somme. The village of Fleury, lying at the mouth of the long Vaux ravine and giving access to the slopes of Souville Fort, became the immediate objective of the enemy's operations.

After a long and intense bombardment, in which Verdun Cathedral was spitefully smitten with salvos of heavy shell, the German infantry was launched on July 7th against the French positions between Thiaumont and Fleury. The Germans took the front French line, but were completely thrown out of it by a French counter-attack, and when night fell the defending front was unbroken. Another prolonged artillery preparation went on for four days. Then on July 11th the hostile infantry made an assault on a large scale, closing upon Damloup Hill, Fumin and Le Chenois Woods, Vaux-Chapitre Wood, Fleury village, and the ground south of Thiaumont.

Costly and vain attacks

General Nivelle and his brilliant lieutenant, General Mangin, had no reason to expose their men to great wastage. They gave ground at last at Damloup, as this position was exposed to flanking fires from Vaux Fort, Vaux, and the eastern plain. It had been held while the shattered wood behind it, Laufée Wood, was strongly entrenched and linked more firmly with the three wooded heights running north-westward and known as Le Chenois Wood, Fumin Wood, and Chapitre Wood. These four woods, seamed with trenches, dotted with redoubts, and lined with deep communicating ways, formed the real defences of the two old forts, Souville and Tavannes, rising immediately behind them. The enemy was badly defeated in all the woodland battles, and though he got a footing in Chenois and Fumin Woods, the French returned in the night and recovered most of the ground, so that the capture of Damloup cost the German commander the best part of two divisions. The enemy was being worn down at Verdun as well as on the Somme, for the losses of the Verdun army were slight when compared with those of the Crown Prince's army.

After the vain grand attack of July 11th the Chief of Staff to the Crown Prince concentrated two fresh divisions for a different kind of attack. He tried a knife-like drive along a very narrow front, at the village of Fleury, directly against Souville Fort. The grey columns massed in the

WELL-MASKED FRENCH GUN ON THE VERDUN FRONT.
Maintaining the guns at points providing the maximum of efficiency with the minimum of exposure was one of the problems on a front where long shelling had destroyed most natural cover. Any such remaining stretch of woodland as this proved valuable for masking artillery from aerial observation.

old formation into the valley where the ruins of the Chapel of Sainte Fine scarcely showed in the chaos of shell-holes below Souville Fort. As brigade after brigade was shattered by shell fire and raked by machine-gun fire, the enemy brigadiers employed an extraordinary method in order to maintain the strength of their attacking front. The method was known as infiltration. It appears to have been first worked out by General von Mudra in the Verdun operations, and it testified to the mechanical perfection of the Prussian drill system.

Each reeling and heavily punished mass, at a signal, re-formed in such a way as to leave lanes running almost straight from the front to the rear. Through these lanes a fresh brigade then advanced in sections and, smartly opening fan-wise at the head of the fighting-line, furiously continued the action. All this was done on a closely engaged front, with both the outworn force and the fresh force maintaining the attack during the manœuvre of infiltration.

This new and remarkable way of driving home an assault at any cost had been prepared by several months of practice. As the British and French did on the Somme, so the Germans did before them at Verdun. They reproduced the hostile positions in great detail on a large practice ground behind their own lines, and also constructed a copy of their own attacking parallel. Then over the model works they continually worked their troops and practised the new infiltration technique of massed attack, until the operation was carried out with mechanical precision.

But on July 12th the French light field-gun and the French machine-gun sadly interfered with the funnels of fresh troops that came through the broken brigades up the slopes to the fort. The inclines were held impregnably, and at the close of the day all that the Germans gained was a little ground at the cross-roads between Vaux and Fleury and around the ruins of Sainte Fine Chapel.

New method of massed attack

This great but fruitless effort exhausted the forces under the Crown Prince. Before his Chief of Staff could arrange another operation the British Army broke the second German line on the Bazentin ridge and compelled Falkenhayn to collect men and guns from Verdun and pour all available shell towards the Somme. Verdun was relieved.

General Nivelle, however, was not yet ready to begin the great counter-offensive. He had to wait for his new 16 in. guns, and build a closer network of two-foot gauge railways, along which little, toy two-funnel locomotives could haul the one-ton shells. This large work of engineering preparation was one of considerable difficulty. An abundance of railway bridges and motor tracks had to be thrown across the gorge of the Meuse at a time when the hostile heavy batteries, including naval guns of enormous range, daily and nightly maintained a bombardment of systematic destruction upon the rear of the French lines.

In spite of the number of guns gradually moved by the enemy from Verdun to the Somme, his gunners remained for months arrogantly superior in striking power to the gunners of the Second French Army. This was seen in the persistence of nocturnal bombardments of great violence regularly undertaken by the Crown Prince's army. Only the stronger side, possessing guns of longer range, systematically fired at night when flames from the gun-pits enabled every principal battery to be spotted. From February, 1916, to October, 1916, the German gunners around Verdun maintained nocturnal bombardments at long range upon the French positions. If the medium heavy French ordnance attempted to reply by night to the German 8 in. batteries, the Germans in turn answered at a secure range with 15 in. cannon and 16·8 in. howitzers. In these circumstances the army of Verdun retired in part to the subterranean shelters of the tunnels beneath the old forts, and left only a thin and flexible line of advanced machine-gun posts to guard against any hostile infantry surprise. When abruptly attacked the advanced French line often withdrew on the principal defensive position.

But, as it withdrew, the French guns prepared for action, and, working with mechanical precision on marked ranges, destroyed the German forces occupying the lost positions. Thereupon, the French infantry returned in strength, and recovered and reconsolidated its line of advanced posts.

In consequence of these flexible tactics of the French Command, only strong and sustained attacks could succeed against the Verdun defences. In making sustained attacks the enemy commander had to expose from twenty thousand to forty thousand of his troops to French shell fire and machine-gun fire to win any considerable ground and retain it. Nothing was to be purchased cheaply from the army of Verdun. Moreover, though the German artillery remained predominant for nearly nine months, its mastery was reduced to a sort of blind, mechanical outburst of power.

French gain air mastery

In the late spring of 1916 General Pétain obtained machines capable of dealing with the Fokker. In the summer of 1916, General Nivelle, profiting by the splendid reorganisation of French aeroplane production, definitely won the mastery of the air at Verdun. He repeated on the Meuse the aerial successes the Allies were winning on either side of the Somme. His airmen brought down the kite-balloons that directed the fire of the heavy German pieces. His fighting pilots swept the Fokkers aside and convoyed scores of large bombing squadrons that shattered every hostile railway centre near Verdun, destroyed the blast furnaces in the Lorraine mine-fields, and attacked the German troop trains.

By the end of July, 1916, the gunners of the Crown Prince's army could do little more than fire by the map against the French rear, and by fire-trench and hill-top observation against the French front. Their observation balloons could only swing low on the horizon for brief periods, when no French planes seemed to be near enough to swoop down with fire-balls. The high positions which the Germans occupied on the Douaumont ridge gave them a wide field of vision over the lower heights the French occupied around Souville; but the French in the valleys and ravines could not be kept under observation by German artillery observers. On the other hand, owing to their recovery of the mastery in the air, the French possessed an entire power of observation over every daylight movement in and behind the German lines.

Arrival of new French guns

General Nivelle and his Staff soon knew more about the disposition of the enemy forces in front of them than was revealed in the operations the Verdun army conducted. The position of practically every German gun was known, especially the long-range guns that seemed to be beyond the reach of a French shell. The new 16 in. French guns arrived secretly by night, and were placed in the pits prepared in advance and then covered up; 16 in. shells arrived also by night, and were accumulated in underground store-places. The telephone system was extended by networks of underground wires, and the little railways threaded all the ravines and went under new tunnels into new centres of distribution.

The much enduring army of Verdun, engaged in alternate spells of navvy work and hand-grenade fighting, knew what was impending, and heartened by the tale of victories on the Somme gained with the new 16 in.

[French official photograph.
POILUS WOUNDED IN THE VERDUN OFFENSIVE.
Duly ticketed with particulars of their injuries, these French soldiers, who had taken part in the great struggle in front of Verdun, awaited at the entrance of a massively-built dug-out the arrival of the ambulance men.

gun, the men went daily into action round Fleury in a cold fury that appalled some of the best German troops.

Even the famous Brandenburg troops, under General von Luchow, faltered when again brought to Verdun. In an order, afterwards found on prisoners, Luchow complained of the way in which his men straggled to the rear when led to the attack, and ordered his officers either to shoot the stragglers down on the spot or punish them sternly by legal sentences. He further ordered that troops should be used in close formation, to keep them from running away, and that all men who strolled from the firing-line should be left without food.

All false pity, all weakness, all pardoning and letting things drift make superior officers accomplices of the criminals (said another German general at Verdun). You must intervene with a hand of iron on all occasions when demoralisation is setting in, or about to set in. Make the men understand that the French regard each bomb of theirs that remains without reply as a sign of mastery, and that every wounded prisoner who falls into their hands is proof of the demoralisation of the German Army.

General von Luchow seems to have become the Commander-in-Chief of the principal forces under the Crown Prince as soon as Falkenhayn was succeeded in the High Command by Hindenburg. The command on the Argonne front was given back to General von Mudra, a capable man of the sound, professional type, who continually emerged as business-manager for the Crown Prince when famous Field-Marshals like Heeringen and Haeseler failed to accomplish the glorious manœuvres they had planned. The position of the Crown Prince became doubtful. All along he had only been a figurehead; every military leader of high reputation on the western front had directed his Fifth Army, and both the former Chiefs of Staff, Moltke and Falkenhayn, had arranged a great campaign with a view to producing a grand and decisive victory on the sector where the descendant of Frederick the Great was in nominal command.

Hindenburg was no courtier. Having the German people strongly behind him, he was more the master of the Hohenzollerns than Bismarck had been. It was an open secret that the conduct and character of the Crown Prince did not please the grim **Hindenburg and the** old Field-Marshal. In his view, military **Crown Prince** considerations had been sacrificed in a perilous manner to dynastic motives. As the salvation of Germany was more important than the prestige of the Crown Prince, Hindenburg decided that he would give no help whatever to the Fifth Army beyond that which Luchow could provide.

It would be going too far to say that Hindenburg engineered the overthrow of the Crown Prince by reducing the Fifth Army to a state of weakness. Military necessities compelled him to withdraw a thousand guns at least from the battlefield of Verdun, and to diminish the troops there by army corps after army corps. The furnace of the Somme had to be fed, and the vast army that the Crown Prince had vainly used before Verdun was the only immediately available store of human and mechanical fuel. Nevertheless, both Hindenburg and his assistant, Ludendorff, by relying upon the calculations of the General Staff which they took over from Falkenhayn, laboured under a disastrous error during the rearrangement of their Verdun forces. **German under-** They reckoned that General Nivelle was **estimate of Nivelle** reduced to a position of permanent weakness. The General Staff had most of the factors carefully tabulated. They knew what forces General Foch had employed on his long line of attack, from Combles to Chaulnes, they could estimate, roughly, the wastage of the French armies on the Somme and at Verdun, and they concluded that France could no more undertake a fresh offensive in the region of Verdun than Great Britain could undertake a new attack on the grand scale in the region of Loos.

It must be admitted that these calculations of the enemy were sound so far as they went. But they only dealt with material factors, and there was an incalculable element in the Verdun situation in the personal genius of General Nivelle. In the course of the war France had produced a brilliant succession of men of genius. Colonel after colonel had become army leader and even commander of army groups. In March, 1916, General Pétain seemed to be the supreme military genius of France. But when he took over the command of the armies of Champagne, and left the task of holding Verdun to the Franco-British officer who had come as a colonel from England in August, 1914, General Nivelle was given the opportunity of proving

FRENCH ARTILLERY THAT MADE THE COUNTER-OFFENSIVE POSSIBLE.
It was owing to their heavier artillery that the Germans got as near as they did to the centre of the Verdun position—it was thanks to their obtaining a superiority in heavy guns that the French were able to carry out their successful counter-offensive.

A MARKET-PLACE THAT BECAME THE KITCHEN FOR A GARRISON.

The covered market-place at Verdun was one of the very few buildings that were not entirely destroyed by the German bombardment which, characteristically, became more spiteful and wantonly destructive as the siege proceeded unsuccessfully. Although considerably damaged, as this photograph shows, it remained more or less weather-proof, and was used as a kitchen by the cooks of the army defending the famous citadel on the Meuse.

himself the master of war that France was seeking. France was running short of men and growing mighty in mechanical power. Her knowledge of military science had been wrought to incomparable acuity by the urgent need, impressed upon all her Staff officers, of accomplishing large results with the utmost economy of human resources. Verdun had been the grand school in the fine French art of winning battles cheaply. General Nivelle, with General Mangin, one of the comrades of General Marchand at Fashoda, with General Passaga, General de Salins and General de Lardemelle, was master of the new method of warfare towards which the leaders of all the belligerent nations of Western Europe had been working. Very patiently did General Nivelle await the opening for a grand counter-offensive, which was being made for him by the terrific Franco-British pressure upon all the German forces. He firmly established the army of Verdun beneath Souville Fort and below the lost ridge of Thiaumont and the Froide Terre Hill. For months the hamlet of Fleury, by the cross-roads to Vaux and Bras, was the scene of hand-to-hand grenade conflicts. The enemy held the eastern ridge by Fleury and Thiaumont, and surveyed from Douaumont and Vaux the uplands that remained in French possession. But he was so weakened by losses and calls for reinforcements from the Somme front that his apparent advantage of working on all the highest ground on the eastern side of the Meuse did not enable him even to hold his own in the hand-bomb, shell-hole battles around Fleury.

After the violent, vain German attack of July 11th, General Nivelle's troops worked back toward Thiaumont by gradual rushes with bombs. All the ground was

General Nivelle's mastery of war

a wild sea of earth, owing to the storms of heavy shell overwhelming both sides during the prolonged and intense action. Cover was therefore abundant, and lines of defence could be rapidly made anywhere by digging in the already ploughed earth between the craters. Rains falling in unusual quantities, succeeded by burning August sunshine, made shell-hole warfare a grievous test of endurance. But the Frenchmen lost none of their ardour of attack, for they could feel the Germans weakening in front of them. Daily they took prisoners, sometimes by rush attacks between Fleury and Thiaumont and sometimes by waiting at night for utterly discouraged men on the other side to creep out and give themselves up.

Between July 15th and July 20th General Nivelle's men took eight hundred prisoners, and carried several important points around Fleury and Thiaumont by means of continual small operations in which scarcely more than a battalion was engaged. On some occasions a single French company suffered comparatively little loss in winning an important redoubt or stretch of trench. By the end of the month this method of little warfare brought the army of Verdun back to the Thiaumont Hill. Thereupon the German commander was compelled to use large forces in a defensive way. After a fierce nocturnal bombardment, on August 1st, 1916, he sent forth columns of assault against the new French positions west and south of the Thiaumont Fort. His massed ranks were completely broken by curtains of shell and streams of machine-gun fire from the alert troops of General Nivelle. Instead of the French losing any fraction of trench, they pursued their shattered foes and bombed them out of part of their line on the southern slope of Thiaumont ridge.

Cumulative effect of little operations

339

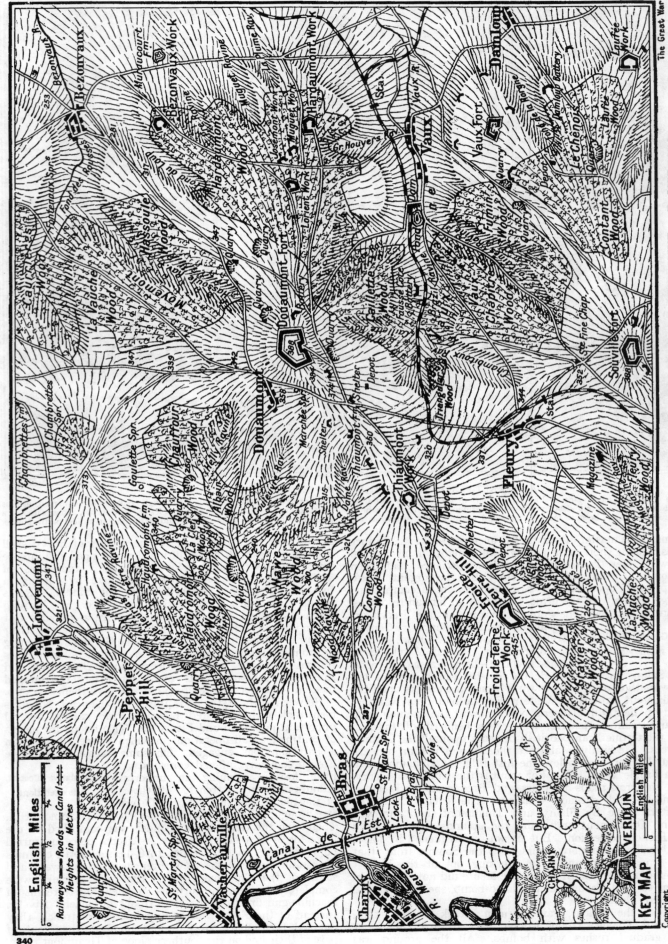

340

MAP SHOWING THE TERRAIN OF THE GREAT FRENCH COUNTER-OFFENSIVE AT VERDUN.

The Great War

Copyright

At the time the Germans made this worse than useless thrust upon the French centre their forces on the eastern wing endeavoured to break through the woods in front of Souville Fort. They maintained the conflict for two days by their new method of infiltration. With gusts of hurricane gun fire and clouds of poison gas the hostile eastern wing tried to balance the Thiaumont defeat by sweeping through the woods right to the inner fortress. In the terrific heat-wave in the first week of August the fight went on. By August 2nd the French lost ground in the woods. They fell back, and, as his men on the eastern side retired, General Nivelle struck out strongly northward, on a wide front from the Meuse to Fleury village. He adopted the échelon form of attack, with the regiments tailing out sideways behind each other, and moving up successively to the wood at Vacherauville and the ridge of Thiaumont. The Germans lost a line of redoubts, eight hundred prisoners, and sixteen machine-guns. Then, as they reinforced the northern front, the French échelons manœuvred eastward and stormed around Fleury village and the railway-station, broke the German line between Thiaumont and Fleury, and finally recovered most of the lost ground in the woods beyond Souville.

Again the German commander was compelled to another action on the grand scale, at a time when his General Headquarters were anxiously asking him for reinforcements for the Somme front. In a night battle of a dreadful kind the army of Verdun stormed back into Thiaumont Fort on August 3rd, and though the victors had to retire owing to the blasting force of the answering German bombardment, they withdrew with eighty prisoners. When day broke the men of Verdun again stormed up the Thiaumont Hill and won the site of the fortress for the second time in twelve hours. Having been driven out of the larger part of Fleury village by another blast of heavy shell, they merely waited until the German infantry occupied the **Desperate fighting for Thiaumont Fort** ruins, then, having something human to attack, they went into Fleury again with bomb and bayonet, and recovered it likewise, except for a clump of ruins on the eastern outskirts.

From the evening of August 4th to daybreak on August 5th the Germans continually attacked Thiaumont with desperate but unavailing courage. Defeated at this point, the German commander swung a fresh force into the eastern woods, and, after having his first assault completely checked by curtain fire, launched another column that reached the French trenches only to be destroyed in a counter-attack of the army of Verdun. Incessant fighting went on day and night on the Thiaumont-Fleury line, and at the close of the first week in August General Nivelle

GENERAL ANDLAUER.
Who was in command of the division which relieved that commanded by General de Lardemelle at the historic Fort Vaux in November, 1916.

was clearly exercising the power of initiative, and forcing the enemy commander to answer his movements and neglect every call for help on the German side of the Somme front. In the afternoon of August 7th the French garrison of Thiaumont Hill moved out in a fresh attack towards the ridge running up to Thiaumont, capturing an important position and several machine-guns.

To this direct challenge the Chief of Staff of the Crown Prince replied with all his available forces. After a furious nocturnal bombardment he sent out, at dawn on August 8th, a succession of large **German artillery's temporary success** masses of men who attacked from Thiaumont to Fleury, under cover of a creeping barrage of a park of 8 in. guns. The French infantry held up all assaults on the Fleury line by means of machine-gun fire, but northward they were driven from the Thiaumont Work, where they only had the cover of shell-holes against the tempest of shell. When, however, the German infantry in turn occupied the shell-holes, the Frenchmen stormed back into Thiaumont and held it until nightfall, when they were again compelled to retire.

This last retirement was brought about by the fact, already remarked, that the German artillery remained superior in range and in weight, and could therefore bombard furiously at night, and either compel the French guns to remain silent while the French infantry suffered, or to reveal their positions by their flash, and engage in a counter-firing combat at a disadvantage. General Nivelle preferred as much as possible not to reveal the position of his guns. Therefore, he withdrew his men from the Thiaumont Work in the night of Tuesday, August 8th.

But he still held firmly to the line running just below Thiaumont to Fleury village, and resuming the little war of company rushes and hand-bomb raids he again worked forward at small expense. At the end of three weeks he had recovered all the ruins of Fleury and made a new line east of the village and along the road leading back to Vaux Fort.

Thus at the beginning of September the German commander was again obliged to make a strong, sudden effort to recover

GENERAL PASSAGA.
Commander of the French infantry division La Gauloise, which won particular glory in the Verdun victory in December, 1916.

the series of important points that had been gained from him bit by bit. On September 3rd he gathered all his remaining forces for a grand assault on the old battlefield below Fort Souville. The woods, the village, cross-roads, chapel, and the slopes south of Thiaumont once more rocked under tornadoes of shell and vanished under smoke and poison gas. The struggle lasted until September 6th. In their first series of rushes the Germans broke into a French salient on the Vaux road, but by a balancing movement the French northern wing scaled the crest running above Fleury to Thiaumont, taking there three hundred prisoners. The Germans then pressed more fiercely upon the Vaux road front and captured another redoubt. When this was recovered by the French the enemy commander ceased to manœuvre on the wings, and, thinking he had at the end of the third day weakened the French centre, he attempted his grand stroke. At eight o'clock in the evening column after column of grey figures charged upon Fleury village. But not a column was able to deploy in the waves of attack. What Germans remained in formation after passing through the curtains of French gun fire were caught by the machine-guns of the Colonial Moroccan infantry. It was the final movement of offensive by the Fifth Germany Army, and it was so weakly or so unskilfully conducted that the attacking forces melted away before they were able to debouch. The next morning the army of Verdun sprang upon the enfeebled enemy, and, thrusting through the woods, captured a mile of German trenches and numerous prisoners. It took the Germans a day to gather troops for a counter-attack, and this flicker of fight ended in the men surrendering by the hundred wherever, with uplifted hands, they were allowed to reach the French line.

There then ensued a long lull on the Meuse, during which the army of Verdun gradually worked forward eastward, and the army of the Crown Prince assumed definitely a defensive attitude. **Germans deceived** Men and guns were removed in increasing **by French finesse** proportion to meet the needs of Falkenhayn on the new Rumanian front and fill the gaps of the enlarged German armies on the Somme. It was in this period of veiled crisis, when Hindenburg was making his final dispositions for the winter season in the west, that General Nivelle was rewarded for the restraint and patience he had displayed. He still allowed the enemy to prevail in nocturnal bombardments, and himself made no infantry movement in force by daylight. Consequently, the Crown Prince in person was convinced that the French forces in front of him were at last permanently weakened by their own long effort of resistance and by all the divisions moved westward since the Iron Division was transferred

[*French official photographs.*

COOLNESS AND COURAGE OF FRENCH SOLDIERS AMID THE RUINS OF FORT VAUX.
Carrying a despatch across the No Man's Land of shell-holes and ruined masonry to the only entrance that was left into Fort Vaux. Above: Three French soldiers who with machine-rifles stubbornly held a shell-hole during an attack before the fort.

PRISONERS OF WAR: THE ONLY GERMAN SOLDIERS WHO SET FOOT IN VERDUN.

For the best part of a year a million and a half German soldiers hammered at the doors of Verdun. A few got in—but only as prisoners of war, and when they passed through the gateway of the Meuse it was on their way to internment. This photograph shows German prisoners lined up in the shattered Place de l'Archeveché while their officers were undergoing interrogation by the officers of the victorious French Army.

to the Somme. This view of the situation agreed with that taken by Hindenburg's Staff and, as Hindenburg did not intend to resume the Verdun offensive, more guns and men were shifted westward.

By the middle of October, 1916, the German batteries on the eastern bank of the Meuse were reduced to one hundred and thirty. It was much less than half the number employed in June, 1916. Great was the

Attenuation of the German forces opportunity offered to General Nivelle, but he refused it. He could foresee from his knowledge of the enemy's require-

ments on other sectors and other fronts that the Crown Prince would be further weakened. All that the French commander did in an active way was to maintain, by means of Adjutant Lenoir and other fine fighting pilots, a complete mastery of the air. By bombing raids on the enemy's artillery positions at Montfaucon and Spincourt, and on all his centres of traffic and distribution, he challenged the German airmen, who were just arriving on the new Halberstadt and Spad machines, to trials of strength. There was proceeding in the French lines an enormous labour of preparation, that needed the utmost secrecy in order to issue in the most astonishing success in the war. Happily, in spite of the new machines the enemy possessed, he was too much preoccupied with his anxieties on the Somme line to make any unprovoked effort to rule the air above the quiet, muddy chaos around Verdun.

Being unable to reconnoitre the field of great activities on the Meuse, the German High Command relied on its sound knowledge of the infantry forces at the disposal of General Nivelle and, on October 20th, took the fatal step of moving two divisions from Verdun to Bapaume. These two divisions had constituted the strategic reserve of the Crown Prince's army and had been held so that they could strengthen any point, from the Argonne Forest to the plain of the Woevre, that was menaced by General Pétain's group of armies. The British forces pressing on Bapaume, and threatening the enemy's lines there at Le Transloy,

were directly responsible for the condition of things at Verdun. They prepared the first great French victory on the Meuse. There was, however, no time for General Pétain to throw fresh forces into Verdun to take advantage of the weakening of the enemy's lines. He could only ask General Nivelle to do all he could with three French divisions that still faced seven German divisions.

But General Nivelle did not require more infantry. Since June, 1916, he had waited only for the new gun— the 16 in. howitzer, with a range exceeding that of the 16·8 Krupp guns at Spincourt. He now possessed the new piece in considerable number, as well as long-range naval cannon of 15 in. calibre. And with abundant machinery, but scarcely more than 30,000 men available, he opened the most remarkable counter-offensive movement of modern times. His preliminary bombardment, started on October 21st, 1916, was an overwhelming surprise to the enemy. To the over-confident and self-flattering Staff of the Crown Prince this sign of the resurrection in greater strength of the army of Verdun was a terrifying thing. The smitten troops in the first zone of defences sent by carrier-pigeon messages praying for instant relief. One pigeon, shot down over the French lines, showed that the German brigadier-generals along the front were fearful their men would not sustain the coming assault.

The thunder of the new heavy artillery increased during the night, imposing for a few hours on the German soldiers the ordeal of blasting fire **Opening of the** that French troops had endured for eight **counter-offensive** months without losing heart or nerve.

When day came, enabling French airmen to direct the guns, the work of destruction went on rapidly under the favouring influence of clear weather. The Germans, kept in uncertainty of the point of the coming attack by the amplitude of the French artillery action, revealed, little by little, all their batteries. One hundred and thirty were traced by the French, and in furious counter-battery firing nearly half of these were silenced. At the same time all the ravines in hostile territory were searched with heavy shell; the Damloup position was wrecked, and the shelters in the quarries of Hardaumont were destroyed or blocked. One of the new French 16 in. shells penetrated the thick concrete of Douaumont Fort and exploded some of the enemy's ammunition, causing a fire and great loss of life.

On October 23rd, when this terrific explosion occurred, the three attacking French divisions were drawn up for the assault in wet, sticky clay, broken into innumerable holes of mud and water and rumples of slippery ground. On the left was a division composed of Zouaves, Sudanese negroes, two companies of Somalis, and a **Dispositions of the attacking French** fine Colonial Moorish regiment that had distinguished itself in the fighting at Fleury. This division of Africa was under the command of General Guyot de Salins, whose objective was Douaumont. On the right of the African division was a French division commanded by General Passaga. It contained contingents from almost every region of France. Then operating on the right was the third attacking division of troops of the line and light infantry from Southern France, under the direction of General de Lardemelle. Altogether there may have been, with a brigade held as a reserve on the left, a total of 33,000 bayonets, directed against nearly double the number of German infantry.

The Germans held their threatened lines with seven divisions. Among them were traced regiments of the 13th Reserve Division and the 39th Active Division, constituting the Seventh Army Corps of the Fifth Army that held the ground about Haudromont and Nawé Wood. From this wood to the Thiaumont Work the lines were held by the 25th Division. From the north of Thiaumont to the north of Fleury the 34th Reserve Division was deployed for action. Chapitre Wood was held by the 9th Division, the positions near the Vaux road

by the 33rd Reserve Division, and finally, the ground in and around Damloup was occupied by the 50th Division. As all these divisions were formed on the new model of only 9,000 bayonets each, the actual strength of the Germans was about 63,000 bayonets to 33,000 bayonets or less.

On the night of October 23rd General Nivelle did not deliver his bombardment with any intensity. He endeavoured to mislead the enemy by withholding the full strength of his artillery for a whirlwind of heavy shell fire on the morning of October 24th. He managed, however, to provoke a reply from the German batteries that led to a great artillery duel in which many German guns were destroyed. But when day broke over the waiting troops it looked as though the attack, that had been fixed for 11.40 a.m., would have to be postponed to another day. For the clear weather had gone, and a thick mist covered all the crests and valleys of the Meuse. But General Nivelle would not alter his plan. Months he had spent in preparing it, and the work had been done with such comprehensive minuteness that many guns could work in the fog in conjunction with the troops, almost as if the field of vision had been clear.

THIAUMONT FARM.
Ruined, devastated, and watered with the blood of thousands shed in almost daily battles for weeks together.

Some of the contact patrols of the French Flying Service went up through the mist and then descended low over the hostile positions, and in continual swoops observed what the enemy was doing. All the French guns began to fire at top speed on targets that had been registered in advance, and, helped a little by some of the low-flying airmen, made terrific shooting in the most difficult of circumstances. At the arranged instant the gunners suddenly lengthened their range, and, with the fog still gathering thickly, the three divisions advanced to their great work.

The action was arranged in two phases. In a single leap forward the troops were to reach

PARTIAL REPARATION: GERMAN PRISONERS MENDING ROADS · IN FRANCE.
German prisoners of war were employed on much useful work in France, but always with strict observance of the settled international rules on the subject. Particularly appropriate was their employment in mending and repairing the roads which their own guns had been mainly instrumental in destroying.

Haudromont Quarries, the northern slope of the Ravine de la Dame, and the entrenchment north of Thiaumont Farm, the battery position on Fausse Côte, and the Ravine of Brazil. They were then to stay for an hour in the positions they had conquered and consolidate them. In the second phase of the operations they were to reach the village and fort of Douaumont and the ridge beyond Fausse Côte, the pond near Vaux village, and the position around Damloup Hill.

The Hill of Douaumont is flanked like a cathedral by a succession of buttresses, formed of lower hills lying westward and divided by deep gorges. The Ravine de la Dame was the first of these cuttings. In the side formed of an angle of dead ground the Germans had excavated a

AFTER EIGHT MONTHS.
Douaumont Fort, captured by the Germans February 25th, 1916, as it was when recovered by the French on October 24th.

WRECKAGE OF LIFE AND LANDSCAPE BY MODERN WAR.
Carrying wounded across exposed ground on a French farm. It is pictures like this—of what was once a prosperous farm surrounded by good timber—that convey some faint idea of the utter devastation wrought in a countryside by hostile invasion.

subterranean city. The armoured caverns were constructed so as to resist the heaviest shell and provided with electric lighting and the conveniences almost of hotel life. Two German battalions, driven underground by the bombardment, were having their mid-day meal and waiting without anxiety for the gun fire to end. But, a few seconds after the shells ceased to fall, a battalion of Zouaves clambered into the trenches and began to explore the subterranean city. Here and there small groups of Germans tried to resist, but a few hand-grenades broke their spirit, and the battalion of Zouaves captured the ravine, with 1,545 men and forty-five officers, at a cost of only fifteen wounded men. The surprised Germans practically surrendered in a body only two minutes after the Zouaves leaped into the ravine at a distance of twenty-five yards behind their barrage.

Having only an hour before they moved forward upon Douaumont, the Zouaves were not able fully to explore the ravine, and a company of Germans, with six machine-guns,

was left untouched in one of the caverns. This led later to an extraordinary incident. A sergeant of the Zouaves, engaged in revictualling duties, lost his way at night in the chaos of shell-holes, and perceived what he took to be a party of Colonial troops. He went up to ask the way, was roughly seized and made prisoner, and pushed down a sap leading to a lighted hall. There some German officers were being served with dinner, and they roughly asked him how he came to be in the German lines. It was clear they knew nothing of the events that had taken place over their heads on that historic day. The sergeant said he had come from Douaumont, and explained that all the ground as far as the fort and village was again French. "I am not your prisoner," said the sergeant; "you are my prisoners." As the sergeant talked, the tone of the German officers became more polite. Finally, the strangely isolated underground force, numbering two hundred men and officers, went with the sergeant, who returned triumphantly to Douaumont, not with the food he should have brought, but with six machine-guns and a column of captives.

All along the line marked for the first **Zouave sergeant's** phase of operations the attack was **remarkable capture** delivered with the same mechanical precision. The only difficulty resided in the nature of the ground, which compelled the advancing troops to work forward very slowly so as not to lose touch in the fog. On the other hand, the fog made the most perfect of smoke-screens for the two leading divisions of attack, who escaped from the hostile shell curtain, and followed their own creeping barrage with extraordinary closeness and with overwhelming surprise effect. Connection with the guns was maintained by carrier-pigeons and optical and acoustic posts, as well as by ordinary and aerial means ; and as all the systems had been worked out in the mists frequent on the Meuse, they operated with practically perfect precision. The Colonial regiment from Morocco, acting with a Senegalese battalion and Somali companies, went over the German line with great driving power and collected below Fort Douaumont.

They were the favourites of General Mangin, who was in immediate control of all the operations as lieutenant to General Nivelle. Mangin **Mangin's faith in** was the most learned of the African school **African troops** of French officers. After he met Lord Kitchener at Fashoda he had made it the object of his life to create from the new colonies of France a black force to supply the lack of equality in men with Germany. Some years before the war, a book by him, " La Force Noir," made him famous in his own country and notorious in Germany ; for he considered that, with proper leading and special tactical dispositions, black and brown troops from the tropics and sub-tropics could be used on the French frontier against the best German infantry—and used with success, in spite of the adverse climatic conditions and the dismaying power of modern massed artillery.

In February, 1916, a Moroccan division, with Senegalese troops, made a fine stand north of Douaumont, until they were caught by terrifying salvos of 12 in. shell. Even then their officers had been able to rally them. And now, with a fine sense of irony, the author of " La Force Noir " gave the fighting men of African races a leading position, alongside the French planters from Algeria, Tunis, and Morocco, in the work of thrusting the Germans from the strong position which their Kaiser had boasted was the pillar of Verdun.

The second phase of operations opened by an enveloping movement by the French infantry division under General Passaga. In a single bound his troops advanced over all the German lines south and east of Fort Douaumont, to a depth of nearly two miles, and took Caillette Wood between Douaumont and Vaux. On the right wing, from Vaux to Damloup, the division under General de Lardemelle met with more resistance, and had to wait on the Vaux road until the artillery hammered the German redoubts there when the fog cleared off. Then the Savoyards carried the Damloup height at a run, while their comrades captured the ravine by Vaux village and cleared the enemy from Fumin Wood.

Meanwhile, the African division went forward with an impetuosity that triumphed over the difficulties of the ground. Slipping, sliding, and falling, with the mud up to their knees, soaked through by rain and mist, in bitterly cold weather, Zouaves and Moorish Colonials and Sudanese

A STUDY AT VERDUN BY A FAMOUS ARTIST.
" A big black man ; round his neck a scarf of brilliant red ; helmet, all dinted, balanced on his head ; body a mass of dirty-yellow cloth shapeless with mud ; a wounded hand wrapped in a white dressing which threw the whole into relief." Sketched by M. Georges Scott.

worked up the hills and along the great ridge, with the shells of their creeping barrage making a line of geysers of mud and smoke in front of them. Every hill and valley flickered with tongues of flame, and from the hogsback of Froide Terre to the dome of Douaumont the line of shell-bursts moved like a heralding cloud of victory, close in front of the white, brown, and black troops.

About 2.30 a wind arose and blew away the mist. Marshal Joffre, who with General Pétain had arrived at Verdun to watch the first great offensive movement of General Nivelle, spied through the rents in the fog the soldiers of France silhouetted, like figures in a shadow play, against the sky-line above the crest of Douaumont. Through field-glasses the figures could be seen approaching the fort on either side, entering the fort, and then returning from it with grey columns of prisoners. It was a Moroccan battalion, commanded by Commandant Nicolai, that won the glory of capturing the famous fort, owing to another battalion, which had been designed to make a direct attack, being held up.

But this grand crowning success was largely due also to the energy and initiative displayed by the subaltern of a Sahara battalion, Second - Lieutenant Abdel-kader Mademba. Lieutenant Mademba was one of the most romantic figures in the French Army. He was the son of King Mademba of the Sahara, who had been a loyal and daring ally of the French in their great desert campaign. The young Sahara prince had fought in France since the beginning of the war, and showed the same gifts of leadership as his father. During the closing attack on the Douaumont height Lieutenant Mademba was at the head of his men, who were in front of the rest of the battalion. Seeing the advance was held up by a nest of German machine-guns on his right, he swung round, shouting to his tribesmen, and, as they followed him, he fell upon the flank of a German redoubt, stormed it, and enabled the general movement to successfully proceed. Afterwards he fell badly wounded.

Generally speaking, however, there was not much fighting around Douaumont. It was not so much a battle as an overwhelming surprise ; and the Germans had so many guns damaged that, **Importance of** when all their positions were lost, nearly **Douaumont** three hours passed before they began in turn to shell Douaumont. The three French divisions had altogether about two thousand casualties, many of them slight, while their prisoners numbered more than six thousand, and included ten battalion commanders. Five heavy and ten light guns were taken, fifty-one trench-mortars, one hundred and forty-four machine-guns, and an enormous quantity of war material. Having regard to the political and moral importance of Douaumont,

"From Verdun": German prisoners being escorted to the rear.

French soldier about to pick up and carry an exhausted comrade.

French wounded coming into a regimental aid post. German prisoners on the right.

SKETCHES MADE BY M. GEORGES SCOTT, THE FRENCH WAR-ARTIST, AT VERDUN, 1916.

WHERE A LOOK-OUT WAS KEPT BEHIND THE VERDUN HILLS.
Observation balloon and mitrailleuse in the Verdun region. The balloon section were preparing to send their "sausage" aloft. The terraced hill, beyond which was the fighting-front, indicates something of the character of the country in this sector, where the Germans maintained long, constant, and continuous pressure.

due to the braggart claims made by the German Emperor in February, 1916, it may fairly be contended that the first great French offensive movement at Verdun was the most brilliant victory won by a belligerent during the war. At a slight cost in men, less than that incurred in many raiding operations, General Nivelle crowned the allied operations on the Somme by a feat of peculiar range and significance.

There was a poetry about the victory of the army of Verdun that was not unlike that of the victories of the Maid of Orleans.

By one of the most poignant of ironic coincidences, the German Staff prepared, a few days before they lost Douaumont, to publish an official account of the operations at Verdun. Its first article appeared on October 25th, alongside the news of the loss of Douaumont, Thiaumont, Haudromont, and Damloup. An opening passage in the account ran :

Verdun is the north-eastern corner pillar of the entire defence system of the East of France. But this is neither the sole nor the principal importance of the fortress. Verdun occupies a far more significant position. It is the French sally-port against Germany. The attempt to break through our front and get in the rear of our forces of Belgium and Northern France was to be renewed from Verdun. In addition to all this, there was a high industrial value attaching to the sally-port, in that it led to the coal-mines and iron-fields of Briey. A French advance from Verdun against Metz would have afforded a possibility of attacking the ironworks of Lorraine and thereby striking at one of the vital points in the German production of munitions for war. Verdun was also a bridge-head guarding the most important road and railways leading from Paris to Metz. Our campaign was planned with the strategic aim of closing completely the sally-port of France, and making use of it ourselves as a wedge for a further thrust into French territory.

Germany's strategic aim

The design, apparently, was to palliate the failures of the Crown Prince by showing that the sally-port of Verdun was such a menace to Germany that it was worth closing at a cost of half a million casualties,

even if at this price it could not be transformed into a new gate of advance towards Paris. Only seven days before General Nivelle made his first attack the Kaiser came to the Verdun front and reviewed the Brandenburg troops that took Douaumont Fort, and received from the commander the public assurance that the men of the Mark were ready for another achievement of the same order.

A week later a mere remnant of the broken Brandenburg division was fugitive, some two miles in the rear of the front it had held, and the "black friends of France," as the Germans had scornfully named the African troops, were chasing German soldiers through the sombre galleries of the great hill fortress.

Four hundred of the men of the garrison of Douaumont surrendered in the afternoon of October 24th, but the work of completely clearing out the underground recesses was not finished until midnight. The German commandant of the fort was captured, and the large stocks of water, food, and bombs and other ammunition were of considerable service to the victors.

The rain that had been falling while the French attack was made increased in the night and the following day. The bad weather told against the enemy while he was frenziedly preparing his counter-attacks. He opened with a movement of blind fury in the morning, and made four efforts to return to Douaumont. He first launched against the fort two frontal assaults, which were broken easily by artillery and machine-gun fire. Then he made his third and chief counter-movement on the flank, from the Wood of Hardaumont. Large forces were employed in four dense waves of attack. But the French guns covered all the ground, and in hurricanes of high-explosive and shrapnel overwhelmed each wave and left only a few broken companies the opportunity of approaching the French lines with uplifted hands and becoming prisoners. The fourth counter-attack was weaker, and vainly directed only against a trench in one of the woods. On October 27th another counter-attack of a feeble kind made on the village of Douaumont was prevented from developing by the fire of the French artillery.

Frenzied German counter-attacks

General Nivelle had sent his men to a line absolutely dominated by his guns, and, as he had temporarily or permanently put out of action nearly half the German batteries, the new French front was less assailable than the old front had been. The only check in the French operations was that which happened to the division under General de Lardemelle around Fort Vaux. The division had been fighting since September in the woods between Vaux and Souville, and therefore knew the ground thoroughly. But the fog hindered the French artillery from shattering a series of fresh machine-gun redoubts, newly built in the enemy's second line, and the infantry had slowly to work round each obstacle that resisted their frontal attack.

All the night of October 24th the struggle with bomb, bayonet, and machine-gun continued in the famous Ravine of Death, running westward from Vaux

RT. HON. D. LLOYD GEORGE.
PRIME MINISTER.

RT. HON. A. BONAR LAW.
CHANCELLOR OF THE EXCHEQUER.

RT. HON. EARL CURZON.
LORD PRESIDENT OF THE COUNCIL.

RT. HON. VISCOUNT MILNER.
WITHOUT PORTFOLIO.

RT. HON. ARTHUR HENDERSON.
WITHOUT PORTFOLIO.

The National Ministry, December, 1916: The War Council of Five.

RT. HON. SIR EDWARD CARSON.
FIRST LORD OF THE ADMIRALTY.

RT. HON. LORD DEVONPORT.
FOOD CONTROLLER.

RT. HON. LORD ROBERT CECIL.
MINISTER OF BLOCKADE.

RT. HON. AUSTEN CHAMBERLAIN.
SECRETARY FOR INDIA.

RT. HON. ROBERT MUNRO, K.C..
SECRETARY FOR SCOTLAND.

RT. HON. DR. ADDISON.
MINISTER OF MUNITIONS.

RT. HON. H. E. DUKE. K.C..
CHIEF SECRETARY FOR IRELAND.

RT. HON. SIR FREDERICK CAWLEY. BART..
CHANCELLOR OF THE DUCHY OF LANCASTER.

RT. HON. SIR JOSEPH MACLAY.
SHIPPING CONTROLLER.

The National Government, December, 1916 : Chie

RT. HON. DR. H. A. L. FISHER.
PRESIDENT OF THE BOARD OF EDUCATION

RT. HON. JOHN HODGE,
MINISTER OF LABOUR.

RT. HON. ALBERT ILLINGWORTH.
POSTMASTER-GENERAL.

RT. HON. LORD WIMBORNE.
LORD-LIEUTENANT OF IRELAND.

RT. HON. SIR ALBERT STANLEY.
PRESIDENT OF THE BOARD OF TRADE.

RT. HON. GEORGE N. BARNES.
PENSIONS MINISTER.

RT. HON. VISCOUNT COWDRAY.
PRESIDENT OF THE AIR BOARD.

RT. HON. LORD RHONDDA.
PRESIDENT OF LOCAL GOVERNMENT BOARD.

RT. HON. SIR ALFRED MOND.
FIRST COMMISSIONER OF WORKS.

rmanent Departments and Special War Ministries.

RT. HON. SIR ROBERT FINLAY, K.C.,
LORD CHANCELLOR.

RT. HON. THE EARL OF CRAWFORD.
LORD PRIVY SEAL.

RT. HON. SIR GEORGE CAVE.
HOME SECRETARY.

RT. HON. R. E. PROTHERO.
PRESIDENT OF THE BOARD OF AGRICULTURE.

RT. HON. A. J. BALFOUR.
FOREIGN SECRETARY.

RT. HON. THE EARL OF DERBY.
SECRETARY FOR WAR.

RT. HON. WALTER LONG.
COLONIAL SECRETARY.

The National Ministry: Chiefs of Government Departments.

village. When clear daylight came at 8 a.m. on October 25th, both the light and the heavy French artillery intervened. The guns smashed a path to the pond of Vaux, and poured upon the fortress promontory above the ravine a torrent of shell. Then, reinforced by two brigades of another division, the troops of General de Lardemelle reached the pond, and stormed a line of redoubts defending the northern corner of the fortress.

Vaux could then have been carried had General Nivelle cared to lose another 2,000 men in order to win another swift and striking victory. But the French commander refused to pay the price that any German general in the same circumstances would have given. He postponed the assault, and for eight days and eight nights turned his 16 in. guns upon the fortress. The result was that the German commandant lost so many men and was left with so demoralised a remnant of the original garrison that—unlike the brave and heroic Frenchman, Major Raynal, in June, 1916—he made no attempt to resist to the last, but evacuated the stronghold.

In the morning of November 2nd the Germans were seen to be leaving the fort, and explosion after explosion occurred which could not be traced to the action of the French shells. The enemy had blown up his stores of ammunition. Very cautiously in the evening a French company surrounded the promontory, while a lieutenant, with searching-parties of engineers, entered the great galleries beneath the ruined superstructure and, finding no enemy and no mine-trap, took possession of the last of the exterior forts of Verdun that the

Tactical value of the fortresses enemy had held. Verdun, the sally-port of France, was re-established in its integrity.

Both Douaumont Fort and Vaux Fort had long since lost all their importance as gun positions. They were designed in 1899 to contain 6 in. guns, and at the outbreak of war were scarcely stronger in striking power than the forts of Liège. Instead of being the pillars of Verdun, they became its points of weakness when the Krupp and Skoda howitzers arrived from Metz. The army of Verdun had to construct entrenchments far beyond the belt of exterior forts, and place cannon and howitzers by the hundred well in front of the old strongholds, in order to defend them. Douaumont and Vaux, however, were built in extraordinary strength. The French engineers were more thorough than the Belgian in their concrete work. None of the monster Krupp guns at Spincourt sent a 16·8 in. shell through the armoured concrete of Douaumont.

When the French, in turn, attacked their own fortress with the 16 in. shell containing a more powerful explosive than the enemy employed, the projectile penetrated only the superstructure. It did not pierce the vaults of the large subterranean galleries that sheltered the garrison. Consequently, the fortresses remained admirable machine-gun redoubts and still more important observation positions. By recovering Vaux the French overlooked the Plain of Woevre, between Verdun and Metz, and thus enabled their long-range artillery constantly to harass the enemy. By recovering the higher northern

WELL-MASKED HILLTOP OBSERVATION-POST NEAR VERDUN.
Where a fissure in the ground on the summit of the hill provided perfect cover the French soldiers raised a natural-seeming screen, from behind which they were enabled to keep close watch over the valley that lay between them and the positions which were occupied by the enemy.

height of Douaumont they prevented the enemy overseeing their lines, and obtained a steady view over his northern front. As outlook towers that no shell could shatter the two fortresses were of high tactical value to General Nivelle.

But the ground he had won required great labour to make it passable. For weeks the troops had to work like pack animals, struggling up to their thighs in mud, at a pace of often less than a quarter of a mile an hour, and carrying on their backs supplies and materials for the new front. The Algerian mules brought stores to the edge of the chaos from which the field-guns fired, but over this chaos only streams of packmen could cross. To organise the ground, forests had to disappear in other parts of France and quarries had to be opened. Yet, in less than six weeks, light railways were running through the zone of shell-pools, mud, and indistinguishable ruins. The horrible ground, from which bodies protruded by the thousand, was drained and made healthy. A great road was driven through it, and branching tracks made to all the recovered heights. This engineering achievement of General Nivelle was as masterly a work as his victory in the field.

He surprised the enemy more by the speed with which he organised the new ground than he did by his attack in the fog. Between the first week of November and the second week of December twenty miles of road were made behind Douaumont and Vaux, with seven miles of light railway line, **Nivelle's organising** and a special log track for hauling siege-**genius** guns close to the German trenches. The immediate consequence of the incomparable display of organising genius on the part of General Nivelle was something that surprised him and the world in general. On November 30th, 1916, the defeated Crown Prince was retired from the personal command of the German forces round Verdun and given the nominal direction of all the German armies from the Oise to Belfort. A few days later the French Government offered General Nivelle the post of Commander-in-Chief, in succession both to Marshal

WHERE THE GERMANS SCORED SOME HITS: INCENDIARY BOMBS FALLING ON VERDUN DURING THE BOMBARDMENT. Shells and considerably from the enemy artillery, which was by no means only directed against the forts. Despite the succession of their obstinate attacks on Verdun and their temporary occupation of some of incendiary bombs were again and again fired into the place, and wrought much damage to property. the surrounding forts, the Germans never effected a footing in the town itself. Verdun, however, suffered

Joffre and General de Castelnau. It was the most dramatic personal incident in the war, excelling indeed in startling rapidity the rise to supreme power of Napoleon. The Third Republic of France, like the First Republic, had produced a brilliant band of great captains. Castelnau had proved his genius in the victory of Nancy; Foch had emerged triumphant on the Marne; Pétain had shown a splendid power of rapid organisation at Verdun and, with Maud'huy on the western heights of the Meuse and Nivelle on the eastern heights, had definitely

Nivelle appointed Commander-in-Chief turned the tide of battle in all the principal theatres of war against the Teutons.

Yet, when all the main machinery of French leadership seemed to have been fully forged in furnace after furnace of battle and finally fixed for the closing offensive, Verdun revealed a new man with a new method and, in a lightning-like movement of appreciation peculiar to the French democracy, he was abruptly promoted to the supreme command. Thereupon, he had again to display the most rapid gifts of organisation—to select, from his former peers and former chiefs, subordinates to carry out his ideas; to change many things; and to arrange his policy with that of the British Command.

By December 13th, 1916, General Nivelle had completed his military arrangements, and on the same day the Briand Cabinet was reorganised, somewhat on the Lloyd Georgian model. The new commander selected General de Castelnau as army-group controller on the northern front, where General Foch had been acting. General Pétain was retained as army-group chief on the central front, and General Franchet d'Espérey, who had fought on the right of the British Expeditionary Force on the Marne and on the Aisne, was made chief of the eastern front. General Mangin succeeded to the command of the army of Verdun, General Lyautey came from Morocco to act as Minister of War, and Marshal Joffre was appointed technical military adviser to the Government.

While engaged in the difficult work of making great changes in the direction of the armies of France, the new Commander-in-Chief speeded-up the preparations for an offensive at Verdun. On December 13th, as he left M. Briand to return to the scene of his October successes, he said to the Prime Minister, pointing to Louvemont and other main positions in the German line: "I am going to attack to-morrow. There are the points I shall reach. It will take me four hours to do it. I don't expect to lose many men and I shall take at least five thousand prisoners. I hope to send you a telegram about two o'clock to-morrow afternoon."

Before the time appointed, M. Briand received the telegram of victory, but the calculation as to prisoners was not entirely correct. Instead of making 5,000 captives, General Nivelle made 12,000, took 120 guns, and drove the enemy back four miles, at a cost of only 1,500 French casualties. The attack was made by two of the divisions that had taken Douaumont in October—the African division under General Guyot de Salins and the French division of the line under General Passaga. With these acted a fresh division under General Muteau, and another fresh division under General Garnier du Plessis. The enemy forces on the front attacked, running from the

Meuse to Bezonvaux village, consisted of five divisions. They were the 14th Reserve Division, the 29th Division, the 10th Division, the 14th Active Division, and the 39th Bavarian Reserve Division. During the six weeks' preparation for battle the Germans dug new trenches, with flanking works in the French style. On Pepper Hill the old organisation was strengthened with wider zones of wire entanglements, concreted galleries, and large sheltered gathering-places, transforming the long down into a huge fortress. The French troops still clung to some of the lower slopes of Pepper Hill, but all their line as far as the Thiaumont Work was overlooked by higher ground, held by the Germans on the crest of Pepper Hill and Louvemont Ridge. The length of front attacked was about six and a half miles, and with his four divisions General Nivelle employed only four men to the yard, in order to break the hostile fortress system.

The weather was again extremely adverse to all operations. It both snowed and rained, making the work of gunnery observation difficult and hindering the French airmen. But in the three days' preliminary bombardment, in the second week of December, 1916, the masses of French guns smashed a path through the German lines and,

GERMAN TRENCHES AND LABYRINTH ABOUT A FRENCH VILLAGE.
Village in the Verdun region, in the neighbourhood of which the Germans made a labyrinth of trenches. These are partly indicated in the photograph by the irregular lines where the earth, turned up to form the trench parapets, shows white against the unbroken surface.

working on by the map during the snowstorm, did terrible execution in the German trenches. In the October battle the Chief of Staff to the Crown Prince had tried to save his men by holding the first line lightly with machine-gun sections and massing his infantry forces in his second and third systems. This method having proved utterly unavailing, the new German commander now held his first line in great strength, and relied on the shelter of his concreted underground galleries for protection against French artillery fire. But **Pulverising effect of French shell** the new 16 in. shell that broke into Douaumont Fort pierced the slighter slabs of German concrete built into the northern ridges. In the evening of December 14th, for instance, seven Germans deserted from the important position of Ratisbon Trench, and said that they were all that existed of a company that had garrisoned the entrenched slope.

At daybreak on December 15th there was improvement in the weather. The sky brightened, and the visibility became excellent. The result was that the German artillery was completely reduced to silence by 9 a.m., and after a whirlwind bombardment the four French divisions went over their parapets at 10 a.m. By this time the French shells formed an impenetrable line of smoke and fire, drawn with mathematical precision across the German front, and at scarcely more than seventy paces behind their moving barrage the attacking troops squelched onward through the deep mud. Thereupon, every undamaged German gun resumed fire ; and, knowing to an inch the range of the front French trenches, the German gunners drenched them in clouds of shrapnel. But the German barrage came five minutes too late. The French troops were well away from their own line, and before their supporting columns passed through the hostile fire curtain, the French siege-guns, directed by a row of observation balloons and low-flying airmen, smashed the German guns in a great counter-battery duel.

French capture Vacherauville Meanwhile, the left French infantry wing, advancing without cover along the low ground by the river, reached the village of Vacherauville. Here every cellar and ruined house was a machine-gun redoubt. The French artillery on both sides of the Meuse covered the assault with great vigour, but in the close village fighting the opposing forces were soon so mixed up that the artillery on both sides could take no part in the battle, but merely played on the opposing routes of approach. Then it was

that General Nivelle's new infantry tactics told with instant effect on the issue of the day. The German division was driven out of the village at little expense in French lives and, forming a stubborn rearguard, it retreated along the road to Beaumont.

South of this road was the high, fortified crest of Pepper Hill. It seemed to be the strongest sector of the hostile front ; but it was the weakest sector. This the enemy commander did not know, but **Conquest of** General Nivelle and General Mangin did, **Pepper Hill** and their plans were made accordingly.

The force attacking Vacherauville was manœuvred slowly and cautiously, in view of the great possibilities afforded by the bare slopes of the hill on their right. Upon these bare slopes the main mass of French artillery fired with horribly destructive power, and the French infantry moved upward quickly to the summit, completely screened by the smoke of their barrages. Suddenly the German gunners seemed to go mad, for they opened a terrific fire of 6 in. and 8 in. shell upon their own troops on the height.

The stricken German infantry sent up signal rockets, and their guns ceased to fire on them. The German gunners, however, had not been so mad as they seemed. One of their aerial scouts may have observed something, and given the range a little too hastily. The extraordinary German barrage was only a few yards short

French official photograph.

POILUS' PLEASANT REST-PLACE : A FRENCH CHATEAU THAT WAR HAD SPARED.

Behind the French front this chateau, which had almost entirely escaped damage, where so many others had been entirely destroyed, served as a pleasant rest-place for French soldiers who had been engaged in the strenuous fighting a few miles away. While many of the men were quietly enjoying their respite in easy attitudes, others were preparing a meal for them in the wayside camp-kitchen shown in the foreground.

of the first storming French waves of attack; and, as the German guns stopped firing on Pepper Hill, the French infantry leaped into the German trenches. At the decisive point on the hill fortress the German lines ran sideways, fronting towards the river and protecting the retiring garrison of Vacherauville from flank attack. As the regiments on this flank were rearguarding their Vacherauville force, they were abruptly assailed in the back by the conquerors of Pepper Hill. Caught unexpectedly with hand-grenades and bayonets, the Germans broke, and the French went down into the valley and drove savagely into the flank of the Germans retreating from Vacherauville.

This was the grand stroke in the battle that upset General Nivelle's estimate of his probable successes, and more than doubled his captures of men and guns. To General Mangin, who executed General Nivelle's plan and gloriously improved upon it in the course of the fighting, the great break-through was due. The Germans on the Beaumont road had been maintaining a gallant rearguard defence. Although they had lost Vacherauville village, they were in strong formation and good heart. But when their flank was broken and their rear threatened, complete panic seized them. Throwing away weapons and equipment, they scattered and fled, with the French in close pursuit, and soon surrendered in thousands.

All Pepper Hill, stretching for a mile and a half towards Louvemont, was turned in less than an hour and a half. Then the victorious wing converged north-eastward towards the Louvemont Ridge, while the French centre moved directly northward, from Thiaumont and Douaumont across a valley and over the trenches seaming the slopes of Louvemont Ridge.

[*French official photograph.*

BRITISH PRINCE DECORATES HEROES OF VERDUN.
Prince Arthur of Connaught decorating General Nivelle and men who so heroically assisted him in the great counter-offensive before Verdun. The ceremony took place outside the Mairie in a town behind the French front, where brave Poilus in heavy marching order provided an appropriate guard of honour.

The ground on this part of the front was extremely difficult. The mud came over the men's knees, and the snow and the night frost, instead of hardening it, had made it as sticky as glue. But winter mud was as powerless to stop the French infantrymen as German guns and German men were. The great ridge was carried practically without a fight, and the village of Louvemont was enveloped and stormed in two hours. Then, as the Germans retreated in disorder from Louvemont village, French airmen swooped down and, raking them with machine-gun fire, so dispersed them that the French centre was able to pass its final objective and continue towards Chambrettes Farm.

Louvemont enveloped and stormed

The troops under General Passaga, forming the right wing of the attack, were the only French force that met with serious resistance. The Passaga division was drawn up between Douaumont, Vaux, and Damloup. In front of it were three wooded heights cut by ravines—Hardaumont Wood, Hassoule Wood, and La Vauche Wood. The ground rose to the level of the dome of Douaumont, affording the enemy observation over the French forces when they descended into the valley in order to attack the forested spurs. Moreover, there were German batteries around the village of Dieppe, flanking the positions which the French stormed and pouring a cross-fire upon the advancing troops. Thus the task assigned to General Passaga's men was by far the most arduous. But though it took long to carry out, it was completed with almost as much success as the drive across Pepper Hill.

In the morning the promontory of Hardaumont, strengthened with numerous fieldworks, was carried through heavy hostile curtain fire coming from the north and east. La Vauche Wood proved an obstacle that delayed the division for some hours, but the remarkable team-work of the French brigade on this sector triumphed over the stubborn resistance of the Prussians. At 3 o'clock in the afternoon all the promontories were carried, together with the great earthwork near Bezonvaux village.

It was at about this hour that the French centre pushed beyond its objective and captured Chambrettes Farm. From this high advanced position, in the middle of their new front, the French forces began to outflank Bezonvaux village and part of Caurrières Wood. All through the evening of December 15th and the morning of December 16th they pressed the Germans on both sides, and captured the village and part of the wood. Having lost one hundred and twenty guns by capture and more than three times that number by counter-battery attack, the Germans took a considerable time in attempting to recover the ground they had lost. In the afternoon of December 15th they were too busy dragging their guns out of reach of the French infantry to help their own fugitive troops on the Beaumont road sector by curtaining the French ground there. The German counter-attack did not occur until the evening of December 17th. Then, after a long and costly bombardment, fresh German forces stormed out against the new French front, but were so overwhelmed by the shell fire and the machine-gun fire of the army of Verdun that they could not reach the new French fire trenches. Only the advanced work of Chambrettes Farm was occupied, and

even this was not held for more than a few hours. After a hurricane bombardment the French troops swept back over the farm, killed or captured the garrison, and firmly consolidated themselves in this advanced position.

"The experiment has succeeded," said General Nivelle as he left his glorious Second Army, to carry on his new work as Commander-in-Chief. "Our method has justified itself. Victory is assured!" Verdun was more than a local success. The gain of four miles of ground, which prevented the enemy from seeing the famous citadel of the Meuse and which gave more elbow-room to the French forces around Douaumont and Vaux, was not of supreme importance, although the territory gained levelled up the two French **Chief significance** sectors on either side the river, and **of the victory** brought the French armies around Dead Man Hill and around Louvemont in line with each other.

From the beginning of the struggle Verdun had been the grand testing-ground between the Gaul and the Teuton. The principal significance of the final French victory was that it showed that the French had gradually elaborated a method of fighting as pregnant with results as the new method by which Napoleon broke the Prussians at Jena. All that Falkenhayn and Hindenburg had produced at Verdun was a new French Commander-in-Chief with new tactics, against which no German defence works could stand. The new method had been tried in several of the later actions on the Somme before it was shown in full perfection at Verdun. It was no secret of General Nivelle, but was practised by the British Staff as well as by the French Staff. In the opinion of good judges, it promised to effect in modern warfare as far-reaching surprises as those created by the Macedonian Phalanx in the age of Alexander the Great and by Spanish infantry tactics in the age of Charles V.

WHERE THE ARTILLERY HAD PREPARED THE WAY BEFORE DOUAUMONT WAS RECAPTURED.
In the Bois de la Caillette, immediately to the south-east of Douaumont. Above: Another scene of desolation before Douaumont, which after having been captured by the Germans in the early part of 1916 was brilliantly retaken by the French before the close of the year.

THE SOCIALISATION OF GREAT BRITAIN AND RISE OF IMPERIAL DEMOCRACY.

By Edward Wright.

Death of Lord Kitchener and End of Era of Individualism—Lloyd George as War Secretary—Development of State Control System—Stagnation of Cabinet and Unceasing Popular Unrest—Pensions Scandal and Reform Work of Mr. Henderson—Lloyd George's Gallant Attempt to Solve the Irish Problem—Lord Lansdowne's Intervention and its Consequences in Australia and America—Middle Europe and the Scheme for Economic War—Allies' Reply by Paris Conference—Cabinet Difficulties in Regard to Execution of Conference Agreements—Marvellous Recovery of British Foreign Trade—Great Rise in Wages and Family Prosperity—Suggestions for a Negotiated Peace with the Enemy—Disasters and Dishonour Underlying the False Humanitarianism—Lloyd George Proclaims a Fight to a Knock-out—Increasing Difficulties in British Food Supplies—The Connoisseur in the Wheat Pit—Reorganisation of Volunteers—Urgent Necessity for More Men for the Army—Struggle Between Lloyd George and Walter Runciman—Admiral Jellicoe Returns to Whitehall—Negotiations between Mr. Asquith and Mr. Lloyd George—A "Times" Leader and the Break-up of the Government—Lloyd George becomes Prime Minister—Labour Party Give their Adherence to the New Government—Germany Offers to Open Negotiations for Peace—The Prime Minister's Reply—Establishment of a System of National Service—The Imperial War Conference—Policy of the Food Controller—Standardisation of Merchant Steamers—State Control of Railways—Speeding-up of British Production—Explosion in a London Munition Works—The British War Loan of 1917.

THE summer of 1916, that opened with the Battle of Jutland Bank and the Battle of the Somme, was a turning-point in the domestic history of Great Britain. The strange death of Lord Kitchener off the Orkney Islands, on June 5th, 1916, marked the end of an old epoch, and the appointment of Mr. Lloyd George as successor to the great captain in the position of Secretary of State for War, on July 6th, 1916, indicated the beginning of a new era. Lord Kitchener was a masterly incarnation of the old English spirit of individualism. He was a man of genius and telling force of character, and it was in large part due to his appeal for volunteers that a great army was available for the Battle of the Somme. But while Lord Kitchener still retained in his strong hands all control of the British land forces, the disasters which occurred at the front through lack of high-explosive shell and heavy ordnance showed that the problems of a war on a Continental scale were not likely to be fully

MINISTERS OF MUNITIONS.   *[Henri Manuel.*
The Rt. Hon. D. Lloyd George, while Secretary of State for War, with the Rt. Hon. E. S. Montagu (centre), and M. Albert Thomas, respectively British and French Ministers of Munitions, an office which Mr. Lloyd George had been the first British statesman to hold.

solved by a dictator of genius of the old school.

The extraordinary complexity of war in modern conditions made the task too heavy for any single soldier, however capable, to bear, and though with undaunted courage he tried to face every difficulty, events were too strong for him. Already, on January 27th, 1916, the strategic control of all British armies had been given to Sir William Robertson as Chief of the Imperial General Staff, which was reorganised towards the tragic close of the Dardanelles expedition. And the earlier appointment of Mr. Lloyd George as Minister of Munitions had diminished the scope of Lord Kitchener's practical dictatorship. No doubt the dilatory party of politicians in the Coalition Cabinet and War Committee impeded the work of Lord Kitchener and, by continually suggesting fears of labour troubles, hindered the great commander from establishing a system of national service. National service, without national control of the main resources of the country, might eventually have proved a cause of trouble.

359

But, though the politicians of the individualistic school could not see it, the nation was rapidly tending, under repeated checks and adversities, towards a policy of general State control.

Mr. Lloyd George succeeded Lord Kitchener as practical dictator, and greatly extended the powers of dictatorship, because he clearly divined the course of public opinion. His early political career as a Radical with Socialistic tendencies gave him large ideas. His later experiences as the most daring of Chancellors of the Exchequer, in which capacity, with the aid of great financial experts, he saved the banking position of Great Britain and the credit system of the world, helped to equip him with the knowledge that was power. Then setting out in a new direction, as an energising but somewhat inexperienced controller of the largest industries in the kingdom, he quickly learnt from his mistakes, and sought the assistance of experts of employers and of men. At the end of a year, as Minister of Munitions, he was one of the strongest minds directing the war in Europe. He could scarcely fire a rifle and he could not train a field-gun, yet as an organiser of the chief instruments of victory he excelled Lord Kitchener, and even extorted reluctant praise from the dismayed and staggering enemy.

If, in the first week of July, 1916, the new Secretary for War had received from his fellow-Liberals in the War Council of the Coalition Cabinet a fuller measure of active and instant help than Lord Kitchener had received, the victory of civilisation might have been achieved under Mr. Asquith's Ministry. But this Ministry was not representative of the new forces in the nation, of which Mr. Lloyd George, with the Labour leaders and several of the Unionist chiefs, was the interpreter and the executor. There had to be a great eruption before the new national forces won room to develop and transform the country. The talent for compromise possessed by Mr. Asquith delayed the eruption for five months. During this period the War Council was in such a state of unstable balance that it could achieve nothing of importance. At every attempt to do something of a decisive nature, the suggestion of a series of resignations led to another depressing compromise. But stagnant as the surface of things seemed during the terrible and glorious months when the British armies on the Somme were advancing from victory to victory, at a cost of a hundred thousand casualties a month, the people laboured in a profound unrest of mind, scarcely knowing clearly what it was they desired.

Delays and discontent A multitude of side issues apparently engaged the full attention of the nation. Nearly everywhere there were things it wanted better done. When the slow-moving Government took steps to remedy some just cause of complaint, the spirit of public discontent burst forth in another direction. A satisfactory national pension scheme for disabled fighting men and the dependents of dead, disabled, or missing soldiers was one of the leading aims of public agitation. At one period it was reported that twenty-two thousand disabled soldiers were in misery, with their regimental pay stopped and no proper pension

supplied to them. The State had never before arrayed an army of millions, and it had no official machinery for providing adequately and nobly for the hundreds of thousands of men that would be broken in its wars.

For nearly a hundred years Great Britain had been a middle-class plutocracy, absorbed in money-making and in profitable colonising adventures. It had despised the warrior, while making more profitable use of him than any other race except the Prussians. Its Government took little or no interest in the broken soldier, whose case was largely left to voluntary charitable organisations. After the Commissioners of the Royal Hospital **Inadequate pension system** for Soldiers at Chelsea had doled out a starvation pittance to disabled soldiers and the dependents of dead or disabled soldiers, various charitable organisations were supposed to investigate each case and supplement the utterly insufficient pension or allowance.

The right and plain course was for the State to look after the soldiers broken in its service, and the women and children impoverished by the death or disablement of their fighting men. But this plain and right course was not taken by the Coalition Cabinet, with the result that the large suffering element in the people chafed in deep anger. A measure, passed in November, 1915, only provided a small contribution by the State to a pension fund mainly collected by charity. Not until October, 1916, did Mr. McKenna agree to increase the Government Pension Fund from £1,000,000 to £6,000,000. By that time, owing to the long delay, the number of pension cases had become unmanageably large, and the various pension authorities further mismanaged the unmanageable. Mr. Arthur Henderson, the Chairman of the Labour Party, was then placed in control of the pension problem. Labour revolt was the nightmare of the Second Asquith Ministry, and as apprehension in regard to the most loyal working class in the world had been used by the party of compromise to cripple the New Army in the making, the same menace was at last turned against the same party, in order to induce it to consent to a just national pension scheme. Mr. Henderson was about to become Minister of Pensions when the overthrow of the Coalition Cabinet enabled him more thoroughly to complete his pension work and make the Labour Party a still stronger reorganising force in the new political era.

Another important problem that threatened to wreck the Coalition Cabinet was the Irish question. After the Sinn Fein rebellion and the visit of Mr. Asquith to Dublin, Mr. Lloyd George was asked to undertake negotiations for a temporary settlement of Ireland. With the unanimous support of the Cabinet, he approached Mr. Redmond and the Nationalist Party and Sir Edward Carson and the Ulster Party. He induced the leaders to accept, for the period of the war, a scheme of Home Rule for Ireland, with the six Ulster counties left out. Sir Edward Carson made a great appeal to the people of Ulster and, in spite of their coldness, induced them to agree, in June, 1916, to the scheme. At a Nationalist conference the temporary

[*Bassano.*]
MRS. H. J. TENNANT.
Director of the Women's Department of National Service.

[*Walter Barnett.*]
MISS VIOLET MARKHAM.
Assistant-Director of the Women's Department of National Service.

The Women's Department of National Service was created in February, 1917, to set up "effective machinery for securing women of the right kind for substitution work and using woman-power of every kind in the most profitable way."

HIS MAJESTY KING GEORGE AND LORD DERBY.
After being Director of Recruiting and deviser of the Derby Scheme " for group enlistment," the Earl of Derby became Under-Secretary of War, and then Secretary for War in the National Ministry in December, 1916.

Home Rule measure was accepted by Mr. Redmond's party. In a signed agreement the leaders of the two parties practically consented to all the Irish Members of Parliament remaining during the war in the House of Commons, and there taking part in the direction of Imperial affairs. The governing idea of the scheme was that Ulster would accept Home Rule when the Irish Parliament had demonstrated its capacity to govern well the rest of Ireland, and when the Irish people proved that they felt it was in their interest to be loyal, and abandoned the policy of separation from Great Britain.

In effect, Mr. Redmond, Mr. Dillon, and Mr. Devlin undertook to deal in their own way with the smouldering fires of the Sinn Fein movement. Their **Attempted Irish** aim was to make Catholic Ireland so **settlement** orderly, loyal, and progressive under the Home Rule experiment that the Presbyterians of Ulster would of their own accord at last be willing to form a United Ireland. It was suggested, in the terms of the agreement, that at the end of the experimental period there should be a conference, representing all the self-governing Colonies of the Empire, to consider the relations of the Dominions to the Home Government, and that in the course of this conference an attempt should be made to work out what the permanent Government of Ireland should be.

It was a generous scheme, and, in the first week of July, 1916, the mediating genius of Mr. Lloyd George and the sympathetic and patriotic understanding of Mr. Redmond and Sir Edward Carson seemed about to open a new era in the relations of Ireland and Great Britain. But almost at the last moment Lord Lansdowne suddenly

intervened as the representative of the British Unionists in Southern and Western Ireland. By a threat of resignation from the Cabinet he compelled some fundamental changes in the draft Bill that had been prepared. All the negotiations were brought to an end by an alteration reducing the number of Nationalist representatives in the House of Commons, so that they could not continue to hold the balance between the Radical-Liberal Party and the Unionist Party. This was in conflict with the terms of the agreement on which the draft Bill was based. The curious explanation offered was that Mr. Lloyd George had not acted as the representative of the Cabinet, but as an agent with limited powers, **Experiment** who could be disowned if the Cabinet **frustrated** did not like the terms he had arranged.

The situation caused by this breakdown was partly saved by the patriotic reticence of Mr. Redmond and the generous conduct of Sir Edward Carson during the debate in Parliament on July 24th, 1916. " It would not be a bad day for this country, or Ireland, or for our prospects in the war," said Sir Edward towards the close of his speech, " if Mr. Redmond and myself were to shake hands on the floor of this house." This offer of personal friendship was generally recognised as symbolic of the new relations between Catholic and Presbyterian Ireland. Though the great experiment was frustrated, yet the fine constructive work of Mr. Lloyd George seemed likely to issue in the future in the greatest achievement of British domestic politics.

In the meantime, the spirit of the Sinn Fein rebellion smouldered on and spread, not only in Ireland, but in every land where Irish emigrants and their descendants

LORD FRENCH, O.M., AND LIEUT.-GEN. SIR FRANCIS LLOYD, K.C.B., D.S.O.
Viscount French was appointed Commander-in-Chief of the Home Forces in 1915, and Sir Francis Lloyd, G.O.C. London District in 1913.

were an important political force. It increased the strength and vehemence of all pro-German movements and intrigues in the United States. But, worst of all, it prevented the second greatest Welsh statesman in the British Empire— Mr. W. M. Hughes, Prime Minister of Australia—from helping on the war by obtaining a vote in favour of conscription. When the Australian referendum was completed in November, 1916, Mr. Hughes' proposal was defeated only by the comparatively narrow margin of 61,000 votes.

During his stay in Great Britain, in the early part of 1916, Mr. Hughes, as the leading Labour Premier of the world, had exercised a telling influence upon the British working classes, and engineered a victorious movement against the octopus activities of German trade and finance. He had broken, by his personal action, some important enemy interests in the Australian key industries, and by public speeches and conversations with representatives of British Labour, he greatly reinforced the movement towards Protection, against which the pro-Germans fought determinedly. Extraordinary as it seems, a considerable party in the Coalition Cabinet remained in favour of Free Trade with Germany after the war. The Teutons, however, had elaborated a great fighting economic system—usually known as Middle Europe—in which Germany, Austria-Hungary, Serbia, Bulgaria, Rumania, Greece, the Ottoman Empire, and the British Protectorates of the Persian Gulf were to be combined in one economic and military federation. In this federation Germany was to be the leading industrial and financial force, with her markets protected from British, American, French, and other allied or neutral competition, by a Middle Europe tariff wall

Trade after the war

Against this formidable scheme the Allies concerted measures at a conference held in Paris in June, 1916. The Marquis of Crewe, Mr. Bonar Law, Mr. W. M. Hughes, Prime Minister of Australia, and Sir George Foster, Canadian Minister of Trade and Commerce, represented the British Empire. France was represented by her Ministers of Commerce and Agriculture and other statesmen of influence. Russia, Italy, Japan, Belgium, Serbia, and Portugal also sent some of their principal Ministers to the Conference. Working together from different points of view, the delegates arrived at a scheme of economic war and economic defence against the Middle Europe Union. They provided for measures to be taken in common during the war, for measures of defence during the difficult period following the conclusion of peace, and, finally, for measures to develop industry and commerce in the allied States during the period of reconstruction, and for permanent defences against the unscrupulous methods of penetration and monopoly which had been employed by the Teutons in the British Empire, Russia, Italy and France, Serbia and Portugal.

On the return of the British delegates to London a committee was appointed to consider the conclusions reached at the Paris Conference, and to work out in detail methods to prevent the resources of the Empire from falling under foreign control, to protect all industries essential for the safety of the nation, and generally develop the resources of the Empire. By July 19th, 1916, the committee, which included many business men who afterwards rose to high political power, began to labour on the plan of the Paris Conference. Some weeks afterwards, at the Trade Union Congress, the representatives of the working classes moved, by a million and three-quarters votes, against half a million votes, for the restriction of foreign goods made by sweated labour. This seemed a significant

indication of a popular movement towards a system of economic defence, such as Mr. Joseph Chamberlain had vainly attempted to establish when he saw the danger of the Teutonic method of penetration. Owing to the influence which the Australian Prime Minister had exercised in Great Britain, the working classes began to see that a protective system would be needed to maintain high wages. The Steel Smelters' Union, in particular, agitated for some tariff or other means of defence against a future disastrous import of German steel. During the debates on the problem of economic defence, a section of Liberals, led by Sir Alfred Mond, Mr. Illingworth, and Sir L. Chiozza Money, abandoned the Free Trade standpoint. But the principal lieutenants of Mr. Asquith, occupying the important positions of Chancellor of the Exchequer and President of the Board of Trade, held to the old policy. Their views directly conflicted with the plans made at the Paris Conference, so that nothing of importance could be done to prepare for common allied action against the Middle Europe federation.

The Coalition Cabinet had become an unworkable instrument. It was rent by divisions on domestic, Imperial, and allied problems of the utmost urgency. Even on the all-important question of the prosecution of the war the Coalition was so divided that it did nothing. Between Mr. Lloyd George, as Secretary for War, and Mr. Walter Runciman, as President of the Board of Trade, there was disagreement of the most fundamental nature—whether

[Elliott & Fry.
MR. WILLIAM MITCHELL-THOMSON, M.P.
Director of the Restriction of Enemy Supplies Department.

the war should be fought to a finish or whether it should be ended in a negotiated peace. Mr. Runciman, with the help of Mr. McKenna, the new Chancellor of the Exchequer, pursued a policy which undoubtedly produced some remarkable results. By exempting men from military service and extending the use of female labour, which Mr. Lloyd George had employed in a large way in munition work, the semi-pacifists maintained a wonderful volume of British commerce. The export trade rose in 1916 to a little over £506,500,000.

This marvellous figure much exceeded British exports in all the years before the war, except 1913. Great Britain had a fleet of 4,000 vessels engaged in military and naval duties, and a million men manning or working for it. She had placed in the field new armies numbering millions, and behind these soldiers she had millions of munition workers, withdrawn from productive labour. Yet in spite of her stupendous naval, military, and munition efforts, which seemed at times as if they monopolised all the human resources of the country, the Island State maintained her export trade close to its highest figure in 1913, when Germany and Austria-Hungary were buying in preparation for war.

The great markets of Germany, Austria-Hungary, and the Ottoman Empire had been lost, and ordinary commerce with Russia was blocked in the Baltic and the Dardanelles. But Great Britain found larger markets in allied countries and in neutral States. And while her blockade slowly destroyed the sea-borne commerce of the German Empire, her own mercantile marine, with its tonnage halved by reason of the needs of the Services, maintained the energising flow of trade in supreme vigour. Considerable credit for this state of things was due to Mr. McKenna and Mr. Runciman.

Expansion of wages

By December, 1916, the wages of some three million British workers were increased by eight shillings a week each. Alongside this expansion of ordinary wages there was an unparalleled development in the income of the family, owing to women, girls, and lads engaging in productive or distributive work. The cost of living rose 45 per cent.

but did not check the prosperity of the working class. The increase in the family income more than balanced the rising price of food.

The middle classes felt the strain of rising prices, and the members of various professions were impoverished. Exceedingly heavy taxation, combined with the great rise in prices and the falling value of many classes of investment, reduced a considerable section of the upper middle classes from a position of luxury to one of bitter poverty. But from a national point of view even this disaster to one class brought compensation. It was estimated that one million men and women, who had been engaged before the war in work of a non-productive nature, were liberated for labour of a directly productive or military kind. In days of peace Great Britain had been generally under-working and largely idling, and families with means had diverted from labour more servants than the nation could properly afford. The stress of the war and the appeal to the patriotism of all classes stripped the race down to its leanest strength, saved it from fatty degeneration of the soul, and gave it an athletic spirit of an incomparable kind.

Masterly as had been the effort made by Great Britain in the Napoleonic Wars, that effort was immensely surpassed by the effort made in the Great War. The British Isles are but a small and detached corner of Europe, **Marvellous expansion** and, in the days of peace, there were times **of industry** when both friend and foe used to think that a series of chances impossible of recurrence under modern conditions, had given the British race so large a dominion over the earth. But by the end of the year 1916 the islanders had excelled all the achievements of their forefathers, and in an unparalleled display of naval power, military power, industrial power, transport power, and financial power they again controlled the destinies of mankind, and controlled them for righteous and noble ends.

This marvellous expansion of British industry and commerce during the violent middle period of the war was not accomplished without sacrifices of a most serious kind. A fearful price was paid for the extraordinary export trade of Great Britain in 1915 in the Battle of the Bazentin Ridge in September, 1916. Had Sir Douglas Haig then possessed an additional hundred thousand well-trained troops, the rupture of the German line would have been a practical certainty. The increase in British commerce cost the country and the Allies another year of war. Then it was that the struggle between Mr. Lloyd George and Mr. Walter Runciman entered on its decisive

CONVALESCENTS AT HEALTHFUL, HELPFUL EXERCISE.
With a view to cultivation of vegetables, wounded soldiers at a Hampstead hospital took readily to the work of digging up the grounds attached to the institution in which they were recuperating.

WILLING SERVICE OF SOLDIERS AS VEGETABLE GROWERS.
Men of the Gordon Highlanders, at the suggestion of Lieut.-Col. Forbes, planted potatoes between the huts at their Reserve camp, and thus utilised to good purpose land that otherwise would have remained idle. Above: Weeding cabbages. Soldier-gardeners stationed at High Wycombe took over the task of tending the allotments of about fifty men who were away with the Colours, and faithfully fulfilled their undertaking.

phase. There was a considerable party of Liberals who did not want the war to continue. Their views were continually suggested, rather than plainly expressed, in the columns of the extreme Radical Press. We cannot, therefore, attempt to explain fully what these views were. But they seemed to be partly based upon the great British achievement in foreign trade and finance, as contrasted with the temporary condition of the enemy's commercial and financial power. The idea was that Great Britain could afford to discuss the terms of " peace without victory." This, it was alleged, Germany was ready to do. It was said, quite indirectly, that she was willing to pay an indemnity to Belgium, to hand part of Alsace-Lorraine back to France, and possibly to make some concession to Russia in the Dardanelles in return for important concessions.

In France there was only a small, insignificant section of Socialists of the German school who were willing to allow

ADMIRAL SIR JOHN R. JELLICOE, O.M., G.C.B.
Sir John Jellicoe, who had been appointed Commander-in-Chief of the Grand Fleet on the outbreak of war and was in supreme command at the Battle of Jutland, May 31st, 1916, became First Sea Lord of the Admiralty on December 4th, 1916.

the Prussians and Bavarians to retain the great iron and coal fields of Lorraine and the enormous potash deposits of Alsace, the latter of which alone were sufficient to pay all the German expenses of the war. Republican France, unjustly attacked when labouring for peace and unprepared for war, was sternly resolute to recover her lost provinces, which were vitally necessary to her industrial and her agricultural strength. Russia also needed a decisive victory to enable her to grow to her full stature. Both for economic and religious reasons the recovery of Constantinople and the expulsion of the Turk from Europe were vital for the Empire that inherited the traditions of the Byzantine Church. Belgium and Serbia needed fuller reparation than their enemies would allow, while victorious Italy still

eyed the Italian cities and Italian territories possessed by her traditional foe, and necessary for her complete command over the Adriatic and for the growth of her power in the Mediterranean.

Of all the Allies, Great Britain, in September, 1916, only could have retired from the war with large material gains. In a purely selfish British point of view, of a low and very short-sighted kind, there may have been some prospect of gain, at comparatively small cost, in the idea of a negotiated peace. The war had increased the strength of the British Empire. Even the losses on the battlefield were counter-balanced by the decrease in emigration. The leading Dominion of Canada had scarcely suffered from the lack of British emigrants, as Americans had flowed across the frontier into her wheat-fields, factories, and expeditionary force. South Africa had greatly enlarged her territory, and being peopled by the fertile Boers as well as by the slower breeding but more enterprising Britons, was firmly established as a dominion that would grow into greatness. New Zealand, the paradise of the world and the greatest laboratory of political experiments, had only to wait until the war was ended in order to obtain a large influx of settlers. And the Commonwealth of Australia, which had also become a great Labour State and a land of high wages, was certain to have her losses in men abundantly replaced when the British national armies were demobilised.

Great Britain had occupied nearly every German colony, created an Army on the greatest Continental scale, and forced the Germans to respect its power. The sea-borne trade of Germany was completely checked, and its re-organisation would take some time, while the export trade of Great Britain was fairly maintained. In these circumstances, it was suggested, with misleading talk about humanitarianism and the ideals of Christian civilisation, that a compromise with Germany was the best way to end the war.

Had the real facts lying behind these suggestions been frankly discussed, the British public would clearly have seen what dishonours and disasters were concealed beneath the false idealism of the new movement. Great Britain was to engineer a peace because she had become stronger **Advocates of a negotiated peace** and more prosperous than her Allies, and thus could afford to treat with her enemies. France was to be left embittered and enfeebled permanently, and perhaps inclining at last to a German alliance, in which Russia would join. Meanwhile, there was to be an attempt to form a new league, with the United States and the British Empire heading it, and with Germany intriguing between the possible Atlantic League and the certain Russian-Japanese Union.

It is unnecessary to attempt to explore all the dark possibilities of a negotiated peace to which a party in the Coalition Cabinet seemed to incline ; for Mr. Lloyd George intervened, and, after a series of partial defeats, broke the scheme and broke the Government with it. After several attempts to palliate and quietly smother the issue between him and his opponents, he unexpectedly turned from Mr. Asquith, who always wanted everybody to temporise over everything. Driving frankly at Mr. Walter Runciman and Viscount Grey and aiming to a less extent at Mr. McKenna, Mr. Lloyd George forced them all out of the War Council, and when Mr. Asquith sided with the semi-pacifists the extraordinary Welshman overthrew the Government he had been trying to reform, and by another remarkable display of power became Prime Minister over a Government of his own making without disturbing the country by a General Election.

In September, 1916, Mr. Lloyd George began openly to fight against the gathering influences making for a settlement without victory. In a remarkable interview with an American journalist, published towards the end of the month, the British Secretary for War warned all neutral States of the danger of interfering, and asserted that the British Empire intended to fight to the finish—"to a knock-out."

Some members of the Coalition Cabinet professed to be sadly shocked at Mr. Lloyd George using a metaphor borrowed from the language of the prize-ring. But their veritable quarrel was not with his diction, but with his policy of fighting to the finish at all costs, and refusing a peace by settlement.

At this period of the struggle the American proposal of intervention in the affairs of Europe by means of a league to enforce peace received some support from certain Radical papers in London and the provinces. Viscount Grey, who had taken a seat in the House of Lords in order to continue, in ill-health, the direction of foreign affairs, favoured the American idea of a league for enforcing peace. In a public speech on October 23rd, 1916, he asked the President of the United States if he would agree to use force to prevent another outbreak of war. Nothing in Lord Grey's speech directly conflicted with Mr. Lloyd George's warning to neutrals not to interfere in the fight to a knock-out. Had there been any clear public disagreement, it would have immediately dissolved the Coalition Cabinet.

Proposed league of peace

Nevertheless, the great difference between the two parties in the Cabinet was known to exist, and the unrest of the nation was felt in continual friction. The half-hearted treatment of the food supply produced in the public the feeling that the Coalition Government had no more clear and vigorous policy in home affairs than in military matters. The demand for the State control of food became urgent when the second German submarine campaign against shipping was clearly seen to be attaining a considerable measure of success. Mr. Runciman, as President of the Board of Trade, had long opposed a demand for State

LORD FRENCH INSPECTING VOLUNTEERS AT NORTHAMPTON.
Field-Marshal Viscount French, as Commander-in-Chief of the Home Forces, greatly encouraged and developed the new Volunteer organisation, in the potential value of which he expressed his firm belief.

control during the war of coal-mines, food, shipping, and other large branches of national activity. Lord Rhondda, the leading colliery-owner of South Wales, had endeavoured to induce the Government to take over the most valuable mines. Only when his proposal was rejected did the Welsh magnate proceed with a scheme of private consolidation of coal resources that tended to grow into a trust of Germanic proportion. Mr. Runciman was son of a ship-owner, and a man of high business ability, and but for his academic cast of Liberalism, with its dogmas of free service and Free Trade, he could have socialised the mercantile marine for the period of the war. He would, at least, have thereby prevented the scandalously large profits made by some shipowners, which were a main source of popular discontent.

Popular anger about freightage

On October 17th, 1916, Mr. Runciman tried to assuage the anger of the public in regard to high freights, by pointing out that the cost of ocean transport was often only a minor item in the general rise of prices. He stated that when bacon, for instance, rose in price ninepence a pound, higher freights accounted only for a halfpenny in the rise. The failure of harvests in many of the agricultural countries, such as the United States and Canada, had increased the price of wheat, oats, and other cereals, making bread dear as well as meat. Although Mr. Runciman did not point this out, the failure of the harvest in many countries abroad had led to enormous speculation, in Chicago and elsewhere, by operators who made huge fortunes out of the rise in crops.

Since the close of 1915 a Grain Committee had sat in London, formed of representatives of Great Britain, France, and Italy, and had arranged wheat purchases for the three

LIEUT.-GENERAL SIR FRANCIS LLOYD INSPECTING ROYAL ENGINEERS AT ESHER.
Sir Francis Lloyd, as the General Officer in Command of the London District, played an effective part in controlling the conditions of the soldiers' life in the metropolis as well as in co-operating in the plans for Home Defence, which were perfected under the Commander-in-Chief of the Home Forces. This photograph shows him inspecting men of the Royal Engineers in the lovely grounds at Esher.

allied countries. But this group of officials and experts was apparently no match for the operators of the United States. If there was a man of the Napoleonic stamp among them, capable of managing the vast financial resources of the Allies, such a man did not get free scope. By the autumn of 1916 the stocks of cereals in Great Britain were so low that the Cabinet Committee of Food Supplies was alarmed at the situation.

In the second week of October, therefore, a Royal Commission was appointed to control all imports of wheat and flour, and prevent any unreasonable increase in price by retailers. The Earl of Crawford, President of the Board of Agriculture, who was appointed as chairman to this Commission, was the high expert selected by the Coalition Government to fight the cunning and experienced "bull" operators in the wheat-pit of Chicago!

Forced onward by the pressure of public opinion, Mr. Runciman finally announced, on November 15th, 1916, that with great reluctance he had agreed to the appointment of a Food Controller, to prevent the coming strain that would fall upon the country in the ensuing year. But in the course of his speech, Mr. Runciman, as President of the Board of Trade, seemed to go out of his way to debate matters with which the President of the Board of Agriculture should have dealt. In particular, he remarked that no more men of the farming class could be spared for the Army, alleging that if three or four further divisions were recruited from the soil the reduction in food supply would outbalance the increase in fighting strength. Then, returning to his own field of survey, he went on to state that conscription had been carried on too far in some trades, and steps must be taken to remedy the matter.

Farmers or fighting men?

That party of Liberals who were working for a peace by compromise developed Mr. Runciman's statement into a plea for a smaller and weaker Army. It was suggested that skilled men should be drawn from the fighting-line in order to increase industry and agriculture, and that the men past military age, who kept their businesses going while acting as a voluntary defence force, should be compelled to undertake practical military duties at home. A raiding invasion by the veteran troops of Germany, so the argument seemed to run, could be defeated by the very patriotic, but old and very amateurish, Volunteers. The suggestion had one good result, in that it led Lord French to improve the equipment and training of the Volunteer Force. The members had to agree to train for a considerable period, and could no longer withdraw on short notice when their businesses required attention. Many younger men, indispensable to the ordinary life of the community and exempted by tribunals from national service, were drafted into the Volunteer Force towards the close of the year. But the military value of this force was still too low to permit it to be the main defence against invasion. The debate on the difficulties of the food supply and the need to obtain more labour for the construction of more merchant ships seemed a manœuvre directed against the Secretary of State for War.

Mr. Lloyd George needed more men for the Army, and he was bent on getting them. He was not greatly afraid that exports in 1917 might drop below the extraordinary record of 1916, as he thought that better organisation might prevent any serious decline in industrial productiveness. He was determined to obtain from the agricultural classes, which contained men of the best fighting stamp, the backbone of another army corps. He thought this might be done without running any serious risk of lessening the home production of food; and in any case he was ready to run the risk. The need for men had been urgent since the middle of September,

1916. In October, Sir William Robertson, who as Chief of the Imperial General Staff was the virtual commander of all the British armies on all fronts of the war, made a speech warning the country that it would not win the war unless more man-power was provided.

One of the objects with which Mr. Lloyd George had mediated between the Catholic Irishmen and the Protestant Irishmen, and brought them to agree upon a partial experiment in Home Rule, was to improve recruiting among the sturdy farming classes of Ireland. Ireland having failed him, the Secretary for War put out every ounce of energy within him to "comb out" of England, Scotland, and Wales the forces required for a fight to the finish.

In the middle of November, 1916, the fierce but hidden

REQUIEM MASS AT WESTMINSTER CATHEDRAL FOR IRISH HEROES.
At Westminster Cathedral, on November 27th, 1916, a Solemn Pontifical Mass of Requiem was held for fallen officers and men of the Irish Guards. Above: The Duke of Connaught (left), who had recently returned after completing his term as Governor-General of Canada, with Lord French (centre), Colonel-in-Chief of the Irish Guards, on the steps of the Cathedral.

struggle in the Coalition Cabinet, in regard to the means and end of the war, was nearing the acute stage. But an open crisis was temporarily postponed by a general attack on the Board of Admiralty. The Liberal Press joined with amazing vigour with most of the Conservative Press in condemning the combination of Mr. Balfour and Admiral Jackson as political and naval chiefs of the Navy. It was widely thought there was not sufficient energy in the combination, and that either Mr. Balfour must be replaced by a politician of active temper, or that Admiral Jackson must retire in favour of some officer fresh from the sea.

The force of this criticism, which had been heard for months, was at last admitted by the Coalition Government. Great changes were made both in the Board of the Admiralty and in the command of the Grand Fleet. For some time the announcement of the changes was delayed for military reasons, but on November 29th, 1916, it was stated that Sir John Jellicoe had been appointed First Sea Lord of the Admiralty, and had been succeeded in his command of the Grand Fleet by Sir David Beatty. The changes were deeply regretted by Admiral Jellicoe. It was the saddest day of his life, he confessed, when he gave over the command of the Grand Fleet to the brilliant young admiral who had proved his genius in handling the cruiser force.

This concession to public criticism in regard to the management of one force

FLAGS FROM THE FALKLAND FIGHT.
Tattered flags from H.M.S. Kent, having been carefully repaired, were on July 1st, 1916, formally dedicated and hung in the nave of Canterbury Cathedral.

IN MEMORY OF JUTLAND.
General Pitcairn Campbell inspecting naval contingent, November 12th, 1916, on the occasion of the dedication in Chester Cathedral of the flag of H.M.S. Chester, on which the boy hero, Jack Cornwell, V.C., fell mortally wounded during the Jutland Battle.

engaged in the war did not prevent the supreme crisis from occurring. Only four days after the changes in the Admiralty and the Fleet had been announced, the Prime Minister advised the King to consent to a reconstruction of the Government. All that was clearly known at first was that Mr. Lloyd George, who had been the ruling agent in the establishment of the Coalition Government, was also the reforming force in the reconstruction of the Government. At the outset he attempted to obtain, by means of a special War Committee, more rapidity and decision in the prosecution of the war to a victorious peace. With this end in view he insisted that his opponents in the old War Council should be replaced by a smaller body of men agreeing with his policy. Mr. Runciman, Lord Grey, and—apparently to a less extent—Mr. Reginald McKenna, were in disagreement with Mr. Lloyd George, who was determined to resign if his scheme were not carried out.

Mr. Asquith at this time still remained poised between his former colleagues. He admitted the dominant power of Mr. Lloyd George, and seemed almost willing to agree to a War Committee composed of Mr. Lloyd George, Sir Edward Carson, Mr. Bonar Law, and Mr. Arthur Henderson. This new War Committee was to replace the Coalition War Council that consisted of Mr. Asquith, Mr. Lloyd George, Mr. Bonar Law, Mr. Balfour, Mr. McKenna, Lord Curzon, and Mr. Montagu, with a long tail of official advisers and ministerial consultants. The reduction of the War Committee to five members was arranged in the last week of November, but on December 1st Mr. Lloyd George felt that military victory would be best assured if the machinery of government were more thoroughly reformed. He proposed that the War Committee should consist of three members, of which Mr. Asquith should not be one, and that the triumvirate should have complete power of directing all matters relating to the war, subject to the control of Mr. Asquith. Mr. Lloyd George, Sir Edward Carson, and Mr. Bonar Law were to constitute the triumvirate, with the Labour leader, Mr. Arthur Henderson, as a possible addition. The main object of this proposal seems to have been to solve the problems of man-power, food control, blockade, and supplies without any interference from Mr. Runciman and his school.

On December 1st Mr. Asquith wrote a letter to Mr. Lloyd George agreeing to changes in the War Committee, but insisting that he, as Prime Minister, must preside at the meetings. Mr. Lloyd George did not agree to this, but December 2nd passed without anything definite happening. This pause in the movement for strong reform was quickly ended. On December 3rd the Unionist members of the Cabinet decided that they would resign if Mr. Asquith did not tender his resignation. Thereupon, Mr. Asquith discussed the condition of affairs with Mr. Lloyd George, and proceeded to the public announcement of a reconstruction of the Government. But strong and sharp differences of opinion in regard to the selection of men for the new War Committee and the position of Mr.

Among the new contingents that were formed as soon as the seriousness of the war was fully realised, those which together formed the University and Public Schools Brigade were particularly notable. Here, with Major Henderson in command, a battalion of these men who rallied to the Colours are seen in the early stages of their training on the slopes of Epsom Downs.

Men of the University and Public Schools Brigade, after undergoing three months of the training which was to fit them to take their place with the new armies in the field. One of the discoveries of the war was the rapidity with which men taken directly from school and University could be trained into steady and efficient soldiers, capable of taking part in operations that might well have tried seasoned veterans.

NEW ARMIES IN THE MAKING: THE UNIVERSITY AND PUBLIC SCHOOLS BRIGADE.

Asquith still divided the Prime Minister and the Secretary for War. After discussion on the main question of the chairmanship of the Committee, Mr. Asquith discussed the following arrangement :

The Prime Minister to have supreme and effective control of war policy. The agenda of the War Committee will be submitted to him ; its chairman will report to him daily ; he can direct it to consider particular topics or proposals, and all its conclusions will be subject to his veto. He can, of course, at his own discretion, attend meetings of the Committee.

Here the matter is said the have been left for further consideration. But the next day, when Mr. Asquith was to have made a written communication on the subject to Mr. Lloyd George, he drew back from the arrangement. He stated that the leading article in the "Times" made him doubt the feasibility of the scheme. "The impression is," he wrote, "that I am being relegated to the position of an irresponsible spectator of the war."

Intervention of the "Times"

The article in the "Times," which either did the mischief or cleared the air, according to the point of view, ran as follows :

Out of a welter of political speculation—some of it calculated, some of it merely misinformed—certain definite facts are already beginning to emerge. The first is that Mr. Lloyd George has finally taken his stand against the present cumbrous methods of directing the war. The second is that he has an alternative scheme of his own, which is not without support among his colleagues. The third is that we are at last within measurable distance of the small War Council, or super-Cabinet for war purposes. On Friday Mr. Lloyd George's decision took shape in the form of written representations to the Prime Minister, and these have since been followed by personal discussion between them. The gist of his proposal is understood to be the establishment forthwith of a small War Council, fully charged with the supreme direction of the war. Of this Council Mr. Asquith himself is not to be a member —the assumption being that the Prime Minister has sufficient cares of a more general character without devoting himself wholly, as the new Council must be devoted if it is to be effective, to the daily task of organising victory. Certain of Mr. Asquith's colleagues are also excluded on the ground of temperament from a body which can only succeed if it is harmonious and decisive. On the other hand, the inclusion of Sir Edward Carson is believed to form an essential part of Mr. Lloyd George's scheme, and it is one which will be thoroughly understood.

The conversion has been swift, but Mr. Asquith has never been slow to note political tendencies when they became inevitable. The testimony of his closest supporters—even more, perhaps, than the pressure of those who have no politics beyond the war—must have convinced him by this time that matters cannot possibly go on as at present. They must have convinced him, too, that his own qualities are fitted better, as they are fond of saying, to "preserve the unity of the nation" (though we have never doubted its unity) than to force the pace of a War Council. Moreover, he can hardly fail to have been profoundly influenced by the attitude of Mr. Bonar Law, who is believed to support Mr. Lloyd George.

This is by no means the first time in the last two years that Mr. Lloyd George has been on the verge of a rupture with his colleagues. Once it was averted by the enforced surrender of the Government over the Military Service Bill. Once the Ministry of Munitions, and more likely the War Office, seemed to provide fresh opportunities even under unsatisfactory conditions, of useful individual service. But from the very beginning he has stood apart from the rest in his unmistakable enthusiasm for vigorous war. The Celtic temperament is apt to concentrate on a single passion, and Mr. Lloyd George has somehow succeeded in impressing even the bitterest of his old opponents with his complete abandonment of every other thought beside the passion for victory. It was only a question of time before he found it impossible to work with the old digressive colleagues under the old unwieldy system. No elaborate theory is needed to account for his revolt. Nor, for the matter of that, is the country at large under any illusions about it.

It may have been given to the leader writer of the "Times" to make history and produce a sudden change in the decision of Mr. Asquith. It is, however, more probable that the newspaper article was merely used as a pretext for abandoning the arrangement, as the Unionists two days before it appeared had decided to resign. Some of Mr. Asquith's principal colleagues were scarcely pleased at the position to which they were being reduced, and were not averse from the policy of their chief resigning and forming a strong opposition, hoping to return to power at an early date after the overthrow of Mr. Lloyd George.

In the meantime, Mr. Bonar Law, after the resignation of Mr. Asquith in the evening of December 5th, was summoned by the King to form an administration. But the Unionist leader, though assured of the cordial support of Mr. Lloyd George, was not able to arrange what he considered a stable Government, as he could not obtain assistance from the main Liberal-Radical group. In these circumstances the King summoned Mr. Lloyd George to form an administration, in the afternoon of December 6th, and the Welsh statesman agreed to undertake the task with the support of Mr. Bonar Law. The Asquith group clearly expected at the end of the first week in December

IN THE TRENCHES—IN HEATON PARK, MANCHESTER.

Convalescent soldiers who had fought in France and Gallipoli constructed in Heaton Park, Manchester, an elaborate system of trenches, a faithful reproduction of those in use at the front. The money charged for inspection of the earthworks was devoted to the benefit of soldiers and sailors blinded in the war.

to return to power in time to arrange the general peace. They thought that Mr. Lloyd George would have difficulties in winning over Lord Curzon, Mr. Chamberlain, and Lord Robert Cecil, and that he would be finally discomfited by the leaders of the Labour Party. But the new and very expectant opposition was not prepared for the extraordinary genius for social reconstruction which Mr. Lloyd George instantly displayed when the opportunity of his life came. By the most astonishing feat of improvisation in history the new Pitt realised the dreams of Disraeli and the visions of Joseph Chamberlain and established a large-based system of Imperial Democracy.

Lloyd George as the new Pitt

The Labour Party held the balance of votes between the Unionists and Liberals. A considerable number of Liberals and Radicals went over to Mr. Lloyd George, but they were not sufficient, even with the Unionists, to outnumber a possible combination of Asquithians, Labour representatives, and Irish Nationalists. Great seemed the difficulties of the new Prime Minister; but happily, the war had completed that long education of the old Conservative school which Disraeli had begun and Chamberlain continued. The experiment of socialising Great Britain, for at least the

ESCAPED RUSSIAN PRISONERS IN LONDON.
In June, 1916, the King received a party of Russian prisoners of war who had escaped from the Germans, and inspected them in Buckingham Palace grounds.

period of the war, was agreed to by the Unionist Party. Thereupon, Mr. Lloyd George had an interview with Mr. Arthur Henderson, Mr. Wardle, Mr. Brace, and Mr. Roberts, on December 7th, and convinced them that the working classes of the kingdom had a supreme opportunity of taking a large and active part in both the conduct of the war and the reorganisation of the country and Empire.

In the afternoon the Labour leaders held, a private meeting at the House of Commons to decide what attitude they should adopt towards the new Government. Mr. Ramsay Macdonald, Mr. Snowden, and other pacifists of the anti-British school naturally denounced the proposal to federate the Trade Unions temporarily with the Conservative and Liberal forces that Mr. Lloyd George was directing. It was because Mr. Lloyd George intended to win the war that the **Decision of the** notorious anti-British sec-**Labour Party** tion in the Labour world endeavoured to prevent the great, practical socialising movement which for years they had been advocating. But Mr. Henderson was strongly supported by Mr. Brace, Mr. Roberts, Mr. Hodge, Mr. George Barnes, Mr. O'Grady and other representatives of the large Trade Unions. By the vote of the majority it was decided to take part in the new Government. In the same afternoon the Liberal War Committee met, under Sir Frederick Cawley, and resolved to support Mr. Lloyd George. The Welsh Liberal representatives also gathered around the first Welsh Prime Minister in history. The result was that, without resorting to a General Election, Mr. Lloyd George obtained in the House of Commons a majority which made him independent of the men whose aim was to defeat him in time to arrange general terms of peace.

The Asquith group retained control of the Party funds, and began to intrigue in England and Scotland to increase their strength in view of a General Election. Wealthy men of position, who had been the social pillars of the Liberal-Radical Party, were approached, with the design to

A ROYAL COMPATRIOT.
Before their reception by King George the Grand Duke Michael inspected the men at the Palace gates.

convert them into instruments against Mr. Lloyd George But the feeling in the country was too strong against the intriguers. It was also too strong for the sinister element in the Independent Labour Party and the Union of Democratic Control. The dispute over war policy and political policy, between Mr. Arthur Henderson and Mr. Wardle on the one hand and Mr. Ramsay Macdonald and Mr. Snowden on the other hand, was clearly decided at the Labour Party Conference on January 23rd, 1917. The delegates, representing more than two million workers and voting by card, gave a majority of 1,542,000 for the new Government. This was a remarkable increase over the vote given the previous year in practical support of the Coalition Government. Mr. Lloyd George and his Labour colleagues obtained a six to one majority vote at the Labour Conference of 1917, as against a three to one majority vote given in 1916 for the new Asquith Administration.

Thus from a sea of difficulties and intrigues Mr. Lloyd George emerged clothed with such power as no modern British Prime Minister ever had. The National Irish Party regarded him at least with sympathy. For, by his previous effort to reconcile Catholic and Protestant Ireland, he had proved himself a great mediator. The leaders of the Trade Unions, who shared his power, trusted him, and felt also trust in the inspiration of social justice that was working through their new colleagues, who represented the land-owning, mine-owning, banking, and industrial classes. If they could but work together, with loyal goodwill, the members of the new Government had it in their power to accomplish, while carrying out their main task of winning the war, a more profound development in social structure than had been achieved in any ancient State in the world.

A promising element in the new administration was the force of experts and business men that Mr. Lloyd George called to his Council. The large and intricate affairs of food control were entrusted to Lord Devonport, formerly Sir Hudson Kearley, M.P., who had shown remarkable talent and firmness in public administration as chairman of the Port of London Authority. He was assisted by Captain Charles Bathurst, a man who had no need for officials to spoon-feed him with knowledge of agriculture.

As President of the Board of Agriculture the Earl of Crawford was replaced by Mr. Rowland Prothero, historian of British agriculture and former agent to the Duke of Bedford,

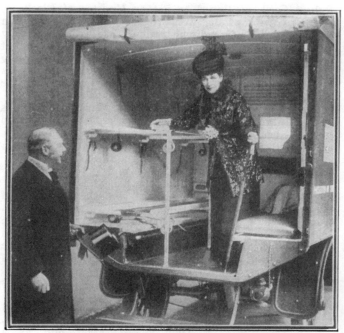

ROYAL INTEREST IN THE SPORTSMEN'S GIFT.
The British Sportsmen's Ambulance Fund was started by a committee of representative sportsmen under the presidency of Lord Lonsdale, to provide a fleet of ambulance cars for the British Red Cross and our Allies. Queen Alexandra inspected one of them at Marlborough House.

whose experimental farm at Woburn was one of the glories of British agricultural science. Even more important than the appointment of Mr. Prothero was the elevation of Mr. H. A. L. Fisher, of the University of Sheffield, to the position of President of the Board of Education. Mr. Fisher was one of the most enlightened leaders of the movement for reform and development of national education. He was without any influence in the political world, and was chosen for his position in the new Government entirely on his merits as an educationist. Even the ranks of Tuscany cheered the appointment of Mr. Fisher.

Quite as revolutionary was the selection of Sir Joseph Maclay for the new post of Shipping Controller. For years Sir Joseph had been the strong Ishmael of the British mercantile marine, having started as a clerk and built up, outside the great lines, a fleet of alert and busy tramp steamers that gave him power and fortune. A man of independence and far-ranging experience, Sir Joseph Maclay seemed to be a shipping controller of great promise. Helping him was Sir L. Chiozza Money, another self-made man, who had acquired in a successful **Some revolutionary** career as commercial journalist and **appointments** writer on economics a remarkable amount of knowledge of all the currents of British commerce. He was of Italian stock, with all the quickness of mind of the race that was working towards another great renaissance while triumphing over its hereditary enemy.

Lord Rhondda, the brilliant magnate of the Welsh coal-fields, who had retired in disgust from politics, returned to a position of authority as President of the Local Government Board. His was a post that offered a pleasant cushion for the languid head of a wealthy and self-contented man. Lord Rhondda had been a champion of the Welsh miners, and, by combining the interests of Labour with efficiency in organisation, he had made the mines he managed more profitable, while increasing his men's wages. Having crowned his fortune with a peerage, he might have rested content with filling, in a highly decorative manner, his position in the Ministry of his fellow-Welshman. But in January, 1917, he began to transform the Local Government Board as Joseph Chamberlain had transformed the Colonial Office. Exercising, for the benefit of the nation,

the fine and original powers of mind he had shown as a colliery-owner, Lord Rhondda quickly became an energetic reformer of the health of the people, and opened his campaign with important measures against the great secret plague and the loss of the most precious of national treasures—child life.

Another man of business genius, Sir Albert Stanley, the managing-director of the London General Omnibus Company and the London Electric Railway system, brought a fresh mind and skilled energy to the directive and fostering work of the Board of Trade. Lord Cowdray, a master contractor, engineer, **New Ministry of** and petroleum magnate, found scope for **Labour** his talents as chief of the Air Board, where he placed the provision of their material under the Ministry of Munitions. Another notable business man, Mr. S. H. Lever, who had been responsible for making of the Munition Ministry a success by reducing the cost of output, was given a still larger field for effecting national economies as Financial Secretary to the Treasury.

New political powers were given to the latest force in British politics—the Labour representatives. A Ministry of Labour was created for Mr. John Hodge, who began to prepare for demobilisation by reorganising and extending the Labour Exchanges, and imparting a different spirit to the officials who had made the Exchanges unpopular with the working classes. Mr. George Barnes was also provided with a new post, the Ministry of Pensions, in the operation of which the working classes were vitally interested. He increased the allowances for children and attempted to find more funds for widows. Two other Labour leaders, Mr. Brace and Mr. G. H. Roberts, had influential positions

DUKE OF CONNAUGHT AND CANADIAN WOUNDED.
The Duke and Duchess of Connaught and Princess Patricia gave great pleasure to the Canadians in the Duchess of Connaught's hospital, near Taplow, by paying them an informal visit shortly after their return from the Dominion in October, 1916.

in the Home Office and in the Board of Trade, while Mr. Arthur Henderson represented the Trade Unions directly in the War Cabinet.

In regard to the relations of the War Committee and the Cabinet, Mr. Lloyd George saw no reason to pursue his old plan for a Committee of Public Safety. None of his new colleagues was likely to oppose him in the conduct of the war as Mr. Runciman had done. There was thus no need for an attempt to reduce the general body of the Cabinet to the position of departmental chiefs. A daily Committee, however, was formed, for direct war purposes, of Mr. Lloyd George as Prime Minister, Mr. Henderson and Lord Milner as Ministers without portfolios, and Lord Curzon as Lord President of the Council and leader of the House of Lords. Mr. Bonar Law became Chancellor of the Exchequer and acting leader of the House of Commons, but, owing to his Parliamentary duties, it was not expected he would be able regularly to attend the War Cabinet.

Sir Edward Carson was made First Lord of the Admiralty and Lord Derby Secretary for War. Mr. Arthur Balfour went to the Foreign Office, while his kinsman, Lord Robert Cecil, continued to act as Minister of Blockade, and Mr. Walter Long went to the Colonial Office. On the whole the new administration was distinguished by intrinsic personal strength. It was a combination of politicians of all parties and expert minds from many important branches of national activity. The politicians had the ear of the country, while the experts had the knowledge necessary for great reforms.

The speed with which the new Prime Minister formed his brilliant administration was very remarkable. The political crisis opened on December 1st and ended on December 7th, 1916. Within a week a clear, fresh, invigorating spirit swept the kingdom and blew over the seas. To France and Italy the news of the end of the long reign of the party of compromise and the beginning of the rule of a truly national British party came as a source of hope and great encouragement. The Italians, who had long been deeply interested in the personality of Mr. Lloyd George, hailed him with the title of "Prime Minister of Europe." To them he was the incarnation of

"Prime Minister of Europe"

the genius of modern Democracy. To the French it was the success of his work as Minister of Munitions that made the new Premier an example of democratic genius. They looked upon him as a greater Carnot—the organiser of victories—and rejoiced he had at last won the control of the war on the British side.

After the political struggle both Mr. Lloyd George and Mr. Asquith suffered under the strain of their conflict, and fell ill. During the illness of the new Prime Minister there occurred the foreseen event that had all along underlain the political crisis. On December 12th the Chancellor of Germany, with a tactless mixture of bluster and bluff, offered to open negotiations for peace. Eight days afterwards the President of the United States intervened between the belligerent nations with a peace Note, suggesting that arrangements should be made for the permanent pacification of the world. Happily, neither Mr. Walter Runciman nor Viscount Grey was in authority to discuss the American idea of a league to enforce peace, or to debate how much backing should be given to France in her demand for the return of all the territories wrested from her in 1870 against the wishes of the population. Mr. Lloyd George was able to speak for the civic majority of the British people, as well as for the fighting men on sea and land who were venturing their lives to the end, and to decide that the war should not end in a draw and a peace without victory.

On December 20th he replied to the German Chancellor's proposal for peace by a telling quotation of the answer made by Abraham Lincoln under similar circumstances: "We accepted this war for an object, a worthy object,

ENROLMENT OF "VICTORY LOAN" CANVASSERS AT THE MANSION HOUSE.
During the raising of the great War Loan at the beginning of 1917 the City of London, as usual, gave a notable lead in taking measures to ensure its success. • The Lord Mayor, Sir William Dunn (on the left), made the Mansion House a headquarters from which an active canvass was carried on for the recruiting of the decisive financial army.

BOARDING THE HOMEWARD-BOUND BOAT
Leave to go home was the real tonic for men worn by active service. The moment when he set foot aboard the homeward-bound boat was one of the great moments in the life of the British soldier.

and the war will end when that object is attained. Under God, I hope it will never end until that time." He went on to state the British terms of peace in the formula made by Mr. Asquith : " Restitution, reparation, guarantee against repetition. Meanwhile," he continued, " we shall put our trust in an unbroken Army rather than in a broken faith." But the most important reply made by the new Prime Minister, in answer to enemy proposals and enemy intrigues, was of a businesslike kind. He announced that a system of national service was about to be established as a counter-movement against the German mass levy organised by Hindenburg. Mr. Neville Chamberlain, the second son of Joseph Chamberlain, and an armament maker and Lord Mayor of Birmingham, was appointed Civil Director of the organisation of the entire human resources of Great Britain.

In practical effect there was to be a British mass levy involving many great changes of life and position to all persons not engaged on work of national value. The prospect might have been a disturbing one in ordinary conditions, but the spirit of the people was wrought to such an intensity that, when Mr. Neville Chamberlain began his work in January, 1917, by calling for volunteers, there was widespread disappointment at the method he was using. The nation was not merely ready to submit to general discipline ; it was eager to do so. The larger part of the manhood of England, Scotland, and Wales was fighting or training for battle or making munitions of war. Nearly every family of size had sons in the trenches or sons on the sea, and fathers engaged on work that was helpful in the war. Many of the daughters were doing what had once been men's work, and often actively assisting in arming the men. Therefore, a majority existed anxious to see the system of national service developed speedily into an effective answer to the German mass levy.

The popular feeling was that what the Teuton could do the Briton could do. If complete national service would shorten the war, and so save the lives of sailors and soldiers, it seemed better to enforce it as fully and rapidly as possible. Indeed, the lapse of time that occurred between Mr. Lloyd George's announcement of national service and the publication of effectual measures by Mr. Neville

Organisation of National Service

Chamberlain, constituted the first disappointment felt by the majority of the people over the new administration. The delay, however, was not due to want of energy, but to a compromise effected with the Labour leaders before they joined the Government. Mr. Henderson and his comrades had from the first insisted that a voluntary scheme should be tried before any general method of compulsion was employed. Thus it was that Mr. Chamberlain began by calling for men and women volunteers, and arranged to sort out all industries and stop those trades which were not required and transfer the workmen to work of more importance.

In all affairs there was displayed the vigour of organisation

GATES OF HAPPINESS : VICTORIA STATION, LONDON.
Crowds gathered at Victoria Station to greet the happy soldiers arriving on Christmas leave. Men of various volunteer regiments were on duty to direct them to the final stage of their journey.

which the Liberal group in the former Coalition Cabinet had lacked. Mr. Lloyd George, with Sir William Robertson and Lord Milner, went to Rome in the first week of the New Year, and, with the Premier and War Minister of France and General Sarrail from Salonika, held a conference with the Italian military and political authorities. This conference was said by the Italian Premier to have resulted in " one of the most important events in the history of the world." It was followed in the last week of January by a similar conference at Petrograd, where Lord Milner, General Sir Henry Wilson, with General Castelnau and the Colonial Minister of France and representatives of the Cabinet and General Staff of Italy, consulted with the leaders of the Russian Government and the Russian Commander-in-Chief. There was also a meeting in London of the military chiefs of Great Britain and France. Nothing was revealed concerning the results of these conferences, but they were of far-ranging effect, and being undertaken, under the direct stimulus of Mr. Lloyd George with a view of welding the Allies together to the prosecution of the war, they were the first-fruits of the new order of things in the British Isles.

While the Prime Minister was absorbed largely in work for the Allies, his lieutenants set out upon their tasks of transforming the Kingdom and Empire. At Christmas an Imperial War Conference was being arranged for the spring of 1917. All the Prime Ministers of the Oversea

Dominions were invited to sit with the War Cabinet, and take counsel with the members in regard to the conduct of the war, the terms on which peace would be granted to the enemy, and the problems that would arise after the cessation of hostilities. Two representatives of India were called to the Conference, which promised to prove in practice a Grand Cabinet of the Empire, in which the oversea democracies would be most **The Imperial** generously represented. It was an historic **War Conference** step in Empire-building, worthy of the man who looked like becoming the new Pitt, and was acclaimed by France and Italy as well as by the British Empire. General Smuts resigned his command in East Africa to attend the Conference; the Premiers of Canada and New Zealand arranged to come in person; the Commonwealth of Australia sent one of her leading statesmen, while India chose as her representatives a native nobleman and a leading administrator.

In home affairs Mr. Rowland Prothero, Lord Devonport, and Lord Derby laboured upon a seemingly impossible work. Lord Derby needed for the Army more men by the hundred thousand. He began by reducing Mr. Prothero to despair, through taking thirty thousand first-rate men

"HYMN OF HATE" IN THE WAR LOAN CAMPAIGN.
Captain Mackenzie Rogan conducted the band of the Coldstream Guards outside the Royal Exchange in the course of the War Loan campaign in February, 1917, and indulged a large lunch-hour audience with the strains of the Prussian "Hymn of Hate."

from agriculture. Then he demanded that every fit man under the age of thirty-one should be removed from civil employment into military work, only skilled engineers, engaged in war factories, shipbuilding yards, and other centres of vital industry being exempted. This extensive scheme was announced on January 17th, 1917. On the following day another great military inroad into agriculture and general labour was made by calling up all lads of eighteen to serve at home for a year, to strengthen the fighting reserves of the Empire.

Yet at this time Mr. Prothero and Lord Devonport were endeavouring by all means to increase the home supply of food and prepare against a possible famine. It was Mr. Prothero's aim to make English agriculture more productive than it had ever been. But he came to power too late in the year to arrest the general decline. There were four million arable acres in the country that had been allowed to become pasture land.

Even in 1916, British wheat-fields had been reduced by a quarter of a million acres, and the general production of home-grown food had fallen twelve per cent. between 1915 and 1916. There was a great shortage of potatoes, and the first food riot occurred at Maryland Market on January 13th, 1917, owing to women wanting potatoes at

a shilling a stone, while the merchants stood out for one shilling and tenpence. The winter wheat for 1917 had been sown, and farmers, owing to the new call for men and lads made by the War Office, were not in a position to plough up more land in the spring to provide the people with bread, potatoes, and other food. In these adverse circumstances Mr. Prothero showed himself a worthy lieutenant of Mr. Lloyd George, and transformed his new difficulties into new opportunities.

First of all, by means of county committees, he surveyed every patch of land that could be improved by manure or tillage. He removed the restrictions that prevented cottagers from keeping pigs, started pig clubs and production committees in every village, and arranged to bring another hundred thousand women on to the land. Then, in return for the agriculturists transferred to the Army, he took out of the ranks every soldier who could manage a steam-cultivator. He raided the munition works and monopolised the principal manufacturers of agricultural machinery, appointing Mr. S. F. Edge, a motor expert and practical farmer, as director of the munitions branch of agriculture. He was able to promise farmers power-machinery and trained hands to till their land and thresh their crops, with a considerable amount of rough, untrained help in harvest-time from large bodies of soldiers.

Three of these soldiers were not worth one trained farm labourer. But the scheme was to supply them in such numbers that the agricultural work could be done. Farmers were promised State loans on the non-existent crops they undertook to grow. Seed wheat, seed potatoes, and other materials of production were to be provided by the Government, and all possible help given in other ways. But the great revolutionary factor in the Prothero campaign was the promise to provide a large amount of State power-machinery and Government hands to replace the manual labour that was going into the Army. Of all men of conservative temper in the world, the British farmer—and the English farmer in particular—was chief. Mr. Prothero's design was to transform abruptly the conservative farmer class into as progressive a body of men as the best Canadian and American agriculturists. The smallness of English fields was a hindrance to the employment of power-machinery in a general way. Nevertheless, the new President of the Board of Agriculture promised the country the greatest revival in agriculture it had ever known.

At the end of 1916, however, there arose a conflict between the farmer and the Food Controller. Lord Devonport had to arrange to feed the people on a stock of wheat which was not large enough. He could not wait until more potatoes were **Difficulties in** grown in the summer of 1917. He had to **food control** do the best he could with the short supplies which were shared with France, Italy, and suffering Belgium. He was, therefore, compelled to establish standard bread in January, 1917. He soon discovered, however, that the stock of wheat was not sufficient even for standard bread, and in the second week of January an order was made that wheat-flour should be diluted with rice, maize, barley, or oatmeal. The consequence was that the public obtained a larger amount of breadstuff of a nutritious kind at the cost of their eggs, bacon, pork, and other meat supplies. For the great poultry and cattle food, commonly known as middlings, went in a large

Mr. Bonar Law, Chancellor of the Exchequer, on January 18th, 1917, addressed a great meeting at St. Andrew's Hall, Glasgow, making an important speech on the War Loan then being raised, in which he urged that the money received would shorten the war and so save lives.

Mr. Neville Chamberlain, Director-General of National Service, at the Central Hall, Westminster, on February 6th, 1917, addressing the public meeting at which he broadly outlined his scheme, and called upon all men up to the age of sixty years to place their services at the disposal of the State.

TWO GREAT PROTAGONISTS OF THE APPEAL FOR MAN-POWER AND MONEY-POWER.

INNS OF COURT O.T.C. AT BERKHAMPSTEAD.
The Inns of Court O.T.C. supplied a large number of useful soldiers to the British Army. They had a camp at Berkhampstead, where they were visited by the King in August, 1916, when his Majesty inspected the trenches they had made and watched them go through various courses connected with their training.

pheasants and other game was prohibited, and measures of great importance were taken to develop the vast fisheries of the Empire.

The grandiose scheme of an Imperial fish monopoly was elaborated by the end of January, 1917. It promised to make the British Empire the purveyor of fish almost to the whole world. The Government already controlled all the whale fishing in the Antarctic Ocean, and thence derived large quantities of whale-oil for the manufacture of high explosives. The State obtained the oil at £38 a ton, as against £300 a ton paid by the German Government for small lots from Scandinavian fishers. Canada was offering to bring fish to Liverpool at a penny a ton, reducible to a halfpenny a ton on large State contracts ; so that, if the consent of the Dominions could be obtained, a British world monopoly in fish, with low retail prices regulated in every town in the kingdom, could be made a matter of practical politics under the new socialising administration.

proportion into bread, and produced a disastrous shortage of pig and poultry stuffs. Before Christmas, 1916, the food had already become enormously dear, causing farmers to kill off their pigs and poultry, and seriously to reduce the meat supply in the country.

But Lord Devonport and Mr. Prothero were an energetic and well-informed couple. In the third week of January the new department of food production turned upon the brewers, and took away from them 286,000 tons of barley and 36,000 tons of sugar, compelling the ouput of beer to be reduced to half the quantity made before the war. In vain did the brewers plead that of the barley they used they returned twenty-five per cent. as food for dairy cows. Mr. Prothero replied that, by giving the barley to millers to be made into war-bread, he would obtain, in addition to the bread meal, forty per cent. of cattle food. About the time that the brewers' interests were further attacked, sweet-makers, milk-chocolate makers and mineral-water manufacturers were subjected to rigorous treatment by the Food Controller.

The making of milk-chocolate was prohibited, the ration of sugar was reduced, no sweets were allowed to be manufactured for sale at more than 2d. an **Sugar, meat,** ounce, and no chocolate at more than **potatoes, and fish** 3d. an ounce. The aim was to save sugar and revive the household industry of jam-making. But private marmalade-making was not encouraged when the Seville oranges arrived ; grocers could not supply the needed sugar. Meals in restaurants and hotels had been restricted, under the Coalition Government, to two courses for lunch and three courses for dinner. The measure, however, had proved an utter failure, as it merely induced the eating of more meat in a single course. It was expected that Lord Devonport would improve upon this piece of Runcimanism ; but in the period up to review he attempted nothing in the matter, but laboured in his task of the control and distribution of staple foods. In conjunction with Mr. Prothero he fixed a price for potatoes, wheat, oats, and other crops. But his maximum price for potatoes had quickly to be changed into a minimum price, in order to encourage growers to develop the 1917 crop. Measures were taken to reduce the deer in the Scottish Highlands and to re-establish the old Scottish sheep farms on ground where sheep could find food. The feeding of

The enterprises of Mr. Prothero and Lord Devonport, with their assistant committees, were favoured by the work of Sir Joseph Maclay, the Shipping Controller. Working in intimate rela- **Co-operation of** tion with the Admiralty, and helped by **shipping control** Sir John Jellicoe, the controller of shipping adopted the new American idea of turning out steamers by the plan on which cheap motor-cars were produced. All the structure, fittings, and engines were standardised, so that any element fitted perfectly into any ship. Cargo steamers were laid down in a quarter of a million tonnage, and turned out piecemeal in different places of the country, the pieces being afterwards assembled somewhat in the manner of a Ford car. Instead of ships being built to the individual taste of each shipowner, they were made in a wholesale manner for State service. In the middle of January, 1917, Sir John Jellicoe addressed the British shipbuilders, warning them that the enemy's new submarine campaign was a serious menace, and that their new work of making standardised steamers was a ruling factor in the issue of the war. " Let there be no question of strikes," exclaimed the famous seaman; "no bad time-keeping, no slacking. Let masters and men remember how great is their responsibility, not only towards the Navy and the nation, but also towards our Allies."

France at the time was held in the rigour of one of the severest winters known for a generation, and in Paris the cost of household coal was 10s. a hundredweight. The sufferings of the urban working classes and lower middle classes of France were partly due to the system of free service favoured by the Liberal Government of Great Britain in the early phase of the war. Miners had gone into the Army and slackers had gone into the mines, with the result that the production of coal had diminished in such a way as to injure both France and Italy. Mr. Lloyd George, again making an opportunity out of a difficulty, used the shortage of coal as a weapon against those Norwegians who were supplying the enemy with food and iron-ore in contravention of the blockade agreement. The export of British coal to Norway ceased for a while. This had the result of giving the Shipping Controller more coal-boats, which he was able to send southward to the assistance of France and Italy. Sir Joseph Maclay

Studies of the winning spirit among the Allies: 1. The Italians on the Isonzo front.

2. *A French recruit among the veterans: Faith, hope, and visions of victory*

3. *British soldier in a conquered enemy trench: Quiet and steadfast and in triumph merciful.*

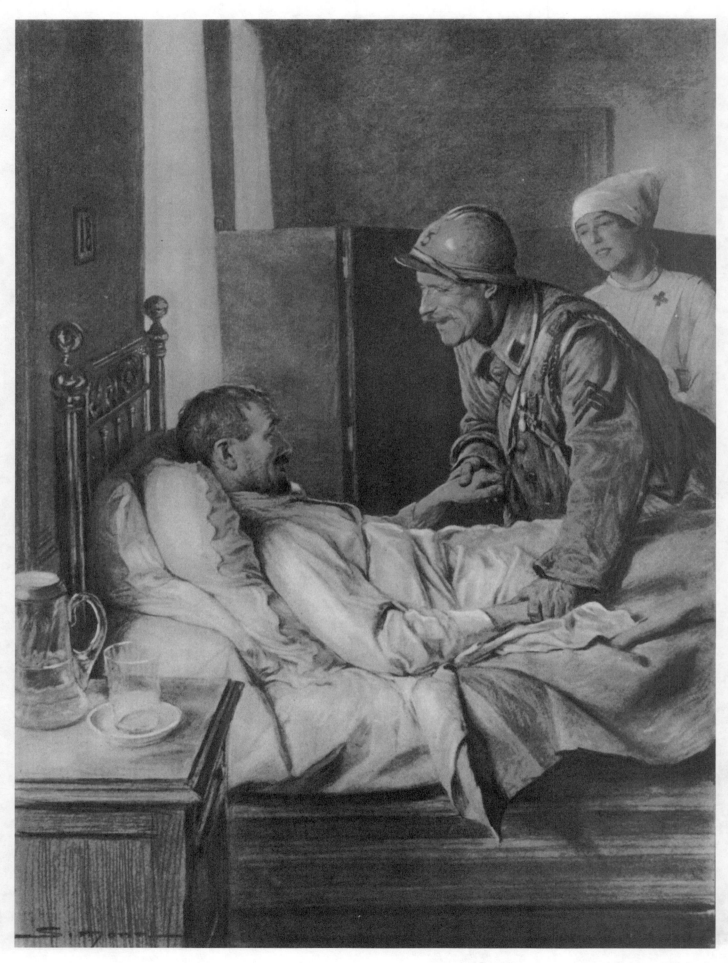

4. *The best tonic for a wounded hero: Word from the battlefield that all goes well.*

also speeded-up the work of discharging and loading cargo steamers, so as to enable ships to be used more frequently. Dock labour was supplemented by bringing up the Transport Workers Battalion to ten thousand men.

This reorganisation of the docks was not, however, sufficient to meet the urgent military needs of the nation. The old Coalition Government had let the vital problem of transport drift, as other things drifted. But when a practical traffic manager, Sir Albert Stanley, succeeded Mr. Runciman at the Board of Trade, there was a revolution of an unexpected kind in the railway system of the country. Sir Albert Stanley, who had worked in the United States before returning to England, bought a Chicago railway and transferred the line, rolling-stock, and bridges to Great Britain, as a cheap and quick method of getting material. Then on January 1st, 1917, he raised all ordinary passenger fares by fifty per cent., and reduced the amount of passenger's luggage to one hundred pounds. Only the holders of workmen's, season, and trader's tickets were exempted from the sudden heavy tax.

Commercial travellers were badly hit, together with many clerks, typists, and shop assistants in Outer London. But the State Controller of Railways went on with his task of restricting public travel, and provoked more agitation by closing a large number of railway-stations. The fact was that the British production of **Restriction of** war material had outrun the ordinary **inland travelling** means of railway transport. In the severe winter all the waterways of Northern Europe froze and stopped traffic. Germany, who relied in a large way upon river and canal transport of war material, was brought nearer to defeat by the ice blockade. England was saved by the earlier enterprise of her northern capitalists, who drove the Great Central Railway southwards in fierce competition against the Midland and Great Northern lines. This recent addition to the English system gave the country adequate railway transport until the enormous new production of the Lloyd Georgian munition factories introduced an unforeseen factor into the situation. The ordinary public service then had to be diminished in order to link the munition works rapidly to the fighting-line in France and Flanders.

There was a danger of munition workers standing idle, because the railways could not carry the material they had made; yet at the same time the Army wanted all that the factories could turn out at top speed. Civilians of all classes had therefore to be checked as much as possible in railway travel, and it was arranged to increase fares, close many stations, and diminish the daily service in order to speed the transport of war material. The munition factories were in a condition of high development, owing largely to the great plans and foresight of Mr. Lloyd George. From the outset he had resolved to pack the entire British front with guns, and help also to pack the French front with heavy artillery, rather than allow the enemy to fight the parallel battle to a standstill. The work he had started in the early summer of 1915 began to mature in the winter of 1916. Thereupon, the people of the United States were utterly astounded by the intervention of a Sheffield armament firm, Messrs. Hadfield, in the supply of munitions for the American Navy. The American Navy had invited

tenders for big shell, and the Bethlehem Steel Works tendered for four thousand shells at a high price, apparently thinking there was no competition to fear. But Messrs. Hadfield, though working under Government control for the British forces, offered to supply the needs of the American Navy at an extremely low price, and obtained the contract. The affair was only a straw showing which way the wind was blowing, but the effect on the industrial circles of the United States was tremendous. It seemed to indicate such a perfecting and speeding-up of British methods of production as was likely to change the course of the world's trade. **Growing expansion** Neutral States had no means of measur- **of industry** ing the work done in Great Britain during the war, as this work was carried out in circumstances of secrecy for all the allied forces. Only such instances as the British tender for the American naval shell revealed, as in a lightning flash, some of the future possibilities of the peaceful expansion of British industries.

There still remained, however, symptoms of indiscipline and selfishness in munition works of the most important order. There were some girls and young men, elated by the high wages they were earning, and deadened by strange and foolish arrogance to their awful responsibilities. Early in January, 1917, a girl working in a fuse hut in the most perilous section of a danger area in the Midlands struck a match to light a cigarette. The match was knocked out of her hand by one of her fellow-workers. But when brought up for trial the thoughtless girl was only fined instead of being imprisoned. Cases of this sort became frequent, and the most deplorable feature about them was that the fines imposed upon the criminals were often paid collectively by the hundreds of persons who had been put in peril of a terrible death.

But a few days after the Midlands incident just referred to, the nation had a ghastly lesson that deeply enforced the need for discipline, carefulness, and sustained sense of responsibility in the most important class of new munition workers. In the evening of January 19th, 1917, London shook under a great explosion, and upon the gloom of the eastern sky-line there rose a flame two miles high. Many persons thought there had been a fight with a raiding Zeppelin; but no load of bursting bombs could have shaken the capital as it was shaken. A fire had broken out in some riverside works where high explosives were being refined. With superb heroism the directing chemist, Dr. Angel, while warning the operatives to seek safety, went to the fire and tried to prevent it reaching the high explosives. Some firemen also arrived, and, though in great peril, stood manfully to their work trying to put out the flames. But as Dr. Angel, who lost his life, and the firemen were trying to prevent the great disaster the explosion occurred. In all there were about four hundred and sixty-nine casualties among men, women, and children. The dead numbered sixty-nine, the seriously injured seventy-two, and the slightly injured three hundred and twenty-eight. In the factory ten women and thirty-eight men were working, but of them nine women and eighteen men were saved by Dr. Angel's warning.

The great British War Loan was inaugurated on January 11th, 1917, in circumstances promising a magnificent success.

[*British official photograph.*]
GREAT GUNS THAT HELD COMMAND OF THE SEA.
Twin guns on a British warship at sea. Untiringly patient and unceasingly watchful, the Grand Fleet and other portions of the Navy held the seas, ever ready to counter any move of the sea-shy enemy.

DR. VON BETHMANN-HOLLWEG, THE IMPERIAL CHANCELLOR, ADDRESSING THE REICHSTAG.

During the early part of 1916 a violent campaign against the Imperial Chancellor was carried on in Germany, largely by the Prussian Conservatives and by means of anonymous pamphlets. He was reviled for not using submarines and airships with sufficient ruthlessness, and for not overthrowing "the chief enemy." Great Britain, forthwith. In June, Dr. Bethmann-Hollweg made a passionate speech in reply to his critics.

THE LIFE OF GERMANY DURING THE YEAR 1916.

By Frederic William Wile, late Berlin Correspondent of the "Daily Mail." Author of "Men Around the Kaiser."

Germany's Economic Distress in 1916 Synchronises with her Supreme Effort to Avert Defeat—The Peace Offer—Vast Food Regulation Scheme—Von Batocki Appointed Food Dictator—Enactment of a Multiplicity of Food Laws—Failure of Organisation Followed by Inconvenience but not Starvation—The Verdun Adventure—Austria's Severe Gruelling—German Naval Activity—Dictatorship of Von Hindenburg and the Mass Levy—Discontent with the Resulting Semi-Serfdom of the Nation—The Frightfulness Campaign—Supersession of Von Tirpitz by Von Capelle—Intensification of the Submarine Campaign—Socialism and the War—The Case of Karl Liebknecht—German War Finance : Loans and Subscribers—The Rumanian Campaign—Winter Sufferings Due to Shortage of Coal, Light, Boots, and Clothes—Preposterous Terms of the German Peace Note to the Allies—Rhetorical Bombast of the German Chancellor—Effect upon Germany of Lloyd George's Appointment to the Premiership—Demand for More Frightfulness—German Plans for a Commercial Armageddon to Begin at the Close of the Armed Conflict—Scope and Functions of the Imperial Board for Transition Economics.

FROM the beginning of the war Germany was guilty of numerous and grotesque miscalculations, but she had no monopoly of them. Her enemies made many, too, and conspicuous among them was their belief that, certainly at the end of two years of war, the economic disintegration of Germany, if not her military defeat, would precipitate her "collapse." Yet the Germans in the first month of the *third* year of war (August, 1916), accepting the challenge offered by the intervention of Rumania on the side of the Allies, launched an entirely new campaign in a remote theatre of operations and carried it through successfully in a miraculously short time. Probably no single military achievement of the entire war outrivalled, to the date of its accomplishment, the conquest of Rumania in a period within four months. It was an event well designed to shock the allied nations in general, and Britain in particular, out of their rosy dreams that the ruthless but highly efficient foe had "shot his bolt."

The year 1916, here under review, though it witnessed the low-water mark of Germany's economic fortunes (food distress), was nevertheless marked by the inception of her supreme effort to stave off defeat : the conferment of something closely akin to a dictatorship upon Field-Marshal von Hindenburg, the national idol, and the coincident

DR. VON BETHMANN-HOLLWEG.
German Imperial Chancellor and Prime Minister of Prussia, who at the outset of the war, described the treaty guaranteeing the neutrality of Belgium as a "scrap of paper."

mobilisation of the nation's whole strength for war purposes under his magnetic supervision. The dawn of "Hindenburgism" synchronised almost to the week, the end of August, with the inauguration of the campaign against Rumania. The rapid victory in which it resulted was called "Hindenburg's very own" (*Ureigenster*), and it inspired Germans to contemplate the future, and to dedicate themselves to it, with renewed confidence in their invincibility.

Yet the end of the third calendar year of the war (1916) was destined to be marked by tell-tale and transparent evidence that, although triumphant in many fields and still in occupation of several hundred thousands of square miles of enemy territory, Germany was conscious that her successes were ephemeral. She asked for peace. She did not sue for it in the generally accepted sense. She "offered" it to her enemies. "Conscious of victory," the Kaiser and his allied fellow-sovereigns invited the Entente Powers to enter into "negotiations for peace," and invoked the good offices of the President of the United States to that end. But no diplomatic dialectics in Berlin could conceal the true inwardness of what the Allies a few days later pilloried as Germany's "sham offer"— viz., that Germany hankered for peace because she knew that, unless she secured it then, there could be no peace, however long delayed, which would find her aught but vanquished. To detail more or less chronologically the course of the fluctuating events which brought the German Government and people to that chastened realisation is the aim of the present chapter.

Food regulation was instituted in Germany as early as February, 1915, when bread tickets were introduced, but as the pinch of the British blockade grew more and more irksome, control of the country's diminishing supplies became increasingly rigid. The 1915 crops had been rather better than normal. The potato supply **Iron regulation** was fairly satisfactory, and the winter of **of supplies** 1915-16 was weathered, not without discomfort and indeed considerable suffering, but without anything approaching either famine or starvation. Rations were enforced by that time for practically every staple necessity of life without exception (even beer), and although short commons was the general rule for meat, bread, butter, milk, eggs, and indispensable fats of all kinds, it was evident that "organisation," the Germans' panacea for all ills, would tide them over the spring and summer into the harvest-time of 1916. They pinned their hopes of "holding out" another year on the prospects of huge crops from the greatest acreage ever planted even in the history of intensive German agriculture.

Constant sapping of man-power from the land for the ravenous and endless demands of the Army sorely denuded German farms of harvest labour. This circumstance, aggravated by the torrential rains which fell during the weeks immediately preceding the harvest, contributed materially towards bringing down the gross yield to a point far below Germany's expectations. Prisoners of war, especially Russians—of whom the Germans claimed to hold 1,500,000— were impressed wholesale into farm labour, but although they relieved the shortage of agricultural workers, advantages derived therefrom were more than wiped out by the disastrous weather. Germany's 1916 crop was a failure. Potatoes, normally harvested to the extent of 50,000,000 or 55,000,000 tons, only yielded something like half the ordinary crop. Early in the

HERR VON BATOCKI.
Herr von Batocki, Governor of the Province of East Prussia. In May, 1916, he became "Food Dictator," or head of the War Nutrition Office then established.

summer, envisaging the approach of calamitous conditions in consequence, the German Government decided to establish an even more iron supervision of foodstuffs than hitherto by organising a so-called "Nutrition Office," and conferring on it autocratic authority.

At the head of the *Ernährungsamt* (Food Ministry) an East Prussian administrator noted for his firmness and executive skill was placed—Herr von Batocki. He was clothed with such plenary powers that he became known forthwith as the Food Dictator. **Von Batocki, the** The Germans are Europe's most **Food Dictator** gluttonous eaters and drinkers, and they gave early and numerous signs that Herr von Batocki's scheme to restrict their appetites and alimentary activities to even a more drastic extent than before would not be easy of accomplishment. Far more serious than individual complaints of hardships which ensued and increased in volume and bitterness were the charges made by South German States like Bavaria and Würtemberg that the Food Dictator, whose authority extended over the whole Empire, was grossly favouring Prussia at the expense of the States which have always been the Cinderellas of the Fatherland.

As graphic indication of their displeasure with what they termed a system of control designed to gorge North Germany and starve South Germany, the Bavarian towns and cities went to the length of announcing that tourists from Prussia must not expect, when visiting South German summer resorts and the like, to be allowed the same rations of meat, bread, milk and other necessaries which were allotted to the natives.

Herr von Batocki, Prussian-like, was adamant to protests, criticism, and abuse alike, and food control from day to day grew in rigidity. By the end of 1916 no fewer than two hundred and fifty-eight new laws, enacted at the instigation of the Nutrition Office or by other departments of the Government, had come into force. They were as follow:

MUNICIPAL FOOD DISTRIBUTION IN CHARLOTTENBURG, A SUBURB OF BERLIN.
By the end of the second year of war the food distress in Germany was acute enough to mean widespread discomfort and inconvenience, but the people had not reached starvation point, though they lacked sufficient nourishment. Queues waited outside the shops and the municipal centres of food distribution. The supplies were often inadequate to the demand represented by the food tickets, but organisation, carried to the utmost limit of Prussian thoroughness, prevailed, and the people, frugal, thrifty, and patriotic by nature, endured the discomfort with fortitude.

Breadstuffs and flour—thirteen laws.
Potatoes and potato products—thirty laws.
Eggs, milk, and cheese—twenty-eight laws.
Sugar-beet, treacle, sugar, and other " sweet " products—twenty-four laws.
Meat and meat products—sixteen laws.
Vegetables and fruits of all kinds—twenty-two laws.
Fish and fish products—eighteen laws.
Coffee, chicory roots, tea, cocoa powder, cocoa, and chocolate—fifteen laws.
Barley, malt, hops, hay, and straw—thirty-six laws.
Fodder and fertilisers—seventeen laws.
Bones, animal oils and fats, soap, soap powders, walnuts, hazelnuts, and washing powders—thirty-nine laws.

In addition to this formidable list of measures, there were nineteen dealing with various other problems directly or indirectly connected with growth or production of food for humans and animals.

In every case these special laws laid down cast-iron rules regarding the import and export of foodstuffs, established maximum prices, fixed rations, determined hours and mode of sale by producer, middleman, and retailer, and in every conceivable way supervised food from the point of origin in the soil or factory to the mouth of the actual consumer, whether man or beast. They represented German organisation and thoroughness carried almost to the uttermost limit. No feature of control was omitted.

RABBIT-BREEDING ESTABLISHMENT AT HANOVER.
Before the war Germans regarded rabbits as vermin, and only the very poorest would eat them. Necessity altered this view, and the breeding of rabbits for food was officially organised and encouraged.

Yet even the most expert of organisers could not make bricks without straw. The Food Dictator might administer two hundred and fifty-eight food laws, but he could not by rescript or edict increase the *supply* of food. Indeed, as 1916 proceeded it became manifest that the Germans were suffering not alone from shortage of food, but from surplus of " organisation." From all quarters of the Empire, in the critical weeks preceding the new harvest, when reserve stocks were low to the point of depletion, came angry cries of distress. Bread continued to be more or less plentiful on the standardised ration scale of four and a half pounds per person per week—sometimes a trifle more, sometimes a little less—but such vital essentials as milk and fats became lamentably and growingly scarce. By the beginning of the winter of 1916–17 Berlin's milk supply, for example, had fallen to a bare one-third of normal. Egg " rations " were at the rate of one per fortnight. Potatoes, which during the summer and autumn had been rationed at eight, nine, and ten pounds per week per person, were cut down to five, six, and seven pounds, and even, as winter approached, to three and four pounds, the rest of the allowance being made up of turnips. Suffering increased in intensity with the arrival of cold weather, which also accentuated the lack of fats. The latter became so scarce throughout the country that it was necessary for the omnipotent Hindenburg to lend his

BERLIN WOMEN WAITING TO BUY MEAT.
Food regulations were instituted in Germany in February, 1915. By the end of 1916 no fewer than two hundred and fifty-eight new food laws were in force, sixteen of which related to meat and meat products.

magic name to a special scheme for acquiring fats, by hook or crook, in sufficient quantities to keep the armies of munition workers in Rhineland-Westphalia, the seat of Krupp's and kindred industries, supplied with indispensable rations of butter, lard, margarine, and dripping. To meet on the one hand the incessant demand of the munition industry for animal and vegetable fats for manufacturing purposes, and on the other hand the equally insistent requirements of working men and women engaged on munitions, was one of the most desperate problems Germany had to confront as 1916 drew to a close. All over the country fats were assembled for shipment to Essen, Düsseldorf, Remscheid, Duisburg, Bochum, Dortmund, Mülheim, Biedefeld **Fat for works and** and other great munition centres. **workers** According to newspaper reports, these commandeered fats were destined exclusively for distribution to artisans engaged in " heavy industry," but it was more than probable that a generous percentage found its way into the maws of munition works rather than munition-workers' bellies.

Though throughout 1916, and particularly in its concluding months, food distress in German towns and cities was aggravated in acuteness, it never reached the stage when the country's condition could be faithfully described as a state of famine or starvation. Inconvenienced, uncomfortable, under-nourished the Germans certainly were. Queues in front of the butcher's, the baker's,

STOCK-TAKING FOR THE DICTATOR.
German pork butchers weighing stock in an inspector's presence. Prussian organisation supervised all food from the point of origin to the mouth of the consumer, checking producer, middleman, and retailer.

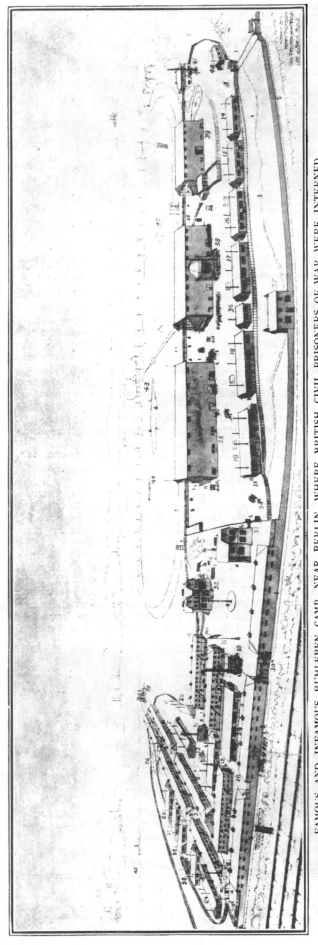

FAMOUS AND INFAMOUS RUHLEBEN CAMP, NEAR BERLIN, WHERE BRITISH CIVIL PRISONERS OF WAR WERE INTERNED.

1-10, Barracks (stables and lofts—heating by steam-pipes inadequate); 13, Negroes' Barracks; 14-18, "Casino," admission by doctor; 33, Kommandant, Post-office, etc.; 35, First Grand Stand (parcels Wooden Huts, heated by coal stoves; 19, Camp Hospital, twelve beds; 20-23, Prisoners' Huts; 24, Soldiers' from home); 37, Guard Post; 38, Second Grand Stand and Kitchen No. 1; 39, Grand Stand, soldiers' mess; Barrack; 25, Wash-house; 26, Prisoners' Lavatory; 27, Guard Post; 28, Wash-house; 29, American 40, Prisoners' Lavatory; 41, Camp kitchen No. 2 and "Tea-house," barrack above; 42, Recreation-ground; Y.M.C.A. Hut; 30, Boiler for heating barracks; 30A, Entrance to camp; 31, Hot-water "Bar"; 32, 43, Imperial Pavilion; 44, Camp rubbish burning-place; 45, River flowing past camp.

and the candlestick-maker's shops became everyday sights everywhere. The suffering of the poor was intense. Even the rich, with money to buy things, found that neither cash nor ration-cards for this, that, and the other commodity were effective, for oftener than not the food for which allowance cards called was not in the market. Yet the tales of sanguinary food riots in Berlin, Munich, Dresden and elsewhere; the tragic yarns of "living skeletons" parading German streets; the stories of wild-eyed women storming the shops in fruitless quest for provisions; the narratives of **Exaggerated tales** "mobs" mowed down by machine-gun **of distress** fire because they demanded "Peace and food" from an impenitent Government—all these accounts were ultimately ascertained to be yarns and stories, and nothing else. In Britain far too willing an ear was lent to these comforting assurances, brought out from the enemy's country with suspicious regularity and circum-stantiality of detail by "neutrals." The net result of such "news" from Germany was in many cases to turn British self-confidence into deceptive over-confidence. The avidity with which people swallowed "starvation' information from Berlin and Vienna was a painful reminder that just as men abroad before the war were inclined to underestimate Germany's power, so were they now dis-posed to exaggerate her weakness.

A fact perhaps not fully appreciated in the countries of her enemies. was that Germany in midwinters during war-time had always to face the serious problem of existing between harvests. One ventured, after thirty months of wrecked predictions on both sides and in all directions, to invade the realm of prophecy about Germany with diffidence bordering on fear; but the sanest students of German affairs seemed agreed at the end of 1916 that, no matter how distressing Germany's food problem during the succeeding six months might become, it alone would not compel her to abandon the war. They recalled that Germans were frugal and thrifty by nature, and highly patriotic besides; that they knew they were fighting with their backs to the wall as well as on underfed stomachs, and that they could hardly fail to put forth a maximum effort to "hold out" until the gathering of another crop.

The "collapse" for which the allied peoples so fervently prayed would be hastened, undoubtedly, by Germany's heartbreaking food shortage, but in the light of her past achievements in surmounting that form of distress, there seemed no really reasonable hope of bringing her to her knees by food exhaustion alone. A nation of 70,000,000 souls, holding in bondage either as supine "allies," or con-quered peoples, another 75,000,000 or 80,000,000 souls, and dominating territory stretching straight across Central Europe from Antwerp to the Black Sea, could not easily be starved into submission.

The year 1916 opened with Germany's military spirits at the top-note. Serbia had been completely subjugated. Bulgaria had become Germany's ally along with Turkey, and the Entente Powers, after grievous losses, had been compelled to beat an ignominious retreat from the Gallipoli Peninsula. The allied offensive on the western front in the autumn of 1915 had demonstrated that the German line was not impenetrable, nor the vaunted Prussian war-machine invincible, but the **Reason for the** line had not been broken nor the machine **Verdun adventure** even approximately wrecked. The German General Staff knew that the supervening months would be restlessly employed by Britain, France, and Russia to gird themselves for a "big push" on all fronts in 1916. It was therefore decided in Berlin, with fidelity to the Moltke principle that the best defence is offence, to attack the Allies at their supposedly most vulnerable spot many weeks before their "big push" could be put into operation. On February 21st, therefore, the Germans, chiefly under the command of the Crown Prince, launched a prodigious assault on the historic position of Verdun, lying astride the Meuse, and on the whole vast defensive scheme in the north-eastern corner of France. To cut the Verdun-Paris railway and again to menace the capital of the Republic as the Crown Prince and Von Kluck had done in the earliest hours of the war, the German Staff concentrated on Verdun the most terrific attack which artillery and human flesh and bone were capable of delivering. As all the world knows, the onslaught failed. Verdun outranked the Marne as Germany's most colossal military reverse thus far during the war. All through the spring and summer the flower of the Kaiser's infantry was hurled in vain against the fortress on the Meuse. Though the fortunes of France, as advanced positions like Douaumont fell into the enemy's hands, seemed more than once to be crumbling, Verdun held. By the end of 1916, after a struggle which had lasted nearly ten months and for sheer ferocity and bloodshed was without equal in military annals, the French had retaken practically all the ground lost at Verdun. Germany's most

CLOSE QUARTERS IN RUHLEBEN INTERNMENT CAMP.
British civil prisoners in their " horse-box " accommodation at Ruhleben, in which camp—between Berlin and Spandau—about four thousand prisoners were interned. Their quarters mainly consisted of the horse-boxes such as that shown, and the lofts above. The prisoners were very harshly treated, and had largely to depend for food upon parcels from home.

ambitious campaign in the west in 1916 had come to an ignominious end. It had cost the Germans many divisions of men in killed, wounded, and captured. (See Chapters cxiii. and cxxxix.)

While the Germans were battering away vainly at Verdun the combined Franco-British offensive on the western front set in. On July 1st the Allies launched on the Somme and on the Ancre a combined assault against the strongly-fortified German lines in that region. Under its impact, characterised by artillery fire of even deadlier

magnitude than that of the German guns before Verdun, the Teutonic line was dented for miles, and immense booty in prisoners and guns fell into the Allies' hands. Germans admitted in their own Press that never in the history of warfare had armies been subjected to the punishment inflicted on their troops in the trenches and dug-outs on the Somme. They said it was not war, but " murder." In that fighting the début of the immortal British " tank " took place. It played a valiant rôle in demoralising the enemy, as did also the magnificent work of British and French aircraft. To all these things enemy newspapers paid unstinted tribute. The Somme offensive did not achieve the complete strategic result which might have been hoped for. But it demonstrated one fact of indelible and far-reaching importance—-viz., the rise of Britain as a land power and the ability of the British, properly equipped and supported, to beat the finest troops in the vaunted German Army and to wreck the most powerful defensive system which had ever been devised by German military science. The lessons which the German generals and common soldiers learned on the Somme were not such as to fill them with much " battle joy " when next they came in contact with the new British armies. It was freely admitted in Germany that her forces in the west had been out-gunned and outshelled by the Allies, and it was laid down as the supreme necessity of the coming winter that German munition production required to be speeded-up even far beyond its previous enormous dimensions

INDOOR GLIMPSE OF VARIED LIFE AT RUHLEBEN.
Counter of a mixed store in Ruhleben internment camp, at which prisoners were able, apparently, to purchase books as readily as groceries. On the further side of the corridor is to be seen a prisoner engaged in making his toilet. Conditions of life at Ruhleben were terrible during the first year, but later became somewhat ameliorated.

if the Kaiser's armies were to be able to hold their own in forthcoming campaigns on the western front. German military moral was never undermined so unmistakably since Jena as it was shattered before Verdun and on the Somme.

While the Germans were being hammered in the west, their decrepit Austrian vassal was subjected to equally gruelling treatment on the eastern front and at the hands of Italy in the Trentino. In Galicia **Brussi'off's** General Brussiloff, at the head of a vast **victorious advance** new Russian host, well equipped with big guns, delivered tremendous strokes against the Austro-Hungarian forces, his capture of prisoners running into hundreds of thousands. Not until the Germans diverted large forces from the Poland front, and such men as could be spared from the harassed lines in the west, were the Austro-Hungarians able to stem Brussiloff's victorious advance. Meantime, the Italians under General Cadorna stormed Gorizia, at which they had so long and gallantly battered. At the end of the summer of 1916 Austria-Hungary presented a most dishevelled appearance

BRITISH OFFICER PRISONERS OF WAR IN GERMANY.
British officers, placed hors de combat by the fortune of war, who sought to keep themselves fit by active service in the tennis-courts. They were at Crefeld, in Rhenish Prussia, about a dozen miles to the north-west of Düsseldorf, where the Germans established a camp for prisoners of war.

from a military standpoint. From the beginning of the war Germany had allowed her to bear the brunt of the punishment so relentlessly inflicted by Russia. It remained one of the miracles of the campaign that, after what she had been compelled to undergo, Austria-Hungary was still able to keep up the hopeless fight. Her sovereignty had long ago become a mere shadow. German generals were in actual, if not nominal, command of her hammered armies, and whenever the latter found themselves in a tight place, German reinforcements were thrown into the breach to save them from utter disaster. It is the custom for Austrian officers when they greet colleagues to salute and say: "I have the honour" (*Ich habe die Ehre*). It is related that when the Austrian Commander-in-Chief one day presented himself at Hindenburg's headquarters he remarked: "I have the honour." Gruff old Hindenburg is said to have replied: "Yes, you have the honour, but I have the work!"

Almost an exact month before the fighting on the Somme

began, the German Navy essayed its boldest stroke. It emerged into the North Sea on what the Berlin Admiralty subsequently described as an "enterprise" (*Unternehmung*). Whatever the "enterprise" was, it was destined to be as great a failure as the Germans' "enterprise" at Verdun. That the German losses were large may be gathered from the fact that for several days, on the grounds of "military reasons," the Berlin Admiralty deliberately withheld from the German public the circumstance that one of the Kaiser's largest and most powerful battle-cruisers, the Lützow, had been destroyed. The Germans called the engagement the Battle of the Skager Rack in contradistinction to the official title conferred upon it in Great Britain—the Battle of Jutland. The one substantial result gained by the enemy was presented to them gratis by the British Admiralty, which stupidly allowed the Germans to circulate the lying version of their "victory" throughout the world a full twenty-four hours before the British report was issued. The British Fleet suffered heavy losses in officers, men, and vessels, but the price paid was in no respect out of proportion to the result achieved—the staggering evidence furnished to the enemy that British command of the sea was inviolate and inviolable.

The three events just narrated—the failure of the attack on Verdun, the irresistibility of the Franco-British offensive on the western front, the wrecked attempt to smash British sea-power—caused the German Government and its High Commands on land and water to institute a sweeping change of régime. Public opinion in Germany was not a factor which the Kaiser and his fellow War Lords were accustomed to consider or to be swayed by. But German knees were set a-quaking so violently in July and August, 1916, that William II. was impelled to take the most drastic step of the war. He decided to transfer the control of the Empire's fighting forces to the one man in whom the country still had unshaken confidence—Field-Marshal von Hindenburg, who had defeated the Russians so decisively in East Prussia and Poland. Though admittedly not a strategic genius, Germans for two years had deified Hindenburg. They looked upon him as a composite of Napoleon and Moltke. They erected a huge iron image of him in Berlin and drove nails into the pedestal for war-charity purposes in the spirit in which Pagan votaries might worship at some shrine. **Hindenburg in** Whatever failures might be achieved by **supreme control** other generals, Germans were obsessed by the conviction that with "our Hindenburg" there was nothing they could not attain. The Kaiser, conscious that a sop to his sorely-tried people was urgently required if their enthusiasm for the war was not fatally to flag, in August appointed Hindenburg Chief of the Great General Staff, with General Ludendorff, Hindenburg's personal aide-de-camp, as Vice-Chief. To make room for "Hindenburg & Co." William II. unceremoniously deposed General von Falkenhayn from the chiefship of the General Staff. Falkenhayn, who enjoyed the repute of being the one military genius Germany's war had produced, was humbled as punishment for the failure of the Verdun campaign, which was personally mapped out and conducted by him

Hindenburg and Ludendorff were forthwith equipped with autocratic power. Their authority was extended even to the direction of the Fleet. Public confidence was vouchsafed them to an unlimited degree. It was understood that they accepted the dictatorship only on condition that they should be monarchs of all they surveyed. Even the Imperial Chancellor's prerogatives, as the premier Minister of the Crown, were transferred, for all practical purposes, to "Hindenburg & Co."

Hindenburg had not been in charge of Germany's destinies many weeks before he evolved the most comprehensive scheme for mobilising a nation for war of which military annals contain any record. At his instigation the Reichstag enacted a so-called "Patriotic Auxiliary Service Law" (*Patriotisches Hilfsdienst Gesetz*), which called up for national service every male person in the Empire between the ages of seventeen and sixty. Women were not

REPRESENTATIVES OF NEUTRAL JOURNALS AT HEIDELBERG.
Neutral journalists were permitted to interview the British prisoners of war interned at Heidelberg. On this occasion the visitors were representatives of a Swedish (left) and an American (right) newspaper

admitted by the beginning of December, 1916, but a more honest estimate would doubtless have placed the figure at 5,000,000 and over. To fill these incessant gaps it became necessary to "comb out" behind the front on a wholesale scale. From railways, mines, and particularly from munition works of all kinds, men had to be ruthlessly withdrawn for actual fighting work. This necessitated filling their places with men or women who had hitherto been employed in civilian occupations not directly connected with the prosecution of the war. The Patriotic Auxiliary Service Law's effect was to enforce conscription of labour in Germany. Its specific intent, as was publicly admitted by a prominent Statesman, was to double the output of German guns and shells, lest the

WOUNDED AND PRISONER.
Second on the left is Lieut. G. S. M. Insall, V.C., captured in the air fight for which he was later awarded the Victoria Cross.

included in the compulsory provisions of the law, but in practice and administration their services were secured on almost as complete a scale as if their labour had been obligatory. Directresses of National Service (to supervise employment of women) were appointed at each Army headquarters throughout the country.

The chief purpose of the "Mass Levy" of Germany's physical strength was to increase the production of munitions. Losses in the field had long been sapping Germany's resources in fighting men. A total casualty list of over 4,000,000 killed, wounded, and missing was officially

TENNIS-COURTS IN THE OFFICERS' INTERNMENT CAMP AT HEIDELBERG.
A poor substitute for the set their brother soldiers were playing in France to strike the Kaiser's crown into the hazard, but a welcome relief from the monotony of enforced idleness.

PACKING FRUIT STONES FOR TRANSMISSION TO CRUSHING MILLS.
German organisation extended to the practical elimination of all waste. Thus the people were forbidden to destroy fruit stones, and in all towns these were collected periodically and taken to mills to be crushed, the oil so extracted being used for many industrial and military purposes.

disadvantages under which the Army fought on the Somme should be repeated the next time the Germans faced the well-equipped hosts of Britain and France.

Though in the Government-controlled Press a vigorous effort was made to convince both the home and foreign publics that Hindenburgism—*i.e.*, the Mass Levy scheme—was enthusiastically supported by Germans, it was notorious that the semi-serfdom which it imposed on the nation was irksome and unpopular. Men did not welcome having long-established businesses of their own summarily closed down in obedience to Auxiliary Service's decree that all " unnecessary " trades and occupations had to be abolished, and the Empire's whole physical effort concentrated on production of man-killing weapons. For instance, in order to " comb out " a given industry and secure more hands for munitions, the authorities would amalgamate two or three works in a certain line of manufacture, and impress the surplus labour which resulted into munitions. Livelihoods, personal convenience, private predilections—everything was subordinated to the one purpose Hindenburg had set himself. A special new department called the " War Bureau "

Hindenburgism the (*Kriegsamt*) was established to administer
" last phase " national service on the new lines. General Gröner was placed in charge of it. In a speech elucidating the purposes of Auxiliary Service, General Gröner said that it must be " ground into the heads and hearts of all Germans that they had to subordinate their wills unquestioningly to the needs and requirements of the Fatherland." The Hindenburg Mass Levy was described by the " Cologne Gazette " as ushering in " the last phase " of the war. What the well-known semi-official journal meant to say, but dared not, was that Hindenburg's determination ruthlessly to seize and use the last ounce of human strength left in Germany represented the Fatherland's supreme effort to stave off defeat.

Throughout 1916 a battle royal raged within Germany itself on the question of submarine warfare. Realising that the weapon they had forged to overthrow Britain—their fleet of battleships, battle-cruisers, and destroyers—

was incapable of achieving that object, the War Party zealots set up the doctrine that the submarine was the heaven-sent instrument with which the hated British could be brought to their knees. Early in 1916 the German Navy, therefore, under the domination of Von Tirpitz, dedicated itself afresh to the task of " sinking everything at sight." The Germans destroyed allied and neutral shipping alike, in the belief that the starvation of the British Isles would inevitably follow in time. The consequence was the recrudescence of a bitter diplomatic controversy with the United States Government.

Meantime, in Berlin two rival camps were set up. One demanded continuance of submarine warfare with all possible " frightfulness," regardless of the dictates of humanity or the susceptibilities of neutrals. Extremists like Count Reventlow particularly clamoured for " relentless " U boat tactics, even at the expense of war with the United States. The head and front of the " Frightfulness " Party was Admiral von Tirpitz himself. He, who had been chiefly responsible for the creation of the modern German Navy as a weapon with which to overthrow Great Britain, realised that unless he could use submarines to that end, it would sooner or later dawn upon German consciousness that the many millions lavished on their Fleet had been money completely wasted. For weeks the issue in Berlin hung in the balance. Finally it was decided by the Kaiser, in March, 1916, that Tirpitz must be dropped and sacrificed on the altar of continued " friendship " with America. A few weeks later the censor blotted Reventlow out of existence as an editorial writer, and for many months afterwards his fiery contributions **Disappearance of Von Tirpitz** were missing from the " Deutsche Tageszeitung," in whose columns he had for years poured forth his gall and spite against everything non-German. He was later restored to favour, and returned to his old " form."

Admiral von Tirpitz, known in Berlin as " Tirpitz the Eternal," because he ruled the Kaiser's Navy autocratically and uninterruptedly for eighteen years, was superseded by Admiral von Capelle as Secretary of State for the Imperial Navy Office, as Germany's " First Lord " is officially known. Admiral von Capelle had been Tirpitz's right-hand man at the Berlin Admiralty for many years. The " pirate chief " had groomed him to be his successor, but, of course, in different circumstances. The accession of Von Capelle was considered abroad as signalising the abandonment by Germany of submarine frightfulness as a " concession " to the United States ; yet, while the shadow of Tirpitz vanished, the substance of frightfulness remained. It not only remained, but became intensified as the months went by and 1917 approached, into the most wholesale frightfulness the Germans had ever practised during the whole war. There were no more Lusitanias, but there was a Britannic ; and history will probably fail to make a very strong distinction between the torpedoing of a Cunard passenger-liner and the submarining of an even larger White Star liner serving the humanitarian purpose of a hospital ship. While the Germans, in other words, contrived to make neutrals believe that ruthlessness at sea had been abolished by them, they were, as a matter of fact, exercising it on a more diabolical scale than ever before. Merchantman after merchantman was sunk in the autumn and early winter of 1916-17—in December alone the pirates gloated over having sent 415,500 tons of allied and neutral shipping to the bottom. Loss of life was comparatively light, as the pirates adopted the "humane" rule of allowing ships' crews to cast adrift in their own lifeboats and to be at the mercy of the elements for long days and nights on end. The popular heroes in Germany in 1916 were young commanders of submarines who with their one craft had sunk as much as 200,000 or 300,000 tons of enemy shipping. Captain Persius, the well-known naval correspondent of the "Berliner Tageblatt," correctly pointed out that, as far **Maximum activity** as the sea was concerned, Germany's cam-**of submarines** paign was not a war of admirals, but of lieutenants and lieutenant-commanders. Persius was referring, of course, to the astonishing "bags" made by German U boat commanders in different seas.

Following the rejection of Germany's peace proposals, there was renewed outcry in the country for acceleration of the process of "starving out" the British Isles by submarines. But nobody knew better than the German Navy's chieftains that U boat frightfulness was already taking place on the largest scale possible. German U boats were as frightful as they knew how to be. The specious cry that they should be permitted to indulge in unrestricted frightfulness was a sheer "bluff," designed to deceive neutrals and enemies into thinking that the Germans were imposing upon themselves a certain self-restraint in deference to outside wishes.

Equally fictitious was the mock strife between politicians in Germany as to the "advisability" or otherwise of intensified warfare at sea and in the air. People both in Germany and abroad were shrewdly led to believe that because Bethmann-Hollweg, the Imperial Chancellor, was not lending his ear to the "demands" of the Frightfulness Party, U boat depredations were being held in check. It was doubtless decided in Berlin by all concerned that Germany's best interests would be conserved by keeping up the frightfulness "controversy" in Press, Parliament, and public, because it actually did create the impression that there were two parties—a humanitarian group and a frightful faction. As a matter of fact, each was frightful. They differed only in their methods. Meantime, U boats ran amok, sinking practically everything within their reach. The only "check" to German

frightfulness was that imposed by the vigilance and gallantry of the British Navy

During the second year of the war the German Social Democratic Party continued to supply constant and unmistakable evidence that it had degenerated as a political force into an aggregation of invertebrates. Opposition to the supine pro-war sentiments of the executive and majority of the rank and file of the party increased during 1916, and eventually took the form of the secession of a number of influential deputies, headed by the former president of the party, Herr Haase. Supported by another Radical named Ledebour, Haase formed a minority group which was christened the Social Democratic Working Community (*Sozialdemokratische Arbeitsgemeinschaft*). It represented, however, only eighteen or twenty members of the Reichstag group of one hundred and eleven Social Democrats. It justified its revolt on the ground that the party had become the impotent tool of the German Government and War Party. The rebels declared that the continued voting by Socialists of credits in Parliament to prosecute a war which had confessedly become a war of aggression, and of which the German nation as a whole was heartily sick, violated all the tenets and principles of Social Democracy, and they asserted they could and would have no more of it. On periodical occasions in the Reichstag, Haase, Ledebour, and their handful of adherents expressed their views on the lines just indicated, but they were ruthlessly suppressed and condemned to remain as voices crying in the wilderness. Later in the year the rebellious "Working Community" was formally expelled from the Social Democratic Party, so that there were at the end of 1916 two Socialist parties in Germany. They re- **Impotence of** mained, however, utterly powerless as far **Social Democracy** as influencing the course of the war was concerned. Their subjugation to the Government's will became so complete that even their former fighting official newspaper, "Vorwärts," earned the obloquy of being known as an outright Government newspaper, as spoon-fed and "inspired" as the "Lokal-Anzeiger," or semi-official "Kölnische Zeitung" itself. For many years prior to 1914 there were people in and out of Germany who imagined that a great European war would find the Social Democrats in that country wielding a force which would paralyse the Fatherland's ability to make war. Instead of bringing about such a state of affairs, the war during 1916 found the Social Democracy more thoroughly enslaved under the boot-heel and domination of Prussian militarism than ever before.

AUSTRIA'S NEW EMPEROR INSPECTS VETERAN GERMAN TROOPS ON A FORMAL VISIT TO THE KAISER.
Charles I. succeeded his uncle Francis Joseph I. in November, 1916, and lost no time in visiting his nominal equal but virtual overlord the German Emperor, to confer with him on the extremely difficult situation in which destiny had placed him. Naturally the two Emperors forthwith inspected German troops, Kaiser Wilhelm wearing Austrian uniform in compliment to his guest.

Only one German Socialist remained consistently true to his political principles to the extent of trying to fight for them—Dr. Karl Liebknecht, a brilliant young Berlin barrister, who represented the Royal borough of Potsdam in the Imperial Parliament and also had a seat in the Prussian Diet. Liebknecht, a son of one of the founders of the Social Democracy, was for years before the war a thorn in the Government and War Party's side. In 1913 he exposed the notorious Krupp bribery scandals, which showed that the gigantic Essen munition firm had been accustomed to subsidise officials of the Prussian War Office, and also newspapers in Germany and beyond its frontiers, for the purpose of keeping war fever alive at home and abroad. When war broke out Liebknecht continued his crusade, and denounced the war and its German authors on every possible occasion. The Government imagined it could effectually gag him by assigning Liebknecht to military service. It actually stuck him into field-grey and put him to work as an Army Service Corps soldier, but he returned to Berlin periodically to take his place in the Reichstag and the Landtag, and unfailingly raised his voice against the objects and the methods Germany was pursuing. He was invariably howled down, but Liebknecht at least left Germany and Europe in no doubt that there was one man in war-crazed Prussia not afraid to speak out his mind.

Meantime, the Prussian authorities anxiously awaited an opportunity and a pretext for ridding themselves of a person who was rapidly becoming a genuine menace to their schemings and plot to keep the German nation muzzled and deaf. His status as a Member of Parliament gave Liebknecht certain immunities from interference, but on "May Day" (May 1st) the Berlin police arrested him on the charge of inciting to public disturbances —taking him in charge in Potsdamer-Platz, the Piccadilly Circus of the German capital, and afterwards justifying his apprehension on the ground that a regularly enlisted A.S.C. soldier on active service had violated regulations by appearing in public in mufti! There was also some cock-and-bull story about Liebknecht having been " caught in the act " of sowing sedition by distributing handbills. Shortly afterwards, following unsuccessful attempts by the Socialist Party in the Reichstag to have their colleague liberated, Liebknecht was placed on trial and duly convicted of treason. He would undoubtedly have been condemned to be shot except that feeling in the country was running high, and his execution, it was feared, would provoke open outbreak of notoriously deep and widespread popular discontent over the war and the hunger hardships it was imposing. Liebknecht, instead of being turned over to the tender mercies of a firing-party, was sentenced to four and a half years' hard labour.

Suppression of Liebknecht
He was also deprived of civil rights, and in consequence was automatically robbed of his two Parliamentary seats. It was not Liebknecht's first acquaintance with Prussian prison walls. Several years before 1914 he served a period of detention in fortress for courageously opposing militarism, the plain purposes of which he saw with no clearer vision than many other Germans, but whose manifest intentions Liebknecht merely attacked with fearlessness.

With Liebknecht safely under lock and key any opposition to the war worthy of the name ceased to exist

HERR BASSERMANN.
Herr Bassermann, leader of the National Liberals, who declared that the German conduct of the war stood " upon a superior plane of civilisation."

in Germany. Men and women complained of the war, " demonstrated " against it when they stood freezing in queues before the butcher's, baker's, and grocer's shops in vain quest for meat, bread, and butter ; but effective protest became a thing of the past when Karl Liebknecht was sent to penal servitude in the late autumn of 1916.

One of the great surprises of the second year of war was Germany's continued ability to finance herself. Assumptions that she would collapse because of money stress proved as illusory as the belief that food shortage would precipitate her disintegration. People abroad forgot that the British blockade had had the effect from the start of making Germany an economically *self-contained*

Augment'ng the gold reserve

nation. The blockade compelled Germans, with minor exceptions, to spend all their war disbursements at home. Money was sent abroad for the purpose of espionage and propaganda, notably to the U.S.A., and for such food shipments as the Germans were able to slip through the Baltic and across neighbouring land frontiers like Holland and Switzerland ; but the overwhelming bulk of the enemy's vast expenditure for war sinews remained in the country. As long as this state of affairs could be maintained—as long as Germany was not required to make heavy payments abroad—she could afford to view with comparative complacency the fall of the mark to the lowest rate of exchange ever recorded—a drop, at times, of as much as 33⅓ per cent. of its normal value (1s.). The "crash" in German finances, under the system of buying practically everything in Germany and paying for it in German paper money to Germans, was therefore not due until the end of the war, when the Germans would require to resume international financial relations and pay for their necessities in gold.

With this end in view, the Imperial Bank of Berlin throughout the year 1916 promoted the policy of conserving gold resources and augmenting its gold reserve by every possible means. The reserve in August, 1914, was something like £62,500,000. It had reached almost double that amount (£125,000,000) by the end of 1916, according to the Reichsbank's statements. Weird expedients were resorted to for the purpose of bringing gold to the bank. Racecourses offered reduced rates of admission to people who paid gate-money in gold and took paper or silver in change. Patriotic women, imitating the historic example of Queen Louise of Prussia, offered their golden trinkets. "Gold Collection Bureaus" were established by municipalities throughout the country.

Hoarding was alleged to be taking place, and to bring forth the hidden money intimation was given that by a certain date all gold coinage in private ownership would be deprived of its legal-tender value.

Up to the end of 1916 the German Empire had made five separate War Loans, aggregating £2,350,000,000 in subscriptions (according to the official reports). The individual details of these loans were as follows :

Date of Issue.		Rate of Interest. p.c.		Price.		Amt. Subscribed (in Millions Sterling).
Sept. 1914	..	5	..	97½	..	223
March 1915	..	5	..	98½	..	453
Sept. 1915	..	5	..	99	..	605
March 1916	..	{ 4½ / 5 }	..	{ 95 / 98½ }	..	535
Sept. 1916	..	{ 4½ / 5 }	..	{ 95 / 98 }	..	534

A particularly noteworthy feature of the German War Loans, in contradistinction to results of the same kind achieved in Great Britain, was the very heavy number of subscribers for small amounts. To the loan issued in March, 1916, there were over 5,000,000 subscribers for amounts ranging from 1s. to £250. To the September, 1916, loan over 3,500,000 persons subscribed for stock, bonds, or certificates, representing investments of 1s. to £250.

Early in the war the German Finance Minister was accustomed to boast that Germany's vast " war investment " would be reimbursed by the heavy indemnities she would extort from her vanquished foes. In pre-war days Prussian war zealots, in communicative moments, would talk of the £20,000,000,000 which they intended to exact from a conquered British Empire.

The advent of the Hindenburg dictatorship at the end of August, 1916, synchronised almost to a week with a very dramatic turn in the military situation—the intervention of Rumania on the side of the Allies. That

Intervention of Rumania

act, long threatened by the Rumanians and eagerly awaited by the Allies, was greeted with justifiable satisfaction in allied countries ; but it was destined to end disastrously as far as their hopes were concerned. Rumania took the offensive in the earlier hours of September, and successfully invaded Austrian territory adjacent to the Danube and in the Carpathian area. But it was not long before Hindenburg contrived to divert a strong force of Germans to assist the Austro-Hungarians, and even to bring up a formidable array of Bulgar and Turkish troops, the whole being under the command of Field-Marshal von Mackensen. Presently General von Falkenhayn, released a few weeks previously to make way for Hindenburg on the General Staff, took the field against Rumania, his own force advancing from one direction while Mackensen's main armies approached from another quarter. The first sign that Rumania's doom was sealed was the fall of her important Black Sea port, Constantsa. The capital, Bukarest, met with the same fate a few weeks later. Then the grain lands and the oil-fields fell into the invader's hands, along with very consider-

Fall of Bukarest

able bodies of Rumanian troops, though the principal army contrived to effect a retreat to the one section of the little country which it was still holding stubbornly, and apparently invincibly, at the end of 1916. Before retiring, the Rumanians carried out a wholesale and systematic destruction of their grain warehouses and oil-wells, thus cheating the Germans of the booty which was their principal incentive in sacking the country. Russian forces co-operated with the Rumanians at various stages of the latter's hapless campaign, but the help received from their powerful ally was not sufficient or timely enough to stem the tide under which the Rumanians were forced to suffer defeat within, roundly, four months of the date they entered the war.

Though the supposed fleshpots of Rumania entirely failed to supply the conqueror to the anticipated degree, the Germans' signal military successes had the effect of bolstering up afresh their confidence in the " invincibility " of their war-machine. They had quite particularly the effect of strengthening Hindenburg's hold on the popular

EMPEROR AND CHIEFS OF THE GERMAN GREAT GENERAL STAFF.

The Kaiser in conference with Field-Marshal von Hindenburg, who is indicating a point on one of the maps spread out before them, and General von Ludendorff, Chief of the Staff. Though admittedly not a strategic genius, Von Hindenburg was regarded by the German people as a composite of Napoleon and Von Moltke, and by the beginning of 1917 his position had become to all appearance that of a dictator.

YY

imagination and of fortifying the country's belief that in him it possessed a leader capable of leading Germany to certain triumph, no matter how long delayed. The Rumanian campaign was supposed to have been planned entirely by Hindenburg and Ludendorff, and they emerged from it with their personal prestige immeasurably enhanced, although no one knew better than themselves that "victory," in the Berlin sense, was in no respect advanced by the Germans' swift triumph over an under-**Hindenburg's** prepared small nation. The people of the **prestige enhanced** unfortunate country found themselves by the end of the year as thoroughly enslaved as the wretched communities under German domination in Belgium, Poland, Serbia, and Northern France.

Military successes in Rumania were cleverly exploited by the German Government and its controlled Press to divert the country's attention from the incessant defeats with which the Army was meeting on the decisive western front. As General Sir Douglas Haig's celebrated despatch on the Somme operations (December, 1916) set forth, the

referred to that inglorious campaign as "the grave." Germans who lived to tell the terrible tale of what they had been called upon to face on the western front in 1916 declared unanimously—in several cases to the writer personally—that "slaughter" was the only description applicable to the fray into which they had been sent as into a shambles. Every German who came out of the Somme and Verdun fighting alive went home to spread the gospel that Germany at last had met her military match in the new British and French armies fighting shoulder to shoulder in the fields of France and Flanders.

From people to whom German soldiers went with their own tales of suffering and terror at the front they heard equally distressing stories of conditions rife in Germany itself at the beginning of the winter of 1916-17. Food distress has been dealt with previously in this chapter. But suffering prevailed in every direction. Germany was plunged as early as November into the coldest winter experienced for many years, only to find that owing to frozen rivers and canals and curtailed railway transport

PRUSSIAN PATRIOTISM MADE TO PAY: STATUES "NAILED" FOR THE GERMAN RED CROSS.

Emden's allegorical figure, with face of Captain von Müller. The charge for nailing this figure was two marks per nail.

Statue of Charlemagne erected at Itzehoe, Schleswig-Holstein. The charge for driving a nail into this great emperor was one mark.

Statue of Saint Martin of Sabaria in Pannonia. This statue was erected at Mannheim, Baden. The price per nail for this figure was three marks.

flower of the German Army had been battered to an extent unprecedented since Napoleonic days by the combined and ceaseless onslaughts of the allied hosts on the Somme and the Ancre. Yet, with effrontery unparalleled, the German General Staff early in December officially declared that the Battle of the Somme might now be considered at an end, and that it had ended in a complete victory for German arms! In announcing this to his people, the Kaiser omitted to supply any details of the "victory" in the form of the tens of thousands of prisoners and hundreds of field-pieces and machine-guns which remained in the Allies' hands; nor did the supreme War Lord dwell on the enormous toll in killed and wounded which his hammered armies had paid for their pretended success. Officers and men who returned to Germany, wounded or on leave from the Somme, were not so reticent as the General Staff at Berlin. In newspapers and in private conversation frequent admission was made that the Somme had been not war but "hell," while survivors of Verdun

facilities there was not nearly enough coal to supply the insatiable demands of war industry and the regular requirements of the civilian population. Schools, hotels, restaurants, theatres, and other places accustomed to shelter crowds of people, were compelled by degrees to shut down altogether because fuel was no longer obtainable, or obtainable to such a limited extent that it was not feasible to open these establishments at all. Dwellers in private houses and flats in **Coal shortage** towns and cities found themselves unable **in Germany** to warm their premises, and living in one room, usually the kitchen, became the order of the day— and night. The hot-water supply ran short simultaneously, so that before the winter was half over the Germans found themselves not only excessively underfed, but uncomfortably underheated as well. It was truly the winter of their supreme discontent.

The coal shortage not only made ordinary living conditions unbearable to the degree of impossibility in many places in Germany, but it had a particularly serious effect on the supply of gas and electricity. Electric tramway services everywhere were disorganised and in many places even had to be abolished entirely. The gas and electricity famine manifested itself chiefly in radical curtailment of illumination of all kinds. Berlin, the gay city of pre-war days and even until the autumn of 1916, became almost as dark at night as Zeppelin-menaced London itself. The police authorities throughout the Empire ordained rigid regulations for suppressing lighting of all kinds. Theatres and restaurants, which used traditionally to keep open until two, three. or four o'clock in the morning, found themselves compelled to put up the shutters and send people home at the unheard-of hours of ten or eleven p.m. Shops were denied the old-time privilege of making elaborate display of electric light outside their premises or in shop-windows, and in the shops themselves lighting was ordered to be reduced to the absolute minimum of actual necessity. The same restrictions were enforced, of course, in private houses,

could not be broken by the further continuation of the war." What the Germanic allies desired, on the basis of their pretended victory, was set forth in the following paragraph of their Note :

> Their aim is not to crush or destroy their enemies. Supported by the consciousness of their military and economic strength, and ready if necessary to prosecute to the utmost the fight forced upon them, but being at the same time inspired by a desire to prevent further bloodshed and to put an end to the cruelties of war, the four allied Powers (Germany, Austria-Hungary, Turkey, and Bulgaria) have proposed to enter forthwith into peace negotiations.

German profession of innocency

Berlin apparently had little faith that this specious offer of peace, on a basis which assumed the victory of the Germanic Powers, would meet with the desired success, for their Note ended with these words:

> If notwithstanding this offer of peace and conciliation the fight should continue, the four allied Powers are resolved to wage it to a victorious end. They repudiate most solemnly all responsibility for the continuation of the war before mankind and history.

Coincident with the sending of the peace " offer " to the

GERMANY'S POPULAR METHOD OF RAISING FUNDS.

The " Iron Hindenburg " at Angeburg. The large iron nails for this statue cost five marks each—and seem not to have been forthcoming in large numbers.   Saint Johann at Hamburg. Patriotism assessed the value of nails for this particular saint at three marks.   The famous statue of Admiral von Tirpitz erected at Wilhelmshaven, by driving nails into which a very large sum of money was raised.

which thus became, by Christmas time, the abodes of people who were underfed, cold, and now condemned to live in semi-darkness. For many weeks previously, shortage of boots and ordinary wearing apparel had been acute, too. Lack of leather, wool. and cotton compelled the State to put footwear and clothing of all kinds on the ration basis. None could be had without permit cards. " Bargain sales " were forbidden, and the Government **Germany's peace offer** even took over the old-clothes trade. This was the setting amid which the Germanic allies launched their impossible and preposterous " offer " of peace on December 12th, 1916, in the form of a Note addressed to the Allies through the Government of the United States. The Note did not dwell on the terrific economic plight in which the Germanic Powers found themselves. It spoke, on the contrary, of their " unconquerable strength," and of their " mighty successes over an enemy superior in number and war material," and declared that their " power of resistance

enemy Powers, the German Imperial Chancellor delivered a defence of it in the Reichstag, in which he elaborated the specious arguments on which it was based. He ended with the following bombastic peroration :

> If our enemies decline, and wish to take upon themselves the world's heavy burden of all those terrors which thereafter will follow, then, even in the least and smallest homes, every German heart will burn in sacred wrath against our enemies who are unwilling to stop human slaughter in order that their plans of conquest and annihilation may continue. In a fateful hour we took a fateful decision. God will be judge. We can proceed upon our way without fear and unashamed. We are ready for fight and we are ready for peace.

History has to record that it was a bare fortnight before Germany thus confessed to all the world her gnawing desire for and need of peace that Britain girded herself afresh for the war by installing a National Government under the dynamic leadership of Mr. Lloyd George. Several days before the formal German peace offer the enemy Press was busily engaged in attempting to diagnose the meaning of Britain's action in breaking with a " Wait and See " policy

Open-air tailors' shop in the prisoners of war camp at Königsbruck, Saxony. The majority of the men shown in this photograph were Russians, whose lot generally while they were held in captivity was harder than that of their French and British comrades in misfortune.

Post-office at the camp for prisoners of war near Giessen, Hesse. Large numbers of parcels of food for French and British prisoners were received here; but for the regular arrival of these many of the unfortunate captives would have well-nigh starved on the rations allotted by Germany.

PARCELS FROM HOME AND OCCUPATION FOR PRISONERS OF WAR IN GERMANY.

in favour of a "Do It Now' régime. What Germany thought of the disappearance of Mr. Asquith and the arrival of Mr. Lloyd George at No. 10, Downing Street, was well epitomised by the "Berliner Tageblatt" when it remarked that: "To all our desires and wishes to end this sacrificial slaughter, our enemy's answer is, unfortunately, Lloyd George!" A few days later "Lustige Blätter," the leading Berlin comic weekly, summarised the country's state of mind about the British Government upheaval by printing the cartoon of a U boat commander who was made to say: "My dearest wish is that Lloyd George were a submarine commander." No crueller blow was ever dealt to German hopes by Britain than the transfer of State leadership at a psychological moment to the most "strafed" Briton of his era.

With their military and naval hopes irreparably blasted by events of the 1916 campaign on land and sea, Germany ended the year with unmistakable realisation that her peace dreams, too, were destined to fail. The outstanding note of the old year, as it faded away, was an increasingly furious demand from practically all quarters that Germany, now baffled in every direction, must have resort to the submarine as the heaven-sent weapon with which to bring to her knees the nation which Bethmann-Hollweg had

MUSIC FOR THE TRENCHES.
A platform was erected amidst the elaborate earthworks that were constructed at Zehlendorff. There the Austrian military bands were able to indulge the national taste for music.

repeatedly described as "our bitterest, grimmest, and most dangerous foe"—*i.e.*, Great Britain. As has already been pointed out in this review, submarine frightfulness was never really checked by the Germans. The only restraint imposed upon pitiless murder at sea was the restraint which came from the British Navy's defensive and offensive activities in that direction. The torpedoing of the British hospital ship Britannic, toward the end of 1916, provided convincing proof that U boat terrorism had not diminished in intensity or moral depravity. But, in order to make savagery look legal, 1917 was ushered in

Unrestricted submarine warfare in Germany amid ferocious cries for "unrestricted warfare" at sea. The speciousness of this demand was illustrated by statistics published early in January, 1917, showing that in December no less than 415,500 tons of allied and neutral shipping had been sent to the bottom.

During the autumn and early winter of 1916 especially outrageous attacks were made on the shipping of Norway —an illuminating commentary on Prussian knightliness toward a nation which had been blighted with the Kaiser's favour in pre-war days to a greater extent than any other country in the world.

No review of Germany in 1916 would be complete without

a reference to her far-reaching plans perfected in that year for waging the war after the war—the commercial Armageddon which was destined to begin in the markets of the world the moment the guns of the armed conflict ceased to bark. In order to meet the conditions which would then ensue, the Germans in the summer of 1916 established what was practically a separate Government to deal exclusively with the industrial, financial, and commercial future. A so-called "Imperial Board for Transition Economics" was set up and clothed with **Germany's commercial designs** the exclusive duty of transferring Germany as soon as possible from a war to a peace basis. Meantime, industrial shipbuilding, navigation, and other business organisations amalgamated more closely than ever before. The great engineering societies of the Empire perfected a league in order to present a more compact front than ever for the forthcoming trade struggle.

The Krupps bought a large interest in the North German Lloyd, and the great A.E.G. electrical works of Berlin purchased shares in the Hamburg-American Line. Aniline-dye manufacturers formed a huge "trust" on American lines in order the better to meet the competition threatened by the Governmental dye industry established in England and by new private enterprises launched in America and Japan to defeat the monopoly in dye-stuffs which had been so long held by the Germans.

Everywhere and in all directions the Germans made it plain that they intended again to enter the trade field throughout the globe more strongly and efficiently organised than ever, and were grimly resolving that however the war ended they were going to establish anew their trade penetration of the world's markets. They left their trade rivals like Britain in little doubt that the fight against German commerce in the future would be no less intensive than it had been in the past. They made it plain that, unless Britain and her friends girded themselves betimes for the war after the war, it would find them as unprepared and unready for that as the Armageddon of 1914 had found them for taking the field against the carefully elaborated and thoroughly organised military machine of the Central Powers.

TRENCH-BUILDING AT ZEHLENDORFF.
Roofed trenches in course of construction at Zehlendorff, in Lower Austria, in preparation for the possible contingency of invasion, of which the Austrian people throughout the war showed acutely nervous apprehension.

Trying bit of road for an artillery team. The troops on the Balkan front had to operate in country of the most varied character, and the men and horses had to negotiate many difficulties such as the sharp bank up which they were taking this gun, the animals gallantly responding to their riders' urging.

British soldiers crossing a pleasant ford in Thessaly. According to an ancient story, it was the distant sight of natives of Thessaly who were on horseback while their steeds were standing with bent heads drinking at a stream that gave rise to the fable of the centaur.

THROUGH A FORD AND OVER ROUGH GROUND IN THE BALKANS.

CHAPTER CLXV.

THE BALKANS: THE ALLIED OFFENSIVE OF 1916, THE CAPTURE OF MONASTIR, AND THE GREEK IMBROGLIO.

By Robert Machray.

A Troubled Story—Equivocal Attitude of Greece Personified in its King—Royalists versus Venizelists—A Growing and Embittered Struggle—Allied Offensive Begins on the Whole Balkan Front—How the British Raided Across the Struma—Horseshoe Hill Gallantly Captured and then Evacuated—Object Accomplished—Serbians Fighting Magnificently in the Moglena Mountains—Heroic Epic of the Storming of Kaymakchalan—Beginning of the Great Contest for Monastir—Fierce Battles near Lake Ostrovo—Defeat and Retreat of the Bulgarians—Florina Taken—Frontal Attack on Kenali Line Fails—General Milne Assists Sarrail—Heavy British Pressure on the Enemy—Extension of the Line Eastward—Violent Encounters on the West in Cherna Bend—Serbs Regain Ninety Square Miles of their Native Soil—Brilliant Fighting Advance of Marshal Misitch—Serbians Across the Cherna—Valuable Strategic Gains—Further British Co-operation has Good Results—The Battle for Monastir—Serbians Continue their Victorious Progress—The Kenali Line Turned—Tremendous Assault by French, Russian, and Italian Troops—Kenali Line in the Hands of the Allies—Fall of Monastir—Sarrail Thanks the Serbians—Situation in Greece Worse for the Entente—Germany Secures a Greek Army Corps—Indignation of the Venizelists—Growth of the National Movement—Venizelos Leaves Athens—Goes to Crete—Lands at Salonika—Becomes Head of the National Provisional Government—Disorder in Greece—Allied Action—Persecution of the Venizelists—Attitude of King Constantine—Increasing Hostility to the Entente—Allied Troops Landed and Treacherously Attacked—Blockade of Greece—Constantine's Evasive Course Ends in Complete Surrender.

ONFUSED and unsatisfactory as ever, the situation in the Balkans continued to be one of embarrassment and difficulty for the Entente Powers; yet, leaving Rumania out of account, some progress could be chronicled by the end of 1916. In Chapter CXLV., which dealt with the Salonika Expedition, the troubled story of the Balkans during the war was brought down to the beginning of September of that year. It was told how, with Salonika as base, a great army of the Allies, comprising British, French, Russian, Italian, and Serbian forces, had been concentrated in Macedonia on a front nearly two hundred miles long. The narrative also commented on the perfidious action of the so-called Neutralist Government of King Constantine in surrendering the strong places of Eastern Macedonia to the enemy, recorded the emphatic protests of M. Venizelos and other Greek patriots, and described the inception of the National movement at Salonika in opposition to the Greek Government.

LORD GRANVILLE.
Lord Granville, grandson of the first Earl, was in January, 1917, appointed British representative to the Provisional Government of M. Venizelos at Salonika, with the title of Diplomatic Agent. He had formerly been Counsellor of the British Embassy in Paris.

One of the crucial things, if not *the* crucial thing, as many thought was the case, in the Balkans during the dark year 1915 had been the equivocal attitude of Greece, as personified by King Constantine and inspired by the pro-German influences with which he was surrounded. The same had to be said, with increased emphasis if that was possible with respect to 1916, after the surrender of Fort Rupel to the Bulgarians in May. As August closed, with Kavalla in the hands of the enemy, plain signs appeared of the sharp division of Greece into two camps, one of which still styled itself neutral, but was permeated with Germanism and enmity to Venizelos and the Entente, while the other was devoted to the Entente and followed Venizelos, though protesting its loyalty to the sovereign and his dynasty. The separation from each other of the two became, however, more and more distinctly marked with the passage of time, as was inevitable because of the irreconcilable antagonism of their ideals and aims. The end of the year saw the two parties sundered by a wide and widening gulf.

WORKING-PARTY MOVING UP TO THE FIRE-TRENCHES.
Leaving a base camp on the Salonika front for spadework in the fire-trenches. Constant labour was necessary in maintaining these trenches, and the rifle had at times to be laid aside in favour of pick and shovel.

[*British official photograph.*
BRITISH FIRING-LINE ON THE SALONIKA FRONT.
Corner of a fire-trench that commanded a roadway. The officers were engaged in "spotting" for the men, whose rifles were ready to utter their stern " No thoroughfare ! " to any enemy that ventured to approach.

At the head of the " Neutralists " stood King Constantine, who, in defiance of the Constitution under which he reigned, and apart from which he had legal authority in no respect whatsoever, had made himself dictator, after the manner of his brother-in-law the German Kaiser. He was able to do this owing to his popularity with the mass of the Greek Army, which still looked on him as the national heroic figure of the First and Second Balkan Wars, and also owing to the debauching of many of his subjects by German money, backed by a powerful and unscrupulous propaganda against Venizelos and the Allies. The Government of Greece was nothing but his creature, submissively registering his decrees and carrying out his orders, the whole tendency of which, when not manifestly hostile, was more or less inimical to the Entente. The journals of Berlin and Vienna did not hesitate to claim him as pro-German, exultingly declaring that by the course he was pursuing he was playing for time—and getting it.

M. Venizelos, who from the very beginning of the war had never concealed his profound sympathy with the Allies, was the natural leader of the Greek Ententists. Previous chapters have described what this splendid statesman, the greatest Greek of his time, did on behalf of the common cause, and how his efforts were rendered nugatory by the opposition of the King. It was well known that Constantine was jealous of him, though it was equally well known that it was he who not only had saved Greece from ruin, but had kept the dynasty on the throne. Yet, taking advantage of the feeling of the King, constant endeavours on the part of the German element in Greece were directed to represent Venizelos to him as an enemy of the dynasty, and were not without effect.

Constantine's jealousy of Venizelos

This was clearly seen when the " Neutralists," formerly termed Skouloudists or Gounarists, as in Chapter CXLV., took to themselves the appellation of Royalists, after the Salonika Provisional Government had been joined by Venizelos, though he expressly maintained its loyalty and that of himself to the Sovereign. The Royalists denounced the Venizelists as traitors, and subsequent events in Athens showed what was the mind of King Constantine towards both them and the Entente.

As regards the Allies, the point had always to be remembered that they had sent their troops to Greece on the invitation of the Greek Government of the day, of which Venizelos was Prime Minister with complete Parliamentary sanction behind him. Though that Government fell, through the unconstitutional intervention of the Greek King, the consequences of its invitation remained in the presence at Salonika of the army of the Entente. From the outset the Greek Government which succeeded that of Venizelos, while professing benevolent neutrality, had done its best to impede, delay, and thwart the plans of General Sarrail, who commanded that army. Other Greek Governments followed under pressure by the Allies, but there was no real change in the position, for there was no real change in King Constantine. During the latter half of 1916 the Greek Government—in other words, the King—showed hostility still more unmistakably, until, in fact, it was plain to everyone

Kaiser congratulates who had eyes to see that the
King Constantine situation was rapidly assuming a dangerous aspect for the Allies, carrying with it a formidable menace to the success of their offensive against the enemy in Macedonia, which had been proceeding since September, and to the security of their forces generally.

From the start Entente action, whether diplomatic or military, in exerting pressure on the various Greek Governments which had held office by the King's pleasure after the fall of Venizelos, had been on the whole halting, inadequate, and apparently easily contented with promises or unsatisfactory concessions. Promises were not kept, or fulfilled only partially. Concessions were made of as little value as possible by underhand tactics, or withdrawn and ignored as soon as it was

thought safe to do so. Evasion, deceit, and treachery marked almost every step of the way of these Greek Governments in their dealings with the Allies. And, after all, these Governments were but the mouthpieces of King Constantine, yet towards him the Entente Powers continued to exhibit a strange and inexplicable tenderness. It was no wonder that Germany, laughing in her sleeve at the Entente, congratulated him on the cleverness with which he contrived to manipulate affairs. Perhaps he was emboldened to throw off the mask by the failure of the Allies in Rumania, but in the beginning of December he went too far, and the long patience of the Entente was exhausted. The close of the year beheld the whole of Greece that was not Venizelist lying under a

[*British official photographs.*]

GETTING BRITISH GUNS INTO POSITION FOR DRIVING BACK THE BULGARIANS.
Mountain battery being placed in position on the British part of the Salonika front. The attitudes of the half-dozen men give some idea of the weight of one of these pieces. Above: Finding the way the wind was blowing in Macedonia. The two non-commissioned officers of the Royal Engineers having filled their small balloon with gas were tying it up before releasing it to ascertain the force and direction of the wind.

rigorous blockade which had been in force for several weeks, and of which there was to be no relaxation till all the demands of the Allies had been satisfied. But meanwhile valuable time had been lost and the allied offensive in the Balkans hindered and checked.

This offensive, of which a beginning had been made in August, and which was designed to support the Rumanians, developed in force on the whole front in the second week of September, 1916. At that time the line **Opening of the allied offensive** held by the Entente forces in Macedonia stretched from the Gulf of Rendena (or Orfano) on the east to Lake Ostrovo on the west. From Chai Aghizi, on the west side of the Struma, where that river enters the Gulf of Rendena, the British stood on the line northward along the right bank of the Struma, of its expansion Lake Tahinos, and of the Struma again, up to Lake Butkova and the Butkova River, whence they occupied the front westward, south of Lake Doiran, to the Vardar, a little north of the village of Smol. From the other bank of the Vardar the line was held by French, Serbian, and Russian troops as far as Lake Ostrovo. A few weeks before the allied front westward had extended to Lake Prespa, but it had been shortened by the Bulgarian offensive under Bojadieff, who had occupied Florina and compelled the Serbians to retire in the middle of August to Ostrovo, where, however, they put up a great fight, and by the end of that month had the situation well in hand in this sector, the enemy being held and then repulsed, while farther north ground was gained in the region of the Moglena—otherwise the Karadjova—Mountains.

No official information respecting the strength of the Allies in Macedonia was forthcoming, but it was popularly stated to amount to something like half a million of men, a figure which probably was a little too high, and an insalubrious climate told heavily on it. The whole army, which the French termed the "Army of the Orient," was under General Sarrail, the French forces on the left and left centre having at their head General Cordonnier, while the British on the right centre and the right were under the leadership of General Milne. On December 6th, 1916, the War Office published a lengthy despatch, dated October 8th, from the last-named general, giving an account of the work done by the British Salonika Army—as the British forces in Macedonia were called—from May 9th, when he assumed command.

After narrating how the British, in co-operation with the French, had gradually extended their front from the Struma to the Vardar by successful fighting, which included the storming of Horseshoe Hill by the Oxford and Bucks Light Infantry at the point of the bayonet on the night of August 17th, General Milne went on to speak of the Bulgarian forces lying over against him on the east side of the Struma—the forces that had occupied Eastern

[British official photograph.
SERBIANS LOOKING TOWARDS THEIR GOAL.
At an observation-station on the Serbian front, when the re-established and re-equipped Army of the heroic, martyred country was beginning that move which resulted in the capture of Monastir.

Macedonia with hardly an effort, owing to the collusion of the Greek Government with Germany. Having alluded to the operations undertaken by British and French troops in the region east of the Struma, with the intention of observing and delaying the enemy's forward movement, General Milne stated :

The Bulgarians continued their advance (in the fourth week of August) into Eastern Macedonia, unopposed by the Greek garrison, and it was estimated that by the end of August the enemy's forces, extending from **Dispositions of the Bulgarians** Demirhissar southwards in the Seres sector of the Struma front, comprised the complete 7th Bulgarian Division, with two or three regiments of the 11th Macedonian Division, which had moved eastwards from their positions on the Beles Mountain to act as a reserve to the 7th Division, and at the same time to occupy the defences from Vetrina-Puljovo northwards. Opposite the Lower Struma was a brigade of the 2nd Division, with a brigade of the 10th Division, in occupation of the coast and the zone of country between Orfano and the Drama-Kavalla road. This brigade of the 10th Division was supported by another brigade in the Drama-Kavalla area. As a result of this advance and of a similar move in the west, General Sarrail decided to entrust to the British Army the task of maintaining the greater portion of the right and centre of the allied line. On the Doiran-River Vardar front there remained, as before, the whole of the Bulgarian 9th Division, less one regiment, a brigade of the 2nd Division, and at least two-thirds of the German 101st Division.

Taking into account the unusual size—upwards of 25,000 men—of a Bulgarian division, the forces opposed to General Milne amounted to at least 120,000 men, the vast majority of whom were combatants and of high military quality. King Ferdinand of Rumania, when speaking of Bulgaria, referred to her "unquestionably courageous Army," and this description was justified. On his side General Milne had the advantage of the active support of a British fleet that shelled the Bulgarians at Kavalla, Neohori, and other points on the coast of Eastern Macedonia, the whole of which, up to the allied line as well as the contiguous Bulgarian coast, was besides kept under a strict blockade.

As September opened, there was almost a lull on the whole of the Macedonian front. On the Struma the Bulgarians were bombarding the bridges at Fitoki and Komarian, south-west of Seres, and British aeroplanes dropped bombs on Angista Station, south-west of Drama, on the railway running from Salonika through Demirhissar and Seres to Dedeagach and Constantinople. On the Doiran-Vardar sectors there was an intermittent cannonade, in the course of which French artillery set fire to the railway-station of Pardovitsa, north of Gevgeli. In the mountains west of the Vardar Bulgarian attacks were repulsed at Vetrenik and near Zborsko, north-east of Kukuruz. In the Lake Ostrovo region the heavy enemy assaults had completely died down. For the moment there was little or nothing of real importance to report. In their tremendous efforts against the Serbians, both on the Ostrovo front and in the Moglena Mountains, the Bulgarians had suffered immense losses, one estimate placing them at 15,000 out of 60,000 men in the Ostrovo fighting. Thus mauled they perforce awaited reinforcements, which, however, were long in coming, because their other troops were required for the invasion of the Dobruja, where Mackensen had planned a great offensive against the Rumanians on the south. The lull, hardly broken by small patrol encounters and exchanges of artillery fire, continued for more than a week. But it was the lull before the storm. It was evidently the turn, the opportunity, of the Allies in Macedonia, and Sarrail began a general offensive on September 10th.

On that date the British, with whom was a French detachment, made raids across the Struma. The British and the French initiated on the east side of the Vardar a systematic bombardment of the enemy's trenches north of Machukovo, south of Gevgeli; and south-west of the latter place delivered a vigorous thrust in the region north of Mayadag, on the west side of the Vardar, which yielded excellent results, all the Bulgarian trenches being carried on a front of 3,000 yards and **Whole Macedonian** a depth of about 800 yards, with the **front engaged** capture of a number of prisoners. On the left of Lake Ostrovo the Serbians displayed great activity with their guns in the neighbourhood of Banitsa, while south-west of the lake they succeeded, after bitter fighting, in capturing some of the enemy's positions, and in the mountain sector more than held their own. Battle was joined on practically the whole Macedonian front in the second week of September, 1916, and continued, with short intervals, well into the following December, when the Greek menace and German

reinforcements for the Bulgarians, combined with incessant bad weather, called a halt.

British operations started with the crossing of the Struma north of Lake Tahinos at five points between Bajraktar Mah and Dragos, while a sixth crossing of the river was effected at Neohori, close to the sea. The country through which the Struma flows is flat and marshy, affording little cover, but on the east side, which the enemy occupied, the Bulgarians had turned into fortified blockhouses the villages that lined the **Initial British** bank. At four o'clock in the after- **operations** noon of Sunday, September 10th, the attacking columns set out, and after encountering fierce resistance, took by storm the villages of Oraoman and Gudeli. The Northumberland Fusiliers gallantly captured Nevolyen, taking thirty prisoners, and driving the enemy out of the place. A battalion took two heights on the east of the Struma at Neohori near the sea. These blockhouse-villages had each been garrisoned by two hundred Bulgarians, who fought desperately. The British were counter-attacked with resolution by the Bulgarian supports, but they easily repulsed the onslaught, inflicting considerable loss on their assailants. According to programme, these villages were evacuated at midnight, there having then been no intention to hold them permanently, the whole undertaking being of the nature of a raiding reconnaissance. When the desired object was satisfactorily accomplished the British retired to the west bank of the river.

Similar operations were carried out by the British five days later. Six small columns crossed the Struma between Lake Tahinos and the bridge at Orliak, and took the

MACHINE-GUNS BEING CARRIED BY MULE TRANSPORT IN THE REGION OF MONASTIR.
Taking machine-guns forward to recaptured Monastir. Mule transport was essential in many parts of the mountainous Balkan front. The French and Serbian forces that reached Monastir had to fight over difficult country before getting to the region in which that town is situated and that comparatively easy stretch through which this well-laden column of men and mules was winding its way in re-occupied Serbian territory.

[French official photograph.

PATHWAY BLOWN THROUGH SOLID ROCK.
Communication-trench made by the Allies through the solid rock of a
hillside in Macedonia. By means of explosives deep ways of safety were
excavated through the seemingly impassable obstructions that were
encountered in the geological formation of parts of this front.

villages of Gudeli, Jami Mah, Ago Mah, and Komarian, which they burned. Some thirty prisoners were
captured. The Bulgarians made several counter-attacks,
which completely broke down under the accurate fire
of the British guns from the west bank of the stream.
Having again made good their prearranged plan, the
British withdrew to their side of the Struma. On
September 23rd a like scheme was somewhat interfered
with by a sudden rise of the river which made bridging
difficult, but in spite of this the enemy's trenches at Yeni
Mah were taken by assault, and three other villages were
raided. In these various expeditions the British received
considerable assistance from the French

Battle of Machine detachment which was commanded by
Gun Hill Colonel Bescoins. Besides harassing the
enemy on this front, these raids yielded
much information which subsequently proved of value.

General Milne's aim to aid the general offensive led to a
battle on the Doiran-Vardar front which reflected the
greatest credit on the British soldier. North of Machukovo,
a little east of the Vardar, the Bulgarians, with whom
were many Germans, held a strongly fortified salient,
like an arrowhead in shape, the tip of which was an eminence
called by the British Machine Gun Hill, and known to the
French as Piton des Mitrailleuses. The position was
not in itself specially remarkable by nature ; it was a
plain grassy ridge, covered with brown lines, but these
lines denoted entrenchments of the most scientific character, with deep dug-outs and communication-trenches,
the whole being protected by rows of formidable wire
entanglements. It might indeed have been a bit cut out

of the German front on the Somme and transferred to the
Balkans. It was attacked in exactly the same way, the
artillery preparation for the assault lasting three days.
From September 11th to 13th the field-guns and mortars
of the British poured thousands of shells upon it, while
their long-range guns played on the enemy artillery behind
the hill and kept it under. High above the field British
aeroplanes circled, directing the fire and noting results.

The attack was ordered for the night of September 13th,
and when scouting-parties had reported that enough of
the wire entanglements had been destroyed, the British
advanced to the assault a little after one o'clock in the
morning of the 14th. In less than an hour and a half
the whole of the trenches that had formed the objective—
all Machine Gun Hill—had been reft from the hands of
the enemy. Of this battle General
Milne, in the despatch alluded to, said　**British purpose**
that the position was occupied after　**achieved**
a skilfully-planned and gallant assault,
in which the King's Liverpool Regiment and Lancashire
Fusiliers specially distinguished themselves. He also
mentioned that more than two hundred Germans were
killed in the work, chiefly by bombing, and seventy-one
prisoners brought in.

At once the British started to consolidate themselves
in the trenches they had won, but the rocky nature of the
ground made rapid organisation extremely difficult.
During the 14th the enemy concentrated a very heavy fire
on Machine Gun Hill from three directions, the bombardment being particularly intense from three o'clock to six
in the afternoon. In the course of a long day of strenuous
fighting the British repulsed several fierce counter-attacks,
but the Germano-Bulgarians succeeded in forcing an
entrance into the work, and all the while they were receiving
strong reinforcements. As it was found impossible in
the circumstances to retain the position, the British were
withdrawn in the evening to their original line, "the
object of the attack," as General Milne stated, "having
been accomplished." Thanks to the effective fire of their
artillery, the British troops suffered very slight loss in
their retirement, and comparatively little in the struggle
itself, while the enemy's losses were very considerable.

On the same front, about a week later, a strong British
detachment, after bombarding the enemy's positions on
the Crête des Tentes, raided and bombed the hostile trenches
and dug-outs, and then withdrew quickly with very few
casualties. North-east of Doljeli a similar raid met with
equal success. As September drew to its end General
Milne issued instructions for operations on a more extensive
scale. He did this " in order further to assist," he said,
"the progress of the Allies towards Monastir" by maintaining such a continuous offensive as would ensure no
transference of Bulgarian troops from the Struma front
to the west (or Ostrovo) front." These words signalised
the great change which had been brought about on the
allied left wing by the victorious advance of the troops
of the Entente, particularly of the brave and intrepid
Army of Serbia, the tale of which was one of the finest
and most stirring in all the fine and stirring tales of the war,
finding a glorious climax in the capture, before the tale
was finished, of Monastir.

On the front immediately west of the Vardar—the left
centre of the Allies—the French contented themselves
with maintaining a heavy bombardment in the region of
Mayadag, which pinned the enemy to his positions in that
sector. It was still farther to the west that the weight
of Sarrail's main offensive was felt, from the Moglena
(Karadjova) Mountains on the north to Lake Ostrovo
on the south, the line then forming the left wing of the
forces of the Entente. At the outset the bulk of the
fighting, which was of the most desperate kind, particularly
on the north, was in the hands of the heroic Serbians on
the whole of this front, but these splendid warriors soon
were supported on the south by large bodies of French

Lieut.-General George Francis Milne, C.B., D.S.O., commanding the British Salonika Army.

Where German intrigue was rampant: General view of Athens as seen from the Acropolis

Allied Fleet anchored off Salamis in September, 1916, to enforce the Allies' demands.

British officers bringing Rumanian gipsies in Macedonia tidings of Rumania's intervention in the war

Ammunition dump of the Serbians fighting in the Allied Army under General Sarrail on the Salonika front.

M. Eleutherios Venizelos, head of the Greek Provisional Government established in 1916.

and Russian troops, who, advancing below Ostrovo, speedily began a great turning movement in the direction of Florina that had a decisive influence on this phase of the campaign and made it memorable.

Upon the rocky slopes and among the high barren peaks of the Moglena range—Kovil, Vetrenik, and Kukuruz—the struggle, which all along had been most **Serbian triumph** bitter and sanguinary since the appear- **at Kaymakchalan** ance of the Serbians on the scene, assumed a greater intensity. French Headquarters at Salonika announced on September 13th that the offensive operations of the Serbian Army actively continued, in spite of the enemy's lively resistance. Northwest of Kovil the Serbians occupied an important position, after an action which cost the Bulgarians heavy losses, and, a little later, carried by charges with the bayonet several lines of entrenchments between Kovil and Vetrenik. They went on gaining, but the difficult nature of the country could not but make their progress slow. Here they were about thirty miles north of Ostrovo. South-west of this region stood the mass of mountains, at the southern end of the Moglena range, of which the highest peak was Kaymakchalan, 8,284 feet above the sea, and a few miles north of Ostrovo. The Bulgarians held Kaymakchalan, and its capture by the Serbians must ever be one of the greatest triumphs of their race.

On September 12th Serbian advanced detachments were fighting hard, and, notwithstanding stubborn opposition, were making some advance towards Kaymakchalan, the position which was essential for the defence of Monastir. It had been strongly fortified, and instructions had been issued by the Bulgarian Command that it was to be held at all costs. The Bulgarians had named it "Mount Boris," as a compliment to their Crown Prince. After a series of fiercely contested actions the Serbs of the Drina Division forced a way to the immediate border of the mountain three days later, but it was not till the 18th that, as a result of several desperate attacks during the preceding night, they occupied the loftiest summit of the mass. The peak had been entrenched and parapeted with stone, and was well provided with guns which had been brought up by a good road from the Bulgarian side, whereas the Serbians had to face enormous transport difficulties, dragging their light guns up the steep, rugged hillsides, and all the while living on as little food as perhaps was possible only to themselves. But they overcame the difficulties and prospered.

When the crisis came, the contest for hours was between man and man, hand to hand, with bayonets and bombs —the latter small weapons of British manufacture and greatly prized by the Serbian soldiers, who handled them in expert fashion. Never was there more deadly, determined fighting, but the Serbians emerged from it triumphantly More than that, on Kaymakchalan they were once more on the sacred soil of Serbia, and here was an earnest of the future. The Bulgarians still clung on to a shoulder of the mass, and they made many great efforts to recapture the lost peak, the greatest of all taking place on the night of September 26th-27th, when, having received large reinforcements, they made a formidable thrust, four times

repeated, at the Serbian trenches, and a fight of the most ferocious nature resulted. How close and bitter was the struggle was shown by the fact that many wounded were taken to hospital with tips of broken-off bayonets still sticking in the flesh, so savagely (said a correspondent) did Bulgar and Serb stab and hack at each other in the darkness of those rocky slopes.

In this attempt to regain the height the Bulgarians began with some success, carrying the Serbian first line, but in the end they were beaten back, their effort failed, and the Serbians kept the mountain. Other attacks were made with almost as much persistence and determination to recapture the position, which Sarrail's growing menace to Monastir had made still more valuable to the enemy, and on September 28th-29th the Bulgarians made a last effort, but it was met with the same valour and success as before, and it ended in a failure so complete that after a Serbian assault they retreated finally from Kaymakchalan. At the beginning of October a Bulgarian communiqué stated that " owing to heavy artillery firing upon the peak

MAP OF THE DOIRAN-VARDAR FRONT, IN MACEDONIA.
On September 10th, 1916, General Sarrail began his general offensive on the Doiran-Vardar front, designing to assist the advance on Monastir by preventing the transference of Bulgarian troops to the Ostrovo front farther west. Machukovo, Mayadag, and Machine-Gun Hill, the last of which was brilliantly carried by the British, were the scene of intense fighting, which served the designed purpose.

and Hill 2,368 " the Bulgarians received orders to withdraw to their main position " in order to avoid unnecessary losses." On October 1st Berlin growled out the reluctant admission that " a strong attack brought the summit of the Kaymakchalan into the hands of the enemy." The Serbian losses in all this fighting were heavy, but those of the Bulgarians were enormous, as was proved by documents found on dead and captured Bulgarian officers, which told of regiments reduced to companies.

While these victorious combats were taking place in the mountains the Serbians, in the region of Ostrovo, had pressed on with their offensive, which made distinct and marked progress from the first. **Clearing the Malka** After adequate artillery preparation they **Nidje range** assailed the Bulgarians west and north-west of the lake, and by violent fighting expelled them from their advanced positions. On the south-west they captured Sorovichevo on September 13th, and next day, at the point of the bayonet, carried Gornichevo, a village midway between the northern end of Ostrovo and the railway to Florina. At the same time they drove the

[*British official photograph.*

ALLIED GENERALS AT SALONIKA. Generals Sarrail and Mahon, the two centre figures, inspecting a gun. General Mahon proceeded to another appointment, and was succeeded by General Milne in May, 1916.

region, gained access to the broad valley in which stood Florina, and, higher up, Monastir. Presently they were before red-roofed Florina itself. Athens, with its usual inaccuracy, announced that General Cordonnier and his Staff entered the town on the evening of the 16th, but the place did not fall to the Allies quite so quickly. French Headquarters at Salonika, on the 18th, told the true story. Not till after a considerable battle was Florina taken.

Determined to make a stand, Bojadieff had rallied his men for the defence of Florina, and held a line which stretched west from Rosna across the railway. The Franco-Russian forces attacked him early on the 17th, and a most bitter struggle ensued that lasted the whole day. The Bulgarians resisted stubbornly, delivering repeated counter-attacks and making several cavalry charges, but without success. Still, they

enemy from the major part of the Malka Nidje range, which extended north and south of Gornichevo. Nor was this all. Serbian cavalry hotly pursued the routed Bulgarians, and seized the village of Ekshisu, having compelled the enemy to retreat precipitately for a distance of more than ten miles. On the 15th the German official telegram had to acknowledge the further success of the Serbians by stating that after fierce fighting the whole of the Malka Nidje ridge had been lost. In the meantime, Franco-Russian forces sweeping south-westward of Ostrovo had completely cleared the region south of the lake, for a distance of upwards of thirty miles, of the hosts of Bulgarian irregulars and Comitadjis who had been infesting the country. Sarrail was in course of executing his turning movement towards the west, the first

Allies capture Florina

objective of which was Florina, and the second, and the more important of the two, Monastir.

Having taken thirty-six guns and much other valuable spoil from the Bulgarians, who continued to fall back in disorder in all directions, the Serbians drove forward on the right flank and the centre, and on September 15th, a few miles west by south of Kaymakchalan, were crossing the Brod, a tributary of the Cherna rising in the Cheganska Planina, and flowing westward above the village of the same name.

On the left the Franco-Russian forces, on the 16th, marched across the passes of the Malareka range, lying north-west of Ekshisu and some ten miles from Florina, and, advancing rapidly, in spite of the natural impediments of the

[*French official photograph.*

A GENERAL WHO LIKED TO SEE THINGS FOR HIMSELF. General Sarrail taking his seat in an aeroplane. The French Commander-in-Chief of the Salonika Army made personal inspection by aeroplane flights both of the Allies' and the enemy's positions on the Bulgarian frontier. These aerial reconnaissances were carried out with great thoroughness.

would not accept defeat, and the battle raged through the following night, and it was not till ten o'clock in the morning of the 18th that the Entente troops could claim that their triumph was complete. But it was a brilliant victory for the Allies, who had conquered only after a desperate conflict. The main body of the enemy retreated in confusion towards Monastir, fifteen miles away to the north. Bulgarian stragglers left behind in the town kept up a savage but vain fight in a few of the houses in Florina for some time, but such as were left alive were finally rounded up and made prisoners. As a result of his defeat Bojadieff was cashiered, and his command was handed over to a German soldier, General von Winckler, who forthwith strengthened the already strong defensive line through Kenali across the valley to the north, which Mackensen himself had selected during the preceding winter for the protection of Monastir against an attack from the south. Florina had been in the occupation of the enemy for exactly a month.

Consequent on the capture of Florina rumour asserted that the Bulgarians were on the point of evacuating Monastir, but this was far from being correct. Strong fortified positions gave them a breathing space and time to concentrate fresh troops. On the side of the Allies it has to be remembered that in their retreat the enemy had destroyed the bridges on the railway, and that other transport facilities were lacking. Further movement in force needed time, but meanwhile Sarrail was extending his left towards Lake Prespa, on the other side of which, in Albania, the Italians were making progress, and coming in his direction from the Adriatic. The advance of the Allies from Florina was not an easy matter unless very strongly supported. Both sides of the valley were walled in by hills from which the Bulgarians swept it with their fire. Yet Sarrail pressed forward, meeting with considerable resistance on the heights north of Pisoderi, midway between Florina and Lake Prespa, and in

Sarrail's slow fighting advance the direction of the Monastery of San Marco, north of the town. East of Florina, in the River Brod district, a Bulgarian counter-attack, in which cavalry took part, was dispersed towards Boreshnitsa by French "75's" before reaching the Serbian lines. But next day, September 20th, the enemy renewing his attempts in this sector, succeeded, after several fruitless assaults, in setting foot in the village, and was then driven out of the place by Serbian bayonets. On the same date the allied troops, in spite of an intense fcg, advanced as far as Hill 1,550, about 5,000 yards north-west of Pisoderi, and took many prisoners. On the 22nd the French announced that the Serbs had reached the outskirts of Vrbeni, north-east of Florina, that, north of Florina, an enemy attack was broken by infantry fire, that all the ground north-west of Armensko, west of Florina, had been cleared, and that, after hard fighting, progress had been made on the heights dominating the

MULE-BORNE STRETCHERS FOR HILLY COUNTRY.
How the Serbians brought their wounded down from the mountains.

[*British official photographs.*

CIVILISED WARFARE WAGED IN THE BALKANS BY THE ALLIES.
German prisoners of war in a Salonika compound filing up for rations. In circle: Serbians bringing wounded Bulgars in on saddle-chairs carried by mules. The Allies' treatment of all wounded, whether friend or foe, and of their prisoners was most humane.

road from Florina to Popli, on Lake Prespa. Bad weather interfered with the operations, but, as reported two days later, they resulted in the repulse of violent assaults near Hill 1,550, with heavy loss to the enemy, and a slight advance north-west of Florina.

At noon on September 24th Sarrail launched a general assault of Serbians, French, and Russians against the Bulgarian positions north of Florina

Northward from Florina The battlefield was a flattish grass plain, bounded on the west by black mountains, and on the east by grassy heights, with Krushograd set in the midst of them. For the most part it was a frontal attack. In the advance the Serbians reached the frontier crest north of Krushograd; French infantry, north-east of Florina, carried the first houses of the village of Petorak after a brisk fight, and on the west the Russians stormed Hill 916, which had been strongly organised by the enemy. In the last-named region a Bulgarian counter-attack was beaten back by French bayonets. South-west of Florina a French observation detachment had lively

"PASS, FRIEND!" BRITISH MARINES CARRYING EQUIPMENT PAST GREEK SENTRIES.
While for reasons which were intelligible, if not convincing, the King of the Hellenes and his Government hesitated to enter definitely into the Great Alliance, the people of Greece were in the majority pro-Ally in their sympathies, and usually her soldiers were on the friendliest terms with ours.

encounters with Bulgarians coming from Biklishta, south of Lake Prespa. On the 26th the French communiqué stated: "East of Florina the French troops, who were violently counter-attacked by considerable Bulgarian forces beyond Armenohor, offered a magnificent resistance to all the enemy's assaults. Mown down by our artillery and infantry fire, the attackers suffered many losses and retired in disorder. West of Florina the Russians, in conjunction with our troops, were engaged in sharp fighting north of Armensko, in the course of which they took fifty prisoners and four machine-guns." Sofia, on the other hand, claimed to have repulsed the Allies, with heavy losses to them. Bulgarians were attacking east and west of Florina on the 27th and 28th of the month. Then for a time the struggle died down to trench warfare and artillery duels. Sarrail was not yet in a position to advance on Monastir. A great deal of work had first to be done.

It was now that the British under General Milne began those more important operations, previously referred to, on

the Struma-Doiran fronts, with a view to giving increased aid to Sarrail's offensive. These were conducted by Lieut.-General C. J. Briggs, C.B., and he began by seizing and holding some villages on the left bank of the Struma, for the purpose of enlarging the bridge-head at Orliak, from which he would be able to threaten a further movement on Seres or Demirhissar. The attacking infantry, on the night of September 29th, crossed below the Orliak bridge and formed up on the left bank of the river. At dawn next morning the Gloucesters and the Cameron Highlanders, under cover of artillery fire, advanced and took the village of Karadjakeui Bala at eight a.m. Almost immediately the Bulgarians opened a heavy and accurate fire on the British, but the remaining two battalions of the brigade—the Royal Scots and the Argyll and Sutherland Highlanders—pushed on against the village of Karadjakeui Zir, though their ranks came under an enfilade. The Bulgarians put up a stubborn resistance, but the place was taken by half-past five in the afternoon. Attempts to bring up enemy reinforcements during the day were frustrated by the British artillery, but during the night the Bulgarians made several strong counter-attacks, all of which failed with heavy losses. Next night they again delivered repeated assaults, but with no better success. The British held their ground firmly, and by the evening of October 2nd the position was solidly organised. General Briggs then turned his attention to the capture of Yenikeui, an important place on the main road to Seres, and one of the Bulgarian centres.

Its assault entrusted to an infantry brigade composed of the Royal Munster and the Royal Dublin Fusiliers, Yenikeui was taken in fine style on the morning of October 3rd. The way had been thoroughly prepared for them by the artillery, which had got the range on the previous day; there was a pause in the firing, the infantry advanced, and, armoured cars co-operating, Yenikeui was occupied, with few casualties to the British, by seven o'clock. It was after that that the heavy fighting began. In the course of the day the Bulgarians launched three heavy counter-attacks. The first came across the plain from Papalova, and at least 3,000 men took part in it, but it withered under the accurate shooting of the British guns, and the Bulgarians retreated without ever reaching the British line. The second also failed under a punishing fire. The third, which took place in the afternoon, was the most serious. Of it, General Milne in his despatch of October 8th said: "At four p.m. the village, the ground in the rear, and the bridges, were subjected to an unexpectedly heavy bombardment from several heavy batteries which had hitherto not disclosed their positions. **Capture of Yenikeui** Following on the bombardment was the heaviest attack of the day, six or seven battalions advancing from the direction of Homondos, Kalendra, and Papalova with a view to enveloping our positions. This attack was carried forward with great determination, and some detachments succeeded in entering the northern portion of Yenikeui, where hard fighting continued all night until fresh reinforcements succeeded in clearing out such enemy as survived." A

TIGHTENING THE HOLD ON GROUND REWON IN THE MONASTIR REGION.

French soldiers digging trenches on Serbian territory from which the invading Germano-Bulgarian forces had been driven. During the steady advance of the Allies over the new ground towards Monastir the troops had frequently to dig themselves in, and were fortunate when they were able to do so in such terrain as that shown, where the sloping ground and scattered shrubs afforded helpful cover during the operation.

correspondent wrote that the whole plain round the two Karadjakeuis and Yenikeui was littered with Bulgarian dead, and added that the losses of the enemy at the former alone were put as high as 3,000 men. Under cover of their artillery the British consolidated their new line, which now formed a satisfactory bridge-head, on the 4th. Next day Nevolyen was shelled, but the Bulgarians evacuated it as soon as the British infantry advanced to the attack—whereupon it was occupied. Pushing on, the British further extended their front, and by the evening of the following day it reached from Komarian on the south, through Yenikeui and Nevolyen, to Elishan on the north.

Though the Bulgarians, stout fighters as they were, had been disheartened by the severe experiences they had undergone, they attempted on the night of September 5th a counter-attack against **Steady British progress** Nevolyen, but the spirit had gone out of them, and it was easily repulsed. Next day a string of five villages fell into the hands of the British—Ago Mah, Komarian, Kristian Kamila (Homondos), Kukuluk, and Elishan, all lying north of Lake Tahinos to a point within three miles of Prosenik, a station on the railway between Demirhissar and Seres. On the 7th a strong cavalry reconnaissance located the enemy on this railway, with his advanced posts on the little River Belitsa, and a considerable force at Barakli Juma, south-west of Demirhissar. Meeting with little opposition, the British continued to advance, and on October 8th they stood on the front Ago Mah-Homondos-Elishan-Ormanli, with mounted troops at Kalendra, near the railway, about six miles due west of Seres.

On the left wing of the Allies—on the west, with Florina as centre—September had closed with long-contested

side of the Cherna from Floka to Petalino. In the course of the afternoon the Serbians to the south-west crossed the River Sakuleva, and came within five hundred yards of Kenali. A French telegram of the 4th stated that the allied forces on the previous night reached the line Petalino, the bend of the Cherna, Kenali, and Negochani, with their left at Pisoderi, at the foot of Mount Chechevo. Berlin confessed that between Lake Prespa and the Nidje Planina the Bulgarians had withdrawn to new positions "in accordance with orders from the Command," but added that on the Nidje fighting was still going on. Sovich, the first of the Serbian villages to be rescued from the foe, was occupied by troops of the Danube Division on October 3rd. Two days later it was calculated that ninety square

SLEIGHS INSTEAD OF CARTS FOR SLOUGHS IN MACEDONIA.

An immense amount of soldier labour went to making the hard roads necessary for transport of guns and munitions in Macedonia. By-roads, however, remained very bad in some parts, and, as shown in these two photographs, the troops sometimes resorted to the use of sleighs instead of carts for light transport, the runners being less liable than wheels to sink into the mud.

miles of Serbian territory had been recovered. On the same date Berlin admitted that the Nidje Planina was in the hands of the Entente troops.

Among the most interesting features of the war, the return to their native land of the Serbians, who had lost and endured so much for the cause, was naturally a subject of cordial congratulation among themselves and the Allies. The reconstitution of the Serbian Army had been more than justified. Nor did it cease to be justified. Now began the crossing of the bend of the Cherna, with all the severe fighting which it entailed, and that figured so frequently in the communiqués for some time. A few miles east of Kenali the Cherna, which comes down through the Monastir plain in a southerly direction, turns

Kaymakchalan in the possession of the Serbians, who, as October opened, advanced a mile and a quarter north of the peak. The conquest of the mountain had immediate important results. Before dawn on October 3rd the Bulgarians evacuated Starkov Grob, a mile west of the mountain, and Floka, three miles north-east. On the same day they abandoned their whole line from the Nidje Planina on the east to Krushograd on the west, and continuing their retirement yielded the region on the east

to the east, makes a wide loop, and then flows on almost due north until eventually it falls into the Vardar above Krivolak. About October 4th the Serbians began to cross the bend in the vicinity of Dobroveni and Brod. Higher up on the east side of the river they advanced to the outskirts of Budimirtsa and Grunishte, north-west of the Nidje Planina. On the 8th they captured Skochivir in the Cherna bend, after rushing two lines of Bulgarian trenches and taking several hundred prisoners with eight machine-guns. More than once the enemy counter-attacked with great violence, but was repulsed on each occasion, and eventually forced back for over half a mile to his third line of entrenchments, which the Serbians began assaulting next day, gaining the position at Slivitsa. A Sofia despatch admitted **Serbians cross the** that the Cherna had been crossed, but **Cherna** said not a word about the defeat of the Bulgarians. Berlin pretended that the Serbians had achieved only small results. On the 10th the Serbians got a footing in the village of Brod, and for many days an intense struggle proceeded, with varying fortunes, between that place and Skochivir. Farther east other Serbian forces—the Second Army, the First and Third Armies being engaged on the Cherna-Kenali front—took by assault on October 6th the height behind Pojar in the Moglena, and on the 7th carried the Dobropolye summit, and from it commanded with their guns the solitary road by which the Bulgarians obtained their supplies in the range.

While all this incessant fighting was being maintained on the right of the Allies' left wing by the Serbians, who were supported by French guns and armed with British hand-grenades, the Entente troops progressed, west of Kenali, on both slopes of the Baba Mountains, and reached Buf and Popli. Kenali Station was in the occupation of the Allies and on both sides of the railway they were assaulting the powerful defensive organisation north across the plain, which had been brought into existence by Mackensen. On October 5th and 6th lively actions were reported along the whole front, and on the 10th the French announced that the offensive continued with

success. But the Kenali line was very strong, and heavy guns were brought to bear upon it in an attempt to batter it down. Besides, the Bulgarians had been reinforced, and fought with the utmost tenacity, trying by all means to keep the Allies out of Monastir. After artillery preparation Sarrail made a general assault, in which French, Serbian, and Russian troops participated, on this main enemy position in the afternoon of October 14th; but the guns had not done enough, or were not sufficiently numerous, to ensure success for the infantry attacks, and the effort, though made with determination and pressed for hours, failed to make an impression. As was to be expected, Sofia exulted in this reverse for the Entente. But the next few days showed how little reason she had for jubilation. Too strong to be taken by frontal assault, the Kenali line was capable of being turned, and turned it was.

Day after day as fierce a struggle as any in the war had been going on in the bend of the Cherna. What the enemy had to say about it was disclosed by the Bulgarian communiqué of October 17th, which read: " In the course of October 14th and 15th the Serbians made unprecedented attempts to break **Bulgarian version** through our front on the Cherna, between **of events** Brod and Skochivir, but all were in vain. On the night of the 15th the Serbians undertook eight successive and very violent attacks in the same sector, but were repulsed with great losses. Our infantry allowed them to approach as far as the wire entanglements in front of our trenches, when they completely repulsed all the eight attacks. We then made a counter-attack, driving the Serbians back

AN ANXIOUS MOMENT FOR THE ARMY SERVICE CORPS. *[British official photograph.*
Fire broke out in a British camp on the Salonika front, and large stocks of supplies of all kinds were threatened. Trains were hurried up as rapidly as possible along the light railway and hastily loaded with stores stacked in the next dump before the latter had time to become involved.

into their original positions." This account, though somewhat confused, at any rate bore witness to the resolution with which the Serbians conducted themselves in the terrible Cherna fighting. At their head was the veteran Marshal Misitch, who had led them to victory against the Austrians in the latter's second invasion of their country, and

New glory for Marshal Misitch

he was convinced that by way of the Cherna would the desired result be obtained. On the 17th he made a sharp thrust forward, and drove the Bulgarians out of the villages of Gardilovo and Velyeselo and took Brod, on the outskirts of which his troops had been for several days. Two cavalry regiments crossed the river, pressed on through Brod, and turned the defeat of the enemy into a headlong rout. All the Serbian forces in this sector got across the river and pushed on. It was another great day for Serbia. Serbian Headquarters announced the capture of seven guns, fifteen machine-guns, and several hundred prisoners, and stated that the strategic importance of the advance which had been made was very great, as facilitating the operations of the Allies farther west. The

[*British official photograph.*]
FIRING A SHOT FOR THE FREEING OF THEIR LAND FROM THE HUN.
Howitzer about to be fired on the Serbian front. Wonderful bravery was shown by the reorganised Serbian Army which took an important part in the forward move through Macedonia and, by way of the heights of Kaymakchalan, reoccupied part of their own country and the town of Monastir.

Serbians had, in fact, outflanked the Kenali line from the east. German reinforcements now arrived for the Bulgarians in this sector, but Misitch went on with his advance, and on the 19th defeated a Bulgaro-German force in the neighbourhood of the village of Baldentsi, some four miles north-west of Brod. Then the weather broke, and to a large extent interrupted the fighting.

The struggle was resumed on October 22nd. The German contingents which had been sent to help the Bulgarians in the defence of Monastir attacked the Serbians, and attempted to regain the positions which had been lost on the 18th and 19th. Some Germans who had been captured in a slight engagement two days before stated that they had come from Koslin, in East Prussia, having been twelve days on the journey; they had previously been on the Galician front. Other Germans captured had been in the Balkans for a year. The Bulgaro-Germans attacking on the 22nd were heavily defeated by the Serbians, who thereupon advanced and carried several of the enemy's trenches to a depth of eight hundred yards, and inflicted heavy losses. During the operations in the bend of the Cherna the Serbians had taken many hundreds

of Bulgarian prisoners. Remembering the cruel manner in which they had treated Serbian prisoners, the Bulgarians were afraid to surrender to the Serbians, thinking they would be tortured and killed. According to a correspondent the Serbians reassured their old foes by having photographs taken of long files of Bulgarian prisoners drawing rations, with loaves of bread under their arms and bowls for soup in their hands. Two thousand copies were printed, and the Bulgarians who had surrendered were invited to write messages on them to their comrades, saying how they had been received. The two thousand picture postcards were then dropped by aeroplanes into the Bulgarian lines. "Since then," the correspondent said, "surrenders have been much more frequent, and prisoners always try to bring with them a copy of the photograph, which they regard as a sort of safe conduct. One man stated that he had paid fifteen francs for his, and carried it always with him in case he should be captured."

In the Serbian communiqué of October 25th, which announced that the Danube and Drina Divisions had taken several heights on the left bank of the Cherna, facing the mouth of the Stroshnitsa torrent, it was stated that four hundred and eighty prisoners and deserters had been taken. The mention of deserters was significant of the new belief of the Bulgarians in the magnanimity of the Serbians. During the closing days of the month there was constant fighting in the Cherna bend, the whole seriously interfered with by bad weather, but generally turning to the further advantage of the heroic Serbians, who proved themselves more than a match for the Germans in this district. As October came to an end the position on the left of the Allies was that a good deal of ground, strategically valuable, had been gained on the Cherna and on the north-east, that the line in front of Kenali on both sides of the railway was stationary, and that progress had been made westward in the mountains looking down on Monastir, and, farther west still, there had been an advance on the shores of Lake Prespa. On October 24th connection had been established between the French and the Italians at Korcha (Koritsa), west of Biklishta and south-west of Prespa, their cavalry detachments having come into touch.

On the right of the Allies the success of General Milne's offensive during the first eight days of October, and of various actions during the rest of the month, of no great individual importance in themselves but cumulatively significant, resulted in the gradual withdrawal of the bulk of the Bulgarians from the valley of the Struma to the mountainous region beyond Demir-hissar and Seres, the enemy retaining only some villages near his old front as advanced outposts. Reconnaissances confirmed that he held Seres in some strength, and his works there were repeatedly shelled by the British guns. West of the place Papalova and Prosenik were occupied, and on October 12th a force of hostile cavalry was driven back two miles south of it. Constant patrol actions took place during the third week of the month, and Barakli Juma, where the Bulgarians were strongly entrenched, was vigorously bombarded. From the sea the fleet co-operated by shelling enemy positions near Neohori and along the coast

Gradual Bulgarian withdrawal

Men of a French machine-gun section returning from their outposts on the Balkan front. Small machine-guns—weapons which the men could conveniently carry for themselves as these men are doing—came to occupy an important prominence among the weapons of the war.

Battery of guns on the French line near the summit of one of the hills in "rolling" country on the Macedonian front. These French guns, sunk in pits and masked by breastworks to lessen the chance of discovery by the enemy, proved of great service in the retaking of Monastir.

FRENCH GUNS, MASSIVE AND MOBILE, ON THE BALKAN FRONT.

to the Meshtian ; on this part of the front Turkish troops had now come up to reinforce the Bulgarians. During the fourth week heavy storms of rain, which caused the Struma to rise several feet, and soaked the terrain, impeded operations. About the 27th-28th Bulgarian attacks in some force on Ormanli and Kalendra were repulsed and broken, with considerable losses to the assailants. On the 31st the British took by storm Barakli Juma, a biggish village, and strategically valuable as it stood in front of the Rupel Pass, one of the chief roads into Bulgaria.

Before October 31st Barakli Juma had been shelled more than once, but early in the morning of that day a bombardment of increased intensity was opened on the Bulgarian defences—it was so fierce that only half an hour afterwards it was discontinued to allow the infantry to advance to the assault, preparation for which had been very thorough, a new bridge having been built over the Struma and advantageous positions secured beforehand. The British pressed on, and as they approached the village the Bulgarians ran out of their trenches and fled back to the shelter of the houses, out of which they were driven with a loss in prisoners of over three hundred men. The Bulgarian resistance was comparatively feeble, and the British had few casualties. The power of the British artillery appeared to have instilled a wholesome fear into the enemy, who attempted no counter-attack for the recovery of the lost ground, and thus permitted easy consolidation of the captured place. On the same day the British moved from Prosenik to Kumli, another village in the same district. On the Doiran front, where Italian contingents were fighting near Lake Butkova, the Allies undertook no operations of importance during October beyond subjecting the enemy's entrenchments to constant artillery fire. A strong Bulgarian assault near Doiran in the middle of the month was repulsed. The Allies made some raids which were successful, but the respective lines remained practically the same as in September.

Effectiveness of British artillery

THE MENACE OF THE FLEET: ALLIED SHIPS OFF SALAMIS.
The Allies treated equivocal Greece with long forbearance, but a composite Fleet under Admiral du Fournet lay off Salamis, west of Piræus, prepared to act forcibly if imperative need arose. That the menace was not by any means an idle one was proved by the establishment of a strict blockade in December, 1916.

Nor was there much change in November on the Struma-Doiran lines, but, continuing to aid the offensive of Sarrail against Monastir, General Milne maintained his pressure on the enemy on both fronts. Having carried by storm the village of Ali Pasha, south-west of Demirhissar, the British ambushed Bulgarian patrols near Salmah, south of Seres, and made repeated raids elsewhere, keeping the enemy occupied and anxious. On November 14th a Bulgarian concentration at Krastali, on the Doiran front, was shelled and dispersed, and about the same date Kakaraska, a village south of Seres on the eastern shore of Lake Tahinos, was carried after a brilliant action. Two or three days later the British captured Barakli, south-west of Demirhissar, and again drove the Bulgarians from Prosenik and Kumli, which had been temporarily evacuated. By this time there had been great developments on the left of the Allies, and the menace to Monastir had become both close and strong.

Bad weather marked the opening of November in the bend of the Cherna and on the Kenali front, artillery duels and slight infantry encounters only taking place. On November 4th the Bulgaro-Germans attempted three separate assaults on the Serbian positions south of

ALLIED TROOPS MARCHING TO THEIR POSITION IN THE FRONT LINE.
In September, 1916, the line held by the Allies, under the supreme command of General Sarrail, stretched from the Gulf of Rendena (or Orfano), on the east to Lake Ostrovo in the west. The French troops under General Cordonnier, with the Serbian Army and a Russian contingent, were on the left, whence the brilliant recapture of Monastir was effected ; the British under General Milne on the right.

WHERE THE ALLIED FLEETS KEPT WATCH ON GREECE.
On board a French warship off Salamis. In 1916 allied warships anchored off Piræus ready to enforce the demands made necessary for safeguarding the Salonika front from threatened Greek treachery.

Next morning the Bulgarians thrice fiercely counter-attacked, but were driven back in disorder, with substantial losses. North of Velyeselo the Serbs also progressed, capturing trenches and prisoners.

The battle in the Cherna bend continued all next day. Sofia reported on November 12th that there had been a lively artillery duel west of the railway, but that east of it all the Allies' attacks were broken, though it went on to state that "the enemy succeeded in holding the heights, making a s lient before our positions north-east of the village of Polog." A French communiqué of the 13th said that the great battle was developing into a brilliant success for the Entente. Supported by the intense fire of the French artillery the Serbians gained a fresh victory in the loop over the Germano-Bulgarian forces, who, after a sanguinary struggle, were compelled to abandon Iyen, fifteen miles east of Monastir, and to fall back for nearly two miles to the north. Five counter-attacks did the enemy deliver with marked ferocity, but not one of them checked the advance of the Serbians, who made free play with their bayonets. Nearer Monastir in the bend Serbo-French troops accentuated their progress north of Velyeselo. The despatch concluded by noting that a thousand prisoners and sixteen more guns had been counted, and that since September 12th, the date on which the general offensive began, the enemy had left in the hands of the Allies 6,000 prisoners, seventy-two guns, and fifty machine-guns.

Budimirtsa and Polog in the Cherna loop, but each of them was easily repulsed. On the 7th the French guns with the Serbians began a tremendous bombardment of the enemy positions in the bend, and three days later the battle for Monastir was commenced by a heavy shelling of the whole hostile front from the mountains on the east, on and across the plain, to the mountains on the west. Perhaps this led the enemy to expect a general attack, but an assault on that day was made alone by the Serbians on the right, the object of which was to oust the Bulgarians from their formidable positions on the heights of Chuke, in the Cherna bend north of Skochivir. After the allied batteries in the early morning had concentrated on the Chuke heights, the Serbians made a converging attack, advancing on a two-mile front from the south and a two-mile front from the west. The Bulgarians held on tenaciously, and even repelled the first waves of the assault, but by two o'clock in the afternoon their outlying trenches were taken by storm, and before the evening closed they had lost one height after another until all were gone. The struggle had been one of the usual desperate hand-to-hand description—a most sanguinary affair. The victorious Serbians pushed on in pursuit and reached Polog, having taken nearly six hundred prisoners, eight guns, nine machine-guns, and much ammunition and equipment.

Fighting in the Cherna bend

Great pressure was brought to bear on the enemy's whole western line on November 14th. On that day the Serbians, continuing their irresistible flanking movement in the Cherna bend on the east, definitely occupied, after violent fighting, all the Germano-Bulgarian positions south of Tepavtsi, among the spoils being over five hundred German prisoners, and then took Tepavtsi and the neighbouring hamlet of Gules, whence they progressed in the direction of Yarashok. That night the enemy, who had brought up fresh troops, made the most resolute efforts to retrieve his fortunes on the Iyen-Yarashok line.

SUPPLIES FOR THE FIRST LINES CROSSING LOW-LYING COUNTRY ON THE SALONIKA FRONT.
Horse convoy of supplies on the way to the Macedonian front. Wonderful organisation was shown in maintaining the allied forces in the diversified country occupied by their armies, varied means of transport being employed, according to the nature of the ground, for good roads were the exception.

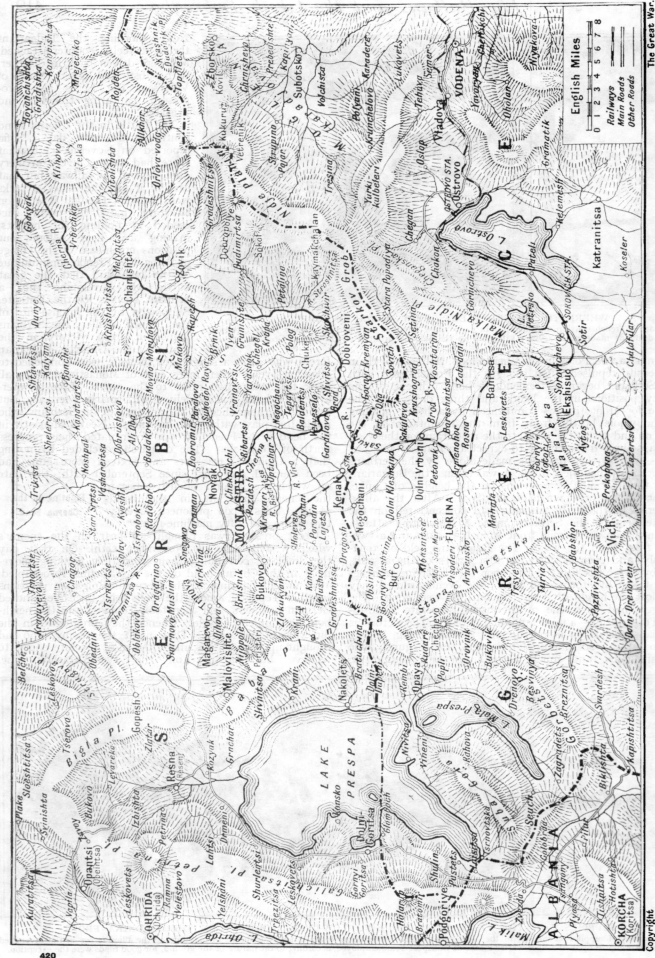

The Great War.

AREA OF THE ALLIED ARMIES' OPERATIONS AGAINST MONASTIR: ACROSS THE BABA RIDGE, CHERNA BEND, AND MOGLENA MOUNTAINS.

ON VIGIL IN THE MACEDONIAN HILLS.
Typical scenery on the Monastir front. The rugged, roadless hill country characteristic of Macedonia was most unfavourable to the movement of modern large armies hampered by much artillery and heavy supply trains.

[French official photograph.

FRENCH OBSERVERS RECORDING ENEMY POSITIONS.
Artillery observation was brought to such perfection during the Great War that gunners firing by the map were enabled to hit the desired object, although it was invisible to themselves, with a single shot.

This line the enemy had fortified long before, but on the 15th the Serbians were able to pierce it at several points and drive him out of Chegel, Negochani, and the Monastery of Yarashok. Meanwhile, during the afternoon of the 14th, Sarrail's French, Russian, and Italian troops, operating west of the Cherna, attacked frontally the strong Kenali line, and despite the most strenuous opposition the French captured the whole system of defence of which that town was the centre, as well as Kenali itself. The official French despatch mentioned that the fighting was desperate at some places, "the men being up to their necks in water and mud." Snow and rain had fallen, and a great part of the fighting occurred during a heavy storm of rain which flooded everything. The Bulgarians, with their German friends, had not yet had enough, and in the night they made strong counter-attacks, recovering part of their trenches, but in the early hours of the 15th, having heard, no doubt, of the triumph of the Serbians on the flank, they abandoned under cover of a fog the whole front line and retired on the River Bistritsa, where they had organised a second line of defence in front of Monastir. The retirement was discovered at dawn, when the Russian troops advanced to assault the village of Lajets, where on the previous day the enemy had made a stubborn stand. The Bulgarians retreated for about five miles to the north, Monastir being four miles farther on. At last, after two months of hard work, the Kenali line was in the hands of Sarrail.

Victory was now in the air, yet there seemed a good deal to be done before it could be realised. The Bulgarian line on the Bistritsa had been prepared for over a month, was well entrenched, and protected by formidable wire entanglements. The weather continued unfavourable, with heavy snow and rain. On the left the Italians fought in the snow, trying to turn the position, while on their right the French at Kanina were held up by machine-guns on a narrow, wretched road by which alone attack there could proceed. The Russians, farther

Sarrail carries the Kenali line

east, forded the Viro River breast-high, but were vigorously opposed, and the French, who came next on the front, were held in check by strong German and Bulgarian forces. It was the action of the Serbians, heroic as ever, in the now famous bend of the Cherna, that finally decided the fate of Monastir. Fierce fighting had been going on daily for possession of the dominating heights north-east of Chegel. On the 15th, Hill 1,212, the central point of the enemy's defence on the Iyen-Chegel-Yarashok front, was captured after prodigious efforts by the Serbians, but was lost again to the Germans. Of this Berlin said that General Otto von Bülow, who was in the middle of the fighting, recaptured the position at the head of the German rifles which stormed it, and that the Kaiser, in recognition of the services of this officer and the men under his command, had promoted him. But on the 17th there was a very different story, for on that day the Serbians once more took the height, and the Germans fled precipitately, abandoning everything. "A large number of machine-guns, very many rifles, an enormous quantity of munitions, and in one spot alone fifty cases of hand-grenades" fell into the hands of the Serbs, according to their official telegram of the 18th. On that day they carried Grunishte, Brnik, and Yarashok, helped at the last-named village by French contingents. They completed their triumph in the Cherna bend by taking by assault all the fortified positions on Hill 1,378, which lay above Hill 1,212, and by driving the enemy out of Makovo as the 19th dawned. The same day several lines of Bulgarian trenches in the direction of Dobromir, north-east of Monastir, were captured by the Serbian troops. Monastir was now completely outflanked, as the

they might fly the French flag, but were told to hoist that of Serbia.

And so Monastir, after being in the possession of the enemy for about a year, became Serbian again; the "Queen City of Macedonia" had been redeemed. It was the first notable success of the Entente Powers in the Balkans. Naturally the Germans did their best to minimise it, but the recapture of Monastir was a heavy blow to them and more especially to the Bulgarians, to whom the permanent occupation of the place was one of their most cherished ambitions. Unfortunately for the Allies the gain of Monastir was more than offset, as events demonstrated, by what was occurring at the same time in Rumania, where the Germans, after defeating the Rumanians in the second **Serbian Army's** Battle of Targu Jiu, had forced their way **achievement** into the Wallachian Plain from the mountains of Transylvania and seized the Craiova-Orsova Railway (Chapter CLIX.). It had been hoped that Sarrail's offensive, with its increasing pressure on the enemy's southernmost line, would have brought effective assistance to Rumania, and with the fall of Monastir this hope gained in strength, but unhappily it proved to be fallacious. Within a month the Germans held Bukarest and practically all Wallachia, the largest and richest part of Rumania.

At the moment the Allies congratulated themselves on possessing Monastir, the taking of which had involved so

EASTERN FRONT OF THE BRITISH SALONIKA ARMY.
In September, 1916, the British eastern line stretched from Chai Aghizi northward along Lake Tahinos and the right bank of the Struma to the Butkova River; thence their Doiran-Vardar front extended westwards.

Serbians commanded the Prilep road behind Monastir, and threatened to cut the enemy line of retreat northward.

Early in the morning of November 19th, under this compulsion, the Bulgarians and Germans evacuated Monastir. No other course was open to them if they were to avoid attack and destruction from the rear. The French communiqué of next day handsomely acknowledged that it was the bold forward movement of the Serbian Army that had brought about this splendid result, and the Berlin despatch of the same date admitted this also when it said that "after the enemy had succeeded in making progress at Hill 1,212, north-east of Chegel, **Recapture of** German and Bulgarian troops occupied a **Monastir** position north of Monastir, and Monastir was evacuated." French troops, hard on the heels of the retreating enemy, entered Monastir at eight o'clock in the morning of November 19th, the anniversary, singularly enough, of the taking of that town by the Serbians from the Turks in 1912. With the French were Serbian cavalry and a Russian infantry regiment, and as they marched along the streets the inhabitants of the town, after hesitating reconnaissances from their barred windows, ventured out and offered them garlands of flowers. Later the citizens sent a deputation to Headquarters asking if

sustained and heavy an effort. The Serbians greatly rejoiced, as they had every right to do. Afterwards General Sarrail, in an Order of the Day in which he addressed each nationality of his soldiers in turn, gave the Serbians the place of honour, saying to them: "You were the first to open the road. You first saw our enemy finally in retreat, and your continued attacks have brought about the fall of Monastir." Telegrams of the heartiest congratulation were sent to the Crown Prince of Serbia, who had taken an active part in the campaign at the head of his Army, and who now took up his residence in the town. It was noticed as a fortunate omen that a perfect rainbow hung over the Serb lines and Monastir on the morning of its capture, and it needed little imagination on the part of those who had undergone such sufferings in the past to see in it a glorious triumphal arch "not made with hands." But though the enemy had lost Monastir he was far from being beaten. Large German reinforcements had been hurried down to this front, probably with the intention of arriving in time to relieve Monastir, but if that was the plan they came too late, and these immediately got into position, offering a most stubborn resistance to the farther advance of the troops of the Entente towards Prilep, some twenty-five miles to the north-east, and their next objective.

Having handed over the administration of Monastir to the Serbians, Sarrail pushed on immediately north of the town and took several villages. On the right the Serbians also captured several villages among the hills, including Novak and Suhodol-Raya, on November 19th, and next day defeated German forces north of Suhodol, north-east of Monastir, and occupied Rapesh, north of Brnik and Iyen. On the left the Italians repulsed violent counter-attacks from the mountainous region of Muza, about six miles south-west of Monastir. The weather again interfered with operations, and the enemy was able to strengthen a line of heights which extended from Snegovo, about two and a half miles from Monastir, to Hill 1,050, south-west of Makovo, some ten or eleven miles east-north-east of that town, and there he made ready to offer an energetic resistance. On the 21st the Allies occupied the villages of Paralovo and Dobromir, and a day or two later the Serbians carried Budimirtsa and held it, notwithstanding mighty attempts of the reinforced Germans to retake it. Bad weather again intervened, and for a while artillery fire alone took up the tale, except on the west, where the Italians made farther progress, pressing their advance in the vicinity of Mount Peristeri and moving on in the direction of Trnova, captured the heights south-west of Nijopole. On the 27th the Serbians, assisted by French Zouaves, gained a valuable strategic position by their capture, after a series of fierce assaults, of Hill 1,050, on which they were opposed by the élite of the German troops, the Chasseurs of the Guard, who had been ordered to hold the hill to the last man. At the same time Sarrail attacked along the rest of this front, but was held up. As

[British official photograph.

M. VENIZELOS AT SALONIKA.

On October 10th, 1916, M. Venizelos landed from the Hesperis at Salonika and definitely joined the Provisional Government that had been established.

[French official photograph.

PATRIOTS WHO WOULD NOT SELL THEIR COUNTRY.
General Zimbrabakis (left) and Colonel Christodoulos, who forcibly resisted the Bulgarian occupation of Seres in September, 1916. The general accepted the position of Minister of War in the Greek National Provisional Government.

the month closed the Germano-Bulgarians were trying in the region north-west of Grunishte to recover the positions which the Serbians had conquered, but met with little success. Then bad weather once more prevailed and hampered the combatants for some days.

Meanwhile the situation in Greece had taken a distinctly unfavourable turn for the Entente Powers, and sinister events which took place on December 1st and 2nd at Athens made matters much worse by suggesting belligerent action against the Allies on the part of King Constantine and his Army, and consequently imperilling Sarrail and his forces in the Balkans, as well as the Provisional Government at Salonika. The story of the shifts and equivocations of King Constantine and his Governments was narrated in Chapter CXLV. as far as the resignation by M. Zaimis of the Premiership, which occurred in the middle of September and was significant of the condition of the country. In the first week of that month, under the pressure of the fleet of the Allies, the Greek Government had agreed that Germans and other foreigners who were **Disturbances in Athens** unfriendly to the Entente should be deported, and the notorious arch-plotter and intriguer, Baron Schenck, with seventy Austrians and Germans, was conveyed by sea to Kavalla from Athens. On the 9th the French Legation was attacked by Greek Reservists, and French bluejackets were landed for its defence. At this juncture there was much disorder in the Greek capital, which was caused by these reservists who, under Gounarist influences,

SCENE OF A GREAT SERBIAN TRIUMPH: KAYMAKCHALAN AFTER ITS CAPTURE FROM THE BULGARIANS, SEPTEMBER 28TH-29TH. 1916.

Kaymakchalan is the highest peak at the southern end of the Moglena range, and is essential for the defence of Monastir. It had been strongly fortified by the Bulgarians, who had orders to hold it at all costs. On September 12th the Serbs began an advance towards it, and after fierce fighting carried the highest peak on the 18th. The Bulgarians clung to a shoulder of the mountain mass and made many determined attempts to recover the lost summit, but finally, on September 28th-29th, they were routed and compelled to abandon the vital position. The Serbian losses in the fighting were heavy, but those of the Bulgarians were enormous.

had formed themselves into leagues or societies in opposition to the Venizelists and the Entente, and who vociferously announced their entire devotion to the King. The Allies demanded the suppression of these organisations, but the Greek Government, though professing compliance, did not suppress them, and in reality encouraged their continued existence.

Posts and telegraphs taken over   Zaimis tendered his resignation to the King on September 10th, but it was not accepted till two or three days later, as Constantine had some difficulty in finding another Prime Minister. The King in vain tried M. Dimitracopoulos, who had been Minister of Justice in the Venizelist Cabinet of 1911, but had subsequently dissociated himself from his old leader. Zaimis was asked to withdraw his resignation, but declined to do so. On the 16th a new Ministry was formed, the Premier being M. Kalogeropoulos, who had held office in previous Governments as Minister of the Interior and Minister of Finance. He declared that personally he was in sympathy with the Entente, but the composition of his Cabinet scarcely accorded with his words, and the diplomatists of the Allies would have nothing to do with him. On the same day the Entente Ministers took over the control of the posts and telegraphs, a thing which had formed part of their demands in their previous Note, presented on September 2nd. Control of the telephone system was next established, and the services were directed by censors appointed by the French.

Throughout all Greece the unrest and dissatisfaction occasioned by the surrender of Eastern Macedonia to the Bulgarians were intensified when about this time it became known that the Fourth Greek Army Corps, which had been stationed at Seres, Drama, and Kavalla, with headquarters at the last-named town, had been carried off to Germany. According to the Berlin account of this unique affair, the commander of this corps asked, on September 12th, for the protection of the German Chief Command in order to prevent the Entente from " forcing these Greek troops to its side, or preparing for them a fate similar to that which befell the overpowered portions of the 11th Greek Division." The German communiqué also said that the commander and his men were threatened with hunger and illness, and, further, that he was unable to communicate with the authorities at Athens. The message cynically added that the corps would enjoy the privileges of guests in Germany until Greece was evacuated by the Allies, and German journals joyfully estimated that this coup would deprive the Entente of the possible support of 25,000 men. This figure, in any case, was an exaggeration. The corps comprised the 5th, 6th, and 7th Greek Divisions, and a large part of the 6th Division under Christodoulos had declared for the Allies. The Greek Army had been partially demobilised, and the total strength of the force appropriated by Germany could not have been above 15,000 men at most. But this extraordinary incident filled the Venizelists and other Greek patriots with dismay and anger, particularly when they heard that on September 12th the 7th Division, with Colonel Hadjopoulos at its head, had really surrendered to the Bulgarians at Kavalla, which important town was thereupon fully occupied by the enemy.

Under its pro-German inspiration the Greek Government tried to justify this disgraceful surrender of the Fourth Army Corps, but when it discovered that general opinion strongly condemned this action it issued a communiqué announcing its disapproval. There was no doubt, however, that the surrender was actually negotiated from Athens, and was connived at, if not ordered, by King Constantine, though on September 23rd the Greek Foreign Minister published a statement that his Government had demanded the return to Greece of her lost army corps, a statement which was the veriest " bluff," and deceived no one. The National movement against the Bulgarian invaders, which had started at Salonika at the end of August, grew in strength under such incitement. Christodoulos with his soldiers reached Salonika on September 15th, and thither, often secretly and by devious ways, went officers and men from all parts of Greece. A spirit of revolt broke out in the islands, and Crete, through her thousands of peasants who were Venizelist to a man, rose up against the Government. The position of Venizelos himself, still hoping the King might change his mind, became more difficult at Athens, where a plot was hatched to kill him, but a bodyguard of faithful Cretans kept him from harm. He saw that at last the time had arrived to take a strong step, and on September 25th he sailed from the Piræus for Crete, accompanied by Admiral Condorioutis and other leading members of his party. He had come to the justifiable conclusion that it was useless to look any longer to the King for a truly National leadership, yet in a proclamation made after reaching Crete he said it would be a happy event if at the eleventh hour Constantine would decide to place himself at the head of the National forces in the country.

The action of Venizelos created a profound impression

MAP OF GREECE, SHOWING THE NEUTRAL ZONE.
As the National movement grew in Greece, so did the friction between the Venizelist and Royalist troops. In October, 1916, a neutral zone, two to five miles in depth, was delimited between them, from Litohoros on the Gulf of Salonika to Grismuni on the Albanian frontier, and from Vrondusa, further north upon the gulf, to Armatovo.

in Athens and in Greece generally, and many of the best elements rallied to him. So strongly did the popular tide set in towards him and his policy that for a few days it seemed as if it might carry all before it ; a report gained ground that Greece would throw off her " neutrality," and the pro-Germans were in despair. General Danglis, a former War Minister, joined Venizelos in Crete. The National movement kept on increasing in strength, but Constantine hardened **National Provisional Government formed** his heart, and the Gounarists, gradually regaining courage, stirred up the Reservist Leagues to attack the Venizelists and provoke disorders in some of the larger Greek towns. On October 4th the Kalogeropoulos Ministry resigned. It had never been recognised by the Entente Powers, but before it quitted office several of its members, including the Prime Minister himself, had come round to think that Greece should abandon neutrality and side with the Allies. They told

The Crown Prince of Serbia and General Sarrail entering Monastir, recaptured November 19th, 1916.

respect to the Greek Fleet the larger units, such as the Kilkis, were to be disarmed, and their complements reduced to one-third, while the smaller units were to be transferred as they were. In addition, two forts commanding the mooring-ground of the allied fleet were to be given to the Entente, and other coast batteries were to be dismantled. The admiral said it was imperative that the breech-blocks of the Piræus batteries should be surrendered to him. The Greek Government was given till one o'clock **Royalists'** next day to reply, but accepted the **pro-German scheme** demands of the Note, though under protest, before the time had expired. The Greek Fleet was transferred to the Allies in the course of the afternoon, and towed to the Keratsini Gulf.

On the 12th, Admiral du Fournet presented a Supplementary Note which demanded allied control of the police in Greece, the prohibition of the dispatch of war material to Thessaly, and the prohibition of the carrying of arms by citizens. The Greek Government again assented. It was high time for the Entente to take drastic measures, for some of the extreme Royalists had made no secret of their scheme, which was that, if the Allies should seek to coerce Greece into joining them, or to force Venizelos upon the King, then Constantine was to proceed to the north with his troops, concentrating them at Trikala in Thessaly, and lie entrenched there till the arrival of a German army, in co-operation with which he would strike at Sarrail. And no sooner were the demands of the Entente accepted than attempts to evade some of them were made, efforts to send further munitions into Thessaly being partially successful. It was significant, too, that there

the King as much, but he replied that the Greek Army was not ready to take the field. Constantine next made efforts to set up another Cabinet, and, after several unsuccessful attempts, induced M. Lambros, a professor of the University of Athens, to form a Government, which came into office on October 9th, and was a collection of political nonentities. Next day Venizelos, after a tour among the islands, landed at Salonika, where he was welcomed by General Sarrail and the Provisional Government in being there—one more dramatic episode in the long and chequered story of that city. With himself, Danglis, and Condorioutis forming a triumvirate at the head of affairs, the Salonika Provisional Government soon afterwards was merged in the National Provisional Government, with a duly constituted administration.

No improvement taking place in the situation at Athens, but, on the contrary, indications that war material was being transported to Larissa, in Thessaly, suggesting action hostile to the Entente, the Allies, on October 10th, through Admiral du Fournet, who was in command of the allied fleet which had been stationed in the Gulf of Salamis since the beginning of September, presented another Note to Greece, which was a virtual ultimatum. In this it was stated that the dispatch of artillery and ammunition into the interior of the country, the movements of Greek ships, and the continued activity of the Reservist Leagues, aroused fears that disturbances might occur at points where the allied fleet was anchored, and might also endanger the security of the troops of the Allies on the Balkan front. Admiral du Fournet therefore demanded the handing over of the Greek Fleet and of the naval yard at the Piræus to the Entente, as well as control of the railway from the Piræus to Larissa. With

Greek Fleet transferred

The Crown Prince and the Commander-in-Chief were interested in the evolutions of an aeroplane over the "Queen City of Macedonia."

[*French official photographs.*]

It was a proud and jubilant Prince who received the congratulations of the Serbian inhabitants of Monastir on the victory that had been gained.

THE RECAPTURE OF MONASTIR, 1916.

(French official photograph.

GREEK VOLUNTEERS AT SALONIKA.
Volunteers flocked to the standard raised at Salonika by
Venizelos. The men were of fine soldierly appearance and
won the enthusiastic admiration of General Roques, the
French Minister of War, who saw them in October, 1916.

French official photograph.

SALUTING THE NEW REGIMENTAL COLOURS.
Colours were blessed and presented to the regiments formed under the auspices
of the new Greek National Government, and after the ceremony, which took place at
Salonika, the colours were borne by the troops past M. Venizelos and General Danglis.

arrived in Larissa at this time, on a tour of inspection, General Dousmanis and Colonel Metaxas,
ex-Chief and ex-Sub Chief respectively of the
Greek General Staff, who, with Dr. Georges Streit,
formed the inner cabal around King Constantine,
and were in such constant and close communication with him that they constituted his private
Crown Council. All three were hostile to the
Entente and Venizelos, who some weeks
afterwards said that if the King would send
them packing there would be some prospect of
a change in his policy, and some hope for the country.

Athens continued in a highly electrical state, and the
Reservist Leagues still actively fomented disaffection.
Admiral du Fournet, on October 16th, landed a naval
force of French and Italians, numbering with reinforcements sent later about 2,000 men, to police the city and
preserve order. The bluejackets occupied the municipal
buildings and the railway-stations at Athens and the
Piræus, though their presence was attended by hostile

**Naval contingent
landed in Athens**

demonstrations, Admiral du Fournet himself being hooted in the streets. But King
Constantine thought it prudent to show a
willingness to meet the demands of the
Allies to some extent, and he declared his readiness to withdraw half the Greek troops concentrated at Larissa, and to
place the Greek Army on a peace footing. Four days
later the Entente Ministers demanded the removal of the
troops in Thessaly to the Peloponnesus, the dismissal of
all effectives, except the 1915 class, and the handing over

of all war material to the Allies. The British and French
Ministers, after the Boulogne Conference on October 20th, and
as a result of it, had audiences with the King, and a satisfactory solution, it was believed, was reached of all outstanding
questions. Constantine received assurances from the
Allies that they had no animosity against himself or
official Greece, and that they regarded the Venizelist
movement as directed entirely against the Bulgarian
aggressor. All the same, it had already been announced
that the Entente had recognised the Provisional Government in Crete, but in Athens it was asserted by the
Royalists that Venizelos had not been recognised,
except in an unofficial manner, and Venizelist circles
in the Greek capital were much disturbed and discouraged.

Among the Allies generally, however, it was thought
that the Greek situation had greatly improved, and a
statement made in Parliament by Lord Robert Cecil,
then Foreign Under-Secretary, on October 31st, took that

view. Reports had reached London that the Venizelists were being prevented from supporting the National movement, but Lord Robert doubted them—wherein he was wrong. Assurances had been given by the King that his subjects would be free to join Venizelos without fear of Government reprisals, but in the last week of October measures were put in force against all who sympathised with him. Officers and men who were about to go to Salonika were thrown into prison or placed under strict surveillance, and it was intimated that officials, as well as officers of the Army and Navy, who adhered to Venizelos would be cashiered. Under a relaxed pressure of the Allies, the Royalists grew exceedingly bold, loudly denouncing Venizelos and his followers as rebels, and cruelly persecuting the latter at every opportunity.

[*French official photograph.*]
TAKING POSSESSION.
French troops entering Monastir. Following on the loss of Kaymakchalan and the brilliant fighting of the Serbian Army in the Cherna bend the Germano-Bulgarians were forced to evacuate the town.

[*French official photograph.*]
FIRST FRENCH ARRIVALS IN MONASTIR.
Though it was the dash and vigour of the Serbians in their fighting to the east of Monastir which hastened its recapture, the gallant French troops were the first who entered the town hard on the heels of the retiring enemy and took possession of it on Serbia's behalf.

Germanism became rampant in Athens and throughout Royalist Greece. In Greek waters a German submarine, which got supplies from Royalists, torpedoed the Angeliki, which was conveying volunteers to Salonika, and sank other vessels. As a protest the seamen of the Piræus went on strike, but the Government tamely submitted to the outrages, and damped down the agitation. Admiral du Fournet sent a Note on November 6th demanding that the destroyers and other light craft of the Greek Fleet in his hands should be used against German submarines, and the King refused compliance —whereupon the admiral next day hoisted the French flag over the ships in question, but found the breech-blocks had been removed from their guns. Also, on the 7th, French troops took possession of the naval arsenal, including the submarine defences and powder magazines, at Salamis.

Meanwhile, news reached England that what had been stated respecting the persecution of the Venizelists was true. The King was then reminded by the Entente that he had definitely promised, on being assured that the National movement under Venizelos was not anti-dynastic, that that movement should receive his support, and that part of the Greek mountain batteries should be handed over to the Allies. But the persecution of the Venizelists continued,

and the batteries were not surrendered. It had come to a veritable duel between the King and the Royalists on the one hand and Venizelos and the Nationalists on the other. At the end of October a collision, with bloodshed, had occurred between the Venizelists and the Royalists at Katerini, on the west shore of the Gulf of Salonika, and to avoid civil war the Allies had garrisoned the town. In spite of persecution the National movement grew. On November 9th Mr. Asquith, then Prime Minister, said at the Lord Mayor's banquet that the British Government was "in hearty sympathy with that great Greek patriot, M. Venizelos," and expressed the pious hope that Greece "might rekindle her lamp and show herself worthy of her immortal past." Royalist Greece had no intention of the sort. Matters drifted on without improvement. On the 14th General Roques, the French Minister of War, who had been at Salonika, and spoke enthusiastically of the troops of the National Army he had seen there, had an interview with the King with the idea of bringing affairs to a head. He demanded the establishment of a neutral zone between the Royalists and the Venizelists, complete liberty of action to all desirous of joining Venizelos, and the use of the Greek railways by the Allies.

A neutral zone was delimited on the 16th. It was from about two to five miles in depth, and extended from **Neutral zone delimited** south of Litohoros, on the Gulf of Salonika, to Grismuni, towards the Albanian frontier, and from north of Vrondusa, above Litohoros, to Armatovo. Nothing further of a substantial character having come out of the interview of General Roques with King Constantine, Admiral du Fournet presented on the 16th another Note, demanding the delivery of eighteen batteries of field-guns, sixteen of mountain-guns, and other munitions, and the Greek Government replied that acceptance would be a breach of "neutrality." While this was being further debated Admiral du Fournet succeeded in ridding Athens of the German, Austrian, Turkish and Bulgarian Ministers. He wrote them a letter ordering them to leave, as it was impossible, he said, for them to remain on the soil of a nation containing people whom their warships intended to attack. The King offered no opposition, and the enemy Ministers and their Staffs departed. In the meantime the Reservists had been stirring up hostility to the surrender of the guns, and the Government persisted in its refusal. On the 24th the admiral told Greece that he must have ten batteries by December 1st and the rest by the 15th, and threatened to take coercive measures in the event of non-compliance.

Fighting in Athens — Two days afterwards the French detachment occupying the Zappeion barracks was reinforced. The situation rapidly became critical. Athens was in a ferment, the Royalists prepared to resist, and the Venizelists were menaced with massacre, their houses and shops being marked with circles in red paint.

As the King—nominally the Greek Government—continued obdurate, allied troops began landing at the Piræus early in the morning of December 1st, and by daylight a French naval force, with British and Italian contingents, or about 3,000 men in all, marched from three directions towards Athens. When the troops approached the city they found Greek forces ready to dispute the ground with them, though King Constantine had passed his word of honour that the Greeks would not offer opposition. Fighting began at 10.30 and

went on till about two in the afternoon, when Du Fournet, at the request of the King, agreed to an armistice. The allied strength had been wholly inadequate to deal with the situation. About three hundred British bluejackets took part in the operations, and eight were killed and many wounded in holding the munition factory. The loss of the French was much heavier, and the Italians also suffered. It was a wanton, unprovoked attack on the part of the Greeks, and the King was personally responsible for it. In the course of the afternoon he offered to hand over six batteries to the Allies. Meanwhile Athens was given over to anarchy—calculated anarchy against the Venizelists, who next day

BULGARIAN AND GERMAN PRISONERS NEAR MONASTIR.   *[British official photographs.*

At first the Bulgarians were terribly afraid of falling alive into Serbian hands, fearing ghastly retaliation. They were treated, however, with most generous forbearance. Above: Interrogating German prisoners near Monastir. A French communiqué, dated November 13th, 1916, stated that since September 12th, when the general offensive began, the Allies had taken 6,000 prisoners.

were murdered or imprisoned and cruelly maltreated throughout the city. The Allies had shown that they were powerless to protect their friends; it was a horrible humiliation for the Entente. About a hundred Venizelists were shot, and on that day and during the ensuing week over 1,800 of them were thrust into prison. The British and other Entente colonies retired to the Piræus, and the Greek Government, having regained control of the telegraphs, sent out false despatches to London and Paris saying that all was well again. But such was not the case. How it really stood was shown by the resignation of the Greek Ministers in Paris and London, who declined to serve King Constantine any longer. Admiral du Fournet was recalled, and his place was taken by Admiral Gauchet, who had been second in command.

Warrant for Venizelos' arrest

An ultimatum was presented by the Entente to the Greek Government on December 14th, stating that, as events had proved that neither the King nor the Government had sufficient authority over the Greek Army, the Allies demanded the withdrawal of the entire Greek force from Thessaly, and that all movements of troops and war material to the north should cease. Meanwhile a blockade had been instituted on the 8th, and it was intimated that this would be maintained until reparation was made for the unprovoked attacks of the Greek forces at Athens, and until adequate guarantees for the future were given. The British and French Ministers had withdrawn to the fleet, and though Greece signified her compliance with the ultimatum they remained afloat. They had at length learned to distrust Constantine, and their attitude was confirmed by the issue at Athens of a warrant for the arrest of Venizelos on a charge of high treason, and by the discovery that the acceptance of the ultimatum contained reservations founded on the Allies' toleration of Venizelist " sedition " in the islands. It was plain that the King and the Royalists were still impenitent. In the last days of the year this was made more apparent by a request of the Greek Government that the blockade should be raised, but the Allies replied in a fresh Note on December 31st, stating that the blockade would be maintained until all Greek troops were removed to the Peloponnesus and the allied control of the Greek services was re-established. At the same time they demanded that the flags of the four chief Entente Powers should be saluted in a public square at Athens, and that Callaris, the Greek general responsible for the attacks on December 1st and 2nd, should be removed. This Note differed from those that had gone before inasmuch

as it was signed by the representatives only of the three Protecting Powers—Great Britain, France, and Russia. It was not well received by the Royalists, whose tone towards the Entente became increasingly hostile and impudent.

Playing for time, the Greek Government—in other words, King Constantine—set forth objections to the Note; but on the morning of January 9th France, Great Britain, Russia, and Italy issued an ultimatum requiring, within forty-eight hours, acceptance in their entirety of its terms. It had been reported that Italy was not in agreement with the other Allies with respect to Greece, but a conference at Rome, in which Great Britain was represented by Mr. Lloyd George, who had succeeded Mr. Asquith as Prime Minister in December, reaffirmed the solidarity of the Grand Alliance. In the ultimatum the name of Italy was a proof of it. On January 10th the Greek Government replied in an unsatisfactory manner.

For a day or two it looked as if Constantine, still hoping for the assistance which Germany was said to have promised, would resist. It was reported that fresh German forces had arrived on the Monastir front, and it was stated that the redoubtable Field-Marshal Falkenhayn was at Larissa. But the promised help did not materialise, and the blockade pressed more and more heavily on Greece. The King was compelled to submit, and on January 16th the Greek Government accepted the demands of the Entente in their entirety without reservation. The Venizelists were released from prison, and compensation was to be given to them. General Callaris was cashiered. The Greek troops were to be withdrawn to the Peloponnesus, fifteen days being allowed for the completion of the process, and the **Greece makes reparation** Allies intimated that the blockade would be maintained till they were satisfied that the withdrawal was sufficiently complete.

The Entente Ministers returned to Athens, where, on January 29th, representative contingents of the four Entente Powers, accompanied by the Ministers themselves and Admiral Gauchet, assembled in the Zappeion Park and had their flags saluted by a large Greek force of all arms. Notable in the march-past was the free and soldierly gesture with which King Constantine's brother, Prince Andrew, saluted as he rode at the head of a detachment of cavalry. This gave a good impression, as the duty might have been so easily delegated to a deputy. The ceremony, which was made most impressive, closed the chapter, Greece's written apology having been presented some days previously.

TEETH DRAWN FROM THE DRAGON'S HEAD OF GERMANOPHIL GREEK ROYALISM.
Greek torpedo-boat destroyers anchored at the Piræus. Admiral du Fournet, who commanded the Allied Fleet, took practical possession of the Gulf of Salamis in September, 1916, to enforce Greek compliance with the requirements of the Allies. Early in October these included the handing over of the Greek Fleet and of the naval yard at the Piræus to the Allies, as well as control of the railway from the Piræus to Larissa.

CHAPTER CLXVI.

MARVELS OF THE BRITISH TRANSPORT SERVICE ON THE WESTERN FRONT.

By Basil Clarke.

Magnitude and Complexity of the Transport Problem Confronting Great Britain—Mobilisation of the Mercantile Marine for Oversea Transport—Institution of the Royal Naval Transport Service—The Army Unequipped to Deal with the Overland Transport Problem—General Principles Underlying the Solution of the Transport Problem in France—Administration: The Quartermaster-General's Branch and the Inspector-General of Communications—Collecting Centres at the Bases—Eighteen Months' Purchases by the British Army—Advance Depots and Dumps—Canals and Barges—Railway Service in France Efficient but Inadequate to the Strain Imposed upon It—Contribution of Personnel, Rolling-Stock, etc., from the British Railways—Divisional Rail-heads —The British Mechanical Transport Service—Repairs and Refit Workshops—Types of Motor-Lorries in Use—Divisional Horse Transport—Separation of Ammunition from Supplies—Sub-Parks and Refilling Points—From Refilling Point to the Front—Reorganisation of Traffic to Meet Army Movements—The Australian Divisional Train—Field Supply Depots—Work of the Battalion and Company Quartermasters—Ration Parties—Upkeep of Roads: Engineering and Labour—Light Railways for Heavy Ammunition: "Antennes" and "Rocades"—Marvellous Organisation at Verdun—Light Vans, Motor-Omnibuses, and Char-à-Bancs—Aerial Railways—Mules, Donkeys, and Dogs—The Postal Service.

GREAT BRITAIN'S transport work in the European War may fittingly rank in history among the victories which it made possible. And when the full record of the many great achievements of the war—the enemy's as well as our own—comes to be drawn up and viewed in one dispassionate perspective, this transport work of Great Britain must hold a prominent place in it.

From none of the greater combatant Powers was such a *tour de force*—especially as regards military transport—so little expected; for in none of these countries at the outbreak of war was to be found so small a means, establishment and personnel, for the undertaking of so huge a task. To Great Britain fell the biggest and most complex transport problem of all. Not only had she longer and more difficult journeys to take her own men, munitions, and other means of war— and in numbers and quantities never previously dreamt of—but in addition she had to play willing handmaiden to a greater or lesser extent to every one of her Allies, making, fetching, and carrying for one and all alike.

The oversea part of this problem was difficult enough, but not inconceivable, because to the British as a sea and shipping nation, sea transport, even for war purposes, was no great departure from their own line of business. By a mobilisation of their mercantile sea-power, a mobilisation which at its apex embraced about 75 per cent. of merchant ships, this side of the war-transport problem was managed at least satisfactorily, if not very adroitly. There was criticism, not a little of it; and astute shipbrokers and others accustomed to the economical freighting and chartering of ships succeeded in proving accusations they had hurled at the naval authorities of over-lavishness in the use of merchant shipping. They pointed out, very truly, that the freighting of ships was a very different thing from the fighting of ships, and that skill in the latter art did not necessarily imply skill in the former.

These criticisms were called for. But the main object was achieved. Nothing went wrong with the armies in the field through faulty sea transport or lack of shipping; and this end, rather than that of strict economy, was the more important consideration at the moment. As an earnest, perhaps, of repentance, and of a wish to remedy their shortcomings in commercial knowledge, the naval authorities instituted in December, 1916, a Royal Naval Transport

---

TRANSPORT ON THE WESTERN FRONT.

This was the amazing record and position of British transport work as it stood in February, 1917. The most remarkable figures given here were obtained specially for "The Great War" from an authoritative source, with permission to use them. No details of the kind had been published previously.

(I.) There had been some 8,000,000 troops conveyed by British sea transport.

(II.) More ammunition was being shipped out of England every *week* than had been made in thirty *years* before the war.

(III.) An average of ten thousand *miles* of telephone wire was being shipped every month.

(IV.) Some 2,000,000 tons of mailbags had been shipped to France alone.

(V.) About twelve thousand tons of supplies were shipped every day. The term "supplies" is used here in the military sense of the word, and comprises only food, forage, light, and fuel. It does not include ammunition, war material, etc.

Service, to which service would be entrusted the duty of studying the business of economical chartering and freighting and allocation of ships.

If the oversea transport problem that faced Great Britain at the sudden outbreak of war was huge, the overland transport problem was colossal. The Navy possessed in their brother sailors and the ships of the British Mercantile Marine a wonderful service, ready-made, to fall back upon for transport work; but **Magnitude of** the Army at the outbreak of war had **the problem** nothing of the sort ready-made—or a mere handful of men and machines at best. To cope with the work before them they had, therefore, men and means to find and to make. To the credit of those responsible be it said that as Great Britain's Army of "more than five million men" grew into being, and as her workshops and factories began to pour out, in quantities that staggered the world, guns, munitions, and supplies for that vast Army and for the Allies' armies, the means of transporting all this output of men and things was evolved at the same time.

It was wonderful work. Waggon-builders, both for horse and for motor vehicles, in all parts of Great Britain and abroad were set to work at fever pace; the world was

[*British official photograph.*]

CAPTURED AND CARRIED OFF TIED TO THE CONQUEROR'S CAR.

German gun captured on the western front being towed away from the field of its past battles by a British motor-lorry. These ubiquitous lorries, of which thousands upon thousands were employed, were utilised in greatly varied ways, besides that of taking up supplies for men and guns at the front.

scoured for horses; the country-side was scoured for drivers and men with a knowledge of horses; the towns were festooned with advertisements for motor-drivers, mechanics, and men with a knowledge of motors; the War Office was beset daily with knots of young men anxious to become officers in this new, vast branch of military service; and, according to their fitness and knowledge, they were allotted to horse transport or mechanical transport, as the case might be.

Nor had railways to be neglected. Men skilled in railway making and working, and in the handling and despatch of goods by rail, had to be found for service in foreign countries through which British transport would be necessary. Such men were forthcoming. British railway engineers and managers who had thrown up positions abroad to come home and help the "Old Country" were garnered in. General managers, traffic managers, locomotive superintendents, constructional engineers, and others earning their thousands a year in railway systems throughout the world, were soon immersed in this great new home undertaking, and standardised under the khaki and red piping and one star of an officer in the Royal

Engineers, Railway Section. And the outcome of it all? It was to be seen at its best in the wonderful organisation that day by day carried men and arms, munitions, food and materials, and a thousand other things, to the trenches, batteries, and billets of our troops fighting so resolutely across the Channel. The same kind of system existed on every other war front, but it was in France and in Flanders that one saw the new British transport organisation at work in fullest capacity.

More than one civilian visitor to the British front, when asked what was the outstanding impression of his visit, replied, "The war transport." It was understandable. If you brought a cultured native from his home in Timbuctoo to see, say, the Tower of London, and asked him what had given him the outstanding impression of his visit, he would probably reply, "London." And just as the Tower is a thing of wonder immersed in a bigger, more conspicuous thing—London—so is war and actual fighting a thing of wonder immersed in a more conspicuous thing— its transport. For fighting is comparatively only the rim, the edge, the selvedge of war. The rest of war is mainly its requisites and transport and the means to them.

In France there was evidence of these things everywhere. On the quays, where men and goods were landed, in the storehouses and depots to which they were first taken, on the railways and the roads and canals that took them thence and right up to trench and battery and billet—here and elsewhere one saw little more than supply and transport in one or other of their many phases. Even the war-weary German prisoners whom one saw working so very leisurely with pick and spade on those busy country roads of France under tolerant British guards— their presence and work there were remoter phases of the great war question of transport, for the maintenance of roads stood in closest relation to the supplying as well as the moving of fighting troops.

At first the ubiquity of stores and men and means of transport to be seen throughout the fighting territory of France and its hinterland to the coast gave one the impression of being designless and chaotic, a medley of work, parts of a system so intricate and complex as to discourage an inquirer from peering into it and trying to grasp the method underlying it all. Fishing-lines and boys' kite-strings get into similar-looking knots, apparently quite unravelable. But a little patience worked wonders, and it was fascinating to find, on closer examination, how interdependently and orderly and methodically these many and conflicting phases of war transport linked together to form one big co-ordinated system. We will try to put in a simple way some of the broader general principles underlying **Complex beauty** the solution of transport problems such **of organisation** as that faced and solved in France.

First as to its general administration. Of the three great branches of the Army, the Quartermaster-General's branch, as is usual in British war organisation, had control of transport, supply, and such things. It was the duty of this branch to be cognisant of the ideas of the Commander-in-Chief of the forces in the field, and to keep him supplied with all requisites for the carrying out of his military schemes. For the sea-transport side of this problem the Quartermaster-General's branch was in close touch with

Nissen huts—an invention which vastly reduced the hardships of the third winter campaign.

On the permanent way: In winter the most practicable road for troops on the western front.

Difficulties of gun transport : Bringing up an 18-pounder through the mud. Man power had to reinforce horse power.

Bavarian battery caught by British gun fire while limbering-up south of the Bapaume road. Only three guns escaped.

Hauling horses out of a mud-filled shell-hole on the western front.

Another transport incident: Digging an artillery horse out of a quagmire.

the Admiralty, and after soldiers, munitions, or goods had been delivered at dock-side in England, responsibility for them passed for the time being from the hands of the Army to the Navy, whose duty it was to see to their safe transport and landing. A naval transport officer was on the dock-side at the port of arrival in France, and also an Army officer, styled " military landing officer," and the naval officer formally handed back to the Army, in the person of the military landing officer, the men or things that had been carried oversea.

From this moment, and until they reached their final destination at the front or elsewhere, they came under the control of that immensely important person in modern warfare, the Inspector-General of Communications. Lines of communication, you remember, are a definite, pre-arranged route, or routes, by which men and supplies reach or leave armies in the field. In a hostile country they may have to be defended by troops specially set apart for this purpose ; but in France, of course, this duty did not amount to much. Lines of communication were maintained to the British front from " bases " at the ports of France—Havre, Calais, Boulogne, Rouen, and elsewhere. The next stage of transport from these " bases " was by railroad or canal.

It will help to a clearer understanding of the transport scheme in this great war area if it be explained that there were separate directors of railway transport, canal transport, and road transport for the lines of communication, all of whose work was linked up under the department of the Inspector-General of Communications, and through him with the Commander-in-Chief and his Staff. And every base on these lines of communication, and every post on them, and every section, had its commandant as representative of the Inspector-General of Communications, with representatives, if necessary, of the directors of railway, road, or canal transport. To the Inspector-General's department, therefore, and his Staff fell immense and important duties. They were responsible for the control and arrangement of everything sent along the lines of communication —men, munitions, animals, supplies, and the rest. (The luckless soldier or civilian found in this area without proper credentials came under the ban of the Inspector-General or his agents.) They also controlled the administrative services on the lines, in addition to regulating transport supply and the hundred activities relating to it.

They were responsible for the disposal of all reinforcements, munitions, supplies, and other materials in the area, and for their despatch to the front when word for them came down ; also for the taking away from the front all that was useful no more. Even the **The Inspector-** removal of wounded came under the ulti-**General's Department** mate, if not the immediate, control of the all-important Inspector-General of Communications. Another of the activities of his vast department was the selection and taking over of sites and buildings for depots of every kind, and all offices, quarters, and materials that might be necessary for the upkeep of the lines of communication and their functions ; also the feeding and housing of all troops living or moving in this area, including prisoners of war. Naturally, so vast a work was split up into many separate departments, each with its own head and representatives ; but the

question of transport touched all alike ; by transport they had their being and carried on their many functions ; by transport they, one and all—just like the fighting men at the front—had to stand or fall.

The bases were the collecting centres for all the commodities needed by every part of the Army. Virtually all of these had to be brought from oversea. France could yield little. The French were busy supplying their own war needs, and even of such things as fresh, home-grown produce, material, and stone for roads Britain had to draw to a large extent on home supplies and carry them overseas. Mr. Balfour mentioned **Some amazing** in 1916 that under the guardianship of **figures** the British Fleet 4,000,000 fighting men, 1,000,000 horses, 2,500,000 tons of stores, and 22,000,00c gallons of oil had passed overseas for Great Britain and her Allies.

The work of the year 1916 is calculable from the colossal figures set out on page 431. The vast bulk of these men and things transported overseas went to France. The bases there, at the foot of our lines of communication, were receiving them day and night.

What hives of activity and of war resources these bases were could be well appreciated after a walk round any one

VILLAGE STREET NEAR VERDUN—FATE OF A FIELD-KITCHEN.
Scene of desolation in the Grand Rue of Fleury, before Douaumont, showing the way in which the cottages were demolished and the roadway reduced to a pool. The field-kitchen, which had slipped into a shell-hole in the middle of this wrecked roadway, had to be abandoned.

of them. A moment's thought as to the quantities and the innumerable kinds of things required by an Army of millions of men—food, ammunition, arms, clothing, fighting and building material, medicaments and surgical appliances, stationery, and a hundred others—will given an idea of the size, number, and variety of the stores and depots at the bases through which all these things had to pass. To help to some conception of their capacity some figures of Army purchases may be given. In eighteen months the British Government bought :

TABLE SHOWING EXTENT OF ARMY PURCHASES.

Boots	20,693,000 pairs		Buttons..	841,913,000
Woollen Cloth	89,818,000 yards		Flannel ..	87,703,000 yards
Tent Duck ..	53,944,000 ,,		Braces ..	10,618,000 pairs
Drawers ..	28,964,000 pairs		Shirts ..	26,340,000
Socks	53,920,000 ,,		Blankets	20,782,000
Brushes ..	43,011,000		Knives and	
Horseshoe			Forks..	23,689,000
Nails .	795,000,000		Pickaxes	2,097,000
Spades ..	3,640,000		Wire Rope	11,394,000 feet
Sand-bags ..	700,000,000		Biscuits	214,718,000 lb
Cheese	69,000,000 lb.		Flour ..	846,564,000 ,,
Jam	176,520,000 ,,		Oats ..	10,368,000 qrs.

[Canadian War Records.

NEWS FROM THE FAR WEST.
Arrival of Canadian mail at a postal centre behind the firing-line on the western front.

These purchases—which represent, of course, only a small part of the many different kinds of things that had to be bought—were up to the spring of 1916. The next year's purchases were on a considerably larger basis, compatible with the great increase during the year in the fighting strength of the nation. An immense proportion of these, as well as a thousand other purchases on a similar gigantic scale, had to pass through the base depots of France to reach the Army in the field and the reserve troops there.

As an illustration of the kind of depot store that was to be found at these bases, one may instance the motor-fittings store at one particular base. In it were to be seen tyres in piles, several feet high and hundreds of feet long. Separate compartments, each as big as a small warehouse, were set apart to contain spare parts for one make of motor-vehicle. Within each compartment inside this place were hundreds of pigeon-holes, each to contain merely one part of this one type of car, and this single part was there in thousands. It was computed early in the war that there were some 500 different types of motor-vehicle used for war purposes, one class of vehicle alone being represented by 20 different types. There were 156 types of solid tyre in use; 679

types of ball bearings; 63 types of magneto. All these and innumerable other parts had to be distributed as required, and at a moment's notice, throughout the war zone from the bases in France.

These depots in turn drew their supplies from huge depots in England, one of which covered many acres underground, and had stocks of tyres, for instance, standing side by side in rows 300 feet long. As with motor " spares," so with all different kinds of war supplies. There were clothing depots—bigger than any clothing emporium ever imagined in ordinary life — provision depots, grocery depots, butchery and meat depots, equipment depots, medical store depots, and a hundred others. From these base depots were fed innumerable smaller depots called advanced depots and field depots, or " dumps," throughout the country. Each of these places would " indent " on base depots for the materials and supplies needed by the troops in its neighbourhood, and the base depots would forward them at best speed.

One begins now to realise the immense work that confronted the transport sections of the Army; their task it was to get all these things—food and clothing and fighting material and ammunition—up to the men in the front lines away from any railway, and to the

[Canadian War Records.

THE FIELD POST: SORTING AND DISTRIBUTING LETTERS FROM HOME.
Canadian mailbags arriving at a distributing centre in France. In circle: Sorting letters from home for distribution. The arrival of the home mail was always eagerly looked for by the men in the field

thousands of other soldiers working in other parts of France.

Should they be sent by road, rail, or canal? Their destination, their character, their urgency had to be taken into consideration before arriving at a decision. Their journey might ultimately prove to be by any one of these three means of transport, or by any two, or by all three. But as a rule the canal's share of the work was limited to the carrying of bulky, non-urgent material such as hay and fodder, pit props for the support of dug-out roofs, planks for the lining of dug-outs, iron roofing, cumbersome and unwieldy machinery parts, and the like. The canal barges were manned by soldier bargees from the rivers and canals of Great Britain and Ireland—very proud of their military status and their military uniform; very good-tempered and jocular, and well able to hold their own against the chaff levelled at them by British soldiers passing along the canal banks. They had only one regret, these quaint water-soldiers, and it was that they never encountered an enemy craft of their own kind. They dreamt, perhaps, of barge warfare, but it never fell their way. Occasionally they came in for shell fire, however.

One excellent purpose of war for which barges were used, both by British and

WOOD FOR TRENCH PROPS. Unloading rough timber that was to be used for props in the trenches.

French, was the moving of wounded men who, through the nature of their injuries, could not stand removal by jolting train or ambulance-waggon. In areas containing navigable rivers and canals, cases that had to be kept very quiet and still were carried by hand on to the barges fitted up as hospitals, and towed quietly down to the coast. The journey was long, but as the barges were fully equipped with beds, nursing staffs, and medical men, the time spent in them was much the same as time spent in a hospital.

The railway was the next great means of transporting men and commodities towards troops in the field. The French railway staffs alone could never have coped with the vast amount of extra work which the presence of millions of British troops threw on the railways of the country. At the outbreak of war the French mobilised more than 200,000 men for railway work, and these men did prodigies of transport in the first few weeks of the war. The Paris to Lyons Railway on August 5th, 1914, for instance, carried 3,000 military trains; the Orleans Railway 1,500.

In 22 days 42 army corps, each needing 142 trains, had been sent along the latter line, and by the end of September, 117,000 tons of food, 66,000 tons of forage, 107,000 cattle, and twice that number of sheep and pigs, had been sent along the same system. Civilian

HOW THE HIGHWAYS WERE MAINTAINED IN THE BRITISH LINES.
Unloading stones for metalling roads during the Somme advance. The work of maintaining good communications with the rear was an important feature of every advance. In circle: Taking up water-pipes along a light railway for establishing a regular water supply to the front line.

BEHIND THE FRENCH LINES ON THE SOMME FRONT: ART'S IMPRESSIVE STATEMENT OF TRANSPORT'S GIGANTIC TASK.

French transport behind the lines on the Somme front. In this suggestive picture the brilliant French artist, M. Georges Scott, presents a wonderful impression of the passing columns of men and materials, of motor, horse, and rail transport, perpetually going and coming to and from that front on which the great decisions of the war were being fought out. In a single glance, as it were, he makes plain to us something of the intricate organisation, the gigantic efforts, necessary to maintain that constant flow of the wonderful tide of transport, in all its miscellaneous manifestations, which was essential to victory.

trains suffered, of course. There was not enough rolling-stock for all. The arrival later of locomotives and rolling-stock saved from the Belgian State Railways when the Germans overran Belgium, added to the French railway resources to a valuable extent, but even then there was little enough for France's own war needs. In addition, the need for men for the French Army became pressing, and after some time nearly a quarter of the number mobilised for railway work were taken away to go into the fighting-lines.

When the railway demands of a huge British Army in France came to be faced, therefore, it was seen that some considerable contribution to the railway resources of France would be necessary if the needs of both these armies in the field, as well as of the civil population of the country, were to be met. It was agreed that the British should undertake certain proportions of the manning and staffing necessary for their own transport work over French railways. One saw on these railways, as a result of this agreement, many British soldier railway servants. Some of the railway sections, more particularly British in their traffic, had even British engine-drivers. Contribution of rolling-stock was also made, and " Le Temps " announced in December, 1916, that Great Britain was shortly to send 10,000 trucks to France, and 10,000 more in the spring of 1917, or earlier ; also some locomotives. Thus was provision made against any overtaxing of the capacities of the French railways owing to the ever-increasing size and demands of the British Army in France.

British railway-men in France A month or so earlier the question of a contribution of steam-tugs for relieving the congestion on the French waterways was gone into. Large quantities of coal were lying both at the pit-heads and in barges on the rivers owing to shortage of tugs. The appointment of M. Clareville as Director of General Transport for all France was a measure aimed at meeting this and similar transport difficulties brought about by the heavy tax the war made on all means of transport in France. Our contributions to the staffing of the French railways included both technical personnel, to deal with the construction, maintenance, working, and repair of railways in the war zone, and railway transport establishment personnel to control the arrangements between the Army and the technical personnel for the transport of troops and war commodities.

It may be said, therefore, that to a large extent the British controlled for their own war purposes the lines or parts of lines that they needed between their bases and their war zone in France. Troops and commodities' were despatched along these railways in special trains to the working of which hardly any French people contributed. Goods trains and ammunition trains were " made up " at the bases by British soldier railwaymen and despatched to the war zone with all the regularity and method employed in a London railway goods-yard. Certain trains left for certain parts of the front at a fixed time every day, and many of them had a fixed load, or one which varied hardly at all from day to day. Of such a kind were the food trains. For, once the Army had settled

POWERFUL " CATERPILLAR " TRACTOR HAULING A HEAVY HOWITZER.
[*British official photograph.*
For moving heavy artillery on the bad surfaces over which they had frequently to be taken to the front in France, the tractor with " caterpillar " movement proved of great value. The odd assortment of boxes and cases for which the tractor provided transport were but a negligible addition to the weight which the tractor had to haul. The horseshoe on the front was presumably mounted as a luck-ensuring charm.

down into well-defined positions, which varied only at long intervals, if at all, it became possible to despatch rations and other requirements fairly regular in character and constant in quantity in similar loads. Troops, of course, who had long journeys to make were sent by train. But troop transport by railway has its difficulties, and in general it was found better in France to move troops by road for all save long-distance journeys, leaving the railways as free as possible to cope with the supply of food and material and ammunition—a tremendous task enough. The nearness to which railway trains could approach forces in the field varied very much in different parts of the war zone, but, at best, they could not approach nearer than six miles or thereabouts, and more often not within double this distance. The points at which they unloaded their freights—of men or ammunition or supplies—were called " rail-heads." These were points on the railway chosen not so much for their nearness to the troops as for their suitability in respect of roads leading thence to the area occupied by the particular troops for whom supplies were meant. For the purposes of transport and supply, an army " division " was treated as the unit—that is to say, that each division organised its own supply and transport, established its own depots and " dumps," and had nothing to **Divisional transport** do with the transport arrangements of **and supply** any other division. Each division had its " rail-head " (though three divisions, making a " corps," might use the same one), and when goods were delivered at these " rail-heads," they were met by divisional transport vehicles of one kind or another for transport to each divisional area. If the troops were a long way distant these vehicles would be motor-waggons and lorries of the " divisional supply column " ; if the troops were not very far away the vehicles might be the horse-waggons of the " divisional trains," * but, in the majority of cases,

---

* Throughout this chapter care must be taken not to confuse divisional " trains," which are horse-waggons, with railway " trains."

BRITISH TRANSPORT LORRIES AND HAND-CARTS PASSING EACH OTHER ON A FRENCH ROAD.

Men of the Middlesex Regiment returning in pouring rain after a spell in the trenches. They were passing a long train of motor-lorries of the British Mechanical Transport Service that were taking supplies up to the front. Though the "Die-Hards" had ponies to draw some of their small carts, the men had to push others over the miry ways, but readily gave their comrades a "lift" on the way back to the rest camp.

the troops were so far distant from "rail-head" that motor transport was necessary.

A "rail-head" at the time of a train's arrival and unloading was quite one of the war sights of France. Railhead might be an old-established goods siding near a town, with loading platforms and warehouses complete, or it might be a bare bit of railway with newly-made sidings in open country miles from any town, and with no more than a farmstead or two to be seen from it. The roads leading from it to the main roads might be of logs laid transversely, called a "corduroy" road, over which horse-waggons and motor-lorries would bump and jolt in liveliest fashion. Motor-vans and horse-waggons might be drawn up against the railway train's side with busy soldiers working in every railway-truck and road vehicle. Or, if the train's load was not for immediate transport to the front, the goods might be piled up on platforms or in adjoining fields, or in any side store space available; for it was an axiom of railway working in France that a train must not be kept waiting; it must be emptied as soon as it arrived, and begin as soon as possible its return journey to the base, carrying any empties or war salvage, or other material that had to be taken down the lines. Vehicles of all kinds beset "rail-head" day and night; the place seemed to have no quiet season. When they were not wanting rations they were drawing ammunition or ordnance stores, or material for working-parties; for road transport from rail-head for these different kinds of requirements was organised separately, even though all might be intended for the same division in the field.

When it is remembered that a division represented possibly as many as 20,000 to 25,000 men and officers, 3,000 or 4,000 horses, guns, both big and small, carts and vehicles innumerable, hospitals, post-offices and the rest, it will be realised what work fell on the divisional transport

Scenes of endless activity

in getting all the requirements for their upkeep and work from "rail-head" to the front, the last stages of the journey being perhaps into inaccessible places where no more than loaded pack-mules could travel, and where even these creatures had to yield up their burden at length to be carried by hand.

A service so big and so thorough as that maintained every day between rail-heads and the front-line troops in France, and especially on the Somme, would never have been possible without some service of road transport of extraordinary capacity and efficiency. This was to be found in the British Mechanical Transport Service. This service of British motor-waggons and lorries was one of the great wonders of the war. People spoke of it as "the" wonder of the war, and it had at least some claim to the appellation. Along the war-zone roads of France, roads that were often execrably bad and execrably narrow, that were sometimes ploughed up by shell, or flooded by rains, or broken and crumbled by subsidence, these fleets of motor-waggons, driven by drivers who a few months earlier had been driving the 'buses and taxi-cabs and commercial motors of Britain, maintained day in day out a service of food and stores and shell in quantities never previously dreamt of in warfare. Night or day they rumbled patiently and methodically along the roads with their heavy loads, overcoming innumerable difficulties and getting vehicles through positions and dangers that would have turned any "nervy" motorist's hair grey. All this they did with a wonderful cheeriness and boyish roguery. There were no more ready jokers on the roads of France than the "M.T." men. They were soldiers, of course, and one noted on every waggon and lorry the rifle slung ready to hand just above the driver's head on his sheltered driving seat. But, except through mishaps and retreats, the motor-lorry drivers did not have much fighting to do. In

The Mechanical Transport Service

the later days of the war, after our advances began, they were fairly safe from actual contact with the enemy, but they came under shell fire at times, and many lost their lives.

These British motor-lorries and waggons in France were to be numbered in their thousands. An official statement made some fifteen months before the war began, and recalled by the "Times" in October, 1914, said that on mobilisation the mechanical transport strength of the various armies would be as follows : Germany, 2,000 motor-"waggon units" (each unit comprising a four-ton lorry tractor with a two-ton trailer) ; France, 5,000 three-ton lorries ; Britain, 1,000 motor-waggons. Without disclosing the full number of British motor-lorries and wagons in use in the war, it may be said that this estimate of 1,000 would not have sufficed for a tithe of the transport work for which motor transport was used. The motor parks in France alone, in which reserves of motor-lorries were stored for the replacement of casualties among the motor-transport waggons, had probably lorries enough to exceed that estimate.

Repair and refit workshops They stood in rows and squares of great size at the base "parks"—brand-new lorries all ready to be drawn upon whenever a new supply column was needed or whenever worn-out or damaged lorries were to be replaced.

The repair workshops and refit workshops for motor-transport vehicles employed thousands of men. They were hives of mechanical industry, often on as big a scale as some of the big railway-engine works at home. In addition, the lines of communication were dotted with sub-depots to which a car could run or be towed to have its defects put right. There were also moving squads of mechanics—"breakdown gangs," as it were—who at a summons by telephone would dash off in their breakdown waggon to the help of any lorry that had met with casualty on the road. These repair gangs were organised in units on military lines. They had their mobile workshops mounted on lorries, and on a country road near the front one might come at any moment upon a broken-down lorry dragged to the roadside or off the road if possible, and round it a swarm of blue-coated soldiers, mechanics, with their lifting tackle and tools and their portable forge roaring pleasantly in the open air to the draught of a hand or foot bellows. Or if the worst had happened, if the lorry had broken down irreparably—as, for instance, when a shell had lifted it off the road and half over the bank, as in one case I saw—the gang at work on it would

be a "motor salvage party." They would burrow among the debris, unscrewing wheels, lamps, horn or anything that was valuable, and before long all that would remain would be the broken chips of the lorry and perhaps a few twisted bits of worthless iron. All else had been lifted into the salvage waggon to be taken away to the local salvage dump, whence it would be transported later to the base.

Special arrangements had been made for dealing with tyre trouble, which was the most common cause of incapacity. Tyre presses were established at different points well inside the war zone to save lorries from having to leave the war area for their repairs. Some of these presses were mounted on special railway trucks. Broken radiators occurred rather often, owing to the crowded state of the roads and rail-heads and the number of times that lorries had to crawl along one behind another, now moving a few yards, now stopping again, and so on. Early in the war this trouble was more common. To men used to the close and crowded traffic of London streets it seemed impossible to get into the way of driving with the regulation thirty paces between each two vehicles. Often they were only a few inches apart, and it needed only a little hole in the road or some unevenness to take the hinder lorry with a bump on to the back of the one before it, a bent or broken radiator being the result. In time, however, the officers managed to eradicate this habit of close driving. To add to the risk of this form of mishap there was sometimes driving to be done at night without lights. As a general rule the lorries were expected to load up at the rail-heads at night, then to "park" by the roadside or in some convenient ground for the night, and to set off on their

Tyre and radiator troubles

HORSE LINES AT A BRITISH AMMUNITION DUMP IN FRANCE.

If the horse came to take a subsidiary part during the protracted trench stages of the war, and was in many respects superseded by the triumphant motor transport, it was yet an essential auxiliary with the guns and waggons in much of the transport work. Above : Scraping the mud from a mule that had been submerged in mire. Mud-filled shell-holes not infrequently proved traps for the transport animals from which rescue was difficult.

FILLING ONE OF THE HOT-FOOD "CONTAINERS."
"Containers" were devised during the war for keeping the
men in the trenches supplied with hot food. One man could
thus carry up the food necessary for many comrades.

journeys with the coming of daylight. But any
little accident on the road might make a lorry late
and prevent its arrival back at "rail-head" before
dark. Night motoring along the roads in the French
war zone was rather speculative work.

The motor-lorries were of many different makes,
British and American, and some makes were
more popular with drivers than others, but no
make that did not prove to possess a very full
degree of efficiency was allowed to form part of a
divisional supply column, which was expected to run
with something of the regularity of a railway train.
The lorries were chiefly of three tons' capacity, and weighed
when loaded some six and three-quarter tons, though there
were also a number of smaller ones. They
had a boarded-up seat, with a hood to
accommodate driver and two other men if
necessary. The lorry sides were boarded
up to a height of perhaps two feet, and from these sides
ran iron rods vertically, bending over the top of the lorry
like the hood of a Cape cart. Over this stretched a tarpaulin cover, generally left open at the back. The lorries
of one supply column were all marked with the same sign.
It might be a red triangle with a white circle inside, or a
hand or a wing, or a white horse, or the ace of clubs, or any
other sign that struck the mind of the man who invented
these things. The sign was conspicuously painted on the
back of the lorry, where it could be seen at a glance.
Numbers and letters were avoided because they were more
tell-tale to any friend of the enemy who watched their
habits and destinations. One man generally rode inside
the lorry, and kept a look-out for any faster-moving

Lorries and their signs

traffic—such, for instance, as a Staff officer's motor-car—
coming up behind him, and on seeing such a car he would
warn his driver by pulling a little bobbin near the top
cover of the lorry, which made some sort of a noise near
the driving seat for the driver to hear. There was a little
secret code between driver and "guard"—one pull for
any ordinary car, and one or more for a brigadier or
divisional commander, with quite a little series for the
Commander-in-Chief himself. And for him, of course,
the ordinary motor-lorry driver got on one side of the road
very quickly indeed.

In the early days of the war the drivers gave their lorries
names, which they painted on them over the driver's hood or
on the sides. Supply columns would take
series of names having one association.
One column might have flower names, or
girls' names; another might have admirals'
names, another names drawn from Dickens' novels—there
was a Stiggins lorry, for instance, a Chadband lorry, and a
Quilp. But it was feared that these names led to a too
close association in people's minds between certain supply
columns and the divisions they served, and an order was
issued that names of lorries must be removed. Unofficially,
drivers still called their lorries by name, but the names were
not painted on.

Life of the motor-lorry crews

SETTING OFF WITH HOT SOUP FOR THE FRONT-LINE MEN.
From a field-kitchen in a conveniently sheltered spot behind the lines the men of the
ration-party got their supplies of hot soup, and with their containers tightly screwed
down, set out thus on the march back to the trenches.

The motor-lorry crews slept for the most part in their
lorries, and at night-time it was interesting to visit a
"column" drawn up at the side of some wide road or in
an open space and see the cunning little arrangements
which the "M.T." crews had devised for their comfort.
The tarpaulin hood of the lorry, spread over its tall
framework of iron rods, made a tent bigger and more
roomy than most tents that fall to the lot of a soldier in
the field. Lit by a candle-lamp or by one of the side oil-
lamps of the motor-lorry and warmed by a paraffin-stove,
a luxury with which many of the lorry crews had provided
themselves, an empty motor-lorry made one of the most
comfortable of billets. Passing soldiers, tramping through
the mud on their way perhaps to dug-out quarters or to
cellar billets, peeped inside the wayside motor-lorries with
envy and chaffed the inhabitants about their "luxurious"
mode of life. Often the homely fragrance of grilling
bacon would float out to these wet and weary "foot
sloggers" from the open flaps of a motor-waggon, and that
seemed always to inspire foot troops to extra irony.

You climbed up to these lorry interiors by the aid of
a small ladder reaching from the back-board to the ground.

Inside you might see the far wall of wood—at the back of the driver's seat—covered with photographs and pictures from the papers. A small hand-mirror might hang there, and possibly a toothbrush, stuck in a small loop of leather. If the load for the following day's journey were on board the accommodation might be very limited. The floor space might be covered with boxes or shell-cases, leaving only very small room available for the occupants. But if there was any room to spare, as was often the case—for the

Caravanning in motor-lorries

lorries were not loaded to their fullest capacity as a rule—a folding-table and a canvas-topped stool or two might form part of the place's furniture. When bed-time came the men could stretch out their blankets on the floor of the waggon or on the cases of goods or ammunition that formed their cargo, but most of them had devised hammock beds made of canvas or sacking, stretched on wooden frames which fitted into grooves cut in the sides of the motor-lorry. These beds were not supplied by the Army, but were home-made. The materials were obtained in many ways that were not orthodox, and the big letters " P.O." on the canvas of one such bed that was seen might have given a hint to the Postmaster-General as to where

HOT RATIONS IN TRANSIT.
Ration-party carrying supplies of hot food along a communication trench to the men in the firing-line.

one of his letter sacks had gone.

The officer in charge of a motor-transport supply column would sleep in billets if his column were parked near its headquarters, but for nights on the road he carried a portable tent, which his servant would pitch at the road-side near his column, and here he would spend the night alone—probably colder and damper than his men with their waggons to sleep in.

The function of motor transport in the war area in France was to serve as the connecting-link between the railways and the horse transport attached to each fighting unit. For motor-lorries, of course, could not take their loads right up to the front-line trenches, nor to within some little distance of them. Instead they took them only to some more

advanced point than " rail-head," to which the divisional horse transport could conveniently come to get them and take them on to the units in the field. A division's horse transport was of considerable strength. The divisional " train," whose duties were connected with food, fuel, light, and other stores, comprised about 160 waggons, 375 horses, and 420 men of all ranks. In addition, a division had its divisional ammunition column of nearly 570 men and some 700 horses. This column was fed by a motor-transport section of 48 motor lorries with 186 men of all ranks. The two services worked on much the same principles but quite separately, for while " supplies " for a division might be a fairly constant load every day, munitions might be a " rush " one week with comparatively little to do the next week. Another factor that made a separate service for supplies and ammunition desirable was the different nature of the commodities handled ; also the fact that as the guns were not so far forward as the infantry and as the shells to be taken to them were so heavy and unwieldy to " tranship," it was desirable whenever possible to run shell lorries right up to the gun positions or to some near point whence shells could be pushed up by hand rail-way or some other such means. Failing

Work of divisional " trains "

this, shells went to the divisional " sub park " (each army corps had an ammunition " park," each division had a " sub park "), to be taken forward later by the divisional ammunition column ; supplies went to a spot called the " refilling point." To this point came every day the divisional " trains " to load up and take back supplies to the three brigades of the division and the " divisional troops "—comprising divisional headquarters Staff and administrative troops not so far advanced in the field as the front-line infantry. Thus " refilling point " was the point at which lines of communication transport and field-transport linked up. " Refilling point," of course, was advanced or retired as the troops which it was intended to serve advanced or retired. Its nearness to the front-line trenches varied very much in different positions, but it might be about ten miles or more.

From " rail-head " to " refilling point " and from " refilling point " to front, the roads of France were always busy. Yet the enormous traffic was wonderfully well

SERVING OUT STEW IN A FRONT-LINE TRENCH.
Company ration-parties, representing each platoon and special section, attended at the battalion " dump " in charge of a corporal, and thence carried the rations to the trenches by hand. The journey was sometimes as long as two miles, and was frequently one of extreme difficulty and danger.

distributed. Supplies and ammunition for different parts of a division had as far as possible their own routes and their own times for being on the road. Some of those road transport services were worked with all the regularity of railway trains at home. Stand at a certain spot on a certain road at a given time and you might depend on seeing one particular unit's "train" pass by. After an interval someone else's ammunition column might come along. The soldier policeman on point duty could tell you almost to a certainty which "trains" were coming along the road at that moment and where they were likely to be. It was seldom that things went wrong. During the vile weather of the early winter of 1916, when the roads seemed literally to rot and disintegrate owing to the great amount of traffic that passed over them in their wet state, one came across serious blocks of traffic at times, but considering the enormous amount of traffic these occasions were surprisingly infrequent.

Road transport regularity

When the Army moved to any considerable extent there was much reorganisation of traffic to be done, but the system was such as to allow of any movement on the part of the Army without throwing out of gear the supply service to it. If there was likely to be any doubt as to a division's position, the divisional supply column motors, on loading up at "rail-head" and turning back towards the front again with their loads, made first for a point on the way technically called a "rendezvous." Here they came in touch with representatives of the actual units for whom their supplies were meant, and if there had been

any change in the position of the troops these men were aware of it and informed the divisional motor transport of any change that might have been made in the position of "refilling point" and acted as guides to it. Whenever the position of the troops became fairly constant, however, these "rendezvous" and their use dropped out, though they were revived at once when the necessity for them again arose.

What the motor-transport supply columns deposited at a "refilling point" was taken away again either immediately or, at latest, before twenty-four hours had expired, by the horse "trains" of the division. It was an inspiring sight to see one of these long "trains" of waggons making its way along the road. In the winter they were yellow mud to the axles, the shaggy hair of their horses was muddy, their riders were muddy, so that at a distance they might have been carved out of mud. Much shouting and encouragement were used to get the horses through the ruts and mud pools in the roads, and a "train" on a bad road, with every driver shouting, waggons jolting, horses slipping and straining, could be heard half a mile away. Everyone used to admire very much the Australian divisional "trains"—the big bronzed men with their wide-brimmed hats, the struggling horses going forward to queer shouts of encouragement that would have been quite foreign words to an English horseman, and to most fearsome cracking of whips. The Australian horsemen, though economical enough in their application of whips, could crack them in most formidable fashion. Rough

Picturesque Australian drivers

GREAT BRITAIN'S WAY WITH PRISONERS OF WAR: TEA AFTER CAPTURE.
[British official photograph.
Germans who fell into British hands had no reason to complain of the treatment they received. In contrast with their own treatment of British soldier prisoners, especially with that meted out in the early days of the war, it was indeed generous to a degree that provoked protest from some people, who thought it would be misinterpreted as due to weakness instead of to proper feelings of humanity.

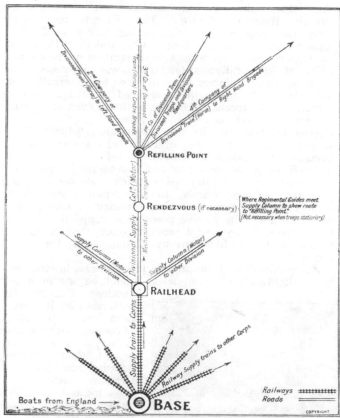

SKETCH PLAN OF TRANSPORT SYSTEM.
Indicating the way supplies were carried from the base to a division.

As far as the "refilling point" transport was all mechanical. From this point onwards to the trenches all transport, as is shown in the second sketch below, was by horse or man power. At the most advanced point that was convenient the food was handed over to each battalion's quartermaster. His men—regimental quartermaster-sergeant and assistants—split up the rations into five parts, one each for the four companies of the battalion, and the fifth for the headquarters of the battalion. The company quartermaster-sergeants were then responsible that the men in the trenches should receive their supplies. Every company quartermaster-sergeant handed over his meat and bacon to his cooks (who, with their cookers, were at the same spot behind the lines), and proceeded to split up his company's rations into parts—one for each company platoon, one for officers, one for machine-gunners, etc. This took him some time, and when he was ready the meat that had been cooking was ready also. This, too, was subdivided, and the whole of the day's rations—cooked meat, bread, tea, jam, etc., was parcelled up in sand-bags, labelled with wooden chips tied on with string. The destination of each **Distribution of** sand-bag was written in indelible pencil **food supplies** on the chip—such and such platoon, or machine-gun crew number so-and-so, or whatever the destination might be. The sand-bags and their contents were then taken nearer to the lines under the superintendence of the company quartermaster-sergeants or their corporals. A cart might be used if the roads were good enough, pack-mules if they were not.

They were carried forward to a selected point which might be as much as a mile or (on the Somme) even two behind the front trenches. Here the company ration-parties, representing each platoon and special section such as machine-gunners, came in charge of their corporals to carry up rations to the trenches by hand. Water-parties, similar to the ration-parties, came also. A water squad had seen to the filling of old petrol-cans (two for each platoon or section) with water, and these and the rations were carried up over the rough country and through the communication-trenches leading to the front trenches.

The journey might be one of extreme difficulty, and it happened not a few times—on the Somme especially—that ration and water parties failed altogether to get their supplies through to their companies. In fact, parties to rescue the ration-parties from the mud had sometimes to be organised. On that day the men in the trenches

roads seemed to cause them no concern. A cart might tilt over to an angle of sixty degrees and yet leave the man inside it still chewing comfortably at his wisp of hay or smoking his pipe as though this was most comfortable travelling. On bad roads the Australians were, perhaps, more expert than our British drivers, but on wet and flooded roads they were at first not so good. The wet and the mud depressed them. They were less used to weather of this kind, but after two years in France they became quite as good "wet-bobs" as the British drivers.

By each divisional horse "train" supplies were taken to field supply depots, or "dumps," near each regimental headquarters, and to the area occupied by the "divisional troops" —that is, the troops such as artillery, engineers, and others whose position was farther from the battle-front than that of the infantry in the line.

Before tracing further the transport of supplies from base to front it may be helpful to show visually, by means of the rough sketch plan above, the progress made so far and the various means of transport adopted, for the whole thing is rather complicated to anyone not familiar with Army transport method and terms.

It will be understood that although on this sketch lines representing routes are drawn straight, the actual routes taken by transport might be, and often were, circuitous; also that no sketch to scale was possible, for distances varied with each "rail-head" and each division and brigade. The idea of the sketch is rather to illustrate the means of supply transport. Ammunition transport followed much the same lines.

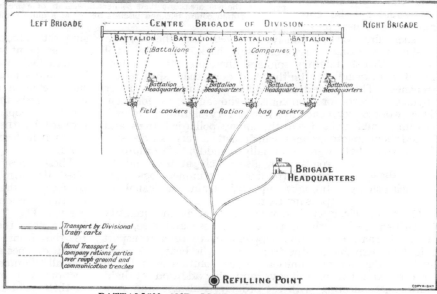

BATTALION AND COMPANY DISTRIBUTION.
Showing how the distribution was effected from refilling point to companies in the trenches.

would have to subsist on any " overmatter " they had in the way of food and water from the previous day. Cases happened of men depriving dead Germans of their water-bottles to help them along till the next day's supplies came up.

The matter of the transport of supplies from base to trench has been gone into in this chapter in close detail because every type of trench and soldier requirement, besides food, had to be taken up by this or very similar methods. Ammunition, weapons, wire, materials, hand-grenades, mine explosives, and a hundred other things threw immense work upon the transport departments of the Army, both regimental and Army Service Corps, and that it was done with so few mishaps is great testimony both to the method and to the men responsible for its working.

The side issues of this tremendous transport work were often very big and important. Remembering the great proportion of the carrying that was done by road it will be evident to everyone that the wear and tear upon roads, and therefore the question of the upkeep of roads, was a very great problem. Not only were the war-zone roads ground to bits by much heavy traffic, rotted and weakened by heavy rains, but near the front they were torn by the enemy's shell, in addition. The work that fell to the road engineers, therefore, was very heavy. They dug great sump-holes by the road-sides to drain off the water, some of these being twelve feet deep and more. Road metal in great quantities was needed, and it was not always readily available, for the stones of France are, for the most part, too soft to make very good road surfaces for heavy traffic.

Labour, too, was a problem. Gangs of German prisoners did some work on the roads away from the front, but the rule that prisoners of war could not be employed in zones liable to shell fire was rigorously observed, and the German prisoners' working areas were well back. It often fell to the British infantry soldiers, therefore, to do their bit of road-mending after they had done their spell in the trenches. They were detailed off in working-parties under engineer officers or non-coms., who acted as foremen. They worked very cheerily, if not very skilfully. French peasants cut sticks from the many pollarded trees and bound them up into fascines, which made a very fair dressing for roads that were especially muddy. " Corduroy " roads were also much in use, and the great " rondins," or trimmed logs, were brought up by train or canal or peasant cart.

Use of light railways

It became clear as time went on, and as the quantity of British shell of the heaviest sorts rose and rose, that some alternative, or some supplement, to road transport might be desirable for the transport of the heavier loads—such as big-gun ammunition. The solution was found in the extension of railways and the addition of light railways, connecting with the ordinary railways and running forward into positions and areas in which ordinary railways would not have been possible. No fewer

than 230 miles of war railways were built by the British Army in France. The French had dealt with the problem of transporting heavy shells in a similar manner with excellent results, and their Decauville railways served as an admirable illustration of the adaptability of light railways for trench-war purposes. The gauge of these railways was only two feet normally, and near the front this might be reduced to little more than a foot, so that trucks might run by hand even along communication-trenches. The rails were riveted together two by two on metal sleepers. These, fastened together and covered with a thin layer of ballast, could

" Antennes " and " rocades "

be put down quickly on almost any existing road or path, and even upon open country. The truck was merely a flat platform on bogie wheels, and it carried a load up to eight tons—the weight-carrying capacity of nearly three motor-lorries. The motive power was supplied by steam locomotives, or by petrol motor-tractors, that could pull a load of twenty-five tons up a gradient of three in a hundred.

A normal rail-head was probably ten miles behind trenches but a light-railway " rail-head " could be within a few hundred feet of the batteries that it served. Care had to be taken, of course, to screen these railways when they neared their batteries, because more than one German battery had been located by allied airmen through seeing the rails that took the shells to it. The light railways were liable to be smashed by shell, of course, but they were so easy to repair—rails for them were all ready pieced together, and needed only to be laid and bolted and ballasted a little — that this risk was not of much consequence.

" ARTHUR " AT THE FRONT.
Coffee-stalls—familiar " Arthur's " in the London streets—were established at many points in the war area, and there soldiers in search of refreshment were able to obtain coffee, tea, and biscuits free or at a quite nominal charge.

[British official photograph.

The light railways linked up with the main railways at convenient points. A junction of this sort might be the simplest affair. The military station, for instance, at the point whence 40,000 men in Champagne were revictualled was an unenclosed space containing a few huts, and a long bank about three feet high running alongside the main rail to serve as a platform. On this were usually carts innumerable, to take away the food supplies for the troops. Ammunition and shells, however, went forward by the light railways, which ran away from the junction in four or five directions to different parts of the front.

These lines were called " antennes " and each supplied its own little section of the front. But it might so happen that an attack in one section might throw on that section's light railway more strain than it could carry. The " antennes," therefore, were intersected at points near the front by light railways running parallel to the front. These were called " rocades." In the event of special stress, ammunition could be sent away by all " antennes " and transferred to one particular section later by the " rocades." The transport capacity of these light railways was shown by the fact that on one day, working twenty-four hours, 1,700 tons of ammunition had been despatched by one of these " antennes " alone.

When ammunition had been unloaded from the main-line railway trucks to the light-railway trucks, a little engine came along and pulled the shell trucks to ammunition depots nearer the front. For each size of gun there was a separate shell shed at the depot. One shed was filled high with stacks of yellow 6 in. shells, another with 8 in., and so on. Telephone connection with every part of the front added to the efficiency of these light railways and the work of the ammunition depots. Extra supplies could be despatched at a moment's notice to any gun position. Occasions might arise, of course, when the expenditure of shell by the guns was such as to overtax the capacity of even the light railways, but on such **Ammunition transport** occasions the motor road transport could **at Verdun** be brought into play again and ammunition supplies could be going both by road and by light rail as well. This happened at Verdun, and working in addition to the light railways was a series of fleets of motor-waggons, comprising in all no fewer than 4,000 waggons carrying shells day and night to the French guns. Nothing like it had ever been achieved in war, or even conceived as possible.

That light railway could supersede road transport altogether was, of course, impracticable. The light railway, though admirable for taking part of the burden off roads, and thereby making more easy their maintenance, and leaving them freer and in better condition for use in periods of special stress, was too inelastic for exclusive use. The motor van and lorry remained the great "stand by" of transport for supplies and ammunition.

There was, on the front in France, a tremendous amount of transport by light vans and motor-cars and motor-omnibuses and chars-à-bancs. The two last named proved very useful for the quick transfer of troops from place to place. The light motor-vans were employed chiefly in motor convoys of the Royal Army Medical Service as ambulances, and the discovery was made that the lighter, cheaper makes of car were more economical to use than many of the more costly makes. Their simpler mechanism seemed less susceptible to damage from the shakings and joltings they received over the rough roads near the front, and several much despised makes of cheap car, American and other, came through their exacting war service with honours while some more famous and better-known makes of car failed with ignominy.

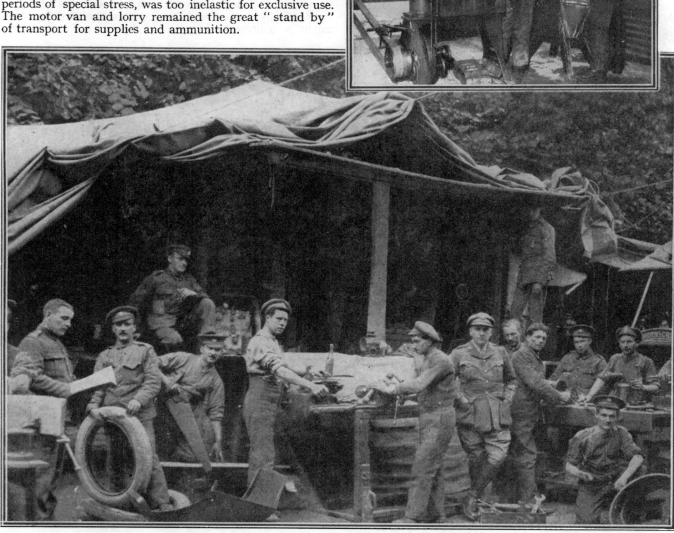

[*British official photographs.*

REPAIR WORKSHOPS FOR MOTOR-TRANSPORT VEHICLES ON LINES OF COMMUNICATION.
Repair and refitting workshops employed thousands of men. In addition, the lines of communication were dotted with sub-depots, to which cars could be towed for repairs, mechanical workshops like the one shown above, and mobile repair shops which could travel to any point. Tyre mishaps and damaged radiators, due to cars running too close to one another on the broken roads, were the most common causes of trouble.
EEE

One of the depots at a base where supplies were received day and night from England and passed on at once up lines of communication.

In very hilly and mountainous parts of France all normal forms of transport by road or by rail were at a disadvantage, and some more satisfactory means of taking up supplies had to be found. Eventually aerial railways were established, consisting of a taut steel wire thirty or more feet above the ground, upon which were suspended small trucks running on a trolly-wheel. They were called "transbordeur" trucks, and they flitted through the air in the queerest fashion, bridging valleys and gullies and ravines that would have been difficult to cross by any other means. Some of these were in full view of the enemy, who often tried by shell fire to upset them, but with little success ; for a wire offered but a slight target, and, as a rule, in places where the wires **Transport in** were visible to the enemy, trucks **mountainous country** were run over only during the night.

For these mountainous districts mules were much used as pack animals. There were, too, a great number of Algerian donkeys—small, whitish, sure-footed beasts of wonderful strength if of equally wonderful obstinacy. The French Colonial troops were almost the only people skilled in the handling of this queer little beast, but under the hands of an Algerian soldier—not always very gentle hands—the donkeys did great work. With shells for field-gun or mountain-gun, packed in wicker cases on their flanks, they could plod their way up or down a mountain side and never lose their feet or their loads. Diminutive railways and trucks were also used for transport purposes in these hilly regions, and harnessed to one of these trucks might be a brace of dogs. Dogs from Canada and Alaska

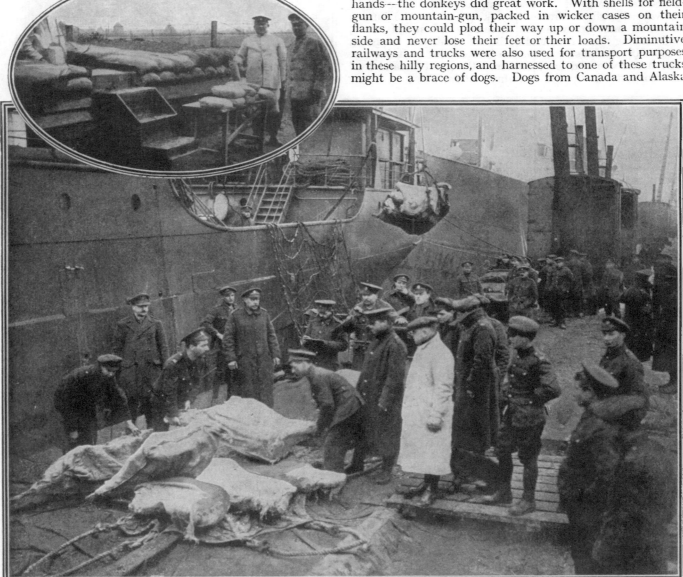

[*British official photographs.*]

Unloading meat from a meat ship on a French quayside and (in oval) a store of yeast for the Army bakers. The daily export of supplies from England for the British Army in France alone was twelve thousand tons, these "supplies" being exclusive of the vast quantities of ammunition, large and small, for artillery, machine-guns, trench-mortars, and rifles.

FEEDING THE BRITISH ARMY IN FRANCE: GLIMPSES OF THE WORK OF THE TRANSPORT SERVICE.

had been imported for the work with special dog-masters of their own. They worked very efficiently. When snow fell their little waggons were fitted with runners and used as sleighs.

The figures given at the beginning of this chapter show to what extent letters and mails increased the transport work of our Army in France. Mails came along to each rail head from the base by railway supply trains having "mail" vans attached. "Mail guards" travelled by the train. At rail-head letters for each division were put into 30 cwt. mail motor-lorries for that division, and these lorries travelled forward, manned by special P.O. staffs, with the M.T. Supply Column to a post-office at refilling point, where the letters were sorted out for forwarding to the respective brigade areas of the division.

Method of forwarding the mails

Each brigade headquarters had a post-office with sub-officer at the regimental headquarters.

The sending back from the front of damaged material and "returnable empties"—such as shell-cases—was another important branch of transport work. At the bases there were huge depots for salvage of this kind, and articles were sorted and separated. One depot was devoted to rifles, water-bottles, bayonets; another to old bicycles, motor-bicycles, and motor-cars; another to clothing, and so on.

Thus to and fro the stream of war transport went, and so long as the war lasted it could never cease. Thousands of men were engaged upon it. To them the war was transport —just transport.

Newly-baked Army bread. The British Government's purchases of flour in the first eighteen months of the war amounted to 846,564,000 lb.

[*British official photographs.*

Lorries loading at a rail-head, and (in oval) putting onions in sacks at a storehouse for entrainment. Vehicles of all kinds beset rail-heads day and night, for it was an axiom of railway working in France that a train must be emptied as soon as it arrived. From rail-head motor-waggons and lorries conveyed the supplies to the divisional area by road.

ONE OF THE WAR SIGHTS OF FRANCE: MOTOR-LORRIES AT A DIVISIONAL RAIL-HEAD.

ARRIVAL OF RUSSIAN HELP FOR THE HARD-PRESSED RUMANIANS.

On the quayside at Braila a cosmopolitan crowd accorded hearty cheers to the Russian transport which brought fresh troops and stores for the assistance of the hard-pressed Rumanians in the time of their great trial. Soldiers, refugees, and a couple of Sisters from the Scottish Women's Field Hospital were among those who enthusiastically welcomed the arrival of help from Rumania's great neighbour and ally.

| CHAPTER CLXVII. |

THE SUPREME DEVELOPMENT OF TEUTONIC-OTTOMAN METHODS OF BARBARISM.

By Edward Wright.

Devilry of German Science—Teutonic Soldiery Soften in Trench Warfare, and are Incited by Slanders on British Troops—Barbaric Treatment of Britons Designed to Provoke Reprisals—Method by which Austro-Hungarians Turned their Men into Devils—Copy of Austrian Order to Perpetrate Atrocities—How the Serbian People were Exterminated by Bulgars, Austrians, and Magyars—Evolution of the Scientific Gorillas of the Latest Darwinian Age—Lettow Fordeck and the Enslavement of British Prisoners in East Africa—Case of Major Howard—Extermination Campaign in Cameroon—Beginning of Slave Raids in Lille—Horrors of Holy Week in North-Western France—French Girls Medically Examined for Most Dreadful Purpose—Thousands of Deportees Starved, Beaten, and Hanged—Germany's Economic War upon Belgium—General System of Slavery Instituted—Economic War Upon Poland and Establishment of Serfdom—Courts of Blood and State Brothels for Polish Girls—Torturing Russian Prisoners of War—Gardelegen and Wittenberg and the Typhus Plot of the Germans—Turks Improve Upon the German Method of Typhus Extermination—How Syria was Dispeopled to Provide More Room for the Turkish Race—Evidence of German Missionaries in Regard to the Ottoman System of Massacres—League of Scientific Savagery between Teuton and Turk—Pitiless Piracy Campaign and Attack on Hospital Ships—How the Children of Germany will Profit by the Racial Extermination Policy of their Fathers.

IN Chapter CX. Mr. Arthur D. Innes gave, from the point of view of an authority on international law, a statement of the most important infractions of the laws and conventions of civilised warfare committed by the Germans in the first period of the war. But after that chapter was written there accumulated so large a mass of fresh evidence of the manner in which the Teutons and their allies conducted war that volumes would be needed to set out even a hundredth part of the matter. The Germans, Austrians, and Magyars excelled in State-directed and organised atrocity all nations with any pretence to civilisation since the Assyrians.

Under the management of Teutonic officers and officials, the Turk was enabled to employ the latest discoveries in bacteriology, in addition to an intensified form of all the older means of extermination he was wont to practise upon Bulgars and Armenians. Typhus, cholera, and anthrax germs were made a part of the armament of the

HIS EMINENCE CARDINAL MERCIER.
The fearless Archbishop of Malines made Christendom ring with his denunciation of German atrocities. In reply to a minatory protest from General von Bissing, Governor-General of Belgium, he declared that the Belgians owed neither obedience, respect, nor devotion to German authority.

enemy, after prussic acid, phosphorus, and chlorine gases were developed by him as weapons of civilised warfare. There are grounds for supposing that inoculation of herds in allied countries with foot-and-mouth disease was attempted by German bacteriologists. German and Austrian men of science, who used in days of peace nobly to risk their lives in the close study of living germs of deadly diseases, were proved to have been guilty of the horrible crime of making cultures in their laboratories with the design of infecting Russians, Rumanians, Italians, and Belgians with the worst of maladies which it was possible artificially to communicate.

Had the power of the Germans and Austrians been as great as their evil desires, the war would have ended by Europe being overwhelmed with some artificially-bred plague. In fine, the bacteriological horrors of Teutonic warfare were such as to cast a lasting obloquy on the whole Teutonic idea of civilisation.

The directors of the Germanic-Ottoman confederacy were brutes

453

of an extreme type, who possessed all the machinery of civilisation without the sentiments on which civilisation had been built. From the generous renaissance of the German spirit in the age of Kant and Humboldt they extracted all the material gains derived from the pursuit of knowledge; but they used these material gains in such a way that their greatest modern man of science, Paul Ehrlich, died broken in spirit in the middle of the war.

The German and Austrian governing classes never sympathised with the glorious work of a disinterested kind that their savants carried on. They shackled many of the best of these men if they tried to work for political freedom as well as for knowledge. They bribed most of the others, by university appointments and social distinctions

GERMAN SLAVE-RAIDERS IN A FRENCH CITY.
Street scene in Lille. Among the barbarities devised by the Germans as occupiers of invaded territory was the wholesale deportation of civilians to do work in Germany in conditions not distinguishable from slavery.

to desert the cause of European democracy and become the technical sub-directors of the great system of military and industrial feudalism on which Germany rested.

The consequence was that many leaders of science in the Central Empires, such as Professor Ostwald, the inventor of the poison gases, degenerated into minds without a conscience. They became human devils; for they had more knowledge than ordinary men, and less conscience than a blood-mad Bavarian peasant who tortured a wounded man before killing him. A certain proportion of the atrocities committed by German and Austrian troops in the movements of invasion in the first period of the war may have been due to nervous strain and cowardice. The inexperienced, overwrought conscripts, drawn by their war-machine into that vast conflict which they had been dreading all their lives, were reduced by the first

battle in which they engaged into a condition of primitive savagery. Their own personal fears overwhelmed the feelings they had acquired as civilised men. As some races are apt to do in a shipwreck or a great fire, they fought with insane savagery, because at heart they were cowards. They tortured their wounded foes because the wounded men were representatives of the nations that were trying to kill them. They ravished and sometimes mutilated girls and women in hostile territories through which they passed as a means of assuaging their angry fear of the armed troops that still opposed them. Had they been confident of emerging alive and victorious from the struggle they might have retained somewhat of the humanity of the truly civilised warrior.

It was worthy of remark that the Saxon troops, who outrivalled the Bavarians in the outrages committed in the first week of the invasion of France, became, some three months afterwards, the least unchivalrous Germans on the western front. When facing British troops they went out of their way to save their enemies from small Prussian surprises, and endeavoured to maintain something of the old standard of chivalry in European warfare. No doubt the exceptional defeat incurred by the Saxon forces on the Marne was largely responsible for the change in their character. Moreover, as they at last recognised that they had met their equals, if not their betters, their fear of the possible treatment of their own civil population inclined them to more civilised ways of fighting.

A veteran soldier has perhaps a steadier frame of mind than a conscript. Having greater control of himself, he is less likely to become a fear-maddened brute. There was **Provocation by German officials** abundant evidence that the Teutonic soldiery became softer in manner when the long struggle in trench lines opened in the west. The German military authorities had to print and publish diabolical lies as to the way in which French and British troops dealt with prisoners in order to revive the ferocity of their own men. It is probable that many of the atrocities which the Germans committed on the western front, such as the tortures inflicted on some wounded Canadians during the first gas attack at Ypres, were designed by German military authorities directly to provoke retaliation upon their own troops. They desired that some of their own rank and file should be maltreated as a means of making their men desperate and cruel, and also of preventing them from surrendering.

This end seems to have been attained by systematically spreading slanders about the manner in which the British soldiers treated their prisoners. In the Battle of the Somme there were parties of Germans caught in a hopeless position and yet afraid to surrender, because they had been told that if the British did not kill their captives out of hand they gouged their eyes out. Happily, in some cases there was one German in the helpless, frightened, desperate group with personal knowledge of the British character. He was often able to convince his comrades that surrender only meant that they would find in England more comfortable quarters and better food than they enjoyed in their own lines.

The Germans who fronted the French also quickly lost the edge of their first wild fury. To provoke them afresh they also were plied with fearful fictions concerning the revengeful ways in which the French treated their prisoners. This method, however, failed of effect. Apparently the Frenchman enjoyed in Germany a character for suavity and mercy superior to that of the Briton. German privates persisted in believing that the French were highly civilised, and always surrendered to them in larger bodies than they did to the British. But the German military authorities were equal to the occasion. They invented the legend of the awful barbarism of the French-African troops, and continually hinted at it in their official communiqués.

As a matter of fact, the Arabs and Berbers, who formed the larger element in the native forces employed by France, were Moslems of a finer caste than the Turk and, by ancient tradition and modern discipline, as chivalrous as the French officers who led them. Most of the Sudanese troops also were Moslems, and though they had negro blood in their veins they were as good men as the negroes who fought in the American Civil War. But the cunning and devilish German authorities succeeded in implanting in the minds of German privates and non-commissioned officers a fear of the inhuman cruelties they would suffer if they surrendered to " the black friends of France." This led, in the struggles around Verdun in February, 1916, and in the fight around La Maisonnette on the Somme in July, 1916, to acts of uncivilised warfare on the part of the Germans which were as bad as anything they had committed in August and September, 1914.

But we can distinguish an important difference between the early and the later German atrocities. In the first period commanding officers in many cases had but to loosen the bonds of discipline in some Belgian, French, or Polish village in order to produce such a scene as Attila might have enjoyed. But in the second period, German soldiers as a whole were tired of atrocity, and somewhat thoughtful of the possible consequence of their acts. They had to be excited by lies, sometimes of so abominable a kind that the statements cannot be put into print for general reading. But even then the larger number of Germans appear to have remained sceptical, and inclined reluctantly to carry out the commands of their authorities. Some of the tales spread among the enemy troops by their own officers, and unfit for publication in a work of this

Dawning fear of consequences

kind, may be read by men in the English translation of the " Reports of the Atrocities Committed by the Austro-Hungarian Army during the First Invasion of Serbia." A neutral authority of Germanic stock, Professor R. A. Reiss, of the University of Lausanne in Switzerland, undertook at the charge of the Serbian Government to inquire into the conduct of the Austro-Hungarian Army. He travelled through a large part of Serbia, and there examined a great number of Austrians and Hungarians and hundreds of Serbians who had witnessed the deeds of the enemy forces. The Swiss professor carried out his work

Austro-Hungarian horrors in Serbia

so thoroughly that his report did not appear in English until the summer of 1916. It arrived in time to effect a great change in the feeling of the British nation, which had ever regarded the Austrian and the Magyar as kinder and more generous in character than the Prussian or Bavarian.

The Austrians are Eastern Bavarians, forming the German advance-guard against the Turks. They learnt to be savagely cruel in their Turkish wars, and by raising regiments of Croatians, who had been brutalised by the Ottomans, they introduced into the wars of religion of the seventeenth century a touch of supreme horror. When they subjugated the Northern Italians they kept down the Lombards with more ferocity than the Prussians afterwards kept down the Poles. When they were driven out of the larger part of Italy and compelled to concede rights to the Hungarians they still continued to be the most efficient race of oppressors in Europe. Being more skilful than the Prussians, they blinded the minds of their subject peoples by preventing them from obtaining a high degree of education or acquiring the rudiments of a spirit of independence. In peace time they kept some races as

A GERMAN SLAVE-RAID IN BELGIUM: DEPORTEES ON THEIR WAY TO EXILE.
On May 2nd, 1916, General von Bissing decreed that all unemployed Belgians should " be conducted by force to the spots where they have to work." This instituted a general system of slavery in Belgium. At least 150,000 Belgians, without distinction of class, were deported and set under the bayonets of German soldiers to work of military importance not only in France, but in mines, factories, and quarries in Germany.

overlords of other races. The Magyars, for instance, did Austrian work by keeping down Rumanian and various Slav peoples, while the Moslems of Bosnia by plundering and ravaging made the Dalmatians and subject Serbs more submissive to the Austrian suzerains.

When the Austrians invaded Serbia they threw off the mask of gentility they had worn before Britons, Frenchmen, Americans, and other representatives of Great Powers. They at once showed themselves, as they had **Austrians use** done in the seventeenth century, superior **explosive bullets** to the Prussians in cold-blooded, calculated ferocity. From the beginning of the war they employed explosive bullets in large quantities. These bullets had been invented by a Swiss as a range-finding device ; but the Austrians and Hungarians used them in machine-gun belts in the proportion of fifteen explosive bullets to ten ordinary bullets. Austro-Hungarian prisoners admitted that their best shots were supplied with explosive bullets for breaking up masses of Serbians. The men were told to use the bullets carefully, and refrain

and that no clear evidence of their general use of explosive bullets and dum-dum bullets would be obtained from the broken, cowed, and silenced mountaineers. If they did not use explosive bullets in a wholesale manner against the Russians in the first week of the war it was because they respected the strength of Russia. But they employed from the outset their vast and secret store of " sighting cartridges " against the small and isolated race of Serbians, on the mistaken calculation that they could conquer the country and terrify the people in time to prevent any considerable outcry.

The Germanic doctrine that savagery in war is the purest form of humanitarianism, because it shortens the conflict by terrifying the opposing nations, was fully practised by the Austrians before it was discussed in theory by Clausewitz. The Austrian military authorities took measures at the outbreak of hostilities to work all their soldiers into a condition of bestial frenzy against the Serbians. The Croats, Dalmatians, Bohemians, Little Russians, and Poles—who formed a large part of the forces of the Empire—were Slavs, and kindly disposed to their fellow - Slavs in the Balkans. But, according to members of these races who were afterwards made prisoners of war and examined by Professor Reiss, diabolical means were employed to induce them to maltreat the Serbians as well as fight them. The men were told that the Serbians did not make war in a civilised way, but mutilated in an obscene manner every wounded man who fell into their hands. Prisoners taken by the Serbs, it was also falsely alleged, would be mutilated after the fashion of Red Indian warfare. The result was, on abundant evidence given by Austro - Hungarian prisoners of war, that wounded Serbians were angrily butchered with knives and bayonets by reason of the ghastly slanders spread by Austrian and Hungarian military authorities.

TOASTING "THE VICTIM": A NEW SENSATION FOR DECADENT GERMANS.
Four German officers, with ingenious refinement of cruelty characteristic of decadents seeking pleasure in new sensations, compelled a Belgian gentleman sentenced to death on the morrow to stand before them while one played Chopin's " Funeral March " and the others drank a toast to " The Victim." M. Dupuy, the artist, effectually perpetuated memory of the atrocity by this very striking picture which he exhibited in the French Salon.

from wasting them where only a single Serb could be aimed at, as the bullets killed two soldiers at a time and inflicted such large wounds that a man who was hit seldom recovered.

Later in the campaign the supply of explosive bullets was apparently increased. For the men of the active Army were then told they could be employed freely against single Serbians as well as against masses. In some companies sixty men of marksman rank were provided with explosive bullets. The order was that these bullets should be used at a range of a thousand metres. This is a distance at which an ordinary bullet goes through the body and makes a small clean wound. But at the same range the explosive bullet, if it did not kill outright, incapacitated a man from further fighting. When the war had been going on for some months the Austro-Hungarians began to manufacture dum-dum cartridges. Cases of them were taken from the enemy as received from the Government factories. The Austro-Hungarians expected they would completely triumph over the Serbians by the end of 1914,

In one case the 53rd Infantry Regiment of Austria, as it was crossing the frontier, was shown a man in Austrian uniform with his ears and forearms cut off. He was led on horseback before the troops, who were told by their officers: " You see what is in store for you if you surrender ! " The Austrians said the man was a Croat, but the Swiss professor found reason for supposing that he was a Serbian, who had been mutilated by the men who paraded him, and then dressed up in Austrian uniform in order to excite the invading troops to **Wholesale massacre** frenzy. In consequence of this infernal **of prisoners** kind of propaganda there were horrible massacres of Serbian soldiers, both wounded and unwounded prisoners of war. In one striking case a large number of Serbian soldiers of the 13th and 14th Regiments surrendered to the Austrians and were massacred by them, and by strange chance the Serbian Government afterwards obtained a photograph of the massacre. Another photograph of a series of official murders was found on a German officer killed in the recapture of Monastir. The scene was at

Forcibly removing French civilians from Lille to German labour colonies. "It was not done by whole families," said one of the sufferers. Men and women, lads and girls were picked out by caprice from unwarned families as though to add torture to the indignities and miseries of slavery.

German "dragooning" in Belgium. But for the distribution of food by the great neutral Commission for Relief the Belgian populace—including over two and a half millions of children—would have starved. The Germans could not even permit this distribution without harsh and brutal interference.

TEUTONIC TORTURE METHODS AS EXEMPLIFIED IN FRANCE AND BELGIUM.

Woman's heavy work in the long journey to the homeland.

Krushevatz, where the mayor of a neighbouring village and five other blameless and wealthy farmers were publicly hanged by a gipsy, while the German officer, for his amusement, photographed the row of gallows. The design was to intimidate the people by slaying their leading men.

The civil population suffered worse than the civil population of Belgium and Northern and Eastern France. Professor Reiss, for example, stated in his report that:

In many of the invaded villages almost all the women from the very youngest to the very oldest were violated. "We were ordered," a man of the 26th Regiment states, "and the order was read out to us, to kill and burn all we met in the course of the campaign, and destroy everything Serbian."

Youth and age returned hand in hand, alike relieved to have got away from the heavy domination of the invader.

The tale of Serbian horrors is too long to republish and impossible to summarise. Children were killed with the bayonet, and villagers were surrounded in their church and slain with butt or steel to save ammunition. Screens of men, women, and children were employed in a more general manner than in Belgium, and the burning of houses, containing old men, women, and children was carried out on a large scale. Some four thousand members of the civil population were estimated to have been killed in the first brief Austro-Hungarian invasion, a considerable proportion being burnt alive or mutilated before their death. As only a small part of Serbian territory was then occupied by the enemy, the percentage of victims was high. Professor Reiss states:

The evidence proves that the manner in which the soldiers of the enemy set about killing and massacring was governed by a system. It was a system of extermination, which was also displayed in the bombardment of open towns with shrapnel and fougasses, and in the systematic way of setting on fire dwellings and farmhouses. It is impossible to regard the atrocities as the acts of a few scoundrels, such as are to be found in every army. My inquiry has proved to me that the overwhelming majority of the civil population most certainly never fired a shot or committed any act of hostility towards the Austro-Hungarian troops. When an army finds itself obliged to execute civilians for taking part in warlike actions, the guilty parties are shot. But almost one half of the victims were bayoneted or clubbed to death, butchered and hanged, burnt alive or even mutilated. The tardy excuses of Austrian officials fall to the ground. Their Army has methodically carried out a mission of extermination, and the butchery of old men, women, and children is part of that mission.

One of the most important documents in connection with

In response to neutrals' efforts the Germans permitted French women and children to be repatriated by way of Switzerland. Pathetic scenes were witnessed on the journey, though the tragic memories revealed in the faces of age had their prophetic contrast in the hopeful smiles of youth.

WOMEN AND CHILDREN REPATRIATED FROM FRENCH TERRITORY IN GERMAN OCCUPATION.

On their arrival at Evian the repatriated families were examined by military representatives of the French and British Armies.

Many of the returned exiles were destitute, and to these the town authorities gave supplies of clothing and refreshments.

the Serbian atrocities is a pamphlet issued by the High Command of the Austro-Hungarian Army, and found in the possession of the men. One passage in it will show how the troops were systematically trained and prepared for the Serbian massacres :

IMPERIAL AND ROYAL 9TH ARMY CORPS.
INSTRUCTIONS REGARDING BEHAVIOUR TO BE ADOPTED TOWARDS THE POPULATION IN SERBIA.

The war is taking us into a country inhabited by a population inspired with fanatical hatred towards ourselves, into a country where assassination, as the catastrophe of Sarajevo has again shown, is condoned even in the upper classes, who extol it as heroism.

In dealing with a population of this kind, all humanity and kindness of heart are out of place. They are **Inhumanity specifically ordered** even harmful, for such sentiments, whose application is sometimes possible in warfare, would here place our own troops in danger.

I therefore give orders that, during the entire course of the war, an attitude of extreme severity, extreme harshness, and extreme distrust is to be observed towards everybody.

Hostages taken in traversing a village are to be brought, if possible, to a passage *en queue*, and they are to be summarily executed if even a single shot is fired at the troops in that locality.

Every inhabitant encountered in the open, and especially in the woods, is to be considered the member of a band which has concealed its weapons somewhere, which weapons we have not the time to look for. These people are to be executed if they appear even slightly suspicious.

Once more discipline, dignity, but the greatest severity and harshness !

It was well known to the Austrians and to all the General Staffs of Europe that Serbia was so exhausted by

Scene in the station-yard at Evian when the repatriated women and children arrived, the worst of their sufferings behind them.

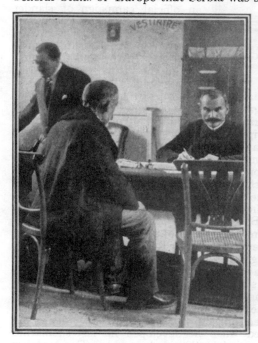

[*French official photographs.*

An information bureau was opened for the use of the poor people who, of course, knew nothing of what had been happening in France. Right : They were given an enthusiastic send-off as they started on their journey to other districts of France.
RELEASED FROM THE CLUTCHES OF THE HUN : EXILES RETURN TO EVIAN, HAUTE SAVOIE.

459

her recent wars that she could provide uniforms only for her active troops and for the smaller part of the men of the second levy. The larger part of the soldiers of the second levy and all the men of the third levy had no uniforms, and therefore fought in their ordinary clothes. But the Austro-Hungarian High Command ordered that all armed Serbians without uniform taken singly or in groups should not be made prisoners, but " be unconditionally executed." These instructions were therefore a downright order to massacre all men of the third levy and the larger part of the second levy.

Extermination the real object It was obeyed rigorously by the invading forces, who also thoroughly pillaged the country.

Moslem peasants from Bosnia were detailed to accompany the troops on the march, and according to the statements of prisoners, the example set by these parties of plunderers and anti-Christians at last stimulated the blood-lust in men who had been kindly fathers of families in private life. What happened in the autumn and winter of 1915, when the rabid Bulgars joined with Austrians, Magyars, and Germans in closing around Serbia and sweeping completely over it, is a tale almost beyond belief. While the territory was still in the hands of the exterminators,

the National Assembly to pass a measure against brigandage, under which the Serbians in Macedonia, Old Serbia, and the Morava region could be executed as bandits. But in the territory held by the Austro-Hungarians the work of slaughter was carried out according to a list of crimes drawn up by the Archduke Friedrich.

Among the crimes entailing death were : (1) Possessing more food in the house than the conquerors allowed ; (2) keeping copper vessels after being twice ordered to give them up ; (3) carrying written messages between third parties ; (4) giving food, shelter, or clothing to escaping prisoners. Denunciation by an informer—usually an envenomed, blackmailing foreign spy—practically meant death, the court-martial being a matter of form. By public executions and the exposure of the dead bodies the Austro-Hungarians endeavoured to terrorise the nation at a time when the people were being gathered by the sixty thousand into slave-gangs for work across the Danube. All prominent men were especially pursued, in order to deprive broken Serbia of her natural leaders and advisers and make her utterly helpless under the combined process of extermination and Babylonian exile.

In Great Britain, France, and Belgium the character of the German became fully known. But, as Professor Reiss remarked, the Austrians—and especially the Viennese—had in times of peace a reputation for charm and good-fellowship. This false reputation, enjoyed by the greatest race of systematic oppressors in Europe, beclouded the general judgment of the Western Allies. In practice there was nothing to distinguish the Austrian from the Prussian, for the reason that the Prussian had reached the Austrian level. The military castes of Austria and Hungary never had anything to learn from the Germans in the matter of atrocities.

They were always more careful and more patient in their preparations. Long before the outbreak of war they maintained an official campaign of slander against the Serbians. The far-reaching effect of this campaign was seen in Mr. Bernard Shaw's early play " Arms and the Man," and in the Viennese comic opera

ROYAL WATCHERS OF AN INTERESTING CEREMONY.

[*British official photograph.*]

Queen Elizabeth of Belgium and her children with the Prince of Wales (right). King George, when visiting the western front in December, 1914, decorated King Albert with the Order of the Garter as a tribute to his personal bravery and a mark of sympathy with the sufferings of his heroic country.

their apparent aim appeared to be to annihilate the independent part of the Serbian race and repopulate the country, so as to have complete and permanent dominion over the vital corridor in the Berlin-Bagdad system. The sufferings of the Serbian nation were, it is no exaggeration to say, beyond all parallel in modern times, and probably much worse than those endured in parts of Germany in the seventeenth century under Austrian savagery. Bulgaria under the Turk never suffered as did Serbia under the Bulgars and Austrians.

The Austro-Hungarian authorities at first seemed to adopt a more humane attitude towards the people of the occupied country than did the frankly murderous Bulgarian authorities. But this appearance of civilisation was designed only to impress those neutral States represented by medical missions, journalists, and other travellers. When conquered Serbia was finally closed to all neutrals, and the American and other medical missions were dismissed, the Austro-Hungarians proceeded systematically to dispeople the land by deportation, internment, and judicial murders. The Bulgarian Government gave some colour of law to their policy of extermination by inducing

founded upon it, " The Chocolate Soldier." The Serbian, as the British Socialist playwright saw him in the light of Austrian propaganda, was a posturing coward whom any European conscript soldier could easily master, especially if he were a conscript of Germanic stock. When, as a result of the early Austrian Press campaign, such an idea obtained in the mind of the most brilliant sophist in the British Isles, the effect produced on the common opinion of Austria was much deeper. But after the **Austrians—real** Balkan Wars the courage of the Serbian **and imaginary** could not be impugned, even by the Austrian Press Bureau and the Shaw-Strauss operatic combination. So a fresh campaign of an abominable nature was begun, with a view, as Professor Reiss reports, of frightening the Austro-Hungarian troops into a frenzy of sadic cruelty.

It must be admitted that the Prussian never showed such diabolical skill of this kind as did the Austrian—the gentlemanly, charming, graceful, waltzing Austrian. The Austrian was the more diplomatic. Acting alone, he would never have driven things to so desperate an extremity as the Prussian reached when he developed his last submarine piracy campaign against the whole world. The Austrian

Timely arrival of the lifeboat at a ship torpedoed near the English coast.

Pulling away from the heavily listing vessel to escape the fatal whirlpool.

(F. G. Mortimer.

From the lifeboat and one of the ship's boats the crew of the torpedoed vessel watch her final plunge.

Camera records of German piracy: Sinking a stately merchantman off the English coast.

British patrol boats racing to the oily ring that marks a German pirate's grave.

Watching the Diomed sink. The pirates jeered at the plight of her crew and abandoned them.

Explosion of a submarine bomb from a patrol where a U boat had been located.

Survivors of the torpedoed s.s. Artist picked up after three days' exposure in a gale.

Callous brutality: Having torpedoed the Karnak, November 27th, 1916, the pirates turned searchlights on to watch her death agony.

always knew when it was to his own interest to stop, and see what he could rebuild out of the wreck of his ambitions. Only against weaker nations did he fully show what a devil he was at heart. When fighting against strong Powers he retained sufficient control of himself to preserve some of the appearances of decency. In the decadence of his Empire he was like a toothless tiger that attacked children, but slunk away from men. It was lack of power, not lack of will, that prevented him from being leader in the work of filling the whole of Europe with horrors like those of the Thirty Years War. Serbia showed what he would have done if he could have ruled on land, as the shell fire which an Austrian submarine poured into an Italian passenger steamer, the Ancona, indicated what he would have done on water had he possessed the full means of murder at sea.

Austria a "toothless tiger"

But by reason of the German's superior power, it fell to him to display on land and sea and in the air the complete character of Teutonic warfare. In the earlier chapter on this subject, Mr. Innes discussed, in sound legal fashion, the enemy's infractions of the laws of nations and the modern conventions settled at The Hague Conference. But the German progressed after that in his evolution into the higher ape and scientific gorilla of the latest Darwinian era. Nothing human restricted him. As his spokesman, Dr. Bethmann-Hollweg, explained to all neutral States, the higher German humanitarianism reconciled good and evil by discovering that inordinate cruelty shortens the period of strife, thus becoming the instrument of all the divine blessings of peace.

The authentic official proclamation of the modern gospel of Germanism only appeared at the beginning of 1917. The fear that the people of the United States had not reached the stage of evolution fitting them to accept this gospel somewhat delayed its State announcement. Also, the weapons for putting it into practice had been rendered almost powerless at first by the fighting seamen and fishermen of Great Britain, and time was needed to prepare stronger instruments. But the doctrine had been practised long before it became an open official policy. It was preached with fire and bayonet in Belgium and France—though there denied at first, by mouth and pen, when the missionaries failed to complete their task of dealing with Paris as they had dealt with Louvain. But even at that time there was, in a distant and obscure part of the world, German East Africa, a German commander, Colonel von Lettow Fordeck, who was openly and energetically reducing the new doctrine fully to practice.

The first British East African campaign, directed from India and badly mismanaged, failed against Lettow Fordeck. The result was that the German commander became the absolute master of a large tract of Equatorial Africa. His prestige over the natives was enhanced by victory, and lines of attack were open to him on the Rhodesian frontier, the Congo State frontier, and the British East Africa frontier. He had an enormous stock of ammunition, thousands of white soldiers, tens of thousands of black troops, and naval guns from the Königsberg. He judged he could never be conquered, and he reckoned the German Empire in Europe would survive all attacks, and that consequently he ran no risk of punishment. Under these conditions the Teuton felt safe in

venting his hatred fully upon the Britons who fell into his hands. British university men, wealthy planters, missionaries, and military prisoners were degraded to the position of slaves, and the treatment of British ladies was barbaric. The ladies had to work as Government serfs for six hours every day, and even elderly and weakly women were threatened with semi-starvation if they objected to perform work of a military nature that directly assisted the enemy.

On one occasion thirty British ladies, with nine Britons and forty natives, were shut in an iron shed for nearly forty-eight hours without any means of sanitation, and for the greater part of the time without even bread and water. Half-drunken guards were set over them, and their sufferings were severe. At other times the British women were deliberately starved, and kept in conditions without decency, when food and separate tents could easily have been obtained. The German Chief of Staff, Captain Willmann, on one occasion gave direct orders that British women were to be kept without food.

The design of the Germans was to destroy the British prestige. To this end, they made both civilian as well as military prisoners perform the lowest kind of work under black foremen. The food provided at one camp was only the waste inferior millet that the blacks would not eat

GERMAN EVIDENCE OF TEUTONIC USE OF THE CROSS.
This irrefragable evidence of Austro-German official crime was found on a German officer killed at Monastir. The scene was Krushevatz, where a village mayor and five other leading local men were hanged, as though in mockery, on cross-formed gallows—merely to intimidate the people of the locality.

and used for beer-making. It produced various kinds of stomach trouble, as it was designed to do, yet proper stores of food were only two hours away. Half-naked British prisoners were set to pull lorries through the streets —work for which the natives were won't to employ oxen— and compelled to clear out the cesspools of native dwellings The natives jeered at the white slaves, who were put on three days' bread and water if they made complaints. The news of the degradation of British men and women was spread for great distances throughout Africa by, of course, German influence.

Major Walter Howard, who was captured by the Germans early in the war, and still a prisoner, sent an account of his treatment through a Russian civilian liberated on parole in November, 1916. Major Howard tried to escape, but after wandering about in the bush for four nights he was found by German native soldiers.

German atrocities in Africa

They all treated him most awfully (wrote the Russian civilian). broke two ribs, smashed his jaw, and he arrived in camp in an unrecognisable state. He was kept confined in cells for many months, with no fresh air, and abused by the white guards as well as by the Askaris. The food we were supplied with was indigestible for healthy constitutions, but poor Major Howard suffered immensely owing to his smashed jaw, as he could not masticate his food. His

At Tabora, where the Rev. Mr. Doulton and the Rev. Mr. Westgate were captured by the Germans, the missionaries were charged with having taught the natives to signal by heliograph. The British native converts were flogged to force them to bear false witness. One native, after receiving one hundred and ten lashes with a hide whip, still held to the truth, and said: "The English have taught us to read and write, and educated us and taught us the things of God. Never anything else." Two converts of the mission lost their courage under the terrible floggings they received, and said they had been taught to signal to the British troops. But a day or

DIGNITY AND IMPUDENCE.
German officers who found fun in jeering at a poor Serbian peasant who had fallen into their power.

military rank was not recognised by the Germans, so he had to work together with the civilians and service men. The work they made us do had only one object—to degrade us in the natives' eyes. In this they succeeded well.

' Most of us had to sleep on the damp ground, and so pressed together were we that we could only take our meals on our beds (dirty grass). In the yard was no shade, and we were supplied with green logs of wood, which we had to chop ourselves. What with the smoke and burning sun above us it was really torture. I can tell you, sir, we looked and felt a miserable lot. We sent to the officer in charge, Major von Orawest, a protest, which Major Howard signed. The next morning he came down in a rage, called us everything bad, and threatened to bring us before a court-martial and have us shot for daring to protest. He stopped us our meat for three days, and we had to live on rice and maize meal. Major Howard wishes you to publish this in influential papers. That is why he begged me to write to you. The slip of paper I enclose is in his own handwriting. He dared not give me more, in case I should be searched and punished. All his diaries have been confiscated, and we dared not have a scrap of paper before a search was made.

Wounded British troops were shot or bayoneted by the Germans in East Africa. The first evidence of this was obtained on September 26th, 1914, when the East Africa Mounted Rifles lost and then recovered the southern slope of the Ingito Hills. Trooper Elliot was shot in the leg, and Lance-Corporal Barridge stood by unarmed to bring him in. The lance-corporal was not seen again, but when the ground was recovered Elliot's body was found with a bullet through his head and a bayonet wound in the neck. Another trooper was found to have been killed by a soft-nosed bullet, and a British Court of Inquiry decided that the Germans were using soft-nosed bullets of the dum-dum type. Mohammedan natives suspected of favouring the British cause were flogged to death or killed in other ways. In some cases their women and young daughters were violated.

Murder of British wounded

DRIVEN FROM HOME BY THE DESTROYING LOCUSTS OF "KULTUR."
Serbian villagers on their way to swell the ranks of refugees from the Kaiser's barbaric emissaries and their fit allies, the Austrians, who had sought by systematic methods to depopulate the country. Few were the possessions left to the peasants of a district into which the Germans penetrated.

two afterwards they, too, stood for the truth, and recanted their enforced and false statement.

In another village a small British column temporarily occupied the country, but was compelled to retire. All the natives were then massacred by the Germans, on the allegation that they had welcomed the British. Colonel von Lettow Fordeck and his Chief of Staff soon established a reign of atrocity over the coloured population, and as the natives saw that the British prisoners were in a state of degraded slavery—cleaning out sewers in the black quarters, pulling carts through the streets, and working under black masters — they lost all faith in British power and justice, and strove to assist the terrifying and victorious Germans. It was not until General Smuts began his enveloping movement around German East Africa that the oppressed black population recovered some independence of character. As in the case of Serbia, the story of Teutonic savagery in German East Africa could only be told after the British and other European prisoners had been released and the lips of the natives unsealed by the complete surrender of the German forces.

There was abundant evidence of Germanic methods of Colonial warfare presented in the Blue Book on German atrocities in Africa, published in July, 1916, and relating mainly to the campaign in Cameroon. The outrages fell, roughly, into six classes. They were: (1) Wholesale murder of natives suspected of favouring the Allies, (2) killing and mutilating wounded soldiers, (3) vile ill-treatment of prisoners of war, (4) employment of expanding bullets, (5) use by German native troops of poisoned arrows, and (6) poisoning of wells. The method pursued against their own subjects by the German authorities was explained by the private secretary to the Governor of Cameroon, Lieutenant von Engelbrechten, in a letter written to another German officer:

There are several cases of Dualas attacking my soldiers and openly helping the British. I have ordered the destruction of all Duala villages. All Dualas met on the road carrying weapons —axes, bows and arrows, and spears, as well as rifles—are to be shot. Prisoners will only be made when they are caught red-handed, and can be legally tried and condemned to death.

Yet all that the British general had then done, in regard to the Dualas and other native tribes, was to employ a few men in British occupied territory as guides. The tribesmen did not help the British, as the Germans alleged, by performing safety and outpost duties, by spying on German movements, or by attacking the Germans. The British general formally protested to the German governor against the manner in which the enemy troops were carrying on the war, but the protest was without effect. Armed bands roved from village to village exterminating the inhabitants. German officers and German privates encouraged their black troops by cutting the throats of wounded British soldiers with knives, shooting down their own non-combatant population, or hanging them, or killing them with axes. The victims in very many cases were women and children who could not flee as fast as the panic-stricken men. Their bodies were often shockingly treated, and the trouble was that this

German barbarism in Cameroon

Germanic method proved, in the case of some tribes, so effective as to increase the ardour and force of the torturers and exterminators.

For some tribesmen accepted the alternative offer made to them and, to escape certain death, attacked the allied forces, using, among other native weapons, poisoned arrows. This was in direct contravention of Article 33 of The Hague Convention, but the German governor and commander had no respect for any customs or conventions of civilised warfare that tended to restrict their striking power. It was only when the Germans in East and West and South-West Africa saw their utter defeat was inevitable that they made an effort to save themselves from reprisals by returning tardily to some of the forms of civilisation. Their attitude throughout was one of consistent barbarism. They gave their demoniacal feelings full play when they thought they could do so without fear of eventual punishment. They afterwards pretended to be the most highly virtuous and chivalrous of warriors when fear of eventual punishment began to weigh upon them. Their character never changed. In their most innocuous guise they were merely cloaking their hellish

Brutality, cowardice, and hypocrisy

SERBIA'S MARTYRDOM: HOSTILE NEIGHBOURS AND HEALERS FROM AFAR.

Troops from Bulgaria—catspaw of the Kaiser—marching through a village in the country which they had invaded. Above: Serbian patients awaiting treatment at a wayside dispensary established by the Stobart Mission. Mrs. Stobart's organisation did wonderful work among the suffering Serbians, and at this dispensary as many as three thousand patients received medical aid and treatment in three months.

COMPULSORY CIVILIAN SERVICE UNDER THE HUNS IN BELGRADE.

Belgrade was the object of several bombardments by the enemy, and when it was captured by them on October 10th, 1915, it had suffered serious damage. The Serbian civilian population of the capital at once became practically the slaves of their conquerors ; and, regardless of any considerations as to class and previous occupation, the inhabitants were set to all kinds of manual labour, including road-mending.

inclinations under a cunning semblance of distressed humanitarianism.

While in Africa the enemy's system of terrorisation was ended or relaxed by the victorious progress of the allied forces, in Europe and Asia it was intensified and extended by the German successes of 1916. And as the Germans reckoned as successes the failure of the Russians to break their front in Galicia and the failure of the Franco-British forces to pierce their line on the Somme, **Atrocities in Europe** their confidence in themselves increased **intensified** as their difficulties augmented. No fear of final defeat checked the Germans, Austrians, Magyars, Bulgars, and Turks in their outrages against humanity. For a while the possibility of the intervention of the United States made the Teutons preserve some vague appearances of legality in their submarine campaign of piracy. Financial considerations in regard to post-bellum commerce were among the chief reasons for the deceptive deference to American opinion.

For the rest, the governing classes of the Central Empires and the larger part of their population were restrained by no fear of consequence from practising practically every atrocity except cannibalism. The German standpoint in the matter was that the war at worst would end in a dead-lock of general exhaustion, and at best in a slow victory by the destruction of British shipping. In either case the Teutons and their allies reckoned that no punishment could be inflicted on them. They therefore harrowed, with diabolical ingenuity, the peoples of the territories they had temporarily conquered. Their conduct was largely based upon the practice of Bismarck, who subjected the northern part of France to methodical ill-treatment in 1870, in the design to make the French public work upon Gambetta and compel him to accept peace on any terms.

In April, 1916, when the attempt to make a sudden break-through at Verdun failed and was succeeded by a slower grinding movement, the German authorities tried to work upon the feelings of the French population by means of the women and girls in the Lille district. In

Holy Week the 64th German Infantry Regiment was released from its fighting work at Verdun and sent, on an order from General Headquarters, to carry out deportations at Lille, Tourcoing, and Roubaix. General von Grävenitz directed the slave-raid ; but the Kaiser with his Chief of Staff and State Chancellor were the deciding authorities in the matter. The industrial region in and around Lille was the richest part of occupied France and the most densely peopled. It was selected as the theatre for the crowning atrocity for the reason that the sufferings inflicted would cause the largest amount of anguish in France.

The German authorities began by issuing an appeal for volunteers to labour for them. As was foreseen, few Frenchmen were willing to work for the enemy and against their own country. Thereupon, the following order was issued and posted on the walls of Lille, on Tuesday, April 18th, 1916 :

All the inhabitants of the house, with the exception of children below fourteen years of age and their mothers and old men, must be ready to be transported within an hour and a half. An officer will finally decide who is going to be taken to the concentration camp. The inhabitants of the house, therefore, must gather in front of their domicile. In case of bad weather they will be allowed to remain in the passage. The door of the house must remain open. All appeals will be useless. No inhabitant, even those who will not be deported, will be allowed to leave his home before eight in the morning (German **The deportations** time). Everyone will have a right to twenty-seven pounds of luggage. If there is any excess **from Lille** weight, everything belonging to that person will be refused without ceremony. The baggage must be separate for each person, and must have a label clearly written and firmly fixed. The address will give surname and Christian name and the number of the identity card. It is absolutely necessary in your own interest to take utensils for eating and drinking, as well as a blanket, good shoes, and linen. Everyone must have his identity card. Anybody trying to escape deportation will be mercilessly punished.

ETAPPEN, KOMMANDATUR.

The townspeople had been prepared for some such action as this. Since the end of March there had been a series of small raids. Tramcars, for instance, would be stopped by a detachment of troops, and three or four of the best-

468

looking girls or able-bodied men would be ordered out, and marched off to unknown destinations. The bishop and the municipal authorities had vainly protested against these small, desultory raids. They arranged a meeting of protest, but while the meeting was being held the general notices were posted on the houses, and three thousand more troops detrained in the city under the direction of General von Grävenitz. At the ends of the streets and at cross-roads machine-gun sections were installed, while the churches were crowded with despairing congregations. Good Friday was spent in prayer by the people and in military preparations by the slave-drivers.

Horrors in Holy Week

Then between midnight and dawn on Saturday the Fives district was attacked. Patrols of ten to fifteen men battered with their bayoneted rifles on the doors of the houses, and ordered the dwellers into the street.

Outside each house hung a list of the occupiers, and after these had been all checked by name, an officer and a non-commissioned officer selected those doomed to slavery, and gave them variously from ten minutes to ninety minutes to take leave of their families.

Terrible scenes of grief and sorrow occurred. In some cases elderly women went mad when their daughters were torn from them. A maddened woman, who lost husband, son, and daughter, turned upon the German soldiers and invoked curses upon their wives, daughters, and race. One woman broke into a sweat of blood when her only child was taken, and after the boy was brought back she could not recognise him, having completely lost her reason. Had entire families been taken the strain would not have been so great, as they would at least have had companionship in suffering. But by a refinement in cruelty each family was broken up; some members going away to an unknown place and other members being left to mourn them and vaguely imagine what had become of them. Twenty-five thousand persons of both sexes, between the ages of sixteen and sixty-five, were torn from their homes and forced to work—or do something far worse than work—for the enemy.

For many good-looking girls and women of all classes were examined by German doctors and then condemned, when found perfectly healthy, to the most awful fate. What happened to them had to be published, in order that the British people might loyally assist the French and Belgian people when the day of retribution should break over

GROSS TRAVESTY OF THE NAME OF FREEDOM: GERMAN TYRANNY IN "LIBERATED" POLAND.
The Polish village children were dragooned and given compulsory lessons in the German language. Above: Hoping to bribe the Poles to fight for them, the Germans proclaimed the "Independence" of Poland; but immediately they occupied the Russian provinces they sent a million Poles into Prussia as slaves, and employed the remaining males, under Landsturm guard, to gather in what crops were left, for the Germans' benefit.

WEAPON EMPLOYED BY THE CIVILISED TWENTIETH-CENTURY TEUTON.
[Italian official photograph.
Type of club found on several Austrian soldiers taken prisoner on the Italian front.   These weapons, suggestive of culture at the stage of cannibalism, had been distributed officially by the Austrian Command.

Germany. After the French girls and women had been medically examined and had passed the test for venereal disease, they were given over to the German soldiery to be used as prostitutes. In plain English, the Kaiser and his Chief of Staff and State Chancellor organised a system of official brothels, and filled these brothels with virtuous French women and girls of all classes of society. In the Scriptural record of the sufferings of the Israelites under the Assyrians there is no such refinement of atrocity recorded. The Assyrian soldiery was no doubt as brutal to women as the German soldiery; but the Assyrian Government did not stoop to systematise violation as did the Christian Government of Germany. Since the distant age of Assyrian deportations the ideal of chastity had been peculiarly strengthened and refined by the long development of Christian civilisation. The French race was eminent for its sense of honour, and the diabolical design of

Organised victimisation of women

the German Government was to torture the entire French nation into submission, by a state-organised attack upon the honour of its virgins and married women. It will be remembered that this attack took place at a time when the best French forces seemed to be wasting away at Verdun, while the British Army seemed to be standing idly between the Yser and the Somme. In these circumstances the enemy hoped to break completely the spirit of the French people by a most horrible campaign of a systematic kind upon the honour and integrity of a highly-strung race.

The other deeds that occurred during the great slave-drives in the spring and winter of 1916 were terrible and yet not so important. Thousands of deportees were starved, beaten, and hung up on trees, with a view to forcing them to work, often being finally murdered. Some were set to labour in the trenches, where they were exposed to the fire of British and French artillery. We cannot measure the extent of the sufferings inflicted upon the enslaved population; but knowing how strong is the spirit of the French democracy and how severe must be the strain under which the French would break down and submit to work as slaves against their own people, we can believe that, could the full secrets of Westphalian mines and Rhine quarries and German railways and fortified lines be revealed, such records of utter human misery would be disclosed as would remain memorable for thousands of years. But above all this welter of bodily pain and mental anguish there will stand, branded in flame upon the entire German people, the history

of the French girls and women who were medically examined and sent away to an unknown destination.

While transforming the occupied territories of France into the scenes of deepest misery that ever overtook her life, the Germans turned upon Belgium and there instituted the same systematic atrocities. After having violated the neutrality of Belgium, murdered more than five thousand men, women, and children, and destroyed twenty-six thousand houses, the Germans reduced the country to ruin and starvation, and then completed their work by carrying the Belgians into slavery. This was not the act of a Government desperately struggling against defeat and wildly casting aside the last vestiges of Christianity and civilisation. It was the act of conquerors, confident of eventual victory and preparing for the

Preparing for a German peace

conditions of a European peace of their own making. Behind the deportations was a policy of spoliation and ruin, carried out with cunning foresight and hard thoroughness, with a view to increasing the economic strength of Germany after the war.

From the beginning of the German occupation the Belgians were plundered by a system of requisitions, confiscations, and seizures that left them famishing and unemployed. Three million German soldiers were fed from Belgium and Northern France, consuming, among other things, nearly half the total quantity of meat eaten in Germany in peace-time. That is to say, Germany saved half her meat supplies by robbing the non-combatant populations of Belgium and Northern France of their food. Then under the direction of Dr. Walther Rathenau, of the General Electric Company, metals, textile products, chemicals, and all materials of direct or indirect military value were collected and sent into Germany if they could not be used on the spot by the German forces. By February, 1915, the Germans had drained from Belgium and Northern France produce and material of the value of £100,000,000. Such was the figure

---

TOMBES
DES
Soldats Français & Anglais

Jusqu'à maintenant j'ai toléré que des petits drapeaux aux couleurs nationales soient placés sur les tombes des soldats français et anglais.

Ma tolérance a été remerciée de la façon suivante. Il y a quelques jours on a placé d'une manière provoquante et sans goût un drapeau tricolore de trois mètres de hauteur sur les tombes des soldats.

J'ai puni les coupables ainsi que le conservateur du cimetière de peines d'emprisonnement et j'ordonne :

Il est interdit de placer sur les tombes des soldats des objets quelconques aux couleurs nationales des puissances alliées contre l'Allemagne, par exemple des drapeaux, des rubans, des cocardes, etc.

Les objets désignés ci-dessus se trouvant encore sur les tombes doivent être enlevés par la police.

Tout contrevenant sera sévèrement puni.

Roubaix, le 24 Mars 1915.

Commandanture de l'Étape.
HOFMANN
Major et Commandant.

Nᵒ 75.

"It is forbidden to place on soldiers' graves anything displaying the colours of Powers allied against Germany—flags, ribbons, cockades, etc."

AVIS

L'Autorité Militaire Allemande a fait fusiller, aujourd'hui, à Hénin-Liétard, deux Officiers Français, les nommés :

Paul THÉRY & Eric BEUTOM

qui, cachés pendant plusieurs semaines à Douai, déguisés en femmes, ont essayé de franchir les lignes allemandes.

Le Gouvernement Militaire Allemand se voit forcé d'attirer, une fois de plus, l'attention du public sur l'article VI. de la Proclamation qui est ainsi conçu :

Tout Officier ou Soldat ennemi rencontré sur le théâtre des opérations ou en arrière des troupes allemandes, ayant quitté son uniforme et revêtu des habits civils, sera considéré comme espion et traité comme tel. La personne qui aura fourni lesdits habits ainsi que les personnes qui, ayant connu le fait, n'auront pas avisé les Autorités Militaires, seront punies comme complices.

Cet article ne sera cependant pas appliqué aux personnes qui, ayant eu connaissance d'un fait dont il est fait mention dans l'article précité, en auront informé l'Autorité Militaire Allemande, jusqu'au Samedi 16 Janvier 1915.

Le 7 Janvier 1915.   **Le Général Commandant l'Armée.**

"The German military authorities have shot two French officers, Paul Théry and Eric Beutom, for trying to pass the German lines disguised."

GERMAN PROCLAMATIONS POSTED IN OCCUPIED FRENCH TOWNS.

given by Dr. Ludwig Ganghofer, a second-rate German poet acting as Royal war correspondent to the Kaiser. In his book entitled, "Travels on the German Front," Ganghofer explained that " an economic war was being waged upon the conquered territories which was leading to the exhaustion of their manufacturing and financial resources." The design was to remove Belgium and Northern France from the list of competitors with German industries, and so to cripple their powers of recovery that they would not be able to enter the markets of the world for a decade after peace was declared. Plants were taken to pieces and distributed among the German munition factories. Then, when the workless Belgians were being kept alive by the American Commission, they were charged with the crime of being unemployed, and requested to volunteer for work in Germany.

STONE-AGE WEAPONS ADAPTED TO MODERN AUSTRIAN USE.
Another of the iron-headed, nail-studded batons issued by the Austrian Government to its soldiers. Many primitive weapons were reintroduced in the Great War, but this was one of the most brutal.

The stagnation of work and industry was complete. Masters and selling agents could not use the Belgian telephone and telegraph systems ; the goods traffic was stopped ; no motor-vehicles were available ; the banks practically stopped payment, and the land could not be cultivated because the enemy had taken the farming horses. By the summer of 1915 one-fourth of the total population of Belgium was without work and without means of living. This was exactly the state of things which the Germans had aimed at producing, and in the name of humanity they offered the Belgians work to keep them alive. In some cases the wages promised were very high, amounting to two pounds a day. But all the work was of a direct or indirect military nature, so that if the Belgians undertook it they would be helping to kill their own countrymen or the allied soldiers trying to liberate them. In these circumstances the Belgians refused the offer, and entered upon a silent, terrible struggle known as " the war with folded arms." They folded their arms and walked out of railway yards, mines, and war factories. The practical effect was that of a great national strike.

The " war with folded arms "

But in April, 1915, the Germans began against the Belgian railwaymen a system of slave-raids that became of general scope as the war went on.

The Belgian workmen were imprisoned and starved, but, despite their sufferings, they could not be cowed to submission. In October, 1915, the Belgian communal authorities were menaced by military proclamations, and were charged with creating difficulties for the German Army. At this time it is estimated that only ten thousand Belgians had been driven by hunger or fear for their families to accept work in German factories. Again Belgium was ransacked of all her remaining material and produce, in order to prevent the communes finding from one to two days' work a week for their unemployed. The communes in Belgian Luxemburg, for instance, drained a quarter of a million acres of marsh, and laid more than six hundred miles of railway track opening up agricultural districts, in order to keep their men at work and lay the foundation of a larger prosperity when peace came. But these far-reaching plans of agricultural development were directly adverse to the German design for permanently weakening the country. Communal work was more dangerous to Germany than private work would have been ; therefore, the slave-drives were organised in a larger way. On May 2nd, 1916, under the direction of General von Bissing, orders were given for all men who seemed to be unemployed to be brought before military tribunals, and if found guilty of having no work to do, the unemployed were " to be conducted by force to the spots where they have to work."

Slavery instituted in Belgium

This decree instituted the general system of slavery in Belgium. Instead of sporadic raids on yards and factories, where highly-trained men could be found, a methodical sweep through the country was laboriously planned and executed. The general deportations began in East and West Flanders, where every person who relied on municipal assistance or public charity was summoned to work for the German authorities under a penalty of three months' imprisonment and £500 fine. This decree was issued on October 3rd, 1916, by Quartermaster-General von Sauderzweig, who was, by the way, the officer directly responsible for the execution of Miss Cavell.

Thereupon, as has already been related by Mr. F. A. McKenzie in Chapter CLVI., the Belgians were carried off into slavery to the number of at least a hundred and fifty thousand men. No real distinction was made

---

VILLE DE CHARLEROI

POLICE

Bâtiments incendiés

Toute personne non régulièrement autorisée qui sera trouvée dans les ruines des maisons incendiées, risque d'être **immédiatement FUSILLÉE**

Des autorisations pourront être accordées aux propriétaires ou à leurs délégués par le Bourgmestre.

Charleroi, le 21 Août 1914.

Le Bourgmestre,
E. DEVREUX

" Any persons who are not officially authorised found in the ruins of burned houses risk being immediately shot." An order posted in Charleroi.

AVIS IMPORTANT !

Le mineur **PAUL BUSIÈRE**, de Liévin, a été fusillé le 23 août, en vertu d'un arrêt du Conseil de Guerre, pour avoir recélé des pigeons voyageurs.

En cette circonstance le Général Commandant l'Armée rappelle à la population civile que :

I.—Toute personne qui détiendra ou recèlera des pigeons ou pigeons voyageurs sera punie de mort.

II.—De la même peine sera passible toute personne qui, ayant trouvé des pigeons voyageurs ou des objets, correspondances ou écritures de n'importe quel genre jetés par un aviateur, les gardera ou les cachera, au lieu de les remettre immédiatement entre les mains du Commandant de place allemand le plus proche.

III.—Dans le cas où des circonstances atténuantes seraient admises, la peine des travaux forcés à perpétuité ou de dix à quinze ans sera appliquée.

IV.—Toute tentative, provocation ou complicité seront suivies des mêmes pénalités.

Le 1er septembre 1915.

Le Général Commandant l'Armée.

" Paul Busiere, miner of Liévin, was shot by order of court-martial for having concealed carrier-pigeons in his possession."

SOME CAPITAL CRIMES UNDER GERMAN CIVILISATION.

between employed and unemployed, except that men of liberal professions were generally, but not always, exempted. What Germany needed were skilled labourers and skilled mechanics of every kind capable of doing work that would release able-bodied Germans by the hundred thousand for the Army. No pity was shown in the selection of the slaves. Fathers of large families were carried off, with the sons of widows and the husbands of women who died during the raid and were unburied. Many deportees were formed into " Civil Working Companies " and set, under the bayonets of the German soldiery, to labour in the German lines in France, making roads, building trenches and machine-gun positions, and constructing new military railways and aviation grounds. Others were sent across the frontier into German mines, iron-works, zinc factories, lime-kilns, and quarries. There they were underfed and ill-treated in a manner in which no enlightened slave-owner would have treated his slaves. An ordinary slave-owner must, in his own selfish interests, see that his human cattle are kept fit enough to continue to work well. But the design of the German murderers of nations was to annihilate the human industrial energy of Belgium and Northern France, so that, in the absence of both labour and material, the economic reconstruction of the countries should be **Prussian slavery** impossible of achievement for at least **in Poland** a generation. Long before the Belgian and French factories were brought back to full productiveness the Germans hoped to have captured all available markets.

In regard to Russian Poland, of which the Teutons pretended to be the redeemers, the same methods of " economic war " were adopted. In the first place, the invading armies were quartered on the country-side and fed upon the meat and corn, causing extreme distress to the people. Then the factories were closed, and much of the machinery and practically all the stocks were requisitioned, and either used by the invaders in Poland or despatched into Germany. The people were left without means of communication and traffic, and, like the Belgians, were forced into a condition of famishing idleness. When it was calculated that their spirit had been broken, they

THE HIGH PRIEST OF FRIGHTFULNESS, HIS CHIEF APOSTLE, AND SOME OTHERS.
The Kaiser, high priest of frightfulness, talking to Von Hindenburg, whose assumption of the military dictatorship was the sign for a renewed outbreak of " ruthless " war on sea and land. The Kaiser's wife, his brother, and his brother's wife are in the background. Above: Von Hindenburg talking to the egregious Crown Prince, assuredly the least martial prince who ever drove soldiers to the slaughter by the hundred thousand.

were asked to volunteer to work for the invaders, who had redeemed them from Russian oppression. A Teutonic party was formed among the Polish gentry, by the influence of some Austrian-Poles, and the people were promised that the ancient kingdom of Poland would be reconstituted by the kind-hearted Teutons if only they would work for their liberators until the glorious peace was made.

But at the time when Hindenburg and Mackensen were "liberating" Poland by ruining and starving it, a considerable part of the Polish people was already kept in Prussian slavery. Before the war about a million Poles used to migrate into Germany every year, and work from winter to harvest in the fields and mines. When war was declared there remained some three hundred and fifty thousand of these migrant men, women, girls, and lads on the estates of the great Prussian landowners. They were detained by the order of the military authorities and reduced to the position of slaves. If they crossed the boundary of the parish in which they were held they were subjected to imprisonment up to twelve months, and all money they possessed was taken from them. The same penalties were inflicted if they refused to work for the Prussian magnates. After the conquest of Po.and, Lithuania, and Courland, the originally large number of agricultural serfs was enormously increased, to allow the Prussian landowners both to work their estates more cheaply and to liberate more men for the Army.

By the autumn of 1916 the remnants of the rural population of the occupied Russian provinces were living on the scanty root vegetables, onions, and turnips remaining in their fields. No peasant had any wheat or potatoes,

BELGIAN DEPORTATIONS: A PULPIT PROTEST WHILE UNDER GUARD.
Priest reading Cardinal Mercier's emphatic protest against the deportation of Belgian workmen to Germany. Even in their churches the Belgians were made to feel the mailed fist of the invader, as is shown by the German soldier standing in grim watchfulness with fixed bayonet by the pulpit stairs.

and tuberculosis and strange starvation diseases sapped what strength in the nation the Teutons had left. Amid this black misery great man-hunts and slave-drives began, on a scale surpassing that of the Belgian deportations. At least a million men were forcibly driven across the frontier to work in mines and munition factories, or to swell the slave-gangs of the Prussian landowners. It is estimated that only eighty thousand men volunteered for

Lure of lying promises

work in Germany under the lure of lying promises. Some of these volunteers were killed by the hardships, and in spite of the censorship on all their messages to their countrymen, the truth about their condition spread through the fields and towns. Nothing then could revive the faith of any Pole in his redeemers. The proclamation of a kingdom of Poland, which was not to include Prussian and Austrian Poland, confirmed the tortured and perishing race in its attitude of passive resistance. Poles refused either to join the new Polish army or to work in their enemy's factories. In Warsaw, for instance, scarcely more

than fourteen hundred volunteers, including Polish-Jews as well as true Poles and Lithuanians, were so spiritually broken down by utter misery as to offer to work or to fight for the invaders.

In these circumstances the Courts of Blood and the slave-hunting forces organised a general system for the destruction and dispersion of the populations of Poland, Lithuania, and Courland. The Courts of Blood were military tribunals with firing-parties attached. Any man who seemed to have the gift of leadership and appeared to be helping to maintain the general spirit of resistance was brought before some Court of Blood, charged with communicating with the enemy, and shot. Thousands of men were thus murdered who often were antagonistic to Russia rather than favourable to her. Their real crime was that they were Poles of independent courage, who laboured for justice to their own race, and thereby hindered the designs of the Teutons.

On Sundays churches were surrounded by German troops, and as the men came out they were collected at

MEN OF THE GALLANT RUMANIAN ARMY THAT SOUGHT TO STAY THE RUTHLESS INVADER.

Group of Rumanian soldiers with a petty-officer of the R.N.A.S. Armoured Cars, which did good service in delaying the further German advance after the fall of Bukarest. The Rumanian Army, heroically as it fought to keep off invaders who had gained so unenviable a fame for behaving like barbarians, was not fitted for withstanding the mass of men and material which the Central Powers had been able to concentrate against it.

the bayonet point and marched to the nearest station, crowded into cattle and goods trucks, and sent under guard to Germany. In the industrial districts the working quarters were usually surrounded at night, and the strongest men and women selected from the houses and placed upon the railway.

There is, unfortunately, reason for supposing that in the winter of 1916 many good-looking Polish girls were not sent to munition factories or agricultural estates, but were medically examined, like the girls of Lille, and reserved for German officers. When this happened the Poles—in Wola, for instance—were already known to be eating their dogs.

The winter was terribly severe, coal was not to be had in the cities, and flour, meat, and potatoes had gone with a large part of the adult population into Germany. The general

Mockery of a free kingdom

misery was such as no civilised people would dare to impose upon its worst criminals. Yet the German and Austrian Emperors, with their principal Ministers, still proclaimed to the world that they had liberated Poland and were making her a free kingdom. The infernal mockery was without parallel in the history of mankind. Poland had more title to fair treatment than even Belgium or Luxemburg had ; for she was not even a neutral State that had stood in the path of the conquerors, but a redeemed country, which they professed to be ready to erect into a buffer territory between the Central Empires and the Russian Empire.

Even from a self-enlightened military point of view the Teutons would have done well to treat the Poles with some consideration, by way of lending colour to their claim to be their liberators. Thereby they might have inflicted great

474

moral damage upon the reactionary party in the Russian bureaucracy, which had prevented the Tsar's proclamation of Polish freedom from being partly carried out in the early phase of the war. But the Teutons were too stupidly atrocious to put on a semblance of humanity in order to win over the discontented Poles. **Stupidity in** They were too greedy for plunder in the **atrocity** first place, and afterwards, when they had stripped Poland bare, they saw no way of retrieving the error they had made except by proceeding to enslave a nation of twelve million people, and wearing it down to death by over-labour, under-feeding, and bodily and mental suffering.

It was, for example, credibly reported that the Poles transported to Weimar and set to forced labour there were paid ninepence a day in the case of men and sixpence a day in the case of women. On these wages they were supposed to feed and clothe themselves. But having regard to the cost of food in Germany in the winter of 1916, sixpence or ninepence a day was not sufficient to buy the means of life. Dutch workers who made £6 a week could not purchase enough food to keep up their strength. What, then, must have been the condition of Polish women who earned 3s. 6d. a week !

But sad as was the condition of the Polish civilian slaves, that of the one million Russian prisoners of war was still worse. In some cases the Russians were harnessed to the plough, together with oxen, and put into the shafts of heavy waggons and made to drag enormous loads. The slightest disobedience was punished in the hardest manner possible, though the apparent slackness was often due to ignorance of the German language. The Russians were put on bread and water, beaten, or lashed by arms and legs to posts for a couple of hours. Their arms and legs were at times put out of joint by this form of crucifixion.

Cossack prisoners, according to the report issued by a Commission of the Russian State Duma, were singled out in internment camps for savage tortures. In some cases the ingenious Germans used strong electric shocks upon Cossacks, after binding them so that they could not move. In other instances the older method of red-hot irons was employed. The Commission traced in detail eighteen cases of burning. No doubt it was because the Germans dreaded the Cossacks more than any other class of Russian soldiers that they more frequently tortured, starved, and hanged them.

British prisoners of war were regarded in somewhat the same way as the Cossacks. The Germans feared the British, and while they were confident they could either win or end the war in a deadlock, they did all they safely could to vent their hatred upon their prisoners of war. In this connection we need not go over the ground already covered in previous chapters. But to continue the record of the things we must specially keep in mind, reference must be made to the later revelations of the horrors of the typhus camps.

On October 24th, 1916, the Committee on the Treatment of British Prisoners of War issued a report upon the camp of Gardelegen. This report was a sequel to the dreadful history of the horrors of Wittenberg Camp, related in April, 1916. In both camps there was a preliminary overcrowding that was probably intentional. At Wittenberg some sixteen thousand prisoners were restricted to ten and a half acres, and kept without proper fuel. At Gardelegen fourteen thousand prisoners were packed into a space measuring three hundred and fifty yards by five hundred and fifty yards. Major P. T. C. Davy, R.A.M.C., who was transferred to the camp just before the epidemic broke out, states :

Horrors at Gardelegen Camp

> The overcrowding was such as I have never before seen or imagined anywhere. The hut contained in the breadth four rows of straw or shaving palliasses, so arranged that laterally they were touching, and only terminally left the narrowest passage-way between. Here men of all nationalities were crowded together. In these huts, devoid of tables and stools, the men lived, slept, and fed. They sat on their bags of shavings to eat their meals ; they walked over each other in passing in and out ; they lay there sick, and, later on, in many cases, died there cheek by jowl with their fellow-prisoners. The atmosphere by day, and still more by night, was indescribably fetid, and this was their sole alternative to going outside in their meagre garments for fresh air.
> I have no hesitation in saying that the diet the prisoners received was not sufficient to keep an adult in a normal state of nutrition. I mean that every man who subsisted on what was issued to him was gradually getting emaciated and anæmic, and was constantly a prey to the pangs of hunger.

Had the German bacteriologists arranged a massacre in the latest scientific manner they could not have improved upon the conditions their military and medical authorities established in the camps. Tens of thousands of prisoners were starved to a condition of extreme weakness in the winter of 1914, when there was no lack of food in Germany. Most of them had their greatcoats taken from them, and though their clothes were so worn that they shivered with the cold, the German authorities would not serve out the new kit that was available. Proper fuel was not provided, and there was only one stand-pipe at Gardelegen for twelve hundred men to wash by, without soap. Most of the men were therefore unable to wash, and the result was that every man was infected with body vermin, swarming in every garment he wore and in every blanket he slept in.

Everybody acquainted with the part that body vermin plays in communicating disease must strongly incline to the judgment that the event that happened was subtly and skilfully designed. A few prisoners suffering from typhus were introduced into the crowded camps, and the lice spread the infection as thoroughly as if each man had been bound and pierced with a hypodermic needle containing the living deadly germ. The only difference between the two methods is that the one the Germans adopted is the more natural and far the easier to carry out on a large scale. While the plague was just beginning to spread the German guards created a reign of terror and brutality. According to the evidence of Major Davy :

Deliberate introduction of typhus

> At the daily roll-call parades men were driven out of their barrack rooms with kicks and blows. The German under-officers were the chief offenders. The German officers, of whom one was in command in each company, were mostly elderly men, who seemed quite in the hands of their under-officers. I never once saw one check an under-officer for the most flagrant bullying.

The Germans clearly knew what was coming at this time, February 11th, 1915. For they brought two British medical officers to the camp, with a small band of French and Russian doctors, in order to release and save their

DURING THE RETREAT OF THE RUMANIAN ARMY ALONG THE DANUBE.
Rumanian soldiers at a point on the Lower Danube. After the united forces of the Central Powers from Transylvania and the Dobruja had swept through Wallachia, and Bukarest had fallen, the Rumanian Army fell back for re-forming on a new defensive line. Above : Two members of the Scottish Women's Field Hospital on the quay at Braila. Their admirable organisation did splendid work in Serbia and Rumania.

own men. Two months previously all the German staff at Wittenberg had left the camp, both military and medical men fleeing and abandoning the sixteen thousand prisoners to their fate. Gardelegen Camp was abandoned in the same manner in February, 1915. The German guards packed and departed ; the German medical officers went ; and in both camps communication with the prisoners was only maintained by orders shouted through the barbed-wire. The insufficient supplies of food and stores were passed in on trollies, worked by winches at either end.

The German guards formed cordons outside the camps, and shot down any men who tried to escape from the plague centres. With the guards were dogs to assist in raising the alarm if any prisoner got through the barbed-wire. No milk, no eggs, or other invalid fare was provided at Gardelegen ; and, though half a cup of milk a day was provided at Wittenberg during the first month, neither camp received the simple drugs it needed, nor any surgical dressings or hospital clothing. Gangrene was common, owing to the fact that many patients lacked the clothing to keep themselves warm. Day after day at Wittenberg a list of medical requisites was sent out, but only a third of the things requested was supplied. At Gardelegen, Major Davy and Dr. Saint Hilaire, the senior allied medical officers, vainly asked for drugs, milk and eggs, and other medical necessities. The German commandant would do nothing. When a new German medical officer appeared the only answer he made to Major Davy's entreaties was to storm at him across the barbed-wire for not saluting properly.

The evident intention was to allow the camps to cleanse themselves of the plague as quickly as the typhus germs could work. The food for the stricken men was acorn coffee and potato bread, potato soup, horse beans, a very little margarine, with sometimes a smell of meat and some-times no meat at all. One kilogramme of bread was the daily ration for ten men, which amounted to less than one-fifth of a pound each. It largely consisted of potato-flour, of low nutritive value, with other inferior ingredients that made it unpalatable. A small quantity of this black bread, with a midday meal of thin potato soup, one raw herring a week, and some thin soup at evening, in which most days the men could not find a trace of meat, formed the diet of thousands of men in an acute and deadly illness.

Some milk was at last obtained at Gardelegen by paying a German non-commissioned officer a commission to induce him to purchase it at the cost of the **Heroic British and** British and French doctors. As these **French doctors** officers lacked gloves and gowns, where-with to safeguard themselves while treating the typhus patients, many of them died, with their orderlies, in nobly trying to fight the disease. This again was no doubt the event the German authorities, when they refused medical supplies, intended to bring about. They desired to see practically all the prisoners of war slain by the pestilence.

The dying men had no beds. They had to lie mostly on piles of shavings or straw mattresses on the ground, while vermin swarmed over them. There they were often soaked and soiled with their own fæcal matter. A Zola could not fully describe the horrors of the scenes in the plague camps. The Black Hole of Calcutta was hot and airless, while at Wittenberg and Gardelegen ice gathered on the dying men, as there were neither bed-pans nor paper for sanitary purposes. The stench, the masses of vermin, the condition of men in delirium, lying in some places packed together on the floor, the dead with the dying, made a spectacle more appalling than that which the barbaric Asiatics created in Calcutta.

Once, at Wittenberg, during the course **The infamous** of the plague, a single German doctor **Dr. Aschenbach** entered the camp. His memorable name was Aschenbach, and he came attired in a complete suit of protective clothing, including an antiseptic mask and rubber gloves. As a reward for his brief and rapid visit he was given the Iron Cross. Yet for months after his inspection the camp continued to be starved of the bare necessities of existence and of the simplest drugs and surgical dressings for the patients' wounds. The answer given by Dr. Aschenbach in person, when asked for only one medical requisite that was urgently required, was, " Schweine Engländer ! "—" You Eng-lish swine ! " Clearly, he was doing all in his power to accelerate the death of the " English swine," and his single visit of inspection was made only to see how the pestilence was spread-ing. Another German doctor, who also entered the camp with great precaution, came to obtain a culture of the typhus germ, to make a vaccine for some German guards, who had caught the disease through selling the prisoners goods across the wire entanglement.

At Wittenberg the German military doctors never en-tered the camp. But in March, 1915, a civilian medical officer, Dr. Kranski, who had been deported from Egypt at the beginning of the war, appeared outside the wire entanglements and did all he could to help. But

BRITISH AND RUSSIAN OFFICERS IN RUMANIA.
Two officers of the R.N.A.S. Armoured Cars with a Russian comrade at a Danube-side station. The figure on the extreme left is one of the Rumanian refugees who were driven from their homes by the invaders.

though he tried to get drugs and dressings, his military superiors prevented him from obtaining them. In April, 1915, Dr. Ohnesorg, of the American Embassy at Berlin, came to the outside of the camp and told one of the British officers there, through the wire entanglements, how favourably impressed he was with the store of meat provided for the patients. The British officer exclaimed there was no meat. It then appeared that the German authorities had exhibited carcases of mutton outside the camp and had carted them back to the town after the American doctor had been impressed by the cunning display. Not a scrap of the meat was sent inside the camp.

By the heroism and devotion of the allied doctors and orderlies the plague was gradually fought down in all the typhus camps by the autumn of 1915. But, terrible to say, at both Wittenberg and Gardelegen the multitudes of prisoners showed more signs of happiness during the pestilence than before the outbreak. For when the German guards and officers fled and abandoned them to their fate, the prisoners, on the evidence of the allied medical men who afterwards saved them, felt a positive relief.

They had been flogged with whips, terrorised by savage dogs, crucified to posts, and continually struck without provocation. Therefore, many of the men looked upon the typhus, with all its horrors, as a godsend. They preferred it to the presence of the German guards. This statement, made by Captain Lauder, R.A.M.C., in regard to Wittenberg Camp, and confirmed by Major Davy in regard to the Gardelegen Camp, tells more than volumes of details could of the methods used by the Germans with regard to British, Belgian, French, and Russian prisoners of war. It consummates the record of atrocities committed on captive soldiers and contained in our earlier chapters.

Turkish barbarism in the Hauran The typhus method of torture and death, which the Germans invented, was afterwards employed by the Turks, under German and Austrian supervision, with a view to exterminating the Syrian and Arab population of the wheat-growing district of the Hauran. The Hauran lies between Jerusalem and Damascus, and was peopled by a mingled race of strong character, upon which the Ottoman yoke sat lightly. The mountainous nature of the country, flanked by the great Syrian Desert, made military operations difficult. But in the autumn of 1916 the Turks and their Teutonic helpers formed a military cordon around that part of the Hauran which was not dominated by the Syrian railway line. Then, among the besieged people, they introduced hundreds of typhus-carriers in the form of Armenian and other prisoners, who had been specially infected in prison, in order to transform them into plague weapons against the independent part of the Syrian population.

In the early period of the war the atrocities in Syria were so shocking to the conscience of the Moslem race as to lead the Arabs of Mecca to revolt against the Ottoman rule. The murder of many Syrian notables set Arabia on fire, with the result that the Young Turks lost all control of the Holy Places of Islam, and became, in spite of their military strength, the practical outcasts of the Moslem world. They lost influence in Afghanistan and in the wilder parts of Mohammedan Africa, and the plan of a Holy War, which they had made in conjunction with the Teutons, utterly failed of effect. By their policy of racial extermination the Ottomans defeated themselves by completely exhausting their religious influence as wielders of the power of the Caliphate.

The full story of the extermination of the Armenians by the order of the Ottoman Government has been told in a large volume of evidence collected by Lord Bryce, edited by Mr. A. J. Toynbee, and presented to Parliament in the middle of December, 1916. The larger part of the evidence was obtained from neutral witnesses residing or travelling in Asiatic Turkey while the events were happening. Another part of the evidence was obtained from natives of the country, and the last part was derived from Germans residing in Turkey and watching the massacres.

The design of the Turks was to kill at least one million Armenian men, women, and children, in order to repeople the country in accordance with a Pan-Ottoman policy. This Pan-Ottoman policy was also directed against the Syrians and many Arabs, all of these being fellow-believers with the Turks. The policy was thus of a political and racial character, being intended to spread the Turkish race by the complete depopulation of fertile territories held by the subject races of the Ottoman Empire. The Armenians were first attacked by the atheistical leaders of the Committee of Union and Progress, not because they were Christians, but because they were a **Extermination of the Armenians** subject race occupying rich territory, holding a great trade route, and in danger of being liberated by the Russian Army of the Caucasus.

The principal massacres began on April 8th, 1915. In each town or village the public crier went through the streets, announcing that every Armenian must present himself at once at the Government building. The men came in their working clothes, leaving their shops and work-rooms open, their ploughs in the fields, and their cattle on the hillside. Without explanation they were thrown into prison, then roped man to man, and marched out and halted at the first lonely place on the road. There

WRETCHED PLIGHT OF RUMANIAN REFUGEES BEFORE THE INVADERS.
Rumanian refugees leaving their homes before the advancing tide of German invasion. The sinister reputation of the Teutons made flight—even by roads ankle-deep in mud—the only course for people in any threatened district, and the consequent misery of the populace was terrible.
HHH

they were butchered. After an interval of a few days the public crier called upon the Armenian women and children to come to the Government building. In droves, varying in size from two hundred to four thousand, the women and children, with the old and sick, were marched along mule-tracks towards the places where the Kurds were waiting for them. On the way the guards violated any woman or girl they pleased, and any Moslem of the country-side was allowed to take what slaves or concubines he wished.

At last the Kurds met the convoys, and the great butchery began. The old men and boys were slain, together with the women the Kurds did not care to carry away. If the women selected as slaves were carrying

LIKELY TO GET A SHORT SHRIFT.
Serbian peasants, suspected of espionage, before the German Headquarters. An order of the High Command said of the Serbian peasants: "These people are to be executed if they appear even slightly suspicious."

babies, the infants were either left on the ground or dashed against stones. Many of the massacres were consummated by the Euphrates, where women and children were driven into the water, and shot if they seemed likely to be able to swim to the farther bank. In the Van district there were no pretences at deportations. The work was done by wholesale massacre on the spot. At Trebizond the Armenians were either drowned at sea or cut down at the first resting-place on the road. Altogether six hundred thousand Armenian men, women, and children were massacred. Another six hundred thousand seemed to have escaped; while a similar number survived, by various methods, the agonies of the long and murderous marches.

The most remarkable evidence was **Corroboration by** obtained from German missionary jour-**German missionaries** nals, which the German censor made strenuous but belated attempts to suppress. For example, the "Allgemeine Missions-Zeitschrift" (or "General Missions Gazette") was allowed, by a mistake on the part of the German Government, to print the following report:

They have marched them off in convoys into the desert on the pretext of settling them there. In the village of Tel-Armen (along the line of the Bagdad Railway, near Mosul) and in the neighbouring villages about 5,000 people were massacred, leaving only a few women and children. The people were thrown alive down wells or into the fire. As it is only the women and children who are sent into exile, since all the men, with the exception of the very old, are at the war, this means nothing less than the wholesale murder of the families.

On May 30th six hundred and seventy-four of them were

embarked on thirteen Tigris barges. A short time after the start the prisoners were stripped of all their money, and then of their clothes; after that they were thrown into the river.

For a whole month corpses were observed floating down the River Euphrates nearly every day, often in batches of from two to six corpses bound together. The male corpses are in many cases hideously mutilated, the female corpses are ripped open. The corpses stranded on the bank are devoured by dogs and vultures. To this fact there are many German eye-witnesses. An employee of the Bagdad Railway has brought the information that the prisons at Biredjik are filled regularly every day and emptied every night —into the Euphrates. Between Diarbekir and Ourfa a German cavalry captain saw innumerable corpses lying unburied all along the road.

Another German missionary reported, in regard to the Mush district:

Harpout has become the cemetery of the Armenians; from all directions they have been brought to Harpout to be buried. There they lie, and the dogs and vultures devour their bodies. In Harpout and Mezré the people have had to endure terrible tortures. They have had their eyebrows plucked out, their breasts cut off, their nails torn off; their torturers hew off their feet or else hammer nails into them, just as they do in shoeing horses. This is all done at night time, and in order that the people may not hear their screams and know of their agony, soldiers are stationed round the prisons, beating drums and blowing whistles. It is needless to relate that many died of these tortures. When they die the soldiers cry, " Now let your Christ help you."

One old priest was tortured so cruelly as to extract a confession that

PITIFUL VICTIMS OF AUSTRO-HUNGARIAN SAVAGERY.
A Serbian refugee tramping the streets with his two little daughters. The civil population of Serbia suffered even worse than the civil population of Belgium and of Northern and Eastern France from the invaders.

HONEST FOLK FALLEN AMONG THIEVES.
Serbians in the hands of enemy troops. Professor Reiss's investigation proved that the Teutons aimed at systematic extermination of the entire Serbian population.

SERBIAN COPPER FOR GERMAN SHELLS.
Young Serbians bringing in all their copper vessels and utensils, which were sent to Germany to be used in munition work. It was death for a Serbian to attempt to retain any of the precious metal, which the invader demanded with uncompromising insistence.

believing that the torture would cease and that he would be left alone if he did it, he cried out in his desperation, "We are revolutionists." He expected his tortures to cease, but, on the contrary, the soldiers cried, "What further do we seek? We have it here from his own lips." And instead of picking their victims as they did before, the officials had all the Armenians tortured without sparing a soul. It is a story written in blood.

The later scenes in Syria, where Moslem populations were massacred in the cause of Pan-Ottomanism, seemed to have been conducted in the same way as the Armenian massacres. The fighting men were first drafted into the Turkish Army, and placed in the forefront of battle against the British and the Russians, for the double purpose of killing them off and disturbing the Allies. When the best fighters were gone and the resistance of the region was thereby weakened, the notable men were executed on

Pan-Ottomanism in Syria trumped-up charges of treason. After these cunning steps had reduced the people into a leaderless and practically unarmed mob, they were harried by extortions and brutal ill-treatment into something that could be represented as a revolt. Thereupon, large military forces were employed against them, and carriers of pestilence were spread among them. By the triple weapons of disease, downright butchery, and starvation the territory was cleared, with a view to it being planted with Turkish peasants.

This was the main difference between the massacre policy of the unregenerate Turk and the enlightened methods of the leaders of the Committee of Union and Progress, who acted always under Germanic influence. The Turks of the new school, who included many renegade Salonika Jews, made uses of the latest discoveries in bacteriology and the latest doctrines of race dominion. Their Pan-Ottomanism was directly inspired by Pan-Germanism.

But, having regard to the way in which the Germans dispeopled Belgium, Poland, Serbia, Northern France, and Rumania, it seems highly probable that the later German methods of deportation were in turn modelled upon the methods of the Pan-Ottomanism. The scientific Teutons and the barbarous Turks amalgamated into a league of scientific savagery, which was utterly without precedent in history. The deeds of Attila and his Huns, the acts of Genghis Khan and his Mongols, were completely eclipsed. For these ancient barbarians only killed by their own hands; they lacked the enormous power derived from scientific researches and modern technical industries.

In the first month of 1917 the enemy abandoned every semblance of respect for the conventions of Christendom, civilisation, and humanity. Possessing at sea, by reason of his submarines, a larger range of power than he exercised on land, he deliberately announced his intention of sinking all hospital ships as well as passenger liners, cargo boats, and the trading steamers of every nation. There was nothing new in the German submarine campaign against the hospital ships of the Allies. On February 1st, 1915, the British hospital ship Asturias was attacked by a German submarine off Havre, and escaped only through the torpedo missing its mark. Again on March 30th, 1916, the Franco-Russian hospital ship Portugal was sunk in broad daylight by two torpedoes discharged from a German submarine off the coast of Eastern Anatolia. On December 21st, 1916, the British hospital ship Britannic was sunk in the Ægean Sea. Within three days, in the same waters, the Braemar Castle, another hospital ship, was also sunk. In the last two cases the evidence was inconclusive, from an official point of view, as to whether mine or torpedo had been employed. But the general opinion was that the two ships had met the same fate as the Portugal.

The evidence, however, was absolutely clear in the cases of the Asturias and the Portugal. Thus, so far as the Allies were concerned, there was no new element of atrocity in the third Teutonic campaign of pitiless piracy which opened on February 1st, 1917. Already non-combatants and neutrals on passenger liners had been killed and wounded by prolonged shell fire, directed both against the steamer and against the small boats in which the passengers were trying to escape. British seamen, who took to their boats after their vessel had been sunk, had been shelled by the enemy submarines. Men had been forced to abandon their ships in midwinter gales and utterly without means of reaching land or succour. Many perished by bitter exposure, having been as clearly murdered as were their comrades who were done to death in German internment camps.

Atrocities of the U Boats

The cold-blooded brutality of the Teutons never varied, in essentials, from August, 1914, to February, 1917. The only difference was that in the first period of the war the human fiends employed cunning as well as cruelty. They covered up their misdeeds as much as possible, in order to maintain good and profitable relations with the United States and other powerful neutral countries. When they were at last so placed that they had to give some evidence of feelings of humanity or lose the financial and commercial support of the most important neutral States, during the difficult period after the war, their blood-fed and blood-blinded passions triumphed over their former prudent policy of money-making

The Lusitania murders, for example, were paralleled, soon after the revival of general submarine piracy, by the torpedoing of another Cunard liner, the Laconia, off the Irish coast, on Sunday night, February 25th, 1917. This act of atrocity was of special historic importance, in that two American passengers, Mrs. and Miss Hoy, lost their lives through the murderous conduct of the enemy, causing such indignation throughout the United States as brought the country nearer to armed conflict with the Central Empires.

Supreme outlaws of mankind

The large majority of Germans, Socialist and otherwise, were inflated with lust for dominion, convinced that they could win in a sharp, short, and profitable war. Therefore, when bearing in mind the incomparable record of Teutonic atrocities, we must remember also that the Germanic races of the Central Empires were responsible for the method of exterminating other races, in the design to outbreed and swamp, by fertility, industrial resources, and riches, the nations they massacred.

It was seen that no peace settlement would be safe or permanent that did not leave the Germans crippled in bodily vigour, in iron power, coal power, and trading opportunities. Had none of these restrictions been contemplated, the Teutons of the younger generation would, even in temporary defeat, have profited at last enormously by the gross crimes of their fathers.

The British blockade promised to level up things slightly by its effect upon the physique of the Germans, Austrians, and Hungarians. But it could not balance the large and mortal injuries done to the peoples of Belgium, Northern France, Poland, Serbia, and Rumania. Only a decisive post-bellum economic policy, loyally carried out for a period of years by the Allies, could make Germany a lasting example to any other nation or nations inclining to exterminating methods of warfare.

Germany held a million Russians prisoners of war, and treated them with a cruelty that was fiendish. The monstrous perverters of all that had been understood as pertaining to culture lashed their victims to posts with their arms drawn tight behind them, bound them naked to trees for hours together, and even tied them to trees with their feet off the ground, so that the whole weight of the tortured body fell on the cutting cords.

INHUMAN HUNS' ILL-TREATMENT OF RUSSIAN PRISONERS OF WAR.

EVERYDAY LIFE ON THE WESTERN FRONT.

By Basil Clarke.

Signs of British Influence Ubiquitous in France—Ships, Railways, Canals, and Roads—How the Language Problem was Solved—Growth of Mutual Understanding between the Two Peoples—Kinds of Environment in which Our Men Lived—Billets with French Families—Huts, Nissen and Others, Tents, and " Shelters "—Cellar Billets—Dug-outs—From Grottoes in Trench Sides to the Elaborate German Works—Chateaux—Migration a Part of the Soldier's Life—Train Journeys and Road Marches—The Sound of the Flute and the "Strombaus Horn "—Life in Rest Billets—Sleep, Kit-Cleaning, and Working-Parties—Daily Life of the Artillery-men—Horrors of Old Trenches Reoccupied—Food and Recreation in Rest Billets—Home Sickness—Food Supply of the British Army—Sugar and Sweets—Clothes and Kit Supply—Life in the Trenches—Old Trenches and New—Learning the Character of the Germans Opposite—Rations—Sentry Duty—Stunts and Raids—Looking Forward to Relief—" A Hot Bath, Clean Clothes, and a Long Sleep!"—Leave—Dinner, Billiards, and an Occasional "Jamboree"—Leave for Home—The Real Tonic for War-Weariness —The Journey to the Boat—Casting Off the Hawsers—One Great Moment in the Life of a British Soldier.

PRECEDING chapters have shown the very definite change for the better that came over the British campaign in the west as a result of the events of July, 1916, and the succeeding months. The close of the year found the offensive still going hardily forward, notwithstanding weather conditions that would have dismayed most troops and reduced many generals to inertia. But, with British moral unimpaired, with British hopes and confidence never so high, British activity also remained unceasing, and till the year's end new gains, if comparatively small ones, accrued almost every day. The enemy, on the other hand, as shown in Chapter CLV., on German moral (which, after being written for this history by an independent witness, was amply confirmed later in a despatch by the British Commander-in-Chief), was losing not only ground and strength and resource, but even hope. The trend of the war by the end of 1916 had become unmistakable—victory for the Allies was dawning, defeat had become impossible.

Leaving the British Army's fortunes in this satisfactory state, we may step aside

for a moment from the main path of the historical survey of that Army's fighting achievements to look in detail into its more personal and domestic doings. What were the daily life and habit and environment of our troops in the west at this time ? How did they live and fare as they so bravely wrought for their country this striking amelioration of her fortunes ?

Thought for a moment of the immensity of Great Britain's enterprises in France and Flanders at the time will enable one the better to realise how varied and multiform were daily life and habit and environment. Had anyone with an eagle's wings and double an eagle's range of vision soared high above Northern France on, say, December 31st, 1916, he could have seen hardly a thing below him that was not either susceptible to British influence in some major or minor degree, or wholly dependent upon it. The ships that he would see —as mere little smoking ellipses on a grey sea—few of them there would be that were not on missions mainly or wholly British. Men, munitions, stores — under one or other head from this comprehensive trinity of war needs could be classified the errand of almost every

CONFIDENCE ON THE WESTERN FRONT.
[*British official photographs.*]
Two British generals conversing on the field of battle. In view of their placid attitude, it is interesting to note that they were under shell fire at the moment this photograph was taken.

OPEN-AIR CONFERENCE: A BRIGADIER-GENERAL GIVING ORDERS TO A COLONEL.

[British official photograph.

It was the ubiquity of British troops in France that most impressed civilian visitors to the war area. Many towns and villages were occupied only by British soldiers:—Generals and their Staffs in the chateaux, others of all ranks in every kind of house and cellar. British soldiers were often the only human beings to be seen in the streets of towns that were anywhere near the British fighting front.

craft—even to that squat, dirty, yellow little ship lurching through the seas with a holdful of British stone, destined for the mending of French war roads.

Or take the railways that this aerial observer would see threading through the land, forking this way, branching that way, like the lines on a palm, and whitened at frequent intervals with moving pennons and swelling dots of steam. He would have been unwise to risk definite statement that anyone of those trains was not carrying British troops or British stores or British munitions, or that it was not being operated by British railwaymen and clerks in soldier garb—or, for that matter, that it was not even being driven by a British engine-driver uniformed for the time being in the blue dungarees and the cap and "R.E." badge of the Royal Engineers, Railway Section.

British soldiers ubiquitous

Many canals, straight and long, would be visible from above, like rods of polished steel. Had that aerial observer's hearing been as keen as the sight with which we have endowed him, he might have overheard exchanges of views between the uniformed crews of these barges shouted out, not in mellifluous French or guttural Flemish, but in the rich, primal vernacular of Wapping, whence not a few of these crews came.

As with the canals and railways, so with the roads; their population of vehicles and people alike might be mainly British. But wherever you looked down upon Northern France upon that day, it would have been difficult to point to any place or object and say definitely that it had no touch with British affairs. Any village you chose might be billeting British troops of one sort or another; any of the many factory chimneys pouring smoke towards you might prove on examination to be part of a British Army machine shop or repair depot, swarming with British soldier mechanics; even the little village school you chanced upon might prove to be harbouring that afternoon —for December 31st was a Sunday—a quiet congregation of British soldiers—fighters or labourers, or miners, or others—singing hymns and listening to the advice of their regimental "padre"—with perhaps Holy Communion to follow.

British soldiers, combatant or non-combatant, were everywhere. They seemed to have permeated in greater or lesser degree the whole scheme of things civil and military throughout the North of France. To survey thoroughly, therefore, the everyday life of this diffused population one would need to peep into every nook and cranny of French affairs. Though the British soldier was in greater or lesser evidence wherever one stopped between coast and front, this chapter will deal with him mainly where he was "spread thickest"—at the front and close behind it.

The signs of British occupancy were unmistakable as soon as you entered a British Army town or village. The policeman, for instance, who stopped you at the cross-roads just outside it, walking out of his little road-shelter with a flag in one hand and the other palm uplifted in the true London police manner, would be a British policeman, though a soldier policeman, wearing the red-and-black badge of the military police on his khaki coat. His colleague in the shelter would be a Frenchman, clothed in pale blue, and together they saw to it that no undesirable or unaccredited person, British or French, passed out of or into that town or village. At night they had a lantern apiece, which they waved to your approaching car as a stopping signal, and with which they examined your papers and passes. It was part of everyday life at the front to have your "papers" handy.

Khaki police at the cross roads

Once past the police wicket, it would be noticed that

new name-boards had been put up for most of the roads and streets, and that the new names were English names. Pall Malls, Rotten Rows, and Piccadillys; High Streets and Church Streets; Station Roads and Cemetery Roads; Sandy Lanes, Love Lanes, and all the rest of the great family of British thoroughfare names were as frequently met with in villages of France as in those of this country. That no time had been wasted, however, in thinking out new English names for French streets and roads was amply testified by the occurrence of such names as Slush Avenue, Porridge Street, Bumpy Road, and Becareful Corner. In some cases, indeed, it would seem that the patience, if not the resource, of the name-finders who rechristened these thoroughfares had quite petered out; for in one busy neighbourhood was to be found a little street called Sausage Street, with a companion street

English names for French streets

parallel to it called Mash Street. Dammit Street also suggested a name-finder short either of time or of patience.

Traffic directions were also posted in English as well as in French along the roads. On the signposts "Drive Slowly" rubbed shoulders with "Ralentir," and "Arrêtez" with "Stop." The only British road travel traditions which our soldier drivers seemed quite to have sacrificed in France were those of reckoning distances in miles and

driving on the left-hand side of the road. After two years in France our drivers were quite as happy to keep to the right side of the road (as do most nations but the British), and hardly one of them would name distances in miles. "Kilomètres" had become the universal standard. One sometimes saw new-comers who had to do little lightning sums in their head or on their fingers before they could reckon a distance; but before long they, too, were thinking quite freely in kilomètres. Miles seemed quite to have

French weights and measures adopted

dropped out of the English vocabulary, so far as wheeled traffic was concerned, though the infantry still clung to "miles," and always marched their "three miles," and not five kilomètres an hour. Pints, quarts, and gallons gave way to some slight extent in favour of "half-litres" and "litres." Pounds and hundredweights, too, grew scarcer, but tons always remained. Our men never left hold of the British ton.

The French people had quickly appreciated our national distaste to speaking any language but our own, and by December, 1916, most of the French shop people who had dealings with our troops had their word or two of English. Many of our men had picked up words of French, and very often a transaction would begin bravely in French, but as difficulties of expression and understanding

[British official photograph.

A STROLL ROUND THE DEFENCE WORKS IN THE FAR FRONT LINE.

A Staff captain making a tour of inspection of the defences in a partially ruined village. An eagle eye was kept upon every point of the defence works, Staff officers, from the brigadier downwards, frequently going round with officers of the regiments holding the trenches to see whether parapets needed strengthening, barbed-wire repairing, trenches deepening, or other work doing to make a position more secure.

ONE "LITTLE GREY HOME IN THE WEST."
Dug-outs varied greatly in degree of elaboration. Many were developed by successive occupants from mere burrows to comparatively comfortable quarters provided with ingenious make-shift furniture.

came along, the language of one or the other of the two negotiants forced itself to the front and held the field

The more self-conscious of the two was generally the Briton, and the conversation ended in English. Here is an example of the kind of thing, taken from real life in a French village shop in Amiens, just before Christmas.

English Soldier (entering) : " Bon jour, monsieur ! "

French Shopkeeper : " Bon jour, monsieur."

E. S. (painfully and carefully) : " Est ce que vous avez des plumes fontaines ? "

F. S. (mystified but polite) : " Comment, monsieur ? "

E. S. (a little less confidently) : " Des plumes fontaines."

F. S. (after a moment's hesitation) : " Ah, monsieur, veut une porte plume ? "

E. S. (waving hands about and looking round shop as though in search of something) : "Non. Mais non. Je voudrai de plume fontaine—er—er—plume fontaine, er—fountain-pen, you know ; fountain-pen for the pocket, you know."

F. S. : " Ah, yes, monsieur ! Foun-

Mutual good-humour in business tain-pen. I have him. What fabrique will you, monsieur ? Fountain-pen automatique ; ze self-fill or——"

E. S. : " Oh, any old sort will do. What are those in the case there ? " etc. (then everything is in English).

A little good-humour on both sides was all that was necessary to make these negotiations pleasant as well as possible, and that grain of good-humour was generally forthcoming. For French civilian and British soldier had come to know one another and to understand one another, and each found the other much more reasonable and intelligible than had seemed the case two years earlier. Our men used the shops and cafés and restaurants without any diffidence, and by this time their presence had come to attract little attention. A peep into any café or restaurant in one of the towns near the British front would have shown you British soldiers and French civilians side by side in perhaps equal numbers and without criticism one for another. This marked an advance, for at the beginning of the war the French people undoubtedly thought our men "queer." Their lack of conventional manners,

the little bowings and neddings and elegances of deportment before strangers that mean so much to the French, made the French regard them as a little hard and unfeeling. And once an idea has got into people's heads it is always easy to find corroborative detail. The French would point to the British soldier's cold way of taking bad news, his easy recovery from it, and his ability to put even the cares of war on one side in a game or a song.

All these things, natural to the British soldier and his race, counted against him at first, and with his plain manners were counted as evidence enough of his utter callousness to the war and to France's troubles. But after two years of the British soldier's presence in their midst the French had learnt to assess these little differences of bearing at their proper worth. An understanding had been established at last, and our men had come to be living on the best of terms with the French civil population. Each recognised the other's good points, and differences of character and manners were seen to be not incompatible with friendship and good feeling. There were quarrels at times, of course. Where would there not be between different communities ? But these were exceptional. British soldiers might get bad treatment from French people, but this was exceptional. For the most part the French, peasantry and townspeople alike, who had the billeting of British troops, undertook their duties in a spirit of friendship rather than of hard business ; they sought how comfortable they could make them rather than how much money they could make out of them.

Billets in French cottages

As almost every British private who had done duty in France between 1914 and 1917 had been in billets with French people at some time or other, it may be interesting to give a picture of one of these billets. Here is a description taken from a letter received from a clever young author, then serving as a private in the Royal Fusiliers : " We have been back (from the line) for ten days, and at present I am billeted with three of our fellows in a French cottage. It is the usual little affair, a brick foundation rising to a height of about three feet, then bent old timber beams and whitewashed plaster as far as the roof, which is of red weather-stained tiles. There is Père Juvenal, a farm worker, his wife and three children, ranging from four years to ten. There is also grandpère, the wife's father, who sits by the fire most of the day, but who feels himself thoroughly important when he is commissioned by Madame to blow the fire with an old and huge pair of bellows. His cheeks puff in and out with every stroke of the bellows, so that between the two of them the fire gets really a double draught. At first we all had the impression that the people did not want us and did not like us. The neighbours certainly used to scowl at us when

PUTTING UP NISSEN HUTS ON THE WESTERN FRONT.
The Nissen hut ranked among the greatest boons devised for the field army during the war. Made of standardised parts, easily portable, and requiring only four men to fit them together, they were used in large numbers and came to be widely appreciated. A full account of them is given on pages 485 and 486.

we went out and washed under the pump in the morning —there was nowhere else to wash — and Mère Juvenal used certainly to keep out of the way and would scurry into their kitchen when she saw us coming in. But the children broke the ice. The baby is a very jolly little soul. I had gone into the kitchen to ask Madame where the village cobbler lived (I wanted a bit of leather). She told me the way coldly enough, and I came out. But the kiddie came running after me and said : ' Eh, mon Dieu ! Tu seras perdu.' (Oh, dear ! Thou wilt get lost.) I laughed and joked with her a bit, and she said in her baby French :

Safeguarded by the baby ' It is necessary that I come with thee to show thee the way and then thou wilt not be lost.' I told her to come along, then, never thinking she would, but she toddled alongside to the gate and came. After a yard or two she looked up at me and said : ' But it is necessary for thee to take care of the carts and the motors. They will surely kill thee. Thou must indeed hold my hand to be quite safe.' And I had to take the little lady's hand to be safe-guarded by her from the village traffic ! In this fashion we went to the cobbler, who was not more than a hundred mètres away, and so we came home. On the way back who should come along but Père Juvenal. He wanted to take the kiddie, but she said ' No.' No, she was ' guarding the English soldier.' She saw me home, and since then she has been many times to see us.

WOODCRAFT IN MODERN WAR.
Fitting a circular saw in a new mill in course of erection on the western front

and my feet have left me with cold, I'll just try to think of—hot milk."

It was probably kindly treatment of this sort that made " billets " with French families one of the most popular forms of housing among our troops in France The various alternatives to " billets " were huts, tents, shelters, cellars, and dug-outs. And this order may be taken as representing their order of popularity and, in inverse ratio, their order of greatest distance from the front. Towards the end of 1916 huts—which earlier in the war were hardly to be seen at all near the front nor in any of the British camps, save those well back—were becoming more common.

Even in camps within range of the enemy's " whistling Percys " (the name given to one of their longest-range guns, which sent a shell with a most unusual and characteristic whistle of its own), a hut or two was generally to be seen. Perhaps the majority were used as offices, but a few were in occupation as living huts, and more were being brought up. " When are your huts coming up ? " was a commonplace of conversation, just as was such a question as " When is your next leave due ? " A hut was something to look forward to. The earlier huts were of the Army pattern usually to be seen in the camps in Britain — darkened timber sides and roof, a little window, and stained wood interior, smelling strongly of creosote. No need to describe these at length.

[*British official photographs.*
WITH A WORKING-PARTY IN A FRENCH FOREST.
Cross-cutting a tree in a wood near the front. The war simply " ate up " timber, and whole forests were laid low to provide balks and flooring for the trenches, posts for the wires, and fuel for the myriad fires.

That was a week ago, and now the old French people cannot do too much for us. They insist on our sitting in the kitchen because it is warmer, and on giving us hot milk at nights, and now and again eggs ; and there is quite a scene if we want to pay for them. During the first week the neighbours hid the handle of the yard pump so that we could not wash there in the morning, but they take no notice now and sometimes stop to have a chat. One of them gave me three apples yesterday morning. Another has given me some home-made ' dubbin' for my boots. She said that only the farming people knew how to make proper dubbin for boots, and she told me the secret of it. But it is quite safe with me, for I could not understand more than a word or two of her recipe. Three days more and we go back into the line. I only wish we could take this old billet along with us. A dug-out, if we are lucky enough to get one this time, will not seem the more comfortable for our having just left this place. But when the wind whistles a note on the edge of my old ' tin hat '

But a totally new type of Army hut began to make its appearance about the end of 1916, and the authorities thought so well of it that they gave large orders for it, and before many months of 1917 had passed there were no fewer than twenty thousand of these huts in France. It was called the Nissen hut, after its inventor, a Canadian officer, who designed it specially to meet the needs of this campaign. Its chief characteristic was that it had no sides, but only a roof and ends and inner flooring. The roof was semicircular, and reached down to the ground on each side, so that there was no need of sides. It was just as though you took a railway arch and boarded up the ends. The arch or roof was of corrugated iron, made in forty-eight sections that fitted one into another, and were all the same size, so that no matter in what order they were fastened together they fitted exactly and made the complete

Description of the Nissen hut

roof. The flooring was also in sections that were interchangeable ; also the ends and the wooden lining for the interior. One type of bolt was used throughout the construction, and the spanner for this bolt was enclosed with the parts. Printed instructions for erecting the hut were sent out with them just as though it might have been a boy's game. No single piece of the hut was heavier than two men could handle easily, and the whole thing could be packed on an Army waggon. Four men could put one together in four hours.

Twenty-four men slept in each hut, and in daytime the beds were rolled to the sides—where the standing room was, of course, least—leaving all the middle, where the roof was highest, available for use as a mess-room. Some fifty men could sit in the hut, even though this number could not walk about very freely. The roof was not shell-proof, but it was a fair protection from splinters. Each hut, by the way, had a stove of the ordinary round Canadian pattern, with a flue-pipe passing through the circular roof. Doors, of course, were at the ends. For warmth and comfort these huts proved to be superior to any other type of field dwelling.

Tents for "moving" units

Tents were next in popularity, though in really cold and windy weather many of our soldiers used to say that they

BRITISH TROOPS ON THE MARCH IN FRANCE.
[*French official photograph.*]
Migration was a great part of the soldier's life in France, and as much as possible the railways were relieved by moving the troops by road. "Loaded heavy," regiments were always on the march, officers on horseback, men on foot and on cycles, stretcher-bearers, baggage-waggons, field-kitchens, and other Army details.

would sooner be in a dug-out, for its warmth. Tents, though to be found in many camps, were most consistently used perhaps by "moving" units, such as telegraph linesmen, pipe-layers, and other working-parties whose work kept them on the move from place to place. Many little camps of merely three or four tents were to be found about the roads of France, and in them were usually small working-parties of this kind. Sometimes solitary tents figured by the roadside, especially at nights. You might look in to find that the occupant was perhaps an officer of motor-transport whose convoy of waggons had been parked for the night in some neighbouring spot, and who had come to spend the night under canvas, the men of the convoy sleeping in their waggons. His servant would be preparing the evening meal on a Primus stove, which served the double purpose of cooking the meal and adding something to the warmth, if not the healthiness, of the tent. For quite often you would find the tent filled with a thick fog, the heat of the stove having turned the moisture of the ground into mist. Little discomforts of this sort passed either unnoticed or merely as object for jest, though in the hospital reports bronchitis and rheumatism figured with unwelcome frequency. Tents, or rather marquees, were

much used at casualty clearing-stations as hospital wards. German prisoners' "cages," too, were usually fitted with tents. Forty or fifty bell-tents inside a high palisading of barbed-wire, with elevated sentry-boxes at each corner, formed the usual equipment of a "cage."

The "shelters" of France struck one as the queerest of all the very queer living places to which the war had given rise. They looked more like habitations fashioned by Rumanian and Hungarian gipsies than by British soldiers. The "shelter" was devoid of definite form, shape, or pattern ; it was a fantasia in architecture. You built it in any shape and of any material. It might be above ground, or half above ground and half under, or all under ground except the roof. If it sank any lower than this it became, of course, a "dug-out." The most orthodox of "shelters" had sides built of sand-bags and a roof of arched iron sheeting, rather stout in structure, dull red or black in colour, and capable of resisting a shell splinter or of turning a bullet. Covered with a foot or two of earth this iron roof became what was euphemistically termed "shell-proof," which means that it would resist damage from any shell save one that hit it directly with all its force. This was the shelter-de-luxe. One saw them sometimes about artillery positions, about other posts that had not been disturbed for some time, and among luxurious people who were able to get iron roofs and sand-bags from the ordnance men. A man who could get iron roofing for his shelter was continually being asked by jealous and facetious friends whether he had an uncle or "papa" in the Cabinet.

From this luxurious type of edifice, shelters tapered down in degrees of respectability nicely graded. A shelter, for instance, might be made of sand-bags after the de luxe model, but the roof might be of clay and logs. The next type might be without the logs. After that may be classified the shelter that had no sand-bags, but merely some substitute such as square oil-cans filled with sand. These made especially solid shelters and were vaunted by their occupants as being even better than the sand-bag variety. Next came the shelter made of odd-sized planks and timbers. Much ingenuity could be exercised in making a house out of planks, no two of which are of the same length or thickness. Then may be scheduled, perhaps, the shelter made of old packing-cases nailed on a framework of planks. This, though not a beautiful structure, might nevertheless be a warm and comfortable one, even though it advertised somebody's milk on its sides, or somebody else's tinned beef.

After that one reached the real stage of makeshift in shelters. A timber framework filled in with clay was a fairly common form of shelter. In dry weather, or in the event of the fire in the shelter drying the clay, it tended to fall out, but the wetness of French weather was generally sufficient to prevent any calamity of that kind.

All-patchwork shelters

The all-patchwork shelter was one of the most common types. For patchwork almost any material would serve. Old tins, cut and stamped out flat, sods of earth, pieces of cloth, particularly old felt and flannel and tarpaulin, and even sheets of thick brown paper. One of the most striking patchwork shelters to be seen in France at this time was probably the one a hundred yards off the Doullens road, south-east of that town. Among the component parts of its walls were two old coats—German—three oil-tins

[French official photograph.

"CHANGING GUARD" ON THE WESTERN FRONT.

French troops marching away from the trenches that had been taken over by their British allies. The line held by Sir Douglas Haig's armies was considerably extended during the winter of 1916-17.

[French official photographs.

COMRADES-IN-ARMS: WHERE THE FRENCH AND BRITISH LINES JOINED ON THE SOMME.

Men of the French and British forces watching a transport train on a roadway in the Somme district. Though the firing-line had been pushed forward, the snapped-off trees show that the road had been well under fire earlier. Above: Another familiar scene where the two armies linked together. French soldiers, to the right, paused to see their British allies marching forward to the task which they loyally shared.

A LITTLE MUSIC AT A DUG-OUT DOOR.
[British official photograph.
If the enemy was quiet, trench duty was sometimes very uneventful. The men wrote letters, ate, and "slacked" till their turn for sentry duty came. Sometimes a banjo solo afforded pleasant amusement.

cut out and flattened, two box sides and two ends, one sack upon which were the tell-tale letters "P.O.," one old umbrella cover, plus part of the frame, two magazine covers, and one pan lid. How the genius who lived in this shelter managed to keep his house parts assembled was a mystery to all passers-by, and much facetious comment was shouted to him from the road by passing troops. Locally it was known to fame as the "Hen Run," but its owner, if asked its name, would roll his eyes dramatically, and with clasped hands would tell you without a smile that it was "My little grey home in the West." I think the truth was that this lonely shelterer—who kept an Army coal-dump by the roadside, or some other unromantic thing of the sort—got so much fun out of the oddity of his house materials that if he had been offered good Accrington bricks to build him a house he would have refused them. Certainly no one ever passed his little domain without a smile, and he was generally in sight to return it.

Cellar billets were much in use at this time, but only within the shell zone and in neighbourhoods close behind it, in which the upper parts of the houses had been destroyed by shell fire. Thus in many of the villages captured from the Germans in our advance during the latter half of 1916 troops were billeted chiefly in cellars. In villages that had come to be out of shell range the upper parts of the houses were made use of if it were possible, but the houses fit for occupation, except in their cellars, were few and far between. A divisional general might be glad to get hold of one. Certainly one of our Colonial generals was housed during

Security in cellar billets

December in a cottage which in peace time might have been occupied by the village postman. If a village were out of shell fire, such upper and ground-floor rooms as could be made weather-tight by patching up with sheeting and ground-sheets were occupied, and the writer spent a pleasant hour one wintry evening in a ground-floor room so patched up. The roof was gone, also the bulk of the ceiling of the ground-floor rooms, but the hole that remained served to let out smoke from the great open fire that had been built in the middle of the "parlour" floor. The men sat round it on planks, laid across two little heaps of brick. Greatcoats were hung on the walls of the room to dry, and also to keep out draughts that came through "leaky" walls. One party played cards on a box by the light of a candle stuck in a wine-bottle, but the bulk were content to sit and talk, or write letters. To sleep, men took off their boots and, rolling themselves in their blankets,

slept on the floor on their ground-sheets with feet towards the fire.

In many villages German shell fire was so frequent that it was not safe to sleep anywhere on or above ground level. To find cellar billets, therefore, saved the trouble of digging dug-outs, and the hunting for cellars was very keen. Officers and men specially told off for this duty would rummage about the ruins of houses, and underneath the most dilapidated and unpromising ruin might be found cellars quite intact. The stone steps leading to them might be blocked up with bricks and plaster and charred ash, but a fatigue-party under a corporal would soon put all this out of the way and lay bare a cellar which would be passed as fit for occupation. Only too often there were gruesome finds in these cellars—from which the Germans had been driven—and if people who die a violent death leave ghosts behind them our men may be said to have slept amid congregations of Teuton ghosts. Not that that seemed to weigh on their minds particularly. They were very much more bothered by the rats. These creatures were almost everywhere, and at first they were generally so hungry as to be ready to feed on anything, from a crust to a Sam Browne belt. But after the soldiers had been in occupation of a cellar for some time the rats picked up so much waste food that they became fat and lazy, and then they would fall an easy prey to the heel of a boot or a well-aimed bully-beef tin.

Fortunately, French village houses are well off for cellars. In some towns, in fact, such as Arras, there were **Varieties of the dug-out**
found cellars extending under great areas, and supported by pillars of stone. They were called "boves," and were said to have been the quarries from which the stone for the houses above them was obtained. In garrisoned villages about Arras were to be found "boves" on a smaller scale, and not a few of them served as quarters for our troops. The ordinary cellar billet, however, was a single cellar, with walls and an arched roof of brick. It was quite dark, and if it happened to have a fireplace and a smoke-flue the occupants counted themselves lucky. Many a cellar billet had no flue or outlet of any sort save the steps, and in these cases our men used often to make a flue out of piping or old tins to carry away the smoke from their little fire. This pipe issued to the upper air by way of the cellar steps, and when these steps were dark you might first learn of the pipe's existence by burning your hand on it. "'Ware stove-pipe" notices were occasionally to be seen at cellar entrances.

The remaining type of dwelling-place used by our troops in France was the "dug-out." These might be deep or shallow, small or big, dry or damp; in short, of all the qualities, good and ill, that a habitation may possibly take to itself the dug-out lacked none; and of evil qualities it might have more than most dwellings. The term "dug-out" was used to cover a big variety of underground works, from the simple little grotto in the side of a trench, which a soldier could burrow out for himself in ten minutes with a trenching tool as some protection from wind and bullet and shell-chip, to the elaborate dug-outs made by the Germans—great underground warrens of passages and rooms and chambers, lighted by electricity, ventilated by electric fans, warmed by kitchen-ranges with tortuous and far-journeying flues.

The simplest kind of dug-out might evolve into quite an elaborate dug-out in the end. The first soldier came along the trench and found his bit of territory very exposed, so he took out his trenching tool and burrowed perhaps three feet laterally into the sand or gravel or white chalk wall of his trench. It was high enough only to admit of his crawling under it, and here, when not on sentry duty,

Little luxuries behind the lines : French children selling chocolate and apples to British soldiers.

Bringing up ammunition under fire in a Somme advance.

In the slough of the Somme: Rescuing a comrade from a shell-hole.

491

Sunday on the western front : An impromptu service under fire

he would lie and sleep, with his feet reaching out uncovered into the fairway of the trench. A day later he might think a larger dwelling would be more comfortable. With trenching tool, therefore, he would enlarge his burrow so that perhaps both he and a mate could crawl underneath it and keep one another warm. Every day and every fresh lot of troops that came into that trench for duty would bring improvements to the dug-out. One man might add a bit of blanket or old coat as a screen door. The next man might feel uneasy as the dug-out shook with the fall of every enemy shell, and add wooden supports to the roof and sides. Soon they might begin to dig downwards; then to add steps; then to scoop out a bigger chamber underground, to add a fireplace, and so on. There is not much doubt that many of the dug-outs used by our soldiers in the trenches were evolved, bit by bit, improvement on improvement, enlargement on enlargement, in the way described, and were not the product of any set and deliberate plan. Some very cosy dug-outs resulted from this evolution.

Other dug-outs on the contrary, were planned and fashioned in their final form. A tunnelling party of miner soldiers would be called in for the excavations, and the timber beams and balks and planks for framework and lining would be brought up and solidly deposited on the building site. Most of the German dug-outs were made in this way, and our men were thankful for the enormous patience and care and skill that had been expended on

Elaboration of German dug-outs them, for thousands of them fell into our hands and served as quarters for our men. To rush forward into a newly-taken position and find dug-outs ready made was a piece of luck that fell to British troops very many times. The position might have been battered by shell fire, but so deep were these German dug-outs, so well lined with timber, and so stoutly made, that after even the heaviest shell fire they were intact. The smaller ones were promptly "bagged" (that was the word) by billeting officers as quarters for their men. The larger ones might be taken for use as battalion headquarters, medical aid posts, advance dressing-stations, and the like. More than one British soldier was cured of a slight wound or sickness without ever seeing daylight once during his "hospital" treatment. Some German dug-outs, which subsequently became British, were fitted with four-poster beds and with panelled sitting-rooms. The writer visited one such dug-out, the walls of which were panelled with white wood. In another room of the same dug-out the wall panels were covered with china-silk drapery. It seemed evident from this and other signs that the wife of the German officer who had occupied the dug-out had been present in it for at least part of the time of his occupancy of the place. It stood near the River Ancre in a part of the line which the Germans had held for two years.

The only other type of dwelling occupied by British soldiers in any numbers—apart, of course, from the barge cabins occupied by the watermen's corps, the railway and station-rooms occupied by the railwaymen, and such special quarters—were the various châteaux occupied by the Staffs and by privileged people such as the war correspondents, among whom the writer had the fortune to be numbered. These châteaux were big French houses taken over furnished from their tenants, and converted to the use of the British occupants. A general and his Staff were usually to be found in one of these châteaux, some of which were of remarkable beauty. You might find a British general sitting in a room surrounded by trench maps, stretched out on drawing-boards placed on easels, and behind them on the walls pictures of age and greatest worth belonging to the family of the house. More than

GUARDS AT "GASPIRATOR" DRILL.

Near the trenches indicators gave notice if the atmospheric conditions were favourable to the enemy sending over gas, and it was then punishable for men to go about without their "gaspirators." A "Strombaus" horn blared an alarm if gas was coming.

one general had his room floor covered with ground sheeting, so that the perfect parquet flooring underneath should not be ruined by the service boots of all the officers who came to see him. Some of these châteaux, unhappily, had not escaped shell fire.

So much for the different kinds of environment on the western front. What daily life in these surroundings was depended, of course, entirely on the unit and on the duty that particular unit was doing at the time. A regiment in huts one week near the coast might be moved up to a village nearer the line the next, and put into tents or cellars. A week or two later might see them in trenches. Migration was a great part, therefore, of a soldier's life. First would come a train journey, and it was one of the frequent sights of the war to see one of those low-built, sombre-coloured trains of the French railways passing painfully and slowly through a village station of Northern France with its barely upholstered carriages packed with British soldiers. In cold weather the train rattled like a ship-riveting yard with the noise of heavy boots stamped on wooden floors to take the chill off innumerable feet. As these trains stood in sidings, with pink, boyish faces, bareheaded, bunched like grapes at every carriage window, French cottars and farm folk would sometimes bring out water or apples and hand them to the travellers with cheery smiles and good wishes. Rations were carried in knapsacks for these train journeys, and at the end of one of them the carriages would present an amazing litter of crumbs and empty tins, chocolate wrappings, and cigarette-ends.

After the train journey would come a **Troops on the** march by road of perhaps many miles **march** —or, if the case was one of especial urgency, a ride by motor char-à-banc. Nothing more moving or picturesque could be imagined than the long columns of British troops one saw marching from "railhead" to war zone, through the yellow sandy roads of France. Here, from a diary, comes a little description written in December, 1916, of troops on the road: "At noon to-day our car pulled up at a pretty spot on the road, and we got out for lunch by the roadside. The chauffeur had pulled the cork out of a bottle of white wine, and M. had handed round the sandwich basket, when the curious, crawling music of a flute band floated up to us from somewhere over the hill-crest behind us. I walked up to the crest to see who was coming, and saw below, in patches, through the trees of the roadside, the rolling wave of a

ALLIED TROOPS FORGATHERED AT A PUMP.
In every land the village pump becomes as it were the natural focal point for the exchange of news and gossip. So in the war did French and British soldiers forgather at the army pumps.

DAILY SCENE AT A WATER-TANK.
Arrangements for a full regular water supply for the troops were wonderful. At every reservoir and tap notices plainly indicated what water was drinkable and what might only be used for other purposes.

line of infantry on the march. Their cap tops caught dully the glint of the light, and made them look like facets of some dull stone, or like the faintly glinting scales of some mammoth snake crawling caterpillar fashion along the road below us. Soon the heads, then the bodies, then the horses of the leading officers rose over the crest of the hill— I had gone back to the car—and hard behind came the troops. The flute band was playing some lugubrious low-pitched melody, and the feet of the marchers were beating on the wet road a rhythmical ' trudge, trudge ' in accompaniment. Why are the lower notes of a **Melancholy music** flute so doleful in the open air ? Fifes are **of the flutes** bright and merry, but flutes on the lower notes ! A flute band playing in a sleet shower might serve to represent the acme of miserableness. Every man was loaded 'heavy': full pack, greatcoats, trenching tool and the rest, with iron shrapnel helmets in little cotton coverings strapped on flat behind. Rifles were being carried anyhow, for it was easy marching. Pipes and cigarettes sent up a thin blue film of smoke, that hung and wreathed like a pale spirit for a moment over the undulating head of the marching column, and then wafted away to the east in long curves. The boys

were talking quietly and naturally as they passed. The sound of their voices made a faint, many-toned hum in the quiet country road.

"Then a sudden booming roar from the west brings an equally sudden stillness in the ranks. Just here and there is a weak and forced laugh, but the majority maintain that quieter, less demonstrative, and truer bravery that neither laughs nor talks, but just ' carries on.' The booming continues and increases ; a sudden tilt or lapse in the wind seems to have brought it closer. These are fine, serious, thoughtful faces that pass one, man after man ; good, clear, steady eyes that look ahead or on the ground, leaning forward to the weight of the pack.

It is a grand sight this line of young **Warning of the** British faces going into battle. They, too, **guns** will be in it to-morrow or soon after. They know this as they march along the road. It will be the first battle to many of them. They are thinking their first thoughts about it all to the near sounding of the guns. The marching line ends. The stretcher-bearers with their little wheeled ambulances come along ; the baggage column with its long-eared mules ; then the field-kitchens, black, oily-looking boilers on wheels, with tiny chimneys emitting yellow smoke, the boilers sending forth steam and the fragrance of a stew. The column halts farther along the road. Packs are unloosed at once (one man taking off another's) and dumped on the roadside. You see men stretching their pained shoulders with sighs of relief. Dinner is served. The men lie on the grass bank by the roadside. Then an order, and they form up once more. But now the khaki caps have been exchanged for iron shrapnel helmets of a dull, pale green. That change is significant. The flutes begin their crawling whimper once more and the men are off—to the front."

One did not need to travel much farther along a road such as this to come upon the quarters of troops who were just " out " or who were just going into trenches. Their place might be some big camp on open ground, once green but now churned to a bright brown mud by the impression of innumerable footmarks and wheel-tracks. The utter disappearance of all grass from around the country-side about field camps was one of their most noticeable features. Field-kitchens would be smoking and steaming away, and here and there about the camp ground might be seen an open-air camp-fire, made perhaps of broken boxes, with a cluster of soldiers standing about it.

Strombaus horns for gas alarms In a prominent position in the camp would be a notice-board with a finger indicator upon it, and underneath it would be a queer apparatus with cylinders and a trumpet mouth. This indicator when pointing a certain way gave to the camp at large the knowledge that the atmospheric conditions were such as to admit of the enemy sending over "gas." With the indicator pointing this way, giving the "gas alert" as it was termed, it became a punishable offence for any man to go about without his gas-mask or helmet—often nicknamed "gaspirator"—ready at hand and in good working order. Press correspondents, too, had to have their gas-masks. When a gas attack began or was seen in advance, the trumpet arrangement, called a "Strombaus horn," blared out with brazen breath—drawn from its twin steel cylinders—a long wail of alarm, not unlike that of a factory buzzer. This was, of course, the signal for the putting on of gas-helmets and for other precautions laid down by the "gas officer," an indispensable official in all encampments within range of the enemy's gas or gas shells. Some of the smaller camps were not possessed of a "Strombaus horn," but in its place had probably an 18-pounder brass shell-case hung vertically by its base rim for use as a gong. Hit with a drumstick or piece of wood, it gave out in good, resonant tone the note ♪ . Every man of the camp knew that note—if not through real gas alarms, at least through frequent practice alarms. The French used their "75" brass shell-cases as gongs in the same way. They gave a note about half a tone higher than the British 18-pounder shell-case. A village might have several of these alarms, and it was an eerie thing to hear them going dong—dong—dong-a-long, like a Chinese festival.

Instead of having a camp in the open the troops might be quartered in a village. It might be a more or less intact village or one which had been shelled. From a shelled village most of the civilian occupants would have departed, leaving the place to the British. **"Back to school once more"** Often it happened that French civilians were in some houses and British soldiers in others, and one or two little public buildings such as schools might be used by French children and British soldiers under a sort of Box-and-Cox arrangement. Schools of this kind were especially used for church service on Sunday afternoons, and it was pretty to see the French children standing at the doors of their school passing

GETTING SUPPLIES OF WATER FROM A REFILLING-PLACE ON THE WESTERN FRONT.
Conserving and regulating the supply of water to the army in the field was of great importance. Special places were marked off on streams and elsewhere, where the troops could get continuous supplies of this prime necessity. Here, where a quick-running stream was crossed by a road, such a point was established, and the petrol-cans, conveniently adapted as water-carrying vessels, could be readily and rapidly replenished.

SYMPATHETIC REPRESENTATIVES OF A NEUTRAL ARMY.   [*British official photograph.*
General Aranaz and Brigadier-General Martinez Anido, of the Spanish Army, visited the western front during the third year of the war.   From a British trench they watched an active bombardment with interest.

[*British official photograph.*
BRITISH NAVAL OFFICER'S VISIT TO THE FRONT.
Captain Guy Gaunt, C.M.G., R.N., British naval attaché at Washington, U.S.A., about to start for a day in the front-line trenches in France.

SOUVENIR OF A VERY FRIENDLY MEETING.   [*British official photograph.*
The Spanish Generals Aranaz and Anido visited General Sir E. H. H. Allenby (centre), commanding the Third British Army in France.   Spain had a number of volunteers serving with the French Army.

jokes with the soldiers who were borrowing it for the time being. "Ah, yes, monsieur soldier," one might say in French, "you come back to school once more ? Yes,? Be good pupil to-day, monsieur soldier." And they loved to pull the forms and desks into position for the service, and to stand out in the road and listen to the English hymn-tunes.

"Rest" billets were to be found behind the line in villages such as this. Any day you might see a regiment or a battalion marching in by the road leading from the front. And they would be very different-looking troops now from those you saw coming up the other way—especially troops that had been through the ordeal of "trenches" during the wet mud days of the Somme battles. With clothes and helmets covered with mud, wet or dry, with feet sore and limping, and eyes hollow with weariness and hardship, they came slowly and painfully along the road without smile or song, and with naught left but their pluck to help them make the last few miles into billets. Just one little fact to enable anyone who did not go through it to appreciate what that march home might mean. A soldier's greatcoat weighed normally about seven pounds. Greatcoats that had been in Somme mud were weighed at some of the R.A.M.C. dressing-stations and they were found then to weigh up to forty-eight pounds. Add to this load the soldier's kit, weighing five or six stones, and you have a big load for even a fresh and strong man to carry. For a man tired and war-worn it was a weary load. The last mile or two of the march into rest billets was often cruel work.

Coming in to rest billets

Sleep and kit-cleaning was their first day's work in "rest," but after that began a round of duties that would seem very far from "rest" to most people. War roads might be so much out of repair that road-parties had to turn out on the second or third day's "rest," under direction of the engineers. If there was one task that came less welcome than another to tired troops it was "plank-carrying for the sappers," as men sometimes called these working tasks. In addition there might be need for working-parties up in the line, and more than one soldier came out of trenches one day only to be sent back again by the night of the next day—not as a fighter in the trenches, but as a member of a working-party working in the No Man's Land between the trenches. Here there was always much work to be done The enemy's shell fire played some trick or other almost every day on the trench defences, especially the barbed-wiring in front of the trenches, and this damage had to be made good. It was work that could not be done in the day, of course, for to be seen outside a trench was to be shot. Night, therefore, was the time always chosen, and working-parties came up "from behind" to do it.

In the quieter villages and neighbourhoods at the back of the front, therefore, you would often see about twilight soldiers quietly assembling in some lane or by the wall of some old barn to make up a working-party to go to the front and work the night in the open. Some would have planks or barbed-wire bobbins or barbed-wire corkscrews (the vertical looped rods of iron through which the barbed-wire . is threaded) ; some would have spades, and others picks or other tools. But in many cases a good number of these men would have naught but rifle and bayonet as usual. These were the escort, whose duty it was to defend the working-party in case of attack. Many pretty fights there were at night between these working-parties and those of the enemy, who, of course, was under the same necesssity to send out night parties. It was often said, in fact, that the Germans sent out more night parties than the British did because they depended more on wiring

Night fighting by working-parties and such things to keep them at bay. They did not like British soldiers to get near enough to begin bayonet and bomb fighting, if they could help it. On some nights our working-parties, finding themselves stalked and hunted, would set out in turn to stalk the hunters, and there were even fights in which men with shovels and picks took their part and made deadly war use of these peace-like weapons. In December, when mist was frequent, working-parties on one or two occasions, owing to a sudden rising of the wind which rolled away the mists, found themselves working within a hundred yards or less of German

MEN OF THE ARMY BEHIND THE ARMY.   *[British official photograph.*
Men of a navvy battalion at work on a road in the Valley of the Ancre. These battalions were perhaps the sturdiest branch of the vast army behind the army which in itself was an amazing contribution that Great Britain made to the cause of the Allies, and through them of civilisation.

working-parties. British soldiers used to say—but whether jokingly or seriously one could not tell—that in these cases no one fired till one party or the other had finished its task, and that this was an understood thing on both sides. If this was the case, one can imagine that work was pretty fast and furious on both sides with a view to getting that triple advantage of which the parodist speaks—" his blow in fust."

The daily life of the artilleryman was perhaps more tolerable than that of the infantryman, if only in that he was seldom in conditions of hardship such as infantrymen in advanced and exposed trenches might have to put up with. But his work was perhaps heavier, and he would probably get a much longer spell of it at one time than the infantryman ; for when the infantry of a division were " taken out " the gunners were often left behind. The gunners were generally well behind the front trenches. First came the field-guns, then the bigger guns, going back and back till the furthest might be six or seven miles away. They were shelled, of course, whenever their positions could be located by the enemy, and shell fire in a gun position was often more dangerous than shell fire in trenches. There was not the same cover, and one unlucky shell might blow gun and gun-crew to eternity. If the enemy's shell fire, however, showed signs of being well on the mark, the firing of that particular battery might be suspended for the time being, and the men could take cover in their dug-outs' and shelters. More often, however, it meant shifting the guns, a tremendous task in " soft " positions. Artillery positions were generally provided with dug-outs or shelters for their crews, but a change of position at a busy time might leave them in new places quite

RUIN LEFT BY THE RECEDING GERMAN TIDE.   *[French official photograph.*
View of the Somme battlefield where the French and British lines joined in 1916, showing the fearful cost to the country-side at which the tide of invasion had been pushed back. Above : A British working-party repairing an important road on the lines of communication in the Somme region.

FLOORING FOR THE SODDEN TRENCHES.
Working-party crossing a frozen canal, bringing up sections of "corduroy" flooring for the trenches—eloquent evidence of the splendid physical condition and high spirit of the troops during the third winter campaign.

FEEDING THE GUNS IN WINTER.
Another working-party had a more strenuous job carrying charges over the slippery ice. Their difficult progress afforded some amusement to themselves and some rather anxious interest to the man watching them.

exposed to any shells that came over. Where the gunners really scored over the infantrymen was in the fact that they were always in better touch with supplies and could run cooking arrangements and fires whereat to get warm and dry for at least some time in a day. It was exceptional for gunners to have to go for days together wet through, cold and unable to get warm rations.

As the forces moved forward in the Somme battlefield, gunners might be moved forward in some positions to old infantry dug-outs, German or British, from which the occupants had moved on. Some of these older dug-outs that fell to the artillery were an acquisition of doubtful desirability, for by this time they were in less good repair, and in addition the rats had had time thoroughly to establish themselves in them. The size and number and fearlessness of these vermin were extraordinary. Even in broad daylight they crawled "fatly" and slowly about the precincts of these underground dwellings, and nothing was safe from

them. In the night they came among the sleepers on the dug-out floors, and even ran over their bodies.

Another dreadful thing about these old trenches and positions, across which battle had raged, was the number of gruesome relics with which the ground was covered. Salvage-parties, burial-parties, and others were at work doing what they could, but after fighting like that of July and August, 1916, there were for a long time arrears of work of this kind to be done, and there were very few old positions at the back of the front—such as those in which artillery might chance to be posted—that had not their grim trophies of some sort. Every heavy rain uncovered new bodies in the innumerable shell-holes. The rats might help the rain, and here and there amid a muddle of wet and mud-stained German uniforms might be seen bones picked white and clean. To walk back to your gun-pits on a cold, grey, bleak afternoon or on a stormy night with the moon dodging in and out of the flying scud overhead, over desolated country-side, past all these grim things, with the rats scooting almost among your very boots, was an experience to make any normal man shudder. Yet the soldiers hardened themselves to such things and worse. Some day, no doubt, a Hogarth or a Dante will arise to show the horrors of this war as they were.

Even though in " rest billets " a soldier might be what he called " legged for a spell of work," and even though " rouser " parades in the early morning and drill and Swedish exercises and inspections were far from being unknown, the " rest " was nevertheless mightily welcome. Here, at least, he did get hot meals and full meals and warmth and comparative dryness, and also a great lessening, if not an elimination, of war risks. It was possible, too, to enjoy in rest billets some of the ordinary amenities of soldier life. There was football, for instance, and any good level field about the rest villages of the war zone of France was pretty sure to have goal-posts. These had been improvised in resourceful fashion of tree branches and rope. But the games were not less keen because the

Gruesome finds in old trenches

ground and the goal-posts were primitive. Regiments would play one another, and different companies and sections of the same regiment might make up matches. Many commanding officers followed, very keenly their men's football and attended the matches. A British general was at tea one afternoon, when his aide-de-camp opened the office door and, saluting, said: "The Gunners are playing the Sappers this afternoon, sir, and they are wondering whether you'll be present." The young man added, with a smile: "It's to be a great game, sir—fur and feathers!" The general looked at his watch. "I'll get over to the field by about half-time," he said, "and see the last half of the game." Soon the shouts of the game and its many spectators were heard from the adjoining field. "Great boys to play are mine," he said appreciatively; adding, after a moment, "and to fight, too." That brigade had not long been out of the front lines, where they had taken a most prominent part in a big advance.

In rest camps and villages music and concerts were often to be had, to which came many leading professional people from home to play and sing and entertain the men. The

Pleasure from the post-office

Y.M.C.A. huts, wherein to write letters, were also a great boon that was not to be enjoyed at the front itself. There would be letters to receive, too—an accumulation of "posts" for all the days that one had spent in trenches. Possibly a parcel as well, with which to make merry with one's friends who had received no parcels. Perhaps the most popular of all the little fatigues that fell to a man to do for the comrades of his billet was to go to the post for letters. There was never any difficulty in finding a man for this job. The local post-office might be no more than a half-ruined barn with a few upturned packing-cases in it to serve as sorting-tables. Or it might be a simple bell-tent in the corner of a field, flying a little red-and-white flag to proclaim its function. But these simple little places and the soldier postmen who presided therein were perhaps the chief purveyors of pleasure in all France. Could their countrymen at home and overseas only have seen the knots of soldiers waiting at these barns and tents "for the mail to come up," and could they have observed the keenness with which each orderly hunted through his bundle, and then the shouting and pleasure with which he was received

back at his billet, they would never have forgotten to write to their relatives and friends at the front.

For among the many hardships of soldiering, home-sickness occupied no mean place. It was a great part of the everyday life of a soldier. To anyone leading the prosy, workaday life of peace, this may sound like an exaggeration; but to go week after week risking life every day, in fact every hour, to know that friends are thinking of you with anxious hearts and prayers and not to be able to see them for a moment, knowing as you did that you possibly might never see them again, was well calculated to bring on a kind of mental sickness worthy of place among the category of serious soldier ailments. A week-end at home set to rights men whom no medicines could cure. Towards the end of 1916 this medicinal value of "leave" was becoming recognised by the authorities, and every effort was being given to make leave more frequent and more general—for there were some men who had gone over a twelvemonth without leave.

Home-sickness and its antidote

"Hot meals and full meals" have been spoken of, and in these things lay undoubtedly the secret of much of our

[*British official photographs.*]

WORK AND PLAY AMID THE SNOWS OF WINTER ON THE WESTERN FRONT.

Men of the mobile motor anti-aircraft guns at a boyish pastime. When winter partially held up operations, British soldiers were ready to maintain their zest for healthy exercise even in the mimic warfare of snowballing.

Above: Artillerymen stacking shells in a snowy "dump" against the time of accelerated activity. Some of the men were wearing the leather jerkins which kept their bodies warm while leaving their arms free.

[*British official photograph.*]

WHERE FRENCH AND BRITISH LINES JOINED: A FRIENDLY TUG-OF-WAR.
Gunners of neighbouring batteries, British and French, who took part in a friendly tug-of-war where their lines joined on the western front. The sergeant in the foreground was evidently engaged in explaining for the benefit of his French comrade the niceties of the game.

of the cream usually sold at home in little brown pots.

Though plenty of jam was to be had, our soldiers often used to say that they missed the sweet dishes they used to get at home. One R.A.M.C. specialist stated that soldiers who did not take alcohol to any great extent were more fond, he had noticed, of sugar than soldiers who took alcohol, and he had an interesting theory that the two things had some common property of which the body of people who worked hard stood in some need. Whether this view is chemically sound need not be gone into; but, in some corroboration of his view, the British Army is a temperate Army, and it is a most "sweet-toothed" Army. The soldiers spent a good deal of their money on chocolate and sweets, and on such things as tinned fruit. The Army canteens sold them, and it was no uncommon sight to see a soldier after a spell in trenches buy a tinful of, say, peaches, or apricots, or pears, prise open the cover with his knife, and eat the tinful without anything with it. The juice of the fruit he would drink from the tin as a beverage.

men's fighting efficiency. The food served out to the soldiers in France was undoubtedly excellent in quality and generous in quantity. In the Army, as elsewhere, could be found cooks, of course, who would spoil any food no matter how good, but in the main the food supply and meals—in all places save in very advanced and exposed positions where cooking was impossible and transport difficult—were good, and there was very little grumbling on the score of bad or insufficient food. In the early morning in these garrisoned villages behind the line it was interesting to stand near the cook-house and watch the mess and billet orderlies coming along with their mess-tins, to be carried away later to their quarters filled with slices of excellent bacon. In the billets or messes, if there were many men, they would file with their plates past a corporal who stood behind the bacon-dish putting so many slices on to each plate. Each man usually carried a piece of bread, which he was allowed to dip in the fat in the dish. Marmalade and jam of excellent quality were also available for anyone who wanted them. A very good butter was served to the troops, though on some occasions margarine was served as substitute. When asked on what system margarine was issued, the men said they could not tell; as a rule they were given nothing but butter, though now and again an odd tin of margarine was issued to them. They did not know why, and as the margarine was very like the butter, they did not trouble to ask. For dinner the best joints were cooked—all fresh meat from England—and there might be puddings. Stews and soups and dumplings were served at intervals. The milk issued to the forces was everywhere well spoken of. It was tinned milk, but neither so thick nor so sticky as the ordinary tinned milk, and from a small hole stabbed through the top of the tin with a jack-knife it would flow quite easily—a white fluid of about the density

Excellent and plentiful food

Nor was it rare to see a soldier eat a whole tin of jam by himself, without bread or anything else. This very noticeable craving for sugar and sweet things on the part of our soldiers may have been partly due to a normal taste for luxuries, but the body has a curious way of its own of asserting its needs by giving the palate a taste for the things needed, and possibly the sugar of the men's diet was not always sufficient to enable them to withstand the cold and the work they were called upon to endure. Certainly the doctors and food specialists of the Army were giving this view some attention at the time.

Craving for sugar and sweets

If the supply of food was good, so also was that of clothes, and though one or two cases had happened during 1916 of quartermasters being unable to get renewals of

[*British official photograph.*]

SERVING OUT A RUM RATION TO MEN OF THE BLACK WATCH.
Soldiers of the famous Black Watch filing up for a warming "go" of rum on the western front. After a hard spell of trench work, or any other labour severely testing either their physical or nerve strength, the men warmly welcomed the serving out of the rum ration.

certain stores from the ordnance people, these were quite exceptional cases, and, as a rule, new tunics, shirts, and other kit could be obtained by any soldier who could prove to the satisfaction of his quartermaster that he needed them. Some people in authority thought, in fact, that clothes and such stores were given out too freely, and towards the end of the year a slight tightening up was noticeable. Some of the soldiers' baths, for instance, had been drawing as many as a thousand new shirts a week for issue, in addition to all those they had received from bathers and washed for reissue to the troops. In the matter of small kit, such as tooth-brushes, pocket-knives, and razors, a new spirit of economy was becoming apparent, and soldiers who could not show that these things had been guarded with due care were invited to pay for any new stores of the kind that they wanted. Keeping trace of one's kit was no small part of the life of the soldier at the front. In makeshift quarters, such as so many of them occupied, and under other such trying conditions of war, it was difficult to account for all the little things missing from one's pack. Especially in trenches was this losing of

Troubles of keeping kit

regiments should go into the line at any particular place and any particular moment, and these were known, as a rule, only to the people who decided the matter, and the men were left guessing as to what they might be. But when orders for "trenches" came along—"proceed to so-and-so, and take over the such-and-such trenches from the such-and-such regiment"—a new note of earnestness came over the men. Speculations began as to whether "the old man," the general, was "sending them in" for a quiet time or for a "strafe"; in other words, did he mean them just to hold the position or had he some "stunt" (a great Army word for special military enterprises) for them to attempt against the enemy? No one knew, of course, and the matter was left, as it began, a subject for speculation.

The such-and-such trenches would be taken over most probably at night. For some short time the old holders of the trenches and their "relief" would be in the trenches together, and in these moments quick summaries of the position and its character and of the character of the Germans opposed to it would be passed from man to man. Any "old scores" against the enemy opposite were sure to be handed on, too. If those Germans were good,

[Canadian official photograph

CANADIANS ON THE WESTERN FRONT: PRACTISING AN ATTACK UNDER COVER OF GAS.
Gas-attack practice under realistic conditions by Canadians. Volumes of smoke having been discharged, as these rolled forth the men plunged forward as though to approach an enemy under its cover. Had they been actual gas-clouds the men would, of course, have been wearing their gas-masks. By such rehearsal troops become "acclimatised" to the conditions of that new weapon which Teutonic savagery had introduced.

things easy. A jack-knife might be laid down for a moment on the ground, and the next minute the mud had engulfed it, leaving no trace even of the spot in which it had been buried. The authorities were fairly tolerant, however, about kit lost in trenches.

As life in the trenches was an all-important part of the life of all infantry soldiers in France it may be gone into more fully.

"Trenches" was an unwelcome but necessary duty that might come to a unit occasionally, or in a long and unpleasing succession. There seemed no rule about it, and for the workaday soldier it was difficult sometimes to see why his regiment or battalion should be "put in" again for a second spell of duty while a friend's unit perhaps was left to enjoy still further rest. They blamed the War Office, or "the Red Hats," as the Staffs were always called, or their colonel, or their member of Parliament—blamed anybody, in fact, but in a genial kind of way, and especially they blamed "their luck." But they went and did the duty well and bravely enough, and to soldiers who did this no one could deny the privilege of a grumble. Many reasons, of course, determined what

"clean" fighters, the fact was made known. If they had done anything "dirty," this fact also was made known, with injunctions to "strafe the blighters good and hard." Then, with wishes of good luck and with happy faces, the older force would move out, leaving the new in possession. The trench might be an old one, with dug-outs, machine-gun posts, saps and the rest, all complete, or it might be a new one with all these things still to be provided, and in the latter case the men just groaned quietly—and set out to provide them.

That night might find them sleeping in a little groove no more than a foot or two high which they had scooped out for themselves in the wall of the trench. And with daylight, or even in the dark hours if the case was urgent, might begin a steady round of work in making that trench more effective for war and more habitable as a dwelling. Uncomfortable days these, and often days of greatest hardship. Some so-called trenches might be no more than a line of shell-holes stretching across a black and barren hillside—shell-holes filled with mud linked up by hillocks of slippery mud. The task of getting rations might be most difficult,

Life in the trenches

[British official photograph.

WHERE BRITISH CAVALRY EAGERLY AWAITED THE SIGNAL WHICH SHOULD GIVE THEM THEIR OPPORTUNITY.

View of British cavalry lines behind the western front. As rumours of each forward move arose it was thought that perhaps at last the long-looked-for chance for the cavalry had come. They had been gradually massed, ready to bear their part in the great task which the Allies had been called upon to perform. In the early months of the war, in the great retreat towards Paris, which Marshal Joffre so dramatically transformed into the forward move from the Marne, the cavalry played a conspicuously notable part. During the long period of trench warfare they could only wait and prepare for the time when they, too, should strike again.

and ration-parties might take seven or eight hours to cross the stretch between the trench and its supplies. Cases were known of these food-parties failing to get back at all. Officers in several cases had to order the opening of "iron rations"—that sacred little tin-case stored in a linen bag and containing beef, biscuits, and tea, which is supplied to every soldier with his kit for use in such emergencies as this. No hot drink might be available—no matter how cold the weather; but most regiments were served out a rum ration when in trenches, and very welcome it was, especially in the early morning.

On the other hand, the trench might be an old one, a dry one, and replete with every trench "luxury"—stout walls of sand or white chalk, a good parapet and parados, dug-outs deep and dry, duck-boards at the trench bottom to walk upon, thereby keeping its holders' feet out of the mud, finger-posts to show one the way, telephones to save long journeys, ammunition stores—and, in fact, all the fittings that had been devised by this time for making trenches more effective and more tolerable as dwelling-places. To this trench it might be possible to bring rations still retaining some of the heat they had when they left the field-kitchens away behind.

If the enemy was quiet, and if your own commander had no particular "stunt" to carry out at the time, trench duty in such a trench as this might be very dull and uneventful. You cleaned your rifle, wrote letters, whittled at little bits of wood with your knife, and ate and "slacked," except when your turn for sentry duty came along. Sentry duty, however, came along very regularly, and at night it could not be done in the cover of the trench with periscopes. Whatever the risk, your head must be kept above the trench and your eyes steadfast on the enemy's lines and the intervening No Man's Land. On clear nights you might feel certain the enemy saw you, but you had to take the risk. Oddly enough, the number of sentries shot on night duty was not considerable in proportion to their numbers. Still, it was solitary work. A two hours' spell was quite long enough.

If the trench happened to be in a place where things were active, as was the case in nearly all the Somme positions, for instance, during the latter half of 1916, trench duty would be anything but peaceful. Saps had to be run out of the trenches in the direction of the enemy, bombing-posts, machine-gun posts, listening-posts, and the like established, and with these tasks and looking out to dodge any shells and bombs and minenwerfen that came over, the infantryman's ordinary day might be a very stirring one indeed. Nor did the waning of daylight necessarily see these tasks finished. A raiding expedi- **Sentry duty at** tion might fall to a soldier's lot on any **night** night. This meant careful preparations, much planning and understanding of detail, and at the time appointed men either crept out of their trench in secret or dashed out of it in the wake of a hurricane of shell fire or trench-mortar fire—it all depended whether the raid were to be a silent and secret one or one prepared by gun fire.

The word "raid," though accurate technically, is a poor one for this type of trench enterprise so much practised by British troops towards the end of 1916. For it has rather a belittling effect, and tends to obscure the extent and the elaborateness of these expeditions as well as to hide their daring and their riskiness. A raid, in fact, was

almost identical with any ordinary attack, with this exception: that whereas in an attack the idea was to take an "objective" and to hold it, the idea of a raid was merely to take a position, hold it for a time, and then to give it up again after killing as many of the enemy, taking as many prisoners, and doing as much permanent damage as possible. Raids were often prepared and prefaced by shell fire just as was an ordinary attack, though the area of it was less. The enemy's machine-guns might have to be faced in just the same way, and there was always the same dangerous movement in the open over exposed ground. For the soldier **Nocturnal raids and** doing trench duty a raid might be as **attacks** dangerous as a general attack; but while attacks provided matter for ample despatches, raids were either ignored or made the matter for paragraphs. In the general perspective of things this was right, of course; but from the point of view of the soldiers taking part in a raid there naturally seemed a great disparity in treatment.

As the time for relief from trench duty drew nearer soldiers began to count the hours, and to tell one another of the things they meant to do as soon as they were "out" and were able to get a few hours' leave. If they had had a hard, "gruelling" time in trenches, as was only too

OPEN-AIR "STABLES" ON THE BRITISH FRONT. [*British official photograph.*

Horses employed on active service near the firing-front, in such primitive "stables" as the ruined country side could provide. The soldiers did their best to keep the animals groomed between their spells of work.

often the case, almost the only "treat" you would hear them promising themselves was a "jolly hot bath, clean 'duds' (clothes), and a long sleep." And when men came out of the Somme trenches in those wet, winter days you might have imagined from their talk—if they were capable of talk—that all the pleasures mankind is heir to lay comprised in that simple recipe—"a hot bath, clean clothes, and a long sleep." They certainly needed all three badly. But the recuperative powers of the British soldiers in those days, as always, were amazing. After that long sleep—it might extend to twenty hours in some cases—little knots of friends would be seen putting their heads together and planning some more elaborate form of enjoyment. Most of their stations, even those near the front, were within travelling distance of some fair-sized town, or at least of some town where there was a good restaurant if nothing more. To get to this town several things were necessary. First, leave. Leave for twelve hours or so was not very hard for "resting" troops to obtain. Next there had to be some means of getting to the town, which might be six miles or more away. Some hardy souls would even set out to walk it, and to these young stalwarts twelve miles or so without a pack would be voted as easy. Often on moonlight nights these walking-parties might be seen returning, all jollity and laughter, to camp along the quiet, tree-lined roads of France.

But more generally it would be possible to get some friendly motor-waggon driver to give a free passage, and the three or four friends would travel to their destination in comfort. Once arrived there the most general thing seemed to be to go to the best restaurant and to order the best possible dinner. It was not so much that any of them had really gone short of food—except in some occasional cases—as that they wanted food of a different kind, served in a fashion that differed from the rough-and-ready soldier way to which they had been subject for so long. They would drink wine with their dinner, very often champagne, which they would pay for jointly, and the sight of three or four privates sitting at dinner, sharing their bottle of Epernay, was quite one of the usual restaurant sights in the towns at " the back of the front." After dinner they could extract all the pleasure in the world from merely walking up and down the dimly-lighted streets of the town watching the passers-by—who very often were only fellow-soldiers from different camps—looking at the shops, buying stationery and picture post-cards, or possibly visiting the local photographer's in a body. After that the café might be visited, and experiments made at the game of French billiards with its giant balls and pygmy tables. Great fun the French experts had watching the Britons' breezy and vigorous play. Quite a new industry sprang up in many of these French towns—namely, that of the afternoon teashop. They often charged scandalous prices—tenpence for a small pot of tea for one person—but to have tea served daintily as at home, out of a china cup instead of a tin mug, our soldiers seemed quite willing to pay this. These visits to town were very orderly. Occasionally they ended in the visitors setting out on a " jamboree," but this was very much the exception. Military police paraded the town, and for the most part they had nothing to do. The townspeople liked these visits, and often disinterested natives were to be seen showing our men the sights of the town—the cathedral, if it had one, or the mairie, or any of its archæological curiosities. The Colonial troops seemed especially interested in these things.

Though these periodical visits to town did a great deal of good by coming as a pleasurable break to a life of great anxiety, hardship and monotony, they **Tasting "life"** were, after all, only a palliative—a sort **on leave** of temporary stimulant rather than a tonic. The real tonic to which each and every British soldier looked forward was " leave "—leave, that is, to go home. Leave was looked forward to by the troops in France as keenly as is water by the thirsty. The wish to get home, even for an hour or two, just to see one's people, became at length a need—a need as pressing as hunger, as uncomfortable as an ache. Men who had gone through every hardship and suffering, every danger and horror, without a murmur might actually shed tears if their leave were unexpectedly cancelled, as

sometimes happened. They had " talked leave " for months, dreamt leave. The only time that the men feared battle and death was when they had been " posted for leave." To be killed on the eve of leave was the only death that was spoken of in terms of real horror and fear. To " go west," as death was sometimes called, was misfortune, a thing that might happen to any man, but to lose your leave was tragedy.

Still all roads have a turning, and, after months of waiting perhaps, a lucky soldier's name would figure on the leave notice-board. " Men posted for leave," an old sergeant of the Grenadiers **When the dream** used to say, " are worse than brides and **came true** bridesmaids waiting for a wedding. They are not fit to live with. They are all on pins and needles, all questions, and all fidgets and anxiety. I'm always glad to see the back of them." Your British soldier, with pack on back and a leave pass in his pocket, would leave his camp.

For the next four hours or so he might be waiting on a bleak station platform " up country " for the leave train to put in an appearance. Then, in a cold, dimly-lighted train, he would pass along to the coast. That train stopped and stopped. It seemed to trickle along its way, by fits and starts, like a rain-drop falling down a window-pane but without the shoot at the end. In the early morning, perhaps, would come the coast. Great trouble! Report to this man; show papers and passes to that man; be in such a place at such a time. There, more examination, more reporting; papers reported upon as being not " strictly in order "; dreadful thoughts and lecture from a corporal one had never seen before on the rules and regulations for a soldier bound on leave, with general comments unasked for on that soldier's paltry brain capacity and general lack of common-

[*British official photograph*]
BILLETED AMID THE DEBRIS OF A WRECKED HOME.
British soldiers in an improvised billet on the western front. Though the scene suggests the after effects of some great earthquake upheaval, the adaptable men appear to have readily made themselves at home.

sense. All this borne patiently. Fall in, march to the boat, and, after it all, with a weary sigh, your soldier bound for leave feels himself at last safe on board ship—all regulations and orders complied with. But not even yet is his anxiety over.

For that naval officer fellow in the blue and gold, on the pier, may even yet come along and stop the sailing of the ship that day on some naval ground or other. Not till the steel hawsers have been cast off the bollards, and the ship's screw is churning the yellow-green waters, not till the muddy, tarry piles of the old French harbour are gliding past is the leave-bound soldier sure that his dream has come true. He is going home at last, going home to mother or wife and children or sweetheart, going home again, alive and well! The wonder of it, after

Being where he has been,
Seeing what he has seen!

That is one of the great moments in the life of a British soldier.

CHAPTER CLXIX.

THE WORK OF THE ALLIED FLEETS: FRENCH, RUSSIAN, AND ITALIAN CO-OPERATION.

By Archibald Hurd, Author of "Naval Efficiency," "German Sea Power," "The Command of the Sea," etc.

EDITORIAL NOTE.—At this stage in the progress of our historical survey of the world-wide events of the war it seems well to introduce a special chapter devoted to the consideration of the naval co-operation given by the Western Allies to the British Fleet during the first thirty months of hostilities. The movements and achievements of the British naval forces in that period have been described with more or less detail in previous chapters, but it has not been possible to say all that the circumstances warranted as to the successful work of Russia in the Baltic, the coastwise service of France, or the able and effective use of the French and Italian Navies in Mediterranean waters. Mr. Archibald Hurd, well known as naval critic of the "Daily Telegraph," has been invited to write this special chapter, and although to some extent familiar ground has had to be covered in the introductory passages, the Editors feel that the circumstances in which the German Navy came into being cannot be too clearly impressed upon British readers, and that a due appreciation of the naval movements which have taken place since the declaration of war is only possible provided the original aims of the Kaiser's naval policy are thoroughly understood.

A JUST appreciation of the work of the allied fleets in the war during the first thirty months of hostilities—August 4th, 1914, to February 4th, 1917—cannot be formed unless an endeavour is made to envisage the conditions which would have existed at sea if the Navies of Russia and France had not been associated with the British sea forces at the very opening of hostilities, and if, later on, two other maritime Powers, Japan and Italy, had not declared themselves on the side of the Allies.

Under the leadership of the Kaiser, who, after Bismarck's dismissal, became virtually the dictator of the policy of Germany in foreign, military, and naval affairs, almost every error was committed against which the great Chancellor warned the young and ambitious ruler during the last years of his life, and from those errors Britain profited when war came. History will record that Bismarck created an Empire which William II. brought to ruin, in the main, because he misread the works of Admiral Mahan, the great American naval historian, and under-estimated the political wisdom of the rulers of neighbouring States.

The wars of 1864 and 1866, against Denmark and Austria successively, gave Prussia Schleswig-Holstein, and thus opened the way to the North Sea. The campaign of 1870 led to the creation of the German Empire. The nerve-centre of Europe was transferred from Paris to Berlin. Bismarck had to determine what course the new Empire should steer, and he came to three definite conclusions. In the first place, a period of peace was essential to enable him to expand the German Army and develop the industries of the new Empire. In the second place, the temptation to found colonies had to be resisted, as they were calculated to lead to a dissipation of strength. In the third place, the German people should not be encouraged to create a great fleet because Germany had obtained ports in the North Sea. In order to mark the relative importance which he attached to the naval and military forces, Bismarck appointed a soldier, Lieutenant-General von Stosch, as Minister of Marine, and kept him there for many years.

RUSSIAN MASTERS OF THE BALTIC.
Admiral Kanin, Commander-in-Chief of the Russian Navy in the Baltic since 1916. Right: The last portrait of Admiral Essen, reorganiser of the Russian Navy and Commander-in-Chief till his death in 1916.

THE TSAR AT KRONSTADT.
Nicholas II. inspecting the crew of a battleship at Kronstadt, the station of the Baltic Fleet.

The Iron Chancellor made no secret of the foundations of the policy which he had marked out for Germany. Germany, he declared, should not plant colonies overseas because they would involve the creation of a great fleet. Germany could provide a dominating navy only at the expense of British friendship. The support of Britain, which Bismarck in the year before his dismissal, 1889, described as Germany's "old and traditional ally," was essential to the Triple Alliance, drawing its strength from military rather than naval power, since Italy, with her exposed coasts, would never place herself in a position of antagonism to the greatest sea Power. Moreover, Bismarck foresaw that the growth of the German Fleet might defeat his aim of keeping Britain and France estranged. Those statements of the basic principles of Bismarckian policy rest on irrefutable evidence.

Lord Odo Russell, who was for a long period British Ambassador in Berlin, in a letter to Lord Granville, in 1873, declared that Bismarck had reached the conclusion that "colonies would only be a cause of **Bismarck against fleet expansion** weakness, because they could only be defended by powerful fleets, and Germany's geographical position did not necessitate her expansion into a first-class maritime Power." Even when, under popular pressure, he abated somewhat his opposition to a Colonial policy, he was careful to consider British susceptibilities and maintained his opposition to fleet expansion. In 1885 he explained that he had determined to acquire Schleswig-Holstein because that province was necessary to Germany if she was ever to have a fleet. "It was a question of national dignity that in case of need Germany should be able to hold her own against a second-rate navy. Formerly we had no fleet. I should consider it an exaggeration for Germany to compete with the French or British Navy."

On another occasion Bismarck uttered a warning against "fantastical plans in connection with naval matters, which might cause us to quarrel with people who are important for our position in Europe." What that cryptic phrase signified in Bismarck's mind may be judged from other statements. He had pointed out years before that "even if we should succeed in building up a navy as strong as that of Britain, we should still have to fear an alliance of Britain and France." That was a development which Bismarck always strove to impede, holding that "these **Menace of Anglo-French alliance** Powers are stronger than any single Power in Europe is or ever can be."

The Chancellor had, moreover, reached the conclusion that "Italy must be able to rely on the assistance of the British Fleet, for the Triple Alliance cannot protect the Italian coast." His conclusion was that "as long as Germany, Austria-Hungary, and Italy are united in the Triple Alliance, and as long as these three States can reckon on the assistance of British sea-power, the peace of Europe will not be broken." Apart from those considerations, Bismarck realised that a German policy of fleet expansion would probably arouse nervous apprehensions in Russia, interested in the balance of power in the Baltic, and might lead that Power to conclude an alliance with France.

MENTIONED IN RUSSIAN DESPATCHES.
A useful unit of the Russian Navy, this little vessel of eighty-five tons, No. 113, was mentioned in the Russian despatches as having done particularly good work in the Baltic.

When William II. took control of German affairs, in 1890, he abandoned Bismarck's policy. The man of blood and iron has left it on record that the Kaiser was hostile to Britain not only when Crown Prince, but during the first years of his rule, when he professed close attachment to the British Royal Family and the British nation. As a youth the Kaiser had spent many years in the Isle of Wight, watching British ships passing in and out of Spithead, and had had the free run of Portsmouth Dockyard. He came to the throne determined at all costs to create a German fleet rivalling that of his grandmother, Queen Victoria. Britain was still pursuing a policy of "splendid isolation," and the young Emperor believed that the animosities which divided the British people on the one hand from France, irritated over Egypt and the Newfoundland fisheries, and on the other from Russia, with her Asiatic ambitions, would persist whatever course Germany might take with reference to naval affairs. That impression was deepened in 1899, when the war in South Africa created a widespread anti-British movement throughout the European continent.

In the light of events, can it be doubted that the Kaiser's telegram to President Kruger, on the occasion of the Jameson Raid, was sent with the intention of fanning the anti-British flame not only in Germany but in other countries? When this dangerous movement was at its height and British resources were suffering from the strain of the long campaign, conducted at a distance of six thousand miles from the home country and therefore resting on sea-power, the Kaiser showed his hand

Since his accession to the throne he had devoted himself to the education of the German people in favour of a great fleet. He had read Admiral Mahan's works and arranged for their translation into German. He had founded the Navy League, and initiated a great Press movement in favour of shipbuilding. In order to undermine the opposition of the Reichstag to his naval ambitions, he had picked out from the Navy an officer with big conceptions of policy, a facile tongue, a pleasant, jovial manner, a *flair* for politics, and an eye for effect. That man was Alfred Tirpitz, then unknown to fame.

The anti-British movement on the Continent at the time of the Boer War supplied the two conspirators with the impulse which was necessary if Germany was to become a first-class naval power. An extremely modest Navy Act had been passed in 1898, on the understanding that it contained a complete exposure of German naval policy for the succeeding six years. Two years later it was determined that the moment had come for a new measure, repealing the one of 1898, and on June 14th, 1900, the

RUSSIA'S BALTIC FLEET UNDER FULL STEAM.
The re-creation of the Russian Navy after the Japanese War was due to Admiral Essen. When war was declared in 1914 the Russian Navy was prepared for it.

Kaiser and Prince Hohenlohe, the Chancellor, put their signatures to an Act which specifically declared that Germany in the future intended to rank as a first-class naval Power. It was declared that "Germany must have a battle fleet so strong that, even for the adversary with the greatest sea-power, a war against it would involve such dangers as to imperil his position in the world." This German Navy Act provided for the construction of a fleet exceeding in strength that of Great Britain.

The Kaiser assumed that the stars in their courses would stand still while he realised his dreams of world domination.

The Kaiser's wrong assumptions His attitude somewhat resembled that of Canute, who is supposed to have commanded the waves to obey his bidding. William II. concluded that, because Britain had hitherto maintained a position of "splendid isolation," she would continue to pursue that policy, and that in accordance with that policy her Fleet would be distributed. That assumption is based upon an admission in the Memorandum of the Navy Act: "It is not absolutely necessary that the German battle fleet should be as strong as that of the greatest naval Power, for a great naval Power will not, as a rule, be in a position to concentrate all its striking forces against us."

At that time the spear-head of the British Navy was in the Mediterranean; squadrons of battleships, cruisers and gunboats were on duty in the outer seas; there was no British naval force in the North Sea, for the old Channel Squadron was mainly a reinforcement for the

Mediterranean. The German Emperor and Grand-Admiral von Tirpitz assumed that political considerations which led to those dispositions of force would persist, and that thus Germany would become the dominating maritime Power in Northern Europe, strong enough to deal Britain a lightning blow. If those anticipations had been realised what would have happened to the British Empire in 1914? Had it been isolated then, with naval responsibilities on the same scale in the Mediterranean, the Far East, and elsewhere, Germany's policy might have been crowned with triumph either as a result of the Great War which convulsed Europe, or, if in that struggle Britain had remained neutral, in a later conflict in which the two countries would have fought to the death on the sea.

For some years it seemed as though the British people would not realise the menace which threatened their every interest. In the five years succeeding the passing of the German Navy Act only fourteen battleships were laid down in British shipyards; during the same period Germany began ten battleships. The British Government also built a large number of armoured cruisers — twenty-one to Germany's four; but the war illustrated the small value attaching to such ships, with their light-armoured belts and medium-calibre guns. During the same period only

RUSSIAN MOSQUITO CRAFT OF THE 4TH DIVISION.
In 1915, particularly, the Baltic Fleet was very busy, and in August of that year, in the Gulf of Riga, the Russian mosquito fleet stung Germany severely, the Novik notably distinguishing herself.

five British scout cruisers were built, apart from eight weak vessels of less than 3,000 tons, and mounting no bigger weapon than the 12-pounder gun ; while Germany laid down in the same period thirteen useful cruisers of high speed—twenty-four and twenty-five knots—and armed them with the 4·1 in. gun, throwing a steel shell of 34 lb. In these years the British Fleet was strengthened by thirty-nine destroyers besides eleven torpedo-boats of limited utility, and Germany laid down thirty destroyers. The course of naval policy in Britain during those five years may well have encouraged the Kaiser and his Ministers to believe that their ambitions would be realised, particularly as British foreign policy, which regulated the disposition of ships, showed for several years no indication of undergoing a radical change.

At last the awakening came. The Russian Fleet had been worsted by Japan, and the balance of power in European waters had thus been upset to Germany's advantage. The crisis was grave, and the British Government made approaches to France with a view to more cordial relations with that sea Power. Simultaneously, Admiral Sir John (afterwards Lord) Fisher, who had been recalled to Britain from the command of the Mediterranean Fleet at the end of 1902, was appointed First Sea Lord of the Admiralty, with freedom to carry out a vast, correlated scheme of naval reforms. A definite alliance with Japan

proved the complement to the Entente with France, that country having already become the ally of Russia.

In these circumstances steps were taken to meet the German challenge. Without fuss or anything calculated to cause irritation in Germany, the main power of the British Navy was shifted from southern to northern waters ; the alliance with Japan enabled vessels to be released from duty in the Far East ; the Entente with France justified a weakening of British strength in the Mediterranean ; closer relations with the United States facilitated a reduction of the forces in the Atlantic. At the same time, projects were under way for strengthening the reserves of the Fleet in home waters. With patience and foresight   **Creation of the** the basis of German naval policy   **Grand Fleet** was slowly undermined, and the Grand Fleet was created, which went to its station in the North Sea when hostilities broke out in the summer of 1914.

In justice to our Allies let it not be forgotten that the vast concentration in the northern mists could never have been carried out had it not been for the splendid co-operation of the Navies of France and Japan, in particular, and for the threat which Russia aimed at Germany in the Baltic. When once the three great sea Powers of Europe were ranged against Germany, the attitude of Italy towards the belligerents was in little doubt. Bismarck's prophecy was fulfilled to the letter. Whatever views the Italian Government may have had —and it is well known on which side their sympathies bent from the first—the fact that Britain, which had been so largely instrumental in effecting Italian unity and still remained the predominant sea Power, was fighting Germany and Italy's traditional enemy, Austria, determined the course of her policy.

The German Emperor and his Ministers reaped as they had sown. In the period of nearly a quarter of a century before the outbreak of the Great War they had deliberately reversed the policy of the great man who

BRITISH, FRENCH, AND ITALIAN WARSHIPS IN THE GULF OF SALAMIS.

[*French official photograph.*

In Southern European waters the allied fleets did an immense amount of work in co-operation, practically clearing the Mediterranean of every enemy flag. The vacillation of the King of the Hellenes necessitated the presence in the Gulf of Salamis of a considerable fleet, which enforced the requirements of the Allies by a blockade of the Greek coast. Above : A gun on one of the Mediterranean islands taken by the Allies.

[French official photograph.

THE ALLIES' IRON HAND.
General view of the Piræus, showing the composite allied fleet of British, French, and Italian warships in possession to prevent the threatened treachery of King Constantine.

[French official photograph.

WATCHING THE ASIATIC EMPIRE OF THE TURK.
On board a French warship off the coast of Asia Minor. The French Navy was strong in ships of the line when war broke out, and these, reinforced by British ships of the cruiser classes, made the allied Mediterranean Fleet a well-balanced force.

created the German Empire. They had stretched forth grasping hands for colonies; they had disregarded Britain's claim to maritime supremacy; they had humiliated France; they had domineered over Russia; they had alienated Japan; they had insulted the United States—all of them sea Powers.

The Kaiser had proclaimed that "Germany's future lies on the water," and his naval ambitions led him from one folly to another. When the awakening came he realised the fruits of a policy which had united all the great naval Powers of Europe against Germany and Austria-Hungary. For a time he professed to believe that the influence of sea-power upon history had been grossly exaggerated.

Sailormen and the Superman He denied the faith according to Mahan, which he had formerly confessed. But, even while these denials were being made, the pressure of sea-power was being exerted. In northern waters as in southern waters, in the Atlantic as in the Pacific, naval influence was being rigorously applied to teach the superman that the sailor had still a share in determining the fate of continents. In this work by sea the Navies of Russia, France, Italy, and Japan shared the honours with the British Fleet.

Ten years before the opening of the Great War, Vice-Admiral Baron Curt von Maltzahn, of the German Navy, wrote a little book on naval warfare. He devoted one chapter to the effect of blockade by sea. He controverted the argument, which was advanced during the agitation in Germany for the increase of the Navy, that shipowners and merchants should bear the cost it would entail, because they alone would benefit by it. Such reasoning, he declared, could appeal only to the ignorant. "For not simply the coasts, but the whole country would suffer if an enemy should blockade our ports." He pointed out the effects which the pressure of sea-power would produce. "It is true that the hostile ships could not proceed farther than the shore-line, but the iron hand of their naval dominion would stretch beyond the limits of the sea. It would knock at the inland office of the merchant, it would hammer at the gates of the factories in the great industrial centres in the heart of the country, and it would rap on the doors of the houses of our working men."

That prophecy was fulfilled in the experience of the German people, and not only their experience, but that of the peoples of Austria-Hungary, Turkey, and Bulgaria. With the support of the allied fleets, which was an essential element to success, the British Navy placed its controlling hand on the heart of Central Europe and once more illustrated the historic truth that the sea controls the land.

I.—The Fight for the Baltic.

When the war broke out Germany was confronted with an embarrassing position in northern waters. Since the close of the war in the Far East the Russian Navy had been re-created, and Germany found herself opposed by the British Fleet in the North Sea and by considerable naval forces under the Russian flag in the Baltic.

So long as it was the fixed policy of the German Empire to remain on friendly terms with Britain the Navy under the ensign of the double eagle could be concentrated at Kiel, which in Bismarck's day was the Fleet headquarters, and the North Sea could be ignored. But in time the Germans began to chafe under the misfortune that they possessed no short route between the Baltic and their North Sea ports, and in June, 1887, when the British people were celebrating the Jubilee of Queen Victoria's reign, work was commenced on a canal to run from Brunsbüttel, at the mouth of the Elbe, to Kiel and Holtenau.

Hitherto vessels proceeding from the Elbe to the Baltic had had to make a **The Kaiser Wilhelm** voyage of nearly six hundred miles **Canal** through somewhat dangerous waters. By constructing the new canal, that distance was to be reduced to sixty-one miles. The new canal—known as the Kaiser Wilhelm Canal—was opened for traffic in 1895. The Germans prided themselves on the fact that the largest ships could pass from one sea to the other in a matter of a few hours. The new waterway was built with a depth of water of 29½ feet, the width on the bottom being 72 feet.

When this connecting-link between the North Sea and the Baltic was opened in 1895, the nations were invited to send men-of-war, and the Emperor delivered a grandiloquent speech, in which he remarked that : " What technique on the basis of its great development has been able to accomplish, what was possible through pride and joy in the work, what finally could be done in promoting the welfare of the numberless workers engaged in the task, in accordance with the principle of the humane social policy of the Empire, has been accomplished in this undertaking."

The Emperor referred to " the significance of the canal for increasing the national welfare and strengthening our defence." In this year, which was marked by celebrations in honour of the twenty-fifth anniversaries of the victories of the Franco-Prussian War, German Imperialism came to the birth. The war between Japan and China was drawing to a close ; Germany decided to have a finger in the pie, and took the lead in preventing Japan from retaining Port Arthur.

In the following year, when the Jameson Raid occurred, the Emperor intervened in South African affairs, sending to President Kruger his notorious telegram. Then, in 1898, Prince Henry of Prussia was despatched to the Far East in command of a naval squadron, to exact **Naval expansion** reparation from China for the murder **and discomfiture** of two German missionaries. " Imperial power," he declared, " means sea-power ; and sea-power and Imperial power are dependent on each other." The Emperor had come to the conclusion that the opening of the Kiel Canal had conferred upon his Fleet strategic freedom, since men-of-war of the largest size could pass swiftly from the Baltic to the North Sea, and he was determined to make the most of the new strength which the canal had given to his naval forces—doubling, as he claimed, the value of his Fleet.

In these circumstances Germany began the work· of fleet expansion. The new navy was to be built to fit the canal. A battleship design on a displacement of about 13,000 tons was adopted. The Kaiser Wilhelm Canal was just big enough for these ships, and, under the Navy Acts of 1898 and 1900, Germany proceeded to build a navy which she was confident would be in a position to operate either in the Baltic or in the North Sea. For some years nothing occurred to disillusion the Germans. But in November, 1905, a mysterious battleship was laid down at Portsmouth Dockyard, and orders were given for three other ships, which were officially described as " armoured

WARSHIP ARRIVING AT SALAMIS.
One of the allied warships arriving at Salamis to put an end to the German intrigues in Greece. At the close of 1916 the attitude of King Constantine made it necessary for the Allies to establish a strict blockade.

cruisers." They were, in fact, the battle-cruisers Invincible. Inflexible, and Indomitable. Several months later, but not before Germany had made considerable progress in the construction of her two 13,000-ton battleships of the 1905 programme, as well as an armoured cruiser, the Blücher, it leaked out first that the British battleship represented a new type, and that the three armoured cruisers were, in fact, swift sisters of the ship of mystery.

The appearance of the Dreadnought, with a displacement of 18,000 tons (nominal), and mounting ten 12 in. guns in contrast with four 11 in. of the German battleships, completely upset all Germany's calculations. It was some time before the German naval authorities, even by bribery, could obtain the plans of the new British battleship. A story is told that, in order to deceive the not very intelligent spies, false plans were prepared and measures taken to see that they reached Germany.

At any rate, what happened was this. First of all the Germans realised that they also had to build Dreadnoughts, and that, if they were to pass from the North Sea to the Baltic, the depth and width

OBSERVATION-BALLOON RETURNING TO PORT.
Kite observation-balloon being towed back to port. These " sausage " balloons proved invaluable for observation purposes over both sea and land. At sea they were " tethered " to their attendant tugs, which took them out, stood by, and when their spell was over towed them back to their shore harbourage.

of the Kiel Canal would have to be increased. Secondly, they were so savage at being outmanœuvred that they accepted the false plan, and laid down four vessels under the impression that they were constructing ships in every way as powerful as the British Dreadnought. The change in the British ship design arrested German battleship building for thirty months, and then those clever people began four vessels, known as the Nassau class, which embodied most of the errors which the British constructors had rejected.

The Germans themselves admit that the British naval authorities proved too smart for them. Writing after the Great War had been in progress for a year, Count Revent-low made a series of confessions pointing to the complete discomfiture which Germany suffered at a moment when she thought her Fleet had acquired complete strategic freedom. He remarked that when the Navy Act of 1900 was passed it was calculated that the rebuilding of the Fleet

Revolution in shipbuilding

would be completed in 1920. " In 1906, however, came the great Dreadnought revolution in shipbuilding, which quickly rendered worthless all ships built before that time (pre-Dreadnoughts),* and compelled tremendous enlargements of wharves, harbours, and canals, gigantic extension of organisation, etc."

In other words, the adoption of the Dreadnought design

---

* In pre-Dreadnoughts of the most recent construction Germany was approaching Great Britain.

by the British naval authorities threw the German move-ment for fleet expansion back for a period of ten years. She was compelled, after an interval during which British yards had been busy, to begin again, and at the same time to undertake what amounted practically to a reconstruction of the Kaiser Wilhelm Canal. Simultaneously, harbours had to be deepened, new slipways constructed, and new docks excavated. Everything had been created on the basis of a maxi-mum ship displacement of about 13,000 tons, and Germany found herself suddenly confronted with a new standard ship of 18,000 tons (nominal).

The Kiel Canal enlarged

Outside the Marineamt in Berlin, probably no one knows the immense sum which Germany had to expend in order to meet the new naval situation. But one detail is known. The Kiel Canal originally cost £8,000,000. In 1908 the work of doubling it was undertaken. The original estimate amounted to £11,000,000, and there is reason to believe that this was exceeded. By this manœuvre, for which Lord Fisher was responsible, German naval progress was arrested, and time was obtained for carrying out the reforms in the British Navy which were essential before it engaged at sea.

The great task of enlarging the Kiel Canal was completed early in the summer of 1914. In preceding years the Kaiser had repeatedly brought the German Empire to the brink of war and had then withdrawn. The explanation was to be found in the vast canal works which were still in progress.

[*French official photograph.*

FUTILE RUTHLESSNESS: GERMANY'S VAIN ATTEMPT TO ESTABLISH AN EFFECTUAL BLOCKADE.

Despite the real gravity of the German submarine campaign in the third year of the war, the men of the Allies' mercantile marine remained quite imperturbed, signing on as freely as usual. What diminution of shipping took place was due to owners' reluctance to incur risk of loss. These wharves at Toulon were constantly crowded with incoming and outgoing Mediterranean shipping, and every French port furnished a similar sight.

They were not completed until June, 1914, when the ceremonies coincided with the Kiel Regatta, and were marked by the presence of the men-of-war of all the Great Powers.

British naval officers were given a particularly cordial reception by the Kaiser and his Ministers, and the Emperor's flag for a time flew from the masthead of the battleship King George V., flagship of Admiral Sir George Warrender. While the festivities were in progress news was received of the murder at Sarajevo of the Archduke Franz Ferdinand and his consort. The assembly immediately broke up. The British ships withdrew, and were joined by other squadrons which had been paying visits of ceremony and friendship in Russian, Danish, and Swedish waters.

Germany by the completion of the Kiel Canal had again obtained strategic freedom. How would she use it? As though to lull all suspicion, the German High Sea Fleet proceeded on a cruise in Norwegian waters, one division remaining in the Baltic to keep an eye on Russia. When the crisis came, in the last days of July, the principal squadrons of the German Fleet were away north in Norwegian waters. Two conclusions are supported by ample evidence. In the first place, Germany believed that the British Government would remain neutral.

In that event, the High Sea Fleet would have been already well on its way round the British Isles, intending to attack France, and thus getting behind the French armies. It was assumed that, at the worst, the British Government would weigh for several days the pros and cons of the situation which had so suddenly developed, and that by the time an unfavourable decision for Germany could be reached the crisis of the war would be over, Paris probably having been occupied, and the French Fleet defeated.

Events did not turn out as Germany anticipated. The British declaration of war synchronised with the invasion of Belgium. Thirty hours before the expiration of the ultimatum, Mr. Winston Churchill at the Admiralty, supported by Admiral Prince Louis of Battenberg, had mobilised the Fleet, and orders were given mobilising the British Army, embodying the Territorials, and putting in motion the machinery for home defence created by the Committee of Imperial Defence.

In the second place these events changed the character of the war, not only in the North Sea and the outer seas, but in the Baltic. Germany had lost the first moves, and she had to recast all her plans in the light of the fact that she was opposed on the one hand by the supreme British Fleet, and on the other by the considerable forces of Russia.

Events had not developed as the Emperor and his Ministers had anticipated, and the Russian Fleet, which they had apparently regarded as a negligible factor provided the British Navy remained neutral, suddenly assumed unforeseen importance as the associate of the supreme naval Power.

Russia was known to possess in those waters four pre-Dreadnought battleships, with a main armament of four 12 in. guns each, besides a quartette of large modern armoured cruisers, two somewhat older armoured cruisers, five light cruisers, thirty-six destroyers, and a number of submarines. Moreover, it was common knowledge that the Russians had nearly completed four powerful ships of the Dreadnought type, displacing 23,000 tons and mounting twelve 12 in. and sixteen 4'7 in. guns each.

The menace of the Russian Fleet, however, resided less in the ships than in the officers and men. The whole spirit of the Russian Navy, as the Germans were soon to realise, had undergone a change since the conclusion of the Russo-Japanese War. The Navy in the Baltic had been re-created under the impulse of Admiral Essen, its distinguished Commander-in-Chief. What this officer had accomplished was revealed by an officer on the Staff of Admiral Kanin, his successor, in an interview published in the "Novoe Vremya" shortly after his death in 1916.

The late Admiral Essen, he declared, worked wonders with the Navy. His fundamental idea was simple— the Fleet must know the entire Baltic, not excluding the most remote rocks; and for this purpose it must cruise for not less than ten months in the year. Formerly this seemed almost impossible! I remember my own younger days. We set out upon a tremendous round-the-world voyage, studied, gained experience, and worked. The decisive moment was the naval inspection after our return from the cruise. Gold, velvet! The inspection over, and suddenly all fell to pieces. And really it could not be otherwise; the wood had rotted, the sails had been devoured by rats. It was necessary to remove this into dry, well-aired store-rooms; otherwise everything would have perished —and it was removed. What was the result? There was, so to speak, a locomotive in all its glory: it was taken to pieces and conveyed in parts somewhere into a shop. This locomotive would be assembled anew, but it would then be another locomotive.

The crew had dispersed and the officers separated. The experience gathered was not passed on to the new people. But now! This is my third year in the same boat. A. M. P. (he pointed to a senior officer) has been here already five years. In such circumstances a man does really begin to know what he has in his hands. Thanks to this, there cannot be any mobilisation for us. We have a term for mobilisation—such and such an hour and such and such a minute. When war was declared we received absolutely nothing from any depot. Perhaps a few things were taken ashore—valuable prizes, relics; but neither stores nor men were required by us; we had everything on hand. In four hours we put to sea. We attained this result solely owing to the fact that the late Admiral Essen refused to have barracks for the crews.

Obverse of the medal which was cynically struck in Germany to commemorate the unjustifiable sinking of the Lusitania, May 5th, 1915, with the legend " No Contraband."

On the reverse Death is figured issuing tickets to the passengers, whom a German is supposed to be warning of the risk they will run from submarines.

MEMORIAL OF A CROWNING INFAMY.

MEMORIAL SERVICE FOR FALLEN GERMANS HELD ON ONE OF THE KAISER'S WARSHIPS.

Officers and sailors on board a German warship who were engaged in taking part in a Memorial Service for their fallen countrymen. A goodly proportion of the men appear to have been more conscious of the contiguity of the camera than of the solemnity of the service at the time that the photograph was taken, judging by the number of heads that were turned round with an evident desire of being included in the picture.

This enthusiastic admirer of Admiral Essen, who rendered conspicuous service in the Russo-Japanese War, proceeded to give some indication of the methods of Admiral Essen in training the Fleet for war.

If a fleet cruises among rocks ten months in the year, the risk, of course, is considerable. I should rather think so! At times one sails alongside absolutely vertical walls. Or, suddenly, as happened recently, a twelve-foot rock is revealed in a spot where not a single pilot is aware that it exists. A reform of that kind cannot be effected without risks; and it was not deemed a crime to run risks. He knew that in the business of risk the exercise of superfluous severity might undermine the moral of any officer. You remember, one admiral was punished for having fired too soon, and another for having done so too late. Essen personally cruised among the rocks. Sometimes we simply dodged through a chink; and the presence of an experienced, universally-loved admiral, of course, did away with all hesitation on the part of the junior officers. The word "impossible" disappeared entirely; everything seemed possible. Essen loved to say that a wreck was reparable; the only thing irreparable was the decline of spirit in the Navy. As a result, of course, the Navy attained a very advantageous position. Here just now we are lying in the ice. If an urgent order should come, we can put out. We are allowed four hours to get up steam and another two or so for the muster. And right away—no matter how severe the cold, we go ahead—we begin to cut the surrounding ice like butter. Only a week ago in a temperature of twenty degrees a battleship came in and moored alongside us. Formerly no one would have believed that such a thing was possible. To me it would have seemed just as preposterous as to manœuvre an army a million strong in a forty-seven-degree frost. But it proves to be possible.

The Russian Navy entered upon the war in the knowledge that it was associated with a force to which it was united by many ancient bonds. When Peter the Great determined to build a fleet for Russia he came to England to learn how ships should be constructed, and on returning to his dominions he took with him naval officers, seamen, and mechanics to assist him in his task. During subsequent years many other officers of the British Fleet joined the Russian Navy. Lord Duffus, Admiral Elphinstone, Admiral Francis Keith, Admiral Greig, Admiral Paddon, Captains William Baker, William Batting, John Deane, John Delap, Edward Lane, Robert Little, John Perry, Andrew Simpson, Sir F. Thesiger, and John Waldron were a few of the many British officers who took service under the Russian naval ensign.

Many other Britons have served from time to time in the civil departments of the Russian Admiralty. Russia's conspicuous naval victory of the eighteenth century was gained by a force trained by British officers. The Russians had obtained command of the Baltic in the early half of the eighteenth century, and Catherine despatched a Russian squadron from the Baltic to the Mediterranean. It was nominally under the orders of Admiral Alexis Orloff; but it was joined in the Mediterranean by reinforcements under Admiral Elphinstone.

In July, 1770, an indecisive battle with the Turkish Fleet was fought in the Levant. At nightfall the Turks cut their cables and, in opposition to the wishes of the more experienced officers, ran into the Bay of Tchesmé, where, "huddled together like birds in a nest," they were blockaded by the Russians. At midnight on the following day four fire-ships, prepared by Admiral Elphinstone, were taken into the bay by Lieutenants Dugdale and Mackenzie, both trained in the British Fleet, the operation being covered by Commodore Greig with four ships of the line and two frigates. In a period of five hours the whole Turkish Fleet, with the exception of one 62-gun vessel and two galleys, had been destroyed.

In later years many other British officers were tempted to join the Russian Fleet, and Sir Samuel Greig, who became a rear-admiral after the Battle of Tchesmé, was eventually appointed Governor of Kronstadt. It is not inappropriate to recall these incidents in the long association of the Russian and British Fleets, since the memory of the past was not without its influence on the course of events when the war-cloud burst in Europe in 1914, and Germany found herself confronted with an enemy in the Baltic and another yet more powerful enemy in the North Sea.

The Germans at once realised that these naval forces offered a threat to Berlin, the capital of the German Empire, situated only just over one hundred miles from the Baltic shores. They remembered that the French had occupied their capital for over two years—1806-8—and that it had been held by Austrians and Russians successively during the Seven Years War. The Kiel Canal, so recently re-opened, had alleviated Germany's difficulty, but had not removed it. The Fleet might try conclusions with the Russians, but any action, it was recognised, must result in losses being incurred, and thus the Fleet would be weakened for the struggle in the North Sea. On the other hand, if battle were accepted in the North Sea, casualties might be sustained which would render the situation in the Baltic even more perilous than it was.

Germany in a dilemma

The Higher Command in Germany no doubt recalled the experiences of the Seven Years War, when Russian sea-power, supported by the Russian Army, forced Frederick the Great to make a peace which certainly did not accord with his early hopes. The course of events is not without interest in shedding light on the position which existed in 1914. At the period of the Seven Years War, Prussia possessed practically no fleet. The Tsaritza Elizabeth had therefore no hesitation in sending a squadron of fifteen sail to blockade the Prussian ports and to bombard Memel, which surrendered to a land force under Fermor; but, after defeating Lewald at Gross Jägerdorf, the Russians recrossed the Niemen. In 1758 Fermor again invaded Prussia, occupied Königsberg and laid siege to Kustrin, on the Oder, which was relieved by Frederick the Great in August. Defeated at Zorndorf, Fermor marched into Pomerania, where he failed to take Kolberg, which was needed as a port of supply.

In 1758 the Russians won the Battle of Zullichau and Kunersdorf, subsequently retiring to Poland for want of provisions. In 1760 a Russian fleet of twenty-seven vessels, under Admiral Mishukoff, with a land force of fifteen thousand men, failed in an attempt on Kolberg; but in October Berlin was bombarded and occupied for four days by a Russo-Austrian army, which retired on the approach of Frederick. In the following year a Russian fleet of forty sail, subsequently joined by a Swedish squadron, blockaded and bombarded Kolberg, which was at the same time besieged by land. On December 16th Kolberg fell, and a new line of sea supply was opened to the Russian armies. The death of Elizabeth occurred on January 5th, 1762, and saved Frederick the Great from the effects of the dual pressure by land and sea. Peter III. at once ceased hostilities.

The Seven Years War

When the Great War began in 1914 the Germans were not unconscious of the danger threatening them in the Baltic. In preceding years defensive measures had been

FRENCH ADMIRAL DISTRIBUTING MEDALS TO MEN OF THE FIRST BRITISH BATTLE CRUISER SQUADRON.
Vice-Admiral Guépratte, of the French Navy (marked x), on board a British battle-cruiser distributing honours awarded by the French Government. These honours were given to officers and men of the First Battle-Cruiser Squadron for the distinguished part which they had played in the defeat of the German Battle Fleet off the Jutland Bank on May 31st, 1916. It was this squadron which began the action at a range of 18,500 yards.

"CLEARED FOR ACTION": THE ITALIAN BATTLESHIP SAN MARCO IN THE ADRIATIC.

View of the guns on the Italian battleship San Marco, ready for any appearance of the enemy. Even as the German Navy remained "bottled up" in its home waters rather than face the British Grand Fleet in the North Sea, so the Austrian Fleet kept in the shelter of its Adriatic ports rather than risk any meeting with the allied fleet—consisting of British, French, and Italian units—which patrolled the neighbouring waters.

taken along the coast; in particular, Kiel had been converted into one of the strongest fortified places in the world, and at other points heavy guns had been placed in order to guard the sea approach to Berlin. Shore artillery can always be employed with advantage against ships at sea, as the Dardanelles operations illustrated in 1915. Germany was also able to utilise to advantage her carefully developed mine-laying service.

In spite, however, of all precautionary measures, uneasiness was felt as to the position in the Baltic, and before the British Fleet had been mobilised the Germans had assumed the offensive. The first act of war in either of the theatres was the bombardment by the German cruiser Augsburg of the Russian port of Libau, which the Russians captured from Sweden in 1701 and definitely annexed towards the close of the eighteenth century. When the Tsar's Government devoted attention to the task of asserting Russian influence in the Baltic, this town, which had already acquired considerable importance, was converted into a naval base for two reasons. In the first place

Bombardment of Libau

it was ice-free and could be used in winter as well as in summer; and in the second place, situated in the Government of Courland, one hundred and forty-five miles by rail south-west of Riga, it offered a threat to Germany.

Before the war in the Far East led to the withdrawal of the major portion of the Baltic forces, it had been intended to make Libau the advanced base of Russia. The misfortunes which overtook the Russians during this campaign rendered it necessary to reconsider the situation in the Baltic, and the Russian Naval Staff came to the conclusion that since the retention of Libau would lead to a dispersion of the limited naval strength at their disposal the port,

menaced by the Germans by sea and by land, could not be defended. The bombardment of Libau was no doubt undertaken by the Germans in full knowledge of the decision to which the Russian naval authorities had come.

The action of the Augsburg was apparently merely a reconnaissance, and many weeks passed without any further development. No doubt in the meantime the Germans were busy making preparations for a determined attack. In November the town was again bombarded. A further interval then occurred, and on March 31st, 1915, German ships again appeared and opened fire. It

From Windau to Riga

subsequently became apparent that the naval forces of the enemy were awaiting the development of the campaign on land. It was only a matter of time when the port would have to be surrendered, and when it fell the position of Windau was menaced, and that port also eventually passed into the hands of the Germans.

If the enemy was encouraged by these successes, he was soon to learn that when he threw himself against strategic points which the Russians were determined to defend, the experience would be far from pleasant. Libau having been seized and Windau occupied, the next objective of the German naval and military forces was the Gulf of Riga.

But the Russians, though their main fleet was concentrated in the Gulf of Finland, had determined to defend this portion of the coast at all costs. Riga, with its direct railway communication with Petrograd, was regarded as the side-door to the Russian capital, and events were to prove that, though our ally had determined not to risk the main fleet in its defence, adequate measures had been taken to prevent the Germans obtaining control of the port, even after the army had advanced to the very outskirts of Riga and dominated a large part of the coastline.

In the early summer of 1915 the German scheme for mastering the Gulf, which had evidently been the subject of considerable thought, was put into operation. Throughout the first days of June the Germans nibbled at the Russian defences, hydroplanes and torpedo craft being employed. This reconnaissance in force was a failure, three of the enemy ships being damaged, if not sunk, by running into mine-fields which the Russians had laid.

Battles for the Gulf of Riga
Undeterred by this experience, the enemy returned to the assault early in July. The Russian cruisers Rurik, Makaroff, Bayan, Bogatyr, and Oleg were cruising between the Island of Oeland and the Courland coast, when they sighted a light cruiser of the Augsburg class, a mine-layer, and three destroyers.

An action developed in circumstances unfavourable to the Russians, who were in superior strength. The sea, according to the Russian official account, was shrouded in a fog so dense that the ships frequently were swallowed up in darkness, and therefore the gun fire was inaccurate. The Russians, attempt-

hour later the enemy began to retreat, while several submarines attacked the Russians unsuccessfully. The Rurik was sent at full speed after the retreating vessels, which were joined by another cruiser of the Bremen class. The Rurik soon had the satisfaction of seeing the effect of her salvos, for the enemy's fire weakened. The Roon's four 8 in. guns were silenced, and fire broke out aboard. Obviously disliking further conflict, the enemy disappeared rapidly in the fog. The Russians sustained trifling damage. No one was killed; fourteen men were wounded. Shortly afterwards the Russians were attacked by torpedoes from submarines, but were protected by Russian torpedo-boats which arrived to reinforce them. One of the torpedo-boats was damaged in driving off the submarine attack.

In the meantime, mysterious submarines had made their appearance in Baltic waters, seriously threatening not only the German Fleet but communication between Germany and Sweden, from which country the enemy was obtaining large quantities of iron ore. Day by day reports reached Berlin of vessels being sunk at sea, indicating that the dangers threatening the German naval forces had been appreciably increased. It soon, however, became apparent that the Higher Naval Command was dominated by the military authorities, who insisted that the control of the Gulf of Riga must be seized at all costs.

The correctness of these assumptions was demonstrated in August when, in spite of the losses already incurred, another and even more determined attack was opened. On August 10th a German force, consisting of nine older battleships, twelve cruisers, and a large number of torpedo-boat destroyers, attempted to break through the mine barrier protecting the Gulf of Riga. On the two previous days the enemy had made tentative attacks evidently intended to cover mine-sweeping operations off Rirben Channel, the only practicable means of approach to Riga. At last, on the 10th, it was determined to make a desperate movement, supported by all the available naval forces. The Russian Fleet operated behind the mine-field, and with the aid of seaplanes drove back the Germans, one cruiser and two torpedo-boat destroyers being damaged. The Germans denied that they had

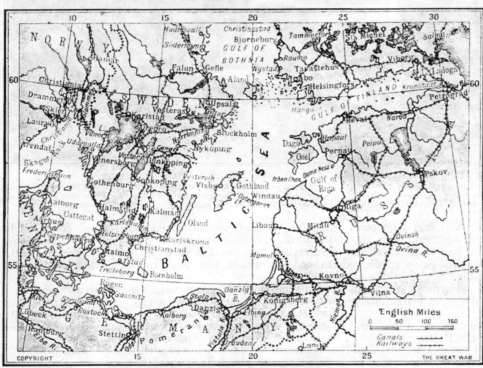

GENERAL MAP OF THE BALTIC SEA.
Early in the war Germany seized Libau and occupied Windau, and then made a determined but vain attack upon Riga, which has direct communication with Petrograd. Severe fighting took place in the Gulf of Riga and later in the Gulf of Finland.

ing to intercept the enemy's retreat, were attacked by the torpedo-boats, but were unharmed. In half an hour the Augsburg cruiser, finding the Russian fire too hot, abandoned her slower consort and fled full speed southward.

The Albatross, the German mine-layer, had begun to show signs of distress, and the torpedo-boats endeavoured to assist her escape, throwing volumes of thick black smoke out of their funnels, thus rendering the fog more dense, but at nine o'clock the foremast of the Albatross was shot away, clouds of steam arose, and the doomed ship began to list to the starboard. Hauling down her flag, she made for the coast. As she was badly damaged, and was entering neutral waters, the Russians ceased firing, and soon she was seen to go ashore behind Ostergarn's Lighthouse. The Russians then cruised northward. At ten o'clock they sighted a squadron of the enemy, including an armoured cruiser of the Roon class, a light cruiser of the Augsburg class, and four destroyers. The Russians immediately joined battle, and half an

suffered any loss, and claimed that the coastal batteries had been silenced and a cruiser of the Makaroff class damaged by gun fire. The German communiqué suggested that the operation had been crowned with success. That claim, however, was soon to be tested, for on August 16th the attack was resumed. Taking advantage of a thick fog, considerable enemy forces managed to penetrate into the Gulf. The Russian ships fell back, firing with effect.

Gallantry of the Sivoutch

The action was continued on subsequent days. During the fighting the gunboat Sivoutch added a glorious page to Russian naval annals. She was an obsolescent vessel of eight hundred and seventy-five tons, with a speed of twelve knots, and carried nothing more formidable than two 4·7 in. guns, supported by a quartette of 12-pounders and three machine-guns. This little vessel became engaged with an enemy cruiser. She was soon wrapped in flames, owing to fires which broke out fore and aft, but she continued to answer shot for shot, until at last she went

Wind-jammers coming up Channel on a flowing sea and before a fast following wind.

Under the White Ensign : Battleships racing past the Rock of Gibraltar on waters dancing under a spanking breeze.

Under the Red Ensign: Merchantmen pursuing their lawful occasions under sail and steam along their broad highway.

Rescuing crew of French battleship Gaulois, torpedoed in Mediterranean, Dec. 26th, 1916.

As the Gaulois made her final plunge the rescued crew raised a cry of "Vive la France!"

down, having previously sunk an enemy torpedo-boat which had intervened in the duel. On the 19th and 20th the engagement was continued with fine spirit by the Russians, and then on the succeeding day the Germans, having suffered heavy casualties, withdrew.

In the Duma the President was able to make the gratifying announcement that the enemy had lost three cruisers and seven torpedo-boats. Under cover of his men-of-war, he had made an attempt to land troops near Pernau, four shallow-draft barges of large size, crowded with troops, being employed. The Russian troops dealt successfully with this attempt to evade the action of the Russian Fleet, "the Germans being exterminated and the barges captured." Thus the whole operation proved a complete and costly fiasco. During the withdrawal of the Germans the battle-cruiser Moltke, a new vessel of 22,640 tons, armed with ten 11 in. guns, besides twelve 5·9 in., and a similar number of 3·4 in. quick-firers, was intercepted by a British submarine, under the orders of Commander Max Horton, who at that time was conducting a reign of terror in Baltic waters. His torpedo went home, but did not strike the Moltke in a vital spot, and she was able to return to port. This was Commander Horton's second considerable success in these waters. This officer, officially described as "a most enterprising submarine officer," had in July torpedoed the German pre-Dreadnought battleship Pommern.

Commander Horton and the Moltke

Apart from the splendid fight of the Sivoutch, this action in the Gulf of Riga provided another dramatic incident. Among the Russian ships which it had been determined to risk in defending the Gulf was the battleship Slava, a pre-Dreadnought vessel of 13,566 tons, armed with four 12 in. and twelve 6 in. guns. Launched thirteen years before, her career as an effective unit of the Russian Fleet may well have been regarded as closed owing to the appearance of the Dreadnought type; but, nevertheless, on this occasion she was to give a good account of herself. The Germans made a dead set against this battleship, which was causing them great inconvenience. On the night of August 17th they sent two of their best destroyers to attack the Slava. Throughout the night these menacing craft endeavoured in vain to get within range of the battleship.

At last the effort was abandoned, and at dawn the destroyers were on their way to rejoin the main force when they encountered the Novik, one of the largest, swiftest, and best armed of the Russian mosquito fleet. The odds were in favour of the enemy, but nevertheless the Novik gave battle. For twenty minutes she maintained the desperate encounter. The leading destroyer had one of her funnels carried away and she suffered other serious damage. The second destroyer came to her assistance, but was driven off, and both ships were soon in ignominious retreat. One of them, it was reported, afterwards sank.

The Germans had again been foiled in their attempt to penetrate the Gulf of Riga and give support to the armies ashore. They had not hesitated to employ large forces and to risk heavy casualties. They had been opposed by an inconsiderable and weak section of the Russian Fleet. The main attack had been preceded, on the German admission, by "several days' difficult mine-sweeping and clearing away net obstructions." When this task had been completed the enemy had evidently concluded that the way had been opened to the domination of the Gulf. Events were soon to undeceive him. Though efforts were made from Berlin to minimise the losses incurred, it was admitted that "three of our torpedo-boats were damaged by mines. One of them sank, one was able to run ashore, and one was escorted to port." The enemy refused to admit the torpedoing of the Moltke at the time, but later on Commander Horton's claim was placed beyond doubt. For the time being the Germans had to admit that the Gulf was impregnable.

Russia dominates the Riga Gulf

Three months later, however, they evidently contemplated another attack. A Russian naval force discovered that the Germans were showing activity at Dome Ness, the promontory forming the western extremity of the Gulf. They were taken completely by surprise by a Russian party which was quickly landed. These daring men, after killing many of the Germans and capturing many others, destroyed the lighthouse, signal stations, and other navigation marks, and removed the beacon and buoys on which the enemy had evidently determined to place reliance when undertaking a further operation in the Gulf. The coastline on either side of Dome Ness was also heavily shelled with good results. The German naval forces, if any were in the vicinity, made no effort to interrupt the operation.

It seemed probable that the enemy had withdrawn his fleet in view of the domination of the Baltic by British submarines and learnt too late of the Russian movement. At any rate, at the time that the Russians were busy on the Courland coast a British submarine intercepted a German squadron, evidently on its way towards Dome Ness. The armoured cruiser Prinz Adalbert, a ship of 8,858

[*French official photograph.*

FRENCH SAILORS' HEROISM IN ATHENS.
French sailors being decorated for the bravery shown by them on December 1st and 2nd, 1916, when the Allies' forces in the Greek capital were treacherously attacked by King Constantine's troops, and many killed.

tons, launched at Kiel in 1901, was struck and almost immediately sank.

This incident illustrates the success with which British submarines in the Baltic co-operated with the Russians in defeating the enemy's plans. But these active British vessels rendered other assistance hardly less important. For some time they conducted an active and successful campaign against German merchant shipping carrying contraband of war from Sweden, and for weeks were able completely to interrupt navigation. One incident may be recalled as illustrative of the influence exerted by these small vessels. Thirteen German merchantmen, under convoy of the auxiliary cruiser Hirman, three torpedo-boats, and a number of armed trawlers, were proceeding towards Germany when at midnight they were thrown into confusion by the appearance of a Russian destroyer flotilla supported by a number of submarines. The Germans were taken completely by surprise, confusion prevailed, the convoy dispersed, and the merchantmen fled towards the Swedish coast. The encounter was short and sharp. The Hirman was torpedoed, only the commander and thirty of the crew being saved; several of the trawlers were disabled; and four or five of the convoy were sunk, the rest taking shelter in Swedish territorial waters.

The Germans were driven to the conclusion, by the sequence of unfortunate experiences in and about the Gulf of Riga, that the operation of seizing this strategic point was one which they could not compass. If, as there is reason to believe, the German naval authorities had throughout acted under the peremptory orders of the Higher Army Command, they had at last to confess to the soldiers that the proposition was not practicable. At any rate, the Gulf of Riga continued to be dominated by the Russian naval forces; Russian ships operated freely, bombarding the western shores to which the German Army held in grim desperation, hoping that in time the German Fleet would come to its rescue. Russian aircraft also assisted materially in increasing the discomfort of the enemy.

The success of the Russians in these operations was a bitter disappointment to the Germans. A correspondent in Petrograd, reflecting the views held by the highest naval authorities, pointed out, after the failure of the enemy, that the success achieved in the defence of the Gulf was ascribed in the main to the experience which had been gained in recent years. The Russians before the opening of the war had come to the conclusion that the holding of the Riga Gulf was essential to the defence of the Gulf of Finland, the headquarters of the main Russian forces. "The Gulf of Finland is regarded as safe so long as the Gulf of Riga remains in Russian possession. The Gulf of Finland on its northern side is fringed with reefs, a well-defined passage exists between these reefs, and Russian naval defence of the Finland Gulf counts largely on using this inside passageway where the depth of water is sufficient for large vessels. Aside from the Finnish reef passage, the waters of the Gulf of Finland are open and there is no block before Petrograd short of Kronstadt."

The Germans at length came to the conclusion that if the Gulf of Riga could not be seized, an effort might be made to pierce the Gulf of Finland. It was apparently conjectured that this operation, if successful, would have a double effect. In the first place, the attack would be upon the main Russian forces and might result in heavy casualties being inflicted, thus reducing the menace offered to German operations in the Baltic. In the second place, it was assumed that any opera- **Germany's material** tions in the Gulf of Finland—the gateway **and moral loss** to Petrograd—would produce a moral effect on the Russian forces holding the other waterway. In these circumstances an attack by comparatively small forces was made upon the Gulf of Finland, but it was repulsed by the Russians with ease.

During these months of war no first-class event occurred, it is true, in the Baltic. But in the encounters between the Russian and German naval forces the enemy suffered not only material, but moral loss. Reference has been made already to the sinking of the battleship Pommern and the armoured cruiser Prinz Adalbert, and the torpedoing of the battle-cruiser Moltke. But those casualties did not exhaust the list. The armoured cruiser Friedrich Karl was lost in the Baltic towards the close of 1914; the protected cruiser Augsburg was sunk by gun fire, together with the somewhat larger ship Magdeburg, and the smaller cruisers Undine and Bremen fell prey to British submarines. It is thus apparent that during the first thirty months of the war the Russian naval forces rendered no mean aid to the Allies.

WHERE THE ITALIAN NAVY KEPT WATCH ON THE ADRIATIC.
Towing Italian naval guns ashore aboard a substantial raft to a Mediterranean island. Lashed alongside a steam-cutter the raft, with its weighty burden, was taken safely to its position. Above: View from an Italian observation-balloon of the boats to which it was roped. The rapidity with which these balloons could be moved is well suggested by the cut-water waves and the foaming wake formed by the towing boats.

ITALIAN SQUADRON IN THE GULF OF TARANTO.
Three warships of the Italian Navy as seen from the deck of a sister ship.
The Italian Fleet had a considerable share in holding the Austrian Navy
inactive in its harbours during a great part of the war.

When hostilities opened the Germans assumed that they could adopt the defensive in the North Sea while taking the offensive in the Baltic. They reached the conclusion that the Navy and Army in co-operation could seize the Gulf of Riga, and that then the German military forces, resting on the sea for supplies, would be able to push on to Petrograd, separated from the Baltic coast by only three hundred and sixty-six miles. The Russian naval and military authorities were well aware of the plans entertained by the enemy, and were well prepared. As Admiral Kanin remarked, " The fundamental strategic picture is amply clear. The Baltic Fleet is a continuation of the extreme flank of the Army ; the task of the Fleet is, as far as possible, to support the movements of the Army, supporting it against envelopment by the German Fleet." He endorsed the suggestion that the two turning points in the war had been the Battle of the Marne and the successful defence of the Gulf of Riga. " Paris was saved on the Marne, while in the Riga Gulf the struggle for the approach to Petrograd terminated in our favour. It is impossible to deny this. What would be the situation of the Army if the Germans now occupied Riga and the entire Gulf of Riga ? Look at the map " (he added to his interviewer) " and you will understand for yourself."

German Navy definitely weakened

In short, the Russians in their operations in the Baltic not only reaffirmed the safety of Petrograd, but they administered to the Germans a series of repulses which had a significant influence on the course of events in the other theatres of naval war. The enemy was definitely weakened for operations elsewhere by the determined, resourceful, and courageous work of the Russian Fleet in this inland waterway, where its operations were splendidly supported by daring British officers in command of a number of submarines.

BATTLESHIPS OF ITALY'S NAVY READY FOR ACTION.
Part of an Italian squadron off Taranto. The Gulf of Taranto has been one of the world's famous naval harbours since the ancient days when the town of Taranto was the Tarentum of the Romans.

II.—In Southern Waters.

During the years immediately preceding the opening of the Great War the fate of British interests in the Mediterranean was often the subject of discussion. Britons remembered that during the Napoleonic War the British Fleet had been obliged to evacuate these waters, leaving the enemy at least in nominal command. In 1796, when Nelson received his orders to leave the Mediterranean, he declared that it was a measure which he could not approve. " Much as I shall rejoice to see England, I lament our present order in sackcloth and ashes, so dishonourable to the dignity of England, whose fleets are equal to meet the world in arms." Would the British Fleet have to

Battleships of the Italian Navy, Pisa class. The Pisa was laid down in February, 1905, and completed in January, 1909. Ships of this class were of little more than 10,000 tons, and carried a complement of five hundred and fifty men. Their armament was thirty guns, including four 10 in.

On board a French transport bound for the East. The gun in the foreground was in readiness for submarines. Only underwater craft of the enemy dared appear in the open waters of the Mediterranean, the Austrian Navy, like that of its German ally, long keeping to the inglorious security of its harbours.

Italian Dreadnought, the Dante Alighieri. This was the first ship of the Dreadnought type to be built for the Italian Navy, having been laid down in June, 1909, and completed during 1912. She carried a complement of nine hundred men, and had a displacement of 18,400 tons.

[French official photograph.

Anti-aircraft gun on board a French warship in the Mediterranean. These guns were kept ever ready against any appearance of enemy aircraft. The French Navy played an important part in policing the Mediterranean during the early part of the war, and in holding the seas against the Central Powers.

SHIPS OF THE FRENCH AND ITALIAN NAVIES THAT TOOK PART IN THE POLICING OF THE MEDITERRANEAN SEA.

withdraw once more? That was the question which men discussed as they watched the rapid development of the navies of the Triple Alliance.

The activity of the Germans in northern waters was reflected in the Adriatic, where Austria-Hungary was busy creating a considerable fleet. The Italian shipyards were also fully occupied in turning out new battleships, cruisers, and mosquito craft. It was common knowledge that no love was lost between the Italians and the Austrians; but, on the other hand, might not Germany by superior power compel Italy to join her unfriendly neighbour? The British naval authorities were not asleep during those years of preparation. An agreement was reached with the French, enabling ships to be withdrawn from the Mediterranean to strengthen the concentration in the North Sea.

In the early years of the century the British fleet in the Mediterranean had embraced twelve battleships, two coast defence ships, thirteen cruisers (large and small), three torpedo-gunboats, and twenty-one destroyers. It was the largest aggregation of naval power ever assembled. In August, 1914, when the war-cloud burst, the White Ensign was represented in the Midland Sea by three battle-cruisers—the Inflexible, Indefatigable, and Indomitable—four armoured cruisers, a similar number of light cruisers, and sixteen destroyers. Fortunately, in the meantime a great accession of French strength had occurred under the impulse of a growing popular movement in France in favour of naval expansion.

A Continental country under democratic rule and with a large Army, appealing to the eye, to support is always at a disadvantage in carrying out its preparations for naval war. On an average the Second Republic had had about one Minister of Marine every year during its existence. Each Minister had brought to his duties ideas of his own, the consequence being that French naval policy often swayed from one extreme to the other; occasionally attention was concentrated on battleships, and then, again,

the battle squadrons were neglected and the money spent upon cruisers and small craft.

During the early years of this century the pendulum swung in favour of battleships, with the result that when war broke out France was strong in ships of the line, but very weak in cruisers. She was able to mobilise four Jean Barts of 23,000 tons, six Dantons of 18,400 tons, and five Patries of 15,000 tons, besides six older battleships. These vessels constituted an imposing battle fleet, but, unfortunately, they were inadequately supported by cruisers. The defect, we may be sure, was not due to any failure on the part of the expert authorities of France, but was traceable to the effect of uninstructed dictation of naval policy by the politician. The main fleet had associated with it seven large armoured cruisers, but only three light cruisers, and these vessels were long past their highest efficiency.

Owing to this defect the French Fleet was "blind," and it was in consequence of that condition that the British naval authorities had assigned to the Mediterranean ships of the cruiser classes. In combination, the Franco-British force represented a well-balanced fleet, far superior in strength to that under the Austro-Hungarian flag.

Down to the day of his death the Archduke Franz Ferdinand, the heir to the Emperor Francis Joseph, had enthusiastically supported the naval movement in Austria-Hungary. It was known that the plans were prepared in consultation with the German naval authorities. The shipyards on the Adriatic had been developed on modern lines. Year by year additional battleships and cruisers had been sent to sea, as fine vessels as were to be found in any fleet in the world. In August, 1914, three Dreadnoughts of 20,000 tons displacement had been completed and another one was almost ready to be commissioned. In addition, the Navy included three powerful battleships of just over 14,000 tons, somewhat resembling the British Lord Nelson type, and mounting four 12 in. and eight 9'4 in. guns.

The Fleet also included three older battleships of 10,430

[Henri Manuel.
VICE-ADMIRAL BOUE DE LAPEYRÈRE.
Vice-Admiral de Lapeyrère, of the French Navy, awarded the Hon. K.C.B. (Military Division) for distinguished services during the Dardanelles campaign.

[Russell.
VICE-ADMIRAL E. C. T. TROUBRIDGE.
Admiral Troubridge, who was leader of the Naval Mission to Serbia in 1915, received the Order of Kara George with Swords, 1915.

[Lafayette.
ADMIRAL SIR A. BERKELEY MILNE.
Commander-in-Chief in the Mediterranean from June, 1912, to August, 1914, when he was nominated Commander-in-Chief at the Nore.

[Russell.
VICE-ADMIRAL SIR G. WARRENDER.
Sir George Warrender commanded the 2nd Battle Squadron, 1912-16. Appointed Commander-in-Chief at Plymouth, March, 1916.

GUNS OF THE SAN MARCO.
Firing the 7'5 in. guns on board the Italian battleship San Marco. This ship, of the San Giorgio class, was completed in 1910.

tons, carrying four 9'4 in. and twelve 7'6 in. guns each. Austria was thus able to concentrate nine battleships, three of them being Dreadnoughts, and, as a reserve, she possessed six obsolescent and small battleships, useful only for purposes of coast defence. It was a fortunate circumstance that the Austro-Hungarian Fleet was also in the position of a fighting man without the normal complement of eyes. Apart from two old ships of little value, Austria-Hungary possessed only one armoured cruiser, the St. George, and of efficient light cruisers for scouting purposes she owned only half a dozen. She was also weak in torpedo craft. In short, the Austro-Hungarian Navy was in no condition to try conclusions with the Franco-British forces.

There was, however, always the possibility that a surprise movement might be attempted in the knowledge that during the early period of the war the British and French admirals would be subject to demands of an embarrassing character. This possibility was accentuated by the presence in southern waters of the German battle-cruiser Goeben, accompanied by the light cruiser Breslau. These two ships had been moved by the Germans from northern waters to the Mediterranean during the Balkan trouble, which had occurred two years before the outbreak of war. It was at first thought that after the peace, which Sir Edward Grey, by conciliatory methods, managed to arrange, these vessels would be ordered back to the Baltic. On the contrary, they remained cruising in the Mediterranean, a source of suspicion and doubt to the Entente Powers.

ITALIAN DREADNOUGHT IN DRY-DOCK.
Italian Dreadnought, Dante Alighieri, in dry-dock. This vessel was laid down in 1909, and completed three years later.

Had the Germans committed an error, and been forced to leave these ships to their fate, or did they form the basis of some secret scheme which had been confided to Vice-Admiral Souchon, who flew his flag in the Goeben, with Captain von Müller, late naval attaché in London, as commanding officer? Of all attachés ever accredited to the Court of St. James's, this officer—who is not to be confused with the famous captain of the Emden of the same name—was probably the most polished in manner and possessed the most perfect command of English.

When war became inevitable, the British and French admirals had other things to think of besides the presence in the Mediterranean of these two ships. The French military authorities urged that convoy must be provided for the Nineteenth Army Corps, quartered in Algeria and Tunis, and urgently required for the defence of France; the British military authorities were not less insistent that the 7th Division of the British Army, distributed between Gibraltar, Malta, and Egypt, should also receive a safe conduct home. At the same time the two admirals were aware that the Mediterranean constituted the lifeline of the British Empire, and that in the course of a few weeks Indian troopships would be passing, taking home to England the 65,000 white troops whom Lord Kitchener had decided to replace with Territorials.

At the moment when the plans for using the Mediterranean for military purposes were being completed, the two German ships gave evidence of their presence. Admiral Souchon had in the meantime been in wireless communication with Berlin, and on August 3rd—that is, the day before the British declaration of war—and at the moment when the French and British troops in and about the Mediterranean were preparing to embark, they put to sea from Messina and proceeded to bombard the Algerian coast. It was only a demonstration, and the ships doubled back at once, the German admiral intending to convey the impression that he was about to steam for the Adriatic, whereas, in company with the storeship General, he purposed endeavouring to reach the Dardanelles and to bring Turkey into the war as an ally of the Central Powers. He first made for Messina to complete his preparations. The order which was issued by Admiral Souchon at mid-day on August 6th, on the eve of sailing from Messina, has since been published. It was in the following terms:

The Goeben and Breslau

News about the enemy is uncertain. I presume his strength lies in the Adriatic and that he is watching both exits of the Mediterranean.

ITALIAN MINE-LAYER SOWING A MINE-FIELD IN SOUTHERN EUROPEAN WATERS.

When Italy came into the war, on May 23rd, 1915, an arrangement was made whereby her Navy became responsible in the main for preventing the enemy from interfering with communications in the Mediterranean. It was so successful in this work that it practically closed the Adriatic to enemy use and reduced the by no means inconsiderable Austrian naval forces to a condition of compulsory and inglorious inactivity.

Object : To break through to the east and reach the Dardanelles. Order of Going : Goeben leaves at five o'clock at seventeen miles an hour ; Breslau follows at a distance of five miles and closes it up at darkness.

I want to create the impression that we are wanting to go to the Adriatic, and in case I so succeed in creating that impression that we are wanting to go to the Adriatic, we shall veer round in the night and make for Cape Matapan, if possible throwing off the enemy.

The steamer General to leave at seven o'clock in the evening, to keep along the Sicilian coast, and to try and reach Santorin. Should she be captured, to try and let me know by wireless. If she receives no further orders from me to ask for them at Loreley (Constantinople station ship).

The responsibility of dealing with these two ships and preventing the German admiral from carrying his plan into effect devolved upon the British Commander-in-Chief, Admiral Sir Archibald Berkeley Milne, with whom was associated Rear-Admiral Troubridge.

The British force, in overwhelming strength, tracked the Germans down to Messina, but failed to bring them to action, though the light cruiser Gloucester put up a plucky fight

THE KAISER WILHELM (KIEL) CANAL.
This waterway between Kiel on the Baltic and Brunsbüttel on the Elbe was opened in 1895. Widened and deepened to take ships of 18,000 tons (nominal), the reconstructed canal was opened in June, 1914.

against them as they proceeded at full speed towards the Dardanelles. An inquiry was subsequently held as to this unfortunate incident, and the Commander-in-Chief was exonerated. Admiral Troubridge then made a claim for a court-martial, and he also was held to be blameless ; so apparently no one was in fault. But, at any rate, the German ships succeeded in getting through the Dardanelles unmolested, and their presence off Constantinople decided Turkey's course, that country declaring war on November 5th, 1914.

Thus hostilities in the Mediterranean opened unfavourably, but, at the same time, the escape of the Goeben and Breslau tended to free the situation from all complications. The British naval authorities felt themselves justified in withdrawing the battle-cruisers, and when Admiral Milne returned home, responsibility for naval affairs in the Mediterranean devolved upon Vice-Admiral Boué de Lapeyrère. That officer some years before had filled the position of Minister of Marine, and had been responsible in no small measure for the movement which was to re-establish France as one of the predominant sea Powers of the world. After a fruitful period of work ashore, he had hoisted his flag as Admiralissmo in the Mediterranean, and when war broke out had for forty months been actively engaged in tuning up the French

Fleet to war pitch. The success of Admiral de Lapeyrère in the months which followed his assumption of responsibility for the defence of allied interests in southern waters is attested, not by a successful battle, but by the very fact that during that period the Austro-Hungarian Fleet lay concealed in its ports, strongly defended by shore guns and mine-fields.

The conditions closely resembled those existing in the North Sea, in that the enemy feared to put his hopes to the venture. Nothing is more irritating to active-minded seamen than a long period of anxious waiting, but the French Fleet supported the test with splendid spirit. The months passed in unbroken silence. When the Dardanelles operations were undertaken our ally was in a position to provide ships to co-operate with the British men-of-war, and paid the price uncomplainingly. That, however, is another story, details of which may be read elsewhere. Our purpose is to deal with the broad issues and to indicate the results which flowed from the success of the Franco-British forces in the Mediterranean in the early and anxious months of the war.

During that period the Mediterranean was thronged with transports, some proceeding from the west to the east, and others from the east to the west. The loss of a single one of these ships at that stage in the war would not merely have represented a material disaster, but would have had unfortunate psychological results. Happily, no untoward event occurred to mar the success which attended the movement of troops by a long sea route on a scale never before contemplated by any Power during a general war in Europe.

At last, on May 23rd, 1915, Italy declared war upon Austria, and the balance of power against the enemy was further increased. Italy brought into action a Navy stronger than that of Austria-Hungary. It comprised four Dreadnoughts completed, and two more in an advanced stage of construction. She also possessed eight older battleships, nine armoured cruisers, ten light cruisers, over a score of destroyers and a large number of torpedo-boats and submarines. An agreement was reached under which the Italian Navy became responsible, in the main, for preventing the enemy interfering with communications in the Mediterranean, and thus the work which had hitherto devolved upon the French Navy was appreciably reduced.

Unfortunately the Italians suffered from two disadvantages. In the first place they were weak in scouting ships, in comparison with the area of operations ; and in the second place they possessed no serviceable harbours in the Adriatic. On the other hand, the Austrians were soon to show that they were able to reap all the benefit flowing from the possession of such well-protected deep-water ports as Pola, Trieste, Cattaro, and Fiume. The Austrian shore is indented with other small ports of great utility as bases for torpedo operations, and is fringed with islands.

Immediately war was declared the Austrians showed that they realised that they possessed considerable geographical advantages, and undertook a raid on the Italian coast in which a number of battleships and other vessels took part. A large part of the enemy Fleet, in fact, put to sea, aeroplanes acting as scouts and also assisting in efforts to damage the Italian towns and villages. In order to appreciate subsequent events, it may be recalled that a statement was issued from Vienna in which the character of this operation was described and the points of attack indicated : (1) Venice, fourteen bombs dropped from aeroplanes ; (2) Porto Corsini Canal raided by destroyer Scharfschütze, supported by cruiser Navara and a torpedo-boat ; (3) Rimini bombarded by armoured cruiser St. George ; (4) Sinigaglia bombarded by battleship Zrinyi ; (5) Ancona bombarded by several ships ; (6) Charavelle balloon shed attacked by aeroplanes ; (7) Potenza River railway bridge bombarded by battleship

Radetsky; (8) Sinarca River railway bridge shelled by cruiser Admiral Spaun; (9) Vieste and Manfredonia, north of Barletta, bombarded by cruiser Helgoland and destroyers Csepel, Tatra, and Lika.

The anticipation that the Austrians intended to make the fullest possible use of their geographical advantages was thus speedily supported by events. The Italians, with five hundred and fifty nautical miles of coast exposed to the enemy, had seriously to consider what means could be adopted to counter the Austrian attack. The Italian Navy was weak in cruisers, and to expose them on a coast-line devoid of harbours was to incur great risk of loss. It was useless to appeal to the civilised world to condemn these attacks on unfortified towns, involving damage to **Coastal railways** property and the murder of unprotected **for mobile defence** civilians. No moral influence, as the British residents on the East Coast of England had learnt, would deter such enemies as Germany and Austria-Hungary from a policy of outrage.

For some time the Italians suffered without being able to hit back, but at last a scheme was evolved which gave promise of success. The scheme consisted in the utilisation of the coastal railway as a means of mobile defence. Armoured trains were fitted out and distributed along the whole littoral. The trains were manned by expert naval gunners, subject to the same discipline and routine as when serving on board ship. As soon as enemy forces at sea were signalled, guns swiftly concentrated on any threatened part of the coast, and thus the policy of outrage and murder was defeated. This simple and ingenious method of defence not only stopped raids by naval units, but also reduced to insignificant proportions the aerial incursions which the Austrians carried out in the early months of the war.

Austria, in entering upon this policy, confirmed the Italians in their belief in the inevitability of the struggle. The enemy had shown that it was indispensable, if Italy was to be defended against outrage, that that **Italy closes** **the Adriatic** portion of the Eastern Adriatic which is Italian in population, language, sentiment, and tradition—namely, Trieste, Istria, and Dalmatia—should become part of the Kingdom of Italy. As the result of this successful adaptation of the coastal railway for purposes of defence, the Austrian naval forces were reduced to inactivity. On the other hand, the Italians continued to exhibit energy in developing the possibilities of the situation. At the opening of the war a blockade of the Adriatic was declared, and a few weeks later the sea was closed to all merchantmen, except such as secured a safe convoy to Italian territory. Moreover, the Italians captured the Austrian town and port of Monfalcone, thus securing an important arsenal and dockyard on the northernmost bay of the Gulf of Trieste, and only fifteen

[*British official photograph.*

ENTHUSIASTIC SCENE ON A FRENCH TROOPSHIP AT THE DARDANELLES.

In the early months of the war the Mediterranean was thronged with transports, the loss of one of which would have represented a material disaster and would have had unfortunate psychological results. Owing to the perfect co-operation of the allied naval forces no untoward event marred the success with which troops were moved by a long sea route on a scale never before contemplated by any Power.

SISTER SERVICES.
British soldiers aboard a British battleship bound for another field of operations.

A NIGHT ON DECK IN THE MEDITERRANEAN.
The troops were billeted for the night on the battleship and camped out on the deck—by no means an unpleasant experience in the Mediterranean at most seasons, though not without a spice of danger when submarines were thought to be about.

miles north-west of the city of that name. The Austrians also found that it was impossible to interfere with the transport of Italian troops, and in this way the Italian Navy was able to co-operate effectively with the Army ashore.

Before leaving this aspect of activity on the part of the allied fleets, it may be appropriate to relate a story which deserves to rank beside the narrative of Jack Cornwell, of the Chester, to whose heroism

Heroism of Castrogiovanni

Admiral Beatty referred in his despatch on the Battle of Jutland. An Italian destroyer, acting as scout to a transport, was suddenly attacked by an Austrian submarine. An engagement ensued between the destroyer and the submarine, in which both were sunk, the transport proceeding in the meanwhile to her destination.

Among the survivors of the Italian destroyer was a young midshipman called Castrogiovanni, who was several hours in the water, floating and swimming as best he could. During this period his cheeriness inspired courage and hope in several of his boat's crew who were gradually getting exhausted. The crew of the Austrian submarine had been able to procure a boat, and, coming upon the young midshipman's little party, offered to take them on board provided they surrendered. Castrogiovanni consulted his men ; none would surrender. " Never ! " he cried. " We prefer to drown rather than become prisoners of Austria."

Several hours later the midshipman and his men managed to land on the Albanian coast, and his first thought was to inform the Italian authorities that a boat containing the crew of the submarine had evidently landed on the same coast. The Austrians were eventually captured as a result of this plucky midshipman's efforts.

If there is any impression that the Austrians exhibited less barbarity than the Germans, it must be dispelled by fuller knowledge, which the Italians possess, of their acts. Reference has been made already to the bombardment of open towns, resulting in damage to property and loss of innocent life. It may be suggested, however, that at any rate, the Austrians were guilty of no such murder as that of Captain Fryatt.

Let the story of an incident of the war in the Adriatic be given as an illustration of the methods adopted by the Austrians. At the outbreak of war, Captain Sauro, who was born at Trieste—three-quarters of the population of which are Italian—offered his services to the country with which, by family association and sentiment, he was in sympathy. Later on he was captured by the enemy, together with the crew of an Italian submarine which was trying to penetrate an enemy port. His mother and sister were at once summoned by the Austrians to greet him. His identity was thus established on the evidence of those nearest and dearest to him. He was forthwith tried and sentenced to be hanged, and in order that the last ceremony might not be wanting in moral atrocity, the woman who bore him and the sister whom he loved were forced to witness the execution.

In the light of this incident and of the bombardment of Italian open towns, the less said about Austrian humanity the better. Nor must it be forgotten that Germany's ally was quite as murderous in her submarine operations. When hostilities began the Austrians possessed less than a dozen submarines. German constructors and German engineers were, however, sent south in order to assist in the creation of new flotillas. Within a few months, supported by German technique, the Austrians were able to send to sea a considerable number of submarines, the commanders of which plumbed as great depths of inhumanity, in proportion to their opportunities, as their " opposite numbers " in the German Navy.

The navies which keep the sea must expect to suffer losses in these days of mines and submarines, and this was

Losses of the Allies

the experience of France and Italy. The latter country had to deplore the destruction of the Dreadnought battleship Leonardo da Vinci, of 22,340 tons displacement, which caught fire and blew up in Otranto Harbour in the autumn of 1916. The old battleship Benedetto Brin and the armoured cruisers Amalfi and Garibaldi also fell victims to Austrian submarines, besides a number of small craft.

The French Navy was robbed of the armoured cruiser Léon Gambetta, which was torpedoed by an Austrian submarine in the Strait of Otranto early in 1915, besides

Ships of the line steaming ahead. The most severe test was imposed on the allied fleets by the long periods of waiting for the enemy to put his hopes to the venture, but it was endured triumphantly. Months passed in unbroken silence, during which the allied fleets kept the seas while the Germans and Austrians remained inactive in the Kiel Canal and in Adriatic ports, and the Turkish fleet was practically wiped out of existence.

Torpedo-boats in a choppy sea. The mosquito craft of all the Allies saw plenty of fighting during the war. This was especially true of the Russians in the Gulfs of Riga and Finland and off the Swedish coast, and of the Italians in the Adriatic. In the North Sea and in the English Channel British torpedo-boats were unceasing in their work, and took part in many encounters besides that of the great Battle of Jutland.

WARSHIPS OF THE ALLIED FLEETS KEEPING THE MASTERY OF THE SEAS.

the cruiser Amiral Charnier. The old battleships Bouvet and Suffren were also lost, the former in the Dardanelles. But, in proportion to the relative strength of the opposing forces, the Austrian Navy suffered at least as seriously as those opposed to it. So far as is known, no Austrian battleship was sunk, but three cruisers were lost, together with a number of torpedo-boats and submarines.

The progress of hostilities in the Sea of Marmora and the Black Sea went on, as it were, behind a veil. From time to time Turkish ships exhibited some activity in the latter waters, but apart from incidental excursions, which cannot be prevented so long as an enemy possesses a single man-of-war, the Russian Fleet in the Black Sea maintained almost undisputed command of that inland waterway, with not unimportant results on operations on shore. The efforts of the Goeben and Breslau to influence the course of events were uniformly unsuccessful, and there is reason to believe that both ships, owing to their unfortunate experiences, were soon reduced

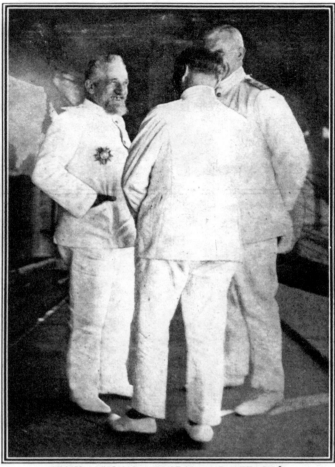

ADMIRALISSIMO, ADMIRAL, AND ATTACHÉ.
Vice-Admiral Boué de Lapeyrère, Admiralissimo in the Mediterranean (left), enjoying a joke with a British admiral. In the foreground is Lieut. C. Millot, French Naval Attache with the British Navy in the Dardanelles.

to a state of inefficiency and uselessness.

It was evident from the first that the Turks, even with the assistance of the two German ships, could make little impression upon the considerable force which the Russians possessed. They were further embarrassed, almost from the entrance of Turkey into the war, by the incursions of British submarines through the Dardanelles right up to Constantinople. By the beginning of 1916 practically the whole of the Turkish Fleet had been wiped out by the united efforts of the British and Russian naval forces.

Turkey, for the first time in her history of many centuries, was reduced to the position of a Power resting on the sea and yet unable to exercise any naval influence on the progress of events.

When, in January, 1917, in a communication to Washington, she announced her "independence of the European Powers," this step was regarded as having been made with a view to enabling her to participate in the peace negotiations apart from any Teutonic control.

GENERAL MAP OF THE SOUTHERN EUROPEAN FIELD OF NAVAL OPERATIONS.
Until May, 1915, the whole responsibility for control of the Mediterranean rested on the British and French Navies under the supreme control of Vice-Admiral Boué de Lapeyrère. Then Italy intervened, taking over the police work and "bottling up" the Austrian Navy in its own Adriatic ports. An allied fleet controlled Greece from the Gulf of Salamis, and the Russian Black Sea Fleet held the complete mastery of the Black Sea.

PANORAMIC VIEW   NEAR MAMETZ.

[British official photograph.

THE ROLL OF HONOUR, 1916.

Aim of the Chapter—Two Changes in Procedure—Examples Thereof—Casualties in 1916—The Various Theatres of War—Monthly Totals—
An Apparent Discrepancy—Grand Total—The Year's Fighting—Comparisons with the Past—A Crescendo of Slaughter— The
Casualties Classified—Killed and Wounded—Percentage of Recoveries— Proportions between Officers and Men—A Heavy Casualty
List Examined—Canadian and Australian Losses—Losses in Various Battalions—How the Infantry Suffered—Naval Casualties—
Classification Thereof—The Jutland Battle—The Total of the Killed—Births versus Deaths—The German Casualties—Absurd
Theories Dispelled—Experts again Wrong—The Somme Battles : A Comparison—British versus German Losses—Tests of Victory—
Missing and Prisoners—Improvement in British Tactics—The Fine Quality of the Dead : Examples—A Typical Obituary List—
Losses among the Aristocracy—Peers and Politicians—Baronets and their Sons—Generals and Colonels—Losses among Naval
Men—The Bar and the Clergy—Oxford's Heavy Loss—Raymond Asquith—Other Scholars Killed—Cambridge Men Killed—The
Public Schools—London University—Chaplains Killed—Losses to Literature and Art—F. S. Kelly and H. Webber— Sportsmen
Killed—Conclusion.

I N Chapter CXVI. (p. 387, Vol. VI.) of THE GREAT
WAR an attempt was made to estimate
in flesh and blood the price which the British
Empire had paid for its temerity in taking
up arms in defence of the rights of the
smaller nations
and the sanctity of the public
law of Europe. The facts and
figures given and discussed
therein took the story down to
the end of 1915, or a little later,
and the present chapter is intended to continue it to the close
of 1916. As before, it is mainly
concerned with the "killed in
action" and the "died of
wounds."

Since the earlier record was
completed two circumstances
have intervened to make the
task of the writer much more
difficult. One is that, on March
2nd, 1916, Mr. Asquith, then
Prime Minister, announced that
henceforward no figures about
the British casualties would be
made public. They would be
recorded and shown, if desired,
to members of Parliament, but
the people and—still more important— the enemy would be
unaware of how the total was
mounting up, and could only
form estimates thereof.

The second change had the
same end in view. Somewhat
later, about the end of March, the
authorities decided that in the
published casualty lists no particulars should be given as to the

BRIGADIER-GENERAL FABIAN WARE, C.M.G.,
Director of Graves' Registration and Inquiries. He was
awarded the Companionship of the Order of St. Michael and St.
George for the efficiency with which he discharged his pathetic
duty to the heroic dead.

battalion to which the injured officer or man belonged,
or the particular theatre of war in which he met his fate.
A comparison of two typical casualty lists will show the
nature of this alteration. On one day, March 3rd, 1916,
before the new regulations came into force, the casualty
list of officers enumerated four
theatres of war wherein fighting
had taken place—France, Mesopotamia, the Balkans, and East
Africa. It gave also the number
of the battalion to which the
killed or wounded officer belonged—6th Shropshire L.I.,
9th Devons, 10th King's Royal
Rifles, and so on. With the men
there was a similar distinction ;
those killed or wounded in France
were given distinct from those
in Mesopotamia, and it was quite
easy to learn that the 9th and
10th Manchesters, for instance,
were then serving in the latter
theatre of war, and the 11th
and 17th Liverpools in France.

To turn now to the official
list of casualties which appeared
in the papers on December 20th,
1916. Therein the officers were
simply classed as "killed," "died
of wounds," "wounded," or
"missing," and so, too—with
additions for "accidentally
killed," "died," and "wounded
and missing"—were the men,
but there was no other division,
no indication whatever whether
the man was serving in France
or the Balkans or Mesopotamia.
Similarly, nothing was said
about the unit to which he

[*Elliott & Fry.* [*Swaine.*

MAJ.-GEN. INGOUVILLE-
WILLIAMS, C.B., D.S.O. Killed.

MAJ.-GEN. M. S. MERCER,
Canadian Forces. Killed in action.

belonged except the bare "Worcester Regt.," "R. Berkshire Regt.," or "R. Flying Corps."

These difficulties, however, are not insuperable. To use a phrase made famous in another connection, "the resources of civilisation are not exhausted," and this chapter will give some idea of the extent and nature of the British casualties in 1916. The figures will not be official, but when the full tale is told, as one day it will be, they will be found to be not far from the truth. They have been obtained by a simple method which is open to all who possess the necessary patience, and which violates no official regulation, either in the letter or the spirit, for the writer is anxious to continue that scrupulous regard for the public interest which the Editors of THE GREAT WAR have consistently maintained from the first.

To January 9th, 1916, the last occasion during the war about which official figures were made public, the total of the British military casualties was 549,467, and this may be taken as the figure for the first seventeen months of the war. Four hundred thousand of these were incurred in France and Flanders, 117,500 in the costly Gallipoli enterprise, and 31,500 in Mesopotamia and the lesser theatres. In addition there were some 13,000 naval casualties.

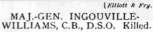
First seventeen
months' casualties

The fighting of 1916, especially since July 1st, was, as one would expect, far more expensive than that of the previous year and a half. The opening of the year coincided almost to a day with the bloodless withdrawal from Gallipoli, but for nearly three months more, as their fate was ascertained, the papers contained the names of casualties under the heading of the Mediterranean Expeditionary Force, the official title for the heroic army of Gallipoli. But a great number of these were headed by the sad legend, "previously reported missing, now reported killed," and others also were in the nature of alterations from the original returns; so, bearing these facts in mind, we

shall be justified in ignoring Gallipoli as far as 1916 is concerned, although a few of the casualties reported therein related to the last days of that campaign.

This increase in casualties did not, it should be remembered, indicate defeat or any falling-off in the fighting qualities of the British troops; rather the reverse. In a moment or two we hope to show, not from mere rumour or hearsay, but from the cold evidence of the casualty lists, that 1916 was a much more successful year for the arms of Britain than was 1915. Here it may be remarked that in 1916 Great Britain had far more men in the field than previously, and that it is almost certain that *in proportion to the numbers employed* the losses showed a decrease, not an **Decreased proportion** increase. It is quite certain that the **of casualties** losses were more fruitful; the British did advance, albeit not a great way, and there was nothing, in lives thrown away for no purpose whatever, to compare with the blunder in Gallipoli. The greatest disaster was Kut, comparatively speaking a minor one.

The mention of Gallipoli brings up another point. In one direction the casualty problem was simpler in 1916 than it was in 1915. A far greater proportion of the total casualties were incurred in one—the main—theatre of war. Mesopotamia yielded a good number during the earlier months of the year, but after the surrender at Kut in April its contribution was negligible. The

[*Lafayette.*

BRIG.-GEN. PHILIP HOWELL,
C.M.G. Killed in action.

BRIG.-GEN. F. J. HEYWORTH,
C.B., D.S.O. Killed in action.

Expeditionary Force at Salonika did little but mark time during the year, and the operations in Egypt and East Africa were on the scale to which older wars had accustomed Britain, rather than on the newer one established by the Great War. Up to February 20th, 1916, it was stated that the total British casualties at Salonika were 57 officers and 1,439 men. That figure included the losses incurred during the retreat from Lake Doiran into Greece in the previous December, and the total casualties of the British contingent cannot have much exceeded 2,500 to the end of 1916.

[*Bassano.* [*Speaight.* [*Speaight.* [*Vandyk.*

BRIG.-GEN. W. J. ST. J. HARVEY.
Died of wounds. Mesopotamia.

BRIG.-GEN. THE EARL OF
LONGFORD. Gallipoli.

BRIG.-GEN. WALTER LONG,
C.M.G., D.S.O. Killed in action.

BRIG.-GEN. C. B. PROWSE,
D.S.O. Killed in action.

Mesopotamia was more costly. In January, and again in March, there was heavy fighting to relieve Kut, and then at the end of April came the surrender of over 2,000 British and 6,000 Indian troops. It will be sufficient, however, to put down the losses there, as far as 1916 is concerned, at 20,000 men, and 5,000 or 6,000 more will amply cover those incurred in Egypt, Greece, and East Africa, leaving the balance for the mighty movements on the western front.

The balance? Day by day the papers contained long lists of names, and to count up the number of these is a simple if tedious task. It has been done; and, thanks to the courtesy of the editor of the "Daily Telegraph," the figures for each of the twelve months are given below.

			OFFICERS	MEN	TOTAL
January	..	..	1,011	17,675	18,686
February	..	..	878	14,822	15,700
March	..	..	993	16,908	17,901
April	..	..	1,211	17,840	19,051
May	..	..	1,623	27,403	29,026
June	..	..	1,740	29,761	31,501
July	..	..	7,071	52,001	59,072
August	..	..	4,693	123,097	127,790
September	..	..	5,403	113,780	119,183
October	..	..	4,366	102,340	106,706
November	..	..	2,312	72,479	74,791
December	..	..	953	39,711	40,664
			32,254	627,817	660,071

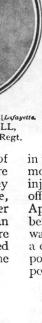

BRIG.-GEN. D. J. GLASFURD.
Died of wounds.

[*Elliott & Fry.*

LT.-COL. D. F. CAMPBELL,
D.S.O., M.P. West Riding Regt.

[*Lafayette.*

In these monthly totals due account has been taken of alterations and mistakes in the casualty lists, and they are therefore as correct as care can make them, although they are not, and make no pretence to be, official. For instance, it often happened that a man was reported killed, and later was found to be alive, or that by some mischance, an unwounded man had been returned as wounded. More frequently, alas! the missing were afterwards reported killed. As soon as the alterations were notified to the Press the necessary corrections were made in the totals.

[*Swaine.* [*Elliott & Fry.*

COL. A. E. SHAW,
Canadian Forces, Ypres.

COL. W. R. MARSHALL,
Canadian Forces.

These monthly figures, it should also be said, represented not the casualties *incurred*, but those *reported* during the period in question. But this fact did not affect the total except to a very slight extent at the end of the year. In the case of officers a week or so usually elapsed between the occurrence of the casualty and the appearance of the name in the papers, and in the case of non-commissioned officers and men a longer period, the difference being due to the fact that casualties among officers, being fewer and more noticeable, were more easily collected and reported than were those among the men.

For instance, the casualties to officers which appeared in the papers on February 10th, 1916, were dated from the base February 3rd, and were probably incurred on the 1st or 2nd. Those of the men were dated from the base January 31st, and occurred doubtless about the 25th or 26th.

Thus the casualties reported during May, let us say, covered, as regards the officers, not the period between May 1st and 31st inclusive, but that between April 23rd and May 22nd, or thereabouts; while as regards the men they covered perhaps the month between April 15th and May 15th.

Explanation of some discrepancies

The same fact accounts for an apparent discrepancy which the sharp-eyed would doubtless detect in the monthly totals above. That was the serious variation in the proportion between officers and men which the various months showed. How else can one explain 7,071 officers injured compared with 52,000 men in July, and only 4,693 officers compared with 127,000 men in August? March and April, too, revealed a like anomaly. It should be remembered, also, that when heavy fighting was proceeding, there was greater delay than usual in recording the casualties, and a comparison between July and August illustrates both this point and the former one. Among the men, a large proportion—probably one-half—of the losses reported in

[*Lafayette.*

LT.-COL. H. H. HARINGTON,
Punjabis, Indian Army.

[*Elliott & Fry.*

LT.-COL. A. R. NETHER-
SOLE, Indian Army.

[*Lafayette.*

LT.-COL. H. C. BULLER,
D.S.O., Canadian Infantry.

[*Elliott & Fry.*

LT.-COL. W. M. O'CONNOR,
R.A.M.C., London Field Ambulance.

[*French official photograph.*

HOMAGE FROM FRANCE.
Wreaths to be placed in the name
of France on the graves of the British
victims of the railway accident.

August occurred in July;
but among the officers the
proportion was much smaller,
probably only a quarter or
less. This meant the ad-
dition of something like
60,000 to the men's figure
of 52,000; and this being
done, the discrepancy be-
tween the two classes of
casualties disappears.

The total of British
military casualties for 1916
may be put down at 660,000
—although, as was explained
in the previous chapter, this
figure does not represent
quite that number of individuals. Many men, as
everyone who has read the
obituary notices knows, were
wounded, not once but three
or four times, and a good
number were first returned as wounded and then as died
of wounds. It is impossible to say with any approach to
certainty how many casualties were affected by this circumstance; the total must have been considerable; it may
have been as high as 100,000, and so reduce our 660,000
casualties to 560,000 individuals or thereabouts.

In January, 1916, it was officially announced that the
total casualties, excluding the naval ones, were, up to the
9th of that month, 549,467. For the succeeding year the
figure was, as we have just seen, 660,071; so that the grand
total for twenty-nine months of war was 1,209,538. In this
computation the first nine days of January are included
twice; but that cannot seriously affect the total, which
we place with considerable confidence at 1,200,000, or
something like 1,000,000 individuals killed, wounded,
missing, or prisoners of war.

The monthly totals given above are a miniature history
of the war. They show us January, when there was a good
deal of activity in Mesopotamia, but little doing on the
western front. In February the operations for the relief

[*French official photograph.*

PUBLIC FUNERAL FOR THE ACCIDENTALLY KILLED.
On January 17th, 1917, a special train full of British officers and men
returning from leave was descending an incline when the couplings broke.
The first section pulled up at Massy-Palaiseau station, near Paris, where
the hind portion ran into it, causing ten deaths and many injuries.

of Kut were partially suspended;
but in March they were taken in
hand again, and in April came the
British surrender. These facts
almost account for the slight
monthly fluctuations, the position
in France being practically
stationary.

With May came a distinct
revival of activity, and henceforward nearly all the casualties
reported were incurred on the
western front. In June there was
still more doing there, and then
came July with its mighty battles.
In August the rate of fighting was
maintained, and September showed
only a slight decline in its ferocity.
October heralded the coming of
winter, and also the exhaustion
inevitable after so tremendous an
effort; while November, and still
more December, proved the truth
of the forecast. A mathematician
would represent the year's casualties by a graph. From January it
would swell out steadily, until
in August and September the
summit of the curve would
be reached. Then to the
end of the year it would fall
away somewhat, leaving off,
however, before it got back
to the level of June.

The year of Minden and
Quebec, 1759, has been called
an *annus mirabilis*, or
wonderful year. What will
historians call 1916? Will
it be known as *annus
cruentus*, the year of blood?
To gain a sense of proportion some figures from the
past may be again recalled:
the Boer War, with its total
casualty list of 38,156;
Waterloo, a "decisive battle," with its 8,000 killed and
wounded; Blenheim, "a
glorious victory," with 670
killed and about 1,500
wounded; and Inkerman,
with 648 and 1,729—less
than 2,500 altogether. It is
probable that in the long centuries between Hastings and
Waterloo, England did not lose 1,000,000 men on the
battlefield altogether.

How different the figures now before us! In February,
the quietest of the twelve months, the losses were over
500 men a day, and in January and February, two months
of comparative inactivity on the part of
her armies, Britain lost nearly as many as **A year of**
during the whole of the Boer War. In May **blood**
she lost just under 1,000 men a day, and
in June just over that number; each day, as it were, one of
her small market-towns—say Calne or Keswick—which in
peace time contained each somewhere about 1,000 men
between 18 and 41 was losing the whole of its able-bodied
men, carried either to the hospital or the graveyard.

But if the losses were serious in June they were far worse
in July and August. Fortunately for chronology, the
Somme battles began on July 1st, just half-way through
the year, and during that month the losses were not 1,000,
but 2,000 a day. In other words, each day was a Blenheim

LT.-COL. EARL OF FEVERSHAM,
K.R.R.C.   Fell leading his battalion.

LT.-COL. THROCK-
MORTON, R. Welsh Fus.
Killed in Mesopotamia.

LT.-COL. H. E. BRASSEY,
D.S.O., R.H.G., att. S. Lancs
Regt.   Killed in action.

LT.-COL. R. L. ASPINALL,
D.S.O. Yorks Regt., att. Cheshires.

LT.-COL. C. E. GOFF,
M.C., Liverpool Regt.   Killed in action.

MAJ. N. E. LECKIE,
Canadian Infantry. Killed
in action.

MAJ. H. E. R. BOXER,
D.S.O., Lincolnshire Regt.
Killed at Hooge.

MAJ. J. R. WARDLE,
Lanarkshire Yeomanry.   Dardanelles.

MAJ. G. E. VANSITTART,
Canadian Field Artillery. Killed in action.

MAJ. VAUGHAN-HARRI-
SON, R.F.A. Killed in action.

MAJ. C. C. DICKENS,
London Regt. Leuze Wood.

MAJ. H. A. CARTER,
V.C., Indian Army.   Killed in action.

MAJ. R. J. MUTRIE,
Canadian Mounted Rifles. Died of wounds.

MAJ. A. L. BICKFORD,
C.I.E., 56th Rifles, I.A.
Died of wounds.

MAJ. E. CAMPION,
Seaforth Highlanders. Died
of gas poisoning.

MAJ. A. A. C. NELSON,
Royal Scots. Died of wounds.

THE ROLL OF HONOUR, 1916.

Photos by H. Walter Barnett, Elliott & Fry, Lafayette, Lambert Weston, Swaine.

COLLECTING THE KITS OF FALLEN MEN WHERE THE ADVANCE HAD PASSED.

British soldiers " cleaning up " after an advance on the western front. Men were told off to collect the kits of the fallen and any impedimenta that the enemy had left behind. Such a party is here seen engaged in this task.

The enemy equipment was separated—as in the heap to the right of the picture—from that belonging to the British, such as was being carried by the laden man on the left, much of which could be utilised again.

or an Inkerman. In August the daily average rose to over 4,000, which we may describe as a Blenheim *and* an Inkerman for every one of the month's thirty-one days, and in September the rate of death and injury was only reduced a little. November had an average of nearly 2,500 casualties a day, and its total was more than that of the first four months of the year combined, while even in December losses were suffered at the rate of well over 1,000 a day. For the whole year the rate of loss worked out at almost exactly 1,800 a day. In other words, every three-quarters of a minute throughout the year,
Daily rate day and night alike, a man, someone of
of loss British race and speech, was either killed or wounded. Mr. Churchill was therefore more than usually accurate when he spoke about a heap of bloody rags carried every minute to the rear.

The casualty list for 1916 is worth examination in some detail, for so far the figures have been totals only, and it will ·be interesting to see how they work out in killed, wounded, and missing. The official returns classified the casualties under quite a number of separate headings. For instance, in January there were fifteen. Killed, died of wounds, died, wounded, missing were, however, the only ones of any size ; the others were, died of gas poisoning (2), drowned (5), accidentally killed (65), suffering from gas poisoning (1), suffering from shock or concussion (256), wounded and missing (137), wounded and prisoners of war (10), missing, believed drowned (1), missing, believed killed (39), prisoners of war (83).

For our purpose many of the headings were superfluous. The dead, in whatever way they met their fate, shall be put together, for all alike have won their place in the Roll of Honour. Those suffering from gas poisoning and shock may be fairly classed with the wounded, and those who were believed to be drowned or killed with the dead ; for, unfortunately, this presumption was usually well-founded. Prisoners of war may be placed in a separate category, as

their return throws a good deal of light on the course of the war.

Classifying the casualties, therefore, under four headings, we have the following figures for the whole year :

	OFFICERS	MEN	TOTAL
Killed	8,560	130,176	138,736
Wounded	21,572	448,786	470,358
Missing	2,040	48,818	50,858
Prisoners	321	3,555	3,876
	32,493	631,335	663,828

The trivial discrepancy between this total of 663,828 and the previous one of 660,071 is accounted for by corrections and alterations from the original lists. For instance, in November 38 officers and 467 men, first returned as either killed, wounded, or missing, were afterwards reported as not killed, wounded, or missing, and there were corresponding figures for each of the twelve months.

Excluding the missing and prisoners, the proportion of killed to wounded, taking officers and men together, worked out at 1 to every 3½, as near as may be. For the previous seventeen months the proportion was 1 to something less than 3—128,138 to 353,283—these being official figures. Whatever reason may be **Proportion of** assigned for the improvement, the result **killed to wounded** was highly satisfactory. Perhaps the men had learned to avoid serious injury more easily ; perhaps the arrangements for attending the wounded had improved ; perhaps the withdrawal from Gallipoli affected the proportion ; probably all three and other reasons contributed. It was the more satisfactory when it is remembered that during the second period the Germans exhausted all the devilish ingenuity of their chemists to wound less and kill more. Clearly they failed.

To what extent did this loss, 660,000 for 1916 or 1,200,000 for the whole period of the war to date, permanently weaken the fighting force ? Some time in 1915 Mr.

Asquith said that 60 per cent. of the wounded recovered sufficiently to return to the front, and in August, 1916, it was stated that 75 per cent. of them returned to duty. The Germans claimed that 70 per cent. of their wounded men returned to the front. There was often a germ of truth in these German statements, and the probable explanation was that the percentage was correct, but referred only to certain classes of the wounded—those slightly injured. It was too much to believe that even German medical science could fit 70 per cent. of *all* the wounded for the hardships of the front.

As regards the British we shall probably be on the safe side if we assume that 50 per cent. of the wounded were able to return to active service, which is a very different thing from being merely fit again for duty. Our calculation is then a very simple one. For 1916, 235,000 of the wounded must be regarded as permanently out of action, and for 1914-15 a further 175,000, making a gross total of 410,000. Add this number to the total of killed, missing, and prisoners, and we obtain 800,000. This was the deduction which must be made from the available man-power, if one wishes to obtain a true estimate of the British resources in this vital direction in 1917.

In Chapter CXVI. something was said about the proportion of casualties as between officers and men, the assumption being made that the Army contained them in the ratio of 1 officer to every 29½ men. It was there stated, in dealing with the returns to the end of 1915, that the killed were 1 officer to every 15½ men; the wounded, 1 officer to every 24 men; and the missing, 1 officer to every 30½. How did the figures for 1916 bear out these proportions? In 1916, according to our figures, 1 officer was killed for every 15 men, and 1 wounded for every 21. Taking the missing and the prisoners together, there was 1 officer to every 22 men.

Ratio of officers to men

The differences between the two sets of figures are slight. The chances that an officer would be killed were still about double those of a private, for if the right proportion were maintained it should be 1 officer to every 29½ men, whereas it was 1 to every 15. Proportionately more officers than men were wounded, but here the ratio was only about 3 to 2, and the same may be said of the missing. Comparing the two periods, 1914-15 and 1916, it may be said that the proportion of officers killed remained stationary, but that the proportion of wounded and missing rose, the wounded a little, the missing considerably—from 3½ per cent. to nearly 5. The reasons for this were probably found in the conditions necessary in an offensive movement, such as the British push on the Somme. The officers must lead off, and the juniors, the leaders of platoons of infantry, suffered more heavily than any other class in the Army. These it was who swelled the total of the missing.

Heavy mortality among subalterns

This point does not need labouring, but an illustration or two may not be out of place. On Monday, July 31st, 1916, the papers contained, as they generally did on a Monday, a very heavy casualty list. This one was heavier than usual, and in officers alone it contained 580 names—that is, more than Kitchener had with him at Omdurman. Of these, 449 were subalterns—lieutenants and second-lieutenants—leaving 131 for captains, majors, colonels, and generals, of whom two appeared in the list. Of 21 officers reported killed on July 7th no fewer than 17 were second-lieutenants, but this proportion was certainly exceptional. Subalterns, therefore, who formed something more than half the officers, suffered more than three-quarters of the total casualties, for the big list of July 31st may be regarded as tolerably representative, and its figures agreed with the conclusions we reached when examining similar returns for 1915.

Another question, which was dealt with in the previous chapter, cannot here be discussed in any detail. This is the nature and extent of the casualties in the different branches of the Imperial forces and in the units composing

BRITISH TROOPS ADVANCING TO THE ATTACK BEHIND BARRAGE FIRE ON THE ANCRE.
Winter morning attack by the British on German trenches in the west. A line of the troops who had just gone "over the top" may be seen advancing in front of the bursting German shells in the foreground. The enemy trenches are dimly visible behind the long cloud of barrage smoke. The steady pressure of the Allies necessitated the enemy making their considerable retreat along the Arras-Soissons line in March, 1917.

those forces. Among the Canadians the casualties officially reported to August 31st, 1916, amounted to 37,861, of whom 8,644 were killed, 27,212 wounded, and 2,005 missing. The autumn fighting added considerably to this, and in December a total of 65,660 was announced. Of these, 10,333 were killed, 5,400 had died of wounds or illness, and 47,187 had been wounded. Probably for the whole year a total of 70,000 would not be far from the mark. Among the Australians the losses were almost as great. Down to the end of 1915, or a little later, they were 24,500, to which a further 6,000 should be added for New Zealand. Their exploits around Pozières during the Somme fighting were marked by conspicuous gallantry, which meant also heavy loss, and so probably 60,000 was not an excessive estimate for the total casualties among the men from the Antipodes. The South Africans, too, did their share. The Indian losses must not be forgotten, so it was not a random guess to assume that of the Empire's 1,200,000 casualties for the whole war to date, 1,000,000 were suffered by the men of the Motherland and the remainder by her children overseas.

As regards the different units the War Office had no desire that their casualties should be known. It would be possible to add together the number returned day by day for each regiment, but such a return would show little

[*British official photograph.*
MENACE OF DEATH UPON THE BALKAN FRONT.
High-explosive shells bursting close to a position held by the British upon the Balkan front. Up to the end of 1916, the casualties of the British with the Balkan Expeditionary Force did not by much exceed 2,500.

unless we knew also how many battalions of that regiment were at the front. Some regiments, those which draw their recruits from populous areas—the Royal Fusiliers, the Manchesters, and the Northumberland Fusiliers, for instance—had twenty or more battalions, while others had only perhaps five or six, and the regiments of Guards not more than four.

In an early despatch of 1916, Sir Douglas Haig mentioned the 20th and 21st Manchesters, and we knew of the 19th Middlesex, the 17th Durham Light Infantry, and many more, but we did not know the number each had at the front, and without this knowledge it is useless to pursue the inquiry. A loss of a hundred men among the Dorsets or the Cameronians might **Battalions which suffered heavily** be equal to one of five hundred among the Liverpools or the Royal Warwicks.

Before the regulations already referred to were introduced in March, 1916, it was possible to discuss this question. We knew then something about the losses of the various battalions, and as each battalion was approximately the same strength, one could say something about its losses. It could be safely assumed that a battalion which lost in a single engagement a hundred or more men killed had suffered severely, for that figure represented an eighth or more of its fighting strength. Such cases were not infrequent

during 1915, and there were a few, mainly from Mesopotamia, reported during the first three months of 1916.

On March 23rd, for instance, 89 of the 2nd Suffolks were returned as killed, and four days later a further 83, with 200 wounded. The 1st Connaught Rangers, then in Mesopotamia, had 100 wounded returned on March 8th, and 80 killed and 108 wounded on the following day. On March 27th, 122 of the 10th Sherwood Foresters were returned as missing, and this battalion lost very heavily indeed in officers and men about that time. Another battalion— Regulars again this time—to suffer heavily was the 2nd Leicesters, in Mesopotamia. On February 15th, 53 of them were returned as killed, **Heaviest casualties among infantry** and a week later a further 86; the wounded, in three days, numbered 238. In January there were big lists of wounded from the 5th West Yorkshires, the 5th York and Lancaster, the 4th Yorkshire Light Infantry, and the 9th Royal Lancasters. Two fine battalions, both in Mesopotamia, which suffered very heavily were the 1st Seaforths and the 2nd Black Watch; day after day they had casualty lists, some of them quite lengthy ones.

As regards the losses in the different arms of the Service, it was still true that the vast majority of these fell upon the infantry. Let us test this assertion by a glance at the casualty list of July 31st, 1916, the one already mentioned. Among the 580 officers, just over 500 were infantry leaders. Of the remainder, 37 were artillery officers, 20 were Engineers, seven were medical officers, six belonged to the Flying Corps, and one was a chaplain. A fair number were described as Machine Gun Corps, but these were infantry rather than artillery proper, and as such we have included them.

The list of casualties among the men, which appeared on the same day, contained 5,770 names. Among the first list of killed—for there were two, one issued on the Saturday and the other on the Sunday—all save five were infantrymen. At the top there were the names of two gunners and two sappers, and at the end that of a man in the R.A.M.C. Between were scores of infantrymen's names, the chief sufferers being the Hampshire, Wiltshire, and two Staffordshire regiments. The "died of wounds" did not contain a single name outside the ranks of the infantry, but the "died" contained those of 3 Hussars, 10 Artillery, 12 Engineers, 4 belonging to the A.S.C., and 6 to the R.A.M.C.

The first of the two lists of wounded pointed still more decisively in the same direction. After 22 names of men in the Flying, Artillery, and Engineer services, nearly two columns were devoted to the names of infantrymen before reaching those of a driver in the A.S.C. and of four men in the R.A.M.C. A column in the "Times" will contain nearly 1,000 of these names, so in this list of wounded we had something like 1,600 infantrymen to just 27 in other arms of the Service.

The second (Sunday's) list was in very much the same proportion. Among the killed there were 16 Artillery and 13 Engineers, all the others, except one of the R.A.M.C., belonging to the infantry. In the "died of wounds," all save nine belonged to the predominant class. The list of wounded, which contained between 2,000 and 3,000 names, had in it 94 Artillery and about the same number of Engineers. This process of examination could be continued indefinitely, but it would only show, broadly speaking,

MAJ. EDWARD COLSON,
Dogras. Indian Army.

MAJ. P. P. BALLACHEY,
Canadian Infantry.

CAPT. GUY DICKINS,
K.R.R.C. Died of wounds.

MAJ. LORD GEO. MURRAY,
Royal Highlanders.

CAPT. A. L. CAY, R.N.,
H.M.S. Invincible.

CAPT. E. P. C. BACK, R.N.,
H.M.S. Natal.

CAPT. C. J. WINTOUR, R.N.,
H.M.S. Tipperary.

CAPT. HON. J. B. CAMP-
BELL, D.S.O., Coldstreamers.

CAPT. J. A. RITSON,
South Lancs Regt.

CAPT. LORD GORELL, D.S.O.,
Royal Field Artillery.

CAPT. H. B. MUDIE,
Remount Service. Accidentally killed.

CAPT. KEITH LUCAS,
R.F.C. Killed in collision.

CAPT. F. S. KELLY,
R.N.V.R.

CAPT. A. G. COWIE,
Seaforth Highrs. Died of wounds.

CAPT. SIR R. FILMER, Bart.,
Grenadiers. Died of wounds.

CAPT. J. W. JACKSON,
South African Infantry.

THE ROLL OF HONOUR, 1916.

Photos by Heath, Elliott & Fry, Lafayette, Russell, Swaine, and Lambert Weston.

CAPT. A. F. HENTY,
Middlesex Regt. Killed in France.

the same results. We may conclude the matter by asserting that in 1916 something like 90 per cent. of the casualties fell to the lot of the infantry. At that time no one, outside the War Office, knew much of the proportions of the different arms in the armies, but it is quite certain that in proportion to their numbers the infantry suffered more heavily than any other class.

The events of the early days of 1917, the German declaration of war on neutral shipping, hospital ships, and all—men, women, and children alike—who go down to the sea in ships, revealed to many, as by a flash of lightning, the debt which not only this country, but the whole civilised world owed to the British Navy, for it alone stood between these bloodthirsty barbarians and their intended victims ; it alone was " a security for such as pass on the seas upon their lawful occasions." In performing this work certain losses in men and material were inevitable, and to the former of these we will now turn.

The price of Admiralty The above figures are exclusive, as we have said, of the naval casualties. It is common knowledge that there was heavy loss of life in the fight off Jutland Bank in May, but it is not so well realised that from the Navy, about which we heard so little, there came a steady tale of death and injury ; two one day and three the next, sometimes rising to fifty or sixty, and altogether making a formidable total, the price of one year of that silent watch and ward which enabled the millions in the British Isles to be fed.

Following the former plan, we will put down the naval casualties in tabular form, month by month, the courtesy of the " Daily Telegraph " being again drawn upon.

	OFFICERS	MEN	TOTAL
January	65	1,006	1,071
February	35	176	211
March	50	208	258
April	31	176	207
May..	63	425	488
June	440	7,376	7,816
July	35	338	373
August	48	321	369
September	58	329	387
October	60	355	415
November	214	398	612
December	69	2,577	2,646
	1,168	13,685	14,853

These totals need little comment. For eight of the months—January, June, November, and December being excepted—they just recorded the losses, in the ordinary work of patrolling the seas, rather more than one officer and about eight men per day. June was the month in which was announced the losses from the great fight of May 31st, and from the disaster in which the crew of the Hampshire perished. December's total told of the price paid by the Royal Naval Division when they took Beaumont-Hamel in November. The same engagement was responsible for November's big total of officers, for many of these, being reported earlier than the men, found their way into the casualty lists some days previously. January's list included the 300 men who went down when the armoured cruiser Natal was sunk in harbour on December 30th.

Taking August as a fairly typical month, one in which no special call was made upon the Navy, it may be interesting to inquire in detail what the casualties were. The official returns classified them thus :

[Elliott & Fry.
CAPT. A. F. WHITESIDE,
Canadian Infantry. Killed in action.

	OFFICERS	MEN
Killed	8	128
Died of Wounds	2	12
Died of Injuries	4	6
Drowned	—	18
Dangerously Wounded	—	12
Severely Wounded	1	4
Wounded	9	82
Slightly Wounded	4	6
Injured	11	—
Missing, believed Dead ..	—	8
Missing	9	44
Prisoners of War	—	1
	48	321

Excepting the four specially noted already, the classification and also the proportions in the rest of the twelve monthly lists were not unlike the one above. In June, of course, the figures were very different. The bulk of the month's losses were incurred in the Battle of Jutland Bank, which, if we deduct the losses in the Hampshire and an average for the everyday work of the Fleet, we may put down at 7,000 officers and men. Adopting the Admiralty classification, we find that 43 officers and 6,024 men were drowned, while 343 officers and 497 men were killed, a further 3 and 57 respectively dying of their

[Bassano.
CAPT. C. T. D. BERRINGTON,
Lancers (I.A.), att. R.F.A. Killed in action.

CAPT. DAVID HENDERSON,
Middlesex Regt.

[Elliott & Fry.
CAPT. HON. R. E.
PHILIPPS, Royal Fusiliers.

Lafayette.
CAPT. WILLIAMS-FREEMAN,
Lincolnshire Regt., att. R. Welsh Fusiliers.

wounds. In a big and costly action it must be extraordinarily difficult to get the details correctly, but if these figures were accurate they revealed rather a curious position—almost as many officers as men were killed. It seems as if in the doomed ships the officers were nearly all killed by gun fire or explosion, while the greater part of the men were hurled into the water and drowned. One hundred and sixty-nine men were returned as prisoners of war, and 4 officers and 60 men as missing—or missing, believed dead.

Attention has frequently been drawn to a vital difference as regards casualties on land and fighting on sea. In the former the wounded far outnumber the dead; in the latter the reverse is usually, almost invariably, the case. A comparison between the naval casualties reported in June and those reported in November and December, when the naval men were fighting on land, gives a further proof of this fact. In June, which for our purpose may be regarded as identical with the Battle of Jutland Bank, the dead, officers and men together, numbered 7,038, and the wounded 778, or 9 killed to every 1 wounded.

Compare with this the figures for November and December. Therein the killed numbered 975 and the wounded 2,283, or 1 killed to every 2½ wounded, a very different result and one quite inexplicable unless one recollects that in the later period the men of the Royal Naval Division were showing their prowess on the Ancre.

CAPT. M. S. RICHARDSON,
Royal Welsh Fusiliers. Died of wounds.

Dividing the casualties among the sailors in the same way as we have done those among the soldiers, the following is the result :

	OFFICERS	MEN	TOTAL
Killed	803	9,140	9,943
Wounded	284	3,248	3,532
Missing	63	1,038	1,101
Prisoners of War	19	267	286
	1,169	13,693	14,862

Again there is a very slight discrepancy accounted for by corrections after the monthly totals had been compiled.

Adding together the naval and military casualties we get the stupendous total for 1916 of 674,933. Of these 148,669 were dead, and even that was not the end. The most perplexing item in the casualty lists was the missing—51,959 altogether. A certain number of these fell, many of them wounded, into the hands of the enemy, but it is practically certain that the vast majority were dead. In the early stages of the war a good many of the British soldiers were taken prisoners by the Germans, but there was no evidence that they took any great number during 1916. They made no claim of extensive captures of men from the British as they did on the eastern front at times, and to a lesser extent at Verdun, and it is quite certain that they would have done so if they could. Regretfully we say that all the evidence pointed to the majority of the missing as dead and not prisoners of war, and we are justified in adding quite 40,000 to our previous total of 148,669. Better, perhaps, to make it the round figure of 190,000.

CAPT. J. D. WADDELL,
Royal Fusiliers. Killed in action.

Those actually returned as prisoners numbered 3,876 soldiers and 286 sailors. June was the only month in which this item was large, 211 officers and 2,251 men being listed as prisoners of war from the Army alone. Most of these, however, referred clearly to the surrender at Kut, for it took several weeks to get the names of the captives into the papers.

In 1916, then, 190,000 men were killed in battle. In 1914, according to the Registrar-General's returns, the excess of births over deaths in England and Wales was 362,354, but in 1915 it fell to 252,201. In 1916 it advanced to 277,277, or not enough to make good the losses in the field, for it must not be forgotten that of the babies born only **War loss and birth rate** about one-half are boys, while the 190,000 were all males. On the other hand, the loss of 190,000 lives fell upon the white population of the whole Empire, not upon England and Wales alone. Taking the British figures as a basis, the excess of births over deaths among the white population of the whole Empire in 1916 would be about 400,000. This provided an excess of males, after meeting the ordinary toll of death, of 200,000, which just about provided for the war loss of 190,000.

This was an important aspect of the world-war in which the Empire was engaged, and the Registrar-General's plain language : "There were 64,569 fewer births and 45,584 more deaths in 1915 (England and Wales only) than in 1914," perhaps helped many to realise something of the far-reaching effects of the struggle on national life.

Here, perhaps, it will not be inopportune to say something about the German casualties, for, after all, the crux of this question is comparison. If the Allies killed off Germans and Turks more rapidly than Germans and

CAPT. F. C. SELOUS, D.S.O.,
Frontiersmen Battalion. Killed in action
in East Africa.

CAPT. H. D. BROUGHTON,
Cheshire Regiment. Killed in
action.

CAPT. HON. R. P. STANHOPE, Grenadier Guards.
Heir-pres. to Earl Stanhope.

CAPT. R. A. SAUNDERS,
R.F.A. and Royal Flying Corps.
Killed in action.

[*Canadian official photograph.*]

GATHERING EQUIPMENT FROM THE BATTLEFIELD.
Salving something of the material wastage of war. Haversacks and belts, bandoliers, and water-bottles, and other of the personal equipment of the men who had fallen or been wounded, was gathered together and sorted out on the field over which the tide of battle had rolled.

Office, having counted and classified these, issued a statement giving the totals. The figures, the authorities said: "do not constitute an estimate by the British authorities, but merely represent the casualties announced in German official lists." It should also be noted that the casualties were those reported during the month in question — not those incurred therein.

In January, 1917, the authorities gave the total of German casualties reported to the end of the previous December as 4,010,160, which should be compared with our figure of 1,200,000, as both were for the whole period of the war down to that date, and both excluded naval losses. The Germans' total was made up thus:

Killed and Died of Wounds	909,665
Died of Sickness	57,459
Prisoners	229,741
Missing	284,115
Severely Wounded	530,991
Wounded	296,564
Slightly Wounded	1,486,020
Wounded Remaining with Units	215,605
	4,010,160

Turks killed off Allies, then the Allies were in a fair way to win the war. If, however, the reverse was the case, then a big change in strategy or tactics was highly desirable.

In this matter let us face the facts without flinching, even if they are not as we anticipated and had been led to believe. In the earlier stages of the struggle people read greedily about the great slaughter inflicted upon the enemy by the British and their Allies, and imaginative soldiers told of the heaps of corpses they had seen in Flanders, or, with still more eagerness, of those they had heard of in Poland. Small wonder that nearly everyone looked for a speedy end to the war, for no nation, however well drilled and organised, could stand such a drain on its man-power. Unhappily, many of these Germans had been, in Kipling's phrase, killed only "with the mouth"; and, after a time, as fresh hordes of them advanced into Poland, Russia, and Rumania, while others kept the British and the French fully occupied in France, it was necessary to abandon the silly theory that they had some secret and inexhaustible store of men for the saner if less pleasant one that their casualties had been much fewer than Britain had been led to believe. At last she looked the facts in the face, a process which those journals—called with rough justice the "hide-the-truth" Press—had done their best to prevent.

This evil, for it was nothing else, was aggravated by the writings and lectures of certain "experts." Drawing large fees for their services, they proved, absolutely and without a shadow of doubt, that by the middle of 1915, or some such date, Germany's last reserves would be exhausted, and her speedy collapse would **Experts discredited** follow. Unfortunately, in 1917, the dates, **by events** whatever they were, had come and gone, and Germany's armies were still unbroken. Gone, too, we hope and believe, had the faith of the people in the "experts."

The German Government, like the British, issued no totals of the casualties in the Kaiser's armies. The names of those killed and injured, however, were published day by day in the Press, and each month the British War

The figures may be accepted as approximately correct, and certainly there was no useful purpose served by exaggerating them, and so deluding the public with the belief that the Germans had lost far more than 4,000,000 men. One remark may be permitted, however. The period to which the figures related is somewhat uncertain. Like the British lists, the German lists were in arrears. For instance, the December **German and** returns referred not to the losses of the **British returns** month of December but to those of some earlier period. There is reason to believe that in the case of Germany the interval between the occurrence and the recording of a casualty was somewhat longer than it was in Britain; some think a great deal longer. However, if we allow it to be two months, thus making the figures under consideration those actually incurred to the end of October, 1916, it would only add something like 200,000, a rough estimate for November and December, to the existing 4,000,000.

On the whole, it will be best to take the figures as they are, and for reasons which were expressed on February 9th, 1916, by the able military correspondent of the "Times," who wrote:

"Can we trust these (*i.e.*, the German) casualty lists? Up to a point we probably can. They are often belated, but so are ours. They contain many errors which are subsequently rectified, but so do ours. They only contain the names of some men who have died of sickness, probably in the Army zone, and omit altogether, as do ours, the names of men invalided, and the floating population of hospitals and sanatoria."

It will doubtless interest some if we bring together the British and the German figures for the three months— July, August, and September—during which the Battle of the Somme was raging. Here they are:

	BRITISH	GERMAN
July	59,072	122,540
August	127,790	240,957
September	119,983	179,884
	306,845	543,381

Storming a trench on the Ancre: Germans surrender before the menace of bomb and bayonet.

Feeding the guns: Rushing up shells for the heavy howitzers during a hot engagement.

During a fight on the Ancre: British wounded bound for dressing station and hospital base.

Passing down prisoners: Officer examining a German before sending him on to internment

Carrying a position: One of the many successful assaults made in the advance to Bapaume.

Searching the depths: What the British found in one of the German dug=outs.

Vision of the Cross: A strange midnight phenomenon seen in France between the opposing lines of combatants.

Altogether the Germans lost nearly double the number that the British did, and that, for two reasons, is about the proportion we should expect. In the first place, as far as we can tell, the Germans had in the field about twice as many men as the British had, and, roughly speaking, we may expect the two armies to suffer about the same proportion of loss. The second point may be illustrated by anticipating a probable criticism. But, say some, the Germans fighting against a ring of foes must obviously have suffered far more heavily than the British operating only on one section of one frontier. To this the reply is that the main burden of the eastern campaigns of 1916 fell upon Austrians, Turks, and Bulgarians, whose losses were not included in the 4,000,000, and that during the period in question the Germans themselves were not heavily engaged except by the British and the French. Moreover, it must not be forgotten that the latter were on the offensive. It is contrary to all experience to suppose that their losses were seriously less than those of the defending armies ; it is far more likely, in spite of the great improvements made in methods of attack, that they were greater. Weighing, therefore, these considerations one with another, everything points to the fact that during those three months Germany lost about 2 men to Britain's 1.

Taking the whole war to the end of 1916 the evidence seems to show that Germany lost 3½ men to Britain's 1.

Balance in Britain's favour — This proportion was both absolutely and relatively in the latter's favour. The population of the German Empire may be put down at 70,000,000, and that of the British at 60,000,000—46,000,000 for the United Kingdom, 8,000,000 for Canada, 4,000,000 for Australia, and the remaining 2,000,000 for New Zealand and South Africa, it being best to omit for this purpose the millions of coloured folk under the British flag. The British were therefore, as regards Germany, in the proportion of 6 to 7, but the losses were only in that of 2 to 7.

A comparison of the two casualty lists went far to prove the superiority of the British fighting man. In this war, at least as far as the end of the period under review, there were no victories as complete as those of Ulm and Sedan, victories which, ending in the surrender of a whole army, left no doubt which was the defeated party. In the absence of such final tests it is somewhat difficult to say what is victory and what is defeat, and each belligerent usually claimed it, adducing the points in his favour and ignoring those against him.

A test which is frequently applied to more or less doubtful battles by military historians is which side remained at the close of the day in possession of the field. Far be it from us to undervalue this consideration. Experience has taught us that it is not to be ignored. Early in the Great War it was loudly proclaimed by anonymous but persistent writers that it was immaterial how far the Germans advanced into Russia or into France. In fact, the correspondent of one prominent London daily went so far as to tell us, not once but several times, that the Russians were retreating through Poland not because they must, but because they wished to lure the foe on to destruction.

AMERICAN AMBULANCE AT WORK NEAR THE FRENCH FRONT.
Removing wounded in an American motor-ambulance. Much valuable work was done by voluntary American organisations, not only in maintaining hospitals for the wounded in France, but also in the active employment of fleets of motor-ambulances for carrying the wounded from the front to the hospitals.

Afterwards, when the Germans had to be driven inch by inch from this occupied territory, we began to see the stupendous folly of this line of argument. How many British lives did it take to regain, in the autumn of 1916, a few square miles on the Somme? How long, it was asked in 1917, was the enemy's presence in Poland and Courland going to add to the length of the war and to the difficulties of the peace?

No ; if the field of battle be the test of victory we must regretfully admit that the Germans had the better of the Allies in 1915 and 1916. But it is legitimate to apply another. Which side took the most prisoners? To do this is clear evidence of superiority, and it was overwhelmingly on the British side. Taking this as a standard, the British beat the Germans in 1916, and the figures prove it completely.

The outstanding feature of the German casualty lists was the number of men returned as missing. Month by month this was considerable, and sometimes, as in December, 1916, it exceeded the number returned as dead. Many of these missing men were doubtless dead, but there was a strong presumption that, alive or dead, the great majority of them fell into the hands of the enemy.

Taking the missing and prisoners together the Germans admitted a loss of 514,000, or just about one-eighth of their total military casualties. In 1916 Britain admitted 54,734 in these two classes, and in 1914-15 a further 68,046, making altogether 122,780, or just about one-tenth, a very much better result. **Missing and prisoners** But the German figure was for fighting on all fronts, and the British ones included the losses, especially heavy in missing, in Gallipoli, so it is desirable to make a closer and more exact comparison. Happily this is possible.

Let us take the figures, placing them side by side, of the prisoners and missing during the second six months of 1916, when for the first time the two nations were at grips on fairly equal terms. Previously, from the battle of Mons onwards, no such comparison was possible, the British being so completely outnumbered.

PRISONERS AND MISSING	BRITISH	GERMAN
July	2,974	16,050
August	13,901	44,674
September	10,125	32,259
October	6,885	44,574
November	6,760	32,150
December	3,404	16,414
	44,049	186,121

Whatever interpretation is put upon these figures they tell in Britain's favour. They may merely mean that Germany's organisation for collecting and burying the dead was less efficient than her rival's. Be it so. More likely it is, however, that they meant the superior efficiency of the British soldier. If it be assumed that half the German forces were engaged against the British on the Somme, and half their losses incurred there, their casualties in prisoners and missing were more than double Britain's. If we give them a point and admit that only one-third of the Kaiser's armies were so employed, and that two-thirds of the above losses were incurred against the Russians and the French, we have still a substantial balance in Britain's favour — 44,049 British against 62,040 Germans. The figures only bear one conclusion. They bear out the opinion, so often expressed by the soldiers themselves, that in 1916 the Briton proved himself a better fighting man than the German. By nature a man of peace, and with little or no previous training in arts of war, he took some time to get into his stride ; but when he did so there was no holding him. Viewing the results of 1915 we might say that there was not much to choose between the two belligerents. But as regards 1916 we can only form one conclusion—the British had improved and the Germans had deteriorated.

This is one of the two proofs of the improvement of the British Army which we undertook to produce from an examination of the casualty lists. Now for the other. The losses among senior officers, generals, and colonels were much lighter, in spite of the heavier fighting in 1916, than they had been in 1914 and 1915. When all goes well, when the Staff plans are carried out with clockwork precision, these officers are, comparatively speaking, out of danger. But when things do not go well it is far otherwise. Colonels hurry up to rally hesitating battalions, or expose themselves to give hasty orders, while generals pay little heed to safety as they make new arrangements for dealing with dangerous and unexpected situations.

The two Battles of Ypres, and still more Loos, afford excellent commentaries on these remarks. Everyone remembers how Hubert Hamilton, leading the 3rd Division, was killed in the first of these engagements, how Generals Munro and Lomax were hit, and how numberless colonels were killed and

[*Elliott & Fry.*
CAPT. BASIL HALLAM RADFORD,
Royal Flying Corps. Popular revue actor.

[*Swaine.*
LIEUT. E. L. ERSKINE LINDOP,
Dogras, Indian Army. Died of wounds.

[*Swaine.*
CAPT. JOHN LAUDER,
Argyll and Sutherland Highlanders.

[*Lafayette.*
LIEUT. R. J. E. TIDDY,
Oxford and Bucks Light Infantry.

wounded. In the Second Battle of Ypres it was nearly as bad, the leaders of the Canadians being particularly unfortunate.

In the Battle of Loos, the most pertinent example, no fewer than three divisions lost their generals—Wing, Capper, and Thesiger—and in the first week of the fighting twenty-eight battalions had their colonels killed, many more were wounded, and the total was considerably increased by losses reported later. These facts told plainly that all had not gone well with the attack, the loss of the three major-generals being especially significant. The unsuccessful attempt to relieve Kut in January, 1916, was another instance of this. Had we known nothing else but the fact that one fairly short casualty list of officers, that of January 27th, contained the names of one general and six colonels, we should have surmised that something had gone wrong.

A study of the casualties in the Somme battles showed a very different result. Therein the total losses were almost equal to those suffered throughout the whole of 1915, and yet only one divisional leader, E. C. Ingouville-Williams, D.S.O., was killed. Neither brigadier-generals nor colonels figured unduly in those long and terrible lists, and we take it that this proved that Sir Douglas Haig's plans worked out far better than had previously been the case, that there were fewer checks and misunderstandings, and that consequently the senior officers had less need to expose themselves.

One hundred and ninety thousand brave men dead ; this is the cardinal fact of our chapter. It would be sad enough if they were the weak and aged, those who, in a few years at most, would pay Nature's debt. It would be still more bearable if they were the thousands who crowd our lunatic asylums and fill our prisons. It is because they were all that these are not—young, healthy, sane, and intelligent—that their loss was so terrible to contemplate. They were in every sense the flower of the race. Take two cases which, although somewhat exceptional, served to bring home the type of man we sacrificed. In January in Mesopotamia there fell Lieutenant C. J. Cockburn, of the 6th Yats. His ancestors had been in the Army for the past one hundred and fifty years ; his grandfather was the first British officer killed during the Indian Mutiny, and his father served under Kitchener in the Sudan. On June 1st Captain Leslie Woodroffe, of the Rifle Brigade, died from wounds received in France. He had been the head of Marlborough and an Oxford scholar before taking up work as a schoolmaster at Shrewsbury. Two of his brothers had fallen before him in the war. One, Kenneth, a cricket Blue at Cambridge, was killed at Neuve Chapelle ; another, Sydney, was awarded the Victoria Cross for gallantry at Hooge, where he was killed ; while Leslie himself had been previously wounded and

LIEUT. DONALD CAMPBELL,
Coldstream Guards. His father, Capt.
the Hon. J. B. Campbell, fell later.

LT. C. H. ABERCROMBIE,
H.M.S. Defence. Well-known
Scottish International footballer.

VISCOUNT QUENINGTON,
Lieut. in the Royal Gloucestershire Hussars (Yeomanry).

CAPT. LORD ELCHO,
Gloucestershire Yeomanry. Eldest son of
the Earl of Wemyss.

LIEUT. HON. V. S. T. HARMSWORTH,
Royal Naval Division. Killed in the
Battle of the Ancre.

SEC.-LT. G. A. ARBUTHNOT,
Grenadier Guards. First served
in a mine-sweeper.

LIEUT. K. L. HUTCHINGS,
Liverpool Regt., att. Welsh
Regt. Famous cricketer.

LIEUT. RAYMOND ASQUITH,
Grenadier Guards. Eldest son of Mr.
Asquith, ex-Prime Minister.

LIEUT. E. H LINTOTT,
West Yorks Regt. Well-known International football player.

LIEUT. T. M. KETTLE,
Dublin Fusiliers. Professor Kettle
was a well-known writer.

SEC.-LT. E. E. EARLY,
Lincolnshire Regt. Killed at
Hohenzollern Redoubt

LIEUT. J. R. DENNISTOUN,
Irish Horse, att. R.F.C. Member of
Scott's Antarctic Expedition, 1910-11.

LIEUT. VISCOUNT CLIVE,
Welsh Guards. Had served earlier in the
Scots Guards.

LIEUT. A. W. LANE-JOYNT,
Motor Machine-Gun Service.
Killed in France.

LT. M. J. VINCENT-JACKSON,
Notts and Derby Regt. (Sherwood Foresters).

CAPT. ARTHUR H. HALES, M.C.,
Wiltshire Regt. Received M.C. for leading
his men though twice wounded.

THE ROLL OF HONOUR, 1916.

Photos by Arbuthnot, Bassano, Elliott & Fry, Hawkins, Lafayette, Swaine

BRITISH TRENCH NEAR FRICOURT WHEN THE TIDE OF WAR HAD PASSED EASTWARD.

Trenches that were established by the British on the western front, near Fricourt, and left deserted when the " big push " had carried the fighting-line farther to the east. Beyond these trenches lay the Mametz Wood, the scene of considerable fighting before it was finally captured. The photograph indicates the vast extent to which sand-bags were employed in the strengthening of trenches and the forming of defensive breastworks.

given the Military Cross. On such men, rather than on the drunkard, the anæmic, or the feckless, did the losses fall.

For the main part those 190,000 were educated men, and so laid mental as well as physical gifts upon the altar. Many of them came from the universities and public schools, and many had been trained for professional life as lawyers, teachers, accountants, and the like. But we do not refer only to these. The rank and file of the fallen included a high proportion of skilled artisans, men who had been accustomed to mix their work with brains, and these also should be included in our category. To put it simply, money had been invested in the education and training of every one of these, and in ordinary circumstances this would have brought a rich return in future years. Now both capital and interest are gone. Keen brains and clever hands, with their most fruitful years before them, have passed for ever from the nation's industrial life; fresh and virile intellects, strengthened by years of training, will add nothing more to its store of scientific discovery; nor cultured and generous minds to the richness of its intellectual and artistic life. Who can assess this loss?

This loss was national. But there was a personal and domestic side to it. From each one of the dead some years of life had been taken, years which should be the most precious and potent of all. But each also, whether as husband, father, son, or brother, left a vacant space in some circle; and it is here, rather than upon the battlefield or even in the hospital, that one realised the incalcul-able amount of misery which the war caused. Any

A loss none can assess

computation thereof is beyond us. We stand outside the bereaved home and its inmates. There the heart knoweth its own bitterness, and a stranger intermeddleth not with its joy.

To bring home to our minds the immensity of this loss, 190,000 men, is not easy. It is so simple to put down the figure, so difficult to visualise the immense array it repre-sents. In 1911 there were in Liverpool, the second largest city in England, 133,551 males between twenty and forty-five years of age, and in Newcastle there were 50,233, so the national loss may be put as equal to all the men of military age in those two cities combined.

It was not only in numbers that the army of killed resembled the men of Liverpool and Newcastle. Like them they were men of diverse and peaceful occupations. Of those killed in 1916 very few indeed were Regular soldiers; over 90 per cent. were by training and inclination civilians. In the first few months of the war the Regulars, officers and men who had adopted the profession of arms from choice, bore the burden of the fighting, but in six months or so there were very few of them left.

As regards the officers this point can be illustrated with comparative ease, but as regards the men it must be taken for granted, although no one will question it, for it can be proved by figures. To the end of 1916 the number of casualties suffered by the British was six times the number of Regular soldiers the country had before the Great War. Even if every one of these Regulars appeared in the casualty lists it would leave something like 1,000,000 names for men who were until the war civilians.

Composition of the new armies

Those who care to turn to the " Times," with its obituary notices of deceased officers, will find ample proof of the diverse callings of the dead. On Monday, October 2nd, there were twenty-four fairly full obituaries. With regard to several there was no indication of what the men did before entering the Army. Of the others, one was a fairly prominent politician and had been a member of Parliament, and another was a professional entertainer. There were two barristers and two bank clerks in the list; another was in the Ceylon Civil Service, and another had devoted himself to architecture and literature. Four only were soldiers before the outbreak of the Great War. Two came from Canada and one from the East to enlist, and two or three others were in business in England. One went straight from school into the Army, and others were at the university in 1914. It was noteworthy that nine of the twenty-four had served in the ranks before obtaining commissions, and that three of them had lost brothers during the war. Taking a number of these notices, say a period of a month, there is hardly a profession or business that is unrepresented; and this, be it remembered, was before the conscripts had entered the field.

In his " Comments of Bagshot," Mr. J. A. Spender remarks that " it is probably a dim instinct of what is for its own good that makes an aristocracy warlike, even in modern times." Be this as it may, there is no doubt whatever that the British aristocracy is warlike, and a glance at the Roll of Honour proves it.

In the 1917 issue of the work, which appeared towards the end of 1916, Debrett gave some interesting particulars about the losses of titled families in the **The warlike** Great War. Up to date, 118 peers and **British aristocracy** baronets had lost their heirs, and in 151 cases the succession to titles had been affected by these and other deaths. Altogether this small class lost 1,450 sons and near relatives; 114 were the sons of peers, 110 the sons of baronets, and 150 the sons of knights, the rest being nephews and other kinsmen. Fourteen peers, 21 baronets, 9 knights, and 9 members of Parliament were among the number.

Speaking in the House of Lords on February 7th, 1917, Earl Curzon carried the story a little further. He said that the death-roll included 6 members of that House, and over 120 of their sons; 62 of the latter were heirs to peerages, and consequently eight peerages were then in danger of extinction.

In our previous chapter we mentioned the names of such peers as were killed in 1914 and 1915, and the narrative may be continued here. The Earl of Longford lost his life while leading the Yeomanry in Gallipoli, in 1915, but his fate was only made certain during 1916, and the same remark applies to Viscount **Losses in the** Crichton, of the Royal Horse Guards, son **peerage** and heir of the Earl of Erne, and to Lord George Murray, a son of the late Duke of Atholl. Lord Lucas, the " Bron " Herbert of former days, was a real hero. During the Boer War he lost a leg, but he qualified as a flying man, and it was while flying that he was killed. To his memory Sir J. M. Barrie paid a noble tribute in the columns of the " Times." Another peer killed was one who, like Lucas, had won his spurs as a politician; the Earl of Feversham, formerly Viscount Helmsley, M.P., was shot in September while leading his battalion, one of the King's Royal Rifles. Later fell Lord Llangattock, one bearing the familiar name of Rolls, and with his death that title became extinct. These three, like a number of others, were men whom great possessions did not deter from service in the field.

Lord Newborough, of the Welsh Guards, died in July from illness contracted when on active service, and after the close of the year Lord Gorell, of the Artillery, was killed. Passing to the heirs to peerages, the Duke of Leinster lost his brother and heir, Lord Desmond Fitzgerald, of the Irish Guards, in March. The Marquess of Bath lost Viscount Weymouth, and the Earls of Powis and Wemyss lost Viscount Clive, of the Welsh Guards, and Lord Elcho, of the Yeomanry, respectively. The death of the Hon. P. R. Stanhope, Grenadier Guards, in September, deprived the earldom of that name of its heir, and another Grenadier to fall was the Hon. E. W. Tennant, Lord Glenconner's eldest son. Viscount Goschen lost his heir, Hon. G. J. Goschen, of the Buffs, in Mesopotamia in January. In July, Lord St. Davids lost his second son, Hon. R. E. Philipps; by the death of the Hon. W. A. Parnell, Lord Congleton lost his heir; by that of Hon. L. E. Johnstone

OUTLOOK OVER THE TRENCH-SCARRED BATTLEFIELD OF THE ANCRE. *[Canadian official photograph.*

Looking towards Contalmaison from the lines which were occupied by the British at the beginning of the forward movement in July, 1916. The Prussian Guard was sent to bar progress near this village; but, despite that fact, Contalmaison was one of the places captured during the series of successes which crowned the " great push " The white lines in the distance indicate the way in which the countryside was scarred with trenches.

in the Jutland battle, Lord Derwent did the same. Later the Hon. F. S. Trench, Lord Ashtown's eldest son, was killed. Lord Stratheden and Campbell, a venerable peer of nearly ninety, had a double loss. On July 19th his grandson and second heir, Donald Campbell, of the Coldstreams, was killed, and a few days later it was known for certain that the peer's eldest son, Hon. J. B. Campbell, also of the Coldstreams, who had been missing since January, 1915, was also dead.

As regards other members of the peerage it would probably be easier to name those families which had not lost a member or members during the war than those which had. The Earls of Sefton and Denbigh each lost a son in the great naval fight of May 31st, as also

Cadets of noble houses

did Lord Glanusk, who had previously been bereaved, and Lord Algernon Percy. The Earl of Selborne and the late Lord George Campbell lost sons, in both cases men of exceptional brilliance, in Mesopotamia, and Lords Auckland and Tennyson suffered in similar fashion. Lord Dewar lost Captain Dewar, of the Camerons, a noted boxer when at Oxford, and Lord Rothermere lost his second son, Hon. V. S. T. Harmsworth, killed while leading the men of the Royal Naval Division on the Ancre. Other losses included grandsons of Earl Brassey and Lords Polwarth and Ashcombe ; nephews of Lords Midleton and Teignmouth,

LIEUT. HENRY WEBBER,
South Lancashire Regt.

[Elliott & Fry.
LIEUT. J. A. MOORE,
South Staffordshire Regiment.

LIEUT. G. E. L. BOWLBY,
Lincolnshire Regiment.

and brothers of Lord Haldon and the Earl of Lanesborough.

The House of Commons had three of its members killed during the year. Viscount Quenington, son of Earl St. Aldwyn, who only survived his loss by a few days, was killed in Egypt ; Captain Hon. Guy Baring, M.P. for Winchester, was killed when with the Coldstreams on the Somme ; and Lieut.-Colonel D. F. Campbell, D.S.O., M.P. for North Ayrshire, died in September while commanding a battalion of the West Ridings. The list of members of the House of Commons who lost sons in the war was headed by Mr. Asquith, whose eldest son Raymond, a lieutenant of the Grenadiers, fell during the heavy fighting of September. The Labour leader, Mr. Arthur Henderson, lost a son, Captain David Henderson, of the Middlesex, and the Unionist leader, Mr. Walter Long, his heir, Brigadier-General Walter Long, D.S.O., in Greece. Sir Gordon Hewart, the Solicitor-General, and Mr. Pike Pease were junior members of the Ministry to suffer a like bereavement.

Private members who experienced this loss in their homes

[Lafayette.
LIEUT. W. A. CLIFF-McCULLOCH,
Irish Rifles.

included Sir Thomas Esmonde, Bart., Mr. T. W. Russell, Mr. Herbert Nield, Mr. A. Strauss, Mr. A. W. Samuels, Mr. John Hinds, Mr. E. R. Turton, Mr. A. W. Soames, Mr. James Boyton, and Sir Robert Williams, Bart. Sir Robert's son was serving as a private in the ranks. Sir Charles Henry and Sir Charles Nicholson, baronets as well as politicians, each lost an only son, and the venerable Mr. Jesse Collings a grandson.

The war left its mark, too, upon politicians who had not succeeded in entering the House, or those who had formerly sat there. In the latter category were Mr. G. A. Arbuthnot, formerly M.P. for Burnley, and the brilliant Irishman, Professor T. M. Kettle, of the Dublin Fusiliers, both killed during the fighting on the Somme. Mr. J. Windsor Lewis and Captain Helenus Robertson were two young Unionists who had attacked strong Liberal seats, and Mr. Hugh Montgomery, killed in September, had been Unionist candidate for Southampton. Lieut.-Colonel F. H. Gaskell, of the Welsh Regiment, had been adopted to fight a seat in Glamorganshire, Mr. C. W. Winterbotham, of the Gloucesters, proposed to attack, in the Liberal interest, Cirencester, and Captain E. L. Boase, of the Black Watch, was Unionist candidate for Dundee. Across the seas, Hon. J. D. Hazen, a prominent Canadian Minister, and Sir J. Allen, a New Zealand politician, each lost a son.

Many of the baronets killed were mentioned in the former narrative, but there are several names to add. Sir R. K. Arbuthnot, commanding the 1st Cruiser Squadron, was killed in the big naval battle of May 31st, and so was Sir C. R. Blane, of the Queen Mary. Blane's two younger brothers had fallen previously, and with his death this title became extinct. Sir Foster H. E. Cunliffe, of the Rifle Brigade, killed in July, was much more than a soldier ; he had been captain of the Oxford cricket team, was Fellow of All Souls College, and owing to his knowledge of military affairs was made the first lecturer on Military History at Oxford. Sir Robert Filmer, of the Grenadiers, was a Kentish baronet whose title dated back to 1674 ; he left no heir. Two others killed were Sir J. H. Jaffray, of the Yeomanry, and Sir E. H. Macnaughten, of the Black Watch. Sir A. A. A. Campbell, killed in May, came over from Nova Scotia and served in the ranks before obtaining a commission in the Cameron Highlanders. Other losses during the year were sons of Sir George Dashwood, an

Losses in the Baronetage

Oxfordshire baronet of ancient lineage, and Sir J. Lulham Pound, making two lost by each of these baronets, while Sir Vere Isham, Sir J. C. Horsfall, Sir Timothy O'Brien, Sir Archibald Edmondstone, Sir William Clarke, and Sir Henry Ewart were among the many who lost their heirs.

As previously explained, the death-roll among the generals was not high during 1916, but neither was it negligible. Among leaders of divisions, the only two to fall were E. C. Ingouville-Williams, D.S.O., and the Canadian major-general, M. S. Mercer, slain during a sudden German attack in May. Those commanding brigades suffered more heavily. Early in the year W. J. St. J. Harvey died of wounds received in Mesopotamia, while in the west the British lost H. G. Fitton, C.B., G. B. Hodson, F. J. Heyworth, of the Guards, Philip Howell, C.M.G., C. B. Prowse, D.S.O., George Bull, D.S.O., L. M.

LIEUT. H. R. ANDREWS,
West Yorks Regt., att. Lancs Fusiliers.

LIEUT. N. A. MORICE,
East Yorks Regt. Died of
wounds.

LIEUT. F. CRATHORNE,
Gen. List, att. R.E. Killed
in action.

LIEUT. J. W. DAVIES,
Royal Welsh Fusiliers. Killed in action.

SEC.-LIEUT. L. J. MOON,
Devon Regt. Died of wounds.

LIEUT. W. DUFF,
Cameronians. Killed in
action.

LIEUT. B. E. HICKS,
Royal Berks Regt. Killed in
action.

LIEUT. E. G. WILLIAMS,
Grenadier Guards. Accidentally killed.

LIEUT. F. L. PUSCH,
D.S.O., Irish Guards. Killed while tending
wounded man.

LIEUT. J. C. MORROW,
Canadian Engineers. Killed
in action.

LT.-SURG. P. J. WALSH,
R.A.M.C. Served with Indian
troops.

LIEUT. C. H. NEWTON,
K.R.R.C. Killed leading his platoon
in Flanders.

LIEUT. A. H. BELL,
Canadian M.R., att. 5th Infantry
Brigade Headquarters.

LIEUT. C. L. MERE,
Royal Lancaster Regt.
Killed in action.

LT. S. R. V. TRAVERS,
Munster Fusiliers. Killed at
Dardanelles.

LIEUT. J. P. PHILLIMORE,
B.Sc., East Kent Regt. (The Buffs).
Killed in action.

THE ROLL OF HONOUR, 1916.

Photos by Bassano, Elliott & Fry, Brooke Hughes, Lafayette, Swaine, Lambert Weston.

Phillpotts, C.M.G., H. F. H. Clifford, D.S.O., C. E. Stewart, C.M.G., D. J. Glasfurd, and one or two others.

The list of colonels killed in action is too long for complete enumeration, but a few outstanding names may be given. Lieut.-Colonel Stewart Macdougall, of the Gordons, had been in the household of Queen Victoria; P. W. Machell, D.S.O., of the Border Regiment, was a

Mortality among colonels

soldier of distinction; E. W. Benson was the only son of Sir Frank Benson, the actor. Those killed in the early part of the year included F. J. Bowker, of the Hampshires, R. W. Fox, of the Devons, H. Maclear, D.S.O., of the Scots Fusiliers, A. B. A. Stewart, D.S.O., of the Seaforths, and R. C. B. Throckmorton, of the Wiltshires.

In the second half of the year the toll taken was heavier. Among many names, the price of the early stages of the "great push," all alike worthy of commemoration, there may be mentioned R. L. Aspinall, D.S.O., of the Cheshires, a famous horseman; Ronald Wood, of the Rifle Brigade, H. Lewis, of the Manchesters, J. A. Thicknesse, of the Somerset Light Infantry, E. A. Innes, of the Warwicks, G. C. Roberts, a Halifax manufacturer, of the Gloucesters; W. Burnett, D.S.O., of the North Staffordshires, C. C. Macnamara, of the Irish Rifles, E. H. Tritton, D.S.O., and W. E. M. Tyndall, D.S.O., of the West Ridings.

The many Canadian colonels killed included H. C. Buller, D.S.O., of Princess Patricia's Own, W. R. Marshall, W. D. Allan, D.S.O., and A. E. Shaw. During July the battalions of one famous regiment, the Northumberland Fusiliers, the " Fighting Fifth," had no fewer than four commanding officers killed— C. C. A. Sillery, one of three brothers to fall, A. P. A. Elphinstone, L. M. Howard,

and W. Lyle. In A. St. H. Gibbons, the Liverpools lost a leader and the world an explorer and a writer, and in A. P. Mack, of the Suffolks, one who had explored the Egyptian Desert. The fighting in the concluding months of the year deprived the Army of such leaders as Lieut.-Colonel J. C. Stormonth-Darling, D.S.O., of the Cameronians, C. E. Goff, of the Liverpools, C. J. W. Hobbs, D.S.O., of the Sherwood Foresters, W. B. Gibbs, of the Worcesters, C. G. Forsyth, of the Yorkshires, W. B. Lyons, of the Munster Fusiliers, and E. T. F. Sandys, D.S.O., of the Middlesex. A few others may be mentioned: F. E. Penn Curzon, of the Royal Irish, J. L. Swainson, D.S.O., of the Royal Lancasters, and C. E. Radclyffe, D.S.O., of the Essex. Of the Royal Naval Division there fell in November—Lieut.-Cols. A. S. Tetley, F. J. Saunders, and W. O. Burge, of the R.M.L.I.

As regards leaders in the Navy, the Battle of Jutland cost the lives of two admirals, Sir R. K. Arbuthnot, already mentioned, whose flag was in the Defence, and the Hon. Horace L. Hood, leading the 3rd Squadron of Battle Cruisers, a sailor bearing one of the great names in

Loss of great seamen

our naval history. Five captains of battleships went down with their vessels on that occasion—Cecil I. Prowse, of the Queen Mary, Charles F. Sowerby, of the Indefatigable, Arthur L. Cay, of the Invincible, T. P. Bonham, of the Black Prince, and Stanley V. Ellis, of the Defence. Another captain to lose his life then was C. J. Wintour, the capable leader of the 4th Flotilla of Destroyers, who was in the Tipperary. Captain E. P. C. Back, with twenty-four of his officers, went down with the Natal in the previous December.

In addition to those already mentioned, the war brought during 1916 sorrow to the homes of many distinguished men. One of the ablest of British seamen, Admiral Sir Percy Scott, lost a son in the Battle of Jutland, and two other admirals, Sir Mostyn Field and Sir Day Bosanquet, suffered a similar bereavement. Particularly sad was the death of Lieut.-General Sir W. N. Congreve's son, Major W. La T. Congreve, of the Rifle Brigade, just after his marriage to the daughter of Mr. Cyril Maude; the Victoria Cross, which his father, too, had won in South Africa, was awarded to the dead officer. Brigadier-General Sir Owen Thomas lost a son, and so did Sir Hallewell Rogers, of Birmingham, Sir J. H. A. Macdonald, Sir A. Scott-Gatty, Mrs. Alec Tweedie, Sir Hugh Clifford, Mr. Stanhope Forbes, R.A., Mr. B. W. Leader, R.A., Sir John Willison, of Toronto, Sir Aston Webb, and Mr. Cecil Aldin, the artist. Sir Edwin Egerton, at one time Ambassador in Rome, did not long survive the fall of his only son.

The death in battle of Mr. J. L. Garvin's only son,

[*Canadian and British official photographs.*

HAVOC CAUSED BY SHELL FIRE IN THE " BIG PUSH " OF JULY, 1916.
German trench which had been demolished by shell fire during the advance on the western front. The foreground dug-out, beneath a formidable barbed-wire entanglement, had suffered from a direct hit. Above: A ruined village near Mametz.

Lieutenant R. G. Garvin, of the South Lancashires, aroused much sorrow and sympathy, as also did that of Mr. Cutcliffe Hyne's son, a subaltern in the Irish Guards. A death in the Battle of Jutland brought the number of sons lost by Mr. J. C. Snead-Cox, of the "Tablet," up to three, and Sir Duncan Baillie, K C.I E., also lost three sons Sir William Vaudrey, of Manchester, and Mr. Lawrence Kellie, the composer, were among the hundreds of fathers who mourned the loss of two. Among the many lawyers to suffer the loss of one were the Hon. J. D. Fitzgerald, K.C., Mr. H. Courthope-Monroe, K.C., Mr. Mark L. Romer, K.C., and Mr. A. R. Ingpen, K.C. The death of Sir Oliver Lodge's son Raymond should not be forgotten, nor should that of Mr. Harry Lauder's only son, a captain in the Argyll and Sutherland Highlanders, because for very different reasons both aroused a good deal of interest. Major C. C. Dickens, of the London Regiment, was a son of Mr. H. F. Dickens, K.C., and a grandson of the great novelist.

The number of sons sent by the clergy into the Army and Navy has often been commented upon, and so it was not surprising to find a large number of them among the fallen. Indeed, it was unusual to see even a small number of obituary notices of soldiers without at least one clergyman's

[*Lafayette.*
LIEUT. H. WYNDHAM THOMAS,
Rifle Brigade.

these so often, both in playing-field and class-room, the leaders of their fellows.

To the end of 1915 Oxford knew that 861 of her sons had been killed in battle, and a year later the total was certainly double that figure, probably more. Those who, like the present writer, were contemporary at Oxford with Raymond Asquith, remembering stories of his almost uncanny brilliance, will not be surprised to see his name mentioned first among those Oxonians who gave their lives for Britain in 1916. As a classical scholar he was in the front rank, and neither Winchester nor Balliol can have trained many who possessed rarer intellectual gifts. Another Fellow of All Souls to fall, Sir Foster Cunliffe, Bart., has already been mentioned.

Leslie W. Hunter, of the Oxfordshire Light Infantry, killed in August, was, like Raymond Asquith, one of Winchester's finest products. When at New College he won practically all the University's classical prizes, and afterwards was made Fellow and Tutor. Another Fellow of New to fall about the same time was Geoffrey W. Smith, a scientist of distinction, who was University Lecturer in Zoology. R. J. E. Tiddy, of the Oxfordshire Light Infantry, was University lecturer in English and a Fellow of Trinity. Captain Guy

[*Elliott & Fry.*
LIEUT. H. C. T. NEALE,
Northamptonshire Regiment.

[*Bassano.*
LIEUT. R. L. KNOTT,
Northumberland Fusiliers.

[*Lafayette*
LIEUT. C. C. HENRY,
Hussars, att. Worcs. Regt.

[*Bassano.*
LIEUT. A. A. WARREN,
Border Regiment.

son in it, and not a rare thing to see quite a number of them in the front page of the "Times" or the "Morning Post." Prominent dignitaries of the Church who in 1916 had sons on the Roll of Honour included Bishop Boyd-Carpenter, the Dean of Ripon; Dr. James Gow, the Headmaster of Westminster School; Dr. Bernard, the Protestant Archbishop of Dublin; the Bishop of Crediton, and many others. Dr. Shaw, Bishop of Buckingham, lost his third son. Three prominent Nonconformist ministers—Revs. W. B. Selbie, of Oxford, Bernard J. Snell, of Brixton, and John Hunter—lost sons, and to these a large number of others could be added, men drawn from a class that does not usually enter the Army, but that did so nobly in the hour of peril.

In the houses of the land it was the intensity rather than the extent of the loss which struck the observer. The dead were counted there by ones and twos, occasionally by threes and fours. To obtain some idea of its extent—of the ravages of war among the youth of the land as a whole—one should turn to the universities and public schools, each with its Roll of Honour, not ones and twos, but hundreds, mounting up to thousands, and

Lafayette
SEC.-LIEUT. R. D. TIBBS,
Indian Army Reserve of Officers.

Dickins, of the K.R.R.C., was Fellow of St. John's, and so was Leonard G. Butler, whose speciality was history. Another loss to St. John's was John Handyside, of the Liverpools, who was made a Fellow of the College in 1908 and was at the time of his death in battle Lecturer in Philosophy at Liverpool University.

In Charles D. Fisher, a brother of the Right Hon. H. A. L. Fisher, Christ Church lost a Tutor, a victim of Jutland, whose influence was remarkable. R. P. Dunn-Pattison, of the Devons, was at one time Lecturer in History at Magdalen; P. Newbold of the Royal West Kents, went from Oriel to become lecturer at Armstrong College, Newcastle-on-Tyne; and R. M. Heath. also of Oriel, won the Newdigate Prize and a Craven Fellowship before entering the Somerset Light Infantry.

Late in 1916 the "Cambridge Review" stated that the losses in killed of the University to date — sometime in the autumn of 1916—were 1,438. Among these men were three who had been Presidents of the Union—G. K. M Butler, of the Yeomanry, a brilliant scholar, as a son of the venerable Master of Trinity should be, Christopher Bethell, and A. D. Barnard, of the Rifle Brigade. Captain H. F Russell-Smith, also of the Rifle Brigade, was a Fellow of St. John's and Lecturer in Political Science; he had been a University prizeman and had taken a double first; Kenneth R. Lewin, of the Duke of Cornwall's Light Infantry, was a scientist of distinction, who had studied at Naples, assisted the Professor of Biology, and worked at Rothamsted; S. B. McLaren was a Second Wrangler, appointed Professor of Mathematics at Reading; G. R. Ray, of the Bedfords, was Fellow and Lecturer in History at Emmanuel College; Captain A. S. Marsh, Somerset Light Infantry, was University Lecturer in Botany. But perhaps the most brilliant of all was Keith Lucas,

Brilliant University men Fellow of Trinity, and also of the Royal Society. He was a physiologist doing research work at Cambridge when war broke out. He then entered the Flying Corps, and had greatly improved the aeroplane compass before he met his death while flying on October 5th. In mental gifts these men were superior to most of their fellows, but, they would be the first to admit, in nothing else. The mass of the fallen from our universities and public schools must here remain unnamed; they gave all they had, powers of mind and body, to the common cause, and are worthy of equal honour with the named.

As regards the other educational centres, a few figures must suffice. In July Sir Henry Miers said that his University of Manchester had lost 90 students and 5 teachers in the war, and Mr. H. A. L. Fisher gave 24 and 2 as the corresponding figures for the smaller University of Sheffield. For Leeds 55 was the total to date. The part played by the Scottish Universities may be seen from the statement, made in 1916, that over 250 students of Edinburgh had fallen.

Of the great schools reports gave 713 as the number of Etonians killed in battle, and over 400 from Harrow. Rugby's total was 364, Marlborough's was 407, Clifton's over 300, St. Paul's 242, Tonbridge's 168, and Rossall's 126. Stonyhurst had 80 names on the Roll of Honour. These figures are merely samples of all, no better and no worse than scores of other schools, and, it should be added, than hundreds of elementary and secondary schools all over the land. These, it is to be hoped, will each have its Roll of Honour drawn up and exhibited, and from it will spring traditions of high courage and fearless endeavour, like to those which are the glory of Eton and Winchester, for such are not of a class but of the race. This may well be one of the great issues of the war, one of its abiding benefits, and, if so, few things will make more for the future greatness of Britain.

Two classes of professional men are not usually found in the ranks of the combatants in war—the doctor and the clergyman. The vacant condition of our medical schools and theological colleges in 1915 and 1916 was, however, proof enough that the spirit of patriotism was as strong in those training for these two callings as it was in those outside, and we cannot say it was less vigorous in those who had entered them.

On November 2nd, 1916, there was a solemn celebration of the Holy Eucharist in the Chapel of King's College, London. It was in memory of those members of the University of London who had fallen in the war, and the list of names as printed is a long one, for it included men from all the colleges which are affiliated to the University,

[*Lafayette.*
LIEUT. HON. G. J. GOSCHEN,
The Buffs (East Kent Regt.).

[*Chancellor.*
SEC.-LIEUT. W. L. ORR,
Royal Irish Rifles.

such as the London School of Economics, the Royal College of Science, and the East London College, as well as King's and University Colleges.

This fact, perhaps, may not strike the casual observer, but he cannot fail to notice the large number of medical men whose names appeared thereon, and London, being the largest medical university, may be taken as a sample of all. Turn over the pages. The different hospitals appear, each heading a roll of names, first for 1914-15 and then for 1916. Some clearly had forsaken, temporarily at least, the art of healing, and had entered other branches of the Service, but the majority had not.

Among the 1914-15 names there were a good number of qualified medical men, but for the full extent of this loss one should turn rather to the names for 1916. St. Bartholomew's Hospital, for instance, had 25; St. Thomas's had 27; Guy's 28, and the London 20, a total of just 100 for these four. Of these, 17 from St. Bartholomew's and 20 from St. Thomas's were qualified men, and the nature of their degrees was given. As regards Guy's and the London the number was less obvious, but it appeared to be 14 from the former and 11 from the latter, making a total of 62 doctors killed. The other hospitals contributed a few, and with the medical schools in other parts of the country, not forgetting Scotland, and the numbers for 1914-15, the medical profession must have many names on its Roll of Honour. One of the most distinguished of these London names was that of Colonel A. E. J. Barker, Professor of Surgery at University College.

Deaths among chaplains are not unknown on the field of battle, and there were a number of such in 1916. At least three clergymen, Captain W. M. Benton, of the Manchesters, R. F. Callaway, of the Sherwood Foresters, and S. F. Hulton, a private, died while fighting as combatants, while among those clergymen killed, when engaged in duties of a more peaceful kind, were the Revs. E. W. Trevor, H. O. Spink, D. M. Guthrie, and F. H. Tuke. The Rev. R. M. Kirwan, at one time the only chaplain with the forces in Mesopotamia, died from hardships incurred there, and a Wesleyan chaplain, Rev. G. T. Cook, was killed in France. It was worthy of note that eight chaplains were among those who went down in the naval fight of May 31st.

Literature and art, which already counted Rupert Brooke and Dixon Scott upon the roll, added thereto during 1916. A. V. Ratcliffe, of the West Yorkshires, was a poet of promise, and so was H. R. Freston, of the Berkshires. Captain Theodore Flatau, an Australian, had written three novels, and **Losses to Literature and Art** edited the "World." The Authors' Club reported sixteen of its members killed. H. N. Dickinson, of the West Kents, was the author of "Keddy" and wrote other stories, and Donald Hankey, of the Warwicks, won a reputation just before his death, on October 12th, by "A Student in Arms." G. S. K. Butterworth, a son of Sir A. K. Butterworth, was a musical composer, and was greatly interested in collecting folk-songs and folk-dances; and H. St. P. Bunbury, of the Artillery, was a painter, one of whose works was hung in the Invalides at Paris. The stage lost Basil H. Radford—better known as Basil Hallam, the creator of Gilbert the Filbert—and Shiel Barry who had played with Sir George Alexander and Lewis Waller. Here may be mentioned the death of a "Punch" artist, Captain Neville Smith,

SEC.-LIEUT. R. W. PHILLIPPS, Grenadier Guards. Killed in action in Flanders.

SEC.-LT. H. ARMSTRONG, East Surrey Regt. Died of wounds.

SEC.-LT. R. G. PECK, Cameronians (Scottish R.) Att. Highland L. I.

SEC.-LIEUT. A. V. RATCLIFFE, West Yorks Regiment. Killed in action near Fricourt.

SEC.-LIEUT. J. F. EGERTON, K.R.R.C. He was killed in action.

SEC.-LIEUT. E. A. STURRIDGE, Yorks Light Infantry. Died.

SEC.-LIEUT. W. J. McCONNOCHIE, R.F.C. Killed in action.

SEC.-LIEUT. J. G. GREGORY, London Regiment. He died of wounds.

SEC.-LIEUT. M. L. PRICE, Middlesex Regt. Killed in action.

SEC.-LT. A. F. BENTLEY, Sherwood Foresters. Died of wounds.

SEC.-LT. D. M. H. JEWELL, Royal Fusiliers, att. R.E. Killed in action.

SEC.-LIEUT. C. P. A. HERSEE, Royal Fusiliers. Killed in action.

SEC.-LIEUT. H. DURANT, Lancers. Killed in action.

SEC.-LT. G. R. A. CASE, Lancs Regt. Killed in action.

SEC.-LT. G. R. JEFFERY, Hussars. Killed in action.

SEC.-LIEUT. H. H. L. RICHARDS, Connaught Rangers. Killed in action.

THE ROLL OF HONOUR, 1916.

Photos by Speaight, Elliott & Fry, Lafayette, Swaine, and Chancellor.

of the Durham Light Infantry, and of one of its literary contributors, Alec L. Johnston, of the Shropshires. Among the journalists to fall was Lieut. I. O. Hutchison, of the "Evening News."

The Civil Service had earned an unenviable notoriety for its reluctance to release suitable men for the Army, but against those who went no charge whatever could be made. Captain R. C. Woodhead, of the Durham Light Infantry, killed in July, was a brilliant Oxford scholar, who had been appointed assistant secretary of the Development Commission. Sir Courtenay Ilbert wrote that three of his clerks in the House of Commons had fallen, and among probationers for the Indian Civil Service the number was four.

Sportsmen who fell

With F. S. Kelly, one of the most remarkable men killed during the Great War, we can pass from art to sport. Kelly, who was killed on November 13th, while serving with the R.N.V.R., and had previously been wounded in Gallipoli, was outstanding in both. As an oarsman he had done nearly everything—stroked the Eton Eight,

MILITARY FUNERAL FOR A BRAVE ENGLISHWOMAN.
Mrs. Harley, sister of Field-Marshal Viscount French, killed by a shell at Monastir, March 7th, 1917, while organising relief for the Serbians, was buried with full military honours. General Milne and Prince George of Serbia accompanied the cortège.

rowed in the Oxford boat, and won the Wingfield Sculls, the Diamond Sculls, and the Amateur Championship of the Thames; he was also a distinguished pianist and composer, one whose talents in that direction had given delight to thousands of music lovers.

Worthy to be named with Kelly, "a goodlie paire of brethren," although as different in externals as two brave men can be, was Lieut. H. Webber, of the South Lancashires. Although sixty-eight years of age, this splendid sportsman, by profession a stockbroker, obtained a commission and went cheerily through the hardships of the campaign until killed at the head of his men on July 21st. Two sportsmen known throughout Britain were killed during the year—F. C. Selous, the hunter, in East Africa, and Kenneth Hutchings, the "hitter," in France.

To mention all the sportsmen killed during the year would be to write down the names of nearly all the 190,000. Among the officers, and to some extent among the men, so many had been in the school eleven or fifteen, had boxed or fenced at Aldershot, or shot at Bisley, or had excelled at running, jumping, rowing, or some other form of sport.

Rugby football, which suffered very heavy losses indeed in 1914-15, had fresh names upon its roll. These included D. D. Howie and Cecil H. Abercrombie, R.N., the Scottish Internationals; C. M. Pritchard, H. W. Thomas, and J. L. Williams, who had played for Wales, and the Rev. R. E. Inglis, a chaplain, Captain R. L. Pillman, of the West Kents, L. A. N. Slocock, and A. F. Maynard, who had played for England. R. O. Lagden, a master at Harrow, was a double blue at Oxford, and so was L. J. Moon, of the Devons; G. Howard Smith won the same distinction at Cambridge. Lieut.-Colonel R. J. W. Carter, Lieut.-Colonel H. E. Brassey, and Major Leslie Cheape were famous polo players. H. G. Bache, a Corinthian, was an English International at the Association game, and E. H. Lintott had also played for England.

University blues of other kinds figured often in the casualty lists. Captain J. A. Ritson rowed in the Cambridge boat, and E. A. L. Southwell and A. H. Hales in the Oxford one. Captain A. G. Cowie played cricket for Cambridge; A. R. Welsh and J. V. Byrne-Johnson were running blues at Cambridge; D. N. Gaussen was President of the University Athletic Club at Oxford. Captain H. B. B. Hammond-Chambers was the Oxford captain at golf. And so the story could be continued almost indefinitely.

Outside the universities the country lost some notable sportsmen. Captain P. G. Graham was a champion swimmer in the North of England; Captain J. G. Davies was one of the best heavy-weight boxers in the Army; Captain R. F. Davies, of the London Regiment, won the King's Prize at Bisley in 1906, and F. Godfrey, of the Royal Fusiliers, held the Army records for the long jump and the hundred yards. G. C. Macleay, of the Camerons, who came from New Orleans to fight, was in 1911 the running champion of the Southern States. Captain W. Booth was the well-known Yorkshire cricketer, and Percy Jeeves the Warwickshire one.

The saving of civilisation

One or two names, which do not fall under any of the above headings, may be mentioned. Commander H. L. L. Pennell was a member of one of Captain Scott's Antarctic Expeditions, and so was J. R. Dennistoun, of the Flying Corps. Captain Douglas Brodie was secretary of the Chartered Company, and Captain H. B. Mudie was a very prominent Esperantist. Major Douglas Reynolds was one of the first to win the V.C. during the war, and in 1916 there fell also Major H. A. Carter, who won it in 1904, and Lieuts. H. R. Martineau and Alexander Young, who won it in South Africa. Captain S. E. Cowan (by an inadvertence described in Chapter CLX. as a second-lieutenant), a son of the chief engineering inspector to the Irish Local Government Board, was presumably killed while flying.

In one of Poe's most powerful stories the narrator tells how he was fleeing in horror from a doomed house. Arrested by a flash of lightning, he turned, and before his startled eyes the vast fabric of the House of Usher crumbled into fragments and disappeared. Had the Germans won the Great War such would have been the fate of our civilisation, built up through long centuries by the toil and pain of millions. That it did not thus crumble to atoms in our sight was due to those who risked death in its defence, and, above all, to those who fell in that holy cause. These we may best leave with those words which, taken from the Apocalypse, have been for nearly four hundred years part of the Office for the Burial of the Dead—"They rest from their labours."

END OF VOLUME 8.